D1520522

Encyclopedia of

MANAGEMENT
THEORY

Editor

Eric H. Kessler
Pace University

Advisory Board

Jean M. Bartunek
Boston College

Michael Hitt
Texas A&M University

Anne Sigismund Huff
National University of Ireland, Maynooth

Paul R. Lawrence
Harvard University

Jeffrey Pfeffer
Stanford University

Andrew H. Van de Ven
University of Minnesota

David A. Whetten
Brigham Young University

Encyclopedia of
MANAGEMENT THEORY

VOLUME ONE

ERIC H. KESSLER EDITOR
Pace University

⑤SAGE reference

Los Angeles | London | New Delhi
Singapore | Washington DC

Los Angeles | London | New Delhi
Singapore | Washington DC

FOR INFORMATION:

SAGE Publications, Inc.
2455 Teller Road
Thousand Oaks, California 91320
E-mail: order@sagepub.com

SAGE Publications Ltd.
1 Oliver's Yard
55 City Road
London, EC1Y 1SP
United Kingdom

SAGE Publications India Pvt. Ltd.
B 1/I 1 Mohan Cooperative Industrial Area
Mathura Road, New Delhi 110 044
India

SAGE Publications Asia-Pacific Pte. Ltd.
3 Church Street
#10-04 Samsung Hub
Singapore 049483

Publisher: Rolf A. Janke
Acquisitions Editor: Jim Brace-Thompson
Developmental Editor: Sanford Robinson
Production Editor: David C. Felts
Reference Systems Manager: Leticia Gutierrez
Reference Systems Coordinator: Laura Notton,
    Anna Villaseñor
Copy Editors: Linda Gray, Patrice Sutton
Typesetter: Hurix Systems Pvt. Ltd.
Proofreaders: Jeff Bryant, Sue Irwin
Indexer: Wendy Allex
Cover Designer: Glenn Vogel
Marketing Manager: Carmel Schrire

Copyright © 2013 by SAGE Publications, Inc.

All rights reserved. No part of this book may be reproduced or utilized in any form or by any means, electronic or mechanical, including photocopying, recording, or by any information storage and retrieval system, without permission in writing from the publisher.

Printed in the United States of America.

Library of Congress Cataloging-in-Publication Data

Encyclopedia of management theory / edited by Eric H. Kessler, Pace University.

v. cm
Includes bibliographical references and index.

ISBN 978-1-4129-9782-9 (hbk.)

1. Management—Encyclopedias. I. Kessler, Eric H., editor of compilation

HD30.15.E493 2013
658.001—dc23   2012039568

SFI Certified Sourcing
www.sfiprogram.org
SFI-00453

13 14 15 16 17 10 9 8 7 6 5 4 3 2

Contents

List of Entries

Editor's Note: Anchor entries are designated with an asterisk.

Reader's Guide

Nature of Management

Functions of the Executive
Humanistic Management
Management Roles
Management Symbolism and Symbolic Action
Managerialism
Organizational and Managerial Wisdom
Practice of Management, The
Principles of Administration and
    Management Functions
Scientific Management

Managing People, Personality, and Perception

Affect Theory
Affective Events Theory
Big Five Personality Dimensions
Causal Attribution Theory
Cognitive Dissonance Theory
Emotional and Social Intelligence
Fairness Theory
Image Theory
Individual Values
Job Demands–Resources Model
Locus of Control
Organizational Commitment Theory
Organizational Identification
Organizationally Based Self-Esteem
Psychological Contract Theory
Psychological Type and Problem-
    Solving Styles
Schemas Theory
Self-Concept and Theory of Self
Self-Fulfilling Prophecy
Sensemaking
Social Cognitive Theory
Social Construction Theory
Social Identity Theory
Social Information Processing Model

Theory of Emotions
Theory of Reasoned Action
Theory of Self-Esteem
Type A Personality Theory

Managing Motivation

Achievement Motivation Theory
Empowerment
Equity Theory
ERG Theory
Expectancy Theory
Goal-Setting Theory
Job Characteristics Theory
Management by Objectives
Needs Hierarchy
Reinforcement Theory
Self-Determination Theory
Theory of Reasoned Action
Two-Factor Theory (and Job Enrichment)

Managing Interactions

Circuits of Power and Control
Conflict Handling Styles
Critical Theory of Communication
Dialectical Theory of Organizations
Dual-Concern Theory
Genderlect and Linguistic Styles
Influence Tactics
Informal Communication and the Grapevine
Information Richness Theory
Organizational Assimilation Theory
Patterns of Political Behavior
Principled Negotiation
Social Exchange Theory
Social Information Processing Model
Social Movements
Social Network Theory
Social Power, Bases of
Strategic Contingencies Theory

Structuration Theory
Theory of Cooperation and Competition
Trust

Managing Groups

Asch Effect
Group Development
Group Polarization and the Risky Shift
Group Punctuated Equilibrium Model
Groupthink
High-Performing Teams
Multicultural Work Teams
Norms Theory
Role Theory
Social Facilitation Management
Social Identity Theory
Social Impact Theory and Social Loafing
Virtual Teams
Work Team Effectiveness

Managing Organizations

Actor-Network Theory
Agency Theory
Behavioral Theory of the Firm
Bureaucratic Theory
Complexity Theory and Organizations
Compliance Theory
Cooptation
Differentiation and the Division of Labor
Dramaturgical Theory of Organizations
High-Reliability Organizations
Knowledge-Based View of the Firm
Matrix Structure
Meaning and Functions of
    Organizational Culture
Multifirm Network Structure
Organic and Mechanistic Forms
Organizational Culture and Effectiveness
Organizational Culture Model
Organizational Culture Theory
Organizational Identity
Organizational Socialization
Organizational Structure and Design
Sociotechnical Theory
Stewardship Theory
Systems Theory of Organizations
Technology and Complexity
Technology and Interdependence/
    Uncertainty

Technology and Programmability
Typology of Organizational Culture

Managing Environments

Business Groups
Contingency Theory
Environmental Uncertainty
Institutional Theory
Interorganizational Networks
Neo-Institutional Theory
Organizational Ecology
Resource Dependence Theory
Social Network Theory
Strategic Alliances
Transaction Cost Theory

Strategic Management

Agency Theory
Balanced Scorecard
BCG Growth-Share Matrix
Business Policy and Corporate Strategy
Competitive Advantage
Core Competence
Diversification Strategy
Dynamic Capabilities
Excellence Characteristics
Firm Growth
First-Mover Advantages and
    Disadvantages
Game Theory
Hypercompetition
Knowledge-Based View of the Firm
Modes of Strategy / Planned-Emergent
Organizational Effectiveness
Product-Market Differentiation Model
Recourse-Based View of the Firm
Resource Orchestration Management
Seven-S Framework
Six Sigma
Stakeholder Theory
Strategic Decision Making
Strategic Flexibility
Strategic Frames
Strategic Groups
Strategic Profiles
Strategy and Structure
Strategy-as-Practice
SWOT Analysis Framework
Tacit Knowledge

Upper-Echelons Theory
Value Chain

Human Resources Management

Attraction-Selection-Attrition Model
Behavioral Perspective of Strategic Human
    Resource Management
Career Stages and Anchors
European Model of Human Resource
    Management
High-Performance Work Systems
Human Capital Theory
Human Resource Management Strategies
Human Resources Roles Model
Knowledge Workers
Model of Occupational Types
Organizational Demography Model
Personal Engagement (at Work) Model
Protean and Boundaryless Careers
Strategic International Human Resource
    Management
Theory of Organizational Attractiveness
Theory of Transfer of Training

International Management and Diversity

Acculturation Theory
Cultural Attitudes in Multinational
    Corporations
Cultural Intelligence
Cultural Values
Diamond Model of National Competitive
    Advantage
GLOBE Model
High- and Low-Context Cultures
Institutional Theory of Multinational
    Corporations
Interactional Model of Cultural Diversity
Managing Diversity
Multicultural Work Teams
Organizational Demography
Social Identity Theory
Transnational Management

Managerial Decision Making,
Ethics, and Creativity

Analytic Hierarchy Process Model
Bounded Rationality and Satisficing
    (Behavioral Decision-Making Model)

Brainstorming
BVSR Theory of Human Creativity
Componential Theory of Creativity
Decision Support Systems
Decision-Making Styles
Escalation of Commitment
Ethical Decision Making, Interactionist Model of
Evidence-Based Management
Experiential Learning Theory and Learning Styles
Garbage Can Model of Decision Making
Image Theory
Interactionalist Model of Organizational Creativity
Intuitive Decision Making
Investment Theory of Creativity
Managerial Decision Biases
Moral Reasoning Maturity
Participative Model of Decision Making
Programmability of Decision Making
Prospect Theory
Stages of Creativity
Strategic Decision Making
"Unstructured" Decision Making

Management Education, Research,
and Consulting

Academic-Practitioner Collaboration and
    Knowledge Sharing
Action Research
Analytical and Sociological Paradigms
Appreciative Inquiry Model
Bad Theories
Critical Management Studies
Engaged Scholarship Model
Evidence-Based Management
Large Group Interventions
Management (Education) as Practice
Multilevel Research
Narrative (Story) Theory
Organizational Development
Positive Organizational Scholarship
Process Consultation
Psychological Type and Problem-Solving Styles
Theory Development
Theory of the Interesting

Management of Operations, Quality,
and Information Systems

Adaptive Structuration Theory
Decision Support Systems

Gantt Chart and PERT
Kaizen and Continuous Improvement
Lean Enterprise
Management Control Systems
Quality Circles
Quality Trilogy
Strategic Information Systems
Technology Acceptance Model
Technology Affordances and Constraints Theory
  (of MIS)
Theory of Constraints (TOC)
Total Quality Management

Management of Entrepreneurship

Discovery Theory of Entrepreneurship
Entrepreneurial Cognition
Entrepreneurial Effectuation
Entrepreneurial Opportunities
Entrepreneurial Orientation
Social Entrepreneurship
Strategic Entrepreneurship

Management of Learning and Change

Action Learning
Business Process Reengineering
Continuous and Routinized Change
Double Loop Learning
Experiential Learning Theory and Learning
  Styles
Force Field Analysis and Model of Planned
  Change
Learning Organization
Logical Incrementalism
Organizational Development
Organizational Learning
Process Theories of Change
Punctuated Equilibrium Model
Quantum Change
Strategies for Change

Management of Technology and Innovation

Architectural Innovation
Dual-Core Model of Organizational Innovation
Innovation Diffusion

Innovation Speed
Lead Users
Open Innovation
Patterns of Innovation
Product Champions
Profiting From Innovation
Sociotechnical Theory
Stages of Innovation
Technological Discontinuities
Technology Acceptance Model
Technology and Complexity
Technology and Interdependence/Uncertainty
Technology and Programmability
Technology S-Curve
Transfer of Technology

Management and Leadership

Attribution Model of Leadership
Authentic Leadership
Charismatic Theory of Leadership
Cognitive Resource Theory
Competing Values Framework
Contingency Theory of Leadership
Leader–Member Exchange Theory
Leadership Continuum Theory
Leadership Practices
Level 5 Leadership
Managerial Grid
Path-Goal Theory of Leadership
Servant Leadership
Situational Theory of Leadership
Substitutes for Leadership
Theory X and Theory Y
Trait Theory of Leadership
Transformational Theory of Leadership

Management and Social / Environmental Issues

Corporate Social Responsibility
Critical Management Studies
CSR Pyramid
Integrative Social Contracts Theory
Moral Reasoning Maturity
Social Entrepreneurship
Stakeholder Theory
Triple Bottom Line

About the Editor

Eric H. Kessler is the Henry George Professor of Management, and founding director of the Business Honors Program, in the Lubin School of Business at Pace University in New York City. As a management scholar, Dr. Kessler holds a PhD in organization management and international business; he has produced over 100 research papers and presentations that span a broad array of management issues and published three critically acclaimed management books: (1) *Handbook of Organizational and Managerial Wisdom,* (2) *Cultural Mythology and Global Leadership,* and (3) *Management Theory in Action: Real World Lessons for Walking the Talk.* As a management educator Dr. Kessler instructs courses and conducts developmental workshops on a range of management levels and topics; in addition he has worked as an executive educator, corporate speaker, and has led numerous global management field studies traveling across six continents. As a management professional, Dr. Kessler is a Fellow and Past President of the Eastern Academy of Management and a long-time member of the Academy of Management; he has served on several management journals' advisory and editorial boards and has worked with a wide variety of large and small as well as private and government organizations. Dr. Kessler has received many academic honors and awards, is a member of Phi Beta Kappa, and has been inducted into national and international honorary societies in business, forensics, economics, and psychology.

Contributors

Eric Abrahamson
Columbia University

Frédéric Adam
University College Cork

Susan M. Adams
Bentley University

Rachida Aïssaoui
University of Memphis

Kleio Akrivou
University of Reading

Ramon J. Aldag
*Wisconsin School of Business,
    University of Wisconsin-
    Madison*

Sarah F. Allgood
Virginia Tech

Sharon A. Alvarez
The Ohio State University

Mats Alvesson
Lund University

Teresa M. Amabile
Harvard Business School

John M. Amis
University of Memphis

Jon Aarum Andersen
Linneaus University, Sweden

Marc H. Anderson
Iowa State University

Siah Hwee Ang
*University of Auckland
    Business School*

Alana S. Arshoff
University of Toronto

James Bailey
George Washington University

Arnold B. Bakker
Erasmus University Rotterdam

Timothy T. Baldwin
*Kelley School of Business,
    Indiana University*

Albert Bandura
Stanford University

Kathleen J. Barnes
East Stroudsburg University

Jay B. Barney
The Ohio State University

Jérôme Barthélemy
ESSEC Business School Paris

Jean M. Bartunek
Boston College

Nigel Bassett-Jones
*Oxford Brookes Business
    School*

Rowan Bayne
University of East London

Max H. Bazerman
Harvard Business School

Lee Roy Beach
University of Arizona

Suzanne T. Bell
DePaul University

J. Kenneth Benson
*University of Missouri-
    Columbia*

John W. Berry
Queen's University

Nicholas J. Beutell
Iona College

Magdalena Bielenia-Grajewska
*University of Gdansk, Poland
    and SISSA, Italy*

Richard S. Blackburn
Kenan-Flagler Business School

George Boak
York St John University

David M. Boje
New Mexico State University

Dianne Bolton
*Swinburne University of
    Technology*

Hyeon-Cheol Bong
*Chunbuk National University,
    Jeonju, South Korea*

Richard E. Boyatzis
*Case Western Reserve
    University*

Chris Brewster
University of Reading

Francesca Bria
Imperial College London

Shelley L. Brickson
*University of Illinois at
    Chicago*

Wayne Brockbank
University of Michigan

Philip Bromiley
University of California, Irvine

Karin Holmblad Brunsson
Uppsala University

Stéphane Brutus
Concordia University

Barbara Benedict Bunker
University at Buffalo

Anthony F. Buono
Bentley University

W. Warner Burke
*Teachers College, Columbia
University*

Lawton Robert Burns
University of Pennsylvania

Lowell W. Busenitz
University of Oklahoma

Gervase R. Bushe
Simon Fraser University

John C. Byrne
Pace University

Kim Cameron
*University of Michigan
Business School*

Laura B. Cardinal
University of Houston

Peter J. Carnevale
*University of Southern
California*

Archie B. Carroll
*Terry College of Business,
University of Georgia*

John S. Carroll
*Massachusetts Institute of
Technology*

Canan Ceylan
Uludag University

Rajeswararao Chaganti
*Fox School of Business,
Temple University*

Alok Chakrabarti
*New Jersey Institute of
Technology*

Artemis Chang
*Queensland University of
Technology*

Jennifer A. Chatman
*University of California at
Berkeley, Haas School of
Business*

Alicia Cheak
*INSEAD Global Leadership
Centre*

Jiyao Chen
Oregon State University

Katherine K. Chen
*The City College of New York
and the Graduate Center,
CUNY*

Raveendra Chittoor
Indian School of Business

Yonjoo Cho
Indiana University

Yoonhee Choi
University of Minnesota

Edward W. Christensen
Monmouth University

Stewart R. Clegg
University of Technology

Charlotte Cloutier
HEC Montreal

David Coghlan
Trinity College Dublin

Aaron Cohen
University of Haifa

Susan Cohen
University of Pittsburgh

Christopher J. Collins
Cornell University

Jay A. Conger
Claremont McKenna College

Leonardo Corbo
University of Bologna

Taylor Cox Jr.
Taylor Cox & Associates

Russell Cropanzano
University of Colorado

Felipe A. Csaszar
University of Michigan

Richard L. Daft
Vanderbilt University

Giovanni Battista Dagnino
University of Catania

Su Mi Dahlgaard-Park
Lund University

T. K. Das
City University of New York

Rein De Cooman
Lessius University College

Edward L. Deci
University of Rochester

Stanley Deetz
*University of Colorado at
Boulder*

Rich DeJordy
Northeastern University

Daniel Denison
*International Institute of
Management Development*

Laurie N. DiPadova-Stocks
Park University

Nancy DiTomaso
*Rutgers Business School–
Newark and New Brunswick*

Stanislav Dobrev
*Eccles School of Business,
University of Utah*

Lex Donaldson
University of New South Wales

Thomas J. Donaldson
*Wharton School, University of
Pennsylvania*

Peter Dorfman
New Mexico State University

Nicky Dries
University of Leuven

Kelly Dye
Acadia University

P. Christopher Earley
Purdue University

Marion B. Eberly
*University of Washington,
Tacoma*

Dov Eden
Tel Aviv University

Thomas V. Edwards Jr.
Pace University

Julia R. Eisenberg
*Rutgers Business School–
Newark and New Brunswick*

Hillary Anger Elfenbein
*Washington University in
St. Louis*

John Elkington
SustainAbility

Amitai Etzioni
*The Institute for
Communitarian Policy
Studies*

Christina Fang
*New York University Stern
School of Business*

Dan Farrell
Western Michigan University

Steven Fellows
Boston University

William P. Ferris
*Western New England
University*

Lorenz Fischer
University of Cologne

Oliver Fischer
University of Oxford

Robert Folger
University of Central Florida

Nicolai J. Foss
Copenhagen Business School

Roseanne J. Foti
Virginia Tech

Nikolaus Franke
WU Vienna

Olivier Furrer
Radboud University Nijmegen

Marylène Gagné
Concordia University

Martin Ganco
University of Minnesota

William L. Gardner
Texas Tech University

Adriana Victoria Garibaldi
de Hilal
*The COPPEAD Graduate
School of Business*

Oliver Gassmann
University of St.Gallen

Ajai Gaur
Rutgers University

Megan W. Gerhardt
Miami University

Simona Giorgi
Boston College

Mary Ann Glynn
Boston College

Don Goeltz
Holy Family University

Timothy D. Golden
*Rensselaer Polytechnic
Institute*

Shanthi Gopalakrishnan
*New Jersey Institute of
Technology*

Jonathan Gosling
University of Exeter

Remzi Gözübüyük
IE Business School

Henrich R. Greve
INSEAD

Bruce Gurd
University of South Australia

Paul J. Hanges
University of Maryland

Jeffrey S. Harrison
University of Richmond

Alex Haslam
University of Exeter

John Hassard
University of Manchester

Oscar Hauptman
University of Western Sydney

Marilyn M. Helms
Dalton State College

James V. M. L. Holzer
*U.S. Department of Homeland
Security*

Robert Hooijberg
IMD

Sean Tsuhsiang Hsu
University of Pittsburgh

Anne Sigismund Huff
*National University of Ireland,
Maynooth*

Lee H. Igel
New York University

Susan E. Jackson
Rutgers University

Mansour Javidan
*Thunderbird School of Global
Management*

Francis Jeffries
*University of Alaska
Anchorage*

Guowei Jian
Cleveland State University

David W. Johnson
University of Minnesota

Roger T. Johnson
University of Minnesota

Stephen Jones
University of Minnesota

William A. Kahn
Boston University

Steven J. Karau
Southern Illinois University at Carbondale

Merel M. S. Kats
Deloitte NL

Theresa F. Kelly
The Wharton School

Eric H. Kessler
Pace University

Manfred F. R. Kets de Vries
INSEAD

Shaista E. Khilji
The George Washington University

Yoo Kyoung Kim
University of Southern California

Brayden G. King
Northwestern University

Peter G. Klein
University of Missouri

David A. Kolb
Case Western Reserve University

Andreas S. König
University of Erlangen-Nuremberg

Richard E. Kopelman
Baruch College

Martin B. Kormanik
O.D. Systems

Tatiana Kostova
University of South Carolina

James M. Kouzes
Santa Clara University

Roderick M. Kramer
Stanford University

Chuhua Kuei
Pace University

Carol T. Kulik
University of South Australia

Stefan Lagrosen
University West

Nancy Lane
IMD

Theresa Lant
Pace University

Gary P. Latham
University of Toronto

Edward J. Lawler
Cornell University

Thomas W. Lee
University of Washington

David Lei
Southern Methodist University

Edward Levitas
University of Wisconsin–Milwaukee

Roy J. Lewicki
The Ohio State University

Leonardo Liberman
Universidad de los Andes, Santiago, Chile

Robert C. Liden
University of Illinois at Chicago

Jeffrey K. Liker
University of Michigan

Robert C. Litchfield
Washington & Jefferson College

Anna Christina Littmann
EBS Business School

Romie Littrell
Aukland University of Technology

Edwin A. Locke
University of Maryland

Christopher P. Long
Georgetown University

Jay W. Lorsch
Harvard Business School

Todd Lubart
Université Paris Descartes

Heather MacDonald
Memorial University of Newfoundland

Joseph A. Maciariello
Claremont Graduate University

Christian N. Madu
Pace University

Ann Majchrzak
University of Southern California

Peter K. Manning
Northeastern University

Lalit Manral
University of Central Oklahoma

M. Lynne Markus
Benley College

Joanne Martin
Stanford University

Mark J. Martinko
Florida State University

Courtney R. Masterson
University of Illinois at Chicago

John E. Mathieu
University of Connecticut

Christina L. Matz
Texas A&M University

Kevin May
George Washington University

Roger C. Mayer
Poole College of Management, North Carolina State University

Abdelmagid Mazen
Sawyer Business School Suffolk University

Mary-Hunter Morris McDonnell
Northwestern University

Raymond E. Miles
University of California, Berkeley

Katherine L. Milkman
The Wharton School

Kent D. Miller
Michigan State University

Marie S. Mitchell
University of Georgia

Terence R. Mitchell
University of Washington

Mario P. Mondelli
Centre for Economic Research

Samantha D. Montes
University of Toronto

Karl Moore
McGill University

Todd W. Moss
Oregon State University

Robert Moussetis
North Central College

Troy V. Mumford
Colorado State University

Susan Elaine Murphy
James Madison University

David G. Myers
Hope College

Karen K. Myers
University of California, Santa Barbara

Anil Nair
Old Dominion University

Dilupa Jeewanie Nakandala
University of Western Sydney

Donald O. Neubaum
Oregon State University

Scott L. Newbert
Villanova University

Tjai M. Nielsen
High Point University

Levi R. G. Nieminen
Denison Consulting

Deborah Nightingale
Massachusetts Institute of Technology

Greg R. Oldham
Tulane University

Miguel R. Olivas-Luján
Clarion University

David L. Olson
University of Nebraska

Joe Peppard
Cranfield School of Management

Theodore Peridis
York University

James C. Petersen
University of North Carolina at Greensboro

Jeffrey Pfeffer
Stanford University

J. Mark Phillips
Belmont University

Nelson Phillips
Imperial College Business School

Pasquale Massimo Picone
University of Catania

Beth Polin
The Ohio State University

Marshall Scott Poole
University of Illinois

Barry Z. Posner
Santa Clara University

Richard A. Posthuma
University of Texas at El Paso

Marlei Pozzebon
HEC Montreal

Michael G. Pratt
Boston College

David J. Prottas
Adelphi University

Prem Ramburuth
University of New South Wales

W. Alan Randolph
University of Baltimore

Devaki Rau
Northern Illinois University

Davide Ravasi
Bocconi University

Barbara Ribbens
Illinois State University

Katherine M. Richardson
Pace University

Ansgar Richter
EBS Business School

Maria Carolina Saffie Robertson
Concordia University

Tonette S. Rocco
Florida International University

Zachariah J. Rodgers
Brigham Young University

Denise M. Rousseau
Carnegie Mellon University

Travis L. Russ
Fordham University

Richard M. Ryan
University of Rochester

Robert Ryan
University of Pittsburgh

Yolanda Sarason
Colorado State University

Saras Sarasvathy
University of Virginia

Carol Saunders
University of Central Florida

Stuart M. Schmidt
Temple University

Marguerite Schneider
New Jersey Institute of Technology

William D. Schneper
Franklin & Marshall College

Randall S. Schuler
Rutgers University

Joanne L. Scillitoe
New York Institute of Technology

Eliot L. Sherman
Haas School of Business, University of California at Berkeley

Katsuhiko Shimizu
Keio University

Dean Keith Simonton
University of California, Davis

David G. Sirmon
Texas A&M University

Sim B. Sitkin
Duke University

Joanne R. Smith
University of Exeter

Charles C. Snow
Pennsylvania State University

JC Spender
Lund University

David Philip Spicer
Bradford University

Gretchen Spreitzer
University of Michigan

Jayakanth Srinivasan
Massachusetts Institute of Technology

Rhetta L. Standifer
University of Wisconsin–Eau Claire

Donna Stoddard
Babson College

James A. F. Stoner
Fordham University

Roy Suddaby
University of Alberta

Mary Sully de Luque
Thunderbird School of Global Management

Kathleen M. Sutcliffe
Ross School of Business, University of Michigan

Paul Szwed
U.S. Coast Guard Academy

Ibraiz Tarique
Pace University

David J. Teece
University of California, Berkeley

Stefan Tengblad
University of Skovde

Deborah J. Terry
University of Queensland

Nicole J. Thompson
Virginia Tech

Pamela S. Tolbert
Cornell University

Maria Tomprou
Carnegie Mellon University

Linda Treviño
Pennsylvania State University

Joanne L. Tritsch
University of Maryland

Bruce W. Tuckman
The Ohio State University

Andrea Tunarosa
Boston College

Dave Ulrich
University of Michigan, Ross School of Business

Andrew H. Van de Ven
University of Minnesota

Rolf van Dick
Goethe University

Hetty van Emmerik
Maastricht University

Jeffrey B. Vancouver
Ohio University

Timothy Vogus
Vanderbilt University

Mary Ann Von Glinow
Florida International University

Victor H. Vroom
Yale University

Nigel Wadeson
University of Reading

Sigmund Wagner-Tsukamoto
University of Leicester

William Wales
James Madison University

Sandy J. Wayne
University of Illinois at Chicago

Howard M. Weiss
Georgia Institute of Technology

David A. Whetten
Brigham Young University

Richard Whittington
Oxford University

Bastian Widenmayer
University of St.Gallen

Joann Krauss Williams
Judson College

Janice Winch
Pace University

Duane Windsor
Rice University

Ingo Winkler
University of Southern Denmark

Jaana Woiceshyn
University of Calgary

Diana J. Wong-MingJi
Eastern Michigan University

Jack Denfeld Wood
IMD

Richard W. Woodman
Texas A&M University

Georges Zaccour
HEC Montréal

Shaker A. Zahra
University of Minnesota

Ting Zhang
Harvard Business School

Lynne G. Zucker
*University of California,
Los Angeles*

Introduction

The word *manage*, according to the *Oxford English Dictionary*, is derivative of the Latin *manus*, or hand and emerges from the Italian *maneggiare*, which refers to the handling or training of horses. Its use has since been expanded to represent a broader concern for the proper handling of things or people, particularly with regard to a company or organization. This is true across multiple levels of analysis. For example, at the most fundamental social unit, the individual, it can be said that people (to varying degrees) manage themselves. We formulate our goals, regulate our behaviors, and allocate scarce physical, emotional, and intellectual resources to our decisions and actions. Further to this, we frequently attempt to manage others; these could include our family, friends, colleagues, coworkers, cohorts, or competitors. We do this through efforts to motivate them, communicate with them, influence them, lead them, and resolve conflicts with them. People also attempt to manage their context and shape their environment; this might represent a group or team, project or venture, formal or informal organization, alliance or network, industry or institution, society or nation state, or perhaps even a transnational global movement. In doing so, there is a common thread to these actions that evidences unmistakable elements of "management": orientation and direction, coordination and control, authority and responsibility, planning and design, and administration and implementation. Thus, in a sense, we are all inexorably managers regardless of whether we are given a business card with the formal title.

Not only does the reach of management run wide, but it also runs deep. That is to say, management is vitally important. It is with rare exception that our personal and professional activities need to be "managed"—implicitly or explicitly, internally or externally, indirectly or directly, proactively or reactively—to sustain efficient processes and achieve effective outcomes. However, highlighting something as important is quite different from saying that it is always done well. To the contrary we are all too often the victims, or perhaps the perpetrators, of poor management. It is simply not enough to cultivate advantageous resources and technologies, develop advanced skills and abilities, or construct superior capital and facilities. Who you are or what you possess (nouns) will only get you so far. We also need to pay attention to management dynamics (verbs). History is filled with countless examples of better managed "underdogs" leveraging their relatively meager means to upend better financed, entrenched, or equipped rivals. And in a world whose playing field has been characterized as increasingly "flat," where resources, access, and opportunities are now more than ever evenly distributed, it is management that is frequently the key differentiator.

Management is also complex. Despite a long history of academic and applied investigations, there are no simple, comprehensive, universally applicable answers to its totality of challenges and conundrums. It should therefore be of little surprise that there are countless "theories" (loosely defined as well as loosely connected) of management. The study of management is almost as broad and diverse as its practice. It encompasses multiple levels of investigation, a wide array of subdisciplines, hundreds of journals, libraries of books, armies of consultants, an eclectic array of researchers and professionals, and diverse education and training programs. For example, focusing solely on the Academy of Management, the preeminent professional organization for management scholars, its ranks comprise nearly 20,000 diverse members from over 100 nations working in over 20 distinct and scarcely integrated academic divisions and interest groups, each with its own particular mores, models, and methodologies. Thus, even in this relatively specialized domain, we still come from different management traditions, practice different management techniques, address different management issues, and speak different management languages—too often scarcely aware of where the "others" are coming from.

Moreover, even when educators artificially narrow the field to discuss a discrete management topic, they often superficially toss out the name of a theorist (Taylor, Simon, Weber, etc.) or make a sideways reference to a specific theory (needs hierarchy, total quality management, etc.) and move on, as if assuming their audience possesses the necessary familiarity to appreciate, evaluate, integrate, and appropriately apply its assumption-based, domain-specific, frequently nuanced insights for improving their particular set of circumstances. Lamentably, this is far from the truth, and as such, management theory more often than not obscures rather than elucidates. Our students, our clients, our practitioners of the craft too often emerge more confused than empowered by these conversations. We hear questions such as, "Which motivation theory should I use?" or "What international strategies work best?" as if any of these tools can be applied without exception or without complement. And more than this, we are regularly presented with a seemingly endless stream of new books and journal articles with the latest fads and theories-of-the-day, professing to have "the answer," yet often scarcely appreciating the theoretical insights that form their foundations, only to ride a brief wave of popularity but fall flat in the end.

In summary, management theory is, on the one hand, (a) elevated by its pervasiveness and importance yet, on the other hand, (b) shackled by its dizzying, disconnected (dis)array of dimensions, perspectives, ideas, voices, and trends.

Rationale for the *Encyclopedia of Management Theory*

It follows from the previous discussion that a common "one-stop" resource for presenting the fundamental characteristics, constraints, explanations, and applications of core management theoretical models and concepts would be of great practical and scholarly use. To date, there is no single definitive source or rigorous, systematic academic collection of the fundamental theories that define the field of management. In response, SAGE Reference decided to publish this two-volume *Encyclopedia of*

Management Theory (*EMT*). I am honored to serve as its general editor.

Herein is the intention of this project—an authoritative compendium of the global landscape of key frameworks that have stood the test of time and whose insights provide the foundation for examining and advising contemporary management practice. The *EMT* is designed to serve as a reference for anyone interested in understanding, internalizing, and applying classical as well as contemporary management theory. Drawing together an impressive team of researchers and educators, it examines the key theories and the theorists behind them, presenting them in the context needed to understand their assumptions, arguments, and strengths and weaknesses. In addition to interpretations of long-established theories, it also offers consideration of cutting-edge research as one might find in a handbook. And like an unabridged dictionary, it provides concise, to-the-point definitions of key concepts, ideas, schools of thought, and major movers and shakers.

For the purposes of this volume, a *theory* is defined as an ordered set of assertions that are predicted to hold true under defined instances. Ideally, theories should posit (a) factors, such as variables, concepts, or constructs, (b) that are related in some systematic way, (c) because of underlying psychological, economic, social, or other dynamics, (d) within temporal, contextual, or otherwise specified boundary conditions. Drawing from the entries Theory Development and Multilevel Research within this volume, we see management theory at its best about attempting to capture the *who, what, how, where,* and *when* but also the *why* to decode and influence a broad range of interdependent phenomena. Yet too often, theories are not well defined or structured. Too often, their explanations ignore critical contingencies. Too often, their central tenets are misunderstood or taken out of context so that they are misapplied, ignored, or overgeneralized. Too often, their baseline assumptions and historical development are underappreciated or obscured. Too often their relationships with complementary frameworks are underdeveloped. These must be corrected if our field is to meaningfully advance, guide research, integrate insights, and successfully contribute to practice. Moreover even among those precursory surveys of management "theories" that do exist, there are few if any filtration systems and coherent distillations that apply a consistent formula to consider their elemental messages and relative importance. This shortcoming also must be remedied. To this end, we will use the following criteria for assessment: *validity times impact*. Validity: The theory has been substantially supported by research and has shown to be accurate in helping understand, explain, and predict management phenomena. Impact: The theory has significant implications for improving management practice and has generated viable applications to produce intended results.

Organization of the Encyclopedia

Inside the *EMT*, the reader will find over 280 signed, cross-referenced entries from an international array of respected management scholars that represent a broad-based coverage of major interest areas and perspectives in the field. Further to this, a "Reader's Guide" was developed to group these entries thematically into the following categories that consider common management questions—yet often proposed different, albeit potentially complementary, answers:

1. What is/should be the nature of management and management thought?
2. How do you manage people's personalities and perceptions?
3. How do you manage people's motivations?
4. How do you manage interpersonal interactions involving communication, power and politics, and conflict?
5. How do you manage group composition, development, and teamwork?
6. How do you manage organizational structure, culture, and systems?
7. How do you manage environmental contingencies, networks, and institutions?
8. How do you manage strategic resources, frameworks, and processes?
9. How do you manage human resources practices, functions, and employee careers?
10. How do you manage within and across international cultures, climates, and other dimensions of diversity?
11. How do you manage decision-making rationality, ethics, and creativity?

12. How do you manage "management" education, research, and consulting?
13. How do you manage operational quality, logistics, and information systems?
14. How do you manage entrepreneurial thinking, creation, and engagement?
15. How do you manage learning, adaptation, and change?
16. How do you manage technology, knowledge, and innovation?
17. How do you manage leadership attributes, behaviors, and styles?
18. How do you manage social issues such as those concerning stakeholders, society, and the environment?

In addition, the *EMT* provides two appendixes that offer unique value for the reader:

- Appendix A (longitudinal): An abbreviated timetable of the "Chronology of Management Theory"—to appreciate the historical, cumulative development of theory within the field,
- Appendix B (cross-sectional): A delineation of "Central Insights" from the aforementioned encyclopedia entries—to encapsulate the major theoretical "take-aways" of the field.

Structure of the Entries

The structure of each individual entry is contingent on its placement in one of three groups, varying in length, based on validity and importance as determined by the editor and advisory board. For each of these categories, standardized author guidelines and checklists were developed that further differentiate this volume from other types of compilations.

Each entry begins with an opening paragraph (*Introduction*) that establishes a framework for the entry to clearly and concisely communicate its intention. It considers the following questions: Definition of the theory: What is the theory's central purpose and premise? Domain of the theory: Why is the theory relevant to the topic of the encyclopedia (i.e., management)? Outline of entry: How will this article be structured?

The first and primary section of all entries (*Fundamentals*) describes the theory to systematically encapsulate its arguments. It considers the following questions customized to the particular nature of the topic: Content of the theory: What are the factors—core elements, variables, concepts, constructs, and so on—that make up the theory? Dynamics of the theory: What are the relationships—systematic ways in which the contents are related? Rationale of the theory: What are the underlying psychological, economic, social, and structural dynamics that explain the relationships? Domain of the theory: What are the temporal, contextual, or otherwise defined boundary conditions in which the theory holds? Context of the theory: What is the connection to similar theories and shared conceptions (general or midrange) of the phenomena?

For longer entries a subsequent section (*Importance*) offers an assessment of the theory to critically evaluate its validity and impact. It considers the following questions, again customized to the particular nature of the topic: To what degree has the theory been substantially supported by research and has proven accurate in helping to understand, explain, and predict management phenomena? How has the theory influenced management scholars and educators? To what degree has the theory provided significant implications for improving management practice and generated viable applications to produce intended results? How has the theory influenced managers?

For select theories that have been designated "anchor entries"—these are highlighted in the entry list with an asterisk—an additional section was requested that bridges the Fundamentals and Importance sections. Here a longitudinal examination (*Evolution*) was requested to dynamically trace its history and development. Significant discretion was allotted to consider in various lengths and approaches the following questions: What are the roots of the theory? What are the major changes, adaptations, tests, and adaptations to the theory that led to its most current form? What were the circumstances—economic, social, cultural, and so on—if any, that influenced its development, and what was their influence? Who are the people who contributed to its development and what was their contribution?

Each entry concludes with cross-references to other related *EMT* entries, to provide additional breadth to the discussion, as well as a list of approximately 5 to 10 supplementary resources (*Further Readings*), both seminal and contemporary, to provide additional depth to the discussion.

The *EMT* Team and Process

Numerous individuals were involved with the *EMT* project at different stages of the process. The Board of Advisors lent considerable expertise and insight to the selection, categorization, and structure of the volume. In many cases, they also wore the hat of entry(ies) author. They rank among the most esteemed luminaries in the management theory field, and I am grateful to them for their support, listed alphabetically: Jean Bartunek, Michael Hitt, Anne Huff, Paul Lawrence, Jeffrey Pfeffer, Andrew Van de Ven, and David Whetten. During the course of compiling the volume Paul Lawrence passed from this world—Paul was a treasured colleague (he was even gracious enough to serve on my doctoral thesis committee) and will be missed. A wonderful group of colleagues at SAGE Publications shepherded this project from conception to completion including acquiring editor Jim Brace-Thompson, developmental editor Sanford Robinson, reference systems coordinators Laura Notton and Anna Villaseñor, production editor David Felts, and marketing manager Carmel Schrire.

The selection of entries and authors for the *EMT* underwent a long, multiphase process. Feedback was solicited from numerous sources, including current and past officers of each Academy of Management division, editorial board members of several of the field's most respected journals, conversations with respected colleagues, and input from the distinguished advisory board. In addition, searches of numerous management databases were conducted as well as reviews of core management research articles, texts, and compilations. From this process, topics were ultimately identified and authors were approached and contracted who were experts in these areas, many of them the principle investigators of the focal theories. Multiple iterations of each entry were drafted, reviewed, edited, revised, and copyedited. Whereas the great majority of authors delivered stellar entries, there were incidences of late drop-outs or quality concerns that necessitated us to remove an otherwise intended contributor or entry. Of course no process of this nature is perfect and there will undoubtedly be some omissions and limitations—as well as emerging research, perspectives, issues, and applications—that we will look to address in subsequent editions.

It should also be noted that within this volume some entries might be seen as more "theoretical" than others. That is to say, there is variability in the extent to which theories can be said to embody what several have put forth are the criteria for a strong theory. In addition, some entries drill down more than others to focus on key concepts or constructs whereas others adopt a more holistic or macro view that entertains different theoretical explanations, categorizations, frameworks, patterns, or perspectives of a focal management phenomenon. Moreover, the reader will also find differences between some entries in their basic assumptions, paradigmatic foundations, intended purposes, and even general intellectual approach. A conscious decision was made to prioritize a path that was more rather than less inclusive; this allowed for a more complete encapsulation of the management theory landscape rather than one that was artificially condensed. Said another way, the volume attempts to avoid the unnecessary rejection of potentially valuable explanations, which could be relatively more dangerous in these circumstances than offering a broader range of theories that vary in their popularity or current level of support and that include potentially but not necessarily more relevant and/or less-compelling insights. In "managing" this trade-off, the intention is to put forth these contributions to management thought in an open and straightforward manner that includes an explicit element of critical review and also invites rather than presupposes consideration by the reader.

Suggestions for Using the *EMT*

As you wade into this volume it may be easy to become disoriented with the great variety of models and perspectives or perhaps vacillate between them becoming an advocate of the most recently read or most persuasively written entry. As editor it is my charge not only to organize, solicit, and shape the entries but also to try to integrate them in some metalogical schemata as to bring the proverbial forest into focus without distorting the view of the trees. The *EMT* Reader's Guide is helpful in this way by offering a thematic categorization of theories, but it should be seen as a beginning and not an end to the conversation. Because management is a relatively new and "soft" science, it is helpful to borrow from those who have walked a similar path—specifically, to consider lessons from the more seasoned domain of theoretical physics, a field that has also seen its share of luminaries and similarly struggled with the

integration of diverse perspectives. Mindful of what Warren Bennis has termed "physics envy," the following discussion selectively adapts two of the strategies communicated by Stephen Hawking that are particularly promising for management in advancing its theoretical precision and practical integration.

The "Trees": Model-Dependent Realism. One of the most useful tools for understanding the trees (i.e., individual theories) within the management forest can be extracted from what Hawking refers to in his 2010 book *The Grand Design* (New York: Bantam Books) as *model-dependent realism.* Per Hawking:

> There is no picture- or theory-independent concept of reality. Instead we will adopt a view that we will call model-dependent realism; the idea that a physical theory or world picture is a model . . . and set of rules that connect the elements of the model to observations. This provides a framework with which to interpret modern science. . . . [D]ifferent theories can successfully describe the same phenomenon through disparate conceptual frameworks. In fact, many scientific theories that had proven successful were later replaced by other, equally successful theories based on wholly new concepts of reality. . . . According to model-dependent realism, it is pointless to ask whether a mode is real, only whether it agrees with observation. . . . A model is a good model if it: 1) Is elegant, 2) Contains few arbitrary or adjustable elements, 3) Agrees with and explains all existing observations, 4) Makes detailed predictions about future observations that can disprove or falsify the mode if they are not borne out. (pp. 42–43, 44, 46, 51)

Let us unpack this. First, theories provide a picture of reality. They supply the categories to label phenomena as well as the map to interpret their relationships. For instance, if one is evoking Maslow's model of reality, then a person's motivations might be seen as striving to fulfill one unmet need or another—for example, internal esteem; alternatively, if one is using Vroom's framework of motivation, then the same actions by the same person might be understood as hedonically attempting to better link outcome with valence. Therefore, it is imperative to recognize that our worldview is shaped by the theories that we employ. Whether we are liberated, or imprisoned, by them is another matter entirely and largely a fate of our choosing.

Second, that there is an evolutionary quality to theoretical development. This might take the form of successive improvements in the way that we see things, such as when new evidence is discovered or new applications are tested, or the advancement of wholly new paradigms for making sense of reality. Both cumulative as well as frame-breaking ideas populate the theoretical space. It is important to recognize not only the theoretical snapshots of management but the cinema and unfolding narrative of its story. Again, whether successive theoretical iterations represent positive enhancements or negative regressions is to be determined. We must be mindful that "newer" does not always mean better and "older" does not always mean classic.

Third, the veracity of management theory is ultimately decided on the shop floor and office space, not in the library or lecture hall. Independent of practical analysis and application, and outside of internal consistency, there is little compelling rationale to determine which competing model is "more real" than another. Management theories perpetuate or fade away (or at least they should) based on their realistic value. That is to say, their acceptance should be a function of the degree to which their predictions agree with and can shape observation. Fourth, and related to the above, the quality of a theoretical modeling is a function of its usefulness to managers. Models are more effective if they are simple, straightforward, broad-based, predictive, and provide tools for action that, if followed, will increase management efficiency and effectiveness. Certainly this is easier said than done, and the tension between criteria recalls Dr. Einstein's pondering of necessary trade-offs that (paraphrasing) a theory can only be two of the following: simple, accurate, and comprehensive. It is therefore important to acknowledge that management is ultimately a professional field and must be judged by the degree to which it offers elucidating perspective, helpful tools, and practical guidance for using them.

Therefore, the first opportunity/challenge for the reader of this volume is to recognize the theories themselves, their language and their limits, and reflect on how they help explain, predict, and impact management dynamics and outcomes. My advice would be the following: Seek to truly understand, on their own terms, the essential insights of these frameworks. Try to customize their lessons and see how they might relate to your particular circumstances. Extract their most useful implications—for

becoming a stronger person, for engaging in more successful interactions, and for constructing more facilitative contexts and mind-sets—to increase your management capacity. Yet do not be satisfied with the information and encapsulated knowledge communicated by the entries; combine them with sound judgment and prudent action to translate your enhanced potential into management "wisdom" for achieving personal and professional success. It is my hope that the *EMT* facilitates this.

The "Forest": (Management) M-Theory. Keeping our focus on the lessons of physics, but now looking not at the trees themselves but at how they relate to each other in the forest (i.e., management theory literature)—or pushing the metaphor farther, perhaps how they can be assembled into a terrarium—Hawking gives us a second vehicle: *M-Theory*:

M-Theory is not a theory in the usual sense. It is a whole family of different theories, each of which is a good description of observations only in some range of physical situations. It is a bit like a map. As is well known, one cannot show the whole of the earth's surface on a single map. The usual Mercator projection used for maps of the world makes areas appear larger and larger in the far north and south and does not cover the North and South Poles. To faithfully map the entire earth, one has to use a collection of maps, each of which covers a limited region. The maps overlap each other, and where they do, they show the same landscape. M-theory is similar. The different theories in the M-Theory family may look very different, but they can all be regarded as aspects of the same underlying theory. They are versions of the theory that are applicable only in limited ranges. . . . Like the overlapping maps in a Mercator projection, where the ranges of different versions overlap, they predict the same phenomena. But just as there is no flat map that is a good representation of the earth's entire surface, there is no single theory that is a good representation of observations in all situations. . . . Each theory in the M-theory network is good at describing phenomena within a certain range. Wherever their ranges overlap, the various theories in the network agree, so they can all be said to be parts of the same theory. (pp. 8, 58)

Let us extract the elements most relevant for our volume. Theories are like maps. They are more or less accurate depictions of a delineated area or landscape. As such, they have limited ranges of application, which are separated by explicitly acknowledged or implicitly active boundary conditions. As Dr. Hawking argues, and most management scholars would readily agree, there is at this time no single theory-of-everything (TOE) that is a good representation of all observations in all situations. Similarly, as inferred by numerous *EMT* entries, it is no easy task capturing the complex configurations of factors that combine to influence organizational success and differentiate the sage management scholar or continuously successful manager from their less distinguished counterparts. It is therefore necessary to "stitch together" (a la image or photo stitching) these depictions to see how each image relates to one another and, in the process, gain a better panoramic perspective of the overarching vista. This suggests that theories need not be seen as necessarily competing visions of reality but instead as representing potentially complementary mappings of different networked components within a multifaceted and multileveled reality. Areas of correspondence represent prospects for theoretical synergy. Areas of divergence represent prospects for theoretical reconciliation and extension (recalling dialectical arguments that a meeting of a thesis and its antithesis has the potential to yield synthesis). Ultimately, they are all contributors to a broader, more inclusive map; that is, they may all be part of the same "Management M-Theory."

What might a Management M-Theory look like? Perhaps overlapping elements of critical and functional perspectives, humanistic and bureaucratic designs, external and internal forces, operational and innovative/entrepreneurial processes, tacit and algorithmic recipes? Integrated individual, interpersonal, group, organizational, environmental, and strategic analyses? Synchronized psychological, sociological, anthropological, political, and economic engines? Amalgamated information-, knowledge-, resource-, and wisdom-based lenses? A harmony of increasingly "high-definition" static management snapshots and dynamic management cinema? The actualization of a Management M-Theory is beyond the scope of this brief introduction. What is important is the general strategy that its idea represents for making sense of the 280-plus entries herein. Therefore, the second opportunity/challenge for

the reader is to understand how the entries—both within and across reader's guide categories—relate to, inform, and influence each other so as to provide the templates for a deeper, more comprehensive comprehension of management theory and an integrated, more effective application of its principles. My advice would be the following: Uncover the underlying theories nested within or derivative of complementary frameworks. Seek to truly understand the specific conditions in which their arguments apply. Actively explore how their focal domains interact with related models and where their conclusions might coalesce. Further, and borrowing from ancient but still relevant philosophical debates, consider how their individually articulated management (lower-case *t*, situation-specific) *t*ruths might be reconciled to help approximate overarching management (capital *T*, overarching) *T*ruth. It is my hope that the *EMT* facilitates this.

In summary, as I conclude this introduction, let me share with you that it has been a wonderful experience constructing the *Encyclopedia of Management Theory*. It has provided me with an opportunity to revisit (and apply) many concepts and explanations, reconnect with valued colleagues and connect with new ones, and learn much from the process. My invitation to you, the reader, is to look at the contents of this volume in a variety of ways. Take a basic look—familiarize yourself with the entries and acquire fundamental information about their models and modes. Take a deep look—really dig into the entries and suggested readings to analyze their logic and comprehend the images and principles that they advance about management reality. Take a hard look—assess the validity and importance of the theories (i.e., the trees) and critically evaluate their usefulness in explaining, predicting, and influencing management dynamics. Take a progressive look—move beyond consumer to use them as a platform for buttressing and extending our field. Take a broad look—see how they relate to each other (i.e., the forest) and might be integrated into a bigger, more holistic picture. Take a reflective look—think about how they can help you on a customized path of personal development and growth. Finally, take a practical look—actively apply them in an integrated, synergistic paradigm to manage for success.

Eric H. Kessler

ACADEMIC-PRACTITIONER COLLABORATION AND KNOWLEDGE SHARING

Academic-practitioner collaboration refers generally to relationships between academics and practitioners in which they share and/or co-construct knowledge with the purpose of creating positive scholarly, individual, and/or organizational outcomes. There are disagreements regarding the extent to which such collaboration can truly succeed. Nevertheless, attempts to create such collaboration take a wide variety of forms, several of which are described below. Academic-practitioner collaboration is particularly important in management. This is due in part to management faculty members serving as sources of managerial training and the multiple consultants who attempt to create bridges between academia and practice. It is also due to the fact that management is by its nature an applied field. It is also important for management theorizing, because the type of knowledge that arises from joint academic-practitioner research can be used for theory testing and building. This entry will include discussion of some barriers to successful collaboration and focus on several methods developed to accomplish it. These methods consist of multiple types of collaborative research approaches as well as bridging institutions, roles, and journals.

Fundamentals

There is ongoing disagreement among academics about the extent to which faculty can truly share research knowledge with management practitioners. There is also ongoing disagreement regarding whether rigorous scholarly research can or should be relevant to managers and other practitioners and whether or not rigor and relevance are mutually exclusive. Further, while both academics and practitioners theorize, the types of theorizing they do differs; academics attempt to create generalizable theorizing and knowledge, while practitioners attempt to create knowledge aimed at helping them succeed in their local situations.

Thus, there is recognition that academics (with regard to their research) and practitioners (with regard to their practice) typically have different aims and different communication systems. This difference is pronounced when the scholarship that academics conduct is based on a positivist epistemological framework. Some scholars believe that the communication systems associated with scientific research are so different from communication systems associated with successful practice that it is not possible to transfer knowledge between them.

Regardless of these tensions and disagreements, multiple means exist for trying to foster collaboration between academics and practitioners. These means rely on the assumption that knowledge truly can be transferred between, or translated across, academic-practitioner boundaries. But in order to accomplish successful translation, most of the means are also based on the assumption that there must be sharing of tacit, not just explicit, knowledge between academics and practitioners. This implies personal relationships between academics and practitioners.

Means that have been developed for academic-practitioner collaboration include multiple research approaches, including action research, insider-outsider team research, Mode 2 research, design science, engaged scholarship, and evidence-based management. The means also include types of bridging functions, including institutions, such as centers, bridging roles, and bridging journals.

Collaborative Research Methods

Action research. Action research is a research method developed originally in the 1940s by Kurt Lewin and colleagues. As originally designed, it involves participants in a social setting collaborating with an intervener, often an external researcher, in diagnosing problems in the setting, jointly constructing ways of assessing the problems and their causes, designing ways to ameliorate these, and assessing the impacts. The original assumption was that in addition to ameliorating the problems, scholarly writing about what had occurred would contribute to academic knowledge. Several means of conducting action research have developed in recent years, including action inquiry, action science, participatory action research, and participatory research. In recent decades, at least within management, focus has tended to be less on scholarly outcomes of action research than on impacts within organizational settings. Also in recent decades, there have been developments of action research, such as appreciative inquiry, that are based on beginning with the positive in a system rather than problems.

Insider/outsider team research. Insider/outsider team research is based on the recognition that insider members of a social setting, whose personally relevant world is under study, typically inquire about the setting differently than external researchers who are primarily concerned about developing generalizable knowledge. In insider/outsider team research insider members of a setting under study collaborate as coresearchers with external researchers throughout the stages of a research project. The assumption is that such heterogeneity in viewpoints and perspectives will contribute to more robust theorizing. Following this approach, insiders and outsiders determine together what should be studied about a setting, develop methods to carry out the study, collect and analyze data, and then communicate the findings in appropriate ways to both academic and practitioner audiences. While such research has been effective in many instances, it may evoke ethical dilemmas, especially if participants in a study do not feel comfortable about insider members of the setting knowing their views. It also requires insider members who are interested in contributing to scholarly knowledge in order to be effective.

Mode 2 research. Briefly, Mode 1 knowledge is what is typically created as a result of scientific research conducted by researchers within one discipline and not expected to have any direct relationship with practice. Mode 2 knowledge, in contrast, is transdisciplinary and emphasizes solutions to practical problems. Characteristics of Mode 2 research in management include knowledge produced in the context of application, transdisciplinarity and diversity among those involved in conducting the research project (including practitioner involvement throughout the project), and decisions about the quality of the research conducted based on how well it responds to the needs of all participants, not just scholars. This is potentially a valuable approach to research, although there are not many examples published in scholarly journals.

Design science. Herbert Simon distinguished between natural sciences and artificial, or design, sciences. He argued that natural sciences are concerned about how things are, while design sciences (including management) are concerned about how things ought to be. Thus, the purpose of design science should be to develop effective means of action. Some have referred to effective means of action as tested and "grounded" "rules" that enable managers and other practitioners to successfully address problems that they regularly encounter in their social settings. Following a design science approach, practitioners, likely collaborating with an external researcher, identify concerns and conduct real time experiments with various types of action that address these concerns. The academics work with the practitioners to compare the effectiveness of the various practices and to determine the underlying reasons that particular practices are more or less effective. On the basis of this analysis, academics and practitioners together develop rules for how to act in response to problems identified. Because design science is particularly concerned with improving practice, the validity of the knowledge developed is considered to be pragmatic. Whether the rules developed help practice is more important than whether they contribute to scholarly knowledge.

Engaged scholarship. Andrew Van de Ven developed engaged scholarship as a participative form of research aimed at obtaining the advice and perspectives of researchers, users, clients, sponsors, and practitioners to understand complex social problems. Various stakeholders may participate in one or more of four research activities that include grounding problem formulation in the real world, developing plausible alternative theories to address research questions, designing and carrying out research to evaluate the alternative models, and applying the research findings to resolve the issue being addressed. Van de Ven considered that informed basic research, informed collaborative research (such as insider/outsider team research), design research, and action research can all illustrate engaged scholarship as long as multiple sets of stakeholders have an opportunity to influence the research and its outcomes. The expectation is that these outcomes will benefit both scholarly knowledge and practice.

Evidence-based management. Building on earlier initiatives in medicine and social science, evidence-based approaches have begun to be developed for management. *Evidence-based medicine* refers to the development of systematic syntheses of what is known or not known about particular phenomena related to some area of medical practice. The syntheses typically build primarily on scholarly publications but also sometimes include skilled clinical judgment. *Evidence-based management* refers to translating principles based on best evidence into organizational practices. Thus, it also begins with the development of systematic syntheses of what is known about particular organizational topics and how what is known might inform effective action. It aims to help "evidence-based managers" make decisions that are informed by social science and organizational research and thus to close gaps between management research and practice.

For collaborative research to occur, organizations need to make participants (perhaps managers themselves, perhaps other organizational members) available to co-conduct research with appropriate academics. They also need to take steps to guard the confidentiality of individuals who contribute data. With regard to evidence-based approaches, they need to develop the capability of using evidence in practice.

Bridging Methods

In addition to these research approaches, there are several bridging functions that serve as links between academia and practice and are aimed at enabling collaboration. These include certain institutional settings, some individual roles, and some journals that consciously aim to bridge academic scholarship and practice.

Bridging institutions. Some centers have been created whose purpose includes linking scholarship and practice. Some that are particularly well known in management are the Center for Creative Leadership and the Center for Effective Organizations (CEO) at the University of Southern California. CEO, for example, conducts research that explicitly involves organizations in assessing how they can be more competitive and effective. It also conducts executive education programs based on the research that has been jointly conducted.

Bridging roles. There are some individual roles that bridge scholarship and practice. One of these roles is that of organization development practitioner, someone who, ideally, is familiar with both scholarly literature pertinent to organizational change and organizational processes as they occur in real time and who can comfortably speak in the languages of both academia and practice. Another role is that of the practitioner scholar. People who identify themselves as such typically work in organizational settings but also have advanced scholarly training, perhaps in executive doctoral programs.

Bridging journals. Some journals attempt to bridge scholarship and practice. One example is *Industrial and Organizational Psychology: Perspectives on Science and Practice.* This journal includes focal papers on topics of interest to both scholarship and practice. Both academics and practitioners respond to the papers. Further, both academics and practitioners publish in journals such as *Action Research* and the *International Journal of Action research.* In addition, *HR Magazine* includes some translations from academic writing to practitioner writing. At the time of this writing, repositories of evidence related to management practice are being developed. A new journal, the *International Journal of Management Reviews,* has begun publishing systematic reviews of research on particular organizational topics, and ways are being developed to provide practitioners access to academic databases.

Managers can take several steps to foster bridging methods. They can, for example, participate in the activities of bridging institutions, and they can read and, potentially, contribute to bridging journals. In some cases it would be appropriate for them to obtain executive doctorates.

Importance

The great majority of the methods described here have appeared and evolved over the course of the past quarter century, and illustrations of such methods expand in frequency yearly. Based on this growth, academic-practitioner collaboration is clearly growing in importance. There continue to be new approaches developed for collaborative research, and an increasing number of academic researchers are recognizing the value to be found in collaborating in research with organizational members.

In terms of bridging initiatives, the number of executive doctoral programs is expanding globally, and more and more managers are involved in evidence-based initiatives. In addition, evidence-based approaches have had impacts on teaching; more evidence-based information is being developed for classes and as reference materials.

Jean M. Bartunek

See also Action Research; Engaged Scholarship Model; Evidence-Based Management; Management (Education) as Practice; Organizational Development; Tacit Knowledge; Theory of Transfer of Training

Further Readings

Bartunek, J. M., & Louis, M. R. (1996). *Insider/outsider team research.* Thousand Oaks, CA: Sage.

Bennis, W. G., & O'Toole, P. (2005). How business schools lost their way. *Harvard Business Review, 83*(5), 96–104.

Kieser, A., & Leiner, L. (2009). Why the rigor–relevance gap in management research is unbridgeable. *Journal of Management Studies, 46,* 516–533.

Mohrman, S. A., & Lawler, E. E. (2011). *Useful research: Advancing theory and practice.* San Francisco, CA: Berrett-Koehler.

Rousseau, D. M., Manning, J., & Denyer, D. (2008). Evidence in management and organizational science: Assembling the field's full weight of scientific knowledge through syntheses. *Academy of Management Annals, 2*(1), 475–515.

Rynes, S., Bartunek, J., & Daft, R. (2001). Across the great divide: Knowledge creation and transfer between practitioners and academics. *Academy of Management Journal, 44,* 340–356.

Simon, H. A. (1969). *The sciences of the artificial.* Cambridge, MA: MIT Press.

Tranfield, D., & Starkey, K. (1998). The nature, social organization and promotion of management research: Towards policy. *British Journal of Management, 9,* 341–353.

Van Aken, J. E. (2004). Management research based on the paradigm of the design sciences: The quest for field tested and grounded technological rules. *Journal of Management Studies, 41,* 219–246.

Van de Ven, A. H. (2007). *Engaged scholarship: A guide for organizational and research knowledge.* New York, NY: Oxford University Press.

ACCULTURATION THEORY

When people of different cultures interact in an organization they bring with them different cultural beliefs and behaviors. These need to be understood and incorporated into organizational policies and practices in order to achieve effective operations. Since all countries (and most organizations) are now culturally diverse, this need for mutual understanding poses challenges that are often rooted in the outmoded belief that culturally different individuals and groups entering the organization are the only ones who need to change. However, the achievement of mutual accommodation requires that all participants accept the need to change; this is a prerequisite for effective operations in culturally diverse societies. This entry begins with an outline of the meaning of the concept and process of *acculturation,* and continues with a discussion of the various ways in which this process is carried out (termed *acculturation strategies*). The long-term outcome of this process is a variable degree of mutual *adaptation* among the individuals and groups in contact. The entry concludes with some implications.

Fundamentals

The core meaning of acculturation refers to the process of cultural and psychological change that takes place as a result of contact between cultural groups and their individual members. Such contact and change occur for many reasons (such as colonization and migration); it continues after initial contact in culturally plural societies, where ethnocultural communities maintain features of their heritage cultures over generations; and it takes place in both groups in contact. *Adaptation* refers to the longer term outcomes of the process of acculturation. Occasionally, it is stressful, but usually it results in some form of mutual accommodation between groups and among individuals. The initial interest in acculturation examined the effects of European domination of colonial and indigenous peoples. Later, it focused on how immigrants (both voluntary and involuntary) changed following their entry and settlement into receiving societies. More recently, much of the work has been involved with how ethnocultural groups and individuals relate to each other, and how they change, as a result of their attempts to live together in culturally plural societies. Nowadays, all three foci are important areas of research, as globalization results in ever-larger trading and political relations. The concept of *psychological acculturation* refers to changes in an individual who is a participant in a culture-contact situation, being influenced both directly by the external (usually dominant) culture and by the changing culture (usually nondominant) of which the individual is a member. There are two reasons for keeping the cultural and psychological levels distinct. The first is that in cross-cultural psychology, individual human behavior is viewed as interacting with the cultural context within which it occurs; hence, separate conceptions and measurements are required at the two levels. The second reason is that not every group or individual enters into, participates in, or changes in the same way; there are vast group and individual differences in psychological acculturation, even among people who live in the same acculturative arena.

A framework that outlines and links cultural and psychological acculturation, and identifies the two (or more) groups in contact, provides a map of those phenomena which need to be conceptualized and measured during acculturation research. At the cultural level, researchers need to examine key features of the two original cultural groups prior to their major contact. It is essential to understand this precontact variation among the groups that are now attempting to live together in a larger society. New settlers bring cultural and psychological qualities with them to the new society, and the existing society also has a variety of such qualities. The compatibility (or incompatibility) in such qualities as religion, values, attitudes, and personality between the two cultural communities that are in contact needs to be examined as a basis for understanding the acculturation process that is set in motion in both groups. It is also important to understand the nature of their contact relationships. It may be one of domination of one group over the other or of mutual respect or hostility. Finally, at the cultural level, researchers need to understand the resulting cultural changes in both groups that emerge during the process of acculturation. No cultural group remains unchanged following culture contact; acculturation is a two-way interaction, resulting in actions and reactions to the contact situation. In many cases, most change takes place in nondominant communities. However, all societies of settlement (particularly their metropolitan cities) have experienced massive transformations following years of receiving new settlers. The gathering of this information requires extensive ethnographic, community-level work. These changes can range from minor to substantial and from being easily accomplished through to being a source of major cultural disruption.

At the individual level, there is a need to consider the psychological changes that individuals in all groups undergo and to examine their eventual adaptation to their new situations. These changes can be a set of rather easily accomplished behavioral shifts (e.g., in ways of speaking, dressing, and eating), or they can be more problematic, producing acculturative stress as manifested by uncertainty, anxiety, and depression. As noted by Ward (2001), adaptations can be primarily internal or psychological (e.g., sense of well-being or self-esteem) or sociocultural (e.g., as manifested in competence in the activities of daily intercultural living). The first refers to "feeling well," the second to "doing well." Much of this research on acculturation can be found in *The Cambridge Handbook of Acculturation Psychology* (2006).

Acculturation Strategies

As noted above, not every group or individual engages the acculturation process in the same way. The concept of *acculturation strategies* refers to the various ways that groups and individuals seek to acculturate. These variations have challenged the assumption that everyone would assimilate and become absorbed into the dominant group. At the cultural level, the two groups in contact (whether dominant or nondominant) usually have some notion about what they are attempting to do (e.g., colonial policies). At the individual level, persons will vary within their cultural group (e.g., on the basis of their educational or occupational background).

Four acculturation strategies have been derived from two basic issues facing all acculturating peoples. These issues are based on the distinction between orientations toward one's own group and those toward other groups in the larger society. This distinction is rendered as a relative preference for maintaining one's heritage culture and identity and a relative preference for having contact with and participating in the larger society along with other ethnocultural groups. These two issues can be responded to on attitudinal dimensions, varying along bipolar dimensions ranging from positive to negative preferences. It has now been well demonstrated that these two dimensions are independent of each other. Hence, these two dimensions are presented orthogonally in Figure 1. On the left side are the orientations held by members of ethnocultural groups; on the right side are the views held by members of the larger society.

Orientations to these issues intersect to define four acculturation strategies. For members of nondominant ethnocultural groups, when these individuals do not wish to maintain their cultural identity and seek daily interaction with other cultures, the *assimilation* strategy is defined. In contrast, when individuals place a value on holding on to their original culture, and at the same time wish to avoid interaction with others, then the *separation* alternative is defined. When there is an interest in both maintaining ones original culture, while in daily interactions with other groups, *integration* is the option. In this case, there is some degree of cultural

integrity maintained, while at the same time seeking, as a member of an ethnocultural group, to participate as an integral part of the larger social network. Finally, when there is little possibility or interest in cultural maintenance (often for reasons of enforced cultural loss), and little interest in having relations with others (often for reasons of exclusion or discrimination), then *marginalization* is defined.

The original definition clearly established that both groups in contact would change and become acculturated. The four terms used above described the acculturation strategies of nondominant peoples. Different terms are needed to describe the strategies of the dominant larger society and are presented on the right side of Figure 1. Assimilation when sought by the dominant group is termed the *melting pot*. When separation is forced by the dominant group, it is *segregation*. Marginalization, when imposed by the dominant group, is *exclusion*. Finally, for integration, when diversity is a widely accepted feature of the society as a whole, it is called *multiculturalism*. With the use of these concepts and measures, comparisons can be made between individuals and their groups, and between nondominant peoples and the larger society within which they are acculturating.

The acculturation strategies (including the ideologies and policies) of the larger society, as well as the preferences of nondominant peoples, are core features in acculturation research. Inconsistencies and conflicts between these various acculturation preferences are common sources of difficulty for those experiencing acculturation. This can occur when individuals do not accept the main ideology of their society (for example, when individuals oppose immigrant cultural maintenance in a society where multiculturalism is official policy or when immigrant children challenge the way of acculturating set out by their parents). Generally, when acculturation experiences cause problems for acculturating individuals, researchers observe the phenomenon of acculturative stress, with variations in levels of adaptation.

Importance

Much research has shown that those seeking the integration way of acculturating (i.e., maintaining a double cultural engagement) achieve the best psychological and sociocultural adaptations, while those who are marginalized have the poorest outcomes. Assimilation and separation strategies are typically associated with intermediate levels of

Figure 1   Acculturation Strategies in Ethnocultural Groups and the Larger Society

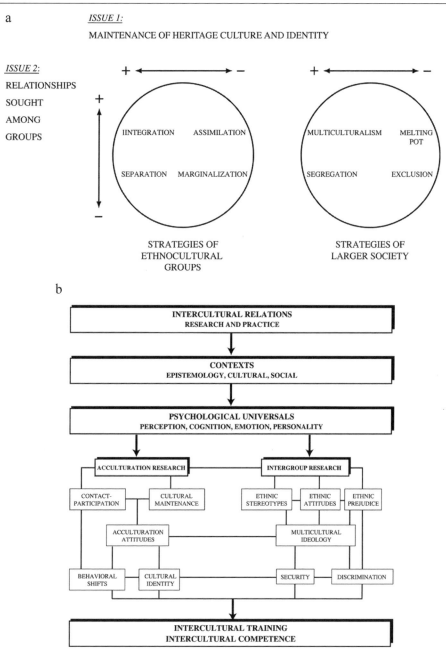

Source: Author.

adaptation. The example of immigrant youth clearly illustrates this pattern.

The implications of knowing about and using the three core concepts (acculturation, acculturation strategies, and mutual adaptation) are that in culturally diverse organizations, these ideas, and the research based upon them, impact on how and how well management and employees engage

each other across cultural boundaries. In particular, knowing the benefits of pursuing and achieving integration, the integration strategy (defined here as the joint involvement in both cultural contexts) is far-reaching for those engaged in intercultural living. Managers and their families who are posted to another country need to be informed of the advantages of the integration acculturation strategy, both prior to departure (through training programs) and during their sojourn (through social and cultural supports). Employees (and their families) who have immigrated to the society can also benefit from being made aware of the benefits of integration. In both cases, there is much to be gained for managing all levels of personnel by creating programs to train and support those who are experiencing acculturation.

John W. Berry

See also Equity Theory; Managing Diversity; Organizational Culture Model; Organizational Culture Theory; Social Identity Theory

Further Readings

Berry, J. W. (2005). Acculturation: Living successfully in two cultures. *International Journal of Intercultural Relations, 29*, 697–712.

Berry, J. W. (2008). Globalization and acculturation. *International Journal of Intercultural Relations, 32*, 328–336.

Berry, J. W., Phinney, J. S., Sam, D. L., & Vedder, P. (Eds.). (2006). Immigrant youth in cultural transition: Acculturation, identity, and adaptation across national contexts. Mahwah, NJ: Lawrence Erlbaum.

Berry, J. W., Poortinga, Y. H., Breugelmans, S. M., Chasiotis, A., & Sam, D. L. (2011). *Cross-cultural psychology: Research and applications* (3rd ed.). Cambridge, England: Cambridge University Press.

Liebkind, K. (2001). Acculturation. In R. Brown & S. Gaertner (Eds.), *Blackwell handbook of social psychology, Vol. IV* (pp. 386–406). Oxford, England: Blackwell.

Redfield, R., Linton, R., & Herskovits, M. J. (1936). Memorandum on the study of acculturation. *American Anthropologist, 38*, 149–152.

Sam, D. L., & Berry, J. W. (Eds.). (2006). *The Cambridge handbook of acculturation psychology*. Cambridge, England: Cambridge University Press.

Ward, C. (2001). The A, B, Cs of acculturation. In D. Matsumoto (Ed.), *The handbook of culture and psychology* (pp. 411–445). Oxford, England: Oxford University Press.

ACHIEVEMENT MOTIVATION THEORY

The achievement motive, as originally framed by David McClelland, refers to a recurrent desire to excel. This achievement motivation theory is important for predicting management success and as such is an essential part of management theory. Such motivation is especially found in managers who are striving for personal accomplishment. As David McClelland suggested, managers scoring high on achievement motivation are managers who are more self-confident, who enjoy taking calculated risks, and who are actively pursuing activities that involve initiating structure, as compared with managers scoring low on achievement motivation. In this entry, the focus is first on how achievement motivation can predict management success. Achievement motivation can be studied from an individual perspective—how it works out for managers. As will be shown, the Thematic Apperception Test (TAT) can be used to measure achievement motivation. Next is an argument that it is also possible to study it from a cultural perspective, and in our globalizing world, it will be increasingly important to know how achievement motivation works out in different cultures. In the final portion of this entry, the focus will be on issues related to acquired motives and how these need be taken into account when designing global selection and assessment practices of managers.

Fundamentals

Achievement motivation goes back to McClelland's theory on acquired motives and has its roots in Henry Murray's needs theory. McClelland's theory focuses on a set of clearly defined motives as they relate to workplace behaviors.

In the acquired motives theory, three basic motives are distinguished: the achievement motive, the affiliation motive, and the power motive. Achievement motivation (nAch) arises from the desire to do something better or more efficiently, to solve problems, or to master complex tasks. The need for affiliation (nAff) comes from the desire to establish and maintain friendly and warm relationships with others. The need for power (nPower) emanates from the desire to control others and to influence their behavior. Whereas managers scoring high on need for power seek to influence others, managers scoring high on achievement motivation are more interested in how well they personally are doing. In this entry, the focus is specifically on one of the three motives from this theory: the achievement motive.

Achievement motivation can indeed predict managerial success later in time. In a longitudinal study, David McClelland and Richard Boyatzis found that the motive to achieve was associated with success at higher levels of nontechnical management. More than 200 managers from the American Telephone and Telegraph Company filled out a survey measuring all sorts of variables, including achievement motivation, and correlated these results with the levels of promotion attained after 8 and 16 years. Indeed, achievement motivation was associated with success. However, the results were not really straightforward. Only at lower managerial levels was it shown that achievement motivation was more important than the ability to influence people to predict managerial success. An explanation for this could be that success at the lower managerial levels is more dependent on individual contributions than it is at the higher managerial levels. Conversely, at the higher managerial levels, upward mobility is more dependent on demonstrated ability to manage others than on achievement motivation.

In developing his theory of human motivation, it was stressed that motives are acquired and can be learned. Hence, David McClelland refers to a language of achievement. In training programs for managerial effectiveness, it is thus important to have managers learn to think and perceive themselves as persons with a high achievement potential. That is, managers need to learn to use the language of achievement so that it signifies their work experiences. Moreover, managers can learn to distinguish achievement goals from other motives to boost their personal effectiveness.

Achievement motivation is not only an individual level construct. Over the past three decades, there has been growing interest in whether (achievement) managerial motivation differs across cultures. For such a concern, studies need to go beyond individual-level analyses of motives and have to examine the cultural embeddedness (at the societal or national level) and aggregate level personality differences underlying acquired motives. Studies of this nature are important because in an increasingly global environment, it is helpful to examine how and under what circumstances motives develop and are nurtured across cultures and how they become salient within organizations and teams. Furthermore, cross-cultural adjustment of employees in the global context may depend on the match between specific individual (achievement) motives on the one hand and personality profiles and cultural embeddedness in countries on the other hand. As a global working

environment becomes the norm, cross-cultural studies of this type become increasingly important and research may help to improve our understanding of the development of acquired motives in different cultures.

In his 1961 *The Achieving Society*, David McClelland extended achievement motivation from the individual to the societal level by arguing that some societies place a far greater emphasis on achievement than others. In addition, he asserted that societies characterized by high achievement motives enjoy higher levels of entrepreneurship and economic development. Despite the intuitive appeal of McClelland's arguments, Geert Hofstede did not conceptualize or measure a corresponding cultural dimension in developing his model of cross-cultural work values. However, more recently, the Global Leadership and Organizational Behavior Effectiveness research project, or GLOBE study, indeed included a measure—performance orientation—that refers to achievement motivation. This dimension is defined as the extent to which national cultures encourage and reward people for superior performance and excellence. Societies that score high as opposed to low on performance orientation tend to emphasize results more than people; reward performance, value assertiveness, competitiveness, and materialism; expect demanding targets; reward individual achievement; and have appraisal systems that emphasize results. Given this conceptualization and its roots in the notion of the achievement motive, the GLOBE study researchers explored the extent to which these constructs are related using the societal level measure of achievement motivation and the GLOBE Performance Orientation Society Practices and Society Values scales. Hetty van Emmerik and colleagues, rather than testing achievement motivation exclusively at the societal level, employed a cross-level model to explore the relationship between societal-level performance orientation and individual-level achievement motives. Specifically, a reciprocal relationship between individual level achievement motives and performance orientation was suggested. That is, the level of achievement motivation reflected by a society relates to the emphasis placed on performance achievements over time. At the same time, because McClelland's theory focuses on motives that are acquired through learning, the emphasis that a society places on performance is posited to shape the achievement needs of its members. Indeed, consistent with expectations, evidence was obtained that managers from cultures that place a high emphasis on performance have relatively high achievement motives. Management scholars are encouraged to broaden this stream of research to consider other characteristics that may account for the emergence and influence of achievement motivation in different cultures.

McClelland's work on assessing motives has employed the Thematic Apperception Test (TAT) or Picture Story Exercise (PSE). The TAT is a projective measure designed to assess the implicit motives of individuals. The PSE, a refinement of the TAT, was developed by David McClelland to assess individual differences in human motivation.

In administering the TAT, respondents are asked to view pictures and write stories about what they see. For instance, in one case, David McClelland showed executives a photograph of a man sitting down and looking at family photos arranged on his work desk. Typically, respondents are presented six or more standard TAT cards. Such TAT cards can depict different situations, for instance, "an architect at a desk," "women in a lab," "ship captain," "a couple by a river," "trapeze artists," and "nightclub scene." When presenting the TAT pictures (called cards), a set of questions guide the respondent in writing a short story. The stories are then coded and the implicit motives are assessed. Although the TAT has received criticism and is time consuming to both administer and score, it was argued convincingly that when the TAT is properly administered, the scores have adequate test-retest reliability.

All TAT stories are to be scored for achievement, affiliation, and power motive imagery by specifically trained scorers with materials precoded by experts and according to the TAT protocol. The TAT protocol is the tool used to interpret the motives revealed via the stories of the respondents. After scoring, the values can be summed for each of the three motives for the six pictures and used for individual managerial assessment.

Proponents of the TAT have argued that the TAT is a valuable measure of achievement motivation. The TAT and PSE have been used at length in many cross-cultural studies, and these measures can be meaningfully used to understand and predict human behavior. However, opponents of the TAT have argued that the TAT is not a valid measure. To solve this controversy, William Spangler conducted two

meta-analyses on 105 selected empirical research articles. He found that correlations between TAT measures of need for achievement and a variety of outcomes were on average positive. Moreover, these associations were sufficiently large for mobility-related outcomes, such as career success, and larger than for survey-based designs.

Importance

McClelland's theory has been used extensively in management and leadership studies of motivation. Many studies have been conducted within managerial, entrepreneurial, and leadership contexts that look at the importance of motives. In addition, the acquired motives theory has also been used in various studies in a cross-cultural context. Consistent with the ideas of acquired needs theory, extensive empirical evidence indeed has demonstrated that achievement motivation is positively related to employees' and managerial job performance, organizational commitment, extrarole behavior, and job involvement. Together, these empirical findings provide support for the notion that achievement motivation is a drive to achieve and excel and may produce higher levels of job involvement, commitment, entrepreneurship, and intra- and extrarole performance at the individual level.

It is important to stress that acquired motives are based on the conceptualization of motives as being learned. Thus, they are posited to vary in strength among individuals as a function of their socialization and as being rooted in a specific culture. Culture shapes the values and norms of its members; these values are shared and transmitted from one generation to another through social learning processes of modeling and observation. Conceptualizing the motives as learned also means that the motives are sensitive to (leadership) training.

Today, mergers across borders, collaborations, and relocation decisions are becoming common experiences for many employees, creating challenges to employee integration within the organization as well as knowledge transfer. However, what has not changed is that people still are attracted to work environments that are compatible with their personality characteristics and that match their own pattern of acquired motives. National culture does matter, and there are likely to be certain circumstances where it matters more and others where it matters less. By considering the interactive effects of national culture and acquired motives, such as achievement motivation, more insight can be gained on how, when, and why motives vary across cultural contexts.

Acquired motives, such as the achievement motivation, are important and to be taken into account when designing global selection and assessment practices of managers. A recent study of Hetty van Emmerik and colleagues showed that acquired motives can be a useful part of personnel selection within a global context. Achievement motivation and other motives then should be considered when designing global selection and assessment practices. Given the relationships of acquired motives to a variety of behavioral and social outcomes, the assessment of motives may be particularly useful in assessing reactions to different situations thus providing a way for organizations to identify potential areas of conflict or concern. However, more work is still welcome on the unexplored relationships between universal motives, such as achievement motivation, and associations with effectiveness in the work situation.

Hetty van Emmerik and Merel M. S. Kats

See also Authentic Leadership; Big-Five Personality Dimensions; Cultural Values; Leadership Practices; Multilevel Research; Social Power, Bases of; Trait Theory of Leadership; Type A Personality Theory

Further Readings

Hofstede, G. (1980). Culture's consequences, international differences in work-related values. Thousand Oaks, CA: Sage.

House, R. J., Hanges, P. J., Javidan, M., Dorfman, P. W., & Gupta, V. (2004). *Culture, leadership, and organizations.* The GLOBE Study of 62 Societies. London, England: Sage.

McClelland, D. C. (1961). *The achieving society.* Princeton, NJ: Van Nostrand.

McClelland, D. C., & Boyatzis, R. E. (1982). Leadership motive pattern and long-term success in management. *Journal of Applied Psychology, 67*(6), 737–743.

Spangler, W. D. (1992). Validity of questionnaire and TAT measures of need for achievement: Two meta-analyses. *Psychological Bulletin, 112,* 140–154.

van Emmerik, I. J. H., Gardner, W. L., Wendt, H., & Fischer, D. (2010). Associations of culture and personality with McClelland's motives: A cross-cultural study of managers in 24 countries. *Group & Organization Management, 35,* 329–367.

ACTION LEARNING

Action learning is a learning approach to developing organizational members' competencies both in content knowledge and process skills in the process of solving real, difficult management issues using teams. Action learning is among the most widely used interventions for leadership and organizational development. The popularity of action learning has been driven by related, tangible outcomes and relevance to real organizational issues using teams in organizations. In this entry will be provided the fundamentals of action learning, the importance of action learning research and practice, and a list for further reading to better understand action learning.

Fundamentals

Action learning's founding father Reginald Revans first used the term "action learning" in published form in 1972, though he had already been implementing action learning since the 1940s. A prime difficulty in researching action learning is the lack of an agreed-upon definition. Revans did not define action learning but described it in terms of what it is not (e.g., a case study, consulting, or a task force), because he believed that to define it would constrain its meaning. As a result, many definitions and variants of action learning have been used, including business-driven action learning, critical action learning, work-based learning, self-managed action learning, and virtual action learning.

Various frameworks have been used to analyze action learning projects; however, many of these focus on the combination of two consistent themes: real, work-based issues and team learning. Action learning is based on the pedagogical notion that people learn most effectively when working on real-time problems occurring in their own work settings. Participants in action learning environments learn as they work by taking time to reflect with peers (learning teams), giving team members opportunity to offer insights into each other's workplace problems. And participants learn best when they reflect together with like-minded colleagues, "comrades in adversity" in Revans's terms, on real problems occurring in their own organizations.

Based on our collective experience in action learning practice and research, we have identified five core elements of action learning that, if seamlessly intertwined, would promote participants' learning and deliver quality solutions as intended. First, action learning is based on team learning. The key to action learning involves participants and teams. A team consists of five to six participants because the team size should ensure diverse perspectives and prevent free riders. Participants' jobs, educational backgrounds, experience, cultures and nationalities, and genders should be factored in to realize diversity in action learning.

Second, action learning revolves around a project to maximize the effectiveness of learning. A project should be something to add value to the organization and should be difficult for participants to solve because adult learners learn best while solving real world problems. There are two types of projects in action learning: individual projects and team projects. In an individual project, participants provide insightful questions, advice, and information to assist other participants with a problem in the problem-solving process and to enhance their learning. In a team project, participants collectively work on one project to solve issues at work for the organization's competitive advantage.

Third, participants enhance their competencies both in content knowledge (information and know-how) and process skills (varied techniques and tools) in the action learning process. Participants learn both explicit and tacit knowledge that are required to solve problems in order to identify customer's needs through the benchmarks of best practices developed by competitors and industries as well as by internal experts. Participants, through teamwork, also learn how to use varied tools and techniques for communication, decision making, problem solving, and conflict management as well as for leadership skills. Many companies in the world, therefore, use action learning for talent development and for preparing future leaders.

Fourth, action learning encourages questioning, reflection, and feedback to generate transformational learning and effective solutions through problem solving in the process. Participants ask questions and reflect on what to know, how to improve teamwork, how to better solve problems, and how to maximize learning in the process. Participants also ensure the quality of learning and the process through peer and external feedback. With respect to the relationship between questioning and knowledge

in action learning, Revans emphasized that learning (L) is maximized if programmed knowledge (P) is combined with questioning (Q). In his action learning formula, "$L = P + Q$," questioning insight is more important than knowledge acquisition. The key to learning is in finding the right question to ask. Questions that help people to get started along this path include: What are we trying to do? What is stopping us from doing it? What can we do about it?

Fifth, internal or external learning coaches are used to provide help for those who are not familiar with problem-solving processes, questioning, reflection, and feedback. Learning coaches are those who oversee the quality of team processes and learning through the use of effective communications, collective decision making, problem solving, and conflict management tools and techniques. Practitioners should limit a learning coach's role to be a process facilitator so that she or he does not intervene in the learning team's content knowledge.

A critical issue involved in action learning regards the balancing act of action and learning in the action learning process. Revans, in 1998, emphasized the need for conceptual and practical balance between action and learning in his well-known remark, "There is no action without learning and there is no learning without action" (p. 83). The real value of action learning that differentiates it from other action strategies is a pragmatic focus on learning for the sake of problem solving. Through a balanced process of action and learning, people often develop skills associated with how to better learn from their experiences. An unbalanced approach to action learning, therefore, is not productive, as action without learning is unlikely to return fruitful longer term results, and learning without action does not facilitate change.

In reality, action learning programs have a tendency either to foster action at the expense of learning or to be oriented to learning instead of balancing learning with action. Ideally, "action" (i.e., outcomes and solutions) in action learning is not the goal, but it should be the means by which learning is achieved. As of late, a greater emphasis has been put on learning-oriented action learning. This latter finding is consistent with that of previous studies indicating that action learning practices are more often perceived to be successful when aimed toward personal growth and learning but not necessarily conducted toward organizational learning and development. Without knowledge about organization-level development and change, action learning practitioners may not consider ways that action learning efforts can be applied to their specific job and organizational contexts.

Despite the lack of an agreed-upon definition of action learning, there are certain basic concepts to be recognized no matter what form of action learning practitioners want to deliver. At the same time, there must be cultural and contextual constraints so that action learning needs to be continually revised and modified. For example, the use of a learning coach that Revans strongly rejected in action learning may be necessary in other cultures where a learning coach is very welcome in the action learning process. The active use of a learning coach fundamentally violates one of Revans's basic principles on the role of a learning coach. Revans made it clear that only in the early stage is a learning coach needed to launch action learning but she or he must eventually get out of the action learning team to avoid getting in the way. However, learning coaches—those who are selected from the talent pool—can enhance their facilitative leadership by tackling organizational issues as well as guiding participants. Selecting competent learning coaches is a key success factor for action learning. As a result, we face a tough challenge that has to strike a balance between continuing Revans's gold standards and customizing action learning in order to meet the requirements of cultural contexts.

Importance

The action-learning balance issue stands out not only as a major consideration for action learning but also as an important lens through which to examine the action learning literature. An examination of balanced action learning approaches can be achieved through evaluation of action learning processes, participant experiences, and the manner in which action learning is framed in the literature. Individuals and organizations are aided by action learning that leads to more effective communication, work climate, cooperation, shared vision, and development at the organization level. When used appropriately in organizational contexts, balanced action learning can be a powerful approach for management development.

When it comes to the improvement of management practice, the impact of action learning can be summarized as follows: First, action learning overcomes fundamental limitations of existing experiential learning methods (e.g., business simulation and role playing) that separate the place where learning occurs and the place where the learning is applied from a learning transfer perspective. Action learning provides a realistic, practical alternative because participants tackle real problems at work in the learning process; it can be more cost-effective in terms of the organization's training investment.

Second, action learning is an outstanding tool for establishing a learning organization through sharing organizational members' experience and know-how. Action learning presents practical approaches for realizing a learning organization or knowledge management in complicated and changing management environments, which will eventually lead to the organization's and organizational members' competitive advantage.

Third, action learning fundamentally changes managers' existing views of learning and of the participants who are attempting to solve the problem. Instead of depending on management consultants to solve problems at work for the organization, organizational members (managers and employees) solve the problems by themselves and build their competencies in the learning process. Participating companies using action learning would slowly decrease their dependence on external consultants.

There are two implications for managers and human resources (HR), both of whom are participating stakeholders in action learning. HR no longer teaches content knowledge, know-how, and information but plays the role of a learning coach or facilitator who would guide and encourage learners to identify problems, use problem-solving tools, and enhance competencies and skills. Participants will build problem-solving and leadership skills in ways that (a) help them learn the problem-solving process by themselves and do not rely on external consultants, (b) allow them to not just propose solutions but also to implement what they've proposed, (c) help them build competencies through questions and reflection, and (d) allow them to enhance their leadership skills by experiencing effective teamwork in the process.

Current practice-based approaches to action learning focus only on face validity for action learning theory; therefore, wider consideration regarding current approaches and their impact is required.

Future research into the processes and outcomes of action learning that strikes the right balance is likely to serve as a catalyst for its diffusion and adoption. Also required is the need to see the cultural differences of action learning practices in order to consider both the continuation of Revans's gold standards and the customization of action learning in diverse contexts.

Yonjoo Cho and Hyeon-Cheol Bong

See also Action Research; Learning Organization; Organizational Development; Organizational Learning; Quality Circles; Strategic Groups

Further Readings

Boshyk, Y., & Dilworth, R. L. (Eds.). (2010). *Action learning: History and evolution.* Hampshire, England: Palgrave Macmillan.

Cho, Y., & Bong, H.-C. (2011). Action learning for organization development in South Korea. In M. Pedler (Ed.), *Action Learning in Practice* (4th ed., pp. 249–260). Hampshire, England: Gower.

Cho, Y., Egan, T. M. (2009). Action learning research: A systematic review and conceptual framework. *Human Resource Development Review, 8*(4), 431–462.

Marquardt, M., & Banks, S. (Eds.). (2010). Theory to practice: Action learning [Special issue]. *Advances in Developing Human Resources, 12*(2), 159–162.

O'Neil, J., & Marsick, V. J. (2007). *Understanding action learning.* New York, NY: AMACOM.

Pedler, M., Burgoyne, J., & Brook, C. (2005). What has action learning learned to become? *Action Learning: Research and Practice, 2*(1), 49–68.

Raelin, J. A. (2008). *Work-based learning: Bridging knowledge and action in the workplace.* San Francisco, CA: Jossey-Bass.

Revans, R. (1972). Action learning—A management development program. *Personnel Review, 1,* 36–44.

Revans, R. (1998). *ABC of action learning.* London, England: Lemos & Crane.

ACTION RESEARCH

Action research (AR) refers to a cycle of data-based problem solving that emerges from the process of scientific investigation. In contrast to traditional scientific research, where the main challenge is to study and understand the problem, action research examines the problem and then develops interventions to solve that problem. Emphasis is placed on collaborative inquiry between researchers and participants that involves a continuously unfolding interplay between data gathering and diagnosis, feedback and joint action planning, action (solution) and assessment, continued data gathering and diagnosis, additional feedback and continued joint action planning, revised actions (solutions), and so forth. The underlying philosophy is that change is successful when the groups and individuals who are involved in a change play an active role in the decision-making process that determines what that change might be and how it might be implemented. Sometimes referred to as participatory action research, the technique is intended to advance theory and practice, contributing to human insights into and understanding of broader organizational dynamics while simultaneously enabling us to improve specific situations. This entry examines the fundamentals underlying the AR process, how it has evolved over the years, and its ongoing influence and importance for contemporary management practice.

Fundamentals

Action research is a holistic approach to problem solving rather than a single method for collecting and analyzing data. The data-gathering phases in the AR process typically involve a combination of methods, from surveys and questionnaires, to interviews and observations, to unobtrusive measures (e.g., archival measures, such as turnover rates, absenteeism, quality statistics). Based on the understanding that all data-collection approaches have strengths and limitations, AR typically involves triangulation across methods and forms of data. For example, while surveys and questionnaires are useful to gauge the attitudes, beliefs, and values of a particular population, since they are typically self-administered, there is no way to probe the information more fully. Thus, follow-up interviews, though more expensive and time consuming, can be used to probe and examine attitudes and opinions about various issues, which can often help to clarify causal relationships. At the same time, what people might say they would do in a particular situation might not necessarily correspond to their actual behavior. Thus, observing people in their work-related roles can provide further insight into those behaviors. Observation, however, is subject to researchers' own perceptual biases—in essence, what humans "see" is influenced by their own feelings and biases. Thus, given these potential problems and limitations, an underlying key is that AR researchers should complement their data-collection efforts, checking the findings generated by one data-collection method with the data presented by another. Emphasis is placed on creating as complete a picture as possible on specific organizational situations, generating data on what organizational members think, feel, and do; drawing out how they work and the tasks they perform and their outcomes; and noting the relationships they develop with their coworkers.

Action research is not intended as a one-time event, which ends when a particular problem is solved and change is brought about. Instead, it is seen as an ongoing process to enhance organizational functioning by generating knowledge that is both valid and vital to the long-term well-being of organizations and their members. It is a progressive problem-solving approach that enables organizational members to develop a deeper understanding of the ways in which a variety of social and environmental forces interact to create complex organizational patterns. By involving participants in the entire process, from the initial design of the project through data gathering and analysis to initial conclusions and actions arising out of the research, AR designers create a foundation for continuous improvement and development. Each iteration adds to our understanding of the group or organization, the way in which it operates, challenges it faces, and ways of achieving its envisioned future.

A key tenet of AR is that human systems can be truly understood and changed only when one engages members of that system in the inquiry process. Within the AR paradigm, knowledge is understood as socially constructed, as assumptions, goals, actions, and outcomes are seen as located within complex social systems. Knowledge, therefore, is inherently social and embedded in practice. It is only through continuous dialogue and reflection among participants that the realities of organizational life can be uncovered and improved.

In addition to AR at the group or organization level, it can also be applied to individual learning. First-person AR takes place within oneself, where the researcher applies the process to him- or herself, examining and reflecting on one's own skills, abilities, knowledge, and identity. This process—raising such questions as Who am I? What frameworks are influencing my thinking? What is happening within me?—is captured in Donald Schön's 1983 notion of the "reflective practitioner," where the researcher develops the ability to reflect both *on* and *in* practice.

AR research is embedded within a system of values—for example, self-awareness, integrity, collaboration, commitment, authenticity, and empowerment—and the process used to create greater convergence between the values we as researchers espouse and those we enact in practice. Underlying the core shared values in the AR process is respect for others' knowledge and insight and the ability of participants to understand and address issues and challenges facing them and their organizations.

In helping to formulate principles of intervention, action research has long served as a core part of the foundation for the theory and practice of organization development (OD). The goal is to enhance group and organizational effectiveness, creating the basis for positive change and healthy work places. Through continuous questioning and reflection—for example, by asking, What is causing the problem? over and over again—the process facilitates the ability of participants to go beyond the tendency to deal with symptoms of problems and move toward the root problem itself. Once this is determined, appropriate interventions—from human process (e.g., team building, intergroup confrontation meetings) and human resource management (e.g., goal setting, performance appraisal) interventions to technostructural (e.g., cross-functional task forces, work redesign) and strategic (e.g., open-systems planning, search conference, large-scale change) interventions—can be determined, tested, and revised as necessary.

Over the past several decades, the AR process has been well documented in a broad range of institutional settings, from industrial workplaces and postindustrial offices to community associations, schools, hospitals and the clergy. It has also influenced the development of a range of related intervention techniques, from action learning and clinical inquiry to community engagement initiatives and appreciative inquiry as well as a general shift to doing research *with* people rather than simply doing research for or on them.

Evolution

Action research has a complex history with contributions from an array of fields and social science domains, including education, psychology, sociology, and cultural anthropology, and a number of traditions within management and organizational research, including T-groups, sociotechnical systems and Eric Trist's work with the Tavistock Institute, and workplace democracy initiatives. The AR method itself has its roots in Kurt Lewin's seminal work on social change during the 1940s as he sought to improve intergroup relations. Lewin stressed the role that research should play in providing the basis for social action, guiding the resolution of social and organizational issues in concert with the individuals and groups experiencing those issues. He conceptualized a science of action based on an iterative and collaborative process of creating change (identifying and solving a problem) through planning, data gathering, action, assessment (fact finding) of that action, feedback to participants, and then using that insight for further planning and action. Emphasizing the application of scientific inquiry in examining both general laws of behavior (group life) and the diagnosis of specific situations, Lewin's work reflected the essence of what is today referred to as actionable knowledge, linking theory development with practical knowing as a basis for improving group and organizational situations and performance. Embedded in this approach is Lewin's conceptualization of the change process, initially "unfreezing" the situation (establishing the need for change, overcoming inner resistance), moving or changing it (influencing new behaviors through cognitive restructuring, re-education), and then "refreezing" the intended change in its broader social context (integration of those new behaviors into social and organizational relationships).

As classical action research was further developed in the 1960s and 1970s, the process developed a basic set of cyclical patterns, embodying the ongoing interaction between behavioral science researchers and their clients, stressing collaboration on identifying problems, collecting valid information on those problems, and analyzing that data to better understand the challenges faced by the organization and its members. Building on Lewin's earlier work, Chris Argyris and colleagues developed the notion of action science, distinguishing between espoused theory, which is conscious and something we are able to articulate when asked (e.g., describing behaviors that we want to emulate), and one's theory-in-use (i.e., those views and perspectives that actually shape our behavior, which we are not fully conscious of because they are so ingrained in us). Focus continued to be placed on change experiments involving real problems in actual social systems, examining a specific issue, seeking to offer assistance to the participants, working with them to resolve the issue, and generating broader insights that would further develop our theories and understanding of group and organizational life. The active and conscious participation of the groups and individuals in the system became more pronounced, especially in terms of their role in planning, data collecting and analyzing, determining specific courses of action, reviewing outcomes, learning from the experience (e.g., what worked, what didn't work), and then revisiting initial plans, further data collecting and analyzing, and so forth.

As our understanding of the underlying process has continued to evolve over the past 30 years, some proponents have suggested that action research reflects more of a life philosophy than intervention technique per se, a theory of social science based on an ongoing commitment to collaborative learning and design, combining action, research, reflection, and reaction in a spirit of co-inquiry. Building on the fundamental principle of collaboration, emphasis is placed on dealing openly with conflict, drawing out its root causes and creating a basis for truly transformative actions. While much of the AR process focuses on past behaviors and events, especially as a way of understanding the present, emphasis is placed on the future and how an understanding of where we are and how we got there can serve as a basis for purposeful action moving forward.

Current practice emphasizes the crucial nature of the partnership between the client and change agent, a spirit of collaborative learning that permeates the relationship, and the processes through which they interact. Focus is also being increasingly placed on the influence and importance of generating and understanding local tacit knowledge as well as an openness and willingness to examine underlying assumptions in the system.

Today, AR practices can best be thought of along a continuum, ranging from the traditional or classical approach of joint problem solving to appreciative inquiry (AI) and its focus on envisioning an ideal future and building on organizational successes (instead of problems), working with the best that groups and organizations have to offer. Described as a "family of practices," variations on the AR model also include action learning (focused on learning and developing through reflection on one's experience while attempting to solve problems in one's own organizational setting), action science (analyzing and documenting patterns of behavior and their underlying rationales in creating causal links and formulating strategies to achieve desired outcomes), and clinical inquiry (when researchers enter an organization at the organization's request, working with the organizational system to enable successful change). Building on a critique of action research as focused on solving organizational problems, for example, appreciative inquiry emphasizes capturing and building on what is already successful in organizational life, creating generative insight for transformative action.

Importance

One of the ongoing challenges in management and organization research is the lingering tension between academic rigor and managerial relevance, undertaking studies that fulfill both the conceptual and methodological demands of scientific inquiry with the practical needs of organizations and their members. Within this context, AR can be seen as helping to close this rigor-relevance gap in management and organizational research. Distinctions, for example, have been made between positivist ("Mode 1") and constructivist ("Mode 2") approaches to research, in which the former emphasizes theory building and testing within the confines of a particular discipline and the latter emphasizes cogenerated knowledge produced in the context of practice. The underlying differences are significant for thinking about organizational research, from the detached, neutral, and context-free nature of Mode 1 research to the engaged, reflexive, and context-embedded nature of Mode 2.

The ideal underlying the AR paradigm reflects Mode 2 research, working collaboratively to create a foundation for both organizational and personal change, with the underlying understanding that theory should not only inform practice but that it can also be generated through practice. As a theory itself, action research is most useful when it is put into practice, attempting to bring about positive organizational change in specific situations. High-quality action research reflects several key characteristics, including the intention of the researcher to effect change in an organization, the understanding that the specific project itself has broader implications beyond the intervention per se, and that the intervention will be used to elaborate or develop theory while being useful to the organization. Theory, in essence, informs the design of the intervention and how it is developed in practice. The process itself is embedded in high standards of rigor and relevance in creating theory as well as empirical testing of relevant propositions within the context of that theory.

One of the keys to the AR process is evaluation, focused on knowing the extent to which (a) intended outcomes were achieved and (b) whether they actually solved the initial problem or concern. The evaluation process, serving as feedback, can also be used to change methods of intervention, suggest alternative ways of approaching the problem, or potentially alter the entire research design. Although validity issues often remain—for example, was the change and its outcomes caused by the change intervention or were other factors responsible (internal validity) and to what extent is the intervention and its outcomes generalizable to other organizational situations (external validity)—the AR process allows for ongoing theory testing and refinement while generating case-specific findings.

As an influential approach to organizational intervention and theory testing, AR is embedded in transparent procedures for decision making, intertwined with a deep respect for humanistic values and democratic ideals, the need to empower group and organizational members as a basis for learning and action, and collaborative theory building and organizational practice. Given today's increasingly turbulent, global environment, the need to understand and appreciate diverse cultures and contexts—including understanding how our own social and cultural orientations play out in the broader global context—have become increasingly important. The 21st century will continue to demand innovations in theory, methods, and interventions to deal with the ever-growing dynamic complexity of human systems. Action research can guide that process. Through AR, organizational members can become researchers—and people learn best, and more willingly apply what they have learned, when they do it themselves, producing knowledge and action that is directly useful to the group or organization. In essence, AR is a guide to practical action from which all managers and organizations can benefit.

Anthony F. Buono

See also Academic-Practitioner Collaboration and Knowledge Sharing; Action Learning; Appreciative Inquiry Model; Force Field Analysis and Model of Planned Change; Organizational Development; Process Consultation; Strategies for Change; Tacit Knowledge

Further Readings

Argyris, C., Putnam, R., & Smith, D. M. (1985). *Action science: Concepts, methods and skills for research and intervention.* San Francisco, CA: Jossey-Bass.

Brydon-Miller, M., Greenwood, D., & Maquire, P. (2003). Why action research? *Action Research, 1*(1), 9–28.

Coghlan, D. (2011). Action research: Exploring perspectives on a philosophy of practical knowing. *Academy of Management Annuals, 5*(1), 53–87.

French, W. L. (1969). Organization development objectives, assumptions, and strategies. *California Management Review, 12*(2), 23–34.

Gibbons, M., Limoges, C., Nowotny, H., Schwartzman, S., Scott, P., & Trow, M. (1994). *The new production of knowledge.* London, England: Sage.

Lewin, K. (1946). Action research and minority problems. *Journal of Social Issues, 2*(4), 34–46.

Reason, P. (1988). *Human inquiry in action: Developments in new paradigm research.* London, England: Sage.

Schein, E. F. (1995). Process consultation, action research and clinical inquiry: Are they the same? *Journal of Managerial Psychology, 10*(6), 14–19.

Schön, D. (1983). *The reflective practitioner.* New York, NY: Basic Books.

Susman, G. I., & Evered, R. D. (1978). An assessment of the scientific merits of action research. *Administrative Science Quarterly, 23*, 582–601.

ACTOR-NETWORK THEORY

Having origins in studies of science, technology, and society (STS), actor-network theory (ANT)—or the "sociology of translation"—is an increasingly popular sociological method used within a range of social science fields. This entry provides a review of ANT, which gains much of its notoriety through advocating a sociophilosophical approach in which human and material factors are brought together in the same analytical view. In attempting to comprehend complex situations, ANT rejects any sundering of human and nonhuman, social and technical elements. The early work of Michel Callon, for example, warns of the dangers of "changing register" when we move from concerns with the social to those of the technical. The methodological philosophy is that all ingredients of sociotechnical analysis be explained by common practices.

Fundamentals

A key ANT notion is that of the *heterogeneous network.* John Law, in 1992, describes this as "a way of suggesting that society, organizations, agents and machines are all effects generated in patterned networks of diverse (not simple human) materials" (p. 380). Law suggests that, while entities, in their broadest sense, are usually conceived of as having stability and uniqueness, ANT, in contrast, advocates that they are essentially a result achieved when different heterogeneous elements are assembled together. As such, the ANT approach suggests that things take form and acquire attributes as a consequence of their relations with others. As ANT regards entities as produced in relations, and applies this ruthlessly to materials, it can be thus understood as a "semiotics of materiality."

As under ANT entities always exist in networks of relations, this approach suggests that it is not possible to conceive of actors as in some way separable from networks, and vice versa. Following Michel Callon, an actor network is "simultaneously an actor whose activity is networking heterogeneous elements and a network that is able to redefine and transform what it is made of" (Callon as qtd. in Farias & Bender, 2010, p. 315). This is so because the activities of actors and networks are interdependent. For example, all attributes usually ascribed as human (thinking, loving, acting, etc.) are generated in networks comprising materially heterogeneous networks that either pass through or have ramifications beyond the body.

In this way, a central feature of ANT is to explain how "ordering effects"—such as devices (e.g., aircraft), organizations (e.g., laboratories), agents (e.g., managers), and even knowledge (e.g., relativity theory)—are generated. Its major focus, at least in its original formulation, is to investigate how entities are performed and kept stable. As a consequence, ANT analyzes the strategies through which entities are generated and held together. It tries to unravel the forces that keep actors "as one," showing in the process how they are networks which need to be reproduced "moment by moment."

Motivated by such concerns, ANT implies that organizations and their components are effects generated in multiple interactions, rather than existing merely in the order of things. Organization is perceived as continuous and unfinished, precarious and partial—a permanent process that generates more or less stable effects, a heterogeneous emergent phenomenon, and a verb. Analyzing organization(s) in this form—stressing that the noun *organization* can exist only as a continuous result of organizing—challenges what mainstream organization structure approaches usually accept as given or taken-for-granted. Thus, analyzing organizing via ANT is to attempt to address by which means a diffuse and complex system composed of humans and nonhumans becomes networked. For this approach, organizations are outcomes and products of continuing process—relations and practices that are materially complex and whose ordering can only be addressed, locally and empirically, as "in the making."

To analyze "ordering in the making" (to quote John Law), ANT has deployed concepts such as *immutable mobiles* and *action at a distance*. Immutable mobiles have the capacity to "fix" knowledge and allow it to be disseminated far beyond its point of origin. They represent, for instance, lengthy processes of translating information (e.g., on location in an ocean, a territory's size and shape, virus behavior) into objects that can be carried while retaining shape (e.g., maps, spatial coordinates, sketches, graphics).

By extension, the possibility of acting at a distance implies "control at a distance" and relies on the alignment of documents, devices, maps, and so on. In so doing, it relies on establishing a materially heterogeneous network, one that permits movement and immutability, simultaneously allowing something previously unknown to become acted upon and controlled. Both of these notions—immutable mobiles and acting at a distance—were central to

well-known early ANT case studies, such as the history of Portuguese maritime expansion and contemporary scientists at work. These were case studies which subsequently influenced a number of early ANT studies on organization, accounting, and information, as in work by Brian Bloomfield and Robert Cooper—studies that suggest issues of organization and control have long been at the heart of ANT.

A final key concept deployed in ANT-inspired analysis is *translation,* or the work through which actors modify, displace, and translate their various and contradictory interests. For Michel Callon, translation is the mechanism by which things take form through "displacements" and "transformations"—such as when actors' identities, the possibilities of their interaction, and the limits of their maneuver are negotiated and delimited. Put basically, translation processes see entities that are, traditionally, categorically differentiated transformed into ones that are in some ways analytically equivalent, thus, representing one of the main epistemological tools used to analyze the establishment of actor-networks.

Evolution

The key ANT notion of translation indeed evolves from the early writings of Michel Callon in which he offers a description of this process. For him, translation is composed of four different "moments"—*problematization* (or the "interdefinition of actors"), *interesssement* (or "how allies are locked into place"), *enrollment* (or "how to define and coordinate roles"), and the *mobilization of allies* (or "who speaks in the name of whom?" and "who represents whom?"). Drawing implicitly or explicitly on this way of portraying translation, a number of case studies on management and organizational issues have been conducted together with a series of kindred studies on information systems and information technology. These studies have appeared regularly in journals such as the *Journal of Management Studies, Organization Studies*, and *Organization*.

A detailed description of translation in Callon's writings, however, can sound rather prescriptive for a reflexive-processual approach, such as ANT. More characteristic perhaps is Bruno Latour's subsequent view that the ANT reflects a philosophy which aims to analyze ordering as complex outcomes of multiple materials, has a strong relational focus that suggests a kind of material semiotics, and declares that a specific ordering process is but one possibility among many. Proposing general rules or aspects of how translation takes place can be seen as imposing a particular view of how actors get assembled into networks, this being particularly problematic when such a model is replicated in case studies. Such a method therefore seems alien to one of the key ANT mandates, namely, the need to follow actors without imposing preconceived templates or definitions on them. The evolution of ANT studies has see the approach criticized for offering what seems to be a "simplistic" way of portraying ordering processes, notably in work by Peter Miller and Olga Amsterdamska. This critique can be clearly linked to translation notions, which appear to provide evidence for a framework that can portray many different cases without "needing adjustment," that is, in terms that appear to explain almost everything from vaccines (in Latour's work) to failed aircraft projects (in Law's research). Without considering how sociological translations can differ, it fails to address any variation among processes of ordering. It has been argued that studies based on the translation notion can, on the one hand, fail to address how the links that constitute translation are made, while on the other, assume similarity among different links thus limiting ANT's capacity to grasp complexity.

As scholars adopting an ANT position have drawn heavily on the translation notion to theorize aspects of organizing, such studies may, therefore, have been underscored by the idea that organizing processes in a variety of empirical settings can be accounted for by simply following Callon's four "moments" recipe. As a result, instead of being thoroughly and richly explained, a variety of specific organizing processes are described (as Peter Miller has suggested) in a "nice and tidy" way, thus, oversimplifying what needs to be explained. Not surprisingly, some writers argue that ANT has often been used as methodological description—as a way to describe and label different actors in a given context. By arguing that actor-networks become irreversible once translation is accomplished, ANT is accused of producing a deterministic approach to networks, as noted by Andrea Whittle and Andre Spicer. Similarly, Vicky Singleton argues that the relative stability of networks depends, not on their coherence, but on their *in*coherence and ambivalence, issues that have been generally neglected in early ANT accounts.

Leigh Star and James Griesemer argue, further, that as translation is from the viewpoint "of one passage point" and this point is usually the manager, the entrepreneur, and the scientist, then this model can lead to a managerial bias, which seems to put ANT in opposition to perspectives that are nonmanagerial and nonperformative (as Critical Management Studies claims to be).

The implication is that key ANT notions lead to a singular representation of ordering at the same time that complexities and differences are disregarded. As such, it is argued by Andrea Whittle and Andre Spicer that this is problematic for the development of "critical" perspectives that seek to explore all the complexities associated with relations that establish order, especially those related to power. As Daniel Neyland suggests, "discussions of ANT and work using ANT has forged the kind of fixed location, well-known theoretical moves, and status as an obligatory point of passage that ANT previously sought to avoid" (2006, p. 30). In effect, not only does ANT proffer several problematic notions, but also, its applications tend to be noncritical. As Jan Harris argues, "Latour's theory has often been reduced to ready acronyms and the unproblematic application of set terms or processes to a given field of study" (2005, p. 176). Consequently, ANT has been accused, as Andrea Whittle and Andre Spicer suggest, of providing an analysis of organization(s) that "naturalizes" organizations themselves.

This simplistic view of organizing has also consequences in terms of how otherness has been addressed in ANT works. Nick Lee and Steve Brown suggest that ANT became a metalinguistic formulation into which any sequence of humans and nonhumans could be encoded. As such, it became a "final vocabulary" that covered everything and risked producing "another ahistorical grand narrative," and Steve Hinchliffe suggests that as a totalizing system, ANT leaves no space for otherness or noncategories—it fails to account for difference, leading to a problematic view of politics, with clear consequences in terms of whether ANT can provide a critical analysis of management and organizations.

Finally, although ANT research has been accused on the one hand of resembling aspects of Marxism and on the other of sharing characteristics with fascism, it has more readily been charged with avoiding a political stance altogether. Olga Amsterdamska, for example, suggests that ANT analyzes the strengths of alliances that make networks but rarely the character of them. This sees ANT concerned with questions of how networks are established in terms of relations, but not with whether these relations are characterized by ethical or unethical means. Donna Haraway argues similarly that as ANT rarely asks for whom the hybrids it analyzes "work," it neglects the role played by inequality in the production of sociological accounts. As such, ANT's seemingly balanced and symmetrical sociotechnical explanations tend to overlook, or even avoid, questions of politics. Further, it has been argued that ANT fails to address how "political" categories, such as gender, race, class, and colonialism, are established; in other words, these categories are not static and a priori but operate as historical modes of conditions that affect relations. Leigh Star, also, discusses ANT's lack of political engagement. For her, even though ANT describes "heterogeneous engineering," it fails to acknowledge that heterogeneity tends to be different for those who are privileged and those who are not. For organization theorist Mike Reed, similarly, ANT ignores how opportunities are unequally distributed in society. And Andrea Whittle and Andre Spicer argue that ANT tends to assume rather than problematize what motivates action and which purposes it serves; it also appears to reproduce, instead of challenge, the networks it describes. In so doing, ANT has been accused of being politically neutral, with critics suggesting it is not an appropriate approach to develop a critical case analysis of organizations.

Importance

Despite such criticisms, for management and organization theory and research, ANT is important because of the novel, relativist approach it offers to the analysis of social and technical phenomena. ANT's suppositions about the transient material-semiotic character of such phenomena see judgments about truth and falsity, good and bad, and right and wrong treated as relative to the context in question. In its early formulations—for example, in the writing of Michel Callon—ANT relativizes cultural differences in assuming, somewhat controversially, that all elements in a network—human and nonhuman—can and should be described in similar analytical terms.

When we consider, for example, the nature of *actants* (human and nonhuman actors) in an actor-network, we assume they take the shape they do by virtue of their "relative" interactions with one another. In its various formulations, ANT exemplifies many of the assumptions of this relativist—or perhaps better, relationist—epistemology. This is reflected in the treatment of multiple material-semiotic actors, or the view that the technical and social coproduce each other, with such analysis being relational both in theoretical and empirical terms. In other words, epistemologically, ANT has been used to conceptualize, simultaneously, relations between (material) things and (semiotic) concepts. When such assumptions are reflected practically in fieldwork, the interactions that researchers examine in an organization involve relations between people, ideas, and technologies, which together can be understood to form a network. As John Law has suggested, entities take their form and acquire their attributes as a result of their relations with other entities. Under ANT, such actor-networks are always contextual and processual phenomena: As they exist only through their continuous making and remaking, it is *relations* that need to be repeatedly performed for such networks not to dissolve.

ANT is important in that it also advances what, for management and organization studies, can be seen as a novel approach to analyzing human agency—a decentered view, notably one in which the social and technical are constituted relationally through simultaneous symbolic and material systems. Under ANT, the human subject appears deprived of the logocentric authority it possessed when analytically "present." In his 1994 work, *Organizing Modernity,* for example, Law discusses how notions of "decentring of the subject" and "heterogeneous materials" inform his "commitment to relational materialism" and thus how his study of a scientific laboratory emphasizes the distributed or heterogeneous character of agency. Discussing *Organizing Modernity* elsewhere, he suggests that theoretically "an organization," a noun, is best not understood as an organization, a noun, at all but rather as a verb, that is, as a process, a continuing process of movement. *Organizing Modernity* is thus a plea to move from nouns to verbs, from things to processes, specifically processes of "ordering." Instead of the laboratory representing an essential phenomenon privileging human existence and intention, Law suggests this organization represents a *materially heterogeneous* set of arrangement processes implicated in and implicating people while also including and producing nonhuman elements such as documents and codes—thus agency does not exclusively belong to people.

Finally, ANT is important for organizational research in advancing prosopects for reflexive methodology. In ANT we find reflexivity expressed both in theorizing and accounts of organizational research. For the former, reflexivity perhaps attains its highest profile in work of Bruno Latour and signally his analysis of the production of scientific facts in *Science in Action,* a 1987 work devoted as much to ontological and epistemological concerns as to the empirical study of technology. Elsewhere, Latour discusses reflexivity in his debate with Ulrich Beck on "reflexive modernization," a discussion which sees Latour explain the unintended consequences and side effects of modernization and how they "reverberate throughout the whole of society" as unruly. Closer to home, in organization studies, Cynthia Hardy and colleagues have deployed ANT to reflexively investigate the role of the researcher and the research community in the production of a research subject, in this case "the refugee." This line of research reveals not only the actions of actors in the refugee system but also, reflexively, their own activities as researchers, as well as those of the broader research community. Above all, the ANT concept of *translation* (after Michel Callon) is deployed to explore the role of actors in the process of social construction that produced refugees as a subject of academic study.

John Hassard

See also Analytical and Sociological Paradigms; Critical Management Studies; Dialectical Theory of Organizations; Social Construction Theory; Structuration Theory

Further Readings

Amsterdamska, O. (1999). Surely you are joking, Monsieur Latour! *Science, Technology, and Human Values, 15*(4), 445–463.

Callon, M. (1986). Some elements of a sociology of translation—Domestication of the scallops and the fishermen of St-Brieuc Bay. In J. Law (Ed.), *Power, action and belief: A new sociology of knowledge?* (pp. 196–223). London, England: Routledge.

Czarniawska, B., & Hernes, T. (Eds.). (2005). *Actor-network theory and organizing.* Malmö, Sweden: Liber and Copenhagen Business School Press.

Farias, I., & Bender, T. (Eds.). (2010). *Urban assemblages.* New York, NY: Routledge.

Harris, J. (2005). The ordering of things: Organization in Bruno Latour. *Sociological Review, 53*(3), 163–177.

Latour, B. (1987). *Science in action: How to follow scientists and engineers through society.* Milton Keynes, England: Open University Press.

Latour, B. (1999). On recalling ANT. In J. Law & J. Hassard (Eds.), *Actor network theory and after* (pp. 15–26). Oxford, England: Blackwell/ Sociological Review.

Latour, B. (2005). *Reassembling the social: An introduction to actor-network-theory.* Oxford, England: Oxford University Press.

Law, J. (1992). Notes on the theory of the actor-networking: Ordering, strategy and heterogeneity. *Systems Practice, 5*(3), 379–393.

Law, J. (1994). *Organizing modernity.* Oxford, England: Blackwell.

Law, J., & Hassard, J. (1999). *Actor network theory and after.* Oxford, England: Blackwell/Sociological Review.

Lee, N., & Brown, S. (1994). Otherness and the actor network—The undiscovered continent. *American Behavioral Scientist, 37*(6), 772–790.

Neyland, D. (2006). Dismissed content and discontent: An analysis of the strategic aspects of actor-network theory. *Science, Technology and Human Values, 31*(1), 29–51.

Whittle, A., & Spicer, A. (2008). Is actor network theory critical? *Organization Studies, 29*(1), 611–629.

ADAPTIVE STRUCTURATION THEORY

Adaptive structuration theory (AST) is concerned with the implementation and use of information and communication technologies (ICT) in groups and organizations. Proposed by Marshall Scott Poole and Gerardine DeSanctis, AST posits that the impacts of ICTs on group and organizational processes and outcomes depend on the structures incorporated in the technology and on the structures that emerge as users attempt to adapt the technology to the tasks at hand. The theoretical grounding of AST can be traced to a number of scholars focused on structuration theory, particularly Anthony Giddens. This entry introduces structuration theory and then discusses concepts added by AST, including the spirit and features distinction and appropriation. Following this, factors that shape structuration are delineated. Finally, the significance of the theory, key findings, and controversies are considered.

Fundamentals

AST was originally applied in the study of group decision support systems, but it has also been used to study enterprise level systems, geographic information systems, electronic billing systems, context aware applications, and mobile systems. It has also been applied to non-ICT topics including leadership, virtual teams, the evolution of standards, and implementation of innovations.

AST posits that social systems, such as groups and organizations, can best be understood in terms of how their members actively structure practices such as decision making. This process of structuring is referred to as *structuration,* defined as the production and reproduction of a social system through members' appropriation of generative rules and resources. Underlying this definition is a distinction between system and structure. A *system* is an observable pattern of relationships among actors, such as a group or organization. *Structures* are the rules and resources that members of the system employ in their activities and interactions that give the system its pattern. Structures are not directly observable, and in fact, the term *structure* is itself a useful reification that is employed for analytical purposes. Structures are dualities in that they are both the medium of activity and its outcome. As members draw rules and resources from tasks, norms, ICTs, and other sources into the activities and interactions that constitute the social system, they are enacting and sustaining these structures and simultaneously making them part of the ongoing organization of the system, that is, reproducing them.

AST argues that the effects of an ICT on group and organizational processes and outcomes depend on the structures embodied in the technology (structural potential) and on the emergent (adaptive) structures that form as members interact with a technology over time. AST distinguishes two elements of ICT structures: spirit and features. *Structural features* are specific types of rules and resources, or capabilities, offered by the system that are embodied in the material ICT artifact—and *spirit* is the general intent with regard to values

and goals underlying a given set of structural features. The spirit of an ICT is the principle of coherence that holds its ensemble of structural features together. As understood by members, the spirit of an ICT provides normative guidelines for applying the ICT, an interpretive scheme for making sense of the ICT and its outcomes, a guide for "filling in" aspects of the ICT that are not explicit, and a degree of control over how the ICT is utilized. An online project management system, for example, may be designed to promote the values of collaboration and efficient use of resources; this spirit, reflected in the overall design of the system, in training, and online help, shapes how users interpret and employ the system. Structural features are rules and resources embodied in the ICT as users encounter and work with it. For example, in the project management system, a budget-tracker tool would incorporate rules for accounting and resource allocation, while a discussion tool might have a space for idea sharing that incorporates collaboration procedures, such as brainstorming. Ideally, spirit and structural features are in alignment, but due to limitations in technology, implementation errors, and unintentional slippage, there are often inconsistencies between features and spirit. The budget-tracker tool, for instance, might display comparisons of project budgets that are meant to be informative but inadvertently create conflicts between members, reducing collaboration.

Structures—spirit and features—are produced and reproduced through structurational processes that occur as members of group and organizational systems appropriate them in ongoing activities. *Appropriation* refers to the process by which members of a social system incorporate structural features into their ongoing activities, literally "making the structure their own." Appropriation involves selection, combination, emphasis, and de-emphasis of elements of the structural potential available to a system. For example, a project team may use some features of the budget tracker and ignore others, leaving the rules and resources in the latter effectively "inert." Each appropriation creates "structures-in-use" that guide system activity and interaction and are unique to the group and organization. A team might appropriate the discussion tool by merging the rules it embodies with some of the rules members use in "offline" discussions. The result is a novel structural ensemble that is tailored to the specific situation in which it is employed.

Structuring processes also draw on external structures from assigned tasks, organizational rules and culture, professions, and other social institutions. Further, they give rise to emergent structures that include outputs of the ICT (e.g., budget reports, lists of ideas) and novel rules and resources that the group or organization creates in the course of its interaction. For instance, a project team might develop a spreadsheet tailored to the strategic goals of the organization to supplement the budget tracker. This spreadsheet carries emergent structures, and if it adds sufficient value that other teams adopt it, then it becomes part of the existing structural potential of the organizational system, to be drawn upon and adapted in the future.

The members' reading of the spirit of an ICT influences its mode of appropriation. For example, if team members come to agree that efficient use of resources is a more important value than collaboration for the project management system, then their use of the system, the external structures they bring to bear, and the structures-in-use they generate and retain will differ from those that would have resulted had they chosen to emphasize collaboration.

A number of *appropriation moves* that represent the particular operations involved in using ICTs in microlevel interaction have been identified. These include bids to use or interpret the ICT in certain ways, to combine it with other structures, and responses to these bids. There are also "metastructuring" actions that direct or channel appropriation moves. Sequences of appropriation moves can be analyzed to identify overall global appropriation of the ICT. A key feature of appropriation is the degree to which it maintains consistency between spirit and features. A *faithful* appropriation occurs when use of structural features is consistent and in harmony with the spirit of the ICT; an *ironic* appropriation occurs when structures are used in ways contradictory to spirit. Some ironic appropriations are deleterious, but others may represent novel and improved ways of using the ICT. Another aspect of appropriation is instrumental use: ICTs may be employed for purposes related to task, process, power, sociality, and exploration, among others.

Several general constructs characterize overall appropriation of an ICT. Degree of use can be assessed in terms of number and frequency of feature use. Degree of understanding refers to how well members grasp the operation of the ICT and its features, as well as its spirit. Degree of consensus on appropriation among users influences the ease with which the ICT is used, consistency of use, and its effectiveness in promoting desirable outcomes; conflicts over the ICT are likely to detract from effectiveness and, if not managed constructively, could lead to power struggles. Finally, appropriations can be characterized in terms of attitudes toward a technology, members' comfort with the ICT, respect for it as useful, and the challenge to work hard and excel that the ICT poses.

Several sets of factors influence the structuring process. Most obvious, *characteristics of the ICT*, including its *restrictiveness* (degree of freedom the user has in applying the ICT), its level of *sophistication* (the degree of intelligence built into the ICT), its *standardization* (the degree to which the ICT is well understood and accepted in the community of which the organization or group is a part), and its *complexity*. A second set of factors external to the system include *task* characteristics, such as difficulty and complexity, and characteristics of the system's *environment*, such as dynamism and hostility. Other external factors such as general technological trends, interorganizational and intergroup dynamics, and social institutions also shape structuration. Third are aspects of the internal system of the organization or group, including group and organizational culture, norms, and leadership.

These three sets of factors are sources of structure, and, just as in the case of ICT structural potential, only a portion of the total constellation of structural elements comes into play. Hence, these factors do not determine group and organizational processes in the traditional causal sense. The system is directly influenced only by those structural elements its members consciously or unknowingly incorporate into the mix of structuring activities.

Outcomes such as effectiveness, efficiency, commitment, learning, and cohesion are the ultimate result of the structurational process. New structures may also result, which influence subsequent interaction. For example, following use of the budget tracker, a team might decide to add a rule that it should analyze multiple-budget scenarios before making significant budgetary decisions, changing prior procedures. These novel structures are then available for the group and organization to use in the future.

Importance

The extensive body of research using AST has yielded a number of generalizations which bear on the validity and utility of the framework as a whole, including the following:

1. Consistent with the theory, differences in the use of the same ICT by different groups and organizations have been observed in multiple studies. The manner in which the ICT is appropriated by groups and organizations has been shown to relate to outcomes including decision quality, member satisfaction, and willingness to use ICT in the future.

2. The relationship between ICT and outcomes is based on a double contingency. To the extent that the ICT is appropriate for the task at hand *and* to the extent it is consensually appropriated by members in a manner appropriate for the task, the group or organization will achieve better outcomes.

3. Users tend to have more trouble with and resist using more sophisticated technologies, but if they appropriate them in a manner consistent with the spirit of the ICT and with the demands of task and context, positive outcomes ensue.

AST has been criticized by some for being overly "positivistic" and hence inconsistent with the interpretive-critical approach Giddens takes. This criticism may be traced to the fact that the theory was developed to bridge quantitative and interpretive approaches in inquiry and emphasizes a priori construct definition and attention to validity of measurement, as well as the earliest exemplars of AST research. However, in addition to quantitative approaches, such as laboratory experiments and structural equation modeling, a number of interpretive studies and even a few critical analyses have been conducted utilizing AST. Several issues are currently under debate. One is the nature of agency and whether ICTs can be agents of some type. A second is how microlevel structurational moves cumulate to yield a more general appropriation of ICTs.

From a practical perspective, AST has generated descriptions and explanations of the processes by which particular structuring processes unfold and strategies for managing ICT implementation. For example, AST studies have found that in supporting users, general heuristics that help users make sense of the ICT as a whole are more effective than training in specifics (provided technical support is adequate). A key skill for ICT managers is learning to "read" the processes of adaptive structuration so that they can channel it in productive directions.

Marshall Scott Poole

See also Innovation Diffusion; Process Theories of Change; Structuration Theory; Systems Theory of Organizations; Technology Affordances and Constraints Theory (of MIS); Transfer of Technology; Virtual Teams

Further Readings

DeSanctis, G., & Poole, M. S. (1994). Capturing the complexity in advanced technology use: Adaptive structuration theory. *Organization Science, 5*(2), pp. 121–147.
DeSanctis, G., Poole, M. S., Zigurs, I., DeSharnais, G., D'Onofrio, M., Gallupe, B., . . . Holmes, M. (2008). The Minnesota GDSS Research Project: Group support systems, group processes, and group outcomes. *Journal of the Association of Information Systems, 9,* 551–608.
Giddens, A. (1984). *The constitution of society.* New York, NY: Basic Books.
Poole, M. S., & DeSanctis, G. (1990). Understanding the use of group decision support systems. In J. Fulk & C. Steinfield (Eds.), *Organizations and communication technology* (pp. 175–195). Thousand Oaks, CA: Sage.
Poole, M. S., & DeSanctis, G. (2004). Structuration theory in information systems research: Methods and controversies. In M. E. Whitman & A. B. Woszczynski (Eds.), *The handbook of information systems research* (pp. 206–249). Hershey, PA: Idea Group.

AFFECT THEORY

This entry describes a general theory about conditions under which the positive affect that people experience when doing tasks with others promotes stronger affective ties to a company or organization. The theory offers guidelines for how to structure tasks, how to frame or define them for employees, and how to make work groups and teams effective at generating a spirit of citizenship and collective orientation in support of the company. The principles of the theory apply to any task that requires people to exchange ideas or information. The theory is inspired by observations that working with others on a task tends to produce positive or negative individual, often private, feelings. If team members work well together, members feel pleased, uplifted, and energized, but if they have trouble coordinating or producing results, members come away feeling down, displeased, or sad. The main idea is that such everyday good or bad feelings shape the affective ties that people develop to their local work groups as well as to the larger organization. Repetition of these feelings is crucial. When people repeatedly experience positive feelings from working jointly with others, they may attribute their feelings to shared relational or group affiliations (e.g., their department or the company). More specifically, the affect theory reveals that people attribute their feelings to groups or organizations especially when they engage in joint tasks that foster a sense of shared responsibility. Individual feelings are essentially transformed into affective group ties. The key result is that individuals are more willing to act on behalf of and make sacrifices for the group or organization. The following entry reviews the main ideas and implications of affect theory.

Fundamentals

There are many theories about affect, or emotion, in psychology and sociology. Most focus on negative emotions (such as fear, anger, and sadness) rather than positive emotions (such as pleasure or excitement). Positive emotions are known to make people view the world more inclusively or broadly, see more options than otherwise, and cooperate more productively with others. Negative emotions tend to narrow people's thinking whereas positive emotions tend to broaden it. Research on groups or teams accords little attention to import of emotions or feelings produced in the course of task interactions. The affect theory of social exchange explains why even mild everyday feelings of pleasure or excitement from task behaviors can have important effects on the ties of commitment people develop to groups or organizations. The emphasis is group level, affective ties rather than interpersonal ties with colleagues.

The affect theory interweaves three broadly applicable ideas:

1. When people accomplish a joint task, they feel good; when they have a joint task but do not accomplish it, they feel "bad." Such emotions inevitably occur when people work with others.

2. If such experiences recur across time, people are likely to interpret their individual feelings as due in part to common group or organizational affiliations.

3. People thus attribute their individually felt emotions to the relevant social unit, which can be a small local group or the larger organization; this in turn leads to affective attachments to the group or organization. The domain of the affect theory is any group or organizational context in which two or more people interact with each other repeatedly in order to exchange things of value (information, knowledge, favors, services) and produce a collective result.

Smaller groups are typically nested in larger groups, and it is plausible that people will associate their feelings more with local, immediate groups than with larger and more distant ones. This is a potential problem for employers. If a work team generates positive affect among its members, they could associate their feelings with the team itself or the larger organization within which the team operates. The affect theory indicates that people attribute their feelings to the local or larger group to the degree that each is perceived as a source of control or efficacy for individuals in the group. If the task structure or content is developed and controlled locally, then the commitment to the local group may be stronger than to the larger organization, whereas if the task is designed and controlled by the larger organization, the attachment or commitment may be stronger to that organization than to the local group. The affect theory suggests some conditions under which organizations foster strong attachments to local units that undermine commitments to the larger organization. This commitment problem is especially difficult for decentralized organizations.

Social-Unit Attributions of Emotion

Social-unit attributions are the process by which individual emotions are transformed into affective ties or commitments to a group. The idea that people can make social group or relational attributions of emotions is new and potentially controversial, because there is a long tradition of research in psychology revealing that people make self-interested attributions for success and failure. In other words, they give themselves credit for task success and blame others or the situation for task failure. The affect theory claims that social-unit attributions of emotions mitigate or counteract such individually centered attributions.

To elaborate, the theory adopts a sharp distinction between global emotions that are immediate (pleasure, enthusiasm) and specific emotions (pride, gratitude) that stem from an interpretation of those global emotions. Global emotions are involuntarily felt as a result of an episode of social interaction. Specific emotions require more thinking or cognitive work (conscious or nonconscious) which interprets the responsibility of self, others, and social units for the global feelings. Different targets (self, others, group) entail different specific emotions. If the positive emotions are attributed to self, the specific emotion of pride is likely (or shame if the emotions are negative); if global feelings are attributed to others, the specific emotions are gratitude (given positive feelings) or anger (given negative feelings); if attributed to the social unit, the specific emotions are group attachment or detachment. The key question for the theory then is, Under what structural or task conditions do people make social-unit attributions for the emotions they feel as an individual?

Joint Tasks and the Sense of Shared Responsibility

The affect theory of social exchange indicates that the most general condition for social-unit attributions is the jointness of the task. A joint task is one in which there is a collective product that members create together through their social interaction. The task cannot be done alone or completed by simply aggregating the performances or contributions of individuals. The degree of task jointness is important because it shapes whether people have a sense of shared collective responsibility for the results. Examples of joint tasks include business partnerships, homeowners associations, and even child rearing.

The jointness of tasks varies not only objectively but also subjectively. An organization or team leader may define the task of a work team in joint or in individual terms and, in the process, highlight

individual or collective responsibility for results. Both the objective task conditions and the subjective definitions put forth to frame the nature of the task are important. The affect theory identifies one main structural (objective) and one main cognitive (subjective) condition for social-unit attributions of individual emotions.

The structural condition is the degree that each individual's contributions to task success (or failure) are separable (distinguishable) or nonseparable (indistinguishable). In some tasks, people cannot distinguish who did what or how much each contributed to the collective product. Tasks that make individual contributions nonseparable or indistinguishable have higher jointness. Such tasks reduce the capacity of individuals to attribute group success to their own individual efforts or to exaggerate their contributions. Overall, tasks that involve adding up or averaging of individual performances or contributions enhance the sense of individual responsibility, whereas tasks that intertwine individual performances should heighten the sense of shared or collective responsibility. Discrete, highly specialized, independent roles in an organization tend to draw attention to individual responsibility, whereas overlapping, collaborative roles highlight shared responsibility.

The cognitive dimension of jointness is the degree that the task promotes the sense of shared responsibility for group success. The argument is that if task interaction in a group or team generates a sense of shared responsibility, people are more likely to interpret their individual feelings as jointly produced in concert with others and, therefore, more likely to attribute their feelings to shared group affiliations. Thus, if employees perceive a shared responsibility for group performance, a work group should generate greater emotion-based cohesion and stronger group-affective attachments. Affective processes can explain the impact of individually versus collectively oriented methods of accountability on group and organizational commitments.

Four Core Propositions

The affect theory is captured by four central predictions:

1. The more indistinguishable the impact of individuals' behavior on task success (or failure), the greater their sense of shared responsibility for results.

2. With greater shared responsibility, people are more likely to attribute their feelings from task activity to the group, that is, to make social-unit attributions.

3. Social-unit attributions of positive emotion generate stronger affective ties to the group resulting in the group becoming valuable as an intrinsic object rather than a purely instrumental one; negative emotions weaken those person-to-group ties.

4. Stronger affective group ties lead members to work harder on behalf of group goals as well as to trust and collaborate with each other. Additionally, the theory predicts that (a) joint tasks and shared responsibility generate the spread of emotions across members in the group (emotional contagion), and (b) commitments to local, immediate groups tend to be stronger in the absence of interventions by the larger organization to claim credit for the positive feelings and experiences of people at the local level.

Importance

Experiments have supported the main ideas of the affect theory. As predicted, repeatedly exchanging valued items with another produces positive individual feelings, and these, in turn, generate perceptions of a cohesive group and various forms of behavioral commitment (staying, cooperation, and altruism); these effects are particularly strong and pervasive if the people are (a) highly dependent on one another, (b) equally rather than unequally dependent, and (c) engaged in a joint task. The research demonstrates that tasks with higher degrees of jointness produce a greater sense of shared responsibility and stronger affective attachments to a group. As expected, social-unit attributions transform individually based feelings into collectively oriented feelings. Moreover, results of research testing the affect theory dovetail with other research in organizational behavior, for example, evidence that positive affect fosters more cooperation and more inclusive mind-sets for processing information. A unique aspect of the affect theory is its attention to emotional pathways by which interdependent task structures generate group and organizational commitments.

The theory has implications for the design of jobs, the structuring of team tasks, and systems of accountability. Highly specialized, precisely defined jobs may create clear expectations and good metrics for performance, but they also may reduce the overall sense of shared responsibility among a set of employees engaging in complementary tasks thereby weakening their affective commitment to the group or organization. Also, the cognitive framing of tasks by leaders can have an impact on whether positive task experiences strengthen or weaken ties to teams or the larger organization and thus how much individuals are prepared to sacrifice for the local group unit or larger organization. Finally, accountability systems that target collective results are likely to promote stronger and more affective ties to the employer organization than those that target only individual accountability.

Edward J. Lawler

See also Causal Attribution Theory; Dual-Concern Theory; Leadership Practices; Organizational Commitment Theory; Social Exchange Theory; Theory of Cooperation and Competition; Theory of Emotions

Further Readings

Lawler, E. J. (2001). An affect theory of social exchange. *American Journal of Sociology, 107,* 321–352.

Lawler, E. J., & Thye, S. R. (2006). Social exchange theory of emotion. In J. Stets & J. Turner (Eds.), *Handbook of the sociology of emotions* (pp. 295–320). New York, NY: Springer.

Lawler, E. J., Thye, S. R., & Yoon, J. (2008). Social exchange and micro social order. *American Sociological Review, 73,* 519–542.

Lawler, E. J., Thye, S. R., & Yoon, J. (2009). *Social commitments in a depersonalized world.* New York, NY: Russell Sage Foundation Press.

Thye, S. R., Yoon, J., & Lawler, E. J. (2002). The theory of relational cohesion: A review of a research program. In S. R. Thye & E. J. Lawler (Eds.), *Advances in group processes* (Vol. 18, pp. 139–166). Oxford, England: Elsevier Science.

AFFECTIVE EVENTS THEORY

Affective events theory (AET) is primarily a framework for studying the nature, causes, and consequences of affective experiences at work. It has been an important influence on the way moods and emotions have been studied in work settings. AET is also a framework for an alternative paradigm for organizational research, one that focuses on within-person variability, the effects of work events on people's work lives, and on the subjective, first-person experience of workers. AET was first described by Howard Weiss and Russell Cropanzano in 1996. This entry presents a brief discussion of its central arguments and applications.

Fundamentals

As an organizing framework for the study of moods and emotions at work, affective events theory is organized around a number of critical distinctions and assumptions. Chief among them are the differences between true affective states, such as moods and emotions, and attitudinal constructs, such as job satisfaction and commitment; the importance of events as proximal causes of affective states and other work outcomes; the delineation of outcomes driven by affect and those driven by attitudes; the episodic structure of work experiences; and the recognition that developing models of within-person variability in affect and performance is as important as developing models of between-person variability.

AET begins by drawing a distinction between job satisfaction and true affective states like moods and emotions. Although this distinction is now well recognized, at the time that AET was introduced, definitions of satisfaction as emotion predominated, causing conceptual confusion among the constructs. In contrast, AET defines satisfaction as an evaluative judgment made *about* one's job, different from but influenced by the variable emotional experiences one has *on* one's job. As described in the original paper and elaborated on by Weiss in later writings, emotions and moods are variable states with relatively definable beginning and endings and carry distinct phenomenal feelings. Satisfaction and other work attitudes are evaluative judgments that, while changeable, are neither "experiential" nor statelike.

A number of key aspects of AET turn on this distinction. For example, consistent with the nature of emotions as states and the basic research on emotional instigation, AET emphasizes the causal influence of events on employees' experiences. Things happen to people, at work and off work, and these events are the proximal causes of affective

states. AET contrasts the focus on events as causal influences with the more traditional focus on work features (pay structures, supervisory styles, etc.) as causal influences. It further suggests that many structural relationships between features of the work environment and affect reports are mediated by the proximal influence of work events. As a result, AET has stimulated research on the nature and consequences of work events.

Following from this, AET makes a distinction between affect-driven behaviors and judgment-driven behaviors, a distinction that helps resolve traditional difficulties in understanding affect- and satisfaction-performance relationships. As described in the AET framework, many aspects of work performance are variable and influenced by being in a certain affective state at a particular moment in time (affect-driven behaviors). Other behaviors are more directly influenced by more enduring attitudes about the job or organization (judgment-driven behaviors). Treating satisfaction as an emotion confuses these two causal processes, leading to the false assumption that satisfaction is a proximal cause of behaviors more likely influenced by momentary affective states and contributing to the ambiguity surrounding affect-performance relationships. In drawing this distinction, AET encourages clarification of proximal causal processes associated with different work outcomes.

Borrowing ideas from Nico Frijda, AET developers and/or practioners describe emotional experiences at work as having an episodic structure, with an emotion episode being a subjectively coherent state extended over time, organized around a coherent theme but potentially including various discrete emotions. The AET framework suggests the importance of studying episodic structures of life experiences generally, and follow-up work has focused on the performance implications of parallel streams-of-emotion episodes and performance episodes.

In sum, AET offers a framework for understanding the within-person causes and consequences of subjective emotional experiences in organizational settings. It describes the nature of affective experiences at work, the episodic structure of such experiences, the influence of affective states on work performance and job attitudes, and the appropriate way to study these processes.

While AET has been an influential framework for studying worker emotions since its presentation, it has also influenced research outside the fields of management and organizational behavior, having been applied to problems of consumer psychology, K–12 classroom effectiveness, and work-family processes. Finally, although AET is best known as a framework for studying emotional experiences, its influence on management research extends beyond this topic. AET's focus on within-person, episodic processes has stimulated more research on the variable nature of work experiences and on the causal importance of work events, and its articulation of the distinctions between attitudes and affective states has helped increase attention to subjective experiences at work more generally.

Howard M. Weiss

See also Affect Theory; Emotional and Social Intelligence; Theory of Emotions

Further Readings

Beal, D. J., Weiss, H. M., Barros, E., & MacDermid, S. M. (2005). An episodic process model of affective influences on performance. *Journal of Applied Psychology, 90,* 1054–1086.

Weiss, H. M. (2002). Deconstructing job satisfaction: Separating evaluations, beliefs and affective experiences. *Human Resource Management Review, 12,* 173–194.

Weiss, H. M., & Beal, D. J. (2005). Reflections on affective events theory. In N. M. Askanasy, W. Zerbe, & C. E. J. Hartel (Eds.), *Research on emotion in organizations: The effect of affect in organizational settings* (Vol. 1, pp. 1–21). Oxford, England: Elsevier.

Weiss, H. M., & Cropanzano, R. (1996). Affective events theory: A theoretical discussion of the structure, causes, and consequences of affective experiences at work. In B. M. Staw & L. L. Cummings (Eds.), *Research in organizational behavior* (Vol. 18, pp. 1–74). Greenwich, CT: JAI Press.

Weiss, H. M., & Rupp, D. E. (2011). Experiencing work: An essay on a person-centric work psychology. *Industrial and Organizational Psychology: Perspectives on Science and Practice, 4,* 83–97.

AGENCY THEORY

Rooted in the field of financial economics and influenced by law, agency theory is used to apply a contractual framework to a vast array of situations in which one party, referred to as the principal, utilizes the services of another party, referred to as the agent. The contractual obligations of the agent to the principal can be negatively affected by the agent's self-interest and result in "agency costs" borne by the principal. However, the principal should anticipate that agency costs might emerge, and he or she can proactively set up controls to keep the costs in check. Agency theory's impact on management theory has been tremendous. Most notably, it is the dominant theory of corporate governance, and indeed agency theory has helped to spur the study of corporate governance. This entry is an exploration of the application of agency theory within the field of management, including some extensions of the theory. It explores why agency theory is so influential, yet at the same time can be so contentious.

Fundamentals

Agency theory provides a parsimonious framework for analyzing transactions or relationships between two parties, the principal and the agent, in which the principal engages the agent to provide a good or service. The theory shows such transactions and relationships as implicit contracts. There are two forces affecting the dyadic contract between the principal and agent: the agent's contractual obligation to the principal and the agent's self-interest, which is assumed to differ from the contractual obligation. The agent is often hired based on expertise or knowledge and is trusted to use this expertise on behalf of the principal. But this gap in expertise indicates that information asymmetries exist between the parties and the agent might have an informational advantage over the principal. Sources of information asymmetry consist of adverse selection, or incomplete precontract information (e.g., the agent is not as competent or experienced as he or she appeared to be), and moral hazard, or postcontract hidden action or hidden information (e.g., the agent takes on too many contracts and fails to service a particular principal well).

As the agent is motivated by self-interest and might engage in adverse selection or moral hazard, "agency costs" can emerge in contract execution and will reduce the outcome to the principal. The term *opportunism* is used to describe the category of self-interest that is characterized by guile. However, a principal can minimize agency costs by assuming that they will tend to occur and employ controls over the agent in order to preempt their occurrence. The two key means for the principal to control the agent are (a) monitoring the agent and (b) creating incentives that align the agent's self-interest with that of the principal, known as bonding. It is thought that when an agent has highly specialized knowledge, monitoring the agent becomes difficult and incentive alignment becomes particularly critical. Monitoring and bonding are not costless and result in additional sources of agency costs that are borne by the principal. However, agency theory espouses that contracts can be structured so that the cost of these preemptive controls is low and will result in greatly reduced resident agency costs due to information asymmetries. In other words, agency theory assumes that managers might run the firm to suit their own interests rather than the interests of their shareholders. However, shareholders can prevail by monitoring and rewarding the managers so that managerial self-interest is then aligned with that of shareholders, and the overarching goal of maximization of shareholder value is achieved.

Per the research paradigms of organization theory put forth by Gibson Burrell and Gareth Morgan, agency theory is clearly in the functionalist paradigm; it regards maintenance of the status quo or the sociology of regulation rather than radical change, and its perspective is one of purported objectivity rather than subjectivity. Along with industrial organization economics and transaction cost theory, agency theory demonstrates the formidable influence of the fields of economics and financial economics on management theory. The theory has been particularly impactful in strategic management, indicating that the foundational influence of economics on the development of this subfield of management has continued in new manifestations. Within the related field of public administration, a variation of agency theory is referred to as public choice theory, which has to do with the accountability of elected officials to their constituents and issues tied to the relative unaccountability of government administrators and bureaucrats, who are shielded by their civil service protection.

Evolution

Corporate governance is an interdisciplinary field, encompassing financial economics, management, accounting, and law. Its definitions range from the rights, responsibilities, and relationships among stakeholders in establishing the direction and performance of the firm, a stakeholder-based definition, to the narrow definition tied to financial economics, which concerns the alignment of control mechanisms to maximize shareholder value. Agency theory rests on the latter definition.

In a powerful seminal work in 1976, the financial economists Michael C. Jensen and William H. Meckling touted agency theory as a theory of the firm, with the firm viewed as a "nexus of contracts." Shareholder wealth maximization is a central assumption of agency theory in this application, as it is an assumption of financial economics. Yet agency theory puts forth the idea that if left to their own devices, managers will tend to overdiversify and overdevelop their firms at the expense of shareholder value maximization. Jensen and Meckling characterized the publicly held or public corporation by its problematic separation of ownership and control, which had been noted several decades earlier by Adolf A. Berle and Gardiner C. Means. In the public company characterized by inactive, diffused ownership, owners or shareholders no longer controlled the firm or its management; instead, corporate managers filled the void by both managing and controlling the firm, a style known as managerialism. While Berle and Means had earlier recognized the issue of the separation of ownership and control, Jensen and Meckling presented a solution to the dilemma; they identified several means by which owners or principals can reduce agency costs and reestablish control over the managers or agents of firms, to reap the rightful benefit of shareholder value maximization.

Eugene F. Fama and Michael C. Jensen then joined the concept of residual claimant status with a nexus of contracts perspective. Agency theorists positioned owners as residual claimants who bear the firm's risk of bankruptcy and are therefore entitled to the firm's profit after all others—namely, its fixed claimants including employees and bond holders—are paid. This agency representation of owners as residual risk bearers and residual claimants further served to advance the primacy of owners and managers' obligations to them through shareholder value maximization.

Yet it must be noted that despite its earlier influence, indeed domination, in financial economics, it was Kathleen M. Eisenhardt's review of agency theory that led to its burgeoning use in management. Eisenhardt differentiated between positive agency theory, focused on governance mechanisms that limit manager-agents' self-serving behavior as exemplified by the contributions of Jensen and colleagues, and the more abstract principal-agent research, focused on the use of logical deduction and mathematical proofs. Eisenhardt took a theory that had little to do with management theory or practice—indeed could be viewed as antimanagement in its assumption that managers have a different attitude toward risk than their shareholders and will tend to make strategic decisions to favor their own attitude, and presented positive agency theory in a manner that illustrated its usefulness in analyzing relationships and testing hypotheses. For example, while agency theory acknowledges the potential for goal conflict, it assumes that conflict resolution lies in the alignment of economic incentives, rather than in the political means of bargaining, negotiation, and coalition building. It is surely much easier for management scholars to test and measure the impact of managerial economic incentives on shareholder value than it is to test and measure the effects of bargaining, negotiation, and coalition building. Agency theory offered management scholars the benefit of parsimonious explanation and strong predictive ability relative to other theories, while ignoring the potential effects of a more realistic range of human motivations and conditions, including the institutional context of the contract as noted by Eisenhardt.

Within the United States and in many other contexts, corporate governance control mechanisms consist of several internal or firm-level forces and several external or contextual forces. The internal control mechanisms are shareholder power, boards of directors, and executive compensation. Agency theory has a prescription for the effective utilization of each internal control mechanism. First, agency theorists' call for shareholder action in aligning managerial and owner interests, which is achieved by the reconcentration of active ownership. Second, according to agency theory, boards of directors exist largely to monitor management and ensure that managers are focused on the overarching corporate goal of maximizing shareholder value; those managers who fail to do so should be replaced by their boards. Third, agency theory has abjectly promoted the use of executive stock options as a mechanism for aligning shareholder and executive interests, with executives rewarded with shares if the firm's stock reaches the option strike price.

There is also the external corporate-control mechanism of corporate takeover, referred to as the market for corporate control, in which underperforming firms whose market value has declined with their performance are acquired by well-performing firms. Whereas there are other external corporate-control mechanisms, or gatekeepers, including industry regulation, credit rating agencies, and auditors, agency theory relies more on internal-control mechanisms, most notably executive compensation, and on the external mechanism of the market for corporate control, assuming that these are more efficacious than the other mechanisms. They are the mechanisms that are most clearly related to economic rather than political means of control.

Importance

Agency theory is surely influential, provocative, and controversial. It attracts some management researchers and provides them with a framework for studying a range of organizational phenomena; it repels others, who critique it; and it challenges a third group, who both revere many of its aspects but revile its shortcomings. Agency theory has also "put a dent in the universe" by affecting business practice through its prescriptions regarding corporate governance mechanisms. This section will first review the application of agency theory within the academic field of management and will then review the effects on business practice that are associated with the influence of agency theoretic thinking.

Impact on Management Theory

Virtually any relationship or transaction can be studied by employing the concept of the principal-agent contract and evaluating the efficacy of mechanisms in controlling the agent and thereby reducing agency costs. Management scholars have applied the theory to a broad range of interorganizational phenomena, including public-private partnerships, supply chain management, and franchising. It has also been employed in intraorganizational phenomena, for example, decision making, employee performance, and corporate entrepreneurship. Yet agency theory's largest area of application within management is corporate governance, which tends to be interdisciplinary and draws from management, finance, law, accounting, and other disciplines. Agency theory has been employed in the study of institutional investment and investor activism and in various aspects of the composition and processes of boards of directors, mergers and acquisitions (referred to as the "market for corporate control"), and executive compensation, generally within the context of effects on organizational performance.

Yet agency theory is also among the most criticized theories within management. Perhaps the most frequent criticism is triggered by its assumption that people are atomistic beings who are primarily motivated by self-interest, rather than socialized beings primarily motivated by norms, professionalism, and/or moral obligation. Despite scholars' claims of its objectivity, agency theory has been viewed as being normative; accordingly, it both advances shareholder primacy as the overarching corporate goal and legitimates self-interest as a motivator. Perhaps the most severe critique of agency theory regards its lack of ethical responsibility in possibly unintentionally promoting corporate corruption and disregard for the societal implications of business practice. The labeling of self-interest as the primary human motivator might unintentionally encourage self-interest, creating a self-fulfilling prophecy.

Some find that the attempt to explain complex, social phenomena through a contractual approach is simply inappropriate and leads to deceptively simplistic solutions. Agency theory is thought to ignore the interdependence and trust that characterizes organizational relationships and teams; and its top-down focus might encourage Taylorism. It diminishes the role of management to that of merely monitoring and rewarding others; and the theory's overemphasis on financial incentives is misguided, as financial incentives can "crowd out" the effects of nonfinancial (and often cheaper and more effective) incentives. Agency theory overstates the case of performance issues due to self-interest while ignoring the difficulties of making managerial decisions within a context of uncertainty, ambiguity, and goal contestation. Certainly, not all suboptimal organizational performance is due to the agency costs of managerial mischief; yet agency theory does not allow for consideration of other sources of suboptimal performance.

There have been attempts to overcome some of the criticisms by melding agency theory with other management theories; these most notably include the behavioral-agency theory of Robert M.

Wiseman and Luis R. Gomez-Mejia, which intertwines some elements of behavioral decision theory; and stakeholder-agency theory, advanced by Charles W. L. Hill and Thomas M. Jones. Luh Luh Lan and Loizos Heracleous boldly apply agency theory from an enlightened stakeholder perspective; in their model, the corporation itself is the principal, and the role of the board expands from monitors to "mediating hierarchs." There have been attempts to reflect greater complexity in the agency contract by conceptualizing multiparty rather than dyadic contracts and to focus on the role of the contract's institutional context in affecting agency costs. The construct of "principal-principal costs" has emerged; it proposes that there is heterogeneity among investors and their interests and indicates that powerful shareholders of a firm (including founding families, those with voting stock, and block holders) can advance their specific interests at the expense of other shareholders. Accordingly, managers can become the pawns of powerful, controlling shareholders.

The abuse of small investors by powerful, controlling investors is a reality in many countries and contexts, and it is interesting that agency theory has been employed to advance this important issue of investor abuse. Perhaps new applications of the theory and new constructs developed from its framework will continue to develop and help to overcome some of the criticism. It cannot be denied that this overly simplistic framework does cause us to focus on the most basic aspects of transacting, which can well be lost in more inclusive theories, and it has generated a groundswell of reaction and new theorizing that might not have otherwise occurred.

Impact on Business Practice

The timing of agency theory's rise to prominence in the 1980s led to its impact on changing actual business practice. Corporate performance was suffering due to the massive overexpansion and diversification of the 1950s to 1960s and was also reeling from the energy crisis, inflation, and global competition. Agency theory presented a series of prescriptions for refocusing corporations by exerting greater control over management.

But many of the prescriptions have either exacerbated the problems or created new problems. First, overreliance on stock options as a means to align managers with shareholders has often backfired, leading to malfeasance including accounting fraud and the backdating of options contracts. It is preferable to use long-term stock grants rather than stock options in executive compensation, so executives bear the downside as well as the upside risk of strategic decisions, as do shareholders. Second, a series of studies indicates that the increased level of monitoring of executives and their more frequent replacement by boards has resulted in even greater compensation levels, due to the resulting heightened executive employment risk. Third, the market for corporate control rarely works as theorized. Often, small, high-performing firms are taken over by large, mediocre firms; the cyclical nature of the activity encourages overpayment for the target, and integration costs negatively affect the deal's rate of return.

Fourth, the movement toward more independent board members hasn't helped, other than in a symbolic way, as the board nomination process remains troubled. Fifth, agency theory promotes the practice of firms completely altering their governance structure by "going private," a process in which firms depart from public stock markets and are then owned by a handful of private equity firms. This trend is troublesome regarding, first, its potentially negative impact on corporate social performance, given newly private firms' abject emphasis on shareholders and shareholder value; and second, its negative effects on employees, bond holders, and other stakeholders, as newly private firms tend to be highly leveraged and are at undue risk of bankruptcy. Sixth, the watchdog mechanism of industry regulation needs revival, as deregulation of banking and other industries—associated with the free-market mantra manifested in agency theory—contributed to the great recession. Perhaps the group of management scholars who both revere and revile agency theory will continue to develop more thoughtful, holistic, and sustainable models, and might "crowd out" the scholars who have utilized the theory without being mindful of its implications for business practice.

Marguerite Schneider

See also Behavioral Theory of the Firm; Management Roles; Managerialism; Prospect Theory; Stakeholder Theory; Stewardship Theory; Upper-Echelons Theory

Further Readings

Berle, A. A., & Means, G. C. (1932). *The modern corporation & private property.* New York, NY: Transaction.

Burrell, G., & Morgan, G. (1979). *Sociological paradigms and organizational analysis.* London, England: Heinemann.

Eisenhardt, K. M. (1989). Agency theory: An assessment. *Academy of Management Review, 14*(1), 67–74.

Fama, E. F., & Jensen, M. C. (1983). Separation of ownership and control. *Journal of Law & Economics, 26,* 301–325.

Heath, J. (2009). The uses and abuses of agency theory. *Business Ethics Quarterly, 19*(4), 497–528.

Hill, C. W. L., & Jones, T. M. (1992). Stakeholder-agency theory. *Journal of Management Studies, 29*(2), 131–154.

Jensen, M. C., & Meckling, M. H. (1976). Theory of the firm: Managerial behavior, agency costs and ownership structure. *Journal of Political Economy, 3*(4), 305–360.

Lan, L. L., & Heracleous, L. (2010). Rethinking agency theory: The view from law. *Academy of Management Review, 35*(2), 294–314.

Schneider, M. (2000). When financial intermediaries are corporate owners: An agency model of institutional ownership. *Journal of Management and Governance, 4*(3), 207–237.

Wiseman, R. M., & Gomez-Mejia, L. R. (1998). A behavioral agency model of managerial risk taking. *Academy of Management Review, 23*(1), 133–153.

ANALYTIC HIERARCHY PROCESS MODEL

The analytic hierarchy process (AHP) is a method for prioritizing among alternatives to facilitate decision making. Developed by Thomas L. Saaty in the 1970s, the AHP provides the decision maker a means to decompose a complex problem into a hierarchy of levels that then allows the decision maker to rank various elements within any particular level using a pairwise comparison scheme. AHP is a relevant topic within this encyclopedia because it has wide appeal and has been used extensively in a variety of managerial decision-making contexts. This entry provides an overview of the generic AHP process, describes some of the supporting notions, explains some of the criticisms, and discusses some of the managerial applications.

Fundamentals

The analytic hierarchy process (AHP) comprises a hierarchy of levels (e.g., goals, criteria, and alternatives). At each level, manager(s) examine each entity on a level across all combination of pairs for the subordinate level. For example, if the goal was to select a car to purchase, one of the criteria for selecting that car might be fuel economy. To determine a priority of cars for a given criterion, each car would be compared to all other alternative cars in terms of that particular criterion. In this case, a hybrid sedan (40 mpg) would be considered more preferable than a midsize sport utility vehicle (25 mpg). This would be repeated for all criteria (e.g., storage space, price, maintenance cost, styling, etc.). Then, each criterion would be evaluated against all other criteria. Once all comparisons have been made (and the rating and ranking have been completed), the range of decisions (choice of cars) will have been prioritized according to the criteria.

The following is the general process by which the AHP is applied in a decision-making context. AHP uses the following basic format to elicit key information about the decision problem:

- Describe the problem to be considered.
- Develop a hierarchy for the problem under consideration. A basic AHP hierarchy might include objectives at the top level, criteria at the next level, and alternatives at the lowest level. There can be more or fewer levels.
- Given this hierarchy, a set of pairwise comparisons are developed (such that for each level of the hierarchy, there are $n[n-1]/2$ judgments to be made using a relative scale). For example, if there are two items being compared, A and B, the decision maker would be asked which element is preferred, more important, etc. Then, the decision maker would indicate the strength of that relationship: equal, moderate, strong, very strong, or extreme (and the following absolute numbers are assigned: 1, 3, 5, 7, or 9, respectively). For example, if A is considered moderately more important than B, it would be assigned the value 3 to indicate that it is three times more important than B. Conversely, B is one third as important as A (the reciprocal). Pairwise comparisons are made for each level of the hierarchy.

Once pairwise-comparison judgments have been made, a solution technique is used to identify the principle eigenvalues for each item in a particular level of the hierarchy. These eigenvalues correspond to the relative weight assigned to each item. The relative weights can be combined across the various levels (e.g., decision criteria) to determine the most preferred alternative (according to the decision-maker's judgments from the pairwise comparisons).

AHP also allows for consideration of what is called a *consistency index,* which examines the coherence of judgments as indicated by the frequency of intransitivies. Such an inconsistency would be evident by the following set of judgments: A is preferred to B, B is preferred to C, C is preferred to A. This consistency index can be used in several ways: It can be used to evaluate the coherence of a particular set of judgments, or it may provide feedback to the decision maker to reevaluate his or her inconsistent judgments.

There are several supporting notions that make this theory possible: A hierarchy may be constructed to represent the decision problem; there are a finite number of items people can effectively consider at one time; at a sufficient level of difference, people can distinguish differences in stimuli between two items; the judged relationships between items can be expressed as ratio scales. Thus, a nearest integer approximation of the ratio between compared values will be revealed by a derived scale, clustering and pivoting can extend the arbitrary scale, the weights are insensitive to small perturbations of judgments under certain conditions, the tangibility of the criteria will dictate the solution method (top-down or bottom-up), and the synthesis is additive in nature.

One of the strongest criticisms of the AHP was that it suffers rank reversal when alternatives are introduced or removed. This has been addressed in several ways including to note that the decision criteria depend upon the alternatives, and accordingly, when alternatives are added or removed, the criteria and also the judgments will necessarily change, and thus, there may be reversals due to this dependence. Other criticisms include concerns when the hierarchy is incomplete and when there is inconsistency in the judgments about paired comparisons and about the particular solution method for finding the relative weights.

Despite these criticisms, due to its simplicity and ability to simplify complex decision problems, AHP has been applied widely in many domains (including private, public, and nonprofit sectors) and across many business functions (e.g., logistics, manufacturing, marketing, strategy). Furthermore, AHP has been integrated with other methods, such as mathematical optimization, quality function deployment, SWOT (strengths, weaknesses, opportunities, and threats) analysis, and data envelopment analysis.

AHP has been used in a wide variety of applications and managerial settings in public, private, and not-for-profit sectors. It has been used in many industry sectors including agriculture, construction, manufacturing, transportation, financial services, retail trade, services, and education.

Paul Szwed

See also Decision Support Systems; Decision-Making Styles; Garbage Can Model of Decision Making; Intuitive Decision Making; Participative Model of Decision Making; "Unstructured" Decision Making

Further Readings

Forman, E. H., & Gass, S. I. (2001). The analytic hierarchy process—An exposition. *Operations Research, 49*(4), 469–484.

Saaty, T. L. (1990). How to make a decision: The analytic hierarchy process. *European Journal of Operational Research, 48,* 9–26.

Saaty, T. L. (2000). *Fundamentals of decision making and priority theory with the analytic hierarchy process, Vol. 6.* Pittsburgh, PA: RWS Publications.

Vaidya, O. S., & Kumar, S. (2006). Analytic hierarchy process: An overview of applications. *European Journal of European Operational Research, 169*(1), 1–29.

ANALYTICAL AND SOCIOLOGICAL PARADIGMS

In the 1970s, Gibson Burrell and Gareth Morgan were young scholars from the United Kingdom who pondered the discordance that characterized the field of sociology in the latter half of the 20th century. Their 1979 book titled *Sociological Paradigms and Organizational Analysis* explored the philosophical traditions that influenced various schools of thought.

In the book, they developed a representation of four distinct schools or "paradigms" within sociology, which embody contrasting assumptions about the nature of society and the appropriate approach to its study. The four paradigms reflect beliefs regarding two issues or dimensions, whether the nature of social phenomena is inherently objective or subjective and whether the study of society should focus on societal regulation (or stability) or on radical societal change. The four paradigms are the functionalist (objective, regulation), interpretive (subjective, regulation), radical humanist (subjective, radical change), and radical structuralist (objective, radical change). At the time of their writing, the functionalist paradigm, which is associated with modernity and the age of science, dominated sociology and organizational analysis; Burrell and Morgan noted that the other paradigms shared the quality of being a response or reaction to functionalism. More than 30 years later, functionalist domination or hegemony continues, though to a lesser degree, in part reflecting the influence of this foundational book in encouraging work within the "reactive" paradigms. While Burrell and Morgan clearly viewed the four paradigms as mutually exclusive, there is continued debate as to whether the paradigms are incommensurate or can be "bridged" and whether bridging would be of benefit. Importantly, these debates are not merely academic exercises but also shape what is studied, learned, thought, expected, and experienced in and about organizations and society. This entry elaborates on the context of the theory's development, its impact, and contemporary debates regarding it.

Fundamentals

Philosophy and Paradigms

Using the language of philosophy, Burrell and Morgan proposed that theories of organizations reflect assumptions that are often implicit and taken-for-granted by theorists and those who are influenced by their theorizing. These assumptions have an ontological nature, meaning that they concern the essence of phenomena and reality: "whether 'reality' is a given 'out there' in the world, or the product of one's mind" (1979, p. 1). They also have an epistemological nature and reflect beliefs about knowledge, namely, what it is, how it is obtained, and if and how it is discerned to be "true." The authors propose that there are also embedded assumptions about the relationship between humans and the social world, namely, if humans are conditioned and become products of their society or if there is a large potential for human action or agency to evoke social change. Last, Burrell and Morgan put forth the idea that beliefs about ontology, epistemology, and human nature shape methodology, or how one should go about investigating social phenomena in order to obtain knowledge.

Burrell and Morgan presented four intellectual traditions or paradigms. Before describing each of the paradigms, it is important to note that the use of the word *paradigm* in this application to sociology and organization theory has a distinct meaning from that of the early work of Thomas M. Kuhn in discussions of the physical sciences. Norman Jackson and Pippa Carter have detailed that according to Kuhn, a paradigm of "normal science" comes to dominate, despite an inability to explain all phenomena. Over time, the incidents of anomalies that cannot be explained by the reigning paradigm increase, leading to new theorizing and development of a new paradigm, which—if successful—comes to replace or supersede the (older) dominant paradigm and becomes the new normal science. So in the Kuhnian view, there is always a dominant paradigm, though dominance shifts from one paradigm to another as new knowledge is gained. Burrell and Morgan instead present their four paradigms as existing simultaneously and in tension with each other. It is also important to note that much of their discussion

of the paradigms in the 1979 book regarded the societal, rather than the organizational, level of analysis, despite the book's title. Some implications for organizations would be forthcoming over the next few decades, most notably in critical management studies.

The Four Paradigms

As seen in Figure 1, the horizontal dimension of the model refers to different representations of management "reality"—as inherently relativistic and dependent on the perspective of the individual, versus comprising tangible elements that are related in regular, relatively predictable ways. The vertical dimension of the model refers to different suppositions of management "focus"—on societal regulation, order, unity, and integration versus on societal tensions, conflict, inequality, and liberation.

The aforementioned dominant functionalist paradigm reflects the assumption that there is an objective reality which is independent of the participant and observer. Social science should follow the principles of normal science derived from the natural sciences; these principles include a researcher who has been formally trained in the scientific method and endeavors to search for knowledge in a manner that is unbiased by personal values. Functionalism believes in the development and progress of society based on a problem-solving approach, with solutions that seek to tweak rather than overthrow the status quo. It stresses that knowledge learned from a particular study can often be applied or generalized

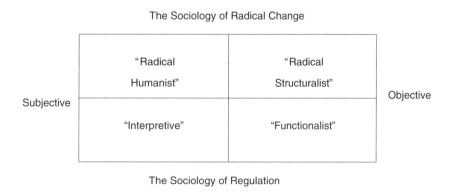

Figure 1   Four Paradigms for the Analysis of Social Theory

Source: From "Four paradigms for the analysis of social theory," in *Sociological Paradigms and Organisational Analysis* by Gibson Burrell and Gareth Morgan (Farnham, England: Ashgate, 1985), pp. 22. Copyright © 1985. Reprinted by permission of the publishers.

to other situations. Based on the application of knowledge to other contexts and development of new knowledge, the social world is seen as characterized by either certainty or predictability. The functionalist paradigm is illustrated by the ubiquitous contingency approach to organizations. Based on the results of previous studies, factors such as its size, age, and technology determine the "best way" for a particular organization to be managed and become efficient and effective.

The second interpretive paradigm is similar to functionalism in stressing regulation or maintenance of the status quo, but it does this largely by default rather than by choice. Great emphasis is placed on the subjectivity of human experience. Here, functionalism's notions of generalizability and predictability have no legitimacy or relevance; instead, the emphasis is on gaining understanding and meaning from the perspective of involved participants, as understanding and meaning of the social world can occur only at the level of subjective experience. Indeed, rather than the subjective experience of an objective reality, according to the interpretive paradigm, reality is enacted or socially constructed by participants. As Morgan stated in 1984, in a reflection on the paradigms, "The whole thrust of the interpretive paradigm is to suggest that the world we inhabit is much more of our own making than we are usually prepared to recognize" (Morgan, 1984, p. 306). Interpretive research is illustrated by the ethnographic, participant-observer approach of John Van Maanen, who once participated in a police training program in order to gain understanding of the socialization process of new police officers and gain insight into their job-related attitudes.

The third paradigm presented by Burrell and Morgan is radical humanism, which is oppositional to functionalism in being both subjective and stressing radical change of status quo. Radical humanists stress human consciousness and the alienation and sense of powerlessness that results from being embedded in social structure (such as organizations). It is associated with the writing of the young Karl Marx and the Frankfurt critical school of philosophy or its critical theory, most notably that of Jürgen Habermas. According to Habermas, knowledge is never neutral but instead serves human interests. Radical humanism assumes that emancipation of the human spirit and fulfillment of human potential can be brought about only by overcoming

learned inaction and enacting radical social change. Reflecting the radical humanist paradigm, John Mingers had advanced that management education should present managing as a broad, important activity that is both "done by all" and is "done to all" and that learning should be viewed as the process of one's self-development related to real-life struggles.

The fourth paradigm of radical structuralism is represented by the later work of Karl Marx. It is committed to emancipation from existing societal power structures and concentrates on power relationships within an objective, realist perspective that is similar to functionalism. Compared to radical humanism, radical structuralism is less about emancipation of the human spirit and more about the potential to generate mechanisms that can reveal and change existing "deep" social structure and the status quo of power. Similar to Marx's radical structuralist position regarding workers, Margaret Blair has advanced that knowledge-age employees "own" much of the firm's intellectual capital but are not adequately compensated for their contributions. But unlike Marx, Blair's solution to employees' experience of injustice maintains a capitalist context; her "mediating hierarchy approach" advocates that employees gain voice in controlling the firm and representing their interests through the means of activist employee ownership. Radical structuralism unabashedly encourages revolutionary change in organizations and governments, which are instruments of domination, by encouraging radical change to social praxis. Power structures in organizations and social divisions in the workplace reflect the broader societal structure.

In summary, social research in functionalism is about capturing and codifying social reality; in interpretism, it reflects on constructing social reality; in radical humanism, social research is about critiquing reality; and in radical structuralism, it is about confronting social reality.

Evolution

The Context and Contribution of Sociological Paradigms and Organizational Analysis

Management is a broad, applied social science that is eclectic in developing from and tapping into a range of basic and applied social science fields. But sociology, namely, the sociology of organizations, is the foundational social science for the field of management. Much of the conceptualization and language of management, including culture, roles, norms, and power, reflects the influence of sociological thought regarding organizations.

In the latter part of the 20th century, sociology was in flux. Talcott Parsons and his adherents, known as the structuralists, had dominated sociology for several decades. Parsonian sociology explains how social order or the status quo is maintained through means including culture, roles, norms, and power. What Parsonian sociology did not explain is how social order is not omnipotent but rather is in tension with sources of disorder and how social transformation can occur. There was little if any recognition of human agency or the human potential to react to imposed structure and generate change in Parsons's writings, leading U.K. sociologist Anthony Giddens to refer to Parsons's view of humans as "social dopes." Giddens's development of structuration theory provided an intellectual basis for understanding how society is indeed not only self-perpetuating but also can and does change through human agency, and it came to eclipse Parsonian sociology.

But the issues with Parsonian sociology exceeded its inability to explain social change. Parsonian sociology represented the American domination of sociology, and as such, it unquestionably viewed the model of normal science developed in the physical sciences by Newton and others as appropriate for the social sciences. Other sociology scholars, particularly some in Europe, were working well outside the boundaries of normal science, developing new theory by in part revisiting the work of Marx and others on emancipation and domination. Yet other scholars were questioning whether results of management studies could be applied or generalized to a range of situations, given the context-specific nature of human existence and organizational life.

Burrell and Morgan entered the fray in 1979. At a superficial level, their book *Sociological Paradigms and Organizational Analysis* contributed by developing a categorization scheme of approaches to sociology. But to view Burrell and Morgan's work at a superficial level is a great disservice, as it is not merely another management theory but rather is a successful attempt at the difficult intellectual task of developing metatheory, or developing theory about theorizing. Their bold attempt to broaden management theory by introducing several nonorthodox, marginalized

perspectives from the periphery to an audience that was previously unaware of the perspectives was a highly successful endeavor. Since then, a number of important research streams have expanded on their thinking or applied their logic in new directions. For example, the radical paradigms are the foundation of the large, influential body of work known as critical management studies (CMS), which was begun in the 1990s by scholars in the United Kingdom who applied critical theory to the domain of management. CMS challenges the view of organizations as a means for attainment of rational, economic-based goals, as this view tends to reduce humans—both managers as well as nonmanagers—to part of the organizational machine. CMS advocates for a less dehumanizing, less corrupt form of management, which would stress the production and distribution of socially useful goods and service and would place emphasis on management's moral and political as well as its technical aspects. Other extensions of the heterodox paradigms include Ken Benson's dialectical theory of organizations and Sumantra Goshal's model of "bad" theories.

Pluralism or Solo Acts, Harmony or Cacophony?

There is a paradoxical quality to *Sociological Paradigms and Organizational Analysis*. First, while Burrell and Morgan successfully articulate the four paradigms, they claim that interparadigmatic research occurs rarely, as it requires that a researcher who can inhabit only one paradigm engage in the seemingly quixotic task of changing his or her paradigmatic assumptions. Yet Burrell and Morgan did so themselves, and quite well. Second, they were also quite neutral in their depiction of the paradigms, which suggests that researchers can indeed achieve a level of objectivity. Third, they refer to as "fact" that the paradigms are mutually exclusive and that a synthesis of them is not possible, given their contradictory assumptions. That researchers who are not in the functionalist paradigm should refer to an aspect of metatheory as fact is a strange juxtaposition of paradigms.

There was a groundswell of critique as well as praise for the book across a range of researchers. Comments included that the authors oversimplified and did not pay adequate attention to the diversity or schools of thought within each paradigm, that researchers can have an affinity to more than one paradigm, and that the book was weakest in the contrast between the two radical paradigms and its rumination about "antiorganization theory." Both radical paradigms focus on the political and exploitative aspects of organizations, and it is somewhat difficult to discern differences between the two of them in Burrell and Morgan's writing. But perhaps the greatest critique and debate regards their strong assertion about the paradigms' mutual exclusivity.

Despite the fact of paradigm mutual exclusivity, researchers have explored the issue of the potential for paradigm commensurability and present a range of thoughts. Norman Jackson and Pippa Carter have defended mutual exclusivity and expressed concern that attempts at commensurability are really attempts at assimilation of the heterodox paradigms into functionalism. Martin Parker and Gerard McHugh unabashedly critique a study involving a cross-paradigmatic approach but then suggest (perhaps in a barb at the reviewed study) that it can be accomplished if integrity of the paradigms is respected. Dennis Gioia and Evelyn Pitre believe that the paradigms are fundamentally incommensurable but do have permeable boundaries and can be bridged, while Gary Weaver and Gioia add that the paradigms can be connected or bridged by researchers who are positioned at points near the center of Figure 1 and diversity or pluralism in paradigms can be maintained despite the bridging. Marianne Lewis and Mikaela Kelemen have outlined an approach for multiparadigm inquiry and suggest that this type of inquiry, based on pluralism and paradox, might yield the new insights.

Importance

There are many broad and encompassing typologies and categorization schemes within management theory, and many are included in this encyclopedia. Of these, Burrell and Morgan's set of paradigms is certainly among the most provocative and influential. Their work forces into consciousness much that is deeply embedded as unquestioned truth. It causes us to think about the nature of social reality, namely, how our training and experiences form a lens through which we experience and interpret social reality; and it develops our sense of epistemology, or what we think of as knowledge about the social world.

On the one hand, from a theoretical perspective, Burrell and Morgan were advocating for future research that would place at the forefront the desire to improve the human condition by radically altering social structure. Yet despite all of the subsequent theorizing, much that is fundamental about our relationship with the paradigms is far from clear. As was said in a review of the book by Orion White in 1983, surfacing paradigmatic commitments could improve theory building. But it is also possible that under some conditions, the unearthing of our paradigmatic tendencies could make us potentially rigid and defensive regarding them or possibly lead us to overly question ourselves and become weakened as researchers, students, and practitioners of management. It is also unclear if and under what conditions we are prisoners, citizens, squatters, converts, tourists, or tour guides of our paradigms.

On the other hand, from an applied perspective, the practical implication of heterodox research—what practicing managers can "learn" from it to improve their organizations and people's experiences of and within them—is underdeveloped. But this critique could also be said of orthodox functionalist research. Yet several implications have emerged from the three heterodox paradigms that have undoubtedly greatly influenced both "orthodox" researchers and management practitioners. These include the important role of subjective experience in affecting one's understanding of a phenomenon, that power and power differentials shape societies and human experience, that the teaching of assumptions regarding human behavior in business programs (i.e., self-interest as a motivator in agency theory) can be interpreted as legitimating these assumptions, and that managerial action should be informed by critical reflection regarding assumptions and lived experiences. The heterodox paradigms bring forth the realization that the body of knowledge known as management is based on deeply rooted assumptions and values as to what is right and what is desirable. The paradigms present us with the possibility that organizations including business firms can become instruments of change that include the attainment of greater social justice among their goals.

Marguerite Schneider

See also Adaptive Structuration Theory; Critical Management Studies; Social Construction Theory; Structuration Theory; Theory Development

Further Readings

Burrell, G., & Morgan, G. (1979). *Sociological paradigms and organizational analysis.* London, England: Heinemann.

Giddens, A. (1979). *Profiles and critiques in social theory.* London, England: Macmillan.

Gioia, D. A., & Pitre, E. (1990). Multiparadigm perspectives on theory building. *Academy of Management Review, 15*(4), 584–602.

Jackson, N., & Carter, P. (1991). In defence of paradigm incommensurability. *Organization Studies, 12*(1), 109–127.

Lewis, M. W., & Kelemen, M. L. (2002). Multiparadigm inquiry: Exploring organizational pluralism and paradox. *Human Relations, 55*(2), 251–275.

Morgan, G. (1984). Opportunities arising from paradigm diversity. *Administration & Society, 16*(3), 306–327.

Morgan, G. (2011). Reflections on *Images of Organization* and its implications for organization and environment. *Organization & Environment, 24*(4), 459–478.

Parker, M., & McHugh, G. (1991). Five texts in search of an author: A response to John Hassard's "Multiple paradigms and organizational analysis." *Organization Studies, 12*(3), 451–456.

Weaver, G. R., & Gioia, D. A. (1994). Paradigms lost: Incommensurability vs. structuralist inquiry. *Organization Studies, 15*(4), 565–590.

White, O. F. (1983). Improving the prospects for heterodoxy in organization studies. *Administration & Society, 15*(2), 257–272.

APPRECIATIVE INQUIRY MODEL

Appreciative inquiry (AI) is a method for studying and changing social systems (groups, organizations, communities) that advocates collective inquiry into the best of what is in order to imagine what could be, followed by collective design of a desired future state that is compelling and, thus, does not require the use of incentives, coercion, or persuasion for planned change to occur. Developed and extended since the mid-1980s primarily by students and faculty of the Department of Organizational Behavior at Case Western Reserve University, AI revolutionized the field of organization development and was a precursor to the rise of positive organizational studies and the strengths-based movement in American management. The following entry describes the principles of AI, the most common methods, and the impact of AI.

Fundamentals

Appreciative inquiry is a response to the centrality of problem solving in managerial work and the classical action research approach to organizational inquiry and change. The originator of AI, David Cooperrider, emphasizes the limitations of problem solving for expanding human horizons and possibilities. Pointing out that the most powerful force for change is a new idea, Cooperrider argues that we need forms of inquiry and change that are generative: They help us discover what could be, rather than try to fix what is. Responding to the postmodernist argument that all social research is inherently biased by the positioning of the researcher, he suggests this is not a reason to give up the pursuit of knowledge. On the contrary, it frees us to take the idea that organizations are made and imagined to its logical conclusion: that what we choose to study and how we study it creates, as much as it discovers, the world. Therefore, a wide field of creative, positive possibility beckons to us.

The AI model is based on the assumptions that organizations are socially constructed phenomena, which have no tangible reality, and that ways of organizing are limited only by human imagination and the agreements people make with each other. It seeks to create processes of inquiry that will result in better, more effective, convivial, sustainable, and vital social systems. It assumes this requires widespread engagement by those who will ultimately implement change.

Principles of Appreciative Inquiry

For the first 15 or so years after the publication of his seminal 1987 paper on appreciative inquiry, Cooperrider resisted calls to write a book on how to do it. Instead, he wanted people to focus on the principles of the model and encouraged widespread innovation in methods. As a result, many ways of doing AI have proliferated, and it is inaccurate to say there is any one way to do it. The initial set of principles for AI was that the inquiry should begin with appreciation, should be collaborative, should be provocative, and should be applicable. Later, Cooperrider and Diana Whitney published a set of five principles that are widely cited and applied.

1. The *constructionist principle* proposes that what we believe to be true determines what we do, and thought and action emerge out of

relationships. Through the language and discourse of day to day interactions, people co-construct the organizations they inhabit. The purpose of inquiry is to stimulate new ideas, stories, and images that generate new possibilities for action.

2. The *principle of simultaneity* proposes that as we inquire into human systems, we change them, and the seeds of change, the things people think and talk about, what they discover and learn, are implicit in the very first questions asked. Questions are never neutral, they are fateful, and social systems move in the direction of the questions they most persistently and passionately discuss.

3. The *poetic principle* proposes that organizational life is expressed in the stories people tell each other every day, and the story of the organization is constantly being coauthored. The words and topics chosen for inquiry have an impact far beyond just the words themselves. They invoke sentiments, understandings, and worlds of meaning. In all phases of the inquiry, effort is put into using words that point to, enliven, and inspire the best in people.

4. The *anticipatory principle* posits that what we do today is guided by our image of the future. Human systems are forever projecting ahead of themselves a horizon of expectation that brings the future powerfully into the present as a mobilizing agent. Appreciative inquiry uses artful creation of positive imagery on a collective basis to refashion anticipatory reality.

5. The *positive principle* proposes that momentum and sustainable change require positive affect and social bonding. Sentiments like hope, excitement, inspiration, camaraderie, and joy increase creativity, openness to new ideas and people, and cognitive flexibility. They also promote the strong connections and relationships between people, particularly between groups in conflict, required for collective inquiry and change.

The Appreciative Inquiry Method

In the late 1990s, the "4D" model emerged and has become strongly associated with AI. This model identifies four phases in AI that occur after the "affirmative topic" is chosen. The affirmative topic is the focus of the inquiry (e.g., increased customer satisfaction, improved health and safety, more effective operations) but phrased in lively, inspiring language (e.g., inspiring fanatically loyal customers).

Discovery. During this stage, participants reflect on and discuss the best of *what is* concerning the object of inquiry. Most often, and this appears to be a key innovation of the AI method, participants are interviewed about their own "best of" stories (e.g., tell me about the time a business most inspired fanatical loyalty in you). Another important innovation has been to have organizational members and stakeholders act as both interviewers and interviewees, that is, to fully engage all affected parties in the act of inquiry itself. Telling and listening to meaningful, personal stories is considered central to creating widespread engagement and building relationships in the early stage of the change process. The affirmative topic is turned into a question (e.g., how do companies inspire fanatically loyal customers?), and answers stimulated by the stories are identified and shared.

Dream. During this stage, participants are asked to imagine their group, organization, or community at its best in relation to the affirmative topic. An attempt is made to identify the common aspirations of system members and to symbolize this in some way. The dream phase often results in something more symbolic, such as a graphical representation, than a mission statement.

Design. With a common dream in place, participants are asked to develop concrete proposals for the new organizational state. Initially, Cooperrider called these "provocative propositions"—a phrase linked to generative theory that still appears in some models. More commonly, social architecture processes are employed where a model of design elements is used to identify categories for participants to organize around and create change proposals, often called possibility statements or design statements.

Delivery/destiny. In the initial four-dimensional, or 4-D, model, the fourth stage was called delivery, but this was subsequently changed by Cooperrider to destiny as he found that delivery evoked images of traditional change management implementation. Exactly what ought to happen in this phase has provoked the most confusion and the least consensus among AI theorists who recognize that using the outcomes of design to create new targets, gaps to fill, and objectives to achieve may be counter to the very philosophy of appreciative inquiry. The most innovative applications have taken an improvisational, as opposed to implementational, approach. Widespread agreement for the design statements are sought, an event is orchestrated where participants make self-chosen commitments to take action consistent with any design element, and leadership makes clear that there will be no action plans or committees—instead, everyone is authorized to take those actions they believe will help bring the design to fruition. Leadership's role is to monitor and support those innovations they want to nurture and create events and processes to energize emergent and self-organizing change.

Many different approaches to AI have been identified, ranging from interventions in which a sole consultant or a small representative group of people do the AI on behalf of a larger group of people to those where most or all of the whole system is engaged in the entire 4-D process in a compressed time span. The majority of published studies of transformational change have been of the latter variety, leading to an increasing emphasis in the AI literature on widespread, synchronous engagement as central to successful AI change efforts. One particular variant, the Appreciative Inquiry Summit, has become the most often advocated form of engagement—ideally a four-day event in which all system members complete all four phases. There are some voices, however, that caution against seeing AI as an "event," however large scale, and argue that it is more effective to think of AI as a long-term process punctuated by events. They suggest that as much or more change comes from daily interactions at work, as people discuss the inquiry, trade stories, and are impacted by new conversations, as it does from new ideas or plans.

Importance

AI has had a profound impact on organizational-development practice around the world in business, nonprofit, and governmental organizations as well as communities. AI produces transformational change without crises or "burning platforms." Hundreds of significant appreciative inquiries have been documented and described at conferences, in journals and books, in the *AI Practitioner* (a quarterly magazine), and through the Appreciative Inquiry Commons (a website). Some outstanding examples include the use of AI to create the United Nations Global Compact; Imagine Chicago, an AI-inspired community-development process copied around the world; and Walmart's use of AI for its global-sustainability initiatives.

Empirical assessments of AI are limited but are more plentiful than for most organizational change strategies. There is a growing body of longitudinal and critical research that is identifying moderating and mediating conditions that affect how AI is best done and under what conditions, opportunities, and limitations. AI does not magically overcome any of the requirements for effective leadership, resourcing, and skilled facilitation of any other organizational-development or large-group intervention. Its unique significance has been in bringing social constructionist theory into widespread consideration in managerial practice, identifying the power of possibility-centric versus problem-centric change strategies, forcing an examination of the impact of positive emotions on change processes, and offering generativity, instead of problem solving, as a way to address social and organizational issues.

Gervase R. Bushe

See also Action Research; Large Group Interventions; Organizational Development; Social Construction Theory; Strategies for Change

Further Readings

Barrett, F. J., & Fry, R. E. (2005). *Appreciative inquiry: A positive approach to building cooperative capacity.* Chagrin Falls, OH: Taos Institute.

Bushe, G. R. (2012). Appreciative inquiry: Theory and critique. In D. Boje, B. Burnes, & J. Hassard (Eds.), *The Routledge companion to organizational change* (pp. 87–103). Oxford, England: Routledge.

Cooperrider, D. L., Barrett, F., & Srivastva, S. (1995). Social construction and appreciative inquiry: A journey in organizational theory. In D. Hosking, P. Dachler, & K. Gergen (Eds.), *Management and organization: Relational alternatives to individualism* (pp. 157–200). Aldershot, England: Avebury.

Cooperrider, D. L., & Srivastva, S. (1987). Appreciative inquiry in organizational life. In R. W. Woodman & W. A. Pasmore (Eds.), *Research in organizational change and development* (Vol. 1, pp. 129–169). Stamford, CT: JAI Press.

Cooperrider, D. L., & Whitney, D. (2005). A positive revolution in change: Appreciative inquiry. In D. L. Cooperrider, P. Sorenson, T. Yeager, & D. Whitney (Eds.), *Appreciative inquiry: Foundations in positive organization development* (pp. 9–33). Champaign, IL: Stipes.

Cooperrider, D. L., Whitney, D., & Stavros, J. M. (2008). *Appreciative inquiry handbook* (2nd ed.). Brunswick, OH: Crown Custom Publishing.

Ludema, J. D., Whitney, D., Mohr, B. J., & Griffen, T. J. (2003). *The appreciative inquiry summit.* San Francisco, CA: Berret-Koehler.

Whitney, D., & Trosten-Bloom, A. (2003). *The power of appreciative inquiry.* San Francisco, CA: Berrett-Koehler.

ARCHITECTURAL INNOVATION

Architectural innovations are those based on linkages between product components rather than significant breakthroughs in the components themselves. The concept can illustrate how product innovation affects organizational procedures and competitive strategy. This entry addresses the details of architectural innovation, how changes in component linkages interact with organizational skills and procedures, and how the concept interacts with market dynamics to produce competitive advantages, and concludes with a discussion of the potential pitfalls facing managers attempting to foster innovation.

Fundamentals

Product architecture is the link that integrates components into a functioning product, whereas architectural innovation changes the architecture or the manner in which the components work together as opposed to changing the components themselves. For instance, the typical coffeemaker consists of housing, filter basket, carafe, power supply, heating element, water reservoir, and water pump. Coffee potency can be adjusted by increasing the contact time between hot water and ground coffee. Therefore, a coffeemaker that controls the flow through the coffee grounds and water pumping rate

could adjust coffee potency; this is an architectural innovation. This illustrates how architectural innovation does not require significant changes in the product components, only in how they are linked together. Components within the architecture may change (smaller, lighter, etc.), but the basic component technology remains the same. In our example, the innovation was enabled by a new pump with an easily controlled flow rate, but the core design concept would still be that of a pump.

Architectural innovation fits into a two-by-two matrix that explains innovation as an interaction between changes in product linkages versus changes in core-component concepts. Innovations relying on changes to the linkages only are the architectural innovations under discussion. Changes that overturn the core-component technology but leave the linkages unchanged are *modular innovation.* For instance, a digital-telephone dialer is a significant component-technology change compared to a digital dialer, but it still accomplishes the same architectural task. Changes which affect neither the linkages nor the core-component technology are *incremental innovations,* and those that affect both are *radical innovations.*

Architectural innovation fits into a spectrum including incremental and radical innovation. Incremental innovation improves component performance without significant architectural change. A radical or disruptive innovation relies on entirely new engineering or scientific principles and can render both component and architectural knowledge obsolete.

Product architecture is often mirrored in the technical skills and managerial procedures of the firms producing the product. Firms manufacturing coffeemakers may have separate departments skilled at molding of housings, producing filter baskets and carafes, and designing power supply, heating elements, and pumping of water to a heating chamber. Firms would also develop procedures and problem-solving routines, so the departments could collaborate. These skills and procedures become the firm's core capabilities, positioning it to exploit incremental-component innovations and react effectively when competitors introduce incremental-component innovations. However, firms may not react well when faced with *architectural innovations.* The warning signs of such innovations may not be recognized due to the very skills and procedures built into the organization around the original product architecture. For instance, the introduction of a coffeemaker that uses a packet containing ground coffee with an integral filter to produce one cup would eliminate the need for a carafe and filter basket. Firms with carafe and filter-basket departments might experience internal resistance in responding to this innovation. Their core capabilities have become core rigidities that inhibit their response to innovation. Firms that excel at building component-core capabilities are often trapped in their original product architecture and suffer competitive failure when the market-accepted architecture shifts.

Architectural innovations have both marketing and technology implications and are often introduced by firms challenging the dominant firm in an industry. The dominant firm is often inhibited from introducing innovative architectures by the lack of appropriate skills and procedures or by being bound to what they know—the existing "successful" mindset. Additionally, the initial architectural innovations are often inferior to incumbent architectures when measured by parameters valued by customers served by the dominant firm. The low value placed on the initial performance of the architectural innovation further inhibits dominant firms from exploiting the innovation. The dominant firm risks a myopic view by being wedded to a specific product and its structure rather than providing value to a broad range of customers.

Challenger firms may introduce architectural innovations into adjacent markets considered unimportant by the dominant firm, but where the innovation has an advantage valued by the market. As the challenger deploys the architectural innovation into the adjacent market, that market develops the expertise and cash flows to steadily improve the new architecture until it is superior to the originally dominant architecture. The dominant firm finds its market position challenged by a superior performing product architecture and could rapidly lose its dominant position to the new entrant with an architectural innovation.

The architectural-innovation model provides insight for practicing managers to build ambidextrous organizations that can nurture both incremental innovations in the dominant architecture and architectural innovations with disruptive potential. Such ambidextrous organizations are inherently unstable, and the more profitable and powerful traditional parts of the firm associated with the dominant architecture will often overpower the younger entrepreneurs that pursue architectural innovations within the firm. It is often necessary to shield architectural innovations in separate facilities with different managers and cultures. Seiko shielded the development of the quartz-watch movement from its dominant culture built around the mechanical-watch movement. Firms can sustain a competitive advantage by actively managing a stream of incremental innovations, fundamentally new innovations, and architectural innovations. Senior management must provide balance between these competing needs for organizational resources and build an organization that can perform both today and in the future.

John C. Byrne and Thomas V. Edwards Jr.

See also First-Mover Advantages and Disadvantages; Innovation Diffusion; Innovation Speed; Patterns of Innovation; Technology S-Curve

Further Readings

Christensen, C. M. (1992). Exploring the limits of the technology s-curve. Part II: Architectural technologies. *Production and Operations Management, 1,* 358–366.

Henderson, R. M., & Clark, K. B. (1990). Architectural innovation: The reconfiguration of existing product technologies and the failure of established firms. *Administrative Science Quarterly, 35,* 9–30.

Leonard-Barton, D. (1992). Core capabilities and core rigidities: A paradox in managing new product development. *Strategic Management Journal, 13,* 111–125.

Levitt, T. (1960). Marketing myopia. *Harvard Business Review, July–August,* 45–56.

McGinn, D. (2011, August 24). The inside story of Keurig's rise—At once unlikely, ultracaffeinated, and occasionally jittery—To a billion-dollar coffee empire. *The Boston Globe Magazine.*

Tushman, M. L., Anderson, P. C., & O'Reilly, C. (1997). Technology cycles, innovation streams, and ambidextrous organizations: Organization renewal through innovation streams and strategic change. In M. L. Tushman & P. Anderson (Eds.), *Managing strategic innovation and* change (pp. 3–23). New York, NY: Oxford University Press.

Ulrich, K. (1993). The role of product architecture in the manufacturing firm. *Research Policy, 24*(3), 419–440.

ASCH EFFECT

Solomon E. Asch conducted a series of experiments on group pressure in the 1940s. The results of these experiments are known in the field of social psychology and organizational management as the Asch effect or the Asch experiments on conformity. The Asch effect is the phenomenon of group consensus and social pressure that influences an individual to change a correct answer in reaction to group members' incorrect answer to the same question. First published in 1952, the experiments' results document the degree to which the experiments' subjects were influenced by the opinions of their fellow participants. This entry highlights the series of experiments that established the Asch effect, along with the general conclusion that social pressure can convince group members to falsify their beliefs in response to even mild social pressure. Beginning with a brief review of Solomon E. Asch's career and his experiments, this entry explores the results of his experiments on group consensus and their implications for management.

Fundamentals

While at Columbia University, Solomon E. Asch began to study social pressure after reading Edward Thorndike's work on the law of effect regarding positive reinforcement. Deciding to test whether group pressure might have an effect on incorrect responses, Asch designed the experiment. The results of these studies have become known as the Asch effect.

Asch began conducting his experiments while teaching at Swarthmore College. The question he sought to answer was how do individuals conform to the opinions of a peer group? To answer the question, Asch designed his experiment to test a group of students who are gathered and seated in a room, where the "subject" is seated toward the back of the room. The entire group is shown two pictures. The first is a picture of a line, and the second is a picture of three different sized lines, only one of which is the same size as the line in the original picture.

After the pictures are shown to the group, the group is asked a series of questions about the pictures. The other participants have been instructed to answer the questions incorrectly by continuing to agree that one of the unequal lines in the second

picture is actually the same size as the original line in the first picture. The experiment tests the single subject's ability to voice his own opinion, regardless of the opinions expressed repeatedly by of those around him.

The subject hears incorrect answers from the other participants. On average, the subject disagrees the first time and responds with the correct answer. For the second trial, the subject usually disagrees again, even though the rest of the group remains committed to their wrong answer. At this point, the subject usually shows visible signs of discomfort. In spite of the subject's own visual perception, a significant number of subjects agree with the crowd. The subjects who agree give several explanations why. The two reasons they give most often for going along with the group is either that they think that the majority has to be correct or that they believe that it is important to the experiment's structure that their answers agree with the group's answers. The responses of the subjects can take three forms. The subjects can always disagree with the group, the subject can always agree with the group, or the subject can switch between disagreement and agreement.

As a follow-up to the experiment, when subjects were tested alone, they answered correctly 99% of the time. When the subjects had been a part of the experiment, the subjects conformed to the group consensus 36.8% of the time by continuing to change their answers in order to go along with the group. Overall in the experiment trials, 75% of the subjects changed at least one of their responses to the experiment's multiple questions, in order to conform to the group consensus. Conversely, 25% of the subjects stayed with their answers and remained committed to their own judgment throughout all of the trials of the experiment.

Asch observed several types of behavior while he was conducting his experiments. He noted that while the subject is actually answering the question correctly, the subject is placed in the position of being evaluated as if he has actually given the wrong answer. This situation sets up a contradiction between the public evidence of the subject's publicly stated opinion and the group consensus. Asch noted several possible behaviors as a result of the situation; however, in only a few of the experimenter's trials did subjects openly identify the group's collusion.

While Asch chose not to draw any firm conclusions about motivations, he came to believe that the experiment tested a key assumption about how we see the world. Asch was equally interested in what caused the subjects to conform to group pressures as he was interested in what caused the subject to resist group pressures for consensus. He concluded that the experiment had implications for both individual values and the formal educational system.

This series of experiments has been re-run many times since it was first reported in the 1950s. The experiments have been redesigned by theorists in order to test many different variables including the size of the overall group and the number of subjects in the experiment, as well as age, ethnicity, country of birth, sex, and subject's social status. In addition, the experiment has been re-run under the same conditions with time the only variable. While there has been variation reported in the results of many of the studies, the primary conclusion stands firm. There is a persistent tendency for people to react to group pressure and to go along with group consensus.

The Asch effect illustrates to managers that colleagues and employees may be tempted to change their voiced beliefs in response to group pressure, in order to achieve consensus. This phenomenon highlights the importance for managers to avoid accepting group decisions without first exploring the process. To avoid suboptimum decision making, managers need to dig below the surface so that different opinions are considered and the best possible solution is achieved.

Joanne L. Tritsch

See also Groupthink; Organizational Identification; Organizationally Based Self-Esteem; Participative Model of Decision Making; Theory of Self-Esteem

Further Readings

Asch, S. E. (1952). *Social psychology.* New York, NY: Prentice-Hall.

Asch, S. E. (1955). Opinions and social pressure. *Scientific American, 193*(5), 31–35.

Asch, S. E. (1956). Studies of independence and conformity: A minority of one against a unanimous majority. *Psychological Monographs, 70*(9, Whole No. 416).

Bond, R., & Smith, P. B. (1996). Culture and conformity: A meta-analysis of studies using Asch's (1952b, 1956) line judgment task. *Psychological Bulletin, 119*(1), 111–137.

Rock, I. (Ed.). (1990). *The legacy of Solomon Asch.* Hillsdale, NJ: Lawrence Erlbaum.

Attraction-Selection-Attrition Model

The attraction-selection-attrition (ASA) model introduced by Benjamin Schneider is a psychological theory that describes why organizations look and feel the way they do. It is a person-based model for understanding the etiology of organizational behavior by considering person effects as the causes of structures, processes, and technology of organizations. The model, in particular, elucidates how individuals join and leave organizations, stating that people are functions of three interrelated dynamic processes: attraction, selection, and attrition. Individuals are attracted to, selected by, and retained in organizations whose members are similar to themselves in terms of psychological attributes. The ASA cycle determines the kinds of people in an organization, which consequently defines the nature of the organization, the structures, processes, and culture. Its focus on the determinants of organizational behavior makes the theory relevant as a general management model. An overview of the fundamental propositions of ASA theory is provided, as are arguments on its validity and impact.

Fundamentals

In the 1980s, the ASA framework originated as a reaction to situational theories that focused on the influence of situational variables (e.g., groups, technology, structures) on organizational behavior. The theory attributes causes to people rather than the results of people's behavior. The first and main assumption posits that organizations are functions of the kinds of people they contain. As Schneider formulated in his seminal paper, attributes of people, not the nature of external environments or organizational technology or organizational structure, are the fundamental determinants of organizational behavior. As such, Schneider reformulated Kurt Lewin's well-known hypothesis (i.e., $B = f [P, E]$), by stating that environments are functions of the persons behaving in them; that is, $E = f (P, B)$. In his second fundamental statement, Schneider emphasizes that people are not randomly assigned to settings. The kinds of people in an organization are the function of an ASA cycle. It is the people who are attracted to, selected by, and remain in a setting, that eventually determine the setting.

Rationale

The framework departs from organizations (not individuals) as the unit of analysis. It attempts to understand interorganizational differences through a focus on the attributes of people. Following the core assumptions, the outcome of the ASA cycle determines why organizations look and feel different from each other. People are *attracted* to, and prefer, matching types of organizations, organizations *select* matching types of individuals (who share many common psychological attributes, although they may differ on some competencies) to join the organization, and nonmatching individuals finally leave the organization by the *attrition* process. The people who become part of the organization and stay based on these processes, in turn, define the nature of the organization and its structure, processes, and culture. According to Schneider, it is, thus, *the people who make the place* rather than the place that makes the people. As dispositional attributes relevant to the ASA cycle, Schneider names personality, attitudes, and values. Since people who fit tend to enter and people who do not fit tend to leave, the people who remain will constitute a more homogeneous group than those who were initially attracted to the setting. Schneider calls this the *homogeneity hypothesis*. The downside of this within-organization homogeneity is that it can be detrimental to long-term organizational viability. Organizations can become so ingrown that they fail to adapt their processes and structure to environmental changes, endangering the organizational survival. According to the ASA model, homogeneity may produce positive consequences in its early stages but negative consequences in later stages.

The propositions of ASA can be summarized as follows:

1. People select themselves into and out of an organization based upon an implicit estimate of the fit between their own characteristics and the attributes of the organization.

2. The people who are attracted to, selected by, and remain in the organization ultimately determine the structures, processes, and cultures that characterize the organization.

3. The ASA cycle produces restrictions in range in the kinds of people in an organization (homogeneity hypothesis).

4. The goals of the organization and the processes, structures, and culture that emerge from them are determined by the characteristics of the founders and those of their early colleagues.

Context

The theory originates from interactional psychology and is part of the larger person-environment fit literature that emphasizes the importance of considering the reciprocal relationships that exist between individuals and their employing organizations. The ASA cycle is closely related to the socialization process that describes how new members fit into specific organizations. However, due to the focus on organizations as unit of analysis, the ASA framework attempts to predict and understand organizational behavior rather than behavior of individuals. Furthermore, the ASA theory builds upon personality research, vocational psychology, and industrial-organizational (I/O) psychology. The first stream of literature lent the idea of the importance of the interplay of personal and situational factors in establishing behavior. The second stream of literature lent the idea that people are differently drawn to environments as a function of their own interests and personality, whereas turnover studies from the third stream of literature offered the idea that people who do not fit an environment will tend to leave it.

Importance

ASA theory stands in dark contrast to the situationist perspective, which is often emphasized in leadership literature (e.g., situational leadership), literature on the dynamics of the external environment (e.g., contingency theory), and job-design literature (job-characteristics model). Although this situationist perspective is often supported by empirical evidence, the person perspective from the ASA theory has also gained support. Schneider's propositions were empirically tested and theoretically discussed in diverse research domains. Theoretically, personality research confirms that people choose themselves into settings that fit their personality, and organizational-demography research confirms that people choose themselves into settings that fit their demographic characteristics (such as gender, age, and educational background). Empirically, several case studies on founders lend support to the role of managers in the long-term culture of organizations. This literature suggests that managers' psychological characteristics are related to the goals and the culture of their organization and that these are reflected in the attributes of the people attracted to, selected by, and retained by the organization. Yet most validity evidence concerns the homogeneity hypothesis. Direct as well as indirect evidence was found in several research domains using diverse measurement techniques. Research based on calculated, objective person-organization fit, such as the Q-sort technique, as well as research based on self-reported perceptions of subjective fit, revealed indirect support. These type of studies confirm that employees are more likely to enter and less likely to leave when the fit of personal values and organizational values is high. Empirical evidence further supports the importance of value congruence between supervisors and subordinates, between managers and their organizations, and between employees and their organizations since it predicts psychological health, positive attitudes, and intention to stay. Anecdotal evidence supports that culture fit rather than competencies fit is used as a basis for hiring—also referred to as the "hiring the right type" syndrome. A final part of indirect support originates from the social-psychological literature which refers to the attraction paradigm and the "similar-to-me" phenomenon. Most studies that directly tested the homogeneity hypothesis used laboratory studies. A few also used field studies, but studies on personality homogeneity are scarce in comparison to studies on homogeneity in demographics. Recently, a couple of personality homogenization studies have suggested that homogenization primarily occurs after the attraction and selection phase assuming that posthire attraction is the major homogenizing force.

Implications for Theory

The ASA theory offers important implications for theory, in particular for personality research and specific domains in organizational behavior theory. First of all, based on the ASA theory, one expects that personality and interest measures are not designed to make fine-grained distinctions within organizations among people who are relatively similar to begin with. Valuable data could be generated by the use of existing personality and interest measures administered to the members of entire organizations. Second, the model is important for

theories on organizational culture in that over time, the ASA cycle leads to the consolidation of organizational culture. People in organizations will be similar to each other. They will start to share attributions of cause, which become the stories and myths by which culture is transmitted and consolidated. Third, the theory is relevant for leadership theory. Different kinds of people are likely to be effective leaders in different kinds of organizations. Different traits will be predictive of leadership effectiveness depending on the kinds of people to be led. Finally, the model offers some valuable insights for job-attitudes theory. Against a situationist interpretation of what causes positive attitudes, according to the ASA model, people in a setting will have the same job attitudes, so the same organizational conditions will be differentially satisfying to people in different work environments challenging several well-known job-design models.

One limitation of the ASA model is its vague specification of what is meant by psychological attributes and fit. ASA tells nothing about precisely which personal attributes are likely to be reflected in which preferences for organizational attributes. This makes it difficult to operationalize and measure the concept of fit. Testing this theory requires analyses at the organizational level and raises the question of how to index homogeneity and measure fit. The earlier used Euclidean distance occurs less often in research as it is replaced by the polynomial regression technique. Furthermore, objective measures compete with subjective perceptions.

Implications for Practice

Although ASA does not present a new technique, test, or training program, it does offer relevant implications for management practice, in particular for organizational change and effectiveness, and personnel recruitment and selection. As regards change management, the ASA model considers increasing homogeneity as having consequences both positive (like psychological well-being) and negative. People are not infinitely adaptable and changeable. Structures and processes will merely change when the behavior of people changes, and the behavior of people will change only when different kinds of people are attracted to, selected by, and stay in the organization. Thus, to ensure long-term viability and competitiveness, organizations should (now and then) bring in newcomers to change the old-timers' dispositions. However, they should make sure that these newcomers share some attributes with those already in the organization, which they are expected to change. As regards recruitment and selection, the ASA model suggests that people join and leave whole organizations, not just jobs. Organizations may, therefore, consider selecting people for organizations not just for jobs, for example, by including organizational diagnosis next to job analysis as a basis for personnel selection. Following the potentially negative consequences related to increased homogeneity, at certain times in an organization's evolution, it may be useful to have good fit, while at other times, it may be useful to promote heterogeneity. Recruitment activities are the best way to bypass self-selection and organizational selection and to yield these "non-right" types required for organizational survival.

Rein De Cooman

See also Managing Diversity; Meaning and Functions of Organizational Culture; Organizational Culture and Effectiveness; Organizational Culture Theory; Organizational Socialization

Further Readings

Kristof-Brown, A. L., Zimmerman, R. D., & Johnson, E. C. (2005). Consequences of individuals' fit at work: A meta-analysis of person-job, person-organization, person-group, and person-supervisor fit. *Personnel Psychology, 58,* 281–342.

Schneider, B. (1987). The people make the place. *Personnel Psychology, 40,* 437–453.

Schneider, B., Goldstein, H. W., & Smith, D. B. (1995). The ASA framework: An update. *Personnel Psychology, 48*(4), 747–773.

Smith, D. B. (2008). *The people make the place: Exploring dynamic linkages between individuals and organizations.* New York, NY: Psychology Press.

ATTRIBUTION MODEL OF LEADERSHIP

The attribution model of leadership describes the interactive processes by which leaders and their employees arrive at causal explanations for employee performance in achievement-related situations and how those explanations in turn determine subsequent leader and employee behaviors and the quality of the leader-employee relationship. The model draws significantly from attribution theory, which identifies how individuals determine causes for events and describes how the resulting attributions determine individuals' emotions, thoughts, motivations, and behaviors. As the success of organizations depends significantly on maximizing employees' performance levels, understanding how leaders and employees react to employee performance is critical to helping leaders manage feedback and performance processes. This entry begins with an explanation of the evolution of the attribution model of leadership over the past three decades. It continues with a summary of the empirical research conducted on the various elements of the models and concludes by offering critical managerial applications.

Fundamentals

In an effort to better explain leader behaviors, the attribution model of leadership—introduced in the late 1970s and early 1980s—focused on leader's causal explanations for employee performance. The model indicated that leaders determine the causes for employee performance on a given task by determining to what extent (a) other employees performed equally well or poorly on the task (*consensus*), (b) the employee frequently performs equally well or poorly on the task across times and situations (*consistency*), and (c) the employee performs equally well or poorly on other tasks (*distinctiveness*). This covariation analysis determines whether the leader attributes the performance level to the employee's internal attributes or to attributes external to the employee thus arriving at either an internal or external attribution. For example, if an employee performs poorly on a certain task, has never performed well on the task (*high consistency*), also does not perform well on other tasks (*low distinctiveness*), but other employees generally perform well on the same task (*low consensus*), then the leader is likely to make an internal attribution and blame the employee's poor performance on aspects such as a lack of ability or skills.

Because this covariation analysis is complex, effortful leaders often take cognitive shortcuts and use causal schemata or categories such as ability, effort, task difficulty, and luck to quickly and economically arrive at causal explanations for employee performance. These four commonly used explanations differ across two causal dimensions: locus of causality and stability. Locus of causality refers to whether employee performance is attributed to internal or external causes while stability refers to whether it is attributed to stable or unstable causes. Ability is an internal, stable cause; effort is an internal, unstable cause; task difficulty is an external, stable cause; and luck is an external, unstable cause.

The attribution model of leadership then suggests that leader attributions for employee performance systematically determine leaders' expectations for future performance and leaders' behaviors toward the employee. In response to their employees' poor performance, leaders are more likely to target their corrective actions toward the employee if they make an internal attribution and toward situational factors if they make an external attribution. Leaders, for example, are more likely to punish employees for their poor performance when they make an internal as opposed to an external attribution. Furthermore, leaders are more likely to expect future performance to be consistent with present performance when they attribute employee performance to stable causes likely to persist over time. For instance, if a given task is difficult and may not be made simpler, the leader expects the employee to continue to perform poorly resulting in possibly severe actions, such as demotion or dismissal. When leaders make unstable, internal attributions (i.e., effort), the rewarding or punishing reactions are particularly strong. Leaders believe effort to be under the control of the employee and therefore punish employees' presumed lack of effort more strongly than when attributing poor performance to less controllable aspects.

Overall, the attribution model of leadership suggests that employee behaviors (i.e., performance) lead to leader attributions, which then lead to leader expectations and behaviors. The model also recognizes that these relationships may be influenced by a variety of different factors such as, among others, personal characteristics of the leader and employee, organizational policies, the quality of the leader-employee relationship, leader's familiarity with the performance task, and leader's expectations for employee performance.

An Interactive Extension of the Model

While the original model focused primarily on leader attributions for employee performance, later research added employees' perspectives to the model by positing that employees similarly make attributions regarding their own performance. Extending the model to the dyadic level suggests that meaningful predictions may be made when knowing the extent to which leaders and employees agree or disagree on their causal explanations. Just like leaders, employees either engage in an effortful covariation analysis or use shortcuts to arrive at internal or external and stable or instable attributions for their own performance, such as ability, effort, task difficulty, and luck.

Interestingly, although leaders and members encounter a similar objective reality, the interactive attribution model of leadership suggests that leaders and employees often arrive at divergent attributions. This is because both leaders' and employees' attributional processes are influenced by perceptual biases, such as the actor-observer bias and the self-serving bias. The *actor-observer bias* demonstrates that actors tend to attribute their own actions to situational factors while observers tend to attribute actors' actions to actors' personal dispositions. The *self-serving bias* suggests that people tend to attribute success to their own personal dispositions while they attribute failures to other people or situational factors. In combination, the two biases predispose employees to attribute their poor performance to external factors (e.g., to coworkers, to the situation) while they predispose leaders to attribute poor performance to employees' internal dispositions (e.g., ability, motivation). Over time and repeated interactions, these divergent attributions can lead to high levels of conflict between leaders and employees. For example, a leader may attribute an employee's poor task performance to a lack of ability while the employee attributes it to an equipment failure. In this circumstance, when the leader reprimands the employee, the employee is likely to be distressed about being blamed for the situation and about the leader not recognizing the equipment problems. Ultimately, this may result in decreased productivity and satisfaction and a deterioration of the leader-employee relationship. When leaders continuously blame members for poor performance, they are more likely to place the employee into their "out-group," resulting in less access to resources and less opportunity for development. Employees may then decide to engage in destructive work behaviors (e.g., theft, harassment) or withdrawal (e.g., absenteeism, quitting).

Another result of contradicting attributions may be learned helplessness in employees defined as feelings of anxiety, stress, apathy, and shame associated with repeated failures that are attributed to stable, internal causes. Helpless employees are more likely to give up, withdraw effort, and ultimately leave their jobs. The attribution model of leadership suggests that leaders may induce such learned helplessness in employees when they attribute employee failures to effort while employees attribute their failures to ability. In that case, the leader is more likely to punish the employee, which the employee will perceive as inappropriate and perceive as yet another uncontrollable failure, raising their sense of learned helplessness. The divergent attributions that leaders and employees commonly arrive at may result in detrimental consequences.

Importance

A significant amount of empirical research has been conducted to examine leaders' attributions for their employees' performance, primarily with regards to poor performance. Generally, this research provided robust evidence for the basic processes between employee behaviors, leader attributions, and leader behaviors across a variety of studies. For example, several empirical studies confirmed the proposed link between the informational cues of consensus, distinctiveness, and consistency and leader attributions and leader behaviors, such as disciplinary actions, training decisions, and feedback delivery. There is also considerable support for the link between the four primary attributional explanations of ability, effort, task difficulty, and luck and leader reactions. For example, in response to their employees' poor performance, leaders who make ability attributions generally react less negatively than leaders who make effort attributions. Similarly, leaders were generally more lenient when attributing poor performance to external as opposed to internal factors. Empirical research also supports the assumptions of the model that other personal or situational factors, such as task interdependence and supervisor control, systematically influence the nature of the proposed relationships.

The interactive extension of the model, including both leader and employee attributions, has received much less empirical attention. There is consistent support for the actor-observer bias and the self-serving bias in the psychological and organizational literature, and research suggests that leaders and employees frequently exhibit these biases in their attributional processes. However, there is only limited empirical research that has examined the interactive dynamics of matching and mismatching leader and employee attributions. The limited research available suggests that when leaders and employees are predisposed to making incompatible attributions due to their divergent attribution styles (i.e., tendencies for similar causal explanations across situations and over time), employees perceive the quality of the relationship with their leader as significantly lower. Newest research suggests that people, in addition to making internal and external attributions, may also make attributions to relationships they have with others (i.e., with their leader). These so-called relational attributions can have a significant influence on the development of leader-employee relationships. This trend to continuously advance the attribution model provides additional evidence for the model's validity and acceptance.

Managerial Applications

Overall, the attribution model of leadership has critical implications for management practice. Since the attributions that leaders make for employee performance influence leaders' choices regarding how to punish, reward, develop, and react to the employee, it is important for leaders to arrive at accurate attributions. Only then are leaders able to address problems appropriately and provide support in a manner that maximizes employees' future performance. It is essential that leaders are aware of biases, such as the actor-observer and self-serving bias, and understand how these may impact their decision-making process. Furthermore, the attribution model of leadership suggests that leaders should be proactive and diligent in their information seeking about possible causes for employee performance to avoid making mistakes. For example, before initiating disciplinary actions resulting in severe consequences for the employee's future, leaders should make sure that they have credible and reliable information regarding the causes for the employee's poor performance. One way to do so is to offer individualized consideration to all employees and to get to know their strengths, weaknesses, and potential personal constraints. For example, a leader may be more lenient with an employee who misses an important deadline when he is aware of the employee's familial problems.

Leaders should also attempt to identify what employees regard as causes for their performance. To ensure open and honest two-way communication, it is critical for leaders to establish a trusting relationship with their employees. Only then will employees feel comfortable sharing their own thoughts and concerns. Ideally, leaders and employees discuss critical events openly together to boost the potential for a common attribution to occur and to maximize employees' buy-in into any corrective actions (e.g., enrollment in skills training, task redesign, job transfer).

Marion B. Eberly and Terence R. Mitchell

See also Causal Attribution Theory; Job Characteristics Theory; Leader–Member Exchange Theory; Managerial Decision Biases

Further Readings

Eberly, M. B., Holley, E. C., Johnson, M. D., & Mitchell, T. R. (2011). Beyond internal and external: A dyadic theory of relational attributions. *Academy of Management Review, 36,* 731–753.

Green, S. G., & Mitchell, T. R. (1979). Attributional processes of leaders in leader-member interactions. *Organizational Behavior and Human Performance, 23,* 429–458.

Martinko, M. J., & Gardner, W. L. (1987). The leader/member attribution process. *Academy of Management Review, 12,* 235–249.

Martinko, M. J., Harvey, P., & Douglas, S. C. (2007). The role, function, and contribution of attribution theory to leadership: A review. *Leadership Quarterly, 18,* 561–585.

Martinko, M. J., Moss, S. E., Douglas, S. C., & Borkowski, N. (2007). Anticipating the inevitable: When leader and member attribution styles clash. *Organizational Behavior and Human Decision Processes, 104,* 158–174.

AUTHENTIC LEADERSHIP

Authentic leadership refers to genuine form leadership through which leaders remain true to their personal values and convictions, display consistency between their words and deeds, and thereby garner high levels of trust and elevated performance from followers. Authentic leadership can be more formally defined as a constellation of leader behaviors that draw upon and promote a positive ethical climate, positive psychological resources, and positive leader and follower development through heightened levels of self-awareness, balanced information processing, relational transparency, and an internalized moral perspective. Importantly, it serves as a "root" construct for other positive forms of leadership, such as transformational, spiritual, servant, and ethical leadership. That is, all of these forms of leadership are enhanced when the leader is genuine with others and true to himself or herself. Given the many favorable leader, follower, and organizational outcomes that are predicted to arise from authentic leadership, it is of special interest to managers seeking to create more supportive and productive work environments. In the sections that follow, the theoretical foundations and components, key research findings, and practical implications of authentic leadership are described.

Fundamentals

Recent interest in authentic leadership has been stimulated by the writings of former Medtronic CEO Bill George, whose books, *Authentic Leadership* and *True North,* have struck a chord with management practitioners and scholars alike. Drawing on his experience as a leader and witness to great leaders, George describes authentic leaders as persons who not only draw upon their natural abilities but also recognize their weaknesses and work hard to surmount them. Such individuals lead with purpose, values, and meaning. They establish enduring relationships with others, and people follow them because they know what to expect. Such leaders are self-disciplined and consistent. They refuse to compromise when their core principles are challenged, displaying the moral courage to stand by their convictions. Finally, they are dedicated to personal development and to working with others to help them achieve personal and professional growth.

Authentic leadership is founded on the underlying construct of authenticity, which is expressed well by the instruction of the ancient Greeks to "know thyself" and Shakespeare's admonition, "to thine own self be true." Modern conceptions of authenticity owe a great deal to the works of existentialist philosophers, such as Jean-Paul Sartre and Martin Heidegger. Psychology has also contributed to the modern conception of the self as a multifaceted knowledge structure, under which people organize information about their personal histories, backgrounds, values, relationships, roles, and identities. Different situations elicit different facets of the self, such that people are driven by a "working self-concept" that guides their behavior in the situation at hand. Thus, a leader's efforts to remain true to the self will depend on the particular self that circumstances invoke. Leaders with complex jobs may be required to assume many different roles, as they move from situation to situation and stakeholder to stakeholder. Despite such diverse demands, they can remain authentic by staying true to the self that is invoked by the role and a set of core underlying values, such as honesty, transparency, trustworthiness, and respect for others, that transcend situational requirements.

While diverse views on authentic leadership have been proposed by management scholars, the literature has coalesced around a four-component perspective advanced by Bruce Avolio, William Gardner, Fred Luthans, Fred Walumbwa, Doug May, and their colleagues. The four components are self-awareness, balanced processing, relational transparency, and an internalized moral perspective.

- *Self-awareness* involves the degree to which a leader is aware of, and owns, his or her thoughts, values, identities, motives, emotions, goals, knowledge, and talents, as well as personal strengths and weaknesses. Self-awareness serves as the foundation for authentic leadership because, without knowledge of one's self, it is impossible to be true to that self.
- *Balanced processing* refers to the degree to which a leader processes positive along with negative and potentially ego-threatening information about the self in a balanced fashion without becoming defensive. That is, the leader seeks accurate feedback about the self to promote self-awareness, while soliciting impartial perspectives on key issues for the purpose of making informed and impartial decisions.
- *Relational transparency* involves the degree to which a leader is open and forthcoming in close

relationships. The leader displays a willingness to disclose personal and potentially sensitive information to close others that may make him or her vulnerable and, thereby, provides the foundation for reciprocal and trusting relationships. That is, the leader presents a genuine as opposed to a "fake" self to others through selective self-disclosure thereby creating bonds of trust and intimacy, while encouraging others to do the same.

- An *internalized moral perspective* refers to an awareness of the ethical components of the leader's decisions and a commitment to behave in a fashion that reflects his or her moral values and beliefs. Thus, the leader's moral conduct is grounded in an internal moral compass that guides ethical choices and provides a commitment to do what he or she deems is right.

The above description of authentic leadership and its components suggests a highly idealized conception of leadership. In reality, however, it is important to recognize that authenticity, and hence authentic leadership, exists on a continuum. That is, no one is completely authentic across all situations and time. Indeed, given the complexity of modern life and the many roles that leaders play, it is unrealistic to assume that they will always be true to themselves regardless of their mood or circumstances. Instead, it is more appropriate to talk about more versus less authentic leaders and situations where leaders are more versus less authentic. In addition, because authenticity is an aspirational goal, people in general and leaders in particular can strive to become more authentic as part of a quest for personal and professional growth.

Authentic leadership does not operate in a vacuum, as the interrelationships with followers and the culture play a key role in establishing authentic leader-follower relationships. Indeed, from the outset, authentic leadership scholars have proposed that the authenticity of followers, which they call authentic followership, is an essential element of the process of authentic leadership. Through positive modeling, positive social exchanges, identification with the leader, emotional contagion processes, and support for self-determination, authentic leaders are seen as fostering authenticity in followers. In addition, followers who exhibit authentic conduct can serve as positive role models for their peers and superiors, thereby contributing to the authentic leadership and authentic followership of others. Finally, a positive ethical climate is assumed to create an atmosphere where self-awareness, transparency, balanced processing, and strong moral principles and conduct are valued and rewarded. Hence, a positive ethical climate can interact with authentic leadership and followership in a reciprocal fashion, such that authentic leaders and followers help to establish and maintain a positive ethical climate, and vice versa.

A major focus of authentic leadership theory has been directed toward the development of authentic leaders and followers. Trigger events, or "moments that matter," can serve to enhance the self-awareness of leaders and hence play a key role in the development of authentic leadership. Surprising feedback from others, a major life event, or a perceived success or failure may serve as triggers that cause one to engage in self-reflection. While such triggers may arise as a natural part of life, researchers have identified a number of practices whereby developmental triggers can be induced through self-reflection and formal training exercises. Developmental readiness, which involves one's sensitivity, capacity, and motivational receptivity to growth opportunities found in the environment, further adds to one's propensity for development as an authentic leader.

Positive psychological resources, including confidence, optimism, hope, and resilience, are posited to contribute to the development of authentic leadership, which in turn, operates to replenish these resources. *Confidence* involves the self-efficacy needed to take on challenging tasks and put forth the effort necessary to succeed. *Optimism* refers to having positive expectations for both present and future success. *Resilience* involves an ability of people to bounce back from problems and adversity to achieve success. *Hope* refers to a positive motivational state whereby one has the willpower to pursue success and the knowledge of pathways for achieving it. Importantly, these resources represent flexible psychological states as opposed to enduring traits. This means they are subject to change and hence open to development.

Importance

Through an extensive research program, Fred Luthans and colleagues have shown that these resources, which they call psychological capital,

or PsyCap, combine to have a synergistic effect on performance. Further, they have demonstrated that training and other developmental interventions can be applied to enhance PsyCap and thereby produce positive gains in job satisfaction, organizational commitment, organizational citizenship behaviors, and individual and organizational performance. Finally, they have confirmed their expectation that authentic leadership and PsyCap are positively and reciprocally related, suggesting yet another avenue for authentic leadership development.

The most extensively used measure of authentic leadership is the Authentic Leadership Questionnaire (ALQ), although the Authentic Leadership Inventory (ALI) was recently introduced as an alternative. The ALQ provides an overall measure of authentic leadership, along with the four components described above, whereas the ALI focuses on the separate components. Although only limited assessments of these measures' psychometric properties are available due to their relatively recent introduction to the field, the preliminary evidence is supportive.

Empirical research indicates that authentic leadership is positively associated with ethical and transformational leadership, leader and follower psychological capital and well-being, follower identification with and trust in the leader, job satisfaction, organizational commitment, work engagement, empowerment, organizational citizenship behavior, employee job performance, and firm financial performance. Overall, this evidence suggests that authentic leadership possesses considerable promise for organizations seeking to foster positive work climates, enhance employee well-being, and elevate individual, group, and firm performance.

A key implication for management practice is that leaders who are true to themselves, show consistency between their words and deeds, and demonstrate moral character and fortitude can simultaneously promote enhanced levels of leader and follower well-being and veritable and sustained performance. Therein lies the cause for much of the excitement about the construct. Rather than forcing people to pursue a "one style fits all" approach to leadership, aspiring leaders are encouraged to look within themselves to find a style of leadership that personally resonates with them and reflects their true self. The opportunity to lead in an authentic fashion is available to all current and prospective leaders, with potential benefits to be accrued by the leader, followers, their organizations, and society at large.

William L. Gardner

See also Charismatic Theory of Leadership; Leader–Member Exchange Theory; Self-Concept and the Theory of Self; Self-Determination Theory; Servant Leadership; Theory of Self-Esteem; Transformational Theory of Leadership

Further Readings

Avolio, B. J., & Gardner, W. L. (2005). Authentic leadership development: Getting to the root of positive forms of leadership. *Leadership Quarterly, 16*(3), 315–338.

Avolio, B. J., Griffith, J., Wernsing, T. S., & Walumbwa, F. O. (2010). What is authentic leadership development? In P. A. Linley, S. Harrington, & N. Garcea (Eds.), *Oxford handbook of positive psychology and work* (pp. 39–51). New York, NY: Oxford University Press.

Gardner, W. L., Avolio, B. J., Luthans, F., May, D. R., & Walumbwa, F. O. (2005). "Can you see the real me?" A self-based model of authentic leader and follower development. *Leadership Quarterly, 16*(3), 343–372.

Gardner, W. L., Avolio, B. J., & Walumbwa, F. O. (2005). *Authentic leadership theory and practice: Origins, effects, and development.* Oxford, England: Elsevier.

Gardner, W. L., Cogliser, C. C., Davis, K. M., & Dickens, M. (2011). Authentic leadership theory and research: A review of the literature and research agenda. *Leadership Quarterly, 22*(6), 1120–1145.

George, W. (2003). *Authentic leadership: Rediscovering the secrets to creating lasting value.* San Francisco, CA: Jossey-Bass.

George, W. W., & Sims, P. (2007). *True north: Discover your authentic leadership.* San Francisco, CA: Jossey-Bass.

Luthans, F., Avolio, B. J., Avey, J. B., & Norman, S. M. (2007). Positive psychological capital: Measurement and relationship with performance and satisfaction. *Personnel Psychology, 60,* 541–572.

Neider, L. L., & Schriesheim, C. A. (2011). The Authentic Leadership Inventory (ALI): Development and empirical tests. *Leadership Quarterly, 22*(6), 1146–1164.

Walumbwa, F. O., Avolio, B. J., Gardner, W. L., Wernsing, T. S., & Peterson, S. J. (2008). Authentic leadership: Development and validation of a theory-based measure. *Journal of Management, 34*(1), 89–126.

B

BAD THEORIES

This entry refers to the corpus of alleged *bad* management theories at the heart of business school curricula that legitimize and promote amoral behavior, corporate misconduct, and many of the Enron-like debacles of the early millennium. According to Sumantra Ghoshal, bad theories may in fact be destroying good management practices. This phenomenon is the by-product of the long-standing shift within management research toward a scientific model of investigation, a shift that has produced two unique and stultifying outcomes in the field of management. First, there is the pretense of knowledge, which removes human intentionality from management research and thus eliminates moral and ethical considerations from management theories. Second, a pessimistic ideology, referred to as *gloomy vision*, permeates theoretical development—a fact that culminates in a biased research lens that focuses on curing negative problems and correcting flaws rather than producing positive outcomes. These two characteristics saturate both management research and business school education and lead to a significant level of claims of truth that are biased and un- or undersupported. Furthermore, the negative assumptions and pretense of knowledge are self-fulfilling, because given their widespread inculcation and resultant beliefs, bad theories are accepted and integrated into management practice even in the face of significant contradictory evidence and available alternative theories. In this entry, the fundamental components of bad theories are provided along with

a discussion of relevant examples and their detrimental effects on business practices. The entry also provides some proposed remedies for bad theories and discusses the implications of such theories for management practitioners.

Fundamentals

Ghoshal's claim regarding bad management theories may best be understood as a response to Milton Friedman's notion of liberalism, which the University of Chicago has espoused and integrated into a broad array of disciplines (e.g., law, economics, and sociology), including management. Here, *liberalism* refers to an ideology that is not only laden with pessimistic assumptions about human behavior but also excludes ethical problem solving from social theory. This ideology has extended its grasp on most management-related academic disciplines, and in doing so, it has tainted management research, pedagogy, and practice with negative assumptions that ultimately prove self-fulfilling.

These assumptions prove self-fulfilling because they have been woven into a pretense of knowledge—an accepted mode of investigation and analysis that takes the posture of a scientific model but that ultimately provides only excessive claims of truth. When such assumptions are implemented without question into a model that purports to produce scientific conclusions, the ideology underlying those assumptions is perpetuated as accepted fact. Ghoshal recognizes this problem as a double hermeneutic, wherein management practitioners who adopt negative predispositions of liberalism ultimately enact policies and treat their employees in ways that prove their assumptions true. By adopting a particular outlook on the nature of the organizational environment or employee behavior, managers necessarily act in a way that communicates that outlook to the organization. As but one example, while transaction cost economics encourages the vigilant oversight of employees to reduce their opportunistic behavior, the very implementation of rigorous monitoring and oversight regimens has been shown to encourage the opportunistic behavior it aims to stem. The manner in which the pretense of knowledge and negative ideology yield negative management practices may best be explained in Figure 1.

Importantly, the proliferation of bad management practices also originates from a growing imbalance in scholarship within the field of management. Drawing on Ernest L. Boyer's work on scholarship, Ghoshal notes that while the four distinct approaches of research, synthesis, practice, and pedagogy were once equally regarded, the past 30 years have witnessed a stark shift in focus toward research at the expense of the other three. This focus marked an end of generalists in the field of social sciences such as management and elevated research to a unique level of exclusivity among scholarly pursuits. This heightened status enhances the truth claims that emerge from management research and further entrenches the ideologically based assumptions on which such claims are based.

Another critical problem in the scholarship of management is its chosen mode of explanation compared with other sciences. While natural sciences may rightly rely on causal and functional explanatory models in their analyses, social sciences such as management should rely on an intentional explanatory model. An intentional explanatory model focuses on individual, purposeful actions as the core unit of analysis because it recognizes the willful behavior of the actor as a primary element of study. This stands in contrast to physics, which may use causal explanatory models of inorganic matter, and biology, which may use functional explanations of organic matter, but that do not recognize intentionality among the objects of study. However, despite the appropriateness of the intentional explanatory

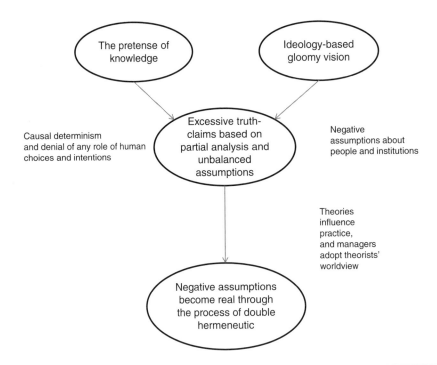

Figure I   The Process of Bad Theories Destroying Good Practice

Source: Ghoshal, S. (2005). Bad management theories are destroying good management practices. *Academy of Management Learning and Education,* 4(1), 75–91. Copyright © 2005 by the Academy of Management. Reprinted by permission.

model for social sciences, management theories routinely incorporate causal and functional modes of explanation. Thus, the human intentions and mental phenomena that lay at the heart of study of management are by and large not included in the theories espoused in the study of management.

In short, academics in the field of business have worked so hard to gain legitimacy for their work on par with the physical sciences that they have overshot their mark. The result is an imbalanced scholarly group of academics who focus the wrong lens on their subjects.

Consequences of Bad Theory

There are many victims of the unfortunate cycle described by Ghoshal. Morality, for one, gets compromised when managers surrender to external forces of the market and competition rather than abiding by their ethics. The near reification of Friedman's maxim that manager's only social responsibility is to maximize shareholder value, for instance, may serve to justify a manager's shirking of his duty to other stakeholders such as employees, the community, or the environment. Common sense also suffers from the promulgation of bad management theories. Managers may well realize that employees contribute more to their company (in terms of ideas, relationships, and reputation) and are more difficult to replace than common shareholders, but they unflinchingly prioritize the value of shareholder contribution and value above employees. This prioritization may culminate in a broad array of management decisions that result in grave consequences for company personnel in return for marginal and fleeting enhancements in shareholder value.

Despite the impact of bad theory on managers' morality and common sense, such theories persist even in light of countervailing evidence. Ghoshal notes that agency theory, which is widely used to support the relationship between shareholder (principals) and managers (agents), would predict the expansion of boards of directors to police managers and the division of roles among chief officers to dilute power, all in the name of increasing performance. Yet studies widely show no support for the impact of such actions on performance, and agency theory still continues to be promoted without question. This continued support for entrenched theories despite a long-standing lack of support (or in some cases, evidence to contrary) reflects the power and pervasiveness of theories widely accepted by business practitioners.

The Cure for Bad Theories

The prescribed remedy for this grand problem is nothing short of a complete overhaul of the focus and practice of business school education. Perhaps the most controversial claim of this theory is that, as the main expositors of bad theories, academics are largely to blame for this self-perpetuating cycle. As such, any meaningful cure must entail a primordial reconsideration and revision of our concept of corporate governance—perhaps examining and applying theories such as stewardship theory with the same rigor and review as agency theory. In this view, a piecemeal or incremental approach to changing business school curricula will not suffice because the strong biases are so firmly entrenched. The primary targets of curriculum overhaul recommended by Ghoshal would include a fundamental review and analysis of those theories on which academics in the field of management most rely.

Another key to reversing this long-standing trend involves regaining a balance in the ideology and assumptions that underlie management research by incorporating positive psychology in the discourse. Positive psychology recognizes the complexity of human beings and organizations but generally calls for a focus on the strengths as well as weaknesses that exist amid such complexity. Invoking positive psychology as the undercurrent of research may counteract the gloomy vision that has held sway for the past several decades.

Implementing these content-related changes to academia would require fundamental changes in the way in which business schools are run. The methods for training PhD students as well as the publication requirements for tenure would have to be reconsidered. The senior leadership at business schools may have to take the lead in forging a new commitment to alternative paths of research—an endeavor that my raise the ire of academics within their own institution and beyond. In addition, peer-reviewed academic journals would have to reexamine their criteria for publication in order to adapt to new and as-of-yet unexamined assumptions and ideologies, as well as a broader, more generalized spectrum of academic contributions.

Importance

Although published relatively recently, Ghoshal's position on bad theories has already had an influence in the literature. Upon its posthumous publication, a number of respected academics, including Lex Donaldson, Jeffrey Pfeffer, Rosabeth Moss Kanter, and Donald Hambrick, among others, all published laudatory responses. The field largely welcomed the pronouncement that bad theories may in fact be encouraging bad management practice, as well as unnecessarily narrowing the focus of business research. However, a number of scholars challenged the assertion that business schools could play such a large role in corporate mismanagement scandals. These scholars agree with Ghoshal's central claims about the central flaws in business school education and with management theories in general, yet they demur on the grounds that academics do not actually wield such power in the practice of management. In short, some feel that Ghoshal's prognosis is correct but business schools are not the sole cause of this malaise simply because they do not have the power to evoke such an outcome. Ultimately, a consensus appears to agree with Ghoshal's call for action—that action being a fundamental review and revamping of the business academic model.

Further response from the academic community may be found in the small but increasing number of conferences and meetings dedicated to the development of positive psychology within business research. Ultimately, Ghoshal called on leading academic journals such as the *Academy of Management Journal* to commit to a new scholarly agenda. And while this may not yet have been formally realized, the issue of the *Academy of Management Learning and Education* in which Ghoshal's work was published and accompanied by numerous responses may serve as an opening salvo in the effort to enact change in accordance with Ghoshal's vision.

Although Ghoshal suggests that both the causes of and cures for bad theories reside primarily within business schools, his theory affects modern managers as well. It is perhaps beyond question that successful business managers must frequently reassess and revise their business models and strategies to remain competitive, but Ghoshal's work suggests they should likewise reassess the basic theories underlying their decision making and corporate governance. Such reevaluation may free modern managers from the firmly entrenched theories that have promoted detrimental behavior in their workplace, as well as open their minds to new conceptions of stakeholder value. Devoting attention to the identification and remediation of the adherence to bad theories may provide modern managers with new tools to deter amoral behavior and business misconduct.

J. Mark Phillips, Kevin May,
and James Bailey

See also Academic-Practitioner Collaboration and Knowledge Sharing; Agency Theory; Engaged Scholarship Model; Firm Growth; Individual Values; Management (Education) as Practice; Managerial Decision Biases; Organizational Development; Organizational Learning; Scientific Management

Further Readings

Boyer, E. L. (1990). *Scholarship reconsidered: Priorities of the professoriate.* Princeton, NJ: Carnegie Foundation for the Advancement of Teaching.

Donaldson, L. (2005). For positive management theories while retaining science: Reply to Ghoshal. *Academy of Management Learning and Education, 4*(1), 109–113.

Friedman, M. (2002). *Capitalism and freedom* (40th anniversary ed.). Chicago, IL: University of Chicago Press.

Ghoshal, S. (2005). Bad management theories are destroying good management practices. *Academy of Management Learning and Education, 4*(1), 75–91.

Hambrick, D. C. (2005). Just how bad are our theories? A response to Ghoshal. *Academy of Management Learning and Education, 4*(1), 104–107.

Kanter, R. M. (2005). What theories do audiences want? The demand side. *Academy of Management Learning and Education, 4*(1), 93–95.

Pfeffer, J. (2005). Why do bad management theories persist? A comment on Ghoshal. *Academy of Management Learning and Education, 4*(1), 96–100.

Popper, K. R. (1968). *The logic of scientific discovery.* New York, NY: Harper & Row.

Weick, K. E. (1989). Theory construction as disciplined imagination. *Academy of Management Review, 14,* 516–531.

BALANCED SCORECARD

The balanced scorecard (BSC) was developed by Robert S. Kaplan, professor at Harvard Business School, and David Norton in the early 1990s. In its early versions, it was a strategic performance measurement system that balanced financial and nonfinancial measures and short run against long run. The system was designed to create visibility of the drivers of value creation in a business rather than just focus on financial outcomes. This was in a context where resources such as people and intellectual assets were becoming more valuable than physical assets in many organizations. There were four dimensions to the original scorecard—Financial, Customer, Internal Business Processes, and Learning and Growth. From its early beginnings in 1992, it has evolved into a tool for strategy execution process. The balanced scorecard intersects with a range of fields in business—innovation, information systems, leadership, marketing and customer value creation, strategy, and learning. The strategy map has become central to the scorecard. This is a schematic of the value creation process integrating the key processes and capital of the organization, especially intellectual capital, in a cause-and-effect relationship. The following section, Fundamentals, explains the development of the balanced scorecard since its inception and the major features of a contemporary balanced scorecard. The Importance section explains the advantages and issues in the use of the scorecard.

Fundamentals

The balanced scorecard is predicated on the notion that performance measures are a powerful influence on members of an organization, particularly if there is a connection with rewards, whether intrinsic or extrinsic. The first mention of the balanced scorecard is in a footnote to a 1989 Harvard case, *Analog Devices,* written about a company that had developed a "Blue Book" with a range of financial and nonfinancial measures. Early scorecards were a collection of measures that balanced financial against nonfinancial and leading indicators that led future performance against lagging indicators. It was a reaction to the relentless pressure by financial markets for ever-increasing returns and the focus on the factors that would affect ongoing profitability, such as customer satisfaction and improved internal processes. There was a recognized connection between the four dimensions of the scorecard, which are as follows:

- *Financial*—The outcome for all profit-making organizations is a financial result for stockholders measured by a range of metrics such as return on capital or net profit margin or growth in revenues.
- *Customer*—In most cases, it is a positive response from the customer that creates value for the organization by profitable sales. The metrics may include sales penetration as well as the level of customer satisfaction and loyalty.
- *Internal Business Processes*—To increase the quality of the customer relationship, operating processes will be continually improved to enhance the quality flexibility while reducing cost of these processes. Measurements may include cycle time, asset utilization, and quality metrics.
- *Learning and Growth*—The driving force of value creation is through the intellectual capital, the ideas, and innovation that bring about new products and services as well as processes, sometimes with rapid discontinuous innovation. It can be measured by the development of human capability, new products to market, and growth of strategic alliances.

For each dimension, the organization identified the key strategic objectives, then the measures that would determine whether the objective had been achieved. For each measure, targets were set and initiatives planned to reach the objectives. The organization needed to clarify its vision and make this the center of the balanced scorecard. The most difficult part of the scorecard was the learning and growth dimension. Implementers of the BSC found great difficulty in this dimension of the scorecard because the areas of intellectual capital and innovation are at the heart of future competitive advantage, yet the drivers are the most difficult to identify.

While some organizations found that the four dimensions worked well for them, others introduced different dimensions. Various fifth dimensions developed, including a social and environmental dimension.

As the BSC spread into the nonprofit sector and government, the financial perspective was no longer the primary goal of the organization and the mission needed to be put as the final outcome. This can be seen in cases developed by Robert Kaplan and David Norton such as Boston Lyric Opera. Nevertheless, there are particular issues in implementing in the nonprofit and public sector because of the significant political context and institutional pressures. Implementing a BSC from the center of a large public sector organization may create significant tensions at the local level where local needs may conflict with the metrics in the BSC.

The BSC has evolved over time, with a series of books whose titles include phrases such as "The Strategy-Focused Organization," "Alignment," and "Strategy Execution Premium." One of the important developments was the explanation of strategy maps, the maps that reflect cause-effect relationships. While these relationships might change over time, it is considered useful for managers to understand the link between drivers of performance. The strategy map becomes a "working hypothesis" of how the organization creates value for its critical stakeholders. Usually the map is driven upward from learning and growth that drove improved business processes, which increased customer satisfaction and led to improved financial results.

Another development of the BSC led to the idea of cascading down the organization. This was the process of linking all departments, and perhaps all employees, to the corporate scorecard so that all sections of the organization would be focusing on strategy and contributing toward it. Individual employee could have their own personal scorecard that reflected their contribution toward the ultimate organizational strategy. This was the key principle in Robert Kaplan and David Norton's 2001 book *The Strategy-Focused Organization.*

Following on from this was the idea of alignment. It was argued that through the use of the scorecard, all parts of the organizations could be aligned around strategic goals. The BSC would be an organizing form that would enable the development of a cohesive strategy that would be communicated to all sections of the organization and achievement of the goals fed back throughout the organization. Although the BSC seems to be built on the planning school of strategy, there is a degree of "emergent" strategy allowed for, as employees would be looking for new opportunities to expand the strategy.

Robert Kaplan and David Norton have now expanded their model to include the BSC as a central part of the strategy execution process—hence, their 2008 book *The Execution Premium.*

Importance

The BSC has become pervasive; it has had an enormous impact on practice and research. After 1992, the idea diffused into larger organizations and was perceived as an important part of corporate governance processes. Now even small nonprofits have a balanced scorecard, at least at a whole of organization level. Although the idea originated in the United States, there are now case studies and surveys of BSC applications into Europe and across Asia. In Europe, there are surveys showing use in Germany and diffusion into Scandinavia. The French have historically used the *tableau de bord,* which has been discussed as both similar in its concept of a balanced structure of measurement and yet distinguished from the BSC. There is increasing evidence of applications of the BSC into Asia, including Taiwan and Singapore, and by 2010 there were over 100 cases of implementations in Chinese hospitals, as just one sector in the Chinese economy.

While the early writings were mainly about the for-profit sector, the BSC is now found in most types of organizations. There are now many books outlining how the BSC might be used in government and nonprofits; Kaplan and Norton have demonstrated how the application may vary with financial outcomes being replaced by mission as the final outcome.

The BSC has generated significant research interest from academics and a thriving debate among practitioners. Since there are alternatives to the BSC, Robert Chenhall came up with the label "strategic performance measurement systems" to encompass all the systems designed to translate strategy into metrics and link operations to the corporate vision.

The research evidence has provided mixed evidence about the effectiveness of the use of BSC. As with most management systems, poor results are often blamed on poor implementations. Rather than focusing on implementation problems, its detractors would argue that it is difficult to implement and does not produce the anticipated benefits, that it is more constraining than enabling and will reduce rather than enhance creativity and innovation.

While the drivers of financial performance are of significant concern to all organizations, the financial outcomes usually dominate the corporate agenda. Even in the presence of the BSC there appears to remain considerable concern at a board level of the short-run financial performance. Indeed, some researchers suggest that the BSC is a shabby substitute for financial performance.

Andre de Waal is one writer who has criticized the BSC as being oversold with a lack of empirical research to demonstrate that it will produce increased performance. Ken Merchant, a well-known writer in management control systems, expressed his belief that statements that the BSC is suitable and beneficial in every organization are unhelpful, nor is there sufficient research to support such claims. Even in cases where there is a correlation between BSC use and high performance, it may indeed be that high-performing organizations use the BSC as a means of drawing together key performance issues rather than the BSC being the driver of that performance.

Others have argued that the BSC, with its four perspectives, has been used as a measurement "straitjacket," which might indeed harm firms by constraining the level of innovation and creativity. Kaplan and Norton have always argued that the scorecard should be seen as a basic structure with plenty of flexibility and that metrics in the innovation area should promote rather than constrain.

There has been specific criticism of the central principle, the cause-and-effect relationship. This is seen as a difficult process. Studies in Austria, Germany, Malaysia, and the United States have shown that more than three fourths of implementers failed to develop these relationships. Claiming causal relationships between perspectives has been seen as quite problematic. These links may be tentative hypotheses, which rapidly change. The time lag is also uncertain; a link between customers and financial outcomes is not unexpected, but the time lags over which this occurs are not really known. The links have been seen as logical rather than causal.

The BSC is designed to encourage external engagement and focus on opportunities as they arise. Kaplan and Norton's description of how Mobil workers might see potential distribution sites is an example. For all this, researchers have suggested that in practice there may be insufficient resources to keep the scorecard dynamic, in which case the scorecard becomes too internally focused, static, and not sufficiently focused on the external environment. Rather than supporting strategy implementation, some researchers have found that in practice, managers struggle to find mechanisms to assist staff to think through responses to the external environment.

Researchers have noted the substantial growth of the intellectual capital literature and compared this with the learning-and-growth perspective of the BSC—often perceived as its weakest aspect. There is a growing literature on intellectual capital and intangible assets, and the nature and formation of these assets is far more complex than the BSC literature might suggest.

The BSC is a management methodology that appears to be here to stay. Many organizations find it a helpful approach to coordinate the development of strategy, its execution, and monitoring of progress and are using it at a board level or a whole-of-organization level. Detailed scorecards cascading down the organization to the departmental and individual levels are less common. Whether organizations will see the BSC as a central tool in strategy execution is not yet clear.

Bruce Gurd

See also Goal-Setting Theory; Learning Organization; Management Control Systems; Modes of Strategy: Planned and Emergent; Strategic Decision Making

Further Readings

Chenhall, R. (2005). Integrative strategic performance measurement systems, strategic alignment of manufacturing, learning and strategic outcomes: An exploratory study. *Accounting, Organizations and Society, 30*(5), 395–422.

Kaplan, R. S., & Norton, D. P. (1992). The balanced scorecard: Measures that drive performance. *Harvard Business Review, 70*(1), 71–79.

Kaplan, R. S., & Norton, D. P. (2001). *The strategy-focused organization: How balanced scorecard companies thrive in the new business environment.* Boston, MA: Harvard Business Press.

Kaplan, R. S., & Norton, D. P. (2004). *Strategy maps: Converting intangible assets into tangible outcomes.* Boston, MA: Harvard Business Press.

Kaplan, R. S., & Norton, D. P. (2006). *Alignment: Using the balanced scorecard to create corporate synergies.* Boston, MA: Harvard Business Press.

Kaplan, R. S., & Norton, D. P. (2008). *The execution premium: Linking strategy to operations for competitive advantage.* Boston, MA: Harvard Business Press.

Neely, A., Adams, C., & Kennerley, M. (2002). *Performance prism: The scorecard for measuring and managing business success.* Upper Saddle River, NJ: Financial Times/Prentice Hall.

Norreklit, H. (2000). The balance on the balanced scorecard: A critical analysis of some of its assumptions. *Management Accounting Research, 11*, 65–88.

BCG Growth-Share Matrix

In the late 1960s, Bruce Henderson, founder of the Boston Consulting Group in Boston, Massachusetts, unveiled an innovative four-cell matrix that would have profound implications for the way corporations manage their business units and product lines. This matrix was created to assist corporations to assess the competitive position of their business units and product lines in relation to their market share and growth; it presents a composite view of the competitive position of each business unit or product line within a corporation. Additionally, it provides senior management with a framework to assess the relative position of each business unit and product line in order to determine how to allocate or reallocate resources. To use the matrix, corporations must assess their business units and product lines—in essence, their business portfolios. Dominating the business world for two decades, the matrix made a significant contribution to strategic planning and continues to be used in Fortune 500 companies today. What became famous as the "Boston Consulting Group (BCG) Growth-Share Matrix" dominated market analysis in the 1970s and 1980s, recasting senior managers as internal bankers, reframing product lines and business units as investments, and naming the product lines or business units themselves "stars," "cash cows," "question marks," and "dogs," depending on their return of the corporation's initial investment. When these cleverly named entities were properly balanced within a company's portfolio, the theory goes, a maximum return on investment was not only achievable, it was an inevitable outcome. The BCG Growth-Share Matrix provided a snapshot of the product line's or business unit's current competitive position but also the analytical framework to predict where they would go. This entry introduces the Boston Consulting Group Growth-Share Matrix and the classic stars, cash cows, dogs, and question marks, along with general conclusions about its current use and some criticisms. Beginning with a historical overview of its development by Bruce Henderson, this entry examines the matrix and its implications for management.

Fundamentals

The BCG Growth-Share matrix was initially developed when Mead Paper Corporation hired the Boston Consulting Group to develop an acquisition strategy. At that time, Mead Paper had six product groups and 45 operating divisions but lacked a strategy for managing the business units and a method to determine which business units or product lines were losing money. Other major U.S. companies at the time, such as General Electric (GE), were also seeking new tools and methods for strategic planning. GE's approach, however, was focused on strategic planning concepts, techniques, and definitions. As a result, their focus helped them define specific product markets, and they coined the term strategic business unit (SBU). Prior to the portfolio-planning matrix approach, a corporation's strategy generally used capital budgeting to evaluate its returns on investments. Capital budgeting is a method first applied in corporate finance in 1951 to determine whether a corporation's long-term investments are worth pursuing.

At the heart of the BCG Growth-Share Matrix is the notion that a company should have a mixture of product lines and business units with different growth rates and market shares. The right combination of high- and low-growth products will balance cash flows in the company's portfolio and, in so doing, ensure the company's success. The matrix itself allows managers to compare the product lines and business units already in their company's portfolio based on the market growth rate and market share. It also provides a framework to allocate resources between the different product lines and business units.

An underlying premise of the BCG Growth-Share Matrix is that the larger a product's market share—or the more rapidly the product's market increases—the more it benefits the company. In the context of the BCG Growth-Share Matrix, four rules influence a product's cash flow: (1) Market share determines margins and cash generated, (2) growth requires additional resources to obtain more assets, (3) market share is earned or bought, and (4) the growth of a product line cannot continue indefinitely. One of the basic assumptions in the BCG Growth-Share Matrix is that a growing market is attractive.

In the BCG Growth-Share Matrix, a corporation's products or business units are plotted in one of four quadrants according to the growth rate of the industry in which it competes and its relative market share. The business growth rate is based on the percentage of the sales of a business unit's product that have increased—in other words, market growth. On the matrix, the vertical (y) axis depicts the growth rate for the next 5 years in percentages of the market on a linear scale. A corporation's business unit or product line is plotted along the horizontal (x) axis, which represents the market share divided by its largest competitor. For example, if Company A has 15% of the market share and its largest competitor, Company B, has 40% of the market share, then the market share of Company A relative to the market share of Company B is 37%, or .37x. In another example, if Company A has 40% of the market share and Company B has 15% market share, the market share of Company A is 266%, or 2.6x. Using this formula, market share of 1.0 or greater indicates the market leader. A "dog" on the other hand is a product line or business unit that has a relative competitive position less than 1.0.

A company's business unit or product line is represented by a circle, the size of which signifies the relative importance of each business unit or product line to the corporation as it relates to assets used or sales generated. Once the company's business units or product lines have been plotted on the BCG Growth-Share Matrix, four categories of business units or product lines may emerge within the corporation's portfolio: (1) stars, (2) cash cows, (3) question marks, and (4) dogs. In the upper left-quadrant of the matrix are stars, which are business units or product lines typically at the peak of their life cycle and that have high growth and high market share. They generally are market leaders that require large amounts of cash to maintain their competitive position, but as market leaders, they should generate large amounts of cash. Stars should be given additional resources if necessary to defend their current market share, as they will eventually become cash cows as long as their market share is maintained. In the lower-left quadrant are cash cows, which are low-growth, high-market-share products that are the foundation of the corporation's portfolio. Cash cows should generate far more cash than is required to maintain their market share. This results in low-growth markets where further investment is not needed. These products should be "milked" for cash as their product life cycle declines, and the company should invest those profits into question marks. In the upper-right quadrant are question marks (also called "problem children" and "wildcats"), which are high-growth and low-market-share products. Question mark products are highly risky and require substantial amounts of money for development in hopes that they will eventually gain enough market share to become a star. When companies cannot increase market shares for question marks and future growth is stopped, these products will eventually become dogs. In the lower-right quadrant are dogs, which are low-growth and low-market-share products. Dogs often lack potential because they are in an unattractive industry. Management should reduce the number of dogs within the company's portfolio by selling them off and carefully managing those that remain. A company's senior management can use these projections of market growth and market share to maintain a balanced portfolio. The company's strategic goal is to have a portfolio that is balanced so that it always has cash, always milking its mature products, and always seeking to develop new products and markets.

Importance

In the 1970s, many U.S. companies faced daunting challenges because of the oil crisis, inflation, and increased global competition that fueled a financial recession. Because of this economic crisis, many businesses were seeking ways to save money and methods to allocate the limited resources on hand. Additionally, many companies were growing more diverse and increasing in size and were confronted with the challenges of managing diverse products across diverse industries. Faced with these challenges, senior managers sought a way to coordinate the activities of their business units and product lines as previous methods appeared no longer to work. The BCG Growth-Share Matrix offered companies an analytical tool to allocate resources between the different product lines and business units to develop strategies to chart this new territory.

The BCG Growth-Share Matrix is not without its detractors. The main criticisms are its (1) narrow focus, (2) basic assumptions, (3) definitions, (4) political process and implementation of subsequent strategies, and (5) operationalization of the strategic statements. The simplicity of the BCG Growth-Share Matrix and its narrow focus has been taken to task as a weakness. Some argue that four cells are too few to represent competitive positioning or market attractiveness. Others argue that the industry's attractiveness is based exclusively on growth rate, which may overemphasize the importance of market share and market leadership. This emphasis may be problematic given that the link between market share and profitability is not necessarily strong.

In addition, its principal assumption—that market share is always desirable—has been criticized. Some critics note that in certain cases, such as stable and predictable niche markets, a product with a low market share in a declining industry can, in fact, be quite profitable. Alternatively, companies may choose to keep dogs since that product line may act as a barrier to competitors. The BCG Growth-Share Matrix has also been criticized for the definitions used, which may contribute to the difficulties already faced by companies to identify product lines and relevant market share correctly. Further, the BCG Growth-Share Matrix has been criticized for not accounting for the political/implementation process. This may be a significant hazard, critics argue, as the unit managers may see any change as a threat or opportunity to distort the perceived market share in self-interest. The BCG Growth-Share Matrix has been criticized for the difficulty in operationalizing its terminology, such as *harvest* and *milk*. Despite these criticisms, one of the main strengths of the BCG Growth-Share Matrix is that it provides senior management a simple analytical tool, based on a single parameter, market share, as the primary indicator of the company's business unit or product line's competitive position.

Although portfolio analysis has waned in popularity since its peak in the 1970s and 1980s—no fewer than five variants of the portfolio-planning matrix were in wide use by major corporations by 1981—the overall influence of the BCG Growth-Share Matrix is significant. More than 40 years after its premiere, it continues to be widely used by Fortune 500 firms to develop strategies to manage cash flow and is regularly taught in business schools across the country. The model's graphic illustration of a given company's financial challenges and opportunities, its relative ease of use, and its straightforward ability to assist corporations to decide easily how to allocate resources ensures its long-term viability.

James V. M. L. Holzer

See also Balanced Scorecard; Competitive Advantage; Strategic Profiles; SWOT Analysis Framework; Value Chain

Further Readings

Collis, D. J., & Montgomery, C. A. (1995, *July-August*). Competing on resources: How do you create and sustain a profitable strategy? *Harvard Business Review*, 118–128.

Hambrick, D. C., MacMillan, I. C., & Day, D. L. (1982). Strategic attributes and performance in the BCG matrix: A PIMS based analysis of industrial product businesses. *Academy of Management Journal, 25*(3), 510–531.

Hax, A. C., & Majluf, N. S. (1983). The use of the growth-share matrix in strategic planning. *Interfaces, 13*(1), 46–60.

Henderson, B. D. (1970). The product portfolio. *Perspectives*, No. 66. Boston, MA: Boston Group.

Henderson, B. D. (1973). The experience curve reviewed, IV. The growth share matrix of the product portfolio. *Perspectives*, No. 135. Boston, MA: Boston Group.

Henderson, B. D. (1979). *Henderson on corporate strategy*. Cambridge, MA: Abt Books.

Mintzberg, H. A., Ahlstrand, B., & Lampel, J. (2005). *Strategy safari: A guided tour through the wilds of strategic management*. New York, NY: Free Press.

Morrison, A., & Wensley, R. (1991). Boxing up or boxed in? A short history of the Boston Consulting Group Share/Growth Matrix. *Journal of Marketing Management, 7*(2), 105–129.

Stern, C. W., & Deimler, M. S. (Eds.). (2006). *The Boston Consulting Group on strategy: Classic concepts and new perspectives*. Hoboken, NJ: Wiley.

BEHAVIORAL PERSPECTIVE OF STRATEGIC HUMAN RESOURCE MANAGEMENT

The behavioral perspective of human resource management (HRM) is one of several alternative theoretical lenses for understanding why firms differ in their approaches to managing employees, and a broad array of consequences that follow from differing approaches to managing employees. The theory's central management insight is that HRM systems are most effective when they are designed to support strategic business objectives. This approach was a departure from previous work that sought to identify the "one best way" to manage employees. The behavioral perspective of strategic HRM asserts that designing effective HRM policies and practices requires understanding the behavioral imperatives of the business objectives and then developing an HRM system to encourage, elicit, and sustain the required behaviors. The behavioral perspective of strategic HRM has been used most frequently in studies of strategic HRM and has been applied primarily for describing and prescribing the links between business strategies, HMR systems, and a variety of stakeholder responses closely associated with employee behaviors. While not generally considered to be a formal theory, the behavioral perspective of HRM provides a framework for understanding how employees contribute to organizational effectiveness. This entry begins with a description of seven defining assertions of the behavioral perspective of strategic HRM. Next, it describes the theoretical roots of the behavioral perspective and its relationship to other recent theoretical approaches driving recent work in the area of strategic HRM. Finally, the entry concludes with a short summary of important contributions that the behavioral perspective of strategic HRM has made to advances in general management scholarship.

Fundamentals

Grounded in role theory, the behavioral perspective of strategic HRM was first articulated by Randall S. Schuler and Susan E. Jackson as a framework for articulating how differences in business strategies might influence the ways employees are managed. Subsequently, the behavioral perspective of strategic HRM has been developed as a framework for analyzing how management policies and practices should be designed to maximize organizational effectiveness, given an organization's specific and unique environmental context and internal organizational conditions. Figure 1 provides a simple schematic illustration of the key concepts of the behavioral perspective and their interrelationships.

Focus Is on Desired Employee Behaviors

As defined by Daniel Katz and Robert Kahn, the term *role behaviors* refers to the recurring actions of organizational members as they interact with their role partners to achieve predictable outcomes. Thus, role behaviors refer to a broad array of employee actions, including those required to perform specific

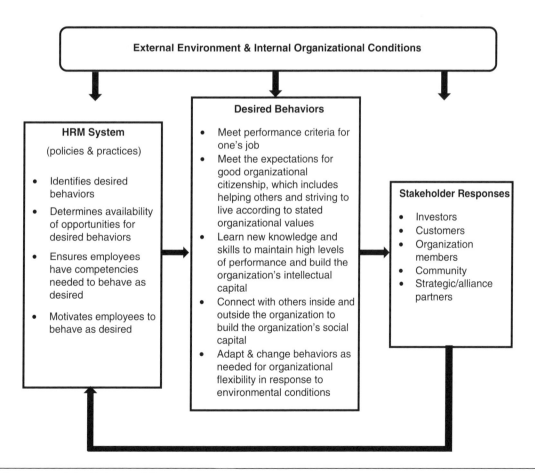

Figure 1   Overview of the Behavioral Perspective

Source: Susan E. Jackson. Copyright © 2012 by Susan E. Jackson. Used with permission.

tasks and jobs as well as behaviors not specified in one's job description but are understood to contribute to the organization's long-term success. As the behavioral perspective of HRM developed, the terminology has been shortened from employee role behaviors to simply employee behaviors.

Different Organizations Need Different Employee Behaviors

The behavioral perspective of HRM argues that different strategies require different role behaviors from employees for those strategies to be implemented successfully. Role behaviors believed to contribute to organizational effectiveness are referred to as "desired" (also referred to as "needed") employee behaviors. Included among this broader set of desired behaviors are activities such as completing tasks that are officially the responsibility of another employee as needed, being adaptive and willing to learn and change as needed, and generally behaving in ways consistent with the organization's stated goals and values. Thus, the behavioral perspective of HRM assumes that management policies and practices influence not only what work gets done in an organization but also how work gets done. The behavioral perspective also makes several other key assumptions, which are briefly described next. The following statement of assumptions also specifies the key concepts that compose the behavioral perspective.

Organizational Effectiveness Improves When Employees Behave as Needed

The behavioral perspective of HRM assumes that the behaviors of employees are one of the major determinants of organizational effectiveness, as judged by the organization's primary stakeholders. Ultimately, stakeholders are an organization's most important role partners; the consequences of employee behaviors are of primary concern to stakeholders. Ideally, employee behaviors are consistent with the long-term needs of the firm, given its competitive strategy and the expectations of others who depend on the employee—including role partners inside and outside the organization. The behavioral perspective recognizes that other factors (e.g., the actions of competitors, economic conditions, industry dynamics) also influence organizational effectiveness, but it focuses on employee behaviors because

it is through behavior that organizational resources are transformed into goods and services that have economic value.

Employee Behaviors Reflect Situational Influences

According to the behavioral perspective of HRM, the desirability of specific behaviors is influenced by a variety of contextual factors inside and outside the organization. Internal contextual factors that influence the behaviors needed for organizational effectiveness are aspects of the particular organization itself—its size, life cycle stage, competitive strategy, technology, structure, and history. External contextual factors that influence the desirability of specific behaviors are conditions outside the organization that affect organizational functioning, including (a) industry dynamics, (b) institutional pressures, (c) economic and political conditions, (d) country cultures, and (e) the action of customers. The behavioral perspective assumes that a comprehensive consideration of these contextual elements is needed to fully determine which employee behaviors are desirable. Thus, determining the desired employee behaviors for a specific organization is the first essential step for effective human resource management.

Management Policies and Practices Shape Employee Behaviors

The behavioral perspective of HRM assumes that employee behaviors are malleable; that is, people are generally motivated to behave in ways that are socially approved of by others, so they are responsive to a variety of informational cues. Two sources of cues emphasized by the behavioral perspective are formal stated policies concerning how employees are to be treated and informal daily practices or the actual ways in which employees are treated.

An organization's formal policies and informal practices for managing employees function together as the HRM system. The many elements of an HRM system include policies and practices for recruiting, selecting, socializing, training, developing, supervising, evaluating, paying, recognizing, promoting, and terminating employees.

Effective Policies and Practices Support Needed Employee Behaviors

All of an organization's many specific management policies and practices operate as a set of interrelated forces that influence employee behaviors. An effective HRM system guides employee behaviors toward desired behaviors by providing opportunities for employees to engage in the behaviors needed, ensuring that employees have the competencies required to engage in those behaviors, and motivating employees to behave as needed. If one accepts the assumption that employees actively interpret and respond to managerial policies and practices, then it follows that an HRM system can direct employee behaviors in ways that increase the likelihood of long-term organizational effectiveness.

For employees to behave as needed, they must have the opportunities to do so. Structural arrangements, job designs, and technology are among the many factors that can create or block opportunities for employees to behave as needed. Given opportunities to behave as needed, employees can best meet the behavioral expectations of role partners if they have the required competencies—that is, the skills, knowledge, and abilities. HRM policies and practices can help ensure that employees have the required competencies by attracting highly competent job applicants, hiring those who are most highly qualified, providing training and on-the-job learning opportunities, and rewarding employees according to the competencies they exhibit. Three components comprising employee motivation are (a) willingness to join the firm and stay with the firm as needed, (b) willingness to exert significant effort toward achieving organizational goals (e.g., working harder, longer, and/or smarter), and (c) willingness to work reliably at the agreed time and place in exchange for an agreed compensation and under agreed working conditions. Policies and practices that influence motivation include the design of work, performance goals and incentives, feedback, and opportunities for advancement, among others.

Effective Organizations Address the Concerns of Multiple Stakeholders

Evaluations of organizational effectiveness must take into account the perspectives of the many stakeholders who are influenced by the actions of employees. Human resource management policies and practices are presumed to be effective when the expectations they communicate and the behaviors they elicit are congruent with the organization's behavioral requirements and satisfy employees' role

partners. To achieve this goal, the HRM policies and practices affecting employees must send clear and consistent messages about the desired role behaviors. The primary stakeholders for most businesses include investors, customers, members of the organization itself (i.e., other employees), members of the broader community, and the organization's strategic or alliance partners. Organizations are considered effective to the degree that they satisfy their primary stakeholders. Thus, to evaluate whether an organization's management policies and practices are effective, the consequences of HRM policies and practices on each stakeholder group should be considered.

Evolution

The general model for understanding HRM that is now referred to as the *behavioral perspective* reflects the influences of several earlier views of organizations. At the same time, when it was first introduced, it represented a major departure from earlier work in the area of HRM and promoted a strategic approach to the study of HRM.

As already mentioned, the behavioral perspective draws most directly on the earlier writings of Daniel Katz and Robert Kahn. In addition, it incorporates Michael Porter's approach to understanding the competitive strategies pursued by firms. The earliest description of the behavioral perspective, offered by Schuler and Jackson in 1987, used Michael Porter's description of competitive strategies as the basis for arguing that different business imperatives should lead organizations to prefer and adopt HRM systems that were congruent with the behavioral requirements of their strategies. Subsequently, after Jay Barney introduced the resource-based view of the firm, the behavioral perspective directed attention to the organizational value of management policies and practices that create and maintain human/behavioral resources that are unique, rare, difficult for competitors to imitate, and valuable.

From "Best" Practices to Practices That "Fit"

When it was first introduced, the behavioral perspective represented a departure from prior approaches to the study of HRM in several ways. Most notably, the behavioral perspective argued that organizations can and often do design HRM policies and practices to achieve their own specific strategic objectives. In the past, HRM scholarship was grounded in a technical perspective, which assumes that some approaches to managing people are generally more effective than other ways of managing people. Thus, the goal for HRM research was to find the "best practices," and the objective of managers should be to adopt those best practices. In contrast the behavioral perspective assumes HRM policies and practices should be designed to fit an organization's specific situation. That is, there is no "one best way" for managing people. Policies and practices that are effective for one organization may not be effective in other organizations because organizations differ in the specific employee behaviors needed to implement the business strategy and satisfy key stakeholders. Subsequently, alternative interpretations of this aspect of the behavioral perspective evolved into several competing theoretical perspectives, including the contingency and configurational perspectives.

From HRM Activities to HRM Systems

The embracing of a systems view for understanding HRM also was a major departure from past approaches. Prior research typically focused on a specific type of HRM activity. For example, studies of how employees responded to particular forms of pay or compensation were conducted without taking into account the influence of other aspects of the total HRM system (e.g., hiring or training policies and practices). Subsequently, HRM scholars embraced the systems view and began investigations designed to understand how employees respond to a few specific types of HRM systems—for example, high-performance systems, high-involvement systems, high-commitment systems, and so on. Consistent with the behavioral perspective, subsequent studies of these HRM system archetypes assumed that employees imbued HRM systems with meaning, which in turn influenced their job-related attitudes and behaviors. However, contrary to the logic of the behavioral perspective, subsequent research on archetypical HRM systems often ignored the assumption that each organization has somewhat unique behavioral requirements that reflect the context in which the organization is situated.

From Employee Outcomes to Organizational Effectiveness as Criteria

A third departure from prior approaches was broadening the criteria used to evaluate the effectiveness of HRM policies and practices. Prior research focused attention on a smaller set of employee outcomes that are of general concern to most employers, especially individual job performance and a few other specific behaviors, such as accepting job offers, absenteeism, and turnover. Consistent with an approach that treats the organization as the focal unit for study, the behavioral perspective also drew increased attention to organization-level outcomes and to the array of role partners with whom employees interact. Thus, HRM scholarship began to investigate the relationships between entire systems of HRM policies and practices and measures of organizational effectiveness, including financial performance, customer satisfaction, and employer reputation.

In a fourth departure from past approaches, the behavioral perspective recognized that employee responses to an organization's HRM system reflect their interpretation of both the organization's formal statements about its practices and the actual behaviors of the organizational agents who are responsible for implementing those practices. Often, responsibility for designing the formal policies for managing employee behaviors lies with human resource professionals, whereas responsibility for implementing those policies lies with supervisors and managers; the actual behaviors of organizational agents responsible for managing employees—that is, managerial practices—constitute the informal element of an HRM system. Formal policies can be thought of as distal stimuli, and informal practices can be thought of as proximal stimuli. Research that investigates the question of how to create alignment between formal policies and informal practices has its roots in the behavioral perspective and highlights the importance of understanding the behavior of *all* employees at all levels in the organization.

Importance

Perhaps the most important contribution of the behavioral perspective has been that it provided a bridge for joining together arenas of managerial scholarship that had previously been unconnected. Traditional HRM research had focused on understanding the behavior of individual employees, with little regard for how employee behaviors related to business strategies or the satisfaction of an organization's multiple stakeholders. Conversely, traditional research into strategic management had largely ignored the implications of strategic choices for managing the firm's employees; when implications for employee behaviors were acknowledged, the focus was on CEOs and other members of top management.

Another contribution of the behavioral perspective is that it provides a logic that can be used to predict and explain various relationships between characteristics of organizations and their environments on the one hand and management practices on the other hand. For example, in one study of several hundred firms, the behavioral perspective was used to develop predictions that HRM systems would differ among firms that placed greater value on innovation (vs. other strategic imperatives, such as cost reduction or quality enhancement). Consistent with predictions based in the behavioral perspective, HRM systems designed to support behaviors needed for innovation, such as risk taking and teamwork, were more likely to be found in firms pursuing competitive strategies that emphasized the development of innovative services and products. Similarly, an investigation of HRM practices in firms that emphasized the delivery of excellent customer service (vs. products) found that the behavioral requirements of customer service (which is relatively intangible and coproduced through interactions with end users) provided an explanation for the differences in HRM systems often found in service versus manufacturing industries. Jackson and her colleagues have also used the behavioral perspective to address the question of how to design HRM systems that encourage and support the behaviors needed in organizations that compete on the basis of knowledge, and to formulate a research agenda for investigating how HRM systems can be used to promote environmental sustainability.

The behavioral perspective also is proving to be important for its ability to provide insights about phenomena at multiple levels of analysis, including individuals, work teams, business units, organizations, and networks of related organizations. For example, a study of top management teams by Collins and Clark found that HRM practices that encouraged executives to build their internal and external social networks were associated with better firm performance, presumably because such networks could be leveraged to achieve organizational goals.

As noted, the behavioral perspective is not a formal theory but rather a general framework that can be applied as a guide for management research and practice. Because the behavioral perspective deals with broad issues and incorporates numerous complex constructs, it is difficult to conduct research to test the validity of perspective. Instead, its value lies in its ability to generate useful questions and provoke analyses that help answer those questions.

Susan E. Jackson

See also Behavioral Theory of the Firm; Contingency Theory; European Model of Human Resource Management; High-Performance Work Systems; Human Capital Theory; Human Resource Management Strategies; Stakeholder Theory

Further Readings

Collins, C. J., & Clark, K. D. (2003). Strategic human resource practices, top management team social networks, and firm performance: The role of human resource practices in creating organizational competitive advantage. *Academy of Management Journal, 46*, 740–751.

Jackson, S. E., Chuang, C.-H., Harden, E., & Jiang, Y. (2006). Toward developing human resource management systems for knowledge-intensive teamwork. In J. Martocchio (Ed.), *Research in personnel and human resource management* (Vol. 25, pp. 27–70). Oxford, England: Elsevier.

Jackson, S. E., Hitt, M. A., & DeNisi, A. S. (Eds.). (2003). *Managing knowledge for sustained competitive advantage: Designing strategies for effective human resource management.* San Francisco, CA: Jossey-Bass.

Jackson, S. E., Ones, D., & Dilchert, S. (in press). *Human resource management for environmentally sustainable organizations.* San Francisco, CA: Jossey-Bass.

Jackson, S. E., & Schuler, R. S. (1995). Understanding human resource management in the context of organizations and their environments. *Annual Review of Psychology, 46*, 237–264.

Jackson, S. E., Schuler, R. S., & Rivero, J. C. (1989). Organization characteristics as predictors of personnel practices. *Personnel Psychology, 42,* 727–786.

Jackson, S. E., Schuler, R. S., & Werner, S. (2012). *Managing human resources* (11th ed.). Mason, OH: Cengage.

Lengnick-Hall, M. L., Lengnick-Hall, C. A., Andrade, L. S., & Drake, B. (2009). Strategic human resource management: The evolution of the field. *Human Resource Management Review, 19,* 64–85.

Schuler, R. S., & Jackson, S. E. (1987). Linking competitive strategy with human resource management practices. *Academy of Management Executive, 3,* 207–219.

Schuler, R. S., & MacMillan, I. C. (1984). Gaining competitive advantage through human resource practices. *Human Resource Management, 23,* 241–256.

BEHAVIORAL THEORY OF THE FIRM

The behavioral theory of the firm (BTF) is the research tradition that builds on and extends the ideas of the book *A Behavioral Theory of the Firm* by Richard Cyert and James March, published in 1963. A key assumption in this work is that managers are boundedly rational, which means that they cannot fully predict the potential consequences of different actions or may not have fully formed preferences about the potential consequences. Its fundamental insight is that managers will behave differently from what is assumed in rational actor views of the organization, both with respect to internal organizational decisions and control and with respect to organizational relations to its environment. Thus, it was intended as a corrective to rational actor views of the firm, and it sought to have an empirically grounded, process-oriented specification of how decisions are actually made. Its domain was initially the most central organizational decisions such as production, price, and inputs of business organizations, but it has since expanded to cover most organizational decision making, and it is also applied to nonbusiness organizations. BTF built on earlier work by March and Herbert Simon that had argued for the importance of individual bounded rationality and organizational structures as tools for understanding decision making, and it made a number of extensions to this work. Collectively BTF and its predecessor and associated work are known as the Carnegie School. In this entry, the fundamentals of the theory are described, followed by a brief discussion of its evolution and importance for the field of organization theory.

Fundamentals

Much of the BTF research has built on "A Summary of Basic Concepts in the Behavioral Theory of the Firm," Chapter 6 of Cyert and March's 1963 book, which discusses its three fundamental concepts (state variables) and four relational concepts (change processes). The fundamental concepts were (1) organizational goals, (2) organizational expectations, and (3) organizational choice. Organizational goals are objectives for the organization created through negotiation among members of the dominant coalition controlling the organization and are not necessarily integrated into a consistent goal system. Organizational expectations are the estimates of future states made by organizational members based on their experience. Organizational choice is made by matching alternatives that are sequentially discovered through search to satisfactory levels on goal variables (i.e., satisficing). Together, these three fundamental concepts outline a form of organizational decision making that makes much lower cognitive and communication demands than do fully rational models; it lets search for alternatives end when an acceptable one has been found, lets different organizational members satisfice on different goals and with different expectations, and lets the organization attend to different goals at different times.

The relational concepts driving action in the model were (1) quasi resolution of conflict, (2) uncertainty avoidance, (3) problemistic search, and (4) organizational learning. *Quasi resolution of conflict* means that decisions with effects on multiple goals are taken in order to meet constraints of minimally acceptable performance on each goal rather than by making explicit trade-offs. *Uncertainty avoidance* means that managers do not explicitly forecast uncertainty in the environment; instead they seek to control the environment through negotiation and react to unanticipated problems. *Problemistic search* means reacting to performance below the aspiration level on a goal variable by searching for solutions "near" the symptom of the problem or the current state of the organization. *Organizational learning* means adaptation of goals, attention, and search processes as a result of experience gained through making changes. The overall model is one of managers seeking to react intelligently to challenges they encounter but in a piecemeal fashion that changes the organization incrementally and not necessarily in the direction of some optimal state.

Work using the concepts developed in BTF is found across a broad range of management research. For example, negotiation of goals is an important element in the theory of intraorganizational power, which has offshoots in research on resource dependence and criticality as sources of power and on the ability of powerful units in the organization to resist change. These are building blocks in resource dependence theory. Organizational expectations and problemistic search are particularly important in research on managerial aspirations for performance, which is known as *performance feedback theory*. In this work, expected performance is a source of an aspiration level, which is defined as the point separating performance that is seen as a problem and performance seen as acceptable. Research on how managers form aspirations has shown regular updating rules that closely resemble those formulated by Cyert and March, and changes have been shown to occur at times consistent with predictions of problemistic search. Combinations of BTF concepts can be found in major research traditions, such as in the use of bounded rationality and uncertainty avoidance as key assumptions of institutional theory, leading to the prediction of mimetic behavior among organizations. Resource dependence theory uses a similar rationale as BTF for its prediction that organizations will seek to co-opt and control environments to avoid making disruptive changes in reaction to environmental demands.

Evolution

Cyert and March's 1963 book was a seminar work in organization theory that had two effects: It (1) set the agenda of research on BTF and (2) introduced key concepts that have been used both directly in BTF research and indirectly as building blocks of other forms of research. Though many influences from key concepts in BTF to current theory can be found, some research traditions are of special interest because they directly address its agenda. The idea of organizations learning from their experience by making enduring changes to their behavioral

patterns is a key insight from BTF that has inspired research on organizational learning, which in turn has a number of branches. Some researchers ask how organizations maintain the lessons of the past experiences and propose that an organizational memory exists in the form of organizational culture, work processes, and networks as well as in individual memories. Others look at effects of different forms of experience on learning and have examined features of the environment such as complexity, proximity to similar organizations, and structure of the competition. This research includes work on how organizations learn from the experiences of their founders. Yet others look for how learning from one's own experience shapes subsequent actions, including "momentum" effects that lead past changes to be repeated because they are still salient action patterns in the organization.

BTF developed the concept of standard operating procedures, which range from managerial decision-making routines to specific routines for performing tasks. Later work focused on task routines and developed theory of routines as a basic object of organizational learning. This work is the foundation of evolutionary theory, which examines how gradual selection and modification of routines can lead to organizational buildup of capabilities. It is an active contributor to ideas on knowledge acquisition, transfer, and use in strategy research, which is concerned with the question of how organizations can display persistent differences in performance. Organizational learning from experience, encoded into routines that may be difficult to transfer or even articulate, has been seen as a potential answer to this question, and this idea is further developed in the resource-based view.

Combining the ideas of routines as the object of learning and problemistic search as the learning mechanism leads to a prediction of incremental changes in response to problems, resulting in the performance improvements at a declining rate seen in the learning-curve literature. This work also looks at how the learning curve is affected by organizational boundaries. The interest in routines has also developed into a research tradition that examines how routines are made and altered, often through direct observation in the field, although experiments and inference from performance consequences is also used. This research shows that routines are remarkably stable but may change in response to a range of factors, including BTF mechanisms such as problemistic search. A related research tradition examines the birth, persistence, and change of organizational rules as a function of organizational problems as well as elaboration of rules and competition among rules. Linda Argote has made central contributions to learning curve research, while Martha S. Feldman and Brian T. Pentland have made important contributions to routines research.

Research on performance feedback has directly examined problemistic search by testing whether organizational performance below the aspiration level leads to changes such as new market behaviors and introduction of innovations. This work assumes influence from other organizations in the adjustment of the aspiration level, which connects the theory with work on how organizational reference groups are formed by similarity, status, or network ties. Conversely, because network ties with other organizations help stabilize the environment, changes in network ties are also an outcome that has been shown to be guided by problemistic search. Much research has combined the problemistic search mechanisms with considerations of managerial risk taking, thus forming a bridge between BTF and prospect theory. It has mainly studied organization-level decisions, but recent work has also found support for problemistic search on unit-level outcomes such as operational safety. This research also examines whether organizations search when they have slack resources, which is also a proposition of BTF. A key feature of the work is tests of whether the performance feedback mechanism from performance to change also includes a sharp drop in the probability of change over the aspiration level, as problemistic search would suggest, especially in organizations that change only with some difficulty. It has generated much evidence to support the BTF propositions. Henrich R. Greve has made key contributions to this research.

The BTF process of quasi resolution of conflict has led to work on how organizations form goals and apply them to specific situations. Unlike the work on performance feedback, the focus is not on how an organization reacts to a specific goal, but rather how one goal or a set of goals become important in a specific situation. One part of this work selects specific contexts for studying political behaviors, such as work on politics among top

managers or between the CEO and the board of directors. Another part examines how the attention of the firm's decision makers changes depending on the decision context. Attention theory can be combined with the performance feedback mechanism to show sequential attention to goals, as predicted by BTF, and can also be applied to work outside the strict boundaries of BTF such as managerial cognition. William Ocasio has made central contributions to this research.

An important concern in BTF was to examine the consequences of the organizational learning resulting from the various mechanisms that were proposed. This has led to a strong stream of research using simulations to model the adaptive consequences of problemistic search in different resource environments, as well as other elements of BTF. The key contributions in this literature concern the trade-offs of different learning mechanisms. Organizations simultaneously learn to execute tasks better and to choose between different tasks, and rapid learning of execution can lead to a competence trap of (long-run) inferior alternatives being chosen. A different version of this trade-off is seen when the organization is modeled as a collective actor rather than a unitary one. Organizations learn from the diverse beliefs of their members at the same time as they socialize the members into the most common beliefs in the organization. Rapid socialization prevents discovery of opportunities, a phenomenon labeled the exploration/exploitation trade-off. Because many organizational mechanisms drive uniformity of beliefs and action, it may be common to see organizations exploit more than they explore. The trade-off between exploration and exploitation has become an important topic in empirical research as well. Recently the modeling tradition has expanded to examine the consequences of decision rules with foresight, such as when a decision maker has a prior belief on which action is the best. James G. March and Daniel A. Levinthal have made important contributions to this research.

Importance

BTF currently exists in the form of a core set of research traditions that follow and build on its central concepts and mechanisms, and these are still very active. There has been notable theoretical and empirical progress in topics such as organizational learning from the experience of others, organizational routines, organizational attention, performance feedback, and adaptation. As one might expect from a theory built on an observational, process-oriented view of organizational decision making, there is a very strong empirical record of support for the main propositions. Much of this support is fairly recent, which may be surprising for a theory of its age, but this is for the simple methodological reason that the theory mostly makes predictions on the likelihood of changes under certain conditions and thus calls for methodologies of dynamic analysis that entered organizational research during the 1980s. Current research takes the central processes discussed above as essentially proven and moves on to elaborations such as introducing conditions moderating the effects, examining specific mechanisms such as sequential attention to goals, and discovering contextual effects such as new outcomes affected by the theory or new contexts that have not earlier been examined. The theory is sufficiently rich that there are still many remaining questions that attract researcher attention.

One reason it is still such an active source of research ideas is that its mechanisms for how organizations change ring true yet have nonobvious consequences for organizational change and adaptation. Many of these mechanisms are valuable targets of investigation even now because advances in methodology or new data sources allow research that was not possible when BTF was originally formulated. In addition to the research that is clearly within the BTF tradition, it has also infused the larger fields of organization theory and strategy with concepts and processes that are integral parts of other theories. Its influence is thus seen broadly through interaction with other kinds of research and narrowly through research that directly develops its main agenda.

Because BTF is closely related to how decisions are made in organizations, it has developed many findings with clear implications for managers. Many of these concern the role of leadership in organizations and informed the leadership course that James G. March taught Stanford MBA students for a quarter century. The lecture notes were later published as the book *On Leadership* (with Thierry Weil), and March's 1994 book on decision making (see Further Readings) is also highly recommended for its didactic value. A central insight in BTF is that organizations are adaptive systems that will take their own path with modest managerial intervention, but these paths are not necessarily optimal. Thus, organizations designed to learn rapidly how to execute strategies may pass up opportunities to discover which strategy is best; organizations designed to rapidly socialize members will fail to update themselves with the new knowledge these members could have brought in, and organizations seeking consistent strategies reduce their strategic flexibility. All these trade-offs have important consequences for performance and survival, and many run counter to lay management advice. Nor do organizations bend to their leader's will as easily as lay management advice assumes. Attempts to control organizations through goal systems encounter the problem that goal proliferation can lead to inaction, while goal concentration produces unwanted side effects. Attempts to control organizations through explicit rules and routines cut off the improvement opportunities in making the routines evolve, while an overly high emphasis on flexibility runs against the tendency of organizations to form and refine routines. Overall, BTF suggests that leadership be exercised with a light touch and with good knowledge on how organizational decisions are actually made.

Henrich R. Greve

See also Bounded Rationality and Satisficing (Behavioral Decision-Making Model); Garbage Can Model of Decision Making; Institutional Theory; Neo-Institutional Theory; Organizational Learning; Resource Dependence Theory

Further Readings

Argote, L. (1999). *Organizational learning: Creating, retaining, and transferring knowledge.* Boston, MA: Kluwer Academic.

Becker, M. C. (Ed.). (2008). *Handbook of organizational routines.* Cheltenham, England: Edward Elgar.

Cyert, R. M., & March, J. G. (1963). *A behavioral theory of the firm.* Englewood Cliffs, NJ: Prentice-Hall.

Gavetti, G., Greve, H. R., Levinthal, D. A., & Ocasio, W. (2012). The behavioral theory of the firm: Assessment and prospects. *Academy of Management Annals, 6*(1), 1–40.

Greve, H. R. (2003). *Organizational learning from performance feedback: A behavioral perspective on innovation and change.* Cambridge, England: Cambridge University Press.

Levitt, B., & March, J. G. (1988). Organizational learning. In W. R. Scott & J. Blake (Eds.), *Annual review of sociology* (Vol. 14, pp. 319–340). Palo Alto, CA: Annual Reviews.

March, J. G. (1991). Exploration and exploitation in organizational learning. *Organization Science, 2*, 71–87.

March, J. G. (1994). *A primer on decision making: How decisions happen.* New York, NY: Free Press.

March, J. G., & Weil, T. (2005). *On leadership.* Hoboken, NJ: Wiley-Blackwell.

Ocasio, W. (1997, Summer). Towards an attention-based theory of the firm. *Strategic Management Journal, 18*, 187–206.

BIG FIVE PERSONALITY DIMENSIONS

People differ from one another in many ways, and these individual differences matter for management theory and practice. The Big Five personality traits (also called the five-factor model of personality) describe five of the most crucial differences between people. An enormous body of research has conclusively established the importance of these five personality dimensions to major topics in management, such as job performance, motivation, leadership, teamwork, entrepreneurship, and strategy. This entry discusses the meaning of the Big Five traits, briefly reviews their history, and highlights their importance for a variety of management topics.

Fundamentals

Personality traits are characteristic patterns of thoughts, feelings, and behaviors. They summarize how people tend to behave across diverse situations. Traits differ from momentary states (e.g., getting upset or being elated) in that they are more stable and enduring tendencies. They highlight both the ways people are similar to others and the ways in which they differ.

The Big Five personality traits are *extraversion, agreeableness, conscientiousness, emotional stability* (also labeled *neuroticism* when reverse scaled), and *openness to experience* (or *intellect*). Each of the Big Five traits is a continuum along which an individual's characteristic tendency is located (e.g., for extraversion, the continuum ranges from extreme

introversion to extreme extraversion). Furthermore, these broad traits encompass a wide range of narrower traits or "facets"; that is, each Big Five trait consists of other traits that fall within its domain. The exact nature of these facets has yet to be established for most of the Big Five, but the facet structure of conscientiousness is fairly well understood.

The trait of *extraversion* distinguishes between people who are described by terms such as talkative, energetic, and bold (on the high end of the continuum) and those who are instead described by terms such as *quiet, shy,* and *withdrawn.* People who score higher on extraversion are more likely to feel comfortable around other people and start conversations, and they don't mind being the center of attention. People who score lower on this trait tend to talk less, keep in the background, and do not like to draw attention to themselves.

The trait of *agreeableness* distinguishes between people who are described by terms such as cooperative, sympathetic, and kind (on the high end of the continuum) and those who are instead described by terms such as *cold, rude,* and *unsympathetic.* People who score higher on agreeableness tend to respect others, treat them as equals, and are concerned about them. People who score lower feel less concern for others, are not very interested in their problems, and are instead focused on their own gain, are demanding, and tend to contradict others.

The trait of *conscientiousness* distinguishes between people who are described by terms such as responsible, efficient, organized, and thorough (on the high end of the continuum) and those who are instead described as disorganized, careless, sloppy, and inefficient. People who score higher on conscientiousness tend to be prepared, pay attention to details, and make and follow schedules. People who score lower are more likely to leave things unfinished, waste time, and need a push to get started on their work. Numerous studies have researched the major components underlying conscientiousness (the facets) and these are now fairly well understood. The four main facets are *industriousness, reliability, orderliness,* and *impulse control.* Several studies have also found a fifth facet called *conventionality.* While each of these facets relates to both the broader conscientiousness trait, as well as the other facets, they sometimes predict outcomes differently.

The trait of *emotional stability* (or *neuroticism*) distinguishes between people who are described by terms such as relaxed and unemotional (on the high end of the continuum for emotional stability or low end for neuroticism) and those who are instead described by terms such as nervous, moody, insecure, and irritable. People who score higher on emotional stability tend to feel comfortable with themselves, seldom feel blue, remain calm under pressure, and are less likely to get frustrated about things. People who score lower (i.e., who score higher on neuroticism) tend to worry about things, become stressed out more easily, and get upset and bothered by events.

The trait of *openness to experience* (or *intellect*) distinguishes between people who are described by terms such as imaginative, philosophical, creative, and deep (on the high end of the continuum) and those who are instead described by terms such as *uninquisitive, unimaginative, unsophisticated,* and *shallow.* People who score higher on openness to experience tend to enjoy thinking about things, such as hearing about new ideas and getting excited by them, tend to have larger vocabularies, and value artistic expression. People who score lower tend not to be interested in abstract or theoretical ideas, avoid philosophical discussions, are less interested in the deeper meaning behind things, and care less about art.

Although the Big Five traits are discussed independently, and clearly have independent effects on various outcomes, it is well known that they are correlated with one another. For example, there is strong meta-analytic evidence that emotional stability is positively correlated with extraversion, agreeableness, and conscientiousness; extraversion is positively correlated with openness to experience; and conscientiousness is positive correlated with agreeableness.

Origins and Boundary Conditions

The question of what is responsible for personality differences has attracted a fair amount of attention. Studies of identical and fraternal twins have conclusively established that genetics are a key part of the answer, with genetic differences accounting for roughly 50% of the variance in each of the Big Five traits. For example, differences in extraversion are known to relate to genes related to the dopamine system. Other work has found that differences in extraversion and emotional stability are correlated with the thickness of specific prefrontal cortex regions of the brain.

Three topics that relate to the boundary conditions and domain of the Big Five are situational strength, cross-cultural validity, and temporal stability. The effects of personality traits are theorized to depend on the strength of the situational pressures acting on the individual in any given context. Scholars have distinguished between strong and weak situations. In strong situations, the expected behavior is generally understood, and deviations from this behavior may have significant negative consequences. In such situations, personality differences matter less. In weak situations, individuals have much greater discretion to decide among behavioral alternatives, because there is no clear expectation regarding appropriate behaviors, and personality differences matter more.

The five-factor model of personality has been found to be valid across an extensive variety of cultures. Although there have been a few studies that have found either fewer or more than five traits and there is at least some evidence that the meaning of the five traits may vary a bit across cultures, these findings are exceptions to what is typically found. Overall, there is clear and strong evidence for the international validity and generalizability of the Big Five.

Personality traits demonstrate relative stability (indeed, some stability is inherent in the definition of personality) but do change over the longer time span of several years. Furthermore, while specific individuals may change in either direction on any of the traits, there are clear trends in the changes among personality over time as people age. Individuals typically increase in conscientiousness, agreeableness, and emotional stability and decrease in extraversion and openness to experience (changes described as reflecting a "maturity principle").

Other Frameworks and Traits

Other frameworks have been proposed to describe the important ways that people differ from one another at a high level. One of the most popular of these historically is the Myers-Briggs Personality Type Indicator, which contained four dimensions that categorized people into one of 16 different personality "types." Research has shown that the four dimensions of this conceptualization are directly related to four of the traits of the Big Five, but that the important trait of emotional stability is missing. While this model has been used in research on personality in the past and has been used extensively for consulting and training purposes (such as helping people appreciate diversity), it has been severely criticized by personality scholars and is no longer seen as an adequate representation of personality.

Perhaps the most viable challenger to the Big Five is the HEXACO model, which includes the Big Five but adds a sixth dimension called *honesty/humility*. This sixth dimension is reflected in adjectives such as honest, modest, and sincere versus greedy, boastful, and sly. Although evidence for this Big Six model of personality is growing, it is too early to tell whether it will become a serious rival to the Big Five model.

Regarding the domain of the Big Five, it is important to recognize that these do not exhaust the ways that people differ; rather, they summarize the major dimensions of difference. A wide variety of other, more targeted personality traits has been shown to relate to important management concerns. Several of the more prominent of these are *self-monitoring* (which is related to extraversion), *core self-evaluations* (part of which is emotional stability), and *need for cognition* (which is related to openness to experience, conscientiousness, and emotional stability). While these and other individual differences are typically related to Big Five traits, they are not completely subsumed by them and are distinct predictors of variables of interest to management scholars.

Evolution

The history of the Big Five begins with attempts in the first half of the 20th century to reduce the many thousands of descriptive terms that differentiate people to a smaller set using the statistical method of factor analysis. For example, Gordon Allport and H. S. Odbert identified 17,953 such terms in the English language from a large dictionary. It was recognized that many of these terms were related or synonymous, but it was unclear how many dimensions were needed to represent the major differences. While early analyses produced a somewhat large number of factors, subsequent reanalyses of these data discovered five factors. By the late 1960s, five different investigations had found strong evidence that five factors described personality at a broad level.

Research on personality then entered a lull because of a highly influential critique of trait psychology, which shifted the focus of researchers toward behavioral approaches and situational forces. In the subsequent two decades, convincing refutations of the critiques on trait psychology were published. By the latter part of the 1980s, an almost overwhelming body of evidence in support of the Big Five personality traits emerged, and its utility for advancing the understanding of the effects of personality on management topics was widely recognized.

Around that time, new scales designed specifically to measure the Big Five were developed. Two that have been extensively used are the copyrighted measures called the NEO-PI (which includes 240 items [i.e., questions] that measure six facets of each of the Big Five traits) and the shortened version of that measure called the NEO-FFI (which includes 60 items). Other published measures were subsequently developed, including widely used measures such as the Big Five Inventory by Oliver John and colleagues (44 items) and Gerard Saucier's Mini-Markers (40 items). More recently, an extensive set of public domain measures have been developed and validated and are available from the International Personality Item Pool; these are increasingly being used by academic researchers.

Importance

The importance of the Big Five traits for personality research is that it identifies the primary differences for researchers to investigate and enables researchers to cumulate findings on traits whose overlap was previously unrecognized. This has enabled scholars to achieve a deeper understanding of the effects of personality traits on management topics.

Job Performance

The most established findings concern the impact of the Big Five personality traits on overall job performance. While it has long been known that individual differences in general mental ability (i.e., intelligence or IQ) predict job performance across essentially all occupations and types of work, it has only been since the advent of the Big Five that researchers had the comprehensive framework of personality necessary to investigate the role of personality. The most consistent finding is that conscientiousness is the Big Five personality trait that best predicts additional variance in job performance across all types of work (with moderately sized effects even after controlling for intelligence). Several meta-analyses have also found that emotional stability affects job performance, although the effect sizes are typically smaller than those for conscientiousness.

In addition to these, extraversion has been found to affect job performance for jobs that involve interpersonal skills (such as sales and managerial positions), and some studies have found that agreeableness and openness to experience predict performance in customer service jobs (although most have found these last two traits to have no relationship to overall job performance). The positive impact of conscientiousness and emotional stability on performance appears to be partially due to greater motivation, as both of these traits have been found to consistently relate to multiple aspects of performance motivation (e.g., goal setting).

When one breaks overall job performance into task performance and contextual performance (or organizational citizenship behaviors [OCBs])—that is, those things not explicitly required to fulfill job requirements but that significantly improve overall organizational functioning), then the impact of the Big Five personality traits changes somewhat. In particular, agreeableness has been shown to relate to "interpersonal facilitation" and is a powerful predictor of extra-role behavior. A recent meta-analysis has found that each of the Big Five traits predicts OCBs and, furthermore, that emotional stability, openness to experience, and extraversion predict OCBs above and beyond the effects of conscientiousness and agreeableness.

While the above research has addressed main effects of the Big Five traits on job performance, there is also a small amount of work that has tested interaction effects between different pairs of the Big Five traits on performance. For example, research has shown that agreeableness and extraversion can moderate the effects of conscientiousness in jobs requiring cooperative and interpersonal interactions with others, such that the effects of higher conscientiousness are stronger for people who score higher on agreeableness or extraversion. These and similar results are intriguing but need to be replicated by future studies.

Other Management Topics

The Big Five are related not only to job performance but also to job satisfaction, turnover, and counterproductive work behaviors. Meta-analytic results have found that emotional stability, extraversion, and conscientiousness are each associated with higher levels of job satisfaction. Furthermore, meta-analytic evidence has found that each of the Big Five is related to reduced turnover. Finally, both conscientiousness and agreeableness have been shown to be negatively related to deviant behaviors such as theft, substance abuse, and disciplinary problems.

A variety of research has examined the role that the Big Five traits play in leadership. Research suggests that people who score higher on extraversion have a greater motivation to become leaders. Furthermore, meta-analytic results have found that extraversion, emotional stability, conscientiousness, and openness to experience each predict leader emergence and effectiveness, and that extraversion has a sizable relationship with transformational leadership behaviors.

A considerable number of studies have examined the role of the Big Five on teamwork and team effectiveness. Unlike research that considers individual-level personality and individual-level outcomes, these studies examine the role of personality at the team level, typically operationalized as the average, minimum, or variance of the team members' individual scores. Meta-analytic results across several studies suggest that team agreeableness and team conscientiousness are the most important traits and that both of these affect team process and performance.

The Big Five personality traits have also been found to play a significant role in entrepreneurship. One meta-analysis reported that entrepreneurs differ from nonentrepreneur managers in being higher on conscientiousness, emotional stability, and openness to experience and lower on agreeableness. Meta-analytic evidence also shows that four of the Big Five (all but agreeableness) are positively related to entrepreneurial intentions and entrepreneurial performance.

Although few studies have examined the roles of the Big Five traits on business strategy and top management team dynamics, there is suggestive evidence that they may play an important role. For example, one suggestive study found that each of the Big Five traits was associated with one or more aspects of top management team dynamics. Another study of CEO personality in small-to-medium Indian firms found that each of the Big Five traits was associated with strategic flexibility (the ability to adapt to environmental changes), which in turn was associated with firm performance.

Given the extensive amount of research showing that the Big Five personality traits affect a broad range of management topics, it seems likely that future research will continue to discover the ways that personality is important to management and organizational behavior.

Marc H. Anderson

See also Emotional and Social Intelligence; Human Capital Theory; Individual Values; Locus of Control; Psychological Type and Problem-Solving Styles; Type A Personality Theory

Further Readings

Bell, S. T. (2007). Deep-level composition variables as predictors of team performance: A meta-analysis. *Journal of Applied Psychology, 92,* 595–615.

Bono, J. E., & Judge, T. E. (2004). Personality and transformational and transactional leadership: A meta-analysis. *Journal of Applied Psychology, 89,* 901–910.

Chiaburu, D. S., Oh, I.-S., Berry, C. M., Li, N., & Gardner, R. G. (2011). The five-factor model of personality traits and organizational citizenship behaviors: A meta-analysis. *Journal of Applied Psychology, 96,* 1140–1166.

Digman, J. M. (1990). Personality structure: Emergence of the five-factor model. *Annual Review of Psychology, 41,* 417–440.

Goldberg, L. R. (1990). An alternative "description of personality": The Big-Five factor structure. *Journal of Personality and Social Psychology, 59,* 1216–1229.

Goldberg, L. R., Johnson, J. A., Eber, H. W., Hogan, R., Ashton, M. C., Cloninger, C. R., & Gough, H. G. (2006). The international personality item pool and the future of public-domain personality measures. *Journal of Research in Personality, 40,* 84–96.

Hurtz, G. M., & Donovan, J. J. (2000). Personality and job performance: The Big Five revisited. *Journal of Applied Psychology, 85,* 869–879.

Nadkarni, S., & Herrmann, P. (2010). CEO personality, strategic flexibility, and firm performance: The case of the Indian business process outsourcing industry. *Academy of Management Journal, 53,* 1050–173.

Witt, L. A. (2002). The interactive effects of extraversion and conscientiousness on performance. *Journal of Management, 28,* 835–851.

Zhao, H., Seibert, S. E., & Lumpkin, G. T. (2010). The relationship of personality to entrepreneurial intentions and performance: A meta-analytic review. *Journal of Management, 36,* 381–404.

Bounded Rationality and Satisficing (Behavioral Decision-Making Model)

The last few decades have witnessed greatly enhanced interest in behavioral decision theory. Unlike traditional decision theory, which is normative or prescriptive and seeks to find an optimal solution, behavioral decision theory (while it yields important practical implications) is inherently descriptive, seeking to understand *how* people actually make decisions. Long considered to be a fringe discipline, and perhaps simply a pesky nuisance to those advocating "economic decision making," behavioral decision theory has emerged as an important and promising domain of research and practice. Two behavioral decision theorists—Herbert Simon and Daniel Kahneman—neither of them economists—won the Nobel Prize in Economics for their work. Further, Cass Sunstein, a leading writer on behavioral decision theory and an advocate of using "paternalistic intervention" to influence decision making, was appointed by President Obama to serve as administrator of the White House Office of Information and Regulatory Affairs. In that role, his views have drawn both applause and condemnation. Popular books such as Thaler and Sunstein's *Nudge,* Ariely's *Predictably Irrational: The Hidden Forces That Shape Our Decisions* and Kahneman's *Thinking, Fast and Slow* have introduced these issues to a broader audience. Behavioral decision theory has been used to offer novel insights into disparate issues such as terrorism futures, road rage, whether to punt, bullet selection, divorce, and organ donation, as well as many management topics. This entry considers (a) rationality and its limits; (b) consequences of such bounds on rationality; (c) the roles of automatic information processing; (d) the relative merits of clinical, actuarial, and clinical synthesis approaches to decision making; (e) controversies relating to paternalistic intervention; and (f) the prospects of statistical groups and prediction markets.

Fundamentals

Rationality and Its Limits

In his 1947 book, *Administrative Behavior,* Herbert Simon wrote that decision making is the heart of administration and that an operational administrative decision is correct, efficient, and practical to implement with a set of coordinated means. *Administrative Behavior* focused on the behavioral and cognitive processes of making rational decisions and served as the foundation for Simon's later work and for much of behavioral decision theory.

In a seminal 1955 article, "A Behavioral Model of Rational Choice," Simon presented what he later called "my chief epistle to the economists," the first major challenge to the concept of rational economic man. He did this not as an intended criticism of traditional economic perspectives but to complement them with a richer, more reality-based view.

The traditional "rational economic man" model of decision making views humans as capable of optimizing. Assumptions underlying that perspective include that the decision maker

- has full knowledge of relevant aspects of the environment, including alternatives, relevant events (states of nature), the probabilities of those events, and the outcomes associated with combinations of alternatives and events;
- possesses a well-organized and stable set of preferences;
- enjoys superb computational abilities capable of optimization;
- is capable of "cool" decision making, not swayed by emotions and stress; and
- has immediate access to costless information.

Simon viewed these assumptions as unrealistic in view of the many constraints facing human decision makers. He presented his view of a "new rationality," one that replaced "rational economic man" with "administrative man." This new rationality includes the following points:

- The classical view of rationality is replaced with "bounded rationality" in which the decision maker tries to find satisfactory solutions within many cognitive, perceptual, situational, and other bounds.
- Aspiration levels are important and dynamic. Success and failure may result in changing levels of aspiration and thus changes in what is deemed acceptable or unacceptable.
- Information acquisition and processing are time-consuming and costly. As such, the question of the ideal level of persistence in pursuit of a goal involves a trade-off between the potential costs and benefits of search.
- Preferences are fluid. For example, preferences may change with time and maturation. In addition, consequences may change one's payoff function. And, of course, we may simply not know our preferences because of lack of experience (and corresponding reluctance to explore alternatives).

Simon reasoned that, in view of the bounds on rationality and associated difficulties, the concept of human decision makers as optimizers is unrealistic. In its stead, Simon proposed that human decision makers *satisfice* rather than optimize. While optimizers seek to determine the best possible alternative in the feasible set, satisficers seek the first acceptable alternative in that set.

While satisficing may seem undesirable (because, for instance, a better alternative may be available than the first acceptable alternative and because it makes the decision maker a slave to the order in which alternatives are available), it recognizes that information search and acquisition are costly. Simon has equated satisficing with finding a needle in a haystack and optimizing with finding the sharpest needle in the haystack, a monumentally more difficult task. Simon reasoned that sometimes just a needle is needed.

Graham Allison used his analysis of the Cuban missile crisis to challenge the economics-based, utility-maximizing rational actor model then dominant in understanding foreign policy decision making. He proposed alternative models recognizing organizational and other constraints (building in part on Simon's work) and top leaders' political actions.

Other scholars have examined the nature and degree of constraints on rationality. For instance, George Miller wrote of "The magical number, plus or minus two," showing that for absolute judgments of unidimensional stimuli such as tones, taste intensities, visual position, loudness, and points on scales, humans are capable of a limited and narrow range of about seven, plus or minus two, absolute judgments of unidimensional stimuli. Thus, human capacity for making unidimensional judgments is limited and varies surprisingly little from one sense to another.

In an early examination of the ability of human decision makers to serve as "intuitive statisticians,"

Paul Slovic reviewed evidence relating to the validity of clinical judgment. He concluded that, in areas such as investment analysis, performance of mutual funds, medical diagnoses, and forecasting, validity was poor and interrater reliabilities were typically low. Further, he came to the "quite disappointing" conclusion that, in general, clinician training and experience have little impact on validity but increase confidence in the decision and reduce willingness to accept external inputs.

Daniel Schacter discussed memory limitations, writing of the "seven sins of memory." His premise was that, though often reliable, memory is also fallible. Schacter identified three "sins of omitting," or types of forgetting. These include transcience, absent-mindedness, and blocking. A second set, "sins of commission," are forms of distortion. These are misattribution, suggestibility, and bias. A final "sin" is the inability to erase intrusive recollections. Schacter argued that these "sins," while troublesome, are by-products of otherwise adaptive features of memory.

Some Consequences of Limits on Rationality

Constraints on rationality result in many heuristics and biases. *Heuristics* are simplifying rules of thumb. One simplifying heuristic—satisficing—was noted earlier. Amos Tversky and Kahneman proposed others, including the following:

Availability is the tendency to estimate the probability of an event on the basis of how easy it is to recall examples of the event.

Representativeness is the tendency to place something in a class if it seems to represent, or "look like," the class.

Anchoring and adjustment is the tendency to use an early bit of information as an anchor and then use new information to adjust that initial anchor. We tend to give too little weight to new information, resulting in insufficient adjustment.

The *default heuristic* is the acceptance of the default presented to us, whether it is the default setting when installing computer software or the default presented on a form. As noted later, this can be a powerful and unobtrusive determinant of decisions.

Constraints on human decision making also lead to a variety of systematic *biases*. These include the following:

Conservatism in information processing occurs when we under-revise past estimates when given new information.

Framing effects. The way information is framed can influence choices. Kahneman and Tversky proposed *prospect theory* to explain some consequences of framing. Prospect theory posits (among other things) that we evaluate alternatives in terms of relative "gains" and "losses" from the status quo rather than in terms of absolute values.

Hindsight bias (or "Monday morning quarterbacking") is the "I knew it all along" phenomenon. This is the tendency for people who learn an outcome of an event to believe falsely that they would have predicted the reported outcome.

Confirmation bias is the tendency for people to seek, interpret, and recall information in ways that confirm their preconceptions.

Overconfidence bias occurs when people's subjective confidence in their judgments is greater than their objective accuracy.

Illusory correlation is the tendency to "see" relationships between variables that do not in fact exist, perhaps because of our stereotypes or expectations.

Gambler's fallacy is the fallacy that if deviations from expected behavior are seen in repeated independent trials of a random process, deviations in the opposite direction are more likely. For example, if five consecutive flips of a fair coin come up heads, the gambler may believe a tail is "due."

Escalation of commitment, or the *sunk cost fallacy,* is the tendency to "throw good money after bad." That is, while the decision to continue to invest in a course of action should be made on the basis of future benefits and costs, we tend to justify further, escalating, investment on the basis of sunk costs, such as the money or lives that have already been expended.

Importance

Heuristics in Continuous Environments

Much of the early research relating to heuristics and biases involved one-time decisions. Such decisions—whether to have chemotherapy or surgery, whether or not to mount an attack on an enemy, or whether to marry one's childhood sweetheart—are common and often critical. Nevertheless, many real-world decisions are in continuous environments, characterized by regular, often redundant, feedback and the opportunity to make incremental adjustments. In such environments, some heuristics may be less troublesome. For example, conservatism in information processing may not be a serious problem in continuous environments since there will be many opportunities to revise.

Fast and Frugal Heuristics

While the overwhelming emphasis on heuristics and biases has been on their dangers, some heuristics, if used consciously and appropriately, may be functional. For example, Gert Gigerenzer has championed use of "fast and frugal heuristics" in an "adaptive toolbox." He notes, for example, that Harry Markowitz, who won the 1990 Nobel Prize in Economics for his work on optimal asset allocation, did not use his award-winning optimization technique for his own retirement investments. Markowitz relied instead on a simple heuristic, the 1/N rule, which states, "Allocate your money equally to each of N funds." Research showed the 1/N heuristic to outperform 12 optimal asset strategies. The optimization models performed better at fitting past data than did the simple heuristic, but there were worse at predicting the future.

Automatic Information Processing

Research also shows that much decision making, rather than being a conscious deliberative process, occurs automatically at nonconscious levels. For example, when we have repeatedly faced a decision situation, we may develop scripts. *Scripts* are models held in memory that specify behaviors or event sequences that are appropriate for specific situations, such as steps in a performance appraisal. Scripts may be effective when dealing with routine situations but may cause problems in novel situations. Research has addressed the benefits and costs of automatic processing, the consequences of conflict between automatic and conscious processing, and the manner and consequences of switching from one mode (automatic or conscious) to another.

Clinical and Actuarial Approaches, Improper Linear Models, and Clinical Synthesis

In view of the many heuristics and biases influencing human decision makers, the *clinical-actuarial controversy* compares accuracy of human (clinical) decision makers to that of actuarial (statistical) models. Research strongly supports the view that actuarial models consistently outperform unaided clinical judgment. Robyn Dawes wrote that there was no research showing clinical judgment to be superior to statistical prediction when both are based on the same codable input variables. That is still the case.

Nevertheless, it is sometimes infeasible to develop a model that optimally relates predictors to outcomes (such a model is termed *proper*). There may, for instance, be too few observations to permit development, or there may be no measurable criterion. In such cases, an improper linear model—one with which the weights of the predictor variables are obtained by some nonoptimal method, such as set to be equal—may be useful. For instance, divorce was significantly predicted by subtracting instances of quarrels from instances of love making, though neither variable was itself a significant predictor. Unit weighting was also used to select a superior bullet for use by the Denver Police Department.

One intriguing form of improper linear model is a *model of man,* so called, with which regression analysis is used to develop a linear model of an individual's decision process. That model is then used to make decisions in place of the individual (this is called *bootstrapping*). It has the important benefit of perfect reliability, enhancing validity. Remarkably, every properly executed study comparing the validity of decisions of individuals to those of their models of man has found the models to be superior.

Despite the overwhelming evidence in support of use of proper and improper linear models, their adoption has been fiercely resisted, even by statistically trained psychologists. Dawes has identified, and attempted to refute, primary causes for such resistance. For example, some critics argue that use of a statistical model rather than, for instance, an interview to choose from among job candidates or a doctor's judgment to diagnose a patient is unfair and dehumanizing. Dawes responds that clinical judgments are seriously flawed and may be self-fulfilling. He notes that some of the worst doctors spend a great deal of time talking with their patients, read no medical journals, order few or no tests, and grieve at the funerals. Also, since the accuracy of statistical models can be assessed and is often low (though higher than that of clinical judges), critics may object to their "proven low validities."

In the face of such opposition to replacement of clinical decision making with use of actuarial models, an alternative—sometimes called *clinical synthesis*—has been proposed in which output of actuarial models is provided to individuals as input to their decisions. The evidence on clinical synthesis is clear: Individuals' decisions are better when they receive outputs from actuarial models, but not as good as if they had simply used that output without modification. One important question, therefore, is to find ways to encourage decision makers to rely more heavily on the recommendations of actuarial models.

Paternalistic Intervention

A recent, important controversy relates to the efficacy and desirability of using knowledge about human cognitive limitations and tendencies in order to "nudge" people toward "desirable" behaviors, a process termed "paternalistic intervention." Two recent books—*Nudge* and *Predictably Irrational*—and numerous articles have highlighted the importance of knowledge of behavioral decision making as well as its controversial implications. The controversy revolves primarily around ethics of use of unobtrusive nudges and the question of who determines what actions are "desirable."

As an example, most states, and many other countries, use an "opt-in" or "explicit consent" form in which people must take a concrete action, such as mailing in a form, to declare they want to be organ donors. In several European countries an "opt-out" rule, also called "presumed consent," is used, in which citizens are presumed to be consenting donors unless they indicate otherwise. Traditional economics would argue that if it is easy to register as a donor or nondonor, the options should lead to similar results. However, in Germany, with an opt-in system, just 12% give their consent, while in Austria, with an opt-out system, 99% do. A simple nudge, in this case manipulation of the default heuristic, has remarkable consequences.

Statistical Groups and Prediction Markets

While there is substantial evidence that statistical models of decision makers (i.e., models of man) outperform those decision makers, those models perform at a level equivalent to that achieved by averaging judges' inputs. This is because averaging across many judges sharply reduces unreliability, one primary benefit of models of man. This suggests that use of *statistical groups*—that is, averaging of group members' judgments—may be useful. In a classic example, Francis Galton examined a competition in which contestants attempted to judge the weight of a fat ox at a regional fair in England. The ox weighed 1,198 pounds; the average guess, from the 787 contestants, was 1,197 pounds. More recently, members of the Society for American Baseball Research were asked in 2004 to predict the winners of the baseball playoffs. In each round of the playoffs, the favored choice of the expert group was correct 100% of the time.

A logical extension of statistical groups is use of *prediction markets* that pool individual judgments to forecast the probabilities of events. In such markets, individuals bid on contracts that pay a certain amount if an event occurs. For instance, a contract may pay $1 if sales of a particular company are above a certain level. If the market price for the contract is $.60, the market "believes" that sales have a 60% chance of exceeding that level. Such markets are being used internally at Google, Hewlett-Packard, IBM, and elsewhere.

Prediction markets such as the Iowa Electronic Markets and InTrade have been remarkably successful in predicting outcomes such as winners of elections and Oscars. The most controversial of these markets (rejected following vitriolic response) was proposed to predict terrorist activities. Critics labeled the proposal as "incredibly stupid" and "a futures market in death." Nevertheless, following the attempt of Umar Farouk Abdulmutallab, the "underwear bomber," to detonate plastic explosives on a Northwest Airlines flight, security experts close to the situation said a prediction market, with its ability to integrate diverse information, could have prevented him from boarding the flight.

In summary, behavioral decision making has dramatically grown in the richness of its insights as well as in its acceptance and impact. It highlights key factors influencing the nature and quality of human decisions, including systematic deviations from the "rational economic man" model of decision making. While inherently descriptive, it suggests important, and sometimes controversial, policy implications for diverse areas such as management, finance, medicine, and foreign policy.

Ramon J. Aldag

See also Decision-Making Styles; Garbage Can Model of Decision Making; Group Polarization and the Risky Shift; Intuitive Decision Making; Managerial Decision Biases; Prospect Theory; Schemas Theory; "Unstructured" Decision Making

Further Readings

Ariely, D. (2009). *Predictably irrational: The hidden forces that shape our decisions.* New York, NY: HarperCollins.

Gigerenzer, G. (2008). Why heuristics work. *Perspectives on Psychological Science, 3*(1), 20–29.

Kahneman, D. (2011). *Thinking, fast and slow.* New York, NY: Farrar, Straus & Giroux.

Kahneman, D., & Tversky, A. (1979). Prospect theory: An analysis of decision under risk. *Econometrica, 47,* 263–291.

Miller, G. A. (1994). The magical number seven, plus or minus two: Some limits on our capacity for processing information. *Psychological Review, 101,* 343–352. (Reprinted from *Psychological Review, 1956, 63,* 81–97)

Schacter, D. L. (1999). The seven sins of memory: Insights from psychology and cognitive neuroscience. *American Psychologist, 54*(3), 182–203.

Simon, H. A. (1947). *Administrative behavior: A study of decision-making processes in administrative organization.* New York, NY: Macmillan.

Simon, H. A. (1955). A behavioral model of rational choice. *Quarterly Journal of Economics, 69*(1), 99–118.

Slovic, P. (1972). Psychological study of human judgment: Implications for investment decision making. *Journal of Finance, 27,* 779–800.

Thaler, R. H., & Sunstein, C. R. (2009). *Nudge.* London, England: Penguin Books.

Tversky, A., & Kahneman, D. (1974). Judgment under uncertainty: Heuristics and biases. *Science, 185,* 1124–1131.

BRAINSTORMING

The term *brainstorming,* as articulated by Alex Osborn in his book *Applied Imagination,* refers to a set of four rules designed to improve creative idea generation. Although first applied in groups, brainstorming rules have also been used extensively to structure individual efforts at idea generation. Because much research on idea generation has used brainstorming rules as a foundational element, time-limited experimental sessions in which all participants are given Osborn's rules are sometimes known as "brainstorming tasks." Perhaps owing to its popularity, *brainstorming* is also often used as a generic synonym for "generating ideas," especially in situations where a block of time is set aside exclusively for idea generation. Brainstorming is relevant to management for its explicit recognition of the importance of creative idea generation and for its potential to increase the likelihood of getting creative ideas in situations where creativity is needed for organizational effectiveness. The theory's central management insight is that efforts at creative idea generation deserve focused attention and can benefit from adopting a formalized structure. The sections that follow describe brainstorming in more detail, provide a brief overview of research assessing its validity and impact, and offer a list of key sources on the topic.

Fundamentals

The four rules of brainstorming are (1) to generate as many ideas as possible, (2) to avoid criticizing the ideas, (3) to attempt to combine and improve on previously articulated ideas, and (4) to encourage the generation of unusual or "wild" ideas. Collectively, the rules may be viewed as a set of goals to strive for when generating ideas. Each rule embodies a separate principle, yet their overall character is also important in the sense that it implicates an underlying logic in which the generation of variation in ideas is maximized (Rules 1, 3, and 4) and separated temporally from the selection and retention of ideas (Rule 2).

The first rule, to generate many ideas, presumes that the likelihood that any single idea will be regarded as creative is low. Osborn's remedy for this was to encourage people to develop a large sample of ideas from which to choose in the hopes of getting at least one that would be regarded as sufficiently creative. The idea that a large sample of ideas is more likely to yield at least one creative idea compared to a small sample is consonant with research that relies on evolutionary theory as a basis for understanding creativity.

The second rule, to avoid criticism, is intended to ensure the separation of idea generation from idea selection. It also signals a safe environment for generating novelty. Osborn observed that idea generation efforts can derail when groups start to argue the merits of each individual idea, and he asserted that creativity would be better served if people refrained from evaluating the merits of individual ideas until after a large sample of ideas had been generated. There are at least two reasons why this rule makes sense from a contemporary perspective. First, the criticism of ideas may affect the types of ideas people generate. In particular, individuals might be reluctant to offer their less obviously practical ideas if they are concerned about criticism. Yet because novelty is a key property of creativity, such ideas may often end up being among the most desirable. Second, criticism may affect the number of ideas people generate. The degree to which this is a problem may have to do with individuals' own reactions to anticipated criticism, but there is reason to think that many people may offer fewer ideas when they expect criticism, and some people's idea production might be severely affected.

The third rule, combining and building on prior ideas, recognizes that creativity often arises from new associations between existing concepts. When ideas are generated in groups, such a rule attempts to provide each person with explicit encouragement to attend to and leverage the cognitive efforts of others. Contemporary theories of cognition in individuals and groups suggest that such efforts might sometimes improve idea generation.

The fourth rule, to encourage the generation of wild ideas, is predicated on the assumption that human idea generation is not completely random. By aiming specifically to generate novel ideas, people may be more likely to generate such ideas. Contemporary theories of creativity and learning suggest that engagement with novelty is likely to produce more novelty in thought.

Used properly, brainstorming rules are proposed to improve the number of ideas produced in a concentrated session of idea generation. Brainstorming rules are also supposed to increase the likelihood of production of one or more ideas later judged to be creative. When used in groups who generate ideas together face-to-face, brainstorming rules have also been proposed to improve satisfaction with idea generation as an activity, feelings of efficacy at generating creative ideas, and willingness to engage in creative idea generation in the future. In organizations, brainstorming rules may also lead at times to competitions for status, opportunities to build an attitude of wisdom, support for organizational memory of prior successes, and skill variety for employees, and they may even afford opportunities to impress clients and generate firm income in professional service organizations.

Importance

Although some of the reasoning supporting the likely utility of brainstorming rules has changed over time, the overall thrust of each of the brainstorming rules remains viable, in theory, as a means to improve creative idea generation. Yet despite decades of research on aspects of brainstorming, conclusions about many aspects of its functioning remain surprisingly tentative. One reason for this equivocation is that relatively little research has directly attempted to assess the contribution of brainstorming rules to idea generation. Instead, the major question of interest to researchers has typically been the relative effectiveness of group versus individual idea generation. With regard to this question, one set of conclusions is fairly clear: under most circumstances, individuals working alone generate more ideas and more creative ideas than individuals working in interacting groups. Researchers aiming to understand why groups do less well than individuals at generating numerous and creative ideas have determined that an important cause of this performance gap seems to be the waiting time between having an idea and verbalizing it within an interacting group setting where not everyone can speak at once.

At the same time, there *are* other possible outcomes of idea generation that may be valuable to management, and some of these may be best accomplished in groups. For instance, individual outcomes related to satisfaction, feelings of efficacy, and interest in idea generation all seem to benefit from group idea generation, as do organizational outcomes such as competitions for status, opportunities to build an attitude of wisdom, support for organizational memory of prior successes, skill variety for employees, impressing clients, and generating income. In general, more evidence is available to support the individual outcomes than the organizational outcomes. Finally, there is beginning to be some evidence that interacting groups can affect the characteristics of generated ideas relative to ideas produced by individuals working alone.

Some research does assess brainstorming rules for their effectiveness in terms of the basic outcomes of the number and creativity of ideas. Overall, this research finds that there is room to improve on any efficacy of brainstorming rules. For instance, there is evidence that both the quantity and novelty rules of brainstorming can be improved by converting them to specific, challenging goals that ask for a specific, difficult number of ideas or a specific, difficult percentage of novel ideas during a fixed time period. Specific, difficult quantity goals have been shown to improve the number of ideas generated relative to "basic" brainstorming rules, and specific, difficult novelty goals have been found to improve novelty and creativity of ideas relative to basic brainstorming rules. Advantages of the specific, difficult goals seem to depend, at least to some extent, on the degree to which people generating the ideas are highly committed to the specific, difficult goals, with higher performance associated with higher commitment. Indeed, research suggests that many individuals may prefer to generate ideas that are less, rather than more, creative.

A variety of other research has also looked at augmenting brainstorming rules with additional rules or procedures. In particular, rules based on how trained facilitators act in groups have shown promise in research. Such rules include exhortations to stay focused on the task, avoid telling stories or explaining ideas, and to keep generating ideas by bringing up previous ideas during a lull. Like the original rules, these additional procedures can largely be used by either interacting groups or individuals working alone. A few procedures, including some electronic idea generation aids and some fairly elaborate paper-based rules, are intended primarily to be used by a group of people generating ideas at the same time either in person or within a technologically mediated space.

The resilience of brainstorming across decades of research and practice is a testament to both the logic underlying its formulation and the need for creative ideas. For managers, perhaps the best advice is that idea generation may benefit from structure. In general, the small base of brainstorming research in applied settings suggests that benefits are more likely to accrue when managers promote careful adherence to brainstorming rules rather than treating them as casual guidelines. For researchers, the many remaining questions surrounding brainstorming suggest that our understanding of creative idea generation and how to improve it remains incomplete.

Robert C. Litchfield

See also BVSR Theory of Human Creativity; Componential Theory of Creativity; Goal-Setting Theory; Interactionist Model of Organizational Creativity; Open Innovation; Patterns of Innovation; Quality Circles; Social Facilitation Management; Stages of Creativity; Stages of Innovation

Further Readings

Diehl, M., & Stroebe, W. (1991). Productivity loss in idea-generating groups: Tracking down the blocking effect. *Journal of Personality and Social Psychology, 61,* 392–403.

Litchfield, R. C. (2008). Brainstorming reconsidered: A goal-based view. *Academy of Management Review, 33,* 649–668.

Litchfield, R. C., Fan, J., & Brown, V. R. (2011). Directing idea generation using brainstorming with specific novelty goals. *Motivation & Emotion, 35,* 135–143.

Nijstad, B., & Stroebe, W. (2006). How the group affects the mind: A cognitive model of idea generation in groups. *Personality and Social Psychology Review, 10,* 186–213.

Osborn, A. F. (1957). *Applied imagination.* New York, NY: Scribner's.

Paulus, P. B. (2000). Groups, teams, and creativity: The creative potential of idea-generating groups. *Applied Psychology: An International Review, 49,* 237–262.

Paulus, P. B., & Brown, V. R. (2003). Enhancing ideational creativity in groups: Lessons from research on brainstorming. In P. B. Paulus & B. A. Nijstad (Eds.), *Group creativity: Innovation through collaboration* (pp. 110–136). New York, NY: Oxford University Press.

Reinig, B. A., Briggs, R. O., & Nunamaker, J. F., Jr. (2007). On the measurement of ideation quality. *Journal of Management Information Systems, 23,* 143–161.

Rietzschel, E. F., Nijstad, B. A., & Stroebe, W. (2010). The selection of creative ideas after individual idea generation: Choosing between creativity and impact. *British Journal of Psychology, 101,* 47–68.

Sutton, R. I., & Hargadon, A. (1996). Brainstorming groups in context: Effectiveness in a product design firm. *Administrative Science Quarterly, 41,* 685–718.

BUREAUCRATIC THEORY

Bureaucratic theory is an essential tool for understanding capitalist democracy. No longer bound by the power of kings, or political or religious leaders, social life is now shaped by the desire to act efficiently toward democratically established ends justified on the basis of scientific knowledge articulated into rules and regulations. The aesthetic of bureaucratic action is "without regard to person," its impersonality. But can bureaucracy's efficiency be reconciled with a livable social life? The gaps between goal-oriented rationality and our hopes for a humane and just society provoke continuing debate. It is easy to talk about bureaucracies, for we all have experience of and opinions about them. But theorizing or evaluating them proves difficult. Some see *bureaucratic* as a derisive or pejorative comment about our helplessness in the face of institutionalized impersonality, with its flavor of a dystopic, dehumanized world. Others see it as a technique for organizing scarce resources efficiently in pursuit of complex social and economic objectives. Despite its vast literature, the theory of bureaucracy remains an unsolved puzzle for social scientists, whether theorists of management and decision making in the private or public sectors, in government, institutionalized religion, or elsewhere. We remain unsure about bureaucracies' nature even as we depend on them more than ever. But recent events have brought bureaucracy's strengths and weaknesses back into view even as many feel Max Weber's analysis more or less put the topic to rest with little more to be said. This entry will summarize the familiar features of bureaucratic theory and also show that, while Weber's work was exemplary, social theories are never more than tools to help us think about our own experiences and activities; they cannot reveal an objective social reality that is independent of us.

Fundamentals

Bureaucracy is an ancient administrative strategy, but it moved to the center of social and political life in 18th-century Prussia under Frederick the Great. Political and economic dominance followed as Prussia's state agencies—the army, national health, education, tax collection, and so on—were reconstructed to eliminate nepotism and corruption and make practical use of "state-istics," facts gathered and analyzed in the service of state efficiency. As a politically active historian, economist, and sociologist, Weber's analysis of the impact of elevating bureaucracy into this central political position remains a superb example of what the social sciences can achieve. As he summarized it, bureaucracy administers public or private policies on

the basis of knowledge—characterized by the six principles he delineated:

1. Policies shall be executed by technically qualified personnel.

2. Occupying offices that shall be defined by (a) learnable rules that give officials specified powers of decision, command, and control and (b) productive and administrative resources that remain the property and purview of the office.

3. Which offices shall be related in a hierarchy of authority and reciprocal communication.

4. The official's decision making shall be rational, impersonal, and based on records and systematically gathered data (statistics).

5. The official's compensation shall be by regular salary and career-determined benefits in the expectation his or her work comprises a fully occupying long-term career.

6. A reciprocal expectation that the official is bound to a "faithful and impartial" execution of his or her organizational-defined duties.

Bureaucratic theory, then, is more than a way of thinking about the world, of preferring science-based facts to human opinion. It is an exploration of the mode of social relations that became increasingly prevalent with the neo-Enlightenment rise of rationalism as a social and personal philosophy. Given our concept of property and its ownership by individuals, economic relations became predominantly rationalized and individualistic. So long as these relations were legally permitted, markets arose. But new nonfeudal, nonreligious, nonmarket relations also arose during capitalism's emergence, especially out of people's preparedness to accept "knowledge work" and the production-related authority of others. At the same time, we have no expectation that any real government or private sector organization could be a "perfect" or "total" bureaucracy. So the value of bureaucratic theorizing may be less in its efficiency-oriented prescriptions than in how it directs the analyst's attention to what it does not illuminate, such as rationalism's impact on society or the employee's personality. Bureaucratic theory is actually an attempt to separate what can be made machine-like, determinable, and uninteresting about human relations from that that cannot be so treated and so remains interesting and germane to the human task of shaping social relations. Against the assertion that bureaucracy is administration on the basis of scientific knowledge, we might deploy bureaucratic theory to explore the consequences of a society's, an organization's, or an individual's "knowledge absences." Thus bureaucratic theory should not be seen as the challenge to balance efficiency against effectiveness, but as a vestige of our attempt to shape the human condition through scientific analysis.

Evolution

While many cite Weber's assertion that bureaucracy was "administration on the basis of knowledge," this really obscures more than it clarifies. It is the usual academic's trick of defining one unknown in terms of another, for knowledge is an even more problematic concept than those citing Weber's comment care to admit. Given our current sociological methods, we presume that the truth value of knowledge is coherent, contingent on "scientific rationality" and on rigorously examined cause-and-effect relations. This is an exceedingly narrow definition of "knowledge." Weber was less constrained and argued for several kinds of rationality, each of which would provide the basis of a certain kind of social knowledge—*zweckrational, wertrational,* affectual, and traditional, which some translate as practical, theoretical, substantive and formal—sometimes abbreviated to *functional* and *substantive.* Weber's "ideal types" arose from his appreciation of the gulf between theorizing organizational relations as logically rational and the historical evidence of more complex forms of social reasoning. Rather than saying, as many do, that an ideal type was an exemplar of social relations that can be explained as rationally determined, Weber was a historian who adopted a more complex methodology—absent which his theory of bureaucracy cannot be properly understood.

Bureaucracy's power lies in how it helps us synthesize many role occupants' specialized expertise and so bring their many different rationalities and specialties to bear on the increasingly complex tasks we humans wish to engage—putting a man on the Moon, curing cancer, preventing the proliferation of nuclear weapons, and so on. Its power arises from (a) the many different kinds of knowledge, scientific and otherwise, that can be related to the

goals chosen and (b) the administrator's capacity to synthesize them into coherent and manageable purposive activity. It is tied up with the division of labor—and knowledge—the demarcating characteristics of the modernist era. But we should also recall Adam Smith's earlier explanation for economic growth, role occupants' ability to focus their imagination on a specific task and raise their productivity without being fully instructed by superiors, something that can only happen when the superiors' rules are incomplete and underdetermining, allowing "space" for the worker's personal agency. Here, Smith advanced an agency-based theory of knowledge growth that was missing from bureaucratic theory, for that has no related theory of learning and, therefore, of scientific or economic growth. Learning and growth, and morality too, lie beyond the bounds of the bureaucratic analysis.

Those who analyze and criticize bureaucratic theory on its own grounds, rather than for its failing to provide them a positivist and deterministic theory of administration, might focus on the contradictions between Weber's social rationalities—wherein lie the subtle "knowledge absences" that real organizational administrators have to address. To illustrate this with a simplified example, "functional rationality" focuses on means, whereas "substantive rationality" focuses on ends—the distinction between efficiency and effectiveness that led Mannheim to argue that the flaw in bureaucratic theory was that functional rationality tended to drive or "crowd out" substantive rationality. In other words, given the specializations and divisions of labor within a bureaucracy, the role occupants' understanding of why they were doing what they were doing was always limited, and they would be only imperfectly aware of the overall goal. This would lead to counterproductive behavior, to their striving to do the wrong thing perfectly rather than do the right thing even imperfectly—what lives on as "the perfect being the enemy of the good"—behavior that is interesting precisely because it springs from knowledge absence. Real administrators have to bridge the distinction between functional and substantive reasoning.

Clearly, we should see every real social relation as "mixed" or "synthesized" in that any compelling analysis must reflect Weber's several rationalities and that a "rigorous" one-dimensional explanation is neither achievable nor sought. The historian's objective is to illuminate social situations and our sense of what might be, or have been, possible. The human actors who synthesize or instantiate action in underdetermined situations can never be detached from the outcome, so at no time can human action be fully "explained" by rational or causal analysis of its circumstances. Hence, it is a profound methodological error to grant a bureaucracy status as an independent nonhuman entity, a thing-in-itself with its own identity, characteristics, and agency—as is our modernist habit. From Weber's point of view, bureaucratic theorizing was about probing the consequences of impacting historically prior modes of social order with an emerging scientific mode. He analyzed the historical development of capitalism, what happened as the ideology of scientific rationality drew economic ideas and objectives into our political process, and even the domination thereof. To think of Weber as an organizational theorist who proposed bureaucracy as a mechanical "one best way" of organizing is to miss his point entirely. On the contrary, his principal concern was how the power and effectiveness of the bureaucratic approach would feed back into complex multirationality of social life and transform or "disenchant" it, promoting the amoral ends-oriented philosophy widely suspected of helping to precipitate the financial crash of 2008.

One important knowledge absence Weber moved beyond the grasp of bureaucratic theory is the process of establishing the bureaucracy's objectives. In the public sphere, goals are outcomes of our collective political process, and we presume that the bureaucratic agency is a neutral instrument of their execution. The bureaucratic approach minimizes the extent to which individual human shortcomings—bounded rationality and bias—deflect the agency from its collectively established purposes. In the private sphere, the entrepreneur (or rather the board of directors) is granted considerable freedom to establish the firm's objectives—which need not be justified as rational or politically chosen—powers attached to the owners' capital.

The crucial knowledge gap between a bureaucracy and the process of establishing its goal(s) is matched by another knowledge gap, between its rules and their execution. In the real world, the bureaucracy's rules are never sufficient to the employee's needs; they are never fully determining. Every situation presents unanticipated challenges because human knowledge is imperfect. Thus, the employee has a measure of discretion in applying the rules and principal-agent issues are always present. Our feeling of helplessness against a bureaucratic process is less toward the rules themselves, given that we accept the bureaucracy's goals as legitimate, than at the bureaucrat's unwillingness to use his or her discretion to our advantage, to find a "workaround" that lets us get what we want. Hence, every employee must contribute from his or her own agency if a rule-based system is to function; there must be an "informal" that complements the "formal." As we puzzle in this direction, we see that bureaucracy is actually about social relations between boundedly rational beings—and those who think it a machinelike social system composed of perfectly rational relations miss the point of Weber's analysis. In Smith's analysis, as opposed to Weber's, the individual operative's agentic contribution is the pivotal seed to the wealth of the nation (and the firm). Weber's analysis focused on how an uncritical rationalism ultimately cripples both the political processes of goal selection and the imagination-based human processes that underpin economic growth.

Bureaucratic theorizing is about modernism and the historical impact of rationalism on our politics, organizations, families, work, and personalities. Weber's analysis was deeply double-edged—to help us identify scientific rationalism's impact and highlight the Faustian compact as we become (a) increasingly dependent on the social and economic efficiencies rationalism offers and (b) correspondingly subordinated to the goals and the means we are forced to choose if we are to reach them. Today, rationalism and rational choice liberalism are under increasing attack, both as a political philosophy and as an approach to economic analysis and social well-being. But bureaucratic theory remains extremely powerful, if only to draw attention to what leaders, politicians, entrepreneurs, and workers must do to bring scientific knowledge into productive relationship with the social world by shaping the goal-setting process and the resulting bureaucratic employees' agency. As Nobel Prize winner Herbert Simon argued, reason goes to work only after it has been supplied with a suitable set of inputs, or premises. If it is to be applied to discovering and choosing courses of action, then those inputs must include, at least, a set of "shoulds," or values to be achieved, and a set of "it's," or facts about the world in which the action is to be taken.

Importance

Weber contrasted bureaucratic administration against "irrational" administration on the basis of family relations or feudal or religious power. Modern capitalist society is marked by increasing rationality, and bureaucracy's spread is just one facet of the historical trend to *modernism,* to prioritizing facts and the scientific attitude over "mere opinion," whether feudally or religiously warranted. It is useful to know that Weber came to theorize rationality and bureaucracy because his doctoral thesis (submitted in 1889) examined the evolution of "private" commercial partnerships in the Middle Ages, a period when family-based administration was being supplemented by rational employment relations, leading to what is now called *principal-agent* problems.

His arguments led us to see rationalism as the proper way to characterize human work—mindful rational decision making or knowledge work—a view readily applicable to both public and private spheres. Even though this was more informative than characterizing work as mere "labor," many shortcomings emerged, framed as the administrative problems or challenges that occupied later scholars and critics. We have the evident "dysfunctions of bureaucracy," such as the Vatican's response to charges of child molestation, the Pentagon's initial failure to armor Humvees in Iraq, or Euromismanagement from Brussels. There is a political angle too—with the growth in the U S. government's share of gross domestic product reaching its highest ever nonwar levels and approaching those of "socialist" European countries, many see state bureaucracies as "cancers on the body politic," an attack on individual freedom and utterly un-American.

On the other hand, the need to raise operational efficiency and reform government agencies and business organizations is taken for granted. British Petroleum's slowness to deal with its Deep Horizon spill led to more oil-industry regulation. The Global War on Terror provoked a massive bureaucracy—the Department of Homeland Security—to eliminate the structural "silo-ing" between agencies that probably contributed to the effective execution of the 9/11 attacks. Likewise developed nations struggle to find appropriate ways of providing and regulating health care, promoting efficiency in hospital, research, and insurance operations, while controlling wasteful tendencies to overtest and overprescribe. Unraveling

our love-hate relationship with bureaucracy draws attention to administrative practice at many levels; we speak of bureaucratic states and organizations or of bureaucratic work, of bureaucrats as individuals, and even of the bureaucratic personality.

But at the deeper level, bureaucracy is about an attitude, a way of looking narrowly at human affairs from the vantage point of the rational pursuit of known goals. It follows that bureaucracy—as a theory of politics, economics, business organization, or work—has come under increasing scrutiny as the modernist project itself has become more questioned, though much of the commentary is pickled with red herrings that academics should know to ignore. For instance, to point to the dehumanizing consequences of being ruled by impersonal facts rather than by "real human beings" misses how complex is the interaction of role and occupant. While the bureaucratic role occupant is defined narrowly by the rules and powers defining the role, no longer treated as a rounded human individual, the employee is also protected against the arbitrary and rule-ignoring authority of those with power in the situation. Likewise, a bureaucratic arrangement protects a policy from the arbitrary views, biases, and interpretations of those charged to implement it. It also creates a relatively objective basis for evaluating their performance. For these reasons alone, an increasing number of people, and percentage of the world's labor force, works in contexts loosely definable as bureaucratic.

Rather than simply dismissing bureaucracy as inhumane, machinelike, or deeply flawed, we might critique it by focusing on its axioms. First, Weber's distinction between *authority* and *power,* alluding to the role occupant's voluntary acceptance of the role's rules, presupposes an unquestioning "faithful" subordination of those implementing the plan to the authority of those choosing its objectives. Reinhard Bendix argued that bureaucracies leveraged ancient psycho-political dispositions such as the acceptance of the power of kings and, absent the citizens' preparedness to bend to another, could not come into existence. We accept state bureaucracies as instrumental servants to our political process only because we accept that process. In the private sector, our capitalist legal system gives entrepreneurs a degree of kingly power that precedes rather than succeeds the formation of private firms. Thus, all bureaucracies stand on aspects of the social and legal order beyond the organization and to argue they "dehumanize" is to overlook our evident willingness to subordinate ourselves to others within certain "legitimate" limits. It follows there are important differences between, say, Chinese and European bureaucratic phenomena. Notably, Ronald Coase argued that employees' willingness to subordinate themselves to the powers of the entrepreneur, within certain limits, was the demarcating characteristic of the Western firm as distinct from a market. Our military, educational, and ecclesiastical bureaucracies clearly stand on quite different social bases with quite different "higher aims" to which occupants subordinate themselves.

To point to a bureaucracy's tendencies to goal displacement to protect itself against change or elimination, to become increasingly sclerotic with the passage of time, and so on presumes the bureaucracy has somehow become an entity unto itself, escaping the hands of those who created it or are its custodians. Thus, a technical question about bureaucracy, as distinct from philosophical criticism of it as an attitude toward the world or as a political comment on the growing impact of rationalism on social thought and action, is whether bureaucratic organizations can acquire agency of their own and, like Frankenstein, come back to haunt those who thought them no more than tools to reach their own objectives. This question raises others, especially (a) about how bureaucratic organizations come into being and (b) how they become legitimate forms of social relation. While Weber saw a bureaucracy growing from the "routinization of the founders' charisma," we now treat bureaucracy as a socially acceptable way of planning and implementing agreed social and economic policies. So long as the objectives are clear and legitimate, we think there should be a rational evaluation and selection of the most efficient means of achieving them—the "knowledge" articulated into the bureaucracy's division of labor and control procedures. Bureaucracy remains the world's administrative system of choice and has yet to be seriously challenged by any other form of administration, largely because our ideas of performance and efficiency are tied up with rational evaluation of goal-oriented activity.

JC Spender

See also Analytical and Sociological Paradigms; Bounded Rationality and Satisficing (Behavioral Decision-Making Model); Dialectical Theory of Organizations; Goal-Setting Theory; Knowledge-Based View of the Firm; Organizational Structure and Design; Principles of Administration and Management Functions; Strategy and Structure

Further Readings

Bendix, R. (1945). Bureaucracy and the problem of power. *Public Administration Review, 5*(3), 194–209.

Collins, R. (1992). *Sociological insight: An introduction to non-obvious sociology* (2nd ed.). New York, NY: Oxford University Press.

March, J. G., & Simon, H. A. (1958). *Organizations.* New York, NY: Wiley.

Mouzelis, N. P. (1967). *Organisation and bureaucracy: An analysis of modern theories.* Chicago, IL: Aldine.

von Mises, L. (1946). *Bureaucracy.* New Haven, CT: Yale University Press.

Weber, M. (1947). *The theory of social and economic organization* (A. M. Henderson & T. Parsons, Trans.). Glencoe, IL: Free Press.

Weber, M. (1978). *Economy and society: An outline of interpretive sociology* (G. Roth & C. Wittich, Trans.). Berkeley: University of California Press.

BUSINESS GROUPS

While the typical image evoked by business is that of a set of independent companies in competition with each other, in many countries large businesses come in groups. Such business groups (henceforth BGs) have various names in different geographies, ranging from Japanese *keiretsu,* Korean *chaebols,* Turkish *families,* and Latin American and Spanish *grupos* to Indian business *groups.* BGs have been defined by Khanna and Rivkin in 2001 as "a set of firms which, though legally independent, are bound together by a constellation of formal and informal ties and are accustomed to taking coordinated action" (pp. 47–48). Since the firms belonging to a BG could be a mix of fully independent public firms and private firms, BGs are somewhat different from conglomerates—single corporations with divisions or subsidiaries in multiple industries. The theory of business groups is concerned with explaining why BGs exist and what are the consequences for a firm of belonging to a BG. BG theory is important for management theory in general because BGs have a significant presence in many economies around the world—in most developing economies but also in many developed economies, such as Sweden and Hong Kong. The following sections of this entry outline some of the predominant explanations for business groups and review the extant body of work in this domain.

Fundamentals

In a review of extant theories explaining the emergence and existence of BGs, Guillen captured three predominant views. The first, which dominates the literature, is the economists' view, based on institutional and transaction cost theories. In this view, BGs emerge in the absence of well-functioning markets or institutions as a strategic response to factor market imperfections in developing economies. Performing the role of missing institutional intermediaries in capital, labor, and product markets, BGs fill the institutional voids by generating their own internal markets for these factors. The second view, primarily advocated by economic sociologists, is that BGs are a manifestation of different social and cultural patterns prevalent in some economies. Consequently, the organizational form of BGs is isomorphic with the social structure surrounding them. In addition to this, the social network perspective emphasizes the benefits that firms realize by virtue of being embedded in an enduring network such as a BG in terms of uncertainty reduction, contract enforcement, and opportunity identification. The third explanation for the emergence of BGs is presented by political or development economists. According to this view, some states or nations actively encourage a few entrepreneurs and facilitate them with incentives to enter new industries, thus creating business groups.

BGs serve the role of strategic networks providing member firms with access to information, knowledge, resources, markets, and technologies. They also provide superior access to the political power structure facilitating BG firms with a richer pool of opportunities. Studies show that BGs also have a positive impact on firm innovation in emerging economies and facilitate a firm's expansion into new geographic markets. In addition to all these benefits, BGs are known to confer some costs on affiliated firms. Most BGs are also characterized by pyramidal ownership structures in which one or more family firms control a set of firms, which in turn control a set of more firms, and so on. Hence, BG firms tend to suffer from conflicts of interests between controlling (typically, family) and minority shareholders. Some BGs have been shown to engage in "tunneling," or moving profits from firms in which they have low cash flow rights to those in which they have higher cash flow rights. There is no firm agreement on whether the net benefit of belonging to a BG is positive or negative.

Recent work on BGs examines the future prospects of business groups, especially in the changing institutional context brought about by a wave of deregulation in the emerging economies. Because BGs essentially provide internal substitutes within the group for weak external institutions, it is argued that BG benefits should be larger in countries with weak economic institutions than in countries with strong institutions and grow smaller within countries with weak economic institutions as the quality of these institutions improves. While some studies have reported evidence consistent with this argument, there is also some contrary evidence, thus hinting at the value addition potential of BGs that goes beyond substitution of institutional intermediaries. In addition, some research is now focusing on how BGs themselves may be evolving over time in response to changes in their environment and also on unearthing the significant heterogeneity that exists among BGs in terms of their differential resource endowments, organizational structures, and interorganizational ties.

The theories of business groups inform managers in the following ways. Managers of transnational corporations would understand some of the unique advantages as well as disadvantages that firms derive from their affiliation with BGs and learn to compete with them better. The same knowledge could help business group owners and managers of BG firms leverage their unique strengths and devise ways to overcome some of the limitations arising from this organizational form.

Raveendra Chittoor

See also Business Policy and Corporate Strategy; Competitive Advantage; Institutional Theory; Resource-Based View of the Firm

Further Readings

Carney, M., Gedajlovic, E. R., Heugens, P. P. M. A. R., Essen, M., & Oosterhout, J. H. (2011). Business group affiliation, performance, context, and strategy: A meta-analysis. *Academy of Management Journal, 54*(3), 437–460.

Chacar, A., & Vissa, B. (2005). Are emerging economies less efficient? Performance persistence and the impact of business group affiliation. *Strategic Management Journal, 26*(10), 933–946.

Chang, S. J., Chung, C. N., & Mahmood, I. P. (2006). When and how does business group affiliation promote firm innovation? A tale of two emerging economies. *Organization Science, 17*(5), 637–656.

Granovetter, M. (2005). Business groups and social organization. In N. J. Smelser & R. Swedberg (Eds.), *The handbook of economic sociology* (2nd ed., pp. 429–450). Princeton, NJ: Princeton University Press.

Guillen, M. F. (2000). Business groups in emerging economies: A resource-based view. *Academy of Management Journal, 43*(3), 362–380.

Hoskisson, R. E., Johnson, R. A., Tihanyi, L., & White, R. E. (2005). Diversified business groups and corporate refocusing in emerging economies. *Journal of Management, 31*(6), 941–965.

Khanna, T., & Palepu, K. (2000). The future of business groups in emerging markets: Long-run evidence from Chile. *Academy of Management Journal, 43*(3), 268–285.

Khanna, T., & Rivkin, J. W. (2001). Estimating the performance effects of business groups in emerging markets. *Strategic Management Journal, 22*(1), 45–74.

Leff, N. (1978). Industrial organization and entrepreneurship in the developing economies: The economic groups. *Economic Development and Cultural Change, 26*, 661–675.

Mahmood, I. P., & Mitchell, W. (2004). Two faces: Effects of business groups on innovation in emerging economies. *Management Science, 50*(10), 1348–1365.

Business Policy and Corporate Strategy

Business policy refers to the roles and responsibilities of top-level management, the significant issues affecting company-wide performance, and the decisions affecting companies in the long run. Corporate strategy is the strategy developed and implemented to the goals set by the company's business policy. As a company-wide strategy, corporate strategy is concerned primarily with answering the question, What set of businesses should the company be in? It should be distinguished from business strategy, which focuses on answering the question of how to build a sustainable competitive advantage in specific business or market. More specifically, corporate strategy can be defined as the way a company creates value through the configuration and coordination of its multibusiness activities. As such, the subject of corporate strategy is the diversified multibusiness corporation. This entry first describes the content of a theory of corporate strategy, then presents the evolution of corporate strategy, and concludes with a discussion of the importance of a theory of corporate strategy.

Fundamentals

From an academic point of view (as opposed to a more managerial or practical point of view), the main objective of a theory of corporate strategy is to understand why such multibusiness firms exist and what is the relationship between diversification and performance. The question of why multibusiness firms exist is particularly important because the neoclassic theory of the firm assumes the sole existence of single-business firms operating in near-perfect markets and competitive equilibrium. The existence of profitable multibusiness firms in the real-world challenges this assumption. Therefore, the reasons for the existence of multibusiness firms require specific theoretical developments. It is also critical for a theory of corporate strategy to explain how the multibusiness firms create value at the corporate level that cannot be created by neoclassic single-business firms or shareholders investing in single-business firms. Such a theory should also explain the roles of corporate headquarters in managing multiple businesses and corporate resources. Thus, corporate strategy has implications for corporate governance and the control of the work of managers. A considerable body of theory has evolved within the disciplines of strategy, economics, finance, marketing, organization theory, and international business that have salient implications for the management of corporate strategies.

Academic interest in developing a theory of corporate strategy has been continuously growing since the rise of multibusiness firms at the beginning of the 20th century. If multibusiness firms were almost unknown in 1900, they are today the dominant type of organizations for the conduct of business activities. In the United States, about 60% of economic output is undertaken by multibusiness firms. The percentage is similar in Western

Europe, while specific forms of multibusiness firms, such as *keiretsu* in Japan and *chaebols* in Korea, are also ubiquitous in other parts of the world. To understand the role of these multibusiness firms and develop a theory of corporate strategy, academic research has emphasized three sets of issues: First, the determinant of firm scope: Why is it that some firms are highly specialized in what they do, while others embrace a wide range of products, markets, and activities? Second, what is the link between scope and performance? Third, what are the implications of this link for the management of multibusiness firms in terms of organizational structure, management systems, and leadership?

The most comprehensive framework presenting the key elements of a theory of corporate strategy has been outlined by David Collis and Cynthia Montgomery. They argue that multibusiness firms exist because they create corporate advantage by aligning four elements: a corporate *vision* about the goals and objectives of the firm, which is then implemented based on the firm's stock of *resources* and portfolio of *businesses*. In addition, the implementation of the corporate vision and its alignment with the firm's resources and businesses should be configured and coordinated through a set of corporate structure, systems, and processes defining the roles of the *corporate headquarters*. When these four elements—vision, resources, business, and roles of the headquarters—fit together, shareholder value is created that cannot be duplicated by financial investors on their own, providing a corporate advantage to the multibusiness firm.

In this framework, nicknamed the *corporate strategy triangle* by the authors, corporate vision refers to the definition of the domain of the firm's activities and is primarily concerned with establishing the boundaries of the firm. The corporate vision should address the question: What set of businesses should we be in? The vision should also outline a set of corporate goals and objectives pertaining to the choice of the firm's main corporate value-creating mechanisms. Michael Porter proposed a classification of four generic mechanisms—sharing resources between businesses, transferring core competences across businesses, creating an efficient internal capital market through portfolio management, restructuring—that should provide the multibusiness firm with a corporate advantage.

Resources constitute the most critical building blocks of corporate strategy, because they determine not what a firm wants to do but what it can do. This is, resources determine in which businesses the firm can have sustainable competitive advantage. By sharing and transferring resources across related business, the firm can achieve synergies and economies of scope, sources of corporate advantage. Moreover, the presence of excess resources that are mobile and fungible provides an incentive for the firm's diversification, as well as a direction for its diversification strategy (which businesses can we enter?).

Businesses refer to the industries or markets in which the firm operates. The composition of the firm's portfolio of businesses is critical for the implementation of the corporate vision and the long-term success of its corporate strategy. The firm's business portfolio influences the extent to which it can share resources across businesses or transfer skills and competencies from one business to the other, as these value-creating mechanisms require businesses to be related. Alternatively, the firm could invest in unrelated businesses to spread risk or move away from declining industries. In addition, the realization of an efficient internal capital market and the implementation of a restructuring strategy require businesses to be somewhat unrelated to lead to a corporate advantage.

To implement a corporate strategy or corporate value creation mechanism, the firm's headquarters plays an important role in coordinating and configuring the activities of the businesses. The corporate headquarters influences business units' decisions through the firm's organizational structure, systems, and processes. The extent of the involvement of the corporate headquarters in the activities of its business units should depend, however, on the corporate vision, the resources the firm possesses, and the level of relatedness between its businesses. This is what Michael Goold and colleagues call a firm's "parenting style." The headquarters should minimize its involvement and delegate most operational decisions to business units, making them as independent as possible to spread risk and minimize overhead costs; alternatively, it can play an important role in the business units' decision-making process to increase coordination across business units in order to force collaboration to achieve a corporate advantage through synergies.

The theory of corporate strategy does not suggest that there should be a single best corporate strategy to create a corporate advantage. Quite the opposite, there exist various strategies that are equally profitable despite the fact that they are based on various combinations of the four elements of the corporate strategy triangle. Several theoretical perspectives have been used to justify the value creation potential of these different combinations: industrial organization theory, transaction cost theory, agency theory, the dominant logic, the resource-based view, strategic contingency and institutional theories, and real option theory. These theoretical perspectives provide the building blocks necessary to explain connections between the elements of the corporate strategy triangle.

From a theoretical point of view, multibusiness firms can exist for many reasons. Principally, a diversification strategy helps increase the firm's corporate value by improving its overall performance, through economies of scope or increased revenues, which is why single-business firms seek to diversify their activities into related and unrelated businesses. Some firms also diversify to gain market power relative to competitors, often through vertical integration or mutual forbearance. However, other reasons for a firm to diversify its activities may have nothing to do with increasing the firm's value. Diversification could have neutral effects on a firm's corporate advantage, increase coordination and control costs, or even reduce a firm's revenues and shareholder value. These reasons pertain to diversification undertaken to match and thereby neutralize a competitor's market power, as well as to diversification to expand the firm's portfolio of businesses to increase managerial compensation or reduce managerial employment risk, leading to agency problems. Incentives to diversify come from both the external environment and a firm's internal environment. External incentives include antitrust regulations and tax laws, whereas internal incentives include poor performance, uncertain future cash flows, and the pursuit of synergy and reduced risk for the firm. Although a firm may have incentives to diversify, it also must possess the resources and capabilities to create corporate value through diversification.

Evolution

More than 50 years ago, corporate strategy was defined by Kenneth Andrews (1971) as "the pattern of objectives, purposes, or goals, stated in such a way as to define what business the company is or is to be in and the kind of company it is or is to be" (p. 28). Following this definition, he argued that the choice of the business(es) the company is or is to be should be based on the twin appraisals of the company external and internal environments. An internal appraisal of strengths and weaknesses of the company should lead to the identification of distinctive competencies, and an external appraisal of the threats and opportunities from the external environment should lead to the identification of potential success factors. However, the corporate strategy of multibusiness firms has undergone enormous change in the last 50 years, affecting both their scope and their organizational structure. The merger and acquisition (M&As) booms in the 1960s and 1980s extended the scope of multibusiness firms, often to the point where corporate value was destroyed by excessive coordination costs and unprofitable use of free cash flows. An emphasis on profitability and the creation of shareholder value became prevalent in response to the economic downturns and interest rate spikes of 1974 to 1976, 1980 to 1982, and 1989 to 1991, which exposed the inadequate profitability of many large, diversified firms. Increased pressure from shareholders and financial markets, including a new breed of institutional investors (e.g., pension funds), led to the rise of shareholder activism and a stricter control of managers' diversification activities. In the 1990s, capital market pressures forced many diversified firms to reassess their business portfolios, the involvement of their headquarters, and the way they coordinated and configured their multimarket activities. For example, a swath of CEO firings in the early 1990s highlighted the increasing power of corporate board members. An even bigger threat to incumbent management was the use of debt financing by corporate raiders and leveraged buyout (LBO) associations in their effort to acquire and then restructure underperforming firms. The lesson to other poorly performing multibusiness firms was clear: Restructure voluntarily and de-diversify or have it done to you through a hostile takeover. As a result of this shareholder pressure, corporate managers increasingly focused their attention on the stock market valuation of their firm. The dominant trends of the last two decades of the 20th century were downsizing and refocusing. Large diversified firms reduced both their product scope by refocusing on their core businesses and their vertical scope, through outsourcing. Reductions in vertical integration through outsourcing involved not just greater vertical specialization but also a redefinition of vertical relationships. The new vertical partnerships typically involve long-term relational alliances that avoid most of the bureaucracy and administrative inflexibility associated with vertical integration. The narrowed corporate scope also has been apparent in firms' retreat from product diversification. More recently, new collaborative structures, such as joint ventures, strategic alliances, and franchising, have become more popular.

Mirroring these changes in firms' corporate strategy, the theoretical lenses and normative prescriptions for corporate strategy theory have evolved over time. From an emphasis on financial performance in the 1960s, to managing the corporation as a portfolio of strategic business units and searching for synergy between them in the 1970s, to the emphasis on free cash flow and shareholder value in the 1980s, to the refocusing on core competencies in the 1990s, and finally, to the industry restructuring in the beginning of the 21st century, corporate strategy theory has continued to change and become more sophisticated. In the beginning of the 21st century, the development and exploitation of organizational capability has become a central theme in strategy research. The recognition has dawned that a strategy of exploiting links (i.e., relatedness) across different business sectors does not necessarily require diversification and that a wide variety of strategic alliances and other synergistic relationships might exploit economies of scope across independent firms.

Importance

The theory of corporate strategy does not have only enthusiastic supporters; skeptics have questioned its importance and relevance, arguing that corporate strategy does not matter. This view largely stems from empirical results derived from a series of early variance decomposition studies that identified negligible corporate effects associated with profitability differences between firms. However, more recently, scholars have reassessed with more sophisticated techniques the relative importance of industry, business, and corporate factors in determining profitability differences between firms and found that corporate strategy accounts for a significant component of performance differences that in some cases approach 25%. These recent results demonstrate that corporate strategy does matter.

Another critic of the theory of corporate strategy is its overreliance on economic theories, such as agency and transaction costs theories, and shareholder value as its ultimate yardstick to measure the success of corporate strategy. These critics argue that these economic theories rely on a key, but controversial, assumption of managerial opportunism. For example, these economic theories assume that managers are often opportunistic and motivated only by self-interest, but this assumption has been subject to frequent challenges. Some scholars hold that most managers actually are highly responsible stewards of the assets they control and do not behave opportunistically. With this alternative view of managers' motives, they propose a stewardship theory, according to which shareholders should install more flexible corporate governance systems to avoid frustrating their benevolent managers with unnecessary and costly bureaucratic controls. The assumption of managerial opportunism also has important implications in the way firms interact with their strategic partners and how headquarters control business unit managers.

By focusing on shareholder value, corporate strategy theory also takes a narrow view on corporate responsibilities. Stakeholder theory broadens this view by arguing that firms and their managers are responsible not only to their shareholders but to a larger group of stakeholders. However, when multiple stakeholders' interests represent ends to be pursued, managers must make corporate strategic decisions that balance these multiple goals rather than just maximize shareholder value. The stakeholder theory of corporate strategy, in turn, proposes that managers' goals should be developed in collaboration with a diverse group of internal and external stakeholders, even if they support potentially conflicting claims. However, if the number of stakeholders to whom firms and managers are accountable increases, the scope of a firm's corporate responsibilities also increases. It has been argued that not one but four types of corporate social responsibilities exist: economic, legal, ethical, and philanthropic. Multibusiness firms' managers' strategic choices therefore must reflect a compromise between various considerations—of which shareholder value is just one.

These recent developments still need to be incorporated into a comprehensive theory of corporate strategy. Such a theory should start to relax some of the main assumptions of the economic theory of corporate strategy, such as managerial opportunism and shareholder value maximization. Mitigating the idea that every manager is opportunistic would require that a comprehensive theory of corporate strategy should build on the developments of stewardship theory. Relaxing the assumption that the ultimate goal of a corporate strategy and managers' sole responsibility is the maximization of shareholder value would require a comprehensive theory of corporate strategy to broaden its perspective to accommodate multiple stakeholders. Finally, expanding firms' corporate responsibilities from making a profit to encompass broader economic, social, and environmental responsibilities would also require new theoretical developments for a theory of corporate strategy.

To summarize, this entry has presented the theory of corporate strategy and its key components. It establishes that corporate strategy encompasses decisions, guided by a vision and more specific goals and objectives, about the scope of the firms in terms of their businesses, resources, and the leveraging of those resources across businesses as well as the role of corporate headquarters for the organizational structure, systems, and processes. There is no single best corporate-level strategy; rather, many value-creating corporate strategies can be developed based on different configurations of the various components of corporate strategy. Firms' corporate strategies and their theoretical rationales have evolved over time in response to the pressures of both the firm's external and internal environments. Diversification is one of the main elements of corporate strategy, such that a firm's level of diversification influences its performance and that corporate strategy matters. However, a theory of corporate strategy encompasses more than the link between diversification and performance. A theory of corporate strategy also incorporates or influences a theory of the growth of the firm, a theory of the organizational structure of the firm, a theory of multipoint competition, and a theory of corporate governance.

Olivier Furrer

See also BCG Growth-Share Matrix; Business Groups; Diversification Strategy; Matrix Structure; Resource-Based View of the Firm; Strategy and Structure; Transaction Cost Theory

Further Readings

Andrews, K. A. (1971). *The concept of corporate strategy*. Burr Ridge, IL: Dow-Jones-Irwin.

Chandler, A. D., Jr. (1962). *Strategy and structure*. Cambridge, MA: MIT Press.

Chandler, A. D., Jr. (1990). *Scale and scope*. Cambridge, MA: Harvard University Press.

Collis, D. J., & Montgomery, C. A. (2005). *Corporate strategy: A resource-based approach* (2nd ed.). Boston, MA: McGraw-Hill/Irwin.

Furrer, O. (2011). *Corporate level strategy: Theory and applications*. London, England and New York, NY: Routledge.

Furrer, O., Thomas, H., & Goussevskaia, A. (2007). The structure and evolution of the strategic management field: A content analysis of 26 years of strategic management research. *International Journal of Management Reviews, 10*, 1–23.

Goold, M., Campbell, A., & Alexander, M. (1994). *Corporate-level strategy: Creating value in the multibusiness company*. New York, NY: Wiley.

Grant, R. M. (2002). Corporate strategy: Managing scope and strategy content. In A Pettigrew, H. Thomas, & R. Whittington (Eds.), *Handbook of strategy and management* (pp. 72–97). London, England: Sage.

Porter, M. E. (1987). From competitive advantage to corporate strategy. *Harvard Business Review, 65*, 42–59.

Rumelt, R. P. (1974). *Strategy, structure and economic performance*. Cambridge, MA: Harvard University Press.

Teece, D. J. (1982). Toward an economic theory of the multiproduct firm. *Journal of Economic Behavior & Organization, 3*, 39–63.

BUSINESS PROCESS REENGINEERING

In his seminal 1990 *Harvard Business Review* article, Michael Hammer challenged managers to do things differently: "Instead of embedding outdated processes in silicon and software, we should obliterate them and start over. We should 'reengineer' our businesses; use the power of modern information technology to radically redesign our business processes in order to achieve dramatic improvements in their performance" (p. 104). Business process reengineering differs from other change initiatives, such as quality or process improvement, because of the radical and holistic nature of the intended change. Subsequently, in the 1993 book titled *Reengineering the Corporation,* Michael Hammer and James Champy defined reengineering as "the fundamental rethinking and radical redesign of business processes to achieve dramatic improvements in critical contemporary measures of performance such as cost quality, service and speed." This entry provides an overview of the fundamentals, evolution, and importance of business process reengineering.

Fundamentals

There are important differences between quality or process improvement initiatives and reengineering or process innovation initiatives.

Process improvement initiatives are more limited in scale and scope; the magnitude of change associated with process innovation or reengineering is more expansive and therefore takes more time. The starting point for process improvement is typically the existing process or function, for process innovation or reengineering is often a clean slate, and the initiative is cross-functional. Finally, whereas process improvement initiatives may be initiated, bottom-up, given the broad scope of change associated with process innovation or reengineering, senior management sponsorship is required.

At the core of business process reengineering are three principles. First, managers should adopt a process view of the business. Second, managers should understand the conditions that enable or inhibit radical process redesign. Third, once the process redesign is complete, managers must be conscious of the tactics and levers they use to manage change. The first two are discussed in this section because they represent fundamental ways of thinking and understanding management reality. The third is more action oriented and underlies the discussion of managerial interventions discussed in the Importance section.

A Process View of the Business

Business process reengineering challenges managers to focus on business processes. A business process typically cuts across traditional functional areas within an organization; it is a horizontal view of the business as contrasted with a more hierarchical view. In his 1993 book, Davenport stated, "A process perspective implies a strong emphasis on how work is done within an organization in contrast to a product focus emphasis on what" (p. 8). A business process is a set of activities that create value for the customer; as such, it typically starts and ends with the customer, and it is something measurable.

Order fulfillment is an example of a process that takes place in many organizations. Order fulfillment involves many traditional departments within the firm, external partners, and the customer. A reengineering initiative focused on an order fulfillment process would involve the redesign of the process where the process is enabled by information technology. In a 1995 Harvard Business School Note, Richard Nolan put forth a strategic reengineering "equation" where Radical Change was seen as equaling New Organization and IT.

The process of making an airline reservation is an example of an order fulfillment process. In the 1990s, airline customers called an airline's reservation desk or a travel agent to make a reservation. A decade later, most customers make reservations on their own, by going to an airline's website or to a travel website. The redesign of this process reduced the need for travel agents and reservation agents who were employed by the airlines, which resulted in significant cost savings to airlines and their customers. The airline reservation example also highlights a shift to self-service, a philosophy whose roots are a by-product of the reengineering era.

In the late 1980s, Otis Elevator leveraged IT to reengineer the process used by its customers to request service of elevators after normal business hours. Prior to the business process reengineering initiative, a customer who experienced a problem with an elevator after hours would call an answering service, which was typically a person working from home, to report an out-of-service elevator. After the business process reengineering initiative, dubbed Otisline, the customer would call a regional or national call center and reach an Otis employee who could troubleshoot and, if necessary, dispatch a technician. With Otisline, the company found they were able to be more responsive to customers and reduce the downtime and "stuck in elevator" situations, thereby increasing customer satisfaction. Later, Otis was able to install sensors in elevators, which sent a signal to the call center. Often, if an elevator was having trouble, technicians could send a software update to the elevator or dispatch a technician before the customer even knew there was a problem. By combining information technology (IT) and organization redesign, Otis Elevator was able to reengineer its customer service process and achieve dramatic results.

It is useful here to highlight several key elements in Michael Hammer and James Champy's definition of reengineering as noted above: "the *fundamental* rethinking and *radical* redesign of business *processes* to achieve *dramatic* improvements in critical contemporary measures of performance such as cost quality, service and speed [italics added]." The first step in any reengineering initiative is to engage in a process that will allow you to envision the future and how to redesign that process. When coaching managers on design projects, reengineering consultants highlight that a team can take one of two approaches: design with a clean slate or design for implementation.

A team charged with redesigning a process can design with a "clean slate"—that is, design as if you were starting from scratch and have no organizational or cultural constraints. Clean-slate designs are often quite radical and, as Tom Davenport noted in his 1993 book *Process Innovation,* may include ambitious plans for new technologies, new skills, and new organizational structures. A clean-slate design will typically result in the most radical design, which can lead to the most radical results.

On the other hand, a team can "design for implementation"; that is, the team can consider the various organizational constraints during its design process. There are a number of typical implementation constraints, including funding, union obligations, culture, organizational structure, and IT systems. A design for implementation approach assumes the existing state and may reflect the constraints that leadership cannot or will not remove. Such a design will be less radical, but it may be easier to implement the change because the less radical design does not disrupt the existing organization culture and structure.

In their 1995 Harvard Business School Note, Donna Stoddard and Sirka Jarvenpaa reported that "Reengineering Design Is Radical; Reengineering Change Is Not!" They argued that organizations that figure out how to combine the two approaches—that is, design for implementation to get started but move toward more radical change—are often the ones who realize the most dramatic results, over time, because they are able to move forward with the change initiative while staying focused on the end goal, the radical design.

Conditions That Can Enable or Inhibit Reengineering

To enable the success of a reengineering initiative, managers must understand the conditions that enable or inhibit radical process redesign. Four factors that managers should consider when embarking on process redesign are the process size, the geographic dispersion of process owners and enablers, recent business performance, and the organization's financial resources. Some of the factors are obvious; small projects are easier to manage than large projects, and one site is easier to manage than multiple sites.

The other two factors may not be so obvious. Recent business performance is a factor that can enable or inhibit a redesign effort. On the one hand, poor performance may create a burning platform and thereby motivate organization members to implement the redesigned business process; on the other hand, it may be difficult to get organization members to embark on a major change initiative if things are going well.

The financial resources of the organization are important to consider when embarking on a major process redesign because it takes time to rethink a process, and time is money. Further, it will take organizational resources to implement the new design since organizational members may have to be retrained, new IT systems may have to be developed, and there may be some period during which people are less productive.

A new IT application or capability may be the trigger for a reengineering initiative. For example, in the 1990s, the proliferation of IT capabilities enabled the self-service phenomenon now commonplace for order entry, banking, and grocery store checkout. Retailers and other corporations benefit from self-service because they need fewer employees per order. Customers like self-service because they can transact business at their discretion—often at any time and or from any place.

Before embarking on reengineering, managers must understand the conditions that will enable or inhibit radical process redesign. With appropriate planning, they can steer the project toward success.

Evolution

Business process reengineering was a very popular management initiative in the 1990s. A number of articles appeared in the popular press and management journals highlighting the promises of reengineering. For example, in 1990, Hammer published his seminal article, "Reengineering Work: Don't Automate, Obliterate" in which he proffered the potential for reengineering to revolutionize the way that companies did work.

In a 1993 article in *Fortune*, Tom Stewart acknowledged the popularity of business process reengineering and referred to reengineering as a fad. He quoted an executive, "If you want to get something funded around here—anything even a new chair for your office—call it reengineering on your request for expenditure." Stewart also stated, that whereas many had tried, few had realized the business process reengineering's promised dramatic improvements; he noted that 50% to 70% of business process reengineering efforts failed to achieve their goals.

In contrast, in his book, Davenport highlighted a number of successful reengineering initiatives. For example, Seimens Rolm reported that because of business process reengineering its order fulfillment processes, its order-to-installation-completion time improved by 60% and its field inventory was reduced by 69%; Cigna Reinsurance reduced operating costs by 40%; and CIGNA reported savings of more than $100 million.

Today, as 21st-century managers look in their rearview mirrors, many pundits will argue that we lost the business process reengineering revolution. Whether one agrees with the pundits or not, most would agree that Michael Hammer, James Champy, Thomas Davenport, and other gurus who espoused the possibilities of business process reengineering charted a course for a new way of thinking about business. The business process reengineering revolution helped managers understand how information technology, when married with organizational change, could revolutionize the way critical businesses processes were accomplished.

Importance

One of the greatest myths of business process reengineering was that it would lead to radical change quickly, or "Big Change Fast." However, implementing change in organizations is hard. As Stoddard and Jarvenpaa argued in their 1993 note, BPR's "Achilles heel" is change management. It takes time to change organization-reporting relationships and culture, to retrain employees, and to develop and implement new IT systems—hence, the longer the time horizon, for the radical change implementation, the better.

When describing the reengineering implementation challenges in their 1995 Harvard Business School note, Stoddard and Jarvenpaa stressed that management must assess the organization and determine the appropriate path for reengineering implementation. Business process reengineering has long been associated with the revolutionary change approach that may result in downsizing, cost cutting, and other abrupt changes that cause significant stress for organizational members. The advantage of the revolutionary approach is that change happens quickly. The disadvantage is that the path may unduly increase project risk. The evolutionary path that seeks the involvement and buy-in of organization members moves at a pace comfortable for employees and is a kinder and gentler approach that promotes change from within the organization. With an evolutionary path, the pace and nature of change is adapted to be comfortable for the current personnel of the organization.

Managers who are leading business process reengineering initiatives must select an implementation approach and implementation tactics that will allow them to realize the intended changes. According to Stoddard and Jarvenpaa, most good managers loathe the revolutionary path for implementation because that approach challenges all that we know about managing and motivating people. "The revolutionary path excludes most of the current organizational expertise, promotes secrecy, supremacy of those selected to create the future vision, unyielding milestones and a simultaneous change of work roles, organization structure and technology" (p. 2). Whereas an evolutionary change approach is deemed to be better for the organization, the major disadvantage of the evolutionary approach is that it takes a long time to accomplish the vision, which must be kept alive and refreshed as market conditions change.

In conclusion, radical process redesign is at the heart of business process reengineering. Managers initiating a business process reengineering initiative must adopt a process view of the business, understand the conditions that enable or inhibit radical process redesign, and select the appropriate change tactics to enable the implementation of the radically redesigned process.

Donna Stoddard

See also Continuous and Routinized Change; *Kaizen* and Continuous Improvement; Strategies for Change; Total Quality Management

Further Readings

Davenport, T. (1993). *Process innovation.* Boston, MA: Harvard Business School Press.

Davenport, T. (1995). Business process reengineering: Its past, present, and possible future (Background note 196–082). Boston, MA: Harvard Business School.

Hammer, M. (1990, *July-August,*). Reengineering work: Don't automate, obliterate. *Harvard Business Review,* 104–112.

Hammer, M., & Champy, J. (1993). *Reengineering the corporation.* New York, NY: Harper Business.

Stewart, T. A. (1993, August 23). Reengineering: The hot new managing tool. *Fortune Magazine,* 41–48.

Stoddard, D., & Jarvenpaa, S. (1993). Business process reengineering: IT-enabled radical change (Background note No. 193–151). Boston, MA: Harvard Business School.

Stoddard, D., & Jarvenpaa, S. (1995). Reengineering *design* is radical: Reengineering *change* is not! (Background note # 196–037). Boston, MA: Harvard Business School.

BVSR Theory of Human Creativity

BVSR theory maintains that creativity depends on the two-step process of *blind variation and selective retention.* If valid, then management theories concerned with invention and innovation must directly incorporate BVSR into their concepts and arguments. In this entry, the original form of the theory is first described, and then subsequent developments in the theory are briefly discussed.

Fundamentals

In 1960, Donald T. Campbell proposed his theory that creativity depended on the two-step process of blind variation and selective retention, or BVSR. Significantly, he believed that BVSR applied to all creative thought as well as to "other knowledge processes," including scientific discovery. Campbell's theoretical presentation was neither highly formal nor intimately based on empirical research,

but rather, he mainly documented the operation of BVSR by extensive quotations from past thinkers, such as the philosophers Alexander Bain and Paul Souriau, the physicist Ernst Mach, and the mathematician Henri Poincaré. Despite the fact that BVSR is often identified as "Darwinian," Campbell did not predicate the theory on any analogy with Darwin's theory of biological evolution. Campbell did not elaborate much on BVSR in his subsequent publications, except to subsume it under a much more extensive evolutionary epistemology. Nevertheless, some researchers took BVSR as the basis for their own theoretical and empirical work. In their hands, BVSR has acquired some claim to providing the most comprehensive and precise theory of human creativity. The comprehensiveness is most apparent in BVSR's capacity to integrate a diversity of phenomena, including the personality traits and developmental experiences of individual creators as well as the organizational and sociocultural contexts in which those individuals create. BVSR's precision is especially conspicuous in combinatorial models of the creative process that have generated predictions that have been subjected to empirical tests.

According to Campbell, creativity begins with the generation of "thought trials," which are then either rejected or selected and retained. Because the ideational variants are not generated with foreknowledge of the outcome, he deemed them blind, albeit sometimes in later writings he would use alternative designations, such as unjustified. The important point is that creators or discoverers often cannot know in advance whether an idea will work until they first generate and test the idea. On the contrary, if the individual can confidently predict whether the idea will be selected or rejected prior to testing, then the idea should signify nothing truly new. Instead, it would most likely represent routine, reproductive, or algorithmic thinking. Campbell then made some effort to describe some of the factors that might enhance BVSR's effectiveness. For example, he pointed out the advantages of what now would be termed multicultural experiences. Persons exposed to two or more cultures would be more likely to transcend cultural constraints on thinking.

Later research has provided both empirical and theoretical support for the BVSR theory. On the empirical side, studies have shown that individual creators possess characteristics that would make them more capable of "thinking outside the box" imposed by expertise, such as the ability or willingness to engage in defocused attention. Likewise, highly creative problem-solving groups tend to consist of members who are unusually heterogeneous with respect to gender, ethnicity, age, and training. This diversity of perspectives increases the odds that the group will avoid imposing unnecessary constraints on the search for the optimal solution. On the theoretical side, BVSR theory has been expanded to encompass a wide range of creative processes and procedures, even including algorithmic methods and combinatorial models. An important aspect of this theoretical expansion has been recent work refining the definition of what constitutes a blind variation, a key term that Campbell had only loosely defined.

The BVSR theory of creativity stimulated considerable controversy over the first 50 years of its existence. The most common criticisms are that (a) it is based on an unjustified analogy with Darwin's theory of evolution by natural selection, (b) it presumes that the creative process is completely random, (c) it denies the important role that domain-specific expertise plays in the creative process, and (d) it minimizes the place of personal volition in creativity. BVSR advocates argue that all four criticisms represent misunderstandings of what the theory actually claims regarding the creative process. BVSR creativity can entail systematic rather than blind methods, take advantage of acquired expertise, and engage conspicuous goal-oriented behavior. With respect to the first criticism, a preliminary version of the theory was actually published in 1855, 4 years prior to the publication of Darwin's theory.

Although BVSR is claimed to provide the best basis for a comprehensive and precise theory of creativity, it remains to be seen whether it will do so. The jury is also still out about the role of BVSR in groups and organizations. For instance, although brainstorming can be seen as involving BVSR at the group level, the efficacy of brainstorming is itself debatable. In addition, it is still unclear exactly how to create an organizational climate that encourages BVSR in the most cost-effective manner.

Dean Keith Simonton

See also Architectural Innovation; Brainstorming; Componential Theory of Creativity; Dual-Core Model of Organizational Innovation; Innovation Diffusion; Innovation Speed; Investment Theory of Creativity; Open Innovation; Patterns of Innovation; Profiting From Innovation; Stages of Innovation

Further Readings

Aldrich, H. E., & Kenworthy, A. L. (1999). The accidental entrepreneur: Campbellian antinomies and organizational foundings. In J. A. Baum & B. McKelvey (Eds.), *Variations in organizational science: In honor of Donald T. Campbell* (pp. 19–33). Thousand Oaks, CA: Sage.

Campbell, D. T. (1960). Blind variation and selective retention in creative thought as in other knowledge processes. *Psychological Review, 67,* 380–400.

Cziko, G. A. (1998). From blind to creative: In defense of Donald Campbell's selectionist theory of human creativity. *Journal of Creative Behavior, 32,* 192–208.

Kantorovich, A. (1993). *Scientific discovery: Logic and tinkering.* Albany: State University of New York Press.

Martindale, C. (2009). Evolutionary models of innovation and creativity. In T. Rickards, M. Runco, & S. Moger (Eds.), *Routledge companion to creativity* (pp. 109–118). London, England: Taylor & Francis.

Nickles, T. (2003). Evolutionary models of innovation and the Meno problem. In L. V. Shavinina (Ed.), *The international handbook on innovation* (pp. 54–78). New York, NY: Elsevier Science.

Schaller, M., Norenzayan, A., Heine, S. J., Yamagishi, T., & Kameda, T. (Eds.). (2010). *Evolution, culture, and the human mind.* New York, NY: Psychology Press.

Simonton, D. K. (2010). Creativity as blind-variation and selective-retention: Constrained combinatorial models of exceptional creativity. *Physics of Life Reviews, 7,* 156–179.

Simonton, D. K. (2011). Creativity and discovery as blind variation: Campbell's (1960) BVSR model after the half-century mark. *Review of General Psychology, 15,* 158–174.

Staw, B. M. (1990). An evolutionary approach to creativity and innovations. In M. A. West & J. L. Farr (Eds.), *Innovation and creativity at work: Psychological and organizational strategies* (pp. 287–308). New York, NY: Wiley.

C

CAREER STAGES AND ANCHORS

Careers are a central construct in the management field, as they reside at the crossroads of individual and organization, of psychology and strategy. In the mid-1950s, at a time when career development theory was dominated by differential psychology and trait-and-factor theory, two important advances were made that would fundamentally change the face of career theory. Career stage theories started to emerge (most notably, Donald Super's career development theory, which laid the foundations for his life-span, life-space theory later on), as well as theories that went beyond career counseling's traditional focus on person-job fit to look at what people actually want from their careers (most notably, Edgar Schein's career anchors theory). Up to that point, the careers literature had been concerned mostly with the prediction of occupational choice and success based on ability and interest tests. Vocational counseling was portrayed as a rather static process that matched people to the "right" occupation. Taken together, career stage and career anchors theories contributed to the understanding of careers by introducing a focus on the dynamics underlying the formation of people's vocational self-concept over time. What follows in the entry is first a bit more background on career stage and career anchors theories and highlighting of central concepts and assumptions in both theories. Then, a discussion shows how the concepts have impacted career research and practice over the years. At the end of this entry are listed some recommendations for further reading.

Fundamentals

Career Stages

Although Super acknowledged the merits of trait-and-factor theory and the matching model to vocational guidance, he felt that they were too static to capture the complex dynamics of adult career development over time. In view of that, he developed a theory of career that conceptualized career development as a lifelong process, rather than a once-in-a-lifetime decision. He identified five consecutive developmental stages, each characterized by its own career concerns:

1. *Growth (age 4 to 13)*. In the growth stage, a child develops his or her capacities, attitudes, and interests. As the child grows older, he or she is confronted with the following career development tasks: becoming concerned about the future, increasing personal control over one's own life, convincing oneself to achieve in school and at work, and acquiring competent work habits and attitudes.

2. *Exploration (age 14 to 24)*. The exploration stage demarcates the transition into young adulthood, in which self-reflection and pursuing (higher) education are central features. Crystallization, specification, and implementation of career preferences are developmental tasks that are typically tackled at this point.

3. *Establishment (age 24 to 44)*. In the establishment stage, the young adult enters his

or her first job and slowly but surely establishes his or her place in the world of work. Career development tasks in this stage involve stabilizing or securing a place in an organization, consolidating one's position, and advancing up the career ladder.

4. *Maintenance (age 45 to 65)*. The maintenance stage is characterized by the aging worker's tendency to hold on to his or her current position, while simultaneously updating work-related skills so as to stay abreast of developments in the field. Career development tasks include holding on to what has been achieved, updating competencies, and finding innovative ways of performing one's job.

5. *Disengagement (over 65)*. Around the age of 65, the disengagement stage sets in. In this stage, most people make active plans to retire. A first developmental task they go through is deceleration (in terms of workload and career centrality in life), followed by retirement planning, and, finally, retirement living.

Traditional linear career stage models, such as the above, make sense mostly within traditional career contexts, such as large bureaucratic organizations. Although many organizations worldwide are abandoning this type of structure—combined with the fact that an increasing number of individuals are enacting their careers across organizational boundaries—this type of stage theory has continued to dominate the literature on careers. Nonetheless, a few recent developments have taken changes in the career environment into account more explicitly. Tim Hall and Philip Mirvis's model of contemporary career development, for instance, centers around ministages of 2 or 3 years containing exploration, trial, mastery, and exit attitudes and behaviors, which individuals "recycle" through across functional, organizational, and other boundaries. Lisa Mainiero and Sherry Sullivan, from their side, developed a "kaleidoscope" model of career development, in which they talk about facets of career that are continually adjusted to best match a person's life situation at any given time, independently of definitions of career success dictated by society.

Career Anchors

Schein's career anchors theory supplements Super's career development theory in the sense that it focuses on the dynamics of people's *internal* career throughout their adult lives. Schein defined career anchors as patterns of self-perceived competence, motivators, and values that guide and constrain career choice:

1. *Autonomy/independence*. Flexibility in terms of when and how to work is seen as of central importance. Organizational rules and restrictions are perceived as bothersome, to the extent that promotion opportunities might be turned down so as to preserve total independence.

2. *Security/stability*. Employment and financial security are main concerns. The focus is less on job content and reaching a high position. Achieving some sort of job tenure is the ultimate goal; compliance is an often-used strategy to achieve it.

3. *Technical/functional competence*. The highest value is placed on the opportunity to apply one's skills and develop them to an ever-higher level. A sense of identity is derived from one's expertise, and being challenged in that area leads to profound satisfaction. Managing others is not seen as inherently interesting, unless it involves project management in the area of expertise.

4. *General managerial competence*. Opportunities to climb the ladder to a position of power are sought after. There is a strong desire to be held accountable for organizational outcomes, and generalist jobs are preferred.

5. *Entrepreneurial creativity*. An important goal is to found one's own company or enterprise while taking risks and overcoming challenges and obstacles. Demonstrating one's abilities (e.g., through financial success) and being recognized for what one has achieved single-handedly are critical motivators.

6. *Sense of service/dedication to a cause*. Important values center around doing work that makes the world a better place (e.g., solving environmental problems, helping people in need, curing

disease). Job offers that do not fulfill these types of values are usually rejected.

7. *Pure challenge.* Solving seemingly impossible problems, succeeding over opponents, and beating the odds are important drivers. Novelty, variety, and difficulty (be it in the field of technology, strategy, or people management) are ends in itself; work situations that lack these features are perceived as mind-numbing.

8. *Lifestyle.* Achieving balance between work and personal life is a principal objective. Integration between personal needs, family needs, and career requirements is aspired to. The main determinant of identity is the person's life as a whole, rather than his or her career. Career opportunities (e.g., international assignments) are gladly declined in exchange for more work-life balance.

Schein was adamant about two points. First, that every person, in essence, has only one career anchor—which lies at the heart of all career decisions the individual will make throughout his or her adult life. Second, that career anchors are shaped by early career experiences and that therefore people who have not had much work experience (i.e., young graduates) do not (yet) have a career anchor. Schein argued that a career anchor is formed when a person's self-image prior to entering the job market (i.e., in the growth stage) is confronted with real-life working experiences (i.e., in the exploration stage), causing crystallization of the vocational self-concept. Once formed, however (i.e., from the establishment stage onward) Schein believed that a person's career anchor would remain stable throughout the further course of his or her life, save in cases where a person's self-image is altered radically by the encounter of unexpected life events or career traumas.

Importance

Research

Both career stages and career anchors theories have been the subject of dozens of empirical studies across the globe. Although, generally speaking, their main assumptions have held over the years, some gaps remain. As for career stage theory, the idea of recycling through career stages, however interesting, has rarely been the object of empirical research. In addition, most studies that have aimed to test the assumptions of Super's career development theory have relied mostly on chronological age and organization, career, or position tenure as indicators of career stage, which goes directly against the idea of career stages being characterized by the level of exploration, establishment, maintenance, and disengagement concerns. Combined with the observation that nearly all career stage studies have been cross-sectional, one might conclude that this this type of approach is measuring types rather than stages. Although recoding continuous data about career concerns into stages may be useful in a counseling setting where an individual's scores are explored in-depth and synergistically, in a research context, this approach is likely to result in oversimplification and loss of data richness. Following Super's notion of minicycles and Hall and Mirvis's idea of overlapping career learning cycles, it may make more sense to study respondents' career concerns using continuous and non-disjoint data formats, while controlling for age and tenure indicators. Career anchors theory was practically unchallenged for 25 years when Daniel Feldman and Mark Bolino published their critique in 1996. Criticism of the career anchors concept has been concerned mostly with its factor structure, as well as with the assumptions of each person having one key career anchor, and its stability over time. Most empirical studies testing the alternative assumptions suggested by Feldman and Bolino, however, have found that Schein's factor structure, although not always optimal, remains the best fit. Evidence was found for some individuals having multiple career anchors. As for the assumption of stability over time, there is a significant need and opportunity for further research adopting longitudinal designs.

Practice

Although the career stage and anchors literatures have primarily spelled out implications for individuals—focusing on individual-level outcomes, such as effective career decision making, career satisfaction, and self-esteem—without a doubt, their impact on management practice has been pervasive. The career anchors literature has taught managers around the world that people with different career anchors desire different kinds of work settings, are motivated by different kinds of incentives and rewards, and are vulnerable to different kinds of career mismanagement. In doing so, it has directly contributed to the rise of realistic job previews (RJP) as a contemporary selection paradigm replacing methods that were focused mainly on "seducing" employees to accept job offers. In the later part of his career, Schein commercialized his knowledge about career anchors in a number of best-selling tools and inventories. The career stage literature, and especially the contributions made by Super, has drastically changed the paradigms used in career counseling practice. Rather than seeing career choice as a one-off decision, it is now perceived as an ongoing journey of exploration and self-construction. Newer career development theories, such as those devised by Hall and Mirvis, and by Mainiero and Sullivan, encourage putting less pressure on early career individuals to make permanent career decisions and avoid early career mistakes at all costs, thus, reducing stress and encouraging lifelong learning and experimentation.

Nicky Dries

See also Individual Values; Protean and Boundaryless Careers; Self-Concept and the Theory of Self; Social Identity Theory

Further Readings

Feldman, D. C., & Bolino, M. C. (1996). Careers within careers: Reconceptualizing the nature of career anchors and their consequences. *Human Resource Management Review, 6*(2), 89–112.

Hall, D. T., & Mirvis, P. H. (1996). The new protean career: Psychological success and the path with a heart. In D. T. Hall (Ed.), *The career is dead—Long live the career* (pp. 15–45). San Francisco, CA: Jossey-Bass.

Mainiero, L. A., & Sullivan, S. E. (2005). Kaleidoscope careers: An alternative explanation for the opt-out revolution. *Academy of Management Executive, 19*(1), 106–123.

Schein, E. H. (1996). Career anchors revisited: Implications for career development in the 21st century. *Academy Of Management Executive, 10*(4), 80–88.

Super, D. E. (1951). Vocational adjustment: Implementing a self-concept. *Occupations, 30,* 88–92.

CAUSAL ATTRIBUTION THEORY

Attributions are causal explanations. Examples of causal explanations include effort, ability, the situation, and luck. The fundamental premise of attribution theory is that people's beliefs (i.e., attributions) about the causes of significant outcomes (e.g., successes and failures) affect their expectations for success, their emotions, and their behaviors. Thus, a student who believes she failed a test because of a lack of ability is likely to expect to fail in the future, feel bad about her performance, and is less likely to study in the future. Attributions are fundamental cognitive processes that affect a wide range of organizational behaviors. Almost all organizational researchers would agree that the reward structures of organizations are critical to the successes and failures of individuals as well as to the success of organizations as a whole. Therefore, attributions about the causes of individual as well as organizational success and failure are critical because they affect the expectations, emotions, and behaviors of organizational members. As will be discussed below, attribution processes are integral to understanding a wide range of organizational phenomena such as leader–member relations, entitlement perceptions, perceptions of abusive supervision, and counterproductive behaviors. The following sections of this entry contain discussions on the theoretical development of attribution theory, basic concepts, research findings, criticisms, and the future of attribution theory in the organizational sciences.

Fundamentals

The origins of attribution theory can be traced back to the work of Fritz Heider, who likened people to naive psychologists, trying to figure out the causes of their outcomes (e.g., successes and failures) as well as the causes of other people's outcomes (social attributions). According to Heider, understanding the dynamics of causation enables individuals to be efficacious in their interactions with other people and the environment. When individuals understand why they are successful, they know what to expect and how to repeat their successes. On the other hand, understanding the causes of failure enables individuals to avoid future failures.

Following the work of Heider, the two most noted contributors to attribution theory are Harold Kelley and Bernard Weiner. Kelley worked on the front end of the attribution process and described how individuals combine different types of information (consensus, consistency, and distinctiveness) to make social attributions about the causes of people's behaviors. *Consensus* information is the result of comparing a person's performance with the performances of others. *Consistency* information is within-person information and is concerned with the stability of the performance. *Distinctiveness* is concerned with the interaction between the person's performance and the situation. Kelley described how the combination of these three sources of information allows observers to attribute a behavior to the person, the situation, or the entity (i.e., the interaction between the person and the situation). Thus, for example, the cause is attributed to the person when consensus is low, consistency is high, and distinctiveness is low.

Weiner focused on describing, explaining, and validating how attributional explanations (e.g., ability and luck) and their dimensions (e.g., internal and unstable) affect the expectancies, emotions, and behaviors of individuals. This early theoretical work as well as the empirical work was grounded in the field of social psychology.

While a few articles addressed attributional processes in the organizational behavior literature in the 1970s, major attention in the organizational behavior literature was not focused on attribution theory until the 1979 publication of an article by Steven Green and Terry Mitchell which explained how attribution processes affected leader–member interactions. Since then, numerous studies have explored the application of attributional processes in organizational contexts. Extensive reviews of this literature have been published by Mark Martinko and his colleagues.

The Basics: Causal Explanations and Dimensions

Typical causal explanations for outcomes such as success and failure include ability, effort, task difficulty, and chance. Underlying causal explanations are the causal dimensions of the explanations. Although numerous causal dimensions have been suggested (e.g., intentionality, controllability, and specificity), the two most common are *locus of causality* and *stability*. An internal locus of causality locates the cause within the individual, while an external locus of causality indicates that the cause is in the environment, outside of the individual. Ability and effort are generally considered to have an internal locus of causality, while task difficulty and luck are considered to have external loci of causality. According to attribution theory, the locus of causality dimension activates emotions. Thus, people generally feel good when they make internal attributions for success and bad when they make internal attributions for failure.

Stability affects expectations. When causes are believed to be stable (e.g., nature of the task and ability), individuals expect the same outcomes in the future. When causes are unstable, different outcomes are possible in the future. Thus, students who believe they failed tests because of deficient ability, which is generally considered to be an internal and stable attribution, are likely to feel bad (internal locus), expect to fail again in the future because the cause is stable, and fail to study (i.e., behave) because of their expectations and feelings. On the other hand, when failure is attributed to effort, which is generally considered to be internal and unstable, students may still feel bad but may be motivated to do better in the future because the cause (lack of effort) is unstable and can be remedied.

Attribution Biases and Styles

The notion of biases and styles is that individuals have innate tendencies and encounter situations that lead to certain types of attributions. Research demonstrates that most individuals display a self-serving bias, which is the tendency to make internal attributions for success and external attributions for failure. This bias is prevalent across most individuals and most cultures.

Another important bias is the actor-observer bias, which is the tendency for actors (people behaving and performing) to make external attributions for their performances, while observers tend to attribute actors' successes and failures to the internal characteristics of the actor. Thus, baseball players tend to attribute their batting performances to the opportunities the pitcher provides (external attributions), while the fans attribute the batter's performances to the characteristics of the batter (e.g., reaction time and strength).

Individuals also display attribution styles, which are tendencies to make the same types of attributions across a variety of situations. Thus, some individuals can be characterized as optimistic, tending to attribute successes to their internal and stable characteristics, such as ability, and their failures to external and unstable causes, such as chance and luck. These types of individuals are generally more resilient in the face of failure. Pessimistic attributions styles are characterized by internal and stable attributions for failure and external and unstable attributions for success. Persistent patterns of pessimistic attributions lead to learned helplessness wherein individuals stop trying even though success may be possible. Alcoholism and drug addiction are often associated with pessimistic attributions styles and learned helplessness. Individuals demonstrate hostile attribution styles when they make external and stable attributions, blaming other people for failures. Research demonstrates that individuals characterized by hostile attribution styles are more likely to report and engage in acts of organizational aggression.

In addition to the styles described above, an almost limitless number of styles can be described by combining attributional dimensions under the condition of success and of failure. Thus, by combining the locus of causality and stability dimensions for success and failure outcomes, 16 different attribution styles for intrapersonal attributions and 16 more styles for interpersonal (social) attributions are possible.

Importance

Attribution Research in Organizations

Since the introduction of attributional perspectives to the field of organizational behavior in the late 1970s and early 1980s, attribution research in organizational settings has proliferated and addressed a wide variety of topics. While a comprehensive review of this research is not possible within space constraints, highlights of some of the findings are provided here to demonstrate the role and importance of attributional processes in organizational behavior.

A substantial body of research has been directed toward confirming the Green and Mitchell model. Numerous studies confirm that Kelley's dimensions of information are related to supervisors' attributions and that, in turn, supervisor attributions are related to disciplinary behavior. Although other situational cues, such as subordinate performance and supervisor-subordinate interdependence, affect disciplinary actions, attributions account for a significant proportion of the variance in supervisors' disciplinary actions.

Considerable research has been done on the self-serving bias. Meta-analyses reveal that the self-serving bias is prevalent in almost all cultures. A series of studies clearly demonstrates that corporate leaders are biased toward taking credit for organizational successes in their annual reports and blaming failures on their environments (e.g., the economy and suppliers). On a more micro level, research demonstrates that both leaders and subordinates demonstrate the self-serving bias in their interactions and that these biases lead to differing perceptions of the quality of their leader–member relations.

There is also support for the actor-observer bias. Multiple studies demonstrate that this bias is prevalent in almost all cultures. The effects of this bias are attenuated when leaders have experience doing the tasks of their subordinates. However, it appears that these biases become more manifest with age. This bias is considered particularly problematic and has been viewed as the cause of inappropriate discipline and training for employees when poor performance is blamed on employee dispositions rather than the actual cause of the poor performance.

Research has also focused on attribution styles. Attributional explanations and attribution styles have been linked to supervisory-subordinate conflict, whistle-blowing tendencies, authentic leadership, entitlement perceptions, abusive supervision, empowerment, learned helplessness, leader–member relations, conflict, bullying, emotions, organizational aggression, victimization by coworkers, alcoholism, drug abuse, depression, emotional intelligence, self-efficacy, self-esteem, negative affectivity, trait anger, impulsivity, impression management, culture, gender, age, feedback, Meyers-Briggs personality types, selection decisions, the employment interview process, the performance appraisal process, ethical judgments, judgments of responsibility, justice perceptions, self- and other-directed counterproductive behaviors, conflict resolution, and a variety of performance related outcomes (e.g., grades, production, and customer relations).

Criticisms

Criticisms of attribution theory have primarily been concerned with the depictions of humans as rational information processers. In particular, critics have asserted that the cognitive effort required to make attributions is too laborious and time consuming to be efficient in everyday routine situations. In response to these criticisms, it is argued that attribution theory is being criticized for claims which it has never made. More specifically, Weiner never stated that people engage in attributions during routine situations. He contended that attributions occur as a reaction to outcomes that are particularly surprising, important, or negative. Thus, many of the criticisms appear to have been generalized to situations that are beyond the scope and applicability of attribution theory.

Applications of Attribution Theory

The potential applications for attribution theory in the organizational sciences have not yet been fully realized. Attributions (i.e., beliefs) about significant outcomes for both organizations and their members are fundamental cognitive processes that affect employee motivation and emotions. Knowledge of employees' attributional processes can help managers correct faulty attributions, leading to optimistic expectancies and positive emotions. In particular, knowledge of attributional processes can be helpful to managers in recognizing, managing, and counseling potentially aggressive employees, entitled employees, and those employees likely to engage in counterproductive organizational behaviors. Knowledge of attributions and attribution styles and feedback can also aid in the selection, training, coaching, and development of productive employees. Because understanding these processes is a critical element for both organizational and individual success, the future for attribution theory is bright.

Mark J. Martinko

See also Achievement Motivation Theory; Affect Theory; Attribution Model of Leadership; Expectancy Theory; Leader–Member Exchange Theory; Social Cognitive Theory

Further Readings

Green, S. G., & Mitchell, T. R. (1979). Attributional processes of leaders in leader-member interactions. *Organizational Behavior and Human Performance, 23,* 429–458.

Heider, F. (1958). *The psychology of interpersonal relations.* New York, NY: Wiley.

Kelley, H. H. (1971). *Attributions in social interaction.* New York, NY: General Learning Press.

Martinko, M. J. (2002). *Thinking like a winner: A guide to high performance leadership.* Tallahassee, FL: Gulf Coast.

Martinko, M. J., Douglas, S. C., & Harvey, P. (2006). Attribution theory in industrial and organizational psychology: A review. In G. P. Hodgkinson & J. K. Ford (Eds.), *International Review of Industrial and Organizational Psychology* (Vol. 21, pp. 127–187). Chichester, England: Wiley.

Martinko, M. J., Harvey, P., & Dasborough, M. (2011). Attribution theory in the organizational sciences: A case of unrealized potential. *Journal of Organizational Behavior, 31,* 1–6.

Martinko, M. J., Harvey, P., & Douglas, S. C. (2007). The role, function, and contributions of attribution theory to leadership: A review. *Leadership Quarterly, 18,* 561–585.

Weiner, B. (1985). An attributional theory of achievement motivation and emotion. *Psychological Review, 92,* 548–573.

CHARISMATIC THEORY OF LEADERSHIP

Some of the most exemplary and influential leaders throughout history have been described as charismatic leaders. In the world of management, renowned entrepreneurs and corporate change agents are often described as charismatic leaders. While popular accounts often ascribe a mythical quality to their charisma, research has shed significant light on the attributes that lead to the perceptions of a leader as charismatic. This entry explores the dimensions that lead to perceptions of charismatic leadership in the eyes of followers. Drawing upon sociologist Max Weber's definition, charisma is "a certain quality of an individual personality, by virtue of which he is set apart from ordinary men and treated as endowed with supernatural, superhuman, or at least specifically exceptional powers or qualities. These are not accessible to the ordinary person, but are regarded as exemplary, and on the basis of them the individual concerned is treated as a leader."

To begin to understand charismatic leadership, it is important to realize that it is an *attribution* based on followers' perceptions and interpretations of their leader's behavior. Because it is an attribution, one follower's charismatic leader may not be another's. In addition, the behaviors associated with charismatic leadership are a constellation. The expression or presence of a single behavior associated with charismatic leadership is rarely sufficient in itself to engender the attribution of charisma. Instead, a critical mass of behaviors must be present. The presence and intensity of individual behaviors, however, are expressed in varying degrees among different charismatic leaders. Certain behavioral components are more critical and effective sources of charisma in some organizational or cultural contexts, but not in others. For example, in some contexts, unconventionality may be less valued as an attribute of charisma than articulation skills, and in other contexts, it may be more valued. Thus, in order to develop a charismatic influence, a leader must have an understanding of the appropriateness or importance of the various behavioral components for a given context. This entry is a description of the attributes by which charismatic leaders are differentiated from noncharismatic leaders. Specifically, these attributes are examined using a three-stage model of leadership and follower influence.

Fundamentals

To understand why certain behaviors are attributed to charismatic leadership, it is useful to think of leadership from a *process* standpoint. Specifically, the process involves moving organizational or societal members from an existing present state toward some future state. This could also be described as a movement away from the status quo toward the achievement of desired longer term goals. To frame and distinguish charismatic leadership, let us consider three stages of this process. In the initial stage, the leader critically evaluates the existing situation searching for deficiencies or poorly exploited

opportunities in the larger environment from which to formulate future goals. In parallel, the leader must assess what resources are available and what constraints stand in the way of realizing these goals. The leader must also determine the inclinations, abilities, needs, and level of satisfaction experienced by followers since they are pivotal to the mission's accomplishment. Following this evaluation comes the second stage: the actual formulation and conveyance of goals or objectives by the leader. Attractive goals must be devised, and they must be articulated in a persuasive manner. Finally, in stage three, the leader demonstrates how these goals can be achieved by the organization or the society. This is accomplished through the leader's and followers' actions and tactics and through expressions of confidence in the followers' capabilities.

It is important to note, however, that the stages just described rarely follow such a simple linear flow. Most organizations and societies face ever-changing environments, and their leadership must constantly be about revising existing goals and tactics in response to environmental changes. This model, however, nicely simplifies a great deal of complexity and allows us to more effectively contrast the differences between charismatic and noncharismatic leadership. The reader should simply keep in mind that a leader is constantly moving back and forth between the stages. We will use these three stages as our framework for distinguishing charismatic leadership from other types.

Stage One: The Charismatic Leader's Sensitivity to the Environmental Context

In the assessment stage, what distinguishes charismatic from noncharismatic leaders is the formers' ability to recognize deficiencies and opportunities in the present context. These leaders actively search out existing or potential shortcomings in the status quo. For example, the failure of firms to exploit new technologies or new markets might be highlighted as a strategic or tactical opportunity. Likewise, a charismatic entrepreneur, such as Steven Jobs of Apple, might more readily perceive certain marketplace needs and address them with new products or services. A charismatic political leader, such as Gandhi, might advocate radical reforms to the existing political system. In addition, the charismatic leader will often perceive organizational deficiencies as platforms for advocating radical change. In contexts of relative tranquility, charismatic leaders play a major role in fostering the need for change by creating deficiencies or finding unexploited important opportunities. In summary, any context that triggers a need for a major change or presents unexploited market opportunities is therefore relevant for the *emergence* of charismatic leadership.

Because of their emphasis on deficiencies or poorly exploited opportunities in markets, organizations and societies, charismatic leaders are always seen as organizational reformers or entrepreneurs. In other words, they act as agents of innovative and radical change. However, the attribution of charisma is dependent not on the outcome of change but simply on the actions taken to bring about change or reform.

In contrast to charismatic leaders, managers often act as administrators who are responsible for the maintenance of the status quo. They influence others through the power of their positions as sanctioned by the organization. While they may advocate change, it is usually incremental and within the bounds of the status quo. Charismatic leaders, however, seek radical reforms for the achievement of their idealized goals and transform their followers (instead of directing or nudging them).

Charismatic leaders are highly sensitive to the constraints in their environments and the availability of resources. They are also sensitive to both the abilities and the emotional needs of followers since these are the most important resources for attaining organizational goals. Such assessments, while not a distinguishing feature of charismatic leaders, are nonetheless particularly important for charismatic leaders because they often assume high risks by advocating radical change. Thus, instead of launching a course of action as soon as a vision is formulated, a leader's environmental assessment may dictate that he or she prepare the ground and wait for an appropriate time and place, and/or for the availability of resources. It is presumed that many a time charisma has faded due to a lack of sensitivity for the environment.

Stage Two: The Charismatic Leader and Visionary Goals

After assessing the environment, a leader will typically formulate goals for achieving his or her mission's objectives. Charismatic leadership can be distinguished from other forms of leadership by the nature of these objectives and by the manner in which the leader articulates them.

First and foremost, the goals of charismatic leaders are characterized by a sense of strategic vision. Here, the word *vision* refers to some idealized goal that the leader wants the organization or society to achieve in the future. The greater the discrepancy of the goal from the status quo, the more likely is the attribution that the leader has extraordinary vision, not just an ordinary goal, and is a charismatic leader. Moreover, by presenting a very discrepant and idealized goal to followers, the charismatic leader provides a sense of challenge and a motivating force for change. Since the idealized goal represents a perspective shared by the followers and promises to meet their aspirations, it is highly attractive to followers despite the challenges it may pose.

A vision and plans for achieving it are, however, not enough. Charismatic leaders must also be able to articulate their vision and tactics in effective ways so as to influence their followers. This involves two separate processes: articulation of the vision within the larger context and articulation of the leader's own motivation to lead. First, charismatic leaders must effectively articulate for followers the following scenarios representing the larger context: (a) the nature of the status quo and its shortcomings or poorly exploited opportunities; (b) the future vision itself; (c) how the future vision, when realized, will remove existing deficiencies, exploit opportunities, and fulfill the hopes of followers; and (d) the leaders' plans of action for realizing the vision. In his or her scenarios, the charismatic leader attempts to create among followers a discontentment with the status quo, a strong identification with future goals, and a compelling desire to be led in the direction of the goal in spite of hurdles.

Besides verbally describing the status quo, future goals, and the means to achieve them, charismatic leaders are also articulating their own motivation to lead. Using expressive modes of action, both verbal and nonverbal, they manifest their convictions, self-confidence, and dedication to materialize what they advocate. Charismatic leaders' use of rhetoric, high energy, persistence, unconventional and risky behavior, heroic deeds, and personal sacrifices all serve to articulate their high motivation and enthusiasm, which then become contagious among their followers.

Stage Three: Charismatic Leadership and the Achievement of the Vision

The final stage of the charismatic leadership process involves building in followers a sense of trust in the leader's abilities as well as clearly demonstrating the tactics and behaviors required to achieve the mission's goals. The charismatic leader accomplishes this by building trust through personal example, risk taking, and unconventional expertise. Generally, leaders are perceived as trustworthy when they advocate their position with thoughtful conviction and demonstrate a concern for followers' needs rather than their own self-interest. However, in order to be perceived as charismatic, leaders must make these qualities appear extraordinary. They must transform their concern for followers' needs into a total dedication and commitment to a common cause they share and express them in a disinterested and selfless manner. So charismatic leaders engage in exemplary acts of commitment that are perceived by followers as involving great personal risk, cost, and energy. The higher the manifest personal cost or sacrifice for the common goal, the greater is the perceived trustworthiness of a leader. In sum, the more leaders are able to demonstrate that they are indefatigable workers prepared to take on high personal risks or incur high personal costs in order to achieve their shared vision, the more they reflect charisma in the sense of being worthy of complete follower trust.

Finally, charismatic leaders must appear to their followers as deeply expert in the means to achieve the vision. Some degree of demonstrated expertise, such as reflected in successes in the past, may even be a necessary condition for the attribution of charisma. That said, charismatic leaders reveal their depth of expertise in large part through the use of unconventional or countercultural means to transcending the existing order. Since attributions of charisma depend on followers' perceptions of their leaders' "revolutionary" and "countercultural" qualities, these qualities also are manifested through the leader's idealized visions. But it is their unconventional, countercultural, and innovative behavior that has the greatest influence. Their uncommon behavior, when successful, evokes in their followers emotional responses of surprise and admiration. Such uncommon behavior also leads to an attribution of charisma.

Importance

What makes charismatic leadership so important a topic is the extent to which followers are mobilized to achieve extraordinary organizational outcomes. Few forms of leadership can match these leaders in motivating human performance. To understand why charismatic leaders are so influential, we turn to James Burns's idea that there are basically two influence processes available to leaders. These are (a) the transactional influence processes and (b) the transformational influence processes.

Under transactional influence, the leader ensures that the followers perform the required behaviors through the use of rewards and sanctions. The success of the transactional influence model is obviously limited to the effectiveness of the "life span" of the commodities offered in exchange. In other words, in the transactional influence mode, followers' compliance is governed by the value-in-exchange of rewards and sanctions.

On the other hand, the transformational mode of exercising influence is explicit in the charismatic leadership. In this case, the leader works to bring about a change in the followers' attitudes and values, as he or she moves the organization toward its visionary goals. This change in followers' attitudes and values is achieved through empowering techniques that increase the self-efficacy beliefs of the followers and affirm that they are capable of achieving the vision. Followers' compliance is the result of two important factors: (a) their internalization of the leader's vision and (b) an increase in their self-efficacy beliefs.

In order to understand the influence dynamics underlying charismatic leadership, we draw on sociopsychological theories of influence processes and empowerment. A leader's influence over followers can stem from different bases of power. Charismatic influence stems from the leader's personal idiosyncratic power (referent and expert powers) rather than from position power (legal, coercive, and reward powers) as determined by organizational rules and regulations. Participative leaders also may use personal power as the basis of their influence. Their personal power, however, is derived from consensus seeking. Charismatic leaders, however, are different from both consensual and directive leaders in the use of their personal power. The sources of charismatic leaders' personal power are manifest in their idealized vision, their entrepreneurial advocacy for radical changes, and their depth of knowledge and expertise. In charismatic leaders, all these personal qualities appear extraordinary to followers, and these extraordinary qualities form the basis of both their personal power and their charisma. Although the use of a personal power base (as opposed to position power base) helps in understanding the charismatics' transformational influence on followers, the leaders' empowerment strategies and the resulting empowering experience of followers are critical ingredients to the success of the transformational influence process. As well, the leaders' identification and commitment, and the exertion of effort to realize the idealized and shared vision, serve as a model to inspire the followers to undergo a self-, or inner, transformation consistent with vision.

The empowerment of followers (building follower self-efficacy and having trust in the leader) is greatly enhanced when charismatic leaders exercise the expert and referent power bases as mentioned earlier. The leader's expert power is effective in exerting transformational influence because followers perceive their leader to possess the knowledge, abilities, and expertise which followers can draw upon and which they see to be necessary for the attainment of the vision. The followers' perception that their charismatic leader possesses the needed expertise makes the leader credible and trustworthy. Similar to expert power, the leader's referent power also lies in the followers' perception of the charismatic leader's commitment to followers' welfare. They perceive the leader's efforts to be selfless and their intent to be altruistic.

Jay A. Conger

See also Attribution Model of Leadership; Influence Tactics; Leadership Practices; Trait Theory of Leadership; Transformational Theory of Leadership

Further Readings

Burns, J. M. (1978). *Leadership*. New York, NY: Harper & Row.

Conger, J. A., & Kanungo, R. N. (1998). *Charismatic leadership in organizations*. Thousand Oaks, CA: Sage.

Conger, J. A., & Kanungo, R. N. (1988). The empowerment process: Integrating theory and practice. *Academy of Management Review, 13*(3), pp. 471–482.

French, J. R. P., & Raven, B. (1959). Bases of social power. In D. Cartwright, (Ed.), *Studies in social power.* (Vol. 6, pp. 150–167). University of Michigan, Ann Arbor.

Weber, M. (1968). *Economy and society* (R. Guenter & Wittich, Eds., Vols. 1–3). New York, NY: Bedminister. (Original work published 1925)

Willner, R. A. (1985). *The spellbinders*. New Haven, CT: Yale University Press.

CIRCUITS OF POWER AND CONTROL

The theory's central management insight is that power is not a thing that people have but a social relation that is dynamic, potentially unstable, and resisted. Stewart Clegg introduced the idea of circuits of power in 1989 to represent the ways in which power may flow through different modalities. The model defines power as flowing through the social relations of daily interactions, organizational practices, and the disciplinary techniques of social structures. Specifically, power is portrayed through relations that flow through three distinct but interacting circuits: the episodic, the dispositional, and the facilitative. In this entry, the three circuits of power will be outlined and implications drawn for managers.

Fundamentals

In the past, power has been thought of structurally as a matter of different levels and types of control, most notably in Steven Lukes's 1974/2006 *Power: A Radical View.* Rather than see power as a structural phenomenon, the central insight of the circuits model is to conceptualize it in a post-structuralist mode as a series of distinctly patterned flows. The most relatively simple circuit entails flows of transitive power, where one agency seeks to get another to do what they would not otherwise do. Power in this sense usually involves fairly straightforward episodic power, oriented toward securing outcomes. The two defining elements of episodic power circuits are agencies and events of interest to these agencies. Agencies are constituted within social relations; in these social relations, they are analogous to practical experimentalists who seek to configure these relations in such a way that they present stable standing conditions for them to assert their agency in securing preferred outcomes. Hence, relations constitute agents that agents seek to configure and reconfigure; agencies seek to assert agency and do so through configuring relations in such a way that their agency can be transmitted through various generalized media of communication, in order to secure preferential outcomes. All this is quite straightforward and familiar from one-dimensional accounts of power.

Episodes are always interrelated in complex and evolving ways. No "win" or "loss" is ever complete in itself, nor is the meaning of victory or defeat definitely fixed as such at the time of its registration, recognition, or reception; such matters of judgment are always contingent on the temporalities of the here-and-now, the reconstitutions of the there-and-then, on the reflective and prospective glances of everyday life. If power relations are the stabilization of warfare in peaceful times, then any battle is only ever a part of an overall campaign. What is important from the point of view of the infinity of power episodes stretching into a future that has no limits are the feedback loops from distinct episodic outcomes and the impact that they have on overall social and system integration. The important question is whether episodic outcomes tend rather more to reproduce or to transform the existing architectonics—the architecture, geometry, and design—of power relations? How they might do so is accommodated in the model: Through the circuit of social integration, episodic outcomes serve to either more or less transform or reproduce the rules fixing extant relations of meaning and membership in organizational fields; as these are reproduced or transformed, they fix or refix those obligatory passage points—the channels, conduits, circuitry of extant power relations. In this way, dispositional matters of identity will be more or less transformed or reproduced, affecting the stability of the extant social relations that had sought to stabilize their powers in the previous episodes of power. As identities are transformed, then, so will be the social relations in which they are manifested and engaged.

System integration also needs to be considered. Changes in the rules fixing relations of meaning and membership can facilitate or restrict innovations in the techniques of disciplinary and productive power, which, in turn, will more or less

empower or disempower extant social relations that seek to stabilize the episodic field, recreating existing obligatory passage points or creating new ones, as the case might be.

Clegg's three circuits interact, are constituted by, and constitute each other, through what Clegg, following actor-network theory, labels as *obligatory passage points*. The reference to such obligatory passage points should not lead us to think that these circuits are "levels," meeting at certain points in time only: The framework is neither "dimensional" nor "structural" because the circuits are mutually implicated in each other. These passage points should rather be understood as points of transitions, in which the taken-for-granted nature of the rules and norms constituting our practices are negotiated and fixed. Clegg thus describes power not as a thing with essential qualities but rather as relations *between* people struggling for meaning. Power concerns decisions made or delayed, certainty established or marginalized, actions taken or ignored, evils tolerated or addressed, privileges bestowed or withheld, and rights claimed or violated. Clegg applies the model to matters of state formation in his 1989 work and has extended it to other substantive areas subsequently. Clegg's model has been used as a theoretical model for numerous organizational studies. Modern managers should be aware that when almost everything they do can be construed as intervening in power relations, that the interpretations that others place on their actions and interests will in all probability differ from those that the managers in question propose, that resistance to power is normal, and that just as one is seeking to configure power relations to one's desiderata so will others be with respect to one in relation to their desiderata. Finally, in any complex set of relations, it is probably foolish and idealistic to assume that these relations, interest, and interpretations can be easily aligned. Power relations are inescapable, entangling, and always capable of destabilization and change. Managers need to manage power's circuitry but should never assume that they control it.

Stewart R. Clegg

Strategic Decision Making; Strategy-as-Practice; Structuration Theory

Further Readings

Backhouse, J., Hsu, C. W., & Silva, L. (2006). Circuits of power in creating de jure standards: Shaping an international information systems security standard. *Management Information Systems Quarterly, 30,* 413–438.

Clegg, S. R. (1989). *Frameworks of power.* London, England: Sage.

Clegg, S. R., Courpasson, D., & Phillips, N. (2006). *Power and organizations.* London, England: Sage.

Davenport, S. & Leitch, S. (2005). Circuits of power in practice: Strategic ambiguity as delegation of authority. *Organization Studies, 26,* 1603–1623.

Lukes, S. (2006). *Power: A radical view.* London, England: Palgrave Macmillan. (Original work published 1974)

Smith, S. (2010). Circuits of power: A study of mandated compliance to an information systems security de jure standard in a government organization. *MIS Quarterly, 34,* 463–486.

Vaara, E., Tienari, J., Piekkari, R., & Santti, R. (2005). Language and the circuits of power in a merging multinational corporation. *Journal of Management Studies, 42,* 595–623.

van Iterson, A., & Clegg, S. R. (2008). The politics of gossip and denial in inter-organizational relations. *Human Relations, 61*(8), 1117–1137.

COGNITIVE DISSONANCE THEORY

Our lives, personally and professionally, are littered with inconsistencies. A manager could believe his employee is a hard worker but find it necessary to lay him off from the company. One could consider oneself a loyal employee but decide to interview at a competing firm. While such inconsistencies are a recurrent part of our lives and the decisions we face, we are driven to maintain consistent cognitions (knowledge) of our beliefs and behaviors. When these cognitions are inconsistent, we experience psychological discomfort known as cognitive dissonance. Situations of dissonance can cause a great deal of mental and physical stress. This experience of disequilibrium has captured the attention of scholars and managers alike for more than 50 years and has been implicated in various important organizational behavior phenomena. Provided in this entry is a brief

history of the development of cognitive dissonance theory, including the fundamentals of the construct, and a discussion of important implications for the theory in today's management practices.

Fundamentals

Leon Festinger introduced the concept of cognitive dissonance while exploring what motivates individuals to reduce inconsistencies in their lives. His formative work attempted not only to define dissonance but also to outline factors that impact the occurrence and magnitude of the experience. Broadly, he proposed that dissonance occurs when people's cognitive elements are not aligned. Cognitive elements refer to the knowledge people hold about what they do, how they feel, what they like, or what they desire. Festinger also suggested that it is rare to never experience dissonance. First, new information from our surrounding environment continually challenges our existing knowledge of what we do, feel, like, or desire. Second, the choices we make are seldom black and white, and as a result, dissonance is a reality of decision making. Although dissonance cannot always be avoided, the magnitude with which we experience dissonance does vary. Specifically, the magnitude of dissonance confronting us corresponds with the degree of discrepancy and the importance of the two competing cognitive elements. The greater the divergence and/or importance of the cognitive elements, the greater the likelihood that dissonance will be aroused. Based on this interpretation of dissonance, Festinger's central argument was that people find dissonance highly aversive and strive to reduce the associated psychological discomfort. Ultimately, as the magnitude of dissonance increases, so does the urgency to reconcile the tension.

Multiple strategies can be executed to mitigate psychological discomfort when it is aroused. One approach includes making changes to either cognitions of behavior or cognitions of attitudes when they are not aligned. Consider the example of a manager who lays off an employee whom he holds in high esteem. The manager likely faces a great deal of psychological discomfort since his cognitions of his attitude (holding the employee in high esteem) and behavior (laying off the employee) are at odds. One approach to reducing this dissonance is rehiring the employee. If he is successful in bringing the employee back to his team, the cognitions of his attitude and his behavior will be positively aligned, mitigating the experienced dissonance. Though such a behavioral change may effectively reduce dissonance, a manager might not be at liberty to rehire the employee. In this case, the manager could alter his attitude toward the employee by calling to mind negative examples of the employee's job performance (e.g., when the employee was late to work, a time when the employee made an error in a report). This change in the manager's attitude will bring greater consistency between his two cognitive elements and reduce the aroused dissonance.

Significantly altering our cognitive elements is not easy; rather, we are constrained by perceptions of our realities, particularly when our cognitions are highly important. Under such circumstances, another method for reducing dissonance is to introduce *new* cognitive elements. For example, the manager, if unable to change the cognitions of his behavior or attitude, might add the cognitions that the employee was likely going to quit soon or that the employee enjoys spending time with his family. These new cognitions have the power to offset the proportion of dissonant elements.

As theories of dissonance evolved, self-consistency became a key explanatory mechanism for cognitive dissonance. Elliot Aronson, one of Festinger's students, proposed that the effects of dissonance are most powerful when a salient self-aspect is threatened. In other words, dissonance is aroused not because cognitive elements do not logically align; rather, dissonance is the result of cognitive elements that challenge the consistency of one's sense of self. Based on these arguments, Aronson suggested that high self-involvement produces a greater need to justify our beliefs or behaviors. Ultimately, such justification enables individuals to maintain a positive and consistent self-concept. To illustrate this point, imagine an individual who believes that being a loyal employee is core to her identity; however, she takes the day off from work to interview at a competing firm. Given the centrality of loyalty to the individual's sense of self, a high level of dissonance is likely to be aroused, resulting in a need to justify the interview. Statements of self-justification may include, "I need to take a job that pays me more so I can pay for my child's college education," or "If I get this new job, I plan to be there until I retire." Such cognitions may enable the individual to maintain her sense of being a loyal employee and alleviate anxiety.

Importance

Festinger's seminal research on cognitive dissonance stimulated substantial interest in the concept among scholars, managers, and mainstream media. In the field of organizational behavior, dissonance theory serves as an important basis for examinations of employees' attitudes and behaviors. Practitioners are intrigued by inconsistencies in beliefs and behaviors among employees, customers, and even themselves. Business journalists are attracted by the power of dissonance theory to explain seemingly inexplicable actions of managers and employees. A greater understanding of the psychological discomfort that individuals and organizational agents face as well as the means of reducing these tensions helps to explain and predict critical management phenomena including decision making, organizational identification, and unethical behavior.

Decision Making

Every day in organizations, we find ourselves in the position to choose or negotiate between two or more options. Dissonance theory can help to explain why people may enter a decision with particular levels of attraction for the available options but dramatically change their attitudes when a decision is made. Preferences are not static; rather, people continually revise their attitudes to be more consistent with the final decision outcome. For example, imagine a recent graduate who must decide between job offers from two companies—a well-established consulting firm and a high-tech start-up firm. Initially, she perceives both positions as highly and equally attractive; however, she cannot work for both firms and accepts the offer from the high-tech start-up firm. While excited about getting her first job, she also experiences a great deal of psychological discomfort since she abandoned an equally attractive offer. In this situation of free choice, the recent graduate will likely feel compelled either to devalue the consulting firm or to inflate her opinion of the high-tech firm. Thus, cognitive dissonance can be valuable in explaining changes in attitude.

Organizational Identification

Issues of dissonance also pertain to matters of organizational identity (features that members deem as central, distinctive, and enduring about their organizations) and organizational identification (the extent to which the organizational membership features in members' own identities). Just as feelings of dissonance are especially troublesome when they involve one's self, or identity, at the individual level, the same seems true at the organizational level. It is problematic when core features of an organization's identity (e.g., "environmental advocate") appear to be inconsistent with other parts of its identity (e.g., "financially driven") or with the organization's actions (e.g., not recycling). Dissonance also tends to accompany changes in organizational identity, problematizing identity change efforts.

Crossing levels of analysis, studies of organizational identification also suggest that individuals are more apt to identify with organizations whose identities are congruent with their sense of self. This alignment between member identity and organizational identity helps to maintain consistency between members' beliefs and the behaviors in which they engage as organizational agents. A desire for individual-organization identity congruence influences individuals' choices in joining and staying at particular organizations. It is also another reason why organizational identity change can be difficult for members and organizations. Consider an example of a doctor who believes that being a top surgeon in his field is core to his identity and has chosen to work at a hospital that defines itself in terms of its prestigious medical staff. However, in an attempt to boost languishing patient satisfaction, the hospital attempts to supplant prestige by patient relationships at the core of its identity. This shift in the hospital's identity from that of prestigious to patient-centered may now conflict with the doctor's sense of self. In order to cope with dissonance arousal, the doctor may alter his current sense of self from that of a top surgeon to a caregiver, decrease his identification with his hospital, attempt to renegotiate the organizational identity back to emphasizing prestige, or switch hospitals.

Unethical Behavior

Theories of dissonance are also quite relevant to exploring issues of unethical behavior. For example, why do individuals who believe that cheating or stealing is wrong participate in fraudulent activities? It is clear that the belief that cheating is immoral is inconsistent with the behavior of financial deception, likely resulting in psychological discomfort. Emerging research shows that, in an effort to reduce dissonance, individuals will alter their beliefs about immoral acts, such as cheating and stealing, through moral justification. This process of rationalization may enable the individual to perceive cheating or stealing as morally acceptable. Ultimately, the more people justify their actions, the more likely they are to continue engaging in such behavior and even gradually increase its scale of risk and consequence.

Shelley L. Brickson and Courtney R. Masterson

See also Ethical Decision Making, Interactionist Model of; Organizational Identification; Organizational Identity; Self-Concept and the Theory of Self; "Unstructured" Decision Making

Further Readings

Aronson, E. (1999). Dissonance, hypocrisy, and the self-concept. In E. Harmon-Jones & J. Mills (Eds.), *Cognitive dissonance: Progress on a pivotal theory in social psychology* (pp. 103–126). Washington, DC: American Psychological Association.

Bendersky, C., & Curhan, J. R. (2009). Cognitive dissonance in negotiation: Free choice or justification. *Social Cognition, 27*(3), 455–474.

Brickson, S. L. (2012). Athletes, best friends, and social activists: An integrative model accounting for the role of identity in organizational identification. *Organization Science.* Advance online publication. doi:10.1287/orsc.1110.0730

Cooper, J. (2007). *Cognitive dissonance: 50 years of a classic theory.* Thousand Oaks, CA: Sage.

Detert, J. R., Trevino, L. K., & Sweitzer, V. L. (2008). Disengagement in ethical decision making: A study of antecedents and outcomes. *Journal of Applied Psychology, 93*(2), 374–391.

Dutton, J. E., Dukerich, J. M., & Harquail, C. V. (1994). Organizational images and member identification. *Administrative Science Quarterly, 39*(2), 239–263.

Festinger, L. (1957). *Theory of cognitive dissonance.* Evanston, IL: Row, Peterson.

Hoshino-Browne, E., Zanna, A. S., Spencer, S. J., Zanna, M. P., Kitayama, S., & Lackenbauer, S. (2005). On the cultural guises of cognitive dissonance: The case of Easterners and Westerners. *Journal of Personality and Social Psychology, 89*(3), 294–310.

Reger, R. K., Gustafson, L. T., DeMarie, S. M., & Mullane, J. V. (1994). Reframing the organization: Why implementing total quality is easier said than done, *Academy of Management Review, 19*(3), 565–584.

Cognitive Resource Theory

Leadership, as a form of interpersonal influence, is most often studied from a leader-centric perspective. Even when early trait approaches to the study of leadership were deemphasized for a time, most conceptualizations of leadership focused on what the leader did. This exclusive focus on the leader was at the expense of any consideration of followers or the context in which the group operated. Cognitive resource theory (CRT) of leadership by Fred Fiedler and Joe Garcia, introduced in 1987, presented a modified approach to the trait theory by considering the contribution of leaders' specific cognitive resources to work group and organizational performance under demanding work environments. This entry is an outline of the premise of CRT and the situations in which individuals may rely on their intelligence over their experience, versus their experience over their intelligence, as well as the reasons why experience is helpful for developing leader's technical skills, leadership self-efficacy, and tacit knowledge.

Fundamentals

General cognitive ability, or intelligence, is said to predict many important life outcomes in addition to managerial and leadership performance. However, within the context of CRT, Fiedler's research in fact found that intelligence did not consistently predict job performance of leaders. Sometimes, intelligence was unrelated or even worse, negatively related to performance. Specifically, while leaders were under stressful situations, intelligence did not contribute to performance; however, in conditions of low stress, a leader's level of intelligence did predict performance. A number of field studies for diverse groups with diverse measures of leader outcomes showed these effects. Also, within the theory, Fiedler and his colleagues examined the effects of many different types of stressful situations (stressors) including situations that produced evaluation apprehension or stressful work events in diverse groups such as the military, firefighters, student groups, and sports teams. The debilitating effects of stress on intelligence could, it was found, lead to increased anxiety and distracted leaders from the task at hand. It was only in situations where leaders behaved in a directive manner could their intelligence contribute to the group's performance—but only when stress was low. Even directive behavior was not enough, however, to utilize the leader's intelligence if stress for the leader was high.

Conversely, Fiedler and his colleagues found a leader's level of experience played an important role in effectiveness in stressful situations. Experience is often defined as the time served in a particular organization, position, or occupational field. Specifically, under conditions of high stress, they found that more experienced leaders performed better than less experienced leaders. Conversely, under low stress, more experienced leaders were not better performing leaders than their less experienced counterparts, and in fact, sometimes performed less well than less experienced leaders.

The task of leadership requires skill acquisition that goes beyond technical knowledge and represents knowledge of an interpersonal and intrapersonal nature that might be gained through years of experience. Fiedler suggested such skills as cognitive, or problem solving skills (including technical experience, or how to do the task), human relations skills (including leadership role experience, or how to organize a group), self-confidence, and understanding oneself and how to satisfy one's own needs. Fiedler's ideas are congruent with the results of a study by Morgan McCall and others in which they asked hundreds of leaders to recall what experiences they thought had made them better leaders. One category of important skills was called *executive temperament* and included the use of self-confidence, power, and persevering through adversity.

In addition to skill acquisition, leadership experience may enhance a leader's ability to cope with stressful situations in a number of ways. First, Fiedler and Garcia suggested that increased experience may act to facilitate performance as it represents the dominant response according to social facilitation theory by Robert Zajonc. As stress increases, the ability to concentrate on the task, especially a novel task, decreases and simple or well-learned responses tend to be elicited. Thus, experience on a task leads to better performance when the person performing the task is under stress. Second, experience may affect the appraisal of a stressful event. Most likely, leaders with a great deal of experience have been exposed to many different types of stressful situations. In other words, another stressful situation may seem like less of a threat because of familiarity with similar situations. Third, experience may work to enhance a leader's belief in his or her ability to cope with a stressful situation. In other words, a leader may see that a particular situation has the potential to be stressful, but the leader's belief in his or her ability to overcome any difficulties in the situation will lead to effective performance. According to Albert Bandura, within the organizational context, high self-efficacy specifically tied to a task is required to deploy one's cognitive resources optimally and to remain task oriented in the face of the many organizational complexities. A measure of leadership self-efficacy developed by Susan Murphy showed that those with greater leadership experience perceived less stress, had higher leadership self-efficacy, and therefore performed better.

CRT has not been without its critics. Criticisms of the theory have focused on the construct of leadership experience: the measures of intelligence used, the measurement of stress, underlying theoretical explanations, and the failure to distinguish the contribution of intelligence and experience to different types of tasks. More specifically, Stephen Zaccaro postulated that leadership experience facilitates the solving of *well-defined* problems because experience allows a person to acquire knowledge that is applicable to these problems but will not facilitate performance for *ill-defined* problems because these types of problems require the generation of novel solutions. Robert Sternberg offers that what a person learns from experience represents the three components of "tacit knowledge": managing self, managing tasks, and managing others. Therefore, years of experience alone will not increase leader effectiveness unless they gain these forms of knowledge.

The implications for a cognitive resource theory of leadership lie in both the selection and training of leaders. Many organizations recognize that training leaders to deal with specific challenging situations improves leadership capabilities. Intelligence as a selection tool will only work if those individuals are also given the opportunity to develop their leadership responses under challenging conditions. Most leader development programs

work to find ways for leaders to draw more from their experiences.

Susan Elaine Murphy

See also Agency Theory; Contingency Theory of Leadership; Emotional and Social Intelligence; Social Cognitive Theory; Social Facilitation Management; Tacit Knowledge; Trait Theory of Leadership

Further Readings

Bandura, A. (1997). *Self efficacy: The exercise of control.* New York, NY: W. H. Freeman.

Fiedler, F. E., & Garcia, J. E. (1987). *New approaches to effective leadership: Cognitive resources and organizational performance.* New York, NY: Wiley.

McCall, M. W., Lombardo, M. M., & Morrison, A. M. (1988). *The lessons of experience.* Lexington, MA: Lexington Books.

Murphy, S. E. (2002). Leader self-regulation: The role of self-efficacy and "multiple intelligences." In R. Riggio, S. Murphy, & F. Pirozzolo, (Eds.), *Multiple intelligences and leadership* (pp. 163–186). Mahwah, NJ: Erlbaum.

Sternberg, R. (1995). A triarchic view of "cognitive resources and leadership performance." *Applied Psychology: An International Review, 44,* 29–32.

Zaccaro, S. J. (1995). Leader resources and the nature of organizational problems. *Applied Psychology: An International Review, 44,* 32–36.

COMPETING VALUES FRAMEWORK

The competing values framework (CVF) has been studied and tested in organizations for more than 30 years. It has been labeled as one of the most influential models ever developed in organizational studies. It emerged from studies of the factors that account for highly effective organizational performance. It was developed in response to the need for a broadly applicable method for fostering successful leadership, improving organizational effectiveness, and promoting value creation. The CVF serves primarily as a map, an organizing mechanism, a sense-making device, a source of new ideas, and a theory of management and organizational performance. From the CVF comes a theory regarding how various aspects of organizations function in simultaneous

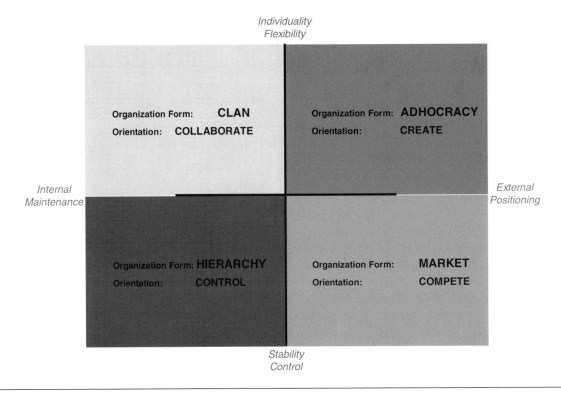

Figure I   Core Dimensions of the Competing Values Framework

Source: Author.

harmony as well as in tension with one another. The framework identifies a set of guidelines that can help leaders diagnose and manage the interrelationships, congruencies, and contradictions among these different aspects of organizations. In this entry, the history and development of the CVF are briefly discussed, the core dimensions of the framework are explained, and the applicability of the framework to organizational culture and performance is considered.

Fundamentals

The competing values framework was developed initially from empirical research on the major indicators of effective organizations, but it has been elaborated to include research on a whole host of other topics—shareholder value, mergers and acquisitions, approaches to learning, organizational culture, leadership competencies, organizational designs, communication styles, organizational virtues, creativity, human resource practices, employee-job matching, financial investments, and information processing. In each case, statistical analyses have confirmed the robustness and applicability of this framework to a

broad array of human and organizational phenomena. That is, the same dimensions that emerged from research on organizational effectiveness also emerged when studying a wide variety of other aspects of human and organizational activities. These dimensions compose the CVF. Figure 1 illustrates this framework.

All organized human activity has an underlying structure. Completely haphazard action, or randomly dispersed elements, is said to be without organization. Organization, by definition, therefore, denotes patterns and predictability in relationships. Identifying the underlying dimensions of organization is one of the key functions of the CVF. It helps uncover the underlying relationships that exist in organizations, leadership, learning, culture, motivation, decision making, cognitive processing, creativity, and so on.

The basic framework comprises two dimensions— one drawn vertically and the other drawn horizontally—resulting in a two-by-two figure with four quadrants. The study of effectiveness in organizations three decades ago revealed that some organizations were effective if they demonstrated flexibility and adaptability, but other organizations were effective if they demonstrated stability and control. Similarly, some organizations were effective if they maintained efficient internal processes whereas others were effective if they maintained competitive external positioning relative to customers and clients. These differences represent the different ends of the two dimensions that makeup the CVF.

More specifically, one dimension of the framework differentiates an orientation toward flexibility, discretion, and dynamism from an orientation toward stability, order, and control. One dimension in the CVF, in other words, represents a continuum ranging from versatility and pliability on one end to consistency and durability on the other end. When referring to individuals, this dimension differentiates people who learn inductively, communicate with animated and speculative ideas, and process information by searching for innovative applications from people who learn deductively, communicate with rational and considered ideas, and process information methodically.

The second dimension of the framework differentiates an orientation toward an internal focus and capability, as well as the integration and unity of processes, from an orientation toward an external focus and opportunities, as well as differentiation and rivalry regarding outsiders. That is, some organizations have value associated with their harmonious internal characteristics; others have value associated with their challenge or competition with entities outside their boundaries. This dimension ranges, in other words, from cohesion and consonance on the one end to separation and independence on the other. When referring to individuals, this dimension differentiates people who learn by examining familiar information, communicate using harmonizing strategies, and process information by analyzing consistencies and congruencies, on the one hand, from people who learn by searching for unfamiliar elements, communicate using confronting strategies, and process information by analyzing uniqueness, aberrations, and discontinuities, on the other hand.

Together, these two core dimensions form four quadrants, each representing a distinct cluster of criteria. The resulting framework represents the way people evaluate organizations, the way they process information and learn about their environments, the way they organize and lead others, the kinds of value created for customers, the clustering of organizational elements, and so on. The framework also defines what people see as good, right, and appropriate. It captures the fundamental values—or culture—that exist in organizations. Importantly, the dimensions produce quadrants that are also contradictory or competing on the diagonal. They highlight one of the most important features of the CVF, namely, the presence and necessity of paradox.

Each of the four quadrants has been given a label in order to characterize its most notable characteristics for creating value. The original formulation of the CVF used terms derived from the scholarly literature in organizational studies to define each quadrant—*Clan* (upper left), *Adhocracy* (upper right), *Market* (lower right), and *Hierarchy* (lower left). In communicating to practicing leaders and managers, however, action verbs are often used that highlight major themes in each quadrant—*collaborate, create, compete, and control*—since these terms contain more practical meaning. The two upper quadrants share in common an emphasis on flexibility and dynamism, whereas the two bottom quadrants share an emphasis on stability and control. The two left-hand quadrants focus on internal capability whereas the two right-hand quadrants focus on external opportunity. What is important to remember is that the quadrants represent clusters of similar elements and similar orientations, but those elements and orientations are contradictory to those in the diagonal quadrant.

Importance

Among the most important aspects and source of the practical utility associated with the competing values framework are the attributes of the four quadrants themselves. Understanding these quadrants has made the framework relevant to a wide variety of phenomena and topics associated with organizations, cognitions, motivations, and so forth. A brief summary of each quadrant follows.

The hierarchy (control) quadrant. The earliest approach to organizing in the modern era was based on the work of a German sociologist, Max Weber, who studied government organizations in Europe during the early 1900s. The major challenge faced by organizations at the turn of the 20th century was to efficiently produce goods and services for an increasingly complex society. To accomplish this, Weber proposed seven characteristics that have become known as the classical attributes of bureaucracy: rules, specialization, meritocracy, hierarchy, separate ownership, impersonality, and accountability. These characteristics were highly effective in accomplishing their purpose. They were adopted widely in organizations whose major challenge was to generate efficient, reliable, smooth-flowing, predictable output. In fact, until the 1960s, almost every book on management and organizational studies made the assumption that a hierarchy was the ideal form of organization because it led to stable, efficient, highly consistent products and services. Because the environment was relatively stable, tasks and functions could be integrated and coordinated, uniformity in products and services was maintained, and workers and jobs were under control. Clear lines of decision-making authority, standardized rules and procedures, and control and accountability mechanisms were valued as the keys to success.

The hierarchy organization, therefore, is characterized as a formalized and structured place to work. Procedures govern what people do. Effective leaders are good coordinators and organizers. Maintaining a smooth-running organization is important. The long-term concerns of the organization are stability, predictability, and efficiency. Formal rules and policies hold the organization together.

The market (compete) quadrant. Another form of organizing became popular during the late 1960s as organizations faced new competitive challenges. This form of organizing relied on a fundamentally different set of assumptions than the hierarchy and was referred to as a market form of organization. The term *market* is not synonymous with the marketing function or with consumers in the marketplace. Rather, it refers to a type of organization that functions on the basis of market mechanisms. The market operates primarily through economic transactions, competitive dynamics, and monetary exchange. That is, the major focus of markets is to conduct transactions (exchanges, sales, contracts) with external constituencies to create competitive advantage. Profitability, bottom-line results, strength in market niches, stretch targets, and secure customer bases are primary objectives of the organization. Not surprisingly, the core values that dominate market-type organizations are competitiveness and productivity.

A market organization, therefore, is a results-oriented workplace. Leaders are hard-driving producers and competitors. They are tough and demanding. The glue that holds the organization together is an emphasis on winning. The long-term concern is on competitive actions and achieving stretch goals and targets. Success is defined in terms of market share and penetration. Outpacing the competition and market leadership are important.

The clan (collaborative) quadrant. A third ideal form of organization is represented by the upper left quadrant in Figure 1. It is called a clan because of its similarity to a family-type organization. In the 1970s and 1980s, a number of researchers observed fundamental differences between the market and hierarchy forms of organization and an alternative form that became popular initially in Asia. Shared values and goals, cohesion, participation, individuality, and a sense of "we-ness" permeated clan-type firms. They seemed more like extended families than economic entities. Instead of the rules and procedures of hierarchies or the competitive profit centers of markets, typical characteristics of clan-type firms were teamwork, employee involvement programs, and corporate commitment to employees.

The clan organization is typified as a friendly place to work where people share a lot of themselves. It is like an extended family. Leaders are thought of as mentors and perhaps even as parent figures. The organization is held together by loyalty and tradition. Commitment is high. The organization emphasizes the long-term benefit of individual development, with high cohesion and morale being important. Success is defined in terms of internal climate and concern for people. The organization places a premium on teamwork, participation, and consensus.

The adhocracy (creative) culture. In a hyperturbulent, constantly changing environment, a different set of assumptions was developed that differed from those of the other three forms of organization. These assumptions were that innovative and pioneering initiatives are what leads to success, that organizations are mainly in the business of developing new products and services and preparing for the future, and that the major task of management is to foster entrepreneurship, creativity, and activity "on the cutting edge." It was assumed that adaptation and innovativeness lead to new resources and profitability, so emphasis was placed on creating a vision of the future, organized anarchy, and disciplined imagination. They have been characterized as "tents rather than palaces" in that they can reconfigure themselves rapidly when new circumstances arise. A major goal of an adhocracy is to foster adaptability, flexibility, and creativity where uncertainty, ambiguity, and information overload are typical.

The adhocracy organization, therefore, is characterized by a dynamic, entrepreneurial, and creative workplace. People stick their necks out and take risks. Effective leadership is visionary, innovative, and risk oriented. The glue that holds the organization together is commitment to experimentation and innovation. The emphasis is on being at the leading edge of new knowledge, products, and services. Readiness for change and meeting new challenges are important. The organization's long-term emphasis is on rapid growth and acquiring new resources. Success means producing unique and original products and services.

A search of the scholarly literature from 2000 to 2009 revealed that the competing values framework was the focus of more than 50 journal articles and 59 doctoral dissertations. The framework was utilized by scholars in diverse disciplines including agriculture, education (primary, secondary, junior colleges, and universities), nonprofits, religious organizations, military, sports, health care (physicians, nurses, hospitals, and nursing homes), government, and business. Its scope is also international, with studies conducted on every continent except Antarctica, including Kenya, the Netherlands, Taiwan, Hong Kong, Singapore, the United Kingdom, Greece, Qatar, Australia, Canada, and across the United States. Empirical support is strong that the competing values framework is empirically validated, theoretically confirmed, and practically useful. It is most likely the most utilized framework in the world for assessing organizational culture and facilitating culture change. The framework is also frequently used to guide management and leadership competency development.

Kim Cameron

See also Organizational Culture and Effectiveness; Organizational Culture Model; Organizational Effectiveness; Typology of Organizational Culture

Further Readings

Cameron, K. S. (1986). Effectiveness as paradox. *Management Science, 32,* 539–553.
Cameron, K. S., & Quinn, R. E. (2011). *Diagnosing and changing organizational culture* (3rd ed.). San Francisco, CA: Jossey-Bass.
Cameron, K. S., Quinn, R. E., DeGraff, J., & Thakor, A. (2006). *Competing values leadership: Creating value in organizations.* Northampton, MA: Edward Elgar.
Quinn, R. E. (1988). *Beyond rational management: Mastering the paradoxes and competing demands of high performance.* San Francisco, CA: Jossey-Bass.
Quinn, R. E., & Cameron, K. S. (1983). Organizational life cycles and shifting criteria of effectiveness. *Management Science, 19,* 33–51.
Quinn, R. E., & Cameron, K. S. (1988). Paradox and transformation: Toward a *framework of change in organization and management.* Cambridge, MA: Ballinger.
Quinn, R. E., & Rohrbaugh, J. (1983). A spatial model of effectiveness criteria: Toward a competing values approach to organizational analysis. *Management Science, 29,* 363–377.

COMPETITIVE ADVANTAGE

The primary objective of a firm's strategy is to identify, create, and sustain a competitive advantage over its industry rivals. A firm is said to possess a competitive advantage if it outperforms its industry rivals over a sustained period of time. Although the scholarly roots of a hypothetical theory of competitive advantage are dispersed across a fragmented management literature, it can be inarguably stated that the primary roots lie in Michael Porter's seminal work on the strategic management of firms—often informally referred to as Porter's theory of competitive advantage. Accordingly, a firm's strategy should identify a unique strategic position within its industry so as to reduce or counter the profit-reducing effect of the competitive forces in that industry. The entry is organized as follows. The next section is focused on the fundamentals of this theory as laid out in Porter's seminal work that provides both frameworks to explain various position-based advantages and prescriptions to achieve and sustain the same. The subsequent section is focused on other developments in the management literature that either were triggered as systematic efforts to provide an alternate explanation for the competitive advantage of firms or extend the concept of competitive advantage to other contexts (e.g., multibusiness firms). This section also shows the conceptual gaps that need to be addressed in order to develop a comprehensive theory of competitive advantage. The final section is a combination of arguments that articulate the internal—and external—environmental perspective on competitive advantage to provide an explanation of how firms create and sustain competitive advantage.

Fundamentals

While the concept of competitive advantage may have originated in the prescriptive literature, its ascendancy as a preeminent theoretical construct is firmly rooted in an interdisciplinary descriptive literature. The prescriptive literature primarily focuses on explaining (to the CEOs) how to create and preserve competitive advantage (to maximize shareholder returns). On the other hand, the descriptive literature focuses on exploring the causality issues from a scholarly perspective. However, a consensus eludes both streams concerning not only the measure of firm performance that reveals competitive advantage but also the factors that contribute to the creation and sustainability of firms' competitive advantage.

Porter's pioneering work in the late 1970s and early 1980s generated both theoretical and prescriptive frameworks to explain the pervasive yet consensus-eluding concept of competitive advantage. In his scholarly articles published in various academic journals, he explains what is now referred to as the positioning-based advantages of firms, and provides the intellectual foundations for a robust field of scholarly inquiry. Porter's best-selling books, *Competitive Strategy* in 1980 and *Competitive Advantage* in 1985, provided not only the intellectual foundations for his theory of competitive advantage but also bridged the divide between the prescriptive and descriptive literature.

Five Forces

Porter's *Competitive Strategy* provides a framework to identify the basis of competitive advantage in a firm's proximate industry environment—referred to as Porter's five forces of competition model. The model predicts the average profitability of an industry in terms of three horizontal and two vertical forces of competition that together determine the structural attractiveness of the focal industry. Basically, the industry structure determines the extent to which the value created by a firm for its customers is competed away (in an unattractive structure) or appropriated by the firm (in an attractive structure). The three horizontal forces of competition that negatively influence industry profitability include the threat of new entrants, interfirm rivalry, and the threat of substitutes. The two vertical forces of competition include the bargaining power of suppliers and buyers. A firm's strategy—informed by an ex-ante analysis of its industry structure—should aim (a) at the very least to cope with these competitive forces, or (b) preferably to counter their negative effects on profitability but (c) ideally to exploit the attractive features of the industrial market.

Generic Strategies

Porter's *Competitive Advantage* prescribes three generic strategies for firms to create competitive advantage: cost-leadership, differentiation, and focus. A firm's choice of one of these generic strategies is influenced by its *ex-ante* choices of competitive advantage (cost-advantage vs. differentiation-advantage) and competitive scope (broad scope vs. narrow scope). A firm's choice of a generic strategy locks it into a clearly identified strategic position and hence is associated with certain risks. Each of these positions is in turn associated with a unique set of activities—through which firms create the chosen value for the customers—and a specified organizational design to accommodate the unique sets of activities. The trade-offs associated with each strategic position renders it impossible or uneconomical for rivals to imitate or enter. Porter's value chain framework is widely employed by firms to identify their activities, analyze the linkages and strategic fit among these activities, and examine the cost-reducing and/or value-enhancing potential of each strategic activity.

Position-Based Advantage

At any time, an industry environment may support one or more competitive positions that are associated with certain advantages and trade-offs. The hypothetical position-based advantages of firms ensure that the value firms create for their customers exceeds the costs of creating that value. Basically, firms' favorable strategic-position contribute to their superior performance vis-à-vis their rivals by (a) lowering the cost of creating and delivering value to the consumers and (b) raising consumers' willingness to pay. For instance, Walmart's substantial cost advantages over its rivals in the discount retail industry allow it to offer comparable value at the lowest prices. Similarly, Apple's differentiation advantage allows it to extract a substantial price premium for most of the high-value products that it sells.

Evolution

The evolution of the concept of competitive advantage can be mapped onto that of the field of strategic management from a normative discipline to a positive science. The "early" strategy literature in the 1970s and 1980s primarily focused on prescriptions for business firms to achieve competitive advantage. In the mid- to late 1980s, the literature began to focus more on explaining the underlying sources of competitive advantage. Toward this effort, the field of strategic management has drawn constructs both from the external- and internal-environment to explain competitive advantage and thereby superior firm performance.

In the 1970s, a few strategy researchers began to build on the conceptual work in theoretical and empirical industrial organization (IO) economics—concerning imperfect competition—to provide structural explanation for the empirical evidence that some firms consistently outperform others. (The concept of imperfect competition developed by IO researchers challenged an important premise in neoclassical economics that any profit differences at the firm-level would be imitated away in perfectly competitive markets.) Further developments in the strategy literature allowed understanding these differences in terms of efficiency of individual businesses rather than industry structure.

In the 1990s, Adam Brandenburger and Harbourne Stuart proposed a value-price-cost bargaining framework regarding a firm's competitive advantage to explain its ability to appropriate the value it creates—for its consumers—as profits. A firm's ability to appropriate this surplus is negatively influenced not only by its rivals but also by its

consumers and suppliers. More specifically, a firm's competitive advantage vis-à-vis its rivals translates into a wider gap between the targeted customers' willingness to pay for its products and the supplier opportunity cost that it incurs to serve those customers.

The concept of competitive advantage remains a touchstone for "sound" strategy even though almost five decades of research have failed to produce testifiable propositions let alone a comprehensive theory of competitive advantage. Together with the concept of strategy, it has fueled the imagination of scholars and practitioners alike, more so than any other area of academic inquiry in management. Yet the field of strategy still awaits a comprehensive theory of competitive advantage that would explain persistence in performance difference across firms in terms of both the systematic difference among firms and their environmental context. More recently, strategy scholars have sought to address several issues toward developing such a comprehensive theory of competitive advantage.

Resource- and/or Capabilities-Based Advantage

At any time, some firms may somehow come to possess specific resources and/or capabilities that confer on them certain advantages over their rivals. Firms are either endowed with certain resources at birth (entry into an industry), or they acquire certain strategic assets from strategic factor markets upon entry, or they internally develop certain capabilities over their life cycle. The advantages conferred by these idiosyncratic characteristics allow the firms to either create superior value for their customers or generate comparable value at a lower cost vis-à-vis their rivals. In summary, the resource-based view of the firm explains a firm's competitive advantage in terms of unique resources that are valuable, rare, imperfectly imitable, and nonsubstitutable. The first-order effect on firm performance—referred to as Ricardian rents—is explained as resulting simply from some firms possessing these resources unlike their rivals. The second-order effect on firm performance is explained in terms of how firms effectively manage these resources vis-à-vis their rivals. The concept of firm capabilities explains why some firms are better able to manage their resources to gain advantage over their rivals who might possess similar resources. A firm may outperform its rivals who possess similar resources by effectively structuring (e.g., acquiring, accumulating, and divesting resources), bundling (e.g., integrating resources to form capabilities), and leveraging (e.g., mobilizing, coordinating, and deploying bundles of resources to exploit market opportunities) its resources. The dynamic capabilities framework explains a firm's competitive advantage in terms of its ability to create heterogeneous resource positions in a dynamically evolving business environment. The effect of dynamic capabilities on firm performance is sometimes referred to as Schumpeterian rents.

Corporate Advantage

Corporate strategy scholars seek to understand whether a firm can leverage (a) its competitive advantage in one market to generate superior performance in another market and (b) its advantages across multiple markets to generate superior performance at the corporate level. While the concept of competitive advantage is useful to address the first issue, it does not really explain superior performance of multibusiness firms. The analogous concept that explains superior performance at the corporate level due to portfolio effects is defined as corporate advantage. The underlying logic of the portfolio effects draws on the resource-based view and transaction cost economics. Hence, corporate advantage accrues to a firm if it can share efficiency-enhancing and/or value-creating resources across two distinct portfolio businesses when it is not possible to exploit those resources through the market.

Demand-Side Dimensions of Competitive Advantage

The extant explanation of cost- and differentiation-advantage focuses on how firms' supply-side activities enable them to capture a greater portion of the value created as profits. While a supply-side explanation of how firms lower the costs of creating and delivering value—by negotiating with their upstream suppliers and/or downstream partners—may be adequate, the same cannot be said about the supply-side explanation of how firms raise consumers' willingness to pay. For instance, typical analyses assume that customers' willingness to pay increases with the performance characteristics and thereby recommend that (say) a car manufacturer should increase fuel-efficiency to provide more value to consumers in order to raise the latter's willingness to pay. In doing so, these analyses ignore the role of firms' demand environment, which in the first place determines the value that is required to be created by the firms. Recent advances in the strategy literature have examined the characteristics of the demand environment that possibly influence firms' differentiation advantage. These include heterogeneity in consumers' (a) preferences regarding product attributes, performance, price, and so on; (b) marginal utility for incremental performance improvements; (c) expectations for (say) interoperability of the basic industry product with a range of complements, and so on.

Endogeneity of Market Structure

Any endeavor toward developing a comprehensive theory of competitive advantage would have to bridge the external- and internal-environment schism that currently forces scholars to ground their theoretical arguments on one side of the divide. Most analytical accounts of sustainable competitive advantage fail to explain how firms' strategic choices influence and are simultaneously influenced by the coevolution of external industry competition and internal firm competences. Strategy scholars need to explain how the endogenously determined contextual conditions (market structure) influence the firms' strategic choices that in turn affect their own competences along with the contextual conditions themselves. Such a theory would explain the complex endogenous processes through which temporally heterogeneous firm (investment) strategies influence and are influenced by the evolution of (a) the industrial market-structure and its determinants—technology, demand, and policy and (b) internal firm-specific characteristics, such as resources, capabilities, and/or dynamic capabilities.

Importance

The extant theories of competitive advantage address two fundamental management issues. First, how do firms create competitive advantage? Second, can firms sustain their competitive advantages? If so, then how?

Creating Competitive Advantage

The literature on position-based advantage explains how a firm's chosen position allows it to deliver a unique mix of value to its customers and thereby enjoy an advantage over its rivals who may have chosen a different position. Hence, a firm's chosen position confers it with an advantage by providing it with an ability to either (a) impose high switching costs on buyers, and/or (b) raise rivals cost of entry, and/or (c) exploit economies of scale and scope, and/or (d) retaliate against later entrants, and so on. An advantageous competitive position allows the occupying firm to create some imperfections in the market and thereby extract monopoly rents. Although the logic of position-based advantage is quite compelling, the complexity of the phenomena—due to the presence of trade-offs and interdependencies among various firm-level activities—has restricted the full analytical treatment of the same. For instance, it is difficult for firms to alter their strategic positions as the industry evolves because of the trade-offs between the positions.

The literature on resource- and/or capabilities-based advantage seeks to explain the firm-level processes through which these advantages first arise. More specifically, it explains various processes through which firms manage their resources to create value for their customers and thereby generate competitive advantage vis-à-vis their rivals. However, it provides *ex-post* accounts of the performance benefits of specific resource management techniques and doesn't seem to have made much progress in terms of developing a framework that could guide the internal firm-specific or the external environmental analyses to inform the *ex-ante* strategic choices concerning resource management. This stream of literature lacks a framework that would inform strategic choices concerning the (a) acquisition, accumulation, or divestment of resources jointly referred to as structuring of resources; (b) improvement and extension of existing capabilities along with development of new capabilities jointly referred to as bundling; and (c) mobilizing, coordinating, and deploying capabilities to exploit new opportunities. In other words, the missing framework would not just inform (say) which resource to acquire and how much to invest and over what time period in order to acquire the said resource that would confer a firm with a particular competitive advantage.

Sustaining Competitive Advantage

A firm can sustain its position-based advantage(s) if its rivals are unable to imitate the underlying sources of advantages due to physical, legal, or economic constraints. Hence, whether a firm can sustain its position-based advantage depends upon the barriers to imitation and entry: scale and scope economies, switching cost of buyers, entry costs, and so on. On the other hand, a firm's position-based advantage is sustainable against innovation by rivals only if it continuously improves so as to enjoy a wider wedge between the value created for its customers and the opportunity cost of its suppliers. However, dominant firms may sometimes exploit away their advantages to maximize profits—under pressure from investors—when forced to choose between exploiting their advantage and investing further to sustain their competitive position.

A firm can sustain its resource-based advantage if the underlying economizing- or value-producing resources are scarce and imperfectly mobile on one hand and inimitable on the other. While scarcity drives up the cost of the underlying resource (e.g., talent) thereby benefiting the owner vis-à-vis the firm which seeks to exploit it, the imperfect mobility of the resource (e.g., location) counters that effect. The literature provides an insight into resource characteristics that serve as isolating mechanisms. For instance, a rival may not want to imitate a rival's particular resource because the cost of accumulating it in the shortest possible time would make it uneconomical. The other barriers to imitation include legal restrictions (e.g., copyrights, trademarks, and patents), superior access to inputs and/or customers, and so forth.

A firm can sustain its capabilities-based advantages against threat of imitation if its rivals are somehow unable to learn the causal mechanism that explains the performance implications of those capabilities. On one hand, combinatorial complexity acts as a barrier to active learning (e.g., learning-by-doing) by rivals thereby serving as a source of sustained capabilities-based advantage. On the other hand, causal ambiguity deters passive learning (e.g., absorptive learning) by rivals and hence even though it is a necessary condition to develop capabilities-based advantage it is by no means sufficient to ensure that such advantage can be sustained. This is because rivals may eventually erode such an advantage by sustained active learning. Finally, a firm can sustain its capabilities-based advantages under threat of innovation by rivals by continuously improving the underlying capabilities before its rivals catch up.

Lalit Manral

See also Diversification Strategy; Dynamic Capabilities; First-Mover Advantages and Disadvantages; Seven-S Framework; SWOT Analysis Framework; Value Chain

Further Readings

Adner, R., & Zemsky, P. (2006). A demand-based perspective on sustainable competitive advantage. *Strategic Management Journal, 27,* 215–239.

Barney, J. B. (1991). Firm resources and sustained competitive advantage. *Journal of Management, 17,* 99–120.

Brandenburger, A. M., & Stuart, H. W. (1996). Value-based business strategy. *Journal of Economics and Management Strategy, 5*(1), 5–24.

Manral, L. (2010). Towards a theory of endogenous market structure in strategy: Exploring the endogeneity of demand-side determinants of firm investment strategy and market structure. *Journal of Strategy and Management, 3*(4), 352–373.

Porter, M. E. (1980). *Competitive strategy: Techniques for analyzing industries and competitors.* New York, NY: Free Press.

Porter, M. E. (1985). *Competitive advantage: Creating and sustaining superior performance.* New York, NY: Free Press.

Porter, M. E. (1996). What is strategy? *Harvard Business Review, 74*(6), 61–78.

Ryall, M. D. (2009). Causal ambiguity, complexity, and capability-based advantage. *Management Science, 55*(3), 389–403.

COMPLEXITY THEORY AND ORGANIZATIONS

Complexity theory is a body of research concerned with explaining emergent patterns in physical properties or social behavior that cannot be explained by studying the individual building blocks in isolation but rather emerge from their interactions. The nonlinear and nonadditive nature of the interactions requires the study of the system as a whole. As a theoretical approach, complexity theory has been proposed to provide a complement to the traditional reductionist approach to science. The theory's central management insight is that managers need to understand how individuals and firms interact and not just how they perform individually. The theory provides a set of tools that facilitate this understanding. This entry will describe the key assumptions, building blocks, and insights of the complexity theory as applied within the context of management research.

Fundamentals

The complexity theory in management is largely based on the Kauffman NK model. Stuart Kauffman, a biologist, designed the model to study how interactions between genes affect the fitness of a species. Within the context of organizations, the model has been used to explain how the interactions among decisions within and across organizations affect organizational performance. The effect of the interactions on organizational performance has been studied within the context of various organizational structures, incentive systems, learning processes, technological regimes, industry characteristics, and environmental dynamics.

The key construct of the model is the notion of interdependence. Interdependence between two decisions exists when one decision influences not only its own performance contribution but also the performance contribution of another decision. The overall organizational performance is assumed to be a function of the performance contributions of all decisions that the organization makes. The organizational performance is conceptualized either as the organizational adaptation or as the ability of the organization to solve a given problem. Superior performing organizations are those that achieve a better fit with the external environment or discover a better solution to a problem. The organizational performance is emergent in the sense that it cannot be deduced from the analysis of each organizational unit in isolation but rather depends on the interactions within the system as a whole. The model is most relevant, and its predictions are most likely to hold, in contexts where the outcomes are driven by the interactions among the decisions as opposed to being dominated by individual decisions.

The model assumes that decision makers within organizational units have bounded rationality. Bounded rationality implies that the decision makers are unable to select the best possible set of decisions but must proceed through an iterative search. An iterative search consists of trial-and-error steps. After each step, the decision makers change a limited number of decisions and observe whether the changes lead to an increase in performance. Typically, only performance-enhancing choices are retained.

The key relationship predicted by the model is that, due to bounded rationality, an increasing density of interdependencies complicates the search of the decision makers. With few interdependencies, changes in a small number of decisions have a small impact on the overall organizational performance. When the interdependencies are dense, however, even changing a small number of decisions can have a dramatic effect (positive or negative) on the overall organizational performance as the focal decision may affect the performance of many other decisions. Limited in their ability to consider a wide range of decisions, the boundedly rational decision makers tend to settle on less than optimal outcomes when facing interdependent choices. A higher density of interdependencies, thus, potentially leads to lower organizational performance. The research has examined a variety of factors that interact with this relationship and could potentially allow the organization to achieve a higher organizational performance. These factors include organizational centralization versus decentralization, differences in the cognitive mechanisms and imitative abilities, and technological modularity and environmental turbulence. The NK model has been recently extended to study the effect of interdependencies across organizational units and entire firms.

Several other complexity theories have made limited inroads into organizational research. First, a complexity theory has been developed to study the dynamic properties of organizational outcomes. This theory is concerned with explaining the differences and transitions between ordered and chaotic sequences of data. The objective is to explain which generative mechanism drives the patterns found in the time series data of organizational outcomes and to study how the number and characteristics of the interacting organizational units as well as the nature of their interactions lead to the ordered versus the chaotic regimes. Second, complexity theory has recently been converging with network theory. Within the context of organizations, network theory focuses on how the network topology (defined as the layout of the connections between network nodes) across and within organizations affects organizational outcomes. As the focus of network theory shifts from the study of a static topology to a dynamic one, the insights gained through complexity theory become more relevant. Even though complexity theory originates in physics and biology, its insights are closely related to some traditional thoughts within management literature. Complexity theory is inherently focused on processes; thus, it is related to the process and the evolutionary theories in management.

The main tool used to generate the insights and predictions based on complexity theory is computer simulations. Nonlinear interactions among a large number of interacting units make studying complex systems using either verbal theorizing or analytical mathematical approaches problematic. The computer simulations used in complexity theory are typically designed as agent-based simulations. An agent-based simulation is constructed by modeling each organizational unit as an agent in the simulation while describing the behavioral rules which the agents will follow. The agents are positioned in a particular topology that defines the agents' interactions. Performance mapping is then used to map decisions that agents make onto performance outcomes. The emergent patterns are observed and analyzed after running the simulations many times (10,000 or more). Predictions and insights can then be deduced by varying the parameter values or model structure and observing statistically significant differences in the observed performance patterns.

Even though complexity theory provides an appealing approach for studying organizational phenomena, empirical studies of complexity models are currently lagging behind theory development. Recently, however, empirical studies appear to be gaining momentum and are expected to grow substantially in the near future.

Managers today can utilize the insights from the complexity theory when designing organizational structures or product architectures or when managing their research personnel. For instance, researchers showed that when designing a modular system, erring on the side of greater integration is associated with lower penalty than erring on the side of higher modularity. Similarly, it has been shown that in cases when few core decisions interact with many peripheral components, broad exploratory search is not needed. Consequently, the complexity theory is starting to provide useful tools that can guide managerial decisions when dealing with interdependent decisions.

Martin Ganco

See also Bounded Rationality and Satisficing (Behavioral Decision-Making Model); Social Network Theory; Systems Theory of Organizations; Technology and Complexity; Technology and Interdependence/Uncertainty

Further Readings

Dooley, K. J., & Van de Ven, A. H. (1999). Explaining complex organizational dynamics. *Organization Science, 10*(3), 358–372.

Ethiraj, S., & Levinthal, D. (2004). Modularity and innovation in complex systems. *Management Science, 50,* 159–174.

Fleming, L., & Sorenson, O. (2001). Technology as a complex adaptive system: Evidence from patent data. *Research Policy, 30,* 1019–1039.

Ganco, M., & Hoetker, G. (2009). NK modeling methodology in the strategy literature: Bounded search on a rugged landscape. In D. Bergh & D. Ketchen Jr. (Eds.), *Research methodology in strategy and management* (pp. 237–268). Bingley, England: Emerald Group.

Kauffman, S. A. (1993). *The origins of order: Self-organization and selection in evolution.* Oxford, England: Oxford University Press.

Levinthal, D. A. (1997). Adaptation on rugged landscapes. *Management Science, 43,* 934–950.

Rivkin, J. W., & Siggelkow, N. (2007). Patterned interactions in complex systems: Implications for exploration. *Management Science, 53*(7), 1068–1085.

COMPLIANCE THEORY

Before the publication of the compliance theory in 1961 in Amitai Etzioni's *A Comparative Analysis of Complex Organizations,* the area of study now known as organization studies was not widely recognized. Instead, studies were organized according to specific kinds of organizations (for instance, industrial sociology, the study of bureaucracies, churches, military institutions, and so on). Compliance theory held that all these units have common features, namely, that organizations are "artificial" social entities that differ from "natural" ones such as the family, clans, and tribes. Organizations have stated goals and are designed to implement them. Hence, the interest in which kinds of power best advance the goals they are meant to serve—and the importance of the orientation of participants that may lead them to undermine or much enhance the organizational goals. This entry is an examination of the ways managers motivate employees, leaders motivate followers, or commanders motivate soldiers to do what must be done. Management to a large extent concerns the management of people. One of the most important questions

is how to find ways that move people to do what must be done—and not reject or resent their duties, indeed, if possible benefit from or enjoy them. Progress can be achieved toward good management by taking into account that different missions require different kinds of commitments and incentives and rewards.

Fundamentals

The research leading to the publication of the compliance theory was carried out by Amitai Etzioni at Columbia University. It drew on a secondary analysis of some 1,100 studies of a large variety of organizations. After its publication, a considerable number of studies tested, modified, challenged, and expanded the theory, which for an extended period of time was very widely cited. A revised edition of *A Comparative Analysis of Complex Organizations* was issued in 1975, which reviewed these studies and showed that the theory was largely confirmed or extended. Arguably the most important extension was the application of the theory to international relations.

The key finding at the foundation of compliance theory is that organizations that differ in the means they use to control their participants (power) and—in the orientations of their participants toward them (involvement) also differ significantly in numerous other ways. Compliance refers to a combined "reading" of both the kind of power employed (of which there are three kinds: coercive, remunerative, and normative) and involvement (which ranges from highly negative to highly positive). Thus, prisons tend to be largely coercive organizations, and their inmates' involvement tends to be negative. In contrast, voluntary associations rely mainly on normative power, and their members' involvement tends to be positive.

Coercive power is defined by the use of force; remunerative power is based on compensation, salaries, wages, fees, and fines; normative power is based on appeals to values people already have, persuasion, and leadership. Involvement refers to attitudes of members of the organization, the rank and file, toward the organization, its goals, and leaders.

While organizations often mix their means of control and draw on two or all three kinds, most rely heavily on one of the three kinds. Thus, prisons rely relatively heavily on coercion, factories rely relatively heavily on remunerative power, and churches rely largely on normative power in dealing with their parishioners. Our second main finding is that most of the lower participants of most organizations display a typical involvement with their kind of organization. For instance, most inmates of most prisons are more hostile toward their prisons than are most workers toward most factories.

In some organizations, the two independent variables (power and involvement) are not congruent. Compliance theory predicts that the resulting tension will lead to changes in either power or involvement, moving these organizations toward compliance equilibrium. Thus, if one tries to draw on normative power in dealing with inmates in a high-security prison, they will not comply, forcing the organization to either use coercive power or find ways to improve the inmates' involvement, for instance, by changing the conditions of confinement and the ways inmates are selected.

The Correlates of Compliance

Organizations where coercion is relatively heavily relied upon and the modal involvement is intensely negative—high-security prisons, for instance—tend rigidly to be divided into two castes, the staff and the inmates, with little expressive contact between them and considerable intercaste tension and open conflict. Mobility from one caste to the other, in effect, does not exist. While one caste controls the other, like an occupation army, it does not, as a rule, provide leadership for the other. The two castes do not make a social whole, though they function within the limits of one organization. Their values are at least in part antithetical.

Organizations where normative power is relatively heavily relied upon and the model involvement is intensely positive—many voluntary associations and the organizations that serve as the core of social movements, for instance—will tend to be integrated into one community, with many expressive contacts across the ranks, comparatively little interrank tension, and mainly latent conflict. Mobility up the ranks is comparatively common. There is a relatively high degree of value consensus among the lower and higher participants. Much leadership "flows" down the organizational structure.

Organizations that rely heavily on remunerative power are "in the middle." The participants in such organizations are often divided into three or more "classes," differing in socioeconomic background, education, and consumption habits; workers,

supervisors, and management are the main ones. While most of the mobility is within each "class," there is cross-class upward mobility. The relationships among the classes vary considerably from factory to factory and from office to office, but on the average, there is less of an expressive split than in coercive organizations and much more instrumental cooperation, but there is much less of an expressive community than in normative organizations. Employees tend not only to have leaders of their own but also to accept some leadership from supervisors.

Differences in compliance structure correlate with numerous other differences such as degree of consensus across the ranks, amount of cross-rank communication and frequency of communication blocks, and the status of lower participants' leaders. In some instances, the relationship between the nature of the compliance structure and such correlates is linear, for instance, the level of cross-rank consensus. In other cases, the relationship is curvilinear, with the dimension—for instance, organizational scope (the degree to which the organization penetrates into various life spheres of the participants)—higher at the two ends of the compliance continuum than in the middle.

International Application

Compliance theory has been applied to international relations. It sees a coercive realm, in which the military forces of nations face one another; a remunerative one, in which nations exchange goods and services and capital and labor flows; and a normative realm, in which values and ideas flow across borders. G. William Skinner and Edwin A. Winckler applied the compliance theory to study the relations between the government and the people in China, finding that different goals required the application of specific kinds of power—and that cyclical applications of the three types of power could be discerned in Chinese history following the revolution. David A. Baldwin categorizes power by what he calls "means of influence," including symbolic means, military means, economic means, and diplomatic means. David Lampton applied the compliance theory to his study of China, finding that it is useful for understanding and describing the "three faces" of China's growing international influence. Lampton organizes his entire volume around the three kinds of compliance, arguing that regimes and other organizations should be "compared and differentiated by the power they possess in various forms" (2008, p. 11), as well as their "preferred 'mix'"—for China, what he calls its "might" (coercive power), "money" (remunerative power), and "minds" (normative power). Recently Joseph S. Nye Jr. employed this approach, referring to military, economic, and soft power.

Amitai Etzioni

See also Action Research; Leadership Practices; Organizational Commitment Theory; Role Theory; Social Power, Bases of

Further Readings

Drummond, H. (1993). *Power and involvement in organizations: An empirical examination of Etzioni's compliance theory.* Aldershot, England: Avebury.

Etzioni, A. (1975). *A comparative analysis of complex organizations* (Rev. ed.). New York, NY: Free Press. (Original work published 1961)

Hornung, S. (2010). Alienation matters: Validity and utility of Etzioni's theory of commitment in explaining prosocial organizational behavior. *Social Behavior and Personality, 38,* 1081–1096.

Lampton, D. M. (2008). *The three faces of Chinese power: Might, money, and minds.* Berkeley: University of California Press.

Skinner, G. W., & Winckler, E. A. (1969). Compliance succession in rural Communist China: A cyclical theory. In A. Etzioni (Ed.). *A sociological reader on complex organization* (2nd ed., pp. 410–438). New York, NY: Holt, Rinehart, and Winston.

Thomas, C. W., Kreps, G. A., & Cage, R. J. (1977). An application of compliance theory to the study of juvenile delinquency. *Sociology & Social Research, 61,* 156–175.

COMPONENTIAL THEORY OF CREATIVITY

The componential theory of creativity is a comprehensive model of the social and psychological components necessary for an individual to produce creative work. The theory is grounded in a definition of creativity as the production of ideas or outcomes that are both novel and appropriate to some goal. In this theory, four components are necessary for any creative response: three components within the individual—domain-relevant skills, creativity-relevant processes,

and intrinsic task motivation—and one component outside the individual—the social environment in which the individual is working. The current version of the theory encompasses organizational creativity and innovation, carrying implications for the work environments created by managers. In this entry, the components of creativity and how they influence the creative process are defined along with a description of modifications to the theory over time. Then, after a comparison of the componential theory to other creativity theories, the theory's evolution and impact are described.

Fundamentals

Creativity is the production of a novel and appropriate response, product, or solution to an open-ended task. Although the response must be new, it cannot be merely different; the nonsensical speech of a schizophrenic may be novel, but few would consider it creative. Thus, the response must also be appropriate to the task to be completed or the problem to be solved; that is, it must be valuable, correct, feasible, or somehow fitting to a particular goal. Moreover, the task must be open-ended (heuristic), rather than having a single, obvious solution (purely algorithmic). Ultimately, a response or product is creative to the extent that it is seen as creative by people familiar with the domain in which it was produced.

The componential theory of creativity was articulated by Teresa Amabile in 1983. A theory designed to be comprehensively useful for both psychological and organizational creativity research, it describes the creative process and the various influences on the process and its outcomes. Two important assumptions underlie the theory. First, there is a continuum from low, ordinary levels of creativity found in everyday life to the highest levels of creativity found in historically significant inventions, performances, scientific discoveries, and works of art. The second, related underlying assumption is that there are degrees of creativity in the work of any single individual, even within one domain. The level of creativity that a person produces at any given point in time is a function of the creativity components operating, at that time, within and around that person.

The Components of Creativity

In the componential theory, the influences on creativity include three within-individual components: domain-relevant skills (expertise in the relevant domain or domains), creativity-relevant processes (cognitive and personality processes conducive to novel thinking), and task motivation (specifically, the intrinsic motivation to engage in the activity out of interest, enjoyment, or a personal sense of challenge). The component outside the individual is the surrounding environment—in particular, the social environment.

The theory specifies that creativity requires a confluence of all components; creativity should be highest when an intrinsically motivated person with high domain expertise and high skill in creative thinking works in an environment high in supports for creativity. Figure 1, from Amabile's 1996 book, *Creativity in Context*, presents a simplified depiction of the theory.

Domain-relevant skills. Domain-relevant skills include knowledge, expertise, technical skills, intelligence, and talent in the particular domain where the problem solver is working—such as product design or electrical engineering. These skills are the raw materials upon

which the individual can draw throughout the creative process—the elements that can combine to create possible responses and the expertise against which the individual will judge the viability of response possibilities.

Creativity-relevant processes. Creativity-relevant processes (originally called creativity-relevant skills) include a cognitive style and personality characteristics that are conducive to independence, risk taking, and taking new perspectives on problems, as well as a disciplined work style and skills in generating ideas. These cognitive processes include the ability to use wide, flexible categories for synthesizing information and the ability to break out of perceptual and performance "scripts." The personality processes include self-discipline and a tolerance for ambiguity.

Task motivation. Intrinsic task motivation is passion: the motivation to undertake a task or solve a problem because it is interesting, involving, personally challenging, or satisfying—rather than undertaking it out

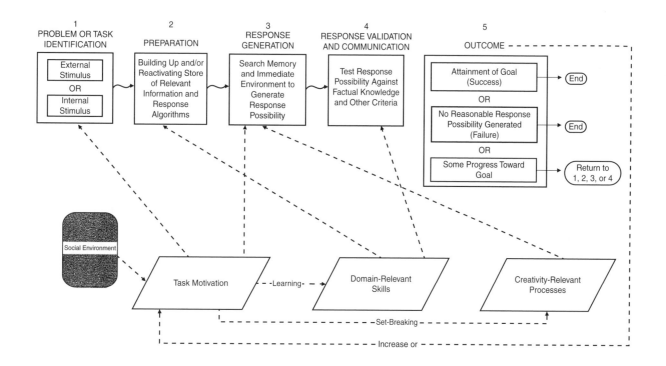

Figure 1 The Componential Theory of Creativity

Source: Amabile, T. M. (1996). *Creativity in Context* (p. 113). Boulder, CO: Westview Press. Copyright © 1996 by Westview Press. Reprinted by permission.

Note: Broken lines indicate the influence of particular factors on others. Wavy lines indicate the steps in the process (where large variations in the sequence are possible). Only direct and primary influences are depicted.

of the extrinsic motivation arising from contracted-for rewards, surveillance, competition, evaluation, or requirements to do something in a certain way. A central tenet of the componential theory is the intrinsic motivation principle of creativity: People are most creative when they feel motivated primarily by the interest, enjoyment, satisfaction, and challenge of the work itself—and not by extrinsic motivators. Because, as research has shown, salient extrinsic motivators can undermine intrinsic motivation, their presence or absence in the social environment is critically important. So, too, is the presence or absence of forces that can support intrinsic motivation.

The social environment. The outside component is the work environment or, more generally, the social environment. This includes all of the extrinsic motivators that have been shown to undermine intrinsic motivation, as well as a number of other factors in the environment that can serve as obstacles or as stimulants to intrinsic motivation and creativity. Research in organizational settings has revealed a number of work environmental factors that can block creativity, such as norms of harshly criticizing new ideas; political problems within the organization; an emphasis on the status quo; a conservative, low-risk attitude among top management; and excessive time pressure. Other factors can stimulate creativity such as a sense of positive challenge in the work; work teams that are collaborative, diversely skilled, and idea focused; freedom in carrying out the work; supervisors who encourage the development of new ideas; top management that supports innovation through a clearly articulated creativity-encouraging vision and through appropriate recognition for creative work; mechanisms for developing new ideas; and norms of actively sharing ideas across the organization.

An Example: E Ink

The story of the invention and early development of the first stable electronic ink serves as an interesting illustration of the components of creativity in an organization. In this instance, two organizations were involved: the Media Lab at the Massachusetts Institute of Technology (MIT) and E Ink, the company that was founded to develop and commercialize the product. Although many people have never heard of this company, most are familiar with the first e-readers, which relied on this product to produce the images of words on the screen: the Sony eReader and the Amazon Kindle.

The devices, marvels of the first decade of the 21st century, used a technology that was notably different from anything that had come before. Once the image was produced by electrical charges moving tiny black and white microcapsules of ink, the image remained stable without drawing additional power. Moreover, the image required no backlighting and could be viewed clearly at any angle—much like words on paper. These two innovative features were unmatched by other electronic inks available at the time.

The concept for this type of e-book, and the original idea for the microcapsules, came from Joe Jacobson, an MIT Media Lab physicist. Jacobson's domain expertise in physics combined with the domain expertise of the two students who worked with him to develop the ink. Barrett Comiskey and J. D. Albert brought their respective skills in the domains of networks and mechanical engineering to the task, gaining expertise in chemistry, optics, and electronics as they went along. Given the responsibility of carrying out most of the experimentation in the lab, Comiskey and Albert relied on their creativity-relevant processes to take a rapid-iteration Edisonian approach; they experimented with multiple variables with great frequency as they attempted to zero in on the correct formulation. From the summer of 1995, when Jacobson had the initial idea, through January 1997, when Comiskey and Albert created the first working prototype, the three were fueled by a strong intrinsic motivation to develop something both astonishing and practical.

The environment of the MIT Media Lab was highly conducive to the team's work. Housing physical and social scientists from a wide array of disciplines, the lab fostered cross-pollination of ideas. There was a high degree of psychological safety, where people spouted "wacky" ideas without fear of ridicule. Moreover, a range of resources facilitated experimentation. Finally, even undergraduates in the lab enjoyed a great deal of autonomy to follow their hunches.

The Components and the Creative Process

As depicted in the figure, all four of the creativity components influence the creative process. The process consists of several subprocesses: analyzing and articulating the exact nature of the problem to be solved, preparing to solve the problem by gathering information and improving any required skills, generating ideas for solving the problem, testing or validating the chosen solution, and communicating that solution to others. This sequence is not rigid; the subprocesses can occur in any sequence and will often recur iteratively until a creative outcome has been attained.

Consider again the example of E Ink. Jacobson was relaxing on a beach one day in 1995 when he finished the book he was reading and realized that he had no additional reading material. This *problem identification* initiated the creative process. Jacobson spent the rest of the afternoon coming up with the basic concept of an electronic book that would wirelessly receive a book's contents in digital form and translate those electrical impulses into images using two-toned conductive particles. This *response generation* was the first in a long series of ideas required for the invention. Jacobson's *preparation*, which enabled this idea, included his entire scientific education. Comiskey and Barrett drew on their own *preparation* in math and engineering and then supplemented that with additional learning in related areas—throughout the entire time they were generating and trying out new ideas in the MIT Media Lab.

Repeatedly, over the months they worked on the problem, Comiskey, Albert, and Jacobson would *test,* and fail to *validate,* an idea. Sensing that they were getting closer, however, they entered into the process again. Repeatedly, they came up with other ideas to try. Occasionally, they even partially *reconceptualized the problem* they were solving. When, at last, they had their working prototype, they *communicated* their success to potential investors whose resources they needed to develop an actual product. The company that they founded, E Ink, brought in more individuals with their own blends of domain-relevant skills, their own creativity-relevant processes, and their own high levels of task motivation. In many ways, the founders also re-created the work environment of the MIT Media Lab that had so strongly facilitated their own initial creativity.

Evolution

The componential theory of creativity was originally articulated in 1983 by Teresa Amabile as "the componential model of creativity." It has undergone considerable evolution since then.

In 1988, Amabile published an extension of the theory to encompass both creativity and innovation in organizations. The basic model of individual

creativity stayed the same, but the assumption was added that the same four components influence the creativity of teams working closely together. More importantly, a parallel set of components was proposed for innovation. According to the expanded theory, innovation depends on (a) resources in the task domain (analogous to domain-relevant skills at the individual level), (b) skills in innovation management (analogous to an individual's creativity-relevant processes), and (c) motivation to innovate (analogous to individual task motivation). These components constitute the work environment impacting individuals and teams.

In 1996, Amabile published a revision of the original model of individual creativity, in a book that included updates by doctoral students and research associates Mary Ann Collins, Regina Conti, Elise Phillips, Martha Picariello, John Ruscio, and Dean Whitney. Research conducted in the first decade after the theory's publication suggested an important modification of one of the theory's most basic tenets: the intrinsic motivation principle. Although many extrinsic motivators in the work environment do appear to undermine intrinsic motivation and creativity, some may not. If rewards or other motivators are presented in a controlling fashion, leading people to feel that they are being bribed or dictated to, the undermining effects are likely to occur. However, if rewards confirm people's competence (for example, by recognizing the value of their work) or enable them to become more deeply involved in work they are excited about (for example, by giving them more resources to do the work effectively), then intrinsic motivation and creativity might actually be enhanced. This process is termed *motivational synergy.*

In 2008, with Jennifer Mueller, Amabile published an additional modification of the theory based on new empirical evidence that the affective state can significantly impact individual creativity. In this modification, affect, which can be influenced by the work environment, in turn influences creativity-relevant processes.

Importance

Recognized as one of the major theories of creativity in individuals and in organizations, the componential theory has been used as a partial foundation for several other theories and for many empirical investigations. Amabile's earliest descriptions of the theory, in a 1983 article and a book the same year, have garnered nearly 2,000 citations in the academic literature. Of all of the theory's tenets, the most heavily disputed has been the intrinsic motivation principle. However, the majority of studies testing that principle have supported it—particularly when the notion of motivational synergy is taken into account. Although certain aspects of the theory remain unexplored empirically, research generally supports the inclusion of all three intraindividual components as well as the socioenvironmental component.

The Componential Theory in Context

The componential theory's basic elements, and the creative process it describes, are similar in the aggregate to other theories of creativity in both psychology and organizational studies, although with different emphases and somewhat different proposed mechanisms. At their core, all contemporary scholarly theories of creativity rely on the definition of creativity as a combination of novelty and appropriateness. Most theories describe a process by which an individual produces creative ideas, and most (but not all) include both skill and motivational elements. Some include the social environment.

The componential theory is distinctive in several respects: (a) its relatively comprehensive scope, covering skills and motivation within the individual as well as the external social environment; (b) its specification of the impact of the components at each stage of the creative process; (c) its emphasis on the social environment and the impact of that environment on the individual engaged in the creative process—particularly the individual's intrinsic motivation. Moreover, unlike other psychologically based theories of creativity, the componential theory was expanded to describe the process of organizational innovation; this expansion was based on a definition of innovation as the successful implementation of creative ideas within an organization. Thus, in later instantiations, the theory became truly multilevel, encompassing creativity in single individuals, teams, and entire organizations.

One shortcoming of the componential theory, as applied to organizations, is its focus on factors *within* an organization. Its failure to include outside forces, such as consumer preferences and economic fluctuations, limits the comprehensiveness of the theory in its current form. Moreover, the theory does not include the influence of the *physical* environment on creativity. Although recent research suggests that the physical environment has a weaker influence on creativity than the socio-organizational environment, the effect is still measurable.

Application in Organizational Settings

Perhaps most importantly for practitioners, many managers have relied on tools and techniques developed from the theory to stimulate creativity and innovation within their organizations.

The theory applies to any realm of human activity, with the basic components and processes and their mechanisms of influence remaining the same. However, certain elements of the model are likely to be particularly distinctive in organizations. The work environment component in organizations contains features such as team dynamics and top management behaviors that are unlikely to be as important, or even present, in nonorganizational settings. And it is likely that the creative process differs across realms of activity. In organizations, for example, the ways in which people identify problems or validate possible solutions are likely to be quite different from the ways in which those activities are carried out in the arts or in basic science laboratories.

Of the three intraindividual components, intrinsic motivation should be the most directly influenced by the work environment. (See Figure 1.) However, it is also important to note that the work environment undoubtedly has effects on domain-relevant skills and creativity-relevant processes, in addition to its effects on intrinsic motivation.

Teresa M. Amabile

See also Brainstorming; BVSR Theory of Human Creativity; Innovation Diffusion; Interactionist Model of Organizational Creativity; Investment Theory of Creativity; Psychological Type and Problem-Solving Styles

Further Readings

Amabile, T. M. (1983). Social psychology of creativity: A componential conceptualization. *Journal of Personality and Social Psychology, 45*, 997–1013.

Amabile, T. M. (1988). A model of creativity and innovation in organizations. In B. M. Staw & L. L.

Cummings (Eds.), *Research in organizational behavior* (Vol. 10, pp. 123–167). Greenwich, CT: JAI Press.

Amabile, T. M. (1996). *Creativity in context.* Boulder, CO: Westview Press.

Amabile, T. M., Conti, R., Coon, H., Lazenby, J., & Herron, M. (1996). Assessing the work environment for creativity. *Academy of Management Journal, 39,* 1154–1184.

Amabile, T. M., & Mueller, J. S. (2008). Studying creativity, its processes, and its antecedents: An exploration of the componential theory of creativity. In J. Zhou & C. E. Shalley (Eds.), *Handbook of organizational creativity* (pp. 33–64). New York, NY: Lawrence Erlbaum.

Dul, J., Ceylan, C., & Jaspers, F. (2011). Knowledge workers' creativity and the role of the physical work environment. *Human Resource Management, 50*(6), 715–734.

Sears, G. J., & Baba, V. V. (2011). Toward a multistage, multilevel theory of innovation. *Canadian Journal of Administrative Sciences, 28,* 357–372.

Simonton, D. K. (1999). *Origins of genius: Darwinian perspectives on creativity.* New York, NY: Oxford University Press.

Sternberg, R. J., & Lubart, T. I. (1991). An investment theory of creativity and its development. *Human Development, 34,* 1–31.

Woodman, R. W., Sawyer, J. E., & Griffin, R. W. (1993). Toward a theory of organizational creativity. *Academy of Management Review, 18,* 293–321.

Conflict Handling Styles

Conflict handling styles are behaviors that people use when they are involved in disputes with others. Conflict handing styles are sometimes called conflict strategies, conflict tactics, or conflict modes. People have preferences and tendencies to use certain conflict styles across different situations. Sometimes, differences between people (e.g., personality, sex, culture, moral development, emotional intelligence, social values) are related to the tendencies to certain conflict styles. However, managers can use any one of a variety of conflict styles that will be most effective given the circumstances. The fundamental aspects of conflict handling styles are described in the next section. It is also shown that thinking about conflict styles has evolved over time and how conflict styles continue to be an important part of management theory.

Fundamentals

The best approach to understanding conflict handling styles is to first understand conflict, then conflict handing, and then conflict management.

Conflict

Conflict exists in situations where one person or group wants something that may be different than what another person or group wants. In the conflict literature, the words *party* or *parties* refer to individuals or groups of people involved in conflict. Conflict exists because two or more parties engage with each other over their differences. There are many situations in the workplace where conflict can arise. For example, conflicts can arise over differences of opinion about how to allocate resources, the level of pay increases, who should be promoted, and so on. In the industrial relations tradition, conflicts arise between employers and labor organizations representing the workers. However, conflicts can also arise between employers and employees even when there is no labor union present. Moreover, conflicts can arise among and between managers at the same or different levels in the organization and among and between employees themselves.

Conflict Handling

Organizations are interested in finding ways to successfully handle conflicts. Sometimes, this is called *conflict management.* Negotiation is one process that can be used to handle or manage conflicts. In negotiation two or more parties voluntarily attempt to reach an agreement to resolve their differences. However, negotiation is a conflict management process but not a conflict handling style. Negotiation is a process during which conflict handling styles will emerge and be observed. Some negotiators may adopt one conflict handing style, and other negotiators may adopt another style.

Conflict Handling Styles

Conflict handling styles are best described as tendencies to engage with others in a particular way. For some scholars, conflict styles are thought of as ways in which parties communicate with others. However, conflict styles can also include nonverbal messages and strategies and tactics that go beyond interpersonal communication. Often, individuals tend to use the same conflict styles across situations and in encounters with different people. However, they can also choose to use different conflict styles in different situations. In fact, experts suggest that certain conflict styles should be used in some situations but not in others.

Although there are several different ways to measure conflict styles, the different methods tend to be based on the same or a similar two-dimensional theoretical perspective. The working definitions for the two dimensions in this perspective are most often derived from the early work of Robert Blake and Jane Mouton. That work theorized that individual management styles could be characterized by two dimensions: a concern for people and a concern for production. Later, those two dimensions morphed into two different concerns: a concern for self and a concern for others. Individuals can have varying degrees of concern (ranging high to low) about the levels of outcomes that they themselves will receive from the dispute. Those with high concern about their own outcomes will care a lot about what they will receive when the dispute is resolved. They tend to be assertive and aggressive. Those with low concern about their own outcomes care very little about what they will receive when the dispute is resolved. They tend not to be assertive or aggressive. Individuals can also have varying degrees of concern (ranging from high to low) about the levels of outcomes that the other person will receive from the dispute. Those with high concern for outcomes for others will care a lot about what the other person will receive when the dispute is resolved. They tend to be cooperative and accommodating. Those with low concern about the outcomes of others care very little about what the other person will receive when the dispute is resolved. They tend to be uncooperative and aggressive. The dominant perspective of conflict styles used by scholars conceptualizes conflict along these two dimensions—(a) concern for outcomes for self and (b) concern for outcomes for others—to identify five distinct conflict styles. Varying terms have been used to describe these five styles, including contend, avoid, compromise, accommodate, and collaborate, which can be summarized using the first letters of each word (CACAC).

Contend (also called contending, competing, forcing, dominating, win-lose). In this conflict style, individuals strive to get what they want, with little or no concern for the other party in the conflict. They are contentious and engage in competitive behaviors and tactics trying to force the solution that they want by dominating the interaction with the other party.

Avoid (also called withdrawing, inaction, avoiding, or lose-leave). In this conflict style, individuals seek to withdraw from or avoid the conflict by not dealing with the other person. They do so even though this may mean that they themselves will not benefit from the dispute. Neither they nor the other party receives a good outcome.

Compromise (also called compromising or sharing). In this conflict style, individuals make concessions and give in on some things in exchange for concessions or compromises from the other party in the dispute. Although the individuals' outcomes are not as high as they could be in either contending or collaborating styles, the parties are striving to achieve some form of mutually acceptable agreement.

Accommodate (also called accommodating, appeasing, obliging, smoothing, yielding, or yield-lose). In this conflict style, individuals yield or give in to the other party's interest and desires. They oblige the other party and appease them by giving them what they want, even though they themselves get very little or nothing in return.

Collaborate (also called collaborating, confronting, integrating, problem solving, or synergistic). In this conflict style, individuals work collaboratively with the other party in the dispute to create solutions which enable both parties to get more. The goal is that both parties can win. This conflict style can be thought of as the golden rule of conflict management since it is consistent with the idea that you should treat others as you would like to be treated.

Scholars have noted that these five CACAC conflict styles have been linked to two different conflict strategies: distributive and integrative. The linkage between conflict styles and distributive and integrative strategies is depicted in Figure 1. That figure shows a two-dimensional graph. The vertical dimension represents the degree of concern that one has for one's own interests and outcomes. The more concern that a party has for one's own interests and outcomes, the higher they are on the graph.

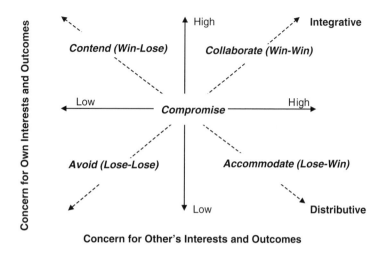

Figure 1   Conflict Styles Matched With Integrative and Distributive Strategies

Source: Author.

The horizontal dimension represents the degree of concern that one has for the interests and outcomes of the other party in the dispute. The further to the right on the graph, the more concern one has for the other party's interests and outcomes. Five CACAC conflict styles depicted on this graph represent the conflict styles that result from the combinations of the levels of parties' concerns for their own and the other party's interests and outcomes.

The dotted diagonal lines represent the integrative (win-win) and distributive (win-lose) dimensions. The Distributive dimension is depicted by the dotted line with two arrows at each end running from the upper left-hand corner to the lower right-hand corner. This dimension represents the degree to which one party wins and the other party loses in the dispute. Thus, if a party has chosen a contend conflict handling style, they are seeking to win for themselves while the other party loses, a win-lose situation. If they adopt a compromise conflict handling style, they would fall in the middle meaning that they would be willing not only to make compromises and get some of what they want for themselves but also to allow the other party to get some of what they want. If they adopt an accommodate conflict style, then they would give the other party what they want while receiving very little for themselves, a lose-win situation.

The Integrative dimension is depicted by the dotted line with two arrows at each end running from the lower left-hand corner to the upper right-hand corner. This dimension represents the degree to which both parties win. Thus, if a party has chosen a collaborative conflict-handling style, they are seeking to win for themselves and also for the other party. This would be considered a win-win situation. If they adopt an avoid conflict style, then neither party receives very much from the dispute, a lose-lose situation.

Evolution

An understanding of conflict styles can be addressed from two perspectives: measurement and normative. From the *measurement* perspective, conflict styles are viewed as categories of strategies or tactics that can typically be summarized into two, three, four, or five styles. Each of these styles can be thought of as multifaceted groups of behaviors that represent that particular conflict style. From the *normative* perspective, conflict styles can be evaluated in terms of the degree of appropriateness given a particular situation. Both the measurement and normative perspectives are discussed below.

Measurement

The earliest measures of conflict styles tended to focus on two or three styles (domination, compromise, and integration; cooperation and competition; nonconfrontation, solution orientation, and control). The 1980s saw the emergence of several models that included four conflict styles (e.g., yielding, problem solving, inaction, contending). However, the most popular and dominant perspective today tends to include a version of the five conflict styles described above.

Early measures required individuals to fill out or respond to questions on a printed questionnaire. More recent adaptations of these questionnaires have enabled individuals to answer questions online. For both the printed and online versions, the responses that individuals provide are typically used to report their preferred or typical conflict styles. One of the earliest and most popular measures of conflict styles follows the dual concerns model. That measure is known as the Thomas-Kilmann Conflict Mode Instrument (TKI). It is widely used in organizational training and managerial development. It is a proprietary instrument, but it can be used by obtaining permission from the TKI's publisher. It uses 30 questions that force respondents to pick one of two statements that they indicate are most like their own typical behaviors. Statements representing each of five conflict styles are matched in pairs with the other styles three times. A scoring metric is used to measure individual tendencies to engage in each of five conflict styles: competing, collaborating, compromising, avoiding, and accommodating. The proponents of this measure note that the forced choice format has the advantage of avoiding problems with social desirability bias by forcing individuals to pick between items. They also point out that the forced choice format was used to measure the relative frequency of the use of different conflict styles.

Another measure also followed the tradition of the dual concerns model and reflects concerns for self and concerns for others. The Rahim Organizational Conflict Inventory–II (ROCI-II) is also one of the most widely used conflict style inventories. Although it is proprietary, permission to use it can be obtained from its author. It has been repeatedly reported to have good psychometric properties (e.g., avoids range restriction, has good test-retest reliability, good Cronbach's alpha internal consistency reliability scores, etc.) and therefore is often used in academic research. It uses five-point Likert response scale anchors ranging from 5 (*strongly agree*) to 1 (*strongly disagree*). It contains 28 questions that are used to identify preferences for conflict styles: dominating, integrating, avoiding, obliging, and compromising.

Other scholars also followed the dual-concerns model to develop a Dutch version of a conflict styles inventory (Dutch Test for Conflict Handling, or DUTCH) that was subsequently published in English as well. This instrument has the advantage of using either 16 or 28 items, and it avoids mention of hierarchical relationships between parties and thereby may be more adaptable to many situations. It is reported to have good psychometric properties. It measures five conflict styles: yielding, compromising, forcing, problem solving, and avoiding.

Though continuing the tradition of the dual concerns model, a different method was used to develop a more parsimonious conflict style measurement instrument. That instrument is called a Conflict Handling Best-Worst Scale (CHBWS). This measurement instrument asks individuals to choose between single items a number of times. The items represent different conflict styles. The items are matched with other items representing different conflict styles. The respondents are asked to identify which of the items are the best and worst descriptions of themselves. A formula is used to calculate a metric score for each of several conflict styles (e.g., avoid, oblige, integrate, and dominate). This scaling procedure is more parsimonious than other methods and takes less time to administer.

Normative

Prior to the 1980s, it was common for scholars to express a normative (perspective) preference for a problem solving, or more collaborative, method as the best approach to conflict. More recent writings, however, stress that the situation will often dictate which conflict style is most appropriate. For example, it may not make sense to engage in problem solving when the other party is unable or unwilling to cooperate because of their current emotional state. Alternatively, in some situations, the issue may be relatively less important to you and therefore not worth fighting about it. In these situations, the best conflict style may be avoiding and not problem solving. Also, depending on the circumstances, competing or forcing might be the best conflict strategy. Thus, a better approach would be to strategically choose the particular conflict style that is most appropriate given the circumstances.

The process called principled negotiations made famous by Roger Fisher and William Ury can be linked to conflict styles in several ways. First, the principled negotiation method encourages parties to focus on interests and not positions. Conflict styles can be linked to interests of self and other as discussed above. Second, the principled negotiations method encourages parties to invent options for mutual gain. This is consistent with the collaborate conflict style. Third, parties often become frustrated or angry with their negotiation opponents, and this causes them to compete when they might be better off using a different conflict style. The problem of negative emotions can be avoided by following the principled negotiation methods of separating people from the problem and using objective criteria. When that happens, it may be more likely that parties will engage in a collaborate or compromise conflict style.

Importance

Conflicts in the workplace are ubiquitous. They occur on a daily basis as managers deal with employees, employees work with each other, and so on. It is in the very nature of human relationships that conflicts will occur as a result of the fact that people have different preferences, needs, and desires. The labor relations perspective illustrates conflict between employers and labor organizations, but that perspective is far too narrow and does not encompass the vast majority of day-to-day conflicts that arise in many workplace encounters.

Given the ubiquity of workplace conflict, it is not surprising to see that the topic of conflict handling styles continues to be important in the management literature. To illustrate the importance of the research regarding conflict styles, a search of major online databases was conducted to search for publications about conflict styles. The search resulted in 8,190 articles that included the phrase *conflict styles* in the text of the article. A Google search using the term *conflict styles* returned about 24 million websites. These websites ranged from university researchers to nonprofit organizations, to consulting firms offering services related to conflict styles and conflict management in the workplace. In addition, conflict styles continue to appear as key components of textbooks on organizational behavior. Many consulting firms use the commercially available conflict style measures, or they have created their own adaptation of these or similar measures for use in their management training and development programs.

Thus, it is clear that conflict styles will continue to be an important topic in the management literature well into the future.

Conflicts, both large and small, are frequent occurrences in the modern workplace. Therefore, the conflict styles model can help modern managers in many ways. First, managers should begin by recognizing that there is more than one way to deal with conflict. Understanding that there are different conflict styles can help managers to better deal with conflict. Thus, it may not always be best to compete or collaborate in every situation. On the other hand, sometimes competing or avoiding may be the best conflict style to use. Other situations may call for different conflict styles. Second, managers should become proficient in using different conflict styles so that they broaden their personal repertoire of managerial tactics. This will enhance their own personal competencies and enable them to effectively choose and use the best conflict style in any given situation. Third, recognizing that there are different conflict styles will enable managers to recognize the styles that are being used against them by others. When managers understand what styles they are facing from their opponents, they will be better able to choose how to effectively respond.

Following are several examples of how managers can benefit by choosing to use the best conflict style. Sometimes, encounters with subordinates will call for the use of collaborative win-win conflict tactics. This could occur during negotiations over wage and benefits. A collaborative solution that meets the interests of both the employer and employees could be to switch from a fixed wage or merit-based pay system to pay based on performance incentives (e.g., commissions, bonuses) so that as performance improves, both the employer and the employees win. However, there may be other times when avoiding or competing are most appropriate. If employees are too demanding or too difficult to deal with, the employer may choose to avoid dealing with them by subcontracting the work to another organization. If employees are requesting something that has a low cost to the employer but is important to employees, such as employee suggestion systems and employee recognition programs, it may be best to simply accommodate the employees' interests and give them what they want. Managers can also use different conflict styles during conflicts with other managers, customers, suppliers, or any stakeholder group. The bottom line is that understanding the conflict styles model gives managers a broader range of options to choose from when engaging in any type of conflict.

Richard A. Posthuma

See also Dual Concern Theory; Managerial Grid; Principled Negotiation; Theory X and Theory Y

Further Readings

Blake, R. R., & Mouton, J. S. (1964). *The managerial grid.* Houston, TX: Gulf.

Daly, T. M., Lee, J. A., Soutar, G. N., & Rasmi, S. (2010). Conflict-handling style measurement: A best-worst scaling application. *International Journal of Conflict Management, 21,* 281–308.

Hall, J. (1969). Conflict management survey: A survey of one's characteristic reaction to handling conflict between himself and others. Canoe, TX: Teleometrics International.

Holt, J. L., & Devore, C. J. (2005). Culture, gender, organizational role, and styles of conflict resolution: A meta-analysis. *International Journal of Intercultural Relations, 29,* 165–196.

Lewicki, R. J., Barry, B., & Saunders, D. M. (2010). *Negotiation* (6th ed.). Boston, MA: McGraw-Hill Irwin.

Ogilvie, J. R., & Kidder, D. L. (2008). What about negotiator styles? *International Journal of Conflict Management, 19,* 132–147.

Putnam, L. L., & Wilson, C. E. (1982). Communicative strategies in organizational conflicts: Reliability and validity of a measurement scale. In M. Burgoon (Ed.), *Communication yearbook* (Vol. 6, pp. 629–652). Beverly Hills, CA: Sage.

Rahim, M.A. (2004). *Rahim organizational conflict inventory.* Bowling Green, KY: Center for Advanced Studies in Management.

Thomas, K. W., Thomas, G. F., & Schaubhut, N. (2007). Conflict styles of men and women at six organizational levels. *International Journal of Conflict Management, 19,* 148–166.

CONTINGENCY THEORY

The core idea in contingency theory is that there is no one best way to lead people or to design an organization including its structure and processes. Rather, the central premise is that the choices which are made must fit the situation faced. This central idea is critically important to leaders and managers who make such decisions, as well as to the scholars who study leadership and organizations. It significantly informs the way they should think about these matters. In essence, they need to consider what actions will fit the situation they confront. The balance of this entry, will explain the basic ideas of this theory and a few of the several variants which have evolved since its introduction in the 1960s, as well as its impact on management theory and practice.

Fundamentals

As the theory was introduced and developed in the 1960s and 1970s, it had two fundamental premises. The first was that a contingent approach was a superior way to understand issues of organization and leadership compared to prior theories which argued that there was one universal approach to such matters (see, for example, Henri Fayol, Lyndall Urwick, or James D. Mooney and Alan C. Reiley). Because the basic contingency idea was investigated and proposed by many different scholars investigating different leadership and organizational phenomenon, the variables identified as important were heterogeneous. This was true with respect to those that were subject to managerial or leadership choice, as well as those variables upon which such choices were contingent.

Two examples illustrate this point. First is the work of Tom Burns and G. M. Stalker. While investigating manufacturing companies in Scotland, they noted that successful firms that were facing conditions of high certainty had organizations that they characterized as mechanistic (formalized structures and procedures, which facilitated the needed routines). However, successful firms that faced conditions that were uncertain (often requiring innovation) had organizations that Burns and Stalker labeled organic (less formality of structures and processes). Thus, in their view, the key determinant of organizational form was the uncertainty the organization faced. The appropriate organizational characteristics to consider were the extent to which the organization was mechanistic or organic.

A second example is the work of Fredrick Fiedler in the United States. It was Fiedler who first used the term *contingency* in describing his theory of leadership. He had used an instrument he developed to study leadership of groups and group performance under a variety of conditions. The conditional factors he looked at were the simplicity or complexity of the task, the preexisting conditions of feelings between the group and the leader in terms of liking or disliking, and the amount of traditional power available to the leader. Without going into detail, his principal finding was that different leadership styles were more effective under different group conditions.

These are but two of the early examples of contingency theory (see *Organization and Environment,* chapter 8, for examples of others). This early work was rapidly followed by other studies using the basic contingency approach. For example, in the realm of leadership, there were studies by Victor Vroom and by Robert Tannenbaum and Warren H. Schmidt, which are discussed below. Similarly, the examination of contingent organizational forms was expanded by the work of Joan Woodward and James D. Thompson. To underscore the diversity of factors which these studies identified as important, Woodward focused on the contingent relationship between manufacturing technologies and organization, and Thompson focused his work on the impact that different types of interdependence among subsidiary units had on other aspects of effective organizations.

While in retrospect all of these individual research efforts can be seen as contributing to what we call today contingency theory, the connections among this stream of work was first made in *Organization and Environment.* In this seminal book, Paul Lawrence and Jay Lorsch first reported on their study of the relationship between the environment and organizations of each of 10 businesses and its connection to business performance. The basic finding was that there was a contingent relationship between the extent to which each business had achieved both the needed differentiation between functional units and the necessary integration among them and business performance. For example, the plastic businesses which were involved in developing new technology needed both greater differentiation among their units, which ranged from research to manufacturing, and tighter integration among them. The study also explained the manner in which processes of conflict resolution and influence contributed to the fit between organizational form and environmental characteristics, such as uncertainty.

While many considered this work important because of the light it threw on matters of organizational design, it was significant also because it recognized that a contingency theory was emerging

to replace the earlier universal theories about leadership and organization. Without using Thomas Kuhn's term *paradigm,* the authors in their review of preexisting theory indicated that there was indeed a new paradigm for thinking about such matters.

This brief history of the foundations of contingency theory reveals first of all the primary commonality among these studies. The appropriate leadership or organization was contingent. Where there was not so much agreement was in the identification of the contingent factors and the choices to be made. In many of these studies and in the general understanding of the theory that has evolved over time, uncertainty of the task or the environment is often identified as the key contingent variable. However, as explained earlier, the different studies in fact also pointed to other contingent conditions. Similarly, while the leadership studies usually identified a continuum of directive to participative leadership style as the behavioral dimension appropriate to different contingencies, they were less uniform in identifying the contingent factors. Similarly, the studies of organizational form identified a wide variety of relevant environmental factors (uncertainty, environmental complexity, type of interdependence, etc.) and different organizational characteristics.

This meant and still means that using contingency theory requires that those who would do so must think carefully about the relevant variables and relationships, which determine the choices they can and should make. In this sense, while it is a theory which seems far superior to the universal theories which preceded it, using it requires a careful diagnosis of the specific situation.

This complexity of application is derived from the fact that the different approaches to contingency theory all have a common root in the recognition that organizations are complex social systems. The behavior of organizational members is shaped by and shapes the nature of the system. But for the organization to succeed, it must be able to meet the demands of the environment in which it exists. If this seems complex, it is!

This underlying notion of organizations as social systems is not unique to contingency theory. It also underlies other recent theories of organizations, such as resource dependence and population ecology. While the later theories are focused on different aspects of organizations and/or use different metaphors to describe organizations, they share with contingency theory the underlying notion that organizations are complicated social systems.

Evolution

In describing the fundamentals of contingency theory above, it was necessary to describe and explain its early history. The evolution of contingency theory has been hindered by the nature of the field of organizational behavior which has been its domain and which, as suggested above, is the study of very complex organizational systems. As the description of the early conceptions suggests, researchers and theorists who study organizational phenomena handle this complexity by being unconstrained in the use of concepts. Rather than using the concepts developed by others, they feel free and in fact rewarded for inventing new concepts. Thus, contingency theory has evolved, the underlying idea of alignment has persevered, and the concepts used have varied and multiplied. Take, for example, contingency theory applied to leadership. The original work was done by Fiedler. It was followed by studies by Tannenbaum and Schmidt and by Victor Harold Vroom and Philip W. Yetten. The later researchers chose to develop their own conceptions of leadership behavior and the variables which were determinants of effective leadership in different settings. In so doing, no attempt was made to build upon or refute Fiedler's work. This is the norm for those who study behavior in organizations. The consequence is that there are competing concepts and frameworks for understanding various phenomena within the broad umbrella of contingency theory.

For example, Tannenbaum and Schmidt saw leadership behavior on a spectrum from boss centered to subordinate centered. At one extreme, the boss made decisions and announced them, and at the other, the boss allowed subordinates to function within limits defined by themselves. The point on this continuum which was the best for effective leadership depended first on the leader's own personality: his value system, his own leadership inclinations, his confidence in his subordinates, and his feeling of security in an uncertain situation. It also depended on forces in the subordinates: their needs for independence, their readiness to assume responsibility, their tolerance for ambiguity, their interest in the problem at hand, the strength with which they identify with the goals of the organization, the necessary experience to deal with the problem,

and their expectations about sharing in the decision making. Finally, it depends on forces within the situation such as the type of organization and members' expectations about participation in decisions affecting their work; the historical effectiveness of the organization; the problem itself, especially its complexity; and the pressures of time.

Like Tannebaum and Schmidt, Vroom and Yetten used a spectrum of leadership, from autocratic to consultative to group based in which the group decided for itself. The contingent variables which determined which style would be most effective were determined by answers to seven questions. While these factors are similar to those used by Tannebaum and Schmidt, they tend to focus more on the nature of the problem itself and less on the nature of the leader or her subordinates. Thus, although both pairs of authors are proposing a contingent relationship between effective leadership and the situation, the specific variables are different. Unfortunately, there has been no work to reconcile and further test these approaches. A similar situation exists in the contingent approaches to organization structure, as we explained above. Different researchers focused on different contingent variables, such as degree of uncertainty, type of technology, and type of inter-unit interdependence. Similarly, they differed on the organizational properties which, if well suited to these externalities, would lead to effective performance.

In essence, the big idea of contingency burst on the field of organization studies in the 1960s, and it persists 50 years later. The problem, however, has been that the only attempt to bring these various studies together into a more unified whole has been the theoretical work of Lex Donaldson. In the broadest sense, Donaldson sees contingency theory as saying that the effect of one variable on another depends upon a third. Thus, if one considers *Organization and Environment*, the performance of an organization (a) in a given environment (b) depends upon achieving the requisite differentiation and integration. Thus, in Donaldson's view, contingency theory is about the relationship among organizational form, the organization's environment, and its performance in that environment, which is consistent with Lorsch's. However, contingency theory also applies to other aspects of organizational behavior, including leadership. Further, Donaldson's approach, which is to try to marry contingency theory with other theories—what he labels as organic theory and bureaucracy theory—may confuse the matter of what is contingency theory. According to Jay Lorsch, bureaucracy (with its roots in Max Weber's work in the late 19th century) was a universal theory—which, it was argued, applied to all organizations. In that sense, it is the opposite of contingency theory. As previously explained, organic theory, which Donaldson attributes to Burns and Stalker, is in Lorsch's judgment one of the earliest sparks of contingency theory. Treating it separately only complicates an understanding of the roots of contingency theory. In spite of these disagreements, Donaldson deserves immense credit for his efforts to explain contingency theory in a manner which he believes will stimulate its future development.

Importance

If one judges the importance of contingency theory in terms of the stimulation of major research studies using this framework, its impact would have to be assessed as modest. There have been few attempts to replicate the original studies just described or to test the theory with field studies of organizations. There are likely two reasons for this. First, scholars in organizations studies often believe they will be best recognized not for building on a prior work but for inventing new concepts. For academics, contingency theory signaled a new perspective on organizations. However, its impact has been moderated by forces in the profession that encourage proposing new theories rather than a systematic, cumulative extension of knowledge. The reasons for this are deeply rooted in the traditions of graduate studies and universities and are beyond the scope of this discussion. Second, the types of studies that led to the development of contingency theory are methodologically and practically hard to pull off. They require access to multiple organizations, the development of new research tools, and most importantly, the most important resource, the time of the researcher(s). For example, the research and writing of *Organization and Environment* required 4 years and at times the efforts of three scholars.

While there have been only limited attempts to launch new studies to refine and improve contingency theory, there are two other ways in which it has had significant impact. First, it has stimulated scholars studying different organizational settings looking for practical answers to view organizations from this perspective. The work of Christopher A. Bartlett and Sumantra Ghoshal in studying multinational companies is one such example; Rosaline K. Gulati's study of organizational design of large corporations is another. Jay Lorsch's work (with Tierney) studying professional service firms in the United States is another (*Aligning the Stars*), as is his investigation of corporate boards (*Back to the Drawing Board,* with Colin B. Carter). In all these examples and many others, contingency theory has been used as the lens through which to view organizational issues. What such work confirms is that contingency theory has become a practically relevant framework for understanding real managerial and organizational issues. Second, and perhaps the most compelling evidence of this fact, is the 7S model developed by the consultants at McKinsey & Company, which explicitly recognizes the importance of achieving an alignment between various internal organizational variables and company strategy for company success. This has since been incorporated in a host of other applied contingency frameworks, such as Robert Burgelman and Andrew Grove's strategy diamond framework, or, as it is sometimes referred to, "rubber-band" theory of alignment. Thus, what began as an academic theory has turned out to be an important practical tool.

This is undoubtedly one reason why, for example, *Organization and Environment* is one of the most widely cited books on organizational studies. Such citations and the studies mentioned above are evidence of what is the greatest importance and significance of contingency theory. Going back to its roots in the 1960s, it represented and still represents a paradigm shift in the way scholars and managers think about organizational theory. It is no longer adequate to look for one best way to solve a leadership, managerial, or organizational problem. One has to first recognize that, more often than not, "it depends," and try to understand the situation from several perspectives then muster the necessary flexibility and appropriate competencies to invent a solution which fits the circumstances. This is from a pragmatic, applied perspective. In essence, contingency theory has become what Fritz Roethlisberger called a "walking stick" for managers to guide them as they make decisions. From this perspective, the precise variables are not as significant as the broad perspective.

Jay W. Lorsch

See also Contingency Theory of Leadership; Expectancy
    Theory; Organizational Effectiveness; Organizational
    Structure and Design; Systems Theory of Organizations;
    Theory of Cooperation and Competition

Further Readings

Bartlett, C. A., & Ghoshal, S. (1989). *Managing across
    borders: The transnational solution.* Boston, MA:
    Harvard Business School Press.

Burns, T., & Stalker, G. M. (1961). *The management of
    innovation.* London, England: Tavistock.

Chandler, A. D., Jr. (1962). *Strategy and structure: Chapters
    in the history of the industrial enterprise.* Cambridge,
    MA: MIT Press.

Lawrence, P. R., & Lorsch, J. W. (1967). *Organization and
    environment.* Boston, MA: Harvard Business School
    Press.

Lorsch, J. W., & Tierney, T. J. (2002). *Aligning the stars:
    How to succeed when professionals drive results.*
    Boston, MA: Harvard Business School Press.

Peters, T. J., & Waterman, R. H. Jr. (1982). *In search of
    excellence: Lessons from America's best-run companies.*
    New York, NY: Warner Books.

Thompson, J. D. *Organizations in action.* (1967). New
    York, NY: McGraw Hill.

Woodward, J. (1958). *Management and technology.*
    London, England: H.M.S.O.

CONTINGENCY THEORY OF LEADERSHIP

The contingency theory of leadership stems from Fred E. Fiedler's extensive work on leadership effectiveness. He described how different types of leadership styles are required for different situations to achieve strong group performance. On the one hand, the theory posited three main contingency variables that shape favorability of the group-task situation for leaders in terms of how much influence or control they have over their followers; these are conceptualized along continuums of affective leader-group relations, task structure, and the leader's position power. On the other hand, leadership style is revealed by how a leader views his or her least preferred coworker (LPC) and is assessed as task oriented or relationship oriented. When these factors are viewed together, the effectiveness of high and low LPC leaders is seen to vary based on the situation

favorability—that is, leaders are most effective when their style fits the context. The contingency theory of leadership offers a midrange theory that is located between the universalist approach of "the great man theory" and individualist perspective with "everything depends." Fiedler's research findings created a significant shift away from universal trait theory's "one best way" approach to a more relative, "it depends" approach that identifies the most appropriate leadership styles for different situations. Research on the contingency theory of leadership grew rapidly with Fiedler's ideas making a significant contribution toward understanding leadership and inspiring additional contingency studies on different organizational phenomenon. Critiques and different research directions also arose as researchers looked to develop a more robust theoretical foundation to understand leadership and expand it into new frontiers. The following section will show highlights of Fiedler's major ideas and major ideas related to the contingency theory of leadership and will show developments focused on leadership behaviors, contingency variables, and their contributions to management research and practical applications.

Fundamentals

Fielder developed the first systematic contingency model for leadership which utilized the idea of a leader's least preferred coworker as a way of defining his or her leadership orientation. The contingency theory of leadership holds two important assumptions—(a) there is more than one best way to organize or behave and (b) any particular way to organize and behave does not apply in the same manner for all situations. An important premise of the contingency theory of leadership is that there is more than one way of leading to achieve positive organizational outcomes as contingency factors influence the need for different leadership behaviors. Fiedler's earlier approach to leadership effectiveness centered on determining leadership behaviors based on how a leader viewed their LPC. A theoretical assumption is that a leader's description of the LPC is a reflection of him or her and the leader's natural, relatively stable leadership style.

Fit is an important idea in the contingency theory of leadership because the definition, whether explicit or implicit, shapes theory development, data collection, and statistical analysis for empirical studies. Fit is a multidimensional concept that can refer to

(a) selection based on natural or managerial actions, (b) interaction based on linear relationship between context and design with impact on performance, and (c) systems based on internally consistent patterns of organizational context and structure to impact performance. The key is that fit between leadership style and contingency variables is positively related to leadership effectiveness and organization performance while a poor fit diminishes performance.

Leader Orientation and LPC Assessment

For Fiedler, leadership orientation is gauged with the Least Preferred Coworker (LPC) Scale assessment. To determine a leader's orientation, the LPC assessment asks the respondents to think of the person that he or she works least well with or had the most difficulty in completing a task and keep the person in mind when responding to 16 eight-point pairs of opposing positive or negative terms to describe the person. Examples of adjectives used to describe the LPC include pleasant-unpleasant, friendly-unfriendly, considerate-inconsiderate, kind-unkind, nice-nasty, and others. The more positively a leader scores his or her LPC, the higher the total score that identifies one as high versus low LPC leader. The scoring is a simple addition of the ratings for each adjective. A high LPC leader is seen as considerate, permissive, and nondirective compared to a low LPC leader who is seen as controlling, managing, and directive. Later, Fiedler shifted theory development from a behavioral to motivational approach to leadership. The high LPC leader employs a relationship approach with concerns for gaining prominence and self-esteem to motivate employees through interpersonal relationships. As a result, the high LPC leader is identified as relationship oriented. The low LPC leader is identified as most concerned with being successful regarding task responsibilities and therefore labeled as having a task-oriented leadership style. The designations indicating relationship-oriented (high LPC score) and task-oriented leadership (low LPC score) styles are presumed to be relatively stable predispositions that do not easily change over time.

Situational Variables

Contingency variables arise from both organizational and interpersonal contexts. Fiedler's leadership contingency model accounts for the group-task situation favorableness with three contextual variables—affective leader–member relations, task-structure, and leader's position power. Combined with leadership orientation, the additional three contingency variables make up eight distinct types of situations for a contingency perspective of leadership. According to Fiedler, the most important determinant of group-task situation, and the resulting impact on team performance, is the relationship between leaders and their followers. When leaders are liked and respected by followers, which inspires trust and loyalty, follow-through is more likely as compared with opposite sentiments, which can lead to apathy or, even worse, revolt under similar circumstances. The second most important dimension is task structure, which refers to the amount of precision in designing and organizing what and how tasks are completed. Four key elements of task structure that affect the favorableness of the situation are (a) degree of clarity in explicit job requirements, (b) variety in ways to complete tasks, (c) feedback of task results, and (d) existence of optimal task outcomes. Last, the dimension of leadership position power is the extent of authority and power a leader can leverage to direct, evaluate, reward, and discipline followers. Fiedler stated that the greatest level of group-task situation favorableness is a combination of good leader–member relations, highly structured tasks, and strong position power, whereas the least group-task situation favorableness is poor leader–member relations, unstructured tasks, and weak position power.

Contingency Relationship of Leader Effectiveness

In a nutshell, the central finding of Fiedler's theory is that task-oriented leaders perform relatively better in either very favorable or unfavorable group-task situations whereas relationship-oriented leaders perform relatively better in situations of moderate favorability. The specifics of the contingency theory of leadership is based on a relational matrix by superimposing continuums of situation characteristics against measures of performance to trace the relationship with different leadership styles and thus delineate the scope of a theoretical model. Fiedler described eight situations as follows (Note: LMX = leader–member exchange):

Situation No. 1: Good LMX, Structured Task Structure, and High Position Power

Situation No. 2: Good LMX, Structured Task Structure, and Low Position Power

Situation No. 3: Good LMX, Unstructured Task Structure, and High Position Power

Situation No. 4: Good LMX, Unstructured Task Structure, and Low Position Power

Situation No. 5: Poor LMX, Structured Task Structure, and High Position Power

Situation No. 6: Poor LMX, Structured Task Structure, and Low Position Power

Situation No. 7: Poor LMX, Unstructured Task Structure, and High Position Power

Situation No. 8: Poor LMX, Unstructured Task Structure, and Low Position Power

Multiple research findings indicated that low LPC leaders achieved positive outcomes in easy or difficulty situations such as shown in number 1, 2, or 8. High LPC leaders achieved positive outcomes in moderate situations such as in numbers 4, 5, and 6. A graphical representation of the eight situations employs increasing favorableness on the horizontal axis with the vertical axis mapping task-oriented to relationship-oriented leader style. A general upside down U-curve association is typically illustrated: starting on the lower left, the least favorable situations are best managed by task-oriented leaders; then, as favorability increases to moderate levels, there is an upward right shift of the curve to instead match relationship-oriented leaders; and finally, as favorability peaks, there is a downward right shift of the curve to again match task-oriented leaders.

Later reformulation of the contingency theory of leadership found that high LPC leaders acted in a task-oriented fashion in favorable group-task situations and in a considerate interpersonal manner in unfavorable group-task situations. At the same time, low LPC leaders acted with considerate interpersonal behaviors in favorable group-task situations but more structuring and task oriented in unfavorable ones. The findings from subsequent studies on the reformulation are mixed, but the developments have significant merit that makes a relevant contribution toward refining the model to better capture the underlying complexities of leadership behaviors.

Evolution

Contingency theory of leadership evolved from at least two significant influences. First, systems thinking shaped management research consideration of organizations as open systems. The concept of open systems drew attention to how contextual factors can impact organizations and, in turn, their leaders. This caused a fundamental shift away from established notions of the great man approach to leadership and its associated growing list of personality traits. Second, management researchers became increasingly skeptical about universal assumptions underlying just one best way for any theory. Fiedler's work stemmed from an industrial organizational psychology background. He had a heavy focus on seeking to understand leadership from data and evidence. Since the late 1960s, his contributions shifted attention from studying leadership traits and personal characteristics to the relationship between leadership styles and situational variables.

In the 1980s, Fiedler and Joseph Garcia built upon the earlier body of research on contingency theory of leadership by integrating two important components of intelligence and experience into cognitive resource theory (CRT). Leaders transmit their cognitive resources, such as intelligence and experience, embedded in plans, decisions, and strategies through directive behavior. Effective transmission is most effective under conditions of low stress and supportive group conditions. In particular, internal stress from the task or situation is more meaningful than from an external source.

Developing key concepts such as fit and context opened the floodgates to many other contingency frameworks and provided opportunities for contingency researchers to strengthen the theoretical foundation of leadership while at the same time expanding the number and scope of variables considered. The idea of fit in contingency theory evolved with expansions to related research streams on person-environment fit and person-supervisor fit. Also, the leader-follower congruence in personal characteristics developed with the notion of dyadic congruence in personality between a follower and a leader which leads to superior work outcomes.

The contingency theory of leadership inspired additional developments of ideas about the leader–member exchange (LMX). Leaders play an important role in shaping the relationship between employee personality and work outcomes. Recently, the dyadic relational approach is focused on the leader-follower behavioral interactions to examine their development process over time that leads to a unique relationship between the leader and each follower. Follower behaviors were accounted for as variations in the contingency relationship. Researchers began examining relational characteristics based on the leader's ability to interact with others. The research on LMX continues to grow with a variety of contingency variables related to role taking, role making, and role routinization. Hence, the contingent factors shift from an external contextual orientation to leadership and followership variables as contingency factors.

In addition to the contingency theory of leadership, Fiedler's stream of research also inspired other contingency theories. Subsequently, Robert House developed the path-goal theory of leadership which identified contingent variables of leadership behavior that are (a) environmental forces identified in task structure to encompass task autonomy and task scope and (b) subordinate characteristics to encompass expectations, role clarity, and satisfaction. Paul Hersey and Kenneth Blanchard developed situational leadership based on followers' task-relevant maturity and psychological maturity. As subordinates increased in their task-relevant maturity, leaders faced a decreasing emphasis on task-structuring leadership behavior and more on consideration type behaviors. Bernard Bass and James MacGregor Burns described transactional leaders who focused on incremental routine task activities and transformational leaders initiated substantial organizational change. Transactional leaders tend to align more with organizations with a defender strategy that have stable environments to reinforce the existing structure, culture, and strategies. Transformational leaders fit more with highly turbulent and uncertain environments and require a prospector or analyzer strategy. The substantial developments of additional contingency theories related to leadership illustrate the significant influence of Fiedler's work.

Importance

Support for the Theory

Over the last several decades, Fiedler's work spawned hundreds of research studies. Early research on the development of the contingency theory of leadership found substantial support in numerous studies with leaders from different professions and industry settings. Research studies drew evidence from groups as varied as corporate presidents, department store employees, hospital supervisors, research chemists, supervisors in electronic manufacturer, large heavy-equipment machinery plant operators, meat cutters in supermarkets, skilled craftsmen, military leadership, educational administrators, and many others. Hence, Fiedler's theory of leadership effectiveness demonstrated generalizability across many different sectors.

Research on the contingency theory of leadership also expanded into a number of related topics such as employee turnover, Maslow's hierarchy of needs, stress in threatening situations, diversity in language and culture, heterogeneous versus homogenous groups, organizational size, organizational climate, interacting and co-acting groups, perceived task competency of the leader and reward dependency of subordinates as well as the interaction of these two, performance evaluation, and many others. Two important topics bear further elaboration. One, threatening situations and stressful conditions create additional pressure for leaders that may alter their normal mode of behaviors. In nonstressful situations, high LPC leaders demonstrated more task behaviors than low LPC leaders, while low LPC leaders demonstrated more interpersonal relationship behaviors. In contrast with stressful situations, high LPC leaders exhibited more interpersonal relationship behaviors, and low LPC leaders exhibited more task behaviors.

A second topic to note is the difference between interacting and co-acting groups. Interacting groups have members engaged in completing tasks with high coordination and interdependent responsibilities, while co-acting groups have minimal interactions and coordination. Examples include interacting groups, such as electronic engineering groups, compared to supervisors in different hospital units. Research findings indicated that the different situations with variations in group-task situation favorableness continue to be consistent for leadership effectiveness for both groups.

Challenges to the Theory

While many research studies found supporting evidence for Fiedler's model of leadership effectiveness, there are criticisms of the theory and research. First, relationship-oriented and task-oriented leadership behaviors are positioned as dichotomous variables, but theoretical consideration is required to examine the two as independent variables from one another. The two are not necessarily opposite ends of a continuum but possibly two separate continuums. Some studies did not find the interpretation of LPC scores related to task versus relationship orientation. In addition, some studies use a sum total LPC score, while others employ an average LPC score. High

LPC scores could also be convoluted by greater cognitive complexity and intelligence, which is currently being explored with cognitive resource theory. Further, there is some debate around whether leaders have one primary, unchangeable style that must be fit to an appropriate situation or if (some) leaders can flexibly alter their style manifesting a range of task- or relationship-oriented behaviors depending on their assessment of the situation.

Second, another concern relates to the lack of consistency in the LPC assessment and the 18-item scale of leader position power across different studies. In some studies, Fiedler's scale for position power was substituted with organizational ranking. As a result, changes in measurement instruments make it challenging to achieve consistency in comparison across studies. Third, tests of statistical significance were frequently not applied to the correlations used to test the model because the number of observations for each of the eight situations tended to be small. Many studies have only three or four situations represented with only a relatively small number that tested for all eight situations of the model. Additional critiques include being too focused on short-run relationships, restrictive analysis of leadership process, lack of flexibility to address additional variables, and lack of integration with new variables.

Applications of the Theory

For practitioners, the contingency theory of leadership has important implications for leader assignments and leadership development. Managers need to diagnose the appropriate fit between leadership type and the needs of particular group-task situations in order to achieve optimal effectiveness. Given that Fiedler posited leadership style as relatively stable and unchanging—basically "fixed"—an important application lies in human resource management processes of attracting, selecting, hiring, and placing leaders with the appropriate orientation for their specific roles and/or adapting roles' descriptions and requirement based on current leadership. That is, managers must match the leader with the situation either by (a) personnel moves: changing leaders to fit the situation-role at hand, or, (b) job redesign: changing (or "engineering") the situation-role itself to fit the leader at hand. However, if a range of leadership behaviors can be learned and mastered, then there are implications for developing leaders with the flexibility and dynamic skill-set to continually evaluate the degree of appropriate fit in order to adapt to varying group-task situations.

Diana J. Wong-MingJi

See also Cognitive Resource Theory; Leader–Member Exchange Theory; Path-Goal Theory of Leadership; Situational Theory of Leadership; Theory X and Theory Y; Transformational Theory of Leadership

Further Readings

Ayman, R. Chemers, M. M., & Fiedler, F. (1995). The contingency model of leadership effectiveness: Its levels of analysis. *Leadership Quarterly*, 6(2), 147–167.

Drazin, R., & Van de Ven, A. H. (1985). Alternative forms of fit in contingency theory. *Administrative Science Quarterly*, 30(4), 514–539.

Edwards, J. R. (2008). Person-environment fit in organizations: An assessment of theoretical progress. *Academy of Management Annals*, 2(1), 167–230.

Fielder, F. E. (1967). *A theory of leadership effectiveness*. New York, NY: McGraw-Hill.

Fiedler, F. E., & Garcia, J. E. (1987). *New approaches to effective leadership: Cognitive resources and organizational performance*. New York, NY: Wiley.

Fry, L. W., & Smith, D. A. (1987). Congruence, contingency, and theory building. *Academy of Management Review*, 12(1), 117–132.

Howell, J. P., Dorfman, P. W., & Kerr, S. (1986). Moderator variables in leadership research. *Academy of Management Review*, 11(1), 88–102.

Jago, G. (1982). Leadership: Perspectives in theory and research. *Management Science*, 28(3), 315–336.

Peters, L. H., Hartke, D. D., & Pohlmann, J. T. (1985). Fiedler's contingency theory of leadership: An application of the meta-analysis procedures of Schmidt and Hunter. *Psychological Bulletin*, 97(2), 274–285.

Strube, M. J., & Garcia, J. E. (1981). A meta-analytic investigation of Fiedler's contingency model of leadership effectiveness. *Psychological Bulletin*, 90(2), 307–321.

CONTINUOUS AND ROUTINIZED CHANGE

Organizational change occurs when an organization makes a transition from its current state to some desired future state. In other words, change routinely occurs in the context of failure of some sort. Managing organizational change is the process of planning and implementing change in organizations in such a way as to minimize organizational inertia, while maximizing the effectiveness of the change effort. Change has been traditionally divided between change that is episodic, discontinuous, and nonroutinized and change that is continuous, evolving, and routinized. Change is also said to be of a quantum nature when many elements change in a major or minor way within a small interval of time. It is discontinuous or revolutionary only when quantum changes radically shape many elements of structure. Change is incremental or evolutionary when it is piecemeal and gradual, that is, when only a few elements transform either in a minor or a major way. The focus of this entry is on the latter form of change which is defined as *continuous and routinized change*.

Fundamentals

In the domains of strategy and organization theory, change is traditionally modeled as a punctuated equilibrium process in which long periods of incremental movement are interrupted by brief periods of cataclysmic adjustment. However, most change in organizations results neither from extraordinary organizational processes, or forces, nor from uncommon imagination, persistence, or skill, but from relatively stable, routine processes that relate organizations to their environments.

The term *continuous change* is used to group together organizational changes that tend to be ongoing, evolving, and cumulative. Such change is often viewed as consisting of small adaptations that, having emerged from improvisation and learning, may or may not accumulate and that occur because systems cannot maintain stability. These small adaptations are often viewed as part of ongoing modifications in organizational processes and practices, but this does not mean that the small changes are necessarily trivial or that they always remain small.

The view of organization associated with continuous change is built around recurrent interactions as shifts in authority—as tasks shift, continuing development of response repertoires, systems that are self-organizing rather than fixed, and ongoing redefinition of job descriptions. Images of organization that are compatible with continuous change include those built around the ideas of improvisation and learning. Literature on improvisation leverages jazz

as a metaphor to describe ongoing acts of adjustment that would permit the organization to be flexible while maintaining some degree of structural stability and routine. The image of organization built around the idea of learning is one of a setting where work and activity are defined by repertoires of actions and knowledge and where learning itself is defined as a variation in an organization's response repertoire. Another important retention-learning mechanism is *organizational routines* defined as repeated patterns of behavior that are subject to change if conditions change.

One of the central issues regarding continuous change is that of continuity itself. Issues of continuity are associated with the concept of organizational culture. Culture is important in continuous change because it holds the multiple changes together, gives legitimacy to nonconforming actions that improve adaptability and adaptation, and embeds the know-how of adaptation into norms and values.

The level at which continuous change occurs provides a dimension for classifying theories about continuous organizational transformation. Incremental or continuous change can be firm level or industry level. Theories of continuous change at the firm level are termed *adaptation theories,* and they maintain that firms track their environments more or less continuously to adjust to them purposively. The two most common mechanisms of adjustment are the *incrementalist approach* and the *resource dependence model.* The former implies that strategists experiment with new products, structures, and processes. Successful variations are institutionalized in firms' structural designs and product-market domains. The latter mechanism of organizational adaptation at the firm level is provided by the resource dependence model. Here, organizational adaptation to environmental uncertainty is reached through active organizational management of resource flows and interdependencies.

Models addressing how industries undergo continuous change are defined evolution models and comprise population ecology and institutional isomorphism. Both models contend that although individual firms are relatively inert, forces within the industry push firms to align to incremental changes which eventually increase the homogeneity of firms over time. The ability to change continuously is also a critical factor in the success of firms. Many firms compete by changing continuously. Rapid and continuous change, especially by developing new products, is not only a core competence, but also it is at the heart of a firm's culture. A classic case is Hewlett-Packard, which changed from an instruments company to a computer firm through rapid, continuous product innovation, rather than through abrupt, episodic change.

In conclusion, the key characteristic of continuous change is the assumption that revolutions are not necessary to accomplish organizational development. Episodic change is driven by inertia and the inability of organizations to keep up, while continuous change is driven by alertness and the inability of organizations to remain stable. Continuous and routinized change can be viewed as an ongoing mixture of reactive and proactive modifications, guided by purposes at hand, rather than an intermittent interruption of periods of convergence.

For managers seeking to achieve effective transformations within their organization, one possible approach is shifting their focus from "change" to "changing." This would imply a switch from a static, event-paced to a dynamic, time-paced approach to change that addresses past, present, and future time horizons and the transitions between them.

Leonardo Corbo

See also Institutional Theory; *Kaizen* and Continuous Improvement; Punctuated Equilibrium Model; Quantum Change; Strategies for Change

Further Readings

Brown, S. L., & Eisenhardt, K. M. (1997). The art of continuous change: Linking complexity theory and time-paced evolution in relentlessly shifting organizations. *Administrative Science Quarterly, 1,* 1–34.

March, J. G. (1981). Footnotes to organizational change. *Administrative Science Quarterly, 26,* 563–577.

Pettigrew, A. M., Woodman R. W., & Cameron K. S. (2001). Studying organizational change and development: Challenges for future research. *Academy of Management Journal, 44,* 697–713.

Tsoukas, H., & Chia, R. (2002). On organizational becoming: Rethinking organizational change. *Organization Science, 5,* 567–582.

Weick, K. E., & Quinn, R. E. (1999). Organizational change and development. *Annual Review of Psychology, 50,* 361–386.

COOPTATION

The word *cooptation* has many definitions, but the most common refers to the election of representatives who, as a result, are absorbed or assimilated by the electing governing body. Cooptation is also used in management and organization studies to describe the influential processes that often lead to outcomes that are neither planned nor desired. Cooptation processes can, moreover, divert an organization's goals in ways that are objectionable to the organization's principals. The principals may be the organization's owners, founders, and/or community representatives who generally control the overall policy making. Typically, other organizational actors, for example, managers, employees, or various external partners, undertake the cooptation process, which may be either formal or informal. The American sociologist Philip Selznick is recognized as the primary developer of cooptation theory. This entry explains its foundation, development, and relevance today.

Fundamentals

Organizations are tools their founders use to achieve certain founder-defined goals. The root word for "organization" is the Greek word for tool: *organon.* However, for many and varied reasons, frequently organizations do not achieve their goals. Their goals may be unrealistic, their competition too stiff, and/or their resources inadequate. Another reason, and the one of particular interest here, is the influence that causes the organization to divert its focus from its original goals. Such diversions may be the result of the process of cooptation when some stakeholder, either external or internal, exerts influence over organizational policy.

There are two main types of cooptation: formal and informal. Formal cooptation may result when external stakeholders, for example, nongovernmental organizations or local communities, have representatives on an organization's board of directors and can thus influence its policies. Informal cooptation may result when internal stakeholders, for example, professional groups, agents, or managers, sidetrack and/or reformulate organizational goals.

The Tennessee Valley Authority (TVA) Case

The theoretical concept of cooptation in management studies builds primarily on Philip Selznick's classic 1949 book, *TVA and the Grass Roots: A Study in the Sociology of Formal Organization*. The U.S. Congress founded the Tennessee Valley Authority (TVA) in 1933 as part of Roosevelt's New Deal. The purpose of the TVA was to address economic, social, and environmental development problems in the catchment area of the Tennessee River. The TVA was a new kind of legislative body based on democratic planning and grassroots participation by poor and underdeveloped regions that suffered from economic underdevelopment, soil erosion, deforestation, and malaria infection.

However, as Selznick described, the grassroots movement had only a modest influence on the TVA. Grassroots participation was instead used as a protective ideology for activities that were more influenced by the nearby land grant colleges and by the U.S. Farm Service Bureau. The former was given responsibility by the TVA for the project's research and education; the latter employed its extensive network of agricultural agents to reach the farmers affected by the TVA programs. Because the interests of these external stakeholders were aligned with the vested and wealthy community interests, directly and indirectly, they exerted a significant influence on policy- and decision making in the TVA.

The cooptation in the TVA was both formal and informal. It was formal in that the external stakeholders held seats on the governing TVA body. It was informal in that some TVA officials had connections with these stakeholders. For example, one TVA executive was a former president of the University of Tennessee. Moreover, some professional groups, in particular the TVA's own department of agricultural experts took an active role in the cooptation with their opposition to the public ownership of land that was a fundamental mission of the TVA. By this opposition, they showed their support for the wealthy farmers of the region.

Consequences and Implications of Cooptation

As an organization, to some extent, the TVA failed to fulfill some of its original goals: the support of farmers' cooperatives and poor Black farmers and the protection of public recreational sites and wildlife areas. Instead, the TVA developed in the postwar period as a specialized utility in the energy sector. With its fifty or so power plants and hydroelectric dams, the TVA continues to be the largest public power utility in the United States after almost 80 years since its inauguration and despite many political controversies.

Although cooptation is generally regarded as an undesirable phenomenon, it can also have positive consequences for an organization. Through fostering commitment and strengthening legitimacy, cooptation may improve relationships and promote cooperation with various stakeholder groups. Thus, cooptation may be the necessary price to pay in order to gain the support of external and internal stakeholders. When Republican administrations criticized the TVA in the 1950s and 1960s, industrialists, bankers, and farmers on power-distributor boards vigorously defended its existence and its operations. Thus, the cooptation process moved in both directions.

One interpretation of Selznick's TVA analysis is that organizational actors may take actions that not infrequently result in unanticipated consequences. Selznick's study, which management scholars and commentators often cite, has brought an actor-oriented perspective to the research on theories on the structure-agency relationship. This perspective suggests that actors are subject not only to structural influence; often, they also reveal skills in agentic action. For students of management, Selznick's book on cooptation helps us understand the difficulty in controlling organizations when managers, professional groups, and/or partners also bring their goals to organizations. The existence and outcome of such co-optive processes deserves special investigation and attention by both management practitioners and management researchers.

Stefan Tengblad

See also Agency Theory; Circuits of Power and Control; Competing Values Framework; Cultural Values; Individual Values; Institutional Theory; Patterns of Political Behavior; Strategy-as-Practice

Further Readings

Couto, R. A. (1988). TVA's old and new grass roots: A reexamination of cooptation. *Administration & Society, 19,* 453–478.

Oliver, C. (1991). Strategic responses to institutional processes. *Academy of Management Review, 16*(1), 145–179.

O'Toole, L. J., & Meier, K. J. (2004). Desperately seeking Selznick: Cooptation and the dark side of public management in networks. *Public Administration Review, 64*(6), 681–693.

Selznick, P. (1949). TVA and the grass roots: A study in the sociology of formal organization. Berkeley: University of California Press.

Suchman M. C. (1995). Managing legitimacy—Strategic and institutional approaches. *Academy of Management Review, 20*(3), 571–610.

CORE COMPETENCE

A broad management term that is often synonymous with what an organization does particularly well, *core competence* in its purest sense is a firm-specific collection of skills, insights, and capabilities that represent the product of long-term accumulated knowledge, organizational learning, and focused investment. Although most often associated with management researchers C. K. Prahalad and Gary Hamel in their 1990 landmark study on enduring, successful organizations to refer to those unique and hard-to-replicate knowledge-based assets that lay the groundwork for competitive advantage, the term *core competence* over the past two decades has become widely used in management jargon and in the popular press to mean almost anything from a profitable core business to a firm's particular way of doing something. As a result, application and use of this term has significantly deviated not only from the pioneering authors' original conceptual intent but also from established nomenclature used in the strategic management literature. This entry is designed to provide an overview of how the term fits within the context of recent research streams on the topic, while also examining some popular conceptions and use of the term. The entry is divided into three sections: anatomy of a core competence, the theoretical evolution of core competence, and the contributions to management theory and practice.

Fundamentals

The origin of the term *core competence* is perhaps best associated with Prahalad's and Hamel's breakthrough examination of how select firms built very deep sources of competitive advantage that endured over time. Around the same time, an emerging management theory known as the *resource-based view of the firm* surfaced in academic studies of firm-based competitiveness. The resource-based view struck a responsive chord among researchers and practitioners because it argued that core competencies are a valuable firm-based resource that enables the organization to distinguish itself from its rivals in important ways. This perspective views each firm as a unique bundle of resources and assets, of which knowledge, skills, and capabilities are among the most important, durable, and less subject to competitor imitation. Although investment in physical assets and new technologies can provide an initial source of competitive advantage, building knowledge-based assets provides more sustainable advantage based on the firm's underlying capacity to learn and apply new insights and skills. In this sense, a core competence emerges from the culmination of a long period of learning and investment that creates an asset which enables the organization to innovate and compete effectively in the marketplace. As such, building core competencies based on knowledge and learning in turn influences the firm's growth, evolution, and even its strategic choices. Some researchers have described this core competence—strategy linkage—as part of a larger evolutionary theory of the firm, whereby earlier competence-building efforts shape and guide the firm's subsequent growth paths.

Although there are numerous research papers that have developed various perspectives on core competencies, ultimately a core competence is composed of (a) the firm's knowledge base, (b) dynamic routines that lay the groundwork for strong firm capabilities, and (c) a high degree of "path dependence" that shapes the firm's evolution.

The Firm's Knowledge Base

A number of researchers from the resource-based view have noted that firms are "repositories" (or "reservoirs") of knowledge that lay the foundation for value creation. In fact, some academic papers have further refined and developed the idea that the economic basis of the firm depends on how well it creates and utilizes such knowledge to achieve distinction from its competitors. This "knowledge-based view of the firm" asserts that the depth of accumulated knowledge is the basis for sustainable competitive advantage and that differences in knowledge among firms can largely explain the differences in firm-level competitiveness. From this perspective, the nucleus of any core competence is a set of insights and knowledge that underpins how the firm approaches innovation of new products, processes, and technologies that build competitive advantage. Presumably, since each firm's core competencies remain distinct from those of its rivals, these assets help erect barriers to imitation from other firms. Over time, firm-specific knowledge and skills enable the organization to apply its core competence in new ways as market opportunities evolve.

In general, the firm acquires knowledge by learning from its external environment and by systematically developing internal insights gained through experimentation and experience. The concept of knowledge is exceptionally broad and can include everything from quality control practices to understanding customers' needs to extremely intricate methods and techniques needed to engineer cutting-edge products and processes. New technologies in themselves, however, do not create competitive advantage; rather, they are the "seeds" that provide the direction for learning and absorbing new types of knowledge. It is important to note that not all types of knowledge contribute to building core competencies equally.

Generally speaking, firms possess two broad types of knowledge: *explicit* (also known as codified) and *tacit*. Explicit knowledge is that which can be written down, explained, and understood by anyone (inside or outside the firm). Explicit knowledge is "transparent" in the sense that it can be widely understood and disseminated anywhere (e.g., blueprints, basic product designs, circuit diagrams, recipes). Tacit knowledge, on the other hand, is highly dependent on organizational context—that is, it is learned and understood by people who work closely with it on a deeply personal manner. Tacit knowledge is insight and experience that is often highly context specific to the firm—in other words, it is deeply rooted in the firm's practices and methods, interaction among members, and cumulative application of ideas to products and processes over time. For example, a particular way of defining and solving problems, craftsmanship, artisan skills, and mastery of a complex technique or method represent various examples of tacit knowledge. In its simplest sense, tacit knowledge is a combination of "know how" with "know why" and is gained through learning-by-doing, rather than through distant or casual observation. Thus, tacit knowledge is deeply rooted in the firm's practices, methods, and interaction among members and is hard for nonmembers to understand, absorb, and duplicate. As a vital component of a firm's core competence, tacit knowledge plays a major role in erecting barriers to imitation and thus building sustainable competitive advantage.

Dynamic Routines and Capabilities

The interaction of explicit and tacit knowledge is unique to each firm and drives the second major component of a core competence—that of dynamic routines and capabilities. Some management researchers have defined *dynamic routines* as recurring, interactive patterns of behaviors or practices within the firm that have become increasingly specialized and understood only by the firm's members. In particular, firms cultivate dynamic routines as they steadily learn and refine their sources of knowledge (increasingly tacit) through "learning by doing" that becomes part of the firm's social fabric. Consequently, dynamic routines represent the culmination of knowledge that is shared and embedded among people and groups within the organization, thus, rendering them context specific also. Thus, the firm's knowledge and experience is then "imprinted" onto dynamic routines that provide the guidance and steps to accomplish important activities. Dynamic routines store accumulated knowledge and help the firm manage highly complex phenomena and in some ways become an automatic response mechanism, such as an organizational algorithm or heuristic, which enables the firm to perform multiple tasks. For example, endeavors such as product development, engineering, building customer intimacy, and quality management all represent value-creating activities—each of which is dependent on numerous dynamic routines to guide and coordinate the tasks of many people. Often, organizational members will be working with one another, working in ways that share ideas, insights, and even metaphors that are all but impossible for nonmembers to truly grasp. As such, dynamic routines are collective in nature, based on shared experiences, and therefore serve to shape many organizational processes.

Dynamic routines, in turn, give rise to a broader construct—that of *dynamic capabilities*. From the academic literature, dynamic capabilities represent an amalgam of dynamic routines that enable the firm to achieve a new strategic posture or configuration in the wake of environmental change. These capabilities reflect the firm's long-term knowledge accumulation and evolution. Thus, dynamic capabilities represent the total sum of the firm's dynamic routines that enable the organization to adapt to industry and market developments to preserve competitive advantage. Knowledge, accumulated and embedded in the firm's people and practices, gives rise to dynamic routines, which correspondingly provide the inputs for dynamic capabilities. These dynamic capabilities provide the substrate for core competence formation and refinement. Core competencies are the cumulative product of knowledge, routines, and capabilities. But competencies by themselves do not automatically confer a long-term advantage; the firm must invest considerable time and sums into organizational learning to reinforce and refresh the firm's knowledge base. While a firm's core competencies drive distinction from rivals, focused learning remains vital to maintain and upgrade the competencies' vibrancy.

Path Dependence

Core competencies are the result of investment and learning that evolved from previous time periods. The accumulation of knowledge and dynamic routines and capabilities thus reflect a highly path-dependent process. *Path dependency* means that firms develop their competencies over a long and specific pattern over time. This process suggests that had a firm undertaken a different path to learn and acquire its knowledge base in earlier time periods, then its core competencies would also have evolved differently. Therefore, competence-building efforts represent a continuous, ongoing, evolutionary process that directly link, past organizational learning efforts and accumulated knowledge from earlier time periods with the state of current core competencies. The strategic implication is that each firm, by cultivating its own unique path of learning and knowledge accumulation, will in turn shape and constrain its evolutionary growth path for the future.

This vital characteristic of path dependence has strong ramifications, especially since competence-building efforts produce an asset that is extremely specialized and durable. Since core competencies are a context-specific, firm-unique mixture of knowledge, routines, and capabilities whose value cannot be easily calculated by outsiders, they are also "opaque" in that it is difficult for competitors to imitate them as well. However, path dependence also suggests that the firm's organizational learning is likely to become more efficient over time as it is focused on new sources of knowledge related to

the firm's competence base. A well-developed and established core competence enables the firm to better understand developments and new technologies related to its knowledge base than a firm that lacks a similar competence. Path dependence thus can enhance a firm's ability to search for new ways to improve its competence's application to future new products and processes.

Evolution

From Rudimentary Idea to a Pillar of Strategic Management

The central notion that an organization should devote its strategic planning and growth to those endeavors that revolve around a distinctive set of activities traces its roots back many decades, at least in the context of the modern management literature. The first stage of knowledge development on core competence has a strong *exploratory* tone to it. Perhaps first discussed at length by Kenneth Andrews in his pioneering work on the concept of corporate strategy, the compelling superiority of a core competence-driven strategy was empirically demonstrated by Richard Rumelt in his landmark 1973 study on corporate diversification strategy. In the early 1980s, the attraction of a competence-driven strategy again manifested itself in Peters and Waterman's 1982 study on excellent companies, whereby a key performance driver is the firm's "sticking-to-its-knitting" in developing long-range plans.

As the academic literature evolved toward rigorous and testable *empirical* analysis, researchers of a series of critical studies further analyzed and dissected corporate-level financial performance. Throughout much of the 1980s, numerous academic studies on corporate strategy and diversification (e.g., the seminal works of Robert A. Pitts, Richard Bettis, Michael A. Hitt, Robert Hoskissonm, and others) tested and reinforced the central notion that corporate strategies based on a sustained and coherent pattern of shared resources and knowledge among business units contribute to superior financial performance. Along a similar vein, these researchers also discovered that firms' internal development of businesses offered greater opportunities to build and reinforce a core competence, as opposed to growth via external mergers and acquisitions.

The late 1980s and 1990s witnessed a further blossoming of academic studies as new theories spawned a *knowledge-based view* of core competence and the firm. Perhaps first initiated by Hiroyuki Itami's 1987 work on the pivotal importance of "intangible assets" and their contribution to sustained organizational performance, the core competence concept served as an integral part of the larger *resource-based perspective* of the firm. The confluence of Prahalad and Hamel's 1990 study with the resource-driven view of Jay Barney triggered a number of invaluable papers throughout the next 10 years. Outstanding works by researchers such as Ingemar Dierickx and Karel Cool, Berger Wernerfelt, David Teece, Gary Pisano (to name just a few) contributed papers that share a common theme—attempting to deepen our understanding of how competences are formed and shaped over time, as well as to study the linkage between competence formation and key organization design parameters. Further incisive research introduced and assimilated a number of related organizational theories to expound on core competence, including tenets from organizational learning, systems thinking, and organizational inertia.

Core Competencies and Core Rigidities

As described earlier, the key characteristics of a core competence—knowledge, dynamic routines and capabilities, and path dependence—make this asset very specialized. A high level of specialization, however, also poses a significant risk that a core competence can become a "core rigidity." In a 1992 seminal paper by Leonard-Barton, a core rigidity represents an overreliance on a capability, technology, methodology, marketing approach, or other former organizational strength that paradoxically can also become a hindrance to organizational change as the firm faces new environmental developments. This inability to adapt is known as *organizational inertia*. As such, because core competencies are deeply interwoven with the firm's dynamic routines and social interactions among members, they can actually impede the learning of new sources of knowledge and skills, especially if new technologies, ideas, or product development methodologies are significantly different or "disruptive" to the firm's existing core competencies. Path dependence that shapes and guides current knowledge accumulation also constrains learning about new technologies and opportunities far afield from the existing core competence. Existing core competencies "locked in" by path dependence also can "lock out" opportunities

to learn new sources of knowledge. As inertia sets in, the value of existing core competencies can decline as rivals develop new sources of knowledge and capabilities that lead to future breakthrough products. If organizational learning efforts become increasingly focused on enhancing the firm's existing core competencies, there is a correspondingly greater risk that the firm can be blindsided by subtle but serious changes in market demand, potential technological obsolescence, or other external challenges to its competitive advantage. Thus, management must strike a careful strategic balance between "exploring" new sources of knowledge that can become new future competencies and "exploiting" existing competencies along well-defined technological trajectories.

Core Competencies, Organizational Learning, and Alliances

Because core competencies are based on knowledge that is often highly tacit, each firm must engage in focused organizational learning that creates its own path dependent, differentiated accumulation of skills and sights. In general, organizational learning can occur through a combination of internal and external efforts. Examples of internal efforts include experimentation with new product designs, formal research and development (R & D) programs, continuous improvement initiatives, as well as the development of proprietary processes and patents that build distinctive sources of advantage. However, external learning through interfirm relationships (e.g., strategic alliances, coproduction agreements) can prove just as valuable in helping firms learn new knowledge and competencies. Because many types of strategic alliances bring firms closer together to jointly develop new products and processes, they can also serve to transfer skills and insights between firms as well. Thus, strategic alliances can serve as vehicles for firms to absorb and internalize knowledge from their partners; external alliances work in tandem with internal developmental efforts to "parallel process" the flow of information and knowledge to accelerate competence-building efforts. Alliances can help a partner "short circuit" the learning process and time required to accumulate its own knowledge and skill set.

The long-term impact and risks of alliances to facilitate competence-building cannot be overstated. In particular, since tacit knowledge is embedded in the dynamic routines and social fabric of the firm, strategic alliances can enable firms to learn their partner's skills through day-to-day contact between managers and key technical personnel. Tacit knowledge cannot be learned through more distant, arms-length relationships, since it is opaque and requires learning by doing. Yet some firms will utilize strategic alliances in an apprentice-like relationship to get very close to their partner's core competencies and to learn as much as they can, often from an unwitting partner. This kind of close and intimate contact generates very significant risks for a firm unaware of its partner's strategic intent and desire to learn. Such close contact enables a partner to gain exceptional access and insight into another firm's internal processes and dynamic routines. A firm's opaque and unique knowledge base becomes "transparent" to a partner that is intricately involved with the firm's operations and organizational processes. In the worst case situation, strategic alliances can ultimately result in one partner "hollowing out" another partner's core competencies and technologies thereby leaving it completely dependent on the predatory partner. For example, many U.S. firms during the 1980s and 1990s ceded technological leadership to their Japanese and South Korean partners in such wide-ranging industries as consumer electronics, automobiles, robotics, machine tools, semiconductors, flat-panel displays, thin-film transistors, and imaging. U.S. companies, for the most part, viewed strategic alliances as convenient outsourcing arrangements from which to gain access to lower cost products and components; their East Asian partners viewed these relationships as opportunities to learn and upgrade their internal competence-building initiatives. Thus, firms that do not conceive strategic alliances as "races to learn" or "competence-based competition" are likely to find that their partners could learn more knowledge from them than they had anticipated. Alliances can result in a shrewd partner becoming a direct competitor after it has absorbed and internalized the firm's distinctive set of knowledge and competencies.

Importance

As noted from the above discussion, core competence captures a very rich, intricate, and complex theory underpinned by a resource or knowledge-based view of the firm. Throughout the past two decades, the term *core competence* has been used in numerous ways such that it has now become part of today's modern business vernacular. In many instances, the term *core competence* has become almost synonymous with any number of different meanings. However, the term *core competence* conjures up a plethora of different concepts for the discerning management reader. For the academic audience, core competence has evolved into a bedrock of strategic management thinking, providing much "gravitas" for both construct development and empirical testing. One cannot think about core competence without considering other vital topics, including innovation, barriers to imitation, resource-based views of the firm, knowledge creation, and other related ideas.

For practicing managers, core competence in some organizations refers to those activities that they perform especially well, even if those activities may be more supporting rather than primary in creating value. Alternatively, core competence may denote profitability in other organizations; that is, a profitable product line or business unit is a core competence. In other instances, a core competence can refer to a large core business upon which senior management decides to refocus its efforts; correspondingly, noncore businesses are seen as peripheral and put on the block for sale. Similarly, core competence may also relate to a central technology or product platform used by an organization to develop specific types or lines of products. For example, high-technology firms look at semiconductors or software platforms as core competencies that spawn end products for customers.

For the academic, the strategic management field has become invaluably richer over the past three decades as new theories and empirical tests provide much discussion and a deeper understanding of organizational performance. Core competence promises to remain a vital field of research and theory development. In the business world, the cultivation and management of core competencies represent an ongoing strategic task for senior managers of any organization. This task requires long-term commitment and focus to build distinctive sources of competitive advantage. Core competencies are as much organizational (patterns of communication, social interaction among members, metaphors, group dynamics) as they are technological (processes, methods, technical specifications). Simultaneously, however, senior management should realize that core competencies built around accumulated knowledge can serve as core rigidities in the wake of environmental change. Erecting barriers to imitation from competitive rivals can also erect barriers to learning new technologies and ideas for future growth.

David Lei

See also Competitive Advantage; Diversification Strategy; Dynamic Capabilities; Excellence Characteristics; Knowledge-Based View of the Firm; Organizational Learning; Resource-Based View of the Firm; Strategic Alliances

Further Readings

Barney, J. B. (1991). Firm resources and sustainable competitive advantage. *Journal of Management, 17,* 99–120.

Eisenhardt, K., & Martin, J. (2000). Dynamic capabilities: What are they? *Strategic Management Journal,* 21(10–11), 1105–1121.

Hamel, G. (1991). Competition for competence and inter-partner learning within international strategic alliances. *Strategic Management Journal, 12* (Summer), 83–104.

Itami, H. (1987). *Mobilizing invisible assets.* Cambridge, MA: Harvard University Press.

Lei, D., Hitt, M. A., & Bettis, R. A. (1996). Dynamic core competencies through meta-learning and strategic context. *Journal of Management, 22*(4), 549–569.

Leonard-Barton, D. (1992). Core capabilities and core rigidities: A paradox in managing new product development. *Strategic Management Journal, 13*(Summer), 111–125.

Nelson, R. R., & Winter, S. G. (1982). *An evolutionary theory of economic change.* Cambridge, MA: Harvard University Press.

Pralahad, C. K., & Hamel, G. (1990). The core competence of the corporation. *Harvard Business Review, 68*(4), 79–93.

Teece, D., Pisano, G., & Shuen, A. (1997). Dynamic capabilities and strategic management. *Strategic Management Journal, 18*(7), 509–533.

Wernerfelt, B. (1984). A resource-based view of the firm. *Strategic Management Journal, 5*(2), 171–180.

CORPORATE SOCIAL RESPONSIBILITY

The basic idea of corporate social responsibility (CSR) is that all businesses have some responsibilities to the societies in which they are licensed to operate that go beyond seeking financial wealth creation on behalf of the owners. At a minimum, businesses should behave ethically and obey laws unless there are sound moral objections to specific public policies. CSR is both a concept and a social movement. Continuing debate about CSR concerns the minimum mandatory requirements and maximum voluntary limits for responsibility activities rather than the basic idea of social responsibility. Even opponents of voluntary CSR accept that there are mandatory legal and ethical duties. They simply argue for those duties to be quite limited. CSR is not restricted to legally defined corporations but rather is synonymous with business social responsibility, or social responsibilities of business, for all enterprise forms. The broader term is reflected in Business for Social Responsibility (BSR), a global network founded in 1992, and the title of Howard R. Bowen's seminal 1953 book emphasizing multiple "social responsibilities." CSR is the label in common usage. Any concept of CSR is a theory of the proper relationship between business and society. How to specify content and test the theory empirically and apply the concept to business strategy and specific decisions is one of the central questions in management research and practice. This entry is structured as follows. The next section explains the fundamentals of the several theories of CSR. The subsequent section assesses the validity and impact of the theories of CSR.

Fundamentals

While businesses practiced aspects of CSR historically, origins of the formal CSR concept go back to Andrew Carnegie's philanthropy proposal in his 1889 essay, "The Gospel of Wealth," and a 1916 article by J. M. Clark in the *Journal of Political Economy.* The Harvard Business School dean W. B. Donham encouraged the idea from the late 1920s. An important exchange in the *Harvard Law Review* in the early 1930s between A. A. Berle Jr. and E. M. Dodd addressed strict fiduciary responsibility versus concern for multiple corporate constituencies. F. W. Abrams in 1951 and H. R. Bowen in 1953 captured the emphasis on social responsibilities of business that developed during the Great Depression and World War II.

Milton Friedman, an economist who received the 1976 Nobel Memorial Prize, launched in the early 1960s an academic counterattack on CSR. Friedman argued that publicly traded corporations should focus on financial wealth creation as the real social responsibility of business. Voluntary CSR activities infringe improperly on government responsibilities and reflect the personal tastes of business managers violating fiduciary responsibility. Private companies have the same status as individuals to practice altruism.

Subsequent CSR literature has been a debate over what became an "essentially contested concept" and efforts by CSR supporters to develop and test a business case for CSR. The basic "pillars" of CSR theorizing can be viewed as Archie B. Carroll's pyramid of responsibilities, the social contract theory of business ethics introduced by Thomas Donaldson, the stakeholder theory of the firm introduced by R. Edward Freeman, and the corporate social performance (CSP) model formalized by Donna J. Wood. The CSP model embeds the CSR principle. Each pillar has a separate entry in this encyclopedia.

The Carroll approach defines four responsibility domains (ordered from base to apex as economic, legal, ethical, and philanthropic) that can be related to different kinds of stakeholders or corporate constituencies. The economic and legal domains are morally infused, such that CSR is always morally principled in approach. U.S. corporation law has long recognized a role for reasonable philanthropy; and obedience to law should be a moral norm. Empirical studies suggest that managers perceive these dimensions as so ordered and weighted relatively approximately as 4:3:2:1 (i.e., proportions of 100%).

The scope of mandatory legal and ethical duties is a continuing debate concerning the merits of relatively free markets versus strong government regulation and social expectations of business behavior. Stakeholder activism helps to drive voluntary business actions concerning philanthropy, environmental sustainability, and human rights. This debate has been sharpened recently by the global financial crisis beginning in 2008. An important literature in recent years has concerned whether the firm's CSR reputation (good or bad) affects its financial performance. Businesses may find that CSR involves profitable or reputation-enhancing opportunities rather than purely costs. If so, then CSR should be considered an integral part of the firm's strategy. This approach links sustainable competitive advantage to CSR. Empirical research reveals that firms combine economic, legal, ethical, and philanthropic activities in different ways. Kinder, Lydenberg and Domini, a social choice investment advisory firm, evaluates selected strengths and concerns for hundreds of publicly traded firms.

Importance

Empirical research has focused on trying to establish a reliable statistical relationship between CSR (and CSP) and corporate financial performance. A generally negative relationship would support Friedman; a generally positive relationship would support a business case for CSR. Meta-analysis of some hundreds of studies tends to suggest a neutral or mildly positive relationship. The absence of a strong business case should not be taken as favoring Friedman. On the contrary, there is no significant risk in CSR; the real risk lies in reputation-damaging misconduct. A recent study suggests the possibility of a curvilinear relationship between CSP (or CSR) and corporate financial performance. While a firm with low CSP may have higher financial performance than a firm with moderate CSP, a firm with high CSP likely has the highest financial performance. This possibility means that responsibility is a joint strategic and values choice, in which CSP and financial performance may work together. A difficulty in empirical testing is the wide range of possible CSR activities.

Despite the academic contest over CSR as a concept and empirically testable theory, there has been increasing institutionalization of CSR guidelines and reporting. CSR is becoming a part of evolving international norms. Many companies, especially multinational firms, now voluntarily issue periodic reports under various titles such as social responsibility, corporate citizenship, sustainability, or social impact. Such reports, typically unaudited presently, are open to charges by activists of highlighting positive achievements, while underreporting negative impacts. The United Nations (UN) Global Compact, a voluntary association of companies and other organizations, promotes 10 principles concerning human rights, labor rights, environmental sustainability, and anticorruption efforts. The International Organization for Standardization (ISO) 26000 standards provide guidance (not certification) for social responsibility activities and reporting. The Global Reporting Initiative (GRI) provides widely used reporting standards for sustainability information in triple bottom line form (economic, environmental, and social dimensions). The Organisation for Economic Co-operation and

Development (OECD) issues OECD Guidelines for Multinational Enterprises and the UN Principles for Responsible Investment. There is a UN Convention against Corruption. The European Commission (EU) has been fostering voluntary CSR, interpreted as a combination of stakeholder participation and sustainability, as part of an EU strategy for growth and jobs. Irresponsibility can prove expensive to corporate wealth; and no company can in today's world seriously assert nonresponsibility. The economic, environmental, social, and corporate costs (to several firms involved) of the Deepwater Horizon catastrophe in the Gulf of Mexico highlighted the point.

As a contested concept with proposed substitutes, CSR has no definitely agreed normative basis or universal definition. However, this condition is largely due to disagreements over the scope of CSR. Key positions advocate restricting CSR to legal and ethical norms, undertaking limited voluntary activities beyond such norms of strategic value to the firm, and broad responsibility to operate in the public interest. A recent reassertion of the Friedman position by Aneel Karnani combined a criticism of voluntary CSR with a call for strong external controls in the form of laws, ethics, and stakeholder activism. The minimum requirements are anchored still in Carroll's pyramid, however interpreted. A financially sustainable company must obey the law and ethical expectations, meet the requirements of its key stakeholders (customers, employees, and owners), and undertake some reasonable set of philanthropic activities—especially those activities positively affecting its reputation with stakeholders. A specific problem arises in conflict of laws across countries. Positive law lacking a normative foundation is not necessarily superior to moral values of business executives and corporate stakeholders. Google operates under constraints in China to which its founders and corporate values are opposed.

Globalization of markets has driven much of the evolution in CSR practices and scholarship. With increased institutionalization and European Commission and United Nations attention, conceptualization, practice, and scholarship concerning CSR continues to evolve and expand. There has been an expansion of the content of CSR to include broadly sustainable development, environmental sustainability, and human rights especially in developing countries. The special representative

of the UN secretary-general (SRSG) on business and human rights has submitted three reports to the UN Human Rights Council concerning a framework for CSR with respect to human rights. Civil lawsuits have been filed in U.S. courts by noncitizens against businesses under the U.S. Alien Tort Claims Act (ATCA) of 1789. An Ecuador court reached a multibillion dollar judgment against Chevron concerning alleged pollution in the Amazon region by Texaco, which was acquired by Chevron. That judgment was appealed by Chevron to U.S. courts.

A recent body of literature has argued that corporate citizenship is superior to CSR as a label and a movement. Ideal citizenship and ideal CSR theories arguably have much the same content. Citizenship, essentially a metaphor, has the advantage of suggesting obligation similar to CSR but the disadvantage of suggesting a corporate citizen's privilege to influence governmental policy in favor of business interests. There have been efforts by scholars to figure out how to combine concepts of CSR, corporate citizenship, business ethics, stakeholder management, and sustainability into a single integrated framework. The most recent version of mainstream stakeholder theory emphasizes entrepreneurial value creation in which economics and ethics are not separable dimensions. Some European scholars have applied the views of the influential German discourse philosopher Jürgen Habermas on law and democracy to CSR. That body of literature argues that firms have a duty to promote internal and external democracy and to help provide public goods where there is governmental incapacity especially in developing countries. This approach is in marked contrast to the conventional view that CSR means voluntary self-regulation by businesses.

Duane Windsor

See also CSR Pyramid; Fairness Theory; Integrative Social Contracts Theory; Stakeholder Theory; Triple Bottom Line

Further Readings

Bowen, H. R. (1953). *Social responsibilities of the businessman.* New York, NY: Harper.
Carroll, A. B., & Shabana, K. M. (2010). The business case for corporate social responsibility: A review of concepts, research and practice. *International Journal of Management Reviews, 12,* 85–105.

Crane, A., Matten, D., McWilliams, A., Siegel, D., & Moon, J. (Eds.). (2008). *Oxford handbook of corporate social responsibility*. Oxford, England: Oxford University Press.

Kemper, A., & Martin, R. L. (2010). After the fall: The global financial crisis as a test of corporate social responsibility theories. *European Management Review, 7*, 229–239.

Porter, M. E., & Kramer, M. R. (2006). Strategy and society: The link between competitive advantage and corporate social responsibility. *Harvard Business Review, 84*(12), 78–92.

Scherer, A. G., & Palazzo, G. (2007). Toward a political conception of corporate responsibility: Business and society seen from a Habermasian perspective. *Academy of Management Review, 32*, 1096–1120.

Schwartz, M. S. (2011). *Corporate social responsibility: An ethical approach*. Peterborough, Ontario, Canada: Broadview Press.

Visser, W., Matten, D., Pohl, M., & Tolhurst, N. (Eds.). (2010). *The A to Z of corporate social responsibility* (Rev. ed.). Chichester, England: Wiley.

Vogel, D. (2005). *The market for virtue: The potential and limits of corporate social responsibility*. Washington, DC: Brookings Institution Press.

Waddock, S. A. (2008). *The difference makers: How social and institutional entrepreneurs created the corporate responsibility movement*. Sheffield, England: Greenleaf.

CRITICAL MANAGEMENT STUDIES

The word *critical* has, of course, a number of meanings. All research is critical in the sense that the researcher is observant and intolerant of weak argumentation, speculative statements, erroneous conclusions, and so on. Critical management studies (CMS), however, go far beyond faultfinding. Its task is the stimulation of a more extensive reflection upon established ideas, ideologies, and institutions in order to liberate from or at least reduce repression, self-constraints, or suffering. Critical research aims to stand on the weaker party's side when studying or commenting upon social relations and organizational conditions involving dominance. There are other stories to tell about management than those emerging from a pro-managerial perspective. CMS is a broad field with no universally agreed-upon core or definition. Given the expanding powers of corporations, management, and leadership, the critical

exploration of management as ideology, function, and practice is increasingly important. This entry will briefly account for CMS's relationship to critical social theorists and traditions like the Frankfurt school, Jürgen Habermas, Michel Foucault and post-structuralism, and the history and development of CMS and then point at some of the research areas and key contributions and challenges for CMS, including its practical relevance.

Fundamentals

The Task of CMS

The central goal of CMS has been to provide inspiration for the creation of societies and workplaces which are free from domination, where all members have an equal—or at least reasonable—opportunity to contribute to the production of systems that meet human needs and lead to the progressive development of all. This sounds quite idealistic. However, the struggle to increase democratic accountability, reduce unnecessary suffering and control, and increase the space for discretion and thoughtful dialogue about goals and means of organizations through critical thinking and liberation from dominant, often taken for granted institutions, interests, ideologies, and identities is often at least a minor part of human life and organizational processes. The task for CMS is to support and strengthen this.

Studies have focused externally on the relation of organizations to the wider society, emphasizing the possible social effects of colonization of other institutions and the domination or destruction of the public sphere. Internally, they have explored the domination by instrumental reasoning, discursive closures, and consent processes within the workplace. Organizations are largely seen as political sites, thus, general social theories and especially theories of decision making in the public sphere are seen as appropriate.

People working in organizations are subjected to, and formed by, administrative demands for adaptability, cooperation, predictability, and conformity. We live in a thoroughly organized society, dominated by large corporations, and this creates particular kinds of subjects in a variety of subtle ways, both as employees and as consumers. The ideal of being well organized is at the core of organizational society.

In a society and working life thoroughly effected by management, everything from structures and strategies to work content, motivation, ethics, career, development, identities, and emotions are incorporated into management regimes where managers, aided by consultants and other experts (on anything from career counseling to testing to diversity to corporate social responsibility and equal opportunity) put strong imprints on human subjects being formed and regulated by management knowledge. CMS then concentrates on what is seen as the darker and often hidden sides of organizations and management. Critical perspectives reject the perhaps most common assumption—held by the public as well as most researchers—that organizations are only or even mainly in the business of producing socially valuable products and services and that management only exceptionally deviates from the norm of fulfilling positive social functions in the interest of most stakeholders. Organizational life and the outcomes of organizational work are far from always positive. Of course organizations contribute to material survival and affluence, job satisfaction and positive social relations, a sense of meaning, and personal development. They also often contribute to stress and bad health: They mean subordination and exploitation; they may encourage people into conformism, excessive careerism, and egoism; prevent them from "free thinking" and free speech; erode moral standards; create or reinforce gender inequalities, and so on. Many corporations in postaffluent society mainly contribute with goods and services that have a far from self-evident consequence in terms of contributing positively or negatively to the environment and human need satisfaction. Many companies are in high-pollution industries. Corporations regularly produce people with consumerist and materialist life orientations through appealing to motives and anxieties around status, self-esteem, and conformism. Fashion, beauty, and luxury industries could exemplify.

CMS operates with understandings of management and organizations being like mental or physical prisons, where formal control and engineering of values and identities lead to suppression. Power and domination, within organizations but also targeting customers, weaker organizations, and to some extent parts of society, are viewed as key elements of organizations. Management knowledge and practices,

such as strategy and leadership, are viewed as discourses that say less about organizational reality or productively informed managerial practice than they function as legitimation of managerial status, interest, and privilege and reinforcement of inequalities between senior people and others.

Critical perspectives also reject the idea that problems normally can be resolved through "better management," taking objectives and "noninstrumental" values for granted. Instead of expansion of technical solutions, issues are seen as calling for political and ethically informed action. Also, advocates of CMS argue that what is understood by gurus, the media, and conventional management theory as better management may create harmful social effects, such as highly disciplined employees and controlled consumers.

Ideology critique shows how specific interests fail to be realized owing partly to the inability of people to understand or act on these interests. CMS researchers' interest in ideologies entails consideration of the difficulties of disadvantaged groups in understanding their own political interest, but it is more often addressed to limitations on people in general, challenging technocracy, consumerism, careerism, and exclusive concern with economic growth at the expense of other values, including ecological concerns and autonomy. Class conflicts and diversity of interests are acknowledged, but the focus is more often on how institutions, ideologies, and identities constrain broad groups of people.

Research Areas of CMS

CMS researchers have emphasized the narrow thinking associated with the domination of instrumental reason and the money code in organizations. Potentially, when wisely applied, instrumental reason is a productive form of thinking and acting. However, in the absence of political ethically informed judgment, critical reflection, and democracy, its highly specialized, means-fixated, and unreflective character makes it strongly inclined to also contribute to the objectification of people and nature and thus to various forms of destruction. This critique has focused on the phenomenon of managerialism; in other words, the celebration and overemphasis of management as a superior and significant force having close to a monopoly on establishing how organizations and work life should be structured and be aimed at and how problems can be resolved.

In the guise of technocracy, management knowledge has pretenses to neutrality and freedom from the value-laden realms of self-interest and politics. It celebrates and "hides" behind techniques and the false appearance of objectivity and impartiality of institutionalized sets of knowledge, bureaucracy, and formal mandates. Not surprisingly, technocracy is promoted by management "specialists" as they claim monopolies of expertise in their respective domains. Human resource specialists, for example, advance and defend their position by elaborating a battery of "objective" techniques for managing the selection and promotion of employees. Strategic management institutionalizes a particular way of exercising domination through legitimizing and privileging the "management" of the organization-environment interface, producing some actors as "strategists" and reducing others to troops whose role is to subordinate themselves and to implement corporate strategies.

Some salient areas of CMS are (a) constrained work conditions where intrinsic work qualities (creativity, variation, development, meaningfulness) are ignored or subordinated to instrumental values and elaborated forms of control; (b) the development and reinforcement of asymmetrical social relations between experts (including management elites) and nonexperts; (c) discursive closures whereby contestation cannot occur in potentially important negotiations of personal identities, knowledge, and values; (d) gender bias in terms of styles of reasoning, asymmetrical social relations, and political priorities; (e) far-reaching control of employees, consumers, and the general political-ethical agenda in society though mass media and lobbying that advocates consumerism and the priority of the money code as a yardstick for values and individual and collective political decision making; (f) destruction of the natural environment through waste and pollution; and (g) the constraints and narrow channeling of ethical issues in business and work and an emphasis on image-management producing a look-good-ethics decoupled from operations.

Evolution

CMS draws inspiration from a range of classical social theorists including Karl Marx, Max Weber, and psychoanalysis. A more specific tradition,

drawing upon these theorists, is the critical theory of the Frankfurt school. This was founded in the late 1920s and gradually developed as one of the most influential intellectual traditions of 20th-century social theory. The most famous names associated with the school are Max Horkheimer, Theodor Adorno, Erich Fromm, Herbert Marcuse, and Jürgen Habermas. Horkheimer formulated the objective of the Frankfurt school in the 1930s as the liberation of human beings from the circumstances that enslave them. The ambition was to identify and critically scrutinize social forms, ideologies, and cultural orientations that prevent people from attaining autonomy and producing social conditions in line with their will and interest. This could range from authoritarian political regimes to cultural masculinity, cultish leadership, and uninhibited commercialism. Of particular interest for management studies is the increasing influence of technocracy and subtle and not-so-subtle forms of control penetrating an expansion of wider sectors of society and organizational life as exposed in classic works such as *Dialectic of Enlightenment* by Horkheimer and Adorno and *One-Dimensional Man* by Marcuse. Modern civilization, it is argued, has become progressively mesmerized by the power of a one-sided, instrumental conception of reason. This is visible in the expansion of business schools and the discipline of management incorporating not just organizational structure and labor process but in making a range of themes and orientations the object of corporate control, including values, identities, and emotions.

A rationale for CMS is offered by Habermas's influential formulation of knowledge-constitutive interests. He distinguishes between three such interests: (a) A technical interest in establishing means-ends relations through controlled experiments and other efforts to establish causal relations is viewed as important and legitimate for mastering nature and is seen as the form of knowledge guiding the natural sciences. It also dominates management studies. (b) A practical (or historical-hermeneutic) interest concerns the understanding of language and culture and aims to create knowledge on ways of creating mutual understanding and human beings in the context of traditions-transmitting institutions. This is the task of the humanities, and the knowledge form here is hermeneutics, and the aim is understanding. (c) An emancipator interest is about developing knowledge about constraints and repression associated with irrational social institutions and ideologies. The task for social science, Habermas claims, is through critical examination to encourage the transformation of these social conditions. Other social researchers, inspired by Foucault, are suspicious about the optimistic and pretentious idea of emancipation, including the possible elitist conception of researchers' knowledge "liberating" the unfree through consciousness. They instead prefer to talk about resistance, viewing this as integral to power; that is, with power, resistance is triggered.

The term *critical management studies* was coined with the publication in 1992 of Mats Alvesson and Hugh Willmott's book with the same name, but critical work in organization studies range back over the decades. In the late 1980s and early 1990s, the trend within critical work on organizations and management moved from the earlier, Marxist-based focus on labor process, over to a stronger interest in culture, subjectivity, and meanings. The great general interest in organizational culture also attracted advocates of CMS. In the 1980s and 1990s also, feminist work started to appear in management and organization studies in some quantities, much of it critically oriented. An initial interest in mainly females was gradually supplemented by an interest, although much more limited, in men and masculinities.

Post-structuralism and postmodernism received considerable attention in critical organizational studies in the 1990s and continue to be influential. Many people earlier interested in a critical-interpretive interest in culture and symbolism moved over into a postmodernistically informed understanding focusing on discourse. Postmodernism is now less of a central theme, but the interest in social constructions and the significance of discourse is strong. Parts of it share with CMS a radical and challenging orientation.

Today, there are debates within the critical perspective(s) between people emphasizing a constructivist and discursive view, influenced by postmodernism, and advocates of critical realism, who emphasize the structures, mechanisms, and objective nature of social reality.

Common among these orientations is an element of questioning established views as true or self-evident. Reality is socially constructed, often in arbitrary and often harmful, repressive ways. CMS tends

to work as a disruption of the ongoing reproduction of the social world. There is, however, seldom a clear agenda, a positive vision, or any powerful questioning of the power effects of social constructions and discourses.

Importance

CMS is for some an esoteric and negative odd bird in the large nest of management studies, while for others, all research includes the critical scrutiny of the subject matters of their discipline, and there is no reason to adapt only or even mainly a pro-corporate stance when studying business and organizations. One can see management studies as the study *of*, not necessarily *for*, management. Irrespective of position, CMS is in the 21st century, a far from marginal tradition in management studies, although more strongly represented in Europe, in particular the United Kingdom, than in North America.

Much CMS literature is conceptual and investigates claims in academic and business literature. There are also good empirical cases but more illustrations than strong studies. The idea of CMS is less to prove how things are than to point at phenomena and aspects that can exercise a repressive impact and need to be countered.

As critical reflection and thinking is a key aspect of any well-functioning modern society and its institutions and professional-occupation groups, so the field of management and the practice of managers also benefit from challenges to more narrow, technocratic thinking and practice. Learning about more or less subtle forms of suppression—and how people may be caught in mainstreaming forms of thinking associated with tradition, fashion, dominant rhetoric, and subordination to authoritarian forms of management—can increase autonomy and encourage efforts to develop more humane and ethic forms of management. A critical distance to various conventions and practices may more generally support reflective professional practice by managers, consultants, and others in corporate settings.

Mats Alvesson

See also Analytical and Sociological Paradigms; Circuits of Power and Control; Critical Theory of Communication; Dialectical Theory of Organizations; Organizational Culture Theory; Social Construction Theory; Structuration Theory

Further Readings

Alvesson, M., Bridgman, T., & Willmott, H. (Eds.). (2009). *Oxford handbook of critical management studies.* Oxford, England: Oxford University Press.

Alvesson, M., & Deetz, S. (2000). *Doing critical management research.* London, England: Sage.

Alvesson, M., & Willmott, H. (Eds.). (2011). *Major works in critical management studies* (Vols. 1–4). London, England: Sage.

Alvesson, M., & Willmott, H. C. (2012). *Making sense of management: A critical introduction.* London, England: Sage.

Deetz, S. (1992). *Democracy in an age of corporate colonization: Developments in communication and the politics of everyday life.* Albany: State University of New York Press.

Jackall, R. (1988). *Moral mazes: The world of corporate managers.* New York, NY: Oxford University Press.

CRITICAL THEORY OF COMMUNICATION

The critical theory of communication's central management insight is that organizations and the various forms of knowledge and the human identities of members are products of complex interaction processes conducted under conditions of inequality. These products and organizational decision making are hence distorted and favor a small subset of interests at the expense of legitimate others. A critical theory of communication is defined as those theories that pose both moral and practical questions to these interaction processes and the forms of inequality. This entry will consider different types of critical theories, review the central questions posed, and detail the impact on management theory.

Fundamentals

All critical theories of communication see *communication* as fundamentally different from what is normally suggested in the ordinary uses of the term. Communication is not seen as one phenomenon among others in organizations. It is not treated as corporate communications nor a management tool, nor even as a term to reference human interaction. Instead, communication is treated as the fundamental process by which organizations exist and as central to the analysis of their production and reproduction.

Several types of critical theories of communication exist. Some are deeply rooted in a Marxist tradition. Much of this work has focused on the political economy of information, ownership of the mass media, communication workers, and the use of communication to advance capitalist interests. This work emphasizes the relations of production, ownership, and material conditions.

Growing out of this has been a second type of critical theories of communication which typically go under the name of *cultural studies.* Researchers for these studies have more often looked at the role of communication in the production and sustaining of a consumption society. Much of the focus has been on the "subjective" side of life, detailing how media messages and advertising produce a particular kind of human being with particular needs.

Each of these can be seen in various management studies. The most central use of the term *critical theory of communication* in management studies, however, has differed somewhat from these traditions. These uses grow out of the development of critical theory as a general social theory in "Frankfurt school" writings in the 1920s and 1930s. Much of this was further developed and recast by Herbert Marcuse in the 1960 in his critique of instrumental reasoning and more completely by Jürgen Habermas in the development of the theory of communicative action. Stanley Deetz took these rather broad philosophical concepts and brought them directly to bear on central issues in management studies and the relation of organizations to society. These concepts have continued to be enriched through their articulation within postmodern theory and various stakeholder theories.

Much of the use of critical communication theory, like critical theory more generally, begins with a careful description of the social historical construction of organizational life. These descriptions detail the arbitrary nature of contemporary institutions and practices and the differential advantages that it affords. Language and communication are seen as central to how these are produced and reproduced across time.

While many constructionists might agree with this, critical work goes a step further. Not only are organizations and their practices constructions that construct, but all construction occurs also under various conditions of inequality and hence serves some people and some interests better than other equally legitimate ones.

Critical studies of communication focus on understanding the relations among power, language, sociocultural practices, and the treatment and/or suppression of important conflicts in decision processes. Generally, those focusing on a critical theory of communication play less attention to direct dominance by power elites in organizations and more to various forms of decisional asymmetry conceptualized as the subtle arbitrary micropractices of power-laden manners of world, self, and other in interaction.

Contemporary critical analyses focus on systems that require organizational members' active role in producing and reproducing their exclusion from meaning making and decision-making processes. Fostering more democratic communication in these terms must look to the formation of knowledge, experience, and identity, rather than merely to their expression. Much analysis has focused on "discursive closures" where open interaction and production is closed off leading organizations to be less adaptive and responsive to social needs.

Critical theories of communication have impacted research regarding organizations through the development of various critical analysis procedures and critical discourse analysis. The focus on better systems of inclusion has impacted corporate social responsibility and stakeholder theory and advanced participatory action research as a stronger form of organization study and intervention.

Critical theories of communication have been very important to the analysis of organizational culture, the development of broader concepts of rationality, and the attempt to include a broader set of values and interests in decision making. They have brought to surface important conflicts that are often suppressed in ordinary interaction in organizations leading to important social and economic benefits.

This work encourages modern managers to develop alternative communication practices that allow greater democracy and more creative and productive cooperation among stakeholders through reconsidering organizational governance and decision-making processes and developing more collaborative management practices.

Stanley Deetz

See also Circuits of Power and Control; Corporate Social Responsibility; Critical Management Studies; Dialectical Theory of Organizations; Fairness Theory; Participative Model of Decision Making; Social Construction Theory; Stakeholder Theory

Further Readings

Alvesson, M., & Deetz, S. (2000). *Doing critical management research*. London, England: Sage.

Deetz, S. (1992). *Democracy in an age of corporate colonization: Developments in communication and the politics of everyday life*. Albany: State University of New York Press.

Deetz, S. (2005). Critical theory. In S. May & D. Mumby (Eds.), *Engaging organizational communication theory: Multiple perspectives* (pp. 85–111). Thousand Oaks, CA: Sage.

Deetz, S., & McClellan, J. (2009). Critical studies. In F. Bargiela (Ed.), *Handbook of business discourse* (pp. 119–131). Edinburgh, England: University of Edinburgh Press.

du Gay, P., & Pryke, M. (2002*). Cultural economy: Cultural analysis and commercial life*. Thousand Oaks, CA: Sage.

Garnham, N. (1995). Political economy and cultural studies: Reconciliation or divorce? *Critical Studies in Mass Communication 12*, 62–71.

Habermas, J. (1984). *The theory of communicative action: Vol. 1. Reason and the rationalization of society*. (T. McCarthy, Trans.). Boston, MA: Beacon.

McClellan, J., & Deetz, S. (2009). Communication. In H. Willmott, T. Bridgman, & M. Alvesson (Eds.), *Handbook of critical management studies* (pp. 433–453). Oxford, England: Oxford University Press.

CSR Pyramid

The issue of corporate social responsibility (CSR) has been debated for decades. The theory behind the concept of CSR is that business organizations have responsibilities to society that extend beyond simply producing goods and services for a profit. Major questions that have driven the debate over this issue have been that of what CSR really means, what those responsibilities are, and how far businesses are expected to go. Though dozens of definitions of CSR have surfaced over the years, an accepted conceptual model of CSR that has become a standard part of management theory is the pyramid of corporate social responsibility. The pyramid of CSR was set forth by Archie B. Carroll in 1991 based on a definitional construct of CSR introduced in 1979. The pyramid was created as a useful way of graphically depicting the four-part definition of CSR by envisioning it as embracing four levels or layers within a pyramidal framework. The four social responsibilities of business were contended to be economic, legal, ethical, and discretionary or philanthropic. The responsibilities were layered from the most fundamental expectation of business profitability at the base of the pyramid extending upward to the most discretionary responsibility at the apex of the pyramid. The CSR pyramid has been relevant to general management theory in that it has posited that businesses have responsibilities to a range of stakeholders other than owners. Other societal stakeholders affected, especially by the legal, ethical, and philanthropic responsibilities, include employees, customers, environment, communities, competitors, and others. In this entry, the fundamentals of the pyramid of CSR are described. This section includes an explanation of the pyramidal metaphor and a brief description of the four types of social responsibility that are depicted in the pyramid. Next is a section on the importance of the pyramid to managers. In this section, it is clarified how the pyramid helps managers to integrate economic concerns into a social performance framework and situate legal, ethical, and philanthropic responsibilities into a coherent structure.

Fundamentals

The pyramid of CSR is built upon the idea that organizations have responsibilities to the public by virtue of society giving them the charter to operate as producers and distributors of goods and services. While historically many business people have expressed the belief that the purpose of business is to make a profit, the pyramid of CSR recasts business purpose into one of meeting the needs and expectations of society's stakeholders in addition to the owners of the businesses. In this light, profitability is seen not as the "purpose" of business but rather as one responsibility it has to the owners or investors who put their resources at risk to start and operate the business. Individuals who start businesses or invest in them may look upon their investments as pursuing profitability. But an institutional or societal perspective would argue that society permits businesses to exist to meet its needs, and profits are the reward or incentive it allows businesspeople for taking risk.

As a metaphor, the pyramid of CSR intends to illustrate that the total social responsibility of business is composed of distinct components that, when taken together, make up the whole. Although the components are treated as separate types for discussion purposes, they are not mutually exclusive and are not intended to juxtapose a firm's economic responsibilities with its other obligations. Rather, the distinct layers seek to explain that the total social responsibility of business comprises four different *types* or *categories* of responsibility. The sequencing of the pyramid's layers, moreover, is ordered from what is thought to be the most fundamental or basic responsibilities of business organizations in order to exist and continue to exist. Thus, if firms do not make a profit, that is, fulfill their economic responsibilities, all the others are moot.

To better understand the pyramid of CSR, it is helpful to consider in more detail the meaning of each of its *types* (levels or layers), beginning with economic.

Economic Responsibilities

First, businesses have economic responsibilities. First and foremost, the capitalistic system calls for business to be an *economic* institution. That is, it is an institution that ought to have the objective of producing goods and services that society wants and to sell them at fair prices—prices that society thinks represent the value delivered and that provides business with profits sufficient to ensure its survival and growth and to reward its owners and/or investors. It can be argued that the economic responsibility of being profitable is "required" of business by society. Economic institutions are not sustainable without ongoing profits.

Legal Responsibilities

Second, businesses have legal responsibilities. Just as society has sanctioned the economic system by permitting businesses to assume the producer and distributor roles, it has also established the ground rules under which businesses must operate—laws and regulations. Legal responsibilities reflect society's view of "codified ethics" in the sense that they embody basic notions of fair practices as formalized by lawmakers. Before a law is created, it likely existed as an emerging ethical issue, one over which some consensus was developing regarding fair treatment of stakeholders. It is business's responsibility to society to comply with these laws and regulations, for they represent consensus expectations regarding fair dealings. Over the decades, laws and regulations have extended into requirements business must meet to respect owners, customers, employees, environments, communities, and so on. On their own, laws and regulations are necessary but not sufficient in terms of transactions with stakeholders. Just as economic responsibilities are required of business by society, so are legal responsibilities.

Ethical Responsibilities

Because laws are essential but not adequate, ethical responsibilities are needed to clarify those activities and practices that are expected or prohibited by society even though they have not been codified into law. The ethical responsibility is unique in that it cuts through all the other levels as well as existing on its own. In the economic responsibility, for example, society has rendered capitalism to be a "good" system (an ethical judgment), and part of this is the notion of investors getting profits. Likewise, before a law was passed, it doubtless originated as an ethical issue, an issue over which some consensus was building about fair treatment of stakeholders by businesses. For example, the civil rights, environmental, and consumer movements that came of age in the 1960s reflected basic alternations in societal values and thus were ethical bellwethers foreshadowing and leading to later legislation.

In this distinct category of ethical responsibilities, reference is primarily made to activities, practices, and conduct residing at a level higher than that required by law or occurring in realms of practice where no laws currently exist. The often repeated observation that "that may be *legal* but it sure isn't *ethical*" is applicable here. It suggests that many laws are inadequate and that society really expects a higher level of behavior and practice out of organizations and its leaders.

Ethical responsibilities embody the full scope of norms, standards, values, and expectations that reflect what employees, consumers, shareholders, and the community regard as fair, just, and consistent with respect for and protection of stakeholder's moral rights. Superimposed on these ethical expectations originating from society and stakeholder groups are the implied levels of ethical practices suggested by the great ethical principles of moral philosophy. These would include the principles of rights, justice, and utilitarianism. It is safe to say

that the ethical responsibilities of business are not required like they are in the economic and legal categories, but they clearly are "expected" of business by society. Many businesses have failed because of their unwillingness to live up to society's ethical expectations of them today.

Philanthropic Responsibilities

Philanthropic responsibilities encompass those corporate actions that are in response to society's expectations that businesses "give back" and be good corporate citizens in the community, nation, and the world. This includes actively engaging in acts or programs to promote human welfare or goodwill. Examples of philanthropy include corporate contributions of financial resources or employee time through volunteerism. Such contributions typically go to support health and human services, civic and community activities, education, and culture and the arts. In recent years, giving in times of crisis has become an expected type of corporate citizenship that would fall into the philanthropic responsibility. Examples of this latter category would include the charitable donations made following Hurricane Katrina. Walmart, Home Depot, and Fed Ex were companies that stood out because of their ability to quickly mobilize and bring quick relief through the donations of supplies. During the Indian Ocean tsunami, businesses donated hundreds of millions of dollars worth of help to suffering communities.

Philanthropic responsibilities may also be thought of as discretionary responsibilities because they are not mandated by law. Some philanthropy is motivated by ethical considerations, but some is motivated more by businesses fulfilling a role that has come to be expected of them by society's stakeholders to be a good corporate citizen. In recent years, strategic philanthropy has become popular among major corporations. Strategic philanthropy is an approach by which corporate giving and other philanthropic endeavors are designed in a way that best fits with the firm's overall mission, goals, or objectives. Therefore, one requirement of strategic philanthropy would be to make as direct a contribution as possible to the financial goals of the firm. Philanthropy has long been thought to be in the best long-range economic interests of business, and the adage of "doing well by doing good" has become a popular way to express business performance in this category of CSR. In recent years, the "business case" for CSR has been advocated, and strategic philanthropy is often thought to be a critical aspect of helping the firm while helping society. In the business case arguments, companies engage in socially responsible activities because of the following reasons: enhanced reputations, competitive advantages, industry trends, cost savings, greater customer loyalty, a more satisfied workforce, and fewer regulatory or legal problems. Though not required of business by society, the philanthropic responsibility is both "desired" and "expected" of business by society.

Importance

No metaphor is perfect, and the pyramid of CSR is no exception. It intends to illustrate that the total social responsibility of business is composed of distinct types or kinds that, when taken together, make up a unified whole. Although the four levels have been treated as separate types of responsibilities for discussion, they are not mutually exclusive. The CSR pyramid holds that businesses are expected to fulfill all four of the responsibilities though they have been depicted in a hierarchical arrangement based on their deep-seated importance to business. The pyramid is not intended to suggest that businesses fulfill their social responsibilities in some sequential fashion, starting at the base. Rather, business is expected to fulfill all its responsibilities simultaneously. Stated in practical managerial terms, the pyramid of CSR is intended to suggest that the socially responsible firm should make a profit, obey the law, be ethical, and be a good corporate citizen via philanthropy.

Two of the most challenging tasks in the field of corporate social responsibility include conceptualizing the concept in understandable terms and in measuring CSR activities and inclinations on the part of managers. The CSR pyramid helps scholars and practitioners to perceive in a comprehensive way what all is involved in the CSR concept. The pyramid brings together different threads of social responsibility concern and illustrates how they constitute a unified whole, which if achieved, address stakeholder concerns ranging from the owners to managers, employees, consumers, and other outside groups. In particular, the conceptual model helps practitioners

to see that social responsibility is not separate and distinct from economic performance. The pyramid integrates economic concerns into a social performance framework and places legal, ethical, and philanthropic responsibilities into a coherent structure. With respect to measurement, the four-part definition of CSR has enabled researchers to develop a means to assess managers' CSR orientations in terms of their prioritizing of the four social responsibility types. Numerous research studies have found that managers do prioritize the four component parts in the same sequence and progression depicted in the pyramidal framework. In research, CSR "orientations" of executives have followed the economic, legal, ethical, philanthropic ordering of priorities.

Archie B. Carroll

See also Corporate Social Responsibility; Ethical Decision Making, Interactionist Model of; Humanistic Management; Stakeholder Theory; Strategic Decision Making; Triple Bottom Line

Further Readings

Aupperle, K. E., Carroll, A. B., & Hatfield, J. D. (1985). An empirical examination of the relationship between corporate social responsibility and profitability. *Academy of Management Journal, 28*(2), 446–463.

Carroll, A. B. (1979). A three-dimensional conceptual model of corporate social performance. *Academy of Management Review, 4*(4), 497–505.

Carroll, A. B. (1991). The pyramid of corporate social responsibility: Toward the moral management of organizational stakeholders. *Business Horizons, 34*(July–August), 39–48.

Carroll, A. B., & Buchholtz, A. K. (2012). *Business and society: Ethics, sustainability, and stakeholder management* (8th ed.). Mason, OH: South-Western Cengage Learning.

Carroll, A. B., & Shabana, K. M. (2010, March). The business case for corporate social responsibility: A review of concepts, research and practice. *International Journal of Management Reviews, 12*(1), 85–105.

Edmondson, V. C., & Carroll, A. B. (1999). Giving back: An examination of the philanthropic motivations, orientations and activities of large Black-owned businesses. *Journal of Business Ethics, 19,* 171–179.

Schwartz, M. S., & Carroll, A. B. (2003). Corporate social responsibility: A three domain approach. *Business Ethics Quarterly, 13*(4), 503–530.

CULTURAL ATTITUDES IN MULTINATIONAL CORPORATIONS

Cultural attitudes refers to a school of thought within international business that explores the relationship between management cognition and the alternative ways multinational corporations (MNCs) respond to the challenge of operating across national borders. The theoretical framework for this approach was introduced by Harold Perlmutter, first in his 1965 *L'enterprise internationale* and next in his famous 1969 article on "the tortuous evolution of the multinational corporation." Drawing on a background in both engineering and social psychology, Perlmutter proposed that the best measure of a firm's internationalization was not some readily available statistic—such as percent of foreign sales—but rather managerial mind-set. Since decision makers vary across MNCs in their beliefs and perceptions about the international environment, organizations end up pursuing fundamentally different solutions to similar situations. Thus, MNC leaders must develop an appropriate managerial orientation, or cultural worldview, if their organization is to achieve long-term financial and operational success. The next section of this entry outlines the basic elements of Perlmutter's theory and describes how it was first adapted by Perlmutter himself and by other early proponents. The entry concludes with a description of this theory's critical place in the development and evolution of international management as a distinctive area of inquiry within management thought.

Fundamentals

Perlmutter originally identified three principal perceptual orientations among top managers in MNCs: (a) ethnocentric, (b) polycentric, and (c) geocentric. In MNCs where an ethnocentric mind-set dominates, people, ideas, and practices from the home country are deemed superior to those from other countries. Decision-making authority resides in the headquarters, and information tends to flow "downward" to national subsidiaries in the form of orders, advice, and counsel. The MNC's identity is closely associated with its country of origin. Recruitment for key positions takes place in the home country, and foreigners often feel marginalized.

The polycentric MNC has been described by the old expression "when in Rome, do as the Romans do." Home-country managers view host-country cultures to be impenetrably difficult to understand, so decision making is delegated to the national subsidiaries. There is comparatively less communication between the headquarters and subsidiaries, or, even between subsidiaries. Consequently, cross-country learning is held to a minimum. Recruitment and training take place at the country level and each subsidiary develops a separate identity.

Within geocentric MNCs, managers seek out the best ideas and opportunities wherever in the world they emerge. Lines of communication and influence are complex, adaptive, and multidirectional. Headquarters and subsidiaries strive for a collaborative approach and pursue goals that are both mutual and global in scope. Subsidiaries often work closely with one another to formulate new ideas and strategies, as well as to transfer best practices. Training and development initiatives are expansive in scope, and key positions are filled by merit rather than nationality. While the geocentric MNC is a truly global entity, organization members still try to identify with local customers and meet their needs. "Globally integrated but locally responsive" is the mantra of the geocentric MNC.

While Perlmutter viewed these three categories as ideal-types, he believed that most MNCs could be categorized meaningfully within this typology. These three managerial orientations were also regarded as a progression. Although firms often start out with a strong ethnocentric bias, they become increasingly polycentric as they expand internationally. Few firms ever become fully geocentric, however, which is treated in Perlmutter's model as a sort of ultimate end state. In later formulations, Perlmutter and his colleagues added a fourth category, labeled *regiocentric*, where the MNC views a broad international region (such as Europe or Asia-Pacific) as a single market. Together, these four managerial orientations are known as the ethnocentric, polycentric, regiocentric, geocentric framework, or *EPRG framework*.

Other factors beyond the MNC's natural evolutionary progression can also shape managerial cultural attitudes. These include individual characteristics such as CEO leadership style and personal biases, as well as organization-level variables including firm size and industry. Theorists also point to the importance of home-country characteristics in determining managerial orientations. MNCs from the United States and other large economies may be more prone to ethnocentricism since home-country environmental munificence offers the latitude to overlook smaller markets. Prior to common market initiatives, European MNCs were especially likely to follow a polycentric approach because of the large number of culturally and institutionally diverse markets within close geographic proximity. New MNCs from developing economies might experience pressures to pursue a geocentric mind-set more quickly due to limited opportunities in their domestic market. In 1993, McKinsey & Company coined the term "born global" to describe MNCs that adopt a global market orientation almost from their inception. Different functional areas within the same MNC can also demonstrate dissimilar managerial orientations. A pharmaceutical company might organize its research and development (R & D) activities based on geocentric ideals but behave in an ethnocentric or regiocentric manner in its sales and marketing efforts.

Importance

The challenge of monitoring and controlling business activities across diverse national institutional environments was one of the first and still most important topics in international management. Business historians attribute the term *multinational corporation* to David Lilienthal (founding director of the Tennessee Valley Authority) who used this phrase in an address given in 1960 to describe corporations with a "home in one country which operate and live under the laws and customs of other countries as well." Lilienthal's speech focused on many of the same issues raised by Perlmutter, and which still captivate international business scholars and managers today. These topics included home office–subsidiary relations; the selection and training of employees for international assignments; problems resulting from national, cultural, and legal differences; and the need to develop a "cosmopolitan" class of managers. Prior to Perlmutter, other early international business scholars, such as Yair Ahroni and Charles Kindleburger, had also explored the impact of managerial cognition on MNC behavior.

The greatest contribution of Perlmutter's approach to MNC cultural attitudes was perhaps his introduction of a formal typology that proved

both relevant and readily adaptable to international business scholars working across a wide variety of subdisciplines. Indeed, few international business frameworks have inspired such a diverse body of research. Researchers in international human resource management point out how Perlmutter's 1969 article was one of the few papers to address international training and staffing issues prior to the 1990s, and that the EPRG framework still serves as the basis for how scholars describe international human resource strategies. The framework holds a similar place of honor within the international marketing field for comparing MNC approaches to new product development and branding strategies among other topics. The cross-cultural management scholar Nancy Adler even drew upon Perlmutter's concepts to distinguish between six types of culture research: (a) parochial, (b) ethnocentric, (c) polycentric, (d) comparative, (e) geocentric, and (f) synergistic. The first four all focus on the behavior of organizations in individual countries, but they differ in the number of cultures being studied and in assumptions about whether theories from one culture are applicable to others. Geocentric studies focus on the behavior of the MNC operating across countries, whereas synergistic research examines cross-cultural interaction within organizational boundaries.

One of the most important and best known adaptations to Perlmutter's framework was formulated by strategic management researchers Christopher Bartlett and Sumantra Ghoshal, who also drew inspiration from John Fayerweather's proposal that international firms must strike a balance between fragmentation and unification. Bartlett and Ghoshal distinguished between (a) multinational, (b) global, (c) international, and (d) transnational companies. Multinationals essentially operate as a portfolio of national companies and may prove effective when there are strong market pressures to be responsive to national differences. By comparison, global firms are more centralized in their operations and decision making. They view their worldwide market as a solitary cohesive whole and tend to be most successful in environments that require cost efficiencies through global integration rather than local responsiveness. International companies seek to transfer knowledge and capabilities from the parent company to its foreign subsidiaries and represent a kind of hybrid form. They are more centralized than multinational firms but allow for more adaptation than purely global entities. Bartlett and Ghoshal proposed that since firms face increased pressures to be both globally integrative and nationally responsive, they should aspire to the fourth category, the transnational approach. This new type requires firms to develop operational units that are globally dispersed, differentiated but interdependent, and create and share knowledge and capabilities on a worldwide basis. They argued that building a transnational organization requires changes to more than just administrative policies and formal organizational structure. Instead, they offered their transnational solution as a new managerial orientation, or state of mind.

Bartlett and Ghoshal's transnational approach and Perlmutter's category of geocentricism share close theoretical ties with the growing body of research on global mind-set. According to Mansour Javidan and Mary Teagarden, global mind-set refers to an individual's ability to influence individuals, groups, organizations, and systems that are unlike his or her own. They contend that this ability depends on three types of capital—intellectual, social, and psychological. The global mind-set construct has been operationalized in a variety of ways including surveys and interviews of senior executives, content analysis of company documents, and assessments of firm behavior. In 2003, P. Christopher Earley and Soon Ang introduced a promising effort to quantify global mind-set through a 20-item survey of cultural intelligence (CQ). This index seeks to measure an individual's ability to perform effectively across diverse cultural settings.

While advocates of cultural intelligence and global mind-set stress the need for MNC managers to adopt a cosmopolitan orientation, cross-cultural researchers often point to the dramatic differences in leadership styles across countries. Societal values in the United States, for instance, encourage managers to stress individual achievement and responsibility, short-term goals, as well as a scientific or rational decision-making orientation. By contrast, the German system of codetermination fosters a more collaborate approach between managers and workers. The Japanese principles of *amae* (dependence), *giri* (obligation), and *gambare* (perseverance) have been argued to contribute to a management system emphasizing reciprocity, hierarchical relationships, and "long-termism." Managers across countries also differ in their degree of power. Managers in the United States, Germany, and Japan normally enjoy a relatively high degree of status. British managers, by

comparison, have not fared as well since their position has traditionally been viewed as an unsuitable vocation for the elite class. Since top positions in most large Chinese firms have historically been held by Communist Party officials, the emergence of professional managers as a unique social class is a relatively new phenomenon in China. Despite changing environments in these and other countries, managers must be mindful of such cultural differences when interacting with stakeholders such as workers, customers, and suppliers in foreign countries.

One recent development within international business research has been a growing movement challenging the view that becoming a "truly global firm" is a strategic imperative. Alan Rugman, for instance, examined the sales activities of the world's largest MNCs and found that the vast majority were either focused on just one region (North American, European, or Asian) or biregional. One of the implications of this finding is that the international management field must place greater emphasis on regional rather than global strategies. In a series of books and articles, Pankaj Ghemawat similarly suggests that business and society is far less globalized than frequently assumed. He cites estimates that 90% of the world's population will never visit a foreign country and still receives an overwhelming share of their news and information from domestic sources. In such a world, it may not be preferable or even possible to achieve both global integration and local responsiveness. He calls on managers to adopt a cosmopolitan orientation where they not only recognize and appreciate national differences but also exercise a healthy caution about them. According to this view, MNCs should not seek out opportunities wherever they emerge without first taking the institutional context into account. Adaptation may not always be possible and is never perfect, so managers must consider cultural, political, legal, economic, and other differences when making market entry and other international business decisions.

William D. Schneper and
Mary Ann Von Glinow

See also Cultural Intelligence; Institutional Theory of Multinational Corporations; Interactional Model of Cultural Diversity; Meaning and Functions of Organizational Culture; Organizational Structure and Design; Strategic International Human Resource Management; Transnational Management

Further Readings

Adler, N. J. (1983). A typology of management studies involving culture. *Journal of International Business Studies, 14*(2), 29–47.

Bartlett, C. A., & Ghoshal, S. (1989). *Managing across borders: The transnational solution.* Cambridge, MA: HBS Press.

Javidan, M., & Teagarden, M. B. (2011). Conceptualizing and measuring global mindset. In W. H. Mobley, M. Li, & Y. Wang (Eds.), *Advances in global leadership* (Vol. 6, pp. 13–39). Bingley, England: Emerald Group.

Kefalas, A. (1998). Think globally, act locally. *Thunderbird International Business Review, 40*(6), 547–562.

Lilienthal, D. (1960). The multinational corporation. In M. Anshen & G. L. Bach (Eds.), *Management and corporations, 1985: A symposium held on the occasion of the tenth anniversary of the graduate school of industrial administration, Carnegie Institute of Technology* (pp. 119–158). New York, NY: McGraw-Hill.

Mendenhall, M. E., Kühlmann, T. M., & Stahl, G. K. (Eds.). (2001). *Developing global business leaders: Policies, processes, and innovations.* Westport, CT: Quorum Books.

Perlmutter, H. V. (1969). The tortuous evolution of the multinational corporation. *Columbia Journal of World Business, 4*(January–February), 9–18.

Peterson, R. B. (Ed.). (1993). *Managers and national culture: A global perspective.* Westport, CT: Quorum Books.

Stahl, G. K., & Björkman, I. (Eds.). (2007). *Handbook of research in international human resource management.* Northhampton, MA: Edward Elgar.

Wind, Y., Douglas, S. P., & Perlmutter, H. V. (1973). Guidelines for developing international marketing strategies. *Journal of Marketing, 37*(2), 14–23.

CULTURAL INTELLIGENCE

International and intercultural work has become the norm for most large companies despite the large challenges confronting global companies. Managers often operate across borders in teams of internationally diverse units. Thus, many large organizations express the need to have managers who can quickly adjust across many cultures and work in a globally diverse context. The result of these pressures has been a need to understand better those characteristics and dynamics that underlie cultural adaptation and adjustment, typically, through some type of human resources training on cultural awareness. An emphasis on understanding others through their related values, beliefs, and practices underlies much current work on cultural training and management education. However, there is a fundamental limitation with a cultural values awareness approach—an awareness of cultural values is not a substitute for more direct knowledge of interpersonal interactions, just as values alone are not solely the predictive feature of behavior. To address these limitations in the face of new global challenges, and supplement the strengths in current approaches, an alternative approach was introduced and discussed that uniquely identifies the specific capabilities of an individual based on a faceted model of cultural adaptation called cultural intelligence, or CQ. This entry is focused on describing a faceted model of CQ consisting of three basic elements: cognitive and metacognitive, motivational, and behavioral CQ for looking at strategic thinking and mental processing, value orientation, and efficacy engagement and actions taken, respectively.

Fundamentals

There are a number of conceptualizations of CQ, the most dominant posed by P. Christopher Earley and Soon Ang as well as D. C. Thomas and K. Inkson. For this entry, the Earley and Ang framework will be focused upon, but the two approaches share many commonalities. CQ consists of three fundamental elements: metacognition and cognition (thinking, learning, and strategizing), motivation (efficacy and confidence, persistence, value congruence, and affect for the new culture), and behavior (social mimicry and behavioral repertoire). To illustrate these facets, take an example of a Thai employee who is seen smiling at his Canadian (expatriate) manager. Relying on direct cues derived from North American culture might lead the manager to assume her employee is happy or pleased. But such an interpretation might be largely overly simplistic and ignorant of social context. The physical action of smiling was once thought to denote a relatively small domain of underlying emotions (positive), but more recent work by psychologists suggests that this view is limited. The attributional mechanisms at work with emotional display are complex and culturally faceted. This idea is illustrated in the example of the "Thai smile" and how this might be best understood by the Canadian manager. First, she needs to observe the various cues provided in addition to the smile gesture itself (e.g., other facial or bodily gestures, significance of others who may be in proximity, the source of the original smile gesture) and to assemble them into a meaningful whole and make sense of what is really experienced by the Thai employee. Second, she must have the requisite motivation (directed effort and self-confidence) to persist in the face of confusion, challenge, or apparently mixed signals. Third, she must choose, generate, and execute the right actions to respond appropriately. If any of these three elements are deficient, then she is likely to be ineffective in dealing with the Thai national. A high CQ *awareness* manager or person has capability with all three facets as they act in unison.

Let us now turn to a more in-depth discussion of the features of cultural intelligence drawn from Earley and Ang's 2003 book *Cultural Intelligence*. First, the metacognitive and cognitive facet refers to information processing aspects of intelligence, and it is conceptualized using self-concept theory. Our "self" is a dynamic interpretive structure that mediates most significant intrapersonal and interpersonal processes. The cognitive facet of CQ can be viewed as the total knowledge and experience of an individual stored in memory concerning cultural adaptation. Knowing yourself is not sufficient, for high CQ awareness does not guarantee flexibility; adaptability of self-concept and ease of integrating new facets into it are, however, associated with high CQ since understanding new cultures may require abandoning preexisting conceptualizations of how and why people function as they do.

Another aspect of CQ is metacognition, and it refers to higher level cognitive processes as part of a person's processing of information, or "thinking about thinking." Thus, metacognition can be broken down into two complementary elements including metacognitive knowledge (what and how to deal with knowledge gained under a variety of circumstances) and metacognitive experience (what and how to incorporate relevant experiences as a general guide for future interactions). Metacognition is a critical aspect of CQ since much of what is required in a new culture is putting together patterns into a coherent picture, even if one does not know what this coherent picture might look like. To do

so requires a higher level of strategy about people, places, and events. A high CQ person must inductively create a proper mapping of the social situation to function effectively. This requires a general but broad foundation of knowledge about cultures and societies similar to the training recommended by an anthropological view covering topics such as economic systems, religious and political institutions, social relationships, and so on.

The second facet of CQ refers to its motivational aspect. It's insufficient to merely have information about how a group of people deal with the world. You must be able (and motivated) to use this knowledge and produce a culturally appropriate response. Cultural intelligence reflects self-concept and directs and motivates adaptation to new cultural surroundings. Psychologist Albert Bandura's self-efficacy idea is that of *a judgment of one's capability to accomplish a certain level of performance*. People tend to avoid tasks and situations they believe exceed their capabilities, and efficacy judgments promote the choice of situations and tasks with high likelihood of success and eliminate the choice of tasks that exceed one's capabilities. A person who does not believe in personal capability to understand people from novel cultures is likely to disengage after experiencing early failures. Highly efficacious people do not require constant rewards to persist in their actions; not only may rewards be delayed, but they may also appear in a form that is unfamiliar.

Efficacy alone is not a full description of the motivational facet of CQ, and an important, and related, addition is psychologist and business professor Edwin Locke's concept of goal setting. Behavior is both goal directed and purposeful. In an intercultural encounter, a challenge is to determine the goals of others coming from a different cultural and personal background. Goals specify the conditional requirement for positive self-evaluation. The process of evaluating the significance of knowledge about what is happening with our personal well-being generates emotions. Goal appraisal is necessary not only for activating a response toward goal attainment but also for generating emotions that are necessary for energizing action. That is, our goals may act as cognitive anchors thereby guiding subsequent actions.

A person's norms and values are an important aspect of the self as they guide attention to unique aspects of the social environment. Values and norms guide our choice of activities as well as help define our evaluation of them. For example, a person having a strong power orientation likely shows deference to authority and engages in a directive style with subordinates. Values are standards that lead individuals to take positions over issues, predispose individuals to favor particular ideologies, guide self-presentations, evaluate and judge ourselves and others, act as a basis for morality and competence comparisons with others, direct individuals concerning what ideas of others should be challenged, and tell individuals how to rationalize beliefs and actions that would otherwise be unacceptable so as to preserve self-image.

Cultural encounters are very different than the context typically experienced by an employee. These encounters challenge a person's thoughts and assumptions about their own culture by contrasting their beliefs about right and wrong with a potentially different system. One reaction to such a challenge is for the individual to isolate himself from the new culture. For example, a person low on motivational CQ who encounters initial frustration of goal attainment (e.g., having an unsuccessful cultural encounter) will have lowered efficacy, negative self-image, and potential disengagement with others.

The third facet of cultural intelligence refers to a person's behavior. Behavioral CQ reflects a person's capability to acquire or adapt behaviors appropriate for a new culture. The behavioral element of CQ suggests that adaptation is not only knowing what and how to do things (cognitive) and having the wherewithal to persevere and exert effort (motivational); it also requires an individual to engage in appropriate actions. Lacking these specific behaviors, a person must have the capability to acquire such behaviors.

A person may know and wish to enact a culturally appropriate behavior but cannot do so because of some deep-seated reservation. For example, imagine a manager who is thrust into an uncomfortable social situation and is not able to control his nonverbal communication cues. This type of response (or lack of it) can be thought of in behavioral terms. Even if a person is able to provide a desired response in a cultural encounter, it remains problematic because the host may detect hesitation and react negatively. Persistence is necessary for the acquisition of new skills and so is a person's aptitude to acquire these new skills. That is, it is not enough to be willing to try and learn new behaviors—a high CQ person has

an aptitude to determine where new behaviors are needed and how to execute them effectively.

Importance

The preceding sections of this entry have introduced and described cultural intelligence and its key elements, metacognitive and cognitive, motivation, and behavior. The utility of this approach is illustrated nicely by an application to a very important problem in global business—running effective global teams. Working on a highly diverse team consisting of members from a range of cultures and backgrounds makes the problem of establishing goals, roles, and rules highly problematic because of the additional complexity added due to cultural differences. Take, for example, the issue concerning rules for interaction within a multinational team. How should members interact and discuss core issues? If disagreements occur, how are they to be resolved? If the team receives limited resources, how should they be distributed? And how might team members decide individual responsibilities? A team member coming from a strong need-based culture might well expect that scarce resources are allocated based on need rather than accomplishment, while a fellow member coming from an equity-based culture might have an opposing view. The unstated assumptions concerning right and wrong, due process, expectations for membership, and so forth are tied to cultural background and experience. So although these kinds of issues are a good starting point for building trusting teams within a single culture, they can easily become contentious issues in the global team.

CQ competencies based on metacognition and motivation are of particularly high importance for the global team. Functioning in such a team requires that members acknowledge their weak overlapping knowledge and focus on the most basic commonality to create a hybrid or synergistic culture that grows out of something more fundamental than distribution of rewards and decision rules. Even though the long-term strength of global teams lies in their diversity and unique experiences as a team, sharing those unique perspectives in a team too early in the group's interactions is risky individually.

Global teams require specific CQ competencies held by members to uncover commonality across its membership, effective and appropriate role allocations, and clearly defined rules for interaction based on the specific needs (i.e., some cultural and some individual) and interests of team members. Metacognitive CQ training addresses these different learning strategies in the way that cognitive CQ training addresses the content differences. Motivational CQ provides the confidence to persist when trying to determine the basis of experienced differences. Behavioral CQ guides appropriate ways of interacting with others from different cultures.

Given the importance of cultural interaction, it remains unfortunate that the dominant approach used in both corporate and educational settings is to provide managers and students with culture-specific knowledge in the case of a targeted assignment (country specific, limited duration assignment, or educational study-abroad program) or culture-general features dominated by a discussion of a limited set of cultural values. Unfortunately, cultural values briefings can easily degrade into a values-based stereotyping of national cultures and provide tenuous, if not downright unfounded, links to actual behavior of cultural participants. CQ represents a new direction for theory and practice that tailors unique facets of capability to each individual. By focusing on these interdependent systems, training and cultural understanding are more easily approached and enhanced.

P. Christopher Earley

See also Cultural Values; Emotional and Social Intelligence; High- and Low-Context Cultures; Organizational Culture Theory; Social Cognitive Theory; Social Information Processing Model; Strategic International Human Resource Management

Further Readings

Bandura, A. (1997). *Self-efficacy: The exercise of control.* New York, NY: W. H. Freeman.

Bhawuk, D. P. (2001). Evolution of culture assimilators: Toward theory-based assimilators. *International Journal of Intercultural Relations, 25,* 141–163.

Earley, P. C., & Ang, S. (2003). *Cultural intelligence: An analysis of individual interactions across cultures.* Palo Alto, CA: Stanford University Press.

Locke, E. A., & Latham, G. P. (1990). *A theory of goal setting and task performance.* Englewood Cliffs, NJ: Prentice-Hall.

Sternberg, R. J. (1985). *Beyond IQ: A triarchic theory of human intelligence.* New York, NY: Cambridge University Press.

Thomas, D. C., & Inkson, K. (2008). *Cultural intelligence: Living and working globally* (2nd ed.). San Francisco, CA: Berrett Koehler.

Triandis, H. C. (1972). *The analysis of subjective culture.* New York, NY: Wiley.

CULTURAL VALUES

In this globalized and multicultural world, there is nearly universal agreement among cross-cultural researchers that values are a key component of culture as demonstrated by a number of important cross-national studies of values. Thus, a number of researchers within sociology, social psychology, and anthropology state that cultural values have a large influence on how people's beliefs, attitudes, and behaviors are shaped. As differences in cultural values are also associated with differences in work-related values, they are of particular interest to academics in the field of management, as well as to practicing managers. Considering that different national cultures have different value systems, the importance and meaning that, for example, Americans, Dutch, Chinese, and Brazilians attribute to work goals, motivation, leadership, communication, hierarchy, and teamwork, just to name a few, may reflect in different and sometimes conflicting attitudes, behaviors, and practices that may be considered legitimate within the same national culture. Building explicitly on the research tradition begun by Geert Hofstede, there is also strong evidence that national cultures and, consequently, values measured at the national level are associated with economic growth, although other factors such as technological progress and governmental policy should also be considered to understand differences in economic performance. This entry will be a review of the nature of cultural values, broach the main cultural frameworks, and show a glimpse at the future faced by scholars and managers in an interdependent world.

Fundamentals

Before introducing the main framework concerning cultural differences in values, it is necessary to explain how theorists have defined *culture* and *values.*

*Culture h*as been explained in various ways. Florence Kluckhohn and Fred Strodtbeck's definition of culture can be synthesized as a shared set of commonly held general beliefs and values that influence people's assumptions, perceptions, and behavior. For anthropologist Clifford Geertz, culture is a historically transmitted pattern—or web—of meanings by means of which men communicate, perpetuate, and develop their knowledge about and their attitudes toward life. For social psychologist Geert Hofstede culture is the collective programming of the mind that manifests itself not only in values but also in more superficial ways such as in symbols, heroes, and rituals.

Values have also been defined in different ways. For Kluckhohn, a value is a conception, explicit or implicit, distinctive of an individual or characteristic of a group, of the desirable which influences the selection from available modes, means, and ends of action. For Milton Rokeach to say that a person "has a value" is to say that he has an enduring belief that a specific mode of conduct or end state of existence is personally and socially preferable to alternative modes of conduct or end states of existence. From these definitions, we can infer that Kluckhohn and Rokeach did not distinguish what is *personally* preferable, desirable, or important from what is *socially* preferable, desirable, or important. In other words, a culture may harbor conflicting values. Such contradictions may exist due to an inconsistency between people's actions and their professed values, which explain why scholars must carefully distinguish between what people do and what they say. So, in Hofstede's view, an important distinction is that between values is the *desired* and the *desirable,* or, in other words, what people actually desire versus what they think they ought to desire. Although the two are not independent, they should not be equated to avoid confusion between reality and social desirability. For sociologist Ronald Inglehart, values change, but historically, the changes are very gradual and reflect changes in the formative experiences that have shaped different generations. As younger generations gradually replace older ones, the prevailing worldview may be transformed. In this sense, values are in a flux that may cause shifts in value systems. Finally, cross-cultural psychologist Shalom Schwartz, a prominent scholar in the study of values across individuals and nations, defines values as conceptions of the desirable that guide the

way social actors (e.g., organizational leaders, policymakers, individual persons) select actions, evaluate people and events, and explain their actions and evaluations.

Hofstede carried out the best known cross-cultural framework in the 1970s, across more than 50 countries, producing four dimensions. It was later revisited, in the 1980s and in 2010, to add two additional dimensions. Before presenting the Hofstede dimensions, it is important to clarify that in studying values, we compare individuals, while in studying culture, we compare societies. Thus, Hofstede clearly stated that in constructing indexes for the national level, researchers ought to make sure that a country's mean scores correlate across countries to avoid the reverse ecological fallacy (it occurs when researchers compare cultures on indexes created for the individual level). Societal cultures reside in (often unconscious) values, in the sense of *broad tendencies to prefer certain states of affairs to others.* For Hofstede, cultures are extremely stable over time, and this stability can be explained with the reinforcement of cultural patterns by the institutions that they themselves are products of the dominant value systems.

In Hofstede's framework, each country is positioned relative to other countries through a score on each comparable dimension. These dimensions, which describe national averages, hold valid as *scores provide not absolute but relative country positions to other countries in the set.* However, this does not invalidate the existence of countries with strong subcultures and more heterogeneous internal dimension distributions (such as Canada with its French Canadian culture that has differences when compared with its English-speaking culture) and of countries with more homogeneous internal distributions (for example, Japan and Argentina). A summarized description of the Hofstede dimensions, extracted from some of his publications, may be useful to better understand their implications.

Power Distance

Power distance has been defined as the extent to which the less powerful members of organizations and institutions (like the family) accept and expect that power is distributed unequally. This represents inequality (more versus less) but defined from below, not from above. It suggests that a society's level of inequality is endorsed by the followers as much as by the leaders. Power and inequality, of course, are extremely fundamental facts of any society. All societies are unequal, but some are more unequal than others. In Hofstede, Hofstede, and Minkov's 2010 edition of *Cultures and Organizations: Software of the Mind,* the Power Distance Index scores are listed for 76 countries (see Table 3.1, pp. 57–58); they tend to be higher for eastern European, Latin, Asian, and African countries and lower for Germanic and English-speaking Western countries.

Uncertainty Avoidance

Uncertainty avoidance is not the same as risk avoidance; it deals with a society's tolerance for ambiguity; it is about anxiety. The roots are nonrational. Human societies at large use technology, law, and religion to deal with uncertainty. Organizations tend to use technology, rules, and rituals. It indicates to what extent a culture programs its members to feel either uncomfortable or comfortable in unstructured situations. Unstructured situations are novel, unknown, surprising, and different from the usual. Uncertainty-avoiding cultures try to minimize the possibility of such situations by strict behavioral codes, laws, and rules. Rules are semirational: It is about trying to make people's behavior more predictable, and because people are both rational and nonrational, rules should take account of both aspects. In the 2010 edition of *Cultures and Organizations: Software of the Mind,* Uncertainty Avoidance Index scores are listed for 76 countries; they tend to be higher in eastern and central European countries, in Latin countries, in Japan, and in German-speaking countries, while lower in English-speaking, Nordic, and Chinese culture countries.

Individualism

Individualism on the one side versus *collectivism,* as a societal, not an individual characteristic, is the degree to which people in a society are integrated into groups. On the individualistic side, we find cultures in which the ties between individuals are loose: Everyone is expected to look after him- or herself and his or her immediate family. On the collectivist side, we find cultures in which people from birth onward are integrated into strong, cohesive in-groups, often extended families (with uncles, aunts, and grandparents) that continue protecting them in

exchange for unquestioning loyalty, and they oppose other in-groups. Again, the issue addressed by this dimension is an extremely fundamental one, regarding all societies in the world. In the 2010 edition of *Cultures and Organizations: Software of the Mind,* Individualism Index scores are listed for 76 countries; individualism tends to prevail in developed and Western countries, while collectivism tends to prevail in less developed, Latin American, and Eastern countries; Japan takes a middle position on this dimension.

Masculinity–Femininity

Masculinity versus femininity, again as a societal, not as an individual characteristic, refers to the distribution of values between the genders, which is another fundamental issue for any society, to which a range of solutions can be found. The assertive pole has been called "masculine" and the modest, caring pole "feminine." The women in feminine countries have the same modest, caring values as the men; in the masculine countries, they are somewhat assertive and competitive, but not as much as the men, so that these countries show a gap between men's values and women's values. In masculine cultures, there is often a taboo around this dimension. In the 2010 edition of *Cultures and Organizations: Software of the Mind,* the Masculinity Versus Femininity Index scores are presented for 76 countries; masculinity is high in Japan, in German-speaking countries, and in some Latin countries, such as Italy and Mexico; it is moderately high in English-speaking Western countries; it is low in Nordic countries and in the Netherlands and moderately low in some Latin and Asian countries, such as France, Spain, Portugal, Chile, Korea, and Thailand.

Long-Term Versus Short-Term Orientation

This dimension was first identified in a survey among students in 23 countries around the world, using a questionnaire designed by Chinese scholars. As all countries with a history of Confucianism scored near one pole, which could be associated with hard work, the study's first author Michael Harris Bond labeled the dimension Confucian work dynamism. The dimension turned out to be strongly correlated with economic growth. As none of the four International Business Machines Corporation, or IBM, dimensions was linked to economic growth,

Hofstede obtained Bond's permission to add his dimension as a fifth to the four. Because it had been identified in a study comparing students from 23 countries, most of whom had never heard of Confucius, Hofstede renamed it *long-term versus short-term orientation;* the long-term pole corresponds to Bond's Confucian work dynamism. Values found at this pole were perseverance, thrift, ordering relationships by status, and having a sense of shame; values at the opposite, short-term pole were reciprocating social obligations, respect for tradition, protecting one's "face," and personal steadiness and stability. In the 2010 edition of *Cultures and Organizations: Software of the Mind,* Michael Minkov, by combining elements of his research with World Values Survey (WVS) items, succeeded in obtaining a new version of long versus short-term orientation, now available for 93 countries and regions. Long-term oriented are East Asian countries, followed by eastern and central European countries. A medium-term orientation is found in South and North European and South Asian countries. Short-term oriented are the United States and Australia and Latin American, African, and Muslim countries.

Indulgence Versus Restraint

The sixth and new dimension, added in the 2010 edition of *Cultures and Organizations: Software of the Mind,* uses Minkov's label *indulgence versus restraint.* It was also based on recent World Values Survey items and is more or less complementary to long versus short-term orientation. It focuses on aspects not covered by the other five dimensions but known from literature on "happiness research." *Indulgence* stands for a society that allows relatively free gratification of basic and natural human desires related to enjoying life and having fun. *Restraint* stands for a society that controls gratification of needs and regulates it by means of strict social norms. Scores on this dimension are also available for 93 countries and regions. Indulgence tends to prevail in North and South America, in Western Europe, and in parts of sub-Saharan Africa. Restraint prevails in Eastern Europe, in Asia, and in the Muslim world. Mediterranean Europe takes a middle position on this dimension.

Evolution

In 2011, Hofstede contextualized his model and included a synthesis on the evolution of concepts and constructs from which we partly borrow.

In the early 1950s, anthropologist Clyde Kluckhohn was the first to argue that there should be universal categories of cultural values. Also in the 1950s, sociologists Talcott Parsons and Edward Shils suggested that human action is determined by five bipolar variables: *affectivity* (need for gratification) *versus neutrality* (restraint of impulses), *self-orientation versus collectivity orientation, universalism* (applying general standards) *versus particularism* (each case is a case), *ascription* (judging others by who they are) *versus achievement* (judging them by what they do), and *specificity* (limiting relations with others to specific spheres such as private and public) *versus diffuseness* (no prior limitation of relations to specific spheres).

From the 1950s to the 1980s, anthropologist Edward Hall published several books with important contributions. He divided cultures according to their ways of communicating into *high-context* (much of the information is implicit, indirect, and you have to read between the lines) and *low context* (information is more explicit, direct, and generally more detailed). Hall is also well known for having identified cultural values related to time, space, and objects and for having introduced other fundamental constructs: *proxemics* (use of space, including personal space and territory) and *monochronic versus polychronic* time (preference to do one thing at a time versus several things happening at once).

In the 1960s, anthropologists Florence Kluckhohn and Strodtbeck, as a result of field studies in small American communities, identified the following value orientations: *an evaluation of human nature* (evil-mixed-good), *the relationship of man to the surrounding natural environment* (subjugation-harmony-mastery), *the orientation in time* (past-present-future), *the orientation toward activity* (being/feeling-controlling, rational-doing/pragmatic), and *relationships among people* (hierarchical-group oriented-individualistic).

In the late 1950s and 60s, sociologist Alex Inkeles and psychologist Daniel Levinson identified three value dimensions, which they called standard analytic issues: *relation to authority, conception of self,* and *primary dilemmas or conflicts* and ways of dealing with them (including the control of aggression and the expression versus inhibition of affect).

Another prominent scholar is Harry Triandis who, during 1980 and 1994, did a good deal of empirical work exploring the *individualism* and *collectivism* constructs. According to his perspective, tendencies toward individualism and collectivism exist within every individual and in every society. In collectivistic cultures, people think of themselves as part of their collectives and, in most situations, subordinate their personal goals to those of their collectives; in individualistic cultures, people are more detached from their collectives, feel more autonomous, and give precedence to personal goals.

Shalom Schwartz, following several theorists (e.g., Hofstede; Kluckhohn & Strodtbeck; and Rokeach), postulates that cultural dimensions of values reflect the basic issues or problems that societies must confront in order to regulate human activity. His theory derives seven types of values on which cultures can be compared, which are postulated to form three bipolar dimensions: *autonomy* (intellectual and affective) *versus conservatism* (approximately equivalent to collectivism), *hierarchy versus egalitarianism* (emphasizing equality, social justice freedom, and honesty), and *mastery* (implying emphasis on ambition and success) *versus harmony* (implying emphasis on unity with nature and protecting the environment).

Sociologist Ronald Inglehart expanded the European Values Survey (now WVS) to cover more than 100 countries worldwide and also areas such as ecology, economy, education, emotions, family, gender and sexuality, and society and nation, among others. Michael Minkov took up the challenge of exploring the potential of the WVS. In 2007, he published a book in which he described three new cross-national value dimensions, which he labeled *exclusionism versus universalism* (which strongly correlates with Hofstede's collectivism versus individualism), *indulgence versus restraint* (which is now the 6th dimension of the Hofstede model), and *monumentalism* (its main facets are pride and self-consistency) *versus flexumility* (a combination of flexibility and humility), which moderately correlates with Hofstede's long and short-term orientation.

Another large-scale project was Global Leadership and Organizational Behavior Effectiveness (the GLOBE), conceived by management scholar Robert J. House in 1991. At first, House focused on leadership, but soon the study branched out into other aspects of national and organizational cultures and produced 18 country scores for each country: nine cultural value dimensions "as is" and nine dimensions "should be." This research has provoked an extensive debate in the literature, but so far, there

seem to have been few applications relevant for practical use by cross-cultural practitioners.

Importance

We live today in an interconnected and interdependent world, where the dimensional cultural value paradigm can help us grasp the internal logic of this changing environment. Different scholars have presented alternative models that have stimulated the debate and the development of cross-cultural research. Dimensions are constructs that help us understand cultural values in order to handle the complex reality of the social world. All models have received support and criticism, but that does not undermine their value and their contribution to knowledge. Even those who advocate that new technologies will make societies more and more similar should consider that cultures with different value systems, or as Geertz put it, with different webs of meaning, will probably cope with technological modernization in different ways. Critics argue that the Hofstede cross-cultural framework is obsolete. However, numerous studies replicating the dimensions have, so far, corroborated their validity, as the scores provide not absolute but relative country positions to other countries in the set.

Finally, cultural dimensions of values, as proposed by Schwartz, reflect the basic issues or problems that societies must confront in order to regulate human activity. As globalization proceeds, new concerns will probably emerge, and the need for new and maybe different theoretical perspectives may rise, but all cross-cultural scholars will have contributed to laying the foundations for the advancement of cultural values research.

For the modern manager operating in a global business context, different cultural value systems in general and the Hofstede value dimensions in particular provide insights to address important issues, challenges, and opportunities that have been mostly exemplified in Hofstede's works as follows:

Power distance (PD) explains *concentration of authority* (for example, the degree of centralization of authority in China vs. the flatter structures with flexible borderlines and empowerment in Denmark). In terms of *preferred managers*, subordinates in low PD countries tend to prefer the consultative type, while subordinates in high PD countries tend to accept autocratic or paternalistic managers. *Management by objectives* can work only if there is room for bargaining between boss and subordinate; consequently, this technique tends not to fit in high PD countries, where *privileges for superiors* are usually normal.

In higher *uncertainty avoidance (UA) cultures,* there is a stronger appeal for rules, so *innovators* tend to feel more constrained by rules and regulations. The appeal of rituals in high UA countries tends to materialize in a need for detailed planning. Coping with uncertainty is also a variable critical to power: In high UA societies, those who control uncertainty tend to be more powerful than in low UA societies, where uncertainty is more easily tolerated. *Competencies* should be more clearly defined in high UA cultures than in low UA cultures and *matrix organization structures* tend to be less acceptable in high UA countries.

In *individualistic cultures,* employees are expected to act rationally according to their own interest, and work should be organized in such a way that this self-interest and the employer's interest coincide; the relationship between employee and employer is primarily a *business transaction.* In a *collectivistic culture,* an employer never hires just an individual but a person who belongs to an in-group, so frequently, trust and loyalty may be considered more important than performance.

In distributing rewards, *feminine cultures* tend to favor *equality and mutual solidarity,* whereas *masculine cultures* tend to favor *equity,* that is, pay according to merit and performance. In more feminine cultures, *resistance against women* entering higher jobs tends to be weaker, so more women tend to be promoted into managerial positions.

Businesses in long-term oriented cultures are usually accustomed to working toward building up strong positions in their markets and they do not expect immediate results. In short-term oriented cultures, the bottom line tends to be a major concern, control systems are focused on it, and managers are judged by it. In long-term oriented societies, having a personal network of acquaintances is extremely important. The relational network lasts a lifetime, and people would not jeopardize it for short-term bottom-line reasons.

In societies that favor indulgence, employees usually consider that striving for happiness is a fundamental component of life, whereas in societies that favor restraint, employees generally attribute a secondary importance to leisure.

Adriana Victoria Garibaldi de Hilal

See also Cultural Attitudes in Multinational Corporations; Cultural Intelligence; High- and Low-Context Cultures; Individual Values; Interactional Model of Cultural Diversity; Multicultural Work Teams

Further Readings

Hofstede, G. (2001). *Culture's consequences: Comparing values, behaviors, institutions and organizations across nations.* Thousand Oaks, CA: Sage.

Hofstede, G. (2011). Dimensionalizing cultures: The Hofstede model in context. *Online Readings in Psychology and Culture, Unit 2.* Retrieved from http://scholarworks.gvsu.edu/orpc/v012/iss1/8/

Hofstede, G., Hofstede, G. J., & Minkov, M. (2010). *Cultures and organizations: Software of the mind* (3rd ed.). New York, NY: McGraw-Hill.

House, R. J., Hanges, P. J., Javidan, M., Dorfman, P. W., & Gupta, V. (Eds.). (2004). *Culture, leadership, and organizations: The GLOBE study of 62 societies.* Thousand Oaks, CA: Sage.

Inglehart, R., & Baker, W. E. (2000). Modernization, cultural change, and the persistence of traditional values. *American Sociological Review, 65*(1), 19–51.

Kluckhohn, F. R., & Strodtbeck, F. L. (1961). *Variations in value orientations.* Westport, CT: Greenwood.

Minkov, M. (2011). *Cultural differences in a globalizing world.* Bingley, England: Emerald.

Minkov, M., & Hofstede, G. (2012). Hofstede's fifth dimension: New evidence from the World Values Survey. *Journal of Cross-Cultural Psychology, 43*(1), 3–14.

Schwartz, S. H. (1994). Beyond individualism/collectivism: New cultural dimensions of values. In U. Kim, C. Kagitcibasi, H. C. Triandis, S. C. Choi, & G. Yoon (Eds.). *Individualism and collectivism: Theory, method, and application* (pp. 85–119). Thousand Oaks, CA: Sage.

Triandis, H. C. (1995). *Individualism and collectivism.* Boulder, CO: Westview.

Decision Support Systems

There are many definitions of a decision support system (DSS). The broadest definition would be any use of readily available computer systems to aid decision makers in making a decision. This entry will review the more academic definitions of DSS.

Decision support system is a term that arose from research conducted at MIT in the 1970s. The definition was commendably broad, including the use of computerized systems to aid human decision makers by providing them better and more timely information, as well as the processing of this data in models. The type of model could range from database query to complex optimization. As the 1970s and 1980s proceeded, divergent views of DSS emerged. In the information systems academic discipline, the focus was on *systems,* providing data from various sources (internal or external), a tool-kit of models, and a user interface that was available in a timely manner. This view is reflected in the earliest DSS texts. Peter Keen and M. S. Scott Morton defined DSS as using computers to (a) assist managers in their decision processes in semi-structured tasks; (b) support, rather than replace, managerial judgment; and (c) improve the effectiveness of decision making rather than its efficiency. Ralph Sprague and Eric Carlson soon followed with another popular text, using this definition—*interactive* computer-based systems that *help* decision makers utilize *data* and *models* to solve *unstructured* problems. At that time, interactive computer access was a new concept. That no longer is the case, so that aspect isn't so important

anymore. DSS is still important to management theory because the other elements of their definition remain useful in distinguishing using computer systems to help humans learn about the implications of the various options available to them, hoping to lead to better, more effective decision making. The term was used early on in connection with commercial software products, a practice that continues to this day. Since the 1980s, there has been more focus on branches of DSS, to include computer system architecture, group communication support, and continued widespread use of the term in connection with models to aid interesting and important decisions. In this entry, fundamentals of DSSs are described in terms of their benefits. Types of DSSs are described, and the importance of DSSs in supporting human decision making is discussed.

Fundamentals

DSSs come in many forms. Their primary feature is harnessing computer power to aid decision maker learning about decision environments. DSSs generally accomplish this through access to data and models appropriate to the decision. There have been literally hundreds of papers using DSS as a keyword every year since 1990 by one incomplete search engine. These papers include many studies of DSS effectiveness. Some of these sources have contributed to the Wikipedia site. Benefits of DSSs include (a) improving personal efficiency, (b) speeding up the decision-making process, (c) increasing organizational control, (d) encouraging decision maker exploration and discovery, (e) speeding up organizational problem solving, (f) facilitating inter-personal communication, (g) promoting learning or training, (h) generating new evidence to support particular decisions, (i) creating competitive advantage, (j) revealing new approaches to thinking about particular problems, and (k) helping automate managerial processes.

There are a number of different types of DSSs. Since the 1970s, the field of operations research has used the term *DSS* liberally whenever they have written articles proposing use of mathematical modeling to aid some specific decision. The difference between a management science analysis and a DSS is often blurry. Over time, the initial success of the approach led to a system that was used by the organization on a regular basis, thus transforming an analysis using data and models to an automated DSS.

D. J. Power has developed a taxonomy emphasizing assisting humans to make decisions. Power classifies at least five types of DSSs:

Communication-driven DSS supports multiple people working on a task. There is a well-developed body of research supporting the idea of group decision support (group support systems, or GSS; group decision support systems, or GDSS, etc.). These systems range from technically focused software such as Lotus Notes through dedicated meeting room software providing support to brainstorming, discussion, voting, and recording. Technology has made the use of cameras connected to desktops (now laptops and cell phones) and Internet telephone connections a cost-efficient means to communicate around the globe. That is not a DSS, but it accomplishes communication-enhancing decision making. Those products that are communication-driven DSSs accomplish much the same thing with the enhancements listed above.

Data-driven DSS emphasizes access to and manipulation of data. Online analytic processing (OLAP) is especially popular commercially. It is used to refer to storage in data warehouses. There are a number of variants:

- ROLAP (relational OLAP) refers to systems retrieving data from relational databases, enabling handling large amounts of data, although with slower response due to use of SQL queries.

- MOLAP (multidimensional OLAP) calls data stored in multidimensional nonrelational databases. This gives faster data retrieval than ROLAP but with the disadvantage that it can practically handle less data.
- HOLAP (hybrid OLAP) seeks to combine ROLAP and MOLAP, using MOLAP storage technology and ROLAP drilling-down processes.
- WOLAP (Web-OLAP) refers to systems accessing data from the Web.
- DOLAP (desktop OLAP) refers to systems accessing data from desktop environments.

Document-driven DSS addresses management, retrieval, and manipulation of unstructured information. This view treats database software as key. Document-driven DSS is focused on text manipulation, as opposed to the data focus of data-driven DSS. The field of text mining would certainly be an example of document-driven DSS.

Knowledge-driven DSS in Power's taxonomy addresses specialized problem-solving expertise (especially tacit knowledge) stored as facts, rules, or procedures. This view can include case-based reasoning. Knowledge-driven DSS overlaps communication-driven and document-driven DSS.

Model-driven DSS emphasizes statistical, financial, or operations research modeling as discussed above. The Institute for Operations Research and Management Sciences has liberally used the term DSS whenever an application of operations research is applied to a decision (which is practically always). Expert systems are the next step once a DSS has been developed, automatically implementing the decision-making process that might be developed within a DSS. The field of data mining (business analytics) is closely related to operations research, applying statistical and artificial intelligence tools to practically every field of scientific and commercial research.

Importance

Our culture has developed the ability to generate masses of data. Computer systems expand much faster than does the human ability to absorb. Furthermore, Internet connections make it possible to share data in real time on a global basis. DSSs are thus needed to cope with masses of data in a dynamic world where new problems challenges old ways of doing things. It is valuable for human decision makers to learn as much as they can about new situations and to explore the expected impacts of their decisions.

There is a clear need for many organizations to be able to process data faster and more reliably. Data mining (different from DSS, but related, as both seek to help humans learn) involves the use of analysis to detect patterns and allow predictions. It is not a perfect science; the intent of data mining is to gain small advantages, because perfect predictions are impossible. But these small advantages can be extremely profitable to business. For instance, retail sales organizations have developed sophisticated customer segmentation models to save sending sales materials to those who are unlikely to purchase products, focusing instead on those segments with higher probability of sales. Banks and other organizations have developed sophisticated customer relationship management programs (supported by data mining) that enable prediction of the value of specific types of customers to that organization and to predict repayment of loans. Insurance companies have long applied statistical analysis, which is extended by data-mining tools to aid in prediction of fraudulent claims. These are only three of many important data-mining applications to business. Models from data mining can be used as DSS models.

The field of operations research used the term to reflect a focus on *models* used to aid decision making (which was the original purpose of management science). This was reflected in many *Interfaces* articles reporting the use of models to aid decision making A search of the INFORMS database through early 2006 identified 46 papers with "DSS" or "decision support system" in the title involving applications to a specific problem, 35 of which were in *Interfaces*. Many other papers include similar applications without the magic words in the title. This is certainly an appropriate use of the term DSS, although it clearly involves a focus on the aspect of modeling. A grant system that continues to encourage implementation of DSSs to specific problems, often over the Internet, has led to many practical software systems were delivered to the public by governmental agencies. Such systems can range from providing farmers tools to design irrigation systems to guides in calculating federal income tax.

In Europe, meanwhile, the idea of decision support focused on development of systems meant to incorporate multiple criteria analysis into *decision aids*. Systems such as analytic hierarchy process (AHP), preference ranking organization method for enrichment evaluations (PROMETHEE), ELECTRE, and others have been marketed as DSSs. Selection decisions are challenging, because they require the balancing of multiple, often conflicting attributes, criteria, or objectives. A number of interesting tools to support selection decision making have been presented. *Expert systems* try to emulate the decisions of an expert in some particular problem domain and include ways to automate decisions in repetitive environments. These are appropriate when rare expertise exists or when complex operations would be improved by precise actions. Rare expertise can be preserved and multiplied. Often, the motivation for an expert system is the computerization of rare expertise. In concept, an individual who is very good at a specific type of analysis can be used as the basis for developing an expert system to replace the expert. In practice, nobody claims to replace the expert but rather to use the computer system to clone and transport the expert throughout the world, recording the expertise in the organizational knowledge base. The difference between an expert system and a DSS is that expert systems are for repetitive tasks, or they wouldn't be worth developing, whereas DSSs in concept were targeted on helping humans learn the complexities of a new problem. DSSs need to be flexible, to respond to changing environments. Expert systems in concept could replace human judgment for well-defined, specific applications.

DSSs can thus appear in many forms. There are many useful systems. Their primary feature is to harness computer power to aid decision makers learn about their decision environment. The original systems in the 1970s were basically spreadsheet models (in a time when spreadsheets had not yet appeared). Interactive Financial Planning System (IFPS) is an example, created by Jerry Wagner. The most persistent and leading texts have been the various editions of Efraim Turban. As modeling tools have evolved, group systems better support communication and collaboration, expert systems enable automation of decision making, and data mining expands the scale of data that can be examined. Decision support has always been an evolutionary field, and will continue to evolve as computer tools and data availability expand.

David L. Olson

See also Bounded Rationality and Satisficing (Behavioral Decision-Making Model); Decision-Making Styles; Image Theory; Knowledge-Based View of the Firm; Learning Organization; Managerial Decision Biases; Organizational Learning; Prospect Theory

Further Readings

Alter, S. L. (1977). A taxonomy of decision support systems. *Sloan Management Review, 19*(1), 39–56.

Burstein, F., & Holsapple, C. (Eds.). (2008). *Handbook on decision support systems.* Heidelberg, Germany: Springer.

Gorry, G. A., & Scott Morton, M. S. (1971). A framework for management information systems. *Sloan Management Review, 13*(1), 56–70.

Keen, P. G. W., & Scott Morton, M. S. (1978). *Decision support systems: An organizational perspective.* Reading, MA: Addison-Wesley.

Power, D. J. (2005). *Decision support systems.* New York, NY: iUniverse.

Sprague, R. H., Jr., & Carlson, E. D. (1982). *Building effective decision support systems.* Englewood Cliffs, NJ: Prentice-Hall.

Turban, E., Sharda, R., & Delen, D. (2010). *Decision support and business intelligence systems* (9th ed.). Englewood Cliffs, NJ: Prentice Hall.

DECISION-MAKING STYLES

Decision-making style is an individual's preferred way of perceiving and responding when faced with a problem-solving situation. This represents a combination of a person's innate personality-driven preferences with his or her learned and habitual responses that have been developed over time and through experience. Scholarly interest in decision-making styles comes from the recognition that individuals can exhibit a particular or dominant behavior in the way they approach decision making, and that an understanding of this and the factors influencing such biases and preferences can help improve the quality and effectiveness of individuals' decision making. This entry outlines two key models of decision-making style (rational vs. intuitive and autocratic vs. group decision-making approaches) and considers their implications and those factors influencing differences in decision-making styles.

Fundamentals

A long-standing distinction is made between rational and intuitive decision-making styles. A rational approach is typified by making decisions in a deliberate and logical manner. This tends to be linked to a structured decision methodologies and reliance on existing concepts and cognitive categories to filter data. An intuitive individual is seen as working on the basis of a hunch or impression of an issue or situation. This is associated with iterative and trial-and-error decision-making approaches, where the individual's focus tends to be on the stimulus for the decision itself. Much of the rhetoric on organizational decision-making tends to focus on the development of and mechanisms for rational approaches, but there is a growing recognition that effective decisions and decision makers combine rational and intuitive approaches. A major financial investment tends to be associated with need for rationality, whereas strong emotional investment tends to be linked with an intuitive bias. Hence, significant decisions such as purchasing a house that contain both financial and emotional elements tend to combine both approaches.

Other work has extended this rational-intuitive model; dependency is seen as a significant approach by a number of authors. Dependent decision makers are seen as requiring the advice, direction, and support of others when making decisions. Although this can be a dysfunctional style, in that it can manifest itself as a reliance on others, it also can be seen positively as a bias toward involving and engaging others in the decision-making process and is therefore an approach that supports employee involvement and engagement. Susanne Scott and Reginald Bruce suggest that individuals in their decision-making styles can, additionally, be either avoidant or spontaneous. An avoidant individual would typically seek to postpone or avoid making a decision. A spontaneous decision maker is likely to be impulsive and prone to making "snap" or "spur of the moment" decisions. Spontaneity is a trait typically valued by organizations, but this is not without the risks associated with undue haste, and while an avoidant approach is also potentially dysfunctional, it also perhaps represents a more considered approach to decision making than the focus on spontaneity encouraged by many organizations.

Victor Vroom and his coworkers have developed a different perspective that focuses on decision participation styles and suggests a continuum from autocratic approaches at one end to a group decision making style at the other. An autocratic style involves minimal input from subordinates (as providers of information), with a manager making a lone decision on the basis of the information available at that time. A group approach is predicated on a high level of subordinate involvement, with the manager delegating the decision to a group. The group then becomes responsible for making that decision through consensus. Between these approaches sits a consultative approach. This involves sharing a decision with subordinates (either individually as a group) to get their views on the decision, but significantly, the decision remains the responsibility of the individual manager and may or may not represent the views expressed by subordinates through consultation. Again group and consultative styles support employee engagement and involvement. Although the nature of the decision and constraints such as time might affect the selection of these choices, a manager's approach will also be influenced by his or her personality, individual preferences, and experiences.

A number of factors are therefore seen as significant in influencing decision-making styles. The availability of information and access to existing knowledge are likely to be significant in influencing the choice between rational and intuitive approaches. Other aspects of the decision environment such as the availability of time and significance of the decision (in individual and organizational terms) are also significant. Organizational factors identified as affecting the choice to use differing styles include structure, culture, and communication. As also suggested, individual differences play a part. An individual's information-processing capacity has been linked to rational versus intuitive preferences, as has the extent to which individuals need structure and tolerate ambiguity. Personality, perception, experiences, and attitudes to involvement and risk have all also been argued as significant factors influencing preferred decision-making approaches.

The preceding outline indicates that when describing decision-making styles, there exist a variety of approaches and a number of self-assessment tools exist that allow individuals to surface and explore their decision-making style preferences. Different styles should not be viewed as better or worse than each other. Alternatives represent a range of attitudes and approaches; individuals may have a tendency to an approach but adopt different styles depending on the decision, its context, and other significant factors. What is important is that individuals recognize the implications of the styles they adopt.

David Philip Spicer

See also Bounded Rationality and Satisficing (Behavioral Decision-Making Model); Ethical Decision Making, Interactionist Model of; Garbage Can Model of Decision Making; Intuitive Decision Making; Participative Model of Decision Making; Programmability of Decision Making; Strategic Decision Making; "Unstructured" Decision Making

Further Readings

Hodgkinson, G. P., Sadler-Smith, E., Burke, L. A., Claxton, G., & Sparrow, P. R. (2009). Intuition in organizations: Implications for strategic management. *Long Range Planning, 42,* 277–297.

Lee, D., Newman, P., & Price, P. (1999). *Decision making in organizations.* London, England: FT/Pitman.

Mintzberg, H. (1976). Planning on the left side and managing on the right. *Harvard Business Review, 54,* 49–58.

Scott, S. G., & Bruce, R. A. (1995). Decision-making style: The development and assessment of a new measure. *Educational and Psychological Measurement, 55,* 818–831.

Spicer, D. P., & Sadler-Smith, E. (2005). An examination of the general decision making style questionnaire in two UK samples. *Journal of Managerial Psychology, 20,* 137–149.

Stanovich, K. E., & West, R. F. (2000). Individual differences in reasoning: Implications for the rationality debate? *Behavioral and Brain Sciences, 23,* 645–655.

Vroom, V. H. (2000). Leadership and the decision-making process, *Organizational Dynamics, 28,* 82–94.

Woiceshyn, J. (2009). Lesson from "Good Minds": How CEOs use intuition, analysis and guiding principles to make strategic decisions. *Long Range Planning, 42,* 298–319.

Dialectical Theory of Organizations

The dialectical view grew out of a critique of existing theory and research. The critique advanced the following arguments: (1) The praxis of rational structuring confined the field to the study of how to make organizations more efficient and effective. (2) The rational and functional explanations legitimized the ideology that existing organizational practices are justified by their rationality or functional necessity. (3) Thinking of organizations in rational and/or functional terms tends to reproduce the existing organizational structures and practices. (4) Rational and/or functional thinking tended to separate organization studies from other fields of inquiry. Organization analysis was seen as a field concerned with organizations seeking to achieve goals in a rational way. (5) The role of internal power and interests in shaping organizations was understated or folded into the rational or functional explanations. (6) The connection of organizations to larger systems of power and domination, both as a contributor to those larger systems and as products of those systems, was neglected. The entry first outlines four arguments fundamental to the dialectical view, showing how these provide a framework for building more specific, testable theories of organizations. These general arguments are on a level of abstraction similar to *structuration theory*, developed by Anthony Giddens. It is argued that people, acting under specific sets of circumstances and structural locations, construct organizational arrangements. They develop ideas and interests and pursue their implementation. They confront contradictions of the structure and opposing sets of interests. Actions and outcomes are affected too by the embedding of organizations in totalities consisting of institutions, networks, and cultures. The dialectic view also calls for a praxis of enlightenment and liberation to guide organization studies rather than a narrow pursuit of effectiveness and efficiency. In the second section, the entry briefly assesses the impact of the dialectical view on the development of organization studies in recent decades. Here, it is shown that a number of different versions of dialectics have been developed and that empirical work guided by these ideas extends to a number of empirical literatures, including power inequalities, gendered practices,

technological choices, policy studies, strategies, and network linkages. Some progress has also been made by various scholars in integrating dialectical theory with other strands of organization theory such as institutionalism.

Fundamentals

In "Organizations: A Dialectical View," Benson outlined four "principles" of a dialectical approach to organization studies, drawing from Marxian and phenomenological theories. Together these provided a framework for thinking about organizations and developing theoretical and empirical work in this field of study. We begin with a restatement of the four fundamental principles of the dialectical view.

Principles of the Dialectical Theory of Organizations

Social construction/production, the first principle, advances the idea that people construct organizations through their ongoing activity, including their social definitions and actions. Partly, they produce the organization purposefully and mindfully, but partly, they produce it through their ongoing practices and interactions. Also, they produce the organization under existing structures, conditions, and circumstances not of their own choosing. The existing social structures, power alignments, and other conditions (e.g., environments and markets) often result in unintended consequences. In this way, the dialectical view challenges the view that organizational structures and practices result from rational choices of the most efficient or effective arrangements.

Benson argued that social construction/production is shaped by the interests and power of the actors both inside and outside the organization, not strictly by the rational pursuit of goals or the fulfillment of needs. Here, he was influenced by Mertonian functionalists Phillip Selznick and Alvin Gouldner; by Ralf Dahrendorf, a critic of functionalism; by Gideon Sjoberg's concept of "contradictory functional requirements"; and by Michel Crozier's study of the power inequalities of departments in a factory.

Contradiction, the second principle, is the idea that opposing tendencies are deeply rooted in organizations. When people act and engage in intended or unintended construction/production, they run into resistance, opposing interests, existing structures, and practices resistant to their actions. The previously produced social arrangements, the opposing projects of social construction, and the entrenched interests and practices resist, stall, deflect, and redirect the process of production. Even the formal structure of the organization, its division into ranks and divisions, creates unintended consequences. People occupying particular positions defend their interests and try to control events in their favor. Power struggles develop and result in negotiations and compromises. There is a sense of irony or paradox in these works. Human action to construct a rational, effective social structure meeting needs or objectives produces a recalcitrant apparatus.

Contradiction has been developed also in the Marxist tradition, where it is theorized that social formations have deeply rooted opposing tendencies. Mihailo Markovic saw the contradictions as both objective structures and collective intentions in the sense of "we contradict" the system by pushing it beyond its limits. Benson held onto both of these meanings while also dealing with contradictions formulated by Claus Offe and Jürgen Habermas. Contradictions bring elements of a system into conflict in a way that threatens its foundations. Offe, for example, argues that commodification of labor power is an essential tendency of capitalism, but its development produces countermovements toward decommodification.

Totality, the third principle, calls for organizations to be understood in their contexts, including both the larger or macro social formation—for example, power structures, cultural patterns, economic systems, globalization, and the meso-structures such as occupations, networks, industries, and fields. In addition, totality demands attention to the emergent social worlds within the organizations—interest groups, gender differences, ethnic solidarities and conflicts, professional divisions, and so on. Alternative realities are constructed within the framework of the official structure of the organization. These alternative forms sometimes become collective projects and social movements challenging the existing order and bringing forth new orders. A dialectical approach brings these alternative worlds into view and examines their potential to reorient the organization. It looks at the possible futures of the organization.

Thinking of the organization as a totality is the opposite of abstracting the organization from its context. Conventional organization theory generated models of organizations as if they were separate entities with distinctive internal social patterns that distinguished them from the larger environment. The dialectical view develops the embedding of the organization in its context, seeing it as an integral part of a social formation. Connecting the organization to the environment requires a theoretical model of that relation. In the Marxist tradition, for example, organizations are understood as parts of the capitalist mode of production. Class conflict, exploitation, and alienation in the organization derive from the contradictions of capitalist systems. Welfare programs, labor market legislation, investment controls, industrial policies, globalization, and other developments have produced different forms of capitalism.

Praxis refers to the commitment of organization studies to the production of forms of social organization. A dialectical approach involves reflexivity—that is, a reflexive understanding and examination of the connection of knowledge to the production of social worlds. In part, this knowledge is critical of the stance of the dominant rational theories that are often engaged in the production of more efficient, more effective organizations without critically examining the uses of organizations. Rationalization of organizations is used not only to make commodities such as automobiles more efficiently but also to establish efficient regimes of social control and domination. In extreme cases, even genocide is efficiently organized by rational bureaucracies. Economic theories and management studies of organizations are often committed explicitly to the implementation of their work through the production of more efficient and effective organizations. There is often a kind of moral commitment to rational structuring in order to produce more goods at more affordable prices, to integrate a country into the capitalist world system, to organize an effective military campaign, and so on. By contrast, the dialectical view advances a praxis of liberation or emancipation of people from systems of domination. An emancipatory praxis does not necessarily lead to abandonment of bureaucracy and resort to totally nonhierarchical, undifferentiated forms of organization. As Stewart Clegg and Wynton Higgins cogently argue, efficient bureaucracies are necessary to implement social reforms and programs of liberation. A praxis of emancipation requires careful analysis of the administrative means of reform and liberation. For example, Wolf Heydebrand and Carroll Seron dealt with the contradiction between the ongoing administrative routinization of the federal district courts and the professional autonomy of federal judges.

Some strands of Marxian thought have addressed these problems. In particular Henri Lefebvre described his position as "possibilist" in the sense that praxis may produce changes in social organization that cannot be predicted or determined in advance; thus, through praxis reforms are possible. The trajectories of development do not form a determined sequence of specific organizational forms. Reforms of capitalism growing out of praxis are possible and may move the system in unanticipated directions. Michael Burawoy has explored some of the varied structures regulating the capitalist labor process. Analysts of state socialist systems have adapted Marxian thought to the critique of those social formations.

Importance

The importance of the dialectical view is that it provides a framework for thinking about organizations that stimulated new thinking by others. The components of the dialectical view are open to development. Scholars cannot "test" the theory per se because there are no predictions; however, other scholars have developed predictions or explanations by elaborating the implications of the view in specific empirical arenas. As such, it has inspired much attention, commentary, critique, and extension. For example, Kenneth McNeil notably critiqued the proposed approach and argued instead for a Weberian perspective. In the mid 1980s Lex Donaldson developed a critique and defended the rational-functional reasoning in contingency theory, whereas around the same time, Michael Reed proposed a somewhat similar dialectical approach based on structuration theory. In recent decades, a number of theories and studies have proposed additional dialectical perspectives. A consensual formulation of dialectical theory has not been produced. Rather, a rich diversity of formulations now exists. Some of these developed directly out of Benson's formulation. Others have different origins.

Political economy is an empirically oriented theoretical approach. Mayer Zald worked on power structures controlling exchanges and negotiations within organizations and on social movements in organizations. The dialectical view provides a way of thinking about and developing political economy theory. It is possibilist rather than determinist. It deals with social construction of the power structures. It deals with contradictions within the political economy and between the political economies of different sectors, industries, and fields. It pushes toward totality, the analysis of the system of political economies—for example, the multi-organizational systems where the contradictions of capitalism are managed through organizational and interorganizational apparatuses. Claus Offe has analyzed the contradictions of such systems. Harland Prechel has developed a historical contingency analysis of public policies affecting the operation of capitalist corporations.

The totality principle might be extended by taking account of *institutional theory and research*. Institutional theory challenges the rational model of organizations and opens up the many unregulated and unrecognized forms of dependence between organizations and their social and cultural contexts. Seo and Creed argue that the dialectical view provides a solution to the theoretical dilemma of embedded agency in institutional theory. Seeing the organization as a process driven by contradictions and opposing interests accounts for the emergence of alternative arrangements. Thus, they reject the coherence model of the organization still embedded in institutional theory. They go on to identify a series of organizational contradictions. Elizabeth S. Clemens and James M. Cook analyze contradictions in the study of political institutions. Proponents of *critical management studies,* Mats Alvesson, Hugh Willmott, and others, analyzed many forms of institutional shaping of organizational practices, including capitalism, gender inequalities, racial discrimination, and others. Robert Thomas showed how professional ideologies and power shaped the selection and development of new technologies in manufacturing firms. Vedran Omanovic showed how the power and administrative structures of a large manufacturing firm in Sweden shaped its implementation of a diversity initiative by focusing it on diversification of ideas rather than on diversity of genders and ethnicities. Karen Ashcraft and Dennis Mumby developed a dialectical approach to the interweaving of gender differences in organizational structures and practices.

The dialectical theory may help broaden managers' decision-making frameworks, challenging the narrow, rational choice perspective and questioning the effectiveness of the strategies and structuring options available to managers. For example, it may challenge the preeminence of "shareholder value" as the primary rationale for managerial decisions and open consideration of other "stakeholders." The dialectical perspective may help illuminate the multiple interests and power structures shaping the organization. The manager may better recognize the limits on the capacity of managerial decisions to shape outcomes. It may also help mobilize a wider range of stakeholders challenging public and corporate policies and organizational structures. Managers may then work in a more democratic political-economic environment that liberates them from the narrow range of options allowed by currently dominating interests.

J. Kenneth Benson

See also Circuits of Power and Control; Critical Management Studies; Institutional Theory; Interorganizational Networks; Social Construction Theory; Structuration Theory

Further Readings

Alvesson, M., & Willmott, H. (Eds.). (2003). *Studying management critically*. London, England: Sage.

Ashcraft, K. L., & Mumby, D. K. (2004). *Reworking gender: A feminist communicology of organization*. Thousand Oaks, CA: Sage.

Benson, J. K. (1977). Organizations: A dialectical view. *Administrative Science Quarterly, 22*(1), 1–21.

Benson, J. K., & Kim, B.-S. (2008). Institutionalism and capitalism: A dialectical and historical contingency approach. In H. Prechel (Ed.), *Politics and public policy: Vol. 17, Research in political sociology* (pp. 67–97). Bingley, England: Emerald Group.

Clegg, S. R. (1989). *Frameworks of power*. London, England: Sage.

Heydebrand, W., & Seron, C. (1990). *Rationalizing justice: The political economy of the federal district courts*. Albany: State University of New York.

Offe, C. (1985). *Disorganized capitalism*. Cambridge, MA: MIT Press.

Omanovic, V. (2009). Diversity and its management as a dialectical process: Encountering Sweden and the U.S. *Scandinavian Journal of Management, 25*(4), 352–362.

Seo, M., & Creed, W. E. D. (2002). Institutional contradictions, praxis, and institutional change: A dialectical perspective. *Academy of Management Review, 17*(2), 222–247.

Thomas, R. (1994). *What machines can't do: Politics and technology in the industrial enterprise*. Berkeley: University of California Press.

DIAMOND MODEL OF NATIONAL COMPETITIVE ADVANTAGE

Casual observations and ample anecdotal evidence support diverse arguments attempting to explain why particular industries in some nations are more competitive than the same industries in other countries. It is hard to argue against the global competitiveness of French perfumes, Italian shoes, German tool and die machinery, or Indian software services. In tackling this issue, the discussion below answers the questions: Why do some nations and their industries outperform others, and what are the implications for individual firms.

To shed light on the questions and provide an alternative to traditional economic theory explanations, a team lead by Michael Porter of Harvard University embarked on an ambitious study of 10 major trading countries and focused on specific industries within these countries that were known to be global leaders. Histories and case studies of 100 industries were developed, and patterns among them were outlined. The results were reported in a major volume of work published in 1990; the proposed diamond of national competitive advantage represents a framework that purports to parsimoniously identify the factors that create the conditions for competitive industries and provide the foundations for globally competitive firms. Ever since its introduction, the model has been debated and elaborated on as much as tested to ascertain the factors validity and their relevance for other countries. In the following few paragraphs, we explore the diamond model, discuss some of the most notable additions and critiques that have been debated since its original presentation in 1990, and consider some of the connections between the model and other related work that attempts to explain and inform the factors responsible for the competitiveness of different industries and nations.

Fundamentals

Four broad national attributes individually, and as a system, constitute what is termed "the diamond of national advantage." Arguably, these attributes determine the conditions and become the catalyst for the competitiveness of individual industries within particular nations. They shape the environment in which local firms compete and determine the advantage bestowed on the firms by their "home base" and place of origin. The diamond presents both the parameters presumed to be responsible for a nation's competitive advantage and the dynamic processes within industries by which such advantage was created. The four attributes are factor conditions, demand conditions, related and supporting industries, and the firms' strategies, structures, and rivalry. Two additional elements address the role of government as an influencer and catalyst of structures and conditions, as well as the reality that many situations occur and critically influence outcomes but are chance events that fall beyond the control of any player in the industry and the market. Within the expanded diamond, each of these attributes plays a determinant role in creating a nation's competitive advantage in a particular industry.

Factor Conditions

Human resources; physical resources such as land, water, mineral deposits, and hydroelectric power sources; knowledge resources and a nation's stock of scientific, technical, and market knowledge; capital resources; and a nation's infrastructure in transportation, communications, and power constitute the factors of production. They represent the inputs to a firm's activities; a nation's endowment plays a pivotal role in the competitive advantage of its firms. Many of these factors are not naturally inherited to a nation but are created through various processes and over time.

Classical economic theory posits that factors of production, such as land, labor, and capital, represent the inputs to a firm's value chain and create the goods and services that the firm sells to its markets. While many of these factors are essentially basic factors in that they are inherited and exist to varying degrees throughout the world, many of the more advanced factors are developed over time through investment and effort. Companies and nations seeking competitive advantage over firms in other

nations must create many of the advanced factors of production, such as technology, skilled labor, and modern infrastructure. For example, a country or industry reliant on innovation requires strong universities, research institutes, and a skilled human resource pool to draw from. These factors are not inherited but are created through investment in industry-specific knowledge and talent. Similarly, the supporting infrastructure of a country, its transportation and communication systems, its banking system, and its power grid as well as its health care system are equally critical and require time and huge investment to get established.

For a nation's competitive advantage, factors of production must be developed that are industry and firm specific. Moreover, while the total pools of resources at a firm's or a country's disposal are on their own right important, the speed and efficiency with which these resources are deployed tends to be more critical for the competitive advantage of the firms and the industry. At times, it is not the abundance but the scarcity of resources that triggers a competitive advantage. For example, Japan has little land mass, rendering real estate prohibitively expensive and forcing firms to reconsider their warehouse and inventory storage needs. Out of necessity, Japanese firms pioneered just-in-time production processes and lean inventory management, creating a resource that yielded competitive advantages over firms in other countries still employing traditional warehousing methods.

Demand Conditions

The composition and nature of home-market demand for the industry's products or services and the pressures exerted by sophisticated customers force firms to design innovative products and responsive product offerings. Such pressures present challenges to a country's industries and in response to these challenges, improvements to existing products and services often result, creating conditions necessary for competitive advantage over firms in other countries. Countries with demanding consumers drive firms to meet higher standards, upgrade existing products and services, and create new offerings. Their industries can better anticipate future global demand conditions and proactively respond to product and service requirements before competing nations are even aware of the need for such products and services. For example, the Danes' environmental awareness has spurred demand for environmentally safe products and has stimulated Danish manufacturers to become leaders in water pollution control equipment, wind energy turbines, and other green energy products that they also successfully export to other nations. Canada's abundance of metals and mineral resources has created a world-renowned mining industry, the world's largest stock exchange for the sector, and a host of industries in mining exploration, engineering, and development, which today successfully compete against the larger nations around the world. Similarly, its vast landmass has always presented unique challenges in bringing people and goods together and has sprung a global industry for telecommunications.

The sheer size of the home market and the complexity of its segments, the rate of growth of home demand, and the early onslaught and saturation of the market contribute to create and amplify the nation's competitive advantage and internationalize the products of the particular industries. The U.S. automotive industry has developed in large measure in response to the early adoption of the car by the masses, the large size of the home market, and Americans' love of their automobiles.

Related and Supporting Industries

The presence of supplier industries and other related industries within the nation and the competitiveness of these industries confer advantages creating stronger firms in the downstream industries that become internationally competitive. Robust suppliers and related industries experiment, innovate, collaborate, develop complementary products, perceive new methods and processes, and identify new applications for their latest technologies. Industries in nations with strong related and supporting industries capitalize early on them to expand internationally and establish a global competitive advantage.

Related and supporting industries enable firms to manage inputs more effectively. Japanese firms draw on the capabilities and skills of exceptional local suppliers of numerical control units, motors, and other components to produce world-class machine tools. Swiss global prowess in pharmaceuticals is closely connected to early achievements in the chemical and dye industries. The international success of Italian footwear is built on a range of related industries

in leather processing and tanning, in specialized machinery and machine tools, and in design services. Italian shoe manufacturers are located near their suppliers. They interact on a daily basis with their leather suppliers and learn about new textures, colors, and manufacturing techniques while a shoe is still in the design stage. The manufacturers are able to prepare their factories for new products long before companies in other nations become aware of the new styles.

Nations with a strong supplier base benefit by adding efficiency to downstream activities. A competitive supplier base helps firms obtain inputs early and rapidly, sometimes with preferential access, using cost-effective, timely methods, thus reducing manufacturing costs. Close working relationships with suppliers provide the potential to develop competitive advantages through joint research and development and the ongoing exchange of knowledge. Arguably, strong local suppliers still benefit downstream industries, even if they themselves do not compete globally. Similarly, related industries offer opportunities for shared activities and technical and information interchanges as well as cultivate new entrants to the focal industry, increasing competition and forcing existing firms to continuously innovate; run tight operations; and develop novel approaches to their business.

Firm Strategy, Structure, and Rivalry

The conditions within a nation governing how companies are created, organized, and managed determine the nation's competitive advantage. A good match between the companies' choices and the various sources of competitive advantage in a particular industry result in a national advantage. The ways in which firms are managed and how they choose to compete are influenced by national context and the particularities of any given country, its culture, its norms, and attitudes toward authority and individualism. Italy's and Israel's global firms are relatively small and family owned, reflecting individualist cultures and strong family ties. German success is usually based on meticulous engineering and technical inclination that produces a constant flow of methodical product and process improvements.

Company goals and corporate governance influence the use of invested capital and the pressures for short-term results versus patient investment in long-term research and innovation. Company goals are set and reflect ownership structures. Shareholders in countries such as Germany, Switzerland, and Japan tend to be institutionally affiliated and have different orientations from those in the Anglo-Saxon countries of the United Kingdom and the United States. In turn, they exert different influences on the affairs of a corporation and favor industries in lower risk contexts, requiring modest initial risk capital and heavy but sustained long-term investment and reinvestment.

Vigorous domestic rivalry is strongly associated with the creation and persistence of an industry's competitive advantage. Rivalry is particularly intense in markets with strong consumer demand, strong supplier bases, and high new-entrant potential from related industries. Such competitive rivalry, in turn, pressures firms to concentrate on the efficiency with which they develop, market, and distribute their products and services. Domestic rivalry also compels firms to innovate and find new sources of competitive advantage. It forces firms to search beyond their national boundaries for new markets, setting up the conditions for global competitiveness. Among all the attributes of the "diamond" of national advantage, domestic rivalry is, arguably the strongest indicator of global competitive success. In numerous examples Porter described in the original book, firms that have experienced intense domestic competition are more likely to have adopted strategies and structures that allowed them to successfully compete in world markets. Intense rivalry from IBM and Hewlett-Packard has spurred companies such as Dell Computer to find innovative ways to produce and distribute their products. Intense rivalry among Japanese automobile manufacturers in their home market has produced a lineage of global competitors in Toyota, Honda, and Nissan.

Government

The role of government in determining national competitive advantages has been debated extensively throughout the international business literature. In the diamond model, the government is not viewed as a determinant, in and of itself, but as an influencer of the four attributes. Government can influence either positively or negatively local demand conditions by establishing standards and regulations and through its vast purchasing power

as a major buyer of many products and services. It can shape factor conditions through subsidies, policies toward the capital markets, education, or protectionism. Government legislation, tax policies, and antitrust laws influence rivalry and firms' strategic orientations, as well as their corporate governance and accountability. Finally, related and supporting industries are affected in innumerable ways through mechanisms such as industrial policies, environmental regulations, and public partnerships.

Chance

While the determinants of national advantage shape the environment for competing in particular industries, the histories of most industries also include many chance events that critically influenced their success and competitiveness. Wars, oil shocks, commodity scarcities, inventions, nature's calamities, and blessings have played major roles in building competitive advantages. Wars have spurred the growth and development of chemical, pharmaceutical, and heavy-metal manufacturing and related industries, which later became global leaders from their home bases in Germany and Japan. Oil shocks hit Japanese industries early and hard because of the country's exclusive reliance on energy imports and forced these firms to take aggressive innovative steps toward energy conservation and lean manufacturing. Yet chance events have asymmetric influences and in and of themselves do not always lead to competitive advantage. Favorable national attributes are also necessary to convert chance events into advantages. For example, insulin was first isolated in Canada, in spite of no particular favorable demand conditions or other circumstances. Subsequently, however, insulin became an international commercial success by Danish and American companies, based in countries possessing specialized factor pools, favorable demand conditions, and other national advantages.

The diamond model posits that economic clusters and co-location of industries are beneficial to achieving global success. Moreover, its author asserts that considering the evolution of diamond, it can explain the competitive development of entire nations. Namely, it argues that economic development is closely tied to competitiveness and identifies four stages of industrial development that correspond to competitive advantages derived from specific conditions. The first stage is "factor-driven," and the industries that are successful are those where companies can compete on the basis of low cost, be that labor or materials. Only one attribute of the diamond offers an advantage. At the second stage, "investment-driven" success arises from heavy investments in factories and infrastructure. Here, three attributes of the diamond are relevant—factor conditions; demand conditions; and firm strategy, structure, and rivalry. At the next stage, the nation finally achieves prosperity, as the full diamond is in place in a wide range of industries and "innovation-driven" competitiveness draws on a host of emerging industries. However, nations are led to decline in prosperity as they move to a "wealth-driven" stage and their citizens' and organizations' interests shift away from creating wealth through investment and innovation to preserving entranced positions and insulating themselves from risk and competition. In consequence, the model can explain success in international trade, account for national prosperity, provide a framework for empirical work, and inform policy prescriptions on national competitiveness.

Evolution

The model's conceptual roots drew from international economics and neoclassical industrial organization economics. The initial appeal and positive reception had as much to do with the author's global standing as one of the most influential scholars in strategic management as it had with the simplicity and directness of the conclusions. The model provided an easy source of relevant answers at a time of major shifts in global business, the opening of many markets, the globalization of trade, the establishment of regions of free-trade agreements, and a heightened awareness for the need of countries, industries, and firms to be globally competitive.

The introduction of the diamond model in 1990 set off a multitude of responses, ranging from glowing endorsements to outright denunciations. Some scholars heralded it as the bridge between strategic management and international economics, a dynamic model that both described and explained the development of globally competitive industries and the ultimate answer to a nation's quest for economic prosperity. Its detractors lamented the many contradictions and ambiguities, the lack of rigor in the logic, the methodological deficiencies, and the circular arguments. Others deplored its limited generalizability and the selective choices of countries and industries to tell a certain story that could not be replicated in other settings.

A number of nations were eager to undertake their own analyses and proceeded to sponsor comprehensive studies of their competitiveness. A series of academic papers were published aiming at testing the model. For the most part, the studies were plugged by methodological challenges that arose from conceptual problems inherent in the model; they offered limited support for or refuted the conclusions of the model. Scholars attempted to augment the original diamond with (a) double diamonds (in the case of Canada and its intertwined automotive industry, which is fully integrated on a North American basis), (b) supranational diamonds (in the cases of Mexico, Austria, New Zealand, or Hong Kong, whose competitive strengths rest on their ability to draw on other countries' diamonds), and (c) proposed additional elements, in some cases expanding the number of attributes to nine.

Importance

No doubt, the diamond model generated substantial discourse and brought to the front many aspects of the debate on national competitiveness. While the diamond model's explanatory and predictive abilities have been undermined by rigorous analysis, it has retained its popularity to a large extent because of its simplicity and intuitive appeal. Whether it possesses the descriptive and explanatory power its author and admirers claim or simply offers commonplace assertions and unfounded, if not dangerous, prescriptions as convincingly have argued its detractors, it has succeeded in being inserted in almost every textbook in strategic management and international business and in being referred to in classrooms, boardrooms, and public policy meetings.

Public policy officials, keen to develop and support globally competitive industries in their jurisdictions, have seen the diamond as a framework that can inform their policies and guide related initiatives. Their attraction toward the model emanates from its commonsensical logic and parsimonious structure. Work on economic clusters and business ecosystems, which provide similar viewpoints, collaborate and complement the prescriptions that arise from the diamond. Both policies that encourage strengthening the factors of the diamond and those that would weaken them are viewed as having implications for the global standing of affected industries. For example, "voluntary" restrictions to imports or high tariffs that shield local firms from global competition, while they may temporary protect these firms, are viewed as undermining their global competitiveness. Moreover, associated prescriptions to managers are equally straightforward suggesting they should make decisions about investments and select locations for their operations on the basis of considerations of these same conditions. Businesses should demand that governments invest in education, infrastructure, and research as well as encourage local competition, and these moves will become the foundations for globally competitive industries.

Theodore Peridis

See also Competitive Advantage; Hypercompetition; Institutional Theory of Multinational Corporations; Theory of Cooperation and Competition; Transnational Management

Further Readings

Davies, H., & Ellis, P. (2000). Porter's competitive advantage of nations: Time for the final judgement? *Journal of Management Studies, 37*(8), 1189–1213.

Dunning, J. H. (1993). Internationalizing Porter's diamond. *Management International Review, 2,* 7–15.

Krugman, P. (1994). Competitiveness: A dangerous obsession. *Foreign Affairs, 73*(2), 28–44.

Porter, M. E. (1990). *The competitive advantage of nations.* New York, NY: Free Press.

Reich, R. (1990). Who is us? *Harvard Business Review, 68*(1), 52–64.

Reich, R. (1991). Who is them? *Harvard Business Review, 69*(2), 77–88.

Rugman, A. M., & Verbeke, A. (1993). Foreign subsidiaries and multinational strategic management: An extension and correction of Porter's single diamond framework. *Management International Review, 2,* 71–84.

DIFFERENTIATION AND THE DIVISION OF LABOR

Division of labor can be broadly defined as the specialization of cooperative labor in specific tasks and related roles or functions. It is a key concept in management and economics and regarded as one of the pillars of the increased productivity of modern and developed industrialized societies. It is also the cause of economic interdependence between different actors in an economy. In this entry, we discuss the development of these concepts from their roots in Greek antiquity to theories that emerged during the industrial revolution to concerns about alienation, exploitation, and class conflict, ending with an account of systems theory.

Fundamentals

The division of labor and the differentiation of tasks and roles can be described on various levels, ranging from division of labor between individuals and groups to that of organizations, states, and societies. Various disciplines take very different views of the phenomenon. In the management literature, particularly when applied to business, it is mainly discussed in terms of: (a) *vertical differentiation,* which is the establishment of defined spheres of authority and responsibility derived from the larger organizational power structure. These are usually represented as differentiated levels of the hierarchy, and (b) *horizontal differentiation,* which is the compartmentalizing of defined areas of engagement derived from the larger organizational domain. These are usually represented as differentiated specializations such as by function (e.g., manufacturing, marketing, research and development, etc.), division (e.g., by product, geography, customer), or business unit.

There is broad consensus about the benefits the division of labor brings for the productivity of an organization as well as the economy as a whole. This is central to the seminal work of Adam Smith, who in his 1776 book *An Inquiry Into the Nature and Causes of the Wealth of Nations* begins in Book 1, Chapter 1 with a discussion titled "Of the Division of Labour" and the argument that "the greatest improvement in the productive powers of labour, and the greater part of the skill, dexterity, and judgment with which it is anywhere directed, or applied, seem to have been the effects of the division of labour." Here, he delineates a framework for understanding these benefits, which arise from what he considers to be three primary factors: (1) *Development of expertise and skill:* When people focus on a narrow set of tasks they acquire greater understanding of and dexterity in performing these tasks. (2) *Increase in efficiency:* Time normally wasted ramping down from one task and ramping up to another (e.g., physical as well as mental transfer time) is reduced. (3) *Greater propensity for innovation:* Increased familiarity and experience in a specialized area allow workers to create advanced machines and methodologies that make their work easier as well as more productive.

Subsequent research has established that as differentiation increases the complexity of production processes and organizations, it also increases the need for coordination, control, and management. When a productive process is segmented into small parts and the individual contributor has only a limited understanding of how the task is related to the end product, integration becomes essential to put the differentiated parts together again. It is also a necessary precondition of any change of the way the work process is structured and organized.

The extent to which certain forms of differentiation can be dysfunctional and detrimental to the development of individuals, organizations, and societies is a matter of debate. Critical analyses argue that the separation of labor and managerial control and power deprive individuals of a meaningful activity, that specialization will lead to an increasingly narrow skill set (de-skilling) on the part of the worker, and that the power structures that underlie these inequalities tend to be rigid, undemocratic, unfair, and self-perpetuating. This view is often identified with Karl Marx and his concept of worker alienation. Similarly, the view of organizations as rationally designed and stable systems has also shifted to one that recognizes the cognitive limitations of decision makers and assumes a high degree of reciprocal dependence of any system and its subsystems with the environment. In a world in which information is limited, decisions take place under uncertainty, and rationality is "bounded." The structure of an organization, if conceptualized as an open system, is no longer seen as the result of a rational process of organizational planning and design but as a cybernetic system whose characteristics reflect of the demands of the environment with which it interacts.

Evolution

Early discussions of the division of labor date back to ancient Greece, when these considerations were a part of philosophy. The focus was mostly on individual characteristics and on how these related to a desirable form of society and the state. Xenophon's biography of Cyrus the Great contains an analysis of how occupations differ in a society; he pointed out how occupational roles can vary depending on the size of the city workers live in. Marx later referred to this as the basis of the idea that specialization is related to the size of a market. Plato's *Republic* contains more explicit references to this topic. The division of labor was, in his view, a natural necessity, given that talents are unequally distributed. In an ideal state, ruled by philosopher-kings, but with common ownership of resources, members of a state would contribute to the best of their abilities. His pupil Aristotle, who was opposed to the concept of the philosopher-king and unification, instead propagated private property as a basis of wealth creation.

Increasing Labor Productivity in Organizations

The division of labor was initially heralded as one of the key achievements of early industrialization. This stage is synonymous with the work of Adam Smith and closely associated with Frederick W. Taylor's scientific management, as well as Henry Ford's mass production of cars in the United States. The concept has developed considerably since then, but in its original stage, it was largely shaped by two authors who published their work during the English industrial revolution. Although they were friends, 18th-century philosopher Adam Smith and historian Adam Ferguson looked at two very different aspects of the division of labor.

In *An Inquiry into the Nature and Causes of the Wealth of Nations* (discussed earlier), Adam Smith used the example of a pin factory to explain the increase in productivity that results from a standardized process in which a holistic production is divided up into small segments. The beneficial effects of the division—or "partition"—of labor had previously been discussed by philosopher David Hume, but not in great detail. In Smith's example, each worker would be responsible for only a single part of the production process and as a result of this form of specialization would be more productive. Ferguson also referred to the pin factory example, much to the outrage of Smith, who suspected his friend Ferguson of plagiarism. However, while Smith saw the division of labor as the driving force of increased productivity and national wealth, Ferguson was mainly interested in the societal consequences and the increasing degree of reciprocal dependence of human beings. His description of the reality of highly differentiated work and social status included phenomena that Karl Marx and others would later discuss under the heading of alienation and exploitation.

Adam Smith's thinking was extended by Frederick W. Taylor in the late 19th century in what he himself later called *The Principles of Scientific Management*. Like Smith, Taylor believed in optimizing labor processes and maximizing productivity by dividing a complex task into easily manageable subtasks, and he also agreed that this increased productivity would be a pillar of the welfare of society as a whole. However, Taylor added that empirical science—instead of rule of thumb and tradition—should be applied to establish the ideal way to accomplish a task. Time and motion studies should help understand and improve production processes and minimize health hazards. Once the "one best way" of accomplishing a task had been identified, it should be communicated as "best practice," standardized quickly, and the implementation of the standard monitored closely. Manual labor and managerial control should be kept separate to maximize the effectiveness of control and to introduce changes more effectively. Taylor argued that the system of scientific management was in the interest of both employers and employees. As production processes were increasingly complex, no single individual could master them in their entirety, and new subtasks could be added where necessary. He recognized that standardized processes could be repetitive and left no freedom for individual variation. This, however, did not represent a problem for him; it meant that objective science and transparency trumped individual preferences and dysfunctional habits. The resulting increase in productivity—including a reduction in accidents—should be reflected in higher wages for the worker so that the interests of employers and employees were in equilibrium. Taylor's work is today often identified with Fordism and mass manufacturing. However, it appears that Henry Ford and his management were unaware of Taylor and simply arrived at similar conclusions at more or less the same time.

Solidarity, Alienation, Exploitation, and Class Conflict

At about the same time, French sociologist Émile Durkheim published his dissertation "The Division of Labor in Society." Instead of optimizing labor productivity, Durkheim was interested in how social order was maintained, and how more "primitive" societies advanced and would eventually become "industrialized." Durkheim suggested that societies were bound together by solidarity. The type of solidarity differs depending on how developed the society is. Primitive societies were kept together by *mechanical solidarity*, with people thinking and acting alike, rooted in a collective conscience. Such a society would be cohesive and integrated because people's personal and working lives are similar. Advanced, capitalist societies, on the other hand, in which labor is differentiated, are bound together by *organic solidarity*. In this case, cohesion results from a higher degree of complementarity and interdependence. Durkheim regarded the division of labor as both risk and opportunity, depending on the state of a society. A high degree of differentiation, he argued, would weaken mechanical solidarity, as people have less opportunity to act in the same way. At the same time, it would strengthen organic solidarity, as people were becoming more interdependent. Modern societies bound by a high degree of organic solidarity and interdependence have the potential for more sustainable cohesion, easier conflict resolution, and a meritocratic distribution of economic benefits. Durkheim believed that the consequences of an increase in the division of labor could be either positive or negative, depending on the state of a society. As societies change toward a more advanced and industrialized stage, the risk of lack of solidarity and appropriate norms—and potentially anomic division of labor—increases. This is where Durkheim's sociological perspective and the work of Smith and Taylor differ fundamentally: Differentiation—and the division of labor and responsibilities—has an effect that goes beyond maximizing productivity. In increasingly complex and urbanized societies, organic solidarity and high interdependence have the potential to avoid and resolve conflict and to maintain social order.

Karl Marx, who had started his work some time before Durkheim, was less optimistic in his assessment of the effects of the division of labor.

In a process he termed *alienation,* workers are expropriated—forcibly deprived of any control over what and how they produce—and become detached from the meaning of the result of their work and the objects they produce. Repetitive activities begin to have a depressing effect on the individual and deprive him or her of the characteristics of meaningful work. Marx pointed out that power was unequally distributed between those who were engaged in the production process and those who controlled the means of production, and—in contrast to Taylor—he argued that the division of labor often reflected this power and status asymmetry more than a technological necessity. Marx therefore drew a distinction between the technical and the social division of labor. While he recognized that some forms of differentiation are technically inevitable, Marx argued that many other forms of division of labor are, at least in part, socially constructed and directly related to status inequalities between the ruling and the working class. The ruling class, however, would use the technical dimension as an excuse to perpetuate status differences. The existing system was, he argued, a necessary evil that would eventually be transcended in a communist society. This is where Marx differed from Durkheim. Marx saw the division of labor as unjust, unfair, and alienating, whereas Durkheim argued that it might enable individuals and societies to become interdependent and more cohesive in the long term. Marx held that it would contribute to the perpetuation of the dysfunctional status asymmetries of the class system rather than foster a system of meritocracy in which each individual could find his or her own place. And unlike Durkheim, he expected a revolution in which the working class would take charge and end the evil of the division of labor rather than a society that is stable in the long term.

Marx's hypothesis of labor and the unequal distribution of power has since been applied to various contexts, ranging from relationships between countries—with imperialism and colonialism being the most obvious examples—to gender settings within organizations and the changing nature of work. There has been much debate about how inequality and injustice related to the division of labor can be self-perpetuating and how phenomena such as the digital divide—a situation in which the underprivileged have less access to digital

technology and therefore find it increasingly difficult to catch up—stabilize such inequalities. However, enthusiasm for Marx's historical determinism—the idea that revolution and a communist society would eventually be inevitable—is limited.

Importance

The impact of the concept of differentiation and division of labor on the theory and design of organizations is significant. Irrespective of the potential effect this might have on the individual, differentiation and division of labor were key features of what classical organization theory would regard as the ideal organization. Max Weber, while conscious of the downsides of bureaucracy, described it as a rational system with clearly defined roles and responsibilities, strict hierarchies, abstract rules that apply universally, and a process of hiring and promotion that would be based on qualifications and performance. Taylor had advocated a separation between labor and control. It was not enough to divide a complex production process into appropriately small elements (differentiation); these elements had to be connected appropriately (integration), and results had to be monitored constantly (control). This is in line with the work of early 20th-century French industrialist Henri Fayol, who was later popularized in the United States by Luther Gulick and Lyndall Urwick. Using the acronym POSDCORB (planning, organizing, staffing, directing, coordinating, reporting, and budgeting), their view of the responsibility of a chief executive officer—or subdivisions responsible for each of these areas—summed up the essence of classic administrative management. The formal structure of authority and the division of labor defined in the organization stage would be integrated in the coordinating stage. Balancing differentiation on the one hand and integration and control on the other are key. Formal organizational structures and processes reflect the need for differentiation, integration, and control in complex environments, where separate departments—and individuals belonging to these departments—are responsible for distinct parts of the total output of an organization, and decisions and activities are integrated on the next higher level of the organizational hierarchy. There are various taxonomies of mechanisms of control, ranging from Harry Braverman's self versus managerial control to Richard Edwards's personal, technical, and bureaucratic control. Modern taxonomies of mechanisms of control, such as by Austin Türk, are structured along the activities of human resource management and separate pre-organizational, social control (early socialization), potential control (selecting, allocating, and educating personnel), and organizational action control (by means of technology, bureaucracy, job design, differentiation, or personal).

Whether organizations should be regarded as rational and whether the formal and highly differentiated hierarchies of modern organizations are the result of an intentional process of organization design is a matter of debate. James March and Herbert Simon argued that, as organizations involve decisions of people who have only limited information and who are cognitively biased, the rationality of organizations is necessarily limited and that they "muddle through" as a result. Organizations were increasingly described as open systems, and the concept of a rational machine that, although it served the outside market, was designed to work in a stable way without reciprocal dependence on the outside world was described as a closed system approach. A system would be commonly defined as a group of elements (e.g., people, equipment, behaviors) that interact, share a common purpose, and are separated from other systems by a boundary. Evidently, biology was one of the most important sources for theory development in this area, and organizations were frequently compared to organisms. In contrast to the closed-systems perspective, the open-system view would regard an organization as an entity that transforms inputs taken from the environment to produce and return output to the environment—and the organization would itself change as a result. The organization, its structure and processes, becomes an integral part of the environment in which it operates. External factors, such as suppliers, distributors, competitors, and the regulatory environment, are more than external constraints; they have an impact on the organization itself. As organizations respond to their environment, their survival is a matter of fit and adaptability, and balancing integration and differentiation is a core element of an organization's ability to respond to changes in the environment. The work Paul Lawrence and Jay Lorsch published in the late 1960s was exceptionally seminal. They introduced a contingency theory of how an organization and its subunits adapt to meet the demands

of their immediate environment. Daniel Katz and Robert Kahn similarly described organizations as open, cybernetic systems, consisting of cycles of events, with a tendency for homeostasis and an inbuilt desire for growth to ensure their own survival. Differentiation on the one hand and integration and coordination on the other are important features of open as well as of closed systems, but design, implementation, and structural changes are viewed very differently. In a closed system, the structure of an organization would be intentionally designed by management, implemented, and then monitored and kept constant. In an open systems view, management is just one of many subsystems of a larger system, and this system has its own goal and is constantly evolving in response to the environment on which this organization is reciprocally dependent. Empirical data support the hypothesis that organizational structures and differentiation vary depending on the complexity of the environment: Lawrence and Lorsch reported that subunits of large organizations in the chemical industry that dealt with complex tasks in rapidly changing environments (e.g., R & D) were less structured and hierarchical, were more focused on the long term, and had a more heterogeneous understanding of the common purpose. Those organizations that operated in a more stable environment (e.g., production; marketing and sales) were more differentiated and hierarchical, focused on the short term and had a clearer understanding of a common goal.

Differentiation and the division of labor are key characteristics of modern management. No reader would envision a work environment without division of labor and structural differentiation. However, there are trade-offs between differentiation on the one hand and individual needs and organizational requirements on the other. It is essential to strike a balance between (a) a useful division of a complex process into manageable subactivities that can be honed to perfection by means of best practices and (b) the degree of fragmentation that entirely detaches the individual from the meaning and deprives him or her of any sense of purpose that can be derived from this activity and its outcome. Similarly, it is important to realize that an increase in differentiation brings with it the need for more integration and control and that these forms of control can become dysfunctional, rigid, and self-perpetuating. As organizations operate in environments that require rapid change to maintain strategic fit, the distribution of labor and structural differentiation will necessarily remain in flux—which limits the degree to which integration and control can be kept constant. Managers as agents of change will be required to retain a high degree of flexibility in how they assign responsibilities, integrate results, and exert control.

Oliver Fischer and Lorenz Fischer

See also Bureaucratic Theory; Contingency Theory; Diversification Strategy; Environmental Uncertainty; Job Characteristics Theory; Managing Diversity; Organizational Effectiveness; Scientific Management

Further Readings

Braverman, H. (1974). *Labor and monopoly capital: The degradation of work in the twentieth century.* New York, NY: Monthly Review Press.

Durkheim, E. (1964). *The division of labour in society.* New York, NY: Free Press. (Original work published 1893)

Katz D., & Kahn, R. L. (1966). *The social psychology of organizations.* New York, NY: Wiley.

Lawrence, P., & Lorsch, J. (1967). Differentiation and integration in complex organizations. *Administrative Science Quarterly, 12,* 1–30.

Marx, K. (1976). *Capital,* Vol. 1. Harmondsworth, England: Penguin. (Original work published 1887)

Pahl, R. (1984). *Divisions of labour.* Oxford, England: Blackwell.

Scott, W. R. (2006). *Organizations and organizing: Rational, natural and open systems perspectives.* Englewood Cliffs, NJ: Prentice Hall.

Smith, A. (1981). *An inquiry into the nature and causes of the wealth of nations* (Vols. 1, 2, R. H. Campbell & A. S. Skinner, Eds.). Indianapolis, IN: Liberty Fund. (Original work published 1776)

Smith, V. L. (1998). The two faces of Adam Smith. *Southern Economic Journal, 65*(1), 2–19.

Taylor, F. W. (1911). *The principles of scientific management.* New York, NY: Harper & Brothers.

DISCOVERY THEORY OF ENTREPRENEURSHIP

The discovery theory of entrepreneurship is particularly based on the work of Israel Kirzner. His theory addresses the working of the price system or, as it is often termed, of the market process. It holds that, contrary to neoclassical economics, markets are in disequilibrium, as the real world is in a state of constant change. This gives entrepreneurs, who are seen as people who are alert to opportunities for profit, a central role in the price system as arbitrageurs. This is reflected in much entrepreneurship literature through a focus on the opportunity as the unit of analysis. Entrepreneurs are said to first discover and then to exploit opportunities. Discovery-related research has addressed why opportunities exist and why some people are more alert to them than others. This entry first summarizes Kirzner's theory and then discusses empirical research on entrepreneurial alertness in addition to alternative views of the functions of the entrepreneur within an economy. It will also discuss creation theory as an alternative to discovery theory.

Fundamentals

Kirzner is an economist of the Austrian school of economic thought. In his writings on the market process, he has built on the work of Ludwig von Mises and of Friedrich Hayek. According to his theory, an opportunity for profit arises whenever any sellers in a market are willing to sell at a price lower than any buyers are willing to pay. Entrepreneurs can then earn profits by acting as arbitrageurs and in so doing push the differing prices together. The entrepreneurs can do so because of their alertness to the profit opportunities of which other market participants are unaware. It is entrepreneurs, therefore, who give predictability to market outcomes by exploiting such opportunities, systematically correcting market errors, and redirecting resources as exogenous shocks take place.

The theory extends beyond pure arbitrage by incorporating production. A profit opportunity exists where the resources required to produce and distribute a product can be purchased more cheaply than the product can be sold. This is often referred to in terms of a "means-end framework," where a recombination of resources is the means by which the end, the production and sale of the product at a profit, can be achieved. Note that, although Kirzner downplays it as not being essential to his aim of addressing the market process, it logically follows that this fundamentally changes the nature of entrepreneurship, compared to pure arbitrage, because commitments to expenditures and the revenues that follow become temporally separated. What was pure arbitrage therefore becomes speculation, requiring subjective judgment; a view has to be taken of possible future sales prices. Entrepreneurs then face the possibility of losses if future prices turn out to be unfavorable.

Kirzner further holds that entrepreneurs do not carry out deliberate searches for opportunities. Rather, opportunities are discovered spontaneously. Hence, those individuals without the alertness required to discover opportunities will fail to exploit them, even though they may have all the information required. The theory is therefore based on an assumption of irrationality, in the form of individuals failing to fully mentally process all their knowledge. Entrepreneurs are those with a superior rationality, in the form of alertness to opportunities.

Note that the Kirznerian concept of entrepreneurial opportunity discovery is based on a functional view of entrepreneurship. In contrast to most work within the entrepreneurship literature, anyone carrying out the disequilibrium-correcting function is an entrepreneur. This could be anyone, such as a corporate executive, and not just one of the more restrictive definitions of the entrepreneur often used in entrepreneurship literature, such as a business founder, small business owner-manager, or self-employed person.

Kirzner provided a theoretical framework designed to analyze the market process. Others have applied key aspects of that framework in the study of entrepreneurship. In particular, this has involved taking the opportunity as the unit for analysis, with opportunities being first discovered and then exploited. Further, not everyone acts as an entrepreneur because only some individuals have the alertness necessary to discover opportunities. Opportunity and alertness are subject to varying definitions, just as is the case with the entrepreneur.

One line of empirical research has investigated alertness in terms of whether business founders do more to position themselves within information flows and use more diverse information than corporate executives. This research stream has produced mixed results. Prior experience, job role, and social networking are also held to be significant to an individual's information flows, so helping to determine their likelihood of discovering opportunities.

Another line of work has been the study of alertness in terms of the cognition of entrepreneurs. This employs theories from psychology. For instance, it has been claimed that entrepreneurs may use different types of mental schemas (i.e., mental models) compared to nonentrepreneurs and that they may be more intuitive. There is not yet a sufficiently large and mature body of empirical research to be able to confidently identify particular characteristics of entrepreneurial cognitions in relation to entrepreneurial alertness or to reject the concept. It may be that the idea has more traction with the case of serial entrepreneurs whose experience leads them to form new cognitive frameworks.

A different line of work, based on informational economics, has investigated whether entrepreneurs deliberately search for opportunities, in contrast to the nonsearch assumption of Kirzner. Hence, this is a separate line of work to those based on Kirznerian alertness and spontaneous opportunity discovery. It has been found that some entrepreneurs do indeed carry out deliberate searches and that those who do so discover more opportunities. Novice entrepreneurs have been found to search widely, while serial entrepreneurs narrow down their search domains. This line of research also claims to offer a means by which people can be taught to be entrepreneurial.

Alternative Approaches

Entrepreneurship based on arbitrage can be contrasted to entrepreneurship based on innovation, although the distinction is not entirely clear cut. Schumpeter described the functional role of the entrepreneur as an innovator. According to Schumpeter, entrepreneurs initiate gales of creative destruction and therefore destroy existing equilibriums, in contrast to the equilibrating role of the Kirznerian entrepreneur. However, Joseph Schumpeter contrasted invention and innovation. We could say, therefore, that someone discovers an opportunity to innovate when they realize that an idea to do something novel can be gainfully exploited, although invention and opportunity discovery may often be simultaneously achieved by the same person. This provides a link to Kirzner's conception of the entrepreneur, at least in cases where the innovation involves dealing with existing markets. However, whereas arbitrage involves buying and selling in existing markets, the introduction of a new product involves market making, as there is no preexisting market for the product. This is therefore an important source of uncertainty for the entrepreneur.

In addition, innovations often involve trial-and-error learning, such as in what have been termed probe and learn processes. The entrepreneur does not always start out with a well-defined idea that stays constant during exploitation. Rather, things can develop in an iterative process of learning and adaptation. A danger with discovery theory, in which the entrepreneur discovers an opportunity and then exploits it, is that such learning and adaptation processes are ignored, the entrepreneur being assumed to exploit a fixed opportunity, or that they become something of a footnote that does not really fit the theoretical framework being used. In fact, this problem also arises in relation to less innovative entrepreneurs; they may also change what they are doing following market feedback.

What has been dubbed the "creation" theory of entrepreneurship in modern entrepreneurship literature gives an alternative theoretical framework to discovery theory that seems compatible with more innovative entrepreneurial processes. Rather than seeing opportunities as existing independently of the entrepreneurs who exploit them, it views entrepreneurs as the creators of the opportunities that they exploit; opportunities are seen as social constructions formed through action as opposed to being formed through exogenous changes in conditions. It stresses iterative decision-making processes that progressively change entrepreneurs' beliefs about opportunities as they interact with the market. The theory posits that there may be very little difference between entrepreneurs and others at the time when they first begin to act entrepreneurially but that they may develop large cognitive differences over time.

A further alternative theoretical framework to discovery theory is that of Frank Knight. Knight also gave a functional view of the entrepreneur. Knight's entrepreneur exercises subjective judgment in the face of Knightian uncertainty, as opposed to risk, in the hope of earning pure profits. Entrepreneurs are seen as being the confident and the venturesome and employers of the doubtful and the timid. Some modern writers on entrepreneurship have claimed that the Knightian view provides a superior theoretical framework to discovery theory. They propose that it is taking action under Knightian uncertainty that truly characterizes entrepreneurship and that a lack

of markets for judgment explains why entrepreneurs exploit ideas themselves. Sometimes such action is described in terms of undertaking an entrepreneurial project in which resources are brought together for a significant duration to exploit an opportunity.

Importance

The adoption of a discovery-based theoretical framework was partly a deliberate attempt to differentiate entrepreneurship from other fields of study. The study of new and small firms was not seen as achieving this aim. Instead, entrepreneurship research could be directed at issues such as how opportunities come into existence and why some people discover and exploit them while others do not. Unfortunately, empirical research into entrepreneurial alertness cannot yet be said to have yielded a convincing set of results. This may be partly because empirical studies take more restrictive views of what an entrepreneur is than the Kirznerian functional view would suggest. It may also be that it tends to be serial entrepreneurs who are particularly alert to opportunities rather than entrepreneurs in general. Indeed, many entrepreneurs are pushed toward founding businesses by circumstances rather than being pulled by strong business ideas. Opportunities also vary widely in nature, some requiring expert and some only basic knowledge to understand them. In some cases, what makes someone interested in pursuing an opportunity may simply be the realization that others have done well out of pursuing similar opportunities—for instance, when considering whether to launch into a competitive industry during a period of growing demand. On the other hand, a highly innovative opportunity requires more of a jump into the unknown. Some scholars have criticized discovery theory and have proposed alternative theoretical frameworks for the study of entrepreneurship. Nonetheless, discovery theory remains a dominant theoretical framework within entrepreneurship literature. Its real-world impact is, however, difficult to assess.

It is not obvious that actual managers and entrepreneurs have been directly affected much by discovery theory. Management courses in entrepreneurship often include some discussion of the problem of discovering opportunities in some form. However, this is often addressed in terms of alternative concepts, particularly creativity and innovativeness. It is possible that being told that one should build up a body of experience and gain information through networking in order to identify opportunities may change a student's subsequent real-world behavior to some extent. However, the idea that superior cognitive abilities are required is of less practical help to the prospective entrepreneur unless means are identified through empirical study by which such abilities can be developed in order to make individuals more alert to opportunities. The market process view of entrepreneurship is, however, important as one of a set of theories demonstrating the economic importance of entrepreneurs whose dynamic economic role is ignored in neoclassical economic theory. Its impact on policymakers is therefore easier to distinguish, having helped to lead to a view of entrepreneurship as being key to economic efficiency and growth as part of supply-side economic policy. Indeed, it is by this route that it could be seen to have most affected management education, in having helped to encourage a more widespread teaching of entrepreneurship courses. It has also helped to lead to wider efforts by governments to encourage entrepreneurial activity.

Nigel Wadeson

See also Entrepreneurial Cognition; Entrepreneurial Opportunities; Entrepreneurial Orientation; Schemas Theory

Further Readings

Alvarez, S. A., & Barney, J. B. (2007). Discovery and creation: Alternative theories of entrepreneurial action. *Strategic Entrepreneurship Journal, 1*(1–2), 11–26.

Busenitz, L. W. (1996). Research on entrepreneurial alertness. *Journal of Small Business Management, 34*(4), 35–44.

Casson, M., & Wadeson, N. (2007). Entrepreneurship and macroeconomic performance. *Strategic Entrepreneurship Journal, 1,* 239–262.

Gaglio, C., & Katz, J. A. (2001). The psychological basis of opportunity identification: Entrepreneurial alertness. *Small Business Economics, 16*(2), 95–111.

Kirzner, I. (1973). *Competition and entrepreneurship.* Chicago, IL: University of Chicago Press.

Klein, P. G. (2008). Opportunity discovery, entrepreneurial action, and economic organization. *Strategic Entrepreneurship Journal, 2*(3), 175–190.

Patel, P. C., & Fiet, J. O. (2009). Systematic search and its relationship to firm founding. *Entrepreneurship: Theory & Practice, 33*(2), 501–526.

Shane, S. (2003). *A general theory of entrepreneurship: The individual-opportunity nexus.* Northampton, MA: Edward Elgar.

Shane, S., & Venkataraman, S. S. (2000). The promise of entrepreneurship as a field of research. *Academy of Management Review, 25*(1), 217–226.

Tang, J., Kacmar, K., & Busenitz, L. (2012). Entrepreneurial alertness in the pursuit of new opportunities. *Journal of Business Venturing, 27*(1), 77–94.

DIVERSIFICATION STRATEGY

Diversification strategy is a firm growth strategy based on expanding the scope of the business segments where the firm competes. With the aim of taking benefit from running a wider business portfolio, governing supplementary resource breadth, and tapping into scope economies, firms attempt to enter into new businesses by a variety of means, such as merger and acquisition deals with an existing firm, internal start-ups and spin-offs, and equity joint ventures or strategic partnerships. The key argument of diversification strategy is that operating more businesses can be a value-enhancing strategy. The purpose of this entry is to review the ideas and key outcomes outspreading from the managerial debates that have progressively unfolded on diversification strategy. We shall then present a discussion of the following key questions: Why do firms diversify? What are the potential traps of diversification strategy? What is the relation between diversification strategy and shareholder value creation?

Fundamentals

Diversification strategy involves two explicit levels of firm strategy: (a) corporate strategy and (b) business strategy. The former entails gathering in the same basket two or more business segments and, therefore, how corporate headquarters is expected to coordinate all the business segments they have chosen to operate. At the corporate level, the challenge is usually to generate synergies among businesses, thereby avoiding the traps of management complexity overload. The latter—that is, business strategy—concerns instead planning and implementing strategic actions to allow each particular business to accrue value and accomplish economic and financial success.

The coordination among business strategies and the role of the corporate headquarters may vary according to the type (or direction) of diversification: *related* versus *unrelated*. Related diversification concerns managing the various value chains of a firm's businesses to allow synergies to emerge, since the value chains between and among business segments are seen as similar or complementary. The potential synergies of related diversification are given by (a) economies of scope, (b) market power, (c) sharing tangible and intangible resources and capabilities, (d) common value chain activities, (e) transferring core capabilities from a business to other businesses, and (f) vertical integration. *Unrelated* (or *conglomerate*) diversification occurs when firms, rather than seeking "strategic fit" and "synergy capture" in the value chains as in related diversification, are motivated to diversify mainly by financial reasons and managerial knowledge and expertise. Consequently, the benefits of unrelated diversification generally do not exceed the ones given by "financial" and "managerial" synergies. While unrelated diversification aims to capitalize on the governance of resources in firms that typically tend to be widely decentralized, conversely related diversification entails an important role for the firm's *headquarters*, which is expected to coordinate and reconnect various business units and swell synergies among them. (Alfred Chandler provides an appealing discussion of the "entrepreneurial" and "administrative" role of the HQ.) In the latter case, the goal of adopting the related diversification strategic option is to perform a more proficient transfer of resources and capabilities between and among businesses than alternative transaction modes do.

Since the seminal works of Igor Ansoff, Alfred Chandler, and Richard Rumelt, for almost four decades, the study of the characteristics instrumental to generate or destroy value in related and unrelated diversification strategies and the inquiry about to what extent diversification strategy is able to allow the firm to achieve performances superior to other strategies have taken a central role in the research agendas of two substantial fields of investigation: corporate finance and strategic management. Here, we concentrate on the underpinnings and impact of views and tools cooked up in the strategy realm.

If we take a step backward, during the 1960s underscoring the good performance of some conglomerate firms, diversification management advocates pushed executives for an increase in the firms'

degree of diversification. In the 1970s, instead, growing interest has gradually coagulated on shaping and applying a few managerial tools supporting strategic portfolio planning of diversified firms. Two diagnostic tools acquired prominence at that time, such as the growth-share matrix and the industry attractiveness-business strength matrix. Forged on the ground of the learning curve in the intelligence workshops of two globally established consulting firms (i.e., respectively, the Boston Consulting Group and McKinsey & Co.), these popular strategy paraphernalia were designed to help balance the cash flows of various businesses at different stages of their life cycles. The matrixes have been (and are still) widely used in consulting and managerial activities. More recently, because of the impact of the core competence movement in the 1990s, diversification strategy trend has reoriented to the issue of *divesting* unrelated businesses to focus on the firm's core business portfolio.

Importance

Understanding the Reasons Why Firms Diversify

To elucidate the key motives for pursuing a diversification strategy, we recall three different, but to some extent complementary, perspectives: (a) diversification as a value-enhancing strategy, (b) strategic flexibility as a driver of diversification strategy, and (c) managerial discretionary power as an antecedent of diversification strategy.

Diversification as a value-enhancing strategy. Diversification strategy, according to Michael Porter, is effective or value enhancing when the following conditions emerge: The industry is attractive in the long run as concerns the size of the market and its projected growth, profitability, competition intensity, and so on; the profit opportunities are higher than the cost of penetrating new markets; and the firm is able to generate synergies between the old business segments in which it operates and the new ones (the so-called better-off test).

The motives that explain why a collection of different businesses can outperform a stand-alone business enterprise and, therefore, the positive value of the better-off test are summarized as follows. The first set of motives to diversify is based on *market power* generated by the benefits of the scope when firms go into new markets. Market power concerns the vertical integration of businesses (i.e., backward or forward vertical integration). Accordingly, under this stream of thought, related diversification is usually preferred to unrelated diversification. Nonetheless, collusive power also supports cross-subsidization among businesses and, hence, the possibility of implementing a predatory pricing strategy. In this case, related and unrelated diversification strategies are deemed both equally applicable with similar results.

The second set of reasons to diversify is based on *the combination and sharing of resources and core capabilities* among businesses. This set of motivations looks at how the resources of different businesses may be suitably connected in the diversification mode and identifies the conditions to assist corporate executives to formulate a successful diversification strategy. More in detail, firms' managers may take advantage of this condition when factor markets are unable to provide resources efficiently to competitors. While the marginal costs of using these resources within a firm are low, the benefits associated to their use are substantial. The firm's goal becomes to take full advantage of the resources liable to market failure by diversifying into businesses other than the one already under reach. Under these circumstances, a related diversification strategy usually outshines unrelated diversification strategy.

The third set of motives to diversify puts emphasis on the benefits of the firm's *internal capital market* in providing financial viability to firm investments, thereby reducing business risk through compensation between positive and negative performances in the different businesses, circumventing transaction costs and the costs of information asymmetry associated with the external financial market and fiscal benefits. Since, in this instance, a diversification strategy's main purpose is to reduce risk, unrelated diversification is preferred over the related one.

Strategic flexibility as a driver of diversification strategy. A second perspective on diversification strategy is linked to a stream of dynamic models of diversification. Firms employ diversification strategy to *switch from businesses that are becoming unattractive to other businesses*. Since the process at hand is highly uncertain and open-ended, firms may decide to pursue a diversification strategy for motives of learning and obtaining an array of new knowledge, resources, and capabilities required to compete in different marketplaces. For signaling reasons, such kinds of diversification strategy can be simply rubricated as sheer experimentation, or in a dissimilar way, firms' corporate managers may purposefully decide to consistently boost up their investments in one or more new businesses.

Managerial discretionary power as an antecedent of diversification strategy. In a different fashion from the foregoing perspectives, agency theory assumes the existence of interests' divergence between the firms' shareholders and managers. According to this approach, the antecedents of diversification strategy are given by the two sides of the same coin: the shareholders' limited information base, as well as the managers' proclivity to pursue opportunistic behaviors. In this instance, the decision to hunt for a diversification strategy is a specific strategic choice taken merely for opportunistic reasons on behalf of the managers or, in other words, for pursuing Weberian power and prestige associated with managing a larger multibusiness firm or for chasing Schumpeterian empire-building strategies and entrenchment and risk reduction. Under this conceptual lens, unrelated diversification is usually preferred to related diversification.

Identifying the Potential Traps of Diversification Strategy

Running a focused firm is universally reputed to be a much simpler task than running a diversified firm. Actually, a larger breadth of businesses portfolio implies a higher level of *managerial complexity*. First and foremost, the strategic variety underlying diversification strategy imposes *multiple dominant logics*. Executives of focused firms mainly pay attention to a relatively narrow set of distinct market and technological stimuli. Therefore, strategic variety has important negative effects on the ability of the CEO and the executive team to manage a firm. In addition, managerial complexity in diversified firms generates the effect of *information overload* that, in turn, increases the intricacies of exercising strategic control over a diverse business portfolio.

Finally, managerial complexity in diversified firms also implies difficulties in assessing the (quality and amount of) creation of value for each business segment and, consequently, to execute an efficient *resource allocation process*. Actually, the typical problems of diversified firms are related to overinvestment and subsidization of loss-making businesses. In addition, unrelated diversified firms frequently suffer from adopting a sheer financial perspective, which favors the pursuit of short-term profit, thus overlooking the possible loss in the firm's long-run competitiveness.

Linking Diversification Strategy and Shareholder Value Creation

As earlier anticipated, two disciplinary traditions—namely, corporate finance and strategic management—have been used to congregate their investigation efforts (heretofore nearly always in an *independent* fashion) on diversification strategy. While studies in these veins display numerous contributions on the nature of the relation between diversification and performance, overall extant results fall short to present conclusive answers on the economic and financial impact that diversification entails.

First, while a few studies in corporate finance inquiry have argued that diversification strategy can create value, the majority of empirical contributions show a negative relationship between the breadth of business portfolio and performance (see Martin and Sayrak for a review). Accordingly, this stream of inquiry estimates the existence of a diversification *discount:* a multiple-segment firm's value below the value imputed using single-segment firm's multiples.

But second, if Athens cries, Sparta doesn't laugh. While the relationship between diversity and performance has received a fragmented answer in strategic management literature, common wisdom bears that related diversification strategy is preferred to a single-business strategy. Actually, conventional empirical inspection, such as the study by Leslie Palich and colleagues, seconds the argument that performance tumbles when firms move from related diversification to unrelated diversification. Therefore, according to strategy literature, the best performance of diversification strategy is generated by the related diversification type or direction.

Third, let us complement the perspectives above with the institutional view of unrelated diversification strategy. A rather eminent research stream has recently argued that the relationship between unrelated diversification and performance is influenced by the institutional environment. In the view of Abhirup Chakrabarti and colleagues, depending on the context of application (more or less developed institutional environments), a well-designed and targeted diversification strategy may facilitate washing out asymmetric information problems and inefficiencies in the external capital market.

Fourth and finally, let us briefly review the main issues concerning variable measurement in diversification strategy. The first issue concerns the *measure of corporate diversification*. The literature presents us with two kinds of measures: (1) measures based on the Standard Industry Code (SIC) and (2) subjective measures of the type of diversification. While diversification measures based on SIC overall fall short of identifying the correlation among different businesses, subjective measures suffer from interpretive bias and are difficult to replicate. The second issue regards the *measure of corporate performance*. Interestingly, while strategic management research usually employs *accounting-based* performance measures (such as return on assets [ROA], typically adjusted for multiple years), assuming the existence of perfect markets, financial studies adopt *market-oriented* performance measures (such as Tobin's Q).

Giovanni Battista Dagnino and
Pasquale Massimo Picone

See also BCG Growth-Share Matrix; Business Policy and Corporate Strategy; Core Competence; Firm Growth; Managing Diversity; Strategy and Structure

Further Readings

Ansoff, I. A. (1957). Strategy of diversification. *Harvard Business Review, 35*(5), 113–124.

Chakrabarti, A., Singh, K., & Mahmood, I. (2007). Diversification and performance: Evidence from East Asian firms. *Strategic Management Journal, 28*(2), 101–120.

Chandler, A. D. (1962). *Strategy and structure: Chapters in the history of the American industrial enterprise.* Cambridge, MA: MIT Press.

Chandler, A. D. (1991). The functions of the headquarters unit in the multibusiness firm. *Strategic Management Journal, 12*(S2), 31–50.

Martin, J. D., & Sayrak, A. (2003). Corporate diversification and shareholder value: A survey of recent literature. *Journal of Corporate Finance, 9*, 37–57.

Palich, L. E., Cardinal, L. B., & Miller, C. C. (2000). Curvilinearity in the diversification-performance linkage: An examination of over three decades of research. *Strategic Management Journal, 21*(2), 155–174.

Prahalad, C. K., & Bettis, R. A. (1986). The dominant logic: A new linkage between diversity and performance. *Strategic Management Journal, 7*(6), 485–501.

Porter, M. E. (1987). From competitive advantage to corporate strategy. *Harvard Business Review, 65*(3), 43–59.

Rumelt, R. P. (1974). *Strategy, structure and economic performance.* Cambridge, MA: Harvard University Press.

Wan, W. P., Hoskisson, R. E., Short, J. C., & Yiu, D. W. (2011). Resource-based theory and corporate diversification: Accomplishments and opportunities. *Journal of Management, 37*(5), 1335–1368.

DOUBLE LOOP LEARNING

Double loop learning (DLL) is an action-oriented theory concerned with helping people and organizations face difficult situations by (a) uncovering serious flaws in the way they learn from their actions and (b) facilitating changes in the underlying values that govern learning in order to reduce defensiveness and produce effective action. DLL has had a significant impact on management theory and practice, because action, learning, and change are fundamental to everything that people and organizations do. This entry contains two main sections. The first section addresses the fundamentals of the broader DLL theory, including the process that produces ineffective actions and interactions among people and how it may be changed to produce DLL. The second section discusses the validity and importance of DLL to management theory and practice.

Fundamentals

DLL theory begins with a straightforward observation: People can assert they have learned something when they can actually *do* what they claim they have learned. Yet the scholarship of action itself has been taken for granted in management on the assumption that once theory is advanced, implementation will be straightforward. In the early 1970s, Chris Argyris and his late colleague Donald Schön began an ongoing inquiry into the nature of practice itself in search for a theory that governs human and organizational action. DLL emerged from this inquiry, which Argyris has continued to refine in the decades that followed. The theory established that learning and action are intertwined and that both are essential for an effective implementation of management theory.

Action and learning. Action is fundamental to individual and organizational lives. People act to produce intended consequences, and they typically express their actions in conversations. Invariably, however, actions produce unintended consequences, particularly in difficult situations. Most learning occurs when people detect and correct mismatches or gaps between the intended and unintended consequences of their actions. This simple process, although prevalent, produces learning that is typically flawed because of hidden designs people hold without being mindful of their limiting effects.

The designs beneath. People act with two types of theories in their minds. The first, called "espoused theory," helps them proclaim to the world what they ought to be saying, believing, or espousing. The second, called "theory in use," is more influential because it informs what people actually do, regardless of their external claims. From examining over 10,000 individual and organizational cases, Argyris has found that the theory in use carries the same basic design across different situations, cultures, races, genders, ages, social statuses, and so on, although manifestations may vary. Notice the emerging promise here: By uncovering the principal structure of the theory in use, we can suggest changes to make learning and action more productive.

The overall structure of the hidden design goes as follows. A set of well-entrenched *governing values* informs the theory in use, which influences the *action strategies* people use to conduct their lives, and most *learning* occurs from detecting and correcting the gap between the intended and unintended consequences of these actions.

Components of the theory in use that describe how action *is* actually implemented are called Model I, which is associated with single loop learning (SLL). Components of the theory in use that prescribe how action *should be* implemented are called Model II, which promotes DLL. Clients should learn to surface and be aware of their use of Model I and its SLL before they are coached toward implementing Model II and its productive DLL. The broader DLL theory, therefore, is both descriptive and prescriptive.

Model I and SLL. The principal governing values of Model I are formed from our early experiences (in childhood, families, schools, etc.), and they govern daily actions with speed and automaticity. These values include internal instructions for people to (a) maximize winning and minimize losing; (b) maintain unilateral control over situations and others; (c) cover up negative feelings to save face, in the name of politeness and decorum; and (d) strive to appear rational. The impact of these governing values on action strategies is rampant, particularly under the threats associated with difficult situations. They lead people to persistently advocate their views over those of others, evaluate actions to support their positions, and make untested attributions about others' intentions. The learning associated with Model I, SLL, aims to change the actions that lead to the unintended consequences, not the hidden governing values. These Model I action strategies produce rounds of misapprehensions, conflicts, and cover-ups, which are exacerbated by the defensiveness inherent in difficult situations. Defensiveness, it turns out, is a hallmark of Model I. Thus, reducing defensiveness is crucial to loosen the grip of Model I and SLL, the predicate to instilling Model II and DLL.

Defensiveness and defensive routines. For the purpose of the current discussion, defensiveness describes a psychological mechanism that people use to "castle-up" and shield themselves from perceived or actual threats or embarrassments. However, because defensiveness is triggered with speed and automaticity, it blocks the reflective learning needed to delve deeper into the root causes of difficult problems. Reflective learning is, therefore, blocked when it is needed most. Organizations create defensive mechanisms as well. Those within an organization imprint their defensive postures on the policies, processes, and cultures they create to protect their working units, and themselves, from potential embarrassments or threats. These imprints solidify over time into defensive routines, which prevent organizations from learning the root causes of their own difficulties. Because learning requires opening up and defensiveness leads to closing down, people facing potentially embarrassing or threatening situations tend to learn very little, if at all. How does it happen?

A four-step mechanism is responsible for arresting productive learning under the stresses of threatening situations. People who are on the defensive tend to (1) say one thing and do another, (2) deny or become unaware of the contradiction, (3) make the denial undiscussable, and (4) make the undiscussability of the denial itself undiscussable and close the matter. The result is a vicious, antilearning cycle that Chris Argyris calls the *doom loop.* Organizational defensive routines initiate a similar process, resulting in mixed messages and a series of escalating cover-ups. For example, a national foreign policy may claim to promote democracy worldwide, while simultaneously supporting some despots in the name of national interest. Policymakers would then design ways to make the contradiction undiscussable and then cover up the cover-ups.

Once managers and leaders are made aware of the intertwined effects of Model I governing values, action strategies, SLL, and defensiveness, the focus would then shift to finding a way out. Enter DLL.

Model II and double loop learning. Human actions will continue to produce mismatches and contradictions. The new Model II paradigm, however, suggests that instead of rushing to change the actions that produced the mismatches (a single loop move), people should first learn to be critical of their Model I values, assess the appropriateness of SLL for dealing with the situation at hand, instill a more effective set of values, and *then* deal with the mismatches based on the new governing values (a double loop move).

DLL, therefore, refers to a reflective learning process enabled by a new set of governing values designed to (a) promote valid, confirmable information about the difficult situations at hand; (b) foster rigorous mechanisms to question the status-quo; and (c) allow free and informed choice for those involved. Simple as it may seem, translating these new values into daily actions and interactions requires patience and tenacity because they would be competing with the well-entrenched, long-practiced Model I values.

With the new Model II regime, people would try to examine difficult tensions for the insights they may contain instead of just pushing their views to win debates and control arguments. They would learn to invite inquiries into the advocacies they make, expose the evaluations they produce to rigorous testing, and substantiate their attributions about others with examples of what led them to their claims. In daily actions, people would practice to (a) be less conclusive and more open to others' views; (b) be more confrontable and less confrontational; (c) adopt a healthy view of vulnerability as a strength, thus not feeling threatened by disconfirmation of their views; (d) minimize psychological distancing from others; and (e) minimize easing-in practices designed to corner others in order to prove a point.

DLL, therefore, is about reflecting on our reasoning process and how it impacts our actions and interactions. It is about both learning new governing values to question the status quo, *and* enabling productive conversations—initially "choreographed" for clients and then mastered with practice—to reduce defensive reasoning and promote effective action.

Four points are worth noting here. First, Model I and Model II should not have to be mutually exclusive. For example, SLL may be used in routine situations and to assess the efficient execution of existing goals, whereas DLL should be practiced to question goal validity and appropriateness, particularly in difficult and challenging situations. Second, DLL is useful for both individuals and organizations. In addition to fostering new interaction patterns, organizations would redesign their policies, procedures, structures, norms, and cultures to encourage rigorous questioning and experimentation on an ongoing basis. Third, genuineness is paramount in practicing Model II and DLL; setbacks will result if people just practice new Model II–like phrases and actions without striving to change the governing values behind them. Fourth, challenging existing Model I governing values may threaten a client's sense of comfort and perceived self-competence; therefore, implementing DLL may initially trigger people's defensiveness. However, as in combating a virus with a vaccine, the defensiveness temperature may have to rise before it subsides.

Importance

The broader DLL theory has had a profound impact on the thinking of scholars and practitioners. Over 10,000 mentions of DLL have been listed in numerous studies covering public and private sectors, including business, medical and health, education policy, classroom learning, and the military. Moreover, the theory has contributed to forging important management perspectives such as system thinking, and its parameters have been used to critique many contemporary management domains, including negotiation, strategy, decision making, communication, teams, diversity, and empowerment. Validating the entire DLL theory in single studies, however, has been less prevalent due in part to the time frame needed to incorporate DLL changes in organizations; still Chris Argyris, Peter Senge, and others have reported on long-term implementations of DLL in various work settings. The main critics of DLL draw attention to its difficult implementation, and stress current productivity levels as evidence that the status quo is acceptable. Proponents of DLL argue that while routine answers to important questions can still help meet existing goals "efficiently," modern competitive work environments accentuate the need for deeper learning that promotes the sense of autonomy and responsibility among employees for them to question the "effectiveness" of those goals and the status quo—a process that DLL facilitates.

DLL can profit modern work environments, which are characterized by an increasing need for higher levels of effectiveness and innovation within an ever-changing cultural milieu and global competitiveness. This rapid pace distinguishes modern managers from their traditional counterparts who often surrender to fire-fighting modes to handle daily problems, only to face them later in more complex forms. In contrast, modern managers adopt a new way of reasoning that is consistent with DLL theory. They search for structures behind and beyond recurring problems, and they strive to create organizational cultures that foster this new way of thinking among their employees. In this transformative culture, managers and employees reflect actively on their own work and behavior. In doing so, they welcome accountability when surfacing and scrutinizing information that may be threatening or embarrassing in order to find long-lasting solutions. DLL offers a direction toward that change and a specific process to deal with the messy and wicked problems of the workplace. The broader DLL theory underscores to the action-oriented manager the importance of scrutinizing action itself and proposes (a) that action is expressed through daily conversations, (b) that action and conversations are influenced by the mental models of those who execute them, (c) that problems occur when espoused visions and thoughts conflict with deeply held structures and assumptions of how the world works, and (d) that the strong influences of mental models and assumption often remain undiscussable. In searching for the undiscussable root causes and structures that lurk behind messy organizational problems, DLL cultivates a questioning mind-set for individuals and organizations alike. To execute this mind-set, DLL provides specific guidelines to modern managers and their employees for expressing actions in genuine daily conversations in order to scrutinize the status quo while simultaneously minimizing defensiveness and maximizing productive learning for individuals and organizations.

Abdelmagid Mazen

See also Action Learning; Action Research; Critical Management Studies; Experiential Learning Theory and Learning Styles; Learning Organization; Management (Education) as Practice; Organizational Learning

Further Readings

Argyris, C. (1992). *On organizational learning.* Cambridge, MA: Blackwell.

Argyris, C. (1993). *Knowledge for action: A guide to overcoming barriers to organizational change.* San Francisco, CA: Jossey-Bass.

Argyris, C. (2010). *Organizational traps: Leadership, culture, organizational design.* Oxford, England: Oxford University Press.

Argyris, C., & Schön, D. (1974). *Theory in practice: Increasing professional effectiveness.* San Francisco, CA: Jossey-Bass.

Diamond, M. A. (1986). Resistance to change: A psychoanalytic critique of Argyris and Schon's contributions to organization theory and interventions. *Journal of Management Studies, 23*(5), 543–562.

Mazen, A. (2000). Like water for chocolate: Action theory for the OB class. *Journal of Management Education, 24*(3), 304–321.

Mazen, A. (2012). Transforming the negotiator: The impact of critical learning on teaching and practicing negotiation. *Management Learning, 43*(1), 113–128.

Senge, P. (2006). *The fifth discipline: The art and practice of the learning organization.* New York, NY: Currency Doubleday.

Senge, P., Kleiner, A., Roberts, C., Ross, R., & Smith, B. (1994). *The fifth discipline field book.* New York, NY: Currency Doubleday.

DRAMATURGICAL THEORY OF ORGANIZATIONS

Theory is a loose and often contradictory matter in regard to explaining the dynamics of formal organization, because it requires an articulation of a substantive matter, "organization," in which forms of rationality conflict with a higher-level abstraction or paradigm called a "theory." A theory of dramaturgical style is a way of seeing or a *perspective* that when applied may include antinomies, contradictions, rhetorical breaches, and indeterminacy. As applied to organizations, dramaturgy is bifocal. It explores the organization as an actor as well as the constraints that organizations place upon actors' demeanor. Dramaturgy and dramaturgical theory reflect the attempts to understand how members of organizations make sense and communicate about the rules, networks, alliances, and career contingencies that shape their lives. Everett C. Hughes has called this the study of systems of interaction that are the setting for the role-drama of work. Erving Goffman, a student of Hughes's at the University of Chicago, developed a systematic analysis of impression management, or dramaturgy, which drew on the work of Kenneth Burke and Émile Durkheim. Organizations are places in which patterned, ongoing interaction occurs, and thus they are places to study the interaction order itself. In 1983, Goffman argued that the key concept for any social analysis is the interaction order itself: "Social interaction can be defined narrowly as that which transpires in social situations, that is, environments in which two or more individuals are physically in one another's response presence" (p. 2). He locates this face-to-face domain as analytically distinct and calls it *the interaction order.* The interaction order is contained within organizations that can be seen as "actors," units who carry out dramas, act out roles, tell stories about themselves, sustain impression management, face-saving, and use many strategies to gain, sustain, and increase their authority. The core idea, dramaturgy's central contribution to management theory, is a metaphor that sees the organization as an acting unit that presents strategies and tactics designed to enhance the power and authority of the organization. The internal dynamics of formal organizations are illuminated by focusing on impression management, leadership and team work, failed performances, and minidramas characteristic of such organizations.

Fundamentals

Dramaturgy is a metaperspective that makes sense of action at several levels whether it is carried out by organizations, groups, or individual actors. Dramaturgy as applied to organizations denotes *analysis* of the social by use of the theatric metaphor and a focus on how performances, especially teamwork, are enacted and with what effect(s). In the context of organizational analysis, dramaturgy takes the organization as an acting unit that can be seen as expressing itself, representing itself, and using symbols and rhetoric in the interest of creating, maintaining, and expanding their fields. Consider the idea of an acting unit, organization as a concept, and some aspects of organizational dynamics.

An acting unit may be a person, group, organization, and any meaningfully coordinated social phenomenon. Organizations, seen in the dramaturgical perspective, refer to a family of ideas: They are social objects that are authoritatively constrained, vertically and horizontally differentiated groups with relatively intense interactions within notable boundaries, technologies, and products. They are actors, or significant "acting units," that perform, seek validation for their actions, manage impressions, compete with other organizations, possess both front and back areas, and manifest teams and teamwork. They produce selectively crafted, persuasive performances before audiences that emphasize or dramatize, overemphasizing some and de-emphasizing other features of action. They build for themselves little dramas, rehearse, and represent them to audiences. They employ strategies and tactics and seek to be trusted. They contain repetitive, common, but situationally and ecologically located and defined activities. Organizations are arenas for collectively situated action organized around tasks and routines. Technology and the material matters are embedded in a network of relations such that to study technology is in fact to study that network in which they are a signifying social object.

Organizations have a life within a network or field of other competing organizations. They must claim and sustain a *mandate* or, as Hughes contends, literally the right to define the proper conduct and ideas with respect to matters concerning their work. This mandate is based on a license, or a validated claim, to carry out tasks rather different from those of other people in exchange for money, goods, or services. The right to carry out these tasks is denied other occupational groups. For this mandate, organizations compete in a network of other organizations-as-actors: Organizations reside in and act in a *web* of similar organizations and audiences. They compete both materially and symbolically to control markets in ideas and money. It is useful, then, to see the mandate as in part based on rhetorical or *presentational strategies* for defending and expanding the mandate; *resource-based strategies* for deploying resources in the interest of sustaining some sort of market; and the *tactics* by which these are actually manifested in action. These rhetorics, strategies, and tactics are modes of dramaturgical action that implicate physical resources, technologies, and personnel. They represent and present the organization as coherent, viable, authoritative, and consistent in its actions, goals, and maneuvers. Organizations are contexts within which sanctioned practices are rewarded and an environment is shaped, defined, and responded to. This representational work goes on in spite of what is known by participants in the organization: the many cliques, vertical and horizontal coalitions, competing for authority and power; the conversation of rationalities brought to the question of ensuring the organization's success; and the often-volatile nature of careers, employment, and markets. Organizations provide the context within which careers are fashioned and made real.

This organizational action, with its strategies and tactics, produces impressions as well as other kinds of information. Such communicating creates a web of social relations between collectivities. Organizational performances generate reactions, positive and negative, or feedback and reciprocity from audience(s), the process by which claims are validated (verbal or nonverbal, written or electronic). Failure to produce feedback and reciprocity requires repair, apology, or re-creation of the exchange. Performances are symbolic action, ceremonies that are multivocal and involve condensed symbols with many facets. Caught up in organizational action, actors "speak" to each other in organizational language by means of imagery, rhetoric, and even nonverbal performances. The performances of concern are the presentations of organizations to their audiences—customers, clients, those served—and their own representation of their mandate. These may or may not be consistent: In times of change; there is often a "gap" between organizational performances for external audiences—stockholders, stakeholders, and customers—and the representation or view of the organization held by those who work there. There may also be contradictions between the messages and performances directed to the various audiences targeted, such as customers, stockholders, employees, and the general public. Organizations deal with these contradictions, as Thurman Arnold notes, by constructing complicated theories.

All mandates, whether in service industries or market-based corporations, are highly ritualized, or embedded in institutional accounts, "reasons why," explanations for, rationales, and mini-ideologies required to minimize the institutional contradictions that arise. For example, police fight crime, but it varies sometimes inexplicably; hospitals provide care, but they must command profits; salaries and bonuses are incommensurate with profit levels. The repeated, often contradictory *bricolage* of an organization's claims—such things as ethical statements, core values, mission statements, and even annual reports—might be called *iterative tautologies* insofar as they echo the rationalizing beliefs held and produced by the top command of the organization. Furthermore, the "bottom line," market criteria for success, which is said to distinguish "service" organizations from businesses, is itself a social construction. What is valued is a social object defined within the conventions of the organization. Some would view hospitals, schools, and universities as "businesses" that should make a profit by serving while exploiting human miseries, curiosities, ignorance, and maladies.

Importance

Internally, organizations rest on compliance and loyalty or visible signs of actors' involvement in the organization's activities. The premise of interaction in Anglo-American formally organized environments is equality; reciprocity that requires deference and demeanor confirming that emotional tone and expression is fundamental to organizational functioning, and its absence leads to sanctioning. This is more likely to be visible in decisions made and dramatized by those residing in higher positions in

the vertical hierarchy of an organization and seen as arbitrary and temporary by those serving below. Reaction to rules, including defining and refining organizational constraints, grants meaning to the formal "rules" of the organization. Rules that bear on organizational conduct are arenas for interpretation and interaction; these situated interactions produce the social objects called "rule following" and "rule breaking." In this way, organizations shape and constrain the situations that actors face. Organizations are home to many rationalities or believed connections between the means employed and the ends sought: Organizations are often overflowing with abundant rationalities—that is, approaches that differ either with respect to means to achieving a given end or differing ends but agreed-upon means or some combination of these, including competing ends and means within an organizational domain. These in turn are the arenas for power struggles. These characterizations of organizational actions are themselves glosses on the processes by which organizations decide. It is useful in this regard to consider organizational deciding as situated rationality, or decisions validated as "rational" at the time they were made or later when they are recorded officially. The transformation of deciding into operating tacit conventions is an important topic for organizational studies in the dramaturgical style.

In effect, much organizational action is backstage, outside the vision of some actors, and almost always outside the view of the external or public audiences. Conversely, there is always a front, or a stylized version of organizational action, and a front stage. When scandals or media events alter the public's understanding and trust of an organization, back and front stage are temporarily elided, out of balance, and must be redefined. Teams and teamwork that maintain the front stage/backstage distinction may be disrupted. Teams are based on a degree of shared secrets, and thus organizations are ensembles of secrets. There may then be conflicts between discrepant members not part of the dominant teams, between teams, and these against or with the dominant coalition in the organization. This is a theme in Goffman's early work.

Finally, the issue for investigation is how the organization constrains situated actions, and how situated actions repeatedly reproduce what is taken to be organizational. These are matters that can be identified, observed, described, and measured: They are features of organizations. The fundamental issue is how in the context of an organization, constraints are managed to sustain what Goffman calls a working consensus. This situated order may well be relevant to the central functions of the organization. Not all that is situated is shaped by structure and vice versa, but *situated collective action* is the primary locus of study for a dramaturgical theory of formal organizations. This focus on collective ordering and deciding requires a consistent focus on what is done—the tasks, practices, and constraints that shape the organization for participants. In a dramaturgical perspective, the organization is a container for observing conventionalized work practices. It is thus more likely to require ethnographic work, close-up observations of organization's workings, and to discount the records, data, reports, and rhetoric of the organization absent such ethnographic materials. Since organizational processes create the meaning of the documents, they are meaningless without an understanding of context within which they were created. The ongoing tension in the field of dramaturgical studies is the question of generalization of the findings across organizations, cultures, and time.

Modern managers might recognize that much of what is carried out in an organization has to do with expressing feelings, connecting to other "team members," telling stories to each other to enhance and maintain status, concealing and revealing information to sanction and control other members of the organization, and finally living out and talking about the "dramas of their organizational lives."

Peter K. Manning

See also Bureaucratic Theory; Dialectical Theory of Organizations; Management Symbolism and Symbolic Action; Meaning and Functions of Organizational Culture; Organizational Culture Theory; Social Construction Theory; Tacit Knowledge

Further Readings

Arnold, T. (1962). *The symbols of government.* New York, NY: Harcourt Brace.

Burke, K. (1962). *A grammar of motives and a rhetoric of motives.* New York, NY: Meridian Books.

Dalton, M. (1959). *Men who manage.* New York, NY: Wiley.

Goffman, E. (1959). *The presentation of self in everyday life.* Garden City, NJ: Doubleday.

Goffman, E. (1961). *Asylums.* Garden City, NJ: Doubleday.

Goffman, E. (1983). The interaction order. *American Sociological Review, 48*(1), 1–10.

Hughes, E. C. (1971). *The sociological eye.* Chicago, IL: Aldine.

Jackall, R. (1988). *Moral mazes.* New York, NY: Oxford University Press.

Manning, P. K. (1977). *Police work.* Cambridge, MA: MIT Press.

Manning, P. K. (2008). Goffman on organizations. *Organizational Studies, 29,* 677–699.

DUAL-CONCERN THEORY

Managers spend a good amount of time negotiating on matters where they need to reach agreement with others, for example, on department budgets, sales contracts, terms of employment such as salary and benefits, to name just a few. Indeed, negotiation is an important part of collective decision making in all walks of life, especially in legal, political, and business settings. It is an important aspect of *dispute resolution,* for example, when labor and management cannot agree about a wage level, as detailed in the classic text on labor negotiation by Richard Walton and Robert McKersie. Other cases of negotiation are about *deal making,* wherein agreement brings value to the parties by establishing the parameters of a commercial partnership or joint venture or through an exchange. In negotiation between a buyer and a seller, for example, the seller may offer to sell an item at X dollars, and the buyer states that she will only buy it at less than X; thus they see a difference of interest on money, and the negotiation proceeds by offers and counteroffers on money and verbal statements designed to influence the other party and reconcile differences and achieve agreement and exchange. It can get complex quickly: There may be many people on multiple sides of a negotiation and multiple negotiation issues, and on each side, instead of an individual, there may be a group or even a larger collective such as an organization or a nation-state. In the latter cases, negotiators act as representatives of other's interests as well as, or instead of, their own. David Lax and Jim Sebenius report that negotiation is a core element of management and the workplace and that it is a core managerial competency. The *dual-concern theory* is defined as a theory of negotiation behavior that posits three fundamental strategies for moving to agreement in negotiation: *yielding* (giving in, making a concession in the direction of the other's benefit), *contending* (holding firm, trying to get the other party to agree on your terms), and *problem solving* (working with the other party to come up with a mutually beneficial "win-win" agreement that is good for everyone). This entry provides a brief overview of the dual-concern theory and a brief explanation of its importance to management.

Fundamentals

The dual-concern theory predicts the occurrence of the three basic negotiation strategies from the intersection of two motivations held by the individual negotiator: (1) *concern* for one's own outcomes (often referred to as *aspirations*) and (2) *concern* for the opposing party's outcomes. Thus, there are two, or dual, concerns. Dean Pruitt and Steve Lewis developed the theory, building on earlier theoretical work by management scholars Robert Blake and Jane Mouton, who had a model of management called the "managerial grid" that argued the most effective management style was one where the manager cared both about the work task and the interpersonal relationships in the workplace, and on related work by Kenneth Thomas on conflict styles, which is about how individuals differ in their response to social conflict.

Rather than viewing self-concern (concern about own interests) as a constant, as did earlier approaches to understanding negotiation behavior—for example, the one developed by Morton Deutsch—the dual-concern theory views it as a dimension running from weak to strong. When this concern is strong, as when one has firm aspirations, one is willing to work hard for outcomes favorable to oneself; when it is weak, one is willing to let one's own interests slip. Other-concern (concern about the other party's interests) is also seen as a dimension that runs from weak to strong. Self-concern and other-concerns are regarded as independent dimensions rather than as opposite ends of the same dimension.

Most theories about negotiation assume an individualistic orientation, when negotiators care only for their own outcomes and are indifferent about the other's outcomes. However, negotiators are often concerned about the other party's outcomes even though this concern is usually not as strong as the concern about their own outcomes. Concern for the other party is sometimes genuine and sometimes instrumental (strategic)—for example, caring about what they want now so the other side will feel obligated to be cooperative in the future. Many of the results of negotiation research do not hold up when negotiators have concern for the other side's outcomes.

The dual-concern theory predicts preferences among the three basic strategies of negotiation from various combinations of high and low self-concern and other-concern. High self-concern coupled with low other-concern is assumed to encourage contending, which are efforts to get the other party to agree on one's own terms (e.g., making a threat such as "Agree to this or we go on strike"). High other-concern and low self-concern is assumed to encourage concession making. High self-concern and high other-concern is assumed to encourage problem solving (e.g., information exchange such as, "That issue is important to me; tell me, which issue is most important to you?"), and the development of creative, integrative, win-win agreements. Low self-concern and low other-concern is assumed to encourage inactivity.

The dual-concern theory posits that the most effective negotiation strategy and the best outcomes will occur when the negotiators care not only about their own outcomes but also the outcomes of the other party. The theory interprets the impact of situations and conditions on negotiation (e.g., accountability to constituents, time pressure, mood) by locating their impact on the relative strength of the two concerns, and it also posits that the conditions that encourage the use of one negotiation strategy will lessen the likelihood of the use of the other strategies. Of course, negotiation is like a machine with many moving parts, and negotiation strategies have many other antecedents in addition to these two concerns, but the dual-concern theory is one basis for making predictions about strategic preference in negotiation.

Experimental evidence for the dual-concern theory comes from studies that independently manipulated self-concern and other-concern. In an important review study, Carsten De Dreu, Laurie Weingart, and Seungwoo Kwon conducted a meta-analysis of 28 studies relevant to the dual-concern theory. The results were clear: When people had a prosocial motive, they engaged in more problem-solving behaviors, fewer contentious behaviors, and achieved better agreements than when they had an egoistic motive; these effects were obtained only when they also had a high resistance to yielding. One criticism of the dual-concern theory is that there are many other motives that can guide behavior in negotiation. Indeed, Peter Carnevale and Carsten de Dreu have written about other motives, such as epistemic motivation, that can guide the desire to understand the issues and the problems faced in negotiation.

The theory's central managerial insight is that managers can often achieve good negotiation outcomes if they not only care about their own interests but also consider other's interests and seek outcomes of negotiation that maximize collective welfare. Modern organizations are more likely to succeed to the extent that managers adopt dual concerns in their negotiating and are able to encourage employees to attend not only to their own interests but to the interests of coworkers as well.

Peter J. Carnevale and Yoo Kyoung Kim

See also Conflict Handling Styles; Game Theory; Influence Tactics; Managerial Grid; Principled Negotiation; Theory of Cooperation and Competition; Trust

Further Readings

Ben-Yoav, O., & Pruitt, D. G. (1984). Resistance to yielding and the expectation of cooperative future interaction in negotiation. *Journal of Experimental Social Psychology, 20,* 323–335.

Carnevale, P. J. (2006). Creativity in the outcomes of conflict. In M. Deutsch, P. T. Coleman, & E. C. Marcus (Eds.), *Handbook of conflict resolution* (2nd ed., pp. 414–435). San Francisco, CA: Jossey-Bass.

Carnevale, P. J., & Pruitt, D. G. (1992). Negotiation and mediation. *Annual Review of Psychology, 43,* 531–582.

De Dreu, C. K. W., Weingart, L. R., & Kwon, S. (2000). Influence of social motives on integrative negotiation: A meta-analytical review and test of two theories. *Journal of Personality and Social Psychology, 78,* 889–905.

Deutsch, M. (1973). *The resolution of conflict: Constructive and destructive processes.* New Haven, CT: Yale University Press.

Lax, D. A., & Sebenius, J. K. (1986). *The manager as negotiator: Bargaining for cooperation and competitive gain.* New York, NY: Free Press.

Pruitt, D. G. (1981). *Negotiation behavior.* New York, NY: Academic Press.

Pruitt, D. G., & Lewis, S. A. (1975). Development of integrative solutions in bilateral negotiation. *Journal of Personality and Social Psychology, 31,* 621–633.

Walton, R. E., & McKersie, R. (1965). *A behavioral theory of labor negotiations: An analysis of a social interaction system.* New York, NY: McGraw-Hill.

Dual-Core Model of Organizational Innovation

The basic premise of the dual-core model of innovation is that many organizations have two primary centers of innovation. Organizations—schools, hospitals, libraries, city governments, welfare agencies, government bureaucracies, and many business firms—are conceptualized as having two cores: a technical core and an administrative core. Each core is a center of innovation with its own employees, tasks, and domain. Innovation can be initiated and adopted in either core. The dual-core approach identifies two distinct processes associated with organizational innovation and change. The original research examined differences in innovation type—technical and administrative—and the initiation of each type of innovation within organizations. The role of organization leaders was also explored. The dual-core name arose to capture the notion of an administrative core that existed along with the technical core identified by James Thompson. Each core plays a distinct role in the innovation process, with initiatives originating at each end of the organization's hierarchy. Administrative innovations trickle down from the administrative core at the top, and technical innovations trickle up from the technical core at the bottom. The dual innovation processes in organizations provide a plausible explanation for inconsistent research findings about the adoption of wide-ranging innovations. In this entry, the two types of innovation are defined, the different leader roles and adoption processes are examined, and the research evidence is reviewed along with organization design characteristics associated with each type of innovation.

Fundamentals

The adoption of innovations is important because innovation is essential for achieving improvements in long-term performance. Innovation is often defined as the adoption of an idea or behavior that is new to an organization. A technical innovation is the adoption of a new idea for a new product, service, or technical production process or service operation. Examples include software that enables greater collaboration among engineers, a new medication dispenser for patients, or developing a new smartphone. Administrative innovation pertains to organization structure, administration and control systems, and human resources and involves procedures, roles, structures, and rules directly related to management of an organization. Examples are the adoption of the balanced scorecard control system, adopting a new online system for recruiting employees, and moving to a virtual organization structure. Technical innovations usually are related to an organization's technology, the output of which touches clients, and administrative innovations are related to the organization's structure and management systems.

The basic dual-core idea is that innovation adoption within an organization will be driven by its respective centers or cores. Each core has its own participants, goals, problems, activities, methods, and domain. Each core is essential to total organization functioning, each taking responsibility for certain sectors of the external environment. People within each core are responsible for the awareness, initiation, and adoption of innovative ideas in their area of expertise. Two separate innovation patterns are proposed to exist in most organizations. Innovation ideas may be moving through the hierarchy in different directions, and the correct direction may increase chances for adoption. Organization members in a specific core will be most knowledgeable and aware of problems, new ideas, and the suitability of innovations in their domain. Experts in the technical aspect of the organization will tend to be those people working on or near the core technology. Upper-level managers are the experts concerning administrative arrangements and will be tuned to new developments that apply to administrative problems. Top managers see the big picture administratively and know what's happening in the environment of similar organizations. Administrative innovations will tend to be proposed and approved near the top of the hierarchy and implemented downward, whereas technical innovations will be initiated upward for approval.

Importance

The distinction between technological and administrative innovation has been cited as one of the most meaningful dichotomies for explaining the process of innovation adoption. Most research articles on organizational innovation report surveys that correlate the number of innovation adoptions with organizational characteristics such as employee professionalism, centralization, formalization, size, and leadership. The innovation research studies that have focused specifically on the types of innovation adopted suggest two general findings. First, administrative innovations are adopted much less frequently than technical innovations. One study reported twice as many technical innovations to administrative innovations, another study reported three times as many, and a broad survey of 342 articles reported 10 times as many mentions of technical innovation as administrative innovation.

Second, the studies support the dual-core idea that technical and administrative innovations are associated with different organizational conditions and internal processes. Technical innovation is typically associated with a looser organic structure and highly professional employees, which allow initiatives to bubble upward from lower and middle levels. Organizations that frequently adopt technology innovations typically have decentralized authority structures and well-educated professional employees. Professional employees have broad networks and awareness of new technical ideas and are more likely to promote adoption. Fewer formal rules and procedures are also associated with technical innovation, presumably because fewer formal procedures encourage creative problem solving and the introduction of new ideas. The structural flexibility and dispersion of power to professional employees facilitates technical innovation.

Frequent administrative innovations, by contrast, have been found to use a top-down process and are associated with a more centralized, mechanistic structure and technical employees of a lower professional level. Organizations that successfully adopt many administrative changes typically have a larger administrative ratio, are larger in size, and are centralized and formalized compared with organizations that adopt many technical changes. The reason is that administrative changes in response to government, financial, competitive, or legal sectors of the environment are implemented top-down. The administrative core can exercise more control over employees in a centralized organization. Formalization of rules and procedures also seems to facilitate administrative changes. If an organization has an organic structure and highly professional employees with freedom and autonomy, those employees may resist top-down initiatives.

The role of leadership is perhaps the most interesting variable because it has been associated with more frequent adoption of both technical and administrative innovations. In the case of administrative innovation, leaders are directly involved in the initiation and implementation of changes. Transformational leaders have the power and authority to initiate changes and could expect less resistance from a less professional workforce. For example, research into civil service reform found that the implementation of management innovation was extremely difficult in organizations that had an organic technical core. The professional employees in a decentralized agency could resist civil service changes. By contrast, leaders in organizations considered more bureaucratic and mechanistic in the sense of high formalization and centralization adopted administrative changes more readily.

In the case of technical innovation, the top leader role is to facilitate and reward the initiation of innovations from the workforce. The ideal leadership style supports an entrepreneurial spirit from below and motivates technical employees to pursue improvements that they may not have otherwise attempted in the form of new services, products, and programs. Thus, leaders who want to support technical innovation can implement a variety of mechanisms, systems, and processes that encourage a bottom-up flow of ideas and make sure the ideas are heard and acted on by top executives. For example, some corporate leaders have held competitions or innovation challenge contests on the company intranet to encourage reserved and introverted engineers to speak up with their ideas for improving the business. Employees vote on their favorites and the winner may take home a cash prize.

Other examples include leaders at companies that have established innovation forums to discuss specific issues about which new technical ideas are wanted. Google leaders famously allow engineers to spend 20% of their time on projects of their own choosing, but managers realized that many ideas from employees were getting lost because the company didn't have processes for reviewing, prioritizing, and implementing the ideas. In response, executives established "innovation review" meetings, where managers present product ideas bubbling up from their divisions to top executives. It's a way to force management to focus on promising ideas at an early stage and provide the resources needed to turn them into successful products and services.

Innovation adoption is important because both academics and practitioners agree that to improve performance and ensure long-term survival, organizations must change and adapt by managing the development and implementation of innovations. The research findings indeed show that innovation and performance are positively related for both administrative and technological innovation. In some organizations, the adoption of one type of innovation was more strongly correlated with performance, depending on the administrative versus technical needs. In other organizations both administrative and technical innovation were positively related to performance. For example, in a sample of 85 public libraries, administrative innovations were adopted to cope with a period of resource decline, and service innovations were adopted in a later period to respond to growing competition from book sales and cable TV.

The lesson of the dual-core theory is that an organization can be led and structured to adopt frequent administrative changes if that is in line with its mission and demands from the environment. Leaders can be expected to initiate administrative innovations implemented through a fairly mechanistic and centralized structure. On the other hand, if frequent technical innovations serve an organization's mission, the leader's role is to facilitate innovations from the bottom-up, and the appropriate structure is more organic and decentralized with employees who are empowered professionals. The different innovation processes based on innovation type makes it important for leaders to understand the type of innovation to be adopted and to seek the correct fit with the organization's design and internal innovation processes.

Richard L. Daft

See also Patterns of Innovation; Process Theories of Change; Stages of Innovation

Further Readings

Daft, R. (1978). A dual-core model of organizational innovation. *Academy of Management Journal, 21*(2), 193–210.

Daft, R. L. (1982). Bureaucratic versus non-bureaucratic structure and the process of innovation and change. In S. B. Bacharach (Ed.), *Research in the sociology of organizations* (pp. 129–166). Greenwich, CT: JAI Press.

Daft, R. L., & Becker, S. W. (1978). *The innovative organization.* New York, NY: Elsevier.

Damanpour, F. (1987). The adoption of technological, administrative, and ancillary innovations: Impact of organizational factors. *Journal of Management, 13*(4), 675–688.

Damanpour, K., & Gopalakrishnan, S. (1998). Series of organizational structure and innovation adoption: The role of environmental change. *Journal of Engineering and Technology Management, 15*(1), 1–24.

Damanpour, F., Szabat, K. A., & Evan, W. M. (1989). The relationship between types of innovation and organizational performance. *Journal of Management Studies, 26*(6), 587–601.

Jaskyte, K. (2011). Predictors of administrative and technological innovations in nonprofit organizations. *Public Administration Review, 71*(1), 77–86.

Keupp, M. M., Palmie, M., & Gassmann, O. (2011). The strategic management of innovation: A systematic review and paths for future research. *International Journal of Management Reviews.* Advance online publication. doi:10.1111/j.1468–2370.2011.00321.x

DYNAMIC CAPABILITIES

Dynamic capabilities are the firm's ability to integrate, build, and reconfigure internal and external resources to address and shape rapidly changing business environments. Since its emergence in the 1990s, the dynamic capabilities framework has attracted a great deal of scholarly interest as a potentially overarching construct for the field of strategic management. The dynamic capabilities framework posits that firms are, to varying degrees, able to adapt to (or even initiate) changes in their environment. The strength of a firm's dynamic capabilities determines the speed and degree to which the firm's idiosyncratic resources and competences can be aligned and realigned to match the opportunities and requirements of the business environment. Strong dynamic capabilities are the basis for the sustained competitive advantage displayed by a handful of firms that have endured for decades even as they have shifted the focus of their activities. Dynamic capabilities contain an important element of creative managerial and entrepreneurial activity (e.g., pioneering new markets) by the top management team and other expert talent. They are also, however, rooted in organizational routines (e.g., product development along a known trajectory) and analysis (e.g., of investment choices). These two facets of dynamic capabilities often work together. At Apple, for example, product development follows an established process but in a way that encourages creative input through, for example, an ad hoc meeting to explore a new idea. Keeping hybrid processes such as this from going off-track is in itself a dynamic capability, rooted in the organization's values and systems. The dynamic capabilities concept provides one of the most comprehensive accounts of what leading firms do to maintain competitive advantage. This entry begins by contrasting ordinary and dynamic capabilities. It presents the intellectual roots of the dynamic capabilities framework and a taxonomy of dynamic capabilities. It concludes with a statement of the central role of dynamic capabilities for dynamically formulating and executing strategies as competitive conditions evolve.

Fundamentals

Ordinary Capabilities

It is perhaps easier to understand what dynamic capabilities are by describing other capabilities that are not dynamic. These ordinary capabilities permit sufficiency (and sometimes excellence) in the performance of a delineated task. They generally fall into three categories: administration, operations, and governance. Ordinary capabilities (also known as competences) become embedded in (a) skilled personnel, including, under certain circumstances, independent contractors; (b) facilities and equipment; and (c) processes and routines, including any supporting technical manuals and the administrative coordination needed to get the job done. Many capabilities can be measured against specific task requirements, such as new product introductions, and benchmarked internally or externally to industry best practice.

A firm's ordinary capabilities enable the production and sale of a defined (but static) set of products and services. But the presence of ordinary capabilities says nothing about whether the current production schedule is the right (or even a profitable) thing to do. The nature of competences, and their underlying processes, is that they are not meant to change (until they have to). The change process is a key part of the exercise of dynamic capabilities. Dynamic capabilities determine whether the enterprise is currently making the right products and addressing the right market segment, and whether its future plans are appropriately matched to consumer needs and technological and competitive opportunities.

Precursors

The intellectual origins of the dynamic capabilities framework can be traced to Joseph Schumpeter and to economic and business historians such as Alfred Chandler and Nathan Rosenberg (for his work on complementary technologies), to Richard Nelson and Sidney Winter (for their work on national systems of innovation and the nature of knowledge), to Oliver Williamson (for his exegesis of asset specificity), and to Edith Penrose (for her work on the sources of growth of the firm). Other intellectual antecedents include (but are by no means limited to) W. A. Abernathy and James M. Utterback (innovation life cycles), Giovanni Dosi (technological change), Israel Kirzner (entrepreneurialism), James March and Herbert Simon (organizational behavior and decision making), Richard Rumelt (isolating mechanisms), and M. L. Tushman (competency enhancing and competency destroying innovation). Behavioral economists such as Daniel Kahneman and Amos Tversky have also provided key insights.

The dynamic capabilities framework builds on that of the *resource-based view* of the firm. Resources are firm-specific, mostly intangible, assets that are difficult, if not impossible, to imitate. Examples include intellectual property, process know-how, customer relationships, and the knowledge possessed by groups of especially skilled employees. They are typically not considered at all in the accounting view of the firm displayed on its balance sheet, except perhaps in a line item for "Goodwill" related to an acquired firm. Resources—particularly intellectual capital—are idiosyncratic in nature and are difficult to trade because their property rights are likely to have fuzzy boundaries and their value is context-dependent. As a result, there is no well-developed market for most types of resources and intellectual capital; in fact, they are typically not traded at all. They are also often quite difficult to transfer among firms simply from a management (let alone transactions) perspective. Competences, the ordinary capabilities described earlier, are a particular kind of organizational resource. The essence of competences (and of all types of capabilities) is that they cannot generally be bought (apart from acquiring the entire organization); they must be built. Valuable differentiating competences may include how decisions are made, how customer needs are assessed, and how quality is maintained.

The resource-based view was an important intellectual leap beyond the prevailing economic view that strategic success is obtained by efficiency and the creation of barriers to entry. The resources approach accorded well with the sense of many practitioners, especially in high-tech industries, that sustainable success came with the laborious accumulation of technological assets and human resources, not from clever strategic positioning. But the approach failed to pursue the questions of how firms develop or acquire new competences and adapt when circumstances change. The dynamic capabilities approach deals primarily with such questions.

Dynamic Capabilities

Dynamic capabilities enable an enterprise to profitably orchestrate its resources, competences, and other assets. They allow the organization (especially its top management) to develop conjectures about the evolution of markets and technology, validate them, and realign assets and competences to meet new requirements. Dynamic capabilities are also used to assess when and how the enterprise is to ally with other enterprises. The expansion of trade has enabled (and requires) greater global specialization.

To make the global system of vertical specialization and co-specialization (bilateral dependence) work, there is a need for firms to develop and align assets within a global value chain so as to develop and deliver a joint "solution" that customers value.

Not infrequently, an innovating firm will be forced to create a market, such as when an entirely new type of product is offered to customers or when new intermediate products are to be traded for the first time. Dynamic capabilities, particularly the more entrepreneurial competences, are a critical input to the market creating (and co-creating) process. The potential changes envisioned in the dynamic capabilities framework go beyond the notion of "fit" seen as optimal in the "adaptation" school of organizational change research, which holds the environment to be exogenous.

Although dynamic capabilities is a framework rather than a full-fledged model, at least some of its assertions and implications are empirically testable. The project of empirical validation is still in its early stages. Careful studies of the successes and failures of specific enterprises have provided a great deal of support already. Supportive statistical evidence includes data showing sustained heterogeneity in firm performance, because dynamic capabilities can support superior long-term returns for some—but not all—companies. Most studies do, in fact, find that differences in profitability persist over time.

Taxonomy of Dynamic Capabilities

Dynamic capabilities can usefully be thought of as comprising three primary clusters of competences: (1) identification and assessment of an opportunity (*sensing*), (2) mobilization of resources to address an opportunity and to capture value from doing so (*seizing*), and (3) continued renewal (*transforming*). Sensing, seizing, and transforming are essential if the firm is to sustain itself as markets and technologies change.

Sensing is an inherently entrepreneurial set of competences that involves exploring technological opportunities, probing markets, and listening to customers, along with scanning the other elements of the business ecosystem. It requires management to build and "test" hypotheses about market and technological evolution, including the recognition of "latent" demand. The world wasn't clamoring for a coffeehouse on every corner, but Starbucks, under the guidance of Howard

Schultz, recognized and successfully exploited the potential market. As this example implies, sensing requires managerial insight and vision—or an analytical process that can serve as a proxy for it.

Seizing capabilities include the design of business models to satisfy customers and capture value. They also include securing access to capital and the necessary human resources. Employee motivation is vital. Good incentive design is a necessary but not sufficient condition for superior performance in this area. Strong relationships must also be forged externally with suppliers, complementors, and customers.

Transforming capabilities that realign the enterprise's resources are needed most obviously when radical new opportunities are to be addressed. But they are also needed periodically to soften the rigidities that develop over time from asset accumulation, standard operating procedures, and insider misappropriation of rent streams. A firm's assets must also be kept in strategic alignment vis-à-vis its ecosystem. Complementarities need to be constantly managed (reconfigured as necessary) to achieve evolutionary fitness, limiting loss of value in the event that market leverage shifts to favor external complements.

The whole notion of management-led transfiguration of the enterprise contradicts the "organizational ecology" school of strategic management research. The ecology approach holds that, as environments shift, incumbent firms face overwhelming inertia and are, as a result, replaced by organizations better suited to the changed context. Although there is considerable empirical evidence of organizational inertia, the dynamic capabilities framework holds that management can overcome evolutionary forces to some degree and the changes that have occurred in the course of the histories of numerous leading corporations, such as IBM and Apple, which suggests that this is true in practice.

Importance

The dynamic capabilities framework is still evolving and has not yet been rigorously tested. Numerous case studies have confirmed the importance of dynamic capabilities in specific instances. There is also a small but growing number of studies that have operationalized various aspects of dynamic capabilities for statistical tests, and these have generally confirmed the importance of specific capabilities for higher firm performance.

Dynamic capabilities provide a basis for competitive advantage because they are embedded in the organization and hard for rivals to imitate. Nontradable assets such as these can provide a solid basis for building long-term profitability. Assets and services traded in a market can be accessed by rivals, which limits the ability to rely on them as a source of competitive advantage. The Internet and other recent innovations have vastly expanded the number and type of goods and services available from efficient, low-cost providers.

Knowledge assets and, more generally, resources, as defined above, remain especially difficult—although not impossible—to trade. In the rare instances when one is able to obtain a resource through purchase, it may be bought for far less than its strategic worth to the buyer because the seller lacks the necessary complements (or vision) to realize the full potential value.

The dynamic capabilities framework encompasses the ability of an enterprise to create, maintain, and manage idiosyncratic, value-supporting intangibles. The framework shows how such assets must be used within a business model for providing value to customers and ensuring the appropriability of some of that value for the firm. The ability to dynamically formulate and execute strategy as conditions evolve is the essential requirement for durable enterprise growth and profitability.

The study of dynamic capabilities teaches the need to look beyond ensuring that a business runs smoothly. Managers at all levels must also be looking around and ahead to detect and respond to opportunities and threats. Strong dynamic capabilities allow an organization or business unit not only to do things right but also to do the right things to stay or become competitive.

David J. Teece

See also Competitive Advantage; Firm Growth; Hypercompetition; Knowledge-Based View of the Firm; Resource-Based View of the Firm; Strategic Alliances; Strategic Entrepreneurship

Further Readings

Di Stefano, G., Peteraf, M. A., & Verona, G. (2010). Dynamic capabilities deconstructed: A bibliographic investigation into the origins, development, and future directions of the research domain. *Industrial and Corporate Change, 19,* 1187–1204.

Eisenhardt, K., & Martin, J. (2000). Dynamic capabilities: What are they? *Strategic Management Journal, 21,* 1105–1121.

Helfat, C. E., Finkelstein, S., Mitchell, W., Peteraf, M. A., Singh, H., Teece, D. J., & Winter, S. G. (2007). *Dynamic capabilities: Understanding strategic change in organizations.* Oxford, England: Blackwell.

O'Reilly, C. A., & Tushman, M. L. (2008). Ambidexterity as a dynamic capability: Resolving the innovator's dilemma. In A. P. Brief & B. M. Staw (Eds.), *Research in organizational behavior* (Vol. 28, pp. 185–206). Oxford, England: Elsevier.

Teece, D. J. (2007). Explicating dynamic capabilities: The nature and microfoundations of (sustainable) enterprise performance. *Strategic Management Journal, 28,* 1319–1350.

Teece, D. J. (2009). *Dynamic capabilities and strategic management: Organizing for innovation and growth.* New York, NY: Oxford University Press.

Teece, D. J., Pisano, G., & Shuen, A. (1997). Dynamic capabilities and strategic management. *Strategic Management Journal, 18,* 509–533.

Winter, S. G. (2003). Understanding dynamic capabilities. *Strategic Management Journal, 24,* 991–995.

E

EMOTIONAL AND SOCIAL INTELLIGENCE

Beneath the many definitions, measures, and concepts, emotional and social intelligence (ESI) is the intelligent use of one's emotions. Neurological research has confirmed that it is difficult to have cognitions that are not using ESI because thoughts are either driven by emotional arousal or in part connected to emotional centers of the brain. A more precise definition of ESI is that it is a set of thoughts, feelings, and behavior driven by a neural circuitry emanating from the limbic system. When Peter Salovey and John D. Mayer first introduced emotional intelligence (EI) into the professional literature, they defined it as a set of abilities in awareness of and handling of your emotions. ESI is crucial as a set of underlying abilities that enable a person to effectively manage and lead others. They are the most direct characteristics of an individual that lead to or cause effectiveness. As such, they are highly relevant to the identification, selection, promotion, succession planning, career path, training, and development of managers. They highlight characteristics and behavior that should be incented and rewarded by the human resource management systems. This entry is an explanation of the concept and how it has evolved and highlights some of the major applications for improvement of management performance.

Fundamentals

An integrated concept of emotional, social, and cognitive intelligence as abilities, self-perception, and the behavioral level of competencies offers a theoretical structure for ESI and links it to a theory of action and job performance. That is, a person's ESI enables him or her to address job demands, functional needs, and role requirements in order to be effective. It enables the person to do these consistent with the internal and external organizational environment. In this sense, ESI is based on a contingency theory of managerial and leadership effectiveness.

Conflict about the definition and theoretical basis of ESI, as well as conflicting operational definitions emerging in various forms of measurement, has plagued the concept and muddied the waters of its potential application in organizations. If defined as a single construct, the tendency to believe that more effective people have the vital ingredient for success invites the attribution of a halo effect. For example, person A is effective, therefore, she has all of the right stuff, such as brains, savvy, and style. The challenge is finding the best "focal point" with which to look at ESI and performance.

The articulation of one overall emotional or social intelligence might be deceptive and suggest a close association with cognitive capability (i.e., traditionally defined "intelligence" or what psychologists often call "g," referring to general cognitive ability. The latter would not only be confusing but additionally would raise the question as to what one is calling emotional and social intelligence and whether it is nothing more than an element of previously defined intelligence, cognitive ability, or personality traits.

A wide variety of publications have linked trait ESI to cognitive intelligence and various forms of performance in academic settings and a few in work settings, using measures such as the Mayer Salovey Caruso Emotional Intelligence Test (MSCEIT). Similarly, a large number of publications have linked self-perception aspects of ESI to personality and performance in academic and work settings, using measures, such as the Emotional Quotient Inventory (EQ-I), Trait Emotional Intelligence Questionnaire (TESIQue), or Wong-Law measure (WLESIS). Special issues of the *Journal of Management Development* in 2008 and 2009, as well as a special issue of the *Journal of Cross-Cultural Management* in 2012, have been devoted to studies showing the link between the behavioral level of ESI (i.e., competencies) and work performance in a wide variety of jobs, sectors, and countries, using measures, such as the Emotional and Social Competency Inventory (ESCI) or coding of behavioral event interviews.

Although data from studies comparing these tests are underway, conceptually we would expect small correlations between these various measures. The MSCEST assesses a person's direct handling of emotions, while the ESCI, which is intended to assess the ESI competencies described earlier, assesses how the person expresses his or her handling of emotions in life and work settings.

Mayer, Salovey, David Caruso, Séphan Côté, Reuven Bar-On, Richard Boyatzis, and their colleagues have shown in various studies that ESI contributes unique variance to criterion measures beyond measures of generalized intelligence and personality.

Although not universally accepted, a number of the primary researchers in ESI contend that the underlying personality theory explains ESI as occurring at multiple levels, such as (a) neural circuits and endocrine (i.e., hormonal) processes, (b) unconscious dispositions called motives and traits, (c) self-image or self-perception, and (c) observed competencies or competency clusters.

The components of ESI as assessed by the three most used measures are the following:

MSCEIT: (a) perceiving emotions: faces, pictures; (b) facilitating thought: facilitation, sensations;

(c) understanding emotions: changes, blends; and (d) managing emotions: emotion management, emotional relations;

EQ-i: (a) intrapersonal: self-regard, emotional self-awareness, assertiveness, independence, self-actualization; (b) interpersonal: empathy, social responsibility, interpersonal relationships; (c) stress management: stress tolerance, impulse control; (d) adaptability: reality testing, flexibility, problem solving; (e) general mood: optimism, happiness; (f) positive impression; and (g) Inconsistency Index;

ESCI: (a) self-awareness: emotional self-awareness; (b) self-management: adaptability, emotional self-control, achievement orientation, positive outlook; (c) social awareness: empathy, organizational awareness; (d) relationship management: inspirational leadership, influence, conflict management, teamwork, coaching and mentoring; and for the university version, two cognitive competencies are added: systems thinking and pattern recognition.

This conceptualization of ESI requires a more holistic perspective than is often taken. When integrating the physiological level with the psychological and behavioral levels, a more comprehensive view of the human emerges.

Evolution

While Edward L. Thorndike and other early psychologists explored an ESI-related concept of "social intelligence" (SI) in the 1920s and 1930s, recent psychologists have appreciated SI's complexity and described it in terms of multiples. Howard Gardner conceptualized this as two of the seven intelligences: intrapersonal and interpersonal. Robert Sternberg called it "practical intelligence" and later "successful intelligence."

The concept of EI was launched onto the world scene by the best seller, *Emotional Intelligence*, by Daniel Goleman in 1995. Peter Salovey and Jack Mayer are credited with first introducing the phrase in a professional journal in 1990. At the same time, others like Reuven Bar-On, were studying these concepts. Although there are differences among the theories and models, these distinctions have more to do with the measurement of ESI with the three most popular instruments, such as the MSCEST (developed by John Mayer, Peter Salovey, and David Caruso), EQ-I (developed by Reuven

Bar-On), and ESCI (developed by Richard Boyatzis and Daniel Goleman), than the underlying theory. Controversy in the field has emerged as to whether there is one concept called ESI, whether it should be called an "intelligence," and how best to measure it. Regardless, the concept of ESI has allowed scholars to create a holistic personality theory, including neuroendocrine processes. It has also provided a label that makes it easy for many to classify the noncognitive characteristics.

Advocates of trait-level approaches often contend that ESI should be seen as a form of intelligence, and as such, it should be associated with traditional intelligence measures. Critics claim that it would not add enough distinctiveness to warrant such elaborate additional measures or even the need for an additional concept.

Professionals advocating self-perception approaches claim it is an internal characteristic, or set of characteristics. Since the characteristics are internal, they are best assessed, the proponents of this perspective claim, by asking persons to assess themselves.

Behavioral approaches or levels of ESI are typically called competencies. The "external," direct consequence to actions in life and work establishes the competencies as forms of intelligence, whether cognitive or emotional. This approach is based on David McClelland's concept of competency. Building on McClelland's 1951 personality theory, Boyatzis offered, in 1982, a scheme as an integrated system with concentric circles. The person's *unconscious motives* and *trait dispositions* are shown at the center. These affected, and were affected by, the next expanding circle of the person's *values* and *self-image*. The surrounding circle was labeled the *skill* level. The circle surrounding it included *observed, specific behaviors*.

The concept of competency-based human resources has gone from a new technique to a common practice in the four decades since McClelland first proposed them as a critical distinction in performance. *A competency* is defined as a capability or ability. It is a set of related but different sets of behavior organized around an underlying construct called the "intent." The behaviors are alternate manifestations of the intent, as appropriate in various situations or times. Competencies require action (i.e., a set of alternate behaviors varying according to the situation) and intent. Boyatzis defined *a competency*

in 1982 as an "underlying characteristic of the person that leads to or causes effective or superior performance." In this approach, an emotional, intelligence competency is an ability to recognize, understand, and use emotional information about oneself that leads to or causes effective or superior performance. Meanwhile, a social intelligence competency is the ability to recognize, understand, and use emotional information about others that leads to or causes effective or superior performance. A cognitive intelligence competency is an ability to think or analyze information and situations that leads to or causes effective or superior performance.

To identify, define, and clarify competencies, an inductive method is typically used. To determine distinctive competencies, a sample of outstanding or superior performers is identified. Then, a sample of "average" or "poor" performers is also identified. Research published over the last 30 years or so shows us that outstanding leaders, managers, advanced professionals, and people in key jobs, from sales to bank tellers, appear to require three clusters of behavioral habits as *threshold* abilities and three clusters of competencies as *distinguishing outstanding performance*. The threshold clusters of competencies include (a) expertise and experience; (b) knowledge (i.e., declarative, procedural, functional, and metacognitive); and (c) an assortment of basic cognitive competencies, such as memory and deductive reasoning.

The distinctive competencies are (a) cognitive competencies, such as systems thinking and pattern recognition; (b) emotional intelligence competencies, including self-awareness and self-management competencies, such as emotional self-awareness and emotional self-control; (c) social intelligence competencies, including social awareness and relationship-management competencies, such as empathy and teamwork.

Recent research in the neurosciences is supporting the observation that neural networks involved in one's emotional self-control and internal reflections are associated with the "executive function." In functional magnetic resonance imaging (fMRI) studies, Professor Tony Jack and his colleagues have shown that when people are engaged in dealing with social situations, a different network is activated, and it is quite similar to the default mode network. The emerging evidence that these two neural circuits are somewhat different suggests further support that emotional intelligence and social intelligence are two different concepts. This difference is supported by endocrine studies.

A major advancement in understanding the effect of competencies on performance came from catastrophe theory, which is now considered a subset of complexity theory. Instead of asking only the typical question, Which competencies are needed or necessary for outstanding performance? David McClelland, in a paper published posthumously in 1998, posed the question, How often do you need to show a competency to "tip" you into outstanding performance? In other words, how frequently should a competency be shown to be sufficient for maximum performance? Using this method, Boyatzis reported significant findings regarding tipping points in an international consulting firm. The profits from accounts of senior partners were analyzed for seven quarters following assessment of their competencies. Senior partners using ESI competencies above the tipping point more than doubled the operating profits from their accounts as compared to the senior partners below the tipping point. The measure of competencies was the average perceived frequency of use of each competency by others around the senior partner, using a 360-degree competency questionnaire. He showed that this method of diagnosing effectiveness was superior to other, more typical methods.

Importance

One of the benefits of the multilevel approach to ESI assessment or competency is that it allows more possibilities of how ESI can be developed in adulthood. The most dramatic results have been shown with the behavioral level of ESI. Under the leadership of Professor Cary Cherniss and Daniel Goleman, the Consortium for Research on Emotional Intelligence in Organizations in a global search of the literature identified only 15 programs that improved emotional intelligence. They showed impact on job outcomes, such as number of new businesses started, or life outcomes, such as finding a job or satisfaction. The few published studies examining improvement of more than one of these competencies show an overall improvement of about 10% in emotional intelligence abilities 3 to 18 months following. The results appear no better from master of business administration (MBA) programs where there

is no attempt to enhance emotional intelligence, as shown in research projects by the American Assembly of Collegiate Schools of Business. They reported that behavior levels of graduating students from two highly ranked business schools, compared to their levels when they began their MBA, showed improvements of only 2% in the skills of emotional intelligence. In fact, when students from four other high-ranking MBA programs were assessed on a range of tests and direct behavioral measures, they showed a gain of 4% in self-awareness and self-management abilities but a *decrease* of 3% in social awareness and relationship management.

A series of longitudinal studies underway at the Weatherhead School of Management of Case Western Reserve University have shown that people can change their complex set of emotional and social intelligence competencies. Richard Boyatzis, Elizabeth Stubbs, and Scott Taylor showed behavioral improvements of 60% to 70% during the 1 to 2 years of the full-time MBA program, 55% to 65% improvement during the 3 to 5 years of the part-time MBA program, and then leveling off at about 50% improvement 5 to 7 years after entry into the part-time MBA program.

In a longitudinal study of four classes completing the Professional Fellows Program (i.e., an executive education program at the Weatherhead School of Management), Ronald Ballou, David Bowers, Richard Boyatzis, and David Kolb showed that these 45- to 55-year-old professionals and executives improved on 67% of the emotional intelligence competencies assessed in this study.

These longitudinal studies are showing that the belief that many of these characteristics cannot be developed (i.e., you have to be born with them) is a result of inappropriate or ineffective development methods.

Because of the consistent validation results from studies of ESI, it is believed that these measures can be used in human resource management and development systems in organizations and in education for development. People can benefit from assessment and feedback on their ESI, and from the behavioral approach, how others see their ESI behavior. It is suggested from some studies, that the use of trained coaches to help a person interpret such feedback and put it to work in improving their performance can help both individuals and their organizations.

Richard E. Boyatzis

Further Readings

Bar-On, R., & Parker, J. (Eds.). (2000). *Handbook of emotional intelligence.* San Francisco, CA: Jossey-Bass.

Boyatzis, R. E. (2009). A behavioral approach to emotional Intelligence. *Journal of Management Development, 28*(9), 749–770.

Boyatzis, R. E., Stubbs, L., & Taylor, S. (2002). Learning cognitive and emotional intelligence competencies through graduate management education. *Academy of Management Journal on Learning and Education, 1*(2), 150–162.

Cherniss, C. (2010). Emotional intelligence: Toward clarification of a concept. *Industrial and Organizational Psychology, 3,* 110–112.

Cherniss, C., & Adler, M. (2000). *Promoting emotional intelligence in organizations: Make training in emotional intelligence effective.* Washington, DC: American Society of Training and Development.

Goleman, D. (1995). *Emotional intelligence.* New York, NY: Bantam Books.

Salovey, P., & Mayer, J. D. (1990). Emotional intelligence. *Imagination, Cognition and Personality, 9,* 185–211.

See also Achievement Motivation Theory; Complexity Theory and Organizations; Contingency Theory; Cultural Intelligence; Leadership Practices

EMPOWERMENT

Empowerment is a popular term that has been used loosely in the business vernacular across different contexts to address a wide variety of issues, resulting in multiple meanings being attributed to it. In the management literature, psychological empowerment focuses on the experience of being empowered and is seen, as per a 1988 article by Conger and Kanungo, as "a process of enhancing feelings of self-efficacy among organizational members through the identification of conditions that foster powerlessness and through their removal by formal organizational and informal techniques of providing efficacy information" (p. 474). *Empowerment* has subsequently been described by Gary Yukl in a 2006 review as "how the intrinsic motivation and self-efficacy of people are influenced by leadership behavior, job characteristics, organization structure, and their own needs and values" (p. 107). Empowerment

is relevant as when workers feel empowered, their personal efficacy expectations are strengthened through developing a "can do" attitude which can be used to socially construct their own reality. This empowerment entry will initially present the fundamentals of empowerment, followed by the evolution of empowerment, its importance, and practical implications and applications.

Fundamentals

Researchers have argued that psychological empowerment is multifaceted and defined as increased intrinsic task motivation manifested in a set of four cognitions reflecting an individual's orientation to his or her work role. The four cognitions, or dimensions, of psychological empowerment are meaning, competence, self-determination, and impact.

Meaning is the value of a work goal or purpose, judged in relation to an individual's own ideals or standards. Meaning involves the perception that a task or activity is of value to oneself. Meaning is also seen as the fit between the requirements of the job tasks and one's own values, beliefs, and behaviors. Meaning is seen as the "engine" of empowerment as it energizes individuals to work.

Competence, or self-efficacy, is an individual's belief in his or her capability to perform work activities with skill. Competence is analogous to agency beliefs, personal mastery, or effort-performance expectancy. Competence also captures the feeling that one is capable of successfully performing a particular task or activity.

Self-determination is an individual's sense of having a choice of initiating and regulating actions over one's own work. This dimension reflects the sense of personal control or influence over one's immediate work situation and autonomy in the initiation and continuation of work behaviors and processes. Self-determination is also referred to as choice which involves "causal responsibility for a person's actions." The degree of choice in the work setting has been described as the crux of empowerment.

Impact is the degree to which an individual can influence strategic, administrative, or operating outcomes at work. Impact is also the belief that one has an influence on organizational-level decisions or policy making, as well as the degree to which individuals perceive that their behavior makes a difference.

Gretchen M. Spreitzer developed a psychological empowerment model based on Kenneth W. Thomas and Betty A. Velthouse's theoretical work, encompassing the meaning, competence, self-determination, and impact dimensions. Spreitzer's model has enjoyed much use in subsequent empirical studies, with several researchers validating Spreitzer's model. However, two research teams proposed that the key dimensions of self-determination and competence, respectively, may not contribute to the understanding of individual empowerment. Additionally, it has been proposed that a three-dimensional model of psychological empowerment—which includes perceived competence, perceived control, and goal internalization—captures an important, overlooked aspect of empowerment, goal internalization, and may be as effective as Spreitzer's four-dimensional model. Finally, concerns have been expressed by one research team about Spreitzer's use of the same data set for all subsequent, related studies.

While there is some disagreement on operationalization of the individual psychological empowerment construct, the four main empowerment dimensions—meaningfulness, competence, self-determination, and impact—have dominated the literature in recent studies.

Antecedents of Empowerment

Antecedents and consequences aid in developing the nomological network of constructs. Antecedents of empowerment can be classified into six categories—individual traits, the task environment, the social structural context, the organizational environment, structural mechanisms, and leadership strategies.

The work context—task environment, social structural context, and organizational environment—has received the most attention and is hypothesized to influence an individual's and a group's sense of empowerment. Task interdependence, responsibility, and core job dimensions (i.e., task identity, autonomy, and feedback) have been seen as task environment characteristics that enable empowerment. Five work-unit social structural

characteristics—low role ambiguity, working for a boss who has a wide span of control, sociopolitical support, access to information, and a participative unit climate—have been consistently found to create a work context facilitating empowerment. Additionally, work units that provide sociopolitical support (i.e., the endorsement, approval, and legitimacy obtained from various constituencies in organizational political networks) and access to information and resources have been shown to enhance team empowerment. Finally, forms of the organization's structure (i.e., opportunity role structure and social structure) have been proposed as empowerment antecedents.

Individuals' traits and conscious behavior have also been viewed as facilitating empowerment. Locus of control and self-efficacy or -esteem were the two individual traits most often seen as empowerment antecedents by researchers. Leader behaviors (e.g., leader–member exchange, rewards, and leadership strategies) have also been seen as precursors to empowerment.

Partial Nomological Network for Empowerment

Managers often face the task of changing employees' attitudes because existing attitudes hinder performance. Although attitudes are often resistant to change, the attitudes can be influenced indirectly through education and training experiences or leadership strategies (i.e., antecedents to empowerment) that change underlying beliefs. The implication is that managers achieve effectiveness and innovation (i.e., consequences of empowerment) by developing generally favorable work attitudes toward the organization and the job (e.g., job satisfaction, organizational commitment, job involvement, and empowerment) in their employees.

While considerable strides have been made toward establishing a common ground across academic and practitioner perspectives on empowerment, there is still work to be done as shown in the diverse approaches to empowerment. The job attitudes' framework provides a useful framework for examining the various approaches to empowerment.

Attitudes represent the cluster of beliefs, assessed feelings, and behavioral intentions individuals hold toward an object. An attitude is a positive or negative feeling or mental state of readiness, learned and organized through experience, that exerts specific influence on a person's response to people, objects, and situations. An attitude, then, is defined as a learned predisposition to respond in a consistently favorable or unfavorable manner with respect to a given object.

Milton J. Rosenberg proposed a structural theory of attitudes that assumes that people have structured attitudes composed of various affective and cognitive components. Attitudes are seen as having three components: affect, cognition, and behavioral intent. Affect is the feeling component of an attitude and contains the feelings one has about a given object or situation. Affect is similar to emotion as it is something over which one has little or no conscious control. The cognitive component of an attitude consists of a person's perceptions, opinions, and beliefs about an object or situation. Cognitions suggest thought processes, especially rationality and logic based on a person's evaluative perceptions of reality. The behavioral component of attitudes refers to a person's intentions or how one expects to act toward someone or something. An intention is a component of an attitude that guides a person's behavior.

The theory of planned behavior builds on the structural theory of attitudes and includes three components: the attitude toward the behavior, a subjective norm, and the degree of perceived behavior control. The attitude toward the behavior refers to the degree to which a person has a favorable or unfavorable evaluation or appraisal of the behavior in question. The subjective-norm social factor proposes a perceived social pressure to perform or not to perform the behavior. The third antecedent of intention, the degree of perceived behavior control, encompasses the perceived ease or difficulty of performing the behavior and reflects past experience as well as anticipated impediments and obstacles. Finally, the various attitude components' interrelatedness means that a change in one precipitates a change in the others.

The behavioral intention model suggests that managers need to appreciate the dynamic relationships between attitudes, subjective norms, and behavioral intentions when attempting to foster productive behavior or employee attitudes (e.g., empowerment). An organization may use leadership strategies (e.g., manipulate structural mechanisms, such as the hierarchical authority, resource control, and network centrality) to attempt to set

goals to increase the productivity and success of the organization. Additionally, employees may feel that the organization's goals are valued (i.e., transformational empowerment) and thus have favorable attitudes toward becoming more energized in their jobs. Their perceived subjective norm might be favorable as they see their coworkers motivated to work hard for the organization (i.e., motivational empowerment approach). Regarding perceived behavior control, employees are completely in charge of thinking about how empowered they will feel in their current work situation (i.e., psychological empowerment) and, hence, in their behavioral work-outcome intentions.

Evolution

There are three major approaches to empowerment which have coevolved—structural, relational, or social exchange; leadership; and motivational perspectives. Despite the diverse approaches to empowerment, psychological empowerment, namely, highlighting empowerment's motivational implications, has emerged as a fundamental way to encompass an individual's personal experience of the various empowerment approaches.

Structural, relational, or social exchange approach. The structural approach focuses on the transfer of power and decision-making authority to lower level organizational members. This approach is used in the largest body of work on empowerment—primarily in the community psychology, social work, and mental health literatures—and is also known as the relational perspective. Power in organizations is the ability to influence organizational outcomes. One-way power can be transferred is through manipulation of structural mechanisms (e.g., hierarchical authority, resource control, and network centrality). This approach implies that organizational actors who have power are more likely to achieve their desired outcomes, while actors who lack power are more likely to have their desired outcomes thwarted or redirected by those with power.

Considered in terms of this perspective, empowerment becomes the process by which a leader or manager shares his or her power with subordinates, such that the emphasis is primarily on the notion of sharing authority. According to the social exchange perspective, as superiors differentiate among subordinates (i.e., in-group and out-group members), they tend to utilize leadership techniques with in-group members and supervision techniques with out-group members. This perspective also focuses on how the sharing of power within an organization is affected by the structures and cultures of the organization and thus emphasizes how the organizational structure should be designed to facilitate the empowerment of its members.

Leadership approach. The leadership approach concentrates on the leadership practices that energize followers to strive toward organizational objectives. When leaders present an exciting organizational vision or a valued goal, leaders invigorate the followers and hence empower them. When subordinates are inspired, the subordinates may be empowered to participate in the organizational transformation process.

The transformational approach, an extension of the leadership approach, captures the psychological effects of empowerment practices (e.g., enhanced efficacy, delegation, and the energizing power of valued goals). Shared vision—consisting of the clarity of organizational expectations, employees feeling responsible to achieve goals, knowing the customer, and feeling responsible to deliver results to the customer—has been seen as an important dimension of empowerment. Empowerment in this perspective is viewed as a cognitive state which is characterized by (a) perceived control, (b) perceived competence, and (c) goal internalization. Perceived control encompasses attitudes about authority, autonomy, and decision-making latitude, while perceived competence embraces feelings of self-efficacy from role mastery. Goal internalization is an indicator of identification with organization goals and captures the energizing aspect of a worthy organizational vision as apparent in transformational, charismatic, and inspiration leadership theories.

Motivational approach. The third approach to the study of empowerment, primarily in the management literature, focuses on empowerment as a motivational construct. This perspective views power as having its base within an actor's motivational disposition. Managerial techniques that strengthen an employee's self-determination need or self-efficacy belief will make that employee feel more powerful, while strategies that weaken an employee's self-determination

need or self-efficacy will increase the employee's feelings of powerlessness. Hence, empowerment, in this motivational sense, refers to an intrinsic need for self-determination or a belief in personal self-efficacy. It is important to note that self-efficacy in the motivational approach shares common ground with self-efficacy in the leadership approach's transformational empowerment. However, self-efficacy in transformational empowerment is developed through competence or role mastery, while self-efficacy in the motivational approach is enhanced through self-determination.

Thomas and Velthouse proposed a multifaceted, cognitive model of empowerment, and defined empowerment as intrinsic task motivation resulting from a set of four task-related cognitions or task assessments or situational assessments pertaining to an individual's work role. The cognitions include meaning (the value of a work goal), competence (similar to self-efficacy), self-determination (choice in initiating and regulating actions), and impact (influence over strategic, administrative, or operating outcomes).

Psychological empowerment, an extension of the motivational approach, focuses on the experience of being empowered and is seen as a process that enhances feelings of self-efficacy among organizational members. Primary vehicles for this include (a) the identification of conditions that foster powerlessness and (b) the removal of these conditions by formal organizational and informal techniques of providing efficacy information. When individuals feel empowered, their personal efficacy expectations are strengthened through developing a "can do" attitude. Inherent in the psychological empowerment notion is the insight that reality is socially constructed. Thus, it is workers' personal interpretations of management job-redesign efforts or intentions that matter most.

Importance

The emphasis on psychological empowerment's four elements—meaning, competence, self-determination, and impact—links it to earlier theory on work motivation, job design, participative leadership, and employee involvement. In general, more empowerment will be felt when the content and consequences of the work are consistent with a person's values, the person has the capability to determine how and when the work is done, the person has high confidence about being able to do it effectively, and the person believes it is possible to influence important events and outcomes.

While empowerment can be particularly important for organizations operating in a team environment, there has been little scholarly attention given to group empowerment. Work by Bradley L. Kirkman and Benson Rosen; Spreitzer; and Deborah Noble, Aneil K. Mishra, and William N. Cooke are notable exceptions. A four-dimensional, team-level model has been proposed which includes group perceptions of the meaningfulness, potency, autonomy, and consequences dimensions, paralleling the individual empowerment dimensions of meaning, competence, self-determination, and impact.

Individuals who find the tasks they perform meaningful, or consistent with their beliefs, attitudes, and behaviors, are more likely to feel empowered. *Group meaningfulness* differs from individual meaningfulness in that beliefs are shared among team members regarding the work; thus, group meaningfulness is a collective belief. Group meaningfulness is seen as a part of the nature of the task necessary for team success and is achieved when the following conditions are met: (a) The group uses a variety of skills, (b) the group's task is a whole piece of work with visible outcomes, and (c) the group receives regular, trustworthy feedback. Without this sense of meaningfulness, when a group's work is routine and unchallenging, of limited importance, and essentially preprogrammed with no opportunity for input or feedback, members are likely to develop negative norms and their performance is likely to deteriorate.

The individual empowerment constructs of competence and self-efficacy are similar to the group *potency* construct. Potency is defined as the collective belief of a group that it can be effective. Potency cannot be measured by summing individual responses to a measure of self-efficacy. Rather, potency concerns group performance, is a belief shared by group members, and is a generalized belief of effectiveness that is more relevant to the complex and widely varied tasks that groups often perform in organizations.

If an individual feels a sense of choice in initiating and regulating his or her own actions, that individual is more likely to feel empowered. At the team level, *team autonomy* has been defined as the degree to which a job provides substantial freedom, independence, and discretion to the team in scheduling the work and determining the procedures to be used in carrying it out. Team autonomy differs from the individual notion of choice as important decisions are made and executed by the group, not the individual, such that autonomy is experienced as a group phenomenon.

The belief that an individual has an *impact* on his or her job and organization can be viewed at the group level. Decisions made by the team can affect team member jobs, other teams, and internal and external organization customers, and team members share this knowledge of impact with other team members. To the extent that teams are able to ascertain their level of impact (i.e., the team knows that its tasks have significant *consequences* for other people), the team can also self-assess its level of empowerment.

Modern managers' efforts to increase employee empowerment often involve organizational programs rather than just an individual leader's actions with direct subordinates. A variety of different empowerment programs have been used, including self-managed teams, democratic structures and processes, and employee ownership of the company. Additional empowerment programs for organizations include selection of leaders for limited terms, active participation in assessing leader performance, implementing formal procedures for making important decisions to give members significant influence over decisions, sharing of leadership responsibilities by members of a small organization, and providing access to accurate information about business performance, plans, goals, and strategies.

Kathleen J. Barnes

See also Decision-Making Styles; High-Performing Teams; Organizational Effectiveness; Participative Model of Decision Making; Social Construction Theory; Substitutes for Leadership; Work Team Effectiveness

Further Readings

Conger, J., & Kanungo, R. (1988). The empowerment process: Integrating theory and practice. *Academy of Management Review, 13*(3), 471–482.

Kirkman, B. L., & Rosen, B. (1997). A model of work team empowerment. In R. W. Woodman & W. A. Pasmore (Eds.), *Research in organizational change and development* (Vol. 10, pp. 131–167). Greenwich, CT: JAI.

Kirkman, B. L., & Rosen, B. (1999). Beyond self-management: Antecedents and consequences of team empowerment. *Academy of Management Journal, 42*(1), 58–74.

Spreitzer, G. M. (1995). Psychological empowerment in the workplace: Dimensions, measurement, and validation. *Academy of Management Journal, 38*(5), 1442–1465.

Spreitzer, G. M. (1997). Toward a common ground in defining empowerment. In R. W. Woodman & W. A. Pasmore (Eds.), *Research in organizational change and development* (Vol. 10, pp. 31–62). Greenwich, CT: JAI.

Thomas, K. W., & Velthouse, B. A. (1990). Cognitive elements of empowerment: An "interpretive" model of intrinsic task motivation. *Academy of Management Review, 15*(4), 666–681.

Yukl, G. A. (2006). *Leadership in organizations*. Upper Saddle River, NJ: Pearson Education.

ENGAGED SCHOLARSHIP MODEL

Engaged scholarship refers to the interconnectedness of the academy's scholarly pursuits and society's most pressing concerns. It is both a historical account of the mission of higher education in America, as well as a call for a return to a more significant relationship between universities and community partners. Ernest L. Boyer argues in *Scholarship Reconsidered: Priorities of the Professoriate* that the full range of academic functions required by professors to achieve the objectives of higher education is not reflected in contemporary faculty reward systems. This disconnect leads many professors to encounter difficulty in balancing and prioritizing their time between teaching, research, and service. To combat this shortcoming, he proposes a broader definition of scholarship which encompasses all the activities required to achieve a university's academic and civic mandates. The result is a set of four diverse yet connected forms of scholarship: the scholarship of discovery, the scholarship of integration, the scholarship of application, and the scholarship of teaching. With a more encompassing definition of scholarship in hand, Boyer provides recommendations for how academics should use these four types of scholarship in his posthumous 1996 article "The Scholarship of Engagement," stating on page 11 that "the academy must become a more vigorous partner in the search for answers to our most pressing social, civic, economic and moral problems, and must affirm its historic commitment to what I call the scholarship of engagement," the fifth and final form of scholarship proposed. In order to obtain this level of engagement, university faculty must partner with professionals in the knowledge economy and citizens in general at local, regional, state, national, and global levels. This enables the mutually beneficial reciprocal-exchange of resources and knowledge between universities and society at large. This type of relationship represents a democratization of scholarship through the involvement of nonacademics in identifying issues and proposing solutions. Such involvement leads to a reduction in the current gap between theory and practice due to the broader involvement of the community, which better equips citizens to be productive and informed participants in a democratic society. In this entry, the fundamental components of engaged scholarship are provided along with a discussion of how engaged scholarship may be used to formulate and evaluate research questions. The entry also provides a discussion of the historical justification of engaged scholarship, some countervailing criticism of the concept, and the implications of engaged scholarship for modern managers.

Fundamentals

The engaged scholarship model is composed of the five forms of scholarship proposed by Boyer in his two previously mentioned works. The scholarship of *discovery* is very similar to what contemporary academics generally refer to as "research" with the distinction that importance is placed not solely on outcomes but also on the process and passion with which one pursues new knowledge. The scholarship of *integration* is the process of giving meaning to the insights drawn from the scholarship of discovery by showcasing how results represent a convergence of disparate research fields, which gives additional perspective to the findings. The scholarship of *application* involves the evaluation of how insights derived from scholarly work can be applied to individuals and/or institutions to better serve the interests of the community at large. The scholarship of *teaching* is not merely the process of transmitting knowledge from professor to student, but rather it is the transformation and extension of that knowledge via class activities, assignments, and discussions. This interaction can inspire students to pursue a career as a professorate, at the same time it spawns innovative new thoughts and directions of the topic on the part of the professor leading the discussion. Finally, the scholarship of *engagement* is the application of these four aforementioned forms of scholarship to the most pressing social, civic, and ethical problems of the day as identified through close collaboration with members of the affected community.

Andrew Van de Ven has taken up Boyer's torch of engaged scholarship and developed a model of how academics can leverage engaged scholarship in their evaluation of such complex societal problems. This model is proposed in an effort to create knowledge that progresses both theory and practice while reducing the gap between the two. The knowledge production model is a continuum of processes that can commence from any stage, but it requires collaboration between key stakeholders in addition to the researcher. The model is iterative, so as new subproblems arise, this method enables simultaneous problem solving of lower level issues within the greater research question at hand.

Problem formulation is a journalistic approach to identifying the relevant who, what, when, where, and how of a particular issue. This is accomplished through discussions with those affected, coupled with a thorough review of the existing relevant literature. Theory building involves dialogue with experts in the field in question, as well as an exhaustive literature review. Subsequently, all forms of reasoning (abductive, deductive, and inductive) are used to create, elaborate, and justify new theory as well as plausible alternative theories. Research design develops the method for evaluating the primary and alternate theories by identifying sources of data and the population of interest for sampling. Problem solving entails the dissemination, interpretation, and application of empirical findings, leading to the validation and selection of one of the theories being tested. This final selection of the most appropriate theory is achieved through a process of writing reports and delivering presentations of research outcomes, the meaning and interpretation of which is vigorously debated in order to reconcile conflicts and arrive at a final consensus.

These steps are evaluated in terms of relevance, validity, truth, impact, and coherence. Problems evaluated using this model should be important and relevant to the intended audience, both in academic and professional circles. At the same time, the research design and execution must remain true to the scientific method required to produce unbiased and genuine outcomes. It represents a recalibration of the way in which researchers ask questions and what they do with the answers they derive as opposed to reworking the process of validating results.

Importance

Boyer weaves a tapestry of examples showcasing the historic commitment of universities to the ideals of engaged scholarship. Over the course of 350 years, from the founding of the American colonies through the latter portion of the 20th century, there are a profusion of such examples. They involve university partnerships to improve communities, practical and relevant research initiatives, and the expansion and democratization of the student body. The colonial colleges, though primarily founded to prepare those entering the ministry, were also a training ground for early civic leaders and were established to ensure health of the commonwealth. Rensselaer Polytechnic Institute (RPI) sought to improve the infrastructure of the budding nation by developing a mastery of all manner of building disciplines, most notably transportation, such as railroads and bridges, and disseminating that knowledge to students who would take up the task of actual implementation. The Land Grant Act, like the founding of RPI, was a mechanism for universities to not only advance technological prowess but also to improve the nation's agricultural and manufacturing capabilities.

At the turn of the last century, representatives from Harvard, Princeton, and Stanford all noted on record the importance of the core aspects of engaged scholarship—practicality, reality, and serviceability. Woodrow Wilson, then a professor at Princeton, additionally warned of the negative effects to society of retreating from this manner of engagement in favor of isolation within the walls of the university. The subsequent decades brought the founding of the largest federal research fund the world has ever seen, the National Science Foundation (NSF), plans for the reconstruction of Europe after World War II (Marshall Plan), and a revamp of American curriculum and creation of summer institutes in response to the successful launching of the Soviet satellite Sputnik—all of which required active participation from universities to solve the most pressing issues facing the nation.

Universities also expanded the base of the student population, giving greater opportunity to more members of society and at the same time receiving new ideas and insights from these students, influenced by their varying experiences and backgrounds. The GI Bill of 1944 initiated this process by introducing roughly 8 million new students to the university system in a short time. Later, affirmative action programs continued this metamorphosis across campuses. Yet at the time of Boyer's work, he found that as this shift from an elite to a mass system of higher education was occurring, the rewards system of the professoriat was narrowing in the favor of specialized research at the cost of educating this new crop of students and solving the next wave of societal problems, which ignited his call for the return to the scholarship of engagement.

Boyer's work, by way of Van de Ven, has not been received without criticism, most notably that of Bill McKelvey. McKelvey takes exception to the concept of engaged scholarship on many levels and questions its promise as a scholarly road map. First and most simply, he does not find it to be a drastic departure from action research, which first appeared in the literature in 1970, and thus does not find this proposal to be novel. He also notes that biases emerge from partnering with firms when evaluating which research questions to ask. A firm has many interests that they will not jeopardize, even in the name of science, most notably their protection of proprietary information. On the other side of the team, the researchers must keep their partners pleased with the relationship in order to maintain the collaboration and thus might be forced to sacrifice the integrity of the research to salvage the relationship, get bogged down in decision by committee, and potentially settle for the lowest common denominator, which could call results into question in the long term. He states the lack of the emergence of any impactful scientific truth from action research as a sign of the lack of results that engaged scholarship will yield. He does, however, offer an alternate solution to narrow the gap between theory and practice. Rather than altering the way research is performed in favor of collaboration, researchers should take a cue from earthquake science and abandon the science of averages in favor of the science of extremes in order to entice practitioners to consume academic publications.

Most of McKelvey's criticism is based on his interpretation of engaged scholarship as a synonym for action research. While the concerns outlined regarding the engaged scholarship model are worrisome, it is presumptuous to assume that research that is created with and to be consumed and integrated by business practitioners will lose its rigor and impact. Boyer himself notes that the most influential social change has been spurred by those external to the professoriat, citing books by Rachel Carson (*Silent Spring*), Ralph Nader (*Unsafe at Any Speed*), Michael Harrington (*The Other America*), and Betty Friedan (*The Feminine Mystique*).

This model of community collaboration is beneficial to managers and practitioners alike as it allows their respective input and needs to drive the research agenda of the institutions of higher learning. The positive results of this symbiosis manifest themselves in two prominent ways. First, research outcomes uncovered through the use of this model will better equip managers to effectively perform their duties and overcome challenges. Second, managers will enjoy improved hiring options from the nascent workforce of university students, as those studying under engaged scholars will be more versed in the most current and pressing business issues.

J. Mark Phillips, Kevin May,
and James Bailey

See also Academic-Practitioner Collaboration and Knowledge Sharing; Bad Theories; Firm Growth; Individual Values; Management (Education) as Practice; Managerial Decision Biases; Organizational Development; Organizational Learning; Scientific Management

Further Readings

Boyer, E. L. (1990). *Scholarship reconsidered: Priorities of the professorate*. Princeton, NJ: Carnegie Foundation.

Boyer, E. L. (1996). The scholarship of engagement. *Journal of Public Service and Outreach, 1*, 11–20.

Kellogg Commission on the Future of State and Land-Grant Universities. (1999). *Returning to our roots: The engaged institution*. Washington, DC: National Association of State Universities and Land-Grant Colleges.

McDowell, G. R. (2001). *Land-grant universities and extension into the 21st century: Renegotiating or abandoning a social contract*. Ames: Iowa State University Press.

McKelvey, B. (2006). Van de Ven and Johnson's "engaged scholarship": Nice try, but. . . . *Academy of Management Review, 31,* 822–829.

Peters, S. J., Jordan, N. R., Adamek, M., & Alter, T. (2005). *Engaging campus and community: The practice of public scholarship in the state and land-grant university system.* Dayton, OH: Kettering Foundation Press.

UniSCOPE Learning Community. (2008). *UniSCOPE 2000: A multidimensional model of scholarship for the 21st century.* University Park, PA: UniSCOPE Learning Community.

Van de Ven, A. H. (2007). *Engaged scholarship: A guide for organizational and social research.* New York, NY: Oxford University Press.

Van de Ven, A. H., & Johnson, P. E. (2006). Knowledge for theory and practice. *Academy of Management Review, 31,* 802–821.

ENTREPRENEURIAL COGNITION

Cognition refers to individuals' (and groups') perceptions, memory, and thinking. By extension, *entrepreneurial cognitions* are informed patterns, inferences, and knowledge that entrepreneurs use to make assessments and decisions regarding new opportunities and their potential commercialization. Entrepreneurial cognitions are ways founders think and make decisions about new opportunities amid the uncertainties that entrepreneurial endeavors face. The study of how people think and interact with those around them has been led by cognitive psychology. This cognitive perspective assumes that what people reflect, say, and do is influenced by their own mental processes. This entry addresses several cognitions, such as alertness, heuristic-based reasoning, and motivation, and their implications for entrepreneurs.

Fundamentals

The environment in which entrepreneurs operate tends to be filled with substantial uncertainty. Emerging technologies may have great potential but, particularly in the earlier stages, problems invariably surface. The pathway to the marketplace is almost always longer than expected because of research and development, unexpected customer problems or acceptance, and the need to acquire needed resources. Resolving and navigating such obstacles often requires the decision makers to draw conclusions and make inferences from limited and sometimes piecemeal information. It is within this entrepreneurial context that the cognitive approach has emerged as an important tool in understanding how entrepreneurs navigate their way through new opportunities.

Entrepreneurial cognition is about understanding how entrepreneurs use mental models to piece together previously unconnected information. Connecting dots that may not necessarily suggest linear pathways can enable entrepreneurs to uncover new opportunities that have not been previously identified or developed. Entrepreneurial cognitions enable entrepreneurs to improvise and piece together the necessary resources to start and grow a business. Identifying the cognitions that entrepreneurs use are becoming useful tools for understanding how they navigate their way through the many uncertainties of the world in which they operate.

We now address several specific cognitions that have received significant attention in the entrepreneurial cognition space.

Alertness to new opportunities. It appears that some individuals are more alert to new business opportunities. Consistent with the Austrian economic perspective, some individuals are more alert to potential business opportunities that most others have overlooked. Alertness is like an "antenna" that facilitates the recognition of gaps in the market that are newly emerging or have previously gone unobserved. A heightened sense of alertness allows an individual to notice features that have not been previously noticed. Entrepreneurial alertness is about those who are able to not only recognize something different but are also capable of noticing disequilibrium situations in the market that may support a new venture opportunity. Unique cognitive frameworks with an eye on opportunities allow entrepreneurs to link previously disparate information and knowledge to connect new opportunities. In sum, alertness to new changes and emerging gaps and being able to perceive some connections to new opportunities hold important potential for understanding the way entrepreneurs work.

Heuristics-based reasoning. Heuristics are simplifying strategies and decision rules used to make decisions more quickly or to compensate for the lack of information and uncertainty. They are often seen as an alternative to rational decision making when full information and risk probabilities are unknown. Heuristics-based reasoning recognizes several things about human decision making. One, there is a subjective aspect to human judgment that is reflected in decision making. Two, beliefs start forming in individuals from an early age based on who they are, patterns within their minds, as well as social interactions and experiences. The resulting beliefs affect decision making. Three, experiences, whether they are successes or failures, tend to form an emerging "theory" about how the world works; thus, when emerging patterns are detected in the present, inferences based on developed patterns from the past are often readily brought forward. These and other human conditions are thought to have a significant bearing on what opportunities get noticed and perceived as well as the ensuing decisions.

Research indicates that entrepreneurs use heuristics in their decision making more extensively than do managers in large organizations. While heuristics are often characterized as leading to errors in decision making, they can be quite efficient and help lead to at least satisfactory decisions. In the entrepreneurial context, this can be quite useful as opposed to the more rational process that is likely to lead to very limited decision making and even paralysis. Heuristics-based logic is also thought to help entrepreneurs make inferences in their thinking, leading to more fresh insights than a fact-based logic would allow. Heuristic-based logic enables entrepreneurs to connect dots and see a pattern even in uncertain and complex situations expediting the learning process and the pursuit of entrepreneurial opportunities.

Motivation, self-efficacy, and other cognitions. The motivation of people to become entrepreneurs has long been thought to play a central role in the desire to pursue entrepreneurial opportunities. Self-efficacy, a dimension closely linked to motivation, is characterized as an individual's belief about their abilities to accomplish a specified activity that they set out to do. A focus of substantial research, self-efficacy has been found to be associated with various tasks and measures of entrepreneurial success.

A couple of additional cognitions that are starting to receive some attention in the entrepreneurial domain are affect and metacognition. Affect draws attention to the influence of emotions on creativity and how entrepreneurs evaluate business opportunities. Affect may well shape evaluations because emotions influence how individuals process information. Metacognition is thinking about thinking. Entrepreneurs tend to be very engaged thinkers who enact multiple cognitive strategies to act (or not) on perceived opportunities. These and other cognitive categories provide us with excellent tools with which to better understand entrepreneurial thinking.

For managers and entrepreneurs, learning about entrepreneurial cognition helps us understand how entrepreneurs think through new opportunities and make decisions. This theory helps explain why entrepreneurs often make new connections, how innovations can emerge from making inferences, and also why entrepreneurs sometimes make decisions that can lead to their venture's demise. Using cognitive shortcuts, such as inferences and heuristics, tends to be quite efficient most of the time but can sometimes lead to errors as well. Without using such cognitive mechanisms, it is usually impossible to pursue entrepreneurial endeavors since full information is rarely available.

Lowell W. Busenitz

See also Bounded Rationality and Satisficing (Behavioral Decision-Making Model); Discovery Theory of Entrepreneurship; Entrepreneurial Opportunities; Intuitive Decision Making; Managerial Decision Biases; Social Cognitive Theory; Strategic Decision Making; "Unstructured" Decision Making

Further Readings

Alvarez, S., & Busenitz, L. (2001). The entrepreneurship of the resource-based theory. *Journal of Management, 6,* 755–775.

Baron, R. A. (2004). The cognitive perspective: A valuable tool for answering entrepreneurship's basic "why" questions. *Journal of Business Venturing, 19,* 221–239.

Baron, R. A. (2006). Opportunity recognition as pattern recognition: How entrepreneurs "connect the dots" to identify new business opportunities. *Academy of Management Perspectives, 20*(1), 104–119.

Busenitz, L. W., & Barney, J. B. (1997). Differences between entrepreneurs and managers in large organizations: Biases and heuristics in strategic decision making. *Journal of Business Venturing, 12,* 9–30.

Gaglio, C. M., & Katz, J. A. (2001). The psychological basis of opportunity identification: Entrepreneurial alertness. *Small Business Economics, 16,* 95–111.

Kahneman, D., Slovic, P., & Tversky, A. (1982). *Judgment under uncertainty: Heuristics and biases.* New York, NY: Cambridge University Press.

Kirzner, I. M. (1997). Entrepreneurial discovery and the competitive market process: An Austrian Approach. *Journal of Economic Literature, 35,* 60–85.

Mitchell, R. K., Busenitz, L., Bird, B., Gaglio, C. M., McMullen, J., Morse, E., & Smith, B. (2007). The central question in entrepreneurship cognition research. *Entrepreneurship Theory and Practice, 31*(1), 1–27.

Neisser, U. (1967). *Cognitive psychology.* New York, NY: Appleton-Century-Crofts.

ENTREPRENEURIAL EFFECTUATION

Effectuation refers to a set of heuristics identified with expert entrepreneurial decision making. The heuristics are nonpredictive in that they do not require the decision maker to rely on information about the future. Instead they allow effectuators to act based on things within their control to reshape their environments and build networks of self-selected stakeholders. Effectual heuristics thus find their greatest use in people-centric, highly uncertain, information-poor, ambiguity-rich decision domains. Derived from the Latin verb *effectuare,* the word *effectuation* literally means "to cause things to happen." Dictionary definitions of the word include the act of implementing (providing a practical means for accomplishing something), carrying into effect, and putting into force or operation. Effectual heuristics differ from the more familiar causal methods in the emphasis on action rather than explanation, human agency rather than physical agency, and a synthetic rather than analytic approach. This entry presents the basic principles of entrepreneurial effectuation.

Fundamentals

The technical use of the word *effectuation* in entrepreneurship and economics began with an in-depth study of expert entrepreneurs and later replicated with novices and expert corporate managers. The studies used think-aloud verbal protocol analysis, a cognitive science methodology, long used to identify the components of expertise in a variety of domains. In this method, subjects are asked to think aloud continuously as they solve problems, typically, complex unstructured problems chosen to closely mimic real-life situations. Studies of effectuation have also been carried out using other methods such as surveys, meta-analysis, counterfactual histories, conjoint experiments, and other subject groups such as private equity investors, research and development (R & D) managers, and social media.

Effectuation inverts the conventional logic that claims more accurate predictions are necessary to achieve control over future outcomes. Instead, to the extent decision makers can control the situation, they don't need to expend energy or resources on trying to predict the future. The five basic principles of effectuation can be presented as straight inversions of predictive strategies as follows:

The bird-in-hand principle: Start with a set of means to create a possible effect. Since other stakeholders also bring their means to the table, this often results in a series of accidental, ad-hoc, and serendipitous events producing a novel effect, both unanticipated and/or unimagined. This inverts the idea that entrepreneurs have to begin with clear goals and/or predefined visions of opportunities and then search for ways and means to achieve those goals or discover and realize the opportunities. The bird-in-hand principle sees the entrepreneurial process as a contingent one and it is responsible for the just-so origin stories of many entrepreneurial enterprises.

The affordable loss principle: Invest only what one can afford to lose and then iteratively push to expand the upside potential of what has just been made possible. Affordable loss is a failure-management principle that encourages a bias for action rather than analysis. This is in stark contrast to causal methods of opportunity assessment that involve predicting future cash flows and seeking to maximize risk-adjusted expected returns.

The crazy quilt principle: Cocreate the enterprise with stakeholders who self-select into the process. This points out a different view of both stakeholders and entrepreneurs. Rather than viewing entrepreneurs as charismatic visionaries and stakeholders as followers, this principle sees the entrepreneurial enterprise as a patchwork effort, where talents, visions, means, and preferences get blended into a one-of-a-kind enterprise. In fact, in the effectual process, the person who chooses to come on board determines what gets built, and not vice versa. The crazy-quilt principle reveals that entrepreneurial efforts are synthetic and bottoms-up, rather than analytic and top-down.

Lemonade principle: Clearly, the effectual process is dynamic, interactive, and iterative. It also assumes and propels unpredictability in the system. Therefore, effectuation entails embracing and leveraging surprises rather than planning and seeking to avoid them. Even negative surprises feed back into the bird-in-hand principle to become inputs into the venture creation process. The lemonade principle encourages the actor to reframe the situation rather than adjust to it. It reveals the entrepreneurial process as not being about clear perception but of opportunistic apperception.

Pilot-in-the-plane principle: This principle spells out the logic of nonpredictive control at the heart of effectuation. It emphasizes the fact that the future is not exogenous to human action, that is, history is not on autopilot. Because human action is capable of intervening and reshaping trends, the pilot-in-the-plane principle argues for not trusting "inevitable" trends. Instead, when an effectuator encounters a probability estimate, she looks for which conditioning assumptions to reify or falsify, not to simply "update" her priors. Effectual logic, therefore, is not Bayesian—a calculus built on effectual probability would be a control engine rather than an inference engine.

Most importantly, effectual action is learnable and teachable. The role of effectual principles can be, and have been, shown in the life histories of hundreds of entrepreneurs and their ventures—for-profit, non-profit, and otherwise. Taken together, these principles offer a way of tackling the fundamental problem of "judgment" at the heart of entrepreneurship—a problem first spelled out in the seminal work of the great economist Frank Knight and also elaborated upon by the school of Austrian economics.

Effectuation also offers mechanisms for understanding sciences of the artificial, a third class of sciences that differ from the natural as well as the social sciences because they take human purpose not as exogenous and peripheral but as intrinsic and central to their problems. According to Herbert Simon, perhaps the preeminent social scientist of the 20th century, artifactual problems are problems of design (creating alternatives) and not simply problems of decision (searching for alternatives and selecting between them). It is precisely in this sense that effectuation recasts entrepreneurship as a science of the artificial.

Finally, effectuation plays a crucial role in ongoing efforts to build an entrepreneurial method analogous to the scientific method. In recent philosophy, the very notion of a "scientific method" has been questioned and criticized. Without taking an ontological stance on the topic, it is historical fact that efforts to build and propagate such a method have enabled the creation of real infrastructure for science and technology and a widening horizon of human progress predicated on that. Efforts to build the entrepreneurial method move us toward widespread access to new solutions and possibilities that are currently available only to effectual entrepreneurs.

Saras Sarasvathy

See also Bounded Rationality and Satisficing (Behavioral Decision-Making Model); Discovery Theory of Entrepreneurship; Entrepreneurial Cognition; Entrepreneurial Opportunities; Programmability of Decision Making; Prospect Theory; "Unstructured" Decision Making

Further Readings

Chandler, G. N., DeTienne, D. R., McKelvie, A., & Mumford, T. V. (2011). Causation and effectuation processes: A validation study. *Journal of Business Venturing, 26*(3), 375–390.

Dew, N., Read, S., Sarasvathy, S. D., & Wiltbank, R. (2009). Effectual versus predictive logics in entrepreneurial decision-making: Differences between experts and novices. *Journal of Business Venturing, 24*(4), 287–309.

Ericsson, K. A., & Simon, H. A. (1993). *Protocol analysis: Verbal reports as data.* Cambridge, MA: MIT Press.

Foss, N. J., & Klein, P. G. (2012). *Organizing entrepreneurial judgment: A new approach to the firm.* Cambridge, England: Cambridge University Press.

Knight, F. H. (1921). *Risk, uncertainty and profit.* New York, NY: Houghton Mifflin.

Read, S., Dew, N., Sarasvathy, S. D., Song, M., & Wiltbank, R. (2009). Marketing under uncertainty: The logic of an effectual approach. *Journal of Marketing, 73*(3), 1–18.

Read, S., Song, M., & Smit, W. (2009). A meta-analytic review of effectuation and venture performance. *Journal of Business Venturing, 24*(6), 573–587.

Sarasvathy, S. D. (2001). Causation and effectuation: Toward a theoretical shift from economic inevitability to entrepreneurial contingency. *Academy of Management Review, 26*(2), 243.

Sarasvathy, S. D., & Venkataraman, S. (2011). Entrepreneurship as method: Open questions for an entrepreneurial future. *Entrepreneurship Theory and Practice, 35*(1), 113–135.

Simon, H. A. (1996). *The sciences of the artificial* (3rd ed.). Cambridge, MA: MIT Press.

ENTREPRENEURIAL OPPORTUNITIES

That entrepreneurs exploit opportunities to create economic wealth is an age-old concept. However, it has not been until recently that the focus on opportunities has become the cornerstone of entrepreneurship research in the field of management. Opportunities, competitive imperfections in product or factor markets, are the distinctive domain of entrepreneurship. This entry reviews the different types of opportunities that entrepreneurs attempt to exploit—recognition, discovery, and creation opportunities—along with the appropriate processes for exploiting them.

Fundamentals

Opportunities, defined as competitive imperfections, exist in markets when information about technology, demand, or other determinants of competition in an industry is not widely understood by those operating in that industry. The existence of competitive imperfections in markets suggests that it is possible for at least some economic actors in these markets to earn economic profits. This definition is derived from neoclassic economic theory, which suggests that economic actors—be they firms or individuals—operating under conditions of perfect competition will not be able to generate economic wealth. Thus, opportunities to generate economic wealth can exist only when competition is not perfect.

To date, at least three opportunity types have been suggested in the literature: (a) recognition opportunities, (b) discovery opportunities, and (c) creation opportunities. Recognition opportunities exist when prices are misaligned across markets, discovery opportunities are formed by exogenous shocks to preexisting markets or industries that entrepreneurs then discover, and creation opportunities are formed endogenously by entrepreneurs who create them.

Recognition opportunities result from a misalignment in prices across two or more markets. For example, if the current price of land is based on its use as farmland and its value if subdivided for residential properties is much greater, then there is an opportunity for an entrepreneur to buy the land at the lower "farm" price and resell it at the higher "subdivision" price. The difference is economic wealth. This kind of opportunity is called a "recognition opportunity" because the main entrepreneurial task is to recognize its existence and then buy (at the lower price) and sell (at the higher price) the asset. This type of opportunity has also been called *entrepreneurial arbitrage.*

Discovery opportunities are assumed to arise from competitive imperfections in markets owing to changes in technology, consumer preferences, or some other attributes of the context within which a market or industry exists. In particular, these opportunities emerge independent of the actions of those seeking to generate economic profits from exploiting them and thus are "objective" and "real" in the sense those terms are used by scholars who adopt a critical realist philosophy. The task of those seeking to exploit discovery opportunities, thus, is to be "alert" to the existence of these objective opportunities and to "claim" those that hold the greatest economic potential. In this view, these actors bring "agency to opportunity."

However, since discovery opportunities are considered by discovery theorists to be objective and real, in principle they could be discovered by anyone operating in an imperfectly competitive market. Of course, not everyone acts on these entrepreneurial opportunities, and so research in this area requires that there are real and objective differences, ex ante, between entrepreneurs and nonentrepreneurs. Without these differences, any actor in an economy could become aware of and then exploit an opportunity—at which point it would no longer be a source of economic profits. However, if those seeking to exploit a discovery opportunity and those not seeking to exploit such an opportunity differ in some fundamental ways, then not all actors in an economy will know about a particular opportunity, or, even if they do, not all will be predisposed to exploit it. Israel Kirzner summarizes the differences between these groups by simply asserting that entrepreneurs are more "alert" to the existence of opportunities than nonentrepreneurs. Entrepreneurial alertness is the ability that some people have to recognize market imperfections that have the potential for generating economic profits.

Creation opportunities are competitive imperfections in factor or product markets that are formed endogenously by the actions of those seeking to generate economic profit themselves. This formation process often begins with little more than a belief that a particular activity may turn into an opportunity. The entrepreneur tests his or her beliefs in an iterative process in the individual's environment, and often after this experimentation, the belief is found wanting, at which time it may be modified and updated or abandoned altogether. Individuals who continue to modify their beliefs about potential opportunities may, in an evolutionary and path-dependent way, end up socially cocreating an opportunity. This opportunity did not exist before the entrepreneur initiated the first actions to form it, and cocreated the opportunity—if successful—with the environment and a now emerging new market.

While differences in opportunity types are important theoretical insights in the field of entrepreneurship, the research promise is in identifying and understanding the different processes used to form and exploit these opportunities. Entrepreneurial action is the manifestation of the entrepreneur's hypothesis about the type of opportunity he or she trying to exploit. If they are accurate and match the opportunity with the correct processes, chances for successful exploitation and wealth creation are increased.

Sharon A. Alvarez

See also Agency Theory; Discovery Theory of Entrepreneurship; Entrepreneurial Cognition; Entrepreneurial Effectuation; Entrepreneurial Orientation; Environmental Uncertainty; First-Mover Advantages and Disadvantages; Sensemaking

Further Readings

Alvarez, S. A., & Barney, J. B. (2007). Discovery and creation: Alternative theories of entrepreneurial action. *Strategic Entrepreneurship Journal, 1*(1–2), 11–26.

Barney, J. (1991). Firm resources and sustained competitive advantage. *Journal of Management, 17*(1), 99–120.
Casson, M. (1982). *The entrepreneur: An economic theory* (2nd ed.). Oxford, England: Edward Elgar.
Gaglio, C. M., & Katz, J. A. (2001). The psychological basis of opportunity identification: Entrepreneurial alertness. *Small Business Economics, 16*(2), 95–111.
Hayek, F. A. von (1948). *Individualism and economic order.* London, England: Routledge and Kegan Paul.
Kirzner, I. (1973). *Competition and entrepreneurship.* Chicago, IL: University of Chicago Press.
Kirzner, I. M. (1997). Entrepreneurial discovery and the competitive market process: An Austrian approach. *Journal of Economic Literature, 35*(1), 60–85.
Mises, L. von (1949). *Human action.* New Haven, CT: Yale University Press.
Shane, S. (2000). Prior knowledge and the discovery of entrepreneurial opportunities. *Organization Science, 11*(4), 448–470.
Shane, S. (2003). *A general theory of entrepreneurship: The individual-opportunity nexus.* Northampton, MA: Edward Elgar.

Entrepreneurial Orientation

Entrepreneurial orientation (EO) is among the most important and established concepts within the field of entrepreneurship and domain of managerial inquiry. The central premise of EO is that an organization can be considered more (or less) entrepreneurial as a collective entity. The notion of firm-level entrepreneurship represents a clear demarcation from the well-established tradition of investigating entrepreneurship as an individual-level phenomenon. The underlying motivation for the concept of EO is the need to theoretically separate firms based upon their entrepreneurial strategy-making processes and behaviors to facilitate scientific research into entrepreneurial phenomenon across organizations. As such, EO allows for distancing the intentions and attitudes of organizational members from the organization's overall behavioral orientation toward entrepreneurship. EO posits that all organizations fall somewhere along a conceptual continuum ranging from conservative (the "low" end) to entrepreneurial (the "high" end). Where an organization places within this conceptual continuum depends upon the extent to which the organization's strategy-making processes have produced a stable firm-level entrepreneurial behavioral pattern. EO research has provided managers with critical insights into how firms may effectively leverage entrepreneurial strategy-making processes and behaviors to achieve important organizational goals, such as growth and renewal. This entry is structured as follows. In the first section, the fundamentals of EO are described. In the next section, the importance of EO research is discussed. In closing, notable further readings are offered.

Fundamentals

The content of EO may be separated into two distinct yet complementary firm-level constructs. The first construct, originally proposed by Danny Miller and later refined by Jeff Covin and Dennis Slevin, defines the concept of EO as the shared positive covariance between three key behavioral dimensions with rich histories of describing what it means for an entity to be considered entrepreneurial, namely, innovativeness, risk taking, and proactiveness. *Innovativeness* reflects a firm's willingness to support new ideas, creativity, and experimentation in the development of internal solutions or external offerings. Generally, innovativeness has been viewed in terms of increased product-market or technological innovation. *Proactiveness* refers to a firm's propensity to embrace pioneering, forward-looking strategic actions which anticipate future market demands. Typically, proactiveness has been conceived in terms of the preemption of competitors within the marketplace. *Risk taking* captures a firm's bold and daring resource commitments toward organizational initiatives with uncertain returns. Risk taking has most often been envisioned in terms of high-risk, high-return strategic behaviors.

The second construct, proposed by Tom Lumpkin and Greg Dess, suggests two additional dimensions. The first is *competitive aggressiveness,* which encapsulates the intensity of an organization's offensive efforts and forceful competitive responses to outperform rivals. The second is *autonomy,* which captures the extent to which an organization supports independent action by its members to bring about new business concepts and new ventures. Additionally, this alternative view of the construct suggests that the dimensions of EO need not strongly or positively co-vary for an EO to be claimed to exist. Rather,

this view suggests that the dimensions which define a firm as being entrepreneurial are those which contribute to the undertaking of new "entry," or venture. Moreover, this conceptualization of EO suggests that within differing organizational and environmental contexts, the dimensions which lead to greater new entry are likely to be different. For example, in the context of limited innovation, "fast followers"—or firms which enter an industry shortly after a market pioneer and choose imitation over innovation—may still be considered to exhibit EO because they are engaging in new entry. Dimensionally, despite their lack of innovativeness, such firms are still aggressively risking organizational resources toward the pursuit of an uncertain new venture opportunity. Thus, the dimensions which capture the essence of EO, according to this alternative view of the EO concept, are defined as those which enable the pursuit of new entry. In short, within this view, differing contexts may have differing profiles of relevant entrepreneurial dimensions.

Both constructs have received significant attention and support within the literature and may be considered equally valid conceptualizations for investigating the phenomenon of an organizational orientation toward entrepreneurial activity. Reflecting upon the first 30 years of EO research, Danny Miller noted that within differing types of firms, it is indeed probable that differing dimensions of EO will manifest with varied consequences. This is notwithstanding the possibility that innovativeness, risk taking, and proactiveness may at all times be theoretically combined as a higher order indicator of firm-level entrepreneurship. Thus, the choice among EO constructs is a research consideration which should be informed by the demands of the research question and context being explored.

The rationale for the EO concept may be traced to the domain of strategic management. Building upon a view that managerial decisions are reflected within the organizations that these individuals lead and thus the behavior that their organizations exhibit presupposes that sustained firm-level entrepreneurial behavioral patterns are generally attributed to the existence of a top managerial decision-making orientation that favors the manifestation of such entrepreneurial activities. Strategy making is thereby central to the definition and domain of EO as a sustained firm-level behavioral phenomenon. Entrepreneurial behavioral patterns emerge from a stable organizational strategy-making orientation favoring entrepreneurial (as opposed to conservative) activities. Entrepreneurial top-management styles and operating philosophies create the behavioral patterns which enable an organization to be recognized as having EO.

The domain and influence of EO depends upon a multitude of contextual and temporal considerations. Contextually, a wide variety of considerations has been demonstrated to influence the value of EO as an organizational phenomenon ranging from organizational (structural organicity, organizational trust, etc.) to strategic (marketing orientation, strategic learning, etc.), to environmental (dynamism, hostility, etc.), to sociocultural (societal individualism, masculinity, etc.) factors. Together, these diverse considerations suggest that the manifestation of EO must be actively managed for the firm-level strategic orientation to fulfill its promise as a driver of increased organizational value creation.

Temporally, behavior is the defining attribute of entrepreneurial firms, and sustained behavior is a necessary condition to claim that an orientation toward entrepreneurial activity exists within an organization. Notwithstanding the possibility that firms may cycle between more entrepreneurial and more conservative orientations over time, periods in which an entrepreneurial orientation is present are defined by an entrepreneurial behavioral pattern being maintained for a period of time which exceeds that of a singular or random entrepreneurial act.

An additional temporal consideration stemming from longitudinal research exploring the phenomenon suggests that the effects of EO upon organizational outcomes increase in magnitude over a period of time. These results suggest that EO can be an effective means of improving long-term organizational performance. Yet high-risk, high-reward strategies also inevitably increase variation in firm performance. Behaving more entrepreneurially implies greater experimentation with business concepts and a commitment of resource to new entries with uncertain returns. These behaviors may produce big losses in addition to big gains over time. In certain firm contexts, for instance, where firm resource "slack" is limited, these losses may tax the organizations already thinly stretched resource bases to where firm discontinuation results. Firm survival is therefore an important consideration when increasing organizational levels of EO.

Moreover, behavior is the central and essential element for defining a firm as being entrepreneurially orientated. Nonbehavioral dispositional attitudes and intentions exist outside of the conceptual boundaries and scope of the phenomenon. Distinctions between nonbehavioral organizational attributes, such as organizational cultural norms and values, and EO as a pattern of sustained strategic actions and behaviors is important because while EO and nonbehavioral organizational attributes are distinct phenomenon, they are often dynamically linked.

Importance

An overview of any foundational managerial concept would be incomplete without a discussion of its validity and impact. To begin, EO has been extensively explored within the managerial literature. In line with the theoretical view of EO as a combined construct, studies have most often investigated the dimensions of innovativeness, risk taking, and proactiveness together and observed these dimensions to exhibit moderate to high correlations with one another in practice. A measurement instrument for capturing EO, offered by Jeff Covin and Dennis Slevin, has been extensively adopted within the literature. The instrument has been scrutinized through numerous validity assessments, and a subscale of the items has been observed to possess strong measurement invariance across differing cultural contexts.

EO has been shown to be a very useful conceptual tool for understanding, explaining, and predicting managerial phenomena. Perhaps owing to its origins within the field of strategic management, the most often investigated dependent variable within EO research has been firm performance. A meta-analysis of the EO-firm performance relationship conducted by Andreas Rauch and colleagues suggests that EO has a moderately large correlation with performance which is robust to different operationalizations of the EO concept as well as both financial and nonfinancial measures of performance. The size of this effect is quite remarkable, comparable to the correlation between taking sleeping pills and having a better night's sleep. To more fully explain the connection between EO and firm performance, researchers have explicated a number of factors which shape the value of organizational entrepreneurial processes and behaviors. Central among these considerations is the role which industry sector or general environmental dynamism may play in increasing the influence of EO on organizational outcomes. In high technology industries, or more dynamic task environments, EO has been observe to exhibit a much stronger influence on positive firm performance.

Scholarly research into EO has shaped managerial thinking through its adoption within prominent business school textbooks and practitioner-focused articles. EO has encouraged organizational managers to think deeply and strategically about their entrepreneurial processes and behaviors—when they are most beneficial—and how to stimulate them. With stronger EO, firms are better able to create and utilize their knowledge-based resources through experimenting with new business concepts and new entry possibilities. Yet EO is a resource-consuming strategic posture with many contextual contingencies which must be considered and ultimately managed if the phenomenon is to fulfill its promise as a positive driver of organizational value creation. In this regard, prior research has offered numerous propositions and issues for practicing managers to consider when enhancing their organization's EO—some of the most useful are the extent to which the organizations structure is organically constructed and the organizations environment is characterized by dynamic, changing conditions. The reader is referred to the related entries within this encyclopedia, listed below, in addition to several particularly insightful studies on the EO concept offered in the following section for further reading.

William Wales

See also Business Policy and Corporate Strategy; Entrepreneurial Opportunities; Strategic Entrepreneurship

Further Readings

Covin, J. G., & Lumpkin, G. T. (2011). Entrepreneurial orientation theory and research: Reflections on a needed construct. *Entrepreneurship: Theory & Practice, 35,* 855–872.

Covin, J. G., & Slevin, D. P. (1989). Strategic management of small firms in hostile and benign environments. *Strategic Management Journal, 10,* 75–87.

Covin, J. G., & Slevin, D. P. (1991). A conceptual model of entrepreneurship as firm behavior. *Entrepreneurship: Theory & Practice, 16,* 7–25.

Covin, J. G., & Wales, W. J. (2012). The measurement of entrepreneurial orientation. *Entrepreneurship: Theory & Practice, 36*(4), 677–702.

Dess, G. G., & Lumpkin, G. T. (2005). The role of entrepreneurial orientation in stimulating effective corporate entrepreneurship. *Academy of Management Executive, 19,* 147–156.

Lumpkin, G. T., & Dess, G. G. (1996). Clarifying the entrepreneurial orientation construct and linking it to performance. *Academy of Management Review, 21,* 135–172.

Miller, D. (2011). Miller (1983) revisited: A reflection on EO research and some suggestions for the future. *Entrepreneurship: Theory & Practice, 35,* 873–894.

Rauch, A., Wiklund, J., Lumpkin, G. T., & Frese, M. (2009). Entrepreneurial orientation and business performance: An assessment of past research and suggestions for the future. *Entrepreneurship: Theory & Practice, 33,* 761–787.

Wales, W., Monsen, E., & McKelvie, A. (2011). The organizational pervasiveness of entrepreneurial orientation. *Entrepreneurship: Theory & Practice, 35,* 895–923.

Wiklund, J., & Shepherd, D. A. (2011). Where to from here? EO-as-experimentation, failure, and distribution of outcomes. *Entrepreneurship: Theory & Practice, 35,* 925–946.

ENVIRONMENTAL UNCERTAINTY

Environmental uncertainty is recognized as a fundamental element of strategic management and entrepreneurship. It is a key concept in various theories such as contingency theory, information process theory, theories of decision making, and theories of entrepreneurship. Environmental uncertainty is a predictor of decision-makers' behaviors and organizational behaviors and structures and also a moderator of the relationship between organizational behaviors and structures and organizational performance. A widely accepted view contends that environmental uncertainty is the key ingredient influencing organizational structure—the more uncertainty resulting from technological and environmental factors, the more the organization will compensate by departing from bureaucratic structure toward a decentralized mode of operation. In this entry, environmental uncertainty is defined, the sources of environmental uncertainty are clarified, theories of environmental uncertainty are described, and the validity and impact of the theories on environmental uncertainty are examined.

Fundamentals

Definition of Environmental Uncertainty

Environmental uncertainty refers to the perceived lack of information about key dimensions of the environment determining a company's performance, such as the unpredictability of the environment, the inability to predict the impacts of environmental change, and the consequences of a response choice.

Environmental uncertainty is a perceptual construct. Though some scholars view environmental uncertainty as an objective attribute, it is generally regarded as a perceptual construct. Perception is a function of contextual factors, individual attributes, and cognitive reasoning. External environmental attributes are sources of perceived environmental uncertainty, which are also influenced by differences in motivation, attitudes, and risk propensity of the perceiver. While dimensions of environmental attributes are often used interchangeably as dimensions of environmental uncertainty, it is important to distinguish the sources and types of environmental uncertainty. Specifying the sources of uncertainty identifies the domain of the environment which the decision maker is uncertain about (e.g., technology or market), while specifying the types of uncertainty focuses on delineating the nature of uncertainty being experienced.

Environmental uncertainty is a multidimensional construct. Environmental uncertainty is classified into three types: state, effect, and response uncertainty. *State uncertainty* represents the inability to predict how the components of the environment are changing. *Effect uncertainty* describes the inability to predict the impact of the change in the environment of the organization. Finally, *response uncertainty* is a lack of insight into response options and/or the inability to predict the likely consequences of a response choice given a changing environment. Such a classification implies a conceptual distinction among different types of uncertainty as a function of lack of information in the different aspects of how environmental change influences organizational

behaviors. The classification also suggests different types of uncertainty have different implications for decision making in an organization.

Sources of Environmental Uncertainty

Research explores the sources of environmental uncertainty from two aspects: environmental components and dimensions of environmental attributes.

Environmental components. Environmental uncertainty can be derived from several environmental components, such as customers, suppliers, competitors, distributors, regulatory factors, union issues, and technology. Among these factors, technology and markets are the best known sources of environmental uncertainty due to ongoing changes and developments within market composition and technology.

Technological uncertainty refers to the degree of familiarity with the given technology or the degree of change in the technologies relative to products developed or manufactured by a company. Technological uncertainty is high where technology is new or rapidly changing.

Market uncertainty refers to ambiguity concerning the type and extent of customer needs. High market uncertainty may result from a fast-changing or emerging market. In such situations, companies are not sure who the customers are, what they want, and how they can be reached.

Dimensions of environmental attributes. There are many dimensions of environmental attributes, including satiability-turbulence (or dynamism, volatility), familiarity-novelty (or newness), simplicity-complexity (or heterogeneousness), and munificence-hostility.

Environmental turbulence refers to the degree in which environmental components act as units of change. It is not change itself—rather, it is unpredictability of the environment that is associated with uncertainty.

Environmental novelty, a related environmental attribute, refers to the degree in which environmental components are new to the decision maker or the frequency with which decision makers take new internal and external factors into consideration. Novelty of environmental components implies decision makers are unfamiliar with such components and are lacking knowledge.

Environmental complexity refers to the heterogeneity of and range of environmental components. A simple environment indicates the components or factors in the decision-maker's environment are few in number and are similar. Complexity indicates the components in the decision-making unit's environment are numerous, dissimilar to one another, and interdependent. Individuals facing a more complex environment need greater information-processing requirements to make decisions and thus perceive greater uncertainty.

Munificence refers to the extent the environment supports sustained growth. Organizations often seek out environments which permit organizational growth and stability. This allows the organization to generate slack resources. Environmental hostility describes the scarcity of critical resources needed by firms. When resources become scarce, firms may have fewer strategic options and experience higher competitive pressures, which may result in unfavorable performance.

Role in Management Theories

Environmental uncertainty is a key concept in various theories. Its role in contingency theory, information-process theory, and theory of entrepreneurship is briefly summarized in the following paragraphs.

Contingency theory and information-process theory.
Environmental uncertainty is the core concept of contingency theory. The central tenet of contingency theory states an organization will be more effective if its structure is adaptive to the demands of internal and external environmental change. Information-process theory provides a mechanism to explain the contingency theory. Studies show that in order to achieve a given level of performance, the amount of information being processed by decision makers depends on the degree of environmental uncertainty the task possesses. The perceived variation in organizational structure is hypothesized as associated with variations in the capacity of the organization to process information. In general, researchers observed two types of organizations: organic and mechanistic. *Organic* organizational approaches possess decentralized decision making, rich and frequent communication, fluidity and flexibility in the task execution process, a high level of organizational integration, and few formal procedures. *Mechanistic* approaches are defined by centralized decision making, formalized procedures, hierarchical structure, and explicit roles and regulations. Researchers suggest the organic form is more effective in highly uncertain environments, while the mechanistic form is effective in stable markets.

Theory of entrepreneurship: Uncertainty and entrepreneurial action.
Entrepreneurship is an uncertain process. Theories of entrepreneurship often support the preventive role of perceived environmental uncertainty in entrepreneurial action. When perceived environmental uncertainty is high, new venture managers may feel unsure about the potential success of their new venture's operations. Environmental uncertainty also influences the assessment of feasibility and desirability of an action. Hence, highly uncertain environments require careful analysis and planning and obstruct entrepreneurial action. Entrepreneurial action can be regarded as the outcome of less perceived uncertainty and more willingness to bear uncertainty. Due to different prior knowledge, motivations, and attitudes, entrepreneurs perceive environmental attributes, such as environmental change, as being less uncertain than nonentrepreneurs. For example, with certain domain-specific knowledge, potential entrepreneurs may recognize an opportunity for a new technology with low uncertainty while others may not. Those who believe an opportunity exists will further consider whether they can win and whether it is worthy of action. Their judgments also depend on prior knowledge, motivations, and attitudes. Entrepreneurs may be willing to bear more uncertainty to act than nonentrepreneurs.

Importance

The validity and usefulness of the theories of environmental uncertainty are examined through three aspects: moderating effect on management systems, the direct effect on entrepreneurial action, and evolving attitudes regarding environmental uncertainty.

Moderating Effects of Environmental Uncertainty

A large number of empirical studies have been conducted on the contingency and information-processing theory. In general, environmental uncertainty has been regarded as a moderator of the relationship between organizational structures and behaviors and their performance at different levels. In fact, according to most empirical studies, environmental uncertainty is possibly one of the most accepted moderators. Accordingly, one-size-does-not-fit-all has become a popular strategic choice for managers. In a highly uncertain environment, firms need to loosen their rules and procedures in order to embrace employees' experimentation, empower employees at a lower level, and even spin off an autonomous team to face the challenges of uncertainty. In contrast, in a stable and mature environment, organizations need to centralize the decision-making power and formalize and standardize the rules and procedures to structure employees' behaviors to improve operation efficiency and yield predictable outcomes.

Studies further suggest different environmental components and attributes have different effects. Therefore, it is necessary to analyze the sources and attributes of uncertainty before any strategy is selected. One study on new product development suggests there are different routes to success under different conditions. When a firm explores an incremental technology change, the firm can and should move rapidly to market. Under conditions of technology newness, it is better to take time to "freeze" the design. When turbulence is high, a firm should develop a new product quickly until diminishing returns are reached. When market newness is high, a firm needs to launch fast and learn quickly in order to capture customer needs in an emerging market.

Direct Effects on Entrepreneurial Action

Entrepreneurial action is determined by the amount of perceived uncertainty and willingness to bear uncertainty resulting from differences in prior knowledge, motivations, and attitudes of individuals. While it is unclear if the two effects can be distinguished, some empirical studies suggest different types of uncertainty (state, effect, and response) and environmental components (technology and market) influence the willingness to engage in entrepreneurial action differently. Moreover, the entrepreneur's expertise reduces the negative effect of entrepreneurial action of effect uncertainty. For example, while response uncertainty has the biggest influence on entrepreneurial action, state uncertainty has the least impact on action. This raises the question, in what setting will environmental uncertainty be meaningful as a predictor of entrepreneurial action? Perhaps

entrepreneurs simply assume a general level of environmental change (state uncertainty) as a given. However, entrepreneurs should not try to predict environmental change, which is out of their control. Instead they should focus on their actions and work to understand, calculate, and create the conditions which reduce the effect of uncertainty.

Evolving Attitudes of Dealing With Environmental Uncertainty

Differences in attitudes affect how institutions view environmental uncertainty. Traditionally, environmental uncertainty has been regarded as a threat due to the challenges it poses to rationality and the detrimental effect on innovative and entrepreneurial action. Hence, the closed system strategy seeks certainty by incorporating only variables positively associated with goal achievement and subjecting them to a controlled network. Most of an organization's actions can be explained by the need to reduce environmental uncertainty. Organizations seek to seal off their technical core from environmental uncertainty through buffering, leveling, or forecasting fluctuations. According to this view, reducing environmental uncertainty becomes one of the key administrative guidelines for practitioners. Thus, traditionally, managers do their best to avoid, eliminate, or reduce environmental uncertainty.

Alternatively, modern managers, particularly innovators and entrepreneurs, can view environmental uncertainty as an opportunity to exploit market opportunities. According to Joseph Schumpeter, the appearance of new and unexpected opportunities is necessary to keep economies moving. Such opportunities include the appearance of unforeseen technological development, unanticipated changes in taste, the development of new users for old products, and the discovery of new sources of raw materials. Basically, such opportunities are a source of environmental uncertainty as well. Without uncertainty, innovative and entrepreneurial activity becomes routine. Such action depends on constraints. There can be opportunities when constraints unexpectedly become relaxed, such as when improvements in technology make transactions easier, or entrepreneurs become more opportunistic.

Entrepreneurial and innovative action depends on the willingness to bear uncertainty. Embracing environmental uncertainty can have a number of benefits—fighting overconfidence, reducing frustration, fostering learning and flexibility, properly framing information, encouraging thoughtful decision making, and cultivating the development of new products, processes, services, and structures. This indicates that modern managers might need to reconsider traditional stances on environmental uncertainty, and embrace it in this fast-changing environment. The ability to cope with, accept, and even embrace environmental uncertainty will enhance their chances of success.

As is apparent throughout this entry, environmental uncertainty is a complex, multidimensional perception. How a business or its management interprets and manages environmental uncertainty will likely determine if they experience positive or negative effects. By exploring its foundations, sources, and importance, a theoretical model of environmental uncertainty allows managers to better understand and manage it.

Jiyao Chen

See also Contingency Theory; Entrepreneurial Opportunities; Strategic Contingencies Theory; Technology and Interdependence/Uncertainty

Further Readings

Chen, J., Reilly, R. R., & Lynn, G. S. (2005). The impacts of speed-to-market on new product success: The moderating effects of uncertainty. *IEEE Transactions on Engineering Management, 52*(2), 199–212.

Duncan, R. B. (1972). Characteristics of organizational environment and perceived environmental uncertainty. *Administrative Science Quarterly, 17,* 313–327.

Lawrence, P., & Lorsch, J. (1967). *Organization and environment: Managing differentiation and integration.* Boston, MA: Harvard University.

McKelvie, A., Haynie, J. M., & Gustafsson, V. (2011). Unpacking the uncertainty construct: Implications for entrepreneurial action. *Journal of Business Venturing, 26*(3), 273–292.

McMullen, J. S., & Shepherd, D. A. (2006). Entrepreneurial action and the role of uncertainty in the theory of the entrepreneur. *Academy of Management Review, 31*(1), 132–152.

Milliken, F. J. (1987). Three types of perceived uncertainty about the environment: State, effect, and response uncertainty. *Academy of Management Review, 12*(1), 133–143.

Thompson, J. D. (1967). *Organization in action.* New York, NY: McGraw-Hill.

EQUITY THEORY

Equity theory provides a framework for understanding how people come to perceive an exchange relationship as being unfair by focusing on the antecedents and consequences of those perceptions. The theory is especially germane to management because the bulk of the research conducted on it has addressed that context. In addition, perceived injustice can have profound effects in organizations. In this entry, the fundamentals of the theory are laid out, its history and development explained, an assessment of the theory offered, and some further readings suggested.

Fundamentals

Equity theory is a concept focused on the reasons why the outcomes of a social exchange might be perceived as unfair because of a lack of correspondence with the inputs to that exchange. Additionally, the theory shows different ways that people might respond when they perceive that lack of correspondence. The lack of correspondence is considered to be unpleasant and hence the source of motivation to be rid of that unpleasantness—to reduce feelings of inequity. The ways to reduce inequity involve bringing outcomes and inputs back into correspondence by making changes to the outcomes or to the inputs or to both. These can be changes in mere perceptions rather than in the actual outcomes and inputs themselves.

An employee's perceived *inputs* might include his or her merit and effort as well as skill, training, education, experience, or seniority. With regard to employees who feel inequitably treated, the relevant inputs are whatever they believe the employer ought to compensate: the perceived contributions to the exchange, for which a fair return is expected. Job-related *outcomes,* therefore, are the kinds of things that employees perceive should be granted in return for what they have contributed to the organization (e.g., salary, bonuses, promotions, benefits, status). This conceptualization stresses that the sense of inequity is a subjective experience based on one's own perceptions. Fairness, like beauty, is in the eye of the beholder.

John Stacey Adams referred to the perceived fairness of outcomes in terms of three possibilities: *equity, disadvantageous* inequity, and *advantageous* inequity. Colloquially, the latter two might be called underpay and overpay. Adams noted how the nature of specific comparisons could affect these. A person making $70,000 per year might feel good about that amount in comparison with someone earning only $20,000 annually, for example, and yet the same person might have an unfavorable reaction if the comparison were to someone earning $200,000 annually.

Consider those salaries on an amount-per-annum basis as not unlike the annual return-on-investment from a mutual fund. What makes for a good return on investment? Suppose you could expect to get a 5% return from mutual fund A ($120 as the outcome for every $100 input). That's "advantageous" relative to a 2% return from mutual fund B but "disadvantageous" relative to a 10% return from mutual fund C. Adams reasoned that comparisons of outcome/input ratios also formed the basis for perceived inequity, whether in its disadvantageous or advantageous form.

If the set of outcomes and inputs designated by A related equitably to those of B, an outcome/input algebraic equivalence is $O_a/I_a = O_b/I_b$. Similarly, disadvantageous inequity is $O_a/I_a < O_b/I_b$, and advantageous inequity is $O_a/I_a > O_b/I_b$. Based on the algebra of ratios, A and B might exist in an equitable relation with A as 4/1 and B as 4/1 (identical terms as exact equality) or with A as 800/4 and B as 400/2 (equivalence rather than the equality of every term) and so on—such as if the numerator were dollars and the denominator were days worked (e.g., A got $800 for 4 days' work, and B got $400 for 2 days' work). By the same token, A with an outcome/input ratio of 20/5 would be in a state of advantageous inequity relative to 15/5 for B; the same 20/5 would create a disadvantageous inequity in A's situation, however, if B's outcome/input ratios were 40/5 or 16/2 and so on.

The use of algebra has important implications. First note that A and B can stand for anything. Adams referred to the two sides of the equation in terms of *Person* and *Other* (he actually used *p* and *a*). He described some of the possibilities in his seminal 1965 article as follows:

> *Other* is any individual with whom Person is in an exchange relationship, or with whom Person compares himself when both he and Other are in an exchange relationship with a third party, such as an employer, or with third parties who are considered by Person as being comparable, such as employers in a particular industry or geographic location. Other is usually a different individual, but may be Person in another job or in another social role. Thus, Other might be Person in a job he held previously, in which case he might compare his present and past outcomes and inputs and determine whether or not the exchange with his employer, present or past, was equitable. (p. 280)

Some descriptions of equity theory (a) fail to note that the exchange can involve three parties, when the comparison is with a coworker (viz., same employer), and (b) claim that a process of *social comparison* guides the search for a *comparison other* as a gauge of outcome–input fairness. As Adams made clear, the comparison could be with yourself. Indeed, the equation would apply if you compared the tax you pay with what people in other countries pay! (Thus, the introduction here of the equation was given in purely algebraic terms by using the letters A and B.)

An example of the $O_a/I_a > O_b/I_b$ equation for advantageous inequity, or overpayment, led Adams to his theory: the result of an experience when he worked for General Electric (GE) in human resources (when the author was a graduate student of Adams). An employee told Adams that he felt overpaid and was working hard to try to deserve what he was paid. Adams decided that just as people can feel angry when they think they get less than they deserve, they might feel guilty about getting more than they deserve. He also reasoned that there would be a psychological motivation to try to make sure that a nonequivalent distribution—unfairness of either type—could be changed into an equivalent one. In short, people dislike inequity and will try to restore justice when an injustice exists; in one way or another, they try to turn inequitable situations into equitable ones.

Because the equation has four terms (inputs and outcomes for A and for B), striving for equity can focus on any of the four: When $18/6 \neq 24/12$, for example, you can change the 18 to 12, the 6 to 9, the 24 to 36, or the 12 to 8. Changing 6 into 9 is like what the GE employee did, namely, working harder (increasing the size of the input term). Neither reducing your outcomes ($18 \rightarrow 12$) nor reducing your employer's inputs ($12 \rightarrow 8$) seems realistic, which shows that not all ways of reducing inequities apply to a given situation. Note that harder work as increased inputs could also increase the employer's outcomes, which shows that more than one term might be changed simultaneously.

Because fairness is subjective, there are four other ways to achieve equity, namely, changing your perceptions of them rather than actually doing anything about them at all! Imagine you get angry about feeling underpaid—but you can't really do anything about it, so you rethink the situation in ways that make your anger somehow evaporate. You could increase your outcomes *perceptually* (psychologically, subjectively, cognitively), for example, by deciding that your work provides you with more than just your pay, because the work is really more enjoyable than you had been thinking about it, you had not taken into account all the friendships it made possible, and so on. You could cognitively reduce your inputs by deciding the work was really easier than you had been thinking. Perceiving your employer's outcomes and inputs differently are also ways that you might make adjustments so that the situation seems more equitable. Adams even included a bailout or "leaving the field" avenue of inequity reduction (e.g., quitting your job).

Inequity reduction is a two-staged process: (a) Certain circumstances cause you to perceive an inequity; (b) you then are motivated to do something (actually or cognitively) to one or more of the four terms of the equation. The point is that you might feel an inequity at first and then later not at all, even though nothing had really changed. You would simply have found a way to justify the input→output relations to yourself, in the same way that dissonance theory describes how people use rationalizations to justify their behavior by changing their attitudes. In other words, Adams said that the experiences of inequity and dissonance are equivalent.

Equity theory also has boundary conditions that are far less constricted than many management theories, and its algebraic formulation is so abstract. Changing imbalance into balance is an abstract idea. Feeling discomfort (Adams called it a state of psychological tension) and wanting to turn that into a more comfortable feeling is a highly abstract way of describing motivation (in fact, it is hard to think of how else to conceive of motivation other than as the desire to make things other than they are now, which means being dissatisfied with how they are now!). The two sides of the equation could represent a variety of things; for example, Person and Other might refer to groups rather than to individuals, as when the outcomes/input ratio of a set of jobs such as toolmakers is out of line with those of jobs such as lathe operators, or when ethnic groups feel inequitably treated relative to one another. It should also be noted that some people are more sensitive than others to the violation of equity.

Evolution

It is possible to think of the first phase of equity theory's history in relation to the theme of boundary conditions. As previously mentioned, at GE, Adams had encountered an instance of "advantageous inequity" firsthand. To him, it seemed counterintuitive. In a subsequent career stage as a professor, he had contact with Leon Festinger (of dissonance fame), which helped provide insights about how perceived inputs and outcomes could be distorted cognitively. The result was that Adams conducted empirical work on equity theory by exploring the overpay case and how people would deal with the "guilt" of an unfair advantage. He was under no illusion that this kind of research would be easy; he had readily acknowledged that dissatisfaction and guilt thresholds differ from one another: the outcome/input ratio will be more deviant from equity before someone feels guilty about being overadvantaged, relative to the deviation it takes for someone to react negatively to feeling underadvantaged. We could say that Adams was trying to push at the boundaries of the theory's predictions in choosing to do research on overpay conditions.

He did that in a series of ingenious laboratory experiments. Although these experiments used college undergraduates and hence might be thought to have limited how much the results would generalize to real organizations, he staged these experiments as if they involved actual part-time work. Students performed identical work while being paid on either an hourly or piece-rate basis in some of the experiments. In others, Adams hired students to do proofreading and made them think that they were (or were not) overpaid because they were (or were not) underqualified. The latter studies showed that the students who perceived themselves as being underqualified reduced their overpayment inequity by doing higher quality proofreading (they found and corrected a greater number of errors than did the members of two other conditions, made to feel equitably paid in either of two different ways). The former studies showed that predictably different ways of reducing overpay inequity were used depending on the way in which the overpayment occurred (viz., on an hourly or on a piece-rate basis).

As the history of research on equity theory evolved, it was these studies that attracted the most attention. They almost immediately produced criticism. Advocates of alternative explanations helped to launch debates that constituted most of the literature on the subject for a few years. Gradually, the interest in the theory itself waned. Scholars of organizational justice eventually became more interested in how the nature of decision-making procedures would influence reactions to outcomes, rather than how the outcomes themselves would have an influence (i.e., interest in what became known as procedural justice).

Disadvantageous inequity received little attention of much note other than for one particularly interesting type of finding in regards to an imaginative way in which the research participants reduced inequity perceptions by using cognitive distortion. Those participants were recruited by Karl Weick, who had them all work on the same task but made one group feel inequitably undercompensated. Weick found that the members of that group responded in a novel way to the task itself: Relative to the other participants, they evaluated their experience in a more glowing way that Weick called "task enhancement." That result is in fact a direct parallel to dissonance studies in which students work on boring tasks but belie their own experience when they are led to make it sound attractive to someone else; they subsequently convince themselves that it was interesting, exciting, and enjoyable.

Perhaps one reason that research on equity theory dissipated was that it was not very easy to predict which such results might be obtained. Here is a boundary condition of another kind: When a theory is so abstract that it can predict almost anything, in practice it can predict nothing! People who feel *underpaid* might distort the experience cognitively, rationalize their way into thinking it was fun, and work that much harder because they now thought they enjoyed it so much—or they might resent the unfairness of it all and instead work less hard (thereby reducing their employers' profitable outcomes). People who feel *overpaid* might work that much harder to get rid of their guilt, or they might rationalize in one way or another that they really

deserved what they were getting, and hence feel no need to increase their work efforts at all.

This problem shows that it takes a careful examination of a given situation in order to figure out whether someone will be motivated in a particular way or not. Research by Robert Folger and colleagues provides an illustration. Based on the connection between equity theory and dissonance theory, it was reasoned that details relevant to the antecedents and consequences of dissonance reduction would have implications for equity theory predictions. By then, a person's choice and sense of responsibility for the consequences of his or her choice (particularly if there were some unattractive features of those consequences) had been determined to be important to dissonance phenomena. Folger and colleagues drew on that logic to design studies in which people "chose" (unknowingly steered by the experimenter) or did not choose to be "overpaid" or "underpaid." Choice/underpayment led to the task-enhancement effect that Weick had found; moreover, the researchers were also able to extend Weick's findings by obtaining enhanced task productivity in that condition. In contrast, no-choice/underpayment participants felt dissatisfied and performed poorly. The reversal of those patterns occurred in the remaining conditions: no-choice/overpay participants worked hard as a function of their undeserved good fortune, whereas choice/overpay participants were like slackers who were "only in it for the money"—they found the task itself to be dull and performed it listlessly.

Importance

Perhaps because research on outcome disparities became eclipsed by developments in procedural justice, the validity and impact of equity theory is not an actively considered issue. It seems safe to say that academic scholars (a) take the basic insights of the theory for granted and (b) do not attempt to pursue it as a research stream of their own—in part because the issue of where the right-hand side of the equation comes from (the "comparison other problem") seems so formidable. The theory has instead been amalgamated into the more generic realm of "distributive justice," alongside considerations of equality and need as other norms of distribution (distributive, procedural, interactional, and informational justice are now considered in conjunction with one another). Managers certainly have some intuitions about the importance of fairness to employees, but it is doubtful that they apply the specifics of the theory itself. Two commentators sum up probably the best evaluations of it. John B. Miner used ratings from experts in the field to assess organizational theories. His results showed that equity scored almost 6 on a scale where 7 was the highest possible, ranking it third among all those evaluated (73 theories in all). At the same time, he gave it only a 3 out of 5 when rating its usefulness in application. Gary P. Latham also gave it high marks on the side of academic endorsement and was more enthusiastic about applicability in saying that he found it useful in his own consulting work. The clearest contribution of the theory, however, has been in the inspiration it provided for the explosion of work in the field of organizational justice more generally, and the value of that more general orientation cannot be denied.

The overall message for modern managers is to note the determinants of fairness perceptions. Some employees will perceive a new job assignment as a positive outcome that makes work more interesting, whereas others perceive it as doing more for the same pay. Some will expect a more extensive education to be an input deserving more pay, whereas others might consider seniority to be more important. Some employees might make internal comparisons to coworkers, whereas others might be focused on this year's raise compared to last year's. Managers should look for signs of perceived inequity, such as increases in turnover and absenteeism, reduced productivity, and so on—then find out what employees think is being rewarded, should be rewarded, and rewarded to what degree and relative to what standards. Managers need to communicate why and how specific inputs and outcomes are important to the organization's functioning. Using clear-cut and well-justified standards (e.g., industry or local wage averages) will help.

The challenge to execute those matters with care is obviously important when it comes to issues such as gender bias and comparable pay, such as biased perceptions that a woman's contribution is not as valuable as the same contribution by a man. Having multiple indicators of those contributions should make it easier to spot that type of discrepancy. That calls for vigilance and periodic review. Under some circumstances, it can be worthwhile to avoid pay

secrecy because rumors or runaway imaginations can create the presumption of inequity where it does not exist—when people overestimate what those around them are getting paid. When and if such transparency is implemented, of course, the "burden of proof" goes up in terms of valid justifications for differentiated outcomes (of any type that might seem to imply special treatment, such as the status of office assignments). If competitive benchmarking and other signs of transparency can be given sufficient publicity and if they receive acceptance as valid, then distorted speculations would be less likely even if salaries themselves were not necessarily open to public inspection.

Robert Folger

See also Cognitive Dissonance Theory; Expectancy Theory; Fairness Theory; Human Resource Management Strategies; Norms Theory; Social Exchange Theory

Further Readings

Adams, J. S. (1965). Inequity in social exchange. In L. Berkowitz (Ed.), *Advances in experimental social psychology* (Vol. 2, pp. 267–299). New York, NY: Academic Press.

Carrell, M. R., & Dittrich, J. E. (1978). Equity theory: The recent literature, methodological considerations, and new directions. *Academy of Management Review, 3,* 202–210.

Folger, R., Rosenfield, D., Hays, R. P., & Grove, R. (1978). Justice versus justification effects on productivity: Reconciling equity and dissonance findings. *Organizational Behavior and Human Performance, 22,* 465–478.

Latham, G. P. (2007). *Work motivation.* Thousand Oaks, CA: Sage.

Miner, J. B. (2003). The rated importance, scientific validity, and practical usefulness of organizational behavior theories: A quantitative review. *Academy of Management Learning & Education, 2,* 250–268.

Mowday, R. T., & Colwell, K. A. (2003). Employee reactions to unfair outcomes in the workplace: The contributions of Adams' equity theory to understanding work motivation. In L. Porter, G. Bigley, & R. M. Steers (Eds.), *Motivation and work behavior* (7th ed., pp. 222–254). Burr Ridge, IL: McGraw-Hill.

Weick, K. E. (1966). The concept of equity in the perception of pay. *Administrative Science Quarterly, 11,* 414–439.

ERG Theory

ERG theory is a needs-based theory of motivation developed by Clayton Alderfer in the late 1960s. ERG stands for the three basic needs—*existence, relatedness,* and *growth*—understood to influence human behavior. Alderfer's theory represents an expansion and refinement of Abraham Maslow's *hierarchy of needs* theory. Like other needs-based theories, Alderfer's theory signifies an important development in our understanding of motivation. Namely, what motivates human beings is a variety of needs that must be satisfied through both extrinsic (external) and intrinsic (internal) means. However, Alderfer's ERG theory is specifically worthy of consideration because its explanation of how different needs categories relate to one another differs significantly from earlier needs theories. What follows is a detailed description of ERG theory, including the needs categories, how these categories relate to one another, and Alderfer's underlying psychological reasoning to explain these relationships. In addition, ERG theory is compared to the aforementioned Maslow's hierarchy, and significant differences are delineated. Next, research into the validity of ERG theory is examined as are ways in which this theory is applicable in practice.

Fundamentals

ERG theory groups human needs into three basic categories—existence, relatedness, and growth. These three types of human needs influence behavior. *Existence needs* refer to fundamental physical aspects a person desires in order to achieve well-being. These include both physiological and material elements required for well-being, such as pay, benefits, safety, and security. *Relatedness needs* reflect the extent to which an individual desires healthy, meaningful relationships with people considered by this individual to be important or significant. *Growth needs* denote the desire a person has to make a meaningful contribution in what they do: to feel involved, to accomplish goals of consequence, and to personally develop and improve.

These needs categories are similar to the ones found in Maslow's hierarchy of needs. Existence needs parallel Maslow's *physiological* and *security* needs, relatedness needs are analogous to Maslow's *social* and *esteem* needs, and growth needs are comparable to Maslow's *self-actualization* needs. Alderfer intended his categories to be a refinement of Maslow's needs sets by eliminating what he viewed as problems in Maslow's theory with overlapping needs and by aligning these categorizations more closely to empirical research on human needs. In his description of ERG theory, Alderfer makes a distinction between relatedness needs and the other two needs categories; unlike the other two categories of needs, relatedness requires *mutuality*—a sharing or interaction with others to satisfy this type of need.

The three categories of needs represent separate, distinct constructs and are not necessarily intended to imply a specific ordering. Instead, Alderfer describes needs categories as running along a continuum according to their level of *concreteness.* Existence needs are considered the most concrete due to the ease with which an individual may determine their fulfillment or their absence. Relatedness needs are thought to be less concrete than existence needs, and growth needs are considered the least concrete. The notion of a continuum instead of a distinct, requisite ordering signifies an important difference between ERG theory and Maslow's hierarchy, which will be discussed later.

According to ERG theory, needs may manifest in the form of complex or *compound* needs comprising multiple-needs categories. For example, a person might desire to be named as project manager, which could result in increased pay (existence need), an opportunity to build different relationships with colleagues (relatedness need), and the chance to develop leadership skills (growth need).

ERG theory is based upon two key elements: *desire* and *satisfaction.* And as such, it is intended to both explain and predict the outcomes of interactions between satisfaction and desire in relation to human needs. *Desire* corresponds to the notions of want, preference, and the strength of such wants and preferences. *Satisfaction* is likened to fulfillment. The theory describes how desire and satisfaction each affects the other. In ERG theory, a person may desire any or all of the three needs categories at any given time. Satisfaction in one category influences the extent to which the person attends to other needs categories. This influence follows the concrete continuum; specifically, once a more concrete category of needs is met, a person's attention turns to the next set of needs category along the continuum.

On the other hand, if a person feels less satisfied with regards to a needs category, that person will regress back to a more concrete set of needs. For instance, if someone's desire is satisfied with regard to existence needs, the desire to satisfy relatedness needs is increased. However, if a person feels less satisfied in terms of relatedness needs, the frustration experienced by that person will cause a regression or refocus back on the more concrete category of existence needs. This is known in ERG theory as the *frustration-regression process*. Additionally, it is worth noting that according to this theory, someone's desire for relatedness and growth needs will continue to increase even when satisfaction is experienced for these categories. This assertion by Alderfer reflects the concepts espoused in classical aspiration level theory. Namely, individuals will raise their aspirations and create new, more challenging goals when they feel satisfied that they have reached current goals. If an employee is pleased with the degree of relatedness experienced at work, it is likely this employee will continue to desire and work toward relatedness. Similarly, opportunities to satisfy growth needs will encourage further development and growth.

As stated earlier, ERG theory and Maslow's hierarchy of needs are similar in that both theories utilize categories of needs. However, ERG theory differs from Maslow's in a number of significant ways. First, ERG includes only three needs categories as compared to Maslow's five. Second, there is the issue of *prepotency*. According to Maslow, lower order needs must be satisfied before higher order needs can emerge. This means that physiological needs must be met before needs such as belonging or self-actualization become salient to the individual in question. In contrast, ERG theory asserts that needs can (and often will) emerge at the same time, described above as compound needs. Although needs are categorized as higher or lower order based on where they fall along the concrete continuum in ERG theory, it is not necessary to fully meet one set of needs before another needs set becomes salient. Finally, ERG theory incorporates the idea of the frustration-regression process. Thus, a person's focus can fall *back* to a more concrete needs set when frustration exists about a less concrete needs set, whereas Maslow's theory allows only for *forward* progression from lower to higher order needs.

Importance

Research on ERG theory has resulted in mixed results, although it is better supported than Maslow's hierarchy of needs theory. Studies support the idea that the desire for needs continues to motivate past the point of satisfaction. The practical implication of this finding is important. Managers who wish to motivate their employees can implement intrinsically motivating programs to encourage continued growth, development, and relationship building with the expectation that these programs represent sustainable motivators. An individual who feels empowered to develop skills and make a meaningful contribution will continue to desire opportunities to further develop and grow. An employee who feels involved and connected within the organization will wish to maintain and build upon these relationships. Support has also been found in favor of the three needs categorizations delineated in ERG theory. Again, this helps inform managers of the general needs types they will most likely encounter among their employees (albeit, in varying degrees). There is also empirical evidence to suggest that satisfying relatedness needs can be a significant factor in job performance, not only for frontline employees but also for managerial employees. Furthermore, results indicate that the satisfaction of growth needs indirectly influences performance through enhanced self-esteem. It should be noted, however, that ERG theory was developed in and for a Western culture, that of the United States. As such, its use should be carefully and mindfully administered in cultures that deviate from Western cultural perspectives.

From a broader, more theoretical perspective it is worth noting that ERG theory, along with other needs-based theories, challenges the behaviorist notion of motivation. As noted by organizational behavior scholars Rober Kreitner and Angelo Kinicki, behavioral theory represents a narrower interpretation of motivation, with an emphasis on the link between reinforcement and behavior. As such, extrinsic motivators overshadow intrinsic options. In contrast, needs-based theories, such as ERG, illustrate how varied human needs may be, acknowledge the complexity inherent in the interaction between desire and satisfaction, and highlight the necessity of both extrinsic and intrinsic motivational options.

For managers, ERG theory explains that different types of needs can occur simultaneously. As such, managers should refrain from directing their attentions to one need set at a time. Managers must also remember that needs are a relative concept; in other words, what fully satisfies the desire of one person with regards to a needs set might not satisfy another person. Also, what motivates individuals and what is most salient and desired by them is likely to change over the course of their lives. For managers, this speaks to the importance of knowing and understanding one's employees. It also illustrates to managers how individualized and varied employee needs can be. This means managers should avoid a one-size-fits-all approach to meeting employee needs and should instead make efforts to customize motivation efforts with their employees' unique desires in mind. Finally, they should make such efforts with the understanding that continued opportunities to satisfy needs will perpetuate desire and result in ongoing efforts by employees for further satisfaction.

Rhetta L. Standifer

See also Job Characteristics Theory; Needs Hierarchy; Organizationally Based Self-Esteem; Self-Determination Theory

Further Readings

Alderfer, C. P. (1969). An empirical test of a new theory of human needs. *Organizational Behavior and Human Performance, 4*, 142–175.

Alderfer, C. P. (1972). Existence, relatedness, and growth: Human needs in organizational settings. New York, NY: Free Press.

Alderfer, C. P. (1977). A critique of Salancik and Pfeffer's examination of need-satisfaction theories. *Administrative Science Quarterly, 22*, 658–669.

Alderfer, C. P., Kaplan, R. E., & Smith, K. K. (1974). The effect of variations in relatedness need satisfaction on relatedness desires. *Administrative Science Quarterly, 19*, 507–532.

Arnolds, C. A., & Boshoff, C. (2002). Compensation, esteem valence and job performance: An empirical assessment of Alderfer's ERG theory. *International Journal of Human Resource Management, 13*, 697–719.

Kreitner, R., & Kinicki, A. (2009). *Organizational behavior* (9th ed.). New York, NY: McGraw-Hill/Irwin.

Maslow, A. H. (1943). A theory of human motivation. *Psychological Review, 50*, 390–396.

Schneider, B., & Alderfer, C.P. (1973). Three studies of measures of need satisfaction in organizations. *Administrative Science Quarterly, 18*, 489–505.

ESCALATION OF COMMITMENT

When a decision maker discovers that a previously selected course of action is failing, she is faced with a dilemma: Should she pull out her remaining resources and invest in a more promising alternative, or should she stick with her initial decision and hope that persistence will eventually pay off? Management scholars have documented a tendency of decision makers to escalate commitment to previously selected courses of action when objective evidence suggests that staying the course is unwise. In these situations, decision makers often feel they have invested too much to quit and make the errant decision to "stick to their guns." This entry describes the nature of "escalation of commitment," its most likely causes, decision characteristics that exacerbate its severity, how it can be prevented, and why it is important.

Fundamentals

Escalation of commitment is a risk whenever a decision maker (a) commits resources to a course of action (thereby making an "investment") in the hope of achieving a positive outcome and (b) experiences disappointing results. Invested resources may take any form from time, money, and labor to mental and emotional energy. For example, an individual risks escalation of commitment across the following diverse circumstances: when deciding between committing more money to bail out a foundering start-up versus investing elsewhere, when choosing between investing in more job training for an underperforming employee versus firing and replacing her, or when weighing whether to invest in marriage counseling versus seek a divorce.

While there are many situations where the best course of action is to commit further resources to a failing investment, the term *escalation of commitment* describes only those situations where objective evidence indicates that continuing with an investment is unwise, and yet an individual chooses to invest further in spite of this.

Explanations for Escalation of Commitment

Self-justification theory. Self-justification theory provides one explanation for why people escalate commitment to their past investments. Feeling personally responsible for an investment that turns sour intensifies the threat associated with failure and increases a decision maker's motivation to justify the original choice to herself. Negative feedback on a past investment decision calls the validity of the original decision into question and is dissonant with a decision maker's natural desire to see herself as competent. Many decision makers attempt to eliminate this conflict by convincing themselves that their failing ventures will turn around if they simply invest more resources. To do so and succeed would prove that the original choice was valid and eliminate the "cognitive dissonance" created by the initial negative feedback.

Confirmation bias. Biased information processing is one way that decision makers reduce the dissonance that arises when their positive self-perceptions conflict with evidence that past investments are under-performing. After committing to a choice, people are far more likely to notice and overweight evidence that supports their decision and ignore and underweight evidence that does not. Furthermore, decision makers actively seek information that confirms the validity of their decisions. This means that decision makers may actually be less aware of problems with their current investments, or, when they *are* aware of such problems, they may underestimate their severity. "Confirmation bias" can therefore cause decision makers to escalate commitment to bad investments.

Loss aversion. When a decision maker receives feedback that her investment is failing, she is faced with the prospect of losing both the potential rewards the investment originally offered and the resources previously committed to it. Past research on prospect theory has demonstrated that the disutility caused by losses is greater than the utility obtained from equivalent gains. For example, the pain of losing $1,000 is more extreme than the pleasure of gaining $1,000. In addition, people become risk seeking in

the domain of losses. Negative feedback on an investment frames the decision about whether to continue with the current course of action as a decision about whether to accept a loss or to take steps to prevent locking it in. This loss framing may lead decision makers to go to great lengths and take unwise risks to avoid losses. Escalation of commitment may therefore occur as a result of loss aversion.

Impression management. Impression management explanations of escalation behavior focus on a decision maker's need to justify her past choices to others. The outcome of an investment is rarely free from external scrutiny, and a decision maker may escalate commitment to her original investment to avoid admitting to others that the venture was a failure or that her decision was flawed. Such admissions might cause others to doubt her competence. Furthermore, people tend to punish decision makers for inconsistency. For example, the term *flip flopper* was effectively used to negatively brand the Democratic candidate John Kerry in the 2004 U.S. presidential election when he updated his views on the second Iraq War. When a decision maker switches from her originally endorsed course of action, observers may take it as a sign of weakness or lack of confidence. Thus, even when a decision maker knows that escalation is not the best option, she may choose to escalate commitment to avoid appearing inconsistent.

Managers should know not only *why* escalation of commitment occurs but also *when* it is most likely to occur and to what degree. Next we discuss factors that influence the likelihood and severity of escalation of commitment.

Factors That Influence the Risk of Escalation of Commitment

Personal responsibility. An individual is more likely to commit additional resources to a bad investment if she was the one who originally endorsed it. In fact, experimental evidence has shown that merely asking people to imagine they were responsible for choosing a failing venture makes them more likely to escalate commitment than asking them to imagine that someone else was responsible for the investment. Furthermore, two of the causes of escalation of commitment that were discussed previously—self-justification and impression management—are driven by feelings of personal responsibility for an investment.

Sunk costs. The more resources that have been spent on an investment, the more likely a decision maker is to escalate commitment. However, because these resources are irrecoverable, it is irrational to factor them into decisions about future outcomes. When considering investment possibilities, a decision maker should ignore these "sunk costs" and choose the alternative that will yield the highest payoffs regardless of the resources that have already been expended. The desire to honor sunk costs is driven by psychological factors including loss aversion (refusing to accept the "loss" of expended resources), self-justification theory (needing to justify past expenditures to oneself) and impression management (wanting to avoid appearing wasteful to others).

Proximity to completion. The closer a project is to completion, the more likely decision makers are to exhibit escalation of commitment. Invested time is one form of sunk cost, so it is more difficult to abandon a project the nearer it comes to completion (i.e., as sunk costs increase). However, there is evidence that proximity to project completion is related to the likelihood of escalation *independent of sunk cost considerations.* Goal substitution theory maintains that, as the end of a project nears, completion-oriented goals begin to supersede the original goals of the project (e.g., profit goals). Because decision makers become caught up in the desire to finish the project, they are more likely to escalate commitment to attain completion goals even when more profitable alternatives are available.

Exogenous explanations for failure. Escalation of commitment is also more pronounced when past investment failures can be blamed on unforeseeable, exogenous events. For example, a business start-up's lack of profits could be blamed on an unexpected economic downturn. Any opportunity to blame a setback on an exogenous source helps a decision maker maintain his positive self-concept and the belief that his original decision was valid, increasing the risk of escalation of commitment. Motivated biased information processing can also lead decision makers to assign excessive blame to exogenous impediments while underweighting flaws

intrinsic to an investment, further exacerbating escalation of commitment.

Group decision making. Past research on escalation behavior in groups has highlighted two countervailing forces that affect the risk of escalation. On the one hand, having multiple decision makers increases the likelihood that someone will recognize the irrationality of investing further resources in a poor venture. On the other hand, adverse group dynamics, such as groupthink (a phenomenon where the desire to avoid intragroup conflict makes group members overly compliant), can artificially reinforce the original decision and override considerations of alternatives. Past research integrating these perspectives suggests that group decision making decreases the likelihood of escalation of commitment; however, when escalation *does* occur in groups, it is more extreme.

Importance

Escalation of commitment has been studied across a diverse set of important business settings. For example, past research on the banking industry demonstrated that senior bank managers escalate commitment to the loans they select by retaining them even after they prove to be problematic. Specifically, executive turnover significantly predicts de-escalation to these problematic loans. Researchers have also shown that radical Wall Street stock analysts become even more extreme in their forecasts about a company's yearly earnings when new announcements reveal the analysts' quarterly forecasts were errant. This pattern of escalation harms analysts' forecasting accuracy and reduces their likelihood of winning prestigious awards linked to increased compensation. Researchers have also documented escalation behavior in managers' personnel decisions. Supervisors of clerical workers in a large public sector organization who originally supported hiring or promoting an employee subsequently provide positively biased evaluations of that employee. Finally, escalation behavior has even been found among professional sports managers: Teams in the National Basketball Association (NBA) escalate commitment to their top draft picks by fielding and retaining these players longer than would be wise based on their performance alone.

Knowing why and when escalation occurs can help managers avoid this common decision bias. The research discussed above suggests several prescriptions for avoiding escalation of commitment, which are listed below (with the source or aggravator in parentheses):

- Actively seek disconfirming information about a chosen alternative (confirmation bias).
- Reframe losses as gains to prevent risk-seeking behavior (loss aversion).
- Structure incentives so that decision makers are not punished for inconsistency (impression management).
- Hand off decisions about whether to commit more resources to an investment to new decision makers (personal responsibility).
- Be careful not to consider expended resources when making decisions (sunk costs).
- Make sure decision makers are frequently reminded of the goals of the investment (proximity to completion).

The field research summarized above highlights that escalation of commitment occurs in diverse management settings and can lead to serious negative consequences for decision makers. For example, it can lead bank executives to retain bad loans, stock analysts to make inaccurate forecasts, managers to retain and promote low-quality employees, and NBA teams to rely excessively on weak players. Accordingly, escalation of commitment is an important bias for managers to be aware of and aim to avoid.

Theresa F. Kelly and
Katherine L. Milkman

See also Cognitive Dissonance Theory; Decision-Making Styles; Groupthink; Managerial Decision Biases; Prospect Theory

Further Readings

Bazerman, M. H., & Moore, D. A. (2009). The escalation of commitment. In *Judgment in Managerial Decision Making* (7th ed., pp. 101–112). New York, NY: Wiley.

Beshears, J., & Milkman, K. L. (2011). Do sell-side stock analysts exhibit escalation of commitment? *Journal of Economic Behavior & Organization, 77,* 304–317.

Schoorman, F. D. (1988). Escalation bias in performance appraisals: An unintended consequence of supervisor participation in hiring decisions. *Journal of Applied Psychology, 73*(1), 58–62.

Sleesman, D. J., Conlon, D. E., McNamara, G., & Miles, J. E. (2012). Cleaning up the Big Muddy: A meta-analytic review of the determinants of escalation of commitment. *Academy of Management Journal, 55,* 541–562.

Staw, B. M. (1976). Knee-deep in the Big Muddy: A study of escalating commitment to a chosen course of action. *Organizational Behavior and Human Performance, 16,* 27–44.

Staw, B. M. (1981). The escalation of commitment to a course of action. *Academy of Management Review, 6*(4), 577–587.

Staw, B. M., Barsade, S. G., & Koput, D. W. (1997). Escalation at the credit window: A longitudinal study of bank executives' recognition and write-off of problem loans. *Journal of Applied Psychology, 82*(1), 130–142.

Staw, B. M., & Hoang, H. (1995). Sunk costs in the NBA: Why draft order affects playing time and survival in professional basketball. *Administrative Science Quarterly, 40*(3), 474–494.

ETHICAL DECISION MAKING, INTERACTIONIST MODEL OF

In the 1980s, a number of ethics-related scandals in business and other organizations were garnering media attention, suggesting that management theorists might wish to attend to the arena of ethical decision-making behavior in a way that they had not previously done. Organizational behavior researchers, borrowing from work by psychologists, were moving beyond debates about person *or* situation effects toward recognizing the importance of *both* individual and situational influences and their interactions on behavior. But there were no explicit models guiding research on ethical decision making and behavior. In 1986, Linda Treviño adopted an interactionist view on ethical decision making in organizations which posited that ethical decision making in organizations results largely not only from the individual's cognitive moral development but also from the interaction of cognitive moral development with other individual differences and contextual features. She offered the model in an attempt to move beyond normative approaches that provide guidance about what people "should" do in ethically challenging situations and beyond less theoretically grounded survey research that had previously identified problems with ethical pressures in organizations but did not offer much in the way of theory that could guide future empirical research. However, other research that had been conducted in the 1970s pointed in the direction of taking into account both individual differences and organizational factors. For example, two laboratory studies by W. Harvey Hegarty and Henry P. Sims found support for the influence of Machiavellianism, rewards for unethical behavior (both increased unethical behavior), and organizational ethics policies (reduced unethical behavior). As noted above, the movement toward an interactionist view also fit with broader trends in organizational behavior. This entry outlines the person-situation interactionist model, describing its essential features. It begins with an overview of cognitive moral development theory, followed by an explanation of how contextual influences and other individual differences are posited to interact with cognitive moral development to influence ethical decisions and behavior.

Fundamentals

An understanding of the model requires a basic understanding of cognitive moral development theory and its proposed direct relationship with ethical decision outcomes. However, because those direct relationships are modest, it is important to consider how other individual differences and features of the contextual environment interact with cognitive moral development to produce ethical or unethical behavior.

Cognitive moral development. Treviño proposed that, in order to understand ethical decision making in organizational context, it would be helpful to begin with Lawrence Kohlberg's theory of cognitive moral development. Beginning in the 1960s, Kohlberg studied boys over time as they developed in their cognitive abilities and their reasoning about ethical issues. His work was later extended to the study of adults. Kohlberg found that people developed through stages that ranged from more self-centered and less autonomous to less self-centered and more autonomous. In his theory, moral

development requires a process called "role-taking" in which the person is able to cognitively put him or herself in another person's shoes. Stages one and two were termed the preconventional level. At Stage 1, individuals are concerned about concrete consequences, obedience to authority figures, and sticking to rules to avoid punishment. At Stage 2, individuals remain self-interested but evolve to consider interactions with others and one-hand-washes-the-other kind of thinking—getting a good deal for oneself. The second level, comprising Stages 3 and 4, was labeled the conventional level. At Stage 3, people look outside to significant others for guidance. They are concerned with living up to expectations of peers and relevant others. At Stage 4, upholding laws and rules becomes important. The third level was labeled *postconventional* or *principled*. At Stage 5, people look more inside themselves for guidance. They also uphold rules, but they do so because the rules serve the greater good and are consistent with values of fairness and rights and with the social contract. Stage 6 was proposed but was found to be only a theoretical stage that applied only to the rare philosopher.

Cognitive moral development and ethical decision making and behavior. Research since the 1980s by Augusto Blasi and James R. Rest and, more recently, a meta-analysis by Jennifer J. Kish-Gephart and colleagues has shown a moderate correlation between cognitive moral development (judgment) and ethical decisions and behavior. Research has also shown that the more principled the individual, the more she or he would resist unethical influence. Because the correlation is only a moderate one, the question becomes, what else influences the relationship between judgment and behavior?

Contextual moderators. Most adults have been found to be at the conventional level, looking outside themselves for guidance in ethical dilemma situations. Therefore, Treviño proposed that these conventional-level individuals would likely be significantly influenced by situational factors, such as organizational reward systems and organizational culture, while those at the principled level would be more likely to do what they have reasoned is the right thing to do regardless of situational factors. Treviño also proposed that cognitive moral development could be advanced by certain types of work that allow the individual to have role-taking experiences that regularly challenge moral thinking. For example, physicians who frequently wrestle with ethical dilemmas are expected to advance in cognitive moral development more than people in more mundane jobs where ethical dilemmas arise less frequently.

Individual difference moderators. Treviño further proposed that individual differences such as locus of control and ego strength would influence the relationship between cognitive moral development and ethical or unethical behavior. For example, ego strength has to do with one's strength of conviction and ability to resist impulses. Therefore, those higher in ego strength are expected to exhibit more consistency between their moral judgment and action than those lower in ego strength. Similarly, locus of control concerns the individual's perception of how much control she or he exerts over events in life. "Internals" see outcomes as the result of personal effort while "externals" see outcomes as resulting from chance or luck. Treviño theorized that internals would therefore be more likely to take responsibility for outcomes and demonstrate more consistency between moral judgment and action than would externals.

Importance

Much research has now been conducted on the factors that influence ethical and unethical behavior in organizations. However, only a small number of studies have tested Treviño's model directly. In 1990, Treviño and Stuart A. Youngblood supported a dual-influences (both individual differences and contextual factors), rather than an interactionist, perspective. The focus was on reward-and-punishment contingencies, and the authors added outcome expectancies as a mediator. The authors found that ethical and unethical decisions were influenced directly by cognitive moral development. Locus of control influenced decision making both directly and indirectly through outcome expectancies, and vicarious reward (recognition that ethical behavior was rewarded in the organization) influenced decisions indirectly through outcome expectancies. Later, in 2002, Jerald Greenberg found support for the interactionist perspective in a study of employee theft. Employees at the lowest (preconventional) level of

cognitive moral development were more likely to steal from their employers if they worked in an environment that did not have an ethics program. Those at the conventional level of cognitive moral development who worked in an environment with an ethics program were less likely to steal. In keeping with Treviño's model, these conventional-level employees were thought to be significantly influenced by the ethics program because of their tendency to look outside themselves to the organizational context for guidance about the right thing to do. Finally, in 2006 Carol Ann Windsor and colleagues also supported the interactionist perspective, using the Treviño and Youngblood simulation in their laboratory study. Subjects made less ethical decisions if they were low in cognitive moral development and also received information that the organization condoned unethical behavior. In that same environment, subjects high in cognitive moral development made more ethical decisions.

A recent meta-analysis of the research on the influences on unethical choice in organizations conducted by Kish-Gephart, David A. Harrison, and Treviño in 2010 found support for the dual influences idea as well. It presented evidence for a direct influence of cognitive moral development and locus of control, as well as other individual differences (Machiavellianism, idealism or relativism). It also found support for a number of situational variables, such as ethical codes that are enforced and ethical climate and culture. The authors called for more research on the interactions among these individual difference and situational variables. Because few studies had tested the interactions proposed in Treviño's model, they could not be assessed in the meta-analysis. Results of the meta-analysis also suggested that future research should attend to the more intuitive/impulsive-affective side of ethical decision making rather than the more deliberative approach represented by cognitive moral development theory and other earlier theories.

Insights from the model can be used by modern managers to understand that the large majority of their employees are looking outside themselves for guidance. Therefore, the management of ethical conduct is essential if ethical behavior in the organization is the goal. Ethical climate, culture, reward systems, and leadership have all been found to have significant influences on employees' ethical behavior and are worthy of managerial attention. It may also be worthwhile to assess employees' level of cognitive moral development and other individual differences such as locus of control because understanding employees' profiles may provide opportunities to target certain employee groups for training or enhanced supervision.

Linda Treviño

See also Decision-Making Styles; Individual Values; Locus of Control; Moral Reasoning Maturity; Organizational Culture Theory; Positive Organizational Scholarship; Reinforcement Theory

Further Readings

Ashkanasy, N. M., Windsor, C. A., & Treviño, L. K. (2006). Bad apples in bad barrels revisited: Cognitive moral development, just world beliefs, rewards, and ethical decision making. *Business Ethics Quarterly, 16*(4), 449–473.

Blasi, A. (1980). Bridging moral cognition and moral action: A critical review of the literature. *Psychological Bulletin, 88,* 1–45.

Greenberg, J. (2002). Who stole the money and when? Individual and situational determinants of employee theft. *Organizational Behavior and Human Decision Processes, 89,* 985–1003.

Hegarty, H. W., & Sims, H. P., Jr. (1978). Some determinants of unethical decision behavior: An experiment. *Journal of Applied Psychology, 63,* 451–457.

Hegarty, H. W., & Sims, H. P., Jr. (1979). Organizational philosophy, policies and objectives related to unethical decision behavior: A laboratory experiment. *Journal of Applied Psychology, 64,* 331–338.

Kish-Gephart, J. J., Harrision, D. A., & Treviño, L. K. (2010). Bad apples, bad cases and bad barrels: Meta-analytic evidence about sources of unethical decisions at work. *Journal of Applied Psychology, 95,* 1–31.

Kohlberg, L. (1969). Stage and sequence: The cognitive developmental approach to socialization. In D. A. Goslin (Ed.), *Handbook of socialization theory* (pp. 347–480). Chicago, IL: Rand McNally.

Rest, J. R. (1986). *Moral development: Advances in research and theory.* New York, NY: Praeger.

Treviño, L. K. (1986). Ethical decision making in organizations: A person-situation interactionist model. *Academy of Management Review, 11,* 601–617.

Treviño, L. K., & Youngblood, S. A. (1990). Bad apples in bad barrels: A causal analysis of ethical decision-making behavior. *Journal of Applied Psychology, 75,* 378–385.

EUROPEAN MODEL OF HUMAN RESOURCE MANAGEMENT

Human resource management (HRM) is contextual. Theories of European HRM focus the subject on stakeholders rather than shareholders and encompass a wide view of the topic. Such theories arise from the unique context of Europe and reflect the conceptual specifics and the internal variety of European HRM. Arguments have been made for the notion of "European HRM" as a conceptually distinct approach. The foundations of a distinctive European approach lie in its approach to "stakeholders" rather than "shareholders." This is reflected in four subsidiary issues: the role of the state, a belief that people have "rights" in and to their jobs, an acceptance that consultation is proper, and a more critical and less "managerialist" agenda going beyond the HRM-organizational performance link. Though none of these elements is unique on its own, the specific combination in Europe leads to conceptual distinction. In this entry, readers will initially explore the fundamentals of European HRM and then each of these four subsidiary topics in turn before identifying the importance of a European approach to HRM for practicing managers.

Fundamentals

Human resource management as a concept developed in the United States. The analysis it provides and the best practices it preaches may not be relevant in regions like Europe. Europe is heterogeneous. For example, the Council of Europe covers 47 nation-states; the European Union (EU) alone has 23 official languages and more than 60 indigenous regional or minority language communities. Centuries-old and often belligerent relationships between European countries created a tradition of tension and rivalry as well as a desire to work together. As noted in the Global Leadership and Organizational Behavior Effectiveness (GLOBE) studies of Robert J. House and colleagues, significant differences exist between cultural clusters—for example, the Nordic, Anglo-Saxon, Roman, and Germanic clusters. There are also important institutional differences in such factors as labor markets, levels of education, legal systems, and trade union membership. The richer countries in Europe have a per capita gross domestic product (GDP) five times the poorer countries. It is no surprise that many of the key studies in varieties of capitalism have been written by scholars from Europe and focused on this region.

Despite all these differences, there is also homogeneity. Factors that are common to European countries and taken together distinguish them from other regions. In particular, the European Union plays a crucial role. Currently, 27 European countries are members of the EU, and Norway and Switzerland also follow the EU's social policy. The EU's four freedoms—the freedom of movement of goods, persons, services, and capital—exemplify this best and have direct implications for HRM. Free movement of persons created new options for labor market mobility and affects HRM especially in areas such as recruitment, career planning, and compensation. The EU also makes deliberate efforts to invest in the human capital available for organizations through programs that support the exchange of people within Europe and create informal networks of understanding and contacts.

Against this backdrop, European does not imply a monolithic context. On the contrary, both commonalities and differences do play a role. Thus, researchers have (a) distinguished HRM in northern Europe from that found in southern Europe; (b) linked differences in HRM to main cultural groupings within Europe; (c) focused on the presence or absence of communitarian infrastructures, finding the Anglo cultures distinct from the rest of Europe; (d) emphasized the importance of the role of the state and differences between countries such as the United Kingdom, Ireland, and the Nordic countries in which the state has a more limited role in industrial relations versus the Roman-Germanic countries, such as France, Spain, Germany, Italy, Belgium, Greece, and the Netherlands, where the opposite is true; (e) used the institutional literature to find differences between the liberal market economies of the United Kingdom and Ireland, the Nordic countries, the collaborative market economies of the central continental European countries (sometimes separating out the flexicurity countries of Denmark and the Netherlands), and the Mediterranean countries.

Unsurprisingly, a more contextual (as opposed to a universalistic "best practice") perspective dominates the academic discussion of HRM in Europe. This focuses on understanding the differences between and within HRM in various contexts and the causes of these differences. Factors such as culture, ownership structures, management decision processes, labor markets, the role of the state, and trade union organization become critical.

Stakeholder Rather Than Shareholder Approach

The emergence of the subject of HRM in the United States in the 1980s was characterized by a stronger emphasis on strategy. The assumption was that the purpose of HRM is to improve the operation of the organization with the ultimate aim of increasing organizational performance, as judged by its impact on the organization's declared corporate strategy or its shareholders.

The European stakeholder perspective challenges this view and acknowledges the greater array of actors within and outside the organization that are relevant to survival as well as for economic success. Groups who have a legitimate stake in the organization include, for example, employees, customers, trade unions, creditors, and nongovernmental organizations (NGOs). The basic argument of the stakeholder approach is that such groups have a collective interest in the organization such as regarding decisions about employment, keeping the environment clean, or acting as a good corporate citizen in the local environment. In some countries, some of these groups have a legal basis for influencing organizational decisions. For example, in the Germanic countries, codetermination through works councils and trade unions is comparatively strong and legally regulated.

The Role of the State

It has been argued that the major difference between HRM in the United States and in Western Europe is the degree to which HRM is influenced and determined by state regulations. Companies have a narrower scope of choice in regard to personnel management than in the United States. Not only does the state have a higher involvement in underlying social security provision and a more directly interventionist role in the economy, but it provides also far more personnel and industrial-relations services and is a more substantial employer in its own right by virtue of a more extensive government-owned sector. For example, most European countries have a substantial share of the 18 to 24 age group in higher education and in addition provide substantial support to employers through state-aided vocational training programs. Equally, in most European countries, much higher proportions of the GDP are spent by the state on labor market programs. This includes training, retraining, job-transition support, job-creation schemes, and programs to help younger people and the long-term unemployed get into the labor market. Substantial proportions of employment (up to 50% in some countries) are in the public sector. The state plays a larger role in HRM partly by being a larger employer than is the case in many other world regions and partly by taking a more controlling and/or supporting role in employment practices. With the state as an employer, a number of basic parameters for HRM change. The time horizon for HRM activities is different, with less pressure for short-term results. In addition, the education and training infrastructure put in place by the state and still mainly state provided in most European countries has a significant impact on organizational HRM. Although human resource development practices vary considerably by country in Europe, in world comparative terms, the provision is extensive and of good quality. State support for posteducation training is also high and gives these countries an advantage in country-level competitiveness.

People's Rights in and to Their Jobs

By and large, the state in Europe accepts and guarantees people's rights in and to their jobs. Legislation is not independent of national values, and it is no surprise therefore to find that the United States, which is characterized by high levels of individualism and comparatively low levels of uncertainty avoidance, has overall comparatively less legislative control over (or interference from, or support for) the employment relationship than is found in most of Europe. There are legislative requirements on pay, on hours of work, on forms of employment contract, rights to trade union representation, requirements to establish and operate consultation or codetermination arrangements—and a plethora of other legal requirements. These are all additional to those few areas such as the legislation on equality or health and safety, which intrude on the employment relationship on both sides of the Atlantic.

The Importance of Consultation and Collective Representation

In Europe, there is frequently a shared understanding that businesses need to be controlled and to treat their employees in a socially responsible way. Consequently, key questions in HRM are about communication and consultation with the workforce. Employee representation, or "voice," may take individual or collective forms. Individually, cultural differences, in particular the influence of hierarchy, will have an impact on the way that managers communicate to their workforce. Organizations across Europe are increasing the amount of communication and consultation in which they involve those employees. Communication with the workforce is higher in the north of Europe than in the south but is everywhere extensive. The collective forms include both union-centred and nonunion mechanisms. In Europe, these tend to be complementary. Legislation in countries such as the Netherlands, Denmark, and, most famously, Germany has for a long time required organizations to have two-tier management boards, with employees having the right to be represented on the more senior supervisory board. In all EU countries, the law requires the establishment of employee-representation committees in all organizations except the smallest. These arrangements give considerable (legally backed) power to the employee representatives.

The legislative status and influence accorded to trade unions is a further core feature of European states. Europe is the continent with the strongest independent trade unions. It is clear that, in general, the European countries are more heavily unionized than most other areas of the world. The unions are in many countries supported by legislation and, at the EU-level unions, management and governments, the "social partners" as they are called, are required to consult with one another.

Importance

European academics have been at the forefront of criticism of the rhetoric of HRM. Studies of HRM in Europe tend to take a more critical view of the topic than is common elsewhere. At the level of the organization (not firm—public sector and not-for-profit organizations are also included), the organization's objectives (and therefore its strategy) are not necessarily assumed to be "good" either for the organization or for society. There are plenty of recent examples where this is clearly not the case. Nor, in this paradigm, is there any assumption that the interests of everyone in the organization will be the same or any expectation that an organization will have a strategy that people within the organization will support. Employees and the unions have a different perspective from the management team. Even within the management team, there may be different interests and views. This leads to challenging the declared corporate strategy and approach to HRM laid down by senior management: asking whether these have deleterious consequences for individuals within the organization, for the long-term health of the organization, and for the community and country within which the organization operates.

In addition, European academic studies are less focused on the policies of a small number of "leading edge" major multinationals and are more likely to study the practices of smaller businesses, public sector organizations, and local workplaces. Here, the objective is less likely to be about achieving the organization's objectives than about understanding the impact of the practices on the various stakeholders involved. Overall, in Europe, HRM is, as a concept, a more contested notion than it is elsewhere.

For practicing managers operating in Europe (and indeed for those elsewhere in the world where there is a stakeholder approach, an enhanced role for the state, and a focus on participation), the European model challenges the received wisdom on best practice HRM purveyed by the consultancies and business schools. In general, this reflects the situation of HRM in the United States, where managers are neither so restricted by nor supported by the state as they are in Europe. However, the messages may be inappropriate outside the United States. In this context, it makes sense for HR managers to have a longer term vision, to spend time on legal compliance, to understand state provision in employment, to work with local communities, and to ensure good working relationships with the trade unions. These are not diversions from strategic HRM but are a proper response to a different set of stakeholders and a different context. In fact, these are the issues that HR managers in Europe do spend a lot of time on— and it is widely believed that they are right to do so.

Chris Brewster

See also Critical Management Studies; Cultural Values; Human Resource Management Strategies; Institutional Theory; Neo-Institutional Theory; Transnational Management

Further Readings

Amable, B. (2003). *The diversity of modern capitalism.* Oxford, England: Oxford University Press.

Bonnafous-Boucher, M., & Pesqueux, Y. (Eds.). (2005). *Stakeholder theory: A European perspective.* Basingstoke, England: Palgrave Macmillan.

Brewster, C. (1995). Towards a "European" model of human resource management. *Journal of International Business Studies, 26*(1), 1–21.

Brewster, C., & Mayrhofer, W. (Eds.). (2012). *A handbook of comparative human resource management.* Cheltenham, England: Edward Elgar.

Brewster, C., Mayrhofer, W., & Morley, M. (2000). The concept of strategic European human resource management. In C. Brewster, W. Mayrhofer, & M. Morley (Eds.), *New challenges for European human resource management* (pp. 3–33). London, England: Macmillan.

Guest, D. E. (1990). Human resource management and the American dream. *Journal of Management Studies, 27*(4), 377–397.

House, R. J., Hanges, P. J., Javidan, M., Dorfman, P. W., & Gupta, V. (Eds.). (2004). *Culture, leadership, and organizations: The GLOBE study of 62 societies.* Thousand Oaks, CA: Sage.

Legge, K. (2005). *Human resource management: Rhetorics and realities.* Basingstoke, England: Palgrave Macmillan.

Sparrow, P., & Hiltrop, J. M. (1994). *European human resource management in transition.* Hempel Hempstead, England: Prentice Hall.

EVIDENCE-BASED MANAGEMENT

Evidence-based management (EBMgt) is the use of the best available evidence to improve the quality of managerial decision making. The concept was coined around 2005 and reflects a broader trend in professions including medicine, education, public administration, and so on for evidence-based practice, that is, the increased and more effective use of scientific findings in practice-related decisions. EBMgt builds on the body of management and social science research to make more systematic decisions that incorporate the best available organizational and scientific evidence. The following sections describe EBMgt's four main components, its importance, and implications for management practice; recommended readings are identified at the end for interested readers.

Fundamentals

EBMgt incorporates well-established scientific findings regarding critical thinking, human judgment, decision making, and learning to aid managers in acquiring quality information and putting it to use. The set of practices that make up EBMgt achieve better quality results in organizations by improving the practitioner's knowledge, judgment, and competencies. It comprises four fundamental activities that can be applied in the everyday exercise of management judgment and decision making: (a) use of the best available scientific findings; (b) gathering of and attending to organizational facts, indicators, and metrics in a systematic fashion to increase their reliability and usefulness; (c) ongoing practice of mindful, reflective judgment and use of decision aids to reduce bias and improve decision quality; and (d) consideration of ethical issues including the short-term and long-term impact of decisions on stakeholders.

EBMgt incorporates scientific findings in two ways. It involves use of scientific evidence when relevant to the specific management decision at hand. It makes use of standard procedures based on what the evidence suggests works. The kinds of scientific knowledge that might be used in making an evidence-based decision are broad ranging, from all areas of management research and beyond, depending on relevance to the managerial decision.

EBMgt practice is not a cookbook or a formula. It is a variety of science-informed approaches that can be adapted to make better quality decisions in the service of organizations, their members, stakeholders, and the public. Evidence is not answers. It is input to the information and processes that help practitioners to make better judgments and decisions. Thoughtful practitioners adapt EBMgt's four facets as needed.

Use of Scientific Knowledge

Scientific knowledge is the bedrock of all evidence-based approaches to practice, from medicine to criminology to education. EBMgt is built on the scientific premise that there is an underlying degree of order in which a common set of basic physical, biological, social, and psychological processes occur. Scientific knowledge is distinct from other forms of knowledge because it is based on controlled observations, large samples sizes (N), validated measures, statistical controls, and systematically tested and accumulated understandings of how the world works (i.e., theory). Scientists are generally subject to the same biases and value judgments of other people. The important difference is that the scientific method provides checks and balances to reduce these biases. The advantage science has over individual experience is that scientific research is essentially a project involving many thousands of people using systematic methods to understand the world. Personal experience is plagued by the problem of small numbers: It reflects an individual's interpretation of events in his or her life. With its scale and scope, science can counter the human tendency to overinterpret small bits of information and underestimate randomness. EBMgt emphasizes the importance of peer-reviewed evidence and the value of systematic reviews of research to address managerial questions.

Use of Business or Organizational Evidence

Making fact-based decisions in organizations is not easy. The basic metrics and indicators used in business decisions start out as raw data generated by the efforts of organization members or people outside the organization. Raw data can omit important information (e.g., counts of errors may not tell whether they were significant). Data are also contaminated in that information may be biased (e.g., underestimates of revenues can make forecasts unreliable). Business facts also need to be interpreted (for example, how much turnover is too much? Some employees might leave positions for "good reasons" such as a lack of fit or because they are reallocated to where they may make stronger contributions); judgments are affected by practitioner roles and background. Facts are also political; the business information on which managers rely can be highly politicized. EBMgt emphasizes the importance of systematic gathering of business evidence, giving priority to its reliability and validity.

Reflective Judgment and Decision Aids

Making decisions based on facts requires a set of supporting practices that increase the reliability and usefulness of available data. EBMgt practices that promote effective decision making include reflective managerial decisions incorporating feedback processes and decision aids, such as logic models, to promote mindful assessment of the circumstances of the decision and available information. A logic model spells out the process by which an organizational intervention, program, or strategy is expected to produce certain outcomes. It is one form of decision aid; others include checklists, process maps, and other tools that prompt recall, reflection, and information gathering. Another process aid is decision tracking, obtaining systematic feedback on the outcomes of certain organizational decisions, which can improve both learning and the decision process.

Making Ethical Decisions With Consideration of Stakeholders

Making ethical managerial decisions is subject to an array of human biases as well as role demands, situational pressures, and conflicting interests. Stakeholder considerations are an inherent feature of systematic decision models and help managers appreciate how their organization fits into its larger environment and how its standard operating procedures affect employees, investors, customers, suppliers, and the public generally. Heuristics and frameworks, like the decision aids described above, can aid making ethical decisions too.

Importance

Evidence of the validity of EBMgt rests largely on the validity associated with its component practices. Validity for the use of specific kinds of scientific evidence in managerial decisions is provided by employment selection decisions based on scientifically established practices, such as structured interviews, work samples directly tied to the content of the job, and certain forms of standardized tests. Similar bodies of evidence are related to managerial decisions associated with performance assessment, employee training and development, negotiation and conflict management, and organizational change. Increasingly, such bodies of evidence are the subject of summary texts (e.g., handbooks) and of systematic reviews to assess the findings the evidence supports.

At the same time, consideration of the depth, consistency, and quality of evidence in managerial research has identified that managerial research domains vary in their current capacity to provide

clear evidence of what works to practice. Both organizational behavior and human resources are subject matter areas with a long history of cumulative research. Entrepreneurship demonstrates several lines of highly cumulative research. In contrast, the study of organizational theory and strategy to date has yielded fewer cumulative research domains and less convergent evidence, with possible exceptions in some topic areas.

The attention that EBMgt brings to the practical implications of managerial research also identifies a shortfall in current management research, the dearth of practice-oriented research. Practice-oriented research examines how practitioners currently practice. It provides information regarding conditions and support practices that make scientific knowledge more useful. At present, EBMgt is limited largely to early adopters and management innovators and is not mainstream organizational practice. Practice-oriented research, by calling attention to problems practicing managers confront, allows specific solutions to be identified as common practice problems, a way of making it more likely that managers will apply EBMgt practices. Practice-oriented research in other areas such as medicine and nursing has eased the adoption of evidence-based practice by identifying required supports while reducing factors that work against their adoption or effective implementation. In medicine, this kind of research has been termed "translation science."

EBMgt is a very different way of thinking and practicing management. The lay view is that management is learned from hands-on experience. The idea that academic research can inform business decisions doesn't fit this tradition. EBMgt introduces new dimensions to what it means to be a manager. Making one's management practice more evidence based can be threatening, feeling both like pressure and loss of control. EBMgt requires engaging in a learning process that can move through the stages of novice to intermediate to expert. It takes time, effort, and good support to become an evidence-based professional manager.

Not every manager is motivated to use evidence. Non-evidence-based practices and personal intuition tend to be the norm for decisions regarding managing people, structuring work, and developing business strategy—and people tend to be comfortable with the status quo. EBMgt appeals to practitioners willing to invest time and effort to expand their knowledge, expertise, and personal depth, drawn to it because of the benefits it offers and intrigued by the personal learning and discipline it involves. It engages managers in a deliberate, life-long effort to develop their professional knowledge, judgment, and impact on organizations.

EBMgt also poses new demands on management educators, to help practitioners develop their ability to think critically, acquire relevant scientific knowledge, and apply evidence-informed methods for better quality decision making. It calls for scholars to pay more attention to the cumulative nature of research and to make their findings more accessible and easier for practitioners to use.

Denise M. Rousseau and
Miguel R. Olivas-Luján

See also Academic-Practitioner Collaboration and Knowledge Sharing; Bounded Rationality and Satisficing (Behavioral Decision-Making Model); Critical Management Studies; Decision Support Systems; Ethical Decision Making, Interactionist Model of; Garbage Can Model of Decision Making; Groupthink; Intuitive Decision Making; Managerial Decision Biases; Programmability of Decision Making; "Unstructured" Decision Making

Further Readings

Donaldson, L. (2010). *The meta-analytic organization: Introducing statistico-organizational theory.* Armonk, NY: M. E. Sharpe.

Locke, E. A. (2009). *The handbook of organizational behavior: Evidence-based principles* (2nd ed.). New York, NY: Blackwell.

Olivas-Luján, M. R., & Rousseau, D. M. (2010, May). Can the evidence-based management movement help e-HRM bridge the research-practice gap? *Proceedings of the Third European Academic Workshop on Electronic HRM, Vol. 570,* pp. 3–33, Bamberg, Germany. Retrieved September 15, 2011, from http://sunsite .informatik.rwth-aachen.de/Publications/CEUR-WS/ Vol-570/paper002.pdf

Pfeffer, J., & Sutton, R. I. (2006). Evidence-based management. *Harvard Business Review, 84,* 62–74.

Rousseau, D. M. (2012). *Oxford handbook of evidence-based management.* New York, NY: Oxford University Press.

Rousseau, D. M., Manning, J., & Denyer, D. (2008). Evidence in management and organizational science: Assembling the field's full weight of scientific knowledge through reflective reviews. *Annals of the Academy of Management, 2,* 475–515.

Sackett, D. L., Richardson, W. S., Rosenburg, W., & Haynes, R. B. (1997). *Evidence-based medicine: How to practice and teach EBM.* London, England: Churchill Livingstone.

EXCELLENCE CHARACTERISTICS

Although the term *excellence* has been defined and used in various contexts and fields during the long history of humankind, the term in relation to management and organizational performance was first introduced and popularized by Peters and Waterman in their best-selling 1982 book *In Search of Excellence—Lessons from America's Best-Run Companies.* Since then, the term became increasingly more popular, and today there are many management frameworks, models, and programs which bear the term excellence in various ways, for example, the European EFQM excellence model and, in the United States, the Malcolm Baldrige Performance Excellence Program. This entry is a review of some identified managerial characteristics of excellence from various management approaches. First, some original ideas as well as definitions are presented, followed by the introduction of some central frameworks, core values, and concepts. The entry ends with a short discussion of the importance of excellence.

Fundamentals

As there are various ways to adopt the term excellence in managerial contexts, there are also many definitions. However, the term excellence is generally associated with meanings of "extraordinarily good" or "performing outstandingly." When something is excellent, then, we can assume that it is in the state of quality, condition of excelling, or in the state of superiority. In this entry, excellence will be delimited to managerial performance. Even here, the definitions vary from context to context. Excellence can be defined broadly as related to an organization or, more narrowly, to aspects of an organization's performance, such as leadership. An example of a definition related to an organization is seen in the EFQM excellence model: Excellent Organizations achieve and sustain superior levels of performance that meet or exceed the expectations of all their stakeholders.

In ancient Greek, the word *arete* is used to denote excellence, and in its earliest usage, the concept included the meaning of living up to one's full potential. Similar meanings about excellence can be found in writings by Confucius (551–479 BCE). Self-control and self-development via lifelong training and education were not only considered to be the methods to realize one's full potential but also the way to achieve harmony in society in general. For this reason, the leader's role was especially emphasized by Confucius. His famous notion, stated in the *Analects,* of *junji,* which can be translated as "superior or excellent man" or "leader" demonstrates this: "The junji (superior/excellent man or leader) makes people's merits grow and demerits to decrease, while the inferior man does the opposite."

From this standpoint, excellence includes doing common, everyday things and is not necessarily determined by comparing one's score or a performance to someone else's. The *pursuit of excellence* comes from doing our best with a view of growing and improving in terms of realizing one's potential. Excellence must then be related to our efforts on how we continuously develop and utilize or mobilize our capabilities throughout our lifetime.

Models/Frameworks of Excellence

Models of excellence can be subdivided into simple models and complex models.

In 1985, Tom Peters and Nancy Austin published a second book on excellence, called *A Passion for Excellence.* The findings from the first book were now simplified into a model with the four criteria, or critical success factors of (1) people who practice excellence, (2) care of customers, (3) constant innovation, and (4) leadership that binds together the first three factors by using "management by wandering around" (MBWA) at all levels of the organizations.

Other simplified models have since been suggested, for example, Dahlgaard-Park and Dahlgaard's 4p excellence model in 1999 and Jeffrey K. Liker's 4p model of the Toyota Production System, published in 2004 (*The Toyota Way),* which was regarded as the leading excellence model of the car manufacturing industry because Toyota, at least until the crisis in 2010 and 2011 related to huge recalls, was perceived as synonymous with excellence.

- Dahlgaard-Park & Dahlgaard's 4p excellence model has the following five criteria: leadership, people, partnership, processes, and products, where it is a leadership responsibility to attain excellence by building excellence into the 4p criteria.
- Liker's 4p model also has four excellence criteria, as follows: philosophy, process, people/partners, and problem solving.

With the worldwide launch of quality award models, from 1988 onward, the concept of excellence became gradually more and more complex and important because the leading quality award models changed their names and/or changed their focus in the late 1990s to have direct relations with well-accepted business excellence criteria. Examples follow:

- The EFQM (European) Quality Award model, launched in 1992, underwent a change in name in 1997 to the EFQM business excellence model, which after the turn of the 21st century became the EFQM excellence model to signal that the new model not only included business excellence aspects but also societal excellence aspects. The European excellence model included from the beginning four results criteria, and the model had from the beginning five enabler criteria and four results criteria, which in the recent revision from 2010 were named as follows: leadership, people, strategy, partnerships and resources, processes, products and services, people results, customer results, society results, key results.
- The U.S. quality award model, called the Malcolm Baldrige National Quality Award, which was launched in 1987, changed the program's name to the Baldrige Performance Excellence Program to reflect the evolution of the field of quality from a focus on product, service, and the customer to a broader, strategic focus on overall organizational quality called *performance excellence.* The original version of the Baldrige model did not include business results because it was believed that achieving excellent results was automatically achieved if the organization could show excellence in the model's six enabler criteria: leadership, strategic planning, customer and market focus, human resource focus, process management and

measurement, and analysis and knowledge management. Today, the business results criterion has been included as the seventh criterion of the model. The Baldrige model emphasizes that the excellence criteria are both context and time dependent, because they have developed three sector-specific versions of the criteria. They are *general, education,* and *health care* criteria, which are revised every 2 years. The award program promotes awareness of performance excellence as an increasingly important element in competitiveness. To receive a Baldrige Award, an organization must have a role-model organizational management system that ensures continuous improvement in delivering products and/or services, demonstrates efficient and effective operations, and provides a way of engaging and responding to customers and other stakeholders. The award is not given for specific products or services.

Core Values and Concepts

The critical success factors for attaining excellence have different names and contents in the various excellence models. For example, in the European model, they are called the *fundamental concepts of excellence,* and in the U.S. model, they are called *core values and concepts.*

The European model has identified the following eight fundamental concepts of excellence: achieving balanced results, adding value for customers, leading with vision, inspiration and integrity, managing by processes, succeeding through people, nurturing creativity and innovation, building partnerships, and building responsibility for a sustainable future.

The U.S. model, by contrast, includes the following 11 core values and concepts: visionary leadership, customer-driven excellence, organizational and personal learning, valuing workforce members and partners, agility, focus on the future, managing for innovation, managing by fact, societal responsibility, focus on results and creating value, and systems perspective.

When assessed as qualified for getting an excellence award or other excellence recognitions, companies' applications are checked for integrating core values and concepts into the excellence model in use. For example, in the European model there is a guideline to follow when checking the eight fundamental concepts with the model's five enabler and four results criteria.

At a general level, Dahlgaard-Park and Dahlgaard recently introduced the code of excellence that consists of five phrases: Excellence can be achieved if people care more than what others think is wise, risk more than what others think is safe, dream more than what others think is practical, and expect more than what others think is possible.

Importance

It follows from these frameworks, models, and programs and the organizations and authors behind them that to attain extraordinary performance organizations should strive to understand, adapt, and implement the criteria or principles of the chosen excellence model.

Peters and Waterman did not provide a definition of excellence, but after having studied and analyzed 62 American firms with outstanding performance, they identified eight characteristics of excellent companies. Several other lists of best excellence practices have since been presented. Such lists typically describe the key enabler characteristics, which differentiate organizations with excellent results from organizations with mediocre or poor results. The British Quality Foundation (BQF) published such a list in a report about business excellence in 1998, and the differentiating characteristics or criteria were as follows: (a) management commitment to the business excellence "journey"; (b) effective strategic planning; (c) an emphasis on people issues through empowerment and training; (d) unprecedented levels of employee participation through effective communication of and involvement in the organization's goals, mission, and objectives; (e) process understanding, management, measurement, and improvement; (f) deliberately avoiding jargon to ensure a seamless integration of business excellence practices; (g) nurturing a culture that focuses implicitly and explicitly on anticipating and serving customers' needs; (h) demonstrating concern for better environmental management; and (i) making the internal spread of best practices contagious.

Lists such as the BQF list or Peters and Waterman's list of eight characteristics concerning *organizational excellence* can be found in several areas of the literature. Such lists may be valuable for organizations that decide to embark on "the journey to excellence," but they may also be misleading. Managers may misunderstand that the list of characteristics is exhaustive, and they may not understand the interrelationships and logical linkages between them, as the lists mix various elements and may not provide a proper guiding framework. Most important is that lists of best practices are always based on the contexts in which the analyzed companies did their business. Any specific company is unique, and hence, the context will vary from company to company. Adaption is for that reason necessary. Simply copying the best practices of other companies may be hazardous.

Su Mi Dahlgaard-Park

See also High-Performing Work Systems; High-Performing Teams; Learning Organization; Organizational and Managerial Wisdom; Organizational Learning; Seven-S Framework; Total Quality Management; Transformational Theory of Leadership; Trust

Further Readings

Dahlgaard-Park, S. M., & Dahlgaard, J. J. (2007). Excellence—25 years evolution. *Journal of Management History, 13*(4), 371–393.

Dahlgaard-Park, S. M. (2009). Decoding the code of excellence—For achieving sustainable excellence. *International Journal of Quality and Service Sciences, 1*(1), 5–28.

Kanter, R. M. (2008). Transforming giants. *Harvard Business Review, 86*, 43–52.

Liker, K. J. (2004). *The Toyota way.* London, England: McGraw-Hill.

Pascale, P.-T., & Athos, A. J. (1981). *The art of Japanese management.* London, England: Simon and Schuster.

Peters, T., & Austin, N. (1985). *A passion for excellence— The leadership difference.* New York, NY: HarperCollins.

Peters, T., & Waterman, R. (1982). *In search of excellence—Lessons from America's best-run companies.* New York, NY: HarperCollins.

Womack, J. P., & Jones, D. T. (1996). *Lean thinking.* New York, NY: Touchstone Books.

EXPECTANCY THEORY

Aligning individual goals with organizational objectives is critical to effective management. Expectancy theory describes the components of successful alignment. In the remainder of this entry, I will describe the theory and its impact on the fields of psychology and management. With the benefit of nearly 50 years of hindsight, I now address the changes that I would make, the research that has led me to these changes, and the ways in which expectancy theory can benefit the practice of management.

Fundamentals

Expectancy theory rests on the assumption that much behavior is motivated and goal directed. Goals induce forces on people to engage in courses of action which they believe will result in their attainment. This was stated formally in two propositions. The first proposition asserted that the force on a person to perform an activity or set of activities is a function of the attractiveness or valence of a goal multiplied by the expectancy that the activity will result in the attainment of that goal. Since there may be multiple anticipated outcomes, some positive and some negative, the valence of each is multiplied by its expectancy and summed over outcomes as shown in the following equation.

$$F_i = f_i\{\textstyle\sum_{j=1}^{n}(E_{ij}V_j)\}$$

Where: F_i = the force to perform act i

E_{ij} = the strength of the expectancy that act i will be followed by outcome j

V_j = the valence of outcome j

This proposition is useful in predicting behavior, such as deciding how much effort and energy to invest in carrying out work. Applied to work motivation, this proposition asserts that the amount of effort that a person puts into the achievement of a performance goal is dependent on two necessary conditions—that the goal is attractive and that the person believes that it can be achieved through effort.

The second proposition asserts that outcomes acquire valence to the degree to which they are believed to be instrumental to the achievement of one's goals. In effect, perceived a "stepping stone" to the achievement of goals become goals, the means become ends. As before, multiple consequences believed to be associated with the stepping stone require summation over outcomes each multiplied by its instrumentality.

$$v_j = f_i\{\textstyle\sum_{1}^{j}(V_k I_{jk})\}$$

Where: V_j = the valence of outcome j

I_{jk} = the perceived instrumentality of outcome j for the attainment of outcome k

V_k = the valence of outcome k

Note that expectancy theory said nothing about the motives or needs that drive human behavior. It has frequently been termed a process theory rather than a content theory, such as those of Abraham Maslow or Clayton Alderfer. The two types of theories potentially complement one another. Content theories address the basic human motives underlying human conduct, while the process theories are concerned with the way in which these motives, and goals based on them, influence people's actions.

Expectancy theory was first published in my 1964 book called *Work and Motivation*. Here, I applied the theory to three aspects of the relationship between people and the work they do: (a) peoples' choices among work, both occupations and jobs, (b) their satisfaction with the work they do, and (c) their effectiveness in performing their work. The theory provided a reasonable explanation for organizing the relevant research on each of these three areas of inquiry. It also identified some gaps in the existing literature and provided an explanation for the frequent finding that measures of job satisfaction and of job performance tend to be uncorrelated.

In applying expectancy theory to work performance, a decision had to be made about the specific behaviors that would be indicative of highly motivated work behaviors. I choose the term *effort*. I did not mean to equate work with "heavy lifting" or to imply that people make conscious decisions about how much effort they would expend in doing their job on a given day or month. However, they do make choices about how much time they spent in doing their jobs, how adequately they prepare in advance for their work, and how persistent they are in overcoming obstacles and distractions. Aggregated over time, such choices influence one's effectiveness. The underlying process is motivation and is represented in the strength of the motivational forces influencing people to use their mental and physical energy in ways that benefit their work performance.

Possibly, the theory's greatest heuristic value stemmed from its prediction that desires have no motivating value unless there is some expectation that their achievement is at least partially under one's control. Valence does not create forces unless expectancy is greater than zero. Motivating people is not just a matter of increasing the importance to them of doing well but also of enhancing their belief in their own capability of doing so. Expectancy is related to what Albert Bandura has termed *self-efficacy*. Motivating people to achieve a performance goal involves both making the goal attractive and strengthening their belief that it is attainable. Consider, for example, the rallying cry of Barack Obama's campaign for the presidency—"Yes, we can!"

Expectancy theory seems to have met a need in industrial psychology. *Work and Motivation* was selected as a Citation Classic by the Committee on Scientific Information and remains in press almost half a century after its initial publication. Its main features have been incorporated into the theorizing of others, and it can be found in most textbooks dealing with the intersection of psychology and management. It has also stimulated considerable research, most of which sought to test its predictions about work performance.

Evolution

Early applications of psychology to improve the effectiveness of organizations dealt largely with the measurement of aptitudes and abilities and their use in selection and placement. It was not until the Hawthorne experiments in the 1930s and the experiments of Kurt Lewin and his colleagues a decade later in the Harwood Manufacturing Company that psychologists began to turn their attention to the role of motivation in work performance. Effectiveness required not only the requisite skills to do the job but also the motivation to carry it out.

As a graduate student in psychology in the mid-1950s, I was caught up in the excitement of this new emphasis on work motivation. It struck me as not only of practical importance but also as of relevance to the discipline of psychology. I was significantly influenced by the writings of Kurt Lewin, who had died almost a decade earlier. His concepts of *force*, *valence*, and *psychological distance* seemed potentially applicable to motivation and work. His admonition that "there is nothing as practical as a good theory" supported my belief that theory can be useful in guiding both research and practice.

I did depart from Lewin on a couple of issues. I avoided his concept of psychological distance, instead substituting the term expectancy, used by Edward Tolman, R. Duncan Luce, Howard Raiffa, and John Atkinson, all notable theorists of the time. A second departure lay in my use of the term instrumentality, which serves to connect goals and subgoals.

Toward a New Expectancy Theory

Despite the success of expectancy theory, there are several things that I wish I had done differently. One involves the use of formal mathematics in the expression of the "two propositions." I suspect that I am guilty of what my colleague, Warren Bennis, has called "physics envy." Without the formalization, I might have better conveyed my conviction that expectancy theory, like Lewin's field theory, should be used primarily for its heuristic value. It provided a language for formulating interesting questions and guiding both practice and research design. I lament the fact that my equations encouraged many investigations seeking to "test" expectancy theory by multiplying questionnaire measures without regard to the ratio-scale properties required by the theory.

I also wish that I had more clearly differentiated between two types of performance goals. In one of the propositions, the valence of a performance goal is seen as dependent on its instrumentality for other outcomes. I had in mind two classes of other outcomes—those that are intrinsic to the task and those which involve the actions of others. Thus, a worker may work exceptionally hard on a task because he or she believed that performance would lead to a promotion and/or because it would lead to feeling good about oneself. The former is frequently referred to as extrinsic motivation since the anticipated rewards and sanctions are the result of actions by external agents. In the second case, performance is instrumental to rewards which are intangible and attributable to processes within the human brain. The distinction is similar to one made by Lewin who contrasted "own forces" with "induced forces."

In the original formulation of expectancy theory, I treated those two sources of motivation as functionally equivalent and interchangeable. The source of the motivation, intrinsic or extrinsic, was irrelevant to work performance. Since the publication of *Work and Motivation,* several streams of research have pointed to the criticality of separating intrinsic and extrinsic motivation.

The first of these pertains to the unstable relationship between intrinsic and extrinsic motivation. Research in the laboratory by Edward L. Deci and by others shows that basing compensation on performance of a task may increase performance in the short run but, over time, decreases intrinsic motivation. Deci has reviewed more than a hundred studies and has concluded that tangible rewards, such as compensation, tend to have a substantially negative effect on the strength of a person's willingness to work hard when the rewards are no longer present.

Note that it is not the receipt of the money that does the damage. The cause lies in its contingent nature; in other words, the fact that it is linked to the level of performance. Monetary compensation changes the meaning of the task from something which is done for personal gratification to something which is done for financial gain. While compensating people for something they enjoy may increase performance, it does so at the expense of the desire to do it "for its own sake."

It should be emphasized that intrinsic motivation is not solely the result of interesting work. It may also reflect the role that work plays in one's self concept and identity. Deci uses the term autonomous motivation, rather than intrinsic motivation, to emphasize this broader conception. For example, extrinsic rewards and punishments may become internalized over time and serve to motivate performance independently of the reward contingencies in the immediate environment. Thus, one may work diligently at one's job because it is the "right" thing to do or because performance influences one's "self-worth."

A second reason for distinguishing these two motivational sources is the evidence that each is best suited to different kinds of tasks. Teresa Amabile has studied creativity in a wide array of groups, ranging from artists and inventors to school children. She has concluded that financial rewards are more suited to repetitive, well-scripted, algorithmic tasks but are likely to reduce performance on tasks regarding creativity and heuristic processing.

In my most recent writings, I have modified the terminology that I had used in writing about expectancy theory. I now use the term *valence* to refer to intrinsic motivation and the term *instrumentality* to refer to extrinsic motivation. In the short run, the two combine in what seems to be an additive fashion, but over time, extrinsic motivation tends to erode its intrinsic counterpart. For the sake of simplicity, I have chosen to ignore this dynamic element in the following equation:

$$\text{Force} = (\text{Valence} + \text{Instrumentality}) \times \text{Expectancy}$$

Importance

From this equation, one can identify three paths to increasing motivation to perform a task or job effectively: (a) basing rewards or sanctions on level of performance (instrumentality), (b) designing the work roles such that effective performance is intrinsically satisfying (valence), and (c) increasing the person's belief that he or she is capable of performing effectively (expectancy). Interventions designed to strengthen expectancy will increase performance to the extent to which either or both valence or instrumentality is positive.

From a practical standpoint, one needs to understand the nature of these three interventions. Expectancy can be enhanced in several ways, including training, coaching, and modeling of effective behaviors. Instrumentality is a straightforward application of the original formulation of expectancy theory—identifying valued rewards and making them conditional on performance. But what about valence? Decomposing this construct constitutes the main challenge confronting a revised expectancy theory.

What is there about people, their work, and the interaction between the two that results in passion and dedication toward one's work? Further, what can be done to create intrinsic motivation? Existing research suggests several promising directions.

Goal setting. The power of goal setting at work was first demonstrated by Alex Bavelas, one of Kurt Lewin's colleagues. He met with groups of sewing machine operators in the management conference room in the Harwood Manufacturing Company. He asked each group if they would like to set a goal for higher production. In most cases, the group agreed, and they proceeded to make a group decision concerning the level of production that they hoped to reach and the length of time in which they would try to reach it. Groups that set goals increased production by an average of 18%.

Goal setting seems to offer much promise for performance management. An extensive study of performance appraisals at General Electric (GE) found that the single most important determinant of performance improvement following an appraisal interview was the setting of performance goals in the interview. An extensive program of research on the practical implications of goal setting is summarized by Locke and Latham.

Job design. Based on a study of accountants and engineers, Herzberg concluded that the content of a job played an exclusive role in motivating people to work. While his findings have been criticized on methodological grounds, subsequent research has supported his view that the way in which jobs are designed plays an important, although not exclusive, role in worker motivation.

J. Richard Hackman and Greg R. Oldham have identified five dimensions of jobs which are associated with their "motivating potential." They are skill variety, task identity, task significance, autonomy, and feedback. They developed a measure called the Job Diagnostic Survey, which has been used to compare jobs in each of the five dimensions. It also serves to identify areas in which jobs might be restructured to increase employee motivation.

The five dimensions are conceptually related to Abraham Maslow's self-esteem and self-actualization needs. These needs, which others have termed "growth needs," sit at the top of Maslow's needs hierarchy and are aroused only when biological and social needs have been satisfied. It follows that economic prosperity and stability of social institutions should make it more important to design jobs which utilize and develop one's skills and abilities.

Connecting work to values. It has frequently been observed that people can be motivated to work not only by the tangible benefits to themselves but also by the opportunity to benefit others, the larger society, or the planet. This is manifest in the tireless, self-sacrificing work of those professionals who leave their careers to work in underdeveloped countries or in parts of the world struck by natural disaster. Charles Handy has argued for making these "legacy issues" an additional level on Maslow's hierarchy of needs, sitting above self-actualization. Most researchers refer to them as values, that is, as, end states which acquire positive valence through their meaning in the larger culture.

James McGregor Burns has coined the term *transformational leadership* to refer to the process by which political leaders have changed institutions by appealing to values which are widely shared among the population. In recent years, the concept has been adapted by the private sector. Leaders are encouraged to motivate their organizations by appealing to a vision of the future which is exciting, promising, and honorable.

Clearly, the belief that one is part of an organization that is adding social value contributes to one's feeling of self-esteem and increases the degree to which work is experienced as meaningful. It is probably less powerful as a motivating force than seeing that one's personal effort has social value. Amy Wrzesniewski and J. E. Dutton have shown that this source of intrinsic motivation is dependent not only on the physical attributes of the job but also on the way in which it is "crafted" by the person. Job crafting has two components. One involves the way in which the employee frames the work that has been assigned. The classic example is that of the two bricklayers, one of whom sees the task as laying bricks, while the other views the task as building a great cathedral.

The second component of job crafting involves customizing one's work to reflect one's unique skills and personality. They have studied these two components of job crafting in many different jobs. For example, they observed a member of a hospital cleaning crew who "framed" his job as helping doctors and nurses care for the sick by providing a germ-free environment. In addition, he took on additional tasks which were not in the job description but which were consistent with both his sense of "self" and his "mission."

In the complex world in which we now live, people are frequently insulated from the results of their labor. Teachers seldom contact their students after graduation, and workers in a manufacturing plant rarely have contact with users of the products which they manufacture. Grant has shown experimentally that work performance can be increased by strengthening the connection between employees and the beneficiaries of their work. In an imaginative set of experiments, he and others have shown large productivity increases by enabling an empathetic relationship with those who are affected by one's labors. For example, people working in a call center seeking to raise scholarship money for worthy students increased their performance after brief contact with a prior scholarship recipient. Similarly, when radiologists were shown a photograph of the person whose imaging scan they were evaluating, they reported more empathy for their patients and did a more effective job of diagnosing their medical problems. These findings echo the original rationale for transformational leadership. When people can see their work or that of their organization as contributing to things they value, whether to specific persons or to societal benefit, the work acquires meaning and elicits more sustained effort. Whether the source of this sense of connection lies in the inspirational role of the leader or in the design of the work itself, the effects on the intrinsic motivation of employees and on the performance of their organizations can be considerable.

A century ago, the scientific management of Frederick Taylor and Frank and Lillian Gilbreth did much to dehumanize work and to destroy intrinsic motivation. To date, researchers studying ways of making jobs more intrinsically motivating have not developed technologies comparable to Taylor's time and motivation study. But there are promising beginnings. One of the most promising of these is a job-crafting exercise developed by Wrzesniewski and her colleagues. It is aimed at helping workers to reorganize, restructure, and reframe their jobs, making them more engaging and fulfilling. It has proven helpful to workers in a wide variety of occupations in shaping how they conduct their jobs and how they think about themselves at work. A large-scale study using this exercise is now underway in a global technology company.

Groups and teams. Finally, we turn to what may be the most powerful source of intrinsic motivation— the small, cohesive work team. If the effort and energy that one puts into productive work can be increased by awareness of interdependencies with external clients and beneficiaries, it is likely that similar forces may emanate from relationships with coworkers.

Tightly knit, highly cohesive groups represent a two-edged sword. They can motivate people to strive for performance or to restrict output. The direction of the motivational force depends on the norms of the group. In the Hawthorne experiments, group-generated forces served to reduce performance in the bank wiring room and to increase it in the relay assembly room.

Over 50 years ago, Rensis Likert wrote an influential book outlining a motivational theory of management. In Likert's view, organizations should comprise not a set of individuals but rather a set of groups. Managers would serve as a linking pin between groups at two organization levels. Likert's theory also required those groups to have high-performance norms. But how were these norms to be created? To answer this question, Likert turned to the work of Kurt Lewin on the motivational effects of democratic leadership style. Through participation in decision making, the goals of workers would become aligned with the goals of their organization.

While Likert never used the term *team* in his writings, his ideas were a harbinger of things to come. Within the last two decades, there has been a widespread movement toward the adoption of teams as the basic building blocks of organizations. Popularized by the success of the Japanese "quality circles," high-performance work teams and self-managed work teams are becoming ubiquitous in organizations in both the public and private sectors. People identify with their teams and work hard to ensure its success. This phenomenon is easily observed on the children's athletic field, where one's worst nightmare is to "let one's teammates down." Similarly, those who have studied troops in battle have reported that great acts of bravery and dedication are typically caused by a desire to help and protect one's "buddies."

Final Reflection

Some may say that I have opened up a can of worms in attempting to incorporate intrinsic motivation as a separate driving force in the motivation to work. Certainly, the issues are complex. People's enjoyment of the work they do is not as simple and straightforward as the mathematical equations in the earlier version of expectancy theory. But the phenomena surrounding intrinsic motivation are increasingly important to the practice of management in a world in which "knowledge work" is becoming paramount. In the last two decades, we have made considerable progress not only in understanding the process but also in identifying specific interventions that managers can make in tapping into this wellspring of energy. In this entry, I have described four promising avenues for increasing intrinsic motivation—goal setting, job design, connecting work to values, and creating work teams dedicated to high performance. They may not have identical effects on all people in all cultures, but all are a reasonable place to begin.

Victor H. Vroom

See also Empowerment; Goal-Setting Theory; High-Performing Teams; Participative Model of Decision Making; Theory X and Theory Y; Transformational Theory of Leadership

Further Readings

Lewin, K. (1938). *The conceptual representation and measurement of psychological forces: Contributions to psychological theory,* Vol. 1, No. 4. Dunham, NC: Duke University Press.
Locke, E. A., & Latham, G. P. (1984). *Goal setting: A motivational technique that works.* Englewood Cliffs, NJ: Prentice Hall.
McGregor, D. (1960). *The human side of enterprise.* New York, NY: McGraw Hill.
Vroom, V. H. (1964). *Work and Motivation.* New York, NY: Wiley.
Vroom, V. H. (2005). On the origins of expectancy theory. In K. G. Smith & M. A. Hitt (Eds.), *Great minds in management* (pp. 239–258). New York, NY: Oxford University Press.

EXPERIENTIAL LEARNING THEORY AND LEARNING STYLES

Management has used experiential learning theory (ELT) to describe the management process as a process of learning by managers, teams, and organizations for problem solving and decision making, entrepreneurial opportunity seeking, and strategy formulation. It has also had a major influence on the design and conduct of educational programs in management training and development and formal management education. Experiential learning theory (ELT) practitioners seek to pass on the legacy of those 20th-century scholars—notably William James, John Dewey, Kurt Lewin, Jean Piaget, Lev Vygotsky, Carl Jung, Paulo Freire, Carl Rogers, and others—who placed experience at the center of the learning process, envisioning an educational system that was learner-centered. ELT is a dynamic view of learning based on a learning cycle driven by the resolution of the dual dialectics of action–reflection and experience–abstraction. It is a holistic theory that defines learning as the major process of human adaptation involving the whole person. This entry is a description of the basic concepts of ELT, the learning cycle and learning style, and how these concepts are used in management today.

Fundamentals

David Kolb created ELT to unify the contributions and insights of these scholars into an explicit and coherent framework based both on the common perspectives they share and the unique contributions they have made to our understanding of experiential learning. ELT integrates the works of the foundational experiential learning scholars around six propositions that they all share:

1. Learning is best conceived as a process, not in terms of outcomes.
2. All learning is relearning.
3. Learning requires the resolution of conflicts between dialectically opposed modes of adaptation to the world.
4. Learning is a holistic process of adaptation.
5. Learning results from synergetic transactions between the person and the environment.
6. Learning is the process of creating knowledge.

The Cycle of Experiential Learning

In ELT, learning is defined as the process whereby knowledge is created through the transformation of experience. Knowledge results from the combination of grasping and transforming experience. The ELT model portrays two dialectically related modes of grasping experience—concrete experience (CE) and abstract conceptualization (AC)—and two dialectically related modes of transforming experience—reflective observation (RO) and active experimentation (AE). Experiential learning is a process of constructing knowledge that involves a creative tension among the four learning modes that is responsive to contextual demands. This process is portrayed as an idealized learning cycle or spiral where the learner "touches all the bases"—experiencing, reflecting, thinking, and acting—in a recursive process that is sensitive to the learning situation and what is being learned. Immediate or concrete experiences are the basis for observations and reflections. These reflections are assimilated and distilled into abstract concepts from which new implications for action can be drawn. These implications can be actively tested and serve as guides in creating new experiences.

Experiential Learning Styles

Kolb's learning styles, describing how individuals learn from experience, are defined by an individual's relative preference for the four modes of the learning cycle described in experiential learning theory—*concrete experience, reflective observation, abstract conceptualization,* and *active experimentation.* These learning styles can be assessed by the Kolb Learning Style Inventory (KLSI). Learning style describes the unique ways that individuals spiral through the learning cycle based on their preference for the four different learning modes—CE, RO, AC, and AE. Because of our genetic makeup, our particular life experiences, and the demands of our present environment, we develop a preferred way of choosing among these four learning modes. We resolve the conflict between being concrete or abstract and between being active or reflective in patterned, characteristic ways. ELT argues that learning style is not a psychological trait but a dynamic state. This dynamic state arises from an individual's preferential resolution of the dual dialectics of experiencing–conceptualizing and acting–reflecting. Stable and enduring patterns of learning style arise from consistent patterns of transaction between the individual and his or her environment. The way we process the possibilities of each new emerging event determines the range of choices and decisions we see. The choices and decisions we make to some extent determine the events we live through, and these events influence our future choices. Thus, people create themselves through the choice of actual occasions they live through. ELT posits that learning is the major determinant of human development, and how individuals learn shapes the course of their personal development. Previous research has shown that learning styles are influenced by culture, personality type, educational specialization, career choice, and current job role and tasks.

Much of the research on ELT has focused on the concept of learning style using the KLSI to assess individual learning styles. While individuals who took the KLSI show many different patterns of scores based on their relative preferences for the four learning modes, years of research on the learning styles of many thousands of individuals have led to the identification of nine types of learning style, each of which is characterized by a specific ability. These learning styles can be systematically arranged around the learning cycle in a grid (as seen in Figure 1).

ELT was developed following Kurt Lewin's plan for the creation of scientific knowledge by conceptualizing phenomena through formal, explicit, testable theory that (a) permits the treatment of both the qualitative and quantitative aspects of phenomena in a single system, (b) adequately represents the causal attributes of phenomena, (c) facilitates the measurement of these attributes, and (d) allows both generalization to universal laws and concrete treatment of

the individual case. Since the first statement in 1971, there have been many studies using ELT to advance the theory and practice of experiential learning. The current Experiential Learning Theory Bibliography includes over 3,000 entries. Since ELT is a holistic theory of learning that identifies learning style differences among different academic specialties, it is not surprising to see that ELT research is highly interdisciplinary, addressing learning and educational issues in many fields, notably management, education, information science, psychology, medicine, nursing, accounting, and law. There are research studies from every region of the world, with many contributions coming from the United States, Canada, Brazil, the United Kingdom, China, India, Australia, Japan, Norway, Finland, Sweden, the Netherlands, and Thailand. These studies support the cross-cultural validity of ELT and the KLSI and also support practical applicability across cultures. The KLSI has been translated into many languages including, English,

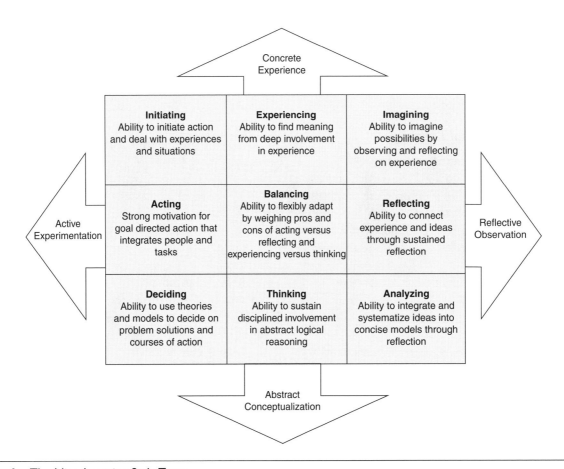

Figure 1   The Nine Learning Style Types

Source: Author.

Spanish, French, Portuguese, Arabic, Russian, Dutch, German, Swedish, Chinese, Romanian, Persian, Thai, and Japanese.

ELT offers a way to study management as a learning process that is dynamic and holistic, operating at the level of the individual, the team, and the organization. When learning is defined holistically as the basic process of human adaptation, it subsumes more specialized managerial processes, such as entrepreneurial learning, strategy formulation, creativity, problem solving, and decision making and leadership. In ELT, these specialized management processes tend to emphasize particular phases of the learning cycle. Entrepreneurial learning tends to emphasize the initiating phase of the learning cycle while strategy formulation tends to emphasize the analyzing phase. Creativity emphasizes the imagining phases, while problem solving and decision making emphasize deciding. Barbara Carlsson and colleagues found that leadership style tends to be related to learning style but is most effective when it moves through the learning cycle and is adaptive to task demands. All of these processes are enhanced when the full cycle of learning is followed. For example, Andrew C. Corbett found that in the opportunity identification phase of the entrepreneurial process, an abstract orientation is helpful in addition to an active orientation. Similarly, Anna B. Adams and associates found that diverse teams that include members with learning styles around the learning cycle tend to be more effective.

David A. Kolb

See also Action Learning; Double Loop Learning; Entrepreneurial Cognition; Intuitive Decision Making; Learning Organization; Organizational Learning; Psychological Type and Problem-Solving Styles; Stages of Creativity; Tacit Knowledge

Further Readings

Adams, A. B., Kayes, D. C., & Kolb, D. A. (2005). Experiential learning in teams. *Simulation and Gaming, 36*(3), 330–354.

Carlsson, B., Keane, P., & Martin, J. B. (1976). R & D organizations as learning systems. *Sloan Management Review, 17*(3), 1–15.

Corbett, A. C. (2007). Learning asymmetries and the discovery of entrepreneurial opportunities. *Journal of Business Venturing, 22,* 97–118.

Gemmell, R. M., Boland, R. J., & Kolb, D. A. (2011, September). The socio-cognitive dynamics of entrepreneurial ideation. *Entrepreneurship Theory and Practice,* 1–21. doi:10.1111/j.1540–6520.2011.00486.x

Kolb, A. Y., & Kolb, D. A. (2009). The learning way: Meta-cognitive aspects of experiential learning. *Simulation and Gaming: An Interdisciplinary Journal, 40*(3), 297–327.

Kolb, A. Y., & Kolb, D. A. (2011). *The Kolb learning style inventory—Version 4.0.* Boston, MA: Hay Resources Direct. Retrieved from http://www.haygroup.com/leadershipandtalentondemand

Kolb, A. Y., & Kolb, D. A. (2012). Experiential Learning Theory Bibliography: Vol. 1(1971–2005), Vol. 2 (2006–2010), & Vol. 3 (2011–2012). Retrieved from http://www.learningfromexperience.com

Kolb, D. A. (1976, Spring). Management and the learning process. *California Management Review, 18*(3), 21–31.

Kolb, D. A. (1984). *Experiential learning: Experience as the source of learning and development.* Englewood Cliffs, NJ: Prentice-Hall.

Osland, J. S., Kolb, D. A., Rubin I. M., & Turner, M. E. (2007). *Organizational behavior: An experiential approach* (8th ed.). Upper Saddle River, NJ: Prentice Hall.

Fairness Theory

Specifically, the theory posits that actions (and someone who has engaged in them, such as decision makers when they choose what to do) seem unfair when people feel that those actions *would* have been better if the relevant person *could* have and *should* have acted differently. This entry provides an introduction to the theory in terms of an illustration about a workplace interaction between a supervisor and her subordinate.

Fundamentals

Fairness theory analyzes why B might hold A accountable for unfair treatment. For example, suppose Alice, Ben's supervisor, publicly ridicules him. If Ben perceives this ridicule as the undesired result of an improper action over which Alice had control, he holds her accountable for unfairness (blaming her for mistreatment he didn't deserve). Fairness theory conceptualizes Ben's reactions in terms of *counterfactual* (contrary to fact) processing. Ben's *actual* situation seems unfair compared with a *fair* treatment counterfactual. (A *worse* counterfactual, on the other hand, would make the actual situation seem better.)

Something can seem undesirable compared to a desirable *Would* counterfactual. Remembering last year's Christmas bonus of $100, for example, makes this year's $50 seem more unfavorable than if last year's had been $25. Indeed, if the counterfactual (alternatively imaginable) condition seems more favorable in certain kinds of ways (e.g., for health and well-being), the more negative-seeming actual condition might even be perceived as harmful. Harm in that sense comes from a contrasting mental representation with the absence of harm. The greater the discrepancy between an actual state and a counterfactual one that *would* feel better, the greater the ease with which the actual state has the potential for feeling harmful—and the more harmful it can feel. The extent to which Ben feels harmed, for example, depends on how the presence of ridicule feels to him relative to its absence. Thus, if Ben has never experienced ridicule before and, in fact, is accustomed to being treated at the very least with politeness and frequently with high praise in a wide variety of contexts, then ridicule will seem to him equivalent to a considerable amount of harm. If Ben is used to being criticized sarcastically some of the time, then ridicule from Alice might seem unfavorable only to somewhat of a degree.

The *Would*-based contrast between feeling good and not feeling good, however, is by itself insufficient as grounds to hold someone accountable for unfair treatment. For example, conditions might seem unfavorable but warranted when losses stem from reap-what-you-sew personal choices (e.g., money lost from bets at Las Vegas). Under such conditions the accountability rests with the person who experiences the unfavorable feelings rather than with anyone else. There are also unfavorable conditions for which no one is accountable, such as those caused by genetic birth defects. Accountable as blame for unfairness will instead require particular versions of *Could* and *Should* counterfactuals.

When a *Could* counterfactual contributes to the possibility that someone might be held accountable for unfair treatment, the language of perpetrator and victim begins to have the potential for becoming applicable (although it will ultimately depend on an additional counterfactual regarding norms of action). The Would counterfactual of a victim involves perceptions of unfavorable conditions. Could counterfactuals refer to perceiving someone as a person whose actions could account for variations in the kinds of conditions that the victim might experience. For example, Alice's actions can vary the conditions that Ben experiences at work because she is his supervisor. Ben perceives that she has a choice about how to treat him and that ridicule is only one of various ways she could treat him. She is in a position to exercise discretion over the courses of action she will take in supervising him. People who have the potential for being perceived as perpetrators, therefore, are those who could have acted so as to prevent the conditions that someone perceives as being unfavorable; other courses of action were available, and at least one of the alternatively available choices would have not led to those conditions. Put another way, the potential victim has one of those alternative choices as a counterfactual action that contrasts with the perpetrator's actual choice.

Finally, the *Should* counterfactual in unfair treatment cases also refers to alternative courses of action but applies normative standards of right and wrong to evaluate them. Just because one person is capable of hitting another does not make it seem like appropriate conduct. In a boxing ring, however, it might very well seem fine—although perhaps not to people who consider the sport too violent. Opponents of abortion make use of Should counterfactuals by denying the moral equivalence of having versus not having an abortion, and anti-abortion billboard campaigns are meant to make very clear (and salient) which of the pregnancy alternatives is the morally superior course of action (viz., bringing a child to full term). On a less contentious level, Ben might apply certain kinds of standards of right and wrong regarding the conduct of supervisors; about ridiculing versus not ridiculing, in particular, he might find the latter the more appropriate. The fairness theory combination of Would, Could, and Should concomitant with assigning accountability for unfair treatment in Ben's case, then, might look like the following: (a) Being ridiculed seems very

unfavorable to him (he can easily think of feedback from supervisors that he Would find more desirable), (b) he is convinced that the ridicule from Alice need not have been given in public (e.g., her access to e-mail comes to his mind as a way that she Could have conveyed feedback privately), and (c) he considers public ridicule to be an unacceptably rude form of conduct when delivered by a supervisor (the appropriate norms of workplace interaction dictate that a greater level of civility Should have been exercised). Altering any of these three counterfactuals makes perceptions of blameworthy treatment less likely (e.g., Ben might instead think that it is acceptable for supervisors to give subordinates public ridicule).

The same counterfactuals apply whether Would is distributive, procedural, or interactional, and counterfactual can occur simultaneously or in any order. Also, counterfactuals can have an influence without conscious awareness. When something seems hot to you, for example, you probably do not have consciously in mind a specific level of cold that you are using for comparison to have a "measure" of *how much* heat (or what level) you are feeling, yet that is still a Would perception.

Fairness theory does not entail that counterfactuals be conscious or in a specific sequence, and it accommodates interactional, distributive, and procedural justice based on the subject of three different Would counterfactuals. Ben's ridicule illustrates an *interactional injustice* Would (i.e., criticism delivered with more respect for Ben's dignity is the counterfactual). Ben might instead (or in addition) experience some dissatisfaction about the size of a bonus because rising gas prices make salient how much better off he would be if the bonus were larger, creating the potential for *distributive injustice* (e.g., if he also believes that the cost of driving Should have been a consideration and that bigger bonuses Could have been awarded because the organization's profits made that quite feasible). Similarly, perhaps Ben experiences some dissatisfaction about the means whereby a decision was made because he realizes how much better he Would have felt if his opinion had been sought (perceived *procedural injustice* if he thinks he Could and Should have been asked for his opinion).

Modern managers can and should use fairness theory to address issues, challenges, and opportunities they face. In particular, they need to be aware of how circumstances can change (a) what employees perceive Would be more desirable than what the organization provides or is doing, (b) what employees perceive that management Could be providing or doing, and (c) what management Should be providing or doing. When a counterfactual puts existing organizational conditions in a negative light (e.g., employees come to perceive that something Could be done differently), management can consider ways to (a) provide alternative counterfactuals (e.g., show that something actually Could *not* be done otherwise) or (b) align organizational practices with prominent counterfactuals (e.g., provide larger rank-and-file bonuses out of substantial profits when gas prices rise; not provide large bonuses to top management when laying off employees).

Robert Folger

See also Equity Theory; Norms Theory; Principled Negotiation; Psychological Contract Theory; Social Exchange Theory

Further Readings

Colquitt, J. A., Scott, B. A., Judge, T. A., & Shaw, J. C. (2006). Justice and personality: Using integrative theories to derive moderators of justice effects. *Organizational Behavior and Human Decision Processes, 100,* 110–127.

Folger, R., & Cropanzano, R. (1998). *Organizational justice and human resource management.* Thousand Oaks, CA: Sage.

Folger, R., & Cropanzano, R. (2001). Fairness theory: Justice as accountability. In J. Greenberg & R. Cropanzano (Eds.), *Advances in organizational justice* (pp. 1–55). Stanford, CA: Stanford University Press.

Gilliland, S. W., Groth, M., Baker, R. C. IV, Dew, A. F., Polly, L. M., & Langdon, J. C. (2001). Improving applicants' reactions to rejection letters: An application of fairness theory. *Personnel Psychology, 54,* 669–703.

LaHuis, D. M., MacLane, C. N., & Schlessman, B. R. (2007). Do applicants' perceptions matter? Investigating reapplication behavior using fairness theory. *International Journal of Selection and Assessment, 15,* 383–393.

Nicklin, J. M., Greenbaum, R., McNall, L., Folger, R., & Williams, K. J. (2011). The importance of contextual variables when judging fairness: An examination of counterfactual thoughts and fairness theory. *Organizational Behavior and Human Decision Processes, 114,* 127–141.

Price, K. H., Lavelle, J. J., Henley, A. B., Cocchiara, F. K., & Buchanan, F. R. (2006). Judging the fairness of voice-based participation across multiple and interrelated stages of decision making. *Organizational Behavior and Human Decision Processes, 99,* 212–226.

FIRM GROWTH

Edith Penrose has had a significant influence on the field of management. This influence occurred primarily through the ideas contained in her 1959 book, *The Theory of the Growth of the Firm*. A recent query in Google Scholar found more than 13,000 citations to the text. The book was written because of her frustration with neoclassical economics' focus on static equilibrium and treatment of the firm as a black box. Although her treatise was addressed to economists, later (to her surprise) it found widest appeal among management scholars. This entry summarizes Penrose's theory of the growth of the firm and identifies its contribution to the field of management.

Fundamentals

Penrose's book analyzed different aspects of firm growth and addressed questions such as these: Why do firms grow? What factors explain the growth trajectories of firms? Is there a limit to growth? What factors determine the rate of growth? What are the different mechanisms of growth? Thus, *Theory of the Growth of the Firm* can be viewed as a collection of arguments that explain how and why firms grow and what factors constrain their growth.

Penrose viewed a firm as a bundle of resources. She argued that because of the indivisibility of resources, they could not be procured in continuous increments. This lumpiness of resources led to availability of excess resources within the firm that provided the inducement to growth. She noted that resources by themselves were useless; it was how the resources were combined—or in her words, "the services generated by the resource"—that created value for the firm. Among the resources she identified as critical to firm growth was the management and administrative structure of the firm. According to Penrose, it was the role of management to choreograph the combination of resources and the services derived from them. Technical and managerial economies, and learning (that increased the management's stock of knowledge), provided additional sources of growth.

It was the different bundles of resources that firms possessed and the different ways that their management combined them that led to heterogeneity among firms. The trajectory of the growth was constrained by the firm's resource inheritance or legacy. As examples, Penrose discussed how research capabilities could lead to development of new products and processes and growth through diversification, while marketing and sales capabilities could create brand awareness and relationship with customers that increased sales of existing products; thus, the two distinct capabilities would produce two different growth trajectories. According to her, the rate of growth would be a function of the ratio of the resources available for expansion to the resources required per unit of expansion. The adverse impact on growth rate of firms because of the cost of developing tacit managerial resources is now known as the Penrose effect. However, Penrose did address how lack of resources (such as experienced management and labor) could be overcome through acquisitions.

While Penrose focused on the "insides" of the firm in developing her theory of growth, she did not dismiss the role of the external environment in firm growth. This acknowledgment of the role of the environment was evident in her discussion of the roles of economic growth rate and competition on firm growth. She viewed the environment not as an objective fact but as the subjective image in the mind of the entrepreneur. Penrose noted that entrepreneurs operated in environments characterized by uncertainties; therefore, their beliefs about the environment became the basis for their actions. While the resources governed the growth trajectory, it was entrepreneurship that provided the motive.

Penrose's book did not have an immediate impact on the field of management. It was several decades later, starting with the publication of Birger Wernerfelt's article in *Strategic Management Journal* in 1984 that the field of strategic management vigorously adopted Penrose's framework. Strategic management is a relatively young field within the management discipline. Academic research in strategic management was initially influenced by the *industrial organization* (IO) economics perspective.

This perspective led to a focus on the external environment and, more specifically, on the structure of the industry in which the firm was embedded. However, many scholars within strategic management felt that the IO perspective offered too aggregate a level of analysis and that it neither explained the heterogeneity among firms within an industry nor offered an understanding of firm dynamics or growth. These critiques and gaps led scholars to embrace Penrose's work. This alternative approach based on ideas contained in Penrose's book came to be known as the *resource-based view* (RBV) of the firm. The RBV became an extremely powerful and popular (based on number of publications and dissertations) framework within strategic management research in the 1990s and 2000s and also spilled over into the broader discipline of management. In the short space of this article, it is impossible to list all the scholars who have refined, developed, and applied Penrose's theory of firm growth to management. However, in addition to Wernerfelt, Jay Barney, Joseph Mahoney, and Margaret Peteraf played critical roles in the development of Penrose's theory and articulating its relevance to management.

In 2001, as the RBV was gaining eminence as a powerful framework to understand firm behavior and competitive advantage, Richard Priem and John Butler published a sharp critique of the RBV in a leading management publication, the *Academy of Management Review*. They asserted that the RBV was based on tautological argumentation, making it difficult to satisfy one of Karl Popper's criteria for a good theory: falsification. Perhaps in anticipation of such critiques, Penrose had acknowledged that testing her theory would be difficult. Despite the critiques, the RBV and its derivative frameworks continue to play important roles in management research and practice. The RBV framework should allow managers to assess their resource structure within the context of their environment to make critical strategic decisions about resource acquisition, divestment, development of core competencies, and outsourcing.

Anil Nair

See also Business Policy and Corporate Strategy; Competitive Advantage; Core Competence; Diversification Strategy; Dynamic Capabilities; Knowledge-Based View of the Firm; Resource-Based View of the Firm; Strategic Alliances; Strategic Groups

Further Readings

Barney, J. B. (1991). Firm resources and sustained competitive advantage. *Journal of Management, 17*, 99–120.

Barney, J. B. (2001). Is the resource-based "view" a useful perspective for strategic management research? Yes. *Academy of Management Review, 26*(1), 41–56.

Lloyd, L. E. (1961). The theory of the growth of the firm [Book review]. *Journal of Marketing, 25*(3), 105–106.

Penrose, E. (1995). *The theory of the growth of the firm.* New York, NY: Oxford University Press. (Originally published 1959)

Pitelis, C. (2002). *The growth of the firm: The legacy of Edith Penrose.* New York, NY: Oxford University Press.

Priem, R. L., & Butler, J. E. (2001). Is the resource-based "view" a useful perspective for strategic management research? *Academy of Management Review, 26*(1), 22–40.

Rugman, A. M., & Verbeke, A. (2004). A final word on Edith Penrose. *Journal of Management Studies, 41*(1), 205–217.

Teece, D. J. (1982). Towards an economic theory of the multiproduct firm. *Journal of Economic Behavior and Organization, 3*(1), 39–63.

Wernerfelt, B. (1984). A resource-based view of the firm. *Strategic Management Journal, 5*(2), 171–180.

FIRST-MOVER ADVANTAGES AND DISADVANTAGES

The first-mover advantage (FMA) is a metaphor that is often evoked to summarize a variety of factors that may contribute to the positive economic performance of early entrants in new or substantially reorganized markets and industries. Because of the commingling of multiple theoretical mechanisms (that may generate or obfuscate an advantage for pioneering firms) under the same umbrella term, the conceptual utility of FMA as a tool for theory building and analysis is unclear. Nevertheless, the metaphor is widely popular among managers and applied strategy researchers, so it is useful to sort the arguments it summarizes even if they are divergent and sometimes contradictory. In this entry, we trace the conceptual origin of the arguments that suggest both advantages and disadvantages for first movers.

Fundamentals

In their 1988 seminal paper on the topic, Marvin B. Lieberman and David B. Montgomery effectively systematized the key drivers of the first-mover advantage: First, economies of learning and experience along with research and development (R & D) investments can produce a technology advantage if the pertinent knowledge can be kept proprietary. Second, first movers may be able to deter entry by acquiring input factors at lower costs than subsequent entrants, by preemptive investment in production capacity, or by positioning in geographic or product markets with limited-scale potential where minimum efficient scale equals market size. Third, timing of entry may afford first movers to develop brand loyalty, which increases switching costs and decreases search costs for consumers. At the same time, first movers may well be at a disadvantage relative to later entrants because of free-riding effects, the emergence of a dominant design and reduced technological uncertainty, abrupt shifts in technology, or lock-in effects arising from early investments in specific assets. In short, there are a good number of reasons to speculate that first movers may succeed or fail as a function of threats and opportunities endemic in time of entry.

Yet rigorous analysis of FMA is greatly constrained by two common biases: First, "success/survivor bias" often leads analysts to select on the dependent variable, in fact making it invariable. Since many first movers may have expeditiously fallen victim to the disadvantages inherent in the first-mover position, they are simply not considered in the risk set. FMA studies thus often are de facto studies of the first successful firms in an industry where success may have little or nothing to do with time of entry; many firms may have entered and failed a market prior to the first successful firm's entry. For example, such logical fallacy often permeates misperceptions of Ford and IBM as first movers in the automobile or personal computer market, respectively. Both firms were the first to succeed in their markets, but neither was a first mover, although they each are the earliest surviving entrant. A second source of bias is "left-censoring" in data collection, which stems from the difficulty in obtaining data dating to the dawn of an industry when many short-lived competitors enter and fail quickly leaving little or no record of their existence. Thus, even if survivor bias is eliminated, the earliest point in time at which record-keeping begins in many industries coincides with the time of institutional visibility, which is typically years later than the entry of first movers. This leads second movers (successful or not) to be mistakenly identified as first movers and again produces flawed causal inferences.

Perhaps the greatest difficulty with garnering theoretical traction from the FMA metaphor is that it is unclear to what extent the purported mechanisms causing the effect are peculiar to time of entry versus pertinent to a specific market structure such as monopoly equilibrium. Advantages stemming from experience, R & D, preemptive investments, brand loyalty, and the like are all easier to realize by a firm that does not face any competitors, at least temporarily, but it is unclear how time of entry itself directly relates to any of these. Note that since a first mover remains the only incumbent until subsequent entry, market concentration is by definition at its global maximum. Would a firm that finds itself in such a monopoly position in the later stages of industry evolution not benefit as much as a first mover would?

Attributing the success of (some) early entrants *solely* to their timing of industry entry may be an oversight. Potential advantages available to early entrants may be only an indirect function of early entry and stem from a firm's ability either to benefit from scale advantage or to extend its prior experience to a new market. The key to a first-mover's success then lays not in being the first to market per se but in the chance to leverage a relevant capability or an experience (often generating an R & D advantage leading to scale economies). That this is easier to accomplish in an empty market is a facilitating condition that does not in itself constitute an FMA. Predictably, empirical research that supports FMA emphasizes the benefits of either large-scale or prior experience, neither of which is directly driven by timing of entry.

While the purported advantages of the first-mover position may not be unique to first movers, its disadvantages certainly appear to be. Technological and market uncertainties in an underdeveloped market are directly tied to timing of entry and may obscure opportunities and increase failure for new entrants. When the first movers are *de novo* firms (i.e., without prior experience), they are particularly sensitive to environmental uncertainty and subject to imprinting. When a social audience does not identify or recognize new organizations as categorically distinct and has no set expectations against which to evaluate their activities, it is unlikely to transact with these organizations despite the merits or appeal of their offerings or the size of latent demand for them. And this "legitimacy vacuum" effect, as Stanislav Dobrev and Aleksios Gotsopoulos term it, is likely to produce a lasting disadvantage for first movers that are new start-ups rather than diversifying entrants.

Studies that focus on the uncertainty associated with entering an unknown, underdeveloped market (in spite of how large its potential may be) unsurprisingly predict FMAs. The key question is, Why are first movers in some industries but not in others able to offset the uncertainty disadvantage by leveraging their own experience and by reaching minimum efficient scale faster than later entrants? The answer to this question requires considerations exceeding the explanation of any single theory. The time it takes for a new organizational form to become taken for granted matters, as does the proportion of new industry entrants who are lateral entrants less exposed to imprinting processes. Or the economics of the business may be such that breaking through scale thresholds requires time to build distribution channels or to leverage positive externalities. And of course, entrepreneurial risk-taking behavior leads to seizing uncertain opportunities in which sheer luck (or the random, path-dependent component of evolution) rewards some entrants at the expense of others. Studies seeking to adjudicate whether first movers benefit or suffer from their timing of entry provide conflicting results. Attempting to solve this inconsistency in simple "advantage versus disadvantage" terms may not be productive. Instead, as Fernando Suarez and Gianvito Lanzolla suggest, it may be more useful to articulate and develop the mechanisms that operate concurrently for new firms in new industries and emphasize the conditions under which the advantages may overwhelm the disadvantages and vice versa.

As Lieberman and Montgomery (1988) admit, "Profits earned by first-movers are fundamentally attributable to proficiency and luck, rather than 'pioneering' per se. But . . . it is often exceedingly difficult to distinguish between proficiency and luck, particularly at the stage where first-mover opportunities are generated. . . . We leave this difficult problem to venture capitalists and extremely ambitious empirical researchers" (p. 49). It seems wise to strongly favor the latter.

Stanislav Dobrev

See also Entrepreneurial Opportunities; Environmental Uncertainty; Firm Growth; Neo-Institutional Theory; Organizational Ecology; Organizational Learning; Organizational Structure and Design; Technology and Interdependence/Uncertainty

Further Readings

Cusumano, M. A., Myloniadis, Y., & Rosenbloom, R. S. (1992). Strategic maneuvering and mass-market dynamics: The triumph of VHS over beta. *Business History Review, 66*(1), 51–94.

Dobrev, S. D., & Gotsopoulos, A. (2010). Legitimacy vacuum, structural imprinting, and the first-mover disadvantage. *Academy of Management Journal, 53,* 1153–1174.

Klepper, S. (2002). Firm survival and the evolution of oligopoly. *Rand Journal of Economics, 33*(1), 37–61.

Lieberman, M. B., & Montgomery, D. B. (1988, Summer). First-mover advantages. *Strategic Management Journal, 9*[Special issue], 41–58.

Lieberman, M. B., & Montgomery, D. B. (1998). First mover (dis)advantages: Retrospective and link with the resource-based view. *Strategic Management Journal, 19,* 1111–1125.

Suarez, F. F., & Utterback, J. M. (1995). Dominant designs and the survival of firms. *Strategic Management Journal, 16,* 415–430.

Suarez, F. F., & Lanzolla, G. (2007). The role of environmental dynamics in building a theory of first-mover advantages. *Academy of Management Review, 32,* 377–392.

VanderWerf, P. A., & Mahon, J. F. (1997). Meta-analysis of the impact of research methods on findings of first-mover advantage. *Management Science, 43,* 1510–1519.

FORCE FIELD ANALYSIS AND MODEL OF PLANNED CHANGE

Kurt Lewin's theory of force field analysis and planned change provides integrated models of management research to enable individual and group behavioral dynamics that enable organizational change toward an intended direction. Force field analysis is a process of organizational intervention that identifies driving influences for and against change. It can be applied to different stages of planned change and conflict resolution. Planned change is an alteration in the form, quality, characteristics, or state of an entity over a period of time, whether the entity is an individual, group, organization, or community. The following discussion traces (a) the origins of the two interrelated concepts and presents an outline of their key processes, (b) the conceptual and practical applications of the two ideas, and (c) their subsequent impact in the discipline of management. Based on the origin of field theory, planned change and force field analysis have enjoyed renewed significance with emerging complexity theories that consider organizations as dynamic, nonlinear, chaotic systems.

Fundamentals

Force Field Analysis

Force field analysis is anchored in field theory developed by Kurt Lewin in the 1940s. The significance of force field analysis lies in its practical application with a democratic-participative approach for collective decision making and action planning that fundamentally contradicted and shifted the prevailing traditional view of management as the ultimate authority over knowledge and decision making. Lewin's theoretical contribution referred to a *field* as the composition of influencing forces and symbolic interactions that structure behaviors in social groups and individual actions.

The notion of *force* is something that propels or hinders movement from one region of a life space to another. On one hand, forces that arise from within are "own forces," which encompass values, thoughts, needs, feelings, beliefs, and any other factors embedded in one's internal composition or within a group's norms and behaviors. On the other hand, "induced forces" arise from the external environment, which include people, events, things, context, and other factors.

Different forces have varying rates of change in their strength to move toward or away from the intended direction or goal. An important heuristic is that proximity to a region of forces is positively related to the strength of the forces' influence. This means that the closer one is to a set of own forces and induced forces, their influences will be stronger in moving toward a particular direction. As an example, to generate induced forces for commitment to customer service among executive ranks, they need to experience the customer service firsthand, as a customer or as an employee, in order to be influenced by induced forces to enable much more rapid changes for improving customer service.

According to Lewin, a field is conceptualized as a space with lines of force. This could be a composition of positive valences that makes up converging forces toward a region or alternatively, a composition of negative valences that makes up diverging forces. This conceptual definition has had relevance to disciplines beyond management to subjects such as sociology, psychology, and even physics. The importance of the field idea centers on being able to map the complexities and dynamics of the forces that encompass human behavior. Changes of the forces in a field lead to changes in social behaviors that then provide feedback to the system in a mutually interdependent fashion. This means there is a quasi-stationary equilibrium as a field is in a constant state of adaptation.

At any point in time, a *force field analysis* may be employed as a practical application of field theory. A force field analysis involves collaboration preferably among diverse stakeholders to represent the range of perspectives in an organizational system. The collaboration involves creating a diagram of different forces in a planned change. The process starts out with a vertical line drawn in the middle to represent the planned change. On one side, a list of key forces driving change has arrows directed toward the vertical line and on the opposite side of the line, forces against or resisting the change with arrows also directed toward the vertical line but in an opposing direction. The length and weight of the arrow sometimes vary to show the different intensity or significance of a force. Both own and induced forces would be represented in the collective diagram. As a result, the diagram from a force field analysis illustrates key forces at play, both in direction and magnitude, in planned change.

Planned Change

For planned change to take place, the driving forces must be greater than the resisting forces. Lewin developed the mathematical formula for behavioral change as a function of the state of a field over time—(dx/dt) where x represents changes in the organization and t represents a specific time period. During the late 1980s, David Gleicher developed a change formula known as $dvf > r$ where d is dissatisfaction with the status quo, v is vision for a positive alternative future state, and f is first steps toward the future vision, and they must be greater than r, which is resistance to change. The process of a force field analysis diagrams the different forces of dissatisfaction, vision, and resistance in planned-change activities in order to identify first steps to increase the forces for change over resistance to change. The collective engagement for a force field analysis is considered essential to the process of problem solving and conflict resolutions in order to move forward with a planned-change agenda.

In conjunction with force field analysis, Lewin also outlined a three-stage theory of managing planned change: unfreezing, movement, and refreezing. First, the *unfreezing* stage is recognizing and generating a degree of urgency for change. This may result from an internal source such as a leadership decision to change strategic direction and/or an external source such as a sudden change in economic climate. The need for change is made explicit in the unfreezing stage. Second, the *movement* stage is the deployment of intervention activities for shifting toward the new, preferred, and intended state. Interventions are intentionally designed organization development activities that may focus on shifting the trajectory of the organizational system, subunits, and/or individuals. Professional coaching, training and development, and organizational restructuring are examples of interventions. Last, the *refreezing* stage is the stabilizing of the new state. After a change alters the prior state, institutionalizing the new state may take place with reinforcements such as new policies, practices, and/or procedures. Planned change is a process that often refers to an organizational level of analysis, but it is also relevant to the individual and group level.

Evolution

Field theory established an important foundation for management research on different levels of analysis such as general and industry environments of organizations and culture, climate, and structure at the organizational level. These levels of analysis give rise to induced forces that are external to an organization's environment. Common induced forces for organizations today include technological innovations, globalization, lifestyle changes, competition, government regulations, and economic fluctuations. For example, economic recessionary induced forces on an organization require adaptation that may involve replacing low-skilled labor with technology or outsourcing or closing of departments. The creation of organizational culture, climate, visions, goals, and values can be attributed to own forces arising from leadership in an organization. Each of these own forces, including leadership, had a rapid growth of management research attention starting in the 1960s. Most of the contemporary developments of these management topics have lost the trail of their research origins to the seminal influences of field theory.

An important caveat in the evolution of field theory is to recognize that (a) fields are embedded in the context of broader forces of fields at different levels of analysis and (b) there are reciprocal dynamics between forces arising from the different fields. At the individual level of analysis, the own forces arise from within a leaders' style, beliefs, values, and worldview, whereas their induced forces come from the both the group and organizational fields. At the group level of analysis, the own forces arise from within the group field, and induced forces originate outside the group at the organizational level and beyond organizational boundaries. The parallel continues for the organizational level too. Field theory contributed significantly to separating the levels of analysis for rapid growth in both management research and education, but more recently, there is increasing recognition for integrated multilevel research and education to address the integrated complexities of contemporary organizational issues.

Whether explicitly or implicitly acknowledged, Lewin's planned change model has had far-reaching influence and impact as a cornerstone for the discipline of management and its related fields. Reflections of the underlying conceptual foundation can be identified in relatively young fields such as strategic management, organizational development, action research, change management, decision sciences, problem solving, and a rapidly emerging practice of professional leadership coaching. Furthermore, specific aspects of planned change attracted significant attention for extensive research. They include topics such as goal setting, decision making, organizational identity, conflict management, strategic planning,

SWOT analysis, motivation theories, organizational learning, training and development, group dynamics and teams, leadership, business communication, and so forth

Andrew H. Van de Ven and Marshall Scott Poole identified planned change as a teleology type of organizational change. They compared teleology in a two-by-two matrix with three other types of organizational change, which were evolutionary, dialectic, and life cycle changes. The two dimensions were unit of change from single to multiple entities and mode of change that spanned prescribed to constructive. Planned change, or teleology, focuses on a single entity and a constructive mode. Another conceptualization of planned change examined content of change and intervention where episodic change in formal structure employed command interventions, change in beliefs employed teaching, change in work processes employed engineering, and change in social relationships employed socializing.

Subsequently, further elaborations of the three stages of planned change involve a recurring sequence of goal setting, implementation, evaluation and feedback, and revisions to the end state. Awareness of significant opportunities, threats, or problems often prompts people to initiate effort and energy for planned change, which relates to the earlier discussion about dissatisfaction in the change formula. Increasing awareness and goal setting make up the first stage of unfreezing in planned change, which relates to a vision of the future. The engagement of key stakeholders to socially construct the preferred future or end state with goal setting is an important first step in the planned-change process. Then implementation with the related actions for organizational change and leadership development form the second stage of movement. The particular interventions for change may involve organizational learning to integrate and adapt with new technology, restructuring organization, team development, dealing with resistance and conflict management, and many other related action items. Evaluation, feedback, revisions, and institutionalization establish the new state at the refreezing stage. The advent of total quality management, *kaizen*, balanced scorecard or dashboards, and related metric monitoring systems for performance improvement became significant for the refreezing stage of planned change.

Importance

From a practical perspective, planned change and force field analysis have an integrated, symbiotic relationship. Force field analysis surfaces qualitative data to support planned change. Significant theoretical developments advanced with planned change in both depth and breadth, whereas force field analysis is more of a practitioner tool. Different types of planned change include contrasting revolutionary change for resolving organizational crisis with evolutionary change for incremental growth and how the two alternate between one another. Another development of planned change can also be found in strategy with intended and realized strategy in comparison with emergent strategy. *Intended strategy* refers to a desired future direction, and a *realized strategy* is what strategic change actually unfolds. Between the two is an emergent strategy that may cause a deviation from what was intended to lead to the realized strategy. Recent organization change also identified a typology of planned change as transformational versus incremental change.

In addition to classifying planned change in terms of their magnitude and complexities, the origins and directions of planned change are important developments that started with a primarily top-down management approach. Today, the sources for planned change can be identified from multiple directions, including bottom-up management or externally stimulated from a variety of induced forces. Regardless of the origin and direction, a force field analysis can be integral to a change process.

Force field analysis may be used by managers at the unfreezing stage to conduct an organizational diagnosis and achieve a shared understanding of the existing dynamics for and against the planned-change initiatives. The unfreezing stage deals with multiple perspectives from different stakeholders in shared situations or conflicted issues. Two key tasks of the unfreezing stage are to generate a socially constructed common reality about the need and urgency for change. For example, a promising innovation can be considered as having potential for new market opportunities, whereas others may consider the same thing as being too risky or not within the scope of the organization's market. At the movement stage, a force field analysis helps to identify significant forces against the intended change and to generate ideas for interventions that can help decrease and/or remove points of resistance. At the refreezing stage, managers practice and sustain the requisite organizational changes. If a force field analysis is used at this point, the focus would be on examining what institutionalizing practices are important and destabilizing forces against the organizational change initiative. The change in context for each stage presents different rationales and contexts for conducting a force field analysis.

A number of important research developments evolved from force field analysis and planned change. One centers on the notion of resistance to change, which unfolded in the late 1940s through to the 1960s. Resistance research started from a systems level concept and then developed to a psychological one. Recent research continues with a psychological focus that addresses meaning making and the social construction of reality for change. Sonnenshein's research study of meaning construction in strategic change implementation traced its influence to Lewin's three-stage model of planned change. But an important development from the study identified the importance of managing paradoxical forces by balancing change dynamics with minimizing uncertainty during the unfreezing stage. Employees often embellish what an organizational change may mean that is in contrast to the intended meanings of managers. Hence, planned change involves multilayered meanings that exist at the same time and are not necessarily congruent with one another but are nevertheless important in an organization development and change process.

An array of factors is necessary to support successful planned-change processes; these include awareness of forces for change, shared goals and process, consensus decision making, real-time challenges to cognitive biases, and appropriate balance of de-escalating challenges. Research also identified the significance of pacing, sequencing, and linearity of change in radical transformations. Within organizational units, change unfolds in a nonlinear manner, which allows for participants' need to develop common norms in collaborative relationships. Densely integrated into planned change is Lewin's foundational impetus for multiple streams of management research in terms of both breadth and depth of related topics.

Research in planned change also led to the development of methods to evaluate the efficacy and impact of change initiatives. The earlier work focused on *alpha changes,* which involve movement along an established measurement instrument; *beta changes,* which involve movement on a measurement instrument that has been recalibrated; and *gamma changes,* which involve assessing change with a redefinition of the domain for change. The latter may happen because the new reality no longer holds the former state. An example to illustrate can be found with shopping where customer service may be measured by how responsive employees are with smiles, professional dress, and friendliness, but the reality no longer exists in an Internet shopping environment. The continued attention to evaluating planned change is important as the research stream continues with a focus on practical organizational problems to align organizational resources on all levels to support its strategy. One of the most significant approaches for managers to assess planned change is with a balanced scorecard or dashboard, which often couples information technology in real time for strategic decision makers and change agents to access organizational outcomes on a range of metrics.

Finally, while earlier research separated levels and units of analysis, a recent theoretical as well as practical development examines the impact of change interventions on multiple levels that include organizational, workplace, individual, and organizational outcomes. These studies draw attention to the complexity of organizational change. Management researchers are in the early stages of grappling with multilevel theoretical and empirical research issues in which planned change would continue to be significant in the foreseeable future. Hence, the last research development discussed here is still emerging with the rise of different but related complexity theories—chaos theory, dissipative structures theory, and theory of complex adaptive systems. Three shared central concepts are the nature of chaos and order, operating at the "edge of chaos," and order-generating rules. Complexity theories consider organizations as natural systems that are nonlinear, self-organizing, and order-generating rules operating at the edge of chaos. In sum, the significance of complexity theories for organizations renews attention and further increases the importance of heeding the insights of Lewin's field theory and planned change model.

Diana J. Wong-MingJi

See also Balanced Scorecard; Complexity Theory and Organizations; Goal-Setting Theory; Organizational Culture and Effectiveness; Organizational Development; Organizational Effectiveness; Participative Model of Decision Making; Strategic Decision Making

Further Readings

Amis, J., Slack, T., & Hinngs, C. R. (2004). The pace, sequence, and linearity of radical change. *Academy of Management Journal, 47*(1), 15–39.

Beckhard, R., & Harris, R. T. (1987). *Organizational transitions: Managing complex change* (2nd ed.). New York, NY: Addison-Wesley.

Burnes, B. (2004). Kurt Lewin and complexity theories: Back to the future? *Journal of Change Management, 4*(4)309–325.

Cronshaw, S. F., & McCulloch, A. N. A. (2008). Reinstating the Lewinian vision: From force field analysis to organization field assessment. *Organization Development Journal, 26*(4), 89–103.

Lewin, K. (1951). *Field theory in social science* (D. Cartwright, Ed.). New York, NY: Harper & Bros.

Robertson, P. J., Roberts, D. R., & Porras, J. I. (1993). Dynamics of planned organizational change: Assessing empirical support for a theoretical model. *Academy of Management Journal, 36*(3), 619–634.

Sonenshein, S. (2010). We're changing—or are we? Untangling the role of progressive, regressive, and stability narratives during strategic change implementation. *Academy of Management Journal, 53*(3), 477–512.

Terborg, J. R., Howard, G. S., & Maxwell, S. E. (1980). Evaluating planned organizational change: A method for assessing alpha, beta, and gamma change. *Academy of Management Review, 5*(1), 109–121.

Van de Ven, A. H., & Poole, M. S. (1995). Explaining development and change in organizations. *Academy of Management Review, 20,* 510–540.

Wooldridge, B., & Floyd, S.W. (1990).The strategy process, middle management involvement, and organizational performance. *Strategic Management Journal, 11,* 231–241.

FUNCTIONS OF THE EXECUTIVE

Chester Barnard's management theory can best be defined as focused on managing individuals in organizations rather on than managing organizations. His theory begins with the psychological need of individuals to meet their goals and aspirations (large and small), their recognition of the inability to meet their goals by their own actions alone, and thus, the necessity to cooperate with others in order to function as they wish. His theoretical contributions are marked by his connecting these assumptions to the formation of organizations and the role of leaders in managing human organizations. Barnard's work has remained significant for nearly a century, during which time scholars and leaders have studied and navigated organizational shifts around the globe. Barnard's *Functions of the Executive*, published in 1938, is remarkable for its comprehensiveness and depth. He details ways in which the human need for association, grounded in biological and physical limitations, expresses itself in cooperative efforts; the dynamics of authority and power and under what conditions individuals follow direction from supervisors without questioning; the prime role of interpersonal and organizational communication; the influence of informal groups; the definition and role of morals in executive leadership and organizational purpose. Clearly, Barnard's work, written during times of turbulence and change in American society, has strong applicability to the relentless global changes of the 21st century. This entry focuses attention on three fundamental factors of Barnard's theory: (a) basic need of individuals for association to meet their goals and aspirations, (b) communication and human interaction, and (c) authority. Following the explication of these key factors, the importance of Barnard's theory is presented.

Fundamentals

The continued relevance of Barnard's work is grounded in the fact that he begins with the individual as his unit of analysis and then builds his theory of organizations around that framework. For Barnard, everything—including authority—starts with the individual at the bottom level rather than at an upper hierarchical level.

Barnard's analysis is inclusive, a brilliant, consistent work that crafts an organizational and societal system based on the needs of individuals. He is often associated with Elton Mayo and others in the human relations movement, which stresses attention to the needs of individuals and groups in the workings and effectiveness of organizations. Barnard's work clearly resonates with Mayo's thinking. However,

Barnard's view of organizations was not based in an existing theory. As a keen observer of people in multiple settings and situations, his conceptualizations emerged from his vast and multifaceted experience dealing with people engaged in organizational/organized settings. These diverse settings represented a variety of institutional purposes from corporate profit to national security to relief to citizens hardest hit by the Great Depression. These direct experiences provided key data that informed Barnard's thinking.

Basic Need of Individuals for Association

Barnard's entire theoretical structure is based in understanding human beings as purposeful individuals with aspirations to improve their situations. Individuals have needs and goals that they cannot fulfill by themselves; human biological and physical limitations prevent them from doing as they would like. While these restrictions curb choices, choices are expanded through cooperation with others to meet desired ends.

Barnard posits in his pivotal work, *The Functions of the Executive*, that organizations begin with two or more people coordinating their efforts and joint action has a purpose. Thus, organizations are inherently *cooperative systems*. The need to cooperate provides incentives for individuals to forge cooperative relations with others. This is the basis for human action and achievement and is manifested in formal organizations as well as in informal groups (within and outside of organizations).

The initial expression of cooperative activity is *informal organizations*. It is here that socialization and learning take place, common understandings are forged, and the basis for the rise of formal organizations are developed. Informal organizations are critical to the development and functioning of the *formal organization* to meet human social needs and enhance the organization's communication structure.

Formal organizations are defined by goals and purpose, arise out of the informal structure, and may build on it. They become complex formal organizations as they grow in size, become more intentional as systems, develop communications structures, become specialized and depersonalized, and contain informal organizations.

Barnard argues that individuals in organizations choose to contribute to them or not, calculating *whether the inducements merit the level of individual contribution.* He might describe the employment contract as one wherein the conditions of employment are defined in terms of performance expectations—what individuals are required to contribute—and inducements, or what organizations provide in the relationship. For example, a person may agree to be hired as department accountant to contribute to the organization by performing requisite accounting tasks. In the hiring process, the organization outlines inducements: working conditions, compensation, benefits, a private office, and so on. If later the department accountant determines that the inducements are not sufficient compensation for poor working conditions or if the employee receives an offer from another company for twice the salary, then the inducements may become insufficient to secure continuing contributions from the individual. In the final analysis, this is a determination made freely by the individual.

Barnard's analysis that the individual, rather than the systems in place, is the starting point is contrary to the work of other theorists. Max Weber, for example, analyzes formal organizations, or bureaucracy, as a system of control and power over individuals.

Communication

As Barnard points out, interpersonal communication and human interaction are fundamental to cooperative activity. Communication is the means through which arrangements and partnerships with others are formed. The importance of this feature in Barnard's work cannot be overstated. While he did not detail specific skills, such as nonverbal communication, active and reflective listening, and other basic communication skills, it is clear that in Barnard's theory, interpersonal and organizational communication is paramount.

Fundamental to Barnard's emphasis on communication is his view that organizations must meet the needs of employees and establish levels of mutual understanding and cooperation. Individuals have free will and can leave the organization if they so choose.

In fact, communication and its systems are regarded as one of the top three executive functions in the organization, along with advancing the purpose of the organization and securing the commitment of individuals to that purpose. Communication is key to the exercise of authority because this is accomplished through communication of directives and other initiatives.

Underlying these functions for Barnard is *moral commitment and a moral code.* As compliance to organizational authority is grounded in clear communication, it is imperative that trust levels be established between organizational actors across levels. This is possible with a sense of morality and responsibility throughout the organization and is initiated and reinforced by the executive leader.

Authority

Barnard recognized the inevitability of authority dynamics whenever individuals come together in relationships and groups. With regard to organizations and other cooperative systems, Barnard views authority as emergent and person focused. One has authority over others to whatever extent that others grant the authority, or by consent. To be clear, Barnard conceptualizes authority as from the bottom-up rather than from the top-down. While one may have authority based on one's position in the organization, for Barnard, genuine (effective) authority is that which has the consent of the individuals. Authority resides in mutual relationships between supervisors and subordinates.

That said, authority is exercised through directives; the supervisor directs the subordinate to perform tasks and actions. What determines if the employee will obey? Barnard conceptualizes this issue through the zone of acceptance, or the acceptance view of authority, and the zone of indifference.

The *zone of acceptance* recognizes that authority is ultimately based on one's acceptance of the authority of the supervisor. The employee will comply with directives from the supervisor if directives are clearly communicated and understood, if directives can reasonably be accomplished (the employee is physically able to do the task), if directives are consistent with the organization's purpose, and if directives are not contrary to the individual's interests.

The *zone of indifference* is the range of directives that the employee regards as legitimate. These are requests with which the employee will comply without considering questioning the authority of the supervisor. An example might be that the supervisor of the accounting department directs the accountants to have the reports completed within 30 days. The employee likely sees such requests as entirely reasonable and within the scope of the supervisor's responsibility and thus would not question the authority of the supervisor in making the request. Barnard points out that expanding this zone of indifference would likely require additional inducements to the employee.

Barnard argues that organizations are *effective* when they meet their goals and accomplish their purpose. He further argues that they are *efficient* if in the process of meeting these goals, the participants cooperated and are satisfied with the process. That is to say, an organization may be effective, but if people are unhappy about how the goals were accomplished or about their lack of participation, then the organization in this regard is inefficient. This critical point advances the long-range view of the importance of employee satisfaction in the ongoing purpose of the organization.

Importance

There is no doubt that the early 21st century has shaped up to be a time of relentless turbulent change. These are fast-paced, extraordinary times. The legitimacy of published sources of knowledge is now constrained by rapid change, with current insights, knowledge, and information appearing on the Internet—much faster than customary publishing.

Traditional governing institutions around the world are demonstrating their limited ability to address daunting issues and challenges that were not known a generation ago. In 2011, the world witnessed the first ever social media-driven revolutions, which were fueled by Facebook, Twitter, and YouTube. The toppling of long-established dictatorial regimes by citizens without the use of weaponry is extraordinary in human civilization.

From the individual point of view, in this century, the future is experienced as increasingly unscripted because of relentless changes touching all parts of life: globalization, technological advances, dynamic employment environment, unexpected fluidity in communications, and even a sense of possibility. Individuals increasingly experience difficulties devising a career pathway toward an expected end. The implications of these changes are both enormous and unknown. Some of them are apparent even now—from the impacts of a global economy to changes in the ways people communicate, to

artificial intelligence (note Watson, the IBM computer that soundly beat two seasoned champions on the TV quiz show *Jeopardy!*), to democratization of knowledge and taking courses on one's mobile device, to international revolutions and self-organizing protests, to nanotechnology that rejuvenates human cells and cures disease, to toxic substances in a small vial of sufficient strength to launch chemical warfare, killing hundreds of thousands. And that is only the beginning.

As human experience becomes more globally connected through technology, and as conditions affecting one part of the world impact the rest of the globe, it is increasingly clear that 20th-century institutional and organizational structures may not be sufficient for the challenges ahead. The future is becoming more individualized rather than institutionalized. With technology, individuals are increasingly empowered. This was demonstrated by the Arab Spring of 2011. News and information are no longer channeled or vetted—everyone with a computer can create content on the Web for all to read. One's individual influence is magnified.

Clearly, Barnard was correct in his assertion that all organizing begins with individual needs. Technology is shaping needs and limitations. Powered now with social media, people are self-organizing into groups all over the world, with no regard to geographic space and political boundaries, to achieve their purposes and aspirations. The physical limitation of space is mediated with Skype, enabling a meeting with someone on another continent without leaving the office.

Currently, the communication factor so prominent in Barnard is magnified as well as ubiquitous. With the Internet available on cell phones, the ease of information retrieval and communicating with multiple people at one time offers new opportunities for collaboration. The importance of basic communication skills is emphasized, along with the need to learn how to reach mutual understandings across mediums, time, cultures, and space.

Barnard's conceptualization of authority is particularly germane for today's self-organizing systems. The clear shift is from the hierarchical model of bestowal to the leveling of consent—from authority bestowed from high in the organization to provide oversight over those below, to authority that people accept because trust is earned. While Barnard did not use this term, the issue becomes one of trust. Earning this level of trust is emerging as a leadership necessity for shaping the new century.

Laurie N. DiPadova-Stocks

See also Bureaucratic Theory; Charismatic Theory of Leadership; Compliance Theory; Cultural Values; Humanistic Management; Leadership Practices; Management Control Systems; Social Power, Bases of; Theory X and Theory Y; Trust

Further Readings

Barnard, C. (1968). *The functions of the executive.* Cambridge, MA: Harvard University Press. (Originally published 1938)

Bell, D. (1973). *The coming of post-industrial society: A venture in social forecasting.* New York, NY: Basic Books.

Friedman, T., & Mandelbaum, M. (2001). *That used to be us: How America fell behind the world it invented and how we can come back.* New York, NY: Farrar, Straus, & Giroux.

Fry, B. R., & Raadschelders, J. (2008). Chester Barnard: Organizations as systems of exchange. In *Mastering public administration: From Max Weber to Dwight Waldo* (2nd ed., pp. 180–210). Washington, DC: Congressional Quarterly Press.

Mahoney, J. T. (2002). The relevance of Chester I. Barnard's Teachings to contemporary management education: Communicating the aesthetics of management. *International Journal of Organization Theory and Behavior, 5*(1&2), 159–172.

Reich, R. (1992). *The work of nations: Preparing ourselves for the 21st century.* New York, NY: Vintage Books.

Zakaria, F. (2011). *The Post-American world 2.0.* New York, NY: W. W. Norton.

GAME THEORY

Game theory is a branch of mathematics that studies strategic interactions between intelligent and rational decision makers, called *players*. Strategic interactions take place anytime a player's payoff depends not only on his or her own decision but also on the decisions made by the other players. Intelligent players fully understand the rules of the game and are able to assess the likely impact of their moves or actions. Given the available information, rationality simply means that players select the strategy that optimizes their payoff. Managers are regularly confronted with situations where the outcomes of their decisions are contingent on how their competitors or partners will react to those decisions. Examples include setting the price of a product, launching a new one, building an industrial plant overseas, bidding for a contract, and negotiating delivery terms with service and input providers. In these examples and in many others—indeed, the list is endless—managers must anticipate the other players' possible decisions when formulating their own strategy, knowing that their competitors are just as sophisticated and are attempting to do the same. In a nutshell, game theory offers a model for thinking strategically in situations involving interdependent gains. As with any model, abstraction, or conceptualization, game theory represents a highly complex reality through a parsimonious model, retaining only those elements that are rationalizable determinants within the context under study. To illustrate, consider a negotiation over wages between a company's management and union representatives. Experts agree that the outcome depends on variables such as the profitability of the firm, wages in similar firms in the industry, the state of the labor market, and both parties' potential losses in the event of a strike. This does not imply that other factors, such as the negotiators' ability, their past relationships, the shape of the room where the negotiations are taking place, and the time at which they start will not play a role in determining the negotiations' outcome. Nevertheless, a game theory model typically ignores these last factors because their impact is too situation specific to be of any general interest. Also, because they are highly perceptual, they can hardly be represented in a conceptually appealing way. To give an analogy, game theory helps determine the best travel route from A to B, but it does not describe the scenery. The remainder of this entry is structured as follows: The elements of a game are defined, and a classification of games is provided; the roots of the theory and its history are discussed, and a brief assessment is given of the impact of game theory, particularly on management and managers.

Fundamentals

Elements of Games

A game involves the following constituent elements:

Players. The agents interacting and competing in the game are called players. A player can be an agent acting solely on his or her own behalf—for example, a chess player or an entrepreneur—or the player can represent a set of individuals presumably sharing the same interest, such as a nation, a corporation, or a political party. In management, players are obviously human, but automata and cells have also been considered in game theory applications in engineering and biology.

Actions. Players have at their disposal a set of possible actions, also called moves or decisions, such as investment in research and development (R & D), price, and advertising budget.

Payoffs. Real numbers measuring the desirability of the game's possible outcomes are payoffs—for example, the amount of money the players (and their organizations) may win or lose, such as raises, revenue, and profits. Other names for payoffs are *rewards, performance indices* or *criteria, utility measures,* and so on.

Pure strategy. A decision rule that associates players' action with the information available to them at the time that they select their move is called pure strategy. So an action—for example, spending advertising dollars, or merging or not with another firm—is a result of the strategy. The word *strategy* comes from Greek (στρατηγία, *strategia*) and has a military meaning. An army general's main task is to design a plan that takes into account (adapts to) all possible contingencies. This is precisely the meaning of strategy in game theory. In a war, as in management, there is no room for "I was surprised by the enemy." This does not mean that it is always possible to design a winning strategy. Sometimes we should be content with a draw or even with a reasonably low amount of loss.

A player may also use a *mixed strategy,* which is a probability distribution defined on the space of a player's pure strategies. It can be viewed as a random draw from a set of pure strategies. The idea of choosing a strategy randomly may be surprising in a theory of rational behavior, but it should not be. The randomization of strategies is a fully rational choice. In some instances, you may put yourself in a vulnerable position if your competitor can guess your strategy. Mixing strategies amounts to keeping a poker face—in other words, not giving out any information about your hand or about whether or not you are bluffing. To illustrate, suppose that a franchisor needs to inspect the franchisees' outlets

for cleanliness and assume that cleaning is costly. Clearly, the franchisor has to surprise the franchisees; otherwise, they will clean only before monitoring visits. By mixing strategies (randomizing over the set of inspection times), the franchisor can induce the franchisees to invest enough in cleaning. Mixed strategies also play an important mathematical role in the proof of existence of a solution to a game.

Classification of Games

In a zero-sum game, a player gains what the other loses. In business and economics, it is seldom the case that the players have fully antagonistic objectives. Even competitors battling for each other's customers will share an interest in enlarging the market. Historically, zero-sum games attracted a lot of attention because parlor games—a source of inspiration for the first generations of game theorists—are zero-sum and because they are easier to deal with mathematically. In addition to this zero-sum/non-zero-sum distinction, games can be classified according to (a) the number of players, (b) the information structure, (c) the mode of play, and (d) the temporal interactions.

Number of players. Games can be designated by the number of players they involve—a one-person game, two-person game, or *n*-person game (with $n > 2$). In a one-person game, the decision maker plays against a nonstrategic (or dummy) player, often referred to as "nature," who makes random decisions. Two-player games focus on one-to-one interactions. Duopolistic competition, management-union negotiations, and politics in the United States are instances that can be modeled as two-person games. Extending the model to *n* players is often conceptually easy but may become computationally challenging because each player needs to guess all the possible sequences of actions and reactions for all players. When the number of interacting players is very large, such as an economy with many small agents, the analysis shifts from individual-level decisions to understanding the group's behavioral dynamics. An illustration of this is traffic congestion: As a first approximation, each agent aims to minimize his or travel time from A to B, but the speed at which any agent can travel depends on the density of other agents in the area. *Population games, evolutionary games,* and *mean-field games* are branches of game theory that study games with large numbers of players.

Information structure. This refers to what the players know about the game and its history when they choose an action. Players have *complete information* if they know who the players are, which set of actions is available to each one, what each player's information structure is, and what the players' possible outcomes can be. Otherwise, players have *incomplete information.* If, for instance, competing firms don't know their rivals' production costs, then the game is an incomplete-information game. The game can also have *perfect* or *imperfect information.* Roughly speaking, in a game of perfect information, players know the other players' moves when they choose their own action. Chess is an example of a perfect-information game. So is a manufacturer-retailer game where the upstream player first announces a product's wholesale price, and then the downstream player reacts by selecting the retail price. The archetype of an imperfect-information game is the *Prisoner's Dilemma,* where (in the original story) the players have to simultaneously choose between confessing and denying a crime. A Cournot oligopoly, where each firm chooses its own production level without knowing its rivals' choices, is another instance of an imperfect-information game.

Commitments and binding agreements are two key concepts related to the information available in a game. A commitment is where players bind themselves to take a future action. This binding and the action itself are known to the other players. In making a commitment, players can persuade (and sometimes force) the other players to take actions that are advantageous to them. Commitment is an absurd choice in an optimization context: Why would a rational decision maker want to reduce his or her set of choices by committing to a course of action? Interestingly, the situation is different when there are strategic interactions. For instance, by committing to investing in a shopping mall in a given location, a big retailer may gain an advantage by preventing the entry of rivals into that market. But clearly, it is not always beneficial to commit. To be effective, a commitment has to be *credible.* A particular class of commitments is *threats.* Credibility means that players will indeed implement their commitment (threat) if the conditions on which the threat rests are fulfilled. Otherwise, the threat is empty. One explanation for the avoidance of a nuclear conflict during the Cold War was that each player (NATO and the Warsaw Pact) firmly believed the other player's commitment

to launch a nuclear response to any nuclear attack, regardless of the cost. In some markets with few competitors, one reason for not engaging in a price war is that each competitor believes that cutting its price too much will almost certainly trigger a cascade of price cuts by competitors, which would result in an individual loss. In a binding agreement, two or more players decide together on restrictions to their possible actions and enter into a contract that forces the implementation of the agreement. Usually, a binding agreement requires an outside authority to monitor the agreement at no cost and to impose sanctions on violators that are severe enough to prevent cheating.

The mode of play and solutions. A game can be played cooperatively or noncooperatively. In the former case, the players can coordinate their strategies and make binding agreements, whereas this option is not possible (or does not make sense) in a noncooperative game. The main solution concept for a noncooperative game is *Nash equilibrium.* An equilibrium point is a vector of strategies, one for each player, with the property that no player can improve his or her payoff by *unilaterally* changing strategy. Conversely, any vector of feasible strategies that is not an equilibrium can be eliminated by a rationality argument; that is, at least one player can do better by adopting a different strategy.

To illustrate, consider a duopoly game where each firm can choose between a regular price and low price for its brand. The resulting payoffs are these: Firm A and Firm B each earn a profit of 4 when both sell at regular price (RP) and a lesser profit of 3 when each sell at low price (LP), but if only one of the firms drops its price then it will earn a profit of 8 (LP) compared to the other's profit of 1 (RP). For this game of imperfect information, the only Nash equilibrium is the pair of strategies (LP, LP), which results in a payoff of 3 to each player. It is easy to verify that no player can improve the payoff by unilaterally changing to the other feasible strategy—that is, to charge the regular price. Although both players would be better off playing the regular price strategy, there is no rational way of achieving this. Indeed, if A thinks that B will play RP, then the best choice is to implement LP strategy and get a profit of 8. Anticipating this rational reaction of Firm A, Firm B will in fact not choose RP. The same reasoning applies for B thinking that A will implement strategy RP. This game is of the

Prisoner's Dilemma variety—that is, a class of games where there is a Pareto optimal (or individually better) solution that, however, cannot be reached when the game is played once and noncooperatively.

Solving a cooperative game schematically follows a two-step procedure. In the first step, the players decide on a common objective to optimize; for example, the weighted sum of stakeholders' benefits or the total cost of treating the solid waste of neighboring municipalities. In the second step, the players have to agree on a way of sharing the dividend of their cooperation. Different solution concepts have been proposed, such as the core, the Shapley value, the nucleolus, and the kernel, each based on desirable properties, such as efficiency, equity, uniqueness of allocation, and stability of cooperation. In any solution, the set of acceptable allocations includes only those that are individually rational. Individual rationality means that players will agree to cooperate only if they can get a better outcome in the cooperative agreement than they would by acting alone.

The temporal interactions. One-shot games are a useful representation of strategic interactions when the past and the future are irrelevant to the analysis; that is, today's decisions affect only today's outcomes for the players and are independent of past moves. When there are carry-over effects and the players can condition their actions on history (and in particular on their rivals' behavior), then a dynamic game is needed. In a *repeated game,* the agents play the same game in each round; that is, the set of actions and the payoff structures are the same in all stages. The number of stages can be finite or infinite, and this distinction has been shown to have a tremendous impact on the equilibrium results. In *multistage games,* the players share the control of a discrete-time dynamic system (state equations) observed over stages. Their choice of control levels, such as investments in production capacity or advertising dollars, affects the evolution of the state variables (e.g., production capacity, reputation of the firm) as well as current payoffs. *Differential games* are continuous-time counterparts of multistage games.

Evolution

Game theory can be seen as the generalization to a multi-agent setting of *decision theory,* which is concerned with determining the optimal behavior of a rational player, possibly in the presence of uncertainty. Decision theory and game theory have heavily relied, at least in some of their areas, on an axiomatic approach—that is, where the players' behaviors are a consequence of some basic principles. For instance, payoffs in games are the translation of the players' preferences, which satisfy the axioms of cardinal utility, which were first introduced by John von Neumann and Oskar Morgenstern. Further, the techniques used to solve games are intimately related to optimization techniques.

The history of the theory of games can be traced back to some key figures, including the following: James Waldegrave in 1713 gave the first known minimax mixed-strategy solution to a two-person game. Augustin Cournot, in his 1838 *Researches Into the Mathematical Principles of the Theory of Wealth,* solved the problem of producers competing in quantity, using a solution concept that is a restricted version of the Nash equilibrium. Charles Darwin, in the first edition of his 1871 book *The Descent of Man, and Selection in Relation to Sex* made the first (implicitly) game-theoretic argument in evolutionary biology. Francis Ysidro Edgeworth proposed the contract curve as a solution to the problem of determining the outcome of trading between individuals, in his 1881 *Mathematical Psychics: An Essay on the Application of Mathematics to the Moral Sciences.* The "core," a fundamental concept in cooperative games, has been shown to be a generalization of Edgeworth's contract curve.

In the period between 1910 and 1930, mathematicians Ernst Zermerlo, Emile Borel, and John von Neumann proved some results for zero-sum games that gave the needed impulse for the theory to take off. The 1944 publication of *Theory of Games and Economic Behavior,* by mathematician John von Neumann and economist Oskar Morgenstern, both of whom fled Nazism in Europe in the 1930s to settle at Princeton University, is considered to be the official birth of game theory. The book was seminal, both for the mathematical ideas it contained and in relating game theory to economics. The relevance of this theory for the social sciences was quickly acknowledged by Herbert Simon in his review of the book in 1945. The 1950s and 1960s were highly prolific periods in terms of breakthroughs such as the concepts of equilibrium and of the bargaining solution (both due to John F. Nash), the value of a cooperative game and the formulation of a stochastic game (both due to Lloyd Shapley), and the core (Donald Gillies), to name only a few. In 1960, Thomas Schelling published the influential book *The Strategy of Conflicts,* and in 1965, Reinhard Selten proposed the subgame-perfect refinement of Nash equilibria. In the mid-1960s, John Harsanyi constructed the theory of games of incomplete information. Many of the developments during that period took place at Princeton University and the RAND Corporation in California, and some were motivated by military applications, in particular, the work of Rufus Isaacs with differential games. Robert Aumann introduced the concept of the correlated equilibrium in 1974. John Maynard Smith's 1982 book *Evolution and the Theory of Games* started the field of evolutionary game theory, which now has applications far beyond biology, where it began.

How has the theory evolved over time? Like many other branches of applied mathematics, the path taken by game theory in the last seven decades can be explained by three driving forces. The first is the intrinsic desire of mathematicians to generalize existing results to other structures, such as noncompact strategy sets and discontinuous pay-off functions. The second driving force has been the need to solve applied problems, which then led to new theoretical developments. The third force is the testing of the theory. Experimental game theory highlighted some discrepancies between the equilibrium predictions and how players actually behave. This was a motivation to relax the assumption of rationality and adopt the milder one of bounded rationality. The theory's vitality is in part due to the significant spillover of ideas that occurs between the communities interested in the mathematical aspects, the applications of game theory and experimentation.

Importance

Since its inception, game theory has tremendously developed and its impact is highly visible in the social sciences, engineering, biology, and computer science. Nowadays, there are learned societies and academic journals that are fully dedicated to game theory. Hundreds of books and lecture notes are available, dealing with different facets of the theory for different audiences (managers, economists, biologists, mathematicians, etc.). Another indicator of its impact is that game theorists were awarded The Sveriges Riksbank Prize in Economic Sciences of Alfred Nobel in 1994 (John C. Harsanyi, John F. Nash, and Reinhard Selten), in 2005 (Robert Aumann and Thomas Schelling) and in 2007 (Leonid Hurwicz, Eric S. Maskin, and Roger B. Myerson). The contributions of the winners in 1994 and 2005 were alluded to above. The most recent award was given "for having laid the foundations of mechanism design theory," which is useful whenever a principal (manager, government) wants agents (employees, firms) who have private information to behave truthfully. Mechanism design is sometimes referred to as a reverse game because the principal is choosing the game structure rather than inheriting existing rules. *Game engineering,* which is defined as the use of game theory to design practical interactive systems, is closely related to mechanism design. A representative real implementation of this part of game theory is the design of auctions for radio waves. The success of game theory comes at a cost. As has happened in the past to other successful fields, game theory has de facto split into subareas, each producing highly sophisticated results that are accessible only to experts. The ever-increasing number of specialized meetings is evidence of this trend.

The scholarly impact of game theory in management can be seen in the literature. Indeed, it is rare that any issue of a top-tier journal does not include at least one article applying game-theoretical thinking. Interestingly, scholars in business schools have not only been consumers of game theory; they have also played an important role in its development. The following are a few of the many topical managerial questions that have been successfully dealt with using game theory: how to coordinate a supply chain; whether a retailer should offer a matching-lower-price clause; how to design incentives to optimize employees' efforts; and how to reorganize a financially distressed company.

Georges Zaccour

See also Agency Theory; Behavioral Theory of the Firm; Bounded Rationality and Satisficing (Behavioral Decision-Making Model); Decision Support Systems; Fairness Theory; First-Mover Advantages and Disadvantages; Strategic Decision Making; Theory of Cooperation and Competition

Further Readings

Dixit, A. K., & Nalebuff, B. J. (2008). *The art of strategy.* New York, NY: Norton.

Fudenberg, D., & Tirole, J. (1991). *Game theory.* Cambridge, MA: MIT Press.

Ghemawat, P. (1997). *Games businesses play.* Cambridge, MA: MIT Press.

Gibbons, R. (1992). *A primer in game theory.* London, England: Harvester-Wheatsheaf.

Haurie, A., Krawczyk, J. B., & Zaccour, G. (2012). *Games and dynamic games.* Series in Business. Singapore: World Scientific-Now.

McMillan, J. (1992). *Games, strategies and managers.* Oxford, England: Oxford University Press.

Straffin, P. D. (1993). *Game theory and strategy.* Washington, DC: Mathematical Association of America.

Von Neumann, J., & Morgenstern, O. (1944). *Theory of games and economic behavior.* Princeton, NJ: Princeton University Press.

Gantt Chart and PERT

The Gantt chart and program evaluation and review technique (PERT) are project management frameworks that are used to schedule, organize, and coordinate activities in a project. Project management has grown in importance due to increased complexity in the development process of goods and services. Membership in Project Management Institute (PMI) has grown from 7,500 members in 1990 to more than 334,000 members in 2010, according to PMI 2010 annual report. The Gantt chart and PERT have become indispensable parts of the contemporary manager's toolbox. The Gantt chart was developed by Henry Gantt, a pioneer in the field of scientific management, as a graphical aid to scheduling jobs on machines in the late 1910s. PERT is a network diagram analysis technique developed in the late 1950s by Booz Allen Hamilton, Inc., under contract to the U.S. Navy for the Polaris Missile Project. PERT is similar to critical path method (CPM), developed around the same time by DuPont and Remington Rand. PERT and CPM both employ the critical path analysis to determine the project completion time and start and finish times of each activity. The difference between PERT and CPM is that PERT gives probabilistic estimates when activity times are uncertain and CPM offers the option of reducing activity times by adding more resources. Today's project management software incorporates features of both approaches, so the distinction between the two techniques is no longer necessary. In the next section, the fundamentals of PERT and the Gantt chart are explained. It is followed by comparison and evaluation of the two methods and suggested readings for further information.

Fundamentals

PERT Network Diagram

PERT network diagram graphically illustrates the following: (a) when the project can be finished, (b) when each activity should be scheduled, (c) which activities are critical (i.e., a bottleneck) that must be started as soon as possible to avoid delaying the project completion, and (d) how long each noncritical activity can be delayed before the project completion time is delayed.

There are two types of PERT network diagrams: activity-on-arrow (AOA) and activity-on-node (AON). In an AOA diagram, the arrow represents the activity, and the node represents events such as the completion of one or more activities. In an AON diagram, the node represents the activity, and the arrow represents the sequencing between activities. Over time, AOA diagrams have lost ground to AON diagrams, which are more easily created with software. An AON network diagram shown in Figure 1 consists of nodes representing activities and arrows connecting the nodes to indicate precedence relationships. Specifically, an arrow from Activity I to Activity J indicates that Activity I is an immediate predecessor of Activity J. This means Activity J can be started only after Activity I is completed. Conversely, Activity J is called an immediate successor of Activity I. Each node contains the following information:

- Activity (task) name
- Activity duration: the length of time an activity will take (in weeks)
- Early start (ES): the earliest time when an activity can start
- Early finish (EF): the earliest time when an activity can finish
- Late start (LS): the latest time when an activity can start without delaying project completion

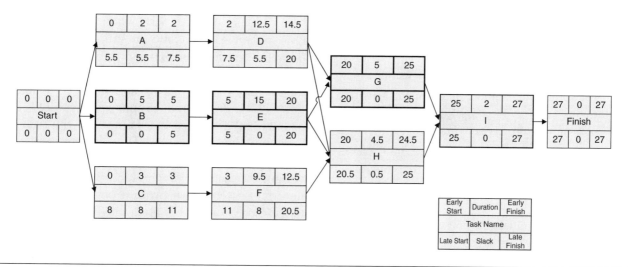

Figure 1 PERT Network Diagram

Source: Author.

- Late finish (LF): the latest time when an activity can finish without delaying project completion
- Slack: the length of time an activity can be delayed without delaying project completion, computed as LS–ES or LF–EF.

The critical path analysis of the project consists of (a) drawing the network with activity name and duration in each node, (b) computing the ES and EF of each activity, (c) computing the LS and LF of each activity, and (d) identifying the critical path in the network. The start and finish nodes mark the beginning and ending of the project and are not real activities. Hence, their duration times are 0. These nodes are optional and are added to clarify the beginning and the ending of the project.

The ES and EF of each activity is computed by making a forward pass through the network, from left to right. Since duration of the start node is 0, its ES and EF are also 0. In general, the ES of each activity is the largest EF of its immediate predecessors. For instance, Activity G can be started only when both of its predecessors, D and E, are completed. D can be finished at 14.5 weeks into the project, and E can be finished at 20 weeks. So the earliest G can start is at 20 weeks. EF is computed by simply adding activity duration to ES. The ES of the finish node is the earliest time that the project can be completed. In this example, it is shown that the project can be finished in 27 weeks.

The next step is to compute LS and LF of each activity by making a backward pass, from right to left. First, LS and LF of the finish node is set equal to the project completion time, 27 weeks. For each activity, LF is computed before LS. The LF of an activity is the smallest LS of its immediate successors. For example, Activity D has two successors, G and H. To ensure both G and H start by their LSs, 20 weeks and 20.5 weeks, respectively, D must be completed by 20 weeks. After the LF is computed, the LS is obtained by subtracting the duration time from the LF.

Next, the critical path is identified in the network. To do this, slack is computed for each activity. It is the difference between the LS and ES (or equivalently, LF and EF). The critical activities are those that have slack of zero, meaning these activities cannot be delayed at all. The critical path is the path from start to finish consisting only of critical activities. In the example, the critical path is B-E-G-I as indicated in bold. The length of the critical path is equal to the project completion time. To illustrate, the length of B-E-G-I is 5 + 15 + 5 + 2 = 27 weeks. Of all the possible paths in the network, the critical path is the longest one. There can be more than one critical path in the network. For example, if duration of H is 5 weeks instead of 4.5 weeks, there will be two critical paths: B-E-G-I and B-E-H-I.

In summary, the critical path analysis of the project in Figure 1 yields the following results:

1. The project can be finished in 27 weeks.
2. The starting and ending times for the activities are indicated by the ES, EF, LS, and LF in the nodes of the project network.
3. The critical activities are B, E, G, and I. These activities must be started and finished as early as possible, according to ES and EF, in order not to delay the project completion.
4. The maximum lengths that the noncritical activities can be delayed are indicated by slacks in the activity nodes of the network.

Gantt Chart

While the PERT diagram illustrates dependence of activities, the Gantt chart shows the timing and the duration of each activity on a bar chart. In the Gantt chart, the length of each bar represents duration of an activity. The location of each bar is based on the ES and EF of the corresponding activity. At any point in time, it is easy to forecast the progress of each activity. For example, at 10 weeks into the project, the Gantt chart shows that activities A, B and C will be finished, and D, E, and F will be in progress. This aids in resource planning. The Gantt chart is simple to understand and is useful for tracking the progress of the project. However, it does not show the dependence between activities, so it is difficult to tell how delay in an activity will affect the project completion time.

A project management software program, such as Microsoft Project, will usually show more details in a Gantt chart. It can show precedence relationships, with arrows connecting Activity A to the left edge of Activity D indicates A is an immediate predecessor of D. Microsoft Project can also highlight the critical activities and track the progress of the project with the progress bar overlaid with the baseline bar.

Probability Estimation in PERT

When the activity duration times are certain, the project completion time obtained with critical path analysis can be taken as a reasonable estimate. If a similar project has not been completed before, the activity duration may be highly uncertain. In that case, the duration of each activity is modeled by a beta distribution with three parameters: optimistic time (a), most likely time (m), and pessimistic time (b). The expected time (t) is a weighted average of the three time estimates, given by $(a + 4m + b)/6$, and the variance of each activity duration is computed as $((b - a)/6)2$. For example, suppose Activity D is estimated to take between 5 and 26 weeks with the most likely time being 11 weeks. Then the expected duration of D is $(5 + 4(11) + 26)/6 = 12.5$ weeks, and its variance is $((26 - 5)/6)2 = 12.25$ weeks. Modeling uncertain activity times with a probability distribution is the feature that distinguishes PERT from CPM.

In PERT, the expected times are used to find the critical path with the usual forward and backward passes. Then the project completion time is modeled by a normal distribution with the mean equal to the length of the critical path, and its variance is equal to the sum of variances of critical-path activities. With these assumptions, probability of finishing by a deadline can be estimated.

Importance

While the Gantt chart and PERT have been most widely used in the construction, information technology, and new product development, they are increasingly being used to manage complex projects in virtually all industries. Some examples are event planning, performing arts productions, underwriting financial instruments, and marketing campaign.

The Gantt chart and PERT are useful in planning a project where time is a limited resource. Both can be used to schedule activities, determine the project completion time, and identify critical activities and activities with slack. The benefits are time savings, facilitation of resource planning, and transparency of the project's progress to the project team members and other members of the organization. To use these techniques, the project team needs to identify the activities of the project, estimate the duration times, and identify dependencies among activities. Typically, these inputs are entered into a project management software program that will produce both the Gantt chart and PERT diagrams.

The Gantt chart is better known than PERT because it is understood more easily by managers.

The advantages of the Gantt chart are as follows: (a) It is easy to create and easy to understand; (b) it can illustrate the current state of a project; (c) it can be used to track progress of the tasks at any point in time; and (d) it can be used to estimate total resources needed at any point in time. The advantages of PERT are as follows: (a) It clearly illustrates interdependence of all activities (although the Gantt chart can be made to show dependencies, too many dependency links can make it difficult to read), and (b) the effect of changes in activity duration can be evaluated easily; it can estimate probability of project completion by a certain date when activity times are uncertain. In general, the Gantt chart is useful for communicating with senior management. PERT is more useful for managing projects with numerous dependencies among activities. In practice, both can easily be created with software.

Janice Winch

See also Decision Support Systems; Scientific Management; Six Sigma; Theory of Constraints; Total Quality Management

Further Readings

Gantt, H. L. (1974). *Work, wages and profit.* Easton, PA: Hive. (Original work published in *The Engineering Magazine,* 1910)

Kerzner, H. (2009). *Project management: A systems approach to planning, scheduling, and controlling* (10th ed.). Hoboken, NJ: Wiley.

Malcolm, D. G., Roseboom, J. H., Clark, C. E., & Fazar, W. (1959). Application of a technique for research and development program evaluation. *Operations Research, 7*(5), 646–669.

Marmel, E. (2010). *Microsoft Project 2010 Bible.* Hoboken, NJ: Wiley.

Pinto, J. K. (2009). *Project management: Achieving competitive advantage* (2nd ed.). Upper Saddle River, NJ: Pearson.

Project Management Institute. (2008). *A guide to the project management body of knowledge* (4th ed.). Newtown Square, PA: Author.

GARBAGE CAN MODEL OF DECISION MAKING

The garbage can model (GCM) is a model within the area of organizational behavior that describes the decision-making process in so-called organized anarchies (organizations facing extreme levels of ambiguity in their decisional environments). The GCM attempts to explain how organizations make choices without having consistent, shared goals and how the organizations' members are involved in these decision-making processes. The decision-making process within the organized anarchies is portrayed as a garbage can into which a mix of problems and possible solutions are dumped, with the particular mix determining the decision's outcomes. The mix is reflected by (a) how many decision areas are handled by the organization, (b) which people in the organization have decision-making power, (c) the organization's decision load, and (d) its resources, time, energy, and attention. This model has been used particularly to describe decision-making processes in the public sector and academic organizations, and it has been tested with computer simulations and real-life decision-making situations. In the following sections of this entry, the fundamental aspects of the GCM are presented, followed by a description of its patterns and decision styles and, finally, a discussion of the model's importance.

Fundamentals

Organized Anarchy

Central to the GCM are the "organized anarchies," which are organizations overwhelmed by extreme ambiguity. This ambiguity appears within three principal areas. First, these organizations are characterized by having multiple, inconsistent, and ill-defined preferences. These organized anarchies tend to rely on a variety of ideas to operate rather than on a coherent systematic structure. They are also likely to find their goals through action rather than knowing them *a priori,* by choice. At the same time, according to the model, the decision makers of these organizations have a limited understanding of the processes, technology, and means being used. This causes trial-and-error-based behaviors or wandering when faced with demands for choice. Through this, decision makers gain residual experience from accidental learning and by creating practical solutions to the issues that they face. A final characteristic of these organizations is the fluid participation of its members. Decision makers capriciously allocate resources, time, and energy to the issues they face, depending on the domain of the organization they are focused on at any particular time, which, in turn, shapes the outcome of the decision-making process. Such a fluid participation adds extra uncertainty to the process as a whole and makes the boundaries of these organizations more volatile.

An important feature of the GCM is the idea that decisions are the result of a chance encounter of four independent streams of events that flow in and out of the organizational decision situations: the problems, the solutions, the participants, and the choice opportunities. The problems within the GCM are the issues and concerns raised by the organizational members, and the solutions are the answers looking for problems. The participants are the organizational members that intermittently pay attention to these issues according to their available time and energy. The choice opportunities are all the situations that call for a decision. According to this model, these four elements are unrelated or only loosely coupled most of the time, and they share only in that they happen to be simultaneously available at a specific point in time. As with a garbage can, problems and solutions are thrown in and become connected with each other by chance, making the decision-making process more a function of random encounters than a rational process. This model emphasizes the fact that solutions, problems, and participants are not connected to each other rationally but arbitrarily, by their mere fortuitous simultaneous occurrence. The consequences that arise from such a particular decision-making process are that in general it is seen as a fuzzy, chaotic process that lacks a clear beginning and end, being the synthesis of a random confluence of disparate streams of events. According to this model, solutions might even be posed when there is no clear problem present, and choices might be made without any problems being solved, and some critical problems within the organizations may persist without being solved.

Patterns and Styles

The GCM has been tested by using a simulation routine in FORTRAN (formula translating system), a programming language. A number of 81 types of organizational situations were obtained by taking all possible combinations of the four streams in a given organization:

1. Access structure (unsegmented, hierarchical, and specialized)
2. Decision structure (unsegmented, hierarchical, and specialized)

3. Energy distribution (important people–low energy, equal energy, important people–high energy)

4. Net energy load of the organization

Considering all the values of the four dimensions, the total number of simulations that were run was 324 in a 20 time-period simulation of organizational decision making. At each of the possible organizational structures generated, the problems, decision makers, and energy levels necessary to make the decisions and solve the problems were assigned. The simulation also considered three different decision styles or ways of solving problems within organizations. First, *by resolution* when some choices solve problems after a period of working on them. The length of time is subject to the number of problems in the queue, waiting to be solved. Second, *by oversight,* referring to the kind of decisions made when decision makers ignore the existing problems when choosing a solution and only invest a small amount of time and energy. In these situations, the choices take place when problems are actually attached to other choices. And third, *by flight,* describing the cases in which some unsuccessful choices are associated with problems until a more attractive choice opportunity with a more successful matching of problems and solutions comes along.

The *net energy load* in the model refers to the energy expenditure in this process, which reflects the decision maker, the movement, and the persistence. Four measures were used to reflect the net energy load in the GCM simulation: (a) the total number of time periods that the decision maker is attached to a particular choice, (b) the total number of times that any decision maker shifts from one choice to another, (c) the total amount of effective energy available, and (d) the total effective energy that is actually used on choices. Apart from these measures, some other aspects of the decision process were also considered in the model, such as the decision difficulty, the problem latency, and activity.

The simulations resulted in some patterns across the different conditions: The most common decision-making styles for problem solving were found to be problem solving by flight or oversight rather than by resolution of problems. The problem-solving process was also found to be quite sensitive to variations in the energy load. The simulations showed that an increase in the net energy load generated an increased problem activity, decision maker activity, decision difficulty, and the use of flight and oversight to a higher degree.

Moreover, another pattern indicated that important choices are less likely to resolve problems than unimportant choices and that unimportant choices tend to be made by resolution.

Importance

The central insight of the GCM is that it captures the complex environment that surrounds organizational decision making and it comes to the conclusion that decisions in such situations tend to be arbitrary, ritualized, and chaotic. By looking into a phenomenon that has been essentially neglected by other models, the main contribution of the GCM is that it adds to the understanding of decision-making behavior in the daily operations of organizations. The model attempts to make sense of the decision-making process in organizations where rational choice models cannot be applied. It represents a point of departure from previous models that assume rational outcomes, consistent sets of preferences, knowledge of alternative solutions, and a full capacity of the decision makers to calculate the probabilities of success of each course of action. The GCM describes the decision-making process in highly ambiguous choice situations where goals and preferences are unidentified, fuzzy, or internally contradictory and the calculation capacity of the decision makers is limited or nonexistent. One strength of the GCM is that it is able to account for much of the seemingly fortuitous and contradictory behavior present in organizational decision making. Another important strength is the fact that the model treats the decision making in organizations not as a mere individual mental process but as a collective phenomenon, adding extra complexity to this process and its understanding. The GCM focuses on several explanatory variables that might affect the decision-making process. It takes into account a wide range of intervening events that influence the decision-making process not considered by other decision-making models.

The GCM emerged as a reaction against the highly structured conceptualizations of organizational decision making within the traditional rational-choice models that dominated the management field at the beginning of the 1970s. The traditional theories of decision making, management, and organization at that point took as a fact the existence of well-defined goals and technology, as well as a substantial participation of the members in organizations' affairs. However, when goals and technology are blurry and participation is fluid, the traditional models of management and decision making tend to fail. In that sense, the GCM expands the organizational decision theory into the little-explored field of organizations that undergo high levels of ambiguity and confusion, as these are not clearly portrayed by the classic theories of decision making.

The GCM also shifts from the earlier focus on decision making as an individual process to a more macro, aggregated, organizational-level decision making.

The GCM abandons the idea that decision making in these organized anarchies would follow a set of linearly defined stages that lead to predictable coherent outcomes: a process that would start with a problem that is clearly defined and isolated and that would end with a solution. Unlike classical decision theory, the GCM, already from the start, disconnects the problems, solutions, and decision makers from each other and depicts both the organizations and decision-making processes as complex, dynamic, and fuzzy phenomena.

The GCM is a significant and often-cited contribution to organizational behavior theory that combines empirical observations, theory, and simulation methodologies. It adds insight into how organizations strive to survive while struggling with ambiguous and multifaceted problems as well as an unpredictable environment. The original GCM has been criticized for amplifying the "anarchic" nature of decision making, focusing on the influence of power and structural constraints. However, according to other studies, institutional theories might complement the GCM by describing how decision making may occur in a slightly more organized manner. Combining the studies that have been carried out to test this model, an important conclusion is that organizational decision making cannot be understood in purely rational terms but would rather need to be analyzed in the context of streams that determine the particular combination of problems, solutions, and participants, in something that might be considered a garbage can.

Leonardo Liberman

See also Participative Model of Decision Making; Strategic Decision Making; "Unstructured" Decision Making

Further Readings

Bendor, J., Moe, T. M., & Shotts, K. W. (2001). Recycling the garbage can: An assessment of the research program. *American Political Science Review, 95*(1), 169–190.

Cohen, M. D., March, J. G., & Olsen, J. P. (1972). A garbage can model of organizational choice. *Administrative Science Quarterly, 17*(1), 1–25.

Olsen, J. P. (1976). Choice in an organized anarchy. In J. G. March & J. P. Olsen (Eds.), *Ambiguity and choice in organizations* (pp. 82–139). Bergen, Norway: Universitetsforlaget.

Olsen, J. P. (2001). Garbage cans, new institutionalism, and the study of politics, *American Political Science Review, 95*(1), 191–198.

Padgett, J. F. (1980). Managing garbage can hierarchies. *Administrative Science Quarterly, 25*(4), 583–604.

GENDERLECT AND LINGUISTIC STYLES

Language is not only a communication tool but also an instrument providing information about the interlocutors, taking into account their gender, culture, and identity, at both the individual and group level. Thus, *a linguistic style* can be described as the set of characteristics that determine one's speaking patterns, whereas a *genderlect* can be defined as the variety of speech shaped by several gender-related features. Linguistic styles and genderlects are important not only for linguists but also for the representatives of other disciplines, including both the researchers and practitioners of management studies and practice. The application of selected linguistic data on styles, dialects, and registers into organizational studies is multidimensional, including the possibility of investigating hierarchies, choosing and adapting marketing and branding strategies, understanding the nuances of intercultural communication, and creating and running effective advertising campaigns. This entry will concentrate on presenting the notions of genderlect and linguistic styles, showing their main features and functions as well as their role in modern management.

Fundamentals

Genderlect is defined as a set of gender-related characteristics of one's speaking. As far as the terminological level is concerned, other terms used for determining the types of gender discourses are registers or styles (e.g., *female registers, women's style*). The term *women's language* was introduced by Robin Lakoff in 1973, and in her later studies, she categorized the way women speak. She discovered that women and men differ as far as specialized vocabulary is concerned; for example, women generally use more names for colors. Moreover, the selection of job-related terminology is also determined by gender. Thus, females have a broader vocabulary about activities generally undertaken by women. As far as expletives are concerned, women rely more often on milder forms, whereas men are rather likely to opt for stronger tools of discursive power, even swear words. Women are also likely to use adjectives representing their emotion, rely on tag question to express uncertainty, and opt for more polite forms in asking for something. In addition, male style is often more impersonal, whereas females prefer more personalized forms of communication. However, apart from the perspectives stressing gender binarism, there are other approaches to genderlects. Since gender is not the only the factor shaping the way one communicates, other parameters, such as class, education, or background are taken into account by researchers to discuss gender variations in broader contexts (groups, communities, companies). The other view is to treat genderlect as a constructional tool of one's identity, with genderlectal linguistic repertoire being the instrument of constructing individual and group personae.

Linguistic style can be defined as the set of characteristics determining one's speaking pattern. Elements of linguistic style include the tone of voice, speed, volume, use of pauses, directness or indirectness, choice of words, credit taking, and the use of questions and jokes as well as the body language that accompanies communication. Taking the cultural perspective into account, linguistic styles can be perceived not only as the set of cultural signals that allows people to communicate their needs, wishes, or feelings but also to understand the message that others want to communicate. In scientific literature, linguistic styles are often associated with one's individual use of language idiolect. However, linguistic styles can be also discussed through the prism of investigating groups or communities (e.g., companies) to study the relations within the grouping as well as the grouping's links with the broadly understood environment.

Both genderlects and linguistic styles are determined by the function they serve (e.g., scientific, technical, business, everyday). As far as management studies are concerned, they vary in terms of the area they are applied to, the type of specialists using them, and the kind of audience toward which they are directed. Thus, the discourse of accounting differs from marketing communication at lexical, syntactic, and pragmatic levels. It should be stressed that the importance of genderlects and linguistic styles is different even within one studied area of management. For example, as far as advertising is concerned, genderlectal elements are strong in the products directed exclusively at female/male users. Moreover, linguistic styles are not only centered on the function they serve; they also mirror the links between those engaged in communication acts and provide information on the inter- and intraorganizational relations between managers, workers, and stakeholders. Thus, linguistic styles are not only used to communicate ideas and exchange opinions, but they also determine the creation and maintenance of relationships. In the use of words and forms of expressions, one shows the attitude to the interlocutor and his or her place and role in conversation. Thus, the way linguistic styles are handled determines organizational communication at both the internal and external level, since they mirror hierarchical relations and organizational communication policy. Moreover, according to the so-called *linguistic style matching* (LSM), the selection of speaker's linguistic tools determines the response of the listener. Thus, linguistic styles are dynamic phenomena, constantly responding to the changing conditions for both the worker and the organization.

As far as knowledge and innovation are concerned, linguistic styles facilitate the exchange of information between management studies and other disciplines. Moreover, they allow knowledge creators not only to inform the potential users on their novel solutions but also receive constructive feedback from broadly understood stakeholders that can later stimulate the development of innovative and effective products or services.

Additionally, the variety of linguistic styles offers managers the possibility of communicating with diversified stakeholders, taking into account their needs and preferences. For example, some groups of speakers prefer direct face-to-face interactions, whereas others opt for written or online communication. Moreover, the selection of linguistic style corresponds to the type of message and the topic of interaction in order to communicate effectively.

Magdalena Bielenia-Grajewska

See also Acculturation Theory; Critical Theory of Communication; Cultural Values; High- and Low-Context Cultures; Individual Values; Informal Communication and the Grapevine; Managing Diversity; Social Power, Bases of

Further Readings

Bakhtin, M. (1986). *Speech genres and other late essays.* Austin: University of Texas Press.

Crawford, M. E. (1997). *Talking difference: On gender and language.* London, England: Sage.

Duranti, A. (2001). *Key terms in language and terms.* Malden, MA: Blackwell.

Gumperz, J. J., & Cook-Gumperz, J. (2007). A postscript: Style and identity in interactional sociolinguistics. In P. Auer (Ed.), *Style and social identities: Alternative approaches to linguistic heterogeneity* (pp. 477–502). Berlin, Germany: Walter de Gruyter.

Lakoff. R. 1973 Language and woman's place. *Language in Society, 2,* 45–79

McGlone, M. S., & Giles, H. (2011). Language and interpersonal communication. In M. L. Knapp & J. A. Daly (Eds.), *The SAGE handbook of interpersonal communication* (pp. 201–237). Thousand Oaks, CA: Sage.

Motschenbacher, H. (2010). *Language, gender and sexual identity: Poststructuralist perspectives.* Amsterdam, Netherlands: John Benjamins.

Niederhoffer, K. G., & Pennebaker, J. W. (2002). Linguistic style matching in social interaction. *Journal of Language and Social Psychology, 21*(4), 337–360.

Sebeok, T. (1978). *Style in language.* Cambridge, MA: MIT Press.

Sims, R. R. (2002). *Managing organizational behavior.* Westport, CT: Quorum Books.

Tannen, D. (2001). The power of talk: Who gets heard and why. In I. G. Asherman & S. V. Asherman (Eds.), *The negotiation sourcebook* (pp. 245–258). Amherst, MA: HRD Press.

GLOBE Model

Pursuing global opportunities is a high priority for most corporations. In a survey of 500 executives at 100 corporations 75% of the respondents' corporations were planning to compete in foreign markets, and 50% expected their corporations to receive more revenue from foreign markets than their domestic markets. The increasing global exposure of corporations increases managerial interest in understanding national cultures and their implications for executives and corporations. In a recent survey, CEOs identified "mobilizing teams and working across cultures" as the top two leadership competencies. There are also compelling academic reasons for considering the impact of societal culture on leadership. The goal of science is to develop universally valid theories. There are inherent limitations in transferring social science theories across cultures. What works in one culture may not work in another. As Harry Triandis suggests, leadership researchers will be able to "fine-tune" theories by investigating cultural variations as parameters of those theories. Furthermore, a focus on cross-cultural issues can help uncover new relationships by including a broader range of variables. The GLOBE (Global Leadership and Organizational Behavior Effectiveness) research program was founded by Robert House in 1991. GLOBE is a multiphase, multimethod, multisample research project to examine the interrelationships between societal culture and organizational leadership. Over 200 scholars from 69 cultures are engaged in this long-term series of studies. The investigators studied over 900 domestic corporations in 62 countries in the first two GLOBE phases and over 1,000 corporations in 24 countries in the third phase of GLOBE. Of the latter 24 countries, 17 were in common with the first two phases, so 69 societies in total were studied. This entry summarizes the main findings of the model and presents some of its most important implications for contemporary management practice.

Fundamentals

Since 1991, the GLOBE research program has continued in three distinct but interrelated phases. Following is a brief description of the major objectives and findings of the program so far. This entry's focus is on the findings with management and leadership implications.

GLOBE Objectives and Findings of Phases 1 and 2

The researchers developed societal measures of cultural values and practices in the first phase of the research project. The investigators surveyed over 17,000 middle managers in 62 cultures and identified nine cultural dimensions briefly described below:

- **Power distance:** The degree to which members expect power to be distributed equally
- **Uncertainty avoidance:** The extent to which norms and rules are relied on to alleviate unpredictability
- **Humane orientation:** The degree to which individuals are encouraged to be kind to others
- **Collectivism I (institutional collectivism):** The degree to which collective distribution of resources is encouraged
- **Collectivism II (family collectivism):** The degree to which individuals express pride and loyalty to their families
- **Assertiveness:** The degree to which individuals are assertive in their relationships with others
- **Gender egalitarianism:** The degree to which gender inequality is minimized
- **Future orientation:** The extent to which individuals engage in future-oriented behaviors
- **Performance orientation:** The degree to which members are encouraged to improve performance

GLOBE defined leadership as the ability of individuals to motivate and enable others to contribute to the effectiveness and success of their organizations. We (the investigators) extended the concept of implicit leadership theory (ILT) to the level of national culture and hypothesized that members of different societies have differing expectations from their leaders, influenced by their cultural values.

The Culturally Endorsed Leadership Theory

We found 21 *primary dimensions* of leadership expectations. A second-order factor analysis of these 21 dimensions produced a set of what we refer to as six *global leadership dimensions*. The six global dimensions and their associated 21 primary leadership dimensions constitute our notion of culturally endorsed leadership theory (CLT) as described below:

Charismatic/value-based leadership. Reflects the ability to inspire and expect high performance outcomes based on firmly held core values; includes six primary leadership dimensions: (a) visionary, (b) inspirational, (c) self-sacrifice, (d) integrity, (e) decisive, and (f) performance oriented.

Team-oriented leadership. Emphasizes team building and implementation of a common purpose; includes five primary leadership dimensions: (a) collaborative team orientation, (b) team integrator, (c) diplomatic, (d) malevolent (reverse scored), and (e) administratively competent

Participative leadership. Reflects the degree to which managers involve others in making and implementing decisions; includes two primary leadership dimensions: (a) nonparticipative and (b) autocratic (both reverse scored).

Humane-oriented leadership. Reflects supportive and considerate leadership and includes compassion and generosity; consists of two primary leadership dimensions: (a) modesty and (b) humane orientation.

Autonomous leadership. Refers to independent and individualistic leadership.

Self-protective leadership. Focuses on ensuring the leader's security through status enhancement and face-saving; includes five primary leadership dimensions: (a) self-centered, (b) status conscious, (c) conflict inducer, (d) face-saver, and (e) procedural.

Universally Desirable and Undesirable Leadership Attributes

The following attributes were found to be universally desirable. Managers in all GLOBE countries believed they contribute to outstanding leadership: trustworthy, just, honest, foresight, plans ahead, encouraging, positive, dynamic, motive arouser, confidence builder, motivational, dependable, intelligent, decisive, effective bargainer, win–win problem solver, administratively skilled, communicative, informed, coordinator, team builder, and excellence oriented.

The following leadership attributes were found to be universally undesirable: loner, asocial, noncooperative, irritable, nonexplicit, egocentric, ruthless, and dictatorial.

Cultural Values as Predictors of Leadership Expectations

There are important relationships between the nine cultural values and six global leadership dimensions. For example, performance orientation as a cultural value predicts all six leadership dimensions. It is a very strong positive predictor of charismatic, participative, and autonomous leadership dimensions. It also positively predicts team-oriented and humane-oriented leadership dimensions and is negatively related to self-protective leadership. Following is a brief summary of how cultural values predict leadership expectations:

- Societies (e.g., United States or Singapore) that value *performance orientation* expect their leaders to be charismatic, participative, autonomous, team oriented, and humane. They do not want their leaders to be self-protective.
- Societies (e.g., Egypt and Ireland) that value *humane orientation* expect their leaders to be charismatic, participative, humane, and team oriented. They do not want their leaders to be autonomous.
- Societies (e.g., Thailand and Taiwan) that value *uncertainty avoidance and rules orientation* expect their leaders to be self-protective, humane, and team oriented. They do not want their leaders to be participative.
- Societies (e.g., Egypt and Malaysia) that value *strong family orientation* expect their leaders to be charismatic and team oriented. They do not want their leaders to be self-protective.
- Societies (e.g., Czech Republic and South Africa) that value *high power distance* more than do other GLOBE countries expect their leaders to be self-protective. They do not want their leaders to be charismatic or participative.
- Societies (e.g., Sweden and England) that value *high gender egalitarianism* expect their leaders to be charismatic and participative. They do not want their leaders to be self-protective.

- Societies (e.g., Canada and Singapore) that value *high future orientation* expect their leaders to be charismatic, team oriented, and humane.
- Societies (e.g., Japan and China) that value *high levels of assertiveness* expect their leaders to be humane. They do not want their leaders to be participative.
- Societies (e.g., El Salvador and Brazil) that value *high levels of institutional collectivism* do not want their leaders to be autonomous.

Objectives and Findings of GLOBE Phase 3

GLOBE Phase 3 has just been completed. The investigators surveyed and interviewed 1,060 CEOs and surveyed their over 5,000 direct reports in 24 countries. The goal was to examine the relationship between national culture, CLT leadership behavior, and leadership effectiveness. In the previous phases, the impact of national culture on managerial expectations of their leaders was examined. In Phase 3, we studied the impact of national culture and CLT on actual behavior of CEOs and their effectiveness. The full description of Phase 3 will be available in the forthcoming book *Strategic Leadership: The GLOBE Study of CEO Effectiveness Across Cultures* to be published in 2012. The following is a brief summary of our findings:

National culture does *not* predict leadership behavior. Contrary to the conventional wisdom, our analysis of the correlation between the nine cultural values and six global leadership dimensions of behavior shows that with a few exceptions, national culture values do not directly predict leadership behavior.

CLT predicts leadership behavior. We examined the correlation between the six CLT global leadership dimensions and their counterpart leadership behaviors. Five out of six CLTs are significantly correlated with their behavioral counterparts, meaning that CEOs tend to behave in accordance to societies' expectations of their leaders.

Leaders who behave according to expectations are effective. The extent to which each leader's behavior is congruent with the culture's CLT counterpart determines the leader's effectiveness. For example, in societies whose CLT expects charismatic attributes, leaders who exhibit these attributes generate strong commitment, effort, and team solidarity among their direct reports.

There are three generic types of global leaders. Our findings show three types of leaders: (1) CEOs whose behavior falls short of the societies' expectations and end up with underperforming corporations and less dedicated direct reports. (2) CEOs whose behavior matches societal expectations and tend to lead reasonably successful corporations and dedicated direct reports. (3) CEOs who significantly exceed their societal expectations and produce superior results. As an example, we found that among 1,060 CEOs, superior leaders' behavior exceeds the societies' expectations. In contrast, inferior CEOs fall drastically short of their societies' expectations.

Importance

GLOBE's 20-year journey has tried to understand the intricate relationship between national culture and leadership expectations, behavior, and effectiveness. We have identified what societies expect from their leaders, how leaders behave in different societies, and what it takes to succeed as a leader in different cultures. This is the first time in the literature that we are able to empirically and scientifically show these complex relationships. Managers can find this information valuable in their efforts to work with and motivate individuals from other cultures. Scholars can use this information to further enhance our scientific understanding of leadership across cultures.

The GLOBE instruments on societal cultural values and practices have shown strong psychometric properties. They are validated as cross-cultural instruments that can be used to compare and contrast the cultures of different countries. GLOBE methodologies and findings are now reported in the latest issues of books focused on cross-cultural and global leadership and management and are being used by various consulting firms who specialize in cross-cultural management.

GLOBE has also received the following awards: (1) American Psychological Association award for *Culture and Leadership Across the World: The GLOBE Book of In-Depth Studies of 25 Societies*. Recipient of the 2008 Ursula Gielen Global Psychology Book Award, given annually by the International Psychology Division (52) of the American Psychological Association to authors of the book that makes the most significant contribution to psychology as a global discipline. (2) Bob House received the Eminent Scholar award for his long years of contributions to the field of leadership. (3) Academy of Management Perspectives (formerly Academy of Management Executive)—best journal paper award for "In the Eye of the Beholder: Cross Cultural Lessons in Leadership From Project GLOBE," by Javidan, M., Dorfman, P., Sully de Luque, M., and House, R. J. (4) Society for Industrial and Organizational Psychology's annual M. Scott Myers Award for Applied Research in the Workplace—awarded to the GLOBE Project team for development, conduct, and application of outstanding practice of industrial-organizational psychology in the workplace (business, industry, government).

Mansour Javidan, Peter Dorfman,
and Paul J. Hanges

See also Cultural Attitudes in Multinational Corporations; Cultural Intelligence; Cultural Values; High- and Low-Context Cultures; Social Cognitive Theory; Social Construction Theory

Further Readings

Dorfman, P., Sully de Luque, M., Hanges, P., & Javidan, M. (2010, August). Strategic *leadership across cultures: The New GLOBE Multinational Study.* Paper presented at the Academy of Management annual meeting, Montreal, Canada.

House, R. J., Wright, N., & Aditya, R. N. (1997). Cross-cultural research on organizational leadership: A critical analysis and a proposed theory. In P. C. Earley & M. Erez (Eds.), *New perspectives on international industrial/organizational psychology* (pp. 535–623). San Francisco, CA: New Lexington Press.

Howard, A., & Wellins, R. S. (2008/2009). Global leadership forecast, 2008/2009. Development Dimensions International Inc. Available online at http://www.ddiworld.com/DDIWorld/media/trend-research/globalleadershipforecast2008–2009_globalreport_ddi.pdf

Javidan, M., Dorfman, P., Sully de Luque, M., & House, R. J. (2006). In the eye of beholder: Cross cultural lessons in leadership from Project GLOBE. *Academy of Management Perspectives,* 20(1), 67–91.

Javidan, M., House, R. J., Dorfman, P., Hanges, P., & Sully de Luque, M. (2006). Conceptualizing and measuring cultures and their consequences: A comparative review of GLOBE's and Hofstede's approaches. *Journal of International Business Studies,* 37, 897–914.

Lord, R. G., & Maher, K. J. (1991). *Leadership and information processing-linking perceptions and performance.* London, England: Unwin Hyman.

Sully de Luque, M., Javidan, M., Hanges, P., & Dorfman, P. (2011, August). Leadership across societies: Universal and culturally specific leadership behavior effectiveness. Paper presented at the Academy of Management annual meeting, San Antonio, TX.

Triandis, H. C. (1993). The contingency model in cross-cultural perspective. In M. M. Chemers & R. Ayman (Eds.), *Leadership theory and research: Perspectives and directions* (pp. 167–188). San Diego, CA: Academic Press.

GOAL-SETTING THEORY

The central management insight of goal-setting theory is that a powerful way to motivate employees is to give them specific, challenging goals. Motivating employees is a core function of management and leadership. A goal is the object or aim of an action. Although the domain of the theory was originally focused on task or work performance, the domain has expanded enormously in recent years. This entry presents the core aspects of goal-setting theory, the mediators (causes) of goal effects, the moderators (boundary conditions) of goal effects, the sources of goals, and the relation of goals to affect (emotions). Also discussed are the issue of multiple goals, goal setting for groups and organizations, the evolution of goal theory, including new developments, and the importance of goal setting.

Fundamentals

The core aspects of goal-setting theory pertain to goal attributes. The highest performance is attained when goals are both specific (usually quantitative) and challenging (difficult). Goals such as "do your best" do not lead to as high performance as specific, challenging goals (with one exception, as noted below). Given sufficient knowledge and commitment, the higher the goal, the higher the performance. Divorced from difficulty, goal specificity decreases variation in performance insofar as it is controllable.

Mediators

Mediators are causal mechanisms. Goals operate through four such mechanisms. They affect attention and effort to goal-relevant knowledge and action at the expense of what is not relevant. They affect effort, in accordance with the difficulty of the goal. They motivate persistence until the goal is attained. The fourth mechanism is more cognitive in nature; goals motivate people to recall and use knowledge of how to perform the task (e.g., task skills, strategies). If people do not have the knowledge, goals motivate them to seek it. However, such searches are not always successful; on new, complex tasks difficult goals may motivate people to blindly try different strategies without discovering the appropriate procedure. In such cases, do-your-best type goals may work better than specific, difficult goals. This is the exception noted above. The solution to this problem is explained in the next section.

Moderators

Moderators are interactions or boundary conditions.

Commitment. If people are not committed to their goals, then goals will have little or no effect on their behavior. Two broad classes of factors affect commitment. One pertains to the importance or value (attractiveness) of the goal. The values may be strictly internal (part of one's personal value hierarchy), external, or external plus internal. For example, monetary incentives may increase commitment if one values money. But money can have a deleterious effect on a person's performance if the goals tied to the money are viewed as impossible to reach and no credit is given for progress toward the goal. Another external factor is leadership. If one admires a leader or views commitment to assigned goals as inherent in the employment contract, that employee will exert effort to attain them. Peer group influence also affects commitment if one values the peer group. Making the goal public increases commitment because it puts one's integrity at stake.

The second factor affecting commitment is confidence. To commit to a goal, one must have the confidence that one can attain it. The key concept here is that of *self-efficacy*, a term coined by psychologist Albert Bandura. Self-efficacy refers to task-specific confidence—that is, how well one can coordinate and carry out a set of actions that will lead to certain performance outcomes. The belief that reaching a goal is important or desirable has little motivating power if one believes that the goal is unattainable. Self-efficacy is based in part on past performance attainments. In addition, it depends on how one interprets one's previous achievements (e.g., the attributions one makes about them) and the context in which they were achieved. For example, if one attributes a past attainment to luck, this will not raise self-efficacy. On the other hand, if one recalls being sick on the day of a poor performance, self-efficacy may not be lowered if progress is not made regarding goal attainment.

Goal commitment is most important when goals are difficult. When goals are easy, commitment is not hard to get as long as there is a reason for taking action. Commitment is most readily measured with a questionnaire (e.g., How committed are you to this goal?). A leading researcher on this topic is Dr. Howard Klein.

Feedback. Goals require feedback so that people can keep track of their progress. Such feedback pertains to how well people are performing. Coaching feedback tells people how to perform better and is valuable in its own right. If people are "behind schedule," the feedback can signal them to speed up or work harder or to try a different strategy. If they are ahead of schedule, the feedback signals they are on the right track. Feedback at the end of a trial or work period can lead people to set higher future goals for themselves. But again, self-efficacy plays an important role in this regard. Self-set goals are most likely to be raised after performing effectively and if self-efficacy is high. Success in itself usually raises one's self-efficacy. After failure, if self-efficacy is low, goals may be lowered or even abandoned.

Task complexity. Goals often have less effect on tasks that are straightforward for a person than on complex tasks. This is most likely caused by the fact that on complex tasks people do not always know or discover effective task strategies or possess the needed skills. If people do have the needed knowledge and skills, specific high goals typically work as well for complex as for simple tasks.

Organizational support. Environmental factors such as supportive leadership, equipment, time, help, and money can affect goal attainment depending on their favorability.

Knowledge, ability. Knowledge, ability, and skill were noted earlier as goal mechanisms because one needs them to attain goals. But these factors are also moderators. This is because people who lack the requisite knowledge or skill will not perform as well with the same goals as people who do possess them.

Goal Sources

There are three main sources for goals. They can be self-set based on one's own values and personal context (e.g., self-efficacy). They can be assigned, typically by an employee's supervisor or by higher management. Assigned goals, in turn, affect self-set goals, as a mediator. Goals can also be set participatively—that is, jointly by the employee and the manager. There is an extensive literature on participation in decision making. In the end, it was found that participatively set goals do not work any better than assigned goals, provided that the assigned goals are not given abruptly or arbitrarily but with a rationale and an expression of confidence that the individual can succeed in attaining the goal. Although participative goal setting is useful as long as goal difficulty level is carefully considered, considerable research reveals that participation seems to be more consistently useful as a method of information exchange (e.g., subordinate to supervisor) than as a motivator.

Goals and Satisfaction

Goals are, at the same time, an objective to shoot for and a standard for evaluating one's performance. These are two sides of the same coin. Goal success leads to satisfaction, and goal failure leads to less satisfaction or dissatisfaction. This means, of course, that people with easy goals are more likely to be satisfied than people with hard goals. This poses the question of how goals that produce less satisfaction lead to higher performance than goals that produce more satisfaction. The answer is implicit in the question. Having a challenging or difficult goal means

that you have to accomplish more in order to feel satisfied. This brings up the question of why people set or accept hard goals. The answer is twofold: First, ceteris paribus, people who accomplish more feel more personal pride than people who achieve less. Students are more proud of getting an A than getting a C. Second, in the real world more practical rewards accrue to those who attain challenging goals. For example, usually (recessions notwithstanding) attaining more education leads to better jobs and a better choice of jobs, more pay, and more job security than does less education. Higher aspirations are harder to attain, but they have a bigger payoff than low aspirations. Ambition means not being satisfied with less. An added benefit of goal setting is that it can increase interest/decrease boredom on tasks that are not always intrinsically interesting.

Multiple Goals

Goal theory has no recommendations regarding how many goals employees should be given. There are many contextual factors involved. These include an employee's ability and knowledge, the time span(s) involved, the causal interconnections between the goals, the ability to delegate some responsibilities, the hierarchy of importance, task complexity, and so on. It is normal for people at work to have more than one goal, but there has been little research on the subject. A few studies show that people can successfully pursue multiple goals at work. There have also been studies in which people are assigned different goals on two different tasks. Typically, whichever goal is given priority has the strongest effect on a person's performance.

Goals Above the Individual Level

There have been many studies of goal setting at the group level. They show that goal setting works equally well at the group level; the same principles noted above apply. Goal effects have also been studied at the organizational unit level within management by objectives programs. In programs in which there was strong organizational commitment, goal setting had a beneficial effect on unit performance.

Evolution

The roots of goal-setting theory lie in biology rather than in electro-mechanical engineering as in the case of control theory. The basic principle involved is that life is a process of goal-directed actions; an organism's survival is conditional on its fulfilling its needs. This applies to single-celled organisms, plants, and animals, including human beings. Much goal-directed action is automatic, built in through evolution (e.g., the root growth of a tree or plant, the internal body systems of animals and humans). The goal of such systems is the survival and well-being of the organism. Among the higher organisms, the faculty of consciousness comes into play, and it is also critical to survival. The organism can perceive the external environment and, responding to its own needs, make choices that guide its actions toward need-fulfilling goals. In human beings, these choices are directly (the choice to think) or indirectly (actions) volitional—that is, not necessitated by prior circumstances.

The first goal-setting study was a laboratory experiment conducted in 1935 in England. But it was not analyzed with statistics. Programmatic goal-setting research was begun in the 1960s. The key method used was in defiance of the policies of contemporary journals, which required that hypotheses be deduced from preexisting theories. In practice, this meant that a lot of theories were "discovered" after the fact to justify the hypotheses. Goal-setting theory was developed by induction, consistent with the way that the hard sciences were developed. Close to 400 studies were conducted by many researchers over a period of some 25 years before the findings were integrated into an actual theory in 1990. Many of these studies were conducted by Edwin Locke and Gary Latham, but others, too numerous to list, did their own studies independently.

Locke and Latham consider goal theory to be an open theory in that new developments to modify, broaden, and refine the theory are expected and welcomed. Since 1990, there have been a variety of new developments and discoveries.

Goals as mediators. There is evidence that goals, along with self-efficacy, mediate or partially mediate the effects of personality traits such as conscientiousness or quasi-traits such as goal orientation. These two variables also mediate the effects of feedback on subsequent performance. Goals and self-efficacy also partially mediate the effects of incentives. Goals mediate the motivational effects of participation in decision making (to the degree that participation

affects goal difficulty level). All this makes sense when the goals are task and situationally specific as well as directive.

Proximal and distal goals. Proximal goals refer to goals that are nearby or close in time, and distal goals refer to goals that are farther away or distant in time. There are no fixed definitions of the actual time spans involved because these vary with the circumstances. For example, in a laboratory experiment, the distal goal might be for the end of the experiment and the proximal goals might be for each trial. In a field experiment (e.g., weight loss), the proximal goal might be for a week and the distal goal for a specific number of pounds to lose in a month. The usual finding is that distal goals work better when they are accompanied by proximal goals. The advantage of proximal goals is that, assuming they are accompanied by feedback, people can see how well they are progressing toward the distal goals. They can change their strategy where necessary to attain the distal goal and/or increase their effort to attain it. Also, nearer goals may be more psychologically "real" than a distant goal over the horizon. In the real world of work, of course, changing circumstances may require changing strategy, even frequent revisions, of both proximal and distal goals. In a dynamic environment, organizations need to be flexible and nimble.

Group versus individual conflict. Goal conflict undermines performance. In a group setting, priorities need to be made clear. If individual and group goals are not consonant, group performance with be undermined.

Learning goals. It was noted earlier that when people are confronted with a new complex task, performance goals may work less well than do-best goals because in a rush to get results people do not develop effective strategies. The solution is to use learning goals. Learning goals ask people to focus not on outcomes, but on learning the best strategies for performing the task. Learning goals may be specific (learn five strategies to perform this task) or general (learn strategies to perform this task). Often, these work better than do-best performance goals and/or specific high-performance goals. This assumes people can learn relevant strategies. A question that arises with learning goals is this:

Do you need performance goals too? In some cases, learning goals work without performance goals because the strategies are good ones and people choose to apply them. But the risk is that learning goals could become ends in themselves and not be consistently and aggressively applied. Some recent research suggests that learning and performance goals can successfully be used at the same time, at least if the task, though new, is not too complex. This is a question that warrants a great deal more research.

Goals and subconscious priming. Recent research in social psychology has found that goals can be subconsciously primed. One way to do it is to give participants sentences to unscramble, many of which include achievement-related words such as *try, achieve, strive, attain.* Then they are given a new task to perform. Another priming method is to show a single picture of a runner crossing the finish line. Primed subjects perform better than nonprimed subjects yet show no awareness of having been primed. This has been found to work even in an employment setting. When conscious goals and priming are done in the same study, both show significant effects on performance.

Enlarging the domain. Goal-setting theory has been used successfully in (a) human resource management, (b) promoting creativity, (c) sports, (d) rehabilitation and promoting health behaviors, (e) entrepreneurship, (f) education, (g) psychotherapy, and (h) the field of bargaining and negotiation.

Importance

Goal theory was formulated based on close to 400 studies, using some 40,000 participants, 88 different tasks, data from eight countries, and time spans from 1 minute to several years; using experimental and correlational designs; in laboratory, simulation and field settings; using self-set, assigned, and participatively set goals; and employing many types of dependent variables, including both performance outcomes and behavior on the job. Meta-analyses have reported effects sizes ranging from $d = .42$ to $d = .82$. Goal-setting theory has been rated as the most important and valid theory in organizational behavior and industrial/organizational psychology. It is widely taught in university courses and appears in

virtually all organizational behavior (OB) and industrial and organizational (I/O) psychology textbooks.

Goal setting is used in some form by virtually all organizations. The General Electric company under Chairman and CEO Jack Welch was influenced by goal theory. Longitudinal studies have shown that goal setting helps to promote organizational growth. Why is this so? Goal setting works because it affects a person's choices; it gives direction to an individual's pursuits. Moreover, a specific, high goal increases a person's effort, prolongs persistence, and cues a search for strategies to attain it. A goal is a regulatory system for monitoring, evaluating, and adjusting one's behavior. Goals provide meaning to otherwise meaningless tasks. They give people a sense of accomplishment. In short, the attainment of specific high goals increases a person's effectiveness, a universal need.

Edwin A. Locke and Gary P. Latham

See also Achievement Motivation Theory; Expectancy Theory; High-Performance Work Systems; *Kaizen* and Continuous Improvement; Management by Objectives; Social Cognitive Theory

Further Readings

Locke, E. A., & Latham, G. P. (in press). *New developments in goal setting and task performance.* New York, NY: Taylor & Francis.

Latham, G. P., & Locke, E. A. (2007). New developments in and directions for goal setting. *European Psychologist, 12,* 290–300.

Locke, E. A., & Latham, G. P. (1984). *Goal setting: A motivational technique that works.* Englewood Cliffs, NJ: Prentice Hall.

Locke, E. A., & Latham, G. P. (1990). *A theory of goal setting and task performance.* Englewood Cliffs, NJ: Prentice Hall.

Locke, E. A., & Latham, G. P. (2002). Building a practically useful theory of goal setting and task performance: A 35-year odyssey. *American Psychologist, 57,* 705–717.

Locke, E. A., & Latham, G. P. (2005). Goal setting theory: Theory building by induction. In K. G. Smith & M. A. Hitt (Eds.), *Great minds in management: The process of theory development* (pp. 128–150). New York, NY: Oxford University Press.

Shantz, A., & Latham, G. P. (2011). The effect of primed goals on employee performance: Implications for human resource management. *Human Resource Management, 50,* 289–299.

GROUP DEVELOPMENT

The central premise of the theory of group development is that, to be most effective, small groups must progress through a series of developmental stages—forming, storming, norming, performing, and ultimately adjourning. Relatedly, the theory's purpose is to inform how groups conceive of and interact during the various stages of group life. In the domain of management, the theory assists both managers and their team members by providing a theoretical lens through which to view the tasks and challenges associated with each stage of group development. I begin by providing a description of the theory and its fundamental elements. Next, I describe how the theory has developed over a period of more than 40 years and added a fifth stage. I then describe the impact of the theory on management scholars and educators, as well as managers themselves.

Fundamentals

The model I proposed of developmental stages for various group settings over time were labeled (1) testing and dependence, (2) intragroup conflict, (3) development of group cohesion, and (4) functional role relatedness. The corresponding stages of task activity were labeled (1) orientation to task, (2) emotional response to task demands, (3) open exchange of relevant interpretations, and (4) emergence of solutions. But I summarized the four stages as forming, storming, norming, and performing. I provided a developmental model of group process by organizing and conceptualizing existing research data and theoretical precepts rather than by presenting original empirical data to support my model.

Only one empirical study could be found to test my hypothesis. Philip J. Runkel and colleagues studied three groups of 15 to 20 college students in a classroom setting. The task of each group was to decide on a project, collect and interpret data, and write a final report. During meetings of the work group, 16 observers, armed with descriptions of my model of stage development, observed the group until something happened that fitted a behavior described by me as belonging to one of the four stages of group structure or task activity. The observers rotated among groups in an effort to reduce observer bias. Ratings from observers supported my theory of group development, dubbed Tuckman's hypothesis. Moreover, I amended my model to include a fifth stage, labeled adjourning. Other researchers such as J. Stephen Heinen and Eugene Jacobson also arrived at the conclusion that groups do appear to develop and grow in an orderly, predictable manner and have tended to follow the same pattern.

It is noteworthy that since 1965 there have been few studies that report empirical data concerning the stages of group development. It is also of interest that most authors, although writing from a theoretical framework, call for further research to verify their hypotheses. A virtually untapped field is the empirical testing of existing models of group-stage development. A major outcome of this review has been the discovery that recent research posits the existence of a final discernible and significant stage of group development—adjourning. The model now stands: forming, storming, norming, performing, and adjourning. A description of the core elements and insights of each stage follows.

Forming. Groups initially concern themselves with orientation accomplished primarily through testing. Such testing serves to identify the boundaries of both interpersonal and task behaviors. Coincident with testing in the interpersonal realm is the establishment of dependency relationships with leaders, other group members, or preexisting standards. It may be said that orientation, testing, and dependence constitute the group process of *forming*.

The core characteristics of the forming stage include orientation, testing, dependence, and establishing group rules and boundaries for interpersonal and task behaviors. Group members must develop awareness of one another's traits and expectations at the outset. By testing rules and boundaries, group members begin to get a sense of where these limits actually lie. Often, eager to take action, group members spend too little time in the forming stage, a deficit that impedes future group progress. As the saying goes, without a strong foundation, the whole house can crumble.

Storming. The second point in the sequence is characterized by conflict and polarization around interpersonal issues, with emotional responding in the task sphere, thus causing resistance to group influence and nonparticipation. These behaviors, serving as resistance to group influence and task requirements, may be labeled as *storming*.

During the *storming* stage, conflict between group members is most apparent. The conflict may take the form of either perceptible behavior, from nonresponsiveness to venting of frustrations, or less noticeable ones, such as disappointment or irritation. In either case, the storming stage is important because it makes apparent which group expectations and requirements need to be addressed for the group to move forward.

Norming. Resistance is overcome in the third stage in which in-group feeling and cohesiveness develop, new standards evolve, and new roles are adopted. In the task realm, intimate, personal opinions are expressed. Thus, we have the stage of *norming*.

During the norming stage, conflicts and issues made apparent during storming become resolved. Group members recognize ways in which the requirements of their group must change, their roles must shift, or both. The revised norms that result are often more nuanced and durable than those established at the outset, because they have been tested by actual conditions and revised based on the realities of the task demands.

Performing. The group then can attain the fourth stage, in which the interpersonal structure itself becomes the means by which task activities take place. Roles develop flexibility and greater functionality, and group energy is channeled into the task. Structural issues have been resolved, and structure can now become supportive of task performance. This stage can be labeled as *performing*.

As a group enjoys the performing stage, they see true progress and productivity. The degree of effectiveness is greater than at any other stage in the process. The group dynamics allow actions to take place, because the actors understand their best roles within the group and have developed commitments to both the task and their collaborators. In this case, the whole is truly more than the sum of its parts, and the history of the group's progress lends momentum to what the members strive to accomplish.

Adjourning. A fifth stage, adjourning, was added to the model in 1977. This stage, explained more in the following section, represents a time when group members depart from the formal group, and often

from one another. *Adjourning* usually occurs as a function of the task itself, such as when the group has accomplished what it initially set out to do. This stage is also referred to as *termination*.

Evolution

As an undergraduate psychology major at Rensselaer Polytechnic Institute in Troy, New York, I focused my senior honors thesis on instruction and learning. This reflected my strong practical interest in how people learn real information in real settings. My interest in the psychology of human learning led to graduate work at Princeton University under the mentorship of the influential learning psychologist Robert Gagne. In 1963, I obtained a PhD in psychology from Princeton. My dissertation study was published in 1964 under the title "Personality Structure, Group Composition, and Group Functioning." The study was supported by the Office of Naval Research and was initially presented at the 1963 meeting of the Eastern Psychological Association. It was designed to examine whether individual personality traits of group members influenced group functioning. This study reflected my interest in group development and specifically recommended further research into the development of emergent group structures.

In June, 1965, some 47 years ago, I published an article in the *Psychological Bulletin* titled "Developmental Sequence in Small Groups." I had just completed my PhD in psychology at Princeton University and had obtained a position at the Naval Medical Research Institute (NMRI) in Bethesda, Maryland. A senior colleague of mine, Irwin Altman, had been collecting research on the topic of small groups and passed it on to me with his blessing. My challenge was to do something productive with it, and I set my mind to work. I located 50 articles from Altman's collection that ranged from therapy group studies, T-group studies, and natural and laboratory group studies and separated them into those descriptive of social or interpersonal group activities and those descriptive of group task activities. I proposed four general stages of development, and the review consisted of fitting the stages identified in the literature to those proposed. In the social realm, these stages in the developmental sequence were labeled testing-dependence, conflict, cohesion, and functional roles. In the task realm, they were labeled as orientation, emotionality, relevant opinion exchange, and the emergence of solutions. A good fit was found between observed stages and the proposed model. Further study of temporal change as a dependent variable via the manipulation of specific independent variables was suggested.

In August 1984, my original article, described above, was featured under the title "This Week's Citation Classic" in *Current Contents* on August 20, 1984. Based on a review of 50 articles describing stages of development in therapy, T-, natural and laboratory groups, a model of small-group development was proposed. Four stages, covering both group interpersonal and task activities, were described and labeled *forming, storming, norming,* and *performing.* The *Science Citation Index* and the *Social Sciences Citation Index* provided an indication that this article has been cited in over 165 publications since 1965. The story of how this came to be is described below.

My first professional job was as part of a small group of social psychologists in a "think tank" setting studying small group behavior as the U.S. Navy prepared for a future of small crew vessels and stations. Nine of us at the Naval Medical Research Institute were busy studying small groups from all perspectives and under all conditions. I was fortunate to have an experienced and talented boss by the name of Irwin Altman, who had been collecting every article he could find on group development. He turned his collection over to me and suggested that I look it over and see if could make anything out of it.

The collection contained 50 articles, many of which were psychoanalytic studies of therapy or T-groups. The task of organizing and integrating them was challenging. After separating out two realms of group functioning—namely, the interpersonal or group structure realm and the task activity realm, I began to look for a *developmental sequence* that would fit the findings of a majority of the studies. I hit on four stages going from (1) orientation/testing/dependence to (2) conflict to (3) group cohesion to (4) functional role relatedness. For these I coined the terms: *forming, storming, norming,* and *performing*—terms that would come to be used to describe developing groups for the next 46 years and which probably account for the paper's popularity.

There still remained the task of getting the paper published, and that was no mean feat.

Lloyd Humphreys, then editor of the *Psychological Bulletin,* turned it down, offering me constructive editorial criticism but concluding that the reviewed studies themselves were not of sufficient quality to merit publication. I was persistent, though, and rewrote the manuscript according to his recommendations and sent it back to him despite his initial outright rejection. I pointed out that I was not trying to justify the collected articles but to draw inferences from them. Humphreys did a complete about-face and accepted my argument and my manuscript and, in short order, it appeared in print.

I ordered, thanks to the Navy, 450 reprints and used them all to fill requests within the first 3 or 4 years after the article appeared. Requests came from all over the world and from a wide range of disciplines, and I have saved some of the more exotic ones. Almost yearly, I received a request from someone to use parts of the article or at least the terms forming, storming, norming, and performing in print. Again, quotability may be the key to success. The labeling of the stages of small-group development had given the group development concept a functional model of how groups advanced through a series of four stages and how those stages could be facilitated.

In 1977, 12 years after the publication of the original *Psychological Bulletin* article, I published by invitation an update of the model in a journal called *Group & Organization Studies*—in collaboration with Mary Ann Jensen. It was labeled "Stages of Small-Group Development Revisited." Mary Ann Jensen joined me in reexamining the stages by looking at published research on small-group development done in the prior 10 years, which would constitute an empirical test of my theory that groups go through the stages of forming, storming, norming, and performing. We reviewed 22 studies that had appeared since the original publication of the model, which we located by means of the *Social Sciences Citation Index.* We set out to directly test this hypothesis, although many other hypotheses could be related to it. These articles, one of which dubbed the stages "Tuckman's hypothesis," tended to support the existence of the four stages but also suggested a fifth stage for which a perfect rhyme could not be found. Following a review of these studies, a fifth stage, adjourning, was added to the hypothesis, and more empirical work was recommended.

Importance

In 2001, my theory of small-group development was included by invitation as part of a special issue on group facilitation. The title of the issue was *Group Facilitation: A Research and Applications Journal*. The editor of the journal, Sandor P. Schuman, included the following statements:

> Although other articles in this special issue suggest the limitations of "stage models" such as this, the memorability and popularity of Tuckman's model make this article required reading for every group facilitator. Were we to conduct a survey to assess the current state of knowledge regarding group development, I suspect that the response we would receive most often would include something about *forming, storming, norming, performing,* and *adjourning.* We owe this memorable characterization of stages of group development to Bruce Tuckman who introduced this oft-cited naming scheme in 1965. We are pleased to reprint his hallmark article.

In February, 2010, *Human Resource Developmental International* published "Perspective: 40 Years of Storming: A Historical Review of Tuckman's Model of Small Group Development," written by Denise A. Bonebright. My model was listed as the one "most predominately referred to and most widely recognized in organizational literature" (Miller, 2003, 122). According to Bonebright, Tuckman's 1965 work was cited in 1,196 articles and Tuckman and Jensen were cited in 544. In 2003, Miller analyzed my model and concluded that there is a high degree of consistency in the description of the stages but numerous theorists who view the developmental process as more complex than can be seen in linear models like my own. Nevertheless, Bonebright saw my model as a useful starting point for team development practitioners because it was "accessible, easy to understand, and flexible enough to apply to many different settings." It became popular in management and practitioner literature. In a survey of professionals, 250 different models were being used in team development practice, of which my model was most commonly mentioned by 16% of respondents.

My model began to appear frequently in the scholarly literature, was regularly listed as a reference on group development theory, and was widely applied to research on work groups. I began to receive frequent requests for permission to use my theory on a daily or weekly basis and most typically granted it. Requests come from all over the world and typically include a visual exhibit of the stages of team development. Book authors write to me, lawyers write to me, professional organizations write to me, instructional designers write to me, colleagues write to me. Requests come from universities, and corporations and organizations all over the world. Doctoral candidates write to me. The Council of Europe wrote to me. The State of Hawaii wrote to me. Pearson Education wrote to me. XanEdu wrote to me. Anyway, I'm sure you get the idea! My fame, if you can call it that, has been and is a mixed blessing. But if nothing else, it does make a wide range of people become aware of and use those now famous words: forming, storming, norming, and performing. And I do get the opportunity to shake someone's hand and say, "Yes, I am the person who coined those famous terms!"

My most recent and possibly last venture into the stages of group development also took place in 2010 when I was invited to write a review of a new book called *Leadership Teams: Developing and Sustaining High Performance.* The emphasis of the book is on working with teams using a six-stage model (rather than a four- or five-stage model with which I am more familiar) and a focus on leadership and teamwork. The first group development stage has four elements: forming the group (sounds familiar!), creativity and innovation (mobilizing goals and objectives), decision making, and allocating resources and ways of working. It sounds a bit like "forming," but with more detail that is based primarily on my ingrained way of thinking. The big question is, "Do I agree with what the leader is asking this group to do?" An illuminating case study runs through the entire book to help answer these questions.

The second group development stage is confrontation. Could that be "storming"? It reflects the inevitability of conflict in complex organizations. This stage is divided into two elements: understanding conflict and managing conflict, and that conflict can be either task conflict or relationship conflict, based on different points of view leading to deterioration and losing sight of the goal. Open criticism, interpersonal conflict, and loss of interest lead to rejection of the leader. The authors recommend that managers should expect conflict but avoid personal attacks and try to improve relationships by managing conflict.

The third stage is coming together, with two elements: work-based relationships (showing the difference between a group and a collection of individuals) and working in groups (building a network of relationships and shifting focus to the group). A detailed list of leadership behaviors is required. Would this be "norming"? So far, we are following the pattern.

The fourth stage changes the linear pattern of the preceding stages. It is called "one step forward, two steps back." Group members are faced with the question, Do I accept the role I will have to play in this group? Group members often resist cultural change, preferring to stick with their own culture. Previous courses of action are taken for granted. The group's slipping back into conflict smacks of confrontation (Stage 2). The process stalls, the group splits into factions, and a leadership battle ensues. It becomes personal. To help group members deal with cultural change, leaders must help them develop competencies required to perform a job and the willingness to apply competencies within a particular context. Enlisting key managers' support becomes a factor.

The fifth stage involves turning a group of people into a team, a "team" being a small number of people with complementary skills who are committed to a common purpose and approach for which they hold themselves personally accountable. The authors list indicators as a benchmark that the team has entered the behaving as one stage (or is this norming?). It includes agreement on a goal, shared and distributed leadership, and a strong leader. Team members need to be part of the decision-making process.

The sixth and last stage is facing the future, meaning managing yourself and developing leaders. It makes me think of "performing." It includes listening, reflecting, taking initiative, reaching out to others, controlling anxiety, not taking criticism personally, building trust, and working to gain credibility and support.

The essential difference between the Sheard model of group development and the Tuckman model, at least as I see it, is that the Sheard model has added a new touch—namely one step forward, two steps back—whereas the Tuckman model offers forming, storming, norming, performing, and adjourning. Without one step forward, two steps back, the two models would appear very similar, but not quite the same. That is why we have options, and options are good things to have!

Bruce W. Tuckman

See also Business Groups; Conflict Handling Styles; High-Performing Teams; Norms Theory; Organizational Development; Work Team Effectiveness

Further Readings

Bonebright, D. A. (2010). Perspective: 40 years of storming: A historical review of Tuckman's model of small group development. *Human Resource Developmental International, 13*(1), 111–120.

Heinen, J. S., & Jacobson, E. (1976). A model of task group development in complex organizations and a strategy for implementation. *Academy of Management Review, 1*(4), 98–111.

Miller, D. (2003). The stages of group development: A retrospective study of dynamic team processes. *Canadian Journal of Administrative Sciences, 20*(2), 121–143.

Runkel, P., Lawrence, M., Oldfield, S., Rider, M., & Clark, C. (1971). Stages of group development: An empirical test of Tuckman's hypothesis. *Journal of Applied Behavioral Sciences, 7*(2), 180–193.

Sheard, G., Kakabadse, A., & Kakabadse, N. (2009). *Leadership teams: Developing and sustaining high performance.* New York, NY: Palgrave Macmillan.

Tuckman, B. W. (1965). Developmental sequence in small groups. *Psychological Bulletin, 63*(6), 384–399.

Tuckman, B. W., & Jensen, M. A. (1977). Stages of small-group development revisited. *Group and Organization Studies, 2*(4), 419–427.

GROUP POLARIZATION AND THE RISKY SHIFT

Group polarization can be defined as an enhancement of group members' preexisting tendencies accomplished through some form of group-induced communication or interaction. Group polarization is most likely to occur in groups in which the members initially hold tendencies that can be defined as leaning toward one or the other end of a continuum. In such cases, group interaction can lead individual members and the group as a whole to move farther away from a middle-of-the-road position and toward a more extreme opinion or intention to act. The term *group polarization* also calls attention to the phenomenon that interacting with others in a group, or merely listening to members of a group interact, can lead individuals to become more committed to and sure of the correctness of their preferences, even as those preferences become more extreme. In this sense, the word *polarization* refers to the tendency to move toward one of the "poles" at either end of a continuum and to become more certain of the correctness of one's position. The fundamentals and importance of group polarization are discussed in the following sections.

Fundamentals

The concept of group polarization has an interesting history. It was first explored in the context of individual and group risk taking by James A. F. Stoner, a student at MIT's graduate school of management completing a master's thesis with his adviser, Donald G. Marquis, a well-known psychologist. While working on a term project in Warren Bennis's course on leadership, Stoner discovered that his own conviction that groups are more cautious than individuals was very widely shared (a "known fact") but did not seem to have been demonstrated experimentally.

To test the hypothesis about the cautiousness of groups, his study compared decisions involving risk by individuals deciding alone and then deciding as members of a group. To assess individual riskiness, he arranged for 91 management graduate students to answer a 12-item questionnaire in which they advised fictitious individuals how much risk to take in a variety of situations. About a week after completing the questionnaire as individuals, 78 of those students were assembled into six-person groups and reached consensus decisions on all 12 questionnaire items. The group decisions were quite different from the initial individual decisions, but the 13 control subjects who completed the same questionnaire again, also after about a week, showed essentially no change in their decisions.

The results were startling. Not only were the group decisions not more cautious, they were strongly more risky on the questionnaire as a whole. Within a few months that "risky shift" was replicated in a study of male and female groups at a Colorado university. And soon a great many other studies replicated and explored aspects of the risky shift in a variety of experimental situations in a variety of countries and with a variety of types of individuals. The risky shift was reliable, robust, and easy to demonstrate in a classroom in 1 hour—a real gift to teachers dealing at that time with another "known fact"—the often voiced student and cultural attitude that "you can't predict human behavior." And it was counterintuitive—"Everyone *knew* groups were more cautious than individuals." But now they were being significantly more risky.

As easy as it was to demonstrate the risky shift in an experimental situation and to show in the classroom that human behavior could be predicted, there was one frequently overlooked anomaly among the 12 items in the original questionnaire. The 12th item involved a couple that was deciding whether or not to get married. They had been advised that a happy marriage was possible "but not certain." The MIT and Colorado male students did not demonstrate the risky shift but actually became significantly more cautious on that decision. But the female groups in Colorado actually shifted in the risky direction, and that shift was also statistically significant.

From Risky Shift to Group Polarization

A series of experiments explored hypotheses about why groups might become more risky. Marquis tested the possibility that there might be a "diffusion of responsibility" but found no support for that hypothesis. M. A. Wallach and his colleagues, on the other hand, did find considerable experimental support for that hypothesis.

However, the possibility of a cautious shift was a particularly compelling challenge to diffusion of responsibility as a general causal factor in risky shifts. Frode Nordhøy, a subject in the first risky shift experiment and another of Marquis's thesis students, demonstrated the possibility of more cautious shifts just a year after the first study. In 1967, Stoner demonstrated both risky and cautious shifts and the possibility that "widely held values" might predict the direction of the "shift": Values favoring risky courses of action would lead to risky shifts in group decisions and values favoring caution would lead to cautious shifts.

The existence of risky and cautious group shifts led to research that suggested the risk/caution aspect of group impacts on decision making were not unique but might be a subset of a larger phenomenon. This larger phenomenon would be a shift to more extreme opinions and decisions in a wide domain of opinions and preferred actions—what Serge Moscovici and Marisa Zavalonni called "group polarization": Discussion typically strengthens the average inclination of group members. A considerable body of experiments has demonstrated such a process in many nations and under a wide variety of topics. Group polarization is now the widely accepted interpretation of the phenomenon originally hinted at in the original risky shift discovery.

Hypotheses About How and Why Group Polarization Occurs

Two current hypotheses about why group discussion among initially like-minded individuals tends to lead to greater polarization of those members' initial tendencies involve the information provided in discussions and the social comparisons the discussants seem to make.

On the first hypothesis, information provided in discussions tends to favor initially preferred alternatives, leading to greater confidence in even more extreme positions. With the content of a group discussion being biased toward initially preferred alternatives, individuals in the group learn additional information that favors their own initial opinions, listen to their own reasons for holding the opinions they hold—thus becoming more confident of those opinions—and discover new ways to deal with facts or perspectives that would argue against or moderate their original position. They become even surer of the correctness of their initial opinion and are inclined to go even further in the direction in which they were originally headed, supported and encouraged by the rhetoric they are creating and sharing with the other like-minded members of their group.

The second hypothesis focuses on individuals' desire to see themselves as different from others on some aspect of life: more "liberal" or "conservative," more risky or cautious, more committed to a course of action, or more rejecting of that course of action. If group interaction leads them to discover they are not as different from others as they had

assumed, they can reestablish their desired distance from others by becoming a bit more extreme in their opinions or preferred course of action. For example in Stoner's early work, individuals frequently thought they were being bold risk takers when they recommended a moderately risky final football play that would guarantee victory if successful but defeat if not successful rather than settling for a safe play that would guarantee a tie for their team. However, when group discussion revealed that their initial position was not as bold as they had thought, they often became advocates of an even bolder play . . . with even less chance of success. The emergent argument that "playing for a tie is for sissies" not infrequently yielded the selection of a play with almost no chance of success.

Importance

The tendency for discussion among like-minded individuals to enhance the initial tendencies of the discussants has been demonstrated in many situations. For example, group interactions have led to (a) increasing French students' initially favorable attitudes toward the French president and their initially negative attitudes toward Americans, (b) increasing the prejudicial statements of initially prejudiced American high school students, (c) increasing the severity of initially guilty traffic accident judgments by Japanese students and increasing the amount of recommended damage awards among jurors initially inclined to award damages, and (d) increasing the willingness of U.K. discussants to discriminate against already disrespected immigrant groups. The phenomenon can also contribute to enhanced benevolence, such as increased concern for social justice and commitment to take positive actions among initially concerned Australians and decreased prejudice among initially less prejudiced individuals. And it can even occur when individuals are merely listening to discussions that are consistent with their initial preferences.

Increased extremity of opinions and increased intentions to act among initially like-minded individuals can occur on subjects where the actions will be healthy for relationships, organizations, and societies. However, the opposite can also be the case. When individuals separate themselves from a diversity of viewpoints and values and surround themselves with only those who hold similar opinions and views of the world, they can become more and more convinced of opinions and actions that become progressively more extreme, leading to the dangers of "groupthink," destructive investment actions rife with "moral hazard," ill-advised business decisions such as Goldman Sachs' decision to construct and sell to its clients securities that were designed by another client to become worthless, business strategies such as Enron's manipulation of the California energy market, and U.S. foreign policy decisions such as the military invasion of Iraq.

Dealing With the Tendencies Toward Polarized Decisions and Actions

The theory of group polarization and the extensive research findings that led to and support the theory are calls for managers to recognize the dangers of insular, isolated, like-minded groups in organizations. The temptation to hire, promote, feel comfortable with, socialize with, and rely on like-minded individuals is a very strong one, and a very human tendency. But it carries with it significant dangers: not just the dangers of making extreme and thus frequently poor decisions—because of their extremity—but the added danger of becoming so sure of those extreme decisions that it is even harder to see and admit when those decisions are yielding progressively worse outcomes.

Too often, the focus on "managing diversity" is seen as addressing and finding ways to handle the complexities and difficulties that occur when nontypical individuals are being incorporated into organizational membership and processes. Beyond any legal or social justice arguments for the need for diversity in organizations, the group polarization perspective suggests that it is exactly those "nontypical" organizational members, with their frequently differing viewpoints, who may be the greatest bulwark against the dangers of groupthink and extreme decisions, perceptions, and actions that like-minded individuals can be so prone to.

In a similar vein, the group polarization phenomenon suggests the advantages of bringing a devil's advocate—a voice of contrary opinions—systematically into managerial decision processes, just as John F. Kennedy is believed to have done, with considerable apparent success, during the Cuban Missile Crisis of 1962.

James A. F. Stoner and David G. Myers

See also Escalation of Commitment; Groupthink; Managerial Decision Biases; Managing Diversity; Social Cognitive Theory

Further Readings

Janis, I. L. (1972). *Victims of groupthink: A psychological study of foreign-policy decisions and fiascoes.* Oxford, England: Houghton Mifflin.

Marquis, D. G. (1962). Individual responsibility and group decisions involving risk. *Industrial Management Review, 3,* 8–23.

Moscovici, S., & Zavalloni, M. (1969). The group as a polarizer of attitudes. *Journal of Personality and Social Psychology, 12,* 125–135.

Myers, D. G. (1978). Polarizing effects of social comparison. *Journal of Experimental Social Psychology, 14,* 554–563.

Myers, D. G., & Bishop, G. D. (1970). Discussion effects on racial attitudes. *Science, 169,* 778–779.

Nordhøy, F. (1962). *Group interaction in decision-making under risk* (Master's thesis). MIT School of Industrial Management, Cambridge, MA.

Ricks, T. E. (2006). *Fiasco: The American military adventure in Iraq.* New York, NY: Penguin.

Stoner, J. A. F. (1961). *A comparison of individual and group decisions involving risk* (Master's thesis). MIT School of Industrial Management, Cambridge, MA.

Stoner, J. A. F. (1968). Risky and cautious shifts in group decisions: The influence of widely held values. *Journal of Experimental Social Psychology, 4,* 442–459.

Thomas, E. F., & McGarty, C. A. (2011). The role of efficacy and moral outrage norms in creating the potential for international development activism through group-based interaction. *British Journal of Social Psychology, 50,* 193–215.

GROUP PUNCTUATED EQUILIBRIUM MODEL

The punctuated equilibrium model (PEM) of group development was first proposed by Connie Gersick in 1988. This model argues that instead of developing gradually over time as proposed by classic linear group development models, work groups progress through long periods of inertia punctuated by concentrated revolutionary periods of quantum change, hence the term "punctuated equilibrium" model. The PEM is one of the most cited group development theories in recent management literature; it represents a paradigm shift from the classic linear models that have dominated the group development literature since the 1950s. The following discussion introduces the fundamentals of the theory, how it differs from the classic linear models, the empirical evidence supporting and refining the theory, and the implication for practice.

Fundamentals

The PEM asserts that groups undergo a two-phase (rather than two-staged) developmental pattern. In Phase 1, groups go through an initial period of inertia, the direction of which is set by the end of the group's first meeting. Phase 1 lasts for half of a group's allotted time. At the midpoint of the group's allotted time, the group undergoes a transition that sets a revised direction for Phase 2, a second period of inertia. In addition, Gersick noted that a group's progress is triggered more by members' awareness of time and deadlines than by completion of an absolute amount of work in a specific developmental stage. Moreover, "halfway" emerges as the most likely moment at which groups will call attention to time or pacing. The midpoint acts as a reminder of the approaching deadline, which interrupts the group's basic strategies at Phase I and facilitates the midpoint transition and thus the onset of Phase II.

Empirical support for the PEM was first presented by Gersick in her initial field study in which she observed eight naturally occurring groups over time and found consistent patterns of two-phase (rather than two-stage) development in these groups. Out of the eight groups observed, Gersick found that (a) every team exhibited a distinctive approach to its task as soon as it commenced and stayed with that approach through a period of inertia that lasted for half of its allotted time and (b) every group then underwent a major transition at precisely halfway between its first meeting and its official deadline, despite wide variation in the amounts of time the eight teams were allotted for their projects (ranging from 1 week to 6 months). During the transition, groups dropped old patterns, renegotiated with outside supervisors, adopted new perspectives on their work, and made dramatic progress. (c) The events that occurred during those transitions, especially

a group's interaction with its environment, shaped a new approach to the task for each group. Those approaches carried groups through a second major phase of inertial activity, in which they executed plans created at the midpoint transitions. This pattern of finding was replicated the following year in a laboratory study using experimental groups with a 1-hour life span. Gersick observed eight groups of MBA students (six groups of three members and two groups of four) designing a commercial advertisement over a 1-hour period of time and found very similar patterns of midpoint transitions. However, the transitions of the laboratory groups were less likely to be influenced by outside stakeholders.

Immediately after the publication of group PEM research, reviewers concluded that this new understanding of change processes challenged the traditional "linear" models of group development, which (a) conceptualized change as a gradual and incremental process, (b) assumed that groups progress through a logical sequence of stages over time, and (c) proposed that groups become more effective as they progress to later stages of development at least until the group moves into the final stage of decline and termination.

Gersick argues that the PEM differs from the traditional gradualist models in the following ways:

- Traditional models (gradualist models) assume that systems can accept virtually any change, at any time, as long as it is small enough. In addition, it is assumed that large changes result from accumulative small changes. In contrast, the PEM suggests that for most of the groups' history, "there are limits beyond which change is actively prevented, rather than always potential but merely suppressed because no adaptive advantage would accrue."
- The PEM disputes the idea that individual systems of the same type (i.e., groups with similar natures) all develop along the same path and that systems develop in "forward" directions, as in stage theories of group development.
- The PEM suggests that conflicting theories about a group's adaptability and rigidity are applicable at different times, depending on whether the group is in a period of equilibrium or transition.
- The PEM suggests that a system's basic organizational principles are varied and

changeable and that we should apply with caution theories based on universal "drivers" such as efficiency. That is, we should apply the appropriate theory that suits the particular "phase" or "transition" a group is in at the time.

In 2003, Artemis Chang, Prashant Bordia, and Julie Duck published a counterview that argued that rather than contradicting linear models of group development, the PEM complements them. They argued that the linear models describe changes at the more micro level within each "phase" of inertia and that a transition marks the shift of a group's behavioral pattern from earlier stages to more structured and productive stages of group development. Incorporating advancement of knowledge in natural sciences (e.g., evolutionary biology) about the PEM, Chang and colleagues contended that groups as systems have multilevels of deep structures and that the level of deep structure at which changes take place determines the observed incremental or revolutionary pattern. In other words, when changes occur in more surface-level structures, incremental changes are observed. On the other hand, revolutionary changes are observed when changes occur at a more fundamental level.

Importance

Subsequent empirical researches found some support for the PEM. Chang and colleagues replicated Gersick's laboratory study with a larger number (25) of groups and reported both linear and punctuated equilibrium patterns of group development, albeit on different dimensions. Specifically, the PEM described changes in a group's time awareness, pacing activities, and task activities over time, whereas the linear model described changes in a group's structure and process on both task and socioemotional dimensions. They also found that the midpoint transition marked the group's resolution of early developmental issues such as leadership and work structure and a move forward in the production phase of the project.

Holly Arrow studied face-to-face and computer-mediated groups over a period of 13 weeks, and these groups experienced planned change both in communication media and in group membership as well as in unplanned changes such as absences. Arrow compared four different change models (robust equilibrium, life cycle, punctuated equilibrium, and adaptive response) and concluded that computer-mediated groups fit the robust equilibrium pattern best, and face-to-face groups fit a bi-stable punctuated equilibrium pattern best.

Stephen Lim and J. Keith Murnighan examined the PEM with groups working on mixed-motive tasks (i.e., negotiation). They found that in a negotiating task, the number of messages and activities displayed by the pairs involved in the negotiation remained constant over time, providing evidence inconsistent with Gersick's model. On the other hand, temporal changes in concessions and pacing followed an exponential curve, which indicated either a sharp increase in these messages right before the deadline or a steady increase over time. Lim and Murnighan suggested that the nature of the task influences the pacing strategies chosen, and in the particular case of negotiation where individualistic motives are important, members might hold on to the individualistic motives until the end when a compromise has to be made for the benefit of the group. Lim and Murnighan concluded that their results did not necessarily challenge Gersick's model; instead, they expanded the model in arguing that the nature of the particular task is important in determining the pacing strategies that a group employs.

Anson Seers and Steve Woodruff conducted two studies. The first investigated whether pacing was a group activity or an individual one. Study 2 compared the PEM against a linear model of group development. In 1997 Seers and Woodruff concluded from these studies that researchers should distinguish pacing activities from group development as a whole: "Pacing appears to be a task deadline-driven process, and group development appears to involve social factors which can extend beyond task-required interactions." Seers and Woodruff proposed that Gersick's model should be identified as a "group task progress" model instead of as a "group development" model. This important distinction converged with Chang's assertion that both punctuated equilibrium and linear developmental patterns of group development can be observed, albeit in different dimensions.

Empirical research largely supports the group PEM, especially when it is used to examine pacing- and task-related activities in teams with limited life spans. However, the significance of the "midpoint" as the most likely point of the transition is yet to be established. The limited research so far suggests that the timing and nature of the transitions may vary depending on the tasks. It is nevertheless important to understand that "timing" is critical when introducing changes to the team. The initial meetings of a team are essential in establishing routine patterns of behaving in newly formed teams; thus it is paramount to invest considerable resources in the planning of the first meeting to give the team the best opportunity to adopt the most effective approach to the task. Second, small internal or external changes can then be introduced to interrupt the group's current state of inertia and create an environment of instability, which will in turn increase the group's propensity for larger scale changes (the PEM). For example, replacing a group member can facilitate the group's examination of current structure and processes and thus provide opportunities for introducing changes to one or both aspects. Once changes have been introduced, early developmental issues might need to be revisited to facilitate effective work under the new working conditions.

In today's business environment, teams with diverse members distributed globally are commonly used to achieve complex organizational goals. It is particular important for the team leader to lead a discussion to establish the expected behavioral norm at project inception in this context. It is also important to set temporal milestones for the groups to review their progress; this will not only pace the group activities accordingly but also provide an opportunity to introduce changes needed to a group's habitual routines. Note that the PEM focuses on pacing and task activities in teams, but we know from other research that trust and relationship management are critical to the success of large and complex projects. New generations of communication technology and the global trend of budget restriction have meant that more globally distributed teams are *not* meeting face-to-face as often. However, meeting face-to-face initially to establish relationships and behavioral norms may still be an important step toward team effectiveness.

Artemis Chang

See also Business Groups; Group Development; High-Performing Teams; Process Theories of Change; Systems Theory of Organizations

Further Readings

Arrow, H. (1997). Stability, bistability, and instability in small group influence patterns. *Journal of Personality and Social Psychology, 72*, 75–85.

Chang, A., Bordia, P., & Duck, J. (2003). Developmental patterns of project teams: An empirical attempt at reconciling the differences between linear progression and punctuated equilibrium models of group development. *Academy of Management Journal, 46*(1), 106–118.

Gersick, C. J. (1988). Time and transition in work teams: Toward a new model of group development. *Academy of Management Journal, 31*(1), 1–41.

Gersick, C. J. (1989). Marking time: Predictable transitions in task groups. *Academy of Management Journal, 32*(2), 274–309.

Gersick, C. J. (1991). Revolutionary change theories: A multilevel exploration of the punctuated equilibrium paradigm. *Academy of Management Review, 16*, 10–36.

Lim, S. G. S., & Murnigham, J. K. (1994). Phases, deadlines, and the bargaining process. *Organizational Behavior and Human Decision Processes, 58*, 153–171.

Pinto, J. K., Sleven, D. P., & English, B. (2009). Trust in projects: An empirical assessment of owner/contractor relationships. *International Journal of Project Management, 27*, 638–648.

Seers, A., & Woodruff, S. (1997). Temporal pacing in task forces: Group development or deadline pressure. *Journal of Management, 23*(2), 169–187.

GROUPTHINK

Irving Janis proposed that highly cohesive groups are likely to suffer from *groupthink*, a strong concurrence-seeking tendency that suppresses critical inquiry and results in faulty decision-making processes and flawed outcomes. He chose the term *groupthink* because of its frankly Orwellian connotation, similar to doublethink and crimethink. Janis discussed as examples of groupthink major historical fiascoes such as the lack of preparedness for the Japanese attack on Pearl Harbor, the escalation of war in Korea, the failed U.S.-sponsored landing of anti-Castro rebels in the Bay of Pigs, and escalation of U.S. involvement in the war in Vietnam. First presented in a 1971 issue of *Psychology Today,* this groupthink phenomenon quickly gained remarkably broad and firm acceptance, dominating the literature on group decision making for decades. Janis reasoned that dealing with vital, affect-laden issues results in "hot" cognitions, in contrast to the "cold" cognitions of routine problem solving. Such situations induce stress, resulting in defensive avoidance, characterized by lack of vigilant search, distortion of the meanings of warning messages, selective inattention and forgetting, and rationalizing. This entry describes the groupthink model and proposed remedies for groupthink. It then summarizes research evidence regarding groupthink, examines the bases for groupthink's remarkable appeal and acceptance, and addresses groupthink's usefulness for managers.

Fundamentals

The Groupthink Model

Janis presented three categories of antecedents to groupthink. First, moderate to high group cohesion is a necessary but not sufficient condition for groupthink. Structural faults and a provocative situational context are secondary antecedents. The structural fault category includes insulation of the group, lack of impartial leadership, lack of norms requiring methodical procedures, and homogeneity of members' social backgrounds and ideologies. The provocative situational context antecedents focus on the role of stress. These include external threats of losses combined with a low hope of finding a better solution than that of the leader and internal stress stemming from temporary low self-esteem attributable to members' recent failures and perceptions that the task is too difficult to accomplish and there is no morally correct alternative.

Janis viewed the antecedents as leading to symptoms of groupthink, including an illusion of invulnerability, rationalization to discount warnings and other negative feedback, belief in the inherent morality of the group, stereotyped views of members of opposing groups, pressure on dissenters, self-censorship, illusion of unanimity, and self-appointed "mindguards" acting to shield the group from adverse information.

Janis saw groupthink as resulting in consequences that interfere with effective group decision making. For instance, the group limits its discussion to only a few alternatives. After a course of action is initially selected, members ignore new information concerning its risks and drawbacks. They also avoid information concerning the benefits of rejected alternatives. Members make little attempt to use experts. And because they are so confident that things will turn out well, they fail to consider what may go wrong and, as such, do not develop contingency plans. These "defects" are seen as leading to impaired performance and other undesirable outcomes.

Proposed Remedies for Groupthink

Janis suggested several methods to prevent or minimize the supposedly dysfunctional consequences of groupthink. These "remedies" include the following: The group leader should encourage all group members to air their doubts and objections; leaders should adopt an impartial stance rather than initially stating their preferences; members should be encouraged to discuss the group's deliberations with trusted associates and report their reactions back to the group; outside experts should be invited to meetings and encouraged to challenge members' views; when a competitor is involved, time should be devoted to assessment of warning signals from the competitor and of alternative scenarios of the competitor's intentions; when considering alternatives, the group should split into subgroups to meet separately from time to time; the group should hold a "second-chance" meeting after a preliminary consensus is reached on a preferred alternative; and the group should consider using dissonance-inducing group processes.

Importance

Forty years after its conception, the groupthink phenomenon retains a remarkably strong intuitive appeal and acceptance. A Google search yielded almost 3 million groupthink "hits." Groupthink is presented as received doctrine in sources ranging from *Educational Gerontology* to the *Utne Reader*, from *The New Criterion* to *Vogue* and is offered as the cause for everything from problems of the Washington Redskins to the U.S. decision to invade Iraq to success of Bernard Madoff's Ponzi scheme. It has a firmly entrenched status with practitioners and continues to be presented as fact in textbooks and to be the subject of theory and research.

Research Evidence Regarding Groupthink

Janis demanded what Ramon J. Aldag and Sally Fuller have called a "strong" interpretation of groupthink, arguing that groupthink is not evidenced if just a few of its symptoms can be detected. Rather, Janis wrote, practically all the symptoms must be manifested, along with the antecedent conditions and signs of defective decision making. However, a "weak" version of groupthink implies that groupthink may be confirmed by the presence of some subset of these characteristics and that the causal ordering posited by Janis may be suggestive rather than necessary. This view sees any partial support, regardless of the number of disconfirming findings, as evidence of groupthink's validity.

One weak interpretation simply views groupthink as overreliance on concurrence seeking. This meaning, which seems to have gained considerable popularity, would grant no value added to groupthink. That is, overemphasis on concurrence seeking was widely recognized decades before Janis presented his model (for instance, by R. L. Schanck in 1932), and the groupthink model simply adopted this element. Another weak interpretation is that groupthink is an undesirable constellation of characteristics resulting from highly cohesive groups. However, research findings convincingly demonstrate that cohesiveness does not regularly lead to negative outcomes. More than 25 years ago, Matie L. Flowers stated that a revision of Janis's theory may be needed, one that would eliminate cohesiveness as a critical variable. Such elimination would, however, largely eviscerate the groupthink phenomenon. Yet another weak view is that groupthink is any set of group processes that precede poor decision outcomes. However, it is not surprising that poor outcomes follow bad things. Further, since many group processes and characteristics leading to poor outcomes have long ago been identified, this meaning, in which groupthink most clearly adopts the form of a metaphor for dysfunction, essentially grants groupthink no status—and Janis no contribution—beyond that of providing a memorable label.

There has been virtually no empirical support for the strong form of groupthink (which, again, Janis demanded as convincing evidence). Most support for groupthink has come from retrospective case studies that have focused on decision fiascoes rather than comparing the decision-making processes associated with good versus bad decisions and that have sought just a sampling of groupthink characteristics as confirmatory. Support for the posited groupings and for links among groupthink characteristics generally derives from anecdote, casual observation, and intuitive appeal rather than rigorous research. There has been no full factor analysis of groupthink variables. Incomplete factor analyses (in which exploratory factor analysis was applied to variables within sets rather than to all variables in the model) support a simpler, and different, model from that presented by Janis. Won-Woo Park's comprehensive

investigation of Janis's model supported only 2 of 23 predictions drawn from the groupthink model. Conversely, 7 of the 23 relationships were significantly *opposite* the direction predicted. Further, Jin Nam Choi and Myung Un Kim examined groupthink in teams facing impending crises. They found groupthink symptoms to consist of two factors. Contrary to groupthink predictions, one of those factors (termed group identity) was significantly *positively* related to team performance, whereas the other (termed concurrence seeking) showed an insignificant negative relationship to performance.

Addressing the most-cited recent example of groupthink, the Challenger disaster, Mark Maier—who developed a popular documentary on the topic—noted in 2002 that new evidence regarding the disaster and further analysis of past evidence convincingly demonstrates that the disaster emphatically is not an example of groupthink. He said two of groupthink's defining features—the conviction of invulnerability and the illusion of unanimity—were conspicuously absent. Maier discussed evidence that the decision to launch was driven by uncertainties rather than perceived infallibility and that certain actions were taken only when it was clear that opinions would not be unanimous.

Bases for Groupthink's Appeal

Writers have sought to understand bases for groupthink's tremendous appeal and acceptance. One explanation is that support for groupthink benefits from availability, with which examples come to mind based on their vividness and reliance on case, as opposed to base, data; a concrete instance of the appearance of groupthink symptoms in a fiasco may be seen as compelling evidence, especially in the absence of base data.

Groupthink is consistent with implicit theories of groups. Individuals observing a situation in which some groupthink characteristics are present may assume the existence of others. Further, feedback about group performance affects the characteristics ascribed to those groups. For example, individuals told that a group has performed poorly are more likely to report instances of "poor" interaction processes, such as lack of willingness to hear other members' views. Thus, focus on poor decision outcomes in groupthink research may lead to reports of poor group functioning.

Also, a focus only on the conjunction of groupthink characteristics and negative outcomes invites illusory correlation. In this sense, the groupthink phenomenon is similar to the "Friday the 13th" phenomenon; only the yes (groupthink/Friday the 13th)–yes (poor outcomes/bad luck) cell is considered. If the yes–yes cell is not empty, support for the phenomenon is inferred. In fact, of course, support for the phenomenon requires examination of all cells.

Further, the negative language of groupthink ("victims of groupthink," "defects of groupthink") and the focus on error invite distortions in responses caused by scale-use tendencies and related psychometric difficulties and may result in framing effects. Individuals presented with negatively framed terminology may adopt the readily available negative frame and respond accordingly.

Groupthink support may also benefit from generalization from a part to a whole, in which a core concept with some validity is incorporated as an element of a broader, renamed concept. Support for the core concept is treated as confirmation of the broader concept and, by association, for its various elements. In the case of groupthink, a core concept with some validity (i.e., the dangers of overemphasis on concurrence seeking) is subsumed in a complex, essentially deterministic model. Subsequent instances of that core concept are then presented as evidence for the validity of the broader phenomenon.

Usefulness for Managers

Groupthink has stimulated research on group dysfunctions; provided links to other literatures, such as stress and vigilance; emphasized potentially important variables in group decision making; and encouraged policymakers to take remedies for excessive concurrence seeking seriously. Indeed, Janis's recommendations for remedies for groupthink offer an excellent compilation of approaches to help preclude group dysfunction. For example, as noted earlier, Janis recommends approaches to encouragement of group members' airing of doubts and objections as well as interaction with trusted associates and outside experts, devoting time to reevaluation of preferred alternatives, assessment of warning signals, and application of dissonance-inducing techniques.

However, while the groupthink model has been valuable in generating interest in group problem-solving processes, it has not incorporated four decades of theory and research, has received limited empirical support, and is restrictive in scope. Recent theory and research, as well as critical evaluation of the model, suggest that more comprehensive models are necessary to guide researchers and practitioners in dealing with group decision phenomena.

It is common for theories to generate initial widespread interest and enthusiasm and to meet with subsequent revision, rejection, or reaffirmation. Groupthink, however, has generally resisted dispassionate reevaluation, perhaps due to its raw intuitive appeal and because studies of groupthink have often been searches for confirmation. Rigorous evaluation of the phenomenon is further rendered difficult by the fact that there are a variety of views of groupthink and contrasting positions on what level of evidence is needed to indicate support. Nevertheless, popular acceptance of groupthink has been extraordinary. Perhaps this is understandable: Groupthink has served as a vivid bogeyman that can be readily summoned to illustrate the dangers of overemphasis on concurrence seeking, and it continues to serve its purpose.

Ramon J. Aldag

See also Group Development; Group Polarization and the Risky Shift; High-Performing Teams; Norms Theory; Schemas Theory; Work Team Effectiveness

Further Readings

Aldag, R. J., & Fuller, S. R. (1993). Beyond fiasco: A reappraisal of the groupthink phenomenon and a new model of group decision processes. *Psychological Bulletin, 113,* 533–552.

Choi, J. N., & Kim, M. U. (1999). The organizational application of groupthink and its limitations in organizations. *Journal of Applied Psychology, 84,* 297–306.

Flowers, M. L. (1977). A laboratory test of some implications of Janis's groupthink hypothesis. *Journal of Personality and Social Psychology, 33,* 888–895

Fuller, S. R., & Aldag, R. J. (1998). Organizational Tonypandy: Lessons from a quarter century of the groupthink phenomenon. *Organizational Behavior and Human Decision Processes, 73*(2/3), 163–184.

Janis, I. L. (1971, November). Groupthink. *Psychology Today, 5*(6) 43–46, 74–76.

Janis, I. L. (1982). *Groupthink* (2nd ed.). Boston, MA: Houghton Mifflin.

Maier, M. (2002). Ten years after *A Major Malfunction* . . . Reflections on "The Challenger syndrome. *Journal of Management Inquiry, 11,* 282–292.

Park, W. (1990). A review of research on groupthink. *Journal of Behavioral Decision Making, 3,* 229–245.

Park, W.-W. (2000). A comprehensive empirical investigation of the relationships among variables of the groupthink model. *Journal of Organizational Behavior, 21,* 873–887.

't Hart, P., Stern, E. K., & Sundelius, B. (1997). *Beyond groupthink: Political group dynamics and foreign policy-making.* Ann Arbor: University of Michigan Press.

H

High- and Low-Context Cultures

Edward T. Hall, in his 1976 book *Beyond Culture*, proposed the idea of *context* to explain differences in communication styles across cultures. Context, understood as the information surrounding an event and inextricably bound up with its meaning, is described as a continuum with high and low context on either end. A *high-context* communication or message is one in which most of the information is either in the physical context or internalized in the persons engaged in communicating, while very little information is in the coded, explicit, transmitted part of the message itself. A *low-context* communication, on other hand, is exactly the opposite; that is, the mass of the information is vested in the code. Here, the communicator is much more explicit, and words are chosen carefully to mean exactly what the communicator is attempting to convey.

Communication is widely recognized as a vital management issue because it contributes significantly to employee morale, behavior, and long-term success of an organization. In particular, as operations have become increasingly globalized and the workforce and clientele have become more diverse and multicultural, the need to communicate effectively has gained prominence. Miscommunication, or inability to convey and interpret meaning of the message as intended, can cost the organization in terms of unnecessary frustration, conflicts, and loss of productivity. Because context is important for how messages are coded and decoded, it is critical that managers develop a clear understanding of high- and low-context cultures in order to improve how they communicate and interpret how others communicate with them. This entry is first a description and explanation of the context model, including its main terms, its importance in cross-cultural management, and its interrelationships with other cultural dimensions. Next, an assessment of the validity and impact of the context model is offered, along with an evaluation of the degree to which it is supported by research and helps to explain management theory and practice. Finally, implications for future research are outlined.

Fundamentals

Context, information, and *meaning* are central terms in Hall's concept and are presented as inextricably associated with each other. Hall has argued that a synthesis of context and information produces meaning, which is socially and environmentally constructed. There is no meaning without a combination of information and context; the same information with an altered context yields a different meaning. Consequently, meaning is the result of a cognitive combination of context and information.

In *Beyond Culture*, Hall argues that the level of context determines everything about the nature of communication and is the foundation on which subsequent behavior rests. This claim, linking context to communication to behavior, has been instrumental in advancing the concept of *high-low context* within cross-cultural management research. As the pace of globalization has increased, the dissimilar communication practices and behaviors that became evident during business negotiations led researchers to conclude that these differences often emerge from contradictory cultural values and beliefs. Hence, high-low context emerged as a critical dimension for categorizing and contrasting national cultures in order to facilitate business communication (along with other dimensions, such as individualism-collectivism, uncertainty avoidance, time orientation, and power distance).

Essentially, the high-low context concept refers to the extent to which communication is carried by explicit, verbally expressed messages or is embedded in the context in which the message is conveyed. Lower context societies attach more meaning to the message itself. They emphasize direct and explicit communication. What is said is what is meant. In contrast, communication in higher context cultures involves subtle meanings embedded behind and around the words spoken. It requires paying much more attention to "reading between the lines" and understanding what the communicator really means through implicit, nonverbal cues. Tone of voice and facial expressions are important elements.

Modes of communication differ between higher and lower context cultures. The mode is implicit, interpretative, and emotional in a high-context culture but explicit, visual, and logical in a low-context culture. This entails difference in the contextualization of messages and the expected roles of the sender and receiver. Higher context cultures rely on the decoding skills of the receiver and focus on nonverbal gestures and cues. Lower context cultures concentrate on the encoding of the message and focus on using words precisely and appropriately.

Hall also emphasizes the difference in worldview of time and space between high- and low-context cultures. He argues that people from higher context cultures function on *polychronic time,* which is in line with their holistic thinking patterns, and those from lower context cultures prefer a *monochronic, sequential time* in line with their linear thinking and direct form of contextualization. This affects their time orientation, as lower context cultures plan and think in the long term, while high-context cultures have a shorter term planning range. Higher context cultures also tend to correlate with cultures that have a strong sense of tradition and history. They exhibit higher uncertainty avoidance and change

little with time. This is in direct contrast with lower context cultures that are low in uncertainty avoidance, hence, relatively more susceptible and open to change.

Higher context cultures are more common in Eastern than in Western cultures. E. T. Hall and Mildred Reed Hall list Japan, Arabic countries, Greece, Spain, Italy, England, France, North American countries, Scandinavian countries, and German-speaking countries in order from high to low context, where some countries were also termed as medium-context countries. It is argued that collectivist cultures, in which group and/or community is valued over the individual, support higher context cultures than an individualistic culture that fosters individual achievement. For example, in Saudi Arabia and China, family, friends, and coworkers have close personal relationships and large information networks. They are generally more collectivist (group oriented) and tend to develop diffuse intersecting relationships where work and personal lives often overlap. Developing trust is a first step to any business transaction in these cultures. Relationships often take precedence over tasks and thus are less governed by reason than by intuition or feelings. Flowery language, humility, and elaborate apologies are typical. On the other hand, lower context cultures, such as Switzerland and Denmark, develop specific compartmentalized relationships at work by maintaining a separation between work and personal lives. Members of these cultures are also more individualistic; therefore, in interacting with others, they require much more detailed information. Tasks often take precedence over relationships, and discussions often end with action. Mediterranean and other European countries are described as medium-context countries.

Importance

Hall's context model is considered to be a major influence in cross-cultural management research. Although there are many prominent and popular conceptualizations of national cultures, including those of Geert Hofstede, the Global Leadership and Organizational Behavior Effectiveness (GLOBE) study by Robert House and associates, and Fons Trompenaars, to name a few, it is only Hall's work that explicitly offers a communication-oriented perspective on culture. Hall contends that culture *is* communication and that no communication by humans can be divorced from culture. In addition, as has been mentioned previously, it can also be used as the basis for explaining other cultural dimensions, such as collectivism, uncertainty avoidance, time orientation, and specific-diffuse relationships.

Over the past few decades, Hall's context model has been used to describe how people in a culture relate to one another, especially in social bonds, responsibility, commitment, social harmony, and communication. Several studies have indicated that (higher or lower) context affects cross-cultural communication, conflict resolution, and negotiations. Hence, it has proven helpful in understanding differences among cultures and for studying the managerial implications of cultural differences. Contemporary managers are increasingly transacting with a culturally diverse assortment of stakeholders, including customers, suppliers, and employees. Communication is a core business activity, which allows organizations to promote a service or product, negotiate a price, sell the product or service, and relay other business-related information to a variety of audiences. In today's intensely competitive and global marketplace, it is important to avoid miscommunication. Understanding the concept of high-low context culture allows managers to be more effective in communicating with others, as well in interpreting what others communicate to them. Making sure you know *how* to say something (or how it is said), in addition to *what* to say (or what is said), is critical. Insights from the low-high context model heighten awareness of cultural nuances and can be used to adapt content and mode of communication to the style and needs of the interlocutor.

Research has expanded classification of high, medium, and low context to countries (beyond Germany, Japan, and the United States) not originally studied by Hall. However, support for such analysis is not universal. Some authors also focused upon validating Hall's context model—empirically analyzing whether countries traditionally assumed to be high context or low context are actually high context or low context in today's globalized environment. This has led to sometimes contradictory and mixed findings. Jane Kassis Henderson has criticized Hall's concept as an analytical tool that is not useful for contemporary global managers as they increasingly experience dynamic and multilingual situations. Others criticized it for bipolarization,

overgeneralization, and lack of empirical foundation. Recently, Markus Kittler and associates performed a systematic review of the studies that have used Hall's concept in the literature between 1991 and 2007. They attribute contradictory findings to several methodological shortcomings of studies subsequent to Hall's research, including an overreliance on quantitative approaches, selection of a convenience (business student) sample, and an exclusive focus upon a United States–Asian comparison. In particular, they show that these studies have used context as a dichotomous variable and neglected the medium-context, despite Hall's original conceptualization of high and low merely as poles of a context continuum. They conclude that a more sophisticated and rigorous approach to Hall's context model is needed in order to revive interest in Hall's context model and to produce work that benefits cross-cultural communication.

Shaista E. Khilji

See also Cultural Intelligence; Cultural Values; Individual Values; Managing Diversity; Meaning and Functions of Organizational Culture; Multicultural Work Teams

Further Readings

Hall, E. T. (1976). *Beyond culture*. New York, NY: Anchor Books/Doubleday.

Hall, E. T., & Hall, M. R. (1990). *Understanding cultural differences*. Yarmouth, ME: Intercultural Press.

Hart, W. B. (1999). Inter-disciplinary influences in the study of cultural relations: A citation analysis of the *International Journal of Intercultural Relations*. *International Journal of Intercultural Relations, 23*, 575–589.

Henderson, J. K. (2005). Language diversity in international management teams. *International Management Studies of Management and Organization, 35*, 66–82.

Hofstede, G. (1980). *Culture's consequences: International differences in work-related values*. Thousand Oak, CA: Sage.

House, R. J., Hanges, P., Javidan, M., Dorfman, P. W., & Gupta, V. (2004). *Culture, leadership and organizations: The GLOBE study of 62 societies*. Thousand Oaks, CA: Sage.

Kim, D., Pan, Y., & Park, H. S. (1998). High versus low context culture: A comparison of Chinese, Korean and American cultures. *Psychology and Marketing, 15*(6), 507–517.

Kittler, M. G., Rygl, D., & Mackinson, A. (2011). Beyond culture or beyond control: Reviewing the use of Hall's high-/low-context concept. *International Journal of Cross Cultural Management, 11*(1), 63–82.

Smidts, A., Pruyn, A. T. H., & van Riel, C. B. M. (2001). The impact of employee communication and perceived external prestige on organizational identification. *Academy of Management Journal, 49*, 1051–1062.

Trompenaars, F. (1993). *Riding the waves of culture: Understanding diversity in global business.* New York, NY: Irwin.

High-Performance Work Systems

High-performance work systems (HPWS; also known as high-commitment practices and high-involvement work practices) refers to a configuration of distinct but related human resource (HR) practices that enhance or increase employees' skills, motivation, commitment, and effort. HPWS is a specific type of HR system. Examples of HPWS practices include formal information sharing programs, formal job analysis, quality of work-life programs, profit sharing plans, extensive training and development, performance based compensation, and formal grievance procedures. HR scholars and practitioners alike have consistently shown, other things being equal, that organizations with rigorous HPWS practices have statistically significant higher levels of individual and organizational performance. In general, research has shown that HPWS is strongly linked to the needs of the business and plays a critical role in how organizations develop and sustain competitive advantage using their human resources. This entry begins with a brief discussion of the characteristics of HPWS, continues by highlighting the current debates in HPWS research, and concludes with a discussion of the implications of HPWS.

Fundamentals

Characteristics of High-Performance Work Systems

The systems perspective. The notion of HPWS is embedded in the systems perspective of managing human resource management (HRM). According to Brian E. Becker and colleagues, this perspective views HR practices as working together to support organizational goals and objectives. Here, the unit of analysis is the entire system rather than the individual HR practices and policies. The various HR practices synergistically complement each other to form unique configurations or bundles that can result in increased performance, both at the individual level (e.g., employee) and the organizational level. For example, research by HR scholars, such as Mark Huselid, has shown that the unique configuration of the HPWS produces high-performance employee behaviors and competencies (individual level) which in turn improve revenue, profits, and ultimately market value (organizational level).

Alignment, or fit. At the heart of HPWS is the concept of alignment, or fit. There are two types of alignment: horizontal and vertical. *Vertical fit* occurs when the entire HRM system fits with all other components of the organization such as business strategy, organizational structure, and organizational culture. An important form of vertical fit is between an organization's business strategy and HRM systems. Over the past two decades, researchers such as Randall Schuler, Susan Jackson, and John MacDuffie have examined (theoretically and empirically) how various configurations of HRM systems relate to different types of business strategies. This stream of research has examined how organizations differ in the configuration of their HR systems and how different bundles of HR policies and practices support their business goals and objectives.

Horizontal fit refers to how various HR policies and practices synergistically support each and enhance one another's effectiveness. As described by John Delery, there are two forms of synergistic relationships among HR practices. First, there can be a positive synergistic relationship among HR practices whereby the whole is greater than the sum of the parts. When HR practices work together (e.g., extensive training practices supporting staffing practices that recruit and select individuals with raw talent), their impact on performance is much greater than the individual practices that made up the system. The second type of relationship occurs when two practices actually work against one another. Becker and colleagues refer to this as a "deadly combination" that produces negative synergy. When HR practices work in deadly combination (e.g., career development programs designed for most valuable employees offered to all types of employees), their impact on performance is much less than the individual practices that make up the system.

Overall an important assumption in HPWS is that organizations that use HPWS have the best possible horizontal and vertical alignments.

Current Debates in High-Performance Work Systems Research

There are currently two important debates related to HPWS for HR researchers and professionals. The first examines the design of the HPWS—how the various HR practices are configured, how the practices within the HPWS work together, and whether there are any subsystems of HPWS. The second area focuses on the process of HPWS—examining the mediating variables between HPWS and firm performance, more specifically on how HWPS affects the knowledge-based human capital (e.g., tacit knowledge domains).

Implications of High-Performance Work Systems

Organizational performance. Over the last two decades, considerable research efforts have been devoted to examining how HPWS practices relate to various measures of individual and organizational performance. Mark Huselid's 1995 study provided strong evidence of the fact that HPWS is related to measures of individual and organizational effectiveness. Huselid's study was focused on both intermediate employee outcomes (e.g., turnover and productivity) and short-term and long-term measures of corporate financial performance. In his study, Huselid also illustrated what HPWS looks like and how the HR practices within the system work together. An important finding from Huselid's work and other strategic HRM is that HPWS systems do not directly impact organizational performance. The HPWS influences intermediate employee outcomes, such as human capital (e.g., knowledge, skills, and abilities), and employee behaviors. These in turn lead to improved performance. This is referred to as the *black box of strategic HRM*.

Talent management. Talent management is an area of HRM that focuses on employees with high level human capital (e.g., knowledge, skills, and abilities). These employees are also known as critical employees,

strategic employees, high-potential employees, and A players. The current trends suggest that HPWS helps organizations attract, develop, and retain talent. Characteristics of organizations that use HPWS to manage talent include focusing more on knowledge workers, providing greater autonomy to strategic employees, extensively using team-based projects, and deploying highly sophisticated technology-based learning systems to develop employees. Due to a critical shortage of talented employees (e.g., easier to develop existing raw talent than to attract talent from external labor markets) HPWS practices are likely to continue playing an important role in how organizations manage talent.

Ibraiz Tarique

See also Behavioral Theory of the Firm; Competitive Advantage; Human Resource Management Strategies; Human Resources Roles Model; Strategic International Human Resource Management

Further Readings

Appelbaum, E., Bailey, T., Berg, P., & Kalleberg, A. (2000). *Manufacturing advantage: Why high-performance work systems pay off.* Ithaca, NY: Cornell University Press.

Arthur, J. B. (1994). Effects of human resource systems on manufacturing performance and turnover. *Academy of Management Journal, 27,* 670–687.

Becker, B. E., Huselid, M. A., Pinckus, P. S., & Spratt, M. F. (1997). HR as a source of shareholder value: Research and recommendations. *Human Resource Management, 36,* 39–48.

Boxall, P. (2012). High-performance work systems: What, why, how and for whom? *Asia Pacific Journal of Human Resources, 50,* 169.

Delery, J. E. (1998). Issues of fit in strategic human resource management: Implications for research. *Human Resource Management Review, 8,* 289–310.

Huselid, M. A. (1995). The impact of human resource management practices on turnover, productivity, and corporate financial performance. *Academy of Management Journal, 38,* 635–673.

Ichniowski, C., Shaw, K., & Prennushi, G. (1997). The effects of human resource management practices on productivity: A study of steel finishing lines. *American Economic Review, 87,* 291–313.

MacDuffie, J. P. (1995). Human resource bundles and manufacturing performance: Organizational logic and flexible production systems in the world auto industry. *Industrial and Labor Relations Review, 48,* 197–221.

Schuler, R. S., & Jackson, S. E. (2005). A quarter-century review of human resource management in the U.S.: The growth in importance of the international perspective. *Management Revue, 16*, 11–35.

Tarique, I., & Schuler, R. S. (2010). Global talent management: Literature review, integrative framework, and suggestions for further research. *Journal of World Business, 46*, 122–133.

HIGH-PERFORMING TEAMS

The ability to work well in teams is undeniably essential in present-day organizations. Across a wide range of organizations, teamwork provides the competitive edge that translates opportunities into successes. High-performing teams are crucial for the effectiveness of organizations, not the least because well-aligned team thinking and goal orientation facilitates dealing with current crises and designing long-term strategies. Yet leaders and scholars too easily overlook the reality that, for most teams, it can be very difficult to generate remarkable synergy and excellent outcomes; instead, many teams become mired in endlessly unproductive sessions and are rife with conflict. Given the importance of teamwork, why do so many teams fail to live up to their promise? The answer lies in the obstinate belief that human beings are purely rational entities. Many team designers or others in positions of leadership fail to appreciate the real complexity of teamwork. They forget—out of denial or simple naïveté—to take into account the subtle, out-of-awareness behavior patterns underlying human interactions, at the interpersonal as well as intrapersonal levels. In other words, individual idiosyncrasies and group dynamics can derail effective team performance if these forces are not examined and, if necessary, addressed. This entry describes the core premises of the clinical approach to individual, team, and organizational studies. The authors then suggest how this paradigm can be applied practically and to great effect within the context of leadership group coaching toward the development of high-performing teams.

Fundamentals

At their best, high-performing teams have a source of collective energy and synergy which allows them to accomplish their goals with great efficiency and effectiveness. Team members possess a shared sense of purpose; they all pull in the same direction at the same time while taking advantage of complementarities in skills and competencies. In such teams, goals and objectives have been discussed and agreed on openly, so each member of the team pursues the same thing. Such teams stick together through highs and lows, taking both the blame and the rewards as something to be shared by all. The team is a source of pride to its members, who derive great pleasure and satisfaction from working together.

Dysfunctional teams, by contrast, are rife with role conflict and ambiguity, unresolved overt and covert conflicts, poor timekeeping and absenteeism. Teams that cannot reach closure have rigid, ritualistic meetings; uneven member participation; tunnel vision; indifference to the interests of the organization as a whole; and a lack of resources, skills, knowledge, and accountability. Within such teams, there is no genuine collegiality, collaboration, or coordination.

In many dysfunctional teams, blaming and scapegoating are some of the major dynamics stalling the organization's productivity and creative process. In these teams, members avoid dealing with conflict, preferring to resort to veiled discussions and guarded comments. Taken to the extreme, such teams become toxic and morph into highly constipated, slow decision-making bodies, underperforming and floundering despite all the resources made available to them. Competitive feelings among team members can result in sabotage of each other's work, unjustified criticism, and withholding of information and resources, contributing to the breakdown of the team's proper functioning. All these dynamics can be very subtle, but they can be very damaging to the organization and its members.

Organizational designers need to realize that, when they create teams, there is more going on than meets the eye. In every human interaction, there are visible, intentional behaviors that are fairly easy to understand, and there are also subtexts, or unconscious motivators, personality quirks, and the emotional life of its team members that influence those actions. A purely cognitive, rational-structural perspective on teamwork will be incomplete if it fails to acknowledge the unconscious dynamics that underlie individual and group motivation and behavior.

Increasingly, organizational studies are starting to pay attention to the emotional life of their members;

they recognize that much of what motivates a person's behavior is beyond his or her conscious awareness. A clinical paradigm brings a more holistic and systemic orientation to organizational studies and interventions by providing a psychodynamic lens for examining the micro, meso, and macro processes of teams—which clinicians can visualize as interwoven individual, group, and organizational interactions.

The Clinical Paradigm

The clinical orientation is solidly grounded in concepts of psychoanalytic psychology, short-term dynamic psychotherapy, cognitive theory, human development, and family systems theory. It is used in conjunction with more traditional organizational development methods as an extremely powerful means to decipher knotty individual leadership, team, and organizational issues. In the case of many incomprehensible organizational situations, a clinical orientation can go a long way toward bringing clarity and providing solutions.

The key premises of the paradigm are the following:

Rationality is an illusion. Behind any irrational act is a rational meaning. Nothing that people do is random. Understanding this rationale is critical to making sense of our own and other people's inner theater—the core themes that affect personality, behavior, and leadership style.

What people see isn't necessarily what they get. Much of what happens to people is beyond their conscious awareness. Most human behavior is driven by unconscious forces. To have a better understanding of these unconscious patterns people need to explore their own and other people's inner desires, wishes, and fantasies; they need to pay attention to the repetitive themes and patterns in their lives and in the lives of others.

The past is the lens through which people can understand the present and shape the future. Like it or not, all people are the product of their past. People are inclined to view the present through the microscope of past experiences. Personality structure is due to a person's genetic endowment and the developmental outcome of the individual's early environment. To make sense of their behavior, people must explore their interpersonal history, including their original attachment relationships.

Applying a clinical paradigm to the study of organizational life can be described metaphorically as entering into an individual's inner theater. Within this inner theater, a rich tragicomedy plays itself out on the stage, with key actors representing the people they have loved, hated, feared, and admired throughout their lives. Some of these early interactions evoke painful memories; others fill people with a sense of well-being. These internal figures are a strong influence on the development of people's values, beliefs, and attitudes, which laid the foundation of their personality, patterns of behavior, preferred leadership styles, and courses of action.

If they want a better understanding of themselves and their behavior in teams, they need to pay attention to the unconscious dynamics of their early relationships (early caregiver, parent, or sibling, for example). These relationships in turn affect not only the way they love, choose their friends, or express themselves, but also they influence patterns of relationships with bosses, colleagues, and subordinates. These relationships permeate all their life experiences and determine the way they make decisions, their preferred leadership style, the way they communicate, and the degree to which they are able to work together closely in teams.

A clinical orientation treats the team or group as a living organism with all its interdependencies and complexities; it moves from the surface of human behavior to a more in-depth analysis of group dynamics so that clinicians may better understand why teams (and the individuals within them) behave the way they do, to identify areas of team dysfunction, to encourage them to loosen their bonds with unproductive past behavior, and to help them see new possibilities in the future.

Importance

Thinking about how to harness the potential force of group dynamics, Manfred F. R. Kets de Vries began, in the early 1990s, to experiment with leadership group coaching in a multi-module program for top executives. Applying the clinical paradigm in these coaching situations, he and his team wanted to help participants confront the underlying forces that prevent them from performing individually and collectively at their best. They believed that by helping senior executives to see below the surface, they would better understand the dynamics (including the resistances) that prevent them from performing at their best and, through the coaching process, identify the changes needed to instill a corporate culture of team-based distributive leadership in their own organizations.

Leadership group coaching is a specific form of intervention that can be carried out strategically with individuals, teams, or an entire organization. Its aim is to direct a group of people (who come from previously existing working groups, or in mixed-function/project groups) toward a specific, mutually determined goal, accelerating organizational progress by providing focus and awareness. By providing a safe space for honest and open explorations and confrontations, teams get a better understanding of the strengths and weaknesses of each of its members. This awareness brings understanding, which in turn builds trust, and opens the path to dealing with the undiscussables, or shadow side, of their team. Through group coaching, team members challenge and reassess their assumptions about themselves and others; in doing so, they understand why they behave the way they do and why the team as a whole behaves the way it does. They undergo a cohesive experience, bringing the team members closer together, not only in terms of resolving conflict and achieving mutual understanding but also by increasing shared accountability and renewed commitment.

When conducted with a strong psychodynamic component, group coaching allows individuals to confront their own dark side and the dysfunctional aspects of their teams. Elucidation and clarification in turn helps induce alignment between the goals of individual group members and accelerates an organization's progress by providing a greater understanding of the team's strengths and weaknesses, which can lead to better decision making. It fosters teamwork based on trust; in turn, the culture itself is nurtured as people become used to creating teams in which people feel comfortable and productive. When they work well, team-oriented coaching cultures are like networked webs in the organization, connecting people laterally in the same departments, across departments, between teams, and up and down the hierarchy.

Operating in today's organizations requires leaders with collaborative, problem-solving, and influencing skills—executives with emotional intelligence, who have an astute understanding of how to analyze complex processes and grasp the intricacies of the company's value chain, who know how to deal with inefficiencies and recognize interdependencies among other stakeholders in the organization, and who are prepared to acquire the emotional know-how to motivate and empower employees and teams to perform at peak capacity. The organizations of tomorrow, more than ever, will need executives who can deal with both the advantages and disadvantages of teamwork and know how to be effective as a member of a team. Today's world of work requires the kind of executive who moves beyond the more cognitive, rational-structural point of view of organizations and pays attention to both the overt and covert forces underlying organizational life.

When dysfunctional group dynamics prevail, teams perform below their capacity, and the price can be considerable. This is one of the reasons why leadership coaching has become such a growth industry. When an organization supports its executives in the development of high-performing teams through leadership coaching programs, the individual, the team, and the whole organization will benefit. Leadership coaching complements existing leadership development programs and makes an essential contribution to the success of any change initiative. What's more, group coaching leads to increased self-awareness and provides a better understanding of the kinds of obstacles that people have to deal with in their journey through life. It gives people a new lens through which to examine deeply confusing personal, team, and organizational problems. Whether these dilemmas are conscious or unconscious, leadership group coaching can help executives create tipping points, to make them more successful at managing their day-to-day responsibilities, meeting their goals, recognizing when they find themselves at crossroads, and, most importantly, creating a fulfilling life.

Manfred F. R. Kets de Vries
and Alicia Cheak

See also Emotional and Social Intelligence; Group Development; High-Performance Work Systems; Needs Hierarchy; Theory of Emotions; Work Team Effectiveness

Further Readings

Crane, T. J., & Patrick, L. N. (Eds.). (2002). *The heart of coaching: Using transformational coaching to create a high-performance coaching culture.* San Diego, CA: FTA Press.

Hackman, J. R. (2002). *Leading teams: Setting the stage for great performance.* Boston, MA: Harvard Business School Press.

Kets de Vries, M. F. R. (2001). Creating authentizotic organizations: Well-functioning individuals in vibrant companies. *Human Relations, 54*(1), 101–111.

Kets de Vries, M. F. R. (2005). Leadership group coaching in action: The Zen of creating high performance teams. *Academy of Management Executive, 19*(1), 61–76.

Kets de Vries, M. F. R. (2006). *The leader on the couch: A clinical approach to changing people and organizations.* New York, NY: Wiley.

Kets de Vries, M. F. R. (2011). *The hedgehog effect: The secrets of building high performance teams.* London, England: Wiley.

Kets de Vries, M. F. R., Guillen, L., Korotov, K., & Florent-Treacy, E. (2010). *The coaching kaleidoscope: Insights from the inside.* New York, NY: Palgrave/Macmillan.

Kets de Vries, M. F. R., Korotov, K., & Florent-Treacy, E. (2007). *Coach and couch: The psychology of making better leaders.* New York, NY: Palgrave/Macmillan.

HIGH-RELIABILITY ORGANIZATIONS

A high-reliability organization (HRO) is an organization that operates in a nearly error-free manner despite facing high levels of social and technical complexity. These organizations need to perform with exceptional reliability because failures have been deemed unacceptable by governmental and/or regulatory bodies. HROs play a key role in management theory because they illustrate the practices and processes through which an organization is able to perform in a highly effective manner under extremely trying conditions. As organizational environments change at an ever-quickening pace, HROs and the management of them serve as a useful model for an increasing number of organizations. In the remainder of this entry, the characteristics of HROs, the processes through which they achieve highly reliable performance, and the ongoing debate between HRO and normal accident theory (NAT) are outlined.

Fundamentals

The scholarly understanding of HROs results from a series of careful, in-depth case studies by a group of researchers at the University of California Berkeley (Todd LaPorte, Gene Rochlin, and Karlene Roberts) who examined aircraft carriers (specifically the USS *Carl Vinson*), the Federal Aviation Administration's Air Traffic Control system (and commercial aviation more generally), and nuclear power operations (Pacific Gas and Electric's Diablo Canyon reactor). Further research on each of these three sites included participation by Karl Weick and Paul Schulman. Later research in this tradition has examined additional HROs, including the fire incident command system, Loma Linda Hospital's Pediatric Intensive Care Unit, and the California Independent System Operator. These diverse organizations share some key characteristics—(a) they operate in unforgiving social and political environments, (b) their technologies are risky and present the potential for (often catastrophic) error, and (c) the scale of possible consequences from errors or mistakes precludes learning through experimentation. Researchers have identified properties of HROs that are similar to other highly effective organizations, including carefully selecting employees to ensure they have the requisite interpersonal and technical skills, continual training to keep skills sharp, and frequent process audits and continuous improvement efforts. Yet other properties of HROs are more tailored to their specific challenges such as a variety of cross-checking mechanisms designed to detect errors before they occur and the development of latent networks of expertise that are activated when an HRO experiences an unexpected event. In addition, the mind-set that characterizes HROs is also unique in that it emphasizes the importance of avoiding misperceiving or misunderstanding emerging threats to reliability.

Defining high reliability has presented some challenges. In an early formulation of high reliability, Roberts proposed that high-reliability organizations are a subset of hazardous organizations that have enjoyed a record of high safety over long periods of time. Specifically, she stated that when an organization could have failed catastrophically but does not on the order of tens of thousands of times, it is an HRO. More recent treatments of high reliability have relaxed this definition in favor of arguing that high reliability merely indicates that some organizations must perform in a nearly error-free manner under very trying conditions, that high risk and high effectiveness can coexist, and that it takes intensive effort to achieve this. This more flexible definition has led a broader set of researchers to contribute to the literature on HROs by expanding it to include reliability-seeking organizations. Reliability-seeking organizations are not distinguished by the human and societal cost of failures but, rather, their need to manage the complexity of their task environment such that they avoid small failures amplifying into organizational mortality.

In an influential review of the case studies of HROs, Weick, Kathleen Sutcliffe, and David Obstfeld provocatively posited that HROs achieve their extraordinary performance through a set of processes known as *mindful organizing*. Mindful organizing consists of preoccupation with failure, reluctance to simplify interpretations, sensitivity to operations, commitment to resilience, and deference to expertise. In other words, HROs are highly reliable because their people spend time discussing what could go wrong (preoccupation with failure), considering the assumptions they make and alternatives to current practice (reluctance to simplify interpretations), attempting to create and share an up-to-date big picture of operations (sensitivity to operations), building capabilities for learning (commitment to resilience), and migrating decision making to the person with the most expertise with the problem at hand (deference to expertise). As such, mindful organizing constitutes actions that forestall and contain errors and crises. This reconceptualization of the literature on HROs led to the development of a mindful organizing scale that has been linked to improving reliability (e.g., reducing medication errors in health care contexts). Mindful organizing's impact on reliability seems to be enhanced when leaders cultivate trust with their employees. Ongoing research on mindful organizing and HROs is focusing on how an organization becomes highly reliable, understanding the conditions under which mindful organizing emerges, and empirically differentiating mindful organizing from other established organizational processes and emergent states (e.g., transactive memory systems).

Research on HROs is often contrasted with, and even seen as a response to, normal accident theory (NAT). NAT asserts that systems that are tightly coupled (i.e., have time-dependent processes that occur in a fixed sequence and limited slack resources) and interactively complex (i.e., parts of the system interact in unexpected ways that are impossible to anticipate and difficult to correct) will inevitably experience accidents, and they will often be catastrophic. The disasters at the Three Mile Island and Chernobyl nuclear facilities are considered representative examples of normal accidents. NAT directly conflicts with HRO in that the former embraces the view that managerial and organizational interventions cannot overcome the tight coupling and interactive complexity whereas the latter suggest that, although very difficult, such organizations can function safely despite the hazards of complex systems. Although the differences between HRO and NAT remain, researchers on both sides of it have agreed that if the recommendations of NAT must be ignored (because a technology is too important), then following the HRO approach to managing the resulting organization is advisable. As a result, research on HROs continues to be of great interest to scholars of leadership, safety, team processes, organizational design, and organizational learning.

Timothy Vogus

See also Complexity Theory and Organizations; High-Performing Teams; Organizational Culture and Effectiveness; Organizational Learning; Positive Organizational Scholarship; Sensemaking; Systems Theory of Organizations

Further Readings

Bigley, G. A., & Roberts, K. H. (2001). The incident command system: High-reliability organizing for complex and volatile task environments. *Academy of Management Journal, 44,* 1281–1300.
LaPorte, T. R., & Consolini, P. M. (1991). Working in practice but not in theory: Theoretical challenges of "high-reliability organizations." *Journal of Public Administration Research and Theory, 1,* 19–48.
Madsen, P. M., Desai, V. M., Roberts, K. H., & Wong, D. (2006). Mitigating hazards through continuing design: The birth and evolution of a pediatric intensive care unit. *Organization Science, 17,* 239–248.
Perrow, C. (1984). *Normal accidents: Living with high-risk technologies.* New York, NY: Basic Books.
Roberts, K. H. (1990). Some characteristics of high-reliability organizations. *Organization Science, 1,* 160–177.

Roe, E., & Schulman, P. R. (2008). *High reliability management: Operating on the edge.* Palo Alto, CA: Stanford University Press.

Vogus, T. J., & Sutcliffe, K. M. (2007). The safety organizing scale: Development and validation of a behavioral measure of safety culture in hospital nursing units. *Medical Care, 45,* 46–54.

Weick, K. E., & Roberts, K. H. (1993). Collective mind in organizations: Heedful interrelating on flight decks. *Administrative Science Quarterly, 38,* 357–381.

Weick, K. E., Sutcliffe, K. M., & Obstfeld, D. (1999). Organizing for high reliability: Processes of collective mindfulness. In B. M. Staw & L. L. Cummings (Eds.), *Research in organizational behavior* (Vol. 21, pp. 81–123). Greenwich, CT: JAI Press.

Weick, K. E., & Sutcliffe, K. M. (2007). *Managing the unexpected: Resilient performance in and age of uncertainty* (2nd ed.). San Francisco, CA: Jossey-Bass.

HR Roles Model

See Human Resources Roles Model

HRM Strategies

See Human Resource Management Strategies

Human Capital Theory

Human capital theory suggests that people are as important as other resources involved in the production of goods and services, and proper investments in human capital can result in improved performance at the individual, group, organization, and country levels. As noted by Gary Becker in the 1960s, investments in human capital provide benefits to individuals, organizations, and societies. This theory is important to management because it guides managers' decisions about investments in training and developing employees. This entry first describes the fundamentals of the theory from a management perspective and goes on to discuss the importance of the theory to the field of human resources management (HRM), in particular strategic HRM and talent management.

Fundamentals

With roots in labor economics, the primary proposition of human capital theory is the notion that an individual possesses human capital, which refers to the knowledge, skills, and abilities acquired from training, development, education, and other types of work and nonwork learning–based experiences. Examples of human capital include cognitive ability, education, work experience, international travel experience, industry experience, and organizational tenure. This human capital is similar to other resources involved in the production of goods and services. Everything else being equal, appropriate investments in human capital can result in increased knowledge, skills, and abilities that in turn can improve performance and productivity at various levels (e.g., individual, group, organizational, and national). As Becker points out, human capital theory can be used to explain the variation in income and productivity across individuals, organizations, and nations.

An important assumption of human capital theory is the proposition that training is an investment from which organizations and individuals expect a return. As described by Becker, investing in human capital is viewed like any other type of investments that are subject to risks and returns. From an organizational perspective, investing in human capital can require extensive resources such as time and labor. Similarly, from an individual perspective, investing in human capital involves significant direct and opportunity costs, such as forgone earning, loss of productivity while in training, and stress and anxiety involved with learning. There are also expected returns for both the organization (e.g., a highly capable workforce) and the individual (e.g., increases in future earnings, job satisfaction, promotions). Another assumption of human capital theory is that (other things being equal), any investment in human capital is likely to add value (e.g., create wealth or increase income) as long as the present value of the benefits exceeds the present value of the costs. In addition, benefits from investment in human capital are future oriented; that is, they occur in the future (e.g., after the learning event has taken place) and need to be discounted or converted to a present value for comparison purposes.

Another important assumption of human capital theory is that there are significant differences between general training and specific training. General training refers to training (or knowledge, skills, and abilities acquired from training) that is transferable across organizations, including within the organization that provides the training or learning experience. Specific training, in contrast, includes training (or knowledge, skills, and abilities) that is limited in transferability to other organizations and is useful to the organization that is providing the training or the learning experience. There are important implications of the differences between general training and specific training for distribution of training costs. With respect to general training, the trained employee benefits more than the organization and hence absorbs the costs of general training. The opposite is true with specific training. The organization benefits more than the employee, hence, the organization providing the specific training or the specific learning experience absorbs the cost of training, not the employee.

An example of a distinction between general training and specific training is on-the-job training (OJT), which is defined as training that takes place at the worksite while the employee is performing work-related activities. According to human capital theory, OJT is effective in providing an employee with job-related knowledge, skills, and abilities. In addition, OJT allows an employee to maintain current levels of knowledge, skills, and abilities. An important point that magnifies the distinction between general training and specific training is that OJT is a type of an investment that is work related and not an institutional investment that focuses on teaching and education.

Another example of a distinction between general training and specific training is the relationship between the type of training and employee turnover. According to human capital theory, the relationship between the employer and the employee becomes stronger with specific training as there are significant separation costs both for the employer and the employee. At the individual level, an employee who receives specific training is less likely to voluntarily leave the organization or quit because he or she will be less attractive to other firms. At the organizational level, the organization that provides specific training is less likely to separate the trained employee from the organization because the organization is likely to incur costs of recruiting and selecting a new employee and then training the new

employee. There are significant costs associated with socializing and training new employees. Overall, specific training is negatively related to voluntary employee turnover.

An interesting proposition of human capital theory is that turnover rate of employees with specific training is most likely lower than for a general trained employee during an economic downturn. According to human capital theory, organizations can do several things to manage the concern with turnover of employees with specific training: (a) get more out of employees who are specifically trained and remain with the organization after training—in other words, increase the rate of return from these employees; (b) offer monetary and non-monetary incentives or premiums to encourage employees to stay with the organization after training. This is a viable option from most organizations that provide specific training because they absorb part or most of the costs associated with providing specific training; (c) offer above market compensation or wages that are higher than alternative employment (e.g., what the employee could earn at any other organization); (d) encourage or ask the employee to share the cost of specific training. Similarly, share the rewards from the specific training with the employee.

There are several other propositions of human capital theory that are relevant to management. First, the ability to acquire or learn a certain level of skill varies with the individual. Some individuals take more time than others. For example, the ability to learn a new language varies from person to person; some people take more time than others to do this. Second, there are significant barriers to entry that prevent people from developing or changing careers. For example, some careers have institutional restrictions, such as licensing and quotas. Third, human capital theory can provide a framework for explaining differences in employee income and compensation levels. For example, certain talented individuals with high levels of human capital earn more than individuals with lower levels of human capital.

Importance

Theodore Schultz, Jacob Mincer, and Becker formalized the theory of human capital in the 1950s and 1960s. Becker's various human capital studies and books in the 1960s developed the theory significantly to address the difficulty at that time of explaining how the traditional factors of production, such as physical capital, affected the growth in income. There was a consensus that the traditional factors of production explained only part of the economic growth and that human capital played an important role in explaining wage differentials. Since its initial development, human capital theory has evolved into one of the most widely used and accepted theoretical frameworks in economics to understand the role of human capital in a variety of contexts. Although the foundation of the theory has not changed much, it has been applied extensively by academics and practitioners to address a variety of issues in a various fields, including general management, strategic management, human resource management, and talent management. A recent Google search of the term *human capital* resulted in over 23 million hits. A search of the ABI/INFORM database using *human capital* as a subject resulted in over eight thousand articles published in the last 60 years. These results show a strong record of scholarship.

The importance of human capital theory can be seen in a variety of fields. The fields of global talent management and strategic human resource management in particular have benefited from this theory and, as such, comprise the focus of the remainder of the entry.

Human Capital Theory and Global Talent Management

If there is one field that has been extensively influenced by human capital theory, it is global talent management. This is a relatively new and emerging area that has benefited from human capital theory. Global talent management focuses on individuals with high levels of human capital. More specifically, global talent management examines how organizations attract, retain, develop, and mobilize talent. Attraction refers to finding and locating talent, retention refers to deterring talent from voluntarily leaving the organization, development refers to preparing talent for critical positions, and mobilizing refers to placing talent in appropriate positions.

Human capital theory provides a conceptual framework to view talent as a form of capital and for understanding the choices organizations can make in terms of attracting, retaining, developing, and mobilizing individuals with high levels of

human capital. Similar to human capital theory, an important assumption of global talent management is that employees with high levels of human capital are useful to the organization to the extent they add firm specific value that is difficult for other organizations to copy and imitate. Investments in practices that attract, develop, retain, and mobilize talent can be viewed as investments in the human capital of the firm. The outcome or return on investments in global talent management practices can firmly be grounded in human capital theory.

Another application of human capital theory can be found in examining the decisions organizations make about how to align high-level human capital with critical or core positions and jobs. An important decision guided by human capital theory is the choice organizations have to make in acquiring high-level human capital either from the external global labor markets or by developing the high-level human capital already within the organization. The assumption behind developing high-level talent internally is that in the context of talent shortages, high-level human capital is an important asset that needs to be developed internally more than recruited externally. This is similar to the argument that firm-specific human capital provides competitive advantage to firms.

Human Capital Theory and Strategic HRM

An important area of research in human resource management (HRM) is the field of strategic HRM, which, among other topics, examines the relationship between HRM systems and effectiveness at various levels (e.g., individual, group, and organization). There is considerable interest in understanding how HRM systems relate to organizational effectiveness—this is referred to as the "black box" of strategic HRM. Recent findings suggest that an important outcome of HRM systems is human capital and that human capital is a mediator in the relationship between HRM and performance.

Another important topic of discussion in strategic HRM is the issue of measuring human capital. This is important to better understand the process through which human capital affects performance measures. Therefore, academics and practitioners alike should use and develop metrics that clearly measure the various forms of human capital.

Ibraiz Tarique

See also High-Performance Work Systems; Human Resource Management Strategies; Human Resources Roles Model; Strategic International Human Resource Management; Tacit Knowledge

Further Readings

Becker, G. (1962). Investment in human capital: A theoretical analysis. *Journal of Political Economy, 70,* 9–49.

Becker, G. (1964). *Human capital: A theoretical and empirical analysis, with special reference to education.* New York, NY: Columbia Press.

Burton-Jones, A., & Spender, J-C. (2011). *The Oxford handbook of human capital.* New York, NY: Oxford University Press.

Flamholtz, G., & Lacey, J. (1981). The implications of the economic theory of human capital for personnel management. *Personnel Review, 10,* 30–39.

Huselid, M., Becker, B., & Beatty, R. (2005). *The workforce scorecard: Managing human capital to execute strategy.* Boston, MA: Harvard Business Review Press.

Lepak, D., & Snell, S. (1999). The human resource architecture: Toward a theory of human capital allocation and development. *Academy of Management Review, 24,* 31–48.

Mincer, J. (1958). Investment in human capital and personal income distribution. *Journal of Political Economy, 66,* 281–302.

Schultz, W. (1961). Education and economic growth. In N. B. Henry (Ed.), *Social forces influencing American education.* Chicago, IL: University of Chicago Press.

Human Resource Management Strategies

Contingency theory, in the context of strategic human resource (HR) management, suggests that systems of HR practices (i.e., an HR strategy) can create competitive advantage and lead to sustained higher firm performance when the system works to create and support the employee capabilities required to support and drive the business strategy of a company or business unit. As researchers seek to understand the how and why of the potential relationship between HR practices and firm outcomes, it is critical to understand that the effectiveness of a particular system of HR practices will be dependent upon the match of this HR strategy to the strategic needs of the organization. This entry presents an overview of the contingency perspective of HR and provides two examples of HR strategies and how they fit with and support specific business growth strategies.

Fundamentals

Strategic human resource management (SHRM) researchers have argued that firms can create competitive advantage when the human resource management strategy is aligned with and supports the strategic needs of the organization. Specifically, when the HR system elicits the workforce characteristics required by the business strategy, organizational performance will be positively affected. Consequently, SHRM scholars have called for research to identify the specific competencies required for success in different strategic contexts and to determine the human resource management approaches which will elicit and support these competencies.

Following research on contingency theory, organizations can drive competitive advantage and higher performance by implementing systems of HR practices that create and reinforce the workforce characteristics consistent with a particular organizational strategy. There are two underlying premises to the contingency-based approach to SHRM. First, different business strategies require unique sets of organizational and workforce competencies and behaviors and in order to drive performance through HR practices, an organization must identify the competencies that are required by its strategy and develop an HR system that effectively elicits and supports these competencies. Second, there is a strong focus on the entire HR system rather than on individual practices. Consistent with these arguments and to provide examples of how particular HR strategies may support specific business strategies, Christopher J. Collins identifies the systems of HR practices most likely to support the underlying workforce characteristics needed to drive and sustain exploration and exploitation strategies—two broad growth strategies that have been articulated for firms and business units.

Exploration and the Engineering HR Strategy

Organizations following an exploration strategy compete through novel innovation aimed at new product or service domains. Firms following this strategy tend to be characterized with a learning orientation focused on experimentation and seeking variation from existing patterns or technologies. To successfully pursue the exploration strategy, firms need access to new knowledge and must create a climate of creativity that is dependent upon the ability to exchange previously unconnected knowledge to produce novel recombinations. Further, firms pursuing this strategy must also create a willingness to take risks, experiment, and experience failures in the pursuit of doing things in novel ways or shifting the technology trajectory.

Underlying these organizational factors are particular workforce characteristics that support exploration. Specifically, employees must be diverse in knowledge, willing to collaborate and exchange knowledge and risk taking. In order to broadly search for and access knowledge, employees must also have expansive external ties and have the opportunities to meet and interact with organizational colleagues to facilitate the exchange and combination of knowledge within the firm. Employees who feel comfortable taking risks are more likely to propose and exchange unusual ideas and experiment with new knowledge.

Following from these arguments, the workforce characteristics most advantageous to a firm pursuing an exploration strategy are flexibility, open and active cross-departmental communication networks, the possession of unique and diverse skill-sets by many employees, and a risk-taking culture that facilitates creative experimentation. Collins argues that the engineering HR strategy is the best fitting HR system to support exploration. James N. Baron and colleagues described the engineering HR strategy as a system of HR practices characterized by selection for specific task abilities, peer-based coordination and control, and employment attachment based on challenging work.

By selecting employees with specific skills and capabilities, this HR strategy will help organizations promote high levels of specialization and the broad base of knowledge required for productive knowledge exchange and combination. Specifically, companies following the engineering model think of employment as an open market for skills which facilitates the addition of new specialized knowledge to broaden the overall knowledge portfolio of the firm. This selection strategy also helps broaden the

connection to external organizations that increases the diversity of knowledge to which the firm has access.

Under this strategy, control and coordination of employees is based on self-management and peer input. Loose guidelines, high levels of coordination, and reliance on attracting highly skilled professionals combine to create a climate in which employees adhere to professional standards and monitor their own as well as their peers' performance. Further, the high degree of autonomy inherent in the engineering model creates the form of employee motivation (i.e., intrinsic motivation) most closely tied to creativity. Finally, employees are more likely to experiment with new ideas and take risks on trying things in new ways when they are empowered to make decisions and determine how to best accomplish their job.

The final aspect of this HR strategy—attachment to the organization based on challenging work—is also complementary to the creation of novel innovation inherent to the exploration strategy. In particular, the focus on increasing attachment by providing employees with exciting and challenging work will create intrinsic motivation in the form of job involvement which fosters creativity. It is likely that employees who take responsibility for and are rewarded based on development within their roles will feel and express higher levels of involvement in their jobs. This strategy also supports internal movement and collaboration and increased trust between coworkers, increasing the likelihood of unique knowledge exchange and recombinations.

Overall, organizations following an engineering HR strategy attract employees with specialized knowledge, increase the flow of knowledge through cross-functional teams and horizontal communication, as well as increase intrinsic motivation for creativity resulting in the exchange of diverse knowledge and unique recombinations of knowledge supportive exploration.

Exploitation and the Bureaucratic HR Strategy

Organizations following an exploitation strategy compete through advantages in quality and/or efficiency and follow a learning orientation anchored in incremental improvements on current technologies and processes. Because competition through the exploitation strategy depends on quality and efficiency in production, exploitative organizations can benefit from depth in knowledge in a particular area which enables the firm to refine and improve existing activities. Organizations can achieve a consistently high level of process improvements and quality improvements through institutionalism and the standardization of work routines.

Consistent with institutionalism and standardization, firms following the exploitation strategy must be able to attract and manage employees who are willing and able to carefully and consistently follow rules and routines and closely comply with managerial direction and rules. Specifically, employees must be committed to following routines, rules, processes, and procedures in order for the firm to maximize the production benefits of standardization. Employees who are rules oriented and motivated to closely comply with processes and procedures are most likely extrinsically motivated. Further, exploitation-oriented firms can facilitate incremental improvement by attracting an employee base with deep rather than broad knowledge. As employees focus their deep knowledge on the tasks and technology at hand, they will be able to identify the incremental improvements and marginal shifts in the existing technology.

Given the importance of institutionalism and work routine standardization and associated employee attributes for firms following an exploitation strategy, it is important to identify how exploitative organizations can effectively align HR practices to support these outcomes. Collins argues that a bureaucratic HR strategy is the best fitting HR system to meet the requirements of the exploitation strategy. The bureaucratic model is guided by a managerial philosophy characterized by formal rules, narrow jobs, tightly held standards, and top-down communication and decision making. Organizations following the bureaucratic HR model follow specific patterns in terms of how they select employees, control employee behaviors and performance, and create employee attachment to the organization.

First, organizations following this HR strategy select employees to fit into the existing production processes based on a narrow set of specific skills, enabling employees to immediately carry out the narrow set of responsibilities tied to a particular job role. Further, employees are assigned specific tasks with tightly delineated responsibilities resulting in little room for variability in the completion of tasks

and assignments. Consistent with this effort, formal rules are likely to dictate training specifications for each job role in the bureaucratic model. With this narrow approach, organizations can ensure that employees are experts with regard to the requirements of their particular job and are more likely able to efficiently and consistently carry out their standardized tasks and focus learning efforts on incremental improvement.

Second, organizations using a bureaucratic HR strategy control employee actions and behaviors through formal management systems, with tight supervision based on rules and documentation. This model uses a standardized performance evaluation system which can help to ensure that employees are completing tasks correctly, efficiently, and according to regulations. In this model of HR, decision making is controlled centrally, leaving little room for discretion and variability at the individual worker level, increasing the consistent execution of activities. By concentrating knowledge flows at the top of the organization, this strategy focuses on the exchange of knowledge within functions or work units in a manner that will support incremental improvements in technologies, products, or processes.

Finally, the bureaucratic strategy stresses rewards and employee attachment based on pay and other forms of extrinsic motivation. For example, promotions and pay raises are tied to employee performance over time, rewarding and retaining those employees who have been most compliant in following the strict processes and procedures set for their job. Further, pay- and promotion-based rewards will help to attract and retain the extrinsically oriented employees who are most likely to be willing and motivated to comply with strict rules and procedures. Additionally, bureaucratic organizations often attract experienced employees by paying higher salaries than competitors, and as stated, promotions provide incentive and rewards for employee performance and development in a particular task domain.

Thus, it has been argued that the bureaucratic HR strategy will support the requirements of the bureaucratic strategy by creating an environment in which employees are more likely to comply with tight rules and procedures and look to direct learning—with incremental improvements based on HR practices oriented toward narrowly defined and tightly controlled job roles, narrow and task specific job skills, vertically controlled decision making and information flows, and extrinsically oriented rewards.

Importance

The field of strategic human resources has long been arguing for following a contingency approach to understand how HR strategies lead to sustained competitive advantage. In recent years, scholars have argued that the best way to identify the HR strategy that is best aligned to support a particular business strategy is to first identify the workforce requirements of the strategic context and then work backward to identify the HR strategy (i.e., the systems of HR practices) that is most likely to drive and support these employee outcomes. Collins, following this line of thinking, has provided two examples of how to use this logic to identify best fitting HR strategies. Specifically, he identifies the engineering HR strategy as the best fitting set of HR practices to support the workforce requirements of the exploration growth strategy and the bureaucratic HR strategy as the best system to support the exploitation growth strategy. Initial research on the contingency approach to strategic HR found mixed support; these early studies were based on generic HR strategies (e.g., high performance HR system) and very generic corporate strategies. Collins believes that following an approach that focuses on more carefully constructed matches between HR and business strategies, as outlined above, will lead to greater consistency in the pattern of findings. Future researchers interested in extending the literature on HR strategies may wish to similarly follow these examples to identify HR strategies and systems that are a fit for other business strategies' strategic contexts.

While there has been a great deal of research examining the effects of high-commitment HR systems, there has been little empirical work that has examined the potential effectiveness of other HR systems. To better understand the complexity of the relationship between HR systems and firm performance and to help the field provide better advice to practitioners regarding the variety of choices on how to manage employees, more research is needed that examines a much wider array of HR systems. The theoretical logic of this entry supports the argument that it is crucial to identify the strategic choices that are specific to a particular industry in order to better understand the workforce requirements inherent to the strategies in that industry.

Christopher J. Collins

See also Behavioral Perspective of Strategic Human Resource Management; Business Policy and Corporate Strategy; Contingency Theory; Dynamic Capabilities; High-Performance Work Systems; Resource-Based View of the Firm; Strategic Contingencies Theory

Further Readings

Amabile, T. M. (1996). *Creativity in context*. Boulder, CO: Westview Press.

Baron, J. N., Hannan, M. T., & Burton, D. M. (2001). Labor pains: Change in organizational models and employee turnover in young, high-tech firms. *American Journal of Sociology, 106*, 960–1012.

Benner, M. J., & Tushman, M. L. (2003). Exploitation, exploration, and process management: The productivity dilemma revisited. *Academy of Management Review, 28*, 238–256.

Collins, C. J., & Smith, K. G. (2006). Knowledge exchange and combination: The role of human resource practices in the performance of high-technology firms. *Academy of Management Journal, 49*(3), 544–560.

Hage, J. (1980). *Theories of organizations: Form, process, and transformation*. New York, NY: Wiley.

He, Z. L., & Wong, P. K. (2004). Exploration vs. exploitation: An empirical test of the ambidexterity hypothesis. *Organization Science, 15*, 481–494.

Kehoe, R. R., & Collins, C. J. (2008). Exploration and exploitation strategies and the equifinality of HR Systems. *Research in Personnel and Human Resources Management, 27*, 149–176.

March, J. G. (1991). Exploration and exploitation in organizational learning. *Organization Science, 2*, 71–87.

Nahapiet, J., & Ghoshal, S. (1998). Social capital, intellectual capital, and the firm advantage. *Academy of Management Review, 23*, 242–266.

Wright, P. M., Dunford, B. B., & Snell, S. A. (2001). Human resources and the resource based view of the firm. *Journal of Management, 27*(6), 701.

HUMAN RESOURCES ROLES MODEL

The roles of human resources (HR) professionals are important because HR practices institutionalize an organization's capabilities and enable the organization to sustain its identity and competitive position. By defining HR roles, managers and HR professionals define expectations of what HR professionals should be, know, and do to deliver value. Line managers are the owners of HR work and HR professionals are architects. A role is an identity as seen in the completion of this sentence: *To deliver value as an HR professional, I must be a _____.* In this entry, five roles that HR professionals play are proposed and described and their importance discussed.

Fundamentals

The myriad of terms, concepts, and metaphors for the HR role tend to dissolve into confusion. Dave Ulrich and Wayne Brockbank propose a simple framework which filters out the noise, synthesizes previous work, and reveals five major HR roles: employee advocate, human capital developer, functional expert, strategic partner, and leader.

Employee Advocate

HR professionals spend about 19% of their time on employee relations issues. The proportion is apt to be higher if working in a service center rather than in a center of expertise. Whatever the context, caring for, listening to, and responding to employees remains a centerpiece of HR work. It requires HR professionals to see the world through employees' eyes—to listen to them, understand their concerns, and empathize with them—while at the same time looking through managers' eyes and communicating to employees what is required for them to be successful. Employee advocacy involves being available and caring while also being able to assimilate and share different points of view.

Some in the field argue that HR should move exclusively to business partnering, to help business leaders define and deliver financial and customer goals. Ulrich and Brockbank disagree. Employee relations are not just window-dressing: Employees really are the primary asset of any organization. The treatment employees receive shows in the treatment of customers and, ultimately, of investors. Indirectly, caring for employees builds shareholder value. HR professionals are the natural advocates for employees—and for the very real company interests they embody.

Advocacy also involves systematic discussion of employee concerns. When strategy is debated among the management team about closing a plant, expanding a product line, or exploring a new geographic market, the HR professional's job is to represent employees. What will this strategy do to employees? What employee abilities will help or hinder execution of this strategy? How will employees respond to this strategy? HR participation in strategy meetings should present the employees' voice—and employees should know that it does so.

Advocacy also involves managing diversity and ensuring mutual respect so that people feel comfortable sharing and discussing various points of view. Dissent with a shared focus on outcomes generates new ideas, encourages innovation, and delivers results. Diversity can be managed through training and communication programs and statistical monitoring or tracking, but it is *created* in the culture—in how leaders make decisions, interact with people, address conflict, and share information. The HR professional's role is to root out discrimination whenever it appears. Had HR professionals countered off-color remarks with, "This is just not acceptable," more than one company would have saved millions in legal fees, settlements, and lost reputations.

Advocacy isn't all sweetness and light. Sharing tough news is also part of this role. When performance is unacceptable, it's essential to act swiftly and decisively to correct the mistake or, if appropriate, to remove the employee. Good performers lose confidence in leaders who fail to act when people perform poorly. And sometimes, even competent and hardworking employees must be let go for reasons beyond the firm's control. The employee advocacy role requires HR to establish a transparent and fair process for reproving and removing employees for whatever reason and then to help implement the process equitably throughout the organization.

Functional Expert

As a profession, HR possesses a body of knowledge. Access to this body of knowledge allows HR professionals to act with insight; lacking it leaves HR professionals wandering aimlessly—seeking best practices but never finding them. With the body of knowledge, HR functional experts improve decisions and deliver results. For example, as executives worry about the competencies of future leaders, they can turn to HR for advice. HR-leadership-development experts who know the theory and research on competencies draw on that research to create a leadership architecture for their organizations. Without a foundation of competency theory, HR professionals act with good intent but bad judgment.

Ed Lawler's research shows estimates that HR professionals spend about 17% of their time doing functional work. Of course, this varies from job to job. Those in centers of expertise spend much more of their time in these areas than do those embedded in the business. Embedded HR professionals have to diagnose business needs and find experts to help them deliver HR practices.

Functional expertise operates at multiple levels. Tier 1 involves creating solutions to routine HR problems. This includes placing HR solutions online through a company intranet or secure Internet site. This first tier requires skills in simplifying complex activities and in turning them into choices that can be self-monitored. Tier 2 work is where HR specialists create menus of choices, drawing on theory, research, and best practices in other companies. The second tier relies on skill in turning knowledge about an HR domain into a program or process. Tier 3 work comes when HR specialists consult with businesses and adapt their programs to unique business needs. The third tier involves skill in diagnosing problems and in creating solutions. Tier 4 work sets overall policy and direction for HR practices within a specialty area. This calls for understanding of strategy and the ability to adapt to a strategic context. While requirements for functional experts may vary across these tiers of work, some general principles apply to all functional specialists.

Functional expertise allows the specialist to create menus of choices for his or her business: what other companies have done, what others in the company have done, what he or she has come up with based on experience. These menus become the template that governs action in the specialist's area of expertise. When a menu item is chosen, he or she is then able to guide its implementation. An expert can adapt the core principles and past practices in this domain to a specific application in the company. This means the specialist will contribute to the evolution of existing theory and practice.

The choices the specialist offers should be designed to shape processes related to his or her area of expertise so as to build the firm's infrastructure and improve its ability to carry out its strategies. Compensation, for example, has processes for setting standards, allocating financial rewards, and allocating nonfinancial rewards. A functional expert should be able to map each process and apply the principles, resources, and tools to upgrade the process to meet current and impending demands.

HR professionals who serve primarily as functional experts often work in either menu design or process implementation. Designers must be HR experts who know trends and applications. Implementers offer operational support as they consult with individual businesses and apply their knowledge to specific settings.

Human Capital Developer

Capital comes from the Latin *caput*, meaning "head." In business, it refers to the head—the chief or primary—assets of a firm (traditionally, its money). Increasingly, people are recognized as critical assets, and HR professionals manage this *human capital*: developing the workforce, emphasizing individual employees more than organization processes. The term has become a catchall for anything related to employees, from individual development to overall assessments such as Watson Wyatt's Human Capital Index. In any case, human capital focuses on wealth created through and by people in the organization.

As human-capital developers, HR professionals focus on the future, often one employee at a time, developing plans that offer each employee opportunities to develop future abilities, matching desires with opportunities. The role also includes helping employees unlearn old skills and master new ones. In the rapidly changing world, employee competencies need constant upgrading. You are responsible for investing resources to shape employees for the future, not the past. At times, these employee development plans may be carried out online through an employee portal where firm opportunities are listed and employees ascertain if they are prepared for the opportunity. At other times, employee development conversations occur through HR programs, such as performance or career management.

Human-capital developers in centers of expertise set up development experiences that employees can access. They also coach leaders, acting rather like sports or music coaches. They focus on both behavior and attitudes, working from an understanding of individual differences to figure out how to motivate desired behavior. For example, in recent years, many

CEOs have been forced out, not because they did not understand the realities of the new economy and requirements of the organization but because they could not govern the organization appropriately. Many others have reshaped their behavior with the help of coaches who observed them in action and helped them change direction. Coaches are not always popular, but they deliver results, and they are accountable for the results they deliver. HR professionals coach by building trust, sharing observations, and affirming changes.

As stewards of human capital, HR professionals assume responsibility for positive team relationships. This may involve formal team building, or it may involve informal dialogues with team members to disclose and resolve differences.

Strategic Partner

HR professionals bring business, change, consulting, and learning know-how to their partnership with line managers, so together they create value. Strategic partners are business-literate and savvy. They partner with line managers to help them reach their goals. Part of this business partnership involves crafting strategies based on knowledge of current and future customers and exploring how corporate resources may be aligned to those demands. They help formulate winning strategies by focusing on the right decisions and by having an informed opinion about what the business needs to do. They focus on execution of strategy by aligning HR systems to help accomplish the organizational vision and mission. They become systems integrators, ensuring that all the different elements of a strategy plan come together in a coordinated way. They also attend to the process of strategy development by ensuring that the right people participate in strategy decisions. In practice, they are members of the management team with a deep expertise in people and organization but with enough business savvy to help shape future business directions.

As change agents, HR strategic partners diagnose organization problems, separate symptoms from causes, help set an agenda for the future, and create plans for making things happen. They have disciplined processes for change and implement those processes regularly in the organization, both with individual projects and with an overall road map for the future.

As internal consultants and facilitators, HR strategic partners advise leaders on what should be done and how, and they help manage the process for change. They become rapid deployment specialists—speed mavens who are not only thought leaders but also practice masters for getting things done. In this, they again resemble coaches, shaping points of view and offering feedback on progress, but doing so for groups rather than just individuals. With their expertise in the management of power and authority in teams, organizations, and alliances, HR facilitators help ensure that people are able to act when necessary without getting caught up in red tape and internecine conflicts.

HR Leader

Leadership begins at home, so HR leaders must lead and value their own function before anyone else will listen to them. And it's easy to go wrong. For example, in one large company, HR experts directed a 2-week leadership development program that spent a few days on each major business dimension—finance, marketing, technology, globalization, and quality—and only 3 hours on HR on Saturday morning. The message was obvious: *Even HR professionals don't think HR matters much.* When confronted with this observation, the organizer said essentially that he did not want to impose HR on business leaders. That meant he did not see HR as central to the business equation; he was not leading from an empowered HR perspective. Business leaders share the natural human tendency to learn more from what they see than from what they hear, so it's essential to set a good example.

At the top of their organization, HR leaders establish an agenda for HR within the firm, both for the way people and organization come together to drive business success and for the way the HR function itself will operate. A well-led HR department earns credibility, and the reverse is also true. HR leaders who do not face up to and implement HR practices on their own turf lose credibility when they present ideas to others. This means that hiring, training, performance management, and communication within the HR function must all be top of the line.

HR leaders also look outward across the organization, helping all functions identify talent and develop capabilities that deliver value. In addition, HR can combine uniquely with experts or executives in other business areas: with finance professionals to create intangible value, with marketing and sales to create customer connections, with manufacturing to ensure productivity, with service to guarantee responsiveness, with sourcing to secure quality, and with information technology to turn data into decisions. HR leaders can also be integrators of the work of other functions. Because HR leaders are rarely contestants for the top executive jobs and because their work is so central to the success of any staff function, they can often be a liaison among the staff groups, ensuring cooperation and consistency.

HR leaders can play an active role in corporate governance, serving as the conscience of the organization and raising and monitoring issues of corporate ethics. They are ideally placed to ensure that legal policies (such as blackout dates for stock transactions for executives with insider information) are understood and followed. They can help the executive team craft and publish values and behavior guidelines and then make sure that they are understood and followed. They can help with Sarbanes-Oxley compliance and other regulatory matters and help their boards be aware of and use proper governance guidelines.

HR leaders maintain and monitor the broader HR community of the organization—both the HR function itself and everyone else who is responsible and accountable for human resource issues. Some companies create separate departments for education, learning, organization design, consulting, or communication, and they restrict HR to traditional areas of people and performance. The authors of this entry believe that HR adds more value when all the elements are combined into one functional organization, but the decision to break them up need not isolate HR. It remains possible for HR leaders to build community even without direct lines of authority. The HR community also includes outside vendors who contract to do HR work and internal administrative staff who perform HR work. Bringing the HR community together is important because those who use "HR services" rarely make distinctions based on where the service comes from. As a community integrator, an HR leader sets broad themes for HR in the company, helps clarify roles, and monitors actions and results.

Importance

The five roles Ulrich and Brockbank suggest synthesize the diverse thinking in the field and represent an evolution of thinking about what an HR professional must do to deliver value. In the knowledge economy and with demographic changes, employees become ever more critical to a firm's success. So, instead of just being employee champions, HR professionals must serve employees both today (employee advocacy) and tomorrow (human capital development). HR functional expertise may be delivered in multiple ways, and HR specialists must not only put HR online but also create innovative HR solutions to business problems. Strategic partners continue to exist, but it's now known with more clarity the multiple roles they play: business expert, change agent, knowledge manager, and consultant. HR leaders also become more visible and central to the roles for HR. The pattern will continue to develop, but for now, these five roles capture what HR professionals do.

These five roles have been supported in Ulrich and Brockbank's 25-year study of HR competencies. At this point, there are data from over 60,000 global respondents (about 40% line managers outside of HR) who reinforce these five roles.

No one plays all five roles to the same degree. Depending on where the HR expert works in the company, different roles have primary or secondary importance. Moving from one area of HR to another (service center to embedded HR, for example) requires changing roles. This shift affects HR careers. Many people choose to stay largely in one area (such as a center of expertise) and develop increasing depth in the roles required for that work. But anyone who moves to another area of the HR department will need to recognize and learn the script for the new role. When HR professionals master these roles and play them well, they add value.

Dave Ulrich and Wayne Brockbank

See also Behavioral Perspective of Strategic Human Resource Management; European Model of Human Resource Management; Human Capital Theory; Human Resource Management Strategies; Theory of Transfer of Training

Further Readings

Ulrich, D. (1996). *Human resource champions*. Boston, MA: Harvard Business School Press.

Ulrich, D., Allen, J., Brockbank, W., Younger, J., & Nyman, M. (2009). *HR transformation*. New York, NY: McGraw-Hill.

Ulrich, D., & Beatty, D. (2001). From partners to players: Extending the HR playing field. *Human Resource Management, 40*(4), 293.

Ulrich, D., & Brockbank, W. (2005). *HR value proposition*. Boston, MA: Harvard Business School Press.

Ulrich, D., Johnson, D., Brockbank, W., Younger, J., & Sandholtz, K. (2008). *HR competencies*. Washington, DC: SHRM.

Ulrich, D., Younger, J., Brockbank, W., & Ulrich, M. (2012). *HR from the outside-in*. New York, NY: McGraw-Hill.

HUMANISTIC MANAGEMENT

Humanistic management is a philosophy of management that emphasizes the interests of the employee in the manager-employee partnership. It is inclusive of a number of more specific theories that place a high value on human growth, potential, and dignity. In fact, humanistic managers don't restrict fair and respectful treatment to employees alone, but rather, they accord this treatment to other stakeholders, such as customers, clients, vendors, and other members of the organizational community as well. They tend to maintain awareness of all organizational stakeholders rather than solely or mainly the shareholders or themselves at the expense of other stakeholders. Humanistic managers care how they accomplish organizational goals. They favor ethical codes for their organizations and pursue policies of global corporate social responsibility, including ensuring the human dignity of their workers in undeveloped countries and protecting the global environment. They work to ensure organizational and interpersonal justice for and among their stakeholders as well. Generally, they seek to belong or attend to professional and global associations with developed standards supporting and upholding human dignity, such as Social Accountability 8000 (SA8000), Fairtrade International, International Organization for Standardization (ISO) 26000, Corporate Accountability International, and others.

They endorse principles of sustainability, such as those promoted by groups like Forestethics or the UN Principles for Responsible Investment (PRI) and Global Compact initiatives. They welcome triple bottom-line reporting of some sort, in reference to the organization's value to stakeholders (people), the global natural environment (planet), and to society at large (profit to society in the sense of economic output exceeds economic input resulting in overall benefit to society). Thus, humanistic management's central insight is that all stakeholders—employees, customers, clients, shareholders, vendors, local and global communities—need to be treated with dignity and sensitivity if economic and environmental sustainability is to exist. However, it is difficult for a manager to operate humanistically unless the entire organization promotes a culture of humanism and organizational learning. This entry is focused on describing the fundamental principles of humanistic management, tracing its origins and the various theories associated with it, and examining its probable future as a management theory for widespread use in the 21st century.

Fundamentals

Humanistic management had its beginnings as a reaction to pre-20th-century management beliefs that one should manage by telling people what to do, monitoring them closely, and punishing them for nonperformance. At its worst, it was not very far removed from the slave labor of the 19th century—conditions could be physically abominable, and workers could be young children or women working 14-hour days at difficult, dehumanized tasks. The more enlightened managers of the day believed they could get the work they wanted from their workers if their messages were phrased properly; however, if they didn't get what they wanted, they were justified in dismissing them. Workers in America thought they had few rights in this situation, and the ones who were immigrants, legal or illegal, English-speaking or not, simply felt that if they wanted to keep their jobs, they should keep quiet and do the best they could. Meanwhile, the father of "modern management," Fredrick Taylor, wrote a book in 1911 titled *The Principles of Scientific Management*, in which he demonstrated through examples and pictures that there was a right way and wrong way to do any physical labor. There was no room for individual differences or considerations among the workers in this view. By timing people and measuring their output, Taylor and other "efficiency experts," like Frank and Lillian Gilbreth, charted and described standardized ways to maximize physical work. Soon afterward, garment workers from New York City and assembly-line workers from Michigan began forming unions and demanding better conditions, better pay, better treatment, and some kind of due process to address perceived grievances.

Following World War I, though, attention began to turn to the effects of work on job incumbents themselves. In their landmark Hawthorne studies, Harvard researchers, including Fritz Roethlisberger and Elton Mayo, discovered several important psychological and sociological variables that impacted workers. For example, to much surprise, there seemed to be no ideal illumination of the factory floor for wire assembly workers. Turn the lights up and performance improved, turn them up higher and performance improved even more, return them to the baseline illumination and performance inexplicably improved the most. Workers were given breaks, and their performances improved, but when the breaks were taken away, their performance went up another notch. Eventually, the team realized that the true key variable responsible for improved performance was the degree of attention being paid to the workers. That they were being treated with interest, listened to, and their words recorded, was what improved performance. Although Mary Parker Follett, the social worker turned management theorist, had a little earlier decried "bossism" and micromanagement during the 1930s and into the 1940s, it was Roethlisberger, Mayo, and associates who became the first academic proponents of humanistic management with the advent of their human relations school of management.

Over the course of the 20th century and the beginning of the 21st century, certain fundamentals of humanistic management have emerged. First, at the level of the individual, a general principle of humanistic management is the recognition of the "human factor" itself—that people are to be treated with respect, listened to, and expected to grow and improve. They all have individual needs, perspectives, emotions, and in general want to be seen as individuals rather than means to an end. Employees, in particular, are not simple extensions of workplace machines or purely economic entities whose univocal behavior is naturally directed and incentivized to gain a wage or salary. Rather, they are holistic, unique beings whose happiness is bound up in opportunities to be challenged, creatively and responsibly. They are not always or exclusively motivated by profit or money but also by the desire to feel good, happy, important, and engaged.

A second key principle of humanistic management is its recognition of and attention to the inevitable social processes between individual employees as well as within work groups. People have relationships with all those with whom they interact personally on a frequent basis. It is important to appreciate their diversity as members of different gender, ethnic, religious, and age groups as well as by skill or profession. Humanistic managers recognize and even celebrate individual differences and diversity in their employees as well as their customers, clients, vendors, and community members. They realize that the complexity of relationships affects the individuals themselves by helping to define realities and determine motivation. At the same time, it brings about conflict and other dynamics that must be managed for the good of the participants and the organization. If a manager does not pay attention to this "informal" level of organization—if cooperative norms and positive social relationships are not established and if individual attitudes and group social patterns are not harmonized with overall objectives—then the whole organization can be brought down.

The third important principle for the humanistic manager involves finding the proper balance between individual happiness at work and overall organizational efficiency. Research has shown that happiness on the job is not necessarily correlated with increasing productivity of workers or the organization. Although job satisfaction is correlated with lower turnover and absenteeism, which themselves are correlated with higher productivity, the history of research on the question is unsettled. There are just too many other variables that can go into productivity, from economic conditions to competitive conditions to the nature of a specific workforce, just to name a few. Yet humanistic managers recognize the inherent value of worker satisfaction and management scholars the validity of satisfaction as a research variable and, as such, seek a synergistic relationship between managerial empathy for others and methods for achieving organizational performance goals.

A fourth fundamental principle of humanistic management is its raised level of ethical concern broadly applied across all stakeholders. Adam Smith's idea that individuals will naturally follow their self-interest and personal desire to help others and that an "invisible hand" will thus guide the organization's welfare positively, all for the benefit of society as a whole and without visible restraint or oversight by formalized governance mechanisms, is not a general belief of the humanistic manager. Instead, humanistic managers believe that they must proactively promote ethical codes and training within the organization, demand accountability of all employees, and ensure that the organization maintains sound social responsibility and citizenship principles within its industrial or organizational group as well as within its local and global communities. It is their duty within the organization to guard against ethical lapses that may hurt others directly or indirectly, for example, negative economic or social consequences, within the society and society as a whole.

Evolution

While the politics of labor had resulted in the creation of the National Labor Relations Board in 1934 and the passing of the Fair Labor Standards Act in 1938 in the United States, both of which protected workers from management practices commonly perceived as unfair, development of management theory was proceeding on various academic paths, many of which were focused on valuing the human dignity of employees. In the aftermath of Roethlisberger and Mayo's work, one major figure in management theory emerged between the mid-1940s and the mid-1960s to extend their thinking. Douglas McGregor, who worked as a supervisor of gas station attendants and a soup kitchen organizer in the 1930s before returning to college and becoming a Massachusetts Institute of Technology (MIT) professor, published a book in 1960 titled *The Human Side of Enterprise,* in which he faced head-on the subject of how managers dealt with their employees through managerial assumptions about them. Theory X assumptions were used by managers who saw their employees as inherently lazy, in need of being watched closely or they would shirk work, children grown larger and looking to cheat their manager and their organization wherever possible. Theory Y assumptions, on the other hand, saw employees as wanting to

do a good job, wanting to do better, interested in challenge, wanting to grow as human beings, seeking responsibility and achievement, and looking to be proud of their accomplishments. Managers who operated primarily under Theory X assumptions tended to use techniques that reflected an expectation of failure among their employees and, as a result, their employees were more likely to fail. When treated under Theory Y assumptions, however, employees were likely to rise to the occasion and do work of which they and their managers were proud. These kinds of employee behaviors may have constituted what Robert K. Merton would a little later call a "self-fulfilling prophecy." The idea that managers needed to look more strongly at the human side of the business equation and consider the significance of their assumptions became quite popular with the advent of McGregor's best selling book in 1960.

McGregor's management book was influenced by the work of a number of psychologists who were writing in a similar vein. Carl Rogers introduced the notion of "unconditional positive regard" as a part of his "person-centered" approach to counseling patients and eventually to teaching students and to treating humans in any relationship where a cooperative end was sought. No matter how poorly someone behaved, the best way to get them to behave better was to assume an attitude of respect and positivity about them. He wrote extensively about treating people with empathy, putting yourself in their place as best you could, and about "active listening," a technique meant to encourage people to say what they were thinking instead of steering them one way or another. In addition, Jack Gibb, a pioneer in humanistic psychology and organizational development, wrote books and articles about trusting people and encouraging a supportive climate to prevent "defensive communication" by following six rules in one's communication: use speech that is descriptive rather than evaluative, be problem-oriented rather than controlling, encourage spontaneity rather than strategizing, be empathic rather than neutral, provide a sense of equality rather than superiority, and be provisional rather than dogmatic.

Contemporaneous with Rogers, motivational psychologist Abraham Maslow wrote several books on his hierarchy of motivation, human potential, values, and self-actualization—the process of achieving one's greatest potential through "peak experiences."

Many others came to make up the humanistic psychology school, publishing their articles in journals such as the *Journal of Humanistic Psychology* and the *Humanistic Psychologist*. Humanistic psychology applied to management eventually led to humanistic management.

Although Maslow's theories would later endure criticism from Geert Hofstede as not appropriate for collectivist cultures and from others such as Clayton Alderfer whose empirical studies suggested they needed modifications, his work had a great influence on several management theorists, including Frederick Herzberg. Herzberg's contribution, later described in what is still the most popular *Harvard Business Review* article ever written, "One More Time: How Do You Motivate Employees," was to utilize Maslow's work to develop "two-factor" or "hygiene" theory. Herzberg's theory suggested strategic directions for managers, who should design jobs and policies to satisfy worker hygiene—such as workplace comfort, pay, security—needs first and then design opportunities for growth through challenge and realizable achievement on the motivator level. He created the term "job enrichment" for this process. Psychologists J. Richard Hackman and Greg Oldham further refined how jobs should be designed or redesigned to achieve maximum motivation potential for those with moderate to high growth needs in the 1970s with their work on the job characteristics model. Meanwhile, Victor Vroom's work, begun in the 1960s on expectancy theory, also helped managers understand work motivation. It posited that the degree of effort that persons put in to effect performance was dependent not only on their desire but also on the strength of their belief (expectancy) that they were capable of successful performance with valued outcomes. Knowing this thought process could presumably help managers coax successful performance, ensure valued outcomes, and eventually lead to executive coaching to help develop leadership skills.

The application in the workplace of all of these theories as well as the ever increasing education level of the workers helped facilitate more dialogue between managers and employees. As managers began to value many employee ideas, and, as they realized the importance of tapping the motivation of their employees to achieve organizational goals, they developed more and more programs for employee involvement in the enterprise. Humanistic managers were learning that trust, authentic communication, and respect could pay off in human and economic terms.

Importance

Recognition of Employees as Valued Human Capital

With increased manager-employee dialogue came continuous improvement programs, profit-sharing and gain-sharing discussions, employee empowerment programs, and team building within organizations as employees became strategic partners across functional areas within the organization and at varying levels with management. Valuing diversity, too, has become an important part of such efforts because of the increasing diversity of the workforce and concomitant legal regulation of the selection process as well as the harm of communication barriers due to diversity issues. Thus, organizations have created departments dedicated to diversity sensitivity and management. It is not uncommon to see even smaller organizations with management titles, such as vice president of valuing differences and vice president of people and culture. In addition, management has not lost sight of the simple fact that in a global economy, its customers are more and more diverse. This entire process of increasing levels of communication has caused management to take more care than ever to protect and develop their "human capital."

In many ways, humanistic management with its more human-centered approach to helping organizations achieve their goals has drawn attention to the functions of selection, training, career development, managing change, and managing feedback that have become the focus of human resource management departments in the modern organization. It has given rise to the study of organizational behavior as a staple of a business education. Although managers and scholars have learned that a happy worker is not always a productive worker unless certain other conditions are present, it has focused new attention on the value of seeking authentic happiness within the organization. Positive organizational scholarship (POS) researchers have begun to find that unlocking the secrets to human resilience, vitality, desire to achieve, creativity, and growth can bring an organization to an uncommon level of excellence. Martin Seligman and others have shown that "well-being theory" can create greater individual happiness in organizations from schools to banks to the military. Empirical studies prove that training for well-being results in increased productivity as employees learn to flourish. In his book, *Flourish*, he points out that the new bottom line of a positive corporation is that profit comes from creating positive emotion, engagement, positive human relations, meaning ("belonging to and serving something greater than the self"), and the opportunity for accomplishment (the first letters of each source spelling PERMA). Ultimately, the goal of a society should be the well-being of its members; corporations would be served well by attending to the same goal.

Role of Corporate Social Responsibility

With the involvement of more communication among all stakeholders in the enterprise, we have entered a time when values, ethics, and social responsibility have become more important in business. There may be many reasons for this, but humanistic management has played an important role. If stakeholders are going to be treated with more respect and dignity than ever before, the relationship must proceed ethically, sincerely, and responsibly. There is a growing realization that organizations have profound responsibilities to the society that has allowed them to exist through its legal registration and incorporation mechanisms. The stakeholder community as a whole must be treated with respect. In the case of organizations of size, the community at issue is normally global. International law and trade organizations as well as local regulations can determine where a company's products will be allowed to be sold in the regional and global marketplace. Decisions are made based on whether a country or region's people will truly benefit from such commerce. If workers are considered to have been exploited in the manufacture of products or the company is considered to be irresponsible with regard to its relationship to the environment in the manufacture of the product, or if the company is considered to be exploiting any of its customers or their intellectual property, permissions will be withheld. This has resulted in ever-growing departments of corporate social responsibility reporting to the highest level within the organization.

Impact on Management Education

Finally, where should U.S. business schools be focusing their curricula according to the humanistic management proponents? Lyman Porter, Lawrence McKibbin, Jeffrey Pfeffer, Christina Fong, and Henry Mintzberg have critiqued current business school education and suggested more humanistic alternatives. The Aspen Institute has become well known for inviting academics and executives to programs on corporate ethics and social responsibility. In a "humanism in business" series of books, many global authors, including members of the Humanistic Management Network, specifically present Humanistic Management Education and Humanistic Business Schools (HUBS) as the way forward. Humanistic management thinkers, writers, and executives have had a major influence on the direction of management research and education beginning from their mid-20th-century roots. The 21st century should see increased attention to its tenets as the economy grows more global, the world grows more populous, resources become scarcer, and cooperation and collaboration become more necessary.

William P. Ferris

See also Corporate Social Responsibility; Empowerment; ERG Theory; Expectancy Theory; Human Capital Theory; Job Characteristics Theory; Positive Organizational Scholarship; Scientific Management; Self-Fulfilling Prophecy; Stakeholder Theory; Theory X and Theory Y; Triple Bottom Line; Trust; Two-Factor Theory (and Job Enrichment)

Further Readings

Alderfer, C. P. (1972). *Existence, relatedness, and growth: Human needs in organizational settings.* New York, NY: Free Press.

Amann, W., Pirson, M., Dierksmeier, C., von Kimakowitz, E., & Spitzeck, H. (Eds.). (2011). *Business schools under fire: Humanistic management education as the way forward.* London, England: Palgrave Macmillan.

Frick, W. B. (1971). *Humanistic psychology: Interviews with Maslow, Murphy, and Rogers.* Columbus, OH: Merrill.

Hackman, J. R., & Oldham, G. R. (1980). *Work redesign.* Reading, MA: Addison-Wesley.

Herzberg, F. I. (1987). One more time: How do you motivate employees? *Harvard Business Review,* 65(September–October), 109–120.

Mayo, E. (1933). *The human problems of an industrial civilization.* New York, NY: Macmillan.

McGregor, D. (1960). *The human side of enterprise.* New York, NY: McGraw-Hill.

Roethlisberger, F. J., & Dickson, W. J. (1939). *Management and the worker: An account of a research program conducted by the Western Electric Company, Hawthorne Works, Chicago.* Cambridge, MA: Harvard University Press.

Seligman, M. E. P. (2011). *Flourish.* New York, NY: Simon & Schuster.

Vroom, V. H. (1964). *Work and motivation.* New York, NY: Wiley.

HYPERCOMPETITION

The term *hypercompetition* is associated with extreme environmental turbulence, with industries and markets where competitive advantage is under constant attack, and with strategies to cope with such environments. The strategic concept of hypercompetition was developed in the mid-1990s, coincident with deepened interest in dynamic external environments and the issues associated with rapid change. Following a brief background, hypercompetition is reviewed here as a macro/external-environment and from a micro-firm strategy perspective. Initial research and recent academic studies are then summarized, followed by open questions and areas for further development.

Fundamentals

Although dynamic environments and intense competition are consistent themes in business literature, the pace of change and competitive pressure has increased over the last several decades. This new environment has been characterized as discontinuous and uncertain, where change is nonlinear and strategic outcomes are less predictable. The most extreme examples of turbulence and competitive complexity are characterized as hypercompetition. In hypercompetitive markets, the traditional goals of cost and quality, timing and know-how, strongholds, and deep pockets have been made less important in an environment where competitive advantages are transient. The pace of change has collapsed the traditional competitive cycle, and equilibrium is impossible to sustain.

The term *hypercompetition* is now generally used to denote all highly competitive and turbulent markets, industries, and competitors. For example, the mobile phone market is often described as hypercompetitive, based on the relentless, rapid introductory cycles of new models and features.

Note that hypercompetition is a relatively broad concept and therefore is difficult to specify and measure. The claims that hypercompetition is widespread remain largely undocumented, and there are moderating forces against hypercompetition, such as opportunities in new, emerging global markets. Use of the term *hypercompetition* continues in the business press, primarily in describing rapid changes in high-technology industries, such as tablet computing, but it has also arisen in disparate markets such as rankings for MBA programs.

Hypercompetitive markets can be better understood by looking at the macro level of external drivers. Externally, hypercompetition is enabled by global integration of markets, rapid change in technology, and the combined effect of these forces on the extended value chain, including buyers, suppliers, and competitors. Globalization changes the quantity and quality of the value chain by dispersing it and then integrating activities across borders. These changes set the stage for hypercompetition on an industry-by-industry basis. As a "feedback loop," intense competition for resources in the value chain and for markets reinforces and accelerates hypercompetitive conditions.

Hypercompetitive markets are also being fueled by rapid changes in consumer demand, the increased knowledge base of firms and workers, the declining height of entry barriers, and the growing number of alliances between firms. Lowered entry barriers affect strongholds, and deep pockets are under attack by cross-border and cross-industry alliances.

At the micro-firm level, a hypercompetitive environment may dictate a new, different strategy. In hypercompetitive environments, the key assumption of a stable market is no longer valid, so the familiar strategic frameworks of positioning in favorable industries or owning valuable and rare resources with the objective of gaining a sustainable strategic advantage may no longer be applicable. Successful strategies in a hypercompetitive market are more akin to the Austrian school of Schumpeter's creative destruction or a high-speed contingency strategy. The concept of dynamic capabilities may also apply in hypercompetitive environments as a means of quickly reconfiguring, acquiring, or shedding resources. But with hypercompetition, any strategic advantage is temporary, so the only viable strategy may be to keep replacing an advantage—including one's own advantage. Hypercompetitive strategies are based on advantages that are created quickly, but a competitive lead is temporary and has to be constantly renewed.

Initial academic studies were concerned with defining the term and establishing hypercompetition as a prevalent condition. In the 2000s, a few researchers addressed how hypercompetitive strategies might differ by industry life-cycle stage. The link between globalization and hypercompetition was also explored, particularly in terms of the effect of a fragmented and competitive global value chain. Recent academic interest has included exploration of the linkage between macro and micro hypercompetitive environments and deeper examinations of competitive dynamics.

These recent studies are addressing the need for a better understanding of hypercompetitive strategy, including dependency on the number of competitors, the individual strategies of the players, the cost of each competitive cycle, the decision speed and aggressiveness of the top management teams, and whether there are complementary products and services. At the macro level, a clearer understanding of the cyclical nature of competition is emerging and recent studies have refined the measurement techniques.

This renewed interest in hypercompetition holds the promise of enhancing the usefulness of the concept and solidifying it as an important field for further academic study. Additional areas for future research include the effects of Internet and computing technologies on hypercompetitive value chains, with the expectation that these technologies will increase the rate of global hypercompetition. Further explorations of competitive dynamics and the link with different external environments would further the understanding of strategic options. Another area for further investigation is the increasing role of small and medium-sized enterprises, as opposed to larger multinational corporations, as technology and an accessible value chain open up the global market to smaller firms. Finally, the link between clusters of production and hypercompetition could profitably be explored in theoretical and in empirical research.

For managers, hypercompetitive markets can cause a focus on short-term advantages and disruptive strategies rather than satisfying customer needs with unique value propositions. When faced with a hypercompetitive market, strategic options include competing on value, finding defensible submarkets, and using vertical as well as horizontal consolidation strategies—or simply outsmarting the competition with dramatic, game-changing strategies. However, margins are squeezed in hypercompetitive markets, and a better path to success may be to avoid the head-to-head hypercompetition altogether.

Don Goeltz

See also Business Policy and Corporate Strategy; Competitive Advantage; Core Competence; Dynamic Capabilities; First-Mover Advantages and Disadvantages; Profiting From Innovation; Strategic Decision Making; Technology S-Curve

Further Readings

D'Aveni, R. A. (1994). *Hypercompetition: Managing the dynamics of strategic maneuvering.* New York, NY: Free Press.

Eisenhardt, K. M. (1989). Making fast strategic decisions in high-velocity environments. *Academy of Management Journal, 32*(3), 543–576.

Grant, R. M. (1996). Prospering in dynamically-competitive environments: Organizational capability as knowledge integration. *Organization Science, 7*(4), 375–387.

Pacheco-de-Almeida, G. (2010). Erosion, time compression, and self-displacement of leaders in hypercompetitive environments. *Strategic Management Journal, 31*(13), 1498–1526.

Wiggins, R., & Ruefli T. (2005). Schumpter's ghost: Is hypercompetition making the best of times shorter? *Strategic Management Journal, 26*(10), 887–911.

I

IMAGE THEORY

Image theory is a cognitive/behavioral theory of decision making. It differs from traditional behavioral decision theory in that it is not based on the analogy between decision makers and gamblers making risky bets. This is because studies of professional decision makers (primarily managers but also firefighters, military officers, and so on) show that they seldom behave like gamblers and they seldom view their decisions as bets. Unlike gamblers, they seldom entertain multiple options. Instead, most of their decisions are about a single option— usually a course of action in pursuit of a specific set of desirable outcomes. Unlike gamblers, they seldom make a decision and passively wait to see what chance will deliver. Instead, they decide on a course of action and work hard to make sure that it yields the results they want. Unlike gamblers, they seldom seek to maximize winnings (profits) to the exclusion of everything else. Instead, they deliberately select goals and take purposeful actions that move them and their organizations toward a valued future. Building on this, image theory's central management insight is that professional managers create an image of what they want their organization's future to be and decisions and subsequent actions are directed toward ensuring that the image becomes reality. In this entry, we briefly review the fundamentals of the theory, examine some of the research deriving from the theory, and describe a version of the theory designed to account for decisions about voluntary employment turnover.

Fundamentals

Image theory defines a decision option, not as a win/ lose gamble but as a plan of action for attaining a goal. Decision making consists of evaluating the compatibility of an option's goal and plan with the decision maker's or organization's values, previously existing goals, and ongoing plans. Options that violate values, contravene existing goals, or interfere with ongoing plans are deemed *incompatible* with the decision maker's and organization's desired future and are rejected. Options that are *compatible* with the desired future are adopted and their plans implemented. Image theory's domain is the actions of individual decision makers, even if they are working in groups. This is because, from a psychological point of view, it is incorrect to speak of groups or organizations as making decisions. Instead, a single agent or, more frequently, a group of agents is entrusted with making the collective's decisions. This means that the individual agent must make a decision and, when other agents are involved, a final decision must be negotiated for the organization as a whole. As a result, in most cases the individual, even a powerful executive, must take into consideration the arguments and the constraints posed by the other parties to the decision.

The theory posits three kinds of cognitive structures, called *images,* and two kinds of decisions, called *adoption* and *progress* decisions, and proposes a model of the decision mechanism, called the *compatibility test.* The key concept is that most of the work of decision making is done by screening out unacceptable options. And because most decisions are about a single option—accept or reject—if the option survives screening, it is accepted. If not, it is rejected and, in many cases, another option is sought to replace it, whereupon the screening process occurs again. When there are multiple options under consideration and only one survives screening, it is accepted. If more than one survives, the least unacceptable is chosen from among them.

Images

Value image constituents are the decision maker's imperatives for his or her behavior and the behavior of the organization as well as criteria for the rightness or wrongness of any particular decision about a goal or plan for attaining that goal. Values as imperatives generate *candidates* for goals to pursue and plans for pursuing them. Values as criteria determine the acceptability of externally generated candidate goals and plans.

Trajectory image constituents are previously adopted goals. The term *trajectory* is used to imply extension in time—the decision maker's vision of the desired future.

Strategic image constituents are the various plans that have been adopted for attaining the goals on the trajectory image. Each plan is a sequence of potential *tactics* leading from goal adoption to goal attainment, a sequence that can be revised in light of information about the changing environment in which implementation is taking place as well as about the success of the plan as it is implemented. Because a plan is inherently an anticipation of the future, it constitutes a *forecast* about what will happen if its component tactics are successfully executed in the course of its implementation.

Decisions

Adoption decisions are about the compatibility of an option's goal and plan with the existing constituents of the value, trajectory, and strategic images. Compatibility leads to adoption of the goal and plan; incompatibility leads to rejection.

Progress decisions are about the effectiveness of an implemented plan in promoting movement toward its goal. This turns on the compatibility of the desired goal and the forecast of what will happen if plan implementation is continued. Compatibility leads to continued implementation. Incompatibility triggers suspension of implementation until the plan can be repaired or replaced with one whose forecast is sufficiently compatible with the goal to warrant its adoption and implementation.

Compatibility Test

The *compatibility test* is the mechanism for assessing compatibility in both adoption and progress decisions. For adoption, the test assesses the discrepancy between the defining features of an option's goal(s) or plan and the pertinent constituents of the value, trajectory, and strategic images. For progress decisions, the test assesses the discrepancy between the pertinent features of the plan's forecast and the defining features of its goal. Compatibility decreases with increases in the number of significant discrepancies. Discrepancies are defined as negations, contradictions, contraventions, preventions, retardations, or any similar form of disparity between what is offered by an option's goal(s) or plan and the decision maker's values or between an implemented plan's forecast and its existing goal.

In its simplest form, the *decision rule* for the compatibility test is that if the sum of the discrepancies exceeds the decision maker's *rejection threshold,* the candidate is rejected; otherwise, it is accepted. The threshold is defined as the sum of discrepancies beyond which the decision maker regards the adoption candidate or implemented plan as incompatible with his, her, or the organization's values, goals, and ongoing plans.

If there is only one option under consideration and it survives the compatibility test, it is adopted. Adoption means that its goals are added to the trajectory image and its plan is added to the strategic image and plan implementation begins. If there are competing options and only one survives the compatibility test, it is accepted. If there are competing candidates and more than one survives the test, the survivors constitute a *choice set* from which the least unacceptable is chosen. In progress decisions, there is only one plan being implemented; if its forecast is incompatible with its goal, implementation is stopped. If its forecast is not incompatible with its goal, implementation continues and is periodically reevaluated for further progress.

Importance

Empirical research has focused on the compatibility test, in both laboratory and organizational settings, and has supported the image theory formulation for both adoption and progress decisions. Among the results for adoption decisions is evidence for the existence of the rejection threshold: (a) the finding that missing information about the features of an option's goal(s) or plan is treated as a discrepancy and lowers the rejection threshold, making it easier to reject options about which too little is known; (b) the finding that when there are no surviving options, decision makers prefer to a search for new ones rather than reassessing those they have rejected, but if no new options are available and reassessment is necessary, they adjust their rejection thresholds so at least one option survives; (c) the finding that decision makers give greater weight to important features when assessing compatibility; and (d) the finding that under time pressure they adjust their rejection thresholds so fewer options are rejected in order to avoid overlooking good ones. Studies of progress decisions show that decision makers are more likely to continue implementation and to commit more resources when progress is being made but that continued progress leads to less careful assessment; more careful assessment is saved for when there appears to be trouble.

In contrast to 30 years of work on adoption decisions, progress decisions, and the compatibility test, until quite recently there has been virtually no work on images. This changed with the reformulation of images as cognitive narratives and the recasting of image theory as a narrative-based theory. Space limitations prohibit description of the new formulation; interested readers are referred to the readings listed in the Further Readings section for this entry.

As a consequence of providing an alternative to the established, gamble-based view of decision making, image theory has allowed both researchers and managers to rethink decision making in a variety of organizational fields: auditing, planning, supervision, job search and job selection, client selection, the effects of organizational culture on decisions, consumer decisions and social responsibility, marketing and communications strategies, and employee turnover. For example, in the past, decisions about voluntarily leaving one's job were conceived of as the result of mentally balancing the risks and payoffs of staying on the job against the risks and payoffs of leaving. Contrast this with the image theory-based model, called the unfolding model of voluntary employee turnover, which, in addition to an important revision of the role of job satisfaction, incorporates image theory's value, trajectory, and strategic images into the job-leaving process. The model posits four decision paths (or prototypical forms) for quitting one's job:

- *Decision Path 1* begins with a jarring negative event that precipitates thoughts of quitting. This prompts a memory probe seeking a preexisting, unimplemented plan for quitting or job change on the strategic image. If such a plan is found, it is implemented and the decision maker quits his or her job. If a plan is not found, one of the other three decision paths is enacted.
- *Decision Path 2* is initiated by a negative event for which the decision maker has no preexisting plan. Instead, he or she incorporates the negative event's implications into his or her forecast about the job and assesses the features of the forecast with the constituents of his or her value, trajectory, and strategic images. If the forecast is compatible with the images, the decision will be to stay in the present job. If the forecast is incompatible, the decision will be to quit.
- *Decision Path 3* also begins with an event, but it can be positive, neutral, or negative. Path 3 is taken when the decision maker has time to be reflective, search for alternatives, and make comparisons. Initially, the compatibility of the forecast about the present job and the three images is assessed. If they are compatible, the decision will be to stay with the present job. If they are incompatible, the compatibility of the forecast for each of the found alternatives is assessed. If only one alternative is found and its forecast is compatible with the decision maker's images, he or she quits and pursues the alternative. If multiple alternatives are compatible with his or her images, the most compatible is then pursued.
- *Decision Path 4* involves no precipitating event and is affectively driven. It typically begins with routine assessment of the compatibility of the decision maker's forecast about his or her present job with his or her value, trajectory, and strategic image. Compatibility is experienced as job satisfaction and leads to the decision to

remain with the present job; incompatibility is experienced as job dissatisfaction. Dissatisfaction prompts a search for alternative job opportunities. Forecasts about found alternative jobs are assessed for compatibility with the images. If the forecasts for none of the alternatives is more compatible with the images than is the forecast for the decision maker's present job, he or she decides to remain with the present job; if the forecast for one alternative is more compatible with the images than is the forecast for the present job, he or she decides to pursue that job; if the forecasts for more than one alternative are more compatible with the images than is the forecast for the present job, he or she decides to pursue the most compatible alternative.

Over the years, substantial empirical support has been reported for this variant of image theory across many different kinds of jobs, companies, industries, and geographic locations.

*Lee Roy Beach, Terence R. Mitchell,
and Thomas W. Lee*

See also Bounded Rationality and Satisficing (Behavioral Decision-Making Model); Decision-Making Styles; Intuitive Decision Making; Prospect Theory; "Unstructured" Decision Making

Further Readings

Beach, L. R. (1990). *Image theory: Decision making in personal and organizational contexts.* Chichester, England: Wiley.

Beach, L. R. (1996). *Decision making in the workplace: A unified perspective.* Mahwah, NJ: Lawrence Erlbaum.

Beach, L. R. (2010). *The psychology of narrative thought: How the stories we tell ourselves shape our lives.* Bloomington, IN: Xlibris.

Beach, L. R., & Mitchell, T. R. (1990). Image theory: A behavioral theory of decisions in organizations. In B. Staw & L. L. Cummings (Eds.), *Research in organizational behavior* (Vol. 12, pp. 1–41). Greenwich, CT: JAI Press.

Lee, T. W., & Mitchell, T. R. (1991). The unfolding effects of organizational commitment and anticipated job satisfaction on voluntary employee turnover. *Motivation and Emotion, 15,* 99–121.

Lee, T. W., & Mitchell, T. R. (1994). An alternative approach: The unfolding model of voluntary employee turnover. *Academy of Management Review, 19,* 51–89.

INDIVIDUAL VALUES

Values are the guiding principles that underpin the way people think, behave, and are motivated. They serve as standards that guide people's action, judgment, and the choices they make, as well as their attitudes and behaviors. Values are generally "stable" and accompany people into every facet of life—societal, organizational, cultural, political, economic, and religious. The general stability in values tends to differentiate them from *attitudes,* which may be more readily altered by events or situations in which people find themselves. For example, a person might have strong values in relation to "equal opportunity." However, in a situation of severe job shortages, the same person might vote in favor of jobs being allocated to "local" employees rather than "foreign" employees, on the basis of the outcome being more beneficial to the local community. This entry explores definitions of the concept of individual values and comments on similarities as well as differences. It provides an insight into well-known value typologies and frameworks used to provide further understanding and enable the measurement of individual values. The entry also draws attention to the impact of cultural values and the need for managers to be cognizant of these values at a time of increasing globalization and intercultural interactions.

Fundamentals

A glance at the literature on individual values identifies an array of definitions and conceptualizations. Despite differences, there is consensus that values are a central determinant in an individual's behavior and motivation in societal, organizational, and work-based contexts. Some researchers, such as Milton Rokeach and Shalom Schwartz, view individual values as "goals." Shalom Schwartz, for example, defines values as desirable and trans-situational goals that vary in importance and serve as guiding principles in people's lives. Milton Rokeach distinguishes between *instrumental* values (which signify desirable modes of conduct) and *terminal* values (which signify desirable end-states of existence), with the two dimensions being interlinked. For example, in his values survey, Rokeach identifies "a comfortable life" as a *terminal value,* while he identifies "being ambitious" or hard working as an *instrumental value* that enables achievement of the terminal value.

A popular definition that captures many facets of individual values is that offered by Robin Williams. He contends that one's values are the standards that we apply in all situations we encounter, not only to determine our action and guide the position we take on various social, political, religious, and other ideological issues but also use to evaluate and judge ourselves, as well as to compare ourselves with others.

Value Types and Frameworks

Rokeach sought to bring consistency in understanding the nature of individual values. He identified five assumptions that could be made: (1) The total set of values that an individual has is relatively small; (2) all people have similar values but to different degrees; (3) values are organized into value sets and systems and are often interrelated; (4) values can be traced to culture, society, and its institutions; and (5) the consequences of human values and actions are widely evident in all phenomena and can be investigated.

The notion of value types is elaborated on by Rob Gilbert and Brian Hoepper, who identify a set of values, each with their own associated concepts. These include the aesthetic (e.g., beauty), economic (e.g., efficiency and productivity), intellectual (e.g., reasoning), political (e.g., justice and freedom), moral (e.g., right and wrong), and environmental (e.g., sustainability).

Schwartz developed a theoretical framework that enabled researchers to systematically identify and measure the value priorities of individuals across societies, organizations, institutions, and cultures. This framework identifies a comprehensive set of 10 motivational value types recognized in 60 nations across all continents of the world. The 10 value types, constructed in a circular structure, reflect the relationships between the values, including elements of conformity and conflict that

we all experience. The value types include power, achievement, hedonism, stimulation, self-direction, universalism, benevolence, tradition, conformity, and security. Schwartz and his colleagues designed a survey instrument, the Schwartz Value Survey (SVS), comprising 57 individual values categorized into the 10 value types. The survey seeks information on how important each value is to the respondent, as a guiding principle in one's life, on a scale ranging from *of supreme importance* to *opposed to my values*. The SVS is widely used to measure individual values across cultures and, in combination with work value surveys, to measure individual values in the workplace and in organizations.

Application to Management

Understanding human values is an ongoing and never-ending process. Consequently, the discussion and debate on how the concept of individual values is defined, how values manifest themselves in people's lives, and how they can be measured and comparatively understood will continue. Rokeach contends that by developing greater self-awareness in relation to one's own and others' values, it is possible to influence the values of people in socially desirable directions. Clearly, this is becoming more evident as the impact of modern technology and the process of globalization intensifies, bringing people closer together, with the accompanying challenge of better understanding one's values and those of others. Given their importance in influencing human behavior, individual values will continue to be fundamental constructs to be further researched and understood.

Modern-day managers can use theoretical insights into basic individual values to better understand the attitudes, behaviors, and motivation of their employees and leverage this knowledge for improved performance in the workplace. The insights can also be used to more effectively fulfill employee aspirations, provide appropriate rewards and incentives, manage diversity in the workplace (including variation in value priorities across factors such as gender, age, educational background, and culture), and create successful cross-cultural or transnational teams—a common feature in modern organizations.

Prem Ramburuth

See also Competing Values Framework; Cultural Values; Emotional and Social Intelligence; Organizational Culture Theory; Role Theory; Work Team Effectiveness

Further Readings

Gilbert, R., & Hoepper, B. (1996). The place of values. In R. Gilbert (Ed.), *Studying society and environment: A handbook for teachers* (pp. 59–79). Melbourne, Australia: Macmillan.

Rokeach, M. (1979). *Understanding human values: Individual and societal.* New York, NY: Free Press:

Schwartz, S., Melech, G., Lehmann, A., Burgess, S., Harris, M., & Owens, V. (2001). Extending the cross-cultural validity of the theory of basic human values with a different method of measurement. *Journal of Cross-Cultural Psychology, 32*(5), 519–542.

Schwartz, S. (1999). A theory of cultural values and some implications for work. *Applied Psychology: An International Review, 48*(1), 23–47.

Williams, R. (1979). Change and stability in values and systems: A sociological perspective. In M. Rokeach, (Ed.), *Understanding human values: Individual and societal* (pp. 15–46). New York, NY: Free Press.

INFLUENCE TACTICS

Influence tactics are the verbal, behavioral, and symbolic actions used by people in organizations when attempting to gain compliance from others. In healthy workplaces, managers, employees, and team members are engaged in exercising influence for a variety of work and personal reasons. Exercising influence in organizations is a continuous social exchange process in which leaders, followers, and peers are both initiators and recipients of influence attempts. A person's influence usage stems from a combination of factors, such as personality, habit, power, desires, roles, setting, and culture. At their essence, management and leadership involve both exercising influence and being open to influence attempts of others. During the past 30 years, researchers developed empirically based categories of influence tactics. Various individual tactics cluster into comprehensive influence strategies, and they, in turn, combine into mixes of influence styles that people use daily in their organizations. These influence strategy categories and metacategories of styles provide a common language

of influence enabling understanding and training and ultimately exercising influence in organizations. In this entry, the seven most commonly used influence strategies are described, followed by descriptions of four influence styles based on mixes of those influence strategies.

Fundamentals

Influence Strategies

The copious array of specific individual influence tactics (e.g., "Please do this," "I need that done," or "Just do it now!") cluster into seven comprehensive influence strategies that have widespread application across numerous cultures. The following descriptions are of the strategies listed in their approximate order of popularity in North American organizations:

Reason. This strategy consists of tactics relying on data, facts, and logical argument to support requests. Reason is the most popular influence strategy used in organizations and involves planning, preparation, and expertise. Reason is a powerful strategy that helps create an image of competence and expertise. The basis for reason is the user's own knowledge, intellect, and ability to communicate.

Friendliness. This strategy relies on creating goodwill toward the user by using flattery, praise, and empathy. Friendliness seeks to create a favorable impression so that the "target" person will be inclined to comply with the user's requests. Using friendliness successfully depends on the user's personality, interpersonal skills, and sensitivity to the moods and feelings of others. Overall, management and employees use friendliness almost as much as reason, because people who are thought well of are often "heard."

Bargaining. This strategy relies on trading benefits and negotiating exchanges. The social norms of obligation and reciprocity underlie bargaining. Users of this tactic rely on exchanges based on the user's own time, effort, skill, or organizational resources desired by another. Although common, bargaining is used less with supervisors than with peers or subordinates

Coalition. This strategy relies on mobilizing other people in an organization to assist the user. The operative principle in using coalition is that there is "power in numbers." The user's power in using this strategy is based on alliances with peers and others in the organization. Coalition is a complex strategy that requires substantial social skill and effort to be successful. However, it is widely used, although less with subordinates than with peers or supervisors.

Assertiveness. This strategy relies on persistence, demands, and being forceful. Often, this means not taking "no" for an answer but without being hostile. Assertiveness creates the impression that the user is "in-charge" and expects compliance with requests. Often, assertiveness incorporates visible displays of emotion and temper. This strategy is used more frequently with subordinates or peers than with those who have more power than the user (i.e., supervisors).

Higher authority. This strategy relies, formally or informally, on gaining the assistance of higher management for support, to apply pressure, or otherwise intervene with a "target" person. The user of this strategy may appeal up the "chain of command" for assistance or request that higher management directly exercise influence on the user's behalf. Higher authority is not widely used and is used substantially less with supervisors than with peers or subordinates.

Sanctions. This strategy relies on rewards or punishments to gain compliance from others. Thus, offering a desirable benefit or an undesirable consequence is perceived as pressure to comply with the user's request. Sanctions are a potentially powerful short-term influence strategy that depends on the user's access to rewards or punishments and on the ability to credibly threaten or actually deliver them.

Influence Styles

Individuals typically mix influence strategies in their organizational relationships with supervisors, peers, and subordinates. The seven distinct influence strategies frequently cluster into four general meta-categories of influence known as influence styles, and they exist in most organizations:

Shotguns. They gain compliance from others by using the full range of influence strategies from reason to sanction with substantial frequency.

Typically, shotguns use assertiveness more than any other strategy, although they frequently use all the strategies extensively. They seek to accomplish much and perceive themselves to have the power to do so.

Bystanders. They employ few influence strategies and have little power or few reasons for exercising influence in their organizations. Social psychologists describe this condition as "learned helplessness."

Tacticians. They substantially rely on reason to influence others, but they employ substantial levels of the other influence strategies. Tacticians have power and have many objectives that they wish to accomplish. They portray themselves as rational and deliberately thoughtful.

Ingratiators. They rely heavily on friendliness to gain compliance from others, especially those they perceive as powerful (i.e., supervisors). Although ingratiators have power and use a variety of influence strategies, they obtain compliance with their requests by attempting to create goodwill and a favorable impression of themselves.

Successful organizational participants, whether management or rank-and-file employees, use influence tactics and styles appropriate to their personality, power, reasons for influencing, who they are trying to influence, and specific organizational culture.

Stuart M. Schmidt

See also Cultural Values; Leadership Practices; Management Control Systems; Organizational Culture Model; *Practice of Management, The*; Social Exchange Theory

Further Readings

Cialdini, R. B. (2009). *Influence: Science and practice* (5th ed.). Boston, MA: Pearson.

Kipnis, D., & Schmidt, S. M. (1988). Upward-influence styles: Relationship with performance evaluations, salary, and stress. *Administrative Science Quarterly, 33,* 528–542.

Kipnis, D., Schmidt, S. M., & Wilkinson, I. (1980). Intraorganizational influence tactics: Explorations in getting one's way. *Journal of Applied Psychology, 65,* 440–452.

Pfeffer, J. (2010). *Power: Why some people have it and others don't.* New York, NY: HarperCollins.

Informal Communication and the Grapevine

Informal communication is premised on the view of organizational communication as systems of information flow with both formal and informal channels. While the formal refers to information flow through official channels, such as newsletters and memos, based on formal organizational and authority structure, the informal refers to emergent, unofficial, and unsanctioned communication among organizational members through informal social contacts. Although there is no overarching model of informal communication, a social network perspective has been a predominant theoretical framework, especially in earlier studies. The focus has been on understanding the informal communication network, also known as the grapevine. Recent theoretical focus has gradually shifted to gossip as a key element of informal communication. The relevance to management in understanding informal communication resides in the various functions it performs in organizations. For example, research reveals that informal communication plays a significant role in administrative and technical decision making, innovation and creativity, power relationships, change management, and socialization. This entry presents foundational theoretical understandings of informal communication in earlier studies followed by a discussion of recent theoretical development and implications for modern management.

Fundamentals

K. Davis's seminal research on informal communication reveals several characteristics of a grapevine. First, grapevine information travels in all directions both across and within chains of command and is transmitted by both organizational members and nonmembers, such as employee spouses. Second, organizational members in the network can be separated into three categories based on the way they handle information: isolates, liaisons, and dead-enders. *Isolates* are those who have a low tendency to receive any information, *liaisons* have a high tendency to both receive and pass on information to someone else, and *dead-enders* have a high tendency to receive information but a low tendency to relay information to others. Studies by Davis and

by Harold Sutton and Lyman W. Porter showed that only a small percentage of organizational members actually perform the liaison function, which proves to be critical to the existence of an informal network. Third, the particular network pattern of informal communication identified by Davis in his data is what he calls a *cluster chain*. In this pattern, an individual passes on information to several individuals (Cluster 1), one of whom shares it with another group of people (Cluster 2); one person in Cluster 2 then passes it on and forms another cluster and so on.

In addition to network characteristics, research by Suzanne Crampton, John Hodge, and Jitendra Mishra identified several conditions that may affect grapevine activities in organizations. These conditions include (1) when the subject matter is widely perceived as important; (2) when formal communications are ambiguous or unclear; (3) when an organizational environment is perceived as insecure, threatening, and/or untrustworthy; and (4) when the future is perceived as uncertain. Under one or more of these conditions, organizations tend to witness heightened levels of grapevine activities.

Recent studies on informal communication give special attention to one of the grapevine's components—gossip. According to Nancy B. Kurland and Lisa Hope Pelled, gossip, which can be positive or negative, is defined as the informal and evaluative talk among a few organizational members about another member who is not present. Social network analysis by Travis Grosser, Virginia Lopez-Kidwell, and Giuseppe Labianca showed that members who share both friendship and workflow ties engage in higher levels of both positive and negative gossip than do those sharing only one type of relationship. In addition, the passing of negative gossip relies heavily on trusting friendship at work but not on task-based relationship.

Mike Noon and Rick Delbridge argued that gossip serves both individual and group functions. At the individual level, gossip functions to gain social influence, understand sociocultural environment, and entertain. At the group level, gossip helps maintain group cohesion and facilitate social control. In particular, research suggests significant implications of gossip on power relationships in organizations. For example, using John French and Bertram Raven's typology of power, Kurland and Pelled conceptually posited that gossip has varied relationships with different types of power moderated by factors such as gossip credibility, relationship quality, and organizational culture. Empirically, Grosser and his colleagues found that highly active gossipers obtain high levels of informal social influence over their peers.

Theories and research on informal communication and the grapevine allow us to see and understand the side of organization or organizing that is emergent, transient, and pervasive but often seems messy, irrational, and out-of-place, as Stewart Clegg and Ad van Iterson keenly pointed out. However, it is within this untidy domain that an organization's cultural undercurrents travel and carve the shifting terrains of our everyday organizational life. Instead of trying to eliminate, or suppress the growth of, grapevine activities from the organizational landscape, managers should first recognize and set up mechanisms to monitor these informal communication activities. Second, managers should incorporate informal communication channels when designing corporate communication strategies. Finally, managers should design messages targeting the informal channels so as to leverage the processes and functions of grapevine activities when communicating critical operational and strategic issues.

Guowei Jian

See also Organizational Culture Theory; Organizational Learning; Organizational Socialization; Sensemaking; Social Construction Theory; Social Network Theory

Further Readings

Clegg, S. R., & van Iterson, A. (2009). Dishing the dirt: Gossiping in organizations. *Culture and Organization, 15,* 275–289.

Crampton, S. M., Hodge, J. W., & Mishra, J. M. (1998). The informal communication network: Factors influencing grapevine activity. *Public Personnel Management, 27,* 569–584.

Davis, K. (1953). Management communication and the grapevine. *Harvard Business Review, 31,* 43–49.

Grosser, T. J., Lopez-Kidwell, V., & Labianca, G. (2010). A social network analysis of positive and negative gossip in organizational life. *Group & Organization Management, 35,* 177–212.

Kurland, N. B., & Pelled, L. H. (2000). Passing the word: Toward a model of gossip and power in the workplace. *Academy of Management Review, 25,* 428–438.

Michelson, G., Iterson, A. van, & Waddington, K. (2010). Gossip in organizations: contexts, consequences, and controversies. *Group & Organization Management, 35*(4), 371–390.

Monge, P. R., & Contractor, N. (2001). Emergence of communication networks. In F. M. Jablin & L. L. Putnam (Eds.), *The new handbook of organizational communication: Advances in theory, research, and methods* (pp. 440–502). Thousand Oaks, CA: Sage.

Noon, M., & Delbridge, R. (1993). News from behind my hand: Gossip in organizations. *Organization Studies, 14,* 23–36.

Rosnow, R. L. (1977). Gossip and marketplace psychology. *Journal of Communication, 27,* 158–163.

Sutton, H., & Porter, L. W. (1968). A study of the grapevine in a governmental organization. *Personnel Psychology, 21,* 223–230.

INFORMATION RICHNESS THEORY

The basic premise of information richness theory (frequently called media richness theory) is that communication media or channels differ in their information carrying capacity, just as pipelines of different sizes and designs have varying capacities for transporting oil. Information richness is defined as the ability of an information exchange to change participant's understanding within a time interval. Information that fits the carrying capacity of its medium more likely will be conveyed and understood efficiently and accurately. For example, a chemist and regulatory attorney for a maker of over-the-counter medicines have to come to agreement about a new product's content and efficacy within government regulations. To set an appointment to meet, they probably would exchange an e-mail. But to integrate the subtleties and complexities of their different perspectives and experiences, they likely will choose to meet face-to-face. They understand intuitively that meeting face-to-face to make the appointment would not be an efficient use of time and trying to negotiate mutual understanding about the drug would be nearly impossible via e-mail. Information is constantly processed within organizations via managers and employees to interpret signals from the environment, handle disruptions, set strategy and goals, monitor performance, coordinate people and departments, and celebrate accomplishments. Managers spend most of their work time communicating via e-mail, telephone, and personal meetings. Information richness theory explains why various communication media are used and how managers and organizations can process information more effectively. In this entry, the underlying components of information richness are defined, the implications for manager communication and coordination are described, and the large body of research evidence is reviewed.

Fundamentals

The theory proposes that two basic elements—media capacity and message content—need to be in alignment for effective communication to occur. The first element—capacity of an information medium or channel—is influenced by three characteristics: (1) the ability to handle multiple cues simultaneously; (2) the ability to facilitate rapid, two-way feedback; and (3) the ability to establish a personal presence or focus for the communication. In order from high to low richness, the basic media classifications are (1) face-to-face; (2) telephone; (3) personal written documents such as e-mails, letters, or memos; and (4) impersonal documents such as rules and bulletins. Face-to-face is the richest medium because it provides immediate feedback so that interpretations can be checked and provides multiple cues via emotions, body language, and tone of voice. Telephone conversations are next in the richness hierarchy. Eye contact, gaze, posture, and other physical cues are missing, but the human voice still carries a large amount of verbal and emotional information. Written or electronic messages lack visual and audio cues but allow for fairly rapid feedback and can be personalized to the recipient. E-mail, text messages, and social networking are increasingly being used for communications that were once handled over the telephone. Finally, impersonal written media, including flyers, bulletins, and standard computer reports are considered the lowest in richness. These channels are not focused on a single receiver, use limited information cues, and do not permit feedback.

The second element of the theory—message content—is gauged by the ambiguity, diverse frames of reference, and equivocality involved for participants to reach shared understanding. Communication messages or transactions that must overcome widely different frames of reference or clarify ambiguous issues to reach understanding are quite different from messages that involve routine, clear, easy-to-understand data.

Manager communications. Information richness theory hypothesizes that manager communication is effective when a rich medium such as face-to-face is used to process information about an ambiguous topic or that involves diverse frames of reference. A medium that is low in richness works best when the transaction involves clear data and shared perspectives. Thus, a senior manager who wants to organize the support of colleagues in favor of a new initiative for which there may be conflicts of interest is predicted to communicate with the other managers face-to-face. A manager who wants to respond to a routine written query from a customer or direct report is predicted to use e-mail for efficiency. The e-mail conveys far fewer cues, but richer cues are not needed to accurately convey a routine message. These media choices are based on the assumption that managers are somewhat rational actors attempting to communicate effectively and use their time wisely.

Organization structure. A substantial body of work describes organizations as information-processing systems. Organization structure and design elements reflect the information-processing needs of an organization. For example, many issues that arise from the environment are fuzzy and ill-defined so that the interpretation of external events cannot be routinized. Typically, managers with different views will converge on a similar interpretation of a key event before responding with a new strategy. Their information processing must have the capacity to reduce ambiguity. Managers discuss, argue, and ultimately agree on a reasonable interpretation that makes action sensible. Organizations in stable environments would likely require less information processing and less use of rich media to interpret the environment.

For example, the newly appointed CEO of a retail chain with 36 stores in 13 cities acted on his belief in strong financial controls and precise analysis. He overturned his predecessor's preference to discuss matters face-to-face and to reach decisions through consensus, visiting stores to see what was selling, breakfast meetings with various people for discussion and planning, and visiting suppliers and fashion shows to stay abreast of new trends. The new CEO requested detailed reports and analyses for every decision, relying on paperwork and computer print-outs for information. He argued that managing a corporation was like flying an airplane. Watch the dials to see if the plane deviates from its course and then nudge it back with financial controls. Personal contact was limited to occasional telephone calls and monthly meetings. Within 2 years, a revolt by board members and vice presidents ousted the new CEO. They claimed that the CEO was hopelessly out of touch with the fast-moving fashion environment, and the retail chain was suffering as a result.

Within organizations, the various subgroups or functional departments must also be coordinated. In uncertain environments, the information-processing requirements to achieve coordination are high. Coordination mechanisms have been organized along a continuum from *group* to *personal* to *impersonal,* which reflects the richness continuum. Cross-functional teams and project and matrix forms of structure use frequent team meetings to achieve coordination and negotiate differences in perspective. Personal coordination mechanisms often rely on individuals for coordination, such as product managers and brand managers or direct contact among employees to bring diverse departments into alignment. Impersonal mechanisms include planning, scheduling, and rules, which typically apply to recurring, well-understood activities and quickly become outdated under conditions of uncertainty and rapid change.

Rich coordination mechanisms deliver faster coordination. For example, during the flight departure process, an airline such as Southwest engages in face-to-face contact among cabin cleaners, gate agents, flight attendants, pilots, caterers, baggage handlers, and mechanics to facilitate task coordination. Southwest is the most efficient airline with respect to a fast departure process partly because other airlines tend to use impersonal means of coordination.

Importance

Seemingly hundreds of studies across several academic fields have investigated media richness. Differences in channel richness have been investigated for human resource recruitment, advertising and marketing, online sales, information systems,

distance education, deception, negotiation, national cultures, knowledge management, business-to-business relationships, and the impact of new media. Within the field of management and organization, variables studied in relation to media selection include geographic dispersion, job categories, social context, symbols, accessibility, job pressure, attitudes, socioemotional content, and task complexity. Within all these studies a few findings stand out.

There is confirming evidence that information media do fit a continuum of richness. Each major medium has a specific capacity for information processing. Moreover, the notion that managers tend to choose a communication medium to fit message content is confirmed for the major media categories of face-to-face, telephone, electronic, and impersonal.

Moreover, evidence has been reported that managers who were "media sensitive" to matching media richness and message content received significantly higher performance evaluations than managers who were "media insensitive." Insensitive managers were rated less effective because they selected communication media almost at random, such as communicating a difficult, emotion-laden message such as telling a subordinate about a demotion through an e-mail or, vice versa, used face-to-face for most routine matters. In addition, senior executives who communicate more frequently face-to-face showed greater mutual agreement. Managers who used less rich communication channels report less agreement about business objectives and planning.

In addition, research also reveals that many factors other than message content influence a manager's selection of a communication medium. Geographical distance, for example, may cause a manager to use telephone or e-mail because the cost to make a cross-country trip is too great to justify a face-to-face meeting. Time pressure has also been shown to influence media choice because the need for an immediate decision may override the luxury of a face-to-face meeting. These factors help explain the rise in videoconferencing, which adds richness to communications for virtual teams.

Other findings show that some managers select a medium for its symbolic meaning rather than to fit message content. A few managers reported that they had chosen the face-to-face medium for a routine communication as a way to signal caring about an employee, the desire for teamwork, to build trust and goodwill, or to convey informality.

In the opposite direction, a few managers would request more data than needed in order to send out a professional-looking written report to symbolize the legitimacy and rationality of a controversial decision. Written media were found to signal authority and legitimacy to other people.

Another finding was that people could develop greater competency within a single medium and thereby effectively communicate both routine and nonroutine messages efficiently through that channel. Channel expansion theory says that personal experience is important in shaping how a manager selects and uses a given channel. Greater experience with a specific channel, with the message topic, with the organizational norms and culture, and with coparticipants enabled the use of a single medium for a greater range of messages. However, there was no correlation of media richness with the analyzability of tasks that people performed, nor was there a clear correlation of message type with the selection of new media or social media. The new forms of media so far have not been classified as appropriate for specific types of messages. Additional research is needed in this area.

The lesson from information richness theory is that the basic idea of a fit between media richness and message content has been supported by research into manager communication and organizational coordination mechanisms. The theory has generated a significant amount of research in several disciplines. Managers and organizations that communicate according to the model tend to be higher performers.

Richard L. Daft

See also Informal Communication and the Grapevine; Matrix Structure; Social Information Processing Model

Further Readings

Brunel, E. (2009). Introducing media richness into an integrated model of consumers' intentions to use online stores in their purchase process. *Journal of Internet Commerce, 8,* 222–245.

Carlson, J. R., & Zmud, R. W. (1999). Channel expansion theory and the experiential nature of media richness perceptions. *Academy of Management Journal, 42*(3), 153–170.

Carlson, P. J., & Davis, G. B. (1998). An investigation of media selection among directors and managers: From "self" to "other" orientation. *MIS Quarterly, 22*(3), 335–362.

Daft, R. L., & Lengel, R. H. (1984). Information richness: A new approach to managerial behavior and organization design. In B. Staw, & L. L. Cummings (Eds.), *Research in organizational behavior* (Vol. 6, pp. 191–233). Greenwich, CT: JAI Press.

Daft, R. L., & Lengel, R. H. (1986). Organizational information requirements, media richness and structural design. *Management Science, 32*(5), 554–571.

Daft, R. L., Lengel, R. H., & Treviño, L. K. (1987). Message equivocality, media selection, and manager performance: Implications for information systems. *MIS Quarterly, 11*(3), 355–366.

Trevino, L. K., Lengel, R. H., & Daft, R. L. (1987). Media symbolism, media richness and media choice in organizations: A symbolic interactionist perspective. *Communication Research, 14*(5), 553–575.

Innovation Diffusion

Management innovations are management entities—ideas, practices, techniques, or organizational forms—perceived as innovations (i.e., as new and improved) by a collectivity. A collectivity is a group of organizations or employees that tend to use the same entities. Theories of innovation diffusion typically advance social mechanisms, originating from *within* collectivities, which cause these collectivities to perceive certain management entities as innovations and adopt them, causing their spread or diffusion across collectivity members. By contradistinction, what distinguishes innovation-diffusion from non-innovation-diffusion theories is that the latter attribute the spread of management entities to forces originating from *outside* collectivities, such as those exerted by government institutions or professional organizations. This entry critically reviews Everett Rogers's influential "diffusion of innovation paradigm" throughout his five reviews published between 1962 and 2005. It then reviews bandwagon and market theories of diffusion and the diffusion literature that emerged after Rogers's paradigm. This entry serves three purposes developed in its three parts. The first part presents Rogers's paradigm and Eric Abrahamson's challenges. This sets the stage for second part, which reviews management studies that have made substantial headway in overcoming the causes of Rogers's paradigm's shortcomings. The third part reviews findings and prescriptions, suggested by recent management research, about how organizations and their managers might adopt more beneficial managerial innovations.

Fundamentals

Rogers's Diffusion of Innovation Paradigm

According to Rogers, the adoption and diffusion of innovations across a collectivity is caused primarily by the gradual communication of information about innovations through channels linking members of the collectivity. When collectivity members learned through communication channels about management entities that were new and improved, they adopted them, thereby channeling information about these entities to other collectivity members that adopted them, causing still more communication and adoptions, ad seriatim.

Adoption sequence. Everett Rogers highlighted a multi-mechanism sequence, emanating from within individual or organizational collectivities, causing the adoption of innovations. The first mechanism accounts for the invention of new management entities whose improvements benefit adopters; the second accounts for the communication of information about such entities' benefits across communication networks; and the third accounts for these entities' adoption. This third adoption mechanism has a sequence of five stages. In the first, potential adopters absorb information about entities. In the second, they review this information to learn whether the entity constitutes what Rogers called an *innovation*—that is, an entity adopters perceive as new, improved, and thereby providing benefits. In the third, adopters' learning persuades them whether to adopt the innovation. In the fourth, adopters persuaded of the innovation's benefits implement it. In the fifth, if they have implemented the innovation they access whether they should continue doing so or, if they have not, whether they should further delay implementation.

Attributes influencing rate of diffusion. Rogers's key policy concern was that innovations should diffuse to members of a collectivity as speedily as possible; this, so that they might benefit from these improvements as long as possible—that is, until older innovations were replaced by the next new and improved management idea, practice, technique, or organizational form. One of Rogers's foci was the characteristics of innovations that influence the *speed* of their adoption and diffusion. Two types of characteristics could affect speed. One pertained to how readily the benefits of an innovation could be learned. An innovation's inherent characteristics might make its benefits easier to perceive (what Rogers called "observability") or to experience through trials ("triability"), as when its real benefits were relatively greater ("relative advantage"). A second class of characteristics, such as an innovation's inherent complexity, or compatibility with other innovations, pertained to the greater speed of their *implementation* (complexity and compatibility). Ceteris paribus, the more the characteristic of a management innovation increased the speed with which individuals or organizations learned about the innovation's benefits and could implement it, the faster organizations would adopt it and it would diffuse.

Cumulative and number of adoptions over time by different adopter types. Since approximately the beginning of the present century, we have known that not every collectivity member adopts at once but do so in suddenly accelerating numbers and sometimes, subsequently, in decelerating numbers. This makes it possible to distinguish five types of adopters that become clear upon observing a diffusion graph: innovators, early adopters, early majority, late majority, and finally laggards. Diffusion frequently produces bell-shaped curves in the number of adopters per time period. It should be noted that there are also what might be called "rejecters" as they reject innovations after adopting them. S-shaped, cumulative-adoption curves characterized by relative few early adopters and a steeper slope of majority adopters denote a higher diffusion speed. Innovation diffusion studies develop measures of adopters' or innovation characteristics to test hypotheses of how they affect adoption or diffusion speed. Moreover, as communication networks channel information about innovations to adopters, researchers such as Jerry Davis in 1991 or David Strang and Nancy Tuma in 1993 developed statistical models and studies about how not only potential adopters' characteristics but also the structure of their information channels alert them to the innovation, influencing whether and how quickly they adopted it. The structure of the channel's network also influences the sequence and timing of adoptions by adopters with different network profiles and the overall speed of diffusion.

Change agents. Change agents are defined by their role, which is to intervene in such a way as to speed up diffusion. Change agents are considered as being within collectivities because they adopt certain innovations whose diffusion they attempt to speed up. These adoptions differ from those of organizations that implement the innovations. Scholars working in Rogers's innovation diffusion paradigm tested hypotheses linking when and how change agents adopt innovations and their effects on overall adoption or diffusion speed.

Abrahamson's Bandwagon and Market Theories of Diffusion

By the time of Rogers's 1995 review, what Rogers defined as innovation-diffusion studies had virtually slowed to a trickle. Abrahamson and Greg Fairchild noted in 1999 that it is not uncommon that when the diffusion of one type of innovation tails off, it triggers the diffusion of a replacement innovation belonging to the same type. As the number of innovation diffusion studies in Rogers's paradigm reached its nadir in 1992, Abrahamson published an article in 1991 that proposed two diffusion mechanisms that challenged Rogers's innovation diffusion mechanism: a bandwagon mechanism and a market mechanism. The bandwagon mechanism specifies social and economic forces causing organizations or individuals to adopt a management entity—regardless of its newness, characteristics, or benefits—because they learn how many and which other organizations have already adopted it. Abrahamson in 1991 and 1996 advanced a second, market mechanism. It specifies how diffusion occurs as a result of the interrelation between supply-side organizations' broadcasting discourse about entities they believed demand-side organizations will perceive as innovative and adopt. Abrahamson developed these bandwagon and market mechanisms in subsequent articles with Lori Rosenkopf and Micki Eisenman.

Evolution

The bell-shaped diffusion in the frequency of published studies in Rogers's innovation diffusion paradigm peaked in 1968, slowing to a trickle by 1992; subsequently, a vibrant management literature has emerged around Abrahamson's and others' theorizing. This section reviews this management literature's research on adoption and diffusion.

Management Techniques

Management techniques, or more exactly *management techniques' labels,* are linguistic strings, such as "business process reengineering." Discourse about management techniques communicates both such management techniques' labels and the business prescriptions these labels denote. *Business prescriptions* are discourse that prescribes certain means to transform organizational inputs into organizational outputs. Organizations or their employees can implement these prescriptions.

Management diffusion researchers today question Rogers's notion that management innovations spring up de novo and diffuse because their inherent benefits are perceived by organizations belonging to a collectivity. If anything, the definition and benefits of management techniques remain very ambiguous for organizations and their participants. Many studies indicate that it is unlikely that there exist precise definitions of management techniques and clear understandings of their inherent innovativeness. It is unlikely, therefore, that management techniques' unambiguous, inherent innovativeness causes their diffusion. Management researchers generally assume that Rogers may have inverted the causality by assuming that management techniques' inherent innovativeness caused their diffusion. Rather, they suggest that diffusion processes determine whether and which management techniques are perceived as innovative and adopted.

Bandwagon Diffusion Mechanisms

When ambiguity surrounds a management technique's definition and innovativeness, organizations take other organizations' adoption of that technique, rather than knowledge about its benefits, as a signal of its innovativeness, and they mimic its adoption. Abrahamson and Rosenkopf's three computer simulations of bandwagon diffusion, published starting in 1991, illustrated how bandwagon diffusion of an innovation could occur because of social conformity or economic risk aversion pressure. Bandwagon resulted from a positive feedback loop: In the first part of the loop, more adoptions caused greater pressures to adopt, whereas in the loop's second part, these greater pressures caused more adoptions. Innovations diffused only as long as the loop cycled, resulting, when it stopped, in different proportions of the collectivities having adopted. This research overcame the single-minded focus on the speed of diffusion. It considered the extent of diffusion as well, as did Abrahamson's market diffusion mechanism.

It is very important to note here a point of frequent confusion. Both bandwagon mechanisms and market diffusion mechanism are not defined by the fact that they diffuse nonbeneficial innovations. They can cause the diffusion of beneficial innovations as well. They are defined by how these mechanisms function. Both bandwagon and market models, however, because they are not based on the assumption that it is innovations' real benefits that cause innovations to diffuse, can explain the diffusion of innovations that had little or no utility for organizations or that caused them active harm.

Management Fashion–Market Diffusion Mechanisms

Researchers using the market diffusion model have paid close attention to both supply-side and demand-side organizations in the market for management innovations. Many researchers, such as Jos Benders, Harry Scarbrough, Krzysztof Klincewicz, Andrew Sturdy, Timothy Clark and Brad Jackson, Margaret Brindle, and Peter Stearns confirmed that consulting firms, books publishing houses, magazines and their publishers, professional associations, and business schools populate the supply-side of the market for management innovations. They promote, through their discourse, techniques that they hope demand-side organizations and their stakeholders will perceive as rational or progressive, will adopt, and will diffuse. Multiple supply-side organizations compete to achieve this end.

Abrahamson's 1996 theory also notes that entities' demand-side potential adopters perceived as new and improved invariably become perceived as old, unsuccessful, or passé, resulting in the diffusion of their rejection. Demand-side organizations include for-profit, nonprofit, governmental, and even military and religious organizations. Total quality management (TQM), for instance, diffused

across all these organizations. Rational management techniques are those that stakeholders believe provide efficient means to important ends. Progressive techniques are those that stakeholders believe are new and improved relative to past rational techniques. The theory of management fashion assumes that demand-side organizations have incipient interests in management entities that are rational and progressive in ways that are not fully clear to them.

As David Strang showed in 2006, only certain supply-side organizations win the competition to launch their management innovations. Winners succeed, either by design or by chance, because the management techniques they promote fit demand-side organizational and stakeholder incipient preferences. Of course, the passage of time undermines demand-side perceptions that management innovations are new and improved. A few of these outdated innovations remain institutionalized, but many are rejected in droves. At this point, supply-side organizations compete again to launch the next management technique that the demand side will perceive as new and improved.

Market Driven Diffusion

Research reveals the existence of three types of market-driven adoption processes, which we examine in turn.

Ceremonial adoption. Certain organizations do not implement the management innovations supply-side organizations supply; they only use the labels denoting these management innovations. They do so to signal to their stakeholders that their organizations are well managed by virtue of having implemented the new and improved management techniques these labels denote; this, even if they have not implemented them. For example, in 1998, Mark Zbaracki's multiple case studies of organizations indicated that when the TQM label and its associated prescriptions reached these organizations, they triggered very limited TQM implementation. What little, halfhearted implementation occurred generally failed. Organizations used the TQM label, however, to communicate to stakeholders stories of successful TQM implementation.

Reinvention. Some researchers note that organizations do not always make only ceremonial use of labels denoting management techniques. Rather, they implement vastly differing variants of the pre-scriptions these labels denote. Consider, for example prescriptions for designing organizations labeled as multidivisional structures (M-form). M-form prescriptions are highly ambiguous. Not surprisingly, a number of researchers found evidence that there existed many variants of M-form organizations, and in 1962, Alfred Chandler, the pioneer of M-form research, noted that many mixed and bastardized versions of the M-form were adopted. What causes these mutations in the adoption of management prescriptions denoted by the same label? Rogers attributes mutation to "reinvention"—a tendency of organizations to reinvent management innovations to serve their idiosyncratic needs. Barbara Czarniawska and Guje Sevon were first to take the next step in 1996 and notice that reinvented innovations were in turn reinvented repeatedly, or translated, as they diffuse across organizations, resulting in any number of technical management mutations. It may not even make sense, therefore, to talk about the diffusion of a single management innovation but rather of how diffusion across organizations is defined by the spread of many mutating management prescriptions whose commonality is that they are denoted by the same label.

Accumulation. Researchers have detected another mechanism causing management innovations to mutate. As noted earlier, management techniques perceived as new and improved become perceived as outdated with the passage of time, causing their widespread rejection. The collapse of outdated management techniques triggered competition among supply-side organizations resulting in the emergence of replacement management innovations, *ad seriatim.* Abrahamson and Eisenman in 2008 showed that series of transitory management innovations had a gradual, yet major effect on management discourse and praxis.

Importance

Making the Adoption Decision

This final section focuses on what we can learn from management studies of the adoption and diffusion of management technique. Several researchers contend that there inheres in Rogers's paradigm a pro-innovation bias—an assumption that only beneficial management innovations diffuse and,

therefore, that management innovations that have diffused must be beneficial. The market and bandwagon mechanisms of innovation diffusion are neutral with respect to the benefits of diffusion for organizations and their managers. Out of inability or self-interest, fashion setters, for instance, may participate in the diffusion of ineffectual management innovations. Likewise, bandwagon processes will cause an entity to diffuse, because others have adopted it, regardless of whether it is or is not new or improved. For these reasons, managers run the risk of adopting ineffectual innovations. When might this be more likely to occur? Two types of adoption—bandwagon and ceremonial adoption—have a higher likelihood of diffusing management techniques that might provide little utility to adopters or that might actively harm them. Two other adoption mechanisms—reinventive adoption and accumulated adoption—have a higher likelihood of benefiting organizations.

Bandwagon and Ceremonial Adoption

Pamela Tolbert and Lynn Zucker's often replicated 1983 study indicates that early organizational adopters of management innovation have needs that tend to make these innovations useful for these adopters. Innovators and early adopters cause bandwagon pressures prompting large numbers of early-majority nonadopters, then late-majority nonadopters and finally laggards to adopt. They would succumb to these bandwagon pressures even though what they adopt would not benefit them. Such findings reveal, in particular, the dangers managers face when they benchmark and imitate other organizations' techniques with little knowledge of these techniques' utility. Abrahamson's 1991 simulation, with Lori Rosenkopf, of bandwagon diffusion also suggests that a few rejections of beneficial innovations could result in their widespread bandwagon rejection. So managers might guard against the risk of abandoning innovations that benefit them, when these innovations are being rejected by many organizations.

Ceremonial adoption processes also seem to have a greater potential to diffuse management innovations of little utility to organizations. In 2000, Barry Staw and Lisa Epstein published a study, replicated by Ping Wang in 2010, providing rigorous evidence of the ceremonial adoptions of management techniques. They found that CEOs' use of ceremonial adoption caused their organizations' reputation and CEOs' compensation to increase. This occurred while the purported adoption of the techniques had little or no effect on these organizations' performance. This suggests that organizational stakeholders should check carefully whether the management innovations that CEOs claim to have implemented were in fact implemented.

Reinventive and Accumulated Adoption

Reinvention occurs when organizations reinvent management techniques to fit them to the idiosyncrasies of their organization. In 1991, Françoise Chevalier's longitudinal study of the implementation of the quality circle (QC) management innovation in eight French organizations revealed two scenarios: one in which organizations followed QC's prescriptions to the letter and another in which they reinvented QCs to fit their organizations. Organizations in the first scenario rejected QCs, whereas in the second scenario they retained and profited from them. This study suggests that managers' reinvention of management innovations to customize them to their organizations may enhance the benefits of adopting such innovations.

Regarding the benefits of accumulation, Robert Cole published a 1999 book in which he examined the series of what he called quality fads—that is, short-lived management innovations designed to enhance product quality. Cole's book makes the compelling case that these quality fads cumulated into major transformation in the quality of U.S. products, putting them on par with those of global competitors. In other words, the benefits of the diffusion of each transitory management innovation may not be apparent. Such benefits become apparent only when managers consider the accumulated result of the adoption of many, short-lived management innovations.

Eric Abrahamson

See also Institutional Theory; Interorganizational Networks; Neo-Institutional Theory; Open Innovation; Social Network Theory; Technological Discontinuities; Technology S-Curve; Transfer of Technology

Further Readings

Abrahamson, E. (1991). Managerial fads and fashions: The diffusion and rejection of innovations. *Academy of Management Review, 16,* 586–612.

Abrahamson, E. (1996). Management fashion. *Academy of Management Review, 21*(1), 254–285.

Abrahamson, E., & Eisenman, M. (2008). Employee-management techniques: Transient fads or trending fashions? *Administrative Science Quarterly, 53*(4), 719–744.

Abrahamson, E., & Fairchild, G. (1999). Management fashion: Lifecycles, triggers, and collective learning processes. *Administrative Science Quarterly, 44,* 708–740.

Benders, J., & Van Veen, K. (2001). What's in a fashion? Interpretative viability and management fashions. *Organization, 8*(1), 33–53.

Clark, T. (2004). The fashion of management fashion: A surge too far? *Organization, 11*(2), 297.

Cole, R. (1999). *Managing quality fads.* New York, NY: Oxford University Press.

Czarniawska, B., & Sevon, G. (2005). *Global ideas: How ideas, objects and practices travel in a global economy.* Malmö, Sweden: Liber & Copenhagen Business School Press.

Rogers, E. (2005). *Diffusion of innovations* (5th ed.). New York, NY: Free Press.

Staw, B. M., & Epstein, L. D. (2000). What bandwagons bring: Effects of popular management techniques on corporate performance, reputation, and CEO pay. *Administrative Science Quarterly, 45*(3), 523–556.

INNOVATION SPEED

Innovation speed generally represents how quickly an idea moves from conception to a product in the marketplace, measuring firms' capabilities to move quickly through the innovation process. Different terms such as time-to-market, cycle time, new product development speed, and speed-to-market have been also used to portray the same concept. Innovation speed is a key component of time-oriented strategy and a pivotal way to achieve time advantage, either first-mover or fast-follower advantage. Time orientation has become the popular choice for most companies to achieve competitive advantage since the late 1980s. This change of managerial focus represents a shift from a more traditional cost orientation, such as management experience curve strategies in the 1960s, portfolio strategies and the strategic use of debt in the late 1960s and early 1970s, and de-averaging of costs in the mid-1970s. Instead of emphasizing the achievement of the most output at the lowest cost, time orientation seeks to achieve the most output in the shortest time frame, more suited for the current fast-changing business environment. Adding it to Michael Porter's three generic strategies of cost leadership, differentiation, and focus, time advantage is being viewed as a new generic competitive strategy. In the following, antecedents and benefits of innovation speed are first discussed and then its trade-offs are addressed.

Fundamentals

Antecedents of Innovation Speed

There are many antecedents of innovation speed, which could be classified into strategy, project, process, and team characteristics. *Strategy characteristics* address the managerial thought and context of innovation in a company at the macro level, consisting of speed emphasis, innovative culture, top management support, strategy synergy, and resource availability. They reflect how top management fosters a favorable climate to facilitate the initiation of new ideas and product development with a specific time-based objective and a clear product concept. Instead of emphasizing cost or quality, a strategic focus on time reflects an innovation strategy that aims to shorten the duration of product development.

Project characteristics refer to the attribute of the innovation projects, resulting from the firm's innovation strategy. Project characteristics that facilitate innovation speed are those that limit uncertainty and complexity of innovation projects. For instance, to shorten development cycle time, firms tend to pursue incremental products and simple projects to reduce design modifications and developmental errors associated with the development of radical and complex products. Project characteristics include product vision, product and technology newness, project complexity, and project size. *Process characteristics* represent the attribute of the innovation process and its execution that affects speed. For instance, although a formal innovation process is necessary to develop new products, the process should be flexible to allow overlap or parallel development of activities. Also, innovation teams would need to learn continuously by taking a probe-and-learn process (i.e., iterating

and testing product concepts) to speed up the innovation process, particularly in developing a totally new product. Process-related factors include the extent to which (a) a formal innovation process and concurrent process are adopted; (b) a probe-and-learn approach are employed; (c) advanced methods and tools are used, such as design-related tools and computer-based tools; and (d) innovation processes are proficiently executed.

Two aspects of *team characteristics*, staff and structure, influence the innovation process. Structure characteristics refer to the integration within and between teams. To accelerate innovation, a sequential process needs to shift to a parallel and integrated process. This new process accordingly requires a new organizational form; that is, team structure should shift from functional teams to cross-functional teams. It requires not only the involvement of different specialists from internal functional departments but also the involvement of external partners to coordinate and integrate with each other toward a common goal. Staff characteristics refer to characteristics such as team leaders' power and expertise and team members' experience and dedication. Team leaders and members are the people who transform valuable ideas, concepts, and specifications into new products; thus, they play a central role in facilitating or impeding process performance, including speed. Only qualified staffs can make a good strategy happen; that is, team members with rich experience, expertise, and skills can effectively execute the time-based strategy and accelerate innovation process.

Benefits of Innovation Speed

Innovation speed is essential for the success, survival, and renewal of firms in turbulent and uncertain environments. By developing products quickly, companies can achieve several important benefits. First, rapid innovation can increase product profitability, margins, and market share. Firms are able to translate time into profits by satisfying their "impatient" customers, who are willing to pay a premium if they can get goods and services very quickly. Second, companies with fast innovation have a greater chance to establish industry standards and may lock up distribution channels. Third, a firm with the capability of developing products rapidly can quickly respond to market demands, improving the timeliness of its product entry and customer satisfaction.

"Trade-Offs" of Innovation Speed

Some researchers and practitioners argue that there are potential trade-offs between innovation speed and other innovation performance indicators, such as speed-quality and speed-cost trade-offs. For example, a strict deadline might make innovation teams slip key processes, trim performance specifications, and/or reduce technological content, which typically undermines product quality. Fast innovation may make managers focus on schedules at the expense of more resources and product performance. Overemphasizing speed may make the innovation process too rigid and unable to respond to competitive and customer-driven changes. Also, under high time pressure, innovation teams may be forced to consider a narrow range of alternatives and have little time to explore ways to improve product specifications.

However, implementing a time-based strategy is not as simple as adding more resources in the innovation process or slipping the key steps or rushing; it is not speeding for speed. Just as Brian Dumaine commented in a *Fortune* magazine article, "The worst way to speed up a company is by trying to make it do things just as it does, only faster. The workers will simply burn out." A time-based competitor is not necessarily better able to finish a single task faster than its competitors are. Time-based competitors have to do something differently, keeping in mind speed as means to success. To implement time-based strategy, a company and its innovation teams should change managerial philosophy to focus on time and make this criterion a priority and, in turn, change the product strategy, innovation process, and organizational structure.

Jiyao Chen

See also Business Process Reengineering; Empowerment; First-Mover Advantages and Disadvantages; *Kaizen* and Continuous Improvement; Organic and Mechanistic Forms; Product Champions; Stages of Innovation

Further Readings

Chen, J., Damanpour, F., & Reilly, R. R. (2010). Understanding Antecedents of new product development speed: A meta-analysis. *Journal of Operations Management, 28*(1), 17–33

Dumaine, B. (1989, February 13). How managers can succeed through speed. *Fortune*. Retrieved from http://money.cnn.com/magazines/fortune/fortune_archive/1989/02/13/71614

Eisenhardt, K. M., & Tabrizi, B. N. (1995). Accelerating adaptive processes: Product innovation in the global computer industry. *Administrative Science Quarterly, 40*, 84–110.

Griffin, A. (1997). Modeling and measuring product development cycle time across industries. *Journal of Engineering and Technology Management, 14*(1), 1–24.

Kessler, E. H., & Chakrabarti, A. K. (1996). Innovation speed: A conceptual model of context, antecedents and outcomes. *Academy of Management Review, 21*(4), 1143–1191.

Stalk, G. J., & Hout, T. M. (1990). *Competing against time: How time-based competition is reshaping global markets.* New York, NY: Free Press.

Zirger, B. J., & Hartley, J. L. (1994). A conceptual model of product development cycle time. *Journal of Engineering and Technology Management, 11*(3–4), 229–251.

INSTITUTIONAL THEORY

Institutional theory is an approach to understanding organizations and management practices as the product of social rather than economic pressures. It has become a popular perspective within management theory because of its ability to explain organizational behaviors that defy economic rationality. It has been used, for example, to explain why some managerial innovations become adopted by organizations or diffuse across organizations in spite of their inability to improve organizational efficiency or effectiveness. The explanation, according to institutional theory, is based on the key idea that the adoption and retention of many organizational practices are often more dependent on social pressures for conformity and legitimacy than on technical pressures for economic performance. In this entry, the core concepts of institutional theory are summarized, its history and evolution are reviewed, and finally, select managerial applications of the theory are discussed.

Fundamentals

Six key concepts form the basis of institutional theory: the infusion of value, diffusion, rational myths, loose coupling, legitimacy, and isomorphism. Each of these is elaborated below.

Infusion of Value

Institutional theory is premised on the observation that abstract social structures—such as family, organization, church—tend to acquire meaning and significance that extends beyond their original purpose. Institutionalization is the process by which, over time, routine tasks, organizational structures, or functional positions acquire surplus meaning or value beyond their intended function. Phillip Selznick first articulated this core idea. Selznick was an American sociologist who, in his 1949 study of the Tennessee Valley Authority (a large federal government organization designed to promote conservation as part of the Roosevelt administration's New Deal) observed that the organization's survival came at the expense of its original purpose. Selznick's study offered two key insights that form the foundation of institutional theory. First, he concluded that organizations become infused with significance (meaning and value) that extends beyond their bare functional utility. Second, he observed that as a result of this infusion of meaning and value, there are often unintended consequences to purposive action. Selznick's work, thus, separated organizational activity into two distinct realms—the technical and rational realm of purposive action and the symbolic and institutional realm of meaning and value.

Diffusion

A related idea is the understanding that new practices are often adopted, not because of their technical outcomes but because they resonate with social and community values. This observation emerged in 1962 through the publication of Everett Rogers's book *The Diffusion of Innovations*. Rogers was a professor of rural sociology interested in understanding why some innovations successfully spread and others did not. He observed that adoption of an innovation often depends less on the objective or technical attributes of the innovation and more on the subjective interpretations of the innovation by the adopter. So for example, an indigenous community may refuse to adopt modern health practices (e.g., boiling drinking water) if the reasons for adoption are not communicated in a way that is consistent with the traditional beliefs of that community. Rogers's identification of different motives for adoption (i.e., technical versus social) and patterns of diffusion of new innovations has been influential in institutional studies of organizations. Researchers have extensively studied the movements of managerial innovations across groups of organizations with the key insight that the adoption of practices often depends on subjective perceptions of conformity to shared values in the broader social or institutional environment within which adoptive organizations exist.

Rational Myths

The foundation of modern institutional theory in management rests on the notion of rational myths published in a seminal paper in 1977 by John Meyer and Brian Rowan titled "Institutional Organizations: Formal Structured as Myth and Ceremony." Meyer and Rowan offered an explanation for prior observations that much organizational activity is unrelated to economic productivity. Organizations, they argue, exist in social contexts in which the rules of appropriate behavior are defined not by economic rationality but rather by *prevailing myths about what constitutes economic rationality*—in other words, taken-for-granted assumptions of what a successful organization should be. Organizations, they observe, can successfully survive by conforming to, or becoming isomorphic with, their institutional environment. The assumption that successful organizations need to have a formal personnel function is one example of a rationalized myth.

Loose Coupling

Related to the idea of rational myths is the observation, by Meyer and Rowan, that organizations often only ceremonially adopt some practices. That is, organizations often must separate and buffer their core productive functions (their technical activities) from functions adopted as a result of institutional pressures. For example, organizations often achieve loose coupling by separating the formal adoption of a practice from its implementation. Thus, during periods of economic contraction, some firms will announce large-scale employee layoffs but fail to implement them. The announcement occurs to conform to social pressures—in keeping with the rational myth that successful corporations are "lean." The failure to implement occurs because the firm recognizes that it would be unable to maintain its current productivity if it fully conformed to institutional pressures.

Legitimacy

Organizations adhere to rational myths and adopt isomorphic practices out of a desire to appear to be a legitimate organization. That is, a central assumption of institutional theory is the idea that organizations improve their odds of survival by conforming to commonly held expectations of what a successful organization should appear to be. Organizations that appear to be legitimate are more likely to access resources than organizations that do not appear to be legitimate. An organization with a formal business plan, thus, is more likely to obtain bank financing than an organization without one. Similarly, an organization with a formal equal opportunity program may be more likely to obtain federal government contracts than an organization without one. Legitimacy is obtained by adhering to the explicit rules and implicit norms of the social environment within which a firm exists.

Isomorphism

Conformity to an institutional environment is, largely, signaled by adopting structures, practices, and behaviors similar to other leading organizations. Organizations who share a common social field, therefore, will be subject to similar institutional pressures and, over time, will become more similar to, or isomorphic, with each other. This core idea was first offered by Paul J. DiMaggio and Walter W. Powell in a key paper published in 1983 and titled "The Iron Cage Revisited: Institutional Isomorphism and Collective Rationality in Institutionalized Fields." They argue that the most significant sources of social pressure to conform arise from the professions and the state. DiMaggio and Powell categorized the types of isomorphism exhibited by organizations into three types. *Coercive* isomorphism is largely political in nature and arises from organizations' need to appear legitimate to other, more powerful actors, such as the state. These rules of conformity are often, but not necessarily, explicitly articulated in the form of rules or laws. *Normative* isomorphism is the need to adopt practices assumed to be right or proper by morally significant actors, such as the professions. These rules of conformity are often, but not necessarily, implicit. Finally, *mimetic* isomorphism refers to the tendency of some organizations to copy other organizations that are perceived to be successful or legitimate under conditions of

ambiguity—that is, when the criteria for or path to success is not apparent.

These six concepts form the foundation of institutional theory in management. Collectively, they provide a model for organizational behavior that stands in sharp contrast to economic or rational choice models of firm behavior. That is, through these concepts, institutional theory suggests that organizations exist simultaneously in two worlds—a technical world where they must attend to material resources such as capital and labor, and a social world where they must attend to symbolic resources such as legitimacy and status.

Evolution

Management scholars sometimes differentiate between "old" and "new" institutionalism. Old institutionalism refers to the detailed qualitative case studies of organizations by organizational sociologists in the 1950s and 1960s. Selznick's classic study of the Tennessee Valley Authority in 1949 demarcates the beginnings of "old" institutionalism. It was followed by publication of *The Organizational Weapon* by Selznick in 1952, a study of a Leninist organization, which focused attention on the process by which organizations become "institutionalized" or take on a character and values distinct from the organizations functional or technical objectives.

New institutionalism is demarcated by the publication in 1977 of Meyer and Rowan's classic paper "Institutionalized Organizations: Formal Structure As Myth and Ceremony," followed closely by DiMaggio and Powell's 1983 paper "The Iron Cage Revisited: Institutional Isomorphism and Collective Rationality in Organizational Fields." The term "new institutionalism" captures a conceptual shift toward a view of institutions as collective cognitions or shared assumptions that, over time, acquire a degree of social concreteness. That is, they become taken-for-granted and, as a result, constrain organizational behavior. There is also a clear methodological distinction between old and new institutionalism. While old institutionalism focused attention on processes that occur inside individual organizations, new institutionalism focused on processes that occur across clusters of organizations that interact frequently with each other—a level of analysis commonly referred to as the *organizational field*.

These two foundational articles initiated an intensive examination of the processes by which institutionalized practices diffuse across organizational fields and, concomitantly, the ways in which organizations become more similar to each other. These "diffusion" studies initially focused on the process by which organizations adopt similar structures—that is, became isomorphic. An early study by Pamela S. Tolbert and Lynne G. Zucker in 1983 established a two-stage model of mimetic adoption in which some organizations initially adopt a practice for technical reasons—that is, the practice improved firm performance. Later adopters, however, do so for reasons of conformity: Adopting the practice did not improve performance but made the adoptive organization look legitimate.

Other studies focused on the mechanisms of diffusion by analyzing the factors that inhibit or promote the adoption of practices across an organizational field. Key agents that have been identified as facilitating or preventing diffusion include the professions, government, management consultants, and interlocking networks of corporate executives. Related research identified the following attributes of organizations that were subject to diffusion: functional positions in organizations, management practices such as total quality management, and strategic decisions such as mergers and acquisitions, downsizing, and long-term incentive plans.

By the early 1990s, theorists began to raise concerns about the core premise of "new" institutionalism. DiMaggio and Powell had framed their paper around the question, Why are organizations so similar? Their answer was that organizations adopt similar practices and structures in an effort to conform to their institutional environment. Critics, however, noted that not all organizations within a common organizational field are the same. Some organizations seem to be able to resist institutional pressures. They also pointed out that highly institutionalized organizational forms or practices sometimes change. Institutional theory, they argued, unfairly depicts organizations as "cultural dopes," overly influenced by collective beliefs, and this, they charged, was inaccurate.

In an early publication one of the founders of new institutionalism, Paul DiMaggio, had accounted for the possibility that institutions might change. DiMaggio identified some actors called "institutional entrepreneurs" with a unique capability of discerning and resisting the powerful influence of collective social beliefs. In a related argument, Christine Oliver observed that some organizations actively engage with and strategically resist institutional pressures to conform.

The idea that actors have the agency to resist institutional pressures and change them generated a new stream of research focusing on processes of institutional change. Early studies had suggested that institutional change could only occur exogenously— that is, by some calamitous event that occurred outside an organizational field. Later research, however, challenged this by demonstrating that marginal actors on the periphery of an organizational field were less subject to conforming pressures and were more likely to initiate change. Subsequent research extended this with the observation that some actors occupy bridging positions between different organizational fields and can initiate change by moving institutionalized ideas across organizational fields.

Scandinavian researchers challenged the notion that institutional ideas move in an intact form across organizations. They observe that institutionalized practices are often translated, or abstracted, in order to move from one place to another and then adapted to local contexts once adopted by individual organizations. Another stream of research focuses attention on the use of persuasive language, rhetoric, or discourse to facilitate change by making new templates appear to be legitimate.

A logical extension of this research has focused attention on "institutional work," or the processes by which actors engage in creating, changing, and maintaining institutions. The core idea of institutional work was introduced by Tom Lawrence and Roy Suddaby in 2006 in a paper titled "Institutions and Institutional Work." The core idea of institutional work is based on the assumption that certain actors in an organizational field acquire a degree of cognitive awareness of their institutional environments as well as a degree of skill or competence in managing or manipulating that environment. The existence of such awareness and skill is premised on the understanding that actors (both individuals and composite actors) are not complete cognitive prisoners of their institutional environment.

In sum, institutional research from the mid-1990s up to and including the present adopted a much stronger focus on agency. Organizations were no longer presented as cultural dopes but rather were seen as actively engaged in the process of adapting to, and in turn influencing, the institutional milieu in which they were embedded. Institutional theory, as a result, has become less associated with notions of blind conformity and ceremonial adoption and more interested in understanding how organizations actively influence their institutional environment.

Importance

As a theory of organizations, institutional theory has demonstrated remarkable resilience. It has transformed from a framework designed to explain organizational similarity and the absence of agency to one designed to explain organizational change and profound agency. Still, even with such a confounding transformation to its core ideology, institutional theory has managed to retain a strong thread of internal coherence. The constant within institutional theory is the assumption that organizational structures and processes acquire meaning and significance that extend beyond their technical purpose. The notion that organizations function simultaneously in technical and institutional environments provides constancy and coherence to this conceptual perspective on organizations.

Institutional theory continues to have a powerful impact on organization theory. It is the single most popular subject for recent submissions to the Organization and Management Theory division of the Academy of Management and has been described (e.g., by Royston Greenwood and colleagues) as the dominant approach to understanding organizations. Yet its impact has been relatively confined within the academy to organization theory and has failed to make a significant impact in strategic management research or in theories of organizational behavior that focus on the individual level of analysis.

Similarly, institutional theory has had relatively little influence on managers and practitioners outside academia. In part, this may be explained by its core assumptions that until recently appeared to diminish the role of management in determining organizational survival. The assumption that managers have no significant role within institutional theory, however, is inaccurate. The managerial implications of institutional theory are not absent from the theory but rather are simply not yet fully articulated. Clearly, the turn toward agency in institutional theory and the ideas around institutional work should focus attention on the idea

that actors can actively manage their institutional environments. Increasingly, managers are engaging in this type of institutional work. So, for example, in the early 21st century, business managers are increasingly engaged in issues of corporate social responsibility, which can be viewed as a way of managers directly engaging with the institutional environment. Similarly, the increasing involvement of corporations in political activity, such as funding political activities and lobbying government and regulators, is another core way in which managers attempt to control their institutional environment. Research has shown, thus, that some organizations are able to actively resist institutional pressures by, for example, shaping the content and diffusion of legal regulations. An emerging stream of studies has also identified ways in which business organizations are increasingly appropriating and internalizing elements of the public sphere—such as corporate universities, corporate armies, and corporate museums—which may also be seen as a means by which business managers are attempting to engage with an organization's institutional environment. Future research will offer a clearer elaboration of these phenomena and the role of management in institutional practices.

Roy Suddaby

See also Innovation Diffusion; Institutional Theory of Multinational Corporations; Interorganizational Networks; Neo-Institutional Theory; Process Theories of Change; Resource Dependence Theory; Social Movements; Structuration Theory

Further Readings

DiMaggio, P. J. (1988). Interest and agency in institutional theory. In L. G. Zucker (Ed.), *Institutional patterns and organizations* (pp. 3–21). Cambridge, MA: Ballinger.
DiMaggio, P. J., & Powell, W. W. (1983). The iron cage revisited: Institutional isomorphism and collective rationality in organizational fields. *American Sociological Review, 48,* 147–160.
Greenwood, R., Oliver, C. K., Sahlin, K., & Suddaby, R. (2008). *The Sage handbook of organizational institutionalism.* London, England: Sage.
Lawrence, T. B., & Suddaby, R. (2006). Institutions and institutional work. In S. R. Clegg, C. Hardy, T. B. Lawrence, & W. R. Nord (Eds.), *Sage handbook of organizations studies* (2nd ed., pp. 215–254). London, England: Sage.

Meyer, J. W., & Rowan, B. (1977). Institutionalized organizations: Formal structure as myth and ceremony. *American Journal of Sociology, 83*, 440–463.

Oliver, C. (1991). Strategic responses to institutional processes. *Academy of Management Review, 16*, 145–179.

Scott, W. R. (2001). Institutions and organizations (2nd ed.). Thousand Oaks, CA: Sage.

Selznick, P. (1949). *TVA and the grass roots: A study in the sociology of formal organization.* Berkeley: University of California Press.

Suddaby, R. (2011). Challenging institutions. *Journal of Management Inquiry, 19*(1), 14–20.

Suddaby, R., & Greenwood, R. (2005). Rhetorical strategies of legitimacy. *Administrative Science Quarterly, 50*, 35–67.

INSTITUTIONAL THEORY OF MULTINATIONAL CORPORATIONS

Scholars are applying the ideas of institutional theory to the study of multinational corporations (MNCs). The boundaries and the content of this area are not well defined, however, as a result of two factors. First, the institutional perspective itself is rather broad and comes in different variations with different foci, sets of constructs, explanatory mechanisms, and levels of analysis. Second, its application to the MNC has been somewhat limited. Thus, it cannot be claimed that a well-specified institutional theory of MNCs exists. However, a growing body of work, primarily in the international management area, has identified important building blocks of such a theory. The institutional perspective advances the central proposition that organizations are socially embedded in their institutional environments. As a result, their actions are not always motivated by economic rationality but are also affected by social considerations of appropriateness. Accordingly, institutional research studies the institutional environments of organizations and the relationships between organizations and their environments. Depending on the particular research focus and the primary discipline on which it draws, the institutional perspective branches out into several areas: institutional economics, comparative institutionalism, and organizational institutionalism, all of which have been applied to the study of MNCs. The next section of this entry provides a brief description of the broad institutional perspective and its three strands. This is followed by a summary of the institutional research in MNCs, including work on the institutional environment, the organization and its relationship with the environment, and on intraorganizational institutional processes.

Fundamentals

At the heart of institutional theory is the concept of institutions, established social structures widely accepted and approved which have achieved a taken-for-grantedness status as a result of the institutionalization process. Institutions consist of explicit rules and regulations, shared social cognitions, and social norms, all of which constrain and shape organizations. This is the deterministic, or "structure" proposition in the theory. While emphasizing the power of the environment, institutional theorists also recognize that organizations may exert some level of "agency"—that is, discretion in their response to institutional pressures. Organizations may even have an impact on their environments by engaging in "institutional entrepreneurship—in other words, facilitating institutional change and developing or promoting new institutional arrangements.

MNCs are organizations that have entities in two or more foreign countries, are actively involved in the management of these foreign operations, and regard those operations as integral parts of the company both strategically and organizationally. The cross-border nature of MNCs brings to the forefront the issue of managing their exposure to multiple and diverse countries and of coordinating their activities across different economic, political, and cultural systems.

With its focus on social embeddedness, the institutional perspective is a natural contender for the study of MNCs. It not only fits theoretically with the nature of these firms, but it also captures their essence and allows for the examination of a wide range of critical issues in MNC management, including internationalization strategies, internal organization, and competitive performance. Furthermore, because of its distinct theoretical features (e.g., institutional multiplicity and complexity), the MNC as an organization challenges institutional theory, highlights certain limitations in its traditional form, and motivates a number of modifications, extensions, and novel theoretical insights.

Institutional economics aims at explaining how the institutional order in a society impacts economic activity. The focus is mostly on the formal aspect of institutions, often defined as the rules of the game in a society (e.g., rules of competition, corruption, government involvement). The explanatory mechanisms are of economic nature. It is argued that societal institutions affect the strategic choices companies make to operate effectively in that society, because the quality of the institutions impacts the costs and risks of doing business. For example, institutional characteristics such as poor regulatory frameworks, weak rule of law, high levels of corruption, arbitrary government intervention, and instability and uncertainty in the regulatory order would negatively affect investment decisions, growth strategies, innovation activities, and performance, among many other indicators of firm outcomes.

Comparative institutionalism also focuses on societal-level institutions. In addition to applying the ideas of institutional economics in a comparative, cross-country fashion, this area also emphasizes a systems view of institutional environments and employs a more diverse disciplinary approach, including political economy and sociology, in addition to economics. It conceptualizes environments as an interdependent set of arrangements in the political, economic, and sociological strata of the society. Over time, the various institutions in a society coevolve and emerge into a relatively tightly interconnected system, captured by terms such as national business systems, national innovation systems, national governance systems, or varieties of capitalism. The primary research interest here is on the cross-country comparison of national institutional systems and the impact of such differences on firms.

Organizational institutionalism focuses primarily on the level of the organization and takes a sociological approach. Institutions are defined as established social structures (e.g., organizational practices and structures) that over time have been "infused with value"; that is, they have acquired a symbolic meaning beyond their technical functionality. Here, institutions are not limited to the formal rules but also include a cognitive and a normative element (i.e., regulatory, cognitive, and normative pillars). Furthermore, organizations face pressures to align themselves with the institutional order because in this way they can achieve legitimacy and ensure their survival and success. The environment exerts its pressures through coercive, mimetic, and normative mechanisms. In response, organizations adopt institutionalized practices and structures; adoption often reflects a desire to appear appropriate to external constituents rather than a rational decision based on cost-efficiency considerations. Organizations' compliance to such pressures leads to similarity, or isomorphism, between organizations and also ensures predictability and stability in social life. While critical for achieving organizational legitimacy, isomorphism is often suboptimal for the economic performance of organizations.

Organizational institutionalism has two distinct strands—old and new institutionalism. "Old" focuses on explaining the emergence of institutions (institutions as outcome) and discusses the role of power and politics, social interaction, value infusion, agency, and processes of institutionalization. "New" treats institutions as independent variables and examines their effects on organizations through the concepts of institutional environments and pressures, isomorphism, and legitimacy. In old institutionalism, institutions are defined at the level of the organization, whereas in new institutionalism, they are defined at the level of organizational fields. Organizational fields consist of a set of organizations typically related through business interactions that through the process of structuration, slowly come to a set of shared institutional arrangements. Recent research on institutional change, institutional entrepreneurship, and institutional work represents efforts at closing the gap between the two strands.

Importance

Understanding the nature of MNCs' institutional environments, the interdependence between MNCs and home and host countries, and the strategic response, choice, or adjustment of MNCs to their institutional context is central to MNC research. All three institutional perspectives have informed this work.

Based on *institutional economics*, scholars have examined the effects of the quality of institutions on various MNC business strategies. Quality of institutions has been measured by a variety of country-level indicators, including economic (e.g., income), political (e.g., democracy), administrative (e.g., ease of doing business), quality of education, banking system, corruption, and others. In addition, scholars have examined the overall degree of institutionalization and development of institutions in a given country or region. Notable is the work on institutional voids, which suggests that many countries, emerging and developing in particular, have institutions that are underdeveloped or inconsistent with each other. Similarly, transition economies are characterized by "institutional imperfections." In the absence of well-developed formal institutions, informal institutions become critical in controlling and coordinating social behavior. Institutional quality impacts a range of MNC strategies. The theoretical reason is that institutions, as "rules of the game," reduce uncertainty by establishing a stable structure for interactions. When the quality of institutions is poor, the cost of exchange and production goes up and organizations react by modifying their strategies. In particular, the institutional quality in MNCs' host countries affects their location decisions, entry mode (e.g., wholly owned subsidiaries and acquisitions in developed countries versus joint ventures in institutionally weak countries), product market strategies, performance, and others. Emphasizing the importance of the institutional conditions, scholars have even proposed an institution-based view of strategy.

Based on *comparative institutionalism,* scholars have examined the national origin of business systems and their institutional features and have provided in-depth comparisons between societies with regard to their business, innovation, governance, and education systems. Most of the work has focused on the comparison between the liberal market model practiced in countries such as the United States and the United Kingdom and on the coordinated market model in Germany. There is also a growing interest in the so-called state model of capitalism followed by Japan and lately China. A robust finding here is that despite the global nature of world markets, country of origin is still a strong factor in shaping organizations. MNCs are imprinted by their home national systems with regard to ownership patterns, property rights, trust in formal institutions, dominant firm type, growth patterns, innovation strategies, and control systems, and these effects are stronger than the host country effects. Furthermore, the differences between national business systems reduce MNCs' ability to transfer practices within the organization. Differences in labor markets, educational systems, and manufacturing processes, reduce MNCs' ability

to implement identical work systems among subsidiaries in different host countries.

Based on *organizational institutionalism,* in particular the conceptualization of institutions as consisting of regulatory, cognitive, and normative pillars, MNC scholars have developed the constructs of country institutional profile (CIP) and institutional distance (ID), measuring respectively the institutional environment in a given country and the difference between the institutional environments between countries. Recognizing that all three pillars are issue specific, CIPs are constructed for specific issues such as quality management, entrepreneurship, and corporate social responsibility. CIP and ID have been found to affect various organizational outcomes, including entrepreneurial activity, entry mode decisions, transfer of organizational practices within MNCs, and difficulty of establishing and maintaining legitimacy. Importantly, the different dimensions of institutional profile and distance have been found to have differential effects on business outcomes. This work has highlighted serious challenges faced by MNCs. One such challenge is the so-called *liability of foreignness* (LOF)—the additional costs incurred by MNCs compared to domestic firms because of unfamiliarity and relational and discriminatory hazards they face in a foreign country. LOF is affected by the institutional distance between home and host countries and changes over time. Possible ways to deal with LOF include ownership strategies when going abroad and isomorphism strategies in host countries. Recent research suggests a possible positive effect of foreignness. Somewhat related is the work on MNCs' political activities. The idea is that that MNCs engage in such activities in host countries to influence the relative dependency and bargaining power between the two sides and the host country's perception of the organization's legitimacy. Emerging research also looks at how MNCs can act as institutional entrepreneurs bringing about institutional change in their host countries.

More generally, recognizing that MNCs are complex organizations, both externally (exposed to multiple and possibly conflicting institutional environments), and internally (having to coordinate diverse sets of units across borders), scholars have advanced new and expanded institutional models for such organizations. MNC complexity challenges the foundational assumption of institutional theory of a well-defined organizational field. Instead, MNCs environments are multiple, fragmented, and possibly conflicting. They include the global meta-environment, the meso-environment where MNC units interact with the local country institutions, and the intraorganizational environment, which itself has a set of institutionalized practices and structures. Under such conditions, there is limited isomorphism in MNCs, as it is partly impossible and partly unnecessary to achieve. To the extent that it exists, it is diverse with regard to the reference class (e.g., host or home country; global meta-environment; and other units in the MNC). MNCs have layers of practices, each of them possibly isomorphic with a different class. This explains the wide variety of practices and structures employed by MNCs and their subunits. It also leads to external and internal tensions, as isomorphism with a particular environment creates inconsistencies with other environments. This brings to the forefront the need to reconcile differences between the different parts of the MNC organization internally as well as with the various external environments. In these conditions, achieving and maintaining legitimacy becomes a complex task. Since legitimacy granting complete isomorphism is not an option, MNCs engage in more proactive behaviors to negotiate their social approval and acceptance by their many legitimating actors.

Thus, the emerging institutional model of MNCs is very different from the one prescribed by mainstream institutional theory. It blends ideas from "new" and "old" institutionalism. It is based on institutional multiplicity and complexity, assumes relative "institutional freedom" and discretion, and includes a significant amount of agency. While still constrained by their institutional environments, MNCs' response to these pressures is not trivial, deterministic, or unitary. Managers have a substantial agency role in this process: to scan the institutional environment of the MNC, make sense of and interpret its characteristics, prioritize conflicting institutional pressures, choose areas of necessary isomorphism, build a portfolio of practices and structures that meet the complex external and internal institutional requirements, reconcile the internal and external tensions, and proactively manage legitimacy of the MNC and its subunits.

Tatiana Kostova

See also Complexity Theory and Organizations; Institutional Theory; Neo-Institutional Theory; Transnational Management

Further Readings

Kostova, T. (1999). Transnational transfer of strategic organizational practices: A contextual perspective. *Academy of Management Review, 24*(2), 308–324.

Kostova, T., & Roth, K. (2002). Adoption of an organizational practice by the subsidiaries of the MNC. *Academy of Management Journal, 45*(1), 215–233.

Kostova, T., Roth, K., & Dacin, T. (2008). Institutional theory in the study of MNCs: A critique and new directions. *Academy of Management Review, 33*(4), 994–1007.

Kostova, T., & Zaheer, S. (1999). Organizational legitimacy under conditions of complexity: The case of the multinational enterprise. *Academy of Management Review, 24*(1), 64–81.

Peng, M. (2002). Towards an institution-based view of business strategy. *Asia Pacific Journal of Management, 19*, 251–266.

Westney, E. (1993). Institutionalization theory and the multinational corporation. In S. Ghoshal & E. Westney (Eds.), *Organization theory and the multinational corporation* (pp. 53–75). New York, NY: St. Martin's Press.

Whitley, R. (2001). How and why are international firms different? In G. Morgan, P. H. Kristensen, & R. Whitley (Eds.), *The multinational firm: Organizing across institutional and national divides* (pp. 27–68). Oxford, England: Oxford University Press.

Zaheer, S. (1995). Overcoming the liability of foreignness. *Academy of Management Journal, 38*(2), 341–363.

INTEGRATIVE SOCIAL CONTRACTS THEORY

The central management insight of integrative social contracts theory (ISCT) is that confronting ethical problems in business demands the integration of universally applicable norms with specific standards that are voluntarily accepted in economic communities. The theory offers a framework for understanding when an economic act, policy, or institution is bad, good, fair, unfair, permissible, or impermissible. ISCT is a form of social contract theory. In other words, it is a theory that establishes a hypothetical social contract that spells out obligations and rights for members of an economic system. The members of the economic institutions of society are thus viewed as hypothetical "contractors," and the contracts they negotiate set the terms for ethics in business. Historically, the idea of a social contract was employed by traditional political theorists such as Thomas Hobbes, John Locke, and Jean-Jacques Rousseau, to offer a framework for understanding *political* obligations in society. ISCT, in turn, applies the idea of the social contract to economic activity, to create a framework for understanding *business* obligations. The theory is called *integrative* because it integrates two principal kinds of social contracts: the micro and the macro. These two principal elements of the theory, the macrosocial contract and the microsocial contract, are presented below.

Fundamentals

ISCT is primarily developed and advocated in the joint writings of Thomas Donaldson and Thomas Dunfee. It integrates the traditional and abstract idea of the philosophical social contract (macrosocial) with the specificity of moral understandings among participants in economic organizations (microsocial). In this manner, ISCT integrates empirical and normative research in business ethics.

Macrosocial Contracts

The *macrosocial contract* is a hypothetical agreement about a broad framework for understanding all economic arrangements. Hypothetical contractors know some things; at least they know their basic preferences and values and thus confront only a partial veil of ignorance—namely one that hides information about their personal economic endowments and roles in society. Contractors recognize the constraints of "bounded moral rationality," which means that they realize that they lack a foolproof moral calculus for sorting out economic conundrums. Second, they recognize the need for some community-based morality that will aid their group endeavors, including economic ones. They understand that such a community-based morality can help optimize their own economic and social preferences.

As a result of making these assumptions, the contractors rationally design a global—that is, macrosocial—contract with the following terms: (1) Local communities may specify ethical norms for their members through *microsocial contracts* (called "moral free space"); (2) norm-generating microsocial contracts must be grounded in informed consent buttressed by a right of community members to exit and to exercise voice within their communities; (3) to be obligatory (legitimate), a microsocial contract must be compatible with hypernorms; and (4) in case of conflicts among norms-satisfying principles 1 through 3, priority must be established through the application of rules consistent with the spirit and letter of the macrosocial contract.

Microsocial Contracts

Economic communities, understood as self-defined groups that carry on economic activity and that are capable of establishing norms of ethical behavior for themselves, generate *microsocial* contracts that establish rules for their members in moral free space. *Authentic norms* are ones that reflect agreed-on attitudes and behaviors of most members of a community. They are the practical ethical rules that guide economic communities. To create binding obligations on community members, norms must be sufficiently authentic to represent consent by the community. This is possible only when a community recognizes appropriate rights to exit and to voice. Exit opportunities should be reasonably available, although they need not be costless. The opportunity to exercise voice needs to be evaluated within the context of organizational environment and decision-making processes.

Even if a norm is authentic to a community, it will not create a binding obligation on community members if it violates universal ethical principles called *hypernorms*. Hypernorms are principles so fundamental that they constitute norms by which all other norms are to be judged. Clues to their existence can be found in the convergence of religious, political, and philosophical thought. When authentic norms are compatible with hypernorms, they become fully legitimate and create morally binding obligations. If incompatible, they are not binding. For example, the norm in a neighborhood that prescribes "Never sell your house to a person whose skin color is X" can be shown to violate the hypernorm of non-discrimination; in turn, the neighborhood norm is illegitimate and thus nonbinding on members of the neighborhood.

ISCT defines three types of hypernorms. *Procedural hypernorms* reflect the consent requirements of the macrosocial and microsocial contracts. *Substantive hypernorms* specify fundamental conceptions of right and wrong and good and bad and are exogenous to both macrosocial and microsocial contracts. Examples of substantive hypernorms include promise keeping, respect for human dignity, and the right to be informed concerning physical dangers in the workplace environment. *Structural hypernorms* recognize rights and principles essential for the establishment and successful operation of just institutions in society. Examples include the right to own property and the "hypernorm of necessary social efficiency."

Individuals making ethical judgments may at times confront conflicting legitimate norms. Many transactions span communities (e.g., a U.S. firm may do business in India) and involve conflicting norms. In such instances, ISCT recognizes a set of six priority rules for sorting among mutually exclusive legitimate microsocial norms: (1) Transactions solely within a single community, which do not have significant adverse effects on other humans or communities, should be governed by host community norms. (2) Community norms indicating a preference for how conflict of norms situations should be resolved should be applied, so long as they do not have significant adverse effects on other humans or communities. (3) The more extensive the community that is the source of the norm, the greater the priority that should be given to the norm. (4) Norms essential to the maintenance of the economic environment in which the transaction occurs should have priority over norms potentially damaging to that environment. (5) Where multiple conflicting norms are involved, patterns of consistency among the alternative norms provide a basis for prioritization. and (6) Well-defined norms should ordinarily have priority over more general, less precise norms. These rules are not meant to constitute a precise calculus. They must be weighed and applied in combination with one another.

Thomas J. Donaldson

See also CSR Pyramid; Cultural Values; Ethical Decision Making, Interactionist Model of; Moral Reasoning Maturity; Norms Theory; Social Identity Theory

Further Readings

Dempsey, J. (2011). Pluralistic business ethics: The significance and justification of moral free space in integrative social contracts theory. *Business Ethics, 20*(3), 253–266.

Donaldson, T., & Dunfee, T. W. (1994). Towards a unified conception of business ethics: Integrative social contracts theory. *Academy of Management Review, 19*(2), 252–284.

Donaldson, T., & Dunfee, T. W. (1995). Integrative social contracts theory: A communitarian conception of economic ethics. *Economics and Philosophy, 11*(1), 85–112.

Donaldson, T., & Dunfee, T. W. (1999). *Ties that bind: A social contracts approach to business ethics.* Cambridge, MA: Harvard Business School Press.

Dunfee, T. W., Smith, N. C., & Ross, W. T. (1999). Social contracts and marketing ethics. *Journal of Marketing, 63*, 14–32.

INTERACTIONAL MODEL OF CULTURAL DIVERSITY

The interactional model of cultural diversity (IMCD) posits that the type and form of diversity in a defined social system, such as a school, a business firm, or a nation, will combine with characteristics of the climate for diversity in that system to impact a variety of individual and collective (e.g., organizational, societal) outcomes. The existence of cultural diversity presents specific challenges and opportunities that, depending on the climate factors, can produce either positive or negative effects on organizational performance or societal well-being. The emphasis on climate factors as determinants or moderators of the relationship between diversity and organizational performance is a key feature of theory. Although this main tenet of the theory is thought to be applicable for understanding the dynamics of cultural diversity at the societal level of analysis, the focus of the theory is on cultural diversity *in organizations*. In addition to this basic tenet, the theory is extended through a series of 44 specific predictions, labeled *propositions*. These theoretical propositions describe how various diversity-relevant concepts relate to one another. Each of these propositions contains a piece of the philosophy about how cultural diversity impacts organizational life. Following this introduction, the fundamentals and evolution segments of this entry explain the concepts and theoretical arguments of the IMCD and how they evolved from previous theory and research. An example of the propositions of the model is given for each diversity factor discussed. Next, the importance segment briefly addresses the contribution and practical utility of the model within the field of the management sciences.

Fundamentals

Before offering a more detailed explanation of the concepts and theoretical arguments of the theory, it should be noted that the IMCD is intended to apply to a wide spectrum of types of diversity; however, the common denominator is that the types of difference must have social and cultural significance in the social system involved. The social dimension highlights the fact that individuals have group affiliations that are meaningful to members of other groups and that add an intergroup component to their life experiences. The cultural dimension means that these differences, to varying degrees, have identifiable norms, values, attitudes, mores, and traditions distinguishable from those of other groups. Therefore, the theory does not attempt to address the implications of *all* human differences. Differences such as height, introversion/extroversion, physical attractiveness, and so on may have effects on the experiences of people in organizations, but the IMCD is focused on those differences that are clearly defined in previous theory and research as social/cultural identity groups.

Diversity

The term *diversity* is defined here as differences of social and cultural group affiliations. The use of the term *affiliation* is deliberately substituted here for identity to convey the key point that people may be linked to specific social/cultural groups by others with whom they interact regardless of whether or not they personally identify with the group or adhere to the cultural norms of the group. For example,

people sometimes say they are Christians or are viewed by others as being Christians and treated accordingly, when in reality they observe few, if any, of the values and cultural traditions of the Christian religion. In the model, the term diversity has two components, type and identity strength. Type refers to the specific categories of difference present. The workforce of an organization is said to be culturally diverse when it contains a mixture of people of different social/cultural groups. The level of diversity is thus a function of the amount of social/cultural group difference that is present. This means an organization can be highly diverse on one dimension, say gender, while very low on another such as national origin. The theory views each type of diversity as having its own stream of dynamics. Thus, the level and form of gender diversity interacts with the climate *for gender diversity* to determine the impact of gender diversity in the organization and so on. Of course, most organizations have many types of diversity present and even single individuals have multiple social group affiliations. Hence there is inevitable overlap and complexity in the application of the model to specific organizational scenarios.

The term *identity strength* in the model refers to the extent to which a particular social group identity is salient in the self-concept of a person. People differ greatly in the extent to which they are conscious of, and enact behaviors based on, specific group affiliations. One of the findings related to this is that social group identity salience for individuals tends to be greater in settings where one's identity group is in the minority as opposed to other settings.

The model predicts that when people identify strongly with a social group affiliation, the climate for that dimension of diversity will have more impact on their experiences at work, their personal work outcomes, and subsequently, on the diversity-related organizational performance outcomes their work affects. It follows then that both the potential benefits and potential costs of diversity are muted to the extent that members do not acknowledge or enact behaviors related to their different group identities.

Sample theoretical proposition: Persons who identify strongly with a minority social/cultural group, to the exclusion of identification with the majority culture, will experience more negative career outcomes than persons with other social group identity structures.

Diversity Climate

The climate of organizations is complex. Here, we are concerned with specific aspects that have been shown in previous research to be especially relevant to the presence of diversity. Eleven factors are identified in the model as forming the diversity climate. Each will be defined and its connection to diversity briefly explained.

Prejudice. Here, prejudice is defined as holding predispositions to dislike or show other forms of negative attitudinal bias toward people based on their membership in a social identity group. The behavioral corollary to prejudice is discrimination.

> *Sample theoretical proposition:* Group identity-related prejudice among employees will hinder effective interpersonal relations and, ultimately, organizational performance.

Stereotyping. Although it can be viewed as a form of prejudice, stereotyping is more specifically a belief system in which individuals are assumed to have certain characteristics, levels of ability, or limitations based on their membership, or assumed membership, in a social identity group. Although theoretically an assumption of superior ability may be due to stereotyping, most stereotypes tend to have negative connotations.

> *Sample theoretical proposition:* Stereotyping behavior is prevalent in organizations, and where present, adversely affects the job performance of stereotyped members and, ultimately, organizational performance.

Personality. Some research that suggests that certain personality traits such as authoritarianism and tolerance for ambiguity are related to the climate for diversity.

> *Sample theoretical proposition:* Higher concentrations of people high on authoritarian personality will adversely affect performance in diverse groups, whereas higher concentrations of people with high tolerance for ambiguity will tend to enhance performance in diverse groups.

Cultural differences. When people of different social/cultural identity groups share a social context, they will share certain cultural traits but also represent differences of culture embedded in their respective cultural backgrounds. East Asians often experience people from Western cultures as being somewhat rude and as being short on respect for authority. Americans and people from many Arab and Asian backgrounds have very different mind-sets about physical space, and men and women tend to have certain nuances of difference in communication styles. These and other differences are based on normative standards of groups, and there is no suggestion that they apply to all individuals within any particular social identity group, but the differences of group norms do matter in some situations. It follows that the more different the cultural traditions and the stronger the identifications with the sub-group, the greater the impact this factor will have on the diversity climate.

> *Sample theoretical proposition:* Ignorance of cultural differences is a source of ineffectiveness in the work performance of diverse workgroups, whereas knowledge of cultural differences will enhance work relationships and work team effectiveness.

Ethnocentrism. Ethnocentrism is a human tendency to view social identity groups with whom one identifies as being more central, more important, or more valid than other groups. It is manifested by in-group pride and favoritism and often also by ostracism of "out-group" members. Mild behavioral forms of this tendency can be seen in organizations in things such as people of the same race or national origin grouping together for lunch or other social interactions. More extreme forms occur when in-group members are blatantly favored for promotions or other important career enhancements.

> *Sample theoretical proposition:* In general, higher levels of ethnocentric thinking and behavior, especially by cultural majority group members, will tend to lessen the potential performance benefits of diversity and increase its potential performance detriments.

Intergroup conflict. In diverse groups tension and conflict sometimes arise specifically because of *diversity-related* phenomena. For example, in a research and development organization, conflict may develop between engineers and scientists due in part to significant differences of language, goal orientations, and ways of approaching problems between the two areas of specialization. Likewise, native-born members of organizations may clash with foreign born members over the use in the workplace of languages other than the majority-group language.

Sample theoretical proposition: In diverse workgroups, the potential for diversity-related conflict between members of different social identity groups can be minimized by (a) reconciling competing goals, (b) increasing resources where possible, (c) ensuring that cultural differences are well understood, (d) ensuring that power is distributed in a representative manner consistent with genuine qualifications, and (e) affirming the identity of minority-group members.

Organizational culture. The culture of organizations consists of values, norms, and modes of operation, or mores. It is almost axiomatic that a strong culture for people in general will be useful for leveraging the potential of diversity. In addition, specific values and norms are especially relevant to cultural diversity. For example, fairness is a common organizational core value that is easily connected to diversity. Similarly, organizational norms and mores in areas such as openness to dissenting views, level of decentralization, and status consciousness are highly relevant to diversity climate.

Sample theoretical proposition: Organizations with cultures featuring norms such as openness to dissent, high decentralization, and a lower level of status consciousness will be more likely to receive the potential performance benefits of diversity than organizations with cultures containing the opposite characteristics.

Acculturation. Organizations cope with gaps between the culture of the organization and that of entering members in different ways. The methods of coping are referred to as *modes of acculturation.* Some level of required conformity in which entering members are socialized to adopt the existing cultural preferences of the organization exists in virtually all organizations. When the level of required conformity is extreme, involving a very wide spectrum of behaviors, the assimilation mode of acculturation is in place. In rare cases, there may little effort made to

conform people to a standard set of norms and values, a form of acculturation sometimes called *separation* or *deculturation.* A third commonly identified mode is pluralism, in which the organization enforces conformity to a set of core values and norms while tolerating differences in behavioral areas considered to be nonessential for the coherent pursuit of organizational goals.

Sample theoretical proposition: Organizations using pluralism as the preferred mode of acculturation in highly diverse settings will reap more of the potential benefits of diversity and avoid more of the potential performance detriments than organizations featuring other forms of acculturation.

Structural integration. The IMCD indicates that the proportional representation of subgroups in organizational settings is an important dimension of the overall climate for diversity. For example, the percentage of women in a defined workforce or other social setting and the gender balance in positions of higher authority are key characteristics of climate that affect the cost-benefit impact of a diverse population.

Sample theoretical proposition: Low proportional representation of an identity group in the workforce of an organization will create obstacles to career success of that group and, ultimately, to the effectiveness of the overall workgroup or organization.

Informal integration. While the structural integration dimension of the model deals with participation in the formal structure of organizations, this dimension recognizes the relevance of the informal organization. The IMCD predicts that access to the informal organization intersects with social identity to produce important dynamics in culturally diverse organizations. Information is shared and social capital is built or diminished in informal settings and relationships.

Sample theoretical proposition: Much of the tendency toward segregation in informal networks is due to cultural ethnocentrism by members of all social identity groups. However, the negative career impact of segregated networks will be greater for minority-group members because of power imbalances in organizations.

Human resource systems. Policies and practices that define the human resource system of an organization must be sensitive to the dynamics of a culturally diverse population. For example, some years ago when fully ambulatory people in one of the author's classes spent a day trying to get around campus in a wheelchair, it opened their eyes to numerous unintended ways in which the environment was insensitive to people who cannot walk. Performance appraisal processes that rely on self-evaluations are inherently unfair to people from cultural traditions that teach modesty. Recruiting processes that rely on a small list of elite schools put young people from lower socioeconomic backgrounds at a distinct disadvantage. These are just a few of numerous ways in which bias related to social identity groups can become institutionalized in the culture of organizations.

> *Sample theoretical proposition:* Organizations that perform HR systems audits to identify and change policies and practices that tend to create culture identity-related bias will be more successful in attracting, retaining, and using human talent than organizations that do not perform such audits.

Evolution

The IMCD is part of a large and growing body of theory and empirical research over the past two decades that has established cultural diversity, and its *management*, as factors of increasing relevance and importance to the effective management of people and the overall understanding of the functioning of organizations. Academically, the theory has its roots in pioneering work in sociology and social psychology, especially social identity theory and intergroup dynamics, and also in work from the field of organizational behavior such as that on organizational culture and equal employment opportunity. A detailed discussion of the streams of work from which the IMCD evolved is beyond the scope of this entry, but a few examples will be cited.

Previous research on social identity makes it clear that differences such as gender, national origin, race/ethnicity, socioeconomic class, religion, age cohort, and area of work specialization have both social and cultural dimensions. The structural integration concept in the model builds on streams of research, including tokenism and affirmative action. The informal organization construct of the model is grounded in the literature on mentoring and social networks; the treatment of acculturation in the model borrows heavily from work on mergers and acquisitions. In addition, the IMCD also builds on writings from the early 1990s on the concept of diversity, including pioneering writers such as Marilyn Loden and Judy Rosener, Roosevelt Thomas, John Fernandez, Lennie Copeland, and Susan Jackson, as well as the author's own earlier writings.

The impetus to create the IMCD derived from a desire to address what many viewed as a significant gap in the management literature, a gap defined by an increasing presence of diversity in the workplace coupled with a dearth of theory and empirical research addressing the impact of diversity on organizational behavior and effectiveness. It was also born of a desire to address a series of interrelated pressing social and economic challenges of our time—namely, the need for a more full use of, and opportunity for, people of all social/cultural backgrounds to reach their full potential and the need to capture the power of diversity to enhance organizational performance and to avoid or minimize its potential to detract from it. In this context, the generic scope of diversity incorporated in the model is paramount. The goals just mentioned were equally relevant for differences of physiological ability, gender, national origin, race, and so on. However, concerns about a better understanding of the impact of differences of race, gender, and national origin were especially potent because of the globalization of the workforce and demographic trends in the workforce of the United States indicating that it was going to be increasingly racially diverse and that women were participating in record numbers. It was in this context that the IMCD was conceived, and although it has undergone minor adjustments over the past nearly two decades, the ideas originally convened in the model remain largely unchanged.

Importance

As noted earlier, the IMCD is grounded in the idea that the climate for diversity, as defined above, moderates or determines the nature and impact of diversity on various outcomes. These outcomes include individual factors such as job mobility and compensation, group-level factors such as the quality of group communications and team problem solving, and ultimately organizational-level factors such as recruiting success, employee turnover, customer satisfaction and market share. In the United States, certain core dimensions of diversity such as race/ethnicity and national origin continue to increase at a high rate of change. Organizations that fail to achieve and maintain a welcoming climate for this diversity will find it increasingly difficult to attract, retain, and receive the full potential of contribution from the best available human talent and to market successfully to a culturally diverse customer base. The interactional model provides a framework for analyzing and changing organizations by identifying the key factors of cultural diversity and making specific predictions about how they relate to one another and to organizational effectiveness. The core model and the propositions derived from it form a comprehensive view of the challenges and opportunities of cultural diversity.

One way to characterize the contribution of the theory is that it summarized in one conceptual framework many critical streams of work and then attempted to extend that work by making new or qualitatively different statements about how concepts from those streams interrelate. Another way to speak about impact relates to the theme that runs through the theory that connects diversity dynamics to organizational performance. Although with some, the proposition remains controversial that the presence of diversity, at least if properly managed, creates a resource that can increase organizational performance, one may fairly point out that it has gained a much larger following as a result of the work described here and a great deal of related work by other authors (see Further Readings list at the end of this entry for examples).

While the sheer complexity of the model makes an empirical test of the full theory impractical, studies conducted both before and after the theory was originally published have confirmed the veracity of various propositions of the theory. The author's research of variables represented in the theory conducted during consulting projects in more than 100 organizations over the past two decades supports the value of the theory to promote understanding of how diversity impacts organizational life and goal achievement.

It is hoped that this revisiting of the IMCD theory will spur even more research and theory construction, as well as assist practitioners in constructing more sophisticated, proactive approaches to leading diverse workgroups. As stewards of our social and economic landscape, it is vital for us to continue to advance our knowledge in this area of management science as we prepare for a future in which cultural diversity will be an ever more salient feature of the world in which we live and work.

Taylor Cox Jr.

See also Competitive Advantage; Fairness Theory; Group Development; Managing Diversity; Organizational Demography

Further Readings

Abrams, D., & Hogg, M. A. (1990). *Social identity theory.* New York, NY: Springer-Verlag.

Blake-Beard, S. D., Finley-Hervey, J. A., & Harquail, C. V. (2008). Journey to a different place: Reflections on Taylor Cox, Jr.'s career as a catalyst for diversity education and training. *Academy of Management Learning & Education, 7(3),* 394–405.

Copeland, L. (1988). Valuing workplace diversity. *Personnel Administrator, 33(11),* 38, 40.

Ely, R. J., & Thomas, D. A. (2001). Cultural diversity at work: The effects of diversity of perspectives on work group processes and outcomes. *Administrative Management Quarterly, 46(2),* 229–273.

Fernandez, J. P. (1991). *Managing a diverse workforce.* Lexington, MA: Lexington Books.

Jackson, S. E. (1992). *Diversity in the workplace.* New York, NY: Guilford.

Konrad, A. M., Prasad, P., & Pringle, J. K. (Eds.). (2006). *Handbook workplace diversity.* London, England: Sage.

Loden, M., & Rosener, J. B. (1991). *Workforce America.* Homewood, IL: Business One Irwin.

Thomas, R. T., Jr. (1991). *Beyond race and gender.* New York, NY: American Management Association.

Williams, K. Y., & O'Reilly, C. A., III. (1998). Demography and diversity in organizations: A review of 40 years of research. In B. M. Staw & L. L. Cummings (Eds.), *Research in organizational behavior* (Vol. 20, pp. 77–140). Greenwich, CT: JAI Press.

INTERACTIONIST MODEL OF ORGANIZATIONAL CREATIVITY

Organizational creativity is commonly defined as the creation or generation of a valuable, useful new product, service, idea, procedure, or process by individuals working together in a complex social system. This definition includes the two key dimensions of creativity or creative behavior: (1) originality, or novelty, and (2) value, or utility. As such, this definition of organizational creativity can be considered an extension of commonly accepted definitions of individual creativity into the organizational context. Similarly, the interactionist model of organizational creativity was developed from an interactionist model of creative behavior at the individual level. The individual level model grew out of a desire to develop a theoretical lens for examining creative behavior that would avoid the fragmentation created by the multiple perspectives on or explanations for creativity that existed in the field. This developmental path has its origins in the notion of an interactionist perspective as a meaningful way to understand human behavior. This entry explores the interactionist perspective on behavior, the origins of the interactionist model of creative behavior, the defining characteristics of the interactionist model of organizational creativity, and the implications of this theory for further research and managerial practice.

Fundamentals

The Interactionist Perspective on Behavior

Personality theorists have had a long tradition of competing explanations for human behavior that have oscillated between extreme positions where personality was considered to be completely determined by heredity versus the notion that the individual differences we think of as personality are explained solely by the environment (the classic *nature versus nurture* debate). In contemporary times, a balance of sorts has become the most commonly accepted position. Most psychologists today, working in the personality arena, argue that personality is determined both by genetics and by the influence of the environment or situation, though they might disagree about the relative contributions of heredity and learning. The "nature versus nurture" debate in personality development finds a parallel in a fundamental dichotomy concerning the origins of human behavior: How best to theorize about the human being? Is behavior largely a function of characteristics and attributes of the person, or is human behavior most readily explained by the situation or context within which the behavior occurs?

As with personality, the *interactionist* position is also the predominant one with regard to the larger issue of human behavior in general. That is, an interactionist perspective on behavior suggests that the behavior of an individual, at any moment, is determined both by the situation within which the individual is behaving and by what the individual brings to the situation, so to speak. In other words, behavior is a function of both characteristics of the person and aspects of the situation or context. Interactionist psychology (sometimes called interactional psychology) has become such a mainstream notion that the terminology has almost disappeared from the literature. One would be hard-pressed to find a behavioral scientist who would argue that an understanding of behavior could rely solely on specifying the "environmental press" or, on the other hand, rely solely on understanding personality and other important individual differences. Simply put, most behavioral scientists view behavior as a function of both person and situation. In the same vein, theorists and researchers concerned with explaining creative behavior have developed a variety of perspectives that have mirrored the theoretical debates occurring with regard to behavior in general.

Individual Creativity From the Interactionist Perspective

The interactionist perspective on creativity is based, most fundamentally, on the notion explained above; that is, all behavior, including creative behavior, is a function of person and situation. Further, the development of the interactionist model of creative behavior, which was the forerunner of the interactionist model of organizational creativity explained below, was informed by the seminal theoretical contributions to the psychological sciences of Hans Eysenck—most specifically, his approach to "modeling" human behavior. Eysenck's work focused very much on understanding the psychology of individual differences and, one suspects, he would have been very surprised to be given any intellectual credit for a theoretical position that is so heavily interactionist. Nevertheless, his approach to understanding human behavior, while emphasizing the attributes and characteristics of the individual, is quite interactionist at some level of abstraction. He advocated exploring all the possible explanatory variation related to a behavioral outcome, certainly including the environmental press or context within which the behavior occurs.

Similar to the ancient parable of a blind man describing an elephant, various theoretical perspectives on creative behavior have tended, historically, to focus on particular sources of explanatory variation to the exclusion of other influences. For example, a theory of creativity developed from the perspective of developmental psychology might explain creativity as most significantly influenced by early life experiences. Most central to our discussion here, many theories of creative behavior have been developed from one of three major perspectives: (1) personality explanations for differences in creativity, (2) cognitive style or ability explanations, and (3) social psychology. Each of these perspectives has demonstrated insight and explanatory power, yet each suffers from the same shortcoming of presenting a partially valid but incomplete explanation for human creativity. Social psychological explanations of creativity are probably closest to the interactionist perspective presented here, in that theories developed from that perspective emphasize the importance of social interaction and typically include a number of social and environmental influences on creative behavior.

The interactionist model of creative behavior incorporates elements of the personality, cognitive, and social psychology explanations of creativity. Creativity is viewed as a complex person-situation interaction that depends on antecedent conditions to the current situation, the current situation, the current state as well as stable attributes of the person, and the interaction of these sources of explanatory variance. Characteristics of the "person" that influence creativity include both cognitive (e.g., information-processing abilities, cognitive "styles") and noncognitive (e.g., personality, beliefs, attitudes) attributes. The "situation" consists of both contextual and social influences (e.g., social interactions with others, work relationships, and so on). In sum, the interactionist model of individual creativity was developed to provide a theoretical lens or framework that would be inclusive, rather than exclusive, with regard to possible sources for or explanations of creative behavior. This interactionist model has been extended into the organizational context.

Organizational Creativity From the Interactionist Perspective

The interactionist model of organizational creativity may be summarized as follows: The creative behavior of organizational participants is a complex interaction influenced by events of the past as well as salient aspects of the current situation (e.g., the "social" context, characteristics of the work setting). Within the person, both cognitive (e.g., knowledge, cognitive abilities) and noncognitive (e.g., personality) aspects of the mind are related to creative behavior. In sum, creative behavior in a complex social system is a function of many aspects of person and situation: cognitive style and ability; personality factors; attitudes and beliefs; motivation; relevant knowledge; influences from coworkers; membership in various groups and teams; contextual influences, including task demands and constraints; and so on. In the organization, the theoretical model assumes that these complex interactions are repeated at each level of social organization. That is, group or team creativity is a function of individual creative behavior "inputs," the interaction of individuals involved, various characteristics of the group that impact creativity, and characteristics of the organization that impact group functioning. The creativity of the organization is a function of the creative inputs of its component groups and teams and of various contextual influences at the organizational level (e.g., organizational culture, reward systems, resource availability) that impact individual and group creativity. The gestalt of creative output (new products, services, ideas, procedures, and processes) for the entire social system stems from the complex mosaic of individual, group, and organizational characteristics and behaviors that occur within the various situational influences (both creativity constraining and creativity enhancing) existing at each level of social organization. Of course, such a description does not richly capture the dynamic nature of reciprocal causation with its many possible feedback loops. Further, creativity, as with all other types and patterns of behavior, represents a process that unfolds over time. The reader is referred to the suggested readings at the end of this entry for a fuller description of organizational creativity from the interactionist perspective.

The basic explanations for creative behavior within an organization can be usefully summed up by three propositions (which provide, perhaps, a more straightforward way of stating the points made in the previous paragraph):

Proposition 1: The creative performance or behavior of individuals in an organization depends on (a) characteristics possessed by these individuals, (b) social influences that enhance or constrain individual creativity, and (c) contextual influences that enhance or constrain individual creativity.

Proposition 2: The creative performance or behavior of groups and teams in an organization depends on (a) the creative performance of group members, (b) aspects of the group or team that enhance or constrain creativity, and (c) contextual influences that enhance or constrain the group's or team's creativity.

Proposition 3: The creative performance of the organization depends on the creative performance of the groups and teams of which it is composed as well as other aspects of the organization that enhance or constrain creativity.

Importance

A number of important implications for both creativity research and the effective management of organizations can be developed from an interactionist perspective on organizational creativity. Space does not permit a detailed exploration of these implications so, again, the reader is referred to the list of suggested readings that accompanies this entry.

Among other things, an interactionist approach suggests that research on organizational creativity must cross levels of analysis. Many of the social and contextual influences on creative behavior represent cross-level influences. For example, characteristics of the organization, such as information flows and communication channels, could either enhance or constrain group or team creativity. Characteristics at the group level—for example, certain group norms—might either enhance or constrain the creativity of individual group members. And so on—the possible examples are legion. Indeed, there is a wealth of accumulated research in the organizational sciences pointing to such cross-level influences. Based on extant knowledge in the field, it appears that a theory of organizational creativity that did not include

such potentially important sources of explanatory variance would be woefully incomplete. Further, the complex person-situation interactions that are central to understanding organizational creativity and the creative process in organizations emphasize the importance of longitudinal field research to advance our understanding of organizational creativity.

With regard to implications for practice, research to date suggests that, in the person-situation interaction that lies at the heart of organizational creativity, possibly the most important managerial focus should be on managing the "creative situation" or context. Understanding characteristics of the person—the cognitive and noncognitive aspects of the mind crucial for understanding creative behavior—will always be important. Still, with the obvious exception of selecting creative "talent" for the organization, it may be less useful to focus on the "person" in person-situation interactions than on the situation, at least from the perspective of managerial action. The argument here is based in part on the notion that it can be quite counterproductive to attempt to manage too closely either creative persons or, at some level of abstraction, the creative process. Both extant research and the interactionist model of organizational creativity suggest that many contextual factors that influence creative behavior and creative outcomes in organizations can be identified. These factors can be conceptualized as essentially either increasing or reducing the probability of creative behavior. From this perspective, the "high-payoff" strategy for management is to design and manage the situation—that is, to design into the situation factors that increase the probability of creative outcomes and to remove from the situation those factors that inhibit or reduce creativity. The situational factors are what we manage rather than creativity *per se.*

Richard W. Woodman

See also BVSR Theory of Human Creativity; Componential Theory of Creativity; Dual-Core Model of Organizational Innovation; Ethical Decision Making, Interactionist Model of; Investment Theory of Creativity; Patterns of Innovation; Stages of Creativity; Stages of Innovation

Further Readings

Amabile, T. M. (1983). *The social psychology of creativity.* New York, NY: Springer-Verlag.

Amabile, T. M. (1988). A model of creativity and innovation in organizations. In B. M. Staw & L. L. Cummings (Eds.), *Research in organizational behavior* (Vol. 10, pp. 123–167). Greenwich, CT: JAI Press.

Eysenck, H. J. (1982). *Personality, genetics, and behavior: Selected papers.* New York, NY: Praeger.

Ford, C. (1996). A theory of individual creative action in multiple social domains. *Academy of Management Review, 21,* 1112–1142.

Shalley, C. E., Zhou, J., & Oldham, G. R. (2004). The effects of personal and contextual characteristics on creativity. *Journal of Management, 30,* 933–958.

Woodman, R. W., & Schoenfeldt, L. F. (1989). Individual differences in creativity: An interactionist perspective. In J. A. Glover, R. R. Ronning, & C. R. Reynolds (Eds.), *Handbook of creativity* (pp. 77–91). New York, NY: Plenum Press.

Woodman, R. W., & Schoenfeldt, L. F. (1990). An interactionist model of creative behavior. *Journal of Creative Behavior, 24,* 279–290.

Woodman, R. W., Sawyer, J. E., & Griffin, R. W. (1993). Toward a theory of organizational creativity. *Academy of Management Review, 18,* 293–321.

Zhou, J., & Shalley, C. E. (Eds.). (2008). *Handbook of organizational creativity.* Mahwah, NJ: Lawrence Erlbaum.

Zhou, J., & Shalley, C. E. (2010). Deepening our understanding of creativity in the workplace. In S. Zedeck et al. (Eds.), *APA handbook of industrial-organizational psychology* (Vol. 1, pp. 275–302). Washington, DC: American Psychological Association.

Interorganizational Networks

An interorganizational network is defined as a set of organizations related through common affiliations or through exchange relations. Examples of such networks include interorganizational joint product ventures, strategic business alliances, supply and distribution channels, industry trade associations, governance councils, or human services networks of education, welfare, police, and hospitals in communities. Interorganizational networks are not defined by a particular theory, nor are they considered a theory themselves; instead, a collection of theories is used to explain their structure and influence. In this entry, three theories that underlie most studies of interorganizational networks are explained: (1) social dependence and exchange theory, (2) brokerage or structural hole theory, and (3) closure or social conformity theory. These theories explain why organizations form relations and how certain structural positions within a network advantage and disadvantage some organizations over others of similar ability. Those in favorable network positions have greater social capital, meaning they can draw on valuable resources or helping behaviors through their network relationships. There is also growing research attention in understanding of how networks evolve over time. These studies explain the formation of present ties and network structures based on past relations and structures.

Fundamentals

Research on interorganizational networks is a subdomain of social network analysis, which includes analysis at levels more micro (e.g., among individuals and groups) and more macro (e.g., industries and nations). Methods of social network analysis are typically used to study the structure and evolution of relations among organizations in a network. This methodology adopts the vocabulary of nodes and ties to represent organizations and relationships among them (respectively). Ties represent a type of connection joining the nodes. Ties may be bonding relationships in which organizations share common affiliations, such as joint ventures, or ties may signify flows of resources, such as information, human capital, goods, or client referrals. Multiplex ties often exist among organizations in a network, which means that ties may involve multiple types of resources or may connect at multiple levels in the organizations, making relationships more complex and more difficult to dissolve. These ties could represent ownership investments, buyer-seller exchanges, or myriad other affiliation or exchange relations.

Social Exchange Theory

According to resource dependence theory, all organizations depend on other organizations in their environment for resources and inputs vital to their functioning and survival. As they establish exchange relationships with and become dependent on other organizations for resources, the latter gain in relative power over the former. This classical view of asymmetric power in social exchange suggests that parties seek to minimize their dependence on other parties and to maximize the dependence of others on them. Organizations seeking external resources from other, more powerful parties try to counteract those parties' power advantage by positioning themselves in a resource network. Specifically, they can enhance their position in the network by establishing numerous ties with potential resource providers (and thereby reduce their dependence by having numerous alternative suppliers) and by restricting or mediating access to resource exchange ties they have that others value.

A less instrumental view of social exchange recognizes the social embeddedness of relationships. As parties interact and negotiate their relationships, they also gain awareness, affiliation and interdependence to shared norms and goals. Following a sense of security that is provided by embedded and closed networks, parties feel less vulnerable to opportunistic behavior. This allows them to focus on the joint (or total) dependencies among parties in a network. It suggests that parties involved in highly interdependent relationships may have a richer and deeper level of interaction that has beneficial outcomes for all parties

Brokerage or Structural Holes Theory

Brokerage or structural holes theory explains how organizations can gain an advantage over others by maintaining a broker, or middle-person, position in the network. The opportunity to broker occurs because networks often possess clusters of organizations that are more densely connected, but these clusters are not attached to one another. The nonexistence of ties between clusters creates a structural hole.

In a brokerage position, an organization can access resources through the bridging tie that other organizations cannot. Brokers can also exploit their position by controlling the flow of resources between otherwise unconnected organizations. Access to and control of resources increases social capital, which advantages the broker. On the other hand, if an organization has many redundant ties—which eliminates the brokerage position—the organization has access to the same resources that other organizations can access. There is nothing unique about the flow of resources among organizations. In such instances, social capital will be relatively homogenous among actors. It is the brokerage position, then, with no redundant ties that gives firms unequal access to and control of resources.

Closure or Social Conformity Theory

Closure exists in dense networks in which organizations have many ties with one another. Closure allows for the accumulation of social capital, both to individual organizations and to the network as a whole. Norms can be enforced since organizations are aware of the actions of all other organizations in the network. If an organization acts roguishly (e.g., it fails to honor an obligation to another organization), other network members will learn of it and sanction the rogue organization (e.g., halt relations with the rogue firm). If closure does not exist, then only the victimized organization can sanction the rogue member, which has less effect. Thus, closure is important for the formation of norms and the development of trustworthiness. Norms or reciprocity and trustworthiness act as a common form of social capital available to all the members of the network.

At the level of individual organizations, social capital is built based on the accumulation of obligations other network members owe an organization. Based on norms of reciprocity, an organization that does something for an alter, such as sharing resources or giving help, accumulates an obligation outstanding. At some future time, the alter must repay the obligation owed to the organization. An actor who accumulates many obligations outstanding is able to recall these when desired. The ability to recall obligations gives the actor greater social capital.

Network Change Over Time

Network change over time is explained both by the dynamics within relations and by structural characteristics surrounding relations. Within a dyad (two organizations with a tie), relations emerge, strengthen, and decay over time through repeated cycles of bargaining, commitment, and execution activities. Relations are more likely to persist when they are viewed as equitable and efficient by both organizations.

A tie between two organizations can be influenced by a third organization—the three together making a triad. Both transitivity and structural balance explain the impact of triads on ties. Transitivity exists in the presence of strong ties. When strong ties exist, it is likely for organizations to associate frequently, to be located close to one another, and to be similar to each other. Time, proximity, and similarity all lead to a greater likelihood that firms with ties to a common third organization will also form a tie.

Structural balance considers whether the ties in a triad are positive or negative—whether organizations are cooperative allies or competitive rivals. The three ties in a triad are balanced if all three ties are positive or if two of the three ties are negative and the other tie is positive. The latter balanced triad represents the familiar proverb, "The enemy of my enemy is my friend." If a triad is unbalanced, then structural balance suggests that one of the ties will change sign (from positive to negative, or vice versa) or a tie will dissolve. Both managers' need to avoid cognitive dissonance, and organizations' strategic moves account for the tendency to move from unbalanced to balanced triads.

Importance

Empirical support has been found in interorganizational networks for each of the theories. However, a number of questions remain for future research, particularly in the area of network evolution and the performance of whole networks. Most network research to date has focused on structure in static ways, and future research needs to explain processes of network formation, development, and dissolution over time. Some informative research at the level of the dyad and triad does exist, but other patterns of network evolution are relatively unexplored. Little is known about the development of interorganizational cliques and status as they evolve over time. Research on the overall patterns of network evolution is also needed to understand how they grow and decline, how they become more closed or open, and how they become more structurally diverse or similar.

Concerning performance, most studies have examined competitive advantage for individual organizations positioned in networks; relatively few have addressed whole network structure and performance. For instance, a set of organizations may be networked together as a supply chain, and they compete against other sets of firms networked together in rival supply chains. The cooperative benefits and vulnerabilities of the collective network of symbiotically related members that compete against other networks need further study. Also, little is known about the part-whole relationship between the performance of individual organizations and the performance of the entire network. Structural hole theory explains how individual organizations gain advantage because of their position in the network. However, research has not yet shown whether the benefits gained by brokers translate into more or fewer benefits for the entire network.

Managers who are aware of the position of their organizations in the larger network can use this understanding to make better-informed decisions. Understanding network position relative to other organizations—both collaborators and competitors—can clarify structural constraints and opportunities that impede and empower organizational action. If managers are cognizant of not only their interorganizational relationships but also the relationships among other organizations, then managers can develop strategies to foster new relationships or alter their existing relationships to change the network structure to their advantage or, in the case of cooperative networks, to increase the welfare of the whole network.

Stephen Jones and Andrew H. Van de Ven

See also Institutional Theory; Multifirm Network Structure; Resource Dependence Theory; Social Exchange Theory; Social Network Theory; Strategic Alliances; Value Chain

Further Readings

Borgatti, S. P., & Halgin, D. S. (2011). On network theory. *Organization Science, 22,* 1168–1181.

Burt, R. S. (1992). The social structure of competition. In N. Nohria & R. Eccles (Eds.), *Networks and organizations* (pp. 65–103). Boston, MA: Harvard Business School Press.

Coleman, J. S. (1988). Social capital in the creation of human capital. *American Journal of Sociology, 94,* S95–S120.

Grannovetter, M. (1973). The strength of weak ties. *American Journal of Sociology, 78*(6), 1360–1380.

Gulati, R., & Gargiulo, M. (1999). Where do interorganizational networks come from? *American Journal of Sociology, 104*(5), 1439–1438.

Pfeffer, J., & Salancik, G. (1978). *The external control of organizations: A resource dependence perspective.* Stanford University Press: Stanford, CA.

Powell, W. W., White, D. R., Koput, K. W., & Owen-Smith J. (1996). Network dynamics and field evolution: The growth of interorganizational collaboration in the life sciences. *American Journal of Sociology, 110*(4), 1132–1205.

Ring, P. S., & Van de Ven, A. H. (1994). Developmental processes of cooperative interorganizational relationships. *Academy of Management Review, 19,* 90–118.

Uzzi, B. (1997). Social structure and competition in interfirm networks: The paradox of embeddedness. *Administrative Science Quarterly, 42*(1), 35.

Zaheer, A., & Soda, G. (2009). Network evolution: The origins of structural holes. *Administrative Science Quarterly, 54*(1), 1–31.

INTUITIVE DECISION MAKING

In the vernacular, intuition is equated with "trusting your gut" and involves knowing something without knowing how you know it. A subject of scholarly discourse for hundreds of years, intuition has become a topic in management primarily in the last few decades. While conceptualizations in philosophy, psychology, and management vary to some degree, Erik Dane and Michael Pratt suggest four characteristics that are fundamental to intuiting. With regard to the process of intuitive decision making, or intuiting, they note that information processing during intuiting is (a) nonconscious, (b) happens quickly, (c) holistic rather than analytic, and (d) affectively charged, from start to finish. With regard to the outcomes of intuiting, we argue that intuiting results in the formation of a judgment. Put plainly, intuition is a relatively fast way to make judgments that involves seeing patterns across data or stimuli. The process of intuition occurs outside conscious awareness; thus, one arrives at a judgment without knowledge of what went into that judgment. Intuiting is also infused with emotions. Researchers suggest that emotions (especially positive ones) can trigger the intuitive process; emotions can be part of the intuitive processing of information; and the intuitive judgment one arrives at also has an affective tint to it (e.g., one might feel positive and confident). This entry distinguishes intuition from other types of decision making, provides an overview of what makes for "effective" intuiting, and discusses some controversies in the field. It concludes by proposing some future research directions as well as practical managerial implications of extant research.

Fundamentals

Intuiting is most often contrasted with rational decision making. The latter is often conceptualized as conscious, deliberate, analytical, and according to some, largely devoid of emotion. Some suggest that intuition and rational decision making may even correspond to different information-processing systems within human beings (e.g., experiential vs. rational, or System 1 vs. System 2). However, the existence of two separate or dual information-processing systems has been questioned in recent years.

Intuition is often confused with "guessing," "instinct," and "insight." Although fast, intuition is different from blind guessing; it involves drawing on deeply ingrained cognitive structures, such as heuristics or schemas, to make affectively charged associations. As a consequence, individuals tend to have more confidence in intuition than in guesses. Intuition is different from instinct in that the former draws on experience, while the latter is based on one's biological "hardwiring," such as automatic reflexes. Intuition is also different from insight, which involves both conscious deliberation (and thus is not totally nonconscious) and an incubation period (which makes it slower than intuiting).

Apart from identifying what it is, much research has focused on when intuition is likely to be effective. Historically, rational analytic approaches are often seen as providing superior outcomes compared with intuition, although this decision-making process is much slower. Hence, some talk about a speed versus effectiveness trade-off in decision making. Intuitions, however, can yield better outcomes than rational models depending on (1) the level of the experience of the decision maker and (2) the nature of the task at hand. Put simply, individuals who have a lot of experience (i.e., experts) in a particular area are primed to be more effective with intuition than rational decision making depending on the type of task they face. By expert is meant someone who has learned domain-relevant information either consciously—through deliberate practice and receiving quick and relevant feedback—or unconsciously (i.e., implicit learning) by paying close attention to one's environment. While there is no "magic number" of practice time needed to become an expert, some estimates place it at 10 years, while others 10,000 hours.

Experts, however, are most effective in their use of intuitive decision making when the task at hand is one where there is more than one right answer (i.e., judgmental) or where the task cannot easily be subdivided and attended to in smaller chunks (i.e., nondecomposable). These types of tasks are common in human resource management, strategic, aesthetic, and investment decisions. In short, intuition is most effective when experts are performing judgmental and holistic tasks.

Importance

As noted, intuition is of critical interest to management scholars given its promise to overcome the trade-off in decision making between speed and effectiveness. While research on intuition in the fields of management and organizational studies has increased in recent years, work in this area has spawned three major areas of concern that have limited its conceptual development and its impact on practice.

Is intuition effective, and if so, when? Intuitions are common, but are they good? Although the conditions for effective intuition are noted above, these arguments are controversial. There has been a historical divide—spearheaded by the work of Nobel Prize winners—on whether or not intuition is an effective means of making decisions. On one side of the divide, research following in the tradition Amos Tversky and Daniel Kahneman has argued that intuitive decision making is often less effective than rational decision making and thus should be avoided. In this tradition, intuitive decision making is linked to the use of relatively simply heuristics (e.g., the representative heuristic) employed in solving highly structured, intellective tasks (e.g., tasks for which one can arrive at a single "right" answer through the application of rules of probability). On the other side, research following in the tradition of Herbert Simon links intuition with complex schemas; consequently, this research argues that certain intuitions, such as those employed by chess masters, can be remarkably effective. The historical controversy has been rendered less controversial as scholars have begun to identify the conditions under which intuition may be most effective. Here, we have named two such conditions: level of expertise of the decision maker and the structure of the task at hand. Some research also finds an interaction between these two conditions, such that expertise brought to bear on judgmental or nondecomposable tasks will lead to the highest level of intuitive decision-making effectiveness.

How many types of intuition exist? A second area of controversy is whether there is one type of intuition or many. While some scholars are adamant that intuition should not be subdivided, others suggest that intuition may be meaningfully divided by the functions it serves: problem solving, moral, and creative intuition. Problem-solving intuition refers to the bulk of research in the area of management reviewed above. The mechanisms underlying problem-solving intuition are pattern matching and recognition.

To illustrate, expert chess players, as studied by Simon and colleagues, are able to make rapid, holistic judgments by matching the chess pieces on the board to elements within their own internalized schemas to ascertain which set of moves to make. While the schema/pattern recognition arguments are common in intuition research, Stuart Dreyfus offers compelling evidence to suggest that learning may result in direct synaptic modification rather than the formation of schemas. But however such experiences are represented or stored, problem-solving intuition is about attending to solving dilemmas.

Another "type" of intuition is moral intuition. Much research in this area builds on the work of Jonathan Haidt's "social intuitionist" perspective (see also the "universal moral grammar" perspective). Moral intuitions are thought to arise from processes similar to those associated with problem-solving intuitions. Both are rapid and involve matching to existing schemas (though they are referred to as "moral prototypes" in this line of research). The biggest difference is that the level of affect associated with moral intuitions (e.g., a feeling that it is always wrong to do *x*) tends to be very intense. Such affective intensity is not necessarily found in problem-solving intuition.

A third and final type of intuition, and the one that is the most controversial, is creative intuition. Unlike problem-solving and moral intuition where a judgment is based on "matching" a situation with an internalized schema, resulting in a convergent categorization (i.e., this is wrong), creative intuition involves more divergent thinking that ultimately results in a solution that is novel and useful—thus moving beyond the preexisting contents of one's schemas. Specifically, creative intuition views intuition—here in the form of synthesizing heretofore unrelated elements into new combinations—as a central contributing factor the creative process. In addition to its more divergent processing, creative intuition often is not immediate. Work by Ap Dijksterhius and colleagues, for example, suggests that this intuition, like insight, may involve an incubation period. While differing on some dimensions, creative intuition is like moral intuition in that it is often associated with relatively intense affective experiences.

How do you measure intuition? A final controversy concerns the measurement of intuition. While the bulk of work on intuition in organizational research remains theoretical, the relatively few attempts to empirically capture intuition showcase some methodological challenges. Some argue that certain individuals have a preference for using intuition and that this preference can be measured as a dependable individual difference. However, these measures do not tend to ascertain the presence of intuiting; rather, they assess one's tendency to trust or rely on intuitions. Others argue that intuition can be prompted, like a behavior, under controlled conditions. These measures, however, fail to measure whether intuition is actually being used by a subject. At the other extreme, advances in neurology and physiology have attempted to directly assess the presence of intuiting through measures such as galvanic skin responses or brain imaging. However, such procedures are costly and often complex, and because of the equipment needed, occur under very artificial circumstances. Some research looking at intuition in moral situations attempts to overcome these shortcomings by using a combination of scenario-based studies and brain imaging; however, these, too, by necessity, occur in artificial situations. In attempts to get at intuition "in the field," some research uses retrospective reports. But these may be suspect because of post-hoc interpretations and recollections. To counter this deficit, one could ask someone to narrate an intuitive decision to a researcher in real time, but this would depend on making a nonconscious process more conscious. In short, there is not yet an agreed-on method for measuring intuition. While many options exist, each carries some significant challenges.

Toward Future Research

As intuition research progresses, especially within the organizational realm, it is likely to continue to probe the contextual conditions that foster intuitive decision making, especially effective intuitive decision making. Research examining problem-solving intuitions, in particular, will likely continue to investigate the types of tasks most amenable to intuiting,

as well as the temporal, social, and knowledge acquisition factors most associated with improving the quality of intuitive judgments. Given recent corporate scandals, research on the use of intuition in moral decision making may also be fruitful. It is interesting that both psychologists and sociologists are converging on a similar conclusion: that the basis for moral intuitions is cultural. That is, societal norms and values become internalized by individuals and form the bedrock for moral intuitions. Research on moral intuitions, therefore, may begin to look at how these norms and values are transmitted to individuals and the degree to which they are "set" even before individuals join organizations. The role of intuition in creativity begs the question of whether creative intuitions are really intuitions at all or whether they are, in fact, some combination of intuitive and other forms of decision making. Future research in this area, as well as in the others, should examine whether and how intuition interacts with analysis, insight, and the like to produce creative, as well as moral and problem-solving, judgments.

Practical Lessons

Neither intuition nor rational analytic decision making is a panacea for managers. But when used by the right people (experts) on the right kinds of tasks (e.g., judgmental), intuition can lead to rapid and effective decisions. For example, given their link to relatively unstructured tasks, intuitions are more likely to be beneficial to managers and those who find themselves faced with task-related ambiguity, equifinality, and uncertainty. However, it is important to note intuition may also be triggered by severe time pressures. While this may be beneficial if making any decision is better than not making one at all or if performed on tasks with a definitive right or wrong answer (e.g., a math-related problem), then intuition may fail to produce good results.

The need for expertise suggests dedicated practice within a specific domain. Such a prescription may run counter to organizational and employee demands for frequent cross-training in very different types of jobs, or for protean careers, especially those that involve moving from industry to industry. What we do not yet know, however, is how similar domains need to be for experience to "transfer" from one to another. Thus, it is unclear whether bringing a CEO into a manufacturing company from a service company will allow for the effective use of intuition.

To close, intuiting is common in organizational life. Moreover, in rapidly changing conditions, it has the potential to lead to superior outcomes when compared to rational analysis. However, theoretical and methodological obstacles continue to influence the development of intuition research and its impact of intuiting on managerial practice. While progress is being made, there is still disagreement over when intuition is effective, whether or not there are certain types of intuiting, and how intuiting should be measured. Thus, there is much room for growth in this area.

Michael G. Pratt

See also Decision-Making Styles; Ethical Decision Making, Interactionist Model of; *Practice of Management, The;* Schemas Theory; "Unstructured" Decision Making

Further Readings

Dane, E., & Pratt, M. G. (2007). Exploring intuition and its role in managerial decision making. *Academy of Management Review, 32,* 33–54.

Dijksterhuis, A., & Nordgren, L. F. (2006). A theory of unconscious thought. *Perspectives on Psychological Science, 1,* 95–109.

Dreyfus, S. E. 2004. Totally model-free learned skillful coping. *Bulletin of Science, Technology & Society, 24,* 182–187.

Epstein, S. (2008). Intuition from the perspective of cognitive-experiential self-theory. In H. Plessner, C. Betsch, & T. Betsch (Eds.), *Intuition in judgment and decision making* (pp. 23–37). Mahwah, NJ: Lawrence Erlbaum.

Haidt, J. (2001). The emotional dog and its rational tail: A social intuitionist approach to moral judgment. *Psychological Review, 108,* 814–834.

Hodgkinson, G. P., Langan-Fox, J., & Sadler-Smith, E. (2008). Intuition: A fundamental bridging construct in the behavioural sciences. *British Journal of Psychology, 99,* 1–27.

Hogarth, R. M. (2001). *Educating intuition.* Chicago, IL: University of Chicago Press.

Kahneman, D., & Klein, G. (2009). Conditions for intuitive expertise: A failure to disagree. *American Psychologist, 64,* 515–526.

Salas, E., Rosen, M. A., & Diaz Granados, D. (2010). Expertise-based intuition and decision making in organizations. *Journal of Management, 36,* 941–973.

Simon, H. A. (1987). Making management decisions: The role of intuition and emotion. *Academy of Management Executive, 1*(1), 57–64.

INVESTMENT THEORY OF CREATIVITY

Robert J. Sternberg and Todd Lubart, in their investment theory of creativity, use concepts from the economic realm to describe the phenomenon of creativity. In particular, it was proposed that creative people are like successful investors in the financial marketplace: they buy low and sell high. Buying low means pursuing new or undervalued ideas that have growth potential—that may be successful for solving one's problem. Selling high means releasing a novel idea on the market when it has gained value and not holding an idea so long that others eventually have the same idea. Rather than producing work that may be good but similar to what others are doing, people who seek to be creative must deviate from the crowd, generating and advancing ideas that may eventually be recognized as new and valuable. In this entry, creative behavior is described as strategic, and the set of resources including human capital that is invested in projects is described. The resulting productions are then valued in a social setting, the marketplace. There are benefits and costs to creative activity, supply-and-demand issues, and the possibility to develop the resources needed for creativity.

Fundamentals

The buy low–sell high principle is partly descriptive of what creative people do naturally and partly prescriptive of a strategy that people may try consciously to implement to improve their creativity; people can develop a buy low–sell high attitude, similar to the "contrarian" attitude advocated for financial investors. Buy low–sell high behavior may involve an analysis of potential of ideas and of the marketplace for launching these ideas, similar to market analysts' tactics. According to the buy low–sell high principle, people fail to be creative because they (a) buy high, pursuing ideas that are already valued or known (perhaps to avoid risk); (b) buy low, pursuing ideas that do not have growth potential; or (c) sell low, exposing an idea before the audience is ready, before the idea has gained in value, or, inversely, hold the idea too long so that it becomes commonplace.

Investment requires capital. Although physical capital and financial capital are relevant, the human capital needed for creativity is the focus of the investment theory. This capital consists of specific intellectual abilities, knowledge, emotion, personality traits (e.g., risk taking), and motivations. Individuals vary on the extent to which they possess each psychological characteristic. For example, one person may be a risk taker, whereas another person is rather risk averse. The resources are hypothesized to develop and change over the life span.

Within the investment theory, each person possesses a portfolio of psychological resources (skills and traits) relevant to creativity. This portfolio may be actively invested in creative projects. From this perspective, the level of creative performance observed depends on (a) a person's level on each of the resources necessary for creativity, (b) a person's active engagement of his or her resources, and (c) the match between the portfolio of resources that a person has and the profile of resources required for creative work in a domain (or a task) (i.e., the market demands).

With regard to the specific resources for creativity, such as knowledge, some fundamental economic principles may account for observed relationships with creative performance. For example, formal education seems to show an inverted-U relationship to creativity, with an intermediate level of education being optimal. Time and energy spent acquiring advanced techniques may lead people to capitalize on their initial investment, favoring the use of existing knowledge. It is expected that people who contribute ideas to a field outside their main line of work will have less vested interest in maintaining the value of extant knowledge in that field and will experience less risk because of their "outsider" status, thus enhancing their benefit-to-cost ratio for proposing a new idea.

Risk taking, generally seen as a key to investment decisions, involves decision making in the face of potential gains or losses when the outcome is uncertain. Generally, people tend to be risk averse. People may underinvest because the potential rewards of a new idea are somewhat ambiguous compared to pursuing technically sound but mundane ideas for which the limited rewards are clear. However, work on risk taking in situations framed in terms of losses shows that people would take risks to minimize potential losses. Thus, creative ideas may be more easily pursued when they represent a possible solution to a bad situation.

Human capital for creativity can be enhanced, at least partially, through training. An investment in creativity training leads to an accumulation of human capital that can later be put to use. The investment in training depends on the marginal utility (value added) to the individual (or business organization if the decision is made by a human resource manager). For example, some occupations may demand creativity more than others, thus modulating the marginal benefits of training.

The decision to pursue creativity training is based on the marginal utility of each unit of training. A person with little human capital for creativity will benefit more than a person who already possesses many resources for creativity. Each of these individuals, however, can be expected to benefit less and less from each additional unit of creativity training, which is the phenomenon of diminishing returns. With regard to the choice of creativity training versus traditional education, David L. Rubenson and Mark A. Runco pointed out that people are more likely to invest in traditional education than in creativity-related education.

At the societal (aggregate) level, there is a supply and a demand for creative activity. The supply of creativity refers to the number of novel, useful productions (ideas, inventions, works) that the members of a social unit (such as an organization or a society) provide. The demand for creativity is the need or desire in a society for creative productions. This demand may vary across topics, domains, and across time. For example, in financially tight periods, there may be a greater market for innovations that propose less expensive alternatives than for bold but costly new products. The demand for creativity also varies from one place to another; some societies value conformity and maintenance of the status quo more than others. Thus, the value of human capital for creativity will itself vary over time, based on the market pull for creative ideas.

Sternberg and Lubart characterize environments—markets—for creativity as ranging from those that are bullish, overtly supporting creative activity, to those that are bearish, hindering creativity. A bullish environment can spark creativity by providing financial and social resources for creativity, encouraging risk taking, tolerating failures, and offering freedom and opportunities for interdisciplinary interactions. Societies and business organizations may influence the supply of creativity by increasing or decreasing incentives (or rewards) to produce new ideas.

Finally, with regard to the market for creativity, Sternberg and Lubart's investment theory highlights the social consensual nature of creativity. Similar to John Maynard Keynes's proposal on the value of stocks based on investors' collective desire to possess the stock, the value of an idea depends on the audience. Thus, ideas (or productions) can appreciate or depreciate in value with time or with a change of audience. We are able therefore to understand better why some creative geniuses are "discovered" posthumously and other "greats" in their day disappear into oblivion.

Depending on whether a person's creative activity fits the market, it may lead to benefits (extrinsic benefits, such as recognition and financial gains; intrinsic benefits, such as satisfaction with one's work and a feeling of accomplishment). However, there are also costs to creative work, such as pecuniary costs of time and resources expended during the work, psychic costs from bearing negative reactions (among others), and opportunity costs concerning the lost benefits of pursuing other, noncreative, alternative projects. At the macroeconomic level, the benefits of creativity include an enhanced quality of life for the society in general, as well as possible stimulation in the economic sphere. Each creative idea may lead to new supplementary products and services, which is consistent with creativity as a motor for economic growth. Societal-level costs include direct financial costs, the use of physical and human resources, and opportunity costs of foregone advancements on other societal projects. The investment theory presentation has focused here on the individual-level creator, but it can apply equally well to creativity at the group level (team creativity) as well as the aggregate business unit or organizational level. Thus, a multilevel approach is possible.

Todd Lubart and Canan Ceylan

See also Brainstorming; BVSR Theory of Human Creativity; Componential Theory of Creativity; Human Capital Theory; Interactionist Model of Organizational Creativity; Stages of Creativity

Further Readings

Romer, P. M. (1993). Idea gaps and object gaps in economic development. *Journal of Monetary Economics, 32,* 543–573.

Rubenson, D. L., & Runco, M. A. (1992). The psychoeconomic approach to creativity. *New Ideas in Psychology, 10*(2), 131–147.

Solow, R. M. (1994). Perspectives on growth theory. *Journal of Economic Perspectives 8*(1), 45–54.

Sternberg, R. J., & Lubart T. I. (1995). *Defying the crowd: Cultivating creativity in a culture of conformity.* New York, NY: Free Press.

Walberg, H. J., & Stariha, W. E. (1992). Productive human capital: Learning, creativity and eminence. *Creativity Research Journal, 12,* 323–340.

Job Characteristics Theory

Job characteristics theory (JCT) attempts to explain how characteristics of the jobs people perform affect their work behavior and attitudes. In addition, the theory identifies the conditions under which these effects are likely to be strongest. The theory's central management insight is that employee effectiveness can be enhanced by designing jobs with high levels of key characteristics and ensuring that employees with appropriate personal qualities are assigned to these jobs. In this entry, I present the basic elements of JCT and discuss its impact on management research, education, and practice.

Fundamentals

JCT posits that five characteristics of the work affect several outcomes via their effects on three psychological states of employees. In addition, the theory argues that these job characteristics have their strongest effects when employees score high on three individual conditions: knowledge and skill, growth need strength, and context satisfactions. The most recent version of the theory is shown in Figure 1. As shown in the figure, the conceptual core of the theory is the set of three psychological states:

- *Experienced meaningfulness.* The degree to which the jobholder experiences the work as inherently meaningful, as something that "counts" in his or her own system of values.

- *Experienced responsibility.* The degree to which the jobholder feels personally accountable and responsible for the results of the work he or she does.
- *Knowledge of results.* The degree to which the jobholder has confident knowledge about how well he or she is performing at work.

JCT posits that the simultaneous presence of these three psychological states results in a number of favorable work outcomes. Specifically, the jobholder should (1) be internally motivated at work (i.e., feel good when performing well and feel bad or unhappy when performing poorly), (2) be satisfied both with the opportunities for personal growth and development at work and with the job in general, and (3) perform effectively at work (i.e., produce work that is both high in quantity and quality). However, if one or more of the psychological states is at low level, fewer of these outcomes should emerge.

The three psychological states are internal to jobholders and therefore do not represent properties of the work that might be designed. JCT identifies five characteristics of jobs that, when present at high levels, increase the chances that a jobholder will experience the three psychological states and, through them, shape the work outcomes identified. The specific job characteristics expected to most strongly influence each of the psychological states are as follows.

Experienced meaningfulness is influenced by skill variety, task identity, and task significance.

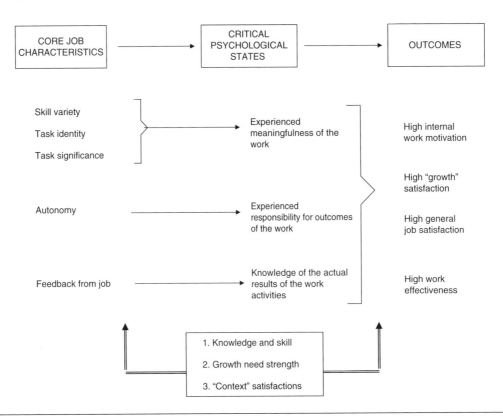

Figure I   Job Characteristics Theory

Source: Hackman, J. R., & Oldham, G. R. (1980, p. 90). *Work redesign.* Reading, MA: Addison-Wesley.

Skill variety is the degree to which the job requires a number of different activities in carrying out the work, which involve the use of a number of different skills and talents of the jobholder. Work that stretches one's skills and abilities should be experienced as more meaningful than work that is simple and routine in nature. *Task identity* is the degree to which the job requires completion of a whole and identifiable piece of work—doing a job from beginning to end with a visible outcome. Putting together an entire product or providing a complete unit of service is inherently more meaningful than being responsible for only a small part of the work. Finally, *task significance* is the degree to which the work has a substantial impact on the lives of other people, whether in the immediate organization or in the external environment. An activity that is consequential for the psychological or physical well-being of others should be experienced as more meaningful than work that makes little difference to anyone else.

Experienced responsibility is shaped by the amount of *autonomy* the job provides. Autonomy is the degree to which the work is structured to provide the jobholder with substantial freedom, independence, and discretion in scheduling the work and in determining the procedures to be used in carrying it out. Thus, as autonomy increases, the employee should feel more personal responsibility for successes and failures that occur on the job and should be more willing to be personally accountable for the outcomes of the work.

Knowledge of results is influenced by *feedback from the job*—that is, the degree to which carrying out job-specified work activities provides the jobholder with direct and clear information about the effectiveness of his or her performance. When the job provides the employee with information about how well he or she is performing (e.g., when a physician treats a patient and sees the patient get healthy) the knowledge of results derives directly from the work activities themselves.

The degree to which a job has high levels of the five characteristics described above, and therefore is likely to prompt favorable work outcomes, is summarized by an index called the Motivating Potential Score (MPS). To produce all three of the psychological states, a job must have a high standing on one or more of the three characteristics that boost meaningfulness (i.e., skill variety, task identity, task significance) and be high on both autonomy and feedback as well. The MPS indicates the degree to which that is the case through the following formula: MPS = (Skill Variety + Task Identity + Task Significance)/3 × Autonomy × Feedback. Thus, a low score on either autonomy or feedback will substantially reduce a job's MPS, since both experienced responsibility and knowledge of results must be present for work outcomes to be high, and those two job characteristics produce the corresponding two psychological states. Conversely, a low score on one of the three job characteristics expected to shape experienced meaningfulness may not necessarily compromise a job's MPS, since a low score on any one of those three attributes can be compensated for by high scores on the others.

As shown in Figure 1, the theory identifies three individual conditions (i.e., knowledge and skill, growth need strength, and context satisfactions) as moderators of the impact of the job characteristics on an employee's responses. Jobholders are expected to respond most positively to jobs high in motivating potential when they score high on all three of these individual conditions.

Knowledge and skill refers to the extent to which the employee has the skills and competencies necessary to complete a job high on the five job characteristics. When individuals have such skills, they have the potential to successfully complete high-MPS jobs and, therefore, to reap the psychological rewards provided by those jobs. By contrast, when employees are missing these skills and competencies they are likely to experience a good deal of frustration on high-MPS jobs, precisely because these jobs offer psychological rewards for effective performance, but the employees are unable to perform well enough to obtain these rewards.

Growth need strength is the strength of an individual's need for personal accomplishment, learning, and development at work. The theory posits that jobholders who have strong growth needs value the opportunities for accomplishment and self-direction provided by jobs high on the five core characteristics and, as a result, respond positively to them. Low GNS jobholders, by contrast, place less value on the

opportunities provided by high MPS jobs and therefore should react less positively to them.

Context satisfactions refers to the extent to which employees are satisfied with major elements of the work context (e.g., pay, job security, coworkers, and managers). JCT posits that when individuals are satisfied with the work context, they are likely to focus their attentions on the properties of a job high in motivating potential and, therefore, appreciate and respond positively to those properties. However, dissatisfaction with the context may distract employees' attention from the work itself and orient their energy instead toward coping with the experienced problems.

Importance

Research Support

More than 200 studies have tested all or portions of JCT. Many of these studies have used the Job Diagnostic Survey (JDS), a research instrument that assesses most of the constructs included in the theory. Extensive reviews of this early research suggest the following conclusions.

Previous research suggests that the five job characteristics have generally positive effects on each of the work outcomes included in the theory. Specifically, results indicate that employees exhibit high work performance and experience high internal motivation, high job satisfaction, and high growth satisfaction when they work on jobs characterized by high levels of autonomy, skill variety, task identity, task significance, and job-based feedback. Moreover, results of early research provide general support for the proposed mediating effects of the psychological states of experienced meaningfulness, experienced responsibility, and knowledge of results. That is, the presence of the five job characteristics increases the experience of the three psychological states as specified by JCT, which then positively influence the jobholder's work outcomes. Recent reviews have also concluded that a single psychological state—*experienced meaningfulness*—is quite effective in explaining the effects of *all* five core job characteristics on the work outcomes. That is, each of the five core properties was found to enhance the extent to which the employee experiences the work as meaningful, which then contributes to the work outcomes included in JCT.

Although research supports many of the basic tenets of JCT, other parts of the theory have received relatively little research support. One of these involves the summary MPS index. Previous studies suggest that the MPS index is *not* more predictive of the work outcomes included in the theory than a simpler index computed by simply adding up scores on the five core job characteristics. Although the MPS index does make conceptual sense, it is likely that these weak results are a function of the psychometric properties of the JDS, which do not allow for the multiplication of variables specified in the formula for the MPS.

The results involving the three proposed moderators were also not completely supportive of the arguments in JCT. First, no studies directly tested the moderating effects of knowledge and skill, so it is unclear if individuals' competencies play a role in how they respond to the five job characteristics. The context satisfactions moderator did receive research attention, but the results of these studies were mixed, and it is not clear that employees respond differently to the job characteristics if they are more or less satisfied with the work context. Finally, reviews of the literature concluded that GNS had little impact on the effects of the job characteristics on the internal motivation and satisfaction outcomes. However, there was some evidence to suggest that employees with high GNS exhibited higher performance on jobs high in motivating potential than did jobholders with relatively low GNS scores.

Implications for Practice

Despite the mixed support for JCT, the theory has a number of implications for the design of jobs in organizations. Specifically, results of previous investigations suggest that improving the standing of the five job characteristics should result in significant improvements in jobholders' work performance, internal motivation, and job satisfaction. There is little evidence to suggest that employees react negatively to these characteristics—even when they are present at very high levels. Thus, applying work redesign practices that have been shown to enhance the job characteristics should have generally positive consequences for the employee and the organization. For example, providing each employee with a larger module of work should boost the skill variety and task identity characteristics. Putting the employee in direct contact with his or her clients and giving the employee continuing responsibility for managing those relationships should enhance

the characteristics of autonomy, skill variety, and feedback. And changes in these job characteristics via the redesign practices just described should foster significant improvements in the psychological states and outcomes included in the theory. Moreover, changes in these job characteristics should result in even higher levels of work performance among employees with relatively high GNS.

Greg R. Oldham

See also Personal Engagement (at Work) Model; Scientific Management; Sociotechnical Theory; Total Quality Management; Two-Factor Theory (and Job Enrichment)

Further Readings

Fried, Y., & Ferris, G. R. (1987). The validity of the job characteristics model: A review and meta-analysis. *Personnel Psychology, 40,* 287–322.

Hackman, J. R., & Oldham, G. R. (1975). Development of the Job Diagnostic Survey. *Journal of Applied Psychology, 60,* 159–170.

Hackman, J. R., & Oldham, G. R. (1976). Motivation through the design of work: Test of a theory. *Organizational Behavior and Human Performance, 16,* 250–279.

Hackman, J. R., & Oldham, G. R. (1980). *Work redesign.* Reading, MA: Addison-Wesley.

Humphrey, S. E., Nahrgang, J. D., & Morgeson, F. P. (2007). Integrating motivational, social, and contextual work design features: A meta-analytic summary and theoretical extension of the work design literature. *Journal of Applied Psychology, 92,* 1332–1356.

Kopelman, R. E. (1985, Summer). Job redesign and productivity: A review of the evidence. *National Productivity Review,* pp. 237–255.

Oldham, G. R., & Hackman, J. R. (2005). How job characteristics theory happened. In K. Smith & M. Hitt (Eds.), *Great minds in management: The process of theory development* (pp. 151–170). New York, NY: Oxford University Press.

JOB DEMANDS–RESOURCES MODEL

Do you know that feeling of tension just before you start a presentation in front of a group? Although your dry mouth and clammy hands feel unpleasant, the tension is very functional. It makes you very concentrated so that you formulate precisely and to the point and your mind does not wander during your talk. However, if the tension becomes chronic and one is confronted with high job demands every day, the functional tension may transform into dysfunctional, chronic stress. In this entry, the focus is on the causes and consequences of organizational stress. Stress is often discussed as an individual-level phenomenon. However, since employees usually work on collaborative goals, they often work in teams of individuals who are exposed to the same work characteristics. This means that we can use team reports of job characteristics and strain to identify the common causes of strain. This entry presents the job demands–resources model as an overall framework to understand organizational stress.

Fundamentals

The Concept of Organizational Stress

Organizational stress is an umbrella term that for some people refers to environmental stressors and, for others, to subjectively experienced strain; yet others use the term *stress* to refer to the consequence of strain. For reasons of clarity, it is important to distinguish between possible causes, consequences, and the phenomenon of strain itself. Generally, scholars use the term *job demands* to refer to possible job-related causes of negative experiences, which can be labeled "job strain." Job demands that are a particular hindrance, such as role ambiguity, role conflicts, and job insecurity, are important causes of strain? Possible consequences of job strain are task-related errors, unsafe work behaviors, and sickness absenteeism. The experience of job strain can be expressed, for example, in the form of fatigue, subjective health complaints, or burnout. Burnout is an often-studied form of prolonged job strain characterized by chronic fatigue and a negative, cynical attitude toward work.

It should be noted that job demands are usually assessed by asking employees for their subjective evaluations of the workload, contacts with clients, and so on. However, in addition to these subjective job demands, researchers have developed techniques to assess job demands more objectively. For example, objective indicators of work pressure could be external observers' assessments of work pressure, the number of units processed per hour, or the number of clients served on a typical workday. According to

the Michigan model, employees need to interpret the objective job demands in order to report subjective job demands. The model proposes that personality may influence the link between objective and subjective job demands, because stable personalities (i.e., those who are emotionally stable, extraverted, and conscientious) would be better able to cope with the demands.

The Job Demands–Resources Model

The job demands–resources (JD–R) model was developed in Europe to understand the causes and consequences of burnout and its opposite—work engagement. Why do some employees lose their energy and become cynical about the content of their work, whereas others remain energetic and enthusiastic? According to the JD–R model, the answer can be found in the work environment. A first assumption of the model is that whereas every occupation may have its own specific risk factors associated with job stress, these factors can be classified in two general categories (i.e., job demands and job resources), thus constituting an overarching model that may be applied to various occupational settings, irrespective of the particular demands and resources involved. *Job demands* refer to those physical, psychological, social, or organizational aspects of the job that require sustained physical and/or psychological (cognitive and emotional) effort or skills and are therefore associated with certain physiological and/or psychological costs. Examples are a high work pressure, demanding clients, and high mental job demands. Although job demands are not necessarily negative, they may turn into job stressors when meeting those demands requires high effort from which the employee fails to recover adequately.

Job resources refer to those physical, psychological, social, or organizational aspects of the job that either (a) are functional in achieving work goals; (b) reduce job demands and the associated physiological and psychological costs; (c) stimulate personal growth, learning, and development. Hence, resources are not only necessary to deal with job demands, but they also are important in their own right. People are motivated to protect and accumulate their resources because they satisfy their basic psychological needs of autonomy, relatedness, and competence. Most individuals want to experience control over what they do, show what they are good at, and share experiences with others. Job resources can satisfy these needs. Job resources may be located at the macro, organizational level (e.g., pay, career opportunities, job security), the interpersonal level (e.g., supervisor and coworker support, team climate), the job level (e.g., role clarity, participation in decision making), and at the level of the task (e.g., skill variety, task identity, task significance, autonomy, performance feedback).

A second assumption of the JD–R model is that two different underlying psychological processes play a role in the development of job strain and motivation. The first is a process of *health impairment*, which suggests that badly designed jobs or chronic job demands (e.g., work overload, emotional demands) exhaust employees' mental and physical resources and may therefore lead to the depletion of energy (i.e., a state of exhaustion) and to health problems. Individuals often use performance protection strategies under the influence of environmental demands (e.g., increased subjective effort) in order to prevent decrements in their task performance. Unfortunately, the long-term effect of such compensatory strategies may be a draining of individuals' energy, eventually resulting in a breakdown. The second process proposed by the JD–R model is *motivational* in nature, whereby it is assumed that job resources have motivational potential and lead to high work engagement, low cynicism, and excellent performance. As follows from its definition, job resources may play either an intrinsic motivational role because they foster employees' growth, learning, and development, or they may play an extrinsic motivational role because they are instrumental in achieving work goals.

Next to the suggested main effects of job demands and resources, a third proposition of the JD–R model is that the *interaction* between job demands and job resources is important for the development of organizational stress. Inherent in the definition of job resources is the assumption that job resources may *buffer* the impact of job demands on job strain, including burnout. The buffering role of job resources is consistent with previously formulated job stress models, such as the demand-control model (DCM) and the effort-reward imbalance model (ERIM). Whereas the DCM states that control over the execution of tasks (autonomy) may buffer the impact of work overload on job stress and whereas the ERIM states that rewards may buffer the unfavorable effects of effort expedition, the JD–R model

expands these views and states that many *different* types of job demands and job resources may interact in predicting job strain. Which job demands and resources play a role in a certain work environment depends on the specific job characteristics that prevail.

A fourth proposition of the JD–R model is that job resources are particularly motivating when job demands are high. Research has indeed shown that job resources are most beneficial in maintaining work engagement under conditions of high (challenge) job demands. For example, skill utilization, learning opportunities, and autonomy are most predictive of engagement when job demands (e.g., workload and emotional demands) are high. This indicates that resources become most salient under demanding conditions. Put differently, job demands become challenges when employees have sufficient job resources available. However, in contrast, job demands become stressors when job resources are lacking.

A fifth and final assumption is that employees are not passive actors but instead may actively change their work environment. The JD–R model proposes that employees may actively change the content or design of their jobs by choosing certain tasks, negotiating different job content, or by assigning meaning to their tasks or jobs. This process of employees shaping their jobs has been referred to as job crafting. Vigorous, engaged workers are most likely to show job-crafting behaviors. They are able to mobilize their job resources, for example, by asking for feedback about their job performance or by asking for help from others (colleagues, supervisor). In addition, engaged workers are inclined to increase their challenge job demands. As a consequence of these job-crafting behaviors, employees may be able to increase their person–job fit and to experience enhanced meaning in their work—thus to prevent job stress and to build their own work engagement. Unfortunately, stressed workers are less likely to craft their work environment. They may get trapped in a downward spiral of job stressors and strain.

Importance

It is important for organizations to prevent job strain and to facilitate work engagement because job stress has been found to lead to impaired functioning on the job. For example, meta-analytic research on the link between burnout and objective performance has shown that burnout leads to impaired in-role performance, reduced organizational citizenship behaviors, and reduced client satisfaction. This means that employees who feel exhausted by their work and who are cynical are less likely to attain organizational goals, to help their colleagues, and to satisfy their clients' needs. In contrast, research has shown that work engagement is predictive of in-role and extra-role performance, improved financial results, and increased client satisfaction.

Whereas engaged workers are active and enthusiastic, stressed workers become passive and they experience negative emotions. The experience of strain seems to impair employees' ability to perform well. People who are burned out by their work have lost their energetic resources to cope with the job demands. In addition, stress undermines openness to experience, and thus burned-out employees do not acquire new skills or knowledge. This reduces opportunities to be creative and find solutions for work-related problems. Organizations should therefore try to prevent organizational stress. The JD–R model can be used to do this in a systematic way. For example, human resources managers could use JD–R questionnaires to measure employees' levels of job demands, resources, and strain. Teams or departments scoring unfavorable on the JD–R questionnaire would need attention: Are certain job demands too high? Do all the teams have sufficient job resources? Interventions could be implemented

and a new round of assessment could ascertain whether the work environment has improved and organizational stress has been reduced.

Arnold B. Bakker

See also Equity Theory; Goal-Setting Theory; High-Performance Work Systems; Human Resource Management Strategies; Job Characteristics Theory; Organizational Commitment Theory

Further Readings

Bakker, A. B., & Daniels, K. (Eds.). (2012). *A day in the life of a happy worker.* Hove, East Sussex, England: Psychology Press.

Bakker, A. B., Demerouti, E., & Euwema, M. C. (2005). Job resources buffer the impact of job demands on burnout. *Journal of Occupational Health Psychology, 10,* 170–180.

Bakker, A. B., & Leiter, M. P. (Eds.). (2010). *Work engagement: A handbook of essential theory and research.* New York, NY: Psychology Press.

Maslach, C., Schaufeli, W. B., & Leiter, M. P. (2001). Job burnout. *Annual Review of Psychology, 52,* 397–422.

Schaufeli, W. B., & Enzmann, D. (1998). *The burnout companion to study and practice: A critical analysis.* Washington, DC: Taylor & Francis.

Sonnentag, S. (2012). Psychological detachment from work during leisure time: The benefits of mentally disengaging from work. *Current Directions in Psychological Science, 21*(2), 114–118. doi:10.1177/0963721411434979

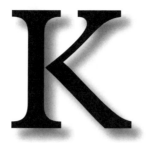

KAIZEN AND CONTINUOUS IMPROVEMENT

Since the 1980s when the "Japanese miracle" of near-perfect quality entered global awareness, the concept of *kaizen* has grown to be part of the international vocabulary of management theory. *Kaizen* represents a vision of an ideal state—improvement everywhere to achieve lowest cost, highest quality, and best service to the customer. As organizations throughout the world have experimented with various incarnations of programs to achieve *kaizen,* such as business process reengineering, total quality management, six sigma, lean management, and theory of constraints, there has been a shift in thinking from viewing *kaizen* as a toolkit to transform processes, to viewing *kaizen* as the essence of a culture focused on striving for excellence across the enterprise. These real-world experiments have led to basic insights into a broad range of issues in management theory, including the nature of bureaucracy, human motivation, how to train and develop people, the skills and roles of leadership, knowledge management, and the relationship between strategy and operational excellence.

Fundamentals

Kaizen means change for the better. Continuous improvement taken literally means everything is getting better all the time. Sometimes a distinction is made between *kaizen,* which is interpreted as small incremental changes, and *kaikaku,* which refers to

big change. This is not necessary since "change for the better" can be big or small. Henry Ford once said, "Nothing is particularly hard if you divide it into small jobs," and if you look closely at big game-changing innovations, they have been achieved through many small steps, some dead-ends, and others' progress toward the vision.

Kaizen is a Japanese word and is often associated with Japanese manufacturing, particularly the Toyota production system (TPS). The book that first popularized the core concepts of TPS was *The Machine That Changed the World.* This book introduced the phrase *lean production* as a new management paradigm as significant as the shift from craft to mass production. Lean production spread as programs first in industry and then into the service sector and has taken on a life of its own with different interpretations by different authors, consulting groups, and organizations. One simple classification is into two categories: tool-oriented lean (mechanistic) and people-oriented lean (organic). The original TPS in Toyota is the latter, and the tools and lean processes highlighted problems that could shut down production, driving active problem solving. The role of people was to think creatively about how to solve those problems, but people had to be developed to have the skills for solving the problems, which Toyota invested in deeply, mostly through on-the-job development with skilled coaches (called *sensei*).

As Toyota globalized, it became clear that there was a need to take the philosophy underlying TPS and make what Japanese members learned on the job explicit so it could be taught in the hundreds of companies in which Toyota had operations and sales offices. The resulting document, *The Toyota Way 2001*, defined two pillars that represent the core philosophy of the company: respect for people and continuous improvement. The underlying principles, more general than manufacturing, have become an aspiration for organizations throughout the world in all sectors, including industry, government, education, defense, health care, mining, and financial services. A related concept is *lean management,* which focuses on eliminating waste from processes. Unfortunately, the concept of *lean* is often misinterpreted as a program led by experts to reduce cost through waste reduction. In reality, lean thinking is virtually synonymous with continuous improvement, or *kaizen,* which requires engaged people, skilled in a discipline problem-solving methodology.

The underlying theory of problem solving evolved from Walter A. Shewhart's concept, taught to Toyota by W. Edwards Deming, which then evolved in Japan into what we now call the plan-do-check-act (PDCA) cycle. Too often, problems are solved by assuming it is clear what the problem is and jumping to solutions with very little follow-up to learn what happened. Daniel Kahneman calls this "fast thinking," as opposed to slow thinking, which takes much more mental effort. In fast thinking, we jump to the first conclusion that comes to mind without thinking deeply or analytically about the problem. As a general principle, he summarizes many cognitive psychology experiments with the conclusion that people seek to minimize mental effort, thus preferring fast thinking. PDCA requires a careful definition of the real problem and then driving to the root cause by deep (slow) thinking and careful study. Only then are possible countermeasures defined, one selected and tried (*do*), and then the results studied (*check*) with further action (*act*) based on the findings.

Mike Rother introduces the concept of *kata* to emphasize that the process of improvement requires a specific skill set and way of thinking that must be learned. *Kata,* a Japanese term often used in martial arts, is a deeply learned routine. He lays out in detail the "improvement *kata*" that drives continuous improvement—that is, a set of routines that need to be repeatedly practiced, with an expert coach as a guide, until they become second nature and the focus can be on the content of the problem instead of on the process steps of problem solving. In essence, one must work hard and practice in a determined way, and it helps to have a coach for

support and motivation, to overcome the tendency toward fast thinking.

Routines bring to mind standardization, which is often thought to stifle creativity. But Adler, studying the TPS at New United Motor Manufacturing (NUMMI), the joint venture between Toyota and General Motors in California, observed an organization filled with bureaucratic standards that were being dynamically adjusted by work teams through *kaizen.* This caused him to question the very nature of bureaucracy and the simple distinction in organizational theory between mechanistic and organic organizations. He concluded there were different types of bureaucracies. He distinguished between *coercive bureaucracy,* in which standards are developed by experts and imposed top-down through a command-and-control structure, and *enabling bureaucracy,* in which standards are best-practice templates owned and improved on by work groups throughout the organization. Enabling bureaucracy actually encourages continuous improvement. In fact, as per Cole, without standardization, individuals learn and may improve what they do, but the improvements are not shared and institutionalized, so organizational learning is not possible.

Let's consider two cases discussed by Jeffrey Liker and James Franz that tried to develop continuous improvement cultures, one through coercive bureaucracy and the other through enabling bureaucracy. A U.S. shipyard that repairs and overhauls submarines and aircraft carriers embarked on a program that taught by establishing a "lean six-sigma" academy. Graduates earned "black belts" and were sent into the shipyard to do projects. While each project showed improvements to the bottom line, there was little change in the culture of the shipyards, little buy-in from people doing the work, and the well-documented changes were only superficially implemented, generally degrading over time—the opposite of continuous improvement. In fact the approach to change reflected the coercive bureaucracy that was at the core of the shipyard rather than changing the culture. A smaller shipyard that had a more team-centered, enabling culture started with deep changes in pilot areas, intensively coaching teams in those areas until they were capable of *kaizen,* then spread the learning work group by work group slowly and patiently and had far more sustainable results with evidence of a good deal of learning. This eventually spread across the yard, and change was deep.

The irony is that over time, due to lack of consistent leadership (leaders were frequently rotated), neither program was able to sustain the journey to continuous improvement.

These case studies illustrate two key points. First, it is far too easy to confuse continuous improvement with a toolkit that can be mechanistically applied to processes presumed to be static. In fact, processes are dynamic and naturally variable and require continuous improvement even to maintain a steady state and even more effort to improve in an innovative way. Second, continuous improvement is 100% dependent on people, and people will not push themselves to keep improving without strong leadership coaching and support. According to Liker and Gary L. Convis, the leaders themselves need to be the first to transform themselves to become skilled at *kaizen* so they can then teach others. Like any life pursuit, such as sports, art, music, or cooking, continuous improvement requires a drive for excellence and continuous practice, and the ideal is always just out of reach.

Jeffrey K. Liker

See also High-Performance Work Systems; Lean Enterprise; Learning Organization; Level 5 Leadership; Organic and Mechanistic Forms; Quality Circles; Sociotechnical Theory; Total Quality Management

Further Readings

Adler, P. S., & Borys, B. (1996). Two types of bureaucracy: Enabling and coercive. *Administrative Science Quarterly, 41*(1), 61–89.

Cole, R. E. (1995). Reflections on organizational learning in U.S. and Japanese industry. In J. K. Liker, J. E. Ettlie, & J. C. Campbell (Eds.), *Engineered in Japan* (pp. 365–379). New York, NY: Oxford University Press.

Deming, W. E. (2000). *Out of the crisis,* Cambridge, MA: MIT Press.

Ford, H. (1988). *Today and tomorrow.* New York, NY: Productivity Press.

Kahneman, D. (2011). *Thinking fast and slow.* New York, NY: Farrar, Straus & Giroux, 2011.

Liker, J. K., & Convis, G. L. (2011). *The Toyota way to lean leadership.* New York, NY: McGraw-Hill.

Liker, J. K., & Franz, J. K. (2004). *The Toyota way to continuous improvement.* New York, NY: McGraw-Hill.

Rother, M. (2009). *Toyota kata.* New York, NY: McGraw-Hill.

Womack, J. P., & Jones, D. T. (2003). *Lean thinking.* Cambridge, MA: Free Press.

Womack, J. P., Jones, D. T., & Ross, D. (1990). *The machine that changed the world.* New York, NY: Rawson.

KNOWLEDGE WORKERS

The rise of knowledge workers, well-trained and specialized professionals, has altered the nature of organizations and their management in fundamental ways. These workers make their living by gaining and using diverse, often specialized knowledge. As such, they have been interwoven with every major organizational function, such as research and development, strategy making, new product design, supply chain analysis, market analysis, and marketing, among others. Knowledge workers have also become influential in production planning and control, logistics, and other traditional manufacturing functions. Peter Drucker was among the very first to note the emergence and growing role of these workers and to systematically examine their effects on companies and their decisions. Drucker concentrated his analyses on the advent of modern information technology as a powerful force that shapes what, how, and when organizations do things. This led Drucker to predict that the growth of these technologies will redefine and even reduce the number of specialized technocrats (knowledge workers). Drucker, one of the most astute observers of management organizations, did not get it entirely right. As technology has become more and more sophisticated and diffused, hordes of knowledge workers have become dominant in today's economy. This entry reviews the fundamental arguments, critiques, and applications of his ideas.

Fundamentals

What Do Knowledge Workers Have in Common?

Despite their varied interests and roles, knowledge workers have several things in common. They tend to be specialists, who have developed a considerable mastery of their respective disciplines through professional training and sometimes practical experiences. As a result, their "disciplinary" focus often shapes their views of key issues confronting their industries, companies, or even their jobs. This is reinforced by the fact they also tend to devote quite a bit of time and energy in acquiring, processing, and using knowledge. Their interpretation of this knowledge is often guided by their prior education and training.

These professional workers also control vast amounts of knowledge that gives them the raw material with which to work through problems, giving them a growing sense of control; some of that knowledge is tacit and therefore cannot be shared easily with others. Yet often this tacit knowledge is the primary source of innovations that can create value. This knowledge is a key source of creativity that results in new products, systems, and processes. It is also a source of new forms of organizing and managing workflow and other employees. In addition, this knowledge makes it easier to acquire new technical skills that make today's organizations more efficient, responsive, and productive. Knowledge workers play an important role in coordinating the various phases of resource assembly, production, marketing, and distribution. They increasingly do so on a global basis as they work for global companies, multinationals, or even local companies that use global supply chains.

Knowledge networks, where discoveries are made, are also global and access to them provides the foundation for innovation of all forms. Knowledge workers use their connections and professional associations to develop links to these knowledge networks, acquire knowledge, and transform it into profitable goods and services. One of the key roles that knowledge workers play in this context is to develop the firm's absorptive capacity—the ability to recognize, value, import, process, assimilate, and use externally generated knowledge in its own operations. Knowledge workers have the expertise and understanding needed to target, import, and transform this knowledge into sources of revenues and profitability. The relatedness of the knowledge these professional employees have helps not only in gaining externally generated knowledge but also in making it possible to use this knowledge productively. The presence of these knowledge employees has been fundamental for the success of the "open innovation" movement, in which companies use discoveries and innovations made by other companies to create new businesses and protect their existing markets.

Principles of Knowledge Worker Productivity

Drucker postulated six principles of knowledge worker productivity that he believed stood in stark contrast to those for manual worker productivity as discussed by Frederick Taylor and others. Knowledge worker productivity demands that (1) because in knowledge work the task does not program the worker but instead the worker defines the task, it is imperative to first ask the question, "What is the task?" to focus attention and effort; (2) the individual knowledge workers themselves be given the autonomy and responsibility for making decisions regarding their own productivity; (3) work is defined to incorporate continuous innovation and this is built into the knowledge worker's job; (4) work is defined to incorporate continuous learning and teaching on the part of the knowledge worker and this is similarly built into the knowledge worker's job; (5) quality of work is held at least as important as quantity in assessing knowledge worker productivity—quality is the "essence of the output"; and (6) knowledge workers are treated as an asset—more importantly, the main asset of an organization or institution—rather than simply a cost. This suggests that they be invested in, attracted and motivated, educated and developed, and managed appropriately.

Fundamental Management Changes

The rise of knowledge workers among the ranks of organizational employees has had a profound, even pervasive, effect on how companies are designed and managed. Work organizations are no longer places where people only make a living but also environments in which they fulfill their growth and "self-actualization" needs. Given that knowledge workers have different needs, organizational designs have to accommodate this diversity through flexibility in compensation, working hours, task assignments, and responsibilities associated with their jobs. Jobs have been redesigned to enhance variety, their motivational potential, and social relevance and impact. The intent was to make jobs more "meaningful" for knowledge workers to capitalize on their growth needs. Knowledge workers value their independence and professional autonomy, a factor that inspired efforts to redesign companies to ensure participatory management practices.

The fact that knowledge workers are trained professionals has led many to view them as a key source of ideas for innovation and entrepreneurship; these ideas often trickle up to senior managers who are no longer viewed as the sole or mainspring of change in the organizations. Ideas and opportunities could be found anywhere in the organization. Knowledge workers also value analysis and use of scientific methods in decision making, a factor that has increased efforts aimed at gathering, analyzing, and interpreting vast amounts of data to guide and shape the firm's decisions.

Knowledge workers value their professional identification, the connection to their profession, and its dominant values and views. Their loyalty to their companies, however, may not be enduring because these knowledge workers move from one company to another to practice their craft. Knowledge workers tend to be cosmopolitan in their outlook, connecting with different groups with different sources of ideas, and experimenting with new things. This cosmopolitan outlook helps link knowledge workers to colleagues in other companies or even professional groups, within and across industries, often transcending geographic distances.

The mobility of knowledge workers creates opportunities for networking as well as forming relationships that transcend organizational boundaries. These networks have become fertile grounds for fermenting, exploring, testing, and refining ideas with the benefit of other members who are bonded to each other by shared professional interests. These networks are increasingly global, transmitting different views and divergent ways of thinking about issues of interest. These ideas and discoveries could be helpful to employers. Alternatively, knowledge workers might opt to become entrepreneurs by creating companies of their own, using the connections and resources their networks make available to them. Some of these newly born companies go international from their inception to capitalize on the supply of knowledge workers, resources, and opportunities that cross borders.

A related but different role that knowledge workers' professional identification plays is *community of practice*. These communities develop around a common issue (e.g., solving a long-standing set of mathematical equations, developing a complicated software program, or diagnosing a rare medical condition). Members of the community share their expertise in solving the issue at hand, knowing well that should they encounter a problem, other members of the community will come to their aid. These communities practice intellectually, interpersonally, and emotionally and engage their members by giving them opportunities to bond, share, learn, and grow.

Importance

Leading Knowledge Workers to Manage Intellectual Capital

The rise of knowledge workers has given birth to a large industry that specializes in connecting and keeping these professionals engaged and current. Numerous professional organizations have come into existence to organize meetings for specialized professionals to share their intellectual interests, research findings, network, and stay abreast of developments in their respective fields as well other fields. Training companies have also become widespread, offering specialized advanced courses and programs for interested knowledge workers. Colleges and universities have also expanded their traditional course offerings to accommodate the growing needs of this expanding population offering degree and nondegree programs. Companies have also invested a great deal in training their employees in order to upgrade their skills and keep them current. Companies have come to view their intellectual capital to be among the most important, valuable, and enduring sources of competitive advantage.

If knowledge is the mainspring of creativity and innovation in contemporary organizations, then managing knowledge workers becomes a major priority. It is no longer sufficient to develop work environments that promote learning to cultivate what knowledge workers know. Management needs to give greater attention to effective ways of motivating these workers and understating their unique needs. This motivation bonds these knowledge workers to their employers. It also stimulates their creativity and even encourages them to take the risks associated with innovation.

Work often determines the identity of these employees, and management needs to design work assignments to capitalize on and reinforce this need. Knowledge workers thrive on doing progressively complex as well as intellectually and organizationally challenging tasks. Therefore, job variety and mobility within the company are essential tools for motivating these knowledge workers. Providing room for exploration and experimentation could also be beneficial to these employees and the companies for which they work. In fact, some companies have learned to give these employees time during their formal work hours to explore projects of interest. While some of these projects may fail, they offer insights into what works and does not work. When they succeed, some of these projects are integrated into the company's overall strategic initiatives.

Knowledge workers' skills and aptitudes form a major part of the firm's organizational memory. The collective knowledge embodied in professional workers provides the foundation for the breadth of that memory. The broader the memory, the more capable the firm is in doing very different things. This breadth allows the firm to cross boundaries and bring very different ideas, learn different skills, and recognize the multiplicity of potential applications. The higher the quality of knowledge these workers have, the deeper the firm's organizational memory. This depth is conducive to radical innovation and seeing connections among different strands of knowledge (which others may not comprehend). Creativity in managing the breadth and depth of this memory can serve very different organizational purposes, such as predicting technological discontinuities, changing competitive dynamics, emerging business models, entry of different types of competitors, and changing customer expectations and needs.

Challenges in Leading Knowledge Workers

Leading knowledge workers is a delicate but demanding act. These workers enjoy professional autonomy, have strong identification with their profession, gain power because of their expertise, and are well connected to others with and outside their companies. Leading knowledge workers requires attention to what they know, how well they know it, and what motivates them to know it by keeping abreast of developments in their fields.

Paradoxically, knowledge workers are loyal to and identify with their professions and peers—rather than their employers per se. They derive their satisfaction and identity from these connections, recognizing that they are likely to change employers several times over the course of their career. This paradox means that companies have to work hard to gain the benefits associated with their knowledge workers—for example, by training and developing them—while realizing that they are likely to move on and work elsewhere.

Another problem companies have encountered is that some knowledge workers learn different skills while working for them and then move to work for their competitors, causing trade secrets to leak quickly and thus disadvantage former employers. Other knowledge workers create their own companies that sometimes compete with their former employers' business. To be sure, some knowledge workers create businesses that complement and collaborate with their former employers, but others aggressively compete with the companies in which they have worked. Given the uncertainty that surrounds knowledge workers' future plans, some employers proceed to divide work into smaller units to which professional employees are assigned. Thus, these employees can become proficient in these narrowly defined tasks without full knowledge of the total process. This fragmentation of work reduces professional workers' motivation and job satisfaction. It could also deprive them of carrying out meaningful tasks, sharing knowledge, learn, and acquiring new skills. The fragmentation of job-related tasks can also complicate the integration needed to develop products, slows down task completion, and raises operational costs. It is also difficult to benefit from the *transactive memory* employees develop as they function as a team, where they "carry forward" those skills and the learning that has occurred in prior assignments.

In sum, knowledge workers populate almost every function in contemporary organizations, occupying central positions that give these workers resources, prestige, and power. Contrary to Drucker's prediction about the demise of knowledge workers, the proliferation of new technologies, especially information-based technologies, has redefined the roles they play. With their central positions throughout the hierarchy, knowledge workers have become the brain, heart, and soul of today's organizations.

Shaker A. Zahra

See also Empowerment; Human Capital Theory; Knowledge-Based View of the Firm; Open Innovation; Tacit Knowledge

Further Readings

Davenport, T. H. (2005). *Thinking for a living: How to get better performance and results from knowledge workers*. Boston, MA: Harvard Business School Press.

Drucker, P. F. (1999). Knowledge-worker productivity: The biggest challenge. *California Management Review,* 41(2) 79–94.

Drucker, P. F. (1999). *Management challenges for 21st century.* New York, NY: Harper Business.

Drucker, P. F. (2001). *The essential Drucker: The best of sixty years of Peter Drucker's essential writings on management.* New York, NY: Harper Business.

Zahra, S. A. (2003). An interview with Peter Drucker. *Academy of Management Executive,* 17(3), 9–12.

KNOWLEDGE-BASED VIEW OF THE FIRM

Many management scholars now view firms as repositories, integrators, developers, and exploiters of various types of knowledge. Proponents of the knowledge-based view (KBV), however, attach primacy to the tacit (inarticulable) capabilities that Penrose argued provide firms with "uniquely valuable" opportunities. The KBV's central argument is that firm-wide tacit capabilities form the firm's core and that cultivation and refinement of these capabilities determines current and future firm vitality. This entry briefly reviews the core elements of KBV perspectives and the relationships predicted among these elements, followed by a brief assessment of the KBV's current impact.

Fundamentals

At the risk of oversimplification, the firm is assumed for the purposes of this entry to consist of two basic elements: (1) resources that encompass any tangible or intangible assets maintained and relatively easily exploitable by the firm and (2) inarticulable or "tacit" capabilities (knowledge) that guide a firm's unique development, maintenance, and exploitation of resources. Learning is viewed somewhat pedantically as the acquisition and development of new and useful types of knowledge. KBV perspectives attempt to describe how capabilities guide a firm's unique positioning—building, acquiring, and dispensing of firm resources—and how learning from experience promotes the modification and evolution of these capabilities. Note that although some disagreement exists about the appropriate level of analysis (i.e., knowledge exists within the individual vs. knowledge exists within the firm), here the focus is on the

firm level because of its preponderance of support. Capabilities define a firm's collective consciousness through which employees view the firm's internal and external environments, and thereby bind and unify various firm entities. More than a mere collection of individuals or transactions, the firm as viewed by KBV theorists is a complex set of social interactions and unwritten rules that form its collective consciousness. These capabilities emerge from the familiarity employees have with one another and evolve from repeated employee interaction as well as attempts at resource positioning. Much like a hockey team whose play is refined and enhanced through continual practice, a firm builds cognizance of, and dexterity with, its resources through recurring exploitation efforts. Capabilities are self-reinforcing as the firm's facility in using and adapting resources to current and future (i.e., expected) environments increases with continued use. Actions (e.g., takeovers, research and development, manufacturing) that first required contemplation at every step become more reflexive or "routinized" as experience mounts and, therefore, require the mobilization of fewer and fewer cognitive resources in subsequent use.

Capabilities also allow for parochial languages and interests (e.g., those of divisions, individual employees, etc.) to be integrated into the firm mind-set. However, KBV perspectives generally do not assume uniformity of knowledge across units or individuals but only that various within-firm knowledge bases are partly composed of firm-wide capabilities. This allows various units or individuals to specialize in specific tasks (thereby encouraging focus and refinement at the employee or unit level) while simultaneously promoting integration of idiosyncratic abilities and efforts with the rest of the firm. In essence, capabilities provide the common knowledge by which local specialized knowledge can be combined into the greater knowledge base. Accordingly, some have pointed to the distinction between "component" and "architectural" capabilities, where the former refers to local (e.g., division, function) task-related skills and the latter refers to the ability to effectively combine and integrate the component tasks and capabilities into a coherent package.

The collective mind-set further enhances efficiency and effectiveness by acting as a lens through which employees and managers rationalize internal and external environments. Although some learning takes place in the minds of individuals, that which each individual learns is a function of what his or her fellow employees (perceive to) know and what is viewed as important by the firm as a whole. Accordingly, through the guidance of firm-wide capabilities, employees and managers distinguish between those resources that are ostensibly crucial to firm success and those that should be discarded. In this way, firm-wide capabilities economize on learning and minimize effects of the bounded rationality of individual employees.

Because a firm is limited in the amount of technologies that it can internally develop, KBV scholars have increasingly focused attention on how firm capabilities promote the absorption of external knowledge. Considerable research suggests that external knowledge acquisition is contingent, at least partly, on previous experience with similar knowledge. Prior experience prompts the firm's development of schema, which can facilitate the rationalization and value assessment of externally available knowledge. When confronted with this knowledge, a firm attempts to identify similarities between novel knowledge and that which it currently possesses. Similarities and discontinuities are identified to provide a bridge to understand dissimilarities. In this way, a firm can engage in "reflection-in-action," whereby prior knowledge acts as a basis on which to "fill in the holes" or transform novel knowledge inconsistencies into usable knowledge. The firm can also estimate the degree to which this knowledge contains potential value from the firm's perspective. In other words, experience provides the basis on which new learning proceeds.

Organizational capability development, therefore, is somewhat localized as exploitation and search practices conform to historically determined paths. Firms tend to search (and will generally be more successful in searching) for productive opportunities in familiar areas or areas closely related to their expertise. The filtering-like action of organization capabilities, as well as the limits to which the firm's reflection-in-action can allow rationalization of highly foreign technologies, necessitates this local character of search. Thus, KBV perspectives tend to be evolutionary where capability development affects and is affected by previous activity, and evolves with exploitation and search. This cycle leads to the firm's in-depth understanding of resource and capability strengths and weaknesses. As suggested elsewhere

in this encyclopedia, such evolutionary tendencies can also lead to inertial tendencies and firm value dissipation.

According to most KBV perspectives, the nature and duration of a firm's competitive position (including competitive advantage) is based on these capabilities. First, as noted, capabilities unite distinct functions within the firm, and the degree to which "architectural" coordination is achieved determines how valuably a firm can exploit, maintain, and build its specialized functions into a coherent organization. Integration of manufacturing, development, and marketing with other areas of the firm, for example, may determine if enough innovative product is produced to meet demand or if volume deficiencies allow competitors to successfully substitute for a firm's product. Furthermore, *future* firm growth depends on the degree to which capabilities allow for and motivate the firm's search for new and valuable ideas. To borrow from Joseph Schumpeter, innovation emerges from the novel recombination of existing technologies, information, and resources. The degree to which capabilities allow various firm entities to identify and establish new connections among one another or to find and absorb externally available technologies (e.g., through collaborations) will determine a firm's future competitiveness. Firms continually confront changing environmental conditions and product obsolescence. The degree to which capabilities continually evolve to confront these threats and promote the exploration and exploitation of new opportunities determines a firm's future vitality.

Future vitality is also a function of the tacitness of these capabilities. Although an employee *possesses* some degree of firm-wide knowledge, he or she cannot *express* it in words. Or to adapt phraseology from Michael Polanyi, an employee "knows more than s/he can tell." Much like one's inability to explain "gut" feelings, a firm possesses in-depth comprehension of resources but cannot effectively codify this knowledge. Again, from Polanyi, the knowledge of (a) the multitude of resources (i.e., experience with employees, fixed assets, cognizance of emotional ties among individuals), (b) the complex web of interactions among resources (e.g., laboratories promote research that in turn is furthered via development units), and (c) the "inexhaustible" possible future configurations among these resources precludes easy description of that which guides firm operations. These three aspects of tacitness emerge from experience but preclude codification. Accordingly, a competitor's comprehension of a firm's capabilities requires the daunting if not impossible task of replicating the firm's path through history. Even in the unlikely case where a competitor could re-create such historical events, the competitor could not compress in a competitively feasible period (e.g., before further capability evolution by the imitated firm) the learning that the firm required decades to develop. Furthermore, since capabilities are rooted not in the mind of any single employee but rather exist within the social fabric of the firm, competitors theoretically could not acquire a firm's capabilities by hiring away firm employees. Even in the case where a competitor hires a significant portion of a firm's employees and management, some KBV theorists might contend that without re-creating the same context within the imitating firm as that which existed in the to-be-imitated firm (i.e., its portfolio of tangible and intangible resources as well as the network on interactions within which they exist), capabilities "acquired" may not conform to the "new" environment.

Thus, capabilities establish the perceived boundaries of the firm through cognitive and emotional (negative or positive) attachment. Nexus-of-contract perspectives (e.g., transaction costs, agency theories) view firms as efficient amalgamations of transactions. From a KBV perspective, however, this would be viewed as overly reductionist. In the same way that a person is more than a mere assemblage of lepton-boson-quark (i.e., subatomic particle) interactions (at least, according to some), defining a firm simply as an assemblage of its constituent parts or transactions fails to capture its true core. Indeed, if one were to reduce two individuals to a count of their various fundamental particles, the two would look remarkably similar. However, because of differences in the two individuals' *organizations* of particles, their personalities may diverge considerably. "Emergent" properties resulting from the complex organization of constituent elements result in creation of capabilities that cannot be created otherwise. A firm, therefore, is not a "substitute" for market governance. Rather, it is a device that creates arenas for unique capability development. As such, organization charts, annual reports, analysts' discussions, and so on provide highly naive and inaccurate depictions of the firm because these don't account for the complex set of interactions (and interactions of interactions) within the firm.

Importance

The KBV has achieved considerable academic support over the past two decades. Yet some find it largely indistinguishable from the *resource-based view* (RBV) of the firm and the research on *dynamic capabilities*. Indeed, apart from instances of pure "luck" (where a firm's current competitive position is determined simply by chance), it is difficult to identify an instance where firm-wide knowledge does not determine competence. Knowledge certainly plays a part in establishing which resources to build and maintain and which to disregard and thus seems central to the message put forth in RBV work. Similarly, apart from level of analysis debates, there does not seem to be a clear demarcation between KBV research and the work on dynamic capabilities.

From an empirical standpoint, capabilities are difficult to operationalize and thus can create difficulties in testing certain aspects of the KBV. Tacit capabilities, by definition, cannot be identified and measured. They are also idiosyncratic to a firm, making techniques used to measure one firm's capabilities (if that were somehow achieved) of limited applicability to measurement of other firm's capabilities. Researchers have attempted to circumvent these difficulties by examining the observable outcomes of capability use. For example, many studies have used patent-derived statistics to assess the dexterity with which a firm's capabilities promote new technologies. This can, to some extent, allow the testing of some KBV prescriptions. However, as implied earlier, a firm's competitive position is not only determined by firm-wide knowledge but also by the complex network of resources that these capabilities guide. Empirical testing under such complexities requires careful consideration of such factors.

KBV perspectives can provide important insights for managers to use when facing critical challenges, opportunities, or both. Manufacturing scale, contracts, intellectual property, star scientists, and other resources are certainly key ingredients in the operations of the firm. But what primarily determines resource value within the firm are the capabilities that guide their use. Acquisition, creation, and disposition of such resources without careful assessment of how such activities influence or can be influenced by tacit capabilities can be quite detrimental to firm value.

In a related vein, executives should remember that cultivating knowledge does not simply entail collecting and organizing information (i.e., that knowledge that is relatively freely and publicly available). Although some scholars view the role of the firm in a knowledge-based economy to be the collecting and analyzing of information, KBV proponents seem to suggest that a firm's chief goal is the *creation* of unique and valuable knowledge. Information must be accessed. But how that information is used and integrated with the firm's other resources will most likely determine the success of a firm's strategy.

Managers should also remember that efficiency can be built within social organizations, even in industries that are not viewed as knowledge intensive. Companies that have considerable scale may not realize efficiencies if the social fabric of the firm creates frictions in knowledge transfer. Thus, returns to otherwise intelligent capital investment without social bonds may be fleeting.

Edward Levitas

See also Competitive Advantage; Dynamic Capabilities; Organizational Learning; Resource-Based View of the Firm; Tacit Knowledge

Further Readings

Cohen, W. M., & Levinthal, D. A. (1990). Absorptive capacity: A new perspective on learning and innovation. *Administrative Science Quarterly, 35,* 128–152.

Grant, R. M. (1997). Toward a knowledge-based theory of the firm. *Strategic Management Journal, 17,* 109–122.

Henderson, R., & Cockburn, I. (1994). Measuring competence? Exploring firm effects in pharmaceutical research. *Strategic Management Journal, 15*[Special issue], 29–44.

Kogut, B., & Zander, U. (1992). Knowledge of the firm, combinative capabilities, and the replication of technology. *Organization Science, 3,* 383–397.

Kogut, B., & Zander, U. (1996). What firms do? Coordination, identity, and learning. *Organization Science, 7,* 502–518.

Nelson, R. R., & Winter, S. G. (1982). *An evolutionary theory of economic change.* Cambridge, MA: Belknap Press.

Nonaka, I. (1994). A dynamic theory of organizational knowledge creation. *Organization Science, 5,* 14–37.

Penrose, E. T. (1959). *The theory of the growth of the firm.* New York, NY: Wiley.

Polanyi, M. (1962). *Personal knowledge: Towards a post-critical philosophy.* Chicago IL: University of Chicago Press

Teece, D. J., Pisano, G., & Shuen, A. (1997). Dynamic capabilities and strategic management. *Strategic Management Journal, 18,* 509–533.

Winter, S. G. (1987). Knowledge and competence as strategic assets. In D. J. Teece (Ed.), *The competitive challenge: Strategies for industrial innovation and renewal* (pp. 159–184). Cambridge, MA: Ballinger.

L

LARGE GROUP INTERVENTIONS

Fundamentals

Large group interventions (LGIs) are a group of organization development (OD) methods for participative change in organizations and communities. These interventions bring representatives of the whole system together to discuss important issues and search for common ground to make decisions. The fundamental premise of these methods is that if you want people in organizations or communities to support a change initiative, you need to involve them in the discussion and decisions about the change—that is, to give people "voice." When this happens, the theory is that they will be more likely to support and sustain the change. In this entry, we briefly describe the history and role of LGIs in OD practice and then present the methods organized by the outcomes they seek to achieve.

LGIs are catalysts in a change process that usually begins with a representative planning committee working with an internal or external OD consultant to manage the change process, including planning event(s) and implementation.

The label "large group" was coined because when the thinking about these methods developed in the 1980s, most organizational change events were managed by experienced facilitators. When Kathy Dannemiller worked with 500 Ford managers in one room, she went against prevailing practice. She managed the large group by creating many small "microcosm" groups. These self-managed groups were composed of about eight people each from a different part of the organization sitting around 5-foot round tables. As they engaged each other in discussions from their diverse perspectives, the whole system began to get to know and understand itself. To allow what was discussed in these small groups to be heard and reacted to by all present, she then used processes such as flip chart reports and sticky dot voting on important issues to make visual the perspectives in the room.

Levels of OD Intervention

OD practitioners select from five levels of interventions: individual, interpersonal, group, intergroup, and system/organization. LGIs are system-level methods specifically designed to get the whole system into the room. The system includes all the stakeholders affected by the issue under discussion. LGIs can involve from 30 people if the whole system is represented to as many as 4,500 when AmericaSpeaks gathered stakeholders to discuss what should happen to the World Trade Center site in New York City in 2002.

LGIs may involve people for a day (America-Speaks; World Café), 2 or 3 days (Future Search; Open Space), or 4 days (The Conference Model; Appreciative Inquiry Summit). Under today's time pressures, however, consultants who design these events are finding creative ways to shorten them or to stretch them out over weeks and even months.

Typology of Methods

Barbara Benedict Bunker and Billie T. Alban created a framework for organizing these methods by three types of outcomes that they aspire to achieve. The first category, Methods for Creating the Future, includes Future Search created by Marvin Weisbord and Sandra Janoff, the Search Conference developed by Fred Emery, Whole Scale Change invented by Dannemiller, and the Appreciative Inquiry Summit of David Cooperrider. These methods involve participants in changes they desire for the future, such as organizational strategy, new products or services, a reduction in community violence, or a new plan for an urban downtown. They are carefully structured using open systems planning as the theory base to lead participants to a concrete outcome. Most are time tested and can be expected to work if used appropriately by persons with some experience. Books are available for each of these methods with details about planning and running the intervention.

The second category is Methods for Work Design. This means examining work flow processes such as how patients are admitted to hospital or steps in a manufacturing process or applying for a bank loan. The people involved in these processes decide what is working and where problems occur. Then, they decide where the biggest payoff would be if the process were redesigned and propose changes. These changes may also require changes in the organization structure. This intervention is often a series of events or conferences that involve analysis, proposals, and decision making. The Conference Model created by Dick and Emily Axelrod, Whole Scale Work Design by Dannemiller, and Fast Cycle, Full Participation Work Design by Bill Pasmore and Al Fitz are examples of these methods. Participative Design by Fred and Merrelyn Emery is a more radical whole organization process that begins with education and then starts at the bottom of the organization with people designing their own work processes.

The third category, Methods for Whole System Participative Work, includes problem solving, discussion, and issue sensing. Open Space Technology created by Harrison Owen is a lightly structured method that allows people to come together to explore a wide range of issues they feel passionate about and create their own agenda for those discussions. The World Café by Juanita Brown is a very flexible method for engaging large groups in discussions. AmericaSpeaks by Carolyn Lukensmeyer creates structured town meetings on public policy issues. Work Out is a problem solving method developed by General Electric to gather stakeholders to analyze and resolve organizational problems within a 90-day time frame. Whole Scale Interactive Events by Dannemiller and Robert W. Jacobs are customized events designed for a specific purpose or outcome. SimuReal, created by Donald C. Klein, is a 1-day organization or community simulation that allows analysis of how things are working or creates a trial run for a new structure.

There are many descriptions of positive change outcomes using LGIs in the literature. However, it is difficult to demonstrate what caused the change when so many factors are involved. Only a few really solid research studies have investigated the processes in LGIs that lead to change. As a result, managers should get the advice of a consultant experienced in several of these methods when considering system wide engagement or selecting a LGI.

Barbara Benedict Bunker

See also Appreciative Inquiry Model; Empowerment; Organizational Development; Organizational Effectiveness; Participative Model of Decision Making; Process Theories of Change; Stakeholder Theory; Systems Theory of Organizations

Further Readings

Bunker, B. B., & Alban, B. (Eds.). (1992). Large group interventions [Special issue]. *Journal of Applied Behavioral Science, 28*(4).

Bunker, B. B., & Alban, B. T. (1997). *Large group interventions: Engaging the whole system for rapid change.* San Francisco, CA: Jossey-Bass.

Bunker, B. B., & Alban, B.T. (Eds.). (2005). Large group interventions [Special issue]. *Journal of Applied Behavioral Science, 41*(1).

Bunker, B. B., & Alban, B. T. (2006). *The handbook of large group methods: Creating systemic change in organizations and communities.* San Francisco, CA: Jossey-Bass.

Holman, P., Devane, T., & Cady, S. (2007). *The change handbook.* San Francisco, CA: Berrett-Koehler.

Weisbord, M. R. (2012). *Productive workplaces: Dignity, meaning, and community in the 21st century.* San Francisco, CA: Jossey-Bass/Wiley.

Worley, C. G., Mohrman, S. A., & Nevitt, J. A. (2011). Large group interventions: An empirical field study of their composition, process, and outcomes. *Journal of Applied Behavioral Science, 47,* 4.

LEAD USERS

Lead users are defined as members of a user population who display two key characteristics: First, they anticipate relatively high benefits from obtaining a solution to their needs—and may innovate as a result. Second, they are at the leading edge of important trends in a given marketplace—and thus experience specific needs far earlier than many users in that marketplace. These lead users are thus able to provide direct input into new product development tasks and have often prototyped new product solutions for themselves or for their communities. The "lead user method" is a managerial tool that allows companies to benefit from the creative potential of lead users. This entry provides a description of the lead user concept and shows how firms can benefit from harnessing the creative potential of this specific user group.

Fundamentals

In a number of studies from the late 1970s and 1980s onward, Eric von Hippel of MIT and several of his colleagues have observed that in very different industries—ranging from high-tech areas such as scientific instruments or thermoplastics to consumer markets such as outdoor equipment or skateboards—a huge percentage of the most important innovations were originally developed by the product users, not by the producing firms. In this context, the term *user* refers to the functional role of the institution and means that with respect to the product or service in question, the institution expects to derive benefits from its own *use*, not from *selling* the artifact. Therefore, "users" may be individual end users such as consumers in the beverages market or firms such as a high-tech manufacturer that uses a specific machine in its internal production process.

The finding that users can be very active in innovation seemed to contradict canonical market research experience from "voice of the customer" techniques, which holds that customers are at best capable of articulating unsatisfied present needs but are hardly able to provide information about future needs or even to provide ideas, concepts, and solutions to match those needs. This puzzle was resolved by the introduction of the lead user concept. Although it may be true that many customers

are unable to provide active input in new product development tasks, there is a specific subgroup of users—the lead users—who are indeed creative and innovative. Lead users are able to provide direct input in new product development tasks and have often prototyped new product solutions for themselves (personally or for the company they work in) or for their communities.

The original theoretical thinking that led to the definition of "lead users" as having (a) high expected benefits from an innovation and (b) a position ahead of an important market trend was built on findings from two different streams of literature.

The "high expected benefits" component of the lead user definition was derived from research on the economics of innovation. Studies of industrial product and process innovations have shown that the greater the benefit an entity expects to obtain from a required innovation, the greater that entity's investment in obtaining a solution will be. The benefits a user expects can be higher than those expected by a producer—for example, if the market is new and uncertain, if customer preferences are heterogeneous and change quickly in the market, or if the costs of innovation are lower for users than for manufacturers because of the "stickiness" of preference information. Component 1 of the lead user definition was therefore intended to serve as an indicator of innovation likelihood.

The second component of the lead user definition—namely, being "ahead of an important marketplace trend"—was included because of its expected impact on the commercial attractiveness of innovations developed by users residing at that location in a marketplace. Studies on the diffusion of innovations regularly show that some customers adopt innovations before others. Classic research on problem solving reveals that subjects are heavily constrained by their real-world experience through an effect known as *functional fixedness:* Those who use an object or see it used in a familiar way find it difficult to conceive of novel uses. Taken in combination, this led to the hypothesis that users who lead a trend would be best positioned to understand what many others will need later. After all, their present-day reality represents aspects of the future from the viewpoint of those with mainstream market needs. Component 2 of the lead user definition therefore indicates the commercial attractiveness of an innovation created by such a user.

Note that these two components of the lead user definition are conceptually independent. They stem from different areas of literature, and they serve different functions in lead user theory. Although they may be correlated in some cases, because a position ahead of the trend may well be accompanied by a high need for innovative solutions, this is not necessarily always the case. Therefore, the lead user construct can be described as consisting of two (formative) dimensions.

In many publications (including this entry), lead users are treated as a specific population or "species," which in essence implies a binary concept. It is therefore important to keep in mind that the lead user construct is distributed over a continuum. There is no natural borderline that objectively distinguishes lead users or non-lead users and empirical assessments show that the distribution of lead "userness" follows a normal distribution and is not bimodal. For matters of stringency, it may hence be useful to talk about lead users; however, it would be more precise to talk about "individuals who display high levels of lead user characteristics."

If lead user innovators are individuals, the question arises as to how they tackle the often-complex task of product development. An individual may well develop an idea, but developing the idea into a functioning prototype often requires diverse and specific knowledge that a lone individual is unlikely to possess. As a result, lead users often organize into communities to complement their capabilities, both in offline communities and in online communities such as open source networks or other forms of virtual institutions. This makes lead users easier to identify for firms seeking to benefit from their creative potential.

The Lead User Method

The lead user method proposed is a managerial heuristic that enables companies to search for commercially attractive user innovations and identify new business opportunities systematically. Usually, this method is described as comprising four phases.

The start phase. The start phase involves defining objectives (e.g., "finding an innovative solution to problem X" or "identifying an innovative product concept in market Y") and setting up a cross-functional team. The latter is important to ensure

that solutions found have sufficient fit with regard to strategy, research and development, and production capabilities and objectives. Also, broad anchorage reduces the risk of "not invented here" problems arising from the fact that solutions external to the company are being sought.

Identification of major needs and trends. In the second phase, the three to five most important trends are selected. This selection is usually based on interviews with experts, information from online forums, and literature research. Their function in the process is to narrow the problem and to allow a systematic search for lead users. The trends are those dimensions in which lead users are far ahead of the mass market.

Identification of users leading those trends. The third phase involves searching for lead users. Earlier studies usually employed a mass screening approach in which a large sample of users (typically from customer databases) was systematically filtered to identify those users who score highest in both lead user dimensions. More recently, lead user studies have increasingly turned to the pyramiding method for the purpose of lead user identification. In the latter approach, researchers start with a few users and ask them who has especially high needs and is leading the trend. Those users are then contacted and asked the same questions, and the process continues until a sufficient level of "lead userness" is achieved (which is usually the case after two or three steps). Recently, experiments have demonstrated the superior efficiency of the pyramiding search strategy compared with screening. Another advantage is the possibility of identifying individuals outside a predefined population or sample. Particularly, analogous markets—that is, markets that are different from the target market but characterized by the same trends—are valuable sources in the search for lead users. Consider the example of a lead user study that aims to find methods of preventing infections in clinical surgery. For this purpose, one important trend would be "methods for increased air purity." Outside of leading hospitals, experts from the analogous field of chip production or CD production may also be able to provide valuable creative input. There are two reasons why it might make sense to ask such people: First, they might possess solution-related knowledge that is worth transferring from the analogous field to the target field, and second, they are less likely to be blocked by existing solutions in the target field.

The lead user workshop. In the fourth and final phase, the lead users identified are invited to a 2 or 3-day workshop in which company members from different functional areas also participate. At these workshops, techniques such as brainstorming, group discussions, and others are used to capitalize on the creativity of the participants. It is important for the company to address the issue of intellectual property rights prior to the workshop and to ensure that the ideas and concepts generated can be commercialized without the risk of legal infringements. Often, this is unproblematic because in many cases it is economically profitable for a users to reveal their innovations freely (e.g., because they expect to profit from the use of the resulting product).

Importance

The lead user concept is helpful for understanding why some users successfully innovate. Its basic propositions—that lead users display a high likelihood of yielding innovations of high commercial appeal—have been confirmed in many academic studies, ranging from case studies and surveys to field experiments and practical applications. In a systematic natural experiment with particularly high validity, the lead user method was compared with other methods of idea generation (such as focus groups). The impressive finding is that, on average, the lead user method resulted in 8 times higher commercial success and provided the basis of a major new product line in all cases, whereas this was the case for only one of 42 non-lead-user projects. This suggests that it is not only a concept of high acceptance among academics but also has substantial practical value.

Recent studies also found that an individual's lead userness with respect to a specific market is correlated with innovativeness, adoption behavior, and opinion leadership. Lead users buy new products earlier and more frequently than average users and influence many other potential buyers' purchase decisions. This suggests that the lead user concept constitutes a valuable approach in other phases of the innovation process as well, such as new product

forecasting, product and concept testing, product design, and the diffusion of innovations.

Nikolaus Franke

See also Entrepreneurial Opportunities; Learning Organization; Open Innovation; Patterns of Innovation; Strategic Entrepreneurship; Technological Discontinuities; Technology and Complexity

Further Readings

Franke, N., von Hippel, E., & Schreier, M. (2006). Finding commercially attractive user innovations: A test of lead user theory. *Journal of Product Innovation Management, 23,* 301–315.

Lilien, G., Morrison, P. D., Searls, K., Sonnack, M., & von Hippel, E. (2002). Performance assessment of the lead user generation process for new product development. *Management Science, 48,* 1042–1059.

Lüthje, C., & Herstatt, C. (2004). The lead user method: An outline of empirical findings and issues for future research. *R&D Management, 34,* 553–568.

Morrison, P. D., Roberts, J. H., & Midgley, D. F. (2004). The nature of lead users and measurement of leading edge status. *Research Policy, 33,* 351–362.

Schreier, M., & Prügl, R. (2008). Extending lead user theory: Antecedents and consequences of consumers' lead userness. *Journal of Product Innovation Management, 25,* 331–346.

Urban, G., & von Hippel E. (1988). Lead user analyses for the development of new industrial products. *Management Science, 35,* 569–582.

von Hippel, E. (1986). Lead users: A source of novel product concepts. *Management Science, 32,* 791–806.

von Hippel, E. (1988). *The sources of innovation.* New York, NY: Oxford University Press.

von Hippel, E. (2005). *Democratizing innovation.* Cambridge, MA: MIT Press.

LEADER–MEMBER EXCHANGE THEORY

Leader–member exchange (LMX) theory was introduced by George Graen and his colleagues during the mid-1970s. Initially referred to as the *vertical-dyad linkage model* of leadership, the theory contends that through a role-making process, some members of a leader's work group become part of the leader's in-group, whereas others compose the out-group. In other words, the leader develops a high-quality relationship with some subordinates (members) and a low-quality relationship with others. The theory proposes that the quality of the exchange relationship between leader and member has a major impact on the attitudes and behaviors of both parties in the dyad. At the time when LMX theory was proposed, it provided an alternative perspective to existing leadership theories that assumed that leaders treat their work group members similarly, called an average leadership style approach. LMX theory is relevant to management because leading others is one of the most critical roles of a manager. Research based on LMX theory provides key insights for managers on how the leader–member relationship develops and how it impacts member, leader, and team outcomes. This entry describes the theory and early research findings, followed by a summary of studies on the antecedents and consequences of LMX. Recent research is discussed that has extended LMX beyond the dyad to the group-level.

Fundamentals

LMX theory is a relationship-based approach to leadership. Originally based on role theory, it was proposed that work in organizations is accomplished through roles negotiated between new members and their leaders. Through this negotiation and role development process, varied interpersonal exchange relationships develop between leaders and their members. A core concept of the theory is that leaders do not develop the same type of relationship with each follower; rather, relationship quality varies widely among members of a leader's work group. Early research described this as resulting in an in-group and out-group within a work group, but subsequently, scholars suggested a continuum of relationship quality, ranging from low to high. More recent studies have applied social exchange theory to understanding leader–member exchanges and suggest that high-quality exchanges are based on social exchange and low-quality exchanges are based on economic exchange. Social exchanges are characterized by unspecified obligations, commitment, trust, and interpersonal attachment, whereas economic exchanges tend to be distinguished by specific, discrete, and tangible transactions.

The first stream of research testing LMX theory focused on determining whether leaders do, in fact, differentiate among members and develop varying exchange relationships. Results confirmed this key contention of the theory. The implication is that to understand leadership in the workplace, studies should focus on the dyadic level and the exchange relationship. Related to this issue is the question of why differentiated relationships develop within a work group. One response is that it occurs through the role negotiation and development process. Extending this explanation, scholars have suggested that leaders have limited time and social resources and thus are able to develop high-quality exchanges with only a subset of members. Although less is known about when and why differentiated exchange relationships develop within a work group, research supports the fact that this is a common phenomenon.

A second stream of research has investigated the consequences of LMX, primarily in terms of member outcomes. Many of these studies are based on social exchange theory and propose that high-quality exchange relationships are associated with desirable outcomes for members because these relationships are characterized by mutual respect, trust, liking, and reciprocal influence. Results of these studies as well as meta-analyses on the relation between LMX and member outcomes indicate that LMX is related to member behaviors, including turnover intentions, actual turnover, organizational citizenship behavior, and job performance. Among attitudinal outcomes, research indicates that LMX is significantly related to organizational commitment and supervisor, pay, and job satisfaction. Perceptions of the work environment have also been linked to LMX. Support has been found for a positive relationship between LMX and member perceptions of justice, empowerment, and engagement. Studies have found a negative association between LMX and member perceptions of politics, role ambiguity, and role conflict. Finally, LMX has been linked to a number of important career-related outcomes, including desirable assignments, promotions, and salary. Overall, the empirical research provides strong support for the critical role of LMX on member perceptions, attitudes, behaviors, and career outcomes.

A third area of research focused on the development of LMX. A limited number of studies addressed questions regarding when the quality of exchange becomes established and whether it is stable. Using longitudinal research designs, these studies examined the development of exchange quality with new leader–member dyads over time. Several key findings emerged. One is that the quality of exchange tends to be fairly stable over time. A second finding is that the quality of exchange that exists within a dyadic relationship tends to be observable; that is, members of a work group tend to know which members have a high- versus low-quality exchange with the leader. A third important finding is that LMX relationships are established fairly quickly, with some studies indicating that this may occur in as little as a few weeks after working together.

Given the strong and consistent findings of the impact of LMX on member outcomes, a fourth stream of research focused on the antecedents of LMX. The primary purpose of the majority of studies on the antecedents of LMX was to identify member characteristics, leader characteristics, and interpersonal characteristics that affect quality of exchange. Similar to the outcomes of LMX, there have been a large number of studies on the antecedents of LMX, resulting in a comprehensive list of significant variables. The member characteristics with empirical support include member competence, personality traits (e.g., agreeableness, conscientiousness, extraversion, positive affectivity, and locus of control), and upward influence behavior. Findings on upward influence behavior suggest that members may proactively manage the exchange relationship that develops with their leader through influence behaviors such as ingratiation and other forms of impression management. Compared to studies on member characteristics, there have been far fewer studies on characteristics of the leader that influence LMX. Support has been found for leader personality (extraversion, agreeableness, and affectivity), leader reward behavior (contingent rewards), and leader expectations of followers. Interpersonal characteristics as predictors of LMX consider both leader and member characteristics jointly. For example, some studies have examined demographic similarity between the leader and member as a predictor of LMX. The findings have been mixed for demographic similarity; however, perceived similarity between leader and member has received support. Similarity in terms of personality traits has also been linked to LMX. Mutual liking and trust have been identified as strong predictors of LMX. In summary, a large number of antecedents of LMX have been identified in the literature. The findings indicate that LMX is not simply based on member competence or performance. Rather, a multitude of member, leader, and interpersonal characteristics predict LMX. Future research is needed to uncover the relative importance of the antecedents depending on the context, as well as how they may interact in predicting LMX.

Much of this review has described empirical research findings. From a theoretical perspective, LMX scholars have offered a multidimensional conceptualization of LMX. Relying on role theory and social exchange theory, four dimensions of LMX have been proposed: contribution, affect (liking), loyalty, and professional respect. A 12-item measure, labeled LMX-MDM, was developed through rigorous scale development procedures to capture the multidimensional nature of LMX. Support for LMX as a multidimensional construct has been found in a number of studies.

While the majority of LMX research has focused on the dyadic level of analysis, recent studies have explored LMX at the group level. When quality of exchange relationships varies widely within a group, this is referred to as high differentiation. The question is whether and how differentiation is related to group performance. Preliminary findings suggest that greater differentiation is associated with higher group performance under certain conditions, such as when task interdependence is high. Another area of research that examines LMX from a group context is studies on relative LMX, which occurs when members compare the quality of their own exchange relationship with the leader to coworkers' exchange relationships with the leader. Results indicate that members' attitudes and behaviors are impacted by not only the quality of their exchange with the leader but also the relative quality of their exchange compared to that of coworkers.

Importance

The key tenants of LMX theory have been strongly supported through hundreds of empirical studies. There is overwhelming evidence that leaders do develop different quality exchange relationships with members of their work groups. Rather than engaging in similar types of behaviors with all subordinates, leaders behave quite differently across subordinates, depending on the quality of the exchange relationship. Research based on LMX theory indicates that the quality of the relationship that develops between a leader and subordinate impacts a number of important individual-level outcomes. The evidence is clear that members who have developed high-quality exchanges with their leaders experience many desirable and beneficial outcomes, such as greater support, desirable assignments, promotions, and so on. In summary, LMX theory is one of the most researched and supported theories of leadership.

In terms of its impact on management scholars, LMX has provided an alternative framework for investigating leadership. Contrary to other leadership theories that assume leaders engage in the same behaviors with all subordinates, LMX theory focused researchers' attention on the dyadic relationship. A multidimensional measure of LMX was developed through rigorous scale development procedures, providing a valid measure of the construct. LMX scholars discovered that the quality of exchange of the dyadic relationship has a significant impact on outcomes that matter to organizations, such as employee commitment, performance, satisfaction, and turnover. Because of these findings, scholars examined predictors of LMX. Applying theories of interpersonal relationships from psychology and sociology, scholars uncovered member, leader, and interpersonal characteristics that influence LMX.

LMX theory has a number of implications for improving management practice. One major implication is that leaders need to consider the quality of the exchange relationship they have established with each subordinate. An exchange relationship that is of high quality and is based on mutual contribution, professional respect, loyalty, and affect is one that will be associated with beneficial outcomes for the member, leader, and organization. It is presumed that leaders who have developed a larger number of high-quality exchange relationships within the work group are more effective leaders. However, this contention needs further investigation in terms of whether this is achievable, given leaders' limited time and resources. An assumption of LMX theory is that some low-quality exchanges within a work group are undesirable yet unavoidable. However, there may be circumstances when dyadic partners prefer a low-quality exchange relationship. This issue has received limited attention as well as how one might change an established low-quality relationship to one that is of high quality.

Another implication for management practice is that leaders and their work group members often have different views of their exchange relationship. That is, LMX studies have found a lack in agreement between member and leader perceptions of their exchange relationship. The implication for managers is that it is important to be aware of the employee's view of the relationship because this affects the employee's attitudes and behaviors and likely differs from the manager's own perceptions of the relationship.

A final implication for management practice is that leader–member relationships develop through an informal, interpersonal process that creates a certain quality of exchange. Characteristics of the member and leader, as well as interpersonal characteristics, influence the development of the leader-member relationship. The relationship is not solely based on member performance or competence. Rather, a broad set of characteristics that either reduce or enhance affect, respect, loyalty, and contribution between the parties result in the quality of exchange. Both parties of the dyad have an impact on the exchange relationship, which develops early in the relationship and tends to be rather stable. The implication is that both the leader and the member need to be proactive and effectively manage the interpersonal exchange relationship so that it leads to desirable outcomes for both and for the organization overall.

Sandy J. Wayne

See also Differentiation and the Division of Labor; Leadership Practices; Role Theory; Social Exchange Theory; Transformational Theory of Leadership

Further Readings

Dienesch, R. M., & Liden, R. C. (1986). Leader-member exchange model of leadership: A critique and further development. *Academy of Management Review, 11,* 618–634.

Graen, G. B., & Uhl-Bien, M. (1995). Development of leader-member exchange (LMX) theory of leadership over 25 years: Applying a multi-level multi-domain perspective. *Leadership Quarterly, 6,* 219–247.

Henderson, D. J., Wayne, S. J., Shore, L. M., Bommer, W. H., & Tetrick, L. E. (2008). Leader-member exchange, differentiation, and psychological contract fulfillment: A multilevel examination. *Journal of Applied Psychology, 93,* 1208–1219.

Liden, R. C., Erdogan, B., Wayne, S. J., & Sparrowe, R. T. (2006). Leader-member exchange, differentiation, and task interdependence: Implications for individual and group performance. *Journal of Organizational Behavior, 27,* 723–746.

Liden, R. C., & Maslyn, J. M. (1998). Multidimensionality of leader-member exchange: An empirical assessment through scale development. *Journal of Management, 24,* 43–72.

Liden, R. C., Sparrowe, R. T., & Wayne, S. J. (1997). Leader-member exchange theory: The past and potential for the future. *Research in Personnel and Human Resources Management, 15,* 47–119.

Liden, R. C., Wayne, S. J., & Stilwell, D. (1993). A longitudinal study on the early development of leader-member exchanges. *Journal of Applied Psychology, 78,* 662–674.

Sparrowe, R. T., & Liden, R. C. (1997). Process and structure in leader-member exchange. *Academy of Management Review, 22,* 522–552.

Wayne, S. J., & Ferris, G. R. (1990). Influence tactics, affect, and exchange quality in supervisor-subordinate interactions: A laboratory experiment and field study. *Journal of Applied Psychology, 75,* 487–499.

Wayne, S. J., Shore, L. M., & Liden, R. C. (1997). Perceived organizational support and leader-member exchange: A social exchange perspective. *Academy of Management Journal, 40,* 82–111.

Leadership Continuum Theory

Robert Tannenbaum and Warren H. Schmidt's leadership continuum theory (LCT) advances an autocratic-democratic continuum model illustrating the degree of power and influence managers assert during decision-making processes. The continuum ranges from manager centered (autocratic) to employee centered (democratic). It is possible for managers to exhibit a hybrid of these approaches. Developed more than 40 years ago, LCT remains relevant for describing, explaining, and predicting how power, authority, and freedom are negotiated and communicated during workplace decision-making processes. This entry outlines the fundamentals of LCT, including a description of the continuum of

decision-making behaviors and the forces that can influence the adoption or avoidance of these actions. Implications of LCT are also discussed.

Fundamentals

LCT proposes that managerial behaviors exhibited during decision-making processes are connected by a theoretical spectrum. As Tannenbaum and Schmidt stated in their seminal 1973 publication,

> Rather than offering a choice between two styles of leadership, democratic or authoritarian, [the LCT continuum] sanctions a range of behavior. . . . The concept does not dictate to managers but helps them to analyze their own behavior. The continuum permits them to review their behavior within a context of other alternatives, without any style being labeled right or wrong. (p. 166)

The behaviors on LCT's continuum are related to (a) the degree of authority that managers choose to exert and (b) the amount of freedom managers grant nonmanagers when making workplace decisions The following describes LCT's continuum of behaviors, ranging from more autocratic (1) to more democratic (7).

1. The manager independently spots a problem, outlines a solution to the issue, and directs nonmanagers in a top-down fashion how to implement the predetermined action plan.

2. The manager independently identifies a problem and solution and attempts to minimize resistance by persuading nonmanagers to accept it as the best course of action (e.g., manager "sells" how the decision personally benefits the nonmanagers).

3. The manager identifies a problem and solution, presents the ideas to nonmanagers, and fields questions to gain a deeper understanding of the implications associated with the predetermined course of action.

4. The manager identifies a problem and solution then presents the tentative ideas to nonmanagers. After soliciting input from nonmanagers, the manager makes the final decision.

5. The manager identifies a problem and solicits input from nonmanagers about the root cause

and potential solutions. After collecting nonmanagers' feedback, the manager makes the final decision.

6. The manager identifies a problem and asks nonmanagers to decide how to resolve the issue given specified parameters.

7. Nonmanagers identify the problem, diagnose root cause, brainstorm potential solutions, and create an action plan for implementing the chosen course of action. Any parameters are imposed by organizational leaders or the environment.

Forces

LCT maintains that there are three forces that managers should consider when deciding which decision-making approach to use: (1) forces in managers, (2) forces in nonmanagers, and (3) forces in the situation.

Forces in managers. Managers' perceptions of problems will inevitably be colored by various internal personality forces. For example, what are managers' value systems regarding the act of involving key stakeholders in making decisions? To what degree do managers feel others are capable and motivated to make workplace decisions? How comfortable are managers with delegating decision-making responsibilities? And to what extent do managers possess tolerance for ambiguity associated with releasing control over decision-making responsibilities?

Forces in nonmanagers. When deciding which approach to use, managers should consider nonmanagers' perceptions and behaviors surrounding decision-making processes. For example, how do nonmanagers expect managers should act? How much involvement in the decision making process do nonmanagers expect? LCT predicts that managers may extend greater freedom if nonmanagers

- possess a relatively strong need for independence,
- demonstrate an appropriate readiness level for assuming greater responsibility,
- have a relatively high tolerance for ambiguity,
- express interest in the problem and understand its importance,
- are aligned with the organization's goals,

- possess the requisite expertise to resolve the problem, and
- expect to participate in making decisions.

Forces in the situation. Situational and environmental forces greatly influence how managers manage the decision-making process. These forces include time pressures, established organizational values and traditions, organizational size and locations, confidentiality issues, interpersonal/group dynamics, and other group variables such as group efficacy in decision making, cohesiveness, permissiveness, mutual acceptance, and commonality of purpose. The scope and essence of the problem will also dictate how much authority managers should delegate to nonmanagers.

Assessment

LCT exhibits a number of strengths and limitations. In terms of strengths, LCT's continuum parsimoniously captures a broad range of approaches for managing decision-making processes. Second, LCT outlines a clear set of predictive conditions for when it is (in)appropriate to delegate greater responsibility to nonmanagers during decision-making opportunities. A third advantage is that LCT exhibits significant heuristic value, advancing a number of robust propositions and relationships ripe for academic testing.

LCT possesses some limitations. For example, LCT does not fully explain the full range of dynamics associated with all types of decision-making processes that occur in all types of organizations. Second, LCT fails to address the consequences and outcomes of the seven proposed leadership approaches and how they might be (in)effective with various types of decisions and organizational changes. Also, LCT fails to take into account how more nuanced human and organizational dynamics (e.g., social bonds or politics) can influence how decisions are really made in the workplace.

Despite such limitations, LCT continues to possess significant utilitarian value to the modern practitioner and organizational scholar. Originally published in the late 1950s, LCT was later reprinted in 1973 with an amendment from its authors. The authors' retrospective commentary began to address some of the aforementioned limitations as well as underscored the persistent relevance of LCT to contemporary organizations. As stated in 1973 by Tannenbaum and Schmidt,

Today's manager is more likely to deal with employees who resent being treated as subordinates, who may be highly critical of any organizational system, who expect to be consulted and to exert influence, and who often stand on the edge of alienation from the institution that needs their loyalty and commitment. In addition, [s]he is frequently confronted by a highly turbulent, unpredictable environment. (p. 166)

Travis L. Russ

See also Contingency Theory of Leadership; Decision-Making Styles; Participative Model of Decision Making; Situational Theory of Leadership; Strategic Decision Making; Theory X and Theory Y

Further Readings

Lewis, L. K., & Russ, T. L. (2012). Soliciting and using input during organizational change initiatives: What are practitioners doing? *Management Communication Quarterly, 26,* 264–294.

Poon Teng Fatt, J. (2004). Leadership styles between technical and non-technical superiors: Guess who will give subordinates more freedom on the job? *Journal of Technical Writing and Communication, 34,* 91–111.

Russ, T. L. (2008). Communicating change: A review and critical analysis of programmatic and participatory implementation approaches. *Journal of Change Management, 8,* 199–211.

Russ, T. L. (2011). Theory X/Y assumptions as predictors of managers' propensity for participative decision making. *Management Decision, 49,* 823–836.

Tannenbaum, R., & Massarik, F. (1950). Participation by subordinates in the managerial decision-making process. *Canadian Journal of Economics and Political Science, 16,* 408–418.

Tannenbaum, R., & Schmidt, W. H. (1958). How to choose a leadership pattern. *Harvard Business Review, 36,* 95–101.

Tannenbaum, R., & Schmidt, W. H. (1973). How to choose a leadership pattern (with retrospective commentary). *Harvard Business Review, 51,* 162–180.

LEADERSHIP PRACTICES

Our leadership framework has its origins in a research project we, the authors, began in 1983. We wanted to know what people did when they were at their "personal best" in leading others. We devised a Personal-Best Leadership Experience Survey consisting of 38-item open-ended questions. In our initial research, we collected and analyzed more than 550 of these surveys, each requiring 1 to 2 hours to complete. We reviewed an additional 80 short-form versions of the questionnaire and conducted 42 in-depth interviews. A thematic analysis of the leadership cases revealed clusters of behaviors that we identified as the Five Practices of Exemplary Leadership®. Our research is ongoing, and to date we've examined more than 5,000 personal-best leadership case studies and over 2 million leadership assessments from around the world. In this entry, we describe the Five Practices, give a brief comment about each from one of the leaders in our studies, present evidence that supports the impact of the Five Practices on constituent engagement and organizational performance, and suggest further reading about our work and that of other scholars and practitioners.

Fundamentals

While each leadership case is unique in its particulars, every story we've collected follows comparable patterns of action. In doing their best, leaders model the way, inspire a shared vision, challenge the process, enable others to act, and encourage the heart. These are the fundamentals of leadership. They remain as relevant today as they were when we first began our studies.

Model the Way

In talking about her personal-best leadership experience Olivia Lai, senior marketing associate at Moody's Analytics (Hong Kong), said to us, "In order for me to become a leader it's important that I first define my values and principles. If I don't know what my own values are and determine expectations for myself, how can I set expectations for others?" The first step on any leadership journey is to *clarify values* and give voice to those values.

Eloquent speeches about common values, however, aren't nearly enough. Actions are far more important than words when constituents want to determine how serious leaders really are about what they say. Exemplary leaders *set the example* through their daily actions, demonstrating deep commitment to shared values. Casey Mork, manager of a new product development team, told us he learned this lesson early on: "You've got to walk the walk, not just talk the talk. Leaders are responsible for modeling behavior based on the values they communicate." As Casey discovered, leading others is about living the values every day.

Inspire a Shared Vision

People described their personal-best leadership experiences as times when they imagined an exciting, highly attractive future for their organization. Nancy Zimpher, chancellor of the State University of New York, for example, said, "Vision trumps everything. Organizations are most effective when a well-articulated and ambitious vision of the future exists." Exemplary leaders *envision the future*. In fact, our data show that focusing on the future is the attribute that most sets leaders apart from individual contributors.

Exemplary leaders also know that they can't command commitment. They have to inspire it by *enlisting others* in a common vision. Just ask Buddy Blanton, a programs manager at Northrop Grumman Corporation. Buddy, wanting to know how he could be more effective at creating a shared vision, asked his team for feedback. They told him, "Help us, as a team, to understand how you got to your vision. We want to walk with you while you create the goals and vision so we all get to the end vision together." This experience taught Buddy that by engaging others in finding common good, unity of purpose can be forged.

Challenge the Process

Challenge is the crucible for greatness. That's precisely what Katherine Winkel, marketing operations manager at Seattle Genetics, observed when reflecting on her peers' personal-best leadership experiences. "The similarity that most stuck out in my mind was that in each story the person described having to overcome uncertainty and fear in order to achieve their best." Every single personal-best leadership case involved a change from the status quo. No one sat idly by waiting for fate to smile upon him or her.

And because innovative change comes more from listening than from telling, exemplary leaders are constantly looking outside themselves and their organization for the clues about what's new or different, and what possibilities others are not seeing. They *search for opportunities* to innovate, grow, and improve.

Exemplary leaders also *experiment and take risks*. But sometimes people are afraid, and one way leaders deal with this reluctance is to approach change through incremental steps, small wins, and continuous learning. When Venkat Dokiparthi was asked to lead a technical development team in India he realized that "I needed to break down the task and make it simple for them to feel successful." Small wins catapult leaders and their team forward and motivate them to move ahead even when times get tough.

Enable Others to Act

No leader ever got anything extraordinary done by working alone. It requires a team effort. That's exactly what Eric Pan, regional head of the Chartered Institute of Management Accountants in South China, told us: "No matter how capable a leader is, he or she alone won't be able to deliver a large project or program without the joint efforts and synergies that come from the team." Leaders *foster collaboration* and build trust by engaging all those who must make the project work. When people are trusted and have more discretion, more authority, and more information, they're much more likely to use their energies to produce extraordinary results.

Exemplary leaders also *strengthen others* so that constituents know they are capable of delivering on promises. They make constituents feel powerful and efficacious. Heidi Winkler, attorney-at-law with Pihl, a privately held construction company in Denmark, learned from her personal-best leadership experience "how much easier it is to achieve shared goals (or even make goals shared) when you involve people in the decisions to be made, trust them to handle the execution, and give them responsibilities and credit along the way."

Encourage the Heart

In climbing to the top, people can become exhausted, frustrated, and disenchanted. They are often tempted to give up. Genuine acts of caring draw people forward. Exemplary leaders *recognize contributions* by showing appreciation for individual excellence. The payoff is explained by Jason Cha, senior manufacturing engineer with Abbott Vacular: "This raises an individual's commitment to excellence because his or her name is associated with a given project."

Leaders also *celebrate the values and victories.* Celebrations and rituals, when done with authenticity and from the heart, build a strong sense of collective identity and community spirit that can carry a group through extraordinarily tough times.

Importance

These are the Five Practices of Exemplary Leadership that emerged from extensive research on what people actually do when they are leading others to greatness. And our research clearly shows that engaging in these practices makes a profoundly positive difference in people's commitment and performance at work.

To assess the impact leader behavior has on engagement and performance, we've correlated responses from nearly 2 million people around the world on the *Leadership Practices Inventory (LPI)*— our 360-degree assessment instrument measuring how frequently leaders engage in the Five Practices— with work attitude and with demographic variables. These scales consist of 10 demographic questions ranging from age and gender to function, industry, and organizational size and another 10 questions about how respondents feel about their leaders and their workplaces.

The conclusion: Those leaders who more frequently use the Five Practices of Exemplary Leadership are considerably more effective than their counterparts who use them infrequently. Statistical analyses reveal that a leader's behavior explains nearly 30% of constituents' workplace engagement. Personal and organizational characteristics of constituents, on the other hand, explain less than 1% of constituents' engagement in, commitment to, and pride in their workplaces. Workplace engagement and commitment is independent of who the constituents are (as related to factors such as age, gender, ethnicity, or education) and of their position, job, discipline, industry, nationality, or the country from which they come.

Many other scholars have documented how leaders who engage in the Five Practices are more effective than those who don't, whether the context is inside or outside the United States, the public or private sector, or within schools, health care organizations, business firms, prisons, churches, and the like. For example, leaders who use the Five Practices more frequently than their counterparts achieve the following:

- Create higher-performing teams
- Generate increased sales and customer satisfaction levels
- Foster renewed loyalty and greater organizational commitment
- Enhance motivation and the willingness to work hard
- More successfully represent their units to upper management
- Facilitate high patient-satisfaction scores and more effectively meet family member needs
- Promote high degrees of involvement in schools
- Enlarge the size of their religious congregations
- Increase fundraising results and expand gift-giving levels
- Extend the range of their agency's services
- Reduce absenteeism, turnover, and dropout rates
- Positively influence recruitment rates

Over a 5-year period, the financial performance of organizations where senior leaders were identified by their constituents as strongly using the Five Practices was compared with those organizations whose leadership was significantly less engaged in the Five Practices. The bottom line? Net income growth was nearly 18 times higher and stock price growth nearly 3 times higher than their counterparts for those publicly traded organizations whose leadership strongly engaged in the Five Practices.

Although the Five Practices of Exemplary Leadership don't completely explain why leaders and their organizations are successful—no model in existence can account for 100% of leader effectiveness—it's very clear that engaging in the Five Practices makes a positive difference no matter who you are or where you are located. How you behave as a leader matters, and it matters a lot.

James M. Kouzes and Barry Z. Posner

See also Authentic Leadership; Cultural Values; High-Performing Teams; Level 5 Leadership; Positive Organizational Scholarship; Transformational Theory of Leadership; Trust

Editor's Note: Portions of this entry are reproduced by permission of the publisher, John Wiley & Sons, Inc., from *The Leadership Challenge, Fourth Edition* by James M. Kouzes and Barry Z. Posner. Copyright © 2007 by John Wiley & Sons, Inc. All rights reserved.

Further Readings

Amabile, T., & Kramer, S. (2011). *The progress principle: Using small wins to ignite joy.* Boston, MA: Harvard Business Review Press.

Burchell, M., & Robin, J. (2011). The *great workplace: How to build it, how to keep it, and why it matters.* San Francisco, CA: Jossey-Bass.

Fredrickson, B. L. (2009). *Positivity: Groundbreaking research reveals how to embrace the hidden strengths of positive emotions, overcome negativity, and thrive.* New York, NY: Crown.

Kraemer, H. M. J., Jr. (2011). *From values to action: The four principles of values-based leadership.* San Francisco, CA: Jossey-Bass.

Kouzes, J. M., & Posner, B. Z. (2003). *Encouraging the heart: A leader's guide to rewarding and recognizing others.* San Francisco, CA: Jossey-Bass.

Kouzes, J. M., & Posner, B. Z. (2006). *A leader's legacy.* San Francisco, CA: Jossey-Bass.

Kouzes, J. M., & Posner, B. Z. (2010). *The truth about leadership: The no-fads, heart-of-the-matter facts you should know.* San Francisco, CA: Jossey-Bass.

Kouzes, J. M., & Posner, B. Z. (2011). *Credibility: How leaders gain and lose it, why people demand it* (2nd ed.). San Francisco, CA: Jossey-Bass.

Kouzes, J. M., & Posner, B. Z. (2012). *The leadership challenge: How to make extraordinary things happen in organizations* (5th ed.). San Francisco, CA: Jossey-Bass.

Wiseman, L. (2010). *Multipliers: How the best leaders make everyone smarter.* New York, NY: HarperCollins.

Lean Enterprise

More than 20 years ago, Toyota became a symbol of business success with a new way to organize automobile manufacturing that became labeled *lean production*. Companies around the world, in many industries, sought to learn from the Toyota production system. Hundreds of books and scholarly papers were written to distill the essential principles and practices, including how work is organized, how human resources are developed and used, and how the system as a whole is managed. More recent studies of Toyota and other organizations have further highlighted the need to expand our understanding beyond the production system to include the application of lean principles to processes and functions that exist both within and beyond firm boundaries, including customers, suppliers and other stakeholders. We refer to this as a theory of *lean enterprise*. In the following section, we will first briefly review the concept of lean and then focus on an enterprise and how an enterprise can be lean.

Fundamentals

The early studies of lean organizations were carried out in manufacturing settings, typified by Toyota, where metrics such as inventory, work in process, and cost could be measured easily. Lean organizations were characterized as having (a) a pull-based system that signals the need for each production step rather than pushing an inventory of work-in-process, (b) standard work flow that promotes efficiency and rapid detection of deviations, (c) a learning system that supports continuous improvement, (d) a human resources system that empowers employees, and (e) a management system that offers support for the process. Over time, lean principles were extended to other aspects of the organization, such as product development, engineering, sales, and billing, and to service industries such as airlines and hospitals. However, the overwhelming majority of lean interventions have focused on the adoption of selected practices rather than as a complete system of change.

In contrast, a lean enterprise can be defined as an integrated entity that efficiently and effectively creates value for its multiple stakeholders by employing lean principles and practices. This definition offers a holistic and broad view that extends beyond an individual department, production line, or company. As a complex, integrated, and interdependent system of people, processes, and technology that creates value as defined by its stakeholders, a lean enterprise develops a value proposition that satisfies multiple stakeholders from various units of the company but also shareholders, suppliers, partners, and customers. For example, a hospital may apply traditional lean practices to deal with an overcrowded emergency room but end up creating more problems for other units in the hospital. An enterprise approach would examine the interdependencies between the emergency department, operating room, pharmacy, suppliers, human resource practices, insurance companies, primary care organizations, and other units within and outside the hospital (including patient expectations and behaviors) that are part of the way value is created for all stakeholders. Even Toyota can be considered part of the Japanese societal ecosystem: The lack of natural resources and the ability to exploit the unique Japanese conception of work were critical catalysts in development of the Toyota production system.

Therefore, a lean enterprise, while exhibiting the features of a lean organization, does so under conditions of complexity (size, stakeholders) and distributed authority (i.e., there is no single authority structure to make decisions and handle conflicts). Existing enterprises that seek to become lean cannot simply mandate new policies and practices, nor can they copy what others have done. Instead, leaders must bring their stakeholders into a new understanding of their interdependence in the creation of sustainable value and trustful relationships while transforming their practices in accordance with lean principles.

Research, based primarily on a small number of large-scale and longitudinal case studies, suggests there are seven principles that characterize lean enterprises. These principles underlie the features of lean organizations mentioned earlier but add new emphasis on holistic thinking and stakeholder value. Essentially, understanding how to *be* a lean enterprise is inseparable from understanding how to *become* a lean enterprise and how to *sustain* the lean enterprise. The first three of these principles can be closely identified with enterprise leadership and leadership responsibilities:

1. *Holistic thinking.* Lean enterprises constantly scan the ecosystem to ensure that they are able to meet the short-term value delivery goals and simultaneously shape the long-term ecosystem within which the enterprise operates. A lean enterprise requires leaders (and others) to take a holistic approach to considering all life cycle, leadership, and enabling processes in an integrative fashion, being careful not to suboptimize the performance of any one area.

2. *Leadership commitment to drive and institutionalize enterprise behaviors.* Leaders play a critical role in setting the vision for the desired future state, communicating it across the

enterprise, and empowering and supporting engagement from all stakeholders. They establish the culture of continuous improvement and create the climate needed for experimentation. Given the emphasis of lean principles on enabling decision making at the lowest appropriate level, leadership necessarily has to be distributed and aligned across the enterprise.

3. *Comprehensive and fair stakeholder value propositions.* An enterprise can be analyzed as a network of value exchange between stakeholders and the enterprise, in which participation is governed by the ability of the enterprise to provide value to key stakeholders. While lean organizations typically focus on a single stakeholder group—the customer—lean enterprises have a fair and comprehensive value proposition that acknowledges and balances the needs of the multiple stakeholders. Furthermore, the value proposition evolves over time to be consistent with the core values of the enterprise.

The next two principles are concerned with the life cycle processes that make up an enterprise, such as sales, product development, and support services:

4. *A focus on effectiveness before efficiency.* The enterprise value proposition has to be constructed to meet both short-term and long-term needs of key stakeholders. It is important to make sure the enterprise is doing the "right things" before doing "things right." All too often, a short-term focus on efficiency becomes a demand for cost and schedule performance that drives out quality, innovation, and long-term value. The focus on effectiveness encourages stakeholders to look across their area of responsibility to see the enterprise value stream as a whole.

5. *Attention to internal and external interdependencies.* Every enterprise is a highly integrated system whose performance is determined by the degree of alignment across the life cycle, enabling, and leadership processes. Often, these processes span functional and organizational boundaries, requiring an understanding of internal and external interdependencies to truly deliver on the enterprise value proposition.

The final two principles focus on enabling processes that support lean enterprise practices:

6. *Stability and flow.* Lean enterprises establish stability to create a baseline against which enterprise performance can be assessed. In the presence of stability, they can then focus on flow to visualize bottlenecks and identify the underlying causes of problems. Information and resources are the key flows that allow products and services to be created effectively and efficiently.

7. *Organizational learning.* Lean enterprises are constantly in motion, as are their environments, so that bottom-up continuous improvement and learning from experience; top-down architecting, reengineering, and transformation; and outward-in benchmarking and sensemaking are continually building enterprise capabilities.

Deborah Nightingale, John S. Carroll, and Jayakanth Srinivasan

See also Business Process Reengineering; High-Performance Work Systems; *Kaizen* and Continuous Improvement; Organizational Effectiveness; Organizational Structure and Design; Stakeholder Theory; Systems Theory of Organizations

Further Readings

Hino, S. (2006). *Inside the mind of Toyota: Management principles for enduring growth.* New York, NY: Productivity Press.

Liker, J. K. (2004). *The Toyota way: 14 management principles from the world's greatest manufacturer.* New York, NY: McGraw-Hill Professional.

Murman, E. M., Allen, T., Bozdogan, K., & Cutcher-Gershenfeld, J. (2002). *Lean enterprise value: Insights from MIT's lean aerospace initiative.* New York, NY: Palgrave Macmillan.

Nightingale, D. J., & Srinivasan, J. (2011). *Beyond the lean revolution: Achieving successful and sustainable enterprise transformation.* New York, NY: AMACOM.

Ōno, T. (1988). *Toyota production system: Beyond large-scale production.* New York, NY: Productivity Press.

Rother, M. (2010). *Toyota kata: Managing people for improvement, adaptiveness, and superior results.* New York, NY: McGraw-Hill.

Shah, R., & Ward, P. T. (2003). Lean manufacturing: Context, practice bundles, and performance. *Journal of Operations Management, 21*(2), 129–149.

Shingō, S., & Dillon, A. P. (1989). *A study of the Toyota production system from an industrial engineering viewpoint.* New York, NY: Productivity Press.

Womack, J. P., Jones, D. T., & Roos, D. (1990). *The machine that changed the world: How Japan's secret weapon in the global auto wars will revolutionize Western industry.* New York, NY: Harper Perennial.

LEARNING ORGANIZATION

In an organizational context, *learning* refers to the process by which organizations notice, interpret, and manage their experience. The outcome of the learning process is typically a change in the organization's knowledge and action repertoires. Knowledge, in this sense, refers to the stock of insights on causal relations (why X leads to Y) and to the process of acquiring knowledge. As it becomes rooted in the organization's routines, practices, and memory systems, the experience related to a specific task or situation can become knowledge, in the form of a cognitive or behavioral transformation or both. Learning, thus, can be thought of as an ongoing spiral; knowledge from past experiences influences the current organizational situation and, in turn, its future. Anchoring the concept of learning in organizational experience solves the tension between two seemingly contradictory views embedded in the learning organization—one that regards learning as a trial-and-error process honed through action and experience and another that emphasizes how cognitive patterns and cause-effect relationships evolve into shared beliefs that are ultimately institutionalized. To examine fundamental processes characterizing the learning organization, this entry reviews (a) four basic characteristics of the learning organization; (b) the evolution of organizational learning theory, including major works that shaped our understanding and our sense of the future trajectory of research; and (c) key research findings on the learning organization, suggesting readings on the topic.

Fundamentals

Learning in organizations is often described as multilevel, meaning that learning can occur at the individual, group, organizational, and interorganizational levels and that learning at one level can affect learning at other levels. The learning that occurs at each level has distinctive characteristics regarding what is learned, how it is learned, and how learning is best accomplished. These differences derive from recognizing that organizations are more than the aggregation of individuals, and therefore, processes such as learning involve more than the accumulation of individual learning. To give a few examples: Context can have a significant effect on individual learning; powerful individuals within the organization can influence what information is transmitted; and social interactions among members of the organization—or with external entities—may increase or decrease the outputs of learning.

In 1990, Peter Senge introduced the concept of the *learning organization* to describe an organization that continually fosters the learning capacity of its members, enhancing its ability to transform itself in the face of changing conditions. He identified five ways in which organizations can enable long-term competitiveness—systems thinking, personal mastery, mental models, building shared vision, and team learning—of which systems thinking is the most important and integrative. Many practitioners followed Senge's footsteps and wrote books with their own models of the learning organization. However, researchers have not yet identified a model of the learning organization that is universally applicable.

Learning is a complex process and thus has been conceptualized in a number of different ways. A simple way to think of it is as a cyclical process that links together four elements: individual learning, organizational learning, organizational action, and organizational context.

Individual Learning

At the individual level, learning involves the conscious or unconscious recognition of patterns that can potentially become opportunities for action. Over time, consensus over shared understandings can develop among organizational members and, through repeated interactions, learning can become embedded in the systems, structures, routines, practices, and infrastructure of the organization. Through institutionalization, the cognitions and/or behaviors that result from the learning process become taken for granted, thus creating a *perceived* reality of the organization and its context. The resulting stocks of knowledge offer individuals an array of resources,

including cognitive and behavioral capabilities, from which actors can draw as needed. Learning that is embedded in the organization influences the way in which individuals interpret subsequent events and experiences and, consequently, shapes the future learning of the organization as a whole.

While organizational learning is often linked to action directed toward change, it can also be directed toward stability by allowing organizations to build on past experiences and maintain the behaviors that were effective. From this perspective, learning can be explained as an evolutionary process of variation, selection, and retention of effective practices, where variation refers to the different interactions by which new knowledge can be generated; selection refers to the processes by which the organization determines what bits of knowledge are viewed as effective; and retention refers to the translation of effective knowledge into institutionalized routines, structures, and practices.

Organizational Learning

The concept of *organizational* learning suggests that the locus of learning does not exclusively reside at the individual level, since learning can result from social interactions and from experiences in particular contexts or situations. Over time, the new repertoire of knowledge and actions can become embedded in the organization's routines and practices. Thus, rather than consisting of the transfer of information from one entity to another, learning materializes through interactions across (or within) any level. Thus, organizational learning can occur internally (from the cognitive patterns that emerge within the organization from repeated interactions) or externally (from the interactions of the organization with its environment). At this level of analysis, the emphasis is less on the content of learning and more on the emergent, processual nature of learning.

Not all organizations have the same ability to become learning organizations. In fact, the rate at which an organization learns is one of the few competitive advantages that remain sustainable over time. The term *absorptive capacity*, coined by Wesley Cohen and Daniel Levinthal in 1990, refers to a firm's ability to recognize the value of new information, assimilate it, and apply it to commercial ends, using the stocks of knowledge and capabilities it already has. An organization's absorptive capacity largely depends on prior knowledge, the variety of organizational experiences, and the ease with which knowledge is transferred across and within subunits in the organization.

The importance of context at the organizational level is reflected in the concept of dynamic capabilities, which describes the set of processes whereby organizations reconfigure their material and knowledge resources to create value under conditions of rapid and unpredictable change. These capabilities are often very similar across organizations and, thus, are popularly referred to as "best practices." According to Kathleen M. Eisenhardt and Jeffrey Martin, an organization's dynamic capabilities vary in relation to the dynamism of its context. Under conditions of moderate or incremental change, dynamic capabilities can be routines that are stable in nature and have predictable outcomes; under conditions of fast-paced change, dynamic capabilities can be simple processes that have unpredictable outcomes and are permanently subject to a strategic modification. This distinction shapes the learning organization: under moderate change, the organization's actions are contingent on existing knowledge, and under fast-paced change, the organization relies on newly created knowledge, and its execution is based on trial and error.

Organizational Action

In 1991, James March introduced the idea that an organization's action can be channeled to either *exploration*, search directed toward new knowledge and competencies, or *exploitation*, search directed toward the better use of existing competencies. In this sense, exploration refers to the search for new, useful adaptations, and exploitation refers to the use and propagation of known adaptations.

For most organizations, balancing exploration and exploitation requires a trade-off between present and future returns. Organizations that rely excessively on just one strategy can fall into dysfunctional learning traps. These traps occur because organizations tend to overlook or overvalue distant times or contexts and ignore failures. Organizations rely on exploitation because it yields more certain and immediate returns; however, it is less likely to yield truly novel solutions and can lead to obsolescence in the long run. Although exploration can enable the discovery of profoundly novel solutions, it also can cause a degradation of performance in the short run because searches for novel solutions tend to fail.

In this context, the speed at which learning occurs acquires particular relevance. For instance, slow adaptation benefits an organization because it encourages the incorporation of new and divergent ideas. In contrast, fast learning tends to drive out alternatives, narrowing the body of knowledge within the organization, which limits the available options and encourages more conservative exploitation in the system. Fast adaptation will tend to exhibit more exploitative behavior, even in situations where the long-run implications of exploration are positive.

Yet learning does not necessarily lead to action. Organizational actions are selected to fit a context. Managers might decide not to carry out a specific behavior or action if they deem the context different from their previous experiences. Attention to noticing and comprehending the context is an important component of the learning process itself.

Organizational Fields, Market Categories, and Industries

The actions of an organization affect its context; simultaneously, however, the context affects how an organization interprets and makes sense of the situation. As interpretations become shared among all the organizations in a field—including competitors, suppliers, buyers, regulatory agencies, and industry associations—patterns of action begin to emerge, thus creating a context that further affects the future experience of organizations. In this way, organizations contribute to the creation of their own environments. The subsequent influence of the context on organizational action emerges as pressures to adopt shared practices regarded as legitimate. Therefore, the goal of learning at this level is more about gaining legitimacy by means of noticing, interpreting, and managing the established "rules of the game" than it is about creating new knowledge. However, scholars have pointed out that learning at the field, or institutional, level can also occur when an organization adopts an idea or business practice later in the diffusion process, driven by the learning experiences of prior adopter organizations for anticipated efficiency benefits.

The interaction of organizational experience and environmental context can lead to learning beyond the organization itself and extend to the level of taken-for-granted rules, norms, and beliefs that characterize the field or industry. At this level, learning occurs when the institutions, or shared understandings, of a particular field change in response to some learning experience. Several mechanisms help explain how institutional learning and change occur, including (a) organizational or individual actions that generate change as a result of unintended consequences; (b) learning processes across organizations and/or populations that are geographically apart or occur in different networks; (c) organizational efforts to imitate other organizations; (d) field-level underperformance and slow adaptation processes; (e) unlearning, disadoption, or negative diffusion caused by factors such as personnel turnover; (f) learning from other organizations' experiences in order to implement best-practices or more efficient routines; and (g) differences in regulation and the organization's responses to regulation and competition.

Evolution

Although the notion of the learning organization can be traced back to the writings of Max Weber on bureaucracies, it was Richard Cyert and James March who, in 1963, first focused attention on learning in the context of organizational routines. Later, in 1978, Chris Argyris and Donald Schön brought attention to the complexities of learning by distinguishing between single-loop and double-loop learning, depending on whether the current rules, frames of reference, or assumptions are held (single-loop learning) or changed (double-loop learning).

Building on this and other work, researchers began to engage a number of different questions. For instance, while some scholars focused on delineating the construct of learning and on differentiating organizational learning from individual learning, others debated the nature of learning as primarily cognitive, associated with knowledge and insights, or primarily behavioral, defined by a change in actual or potential actions. Related streams of research took divergent paths: some aimed at delineating the boundaries between organizational learning, organizational change, and adaptation; others emphasized adaptive learning and modeled organizations as target-oriented, routine-based systems; and still others paid more attention to the processes

of knowledge development by focusing on the content produced by learning.

Another notable distinction is that between researchers who studied organizational learning as an outcome in and of itself and those who built on the findings of organizational learning to explain other organizational phenomena, such as innovation, adoption of best practices, and creation of strategic alliances. In particular, organizational learning became very popular within the field of strategy, where researchers studied the relation of learning to performance and introduced terms such as absorptive capacity, stickiness, and dynamic capabilities.

Over time, traditional conceptualizations of human cognition shifted from emphasizing the "what" or the object of learning to the "how" or the process of learning. The traditional view conceived of learning as a process of knowledge transfer that occurred in and across individual minds. Yet as different factors, including the organization's identity, the flexibility of its strategy, and the characteristics of the field or industry, were found to enable or constrain the process of learning, a sociocultural perspective emerged, in which learning is conceived as a socially embedded process dependent on the uncertainty, munificence, and richness of the context in which it occurs. This will likely spur future inquiries into the learning organization, along with a more nuanced perspective on how the interaction of organizational experience and environmental context affect the creation of knowledge, and a more thorough exploration of organizational learning subprocesses, including the creation, retention, and transfer of knowledge.

Importance

These different perspectives on organizational learning have enriched our understanding of the learning organization. Empirical work has shown how, under conditions of high uncertainty, organizations benefit from directing resources to processes of exploration, while under lower uncertainty, organizations tend to rely on exploiting their available knowledge stocks. Moreover, learning can have both positive and negative effects: Organizational performance can improve with experience as a result of learning, yet it can suffer from incorrect inferences or erroneous causal beliefs, particularly when organizations operate in ambiguous environments in which the interpretation of the available information can lead to different and often inaccurate assumptions.

Much of the current research focuses on (a) understanding the mechanisms by which learning occurs, (b) when it is that learning leads to improved performance, (c) why it is that some organizations are better at learning than others, and (d) how the context in which organizations operate affects learning. In addition, work has focused on understanding the relationship between organizational learning and organizational action, building on findings that show how the availability of resources, the structure of the organization, the internal and external politics, and the degree of environmental complexity can influence whether or not learning is translated into action.

Another area of inquiry focuses on the relationship between learning and knowledge and has demonstrated that organizations store knowledge in various ways, including the know-how of individual members and the structures, routines, and practices of the organization. Researchers have enriched our understanding of the collective memory systems through which organizations codify, store, and retrieve knowledge regarding the expertise of its members and the processes required to access this information.

New lines of research that have important practical implications are exploring the mechanisms by which organizations learn through rare events, the effects of social networks on knowledge creation, and the consequences of mindful (attentive) or less mindful learning subprocesses on the outcome of knowledge creation, transfer, and retention.

In conclusion, the learning organization continues to be a key concern today. For managers, achieving short- and long-term goals largely depends on the organization's ability to continuously learn and adapt to the environment. However, the challenge of creating a learning organization is not only establishing the appropriate systems for acquiring cognitive and behavioral capabilities but also to ensuring that these capabilities are retained and easily retrievable. Based on current theories, it is important for managers to acknowledge that learning at the level of the organization is more than the mere aggregation of individual knowledge and behaviors. When learning is viewed as tied to specific contexts and constructed through the ongoing interactions of organizational members, the question becomes less about *what* individuals are learning and more about *how* the

interpersonal and behavioral connections can enable organizations to better navigate the complexities of the environment.

*Mary Ann Glynn, Simona Giorgi,
and Andrea Tunarosa*

See also Double Loop Learning; Dynamic Capabilities; Experiential Learning Theory and Learning Styles; Multilevel Research; Tacit Knowledge

Further Readings

Argote, L., & Miron-Spektor, E. (2011). Organizational learning: From experience to knowledge. *Organization Science, 22,* 1123–1137

Argyris, C., & Schön, D. A. (1978). *Organizational learning: A theory of action perspective.* Reading, MA: Addison-Wesley.

Cohen, W. M., & Levinthal, D. A. (1990). Absorptive capacity: A new perspective on learning and innovation. *Administrative Science Quarterly, 35*(1), 128–152.

Cyert, R., & March, J. G. (1963). *A behavioral theory of the firm.* Englewood Cliffs, NJ: Prentice-Hall.

Eisenhardt, K. M., & Martin, J. A. (2000). Dynamic capabilities: What are they? *Strategic Management Journal, 21,* 1105–1121.

Fiol, M., & Lyles, M. A. (1985). Organizational learning. *Academy of Management Review, 10*(4), 803–813.

Glynn, M. A., Lant, T. K., & Milliken, F. (1994). Mapping learning processes in organizations: A multi-level framework linking learning and organizing. In C. Stubbart, J. R. Meindl, & J. F. Porac (Eds.), *Advances in managerial cognition and organizational information processing* (Vol. 5, pp. 43–83). Greenwich, CT: JAI Press.

Levinthal, D. A., & March, J. G. (1993). The myopia of learning. *Strategic Management Journal, 14,* 95–112.

March, J. G. (1991). Exploration and exploitation in organizational learning. *Organization Science, 2*(1), 71–87.

Senge, P. M. (1990). *The fifth discipline: The art and practice of the learning organization.* New York, NY: Currency Doubleday.

LEVEL 5 LEADERSHIP

Level 5 leadership is an evidence-based theory that describes a set of five kinds of managerial leadership styles for increasing effectiveness of executive management of large companies. The theory is an important addition to the study and practice of management through wide interest and response by practitioners and a multifaceted set of responses from academia. James C. (Jim) Collins III has been the driver of the theoretical development and operates an influential management and consulting laboratory for defining leadership and training managerial leaders. In his 1994 book, *Built to Last: Successful Habits of Visionary Companies,* Collins and coauthor Jerry I. Porras looked at how to build an enduring great company from the ground up. Developing the ideas, a second project was initiated to attempt to discover how companies that had been operating at an "ordinary level" quickly developed into exceptional performers in their industries—went from good to great. In the research for the 2001 book *Good to Great: Why Some Companies Make the Leap . . . and Others Don't,* Collins sought processes and outcomes that would allow him to look empirically at the question of how a decent company could become a great one. In this study, he presented a framework for Level 5 leadership. This entry provides an overview of the definition and evolution of the theory.

Fundamentals

James C. Collins earned degrees in business administration and mathematical sciences from Stanford University and taught at Stanford in the 1990s. In 1995, he founded his management laboratory in Boulder, Colorado, for research and education on how great organizations become that way and do or do not stay great and for providing insight and guidance to leaders and those charged with hiring leaders. Collins has worked in the business sector as a senior executive at CNN International and with social sector organizations, such as the Johns Hopkins Medical School and the Girl Scouts of the USA, among other nongovernment and government organizations. Collins has been engaged in a series of research projects to distinguish companies that are sustainably great from others. For the publication of *Good to Great,* Collins and his staff identified 11 great companies and compared them to 11 unexceptional companies. They identified the distinguishing feature of the great companies as a new CEO who took charge of the organization and then improved its performance. These 11 CEOs all shared the same two characteristics: They were modest and humble,

as opposed to self-dramatizing, self-aggrandizing, and self-promoting, and they were phenomenally, almost preternaturally, persistent in driving the companies toward prescribed goals.

Collins's Hierarchy of Leader Characteristics

At the time, these findings were contradictory to the business literature that promoted the cult of the charismatic CEO. *The Level 5 leader* refers to the peak of a five-tier hierarchy of leader characteristics. A Level 5 leader is someone who embodies personal humility and strong and willful persistence in pursuing formulated goals and objectives. Collins's leadership level hierarchy consists of

- Level 1: the highly capable individual—a productive contributor with exceptional individual talents and skills,
- Level 2: contributing team member—works effectively and contributes to achieving team goals,
- Level 3: competent manager—efficient and effective pursuit of goals through planning and organizing,
- Level 4: the effective executive—clear and compelling vision encourages high performance,
- Level 5: the leader—personal humility and professional resolve allows development of a great organization.

In the book *Good to Great,* Collins describes Level 5 leaders as not exhibiting a strong charismatic personality but holding a sense of purpose to serve the common good above personal gain. The idea is supported by another evidence-based theory, that of James Kouzes and Barry Posner, in the 2007 fourth edition of *The Leadership Challenge.* They similarly note that the credibility of a leader is built on his or her character: a willingness to define and live personal values and to strive for a higher purpose that appreciates the diversity and role of constituents in shaping the future.

Frequently, the lack of public prominence of Level 5 executive leaders is obscured by Level 4 types—CEOs who do have effective leadership skills but are often more committed to self-aggrandizement than the sustained future of the enterprise. Celebrity leaders often succeed for a time but can be damaging in the long run because they don't create sustainable results. Collins often refers to Lee Iacocca as a prominent example of a Level 4 executive. Iacocca did improve the fate of Chrysler while he was CEO, but he did not establish and implement a long-term vision for the company. Chrysler, according to Collins, is an example of "good-to-great-to-imploding," a more common example than sustained good-to-great company. According to Collins, we live in a culture that does not pick Level 5s as subjects of admiration; we pay attention to the 4s.

Collins employs a parable he calls "the Window and the Mirror." Level 5 leaders tend to look in the mirror and blame themselves for mistakes. But when things are good, they look out the window and proclaim either how everyone in the company is wonderful or how good fortune caused success. Collins comments that when he asked Circuit City's Alan Wurtzel about his company's success, Wurtzel replied that 80% to 100% was because "the wind was at our backs." Collins faxed him charts showing how much better his company did than others in the field. "I told him they all had the same wind," said Collins. "'Gee,' was his response. 'We must have been really lucky.'"

Practices of the Level 5 Leader

Collins identifies key practices associated with Level 5 Leaders in his list of great companies: *Get the right people on the bus;* successful staffing must be in place before the leader can decide what decisions are taken. Enterprises can change if the right people are in place, and the wrong people will certainly make the enterprise fail. *Confront the brutal facts;* don't ignore reality in favor of hopes, and only by having accurate facts can you achieve success. *The hedgehog concept;* having a single, simple, extremely clear concept of what is the business of the enterprise, which must be something the business can make money at, be passionate about, and be the best in the world at. As the ancient Greek poet Archilocus noted, "The fox knows many things, but the hedgehog knows one big thing."

Additionally, Collins identifies *the three circles:* (1) A culture of self-discipline is critical, and the hedgehog concept creates a defined system within which to act. (2) Technology is an accelerator, not an impetus for or agent of change. Good companies use it to facilitate execution of processes, but it won't save a failing company. (3) *The flywheel* refers to the idea of momentum; keep pushing in the one correct direction, and the company will build up a lot of momentum that will help overcome obstacles. Momentum is built a bit at a time, through constant, diligent work.

Most of the executive leaders of great companies discussed luck as an important factor in their success. Level 5 leaders are not the kind of people who want to point to themselves as the cause for an organization's success.

As time passed, CEOs changed, and the great companies' performances changed. However, because some of the great companies profiled in *Good to Great* and *Built to Last* had subsequently lost their positions of prominence does not invalidate what we can learn by studying that company when it was at its historical best. In Collins's 2009 book, *How the Mighty Fall: And Why Some Companies Never Give In,* he revisits the company histories, seeking the seeds of destruction leading to serious performance stumbles for both the successful and the comparison companies. He identifies the five stages of progressing from great to destruction:

Stage 1: Hubris born of success. Level 5 Leaders never presume they have reached ultimate understanding of all the factors that brought them success; they retain a somewhat irrational fear that perhaps their success stems in large part from fortuitous circumstance and thereby worry incessantly about how to make the enterprise stronger and better positioned for the day the good luck runs out.

Stage 2: Undisciplined pursuit of more. Violation of the hedgehog concept—companies stray from the disciplined creativity that led them to greatness in the first place, making undisciplined leaps into areas where they cannot be great or growing faster than they can achieve with excellence or both.

Stage 3: Denial of risk and peril. Leaders discount negative data, amplify positive data, and put a positive spin on ambiguous data. Those in power start to blame external factors for setbacks rather than accept responsibility. The vigorous, fact-based dialogue that characterizes high-performance teams dwindles or disappears altogether.

Stage 4: Grasping for salvation. The cumulative peril and risks gone bad at Stage 3 assert themselves, throwing the enterprise into a sharp decline visible to all. Those who grasp for salvation have fallen into Stage 4. *Saviors* sought include a charismatic leader, a bold but untested strategy, a radical transformation, a dramatic cultural revolution, a hoped-for blockbuster product, a game-changing acquisition, or any number of other silver-bullet solutions. Initial results from taking dramatic action may appear positive, but they do not last. According to Collins, leaders atop companies in the late stages of decline need to get back to a calm, clear-headed, and focused approach. If you want to reverse decline, be rigorous about *what not to do*.

Stage 5: Capitulation to irrelevance or death. The longer a company remains in Stage 4, repeatedly grasping for silver bullets, the more likely it will spiral downward. In Stage 5, accumulated setbacks and expensive false starts erode financial strength and individual spirit to such an extent that leaders abandon all hope of building a great future. In some cases, the company's leader just sells out; in other cases, the institution atrophies into insignificance; and in the most extreme cases, the enterprise simply dies outright.

Importance

As an evidence-based theory, the Level 5 leadership model has been criticized for using data-mining techniques that could lead to conclusions based either on random patterns or on patterns that exist only in the sample firms for a particular time period studied. The studies are also criticized for survivorship bias or survivor bias, an effect in a study where comparisons of companies that have an unusually high and consistent record of success are compared with a historic population average. This is not a flaw in Collins's work but in the design. The highly successful companies are outliers. Given the relatively high turnover of CEOs, it is possible that the market selects CEOs with high skills, and these CEOs build companies that can survive a few decades of inept executive leadership, assuming they are not succeeded by another Level 5 leader.

Level 5 leaders' propensity for humility has led to their attribution of success to luck or forces external to themselves; in Collin's 2011 book with Morten Hansen, *Great by Choice: Uncertainty, Chaos, and Luck—Why Some Thrive Despite Them All*, emphasis is on the choices leaders make as determining success, confirmed in paired comparisons of great and ordinary companies. Executive leaders of great companies combined creativity with discipline so

that the discipline amplifies the creativity rather than dampening it and are "productively paranoid" so as to create a company that can deal with big, unexpected shocks. The Level 5 leader demonstrates (a) *fanatic discipline* through consistency of action, not overreacting to changes in circumstances; (b) *empirical creativity* through bold initiatives directed by sound empirical information; and (c) *productive paranoia*—continual search for threats, especially when things are going well. The paranoia is channeled into preparation, contingency plans, and building margins of safety.

As an indicator of the influence of the Level 5 concept, *Good to Great* was listed in *Forbes* magazine's list of the 20 Most Influential Business Books from 1981–2000 and in Covert and Sattersten's *The 100 Best Business Books of All Time*. Harzing's *Publish or Perish* citation search software shows that Collins's specific Level 5 publications average some 81 citations per year.

As to whether Level 5 leaders are born or made, Collins concludes that many people probably have seeds of abilities and attitudes necessary to attain that status. Collins's work provides managers today with a set of managerial processes derived from empirical studies of companies of varying degrees of success that can be relatively easily implemented by executives with the authority to do so. Those with lesser authority can apply the techniques within their organizational parameters defending their initiative from Collins's evidence and, hopefully, their own success. Additionally, Collins's company provides formal training.

Romie Littrell

See also Behavioral Theory of the Firm; Business Policy and Corporate Strategy; Charismatic Theory of Leadership; Contingency Theory of Leadership; Evidence-Based Management; Influence Tactics; Organizational Culture Theory; Self-Fulfilling Prophecy; Transformational Theory of Leadership

Further Readings

Collins, J. C. (2001). *Good to great: Why some companies make the leap . . . and others don't*. New York, NY: HarperCollins.

Collins, J. (2001). Level 5 leadership. *Harvard Business Review, 79*(1), 66–78.

Collins, J. C. (2009). *How the mighty fall: And why some companies never give in.* New York, NY: HarperCollins.

Collins, J. C., & Hansen, M. T. (2011). *Great by choice: Uncertainty, chaos, and luck—Why some thrive despite them all.* New York, NY: HarperCollins.

Collins, J. C., & Porras, J. I. (1994). *Built to last: Successful habits of visionary companies.* New York, NY: HarperCollins.

Covert, J., & Sattersten, T. (2009). *The 100 best business books of all time: What they say, why they matter, and how they can help you.* New York, NY: Portfolio/Penguin.

Harzing, A. W. (2007). *Publish or perish* [Computer software]. Available from http://www.harzing.com/pop.htm

LMX Theory

See Leader–Member Exchange Theory

Locus of Control

Locus of control, referring to the concept of internal versus external control of reinforcement, developed out of social learning theory. Locus of control is the source of perceived power to affect an outcome. An internal locus of control reflects the belief that power resides within the individual, while an external locus of control reflects the belief that power resides in outside forces. The individual's perception moves somewhere on a continuum between internality (i.e., control by self) and externality (i.e., control outside of self). Organizational change initiatives can be more efficient and effective when managers consider locus of control. Understanding an individual's perceived locus of control is important for managers' ability to lead or influence, because the employee's reaction to change will likely depend on the employee's locus of control. Managers who understand that subordinates with an internal locus of control respond differently to organizational change initiatives than do those with an external locus of control can improve employees' commitment and reduce negative behaviors such as turnover. Although also relevant to other contexts (e.g., psychology, adult development, education, and learning theory), this

entry focuses on the application of locus of control in the context of management of planned organizational change.

Fundamentals

In 1954, Julian Rotter put forth the concept of internal versus external control of reinforcement in a seminal text on social learning theory. Social learning theory represents a synthesis of Clark Hull's stimulus-response theory and Edward Tolman's cognitive interactionist theory. The major difference between stimulus-response and cognitivist learning theory centers on the use of the concept of reinforcement (i.e., goal, objective, outcome). The premise of social learning theory is that an individual's actions are predicted on the basis of the individual's expectations for reinforcement, the perceived value of the reinforcement, and the situation in which the individual finds himself or herself. Expectancy requires that the individual value the outcome, have self-efficacy, understand and trust the reward system, and avoid negative or unacceptable outcomes.

Although Rotter's social learning theory attempted to integrate stimulus-response and cognitive interactionist learning theories, he is more commonly viewed as a leading contributor to the study of linear cognitive interaction. Perhaps this view is based on his notable emphasis on the cognitive-field interactionist learning theory of Kurt Lewin rather than on B. F. Skinner's theory of conditioning through reinforcement. Social learning theory embodies the idea of continuous learning and making meaning within a collective context through interaction with one's environment. In other words, personality, which is internal to the person, cannot be viewed as existing in isolation from the environment. To understand behavior the individual and environment must be considered together. The concept of locus of control is focused on the individual's perception of whether the locus of control or power is centralized in the person or in the environment.

Rotter conceptualized locus of control as a predisposition in the perception of what causes reinforcement (i.e., reward, favorable outcome, goal accomplishment). A predisposition for internal locus of control (i.e., internality) results from the perception that reinforcement is contingent on one's own behavior or one's own relatively permanent characteristics or traits (i.e., personality). Perception that reinforcement is due to luck, chance, fate, or factors beyond one's control indicates an external locus of control (i.e., externality).

Rotter suggested that personality is a learned behavior compared to Carl Jung's philosophy that personality is a heritable characteristic. Change in locus-of-control orientation is, therefore, expected because learning can occur. One aspect of an individual's personality is the equilibrium between the individual's respective drives for autonomy, control, and social acceptance. This equilibrium contributes to the individual's locus-of-control orientation. Social learning theory suggests that locus-of-control orientation can change because of changes in reinforcement, the value of the reinforcement, or the situation itself. The implication is that an individual's locus-of-control orientation will change with life's experiences.

In 1976, Herbert Lefcourt provided a slightly different perspective on the concept of internal versus external control of reinforcement. Perceived control is a generalized expectancy for internal control of reinforcement. Reactions to unpleasant stimuli are shaped by the individual's perceptions of the stimuli and by the individual's perceptions of ability to cope with the stimuli. In 1984, Patricia Gurin and Orville Brim provided another perspective on the construct. Sense of control is a function of causal reasoning. Expectancy is a probability assessment, tied to causal questions. An individual understands that a certain condition results in a certain outcome, and the individual has or can produce the certain condition. Albert Bandura defined this latter component as self-efficacy.

The first scholars to have used the term *locus of control* in reference to the construct of internal versus external control of reinforcement appear to be Rue Cromwell, David Rosenthal, David Shakow, and Theodore Zahn in 1961. Although hundreds of studies have investigated the construct, it was not until the early 1970s that *locus of control* regularly appeared in the psychology literature. Another decade passed before the term entered common usage in the management literature in reference to the construct of internal versus external control of reinforcement in the context of organizational change.

Measuring Locus of Control

Rotter provided a 29-item Internal-External (I-E) scale for identifying one's locus of control. This forced-choice questionnaire assesses whether people believe that events are contingent on their own behavior or their own relatively permanent characteristics or traits (i.e., internal predisposition) or whether people believe that events are contingent on luck, chance, fate, or factors beyond their control (i.e., external predisposition). One point is given for each external response to a question; therefore, the more points a respondent receives, the greater his or her perception of external locus of control. Frequently, this scale is reverse coded, resulting in higher scores equating to higher perceptions of internality. Measurement of the locus-of-control construct has been debated. Lefcourt identified nine different instruments for assessing locus of control and cautioned using any of the scales with a discerning eye. Instruments using a forced-choice format (e.g., Rotter's I-E scale; Reid-Ware Three-Factor I-E Scale) or a binomal format (e.g., Bialer's Locus of Control Questionnaire), rather than Likert format scales, have tended to be used more consistently by researchers.

The multidimensionality aspect of the locus-of-control construct has been a source of interest in the arena of measurement. Factor analysis empirical research of Rotter's scale has produced subscales with statistically significant criterion validity for measuring the locus-of-control construct. Alternately, studies have shown Gurin and associates' 13-item scale's validity for measuring the core construct of internal versus external control of reinforcement.

Importance

The initial grounded theory established generalized expectancies for locus of control. Confusion and misuse of the construct has led to clarifications, including the need to maintain generalized expectancy, treat the value of the reinforcement variable as a separate variable, and avoid unidimensionality. Some researchers erroneously attempted to use the I-E scale to predict specific behaviors. Although the theory allows prediction in a large number of different situations (i.e., generalized), prediction is at a low level. A second area of clarification centered on the three variables in social learning theory: the individual's expectations for reinforcement, the perceived value of the reinforcement, and the situation in which the individual finds himself or herself. Some researchers, however, failed to treat reinforcement value as a separate variable. This is particularly important to consider in social action situations. A third area of clarification centered on the multi-dimensionality of the construct. Investigators frequently referred to subjects' unidimensionality as internals or externals, with internals being viewed more favorably. Rotter reiterated that the I-E scale represented a multidimensional continuum, with an individual's position on the continuum as dynamic and neither good nor bad.

The general implications for a manager center on understanding employees' perception of locus of control around the organizational change. With those employees whose locus of control leans toward internality, the manager should leverage these employees' sense of empowerment by *coaching* them to move forward on the change. Have these employees identify actions they individually can take to support the change, lead in taking those actions, and support their external-locus-of-control coworkers in adjusting to the change. With those employees tending toward an external locus of control around the organizational change, the manager should *coax* them to move forward on the change. Help these employees identify aspects of the change over which they might regain a sense of control, consider aspects to which they can adapt, and take steps to let go of their reluctances.

Rotter's initial conceptualization of the construct focused on control over reinforcement (i.e., goal attainment, outcome). Some investigators, on the other hand, have interpreted this conceptualization as control over the individual's *environment*. The latter perspective appears faulty. For example, one cannot control whether it is going to rain (i.e., environment), yet one *can* control how wet one gets in the downpour (i.e., outcome). In a planned-change instance of downsizing, employees may not be able to control whether the organization goes through with it, yet they can exercise control over how the downsizing impacts their career. The manager should enhance employee internality by routinely creating opportunities for employees' proactive career development, helping employees see alternative options when downsizing occurs, and encouraging those who tend toward externality to regain some sense of control over their future in spite of the downsizing.

Locus-of-control research has proven especially relevant for managers engaged in planned organizational change. On the results of a study in which locus of control was an independent variable, after receiving feedback, individuals with an internal locus of control exhibited more behavioral change than individuals with an external locus of control. In a study on turnover intentions (TI), the results indicated individuals with a locus of control toward internality had a stronger influence of job satisfaction on TI and organizational commitment (OC), while those with locus of control toward externality had a stronger influence of perceived organizational support (POS) on job satisfaction and OC. The results suggested administering instruments measuring locus of control to differentiate internals from externals, then consulting with the externals to boost their confidence, which, in turn, will increase their POS, job satisfaction, and OC and lower their TI.

Organizational change results in a disorienting dilemma for many employees. Employees' sense of control is an issue in the reluctance of employees to embrace organizational change. One of the earlier studies of the locus-of-control construct showed that internality enhances information seeking, while externality reduces information seeking. Within the context of social learning theory, information seeking would be viewed as a function of the value placed on the objectives to which the information-seeking behavior is related and the expectancy for success in achieving those objectives. Lanny Blake's 11-step plan to simplify the change process and the change agent's role includes fostering a sense of control over the process by involving employees in the change planning and implementation stages. A greater sense of employee control comes from involvement and communication to build cohesiveness, collaboration, community norms of acceptance, involvement in problem solving and decision making, and participatory intervention.

The issue of control becomes relevant when an event is so significant that it makes uncertainty a concern. For example, the upheaval of reorganization causes an increase in employees' externality. Conventional wisdom suggests that management should notify employees of a pending layoff at the last possible moment, to minimize the response of dysfunctional employee behavior. The findings of one study showed no difference in behavior of employees notified at an earlier time. Instead, knowledge of an imminent layoff allowed employees to take control or at least maintain a sense of control of their lives (i.e., gain a greater sense of internality).

Jay Conger and Rabindra Kanungo identified two different approaches—relational and motivational—to the development of the empowerment construct, which viewed individuals' locus of control as static rather than fluid or changeable. Empowerment as a relational construct occurs through movement toward participative management, where organizational decision making is shifted to lower levels for inclusion of a larger number of employees. Empowerment as a motivational construct occurs when management enables employees by helping employees perceive they have power and control—that is, enhanced internality.

Martin B. Kormanik and Tonette S. Rocco

See also Causal Attribution Theory; Empowerment; Expectancy Theory; Personal Engagement (at Work) Model; Reinforcement Theory; Social Cognitive Theory; Theory of Self-Esteem; Type-A Personality Theory

Further Readings

Bandura, A. (1977). Self-efficacy: Toward a unifying theory of behavior change. *Psychological Review, 84,* 191–215.

Conger, J. A., & Kanungo, R. N. (1988). The empowerment process: Integrating theory and practice. *Academy of Management Review, 13*(3), 471–482.

Gurin, P., & Brim, O. G. (1984). Change in self in adulthood: The example of sense of control. In O. G. Brim (Ed.), *Life-span development and behavior* (Vol. 6, pp. 281–334). New York, NY: Academic Press.

Joe, V. C. (1971). Review of the internal-external control construct as a personality variable. *Psychological Reports, 28*(2), 619–640.

Kormanik, M. B., & Rocco, T. S. (2009). Internal versus external control of reinforcement: A review of the locus of control construct. *Human Resource Development Review, 8*(4), 463–483.

Lefcourt, H. M. (1972). Recent developments in the study of locus of control. In B. A. Maher (Ed.), *Progress in experimental personality research* (Vol. 6, pp. 1–39). New York, NY: Academic Press.

Lefcourt, H. M. (1976). *Locus of control: Current trends in theory and research.* Hillsdale, NJ: Lawrence Erlbaum.

Reid, D., & Ware, E. (1974). Multidimensionality of internal versus external locus of control: Addition of a third dimension and non-distinction of self versus others. *Canadian Journal of Behavior Science, 6,* 131–142.

Rotter, J. B. (1966). Generalized expectancies for internal versus external control of reinforcement. *Psychological Monographs, 80*(1, Whole No. 609).

Rotter, J. B. (1975). Some problems and misconceptions related to the construct of internal versus external control of reinforcement. *Journal of Consulting and Clinical Psychology, 43*(1), 56–67.

Logical Incrementalism

In the 1950s, Charles Lindblom studied decision-making processes in public administration. He observed that the objective was rarely to achieve a long-term strategy. Decisions were primarily made to solve short-term problems. In many instances, there was no connection at all between the decisions. Many actors were involved and there was no central coordination. Lindblom refers to such decision-making processes as "disjointed incrementalism." In the late 1970s, James Brian Quinn began a large research project that documented the processes used to formulate and implement strategy in 10 large and diversified firms. The sample included firms from a variety of industries and countries (e.g., Chrysler, Exxon, General Mills, Pilkington, Pillsbury, Xerox). The result of Quinn's research project was a landmark book titled *Strategies for Change: Logical Incrementalism.* Like Lindblom, Quinn found that decision-making processes were incremental. Unlike Lindblom, however, he did not conclude that they were disjointed. According to Quinn, top executives in firms do not "muddle"; they seem to direct decision-making processes toward a long-term goal. Because of this underlying logic, he coined the expression: *logical incrementalism.* In 1980, Quinn defined logical incrementalism as an approach in which a manager "probes the future, experiments, and learns from a series of partial commitments rather than through global formulation of total strategies" This entry presents the fundamentals of the concept and concludes with an assessment of its validity and its impact on the management literature.

Fundamentals

Two major approaches are generally used to describe how managers formulate and implement strategy: the formal planning approach and the power-behavioral approach. Logical incrementalism is different from the formal planning approach. In the formal planning approach, the full strategy is formulated before it is implemented. Thus, the formulation and implementation of strategy are sequential activities. In logical incrementalism, strategy formulation and strategy implementation take place simultaneously. In addition, logical incrementalism emphasizes qualitative and organizational factors, whereas the formal planning approach focuses on quantitative analysis. The underlying rationale is that quantitative analysis is less useful for nonroutine activities (such as the development of a new strategy) than for routine activities. Logical incrementalism is also different from the power-behavioral approach. The power-behavioral approach focuses on negotiation processes and the practice of "muddling" in public administration. While logical incrementalists negotiate with stakeholders, they also have a clear sense of direction.

As Quinn made clear, successful strategies are rarely brought about deliberately through a process of formulation followed by implementation. They often emerge over time as managers proactively develop a course of action and reactively adapt to unfolding circumstances. The implications are straightforward. Instead of setting a course of action in advance, managers should proceed incrementally. Initially, the strategy is likely to be broad and vague. As more information becomes available, it will become more precise. Interestingly, there are two potential uses of logical incrementalism. Although logical incrementalism can be used as a process to formulate a strategy, it can also be used as a process to implement a strategy that already exists in the mind of top managers. In that case, the implementation of strategy (rather than the formulation of strategy) is incremental.

Logical incrementalism suggests that subsystems play a key role in the emergence of strategies. Large firms have different subsystems. They typically include the diversification subsystem, the divestiture system, the major reorganization subsystem, and the external relations subsystem. In the formal planning approach, strategies are formulated by the top management before being implemented in the subsystems. According to logical incrementalism, top managers should encourage employees working in the subsystems to contribute to strategies. A major advantage of small-scale experiments is that they face little opposition. In addition, failures do not have important implications for the firm. Because each subsystem focuses on a particular type

of strategic issue, however, decisions made at the subsystem level may be inconsistent. Therefore, it is crucial for top managers to maintain some consistency among them. At the subsystem level, Quinn also makes an important distinction between "hard-data" and "soft" decisions. Examples of hard-data decisions include make-or-buy decisions and various resource allocation decisions. The use of a particular management style in a firm is a good example of soft decision. Unlike hard-data decisions, soft decisions cannot be made using quantitative analysis. However, they often have more important implications for the firm than do hard-data decisions.

Importance

Quinn suggests that logical incrementalism is the best way to develop successful strategies. As he put it, logical incrementalism "is so powerful that it perhaps provides the normative model for strategic decision-making" Logical incrementalism has many advantages. First, the cognitive abilities of managers are limited and the environment that surrounds the firm is uncertain. With logical incrementalism, managers act in small steps and gather feedback. Thus, adaptations can be made over time and major mistakes can be avoided. Second, decisions made incrementally are easier to implement because they tend to be consistent with the culture, resources, and capabilities of the firm. Third, employees frequently have vested interests. Using an incremental approach can help overcome some of these vested interests.

The story of IKEA as told by Jérôme Barthélemy provides some evidence of logical incrementalism at work. IKEA is currently the world's largest furniture retailer. IKEA's success can be attributed to the fact that it redefined organizational practices in the furniture business. How did IKEA's highly successful strategy come about? An in-depth examination of the history of IKEA reveals that its strategy was not brought about deliberately through a process of formulation followed by implementation. Consistent with logical incrementalism, IKEA's strategy emerged as Ingvar Kamprad (IKEA's founder) shaped a course of action by adapting to unfolding contingencies. For instance, global sourcing is a key driver of IKEA's low-cost structure. Kamprad made the pioneering decision to source furniture from communist Poland as early as 1961. Because manufacturing costs were 50% lower in Poland than in Sweden, this decision looks brilliant in hindsight. However, it was not deliberate. In the 1950s, Swedish furniture retailers and manufacturers had an agreement to keep prices high. Because IKEA's strategy consisted in selling furniture at considerably lower prices than its competitors, the Swedish retail cartel gave local furniture manufacturers the following ultimatum: *"If you sell to IKEA, we will no longer buy from you."* Most manufacturers didn't dare defy the retail cartel and refused to do business with IKEA. Thus, looking for suppliers outside Sweden was the only way for Kamprad to overcome a boycott that could have led IKEA to bankruptcy. At that time, doing business with communist countries was unusual and risky. In fact, most of IKEA's strategy emerged through experimentation. Ingvar Kamprad tested a large number of different approaches on a small scale. Originally, IKEA was a mail-order company that used to sell goods such as Christmas cards, pens, and picture frames. Kamprad introduced the first piece of furniture in his mail-order catalog to imitate a successful competitor. It is only because the "test furniture" was a huge success that he decided to focus on furniture and ended up discontinuing all other products. On the other hand, if an approach did not work, he refrained from using it again.

As Quinn put it, "strategy deals with the unknowable." Therefore, proceeding incrementally is likely to be better than trying to plan everything in advance and implement this plan.

However, logical incrementalism is not a panacea for several related reasons. First, managers do not always anticipate the consequences of the decisions they make. Internal or external events over which managers have no control may precipitate a series of decisions that do not fit together and lead to confusion. Second, developing a strategy using logical incrementalism is a safe but relatively slow process. When decisions need to be made quickly, logical incrementalism may not be the best option. Third, logical instrumentalism remains more descriptive than normative. Although Quinn describes how managers deal with ill-structured issues, he

offers little information about how to manage decision-making processes (and eventually enhance performance).

In general, research on strategic decision making can be divided into two categories: content research and process research. While content research deals with the actual content of strategic decisions, process research focuses on how they are made and implemented. Logical incrementalism is a major theory in the process research literature. The concept is referenced in most academic literature reviews, which clearly suggests that is of interest to academics. It is also referenced in most management textbooks, which indicates that it is relevant for managers (and future managers). On the other hand, it can be noted that few empirical studies have actually used it. A potential explanation is that empirical research agenda has been dominated by content issues rather than by process issues. Another potential explanation is that Quinn's empirical study provided sufficient evidence of the usefulness of logical incrementalism.

Jérôme Barthélemy

See also Decision-Making Styles; Modes of Strategy: Planned and Emergent; Process Theories of Change; Programmability of Decision Making; Strategic Decision Making; Strategy-as-Practice; "Unstructured" Decision Making

Further Readings

Barthélemy, J. (2006). The experimental roots of revolutionary vision. *Sloan Management Review, 48*(1), 81–84.

Lindlbom, C. (1959). The science of muddling through. *Public Administration Review, 19,* 79–88.

Mintzberg, H., & Waters, J. (1985). Of strategies, deliberate and emergent. *Strategic Management Journal, 6,* 257–272.

Quinn, J. B. (1978, Fall). Strategic change: Logical incrementalism. *Sloan Management Review, 20*(1), 7–21.

Quinn, J. B. (1980). *Strategies for change: Logical incrementalism.* Homewood, IL: Irwin.

MANAGEMENT (EDUCATION) AS PRACTICE

This entry explains why educating *practicing* managers is important and the main factors to bear in mind when doing so. Management cannot be taught in a classroom. Actually, it probably can't be *taught* at all, but people can *learn* how to manage, to get better at it, and to take on more complex assignments, by reflecting on experience in the light of concepts. Management is a bundle of functions performed on behalf of an enterprise, and the term also refers to a specific group of people whose main role is to perform these functions. There is not always a perfect overlap between these two—not everything that managers do is really "managing"; nor is all management performed by people who are designated "managers." This entry is concerned with education for people who manage, whatever their job title, particularly with education that makes use of that experience and relates directly to it. Consequently, it will not address education for people who want to be managers but so far have no experience of the work, or, people who research management but have no intention of doing it.

Fundamentals

Education for practitioners has a long history: Military training has often involved periodic reflection and reassessment of tactics and behaviors. In modern industrial settings, *action learning* is the term most often employed to describe an approach

to learning from the experience of managing, while continuing to do the job. Action learning combines three kinds of inputs: participants' current managerial challenges, the opportunity to discuss and compare with peers, and analysis and interpretation in the light of theoretical models. Groups of managers engage in "action learning sets," committing to share their challenges and discuss their implications at regular meetings, face-to-face, or virtually. The approach was first articulated by Reg Revans in Manchester, England, in the 1960s and has evolved in numerous settings—within companies, in master of business administration (MBA) associations, and across communities, as the basis for emerging social reforms. In Revans's original version, participants would work together without any outside interference, although many groups prefer to employ a professional facilitator but still follow an agenda that arises from the specific situations faced by members. Others are more structured, covering a curriculum with required papers leading to award of diplomas by universities or associations. These differences imply a significant question: Who determines what is legitimate learning, and what are acceptable outcomes? In the pure model, it is entirely down to the set members to evaluate each others' contribution, and for each individual to make use of the outcomes in their own work. Facilitated groups may look to the professional facilitator to ensure quality of participation. Frequently, formal university accreditation is valued by participants, so they find ways to embed the evaluation of learning in assessment and examination processes. This is not necessarily a bad thing, as it can push people to think more deeply, broadly, and critically about their own sensemaking; to subject common sense notions to rigorous analysis; and to pursue a structured path of gradually more complex and challenging ideas.

Common to all these approaches is shared reflection on experience in the light of concepts, with the intent to apply insights in one's own managerial practice; this is different from studying cases of other businesses, perhaps imagining oneself to be the CEO facing a tough decision. When the situation is one of facing oneself, it is far harder to succumb to wishful thinking or grand strategic gestures, because in reality, implementation is more difficult than one might imagine in a typical MBA classroom, for example. More importantly, when someone learning about management knows that he or she will be responsible for really following up on recommendations made in a discussion group, the individual knows him or herself to be a moral agent, responsible for whatever he or she does. This is the best basis for responsible management education: embedding it in real responsibilities, not working through simulations. This is based on an understanding of learning articulated for managerial settings by Chris Argyris and Donald Schon in the 1970s, drawing on ideas of earlier professional educators, such as John Dewey.

Advocates of this approach to management education criticize typical MBAs for teaching the wrong things to the wrong people in the wrong ways. Henry Mintzberg argues that management is more than the simple accretion of business functions; it can't be learned by people with no experience of managing and certainly not by sitting in a classroom absorbing techniques and models or pretending to be a character in a case study. Mintzberg suggests that managing is effected through various kinds of work: communicating, linking, and dealing in the organization and its wider environment and controlling, leading, and doing within a unit. These kinds of work might draw on skills and knowledge about finance, markets, organizational behavior, and innovation; but technical knowledge is necessarily subordinate to the interactive practicalities of managing. Jonathan Gosling and Mintzberg suggest that managing involves working in at least five distinct mind-sets: action, reflection, worldliness, collaboration, and analysis. Taking action is crucial, but one is only really managing (rather than reacting) when action is informed by reflection on ends and means: Are they worthwhile and

effective? This requires analysis, and, not just from one point of view because managing always involves collaborating with others, which is only effective if one is able to get into their way of seeing things, with the worldly wisdom to know what will work for them. Educating practicing managers requires strengthening the ability to work in each of these mind-sets and to weave them together in each manager's specific context. Educational methods should, in this view, be designed to enhance reflectiveness, worldliness, analytical ability, action orientation, and collaboration.

This approach can be summed up in seven tenets for educating practicing managers: (a) Management education should be for practicing managers; (b) they should stay in the jobs so they weave learning through their practice; (c) management education thus leverages life experience as fully as possible; (d) the key to learning is thoughtful reflection, mostly with peers, interpreted in the light of concepts from relevant theory; (e) from this reflection follows impact at work; (f) all together, education becomes interactive learning; and (g) the physical architecture, faculty, and pedagogy of management education therefore has to be facilitative of this process.

Note that working with experience is not the same as "experiential" education, which refers to having experiences that are concocted to surprise, challenge, stretch, or focus attention on something new. Experiential education includes a huge range of activities, such as outdoor adventures, T-groups, work shadowing, community service, and business simulations. All of these can contribute valuable learning in the context of a well-designed educational program. But here we are concerned with the even wider context in which such a program takes place—specifically, a context in which the learner is primarily holding a managerial role and responsible for what happens as a result of the way she or he behaves in that role.

Importance

The workplace, where most managing takes place, offers many opportunities for learning if appropriate reflective practices are built into it. Management education, distinguished from management development by its attention to a broader context, is deepened when participants analyze and interpret their current and impending responsibilities as "live case studies."

Classroom activities can contribute if adapted to encourage discussion as well as presentations, but they need to be configured appropriately in their pedagogy and physical layout (movable seating in a flat room, for example). Lectures and concocted experiences can play a part by providing new perspectives, reconfiguring group dynamics, and demonstrating techniques, but all should be related back to the real and current responsibilities of participants. In this way, learning remains rooted in the moral agency of managers, valuing their human resourcefulness and recognizing that they offer more than mere technical competence in the functional disciplines.

Curricula should thus be organized in ways that enhance understanding of the complex interplay of personal motives, skills, competences, collective beliefs, technical procedures, group dynamics, political wrangling, argument, and persuasion by which managing is accomplished—and also enhance the participants' readiness to act appropriately. This is unlikely to be achieved by a series of courses in business disciplines, such as finance, marketing, accounting, and so forth, however convenient it might be for teachers whose research careers and identities are organized in these silos.

An alternative is to design a curriculum according to various kinds of problems that managers face—problems of organizing, managing, working internationally, setting direction, and so on. Another logic, compatible with this, is to adopt pedagogies that draw participants into different ways of thinking, because managing involves fluency in a number of distinct mind-sets. For example, some argue that managers need to be able to work reflectively, analytically, collaboratively, with worldly wisdom, and oriented toward action. Each of these is rather different but must be woven together in the doing of managerial work. Educational activities can develop all of these mind-sets at the same time as teaching useful techniques and addressing important problems. These three approaches to curriculum and pedagogic design differ as follows:

1. Formulae, models, and techniques can be transferred to learners, who simply have to receive and absorb.

2. Case studies provide examples of real problematic situations and become especially useful if drawn from the experience of those taking part. This requires a discursive approach to learning spaces—not the combative arena of typical case-teaching classrooms, but round tables and a flexible agenda.

3. Ways of thinking—mind-sets—make available different kinds of awareness. Most experienced managers know this intuitively, and management education can enhance their familiarity and application of these mind-sets.

The point is that education that enhances practice should do more than impart knowledge and technical skill; it should enable people to think, see, and feel in different ways that are related to the work they do.

The ideas described in this entry have had a large and increasing impact on management education worldwide. The rise of business schools and the MBA degree in the latter part of the 20th century disguise the facts that (a) MBAs are a small part of the total management education market and (b) most countries (the United States excepted) will not accept people into MBA degree programs unless they have 3 to 7 years work experience. The United Kingdom has been a particularly intense site of innovation, where action-learning approaches are almost ubiquitous in most sectors of the economy and built into many MBAs. In the 1990s, many of these ideas were brought together in a program called the International Masters in Practicing Management (IMPM), a collaboration of five business schools in five countries, with participation from managers sponsored by their employing companies. The IMPM acted as a spur to many other business schools to move their provision more toward this style, and the original model of action learning, managers learning from each other in discursive groups without interference, has been adapted for the Internet age. A further development has been coined as "close learning," in contrast to "distance learning." In the latter, the student is distant from the supposed source of knowledge—the university. But close learning recognizes the opportunity to learn from day-to-day managerial experience, and it uses Internet technologies to bring all the elements so far discussed close to the manager—disciplined reflection and analysis of experience, group discussions with other managers, and theories and concepts with which to challenge common-sense interpretations.

At the margins, some are now predicting the end of the "banking" model of management education (in which the university acts as repository of stored knowledge that users might draw on), and a shift toward a "wiki-school," in which practicing managers, researchers, and teachers cocreate knowledge, insight, and understanding by working collaboratively on current managerial work over the Internet and other mobile technologies.

Jonathan Gosling

See also Academic-Practitioner Collaboration and Knowledge Sharing; Action Learning; Experiential Learning Theory and Learning Styles; Learning Organization; Management Roles

Further Readings

Argyris, C., & Schon, D. A. (1978). *Organizational learning.* Reading, MA: Addison Wesley.

Gosling J., & Ashton, D. (1994). Action learning and academic qualifications. *Management Learning, 25*(2), 263–274. Thousand Oaks, CA: Sage.

Gosling, J., & Mintzberg, H. (2003, November). The five minds of a manager. *Harvard Business Review,* 54–63.

Gosling, J., & Mintzberg, H. (2006). Management education as if both matter. *Management Learning, 37*(4), 419–428.

Ladkin, D., Case, P., Gaya Wicks, P., & Kinsella, K. (2009). Developing leaders in cyber-space: The paradoxical possibilities of on-line learning. *Leadership, 5*(2), 193–212.

Mintzberg, H. (2004). *Managers not MBAs.* San Francisco, CA: Berret Koehler.

Mintzberg, H., & Gosling, J. (2002). Educating managers beyond borders. *Academy of Management Learning and Education, 1*(1), 64–76.

Raelin, J. A. (2000). *Work-based learning: The new frontier of management development.* Upper Saddle, NJ: Prentice Hall.

Revans, R. A. (1971). *Developing effective managers.* London, England: Longman.

Reynolds M. (1998). Reflection and critical reflection in management learning. *Management Learning, 29*(2), 183–200.

MANAGEMENT BY OBJECTIVES

Management by objectives, known in the private and public sectors as MBO, was initially developed and promulgated by Peter Drucker, Douglas McGregor, and George Odiorne. MBO is a system for uniting employees in the pursuit of their organization's objectives. A key differentiator of MBO is its emphasis on *cascading objectives* from the CEO to the hourly employee. The objectives an employee is striving to attain are those that support the attainment of the objectives of the first-line supervisor whose objectives, if attained, support the attainment of the middle manager to whom he or she reports. Similarly, the objectives set and attained by the middle manager support the attainment of the objectives by a top manager whose objectives reflect one or more dimensions of the organization's strategic plan. The result is everyone knowing and understanding what is expected of them as individuals to increase their organization's effectiveness. In summary, goal attainment at each level in the management hierarchy facilitates the attainment of the objectives set by a manager at the next-highest hierarchical level. Because MBO is used in one or more forms by most organizations, this entry focuses on six aspects of MBO: (a) the core variables that constitute this procedure, (b) the relationships among these variables, (c) the implementation of MBO, (d) the boundary conditions for its effectiveness, (e) criticisms of MBO, and (f) the benefits of implementing MBO.

Fundamentals

MBO has a solid foundation in the behavioral sciences. Its effectiveness is due primarily to its emphasis on three core variables that are critical for motivating employees in work settings, namely, goal setting, performance feedback, and participation in decision making. More than 1,000 empirical studies in organizational psychology on goal setting show that specific, high goals lead to significantly higher performance than not setting goals or setting a vague one such as urging employees to do their best. Goals serve a dual function. First, they are motivating in that employees exert effort and persist until the goals are attained. Second, they serve as standards for performance evaluation. Interestingly, having a large number of goals has not been found to lead to negative results. In fact, employees who worked for supportive managers reported greater effort with increased number of goals. The setting of priorities is related to positive feelings about an MBO program and improved relations with one's manager. Hence, many organizations use MBO to conduct performance appraisals of individuals, teams, or both.

Hundreds of studies in both experimental and organizational psychology have shown that feedback on one's performance is necessary for both learning and motivation. Specifically, feedback allows employees to determine what they must start doing, stop doing, or be doing differently to attain their respective goals. Research shows that people who receive feedback are motivated to solve problems and are more likely to do so. Feedback can also increase an employee's self-efficacy that an objective is attainable. Given that the feedback is provided in a supportive manner, it is typically interpreted by an employee as interest and concern by the person's supervisor. Feedback given in a negative manner typically lowers job performance. Participation with one's supervisor on the goals that should be set, and the ways to attain them, increases an employee's understanding of his or her boss's expectations, and the appropriateness of the goals that are chosen. It also has been found to increase job satisfaction, particularly for employees who have a high need for certainty.

Interrelationships Among Variables

Goal setting is not effective unless feedback is provided on goal progress. Feedback is not effective unless it leads to the setting of and commitment to specific high goals. Performance feedback in itself is only information. It is useful only if it is acted upon. Employee participation in the setting of objectives is important because as noted earlier, it increases the likelihood of understanding expectations. It also increases the likelihood of understanding why an objective is important for an organization's effectiveness. This typically leads to discussions of ways to attain it. Finally, there is evidence that participation in the goal-setting process leads to higher goals being set than is the case when they are assigned. Goal-setting theory states, and empirical research shows, that the higher the goal, the higher an employee's performance.

Implementation of MBO

Implementing MBO is typically a four-step process. First, specific organizational objectives are set. Second, "cascading" supporting goals are established for employees in each hierarchical level, and plans for attaining these objectives are agreed upon. Third, dates are agreed upon for reviewing goal progress. The fourth step is the "final review" regarding goal accomplishment and the setting of new objectives. Meta-analyses reveal that the success rate of implementing MBO ranges from 90% to 97%.

Boundary Conditions

Factors inherent in the employee, the job, and the organization can enhance or diminish the effectiveness of MBO. Employees with a high level of interest in their job want their boss to be minimally involved in setting their objectives. Those who are high on need for certainty and structure in their jobs do want their boss to be extensively involved in setting objectives. For all types of subordinates, a manager should make sure the objectives focus on areas of importance for the subordinate's, the department's, and the organization's success. Frequency of job change influences the effectiveness of MBO. In changing job situations, effort by the supervisor to clarify and prioritize goals is important. For individuals in stable jobs, high levels of supervisory involvement is sometimes perceived by employees as unnecessary and could be interpreted by the employee as the supervisor having problems with that individual's performance. An organizational factor that influences the effectiveness of MBO is the support given to it by senior managers. An organization's productivity increases when top management is committed, and is seen as committed, to MBO being taken seriously. When top-management commitment is high, gains in productivity are substantially higher than when top-management commitment to MBO is low.

Importance

MBO, with its emphasis on cascading objective setting, typically increases the amount of communication between management hierarchies, and between employees and their immediate supervisor, on the action steps necessary to implement the organization's strategic plan. This communication reduces goal conflict among individuals. By rewarding progress toward goal attainment, the driving forces needed for an organization to be successful in its operating environment are focused on the "right things." Moreover, studies show that as a result of MBO, employee attitudes toward the job, as well as their performance, increases as does organizational commitment.

In addition to increasing an employee's performance, studies have shown that the introduction of MBO programs improves an organization's performance. The impact of MBO programs on productivity is further strengthened when the level of top-management commitment to them is high. When top-management's commitment is high, gains in productivity are substantially higher than when top-management commitment is low. In short, top-management commitment plays an essential role throughout the entire process of MBO, including the setting of specific, high goals; providing feedback; and including employee participation in the decision-making process.

No management system or technique is immune to criticism. A major criticism of MBO is its focus on "bottom-line" cost-related measures. These measures (e.g., revenue generated, cost reduction targets) are sometimes excessive in that they are affected by factors that are beyond an individual's control (e.g., currency fluctuations). Such objectives can lead to a "results at all costs mentality," which in turn can foster unethical behavior. Moreover, bottom-line measures are often deficient in that they do not take into account factors for which an individual should be held accountable (e.g., team playing within and between divisions). The solution is to make explicit, and then assess, the behaviors an individual is to exhibit in attaining bottom-line objectives.

A second frequently heard criticism is that MBO implicitly encourages smart people to find ways to make relatively easy goals appear difficult to their boss. This sometimes occurs when MBO is used as the basis for making performance appraisals. This is especially likely to occur when monetary bonuses and salary increases are tied to goal attainment. A solution is to reward increments in goal progress rather than make money an "all or none" result of goal attainment or failure.

MBO is a performance management tool that allows managers to monitor the levels of productivity and performance in their organizations. MBO provides managers with important information to improve the performance of their employees. In terms of the modern management context in which organizations are faced with intense competitive pressures, it is important for managers to consider the negative implications of MBO. Managers need to ensure that using MBO as a performance management system does not create a results at all costs mentality in the organization or does not negatively influence the ethical standards in the organization. Managers should achieve this by monitoring the ways in which employees strive to achieve their goals and use this information in the appraisal process.

Gary P. Latham and Alana S. Arshoff

See also Goal-Setting Theory; High-Performance Work Systems; Human Resource Management Strategies; Learning Organization; *Practice of Management, The*; Quality Circles; Scientific Management

Further Readings

Carroll, S. J., & Tosi, H. L. (1973). *Management by objectives: Applications and research.* New York, NY: Macmillan.

Drucker, P. F. (1974). *The practice of management.* New York, NY: Harper & Row.

Ivancevich, J. M. (1974). Changes in performance in a management by objectives program. *Administrative Science Quarterly, 19,* 563–574.

Kondrasuk, J. N. (1981). Studies in MBO effectiveness. *Academy of Management Review, 6,* 419–430.

Locke, E. A., & Latham, G. P. (1990). *A theory of goal setting and task performance.* Englewood Cliffs, NJ: Prentice Hall.

McGregor, D. (1960). *The human side of enterprise.* New York, NY: McGraw-Hill.

Odiorne, G. S. (1968). *Management by objectives: A system of managerial leadership.* New York, NY: Pitman.

Pringle, C. D., & Longnecker, J. G. (1982). The ethics of MBO. *Academy of Management Review, 7,* 305–312.

Rodgers, R., & Hunter, J. E. (1991). Impact of management by objectives on organizational productivity. *Journal of Applied Psychology, 76,* 322–336.

Rodgers, R., Hunter, J. E., & Rogers, D. L. (1993). Influence of top management commitment on management program success. *Journal of Applied Psychology, 78,* 151–155.

MANAGEMENT CONTROL SYSTEMS

Organizational control is defined as any mechanism or process that managers use to align attention, attitudes, behavior, and outcomes of organizational members with an organization's goals. The concept of organizational control describes both formal control (such as structures, procedures, and rules) and informal control (such as norms, practices) mechanisms, as well as the systems of control mechanisms used in predictable configurations. From their earliest writings, organizational scholars have emphasized the relationship between control application and goal attainment and have depicted organizational control as one of the four primary functions (i.e., controlling, coordinating, organizing, and planning) of management. Most conceptualizations of organizational control rest on theories of cybernetic systems where inputs are transformed through processes into outputs. In implementing these systems, managers plan, measure, reward, and provide feedback on achieved performance. Control systems evaluate inputs, processes, and outputs to assess the attainment of specific production standards. If standards are satisfied, work proceeds unabated. If not, managers alter the inputs, processes, or outputs employed by the system until desired standards are achieved. The information processing theory of organizations was synthesized into the core idea that control is based upon the programmability of tasks and the measurability of outcomes. Contemporary organizational research presents two primary streams of control research. One influential body of work examines individual elements of control. A second prominent body of work investigates ideal types of control arrangements. Together, these two streams provide the foundation for control research; each is briefly summarized in this entry.

Fundamentals

Analyzing Individual Control Mechanisms as Single Elements

Research on individual mechanisms of control has greatly influenced theory and research over the last two decades. This work has identified and classified *single controls* as control mechanisms (i.e., individual units, such as standards, rules, procedures, policies, routines, and norms) used to manage organizational functions, such as socialization processes, principal-agent relations, and performance evaluations. The individual control mechanism perspective has emphasized the use of formal controls which describe officially sanctioned mechanisms that are executed through explicit, written codified rules,

procedures, policies, and systems. Researchers have also emphasized informal controls that describe norms and beliefs that guide behavior. These mechanisms are developed and applied through direct (face-to-face) personal contact, shared experiences, organizational stories, rituals, and other culturally based processes.

Empirical research has classified individual control mechanisms according to the target of control. Arguably, the most widely used classification scheme groups mechanisms based on the segment of the organizational transformation process to which they are targeted: inputs used in production, processes involved in performing work, and outputs that represent product quality or quantity. Managers select input targets ("input control") to direct the flow of human, material, and financial resources into the firm. Managers choose behavioral targets (referred to as "behavior control" or "process control")—such as rules and norms—to determine how work gets done. Finally, managers employ output targets, such as profits, customer satisfaction levels, and production volumes and schedules—to regulate the product and service results that are achieved.

Examining Control Mechanisms in Clusters or Configurations

Researchers have observed that, in practice, sets of individual control mechanisms tend to predictably cluster into control systems and that studying each control element in isolation does not adequately reflect the complexity of organizational control use. This recognition has led researchers to focus greater amounts of their attention on evaluating the effectiveness of different control system configurations, how such control systems evolve over time, and the relationships between control systems and other important organizational phenomena (e.g., innovation, trust).

A second and distinct stream of control research has emerged that adopts a typological perspective in examining ideal types of control systems. Perhaps the most well-known typology of control systems was proposed in the late 1970s by William Ouchi (building on the work of Oliver Williamson). Ouchi's "markets, hierarchies and clans" approach defined three distinct types of control systems, each comprising different clusters of individual control elements. Managers within market control systems primarily focus on evaluating specific transaction outcomes; the most common of these is the price or cost of each transaction (e.g., a piece rate for production workers or a performance-based bonus for an executive).

A second form, referred to as the bureaucratic or legalistic control system, attempts to address how individuals adhere to organizational rules or norms. Managers within bureaucratic control systems apply formal procedures, rules and regulations, job specialization, and hierarchical authority to direct the processes and procedures that their subordinates use in performing work tasks. A third form, referred to as the clan control system, is composed of informal, norm-based social control mechanisms to ensure selecting the "right" people and doing things "properly." In clan control systems, managers focus on selecting, motivating, monitoring, and rewarding based on adherence to the organization's cultural norms as expressed through particular values, behaviors, and attitudes.

Recently, researchers have extended this control system classification by assessing the extent to which actors within each control system emphasize formal and informal mechanisms. These dimensions can be crossed to form a two by two table where low formal and informal control characterize the market control system and where high-low combinations characterize the "bureaucratic" (high formal, low informal) and "clan" control systems (high informal, low formal). This classification scheme has helped scholars identify the *integrative* control system as a fourth type, comprising high levels of both formal and informal controls. The incidence of each of the types of systems and how they evolve and change form over time is still not well understood, but research is being done to explore these fundamental questions.

Organizational control research has historically been manager focused and has stressed the use of singular control mechanisms in isolation. More recently, researchers have moved away from studying singular forms of control and embraced the study of multifaceted control systems. These two trends build on the seminal works on organizational control while reflecting the complexity needed to better understand how modern organizations function.

While organizational control theory spans decades and is no longer conceptualized as being only administered top-down, executed formally, and directed toward output through the use of reward and punishment levers, it is more important than ever to organizational success in uncertain and changing environments. Modern managers must recognize that control usage varies by organizational units and levels and is multifaceted and dynamic. The effective implementation of control by managers should seek to use multiple controls to balance and adapt configurations of control to promote the commitment and achievement of organizational goals. Thus, managers can continually reassess control usage across hierarchical levels and time.

*Laura B. Cardinal, Sim B. Sitkin,
and Christopher P. Long*

See also Agency Theory; Balanced Scorecard; Contingency Theory; Organizational Culture Model; Organization Culture Theory; Organizational Structure and Design; Strategy and Structure

Further Readings

Anthony, R. N. (1952). *Management controls in industrial research organizations*. Cambridge, MA: Harvard University Press.

Cardinal, L. B., Sitkin, S. B., & Long, C. P. (2004). Balancing and rebalancing in the creation and evolution of organizational control. *Organization Science, 15,* 411–431.

Fayol, H. (1949). *General and industrial management* (C. Storrs, Trans.). London, England: Pitman.

Ouchi, W. G. (1979). A conceptual framework for the design of organizational control mechanisms. *Management Science, 25,* 833–848.

Ouchi, W. G. (1980). Markets, bureaucracies, and clans. *Administrative Science Quarterly, 25,* 129–141.

Sitkin, S. B., Cardinal, L. B., & Bijlsma-Frankema, K. (2010). *Organizational control: New directions in theory and research*. New York, NY: Cambridge University Press.

MANAGEMENT ROLES

The concept of management roles refers to how managers behave at work. These roles are popularly described as what managers "do": their performance in predictable roles that specify rights, duties, expectations, and norms. Thus, management roles are highly influential in the field of management since what managers do depends to a great extent on how they perceive these roles. The following three sections of this entry describe the concept of management roles, trace the development of management role theory, and evaluate the contributions of that theory. The concluding section lists suggestions for further reading and provides cross-references to related entries in this encyclopedia.

Fundamentals

Because management is difficult to define, it is not always possible to draw clear distinctions between managerial and nonmanagerial work. Tasks considered managerial in one country or a sector may be categorized as employee tasks in other countries and sectors. However, as researchers, if we look at the roles managers perform, we may reach a better understanding of how managerial work differs from nonmanagerial work. From the lowest supervisory level to the highest executive level, managers lead other people, often assuming interpersonal, economic, and operational responsibilities. These responsibilities have an important impact on various management roles.

Before describing these management roles, it is useful to briefly discuss roles and role theory as developed mainly in the fields of sociology and social psychology. In role theory, the role concept is associated with the division of labor that assigns heterogeneous and specialized tasks to (work) roles. There are many work roles other than management roles, for instance, teachers, nurses, police officers, and sales persons, all of which are unique work roles.

In all such work roles, in addition to prescribed rights and duties, there are expectations and norms of appropriate behavior. For example, it is assumed managers will take leadership responsibility competently and authoritatively. Yet as the ongoing discussion about management roles indicates, the specific expectations and norms are rarely static. Managers are change agents. Therefore, as they help their organizations change, they too are required to adapt to new expectations and norms.

There are several ways to look at how expectations and norms associated with management roles are shaped. Evaluations are influential. People (other managers and/or employees) evaluate managers' performance, and managers evaluate their own

performance. Is he or she acting competently in this situation? And what about oneself? Such self-evaluation is strongly related to identity regulation. In addition, the responsibilities and obligations of work tasks influence the expectations and norms of managerial roles.

In his 1973 book, *The Nature of Managerial Work,* Henry Mintzberg presented what is now the most renowned model of managerial roles. The model consists of 10 roles divided into three categories: interpersonal roles, informational roles, and decisional roles. These 10 roles are summarized next. The term *organization* is used here in a general sense to mean the entity, the unit, the department, and so on.

Interpersonal Roles

- *Figurehead:* A manager who represents the organization. These work tasks typically have a ceremonial character.
- *Leader:* A manager who creates a positive atmosphere and motivates subordinates. Work tasks include employee hiring and compensation.
- *Liaison:* A manager who is the contact link between peers and outsiders. In modern management literature, this work task is often described as networking.

Informational Roles

- *Monitor:* A manager who is knowledgeable about various conditions related to the organization. Such conditions include environmental issues, technological developments, and cultural trends.
- *Disseminator:* A manager who circulates information (both factual data and value-based opinions) in the organization.
- *Spokesperson:* A manager who publicizes information externally that is in the best interest of the organization, for example, in order to persuade consumers or to establish or reestablish external legitimacy.

Decisional Roles

- *Entrepreneur:* A manager who initiates change that exploits opportunities and improves operations, for example, by increasing productivity using new technology.
- *Disturbance handler:* A manager who deals with negative events in the organization, such as

product quality problems, workplace conflicts and accidents, and poor employee job performance.

- *Resource allocator:* A manager who makes decisions or approves and/or disapproves decisions related to the allocation of financial and personnel resources and to the authorization and scheduling of various activities.
- *Negotiator:* A manager who mediates between the organization and union representatives, customers, and business partners.

Another leading management researcher is Rosemary Stewart, a business theorist who has written extensively on managerial work. In her 1967 book, *Managers and Their Jobs,* she identified five managerial groups. In profiling these groups (listed next), Stewart presented another categorization of management roles.

- *Emissaries:* Managers who travel widely and spend much of their time away from the organization.
- *Writers:* Managers who read, analyze, and write.
- *Discussers:* Managers who work mainly through staff meetings.
- *Troubleshooters:* Managers who work mainly with disturbances, including operational problems.
- *Committee members:* Managers who work with committees that consist of members from various organizational areas.

Fred Luthans, Richard M. Hodgetts, and Stuart A. Rosenkrantz present a third conceptualization of management roles. In their 1988 book, *Real Managers,* they identified and quantified the following 11 kinds of activities performed by managers. Percentages are averages for the 248 managers in their study.

- Exchanging information (15%)
- Handling paperwork (14%)
- Planning (13%)
- Decision making (11%)
- Interacting with outsiders (10%)
- Socializing and politicking (9%)
- Controlling (6%)
- Training and developing (6%)
- Staffing (5%)
- Motivating and reinforcing (5%)
- Managing conflict (4%)

A second important topic in the research on management roles is managerial behavior (i.e., what do managers do?). A constant finding in this research is that face-to-face meetings consume a significant amount of the manager's workday (even with the arrival of smart phones, e-mail, and other forms of electronic communication in the past decade). Managers typically spend between one half to two thirds of their workdays in meetings in which the most time-consuming activity is information processing (e.g., listening, talking, and reviewing). Despite the popular image of managers as sovereign decision makers, in reality, they work cooperatively with others.

Another common finding is that, because of the unpredictability of their work demands, managers are mostly involved with unscheduled activities, often in fragmented ways. A typical workday involves dealing with a series of unrelated tasks, some of which must be addressed simultaneously. This work pattern is especially evident for managers who are closely involved with production processes.

Managers have work challenges that are often daunting, particularly in large organizations. Sometimes, managers who are confronted with ambiguous goals are rarely sure of the results their decisions will achieve. For instance, serious problems may arise in a project that initially seemed promising, or a key employee may leave the organization, or an important supplier may fail to meet delivery terms. Successful managers must be flexible in adapting to new circumstances that require dealing constructively with the stress of such heavy and changing workloads. It is exhausting work. The following quote from Linda Hill's 1992 book, *Becoming a Manager: Mastery of a New Identity,* reveals a common frustration managers have about their work:

A lot of days, I'm here early and out late. Still I accomplish nothing that I was supposed to accomplish. I have so many interruptions and have to keep shifting my priorities. By the end of the day I feel drained, with nothing to show for all my work. (p. 192)

To deal with this organizational maze, managers follow both formal and informal paths. They are involved in numerous informal activities, both at work and outside of work. Such activities include building personal alliances, gossiping with peers and others, and exchanging tricks-of-trade with other managers. Formal activities have a more symbolic aspect, and this means that while they are treated as significant activities they are in reality not so important for the determining the future of the organization. Examples are participation in conferences where decisions have been made a priori or where managers have to show compliance with particular policies, even if they may be largely irrelevant to their own concerns.

The manager who follows the rules and supports the customs and values of the organization is perceived as a competent role performer. The unconventional manager who wears Bermuda shorts to board meetings or who is unwilling to monitor costs will not last long in the role (provided he or she is not an owner). However, it is not enough to merely play the role of the "organization man" or woman. Successful managers must find creative solutions to problems. Unlike many nonmanagerial positions, management positions allow room for individual influence. According to Stewart, choice in management roles arises in the space between job demands (what has to be done) and job constraints (what cannot be done). She concludes that even managers in similar positions may interpret their areas of choice very differently.

Evolution

The concept of work roles can be traced back to the German sociologist Max Weber and his writings about bureaucracy. Weber described how bureaucracies could act in a rational way if the work holders, here called role occupants, were able to differentiate between personal values and work-specific norms and rules. Weber's writing has stimulated a vast literature on the role of the bureaucrat or administrator; a notable critique to the notion of the rational administrator has been made by Herbert A. Simon.

The research on management roles is generally acknowledged to originate with Sune Carlson's 1951 classic book, *Executive Behaviour*, a study of 10 Swedish top executives. Inspired by the work-study tradition in the scientific management movement, Carlson studied executive behavior, in particular the executives' workloads and work methods. Later studies, patterned after Carlson's study, have replicated his findings. The work behavior of top

executives, with their excessive workloads, is fragmented and reactive. It is difficult for them to find time to deal with long-term issues and company policies.

In the 1950s and the 1960s, researchers in the United States and England focused on the management roles of the foreman and the middle manager. Besides Stewart's research (see above), there were several other studies. Melville Dalton's *Men Who Manage* and Leonard Sayles's *Managerial Behavior* examined the informal aspects of managerial work, including its complexity. Sayles also identified several management roles (e.g., the liaison, the disturbance handler, and the negotiator) that Mintzberg made use of in his model.

Daniel Katz and Robert L. Kahn integrated role theory within an open-system organizational framework in the 1960s, and they identified three different managerial roles:

- *Technical role:* Work activities make use of specialized and functional techniques, that is, budgeting, market research, and analytic tools.
- *Interpersonal relations:* Work activities relate to human relations and people management, for instance, motivating and conflict resolution.
- *Conceptual role:* Work activities relate to complex problem solving and the ability to take a broad and long-term perspective.

In addition to articulation of his 10 management roles, Mintzberg in his 1973 book (see above) summarized what researchers of that time had learned about managerial work. According to Mintzberg, the research concluded the following: (a) Managers work at a demanding and unrelenting pace; (b) managers work in situations where brevity, variety, and fragmentation are the norm; (c) managers prefer to focus on live action (i.e., current rather than historical events); and (d) managers prefer face-to-face meetings and telephone conversations rather than written communications. These four points still seem a valid description of the nature of managerial work.

In the same book, Mintzberg described an observational study of chief executives that he also wrote about in the now-classic 1975 article titled "The Manager's Job: Folklore and Fact." In the article, Mintzberg criticized the popular view of the manager as the decision maker who makes a careful evaluation of various alternatives before taking action. In the article, Mintzberg also broke from the traditional view that management action requires systematic analysis.

John Kotter developed these ideas in his 1982 book, *The General Managers*. Kotter showed that managers could take advantage of fragmented and emergent work situations by using personal networks to advance their agendas. Kotter concluded that even chaotic discussions could be highly effective and that short-term and reactive behavior could benefit long-term objectives.

There is also research on management roles that deals with other informal aspects of management behavior, in particular the involvement of managers in organizational politics. For example, Rosabeth Moss Kanter's 1977 book, *Men and Women of the Corporation*, describes how senior executives are more comfortable hiring men, and considers female managers as too emotional and as odd members in peer networks. This attitude prevented women from advancing in companies. There are also studies that show how managers use their personal networks to advance their careers and avoid the perils of reorganization and downsizing.

More recent research highlights the emotional demands and stress experienced by managers in their work. As this research shows, some managers become disillusioned and cynical as far as their management roles. An example of such research is Tony J. Watson's 1994/2001 book, *In Search of Management*. In describing the chaos, uncertainties, ambiguity, and contradictions that surround managers, Watson shows how upper managers influence the work of middle managers by introducing change and restructuring programs. Yet as Watson argues, these measures seem mostly to produce unexpected and unplanned-for results in the paradoxical and complex world of management.

To conclude, the research on management roles tells us that managers do not always behave in the ways management textbooks describe (and promote). Researchers of management roles do not necessarily find that managers are poor practitioners. Instead, they find that the simple prescriptions for effective management behavior and the one-dimensional descriptions of management roles are of limited use in actual managerial work environments.

Importance

Despite the existence of research on management roles, it is much more common for researchers, past and present, to focus on managerial functions in organizations. The functional approach has dominated in such studies since the early 20th century. The result of the popularity of this approach is that management researchers have narrowed their objects of study to specialized areas that deal with particular functions, for example, management accounting or marketing strategy. With such foci, it is possible to develop recommended work practices for specialized areas.

However, the functional approach fails to take a broad, large-scale perspective on management roles. Managers have to oversee a large number of functional activities in order to make a somewhat coherent assessment of them. It is not certain, for example, that the accountant's control measures motivate subordinates who may have different views. Although it may be argued that the functional approach has influenced management roles research (e.g., Mintzberg's ten roles model), not all managers' actions have functional purposes. More importantly, managers rarely use (or use differently than described) the managerial functions found in textbooks. One explanation may be that formal and rational decision making is too time consuming and too intellectually demanding.

Despite the modest attention given to them by researchers in other subfields of management research, the management roles research has identified many ideas worthy of continued examination. Perhaps the most important of these ideas is that managers perform their roles in complex and often unstructured work settings where outcomes are uncertain, behaviors have symbolic meaning, and stress, overwork, and frustration are commonplace. Gradually, this practice approach, which looks at what managers really do, has begun to establish itself as a research method that rivals the traditional functional approach. Examples of the latter are the strategy-as-practices approach and the behavioral decision-making approaches (see the links at the end of this entry). There are good possibilities for cross-fertilizations between these approaches and the managerial roles research.

Management roles research benefits from its strong empirical base. The findings from this research derive from fieldwork in which managers' activities are observed and time measured. Moreover, support for management roles research, which has been conducted in various contexts (sectors and countries) and at different hierarchical levels, is strengthened by the findings of both similarities and differences in managerial work behavior.

Management roles research has been less successful in its effort to name the definitive management roles. As previous research has shown, there are numerous ways to categorize these roles. It seems impossible to identify a set of roles that apply to all managers in all contexts. As noted above, Mintzberg's ten roles model has a functional bias and does not capture all roles that managers play. Like leadership research, which struggles to define the definite traits of a good leader, management roles research is in danger of producing a plethora of categorizations.

Management roles research also faces the practical challenge of convincing managers (and educators) of its findings on what managers *actually* do. These empirical studies of management roles may not align with cultural understandings of what managers *should* do. Overcoming this resistance is a task for future researchers of management roles. Scientific fact should be treated as more important than cultural beliefs, but this is often not the case.

Knowledge about managerial role theory can be used in many different settings. It can be used for identifying what kinds of knowledge, skills, and abilities are needed to be successful in senior management positions; to help managers cope with work situations characterized by complexity, uncertainty, and ambiguity; and not least to understand the realities of management.

Stefan Tengblad

See also Behavioral Theory of the Firm; Complexity Theory and Organizations; Garbage Can Model of Decision Making; Intuitive Decision Making; Management (Education) as Practice; Organizational and Managerial Wisdom; Strategy-as-Practice; "Unstructured" Decision Making

Further Readings

Hill, L. A. (1992). *Becoming a manager: Mastery of a new identity.* Boston, MA: Harvard Business School Press.

Kotter, J. P. (1982). *The general managers.* New York, NY: Free Press.

Luthans, F., Hodgetts, R. M., & Rosenkrantz, S. A. (1988). *Real managers.* Cambridge, MA: Ballinger.

Mintzberg, H. (1973). *The nature of managerial work.* New York, NY: Harper & Row.

Mintzberg, H. (2009). *Managing.* San Francisco, CA: Berrett-Koehler.

Stewart, R. (1982). *Choices for the manager.* Englewood Cliffs, NJ: Prentice Hall.

Tengblad, S. (Ed.). (2012). *The work of managers: Towards a practice theory of management.* Oxford, England: Oxford University Press.

Watson, T. J. (1994/2001). *In search of management: Culture, chaos and control in managerial work* (Rev. ed.). London, England: Thomson Learning. (Original work published 1994)

MANAGEMENT SYMBOLISM AND SYMBOLIC ACTION

Management symbolism and the focus on symbolic action within the field of organization and management studies can be labeled as one result of the so-called cultural turn within organization studies. During the 1980s, organization and management scholars shifted their attention from understanding organizations as rational-authoritative machines or information-processing computerlike entities toward organizations as populated by human beings who bring with them interests, norms, values, and expectations in their search for creating meaning from the world around them. As a result, the experiential world of the organizational members and how they create and interpret organizational reality became the center of academic and managerial interest. This entry first outlines the fundamental ideas behind this approach before turning toward leadership studies and the symbolic management approach as two particular examples of how the symbolic perspective on management and organization has influenced research and practice.

Fundamentals

Approaching management from a symbolic perspective involves referring to the category of meaning within organization and management studies. Focusing on symbolic action implies an understanding of organizations as being constituted and enacted by all organizational members, bringing acts of sensemaking to the forefront of any activities in order to develop insight. Following this, the meaningful world of organizations is conceptualized as the result of numerous and ongoing social interactions, creating, maintaining, and changing what is understood as organizational reality. This reality provides organizational members with a common understanding and a frame of interpretation. This frame offers information about status, power, commitment, motivation, and/or control and in this sense informs about the social order. For example, it serves as the background in understanding the employees' role within the organization, interpreting the various discourses within the organization, or perceiving an action as management action.

Understanding organizational reality and management as being infused with meaning implies a rejection of the existence of factual or objective actions and outcomes. Instead, phenomena such as organizational structures and processes, strategies, management decisions, leader behavior, or employee deviation make sense only when the meaning that organizational members attach to these phenomena is understood. Thus, structures, concepts, material objects, acts, and forms of communication are seen as symbols that need to be interpreted in order to comprehend their meaning.

Paying attention to symbols (i.e., phenomena and attached meanings) means to consider the following three characteristics. First, symbols vary in their degree of complexity. Plain symbols, such as the size and furnishings of a manager's office, straightforwardly signify the responsibility and importance of this person. However, a language specific to an organization or a profession (e.g., the language of information technology specialists) constitutes rather complex symbolic systems that demand a higher effort of interpretation in order to make sense of them. Second, symbols within organizations both unconsciously emerge and are intentionally created. Organizations consciously create a certain picture of themselves for their employees in order to achieve various effects. For example, to issue a house journal is one means to communicate the organization in a certain—usually favorable—way to its members. With regard to emerging symbols, a manager's efforts to prepare himself or herself for all kinds of

unexpected situations, by establishing various action plans, symbolizes something about this person's way of dealing with difficult situations. Third, although symbols are constituted in social interaction, their meaning is not shared by all organizational members in every case. For instance, to receive an award for longstanding service within the organization is interpreted as a great honor by some, yet it is understood by others as a symbol for excessive subordination and loyalty ("25 years of subjugation for a distinguished service award").

The latter aspect already suggests an important note embedded in the understanding of organizations as symbolic systems or, more precisely, systems of shared meanings. Although organizations are conceived as meaning systems, the degree to which meaning is shared varies due to organizational subunits having their own interpretations. Arguably, the management and workers of a company would each have a different understanding of a labor dispute and, thus, each party's approach to resolve such a dispute would vary. Another example would be the implementation of a strategy focused on the customer, which could be perceived as more welcoming by the marketing department than by the controlling unit. Consequently, although organizational reality provides the members of an organization with a frame for interpreting their experiences at work, this should be understood only as an orientation toward possible perspectives and points of view. The particular meaning attached to, for example, the decision to outsource elements of the production process or to switch to flexible labor is informed by the organizational context and other interpretative resources such as individual and group interests, socialization, social class, and organizational position. In fact, a symbolism-based account of management and organization implies learning about the ongoing processes of cocreating meaning out of the organizational members' lived experiences at work.

Furthermore, organizations do not exist independently from their surroundings. Hence, the meaning of organizational aspects is also informed by, for example, the broader society. Symbolic action within an organization is infused with meaning from other symbolic systems. To understand organizations one has to learn about the interpretative resources of organizational members as well as how their interpretations are informed by sources located both inside and outside the particular organizational context. In this sense, to grasp how decisions are made on the one hand requires reconstruction of the different interpretations of the people contributing to the decision-making process. On the other hand, the influence of societal symbolic structures, for instance, the relationship between men and women, professionals and nonprofessionals, or old and young people needs to be considered, as these symbolic aspects transcend the boundaries of organizations and may also influence decision-making processes.

Importance

Management symbolism and symbolic action acknowledges the interacted social reality in organizations and, thus, provides a useful framework for management research focusing on cultural and symbolic issues. In particular, management is conceptualized as a collective sensemaking process with all parties of the organization involved. In this sense, the meaning associated with structures, processes, and actions cannot be prescribed by an authoritative sender (e.g., the management) but has to be continually negotiated with the receiver (e.g., the workers).

The symbolism approach to management and organizations has significantly influenced management knowledge. This influence can be observed in both academic studies and applied management. Two examples to be referred to here are leadership studies and the perspective of management as a symbolic action.

The study of leadership is a field that is impacted by the ideas of symbolism. Symbolic leadership approaches concentrate on studying values, meaning, interpretation, history, and context in addition to other symbolic elements of the leadership process. On the one hand, leaders do not directly influence followers in a sort of objective and unidirectional way. Leaders are themselves symbols, and their actions are symbolic actions that are subject to interpretation by followers. What leaders are, what they do, and essentially what leadership means in a particular organization is manufactured within the social interaction between leaders and followers. Leadership, then, becomes conceptualized as a collective effort of participants to co-construct, co-maintain and co-change their understanding of the social order. Studying leadership, hence, involves developing insight into processes of symbolic action

and the negotiation of joint meaning. To understand leadership implies to learn about the various codes members of an organization use for interpreting perceived reality and to decode the numerous linkages within the symbolic systems at play. On the other hand, this account of leadership research does not conceive leadership as independent from the organizational context. Rather, leadership is embedded in organizational language, material artifacts, and social structures and rules. Consequently, employees are influenced by the actions of leaders as well as by reward systems, organizational principles and rules, work content, and practices. Leadership becomes defined as a distinct kind of social practice that receives its meaning only in relation to other social practices within the process of organizing. Hence, the context needs to be taken into consideration as it is only through the relation between leadership processes and the context that one can make sense of the leadership phenomenon studied.

The so-called symbolic management approach is another example of how the turn toward understanding meaning and sensemaking in organization and management studies has influenced management knowledge. At the heart of this approach lies the proposition that to manage organizations successfully one should not concentrate on managing human resources, organizational structures, or financial resources but should focus on the meaning attached to these organizational aspects. In this sense, management becomes the management of meaning, which means to provide and negotiate a sense of what is going on in the organization. Symbolic resources—that is, sources to make sense of what is going on, are understood as the primary source in the process of influencing attitudes, values, and emotions. Thus, two principles are constitutive of symbolic management.

First, symbolic management implies an understanding that meaning is not manageable. One cannot create, control, or manipulate the meaning associated with managerial acts, incentive systems, or flat structures. Rather sensemaking is a process of cocreation with those affected by managerial decisions playing an important part. Hence, symbolic management should concentrate on providing the sense behind organizational processes and structures; therefore, managers should actively involve themselves in the process of negotiating joint meaning. This account turns management processes into creative and participatory undertakings aiming to establish reflections about organizational culture and, thus, values, principles, and behaviors. A dialogue is favored in order to enable all participants to grasp the nature of the organization's culture and to understand its symbolic reality.

Second, symbolic processes possess their own logic. To influence the meanings contributing to organizational members' sense of their organization is difficult, and it takes time. Organizations as systems of shared meanings develop their own logic that cannot be simply changed by one member or one group. Additionally, as organizations form rather complex symbolic systems, they cannot be understood from a single point of view. In this sense, managerial actions, for example, the changing of the organizational logo, or announcing that "from now on we are working in teams rather than groups," or proposals that starting next year the organization will become more service oriented, won't necessarily affect employees' interpretations in the intended way. Employees will make their own sense of these changes, which may consequently result in rather unexpected behavior. Thus, symbolic management implies an understanding of the symbolic logic of the organization, not to be able to successfully manipulate it but to better understand the social consequences of management, including unexpected developments or unwanted effects.

Some authors argue that engaging in the management of meaning appears to have no direct impact on behavior, and as such, it has led managerial research and practice to partly swing back to more functionalist approaches. Nevertheless, one can conclude that management symbolism and the focus on symbolic action nowadays constitutes an important and influential part of management studies and organizational design.

Ingo Winkler

See also Narrative (Story) Theory; Organizational Culture Model; Social Construction Theory

Further Readings

Alvesson, M., & Berg, P. O. (1992). *Corporate culture and organizational symbolism*. New York, NY: Walter de Gruyter.

Hatch, M. J. (1997). *Organization theory: Modern, symbolic and postmodern perspectives*. Oxford, England: Oxford University Press.

Jones, M. O. (1996). *Studying organizational symbolism: What, how, why?* Thousand Oaks, CA: Sage.

Pfeffer, J. (1981). Management as symbolic action: The creation and maintenance of organizational paradigms. In T. G. Cummings & B. M. Staw (Eds.), *Research in organizational behaviour* (pp. 1–52). Greenwich, CT: JAI-Press.

Pondy, L. R., Frost, P. J., Morgan, G., & Dandridge, T. C. (Eds.). (1983). *Organizational symbolism*. Greenwich, CT: JAI-Press.

Smircich, L., & Morgan, G. (1982). Leadership: The management of meaning. *Journal of Applied Behavioral Sciences, 18*(3), 257–273.

Turner, B. A. (Ed.). (1990). *Organizational symbolism*. New York, NY: Walter de Gruyter.

Turner, B. A. (1992). The symbolic understanding of organizations. In M. Reed & M. Hughes (Eds.), Rethinking organization. New *directions in organization theory and analysis* (pp. 46–66). Thousand Oaks, CA: Sage.

MANAGERIAL DECISION BIASES

Decision biases are systematic and predictable deviations from rational thoughts and behaviors. Such biases span all steps of the decision-making process, from defining the problem to weighing the criteria to computing the optimal solution. Within the past five decades, the study of decision biases has taken primarily a descriptive approach toward understanding ways in which individuals are biased. Herbert A. Simon's research on bounded rationality established one of the earliest frameworks on biases in decision making, suggesting people's judgments depart from rationality due to three main factors: (a) a dearth of crucial information or criteria for understanding the problem, (b) time and cost constraints in obtaining higher quality information, and (c) perceptual errors that limit accuracy in calculating a solution. Since then, researchers have focused on how individuals are biased by the use of heuristics. This entry provides an overview of that work and also gives attention to more recent work on bounded decision making, misattribution, emotions, and recent attempts to prevent or eliminate such biases.

Fundamentals

Heuristics

Perhaps the most widely researched biases stem from the study of heuristics, which are mental guidelines, or "rules of thumb," used to reach a solution, particularly when an exhaustive search is impractical. Daniel Kahneman and Amos Tversky noted that three main heuristics—availability, representativeness, and anchoring—can lead to irrational, suboptimal, and sometimes contradictory decisions. The availability heuristic suggests that individuals assess the frequency, probability, or likely causes of an event based on the degree to which instances or occurrences of that event are readily available in memory. In particular, events that are more recent, vivid, or easier to recall can heavily influence subsequent decisions. For instance, human resource managers may be more likely to hire memorable individuals, who tend to have a background, culture, and education similar to their own.

The representativeness heuristic encapsulates how people tend to look for traits that correspond to previously formed stereotypes and use this similarity as a proxy for misguided probabilistic thinking. Dependence on similarity to make inferences may lead to insensitivity to base rates and small sample size, misconceptions of chance and regression to the mean, and the conjunction fallacy. Entrepreneurs ignoring base rates will overestimate the probability of their businesses achieving success because they do not take into account the base rate for business failure. The belief that small sample sizes are sufficient to draw inferences about a larger population is another bias that results from use of the representativeness heuristic. As a result, managers testing a product with a small sample of individuals may overestimate the degree to which the small sample is representative of the entire population of consumers and, thus, may too readily make product decisions based on this inference.

Begetting misconceptions of chance, the representativeness heuristic often results in faulty predictions about future events. Individuals may believe that the sequence of coin flips H-H-H-H-H-H is much more likely than the sequence H-T-H-T-H-T, even when the probabilities of both sequences are identical, because the latter appears more random and also has an equal representation of both heads and tails. Furthermore, ignoring that each flip is independent of every other, individuals are much more likely to predict that the subsequent flip will be tails when asked about the first sequence than the second sequence. These misconceptions of chance are seen especially in many sports fans' belief in the "hot hand" phenomenon: Players have a better chance at making a shot or scoring if they have had a consecutive series of shots or points. However, such a phenomenon does not exist, as research has shown that the immediately prior shot does not affect the outcome of the subsequent shot. Biases in predictions may also result from neglecting the principle of *regression to the mean*. That is, individuals overweigh data from past performance in making their predictions of future performance, which is particularly problematic for outcomes that are heavily dependent on chance. Investment managers may mistakenly expect that funds that have done well in the past may continue to do well in the future.

Using similarity or representativeness to judge the probability of an event can also lead to the conjunction fallacy, which occurs when individuals believe the subset is more likely than the larger set. This fallacy typically arises when the conjunction of multiple events or qualities is more vivid than any one of the qualities alone and biases judgments in all fields from international relations to medicine. For instance, when individuals are asked to estimate the incidences of earthquakes in California versus North America, their answers likely imply that California has more earthquakes than North America, a statistical improbability.

Research has shown that anchors, including defaults, frames, and reference points, also serve as heuristics, biasing individuals' answers to questions even when the anchors are irrelevant to the questions at hand. Once individuals encounter these anchors, individuals generally fail to adjust sufficiently, even if these anchors are irrelevant to the context. Such effects are particularly well documented in literature on negotiations that show the initial offer to the opponent anchors the final deal, especially when there is ambiguity from the opponent's perspective over the true value of the negotiated object.

A number of other biases have also been summarized from this literature, including the confirmation bias, which is based on individuals' natural tendency to prove a hypothesis by searching only for confirming evidence, not disconfirming evidence. The Wason selection task illustrates this bias: Participants are shown four cards, two cards with the numbers 3 and 8 and two cards with red and brown colors facing upward, and they are asked to provide the two cards that can sufficiently test the statement that if a card shows an even number on one face, then its opposite face is red. While most individuals are correct to pick 8, they are usually incorrect in picking red—instead of brown—as the second card, neglecting evidence that could invalidate the statement. Hiring managers often face problems that arise from confirmation bias as they follow up only on the performance of those they hired, not those they did not hire.

Bounded Awareness, Ethicality, and Willpower

Whereas research on bounded rationality and heuristics generally focuses on how individuals depart from rationality when they are aware of the information provided, research on bounded awareness targets how people fail to notice or focus on useful, observable, and relevant data. In auction scenarios, bidders often fail to realize that placing the highest bid in order to win an auction item may in fact be a curse as the winning bid is likely greater than the item's true value. Inattentional blindness refers to the phenomenon in which individuals do not see what they are looking for, even when they are looking directly at it. Similarly, individuals are subject to change blindness, which describes how individuals fail to notice changes in their environment, particularly when the change is gradual. In the domain of ethical decision making, individuals are more likely to make unethical decisions when the ethical degradation is gradual, rather than sudden.

Bounded ethicality refers to the psychological processes that lead people to engage in ethically questionable behaviors without being aware that they are doing anything wrong. Research suggests that individuals often implicitly associate positive characteristics to in-groups and negative characteristics toward out-groups, or groups to which these individuals do not belong. Such research may be particularly relevant for hiring managers, who may be expressing favoritism toward their in-group members and as a result, unknowingly and indirectly

discriminating against applicants outside the in-group. Additional research on bounded ethicality suggests that individuals who were depleted of their self-regulatory resources were more likely to cheat impulsively than individuals who were not depleted.

Beyond ethics domains, other biases stem from individuals' bounded willpower, which refers to the overweighting of the present and near future, and underweighting of future states. Because individuals often discount the future, they consequently take actions that directly conflict with their own long-term interests. Such bounds in willpower help explain the reason individuals procrastinate or neglect to save for the future. Research suggests that organizations also exhibit bounded awareness when they fail to use cost-efficient building materials because they are expensive in the short run.

Misattribution

Misattribution refers to individuals' biased judgments about the causes or associations of social phenomenon. The fundamental attribution error describes individuals' tendency to judge others' behaviors as a reflection of their stable disposition and one's own behaviors as a result of situational factors. Additionally, individuals generally attribute positive behaviors to dispositional factors and negative behaviors to situational factors for people they like; for those they dislike, individuals are more likely to attribute positive behaviors to situational factors and negative behaviors to immutable dispositional factors. Individuals also tend to believe that their own behaviors are more variable than others' behaviors. Such errors in judgment could exacerbate conflict among individuals in organizations, especially if individuals perceive others' negative behaviors as part of their immutable disposition. Another form of misattribution bias is the self-serving, or egocentric bias, which describes how people claim to have taken more responsibility than other contributors attribute to them. As a result, individuals in a team setting are likely to overclaim credit for the work they have accomplished, particularly when the outcome is positive.

Emotions

Just as heuristics and bounded awareness can lead to biases, emotions can also greatly impact the decision-making process and can lead individuals to make irrational or suboptimal decisions. Research on negative emotions suggests that fear triggers risk-averse behaviors, whereas anger incites risk-seeking behaviors and leads individuals to be overconfident and optimistic about risky decisions. Ironically, those who are angry perceive themselves to have lower risk of health issues, such as heart disease, even though they are actually the individuals who are at heightened risk of heart disease.

Research on how emotions affect managerial decision biases is particularly relevant in the context of negotiations, where outcomes can vary widely. For instance, anger is one of the main explanations for rejecting unfair offers, even if accepting the unfair offer is monetarily more optimal than the alternative. Findings on positive emotions suggest that managers strategically displaying positive emotions are more likely to close a deal and gain concessions from the other party in distributive settings. Even though negotiators make more extreme demands when facing an opponent strategically displaying negative—rather than positive or neutral—emotions, these negotiators are also more likely to concede to an angry opponent than to a happy one.

Importance

Although research on managerial decision biases often focus on negotiation and hiring decisions, scholars have shown that biases exist in almost every area of managerial life, including, but not limited to, employee evaluations, team performance, and strategic planning. For example, managers can overestimate sales of a particular product due to the desire to look for confirming evidence of product success or overattribute work to the individual who is most visible on a particular project. Studying these biases is particularly important within the management field as decision biases are pervasive and can have a large impact on the structure, function, and composition of organizations.

Given that biases are widespread, how can modern managers prevent them from influencing the decision-making process? In recent years, a growing number of researchers have been focusing more on how to design choice sets that ultimately nudge individuals toward the more optimal choices. For example, if enrollment in 401(k) plans is suboptimal, then managers could make enrollment in these plans the default option. However, designing the optimal plan is not straightforward. Default enrollment into

401(k) plans for employees appear to dramatically increase enrollment numbers; however, these plans can also lead employees to anchor at low, suboptimal default savings rates, especially problematic for those who would have otherwise chosen high savings rates under a system without a default choice. Such findings illustrate that further research is needed to determine exactly how choice architectures can be optimally designed, especially when the best decision differs for each individual. Future directions of this research could be particularly relevant for managers as they design the choice architecture to curtail the rate of errors in decision making within their organizations.

Beyond choice architecture as a means of reducing bias in decision making, scholars suggest that obtaining the perspective of an outsider who does not have an economically or emotionally vested interest in obtaining a particular outcome can curtail irrational decision making. Furthermore, there is some evidence that simply being aware of how individuals are biased can lead managers to make more rational decisions.

Ting Zhang and Max H. Bazerman

See also Bounded Rationality and Satisficing (Behavioral Decision-Making Model); Decision Support Systems; Decision-Making Styles; Intuitive Decision Making; Strategic Decision Making; "Unstructured" Decision Making

Further Readings

Bazerman, M. H., & Moore, D. A. (2008). *Judgment in managerial decision making* (7th ed.). Hoboken, NJ: Wiley.

Einhorn, H. J., & Hogarth, R. M. (1978). Confidence in judgment: Persistence of the illusion of validity. *Psychological Review, 85*(5), 395–416.

Gino, F., & Margolis, J. D. (2011). Bringing ethics into focus: How regulatory focus and risk preferences influence (un)ethical behavior. *Organizational Behavior and Human Decision Processes, 115*(2), 145–156.

Lerner, J. S., & Keltner, D. (2001). Fear, anger, and risk. *Journal of Personality and Social Psychology, 81*(1), 146–159.

March, J. G., & Simon, H. A. (1958). *Organizations.* New York, NY: Wiley.

Milkman, K. L., Chugh, D., & Bazerman, M. H. (2009). How can decision making be improved? *Perspectives on Psychological Science, 4*(4), 379–383.

Ross, M., & Sicoly, F. (1979). Egocentric biases in availability and attribution. *Journal of Personality and Social Psychology, 37*(3), 322–336.

Simon, H. A. (1957). *Models of man: Social and rational.* Oxford, England: Wiley.

Thaler, R. H., & Sunstein, C. R. (2008). *Nudge: Improving decisions about health, wealth, and happiness:* New Haven, CT: Yale University Press.

Tversky, A., & Kahneman, D. (1974). Judgment under uncertainty: Heuristics and biases. *Science, 185*(4157), 1124–1131.

Managerial Grid

Leadership theories can be grouped into three main categories: (a) leadership as personality, (b) leadership as behavior and action, and (c) leadership as symbol. *Leadership style* denotes the behavior or behavioral pattern of leaders. Robert R. Blake and Jane S. Mouton's managerial grid theory is among the most well known in the field of leadership style. The leadership grid theory is based on a large number of studies performed by Blake and Mouton, among others such as Anne Adams McCanse. There are also two kinds of theories on leadership effectiveness. The *universal* theorists claim that there is one best way to lead, while the *contingency* theorists claim that leadership effectiveness is dependent on the situation. The managerial grid theory represents the strongest argument for the former. The managerial, or leadership, grid provides a framework for understanding and executing effective leadership. The grid theory has been applied all over the world, to private, public, and voluntary organizations.

Blake and Mouton's first book on their theory appeared in 1964. Over the years, they applied the theory numerous times and developed it, refining its theoretical basis and steadily adding to the documentation of its practical use. The key behind the success of the grid theory lies in the focus on style (behavior). Blake and Mouton rejected the notion that leadership style has its basis in personality. This entry presents the two dimensions of leadership style and defines the five leadership styles. Additionally, the explanation of the leadership behavior is also presented as well as how Blake and Mouton measured the styles. The entry also stresses the argument that there is one best way to lead—team

management—and the logical and empirical support for this universal theory of leadership.

Fundamentals

The Two Dimensions of Leader Behavior

Blake and Mouton stated that the process of achieving organizational purpose through the efforts of people results in some people attaining the authority to set the direction and to coordinate effort, that is, to exercise the responsibility for the activities of others. The foundation for understanding leadership consists in recognizing that a boss's actions are dictated by assumptions on how to use authority to achieve organizational purpose with and through people. According to Blake and Mouton, the processes of leadership involve the achievement of results with and through others. Whether it is called management, supervision, or administration, the underlying processes establish direction and permit coordination.

The basis for Blake and Mouton's grid theory is simple but fundamental. There are two dimensions (orientations) in all leaders' behavior. One dimension covers managers' concern with solving the task and the other their concern for the people under them. These dimensions are the same as those used by the Ohio State Leadership Studies, presented as "Consideration" and "Initiating Structure," and the dimensions of "employee-centered" and "production-centered" from the Michigan Studies. Blake and Mouton make numerous references to the Ohio State studies, which found that some managers are more concerned with solving tasks while other managers are more occupied with their relationships with subordinates. Additionally, some managers exhibit the same degree of focus on both dimensions at the same time.

This framework presents leadership style as a combination of the emphases that managers put on achieving results (task orientation) and on the relationship with the subordinates (people orientation). The theory regards the two elements in leader behavior as being independent of each other. Consequently, the emphasis that one manager puts on one dimension does not determine how much emphasis he or she puts on the other. Leadership style can, therefore, be presented as areas in a two-dimensional system. The grid consists of a quadrate with Concern for Production on one axis and

Concern for People on the other. Blake and Mouton did not intend the leadership style to cover all aspects of leader behavior. Rather, they sought to provide clear patterns in the basic behavior of leaders. For the sake of simplicity, the axes are ranked into areas from one to nine. However, Blake and Mouton describe only five of these styles, which they regard as the most basic ones. A deliberate and important omission is the lack of a zero point. A minimum of concern on both axes is mandatory because leadership would collapse if a manager were not to exhibit any concern for the production or the people, or both. Blake and Mouton emphasize that the exercise of leadership involves a task to be accomplished and people to do it. These two concerns are interdependent; one cannot be had without the other.

Leadership Style

Blake and Mouton define style as "patterns of basic behavior." These patterns are described by two orientations:

> Concern for production. This concept must be related to the nature of the organizations and the products and services rendered. Production refers to whatever an organization hires people to accomplish. Concern for production does not indicate the amount of actual production achieved but instead the character or strength of assumptions behind the concern.
>
> Concern for people. Concern for people is revealed in many different ways. It may manifest itself as efforts to induce subordinates to like the manager or to ensure good working conditions, or it may involve the manager trusting the subordinates and giving them responsibility. Depending on the character of the concern, subordinates may respond with enthusiasm or resentment, with involvement or apathy, and so on. Once again, concern for people does not measure what the managers achieve but indicates the character or strength of assumptions behind the concern for them.

Blake and Mouton present an overview of research and theory which describes behavior on the basis of these two dimensions. Factor analyses have strengthened the conceptual analysis, confirming that most of the variance in behavior can be explained by these two dimensions. Blake and Mouton concluded, therefore, that a framework

for analyzing leadership behavior based on these dimensions is sufficient for understanding managers' assumptions and actions. The five basic leadership styles are as follows.

- *Authority-obedience.* This style is characterized by a manager who displays maximum concern for production combined with a minimum concern for subordinates. This kind of manager concentrates on maximizing production by exercising power and authority and by achieving control over people by indicating what they should do and how they should do it.
- *Country-club management.* A manager with this style has maximum concern for his or her people combined with a minimum concern for production. Primary attention is placed on amiable feelings among colleagues and subordinates, even at the expense of results.
- *Impoverished management.* This style is characterized by a manager with minimum concern for both production and people. This kind of manager does only the minimum required to remain in the organization.
- *Organization-man [sic] management.* This style is characterized by a manager who holds "go-along-to-get-along" assumptions, which are revealed by his or her conformity to the status quo.
- *Team management.* This style integrates concerns for both production and people. It is a goal- and team-oriented approach that seeks to gain optimum results from everyone who can contribute through participation, involvement, commitment, and conflict solving.

Importance

Explanations and Measurement of Leadership Style

When managers face a situation or problem they will act on the basis of a subjective assessment of what is at hand. This assessment includes assumptions of what the facts and possibilities are and of what are reasonable courses of action. These assumptions become part of a manager's beliefs or attitudes, and they guide and shape behavior. A theory of leadership is possible because there are only a limited number of assumptions on how to achieve results with and through other people. The dominant leadership style may be explained by the manager's personal background and work experiences.

It is not clear from Blake and Mouton's writings whether assumptions cause beliefs and attitudes or vice versa. Although Blake and Mouton state that managers' actions stem from their basic attitudes, the use of concepts is inconsistent; Blake and his later collaborator McCanse claim that the grid model describes attitudes and behavior. A reasonable interpretation is that Blake and Mouton regard attitudes as forming the basis for the leadership styles. In relation to leadership style, it captures the attitudes to elements highly relevant to the manager, that is, how important it is for the manager to exhibit concern for the subordinates and for solving the tasks. Blake and Mouton stress that the style variables are attitudinal and conceptual, with behavioral descriptions derived from and connected with the thinking that lies behind action.

For educational or training purposes, Blake and Mouton developed a questionnaire to measure leadership styles. The questionnaire is not, however, extensive, and the items are phrased in such a way that the managers are tempted to respond dishonestly. In fact, Blake and Mouton warn the respondents against self-deception when they are answering the questionnaire. Blake and McCanse presented a revised version of the questionnaire, but they do not provide the data regarding the reliability and validity of this instrument.

Leadership Style and Effectiveness

Blake and Mouton and Blake and McCanse offer no definition of effectiveness, and they use the concepts of effectiveness, productivity, goal attainment, and performance indiscriminately. The concept of career has also been used as a criterion. It is evident that Blake and Mouton considered goal attainment to be the most central, as it is part of their definition of leadership, namely, the attainment of the organization's goal. It is perhaps telling of their focus on the consequences of leadership styles that the subtitle of their 1985 book *The Managerial Grid III* states: "A new look at the classic that has boosted productivity and profits for thousands of corporations worldwide."

Blake and Mouton are the most vocal advocates for a *universal* leadership theory. They insist that there is one—and only one—leadership style that

is best: team management (9, 9 style on the grid previously mentioned).

The managerial grid theory got caught up in the crossfire between the universal and the contingency theories. Drawing from their 15 years' experience as participants and observers in groups linked to research institutions, Blake and Mouton became convinced that there is one best way to lead. They formulated this claim through the years with varying degrees of specificity and rigor and maintained forcefully that effective leadership is *not* contingent on the situation, directly in opposition to Fred E. Fielder. Blake and Mouton's own research provides scientific support for their stance, and they have presented strong logical arguments for the prominence of the 9, 9-leadership style.

Blake and Mouton have also referred to investigations which show that the 9, 9 style is superior to other kinds of behavior. Other researchers, especially P. E. Mott, have also supported their conclusions. Research indicates that a leader can influence the performance of subordinates positively by increasing the concern for both production and people. Blake and McCanse claimed that the strength of the grid model lies in the facts that it is possible to link observable behavior together with inherent assumptions and that the behavior is linked to its consequences. In that way, it is possible to claim that the grid model describes, explains, and predicts the effects of leader behavior.

Blake and Mouton do not explicitly describe how their theory was generated. However, the Ohio State studies did influence them strongly. It is evident that Blake and Mouton did not perform empirical studies to generate the two dimensions but instead synthesized the works of others and combined them with their own experiences. David J. Cherrington has claimed that there is no consistent support for the grid model and that its positive reception is actually based on well-known research that has been generously interpreted to support their theory. The managerial grid theory does not describe the five leadership styles on a sound scientific basis, and the antecedents behind the style behavior leave much to be desired.

Blake and Mouton are ardent proponents for a *universal* leadership theory, claiming that team management (9, 9) is the best leadership style. The universal theories were contested when Fiedler presented his theory of contingency. It is perhaps the irony of fate that the universal stance has regained precedence owing to first the work of David C. McClelland and especially the transformational leadership theory. Both of these contributions use the same argument: There is one best way to lead. Is it team (9, 9) managers, or power-motivated managers, or transformational managers? Whatever the answer may be, the managerial grid theory is one of the most influential theories of leadership and has influenced millions of managers around the world.

Jon Aarum Andersen

See also Contingency Theory of Leadership; Organizational and Managerial Wisdom; Organizational Effectiveness; Situational Theory of Leadership; Trait Theory of Leadership; Transformational Theory of Leadership

Further Readings

Blake, R. R., & McCanse, A. A. (1991). *Leadership dilemmas, grid solutions.* Houston, TX: Scientific Methods/Gulf.

Blake, R. R., & Mouton, J. S. (1964). *The managerial grid.* Houston, TX: Gulf.

Blake, R. R., & Mouton, J. S. (1978). *The new managerial grid.* Houston, TX: Gulf.

Blake, R. R., & Mouton, J. S. (1982a). A comparative analysis of situationalism and 9, 9 management by principle. *Organizational Dynamics, 10*(4), 20–43.

Blake, R. R., & Mouton, J. S. (1982b). Theory and research for developing a science of leadership. *Journal of Applied Behavioral Science, 18*(3), 275–291.

Blake, R. R., & Mouton, J. S. (1985). *The managerial grid III.* Houston, TX: Gulf.

Cherrington, D. J. (1989). *Organizational behavior: The management of individual and organizational performance.* Boston, MA: Allyn & Bacon.

Fiedler, F. E. (1967). *A theory of leadership effectiveness.* New York, NY: McGraw-Hill.

McClelland, D. C. (1975). *Power: The inner experience.* New York, NY: Irvington.

Mott, P. E. (1972). *The characteristics of effective organizations.* New York, NY: Harper & Row.

MANAGERIALISM

Managerialism refers to the power and control of managers and administrators within and over the organizations that employ them and, from a historical perspective, to the era of capitalism characterized by managerial power and control. While *managerialism* is sometimes used to describe managerial power, the term is inherently normative and is couched in a sense that managers are powerful relative to others and might misuse this power if there is insufficient control over them. Managerialism provokes an examination of the purpose of the corporation and the instrumentality of corporate management in achieving this purpose. This entry reviews the emergence of managerialism and sketches the range of existing responses to it.

Fundamentals

According to management theory, management positions—most notably executive positions—are rightfully and necessarily power laden. Executive managers must exercise power in order to execute their responsibilities within a context of uncertainty and competing interests. As those occupying executive positions are entrusted with decisions that are complex, nonprogrammable, and significant in their impact; the criteria for selecting executives should include the requisite judgment needed to make such decisions. Those in executive positions should therefore understand the nature of their responsibilities and should meet these responsibilities through the execution of sound judgment and the appropriate use of power. Also, according to management theory, executives should be accountable for their decisions and actions, and their discretion or latitude is limited by a series of exogenous (i.e., legal, ethical) and endogenous (organizational, personal) factors. Therefore, managerial power should be substantial but should also be limited by checks, balances, and constraints.

In the early 20th century, Adolf Berle and Gardiner Means detailed the emergence of a force that challenged the assumption of adequate checks and balances. Many large U.S. corporations, which had started as private entities owned by a few, had become "modern," publicly held corporations whose stock was traded in public equity markets. With public market trading and the liquidity it offered in the buying and selling of stock, there were now many owners of a given corporation, with many owning relatively few shares of its stock. Corporate ownership had become passive and diffused. As the concentration of ownership among a few large owners or block holders indicates active, controlling ownership, an implication of the diffusion was that owners had much less ability to control the firms in which they had invested. Ownership and control had become separated, and something was awry in terms of checks and balances on corporate management. Those employed as corporate managers were often managing and controlling the firm, and the age of managerialism had begun.

The concept of managerialism is inherently normative; it is embedded in the legitimacy of managerial power and control relative to others. Responses to managerialism regard how executives should prioritize the interests of various constituents and their own self-interest in managing the corporation. The response to managerialism based on agency theory rests on reestablishing the dominance of owner control over manager-agents. Agency theory puts forth that if left to their own devices, managers will overly diversify and overly grow their firms at the expense of shareholders and shareholder value maximization. Agency theory-based solutions to managerialist tendencies include monitoring managers, incentivizing them to think like shareholders, and empowering boards of directors to replace errant executives. Agency theory assumes that the corporate control system will continue to evidence a tendency toward managerial self-interest, as self-interest is a basic assumption about human behavior. Yet agency theory espouses that maximizing shareholder value is the appropriate overarching corporate goal and corporate governance mechanisms, such as executive compensation, and the board of directors can keep management on track toward achieving it.

Another response to managerialism is associated with critical management studies (CMS). Here, managers are thought to be a powerful class or elite. Managers are trained to view themselves as such in their business degree programs, in which agency theory dogma about the behavioral assumption of self-interest is used to rationalize and perpetuate managerial self-interest. Some CMS adherents view managerialism from a Marxist perspective; that is, those entrusted to manage large organizations are not trustworthy, and the realignment of corporations to maximize shareholder value as an overarching goal is illegitimate. Other CMS advocates are a bit less radical and are somewhat in sync with stakeholder theorists about improving, rather than abandoning, the corporate system and redirecting managerial power.

According to stakeholder theorists, while shareholders contribute their financial capital to the firm and are to be rewarded for doing so, the human capital of employees also matters very much to the firm's value creation. Here, the perspective is to evolve firms further, so that employees, those who invest their human capital in the firm, will become a larger force in strategic decision making relative to their historic and current roles. And the responsibilities of the corporation to society also deserve greater prioritization by corporate management, as had been noted decades ago by Berle and Means.

But stakeholder theory has yet to articulate well how various stakeholders' interests, including managerial self-interests, might or should fit together to best affect the firm and its strategy. There is concern that if managers are granted more discretion to serve as stewards of the corporation rather than as shareholders' agents, they might instead engage in a greater level of managerialism. Others contend that institutional and other large block holders could come to represent a broader set of stakeholder interests, as public pension plans now do in the United Kingdom, and in so doing establish and legitimate shareholder control over the 21st-century corporation. Although managerialism was detected decades ago, there is further work to do in developing a workable solution to it.

Marguerite Schneider

See also Agency Theory; Critical Management Studies; Stakeholder Theory; Stewardship Theory; Upper-Echelons Theory

Further Readings

Berle, A. A., & Means, G. C. (1932). *The modern corporation & private property*. New York, NY: Transaction.

Blair, M. M. (1995). *Ownership and control*. Washington, DC: Brookings Institution.

Cheffins, B., & Bank, S. (2009). Is Berle and Means really a myth? *Business History Review, 83,* 443–474.

Delbridge, R., & Keenoy, T. (2010). Beyond managerialism? *International Journal of Human Resource Management, 21*(6), 799–817.

Locke, R. R., & Spender, J.-C. (2011). *Confronting managerialism*. London, England: Zed Books.

Mizruchi, M. S. (2004). Berle and Means revisited: The governance and power of large U.S. corporations. *Theory and Society, 33,* 579–617.

Post, J. E., Preston, L. E., & Sachs, S. (2002). *Redefining the corporation*. Stanford, CA: Stanford University Press.

Raelin, J. A. (2010). The end of managerial control? *Group & Organization Management, 36*(2), 135–160.

Managing Diversity

Managing diversity is an umbrella term for the strategies and practices organizations use to manage a diverse workforce. The term originated in North America but is now used in many different parts of the world. Managing diversity initiatives usually target diversity dimensions that are visible in employees' physical characteristics (e.g., differences due to gender, race, age, and some disability conditions), but sometimes they encompass other, less visible dimensions (e.g., differences due to personality, hidden disability conditions, parental status, or cultural values). As organizational workforces become more diverse in terms of gender, race, age, and other demographic characteristics, organizations can experience both positive and negative effects. Demographic diversity may increase organizational innovativeness and productivity, because diverse employees bring a greater range of perspectives to bear on organizational decision making and are more likely to reach a wider range of customers in a diverse marketplace. However, diverse organizations also experience less employee commitment, more employee dissatisfaction, higher turnover, and greater intergroup conflict. As a result, organizations are increasingly investigating strategies designed to manage diversity and help them to achieve the best possible outcomes from a diverse workforce. The following entry will present the alternative diversity perspectives that organizations adopt in their diversity management efforts and describe three diversity practices (diversity recruitment, diversity training, and mentoring) that organizations can use to attract, develop, and retain a diverse workforce.

Fundamentals

Managing diversity is generally viewed as having two distinct components. One component involves the organization's overall philosophy or perspective on diversity. Organizations may adopt one of three distinct perspectives reflecting management's beliefs about the best way to manage diversity: discrimination-and-fairness, access-and-legitimacy, or integration-and-learning. The second component involves the specific practices or initiatives that the organization uses to manage diversity. Managing diversity practices are usually voluntarily adopted by organizations, and these efforts are often broader and more proactive than the requirements imposed by equal opportunity legislation. Three of the most common diversity management initiatives are diversity recruitment, diversity training, and mentoring programs. The two components of managing diversity are related, because an organization's diversity perspective is likely to drive the organization's choice among alternative diversity management practices.

Diversity Perspectives

The *discrimination-and-fairness perspective* focuses an organization's attention on providing equal opportunities in hiring and promotion, suppressing prejudicial attitudes, and eliminating discrimination in its practices. In this perspective, the organization consciously dismantles hurdles that might constrain its ability to attract a diverse workforce. But once in the organization, diverse hires are expected to assimilate into the dominant organizational culture. Therefore, the organization is more likely to adopt identity-blind practices that can be applied to all employees, rather than identity-conscious practices that focus on particular groups. For example, a discrimination-and-fairness organization might be more likely to develop a general mentoring program designed to develop junior staff and prepare them for promotion and less likely to develop a mentoring program targeting junior female staff with a focus on the unique problems experienced by female employees.

An *access-and-legitimacy perspective* is based on an organization's recognition that its markets and customers are diverse. Therefore, it is beneficial for the organization to match that customer diversity with diversity in its workforce. Organizations adopting this perspective increase employee diversity but may concentrate on sales and service positions where diverse employees have direct contact with customer markets. As a result of this focus, an access-and-legitimacy consumer products organization might have high racial minority representation among its salespeople but might not experience parallel levels of diversity among middle and upper level management.

The *integration-and-learning perspective* suggests that the insights, skills, and experiences employees acquire due to their demographic group membership are valuable resources that the organization can use to rethink its primary tasks and redefine its business practices in ways that will advance its mission. Organizations adopting this perspective are motivated to find opportunities for diverse employees to influence one another and impact the organization as a whole. For example, if an integration-and-learning organization learned that older salesclerks had a particular approach to working with older customers that improved sales, the older sales clerks might be urged to teach their sales techniques to their coworkers, and the coworkers would be encouraged to try the new techniques across a broad range of customer groups.

Diversity Management Practices

In *diversity recruitment, organizations are primarily* concerned with increasing the diversity of their current workforce. Organizations strategically modify their recruiting activities to attract individuals with particular demographic characteristics. Usually, these modifications are designed to signal to prospective job applicants the high value the organization places on employee diversity. Some modifications focus on the content contained in recruitment materials. For example, an organization might include employee photos in their recruitment materials to highlight the demographic diversity within their current workforce or present pro-diversity statements in their recruitment materials. An organization might also advertise benefits that it thinks might be particularly appealing to certain demographic groups (e.g., highlighting part-time hours to attract retirees or promoting its on-site child care program to attract young mothers). Other modifications focus on recruitment channels. For example, an organization might work with community retirement groups to attract retirees or place its ads in a publication targeting new mothers.

Diversity training is a strategy designed to improve relations among organizational members, particularly between members of different demographic groups (e.g., female and male employees, younger and older employees, or racial majority and minority employees). The training may take several different forms. Awareness training is intended to make employees more aware of the cognitive processes that may lead to discrimination and differential treatment. Skill training is intended to provide employees with specific skills (e.g., conflict management, team building, or decision-making) that will equip them to work effectively in a diverse workforce. The two types of training may be administered in combination or in sequence, but because most organizational diversity training is offered as a short-term stand-alone program, awareness training is more common in practice.

Finally, formal *mentoring programs* are designed to retain diverse employees and help them to advance in the organization by developing cross-level relationships within the organization. Informal mentoring results when senior managers provide developmental support to more junior members of the organization, and research suggests that senior members are more likely to provide support to junior people who are demographically similar to themselves. As a result, employees from demographic minority groups may be less likely to attract mentors (especially senior-level mentors) and receive less mentoring attention. In formal mentoring programs, organizations deliberately pair senior and junior members in a mentoring relationship for a specific period (e.g., 6 months or a year) in order to develop the junior member's skills and help the junior member to advance. Some organizations are also experimenting with group mentoring programs and employee network groups that facilitate relationship building among peers rather than across organizational levels. Employee network groups are employee-initiated groups organized around a demographic characteristic that receive organizational support and recognition. For example, an employer might provide a meeting room for a small group of employees to assemble once a month to discuss the challenges associated with being a racial minority within the organization.

Linking Diversity Management Perspectives With Diversity Management Initiatives

An organization's diversity management perspective is expected to impact the choice among these initiatives. Diversity recruitment, for example, is designed to increase diversity within the organization, a primary objective of access-and-legitimacy organizations. Diversity training may help to reduce discrimination within the organization, an important goal for legitimacy-and-fairness organizations.

Organizations hoping to improve productivity across the entire organization (the objective of learning-and-effectiveness organizations) are encouraged to develop an integrated diversity management program that includes multiple diversity initiatives, because individual initiatives focus on different aspects of an employee's employment. Diversity recruitment strategies might attract segments of the labor market that are currently underrepresented in the organizational workforce. However, as the workforce becomes more diverse, there is more potential for intergroup conflict, and so the organization is likely to adopt diversity training strategies to help diverse employees work effectively together. Further, because organizational diversity is frequently associated with higher turnover among both majority and minority employees, organizations may need to complement diversity recruitment strategies with retention strategies. Mentoring programs can play a useful role in employee retention because they encourage employees to develop extended networks that embed them within the organizational context.

Importance

A large body of research has examined the effectiveness of each individual diversity management practice.

Diversity Recruitment Effectiveness

Including pictures of diverse employees and statements about the organization's commitment to diversity in recruitment materials generally increases applicant attraction among women and racial minorities. However, these strategies seem to have no effect on applicant attraction among men and Whites. Therefore, these diversity recruitment strategies appear to be effective (and low-cost) strategies for organizations to use to increase the diversity of their workforces. They attract minority group members without discouraging major group members, enabling the organization to use the same recruitment advertisements to appeal to a broad labor market. However, most of the research on diversity recruitment has been conducted in experimental settings, so it is unclear whether recruitment ads targeting particular demographic groups will directly translate into greater organizational diversity. In addition, researchers have cautioned organizations against presenting an unrealistic picture of the organization—applicants who are attracted to an organization because of a pro-diversity message in its recruitment materials will be disillusioned if the organization does not deliver on that message on the job.

Diversity Training Effectiveness

Diversity training has received much criticism in the literature, but most of the criticism has been leveled at awareness training. There is little evidence that short-term awareness training has a sustained impact on employee stereotyping or discrimination. Diversity skill training, in contrast, has been demonstrated to deliver skill improvements. Unfortunately, most of the research on diversity training effectiveness has focused on short-run impacts, so it is unclear whether the diversity skills trainees exhibit during a diversity training program will be effectively transferred to the job.

Formal Mentoring Effectiveness

Research suggests that formal mentoring programs help diverse employees to achieve higher job and career satisfaction, larger salaries, and faster promotion rates. However, the research also suggests that employees with formal mentors experience less career success than employees with informal mentors. In other words, formal mentoring programs achieve only some of the positive effects associated with informal mentoring based on demographic similarity. The early research emerging on employee network groups suggests that they may be effective in reducing turnover among minority employees. Employee network groups facilitate relationships among minority employees that help to reduce the sense of isolation that might otherwise occur in a diverse organization. Employee network groups require little administrative or financial commitment from the organization, so they may be an inexpensive but useful option to include within an organization's diversity management program.

Diversity Management Effectiveness

Unfortunately, while many studies have examined the effectiveness of diversity recruitment, diversity training, and formal mentoring as stand-alone practices, very little research has examined the effectiveness of these initiatives when they are "bundled" into an overall diversity management strategy. In addition, very little research has examined how an organizational diversity perspective impacts overall organizational productivity. A few studies, largely case study analyses of individual organizations, suggest that an organization's diversity perspective drives its initial choice of diversity management practices. Over time, as an organization becomes more diverse, and experiences more diversity-related challenges, it expands its portfolio of diversity management strategies and develops more effectiveness in diversity management.

Carol T. Kulik

See also Human Resource Management Strategies; Interactional Model of Cultural Diversity; Organizational Demography; Social Identity Theory; Theory of Organizational Attractiveness; Theory of Transfer of Training

Further Readings

Allen, T. D., Eby, L. T., & Lentz, E. (2006). The relationship between formal mentoring program characteristics and perceived program effectiveness. *Personnel Psychology, 39,* 125–153.

Avery, D. R. (2003). Reactions to diversity in recruitment advertising: Are differences Black and White? *Journal of Applied Psychology, 88,* 672–679.

Ely, R. J., & Thomas, D. A. (2001). Cultural diversity at work: The effects of diversity perspectives on work group processes and outcomes. *Administrative Science Quarterly, 46,* 229–273.

Friedman, R. A., & Holtom, B. (2002). The effects of network groups on minority employee turnover intentions. *Human Resource Management, 41,* 405–421.

Jayne, M. E. A., & Dipboye, R. L. (2004). Leveraging diversity to improve business performance: Research findings and recommendations for organizations. *Human Resource Management, 43,* 409–424.

Kulik, C. T., & Roberson, L. (2008). Diversity initiative effectiveness: What organizations can (and cannot) expect from diversity recruitment, diversity training, and formal mentoring programs. In A. P. Brief (Ed.), *Diversity at work* (pp. 265–317). Cambridge, MA: Cambridge University Press.

Lankau, M. J., Riordan, C. M., & Thomas, C. H. (2005). The effects of similarity and liking in formal relationships between mentors and protégés. *Journal of Vocational Behavior, 67,* 252–265.

McKay, P. F., & Avery, D. R. (2005). Warning! Diversity recruitment could backfire. *Journal of Management Inquiry, 14,* 330–337.

Roberson, L., Kulik, C. T., & Pepper, M. B. (2003). Using needs assessment to resolve controversies in diversity training design. *Group and Organization Management, 28,* 148–174.

Thomas, D. A., & Ely, R. J. (1996, September/October). Making differences matter: A new paradigm for managing diversity. *Harvard Business Review,* 79–90.

MATRIX STRUCTURE

Matrix management encompasses a series of efforts to lay one or more new forms of departmentalization on top of an existing form. Matrix approaches extend the classical school of administration's analysis of organizational structure and offer a set of solutions to well-known and central organizational problems of task coordination and information processing. This entry describes the configuration of matrix structures, the purposes they serve, their strengths and weaknesses, their constituent elements, their relationship to other coordinative devices, and their utilization by large firms.

Fundamentals

Firms are typically structured around different forms of departmentalization: functions (e.g., sales, marketing, manufacturing, and research and development, or R & D), projects, product lines, geographic areas, customer segments, and so on. Matrix management encompasses a series of efforts to lay one or more new forms of departmentalization on top of an existing form (e.g., function by project, function by product line). Thus, if the existing form is the vertically organized functional organization, the new form of departmentalization is a horizontal overlay of project teams or product lines on top of the vertical hierarchy. As the new form of departmentalization grows more elaborate (e.g., as projects increase or product lines proliferate), the grid becomes more dense, and the structure approaches a full matrix structure.

The decision to adopt a matrix structure is strongly motivated by the desire to have the best of two or more forms of departmentalization used. Thus, in a typical function-by-product line structure, the firm seeks to maintain the advantages of functional organization (e.g., specialization, efficient use of resources, scale economies, focus on in-depth skill development, strategic control kept at the top of the firm) with the advantages of product line organization (e.g., coordination between functions, product focus and accountability, development of greater breadth in managerial training, flexibility in adapting to changing product needs, and maintaining proximity to the customer). The matrix is further adopted to solve problems of information processing and communication across functional personnel in firms with multiple ongoing projects, product lines, geographic segments, and so forth.

Of course, the matrix also possesses some of its own weaknesses. These include possible confusion over who is responsible for what, conflicts resulting from two competing hierarchies with authority over personnel, power struggles between functional and product line managers, the premium placed on teamwork and interpersonal skills, and development of common ground and goals across the multiple hierarchies. Robert Ford and W. Alan Randolph include a full review of the strengths and weaknesses of the matrix structure, and Thomas Sy and Laura D'Annunzio articulate the challenges of managing matrix organizations.

Matrix structures vary in terms of the structural and administrative elements that build upon one another to form more dense grids. The new departmentalization form can be *structurally differentiated* from the existing form, using a matrix director and matrix department. The two forms of departmentalization that the matrix comprises can exert *dual authority* in terms of supervision of shared subordinates (e.g., two-boss managers). Managers in the new form of departmentalization can have formal *decision-making authority* for administration, budgeting, and policy making. The matrix structure can also possess *dual support systems* (information systems, planning). Matrix structures are commonly linked with project management and project organization. Reviewing past uses of the term, Ford and Randolph in 1992 summarized the matrix as "cross-functional overlays that create multiple lines of authority and that place people in teams to work on tasks for finite periods of time" (p. 272).

The matrix structure is commonly viewed as the end point in a sequence of lateral coordinative arrangements. Long ago, Paul Lawrence and Jay Lorsch, and, Jay Galbraith proposed that these arrangements formed a Guttman scale in which the matrix elements build cumulatively upon one another. As firms seek to coordinate their internal activities, they sequentially install liaison roles, task forces, teams, integrators, integrating departments, and finally the pure matrix structure with cross-cutting forms of departmentalization. This series of coordinative mechanisms increases the firm's capacity to handle uncertain tasks and their high information-processing demands. The more developed arrangements are appropriate for higher levels of task uncertainty and task diversity.

At the same time, matrix structures are not a typical end point in organization design but, rather, the midpoint between the two extremes of functional departmentalization and product departmentalization. The matrix is often a way station as firms (a) decentralize (move away from functional groupings) toward a product line structure and (b) centralize (move away from product lines or customer groupings) back toward the functional structure. Firms thus experiment with the matrix structure (for perhaps as much as 10 years) before shifting to a more dominant form of departmentalization.

There is very little empirical research on matrix structures but rather a lot of anecdotal and opinion-based articles. Lawton R. Burns confirmed that matrix arrangements do build upon one another in a Guttman scale, but he did not find evidence that matrix complexity is tied to the firm's task diversity and uncertainty. Burns and Douglas Wholey found instead that the adoption of matrix structures is heavily influenced by institutional pressures (mimicry of opinion leaders) rather than technical forces. There is a good deal of descriptive information on the functioning of matrix structures. One of the best known illustrations is Asea Brown Boveri (ABB), a global matrix firm (organized around business areas and countries) in the 1990s. ABB attempted three balancing acts simultaneously: be global and local, big and small, and centralized and decentralized. The case illustrates many of the managerial techniques utilized by ABB to make matrix structures work effectively.

Managerial thinking about matrix structures has evolved beyond two-dimensional grids of departmentalized forms to emphasize the inherent "ambidexterity" of matrix structures like ABB. Michael Beer and Nitin Nohria suggest that firms need to simultaneously balance multiple dimensions, such as a short-term focus on efficiency and exploitation (theory E) with a long-term focus on R & D and exploration (theory O). The focus on ambidextrous thinking has now joined matrix structures as a popular way to conceptualize cross-cutting dimensions.

Lawton Robert Burns

See also Bureaucratic Theory; Differentiation and the Division of Labor; Organizational Structure and Design; Principles of Administration and Management Functions; Strategy and Structure; Technology and Complexity

Further Readings

Beer, M., & Nohria, N. (2000). Resolving the tension between theories E and O of change. In M. Beer & N. Nohria (Eds.), *Breaking the code of change* (pp. 1–33). Boston, MA: Harvard Business School Press.

Burns, L. R. (1989). Matrix management in hospitals: Testing theories of matrix structure and development. *Administrative Science Quarterly, 34*, 349–368.

Burns, L. R., & Wholey, D. R. (1993). Adoption and abandonment of matrix management programs: Effects of organizational characteristics and interorganizational networks. *Academy of Management Journal, 36*(1), 106–138.

Davis, S., & Lawrence, P. (1977). *Matrix.* Reading, MA: Addison-Wesley.

Ford, R., & Randolph, W. A. (1992). Cross-functional structures: A review and integration of matrix organization and project management. *Journal of Management 18*(2), 267–294.

Galbraith, J. (1972). Organization design: An information-processing view. In J. Lorsch & P. Lawrence (Eds.). *Organization planning: Cases and concepts* (pp. 49–74). Homewood, IL: Irwin.

Ghoshal, S., & Bartlett, C. (1997). *The individualized corporation.* New York, NY: HarperBusiness.

Knight, K. (1976). Matrix organization. *Journal of Management Studies, 17*(2), 111–130.

Lawrence, P., & Lorsch, J. (1967). *Organization and environment.* Cambridge, MA: Harvard University Press.

Sy, T., & D'Annunzio, L. S. (2005). Challenges and strategies of matrix organizations. *Human Resource Planning, 28*(1), 39–48.

MEANING AND FUNCTIONS OF ORGANIZATIONAL CULTURE

Theories of organizational culture explain patterns of behavior within organizations in terms of relatively shared mental structures that influence how people make sense of their workplace reality and of the symbols and symbolic practices that maintain and reproduce these understandings. In 1983, Laura Smircich drew connections between different research themes on organizational culture and different concepts of culture rooted in anthropological research. This entry combines Smircich's analysis with insights from later work to outline a socio-anthropological theory of what organizational culture is and how it affects organizational behavior. Understanding cultural processes in organizations is important to correctly interpret organizational phenomena and anticipate collective responses to managerial action.

Fundamentals

The notion of organizational culture draws on different research traditions in anthropology and sociology. By this term, organizational theorists generally refer to a pattern of belief structures that members of an organization share to varying degrees, which influences how they make sense of their reality and underpins the written and unwritten norms that regulate behavior in the organization. Among these belief structures, theorists often distinguish between *basic assumptions* and *espoused values.*

The former refers to deep understandings about appropriate ways of addressing fundamental problems in organizations: how to relate to the external environment and to the various stakeholders of the organization, and, how to regulate social interaction among its members. Examples of these understandings can be found in the degree of confrontation or in the level of intimacy that are considered acceptable within the organization. Basic assumptions tacitly operate below the threshold of consciousness: They are so deeply ingrained in our cognition that we take them for granted as a "natural" way of handling organizational problems.

Comparative research on cross-cultural management suggests that these assumptions often reflect the culture of the broader national or regional context within which the organization is embedded.

National cultures differ along several important dimensions, including the degree of inequality in the distribution of power that they consider desirable, their relative aversion to risk, their inclination toward collaborative versus competitive forms of interaction, and their preference for material versus expressive rewards. These differences tend to reflect on the way people design organizational structures and incentive systems, exercise leadership, and, more generally, exercise the forms of interaction that they consider appropriate in the workplace.

In organizations, some basic assumptions are occasionally brought to the surface as espoused values—conscious definitions of appropriate and inappropriate behavior, made explicit in conversations and organizational communication. Ideally, espoused values correspond to assumptions that members perceive as essential—that is, as central to the preservation of the integrity and viability of the organization—and distinctive compared with other organizations. Essential and distinctive values reflect members' understanding of the "identity" of their organization. It may happen, however, that some of these values embody ideal, rather than current, cultural traits and do not really correspond to observed behavior. These values may rather manifest the need of members to feel good about themselves. Or they may reflect the attempt of organizational leaders to stimulate changes toward an envisioned new culture, or, to project an image appealing to external stakeholders.

Espoused values can therefore be misleading when it comes to capturing the fundamental assumptions that really influence behavior within an organization. Espoused values, however, are not the only manifestations of these assumptions. Members' assumptions about appropriate ways of handling social interactions are also reflected in the organizational jargon they use, the stories they tell, the rites they engage in, the way in which they organize and furnish office space, and so on. All these visible, tangible, and audible manifestations of the organizational culture are usually referred to as *organizational artifacts*. In organizations, material, discursive, and behavioral artifacts not only express less visible values and assumptions but also contribute to their reproduction by structuring and constantly reconstituting social relationships and interaction.

Building on the hermeneutic tradition in cultural anthropology, some organizational theorists have highlighted the symbolic properties of these artifacts and drawn attention to the way in which the underlying meaning structures that constitute the basic assumptions of a culture are revealed and maintained by a system of symbols and symbolic practices. A symbol is an artifact that stands for a broader, more abstract concept or meaning. Organizational symbols usually include—but are not limited to—logos, buildings, visual images, and, often, milestone products. Even stories, slogans, and the organizational language itself perform an important symbolic function by sustaining the system of meanings that constitute the culture of the organization.

While a symbolic perspective on cultural analysis tends to envision members as "suspended in a web of meaning" of which they are only partially aware, recent research in cultural sociology has advanced the idea of culture as a "repertoire" or "toolkit" of resources that members can purposefully draw upon to pursue individual interests. This perspective on culture emphasizes individual agency in making flexible use of language, stories, symbols, rites, and other cultural material to inspire, enact, and justify different strategies of action. Applications of these ideas to organizations have emphasized how cultural change occurs as members are exposed to new and different resources that expand the repertoire that they can draw upon to formulate and implement new strategies.

Finally, while some organizational theorists view culture as an important lens—or "root metaphor"—through which to analyze organizations, others view culture as a resource in itself—a powerful tool to manage organizations. These scholars consider culture an important variable in the organizational system, along with strategy, structure, and system. Researchers in this tradition argue that shared values and assumptions influence employees' commitment to the organization and support to its strategy, and it points to the opportunity for organizational leaders to influence these values and assumptions by engaging in various forms of symbolic action (communication, role modeling, punishing, and rewarding, etc.). Organizational artifacts are considered as symbolic devices that leaders can and should manipulate to shape deeper belief structures. The preferential use of the term *corporate* (rather than "organizational") culture attests to the pragmatic, managerial perspective these scholars adopt, as they encourage leaders to build strong cultures to sustain corporate success. According to these scholars, cultures are "strong" when they are characterized by norms and values that are strongly held and widely shared throughout the organization. Available evidence from large-scale research, however, indicates only how strong cultures are associated with reliable performance (low variation over time) in relatively stable environments. In rapidly changing environments, instead, the strength of a culture is relatively less important than the adoption of norms and values that make the organization adaptable to change.

Whether organizational cultures are really as easily "manageable" as this literature optimistically suggests, however, is still questioned, because the fundamental functions that culture performs in organizations tend to make it intrinsically resistant to deliberate change.

Importance

The importance of culture in shaping the functioning and adaptability of an organization—but also its resistance to deliberate attempts at manipulation and change—is related to the fundamental functions it performs. In organizations, culture acts as a sensemaking device that guides members' interpretation of events (and their response to them): It facilitates coordination and maintains social order, it acts as a social control mechanism, it conveys a sense of identity, and it provides resources to justify and give sense to organizational action.

The system of belief structures that constitutes a culture helps its members organize their experience of the world. It tells them whether an event is worth paying attention to, how to *make sense* of this event, and how to respond to it. It helps them classify people, and it suggests appropriate behavior when interacting with them. When exposed to different cultures, surprise, puzzlement, or irritation may arise from situations that our system of beliefs cannot comprehend or bring us to interpret in misleading ways. While the sensemaking function of culture helps reduce uncertainty about how to "perceive, feel, and act" in most situations, it also induces resistance to change, in that cultural changes require members of an organization to modify their definition of their workplace reality.

By defining appropriate ways to interpret and handle social relations and interactions, culture is important in the maintenance of *social order*. In organizations, cultural beliefs underpin the role systems,

and the internal allocation of resources to different tasks (i.e., who does what, and, with what objectives and resources). It legitimizes the distribution and the exercise of authority and power (i.e., who has the right or is allowed to decide what). People will accept a given distribution of tasks, resources, and power in an organization to the extent that it conforms to deeply ingrained cultural beliefs. Organizational changes that disrupt this social order may encounter resistance, not only because they alter the material conditions within which resources are allocated and power is exercised but also because they run against the deep assumptions that justify this equilibrium.

By indicating desirable goals and appropriate codes of conduct in different situations, culture also acts as a *social control mechanism,* encouraging certain types of behavior, and discouraging others in addition to the formal rules and structures of the organization. Culture, as a control mechanism, operates at two levels. Internally, in ordinary circumstances, culture brings us to act in relatively predictable ways, following taken-for-granted beliefs and norms that lie under the threshold of awareness. Deviance from these responses tends to be inconceivable, and, if considered, it tends to induce feelings of guilt or discomfort. Externally, culture subjects members to social control manifested in the embarrassment, disapproval, or outright punishment that the violation of cultural norms and values is likely to elicit. Social control is particularly intense in strong cultures, where conformity to collective norms and expectations is constantly reinforced by formal mechanisms and informal peer pressure.

Organizational cultures also perform an important expressive function in that some of the more visible manifestations of a culture—its symbols, its stories, its rites, its myths—help maintain a collective *identity*. Organizational culture supplies members with important cues for making sense of what their organization is and stands for. The underlying values that these symbols, stories, and myths allude to instill members with pride in the organization, its past accomplishment, and its distinctive traits. By doing so, they stimulate their identification and reinforce their commitment. Highly identified members, in turn, will be more cooperative and supportive of organizational strategies. While the loyalty and discipline of highly identified employees may increase their willingness to implement organization changes, however, these employees may also strongly oppose changes that they perceive as violating their understanding of the identity of the organization.

The four functions of culture highlighted so far all address the intrinsic need of people and groups for stability and predictability—in their cognition, in their system of relationships, in their behavior, and in their sense of self. As the notion of "cultural toolkit" reminds us, however, culture does not act exclusively as a set of constraints, but also provides individuals with a more or less vast reservoir of "resources" that they can draw upon to justify and *give sense* to acts that may or may not conform to prevailing patterns of thought and action. In most cultures, the correspondence between symbols, stories, myths, and espoused values on the one side, and actual patterns of behavior on the other side is not perfect. Some artifacts may be remnants of the past, manifestations of latent or drifting values with little or no connection with currently dominant beliefs. Others may be open to multiple interpretation to suggest different implications for practice. It is this sense-giving function of culture that established or emerging organizational leaders may draw upon to induce changes in the culture itself, by drawing on this reservoir the symbolic resources they need to present proposed changes as reviving traditional values or as consistent with the cultural heritage of their organization.

Davide Ravasi

See also Competing Values Framework; Cultural Values; Management Symbolism and Symbolic Action; Organizational Culture Theory; Organizational Culture and Effectiveness; Organizational Culture Model; Organizational Identity; Typology of Organizational Culture

Further Readings

Hatch, M. J. (1983). The dynamics of organizational culture. *Academy of Management Review, 18*(4), 657–693.

Morrill, C. (2008). Culture and organization theory. *Annals of the American Academy of Political and Social Science, 619,* 15.

O'Reilly, C., & Chatman, J. A. (1996). Culture as social control: Corporations, cults, and commitment. *Research in Organizational Behavior, 18,* 157–200.

Ravasi, D., & Schultz, M. (2006). Responding to organizational identity threats: Exploring the role of organizational culture. *Academy of Management Journal, 49,* 433–458.

Rindova, V., Dalpiaz, E., & Ravasi, D. (2011). A cultural quest: A study of organizational use of new cultural resources in strategy formation. *Organizational Science, 22,* 413–431.

Schein, E. (2010). *Organizational culture and leadership (4th ed.).* San Francisco, CA: Jossey-Bass.

Smircich, L. (1983). Concepts of culture and organizational analysis. *Administrative Science Quarterly, 28,* 339–358.

MODEL OF OCCUPATIONAL TYPES

See Occupational Types, Model of

MODES OF STRATEGY: PLANNED AND EMERGENT

The planned versus emergent modes of strategy can be traced back to the work of Henry Mintzberg and James Waters, in which they sought to distinguish between these two forms of strategy. In essence, planned strategy is one in which the ultimate intention of the strategy is explicit and clearly articulated. This strategy is crafted by the top management and gets communicated throughout the organization. The strategy is always in control, and as such, external forces have little effect on the outcomes of the planned strategy. The emergent strategy, on the other hand, does not have any intention relating to it. It relies on the flexibility of the organization and the environment (changes) to lead the organization to where it may be going. These two modes of strategy are now understood as a continuum, and organizations today often use both modes in complementarity. As such, it is critical to know the fundamentals, assumptions, and challenges of using these two modes of strategy, which is what this entry will show. Below, the background, applications, and contemporary research on both planned and emergent strategies are highlighted.

Fundamentals

The planned strategy mode is grounded in the *design school of strategy.* The design school emphasizes strategy formulation—that firms analyse both their internal and external environments to help to determine their strategies at the corporate, business, and functional levels. Subsequently, the strengths-weaknesses-opportunities-threats (SWOT) analysis is commonly used to prescribe the strategic choice. The fact that the planned strategy mode assumes that an organization has complete control of its plan over time toward its desired intention has resulted in criticisms. For example, Mintzberg questions if an organization can accurately assess its own strengths and weaknesses when engaging in new activities that it does not have prior exposure to. He also questions why strategy should necessarily precede structure as prescribed in the planned strategy mode. Moreover, while making strategy explicit will allow all levels in the organization to align their goals, it is likely to cause inflexibilities when executing the strategy. The allowance of separation of formulation from implementation in this school can also be problematic—as the formulators need not be the implementers, which can cause alignment issues.

The assumption of complete nonintention of emergent strategy mode makes it hard to imagine any organization using a pure emergent strategy. Extensive work on the relative effects of industry and firm attributes on firm performance also suggests that a firm's strategy and resources at best explain 30% of firm profitability, with industry explaining about 10 to 20%. This leaves about 50% of firm profitability unexplained. This literature thus lends some support to the argument that planned and emergent strategy modes are the two extremes of a continuum, and organizations adopt a combination of the two. Thus, the realized strategy of any organization is the outcome of realized planned strategy (a portion of planned strategy) and emergent strategy.

The *process school of strategy* posits that strategy evolves over time as both internal and external environments of an organization change. In this school of thought, more attention is given to market processes, such as strategic interactions and learning. As this school looks at both historical development and observes the pace and path of change, it is commonly associated with the emergent strategy mode. Advocates of the emergent strategy mode argue that the boundaries set in the planned strategy mode are highly unrealistic—that key stakeholders and managers need to be involved in setting organizational strategy, that communications and commitment are drawn from all levels of the organization,

and that every aspect of the strategy is planned and controlled in a particular direction without disruptions. Organizations should instead have a flexible view and structure to cater to unforeseen circumstances that arise during the course of the execution of any intended strategy.

As learning and experiential learning take center stage on the strategizing processes, emergent strategy mode is argued to be becoming more prominent in today's strategy understanding. For example, it is a good planned strategy to engage in a strategic alliance, yet an emergent strategy has to be in place as partners would have to learn and adapt to each other once the alliance is formed. More recent work in the planned-emergent strategy mode discussions has suggested that while prediction characterizes researchers' understanding—that what can be predicted can be controlled—we need to recognize that when the market is highly uncertain, prediction does not necessarily mean control. This latest differentiation is still in its infancy but will extend our understanding of the planned-emergent strategy modes significantly.

The comparison of planned and emergent strategy modes also raises questions to research on the decentralization of decision making, planning horizons, environmental scanning and uncertainty, and internal organizational structure that enhances flexibility. In each of these fields, researchers need to find balance in accommodating an environment that is predictable in some dimensions but unpredictable in others. It is important to note that Mintzberg and Waters further suggest that there are other forms of strategy modes that come in between the planned-emergent continuum. Those proposed include entrepreneurial, ideological, umbrella, process, unconnected, consensus, and imposed strategy modes, but they are by no means exhaustive.

Siah Hwee Ang

See also Environmental Uncertainty; Management by Objectives; Strategic Decision Making; Strategies for Change; Strategy-as-Practice

Further Readings

Burgelman, R. A. (1994). Fading memories: A process theory of strategic business exit in dynamic environments. *Administrative Science Quarterly, 39,* 24–36.

Grant, R. M. (2003). Strategic planning in a turbulent environment: Evidence from the oil majors. *Strategic Management Journal, 24,* 491–517.

Mintzberg, H. (1990). The design school: Reconsidering the basic premises of strategic management. *Strategic Management Journal, 11,* 171–195.

Mintzberg, H. (Ed.). (2007). *Tracking strategies: Toward a general theory.* New York, NY: Oxford University Press.

Mintzberg, H., & Waters, J. A. (1985). Of strategies, deliberate and emergent. *Strategic Management Journal, 6,* 257–272.

Shaver, J. M., Mitchell, W., & Yeung, B. (1997). The effect of own-firm and other-firm experience on foreign direct investment survival in the United States, 1987–92. *Strategic Management Journal, 18,* 811–824.

WiltBank, R., Dew, N., Read, S., & Sarasvathy, S. D. (2006). What to do next? The case for non-predictive strategy. *Strategic Management Journal, 27,* 981–998.

MORAL REASONING MATURITY

The primary aim of theories of moral reasoning maturity is to facilitate scholars' understanding of the ways in which people form moral judgments in regard to issues involving ethical complexities. These theories form part of the broader theoretical domains of moral psychology and descriptive ethical theory, which emphasize individual factors in ethics and morality, and are guided by the view that questions of ethics are subjective and contextually sensitive. Their reliance on abstract reasoning (like most moral psychology theories) places considerable emphasis on reason, in contrast to affective or intuitive processing, as the main form of cognitive process which affects moral judgment. These theories are heavily based on, and continue to draw from, the long Western tradition in European philosophy from the ancient Greek to moral philosophers of more recent times (primarily Immanuel Kant and John Rawls). Theories of this type have two central premises. First, it is assumed that certain intrapersonal dynamics, tied to capacities of cognitive maturation, affect a person's moral reasoning when confronted with a moral dilemma in a given context. These theories are part of a larger body of work of cognitive developmental theory in moral, developmental, and social psychology. They assume a link between cognitive maturity and moral reasoning, and between moral reasoning and subsequent moral action. The second assumption lies in its conception of a staged process of development. The path toward maturation is seen as unidirectional, and development is formulated as an incremental progression from lower to higher stages of moral maturation. Particular regard is paid to the ethical and psychosocial maturity of the individual, as manifested in their cognitive patterns of reasoning. Accordingly, theory in this area examines the individual dynamics that affect both moral awareness and moral decision making, as distinct and complementary domain to situational descriptive ethical theories. These theories outline an approach to problems of management morality and business ethics. They usefully inform various debates in areas that share a common interest in the ways in which individual factors impact management ethics and morality, from public policy to healthcare, corporate governance, and stakeholder agency problems. This entry continues with an examination of the most prominent theories that have influenced thought and practice in this area, these being Lawrence Kohlberg's cognitive moral development theory and Jane Loevinger's theory of ego development. The second section outlines the contribution of Jean Piaget to the development of this theory, with particular reference to subsequent adaptations, leading thinkers, and the circumstances that influenced the growth of these theories. The final section surveys some seminal works in this area that continue to contribute to the development of the theory.

Fundamentals

Broadly speaking, there are two prominent cognitive developmental theoretical frameworks of moral reasoning and maturity, both of which are post-Piagetian. Each focuses on the dynamics of cognitive meaning making that motivate certain kinds of reasoning to inform moral judgment or broader decision-making practices. The first of these, Lawrence Kohlberg's cognitive moral development theory (CMD), focuses more narrowly on the development of a person's capacity for understanding moral dilemmas and reaching moral judgment via moral reasoning. The second, Jane Loevinger's theory of ego development, evolved as the core constructivist post-Piagetian cognitive developmental theory, and focuses on a broader examination of the cognitive structures of meaning making that guide adult psychosocial maturation. The scope of Loevinger's theory thus extends to incorporate a broader range of issues that involve more judgment via reasoning than morality dilemmas alone. It assumes that moral issues are indirectly involved in the broader question of how the self relates to others and its inescapably social nature. Loevinger (and a number of other prominent developmental psychologists in the United States) made significant contributions to the development of ego stage theories, building directly on the work of Anna Freud after her move to America. Accordingly, Loevinger's theory is heavily influenced by Freudian psychoanalytic psychology: its concern regarding the destructive role of unconscious emotional processes and the optimistic belief that evolution of reason segues to superior moral judgment and superior moral action. A primary concern of both theories is the need to respond to the increasing subjectivity and relativism of adult social relations as moral beings. Consequently, they are especially concerned with understanding how to balance the need for autonomous agency and identity independence with the interests of others, and the dominant cultural moral norms embedded in social relations that regulate behavior and expectations.

Kohlberg's theory initially defined six developmental stages of moral reasoning, based on the development of moral cognitive structures as per the Piagetian concern with the role between accommodation and assimilation in cognitive maturation. These stages can be grouped into three levels of cognitive moral reasoning: preconventional, conventional, and postconventional. A concise breakdown of Kohlberg's seven stages might be considered as follows. The first two levels, preconventional and conventional, both comprise two consecutive stages. In Stage 1 of the *preconventional stage,* the resolution of moral dilemmas is facilitated primarily through obedience and the avoidance of punishment. In Stage 2, resolution is founded on narrow and self-interested moral calculation. Stages 3 and 4, composing the *conventional level,* are oriented toward conformity, with morality predicated on respect for authority and the maintenance of the status quo. The *postconventional level in* Kohlberg's theory initially comprised two stages, before the addition of a final stage of moral maturity in his later work, bringing the number of stages in this theory up to seven. Stages 5 and 6 describe morality oriented

toward the common good and the establishment of a social contract, alongside a broader concern for autonomous action oriented toward adherence to universal human ethical principles, rather than consensus. These stages can therefore be characterized by choices of moral action that are at odds with the current status quo and authority. Kohlberg's seventh stage has been seen as an attempt to go beyond an exclusively cognitivist-rationalist approach to morality by reintegrating intuitive responses to moral dilemmas, thus including natural law and intuitive approaches to morality. This integration is known as *dual processing moral reasoning.*

Central to Loevinger's theory of the key dynamics of ego development are the constructs of differentiation and integration. Loevinger's work has been considerably influenced by biological observations of evolution, in which the growth and development of living organisms is predicated upon their ability to differentiate themselves from their surroundings and other organisms. Loevinger's seven stages represent hierarchically layered plateaus, or equilibria, of increasing cognitive differentiation in an individual's capacity for reasoning. As such, each stage constitutes a distinct way in which the individual interprets social reality and makes judgments that produce socially meaningful action. Constructivist stage theory posits that each stage of global meaning making represents a different epistemology, or way of knowing. Loevinger's formulation avers the importance of structuralist approaches to cognitive development. The Sentence Completion Test (SCT), published by Loevinger, Le Xuan Hy, and Kathryn Bobbitt in 1998, is the core measure in this theory.

A concise breakdown of Loevinger's seven stages might be considered as follows: (one–two) the presocial and self-protective stages, in which reasoning is often based on stereotyping and conceptual confusion; (three) the conformist stage, characterized by a dependence on clichés and simpler cognitive patterns; (three–four) the conscientious-conformist stage, in which reasoning exhibits increasing conceptual multiplicity but lacks complexity; (four) the conscientious stage, with increased conceptual complexity and patterned reasoning but with particular concern for decisions that value communication; (five) the individualistic stage, characterized by a cognitive style that acknowledges the distinction between process and outcome but exhibiting a concern that decisions creating dependence and interdependence are problematic; (six) the autonomous stage, with high conceptual complexity, reasoning oriented toward complex patterns, broad scope, objectivity, toleration for ambiguity, and an awareness of the broader social context; and (seven) the integrated stage.

The concept of integration is a central premise of moral development theory, but there have thus far been few inquiries into the nature of its core mechanisms, and questions remain as to what precisely is being integrated. In Loevinger's theory, integration refers primarily to the reintegration of affect and intuition with reason. Loevinger's seventh stage is therefore defined by a capacity for reason and the navigation of the social world based on a "dual knowledge epistemology," as with Kohlberg's seventh stage. This advanced capacity for cognition is based on an integrated intuitive and rational dual processing that gives rise to a processual capacity for morality, enabling authentic action and a nuanced approach to problems of morality and relatedness. Integration, therefore, represents a significant departure from the earlier autonomous stage, in which, with recourse to reason alone, an individual may not be able to overcome an obligation to reproduce expected social or cultural norms in a given context. While reasoning may be sound in these latter cases, it may not be translated into congruent action; the course of action chosen is incompatible with less conscious inner feelings. In such cases, the obsessive pursuit of reason in instances of moral judgment is seen to trigger various defense mechanisms caused by suppressed or unexplored affect. For Loevinger, integration is an advanced stage of character and identity maturation that enables what William Perry in his work conceptualized as a capacity for developing committed action in the midst of relativism.

Evolution

Theories of moral reasoning maturity are heavily rooted in the Piagetian contribution to developmental and moral psychology. Jean Piaget (1896–1980) is one of the most influential theorists in developmental psychology and continues to influence theory in a number of cognate disciplines, including moral theory and applied moral theory, psychology and adult development psychology, theory on learning, educational theory, and organizational behavior. It was Piaget who showed that both the psychological and epistemological progression of knowledge and morality is structured in hierarchically layered stages of continuous development. The development from the least to the highest stage of moral and psychosocial maturation is marked by three levels of achievement: the development of formal operations, the development of abstract critical thinking, and mastery. This theory holds that development toward formal operative cognition is a result of the interaction of two processes: accommodation and assimilation. The achievement of formal operations takes place in early adulthood but no later than the 24th year of age.

The work of Loevinger has in turn influenced a number of more focused studies, including William Perry's theory of intellectual and ethical development during college years, Theodor Adorno's typology of prejudiced and unprejudiced meaning making, Erich Fromm's ego types, and Lawrence Kohlberg's ego, moral, and cognitive stages of development. The theories of Loevinger and Kohlberg make epistemological assumptions that extend across a number of theoretical domains ranging from philosophy to biology. These traditions all emphasize the construct of integration and the importance of the relationship between differentiation and integration, as a core mechanism underlying the growth from lower to higher stages of maturity.

Kohlberg's theory informs the work of James Rest on the underlying cognitive process for moral decision making, including his Defining Issues Test (DIT), a highly reliable and respected measure for moral judgment, which is an alternative measure for Kohlberg's stages of moral reasoning. Rest's work has sparked further advances in theory on moral reasoning, and questions the primacy of the effects of individual factors on moral reasoning versus those of culture, in a way reminiscent of Kohlberg's own addition of a seventh stage of morality in his later work, which focuses on a dual processing between reason and intuition. Critics of Kohlberg maintain that his theory unduly prioritizes a concern for justice as the key variable to the exclusion of other important moral values in adult cognitive moral development. Furthermore, some critics have identified that the empirical testing on which it is based is overwhelmingly based on males. Carol Gilligan has since developed a complementary theory, showing that often women's moral maturation proceeds in a sequence strongly reminiscent of Kohlberg's but in content oriented toward reasoning based on a concern for care rather than justice.

Important early works included that of William Perry on moral and intellectual development during college years. More recent influential work has been done by Robert Kegan and Lisa Laskow, building upon the foundation laid by Loevinger in bridging between upper end stages of developmental cognitive psychology with postmodern self theory. An impressive theoretical study evolving out of the work of Loevinger and that of other developmental theorists that seek to understand the processes involved in the upper end, or postconventional, stages of moral development has been undertaken by Suzanne Cook-Greuter. This work reviews a number of specialized stage theories that are congruent with those of Loevinger and Kohlberg in their focus on hierarchical complexity (work emphasizing structural aspects of higher level cognition) and dialectical thinking as meta-systematic cognitive organization forms.

Most of the theories of moral reasoning maturity have been profoundly impacted by an assumption about the foundation of ethics lying in rationality. A cognitivist approach to moral maturation is still the predominant approach in moral psychology. These have been linked with assumptions on ethics and morality based on an idealized quest for identity autonomy rooted in modernity. Some of these assumptions have been profoundly critiqued and rejected by contemporary postmodern moral philosophers, such as Judith Butler. And yet much of the recent work to develop theory on the highest stages of postconventional morality seem congruent with trends in postmodern moral philosophy, though this as yet lacks theoretical clarity.

Importance

The impact of these researches has thus far been largely confined to the theoretical sphere. This is likely due to the conceptually dense nature of the constructs and processes involved in both Kohlberg and Loevinger's highest stages of moral and psychosocial maturity (a fact Loevinger herself acknowledges). These theories remain difficult for nonspecialists to understand and are to a large extent underexploited by management and organizational researchers and practitioners alike. Regarding the highest stages concepts of moral maturity in Kohlberg and Loevinger, it is worth noting their being in harmony with the latest social intuitionist theorists, such as Jonathan Haidt, who argue on the primacy of intuitive moral processing, influenced by David Hume and Scottish philosophy of the 18th century.

In recent years, there has been a burgeoning effort to understand the ways in which managers approach moral dilemmas and, importantly, the degree to which the decisions they make evidence their moral awareness and patterns of cognition. Through several decades of such research, empirical findings consistently show that for a majority of managers, moral reasoning dilemmas are being resolved predominantly at the conventional stages of moral reasoning (earlier than stage five). In the wake of the abundance of corporate corruption scandals involving immoral or amoral management after the 1990s, various areas of organizational and management research have shown a renewed desire to understand why so few adults and managers demonstrate postconventional stages of reasoning. A respectable body of empirical research on constructivist stage development shows that the highest stages of development have unfortunately been supported with little evidence as to how and why only a minority of adults proceeds from conventional to postconventional moral reasoning, with some researches placing the rate of postconventional maturation at 1/100. Thus, critique has focused on the practical usefulness of these theories, as moral maturation is increasingly recognized as the complex process that it is. Not unrelated to these critiques are increasing doubts as to whether the basic theoretical premise of the stage-type evolution of moral maturity, with its implication that an adult can arrive at a higher level of moral responsibility only after passing through all lower stages, is an altogether sound assumption. Competing noncognitivist theorists on moral judgment have pointed out that empirical data show a weak link between cognitive moral judgment and actual behavior, while others argue that these staged developmental models underplay the role of intelligence in higher moral reasoning capacity. These critiques have motivated considerable inquiry to validate further the core stage assumption of this theory.

Moral development theory has profoundly influenced research, knowledge creation, and the development of learning interventions in higher education by a number of prominent theorists in learning and education. Notable are David Kolb's experiential theory of learning and development, Baxter

Magolda's quantitative measure of self-authorship, drawing from the work of Robert Kegan, and theory on the development of reflective judgment. In addition to its contribution to management education, through various frameworks for student development in management studies and the teaching of business ethics, these theories have also influenced research into leadership and leadership development. The empirically researched and theoretically rigorous contribution of Bill Torbert and associates is based on constructivist development psychology rooted in Loevinger, but it is adapted to be easily understood and relate to various role challenges in the managerial job family. While it is not unusual for managerial development interventions to be theoretically informed by Kohlberg's moral cognitive development theory, the pool of insights and approaches that this body of theory offers has yet to be fully exploited by the practitioner community.

Kleio Akrivou

See also Ethical Decision Making, Interactionist Model of; Experiential Learning Theory and Learning Styles; Fairness Theory; Intuitive Decision Making; Management (Education) as Practice; Organizational and Managerial Wisdom

Further Readings

Akrivou, K. (2008). *Differentiation and integration in adult development: The role of self-complexity and integrative learning in self-integration.* Cleveland, OH: Case Western Reserve University, Department of Organizational Behavior.

Alexander, C. N., & Langer, E. J. (1990). *Higher stages of human development.* Oxford, England: Oxford University Press.

Cook-Greuter, S. R. (1999). *Postautonomous ego development: A study on its nature and its measurement.* Boston, MA: Harvard University, Graduate School of Education.

Haidt, J. (2001). The emotional dog with its rational tail: A social intuitionist approach to moral judgement. *Psychological Review, 108*(4), 814–834.

Kegan, R. (1994). *In over our heads: The mental demands of modern life.* Cambridge, MA: Harvard University Press.

Kohlberg, L. (1969). Stage and sequence: The cognitive-developmental approach to socialization. In D. A. Goslin (Ed.), *Handbook of socialization theory and research* (pp. 347–480). Skokie, IL: Rand McNally.

Kohlberg, L., & Ryncarz R. A. (1990). Beyond justice reasoning: Moral development and consideration of a seventh stages. In N. Alexander and E. J. Langer (Eds.), *Higher stages of moral development* (pp. 191–207). New York, NY: Oxford University Press.

Loevinger, J. (1976). *Ego development: Conceptions and theories.* San Francisco, CA: Jossey Bass.

Piaget, J. (1962). *The moral judgement of the child.* New York, NY: Collier Books.

Piaget, J. (1971). The theory of stages in cognitive development. In D. Green (Ed.), *Measurement and Piaget* (pp. 1–11). New York, NY: McGraw-Hill.

MULTICULTURAL WORK TEAMS

Multicultural work teams are a means of organizing work where two or more individuals from different cultures work together to achieve a common goal. Globalization, the rise of multinational organizations, and the general need to cross international borders in order to conduct business contribute to the prevalence of multicultural work teams. Multicultural work teams are uniquely positioned to provide benefits to organizations such as extensive knowledge of product markets and cultural savvy in how to conduct business in the local cultures. Research on multicultural work teams is focused on how to realize the benefits of culturally diverse teams while effectively managing the challenges they face such as distributed communication, differences in work norms, and language fluency issues. Theories explicating multicultural work team effectiveness and key characteristics of multicultural work teams are discussed in the following sections of this entry.

Fundamentals

The idea that cultural diversity can enhance team performance is based on cognitive resource theory. Cognitive resource theory suggests that diversity in a team can serve as an indicator of available knowledge and differing perspectives. The cultural diversity of multicultural work teams can indicate an important breadth of cultural knowledge, perspectives, cognitions, and languages needed for the team to meet its objectives. As an illustration, a multicultural product team may have an engineer at company headquarters in Germany, a marketing professional in the United States where the product will be sold, and a procurement specialist at the manufacturing facility in Mexico. These culturally diverse team members may have important insights into the local cultures involved with getting the product to market. The procurement specialist may have an in-depth understanding of shipping and procuring product parts in Mexico. The marketing professional may have an in-depth understanding of the U.S. consumer market. The engineer may be able to navigate the culture of the organization and ensure the product is consistent with the organization's standards and values. The cultural diversity of the team helps the organization effectively design, manufacture, and market a product in a global environment.

Cultural diversity may signal the availability of relevant knowledge and differing perspectives, but effective information elaboration is needed for the team to benefit from the diversity. Information elaboration involves information exchange and knowledge integration. Factors such as a shared understanding of the task, team trust, and culturally intelligent leadership help support the information elaboration process.

While cultural diversity is the strength of multicultural work teams, it can also present challenges. Similarity-attraction theory and social categorization theory suggest potential difficulties as diverse team members interact. The similarity-attraction theory suggests that culturally homogeneous teams should be more productive than culturally diverse teams because of the mutual attraction shared among team members with similar backgrounds. Real or perceived differences in cultural values, such as work norms and respect for hierarchy, and the use of different styles of communication (e.g., low or high context) may lead to less efficient team processes, decreased social cohesion, or increased conflict. Similarly, social categorization theory suggests that team members categorize other team members into subgroups, which can form the basis for an in-group–out-group distinction. Team members may develop an intergroup bias in some conditions and favor and cooperate with members of their in-group more than with members of an out-group. As such, team members from the same culture rather than different cultures may be more attracted to and cooperate more with one another, making cross-cultural collaboration difficult. For example, team members

fluent in the same language may be prejudiced toward those from other backgrounds and may preferentially provide opportunities for development or assign a coveted task to those who share the same primary language or accent. Acknowledging team member differences, emphasizing team goals, and fostering a shared team identity are some of the ways the negative effects of similarity-attraction and social categorization can be mitigated.

Finally, multicultural work team members are often distributed across time zones and locations, which can complicate team member coordination. Multicultural work teams often meet virtually and rely on communication technology to bridge distances and time. Trust between team members can be difficult to develop and more fragile in virtual teams. Occasional face-to-face meetings, explicit time and goal management, and emphasizing the team's shared goals are common in high-trust virtual multicultural work teams.

Multicultural work teams are not a panacea. Potential coordination difficulties between team members separated by culture, distance, and time zones need to be addressed and actively managed for optimal multicultural work team performance. However, when organizations have a specific business purpose that requires the diverse understanding and knowledge of different cultures, multicultural work teams can provide an attractive means of structuring work.

Suzanne T. Bell

See also Cognitive Resource Theory; Cultural Values; Managing Diversity; Virtual Teams; Work Team Effectiveness

Further Readings

Behfar, K., Kern, M., & Brett, J. (2006). Managing challenges in multicultural teams. In E. A. M. Mannix, M. Neale, & Y. Chen (Eds.), *Research in managing groups and teams: Vol. 9. National culture and groups* (pp. 233–262). Oxford, England: Elsevier Science Press.

Earley, P. C., & Gibson, C. B. (2002). *Multinational work teams: A new perspective.* Mahwah, NJ: Lawrence Erlbaum.

Earley, P. C., & Mosakowski, E. (2000), Creating hybrid team cultures: An empirical test of transnational team functioning. *Academy of Management Journal, 43,* 26–49.

Hofstede, G. (2001). *Cultures consequences* (2nd ed.). Thousand Oaks, CA: Sage.

Jarvenpaam, S. L., Knoll, K., & Leidner, D. E. (1998). Is anybody out there? Antecedents of trust in global virtual teams. *Journal of Management Information Systems, 14*, 29–64.

Montoya-Weiss, M. M., Massey, A. P., & Song, M. (2001). Getting it together: Temporal coordination and conflict management in global virtual teams. *Academy of Management Journal, 44*, 1251–1262.

Van Knippenberg, D., De Dreu, C. K. W., & Homan, A. C. (2004). Work group diversity and group performance: An integrative model and research agenda. *Journal of Applied Psychology, 89*, 1008–1022.

Von Glinow, M. A., Shaprio, D. L., & Brett, J. M. (2004). Can we talk, and should we? Managing emotional conflict in multicultural teams. *Academy of Management Review, 29*, 578–592.

MULTIFIRM NETWORK STRUCTURE

Firms in many industries choose to focus on their core activities and outsource noncore activities to external providers. As a result, many products and services in the global economy are designed, produced, and distributed by multiple firms hooked together into a type of organization called a *multifirm network*. The main benefits of the multifirm network structure are flexibility, the variety of capabilities that can be assembled, and the economies of scale and experience that can be leveraged in each activity. The typical multifirm network organization is hierarchical, centered on a lead firm that organizes and manages its suppliers and partners to produce and deliver products or services. Examples of firms that use hierarchical multifirm network structures are Toyota (automobiles), Walmart (retailing), and Li & Fung (apparel manufacture). Recently, multifirm networks have been used inside collaborative communities of firms to develop complex, knowledge-intensive products. Collaborative innovation networks, such as those used by Blade.org in the computer server industry, are temporary, voluntarily formed structures that are self-managed rather than hierarchically managed. This entry describes how the organization of economic activity has gradually changed from the atomistic firm as the key building block to groups of specialist firms operating collectively in a network.

Fundamentals

Prior to the 1970s, most American firms were self-reliant—they tended to use only their own resources and capabilities to conduct their businesses. During much of the 1970s, large firms were widely criticized by the business press for being uncompetitive compared with major Japanese companies, such as Sony, Toyota, and Honda. In their attempts to become more flexible and adaptive, American firms began to change how they were organized. Many firms downsized to reduce costs. Some firms removed layers of middle managers from their hierarchies in order to speed up decision making and resource allocation. Others began to subcontract activities—first production and later other business functions—to firms that were specialists in that particular activity. Gradually, the multifirm network structure took shape. Networks composed of multiple specialist companies as their main actors have been called *modular* organizations. Multifirm networks that change their shape frequently are called *virtual* organizations.

A multifirm network organization is different from a traditional (self-contained) organization in several respects. First, instead of holding in-house all the resources required to offer a product or service, multifirm networks use the collective resources of many firms. Each firm in the network specializes in a set of activities that constitute a portion of the total business. Second, multifirm networks rely heavily on market mechanisms in addition to administrative mechanisms to manage resource flows. In order to maintain its position in the network, a firm must behave efficiently and reliably—just as it would have to behave if it wanted to be successful in open markets. Third, lead firms in many multifirm networks expect their suppliers to contribute proactively, to engage in behaviors that improve the network rather than simply fulfilling a contractual obligation. Doing so can help the whole network to learn, improve, and adapt. Last, a multifirm network can be more flexible and scalable than a traditional organization. It can increase or decrease in size relatively quickly, and it can more easily expand its scope than a traditional organization.

A network is a set of actors connected by ties. The network perspective has been used to study how firms connect themselves in order to engage in economic activity, how the resulting multifirm organization can be controlled and coordinated, and why and how networks change over time. Over the past two decades, network research has shifted toward an "agency" view in which lead actors take the initiative to design and build multifirm networks to accomplish corporate objectives. The most visible multifirm network organizations today are global supply chains. Supply chains, the network of firms that contributes both inbound and outbound products and services along an industry value chain, dominate many sectors of the global economy. In early supply chains, a lead firm would link to specialist providers in the industry to create an integrated multifirm organization called an *extended enterprise.* Often, the motivation for forming such a supply chain was cost reduction and efficiency. The automobile industry provided many of the early examples. In some supply chains, lead firms recognized that their suppliers had knowledge and expertise that was being underutilized, and they began to collaborate with those firms not only to reduce costs but also to improve products and develop new markets. Those supply chains had the capacity to learn and grow, supported by management techniques, such as benchmarking, business process reengineering, total quality, and best practices programs.

The logic driving supply chain evolution—leveraging knowledge and other resources held by network partners—has produced the latest manifestation of multifirm networks: collaborative innovation networks. Such networks can be found in collaborative communities of firms. For example, Blade.org is a collaborative community of more than 200 firms in the computer server industry. This organization was designed and built by International Business Machines (IBM) Corporation and seven other founding firms, and during 2005 to 2011, Blade.org developed many new products for the growing blade-based computer server market. Blade.org used protocols, processes, and infrastructures to enable its member firms to form temporary multifirm networks to develop and commercialize products. These self-organizing networks do not rely on hierarchies for control and coordination, demonstrating the versatility of the network structure.

Charles C. Snow and Raymond E. Miles

See also Actor-Network Theory; Interorganizational Networks; Organizational Structure and Design; Strategic Alliances

Further Readings

Barabasi, A. L. (2002). *Linked: The new science of networks.* New York, NY: Perseus.

Borgatti, S. P., & Foster, P. C. (2003). The network paradigm in organizational research: A review and typology. *Journal of Management, 29,* 991–1013.

Miles, R. E., & Snow, C. C. (1986). Network organizations: New concepts for new forms. *California Management Review, 28,* 62–73.

Nohria, N. (1992). Is a network perspective a useful way of studying organizations? In N. Nohria and R. G. Eccles (Eds.), *Networks and organizations* (pp. 1–22). Boston, MA: Harvard Business School Press.

Powell, W. W. (1990). Neither market nor hierarchy: Network forms of organization. In B. Staw (Ed.), *Research in organizational behavior* (pp. 295–336). Greenwich, CT: JAI Press.

Snow, C. C., Fjeldstad, Ø. D., Lettl, C., & Miles, R. E. (2011). Organizing continuous product development and commercialization: The collaborative community of firms model. *Journal of Product Innovation Management, 28,* 3–16.

Thorelli, H. B. (1986). Networks: Between markets and hierarchies. *Strategic Management Journal, 7,* 37–51.

MULTILEVEL RESEARCH

The essence of multilevel research in management is that any outcome of interest is the result of a confluence of effects emanating from different levels of analysis. The overall logic is that individuals are nested in teams or work groups, which in turn are nested in larger organizational units, such as departments, districts, or strategic business units (SBUs), which in turn are nested in organizations. Further, organizations are arranged in strategic business groups or perhaps interorganizational networks, which in turn are nested in industries or overall performance environments. These multilevel arrangements have important implications for the development of theory, research, and application. This entry outlines the three cornerstones of the multilevel paradigm in terms of levels of theory, measurement, and analysis, highlighting how this approach pertains to all areas of management and how it changes our thinking and opens up doors for multidisciplinary advancements.

Fundamentals

Multilevel investigations simultaneously consider the relationships between predictors and criteria variables at two or more levels of analysis. Although most applications consider two levels of analysis, other than the complexity of doing so, there is nothing to preclude one from embracing three or more levels of analysis. The variables included within each level may be different or similar to one another across levels. Situations where variables are conceptually comparable across levels (e.g., efficacy, cooperation, competitiveness) are referred to as *isomorphism*. Instances where the relationships linking variables within levels are comparable to similar ones across different levels are referred to as *homologous*. *Cross-level* relationships describe instances, whereas predictor variables from one or more higher levels exert influence on lower level processes or outcomes.

Given the inherent nesting arrangement of multilevel models, the degree of linkage across levels is referred to as *bond strength*. The general rule is that the relative strength of bonds across levels of phenomena increases with proximity and inclusion, and decreases with distance and independence. For example, the notion of *proximity* suggests that individuals are most likely to be influenced by their personal attributes, followed by team-level variables, and then by variables from more distant levels, such as industry characteristics. At issue is that, all else being equal, variables residing within a given level are likely to have the strongest bonds, followed by forces from adjacent levels, and to a lesser extent influences from more distant or removed levels from the focal level. Whereas this general pattern is likely to be widely applicable, it does not preclude the possibility of a distant variable exerting a more direct or immediate effect should a theory warrant. For example, individuals may be directly susceptible to events occurring in the far-removed performance environment.

The notion of *inclusion* refers to how neatly the level entities are hierarchically arranged. To the extent that lower levels are wholly contained in higher level units, bond strength increases. To the extent that lower level entities bridge higher level collectives (e.g., team memberships that span organizations or organizations that are members of multiple strategic groups), the bond strength across levels weakens. *Embeddedness* describes how lower

level phenomena are aligned with higher level factors and processes, such that greater alignment generates stronger bonds or inclusion across levels. The idea here is that higher level variables serve as a context or constraint within which lower level phenomena operate. Finally, *entrainment* refers to the rhythm, cycles, synchronicity, and pacing of organizational phenomena. As a general rule, the rate at which higher level phenomena (e.g., team cohesion) evolve and change is slower than those of lower level phenomena (e.g., individuals' motivations and attitudes).

Collectively, the notions of bond strength, inclusion, embeddedness, and entrainment suggest that higher level variables (e.g., environments or industries) are far more likely to influence lower level variables (e.g., organizational structure or team arrangements) than the reverse. While this perspective does not preclude the possibility of upward and reciprocal influences, the prevailing logic in management research is that the larger context within which lower level processes are nested generally exerts greater downward influences than lower level variables exert on the higher level context. Research is beginning to explore upward influences where, for example, a single toxic employee might undermine group morale or a particularly effective unit might alter an organizational strategy. Generally speaking, upward influences are more likely in situations where higher level phenomena have yet to fully crystallize or form, such as during socialization periods, early team interactions, following a major organizational intervention, and so forth.

While variables from more proximal layers are likely to exert greater influence on some focal outcome than are variables from more distal layers, there are likely *cross-level mediational relationships* that provide linkages across levels. For example, features of a competitive environment may well place a premium on certain organizational designs or practices. In turn, the organizational arrangements may drive subunit operations and whether employees are arranged in teams or not. In short, there is often a filtering effect as distant forces make their way through intermediate levels to a given focal variable. The intervening levels may act to neutralize or accentuate the distal influences and, thereby, also operate as *cross-level moderating effects*. Naturally this does not preclude *direct cross-level effects* of variables from distal layers on the focal variable. Across layers, influences may be positive (e.g., munificent environment, empowered units) or negative (e.g., resource impoverishment, dysfunctional group conflict), or exhibit complex interactions. Notably, the knowledge, skills, abilities, and other characteristics (KSAOs) associated with entities also can exert both direct effects and potentially moderate relationships within and across layers in this model. In this context, KSAOs may refer to individual differences, team composition, or an organization's human capital.

Importance

The multilevel framework is important because it forces scholars and practitioners to formally consider factors from outside of their focal level. For example, while team effectiveness is a function of how well members coordinate their efforts, their task design, and so forth, it is also driven by members' characteristics and the extent to which an organization supports teamwork initiatives. These latter features come from lower and higher levels of analysis, respectively. Multilevel investigations are guided by three important interrelated issues, namely, the level of (a) theory, (b) measurement, and (c) analysis, for the constructs included in an investigation. Level of *theory* refers to the focal level to which generalizations are designed to apply. Level of *measurement* refers to the unit(s) from which data are collected, whereas the level of *analysis* refers to the unit(s) to which data are assigned for substantive analyses. An important point is that these three facets must be aligned in order to minimize levels-related confounds, or *fallacies of the wrong level*.

Level of Theory

An important feature of the level of theory is the notion of *focal unit*—which are the entities that scholars wish to make generalizations about. In other words, variance exists in whatever level of entity researchers wish to predict (e.g., individuals, subunits, firms). The nesting assumption of modern-day multilevel theories implicitly assumes that entities are members of one, and only one, collective at a particular level of inquiry. Once the focal unit for generalizations is identified, a multilevel theory can be built. Multilevel theories begin with a specification of the outcome variable(s) of interest, and the level(s) at which they reside. Theorists should then specify, a

priori, the level of each predictor construct and the processes by which higher level constructs form and are related to the focal outcome(s) of interest.

Level of Measurement

The level of measurement refers to the level at which the raw data were collected. The key principle here is that whenever the level of measurement differs from the level of analysis, some justification for the aggregation of data is warranted. Therefore, we need a theory and rationale and supporting psychometric evidence, to justify aggregating data from one level of analysis to represent a higher level construct, for example, if researchers collect data from individual team members and wish to use these to index team-level variables (e.g., demographic diversity, cohesion); they need to advance a theory as to how those data combine to represent the higher level construct. Generally speaking, there are two types of aggregation principles: composition and compilation. *Composition* refers to situations where simple descriptive statistics (such as the mean or variance of scores in a collective) adequately represent the processes that associate lower level data with higher level constructs. That is, each lower level entity implicitly contributes equally to the higher level index in a fairly straightforward manner. In contrast, *compilation* refers to instances where measures collected from lower level entities combine in nonlinear complex ways to generate a gestalt, or whole, that is not reducible to its constituent parts. In effect, compilation suggests that not all lower level scores contribute equally to the aggregate phenomenon and that such weighting may change over time.

A typology of multilevel constructs has developed over the years, which includes at least six different types: (a) selected score (e.g., most anxious member), (b) summary index (e.g., members' social capital), (c) consensus (e.g., affective tone), (d) referent shift or alignment (e.g., collective efficacy), (e) dispersion (e.g., functional diversity), and (f) aggregate (e.g., industry munificence). Importantly, depending on the nature of the higher level construct, it is incumbent upon researchers to provide different types of psychometric evidence to support aggregation.

Level of Analysis

The level at which data are analyzed must be aligned with the level of theory for the constructs involved. To the extent that the two facets are not aligned, misspecifications of various forms will arise—often referred to as fallacies of the wrong level. Because lower level entities are not independent in multilevel designs, traditional single-level analytic techniques, such as multiple regression, are not applicable (because they employ the wrong error terms). Fortunately, recent developments have produced statistical techniques that account for such nonindependence and can accurately analyze relationships that traverse levels of analysis. Generically referred to as *random coefficients analysis* (RCM) or *hierarchical linear modeling,* multilevel analyses can test three types of relationships. First, there are potential *lower level direct influences,* such as between individuals' personality variables and their attendance. Second, there may be *direct cross-level influences,* such as the effects of group cohesion on members' average attendance. And third, there may well be *cross-level interactions* whereby the relationships between lower level predictors and outcomes differ as a function of higher level factors. For example, the relationship between individuals' need for affiliation and their attendance might be accentuated to the extent that they are members of groups with high attendance norms. Naturally, interactive relationships among variables from within any given level may be incorporated as well.

These basic types of relationships can be extended to test mediational and longitudinal relationships, and RCM has been extended into the realm of multilevel structural equation modeling, and it has been integrated with growth modeling and longitudinal techniques. Yet many challenges remain to be addressed, including adequate methods for estimating the power of various multilevel parameter tests, measurement models that traverse levels of analysis, centering of data, and a myriad of sampling-related issues. Whereas the multilevel framework offers great promise for advancing the science, it also provides a valuable diagnostic lens for practice. For example, a dysfunctional group might not be attributable to poor team factors, such as communication or coordination breakdowns, but rather to the poisonous influence of an individual member or perhaps to an organizational climate that is nonsupportive of teamwork. The multilevel framework helps to guide managers to consider the root causes underlying organizational successes and failures.

John E. Mathieu

See also Business Groups; Multifirm Network Structure; Organizational Structure and Design; Systems Theory of Organizations; Work Team Effectiveness

Further Readings

Chen, G., Mathieu, J. E., & Bliese, P. D. (2004). A framework for conducting multilevel construct validation. *Research in multilevel issues: The many faces of multilevel issues, 3,* 273–303.

Hitt, M. A., Beamish, P. W., Jackson, S. E., & Mathieu, J. E. (2007). Building theoretical and empirical bridges across levels: Multilevel research in management. *Academy of Management Journal, 50*(6), 1385–1399.

Holcomb, T. R., Combs, J. G., Sirmon, D. G., & Sexton, J. (2010). Modeling levels and time in entrepreneurship research: An illustration with growth strategies and post-IPO performance. *Organizational Research Methods, 13*(2), 348–389.

Hox, J. J. (2010). *Multilevel analysis: Techniques and Applications* (2nd ed.). New York, NY: Routledge.

Klein, K., & Kozlowski, S. W. J. (2000). *Multilevel theory, research and methods in organization.* San Francisco, CA: Jossey-Bass.

Mathieu, J. E., & Chen, G. (2011). The etiology of the multilevel paradigm in management research. *Journal of Management, 37,* 610–641.

Rousseau, D. M. (1985). Issues of level in organizational research: Multilevel and cross-level perspectives. *Research in Organizational Behavior, 7,* 1–37.

Short, J. C., Ketchen, D. J., Palmer, T. B., & Hult, G. T. M. (2007). Firm, strategic group, and industry influences on performance. *Strategic Management Journal, 28*(2), 147–167.